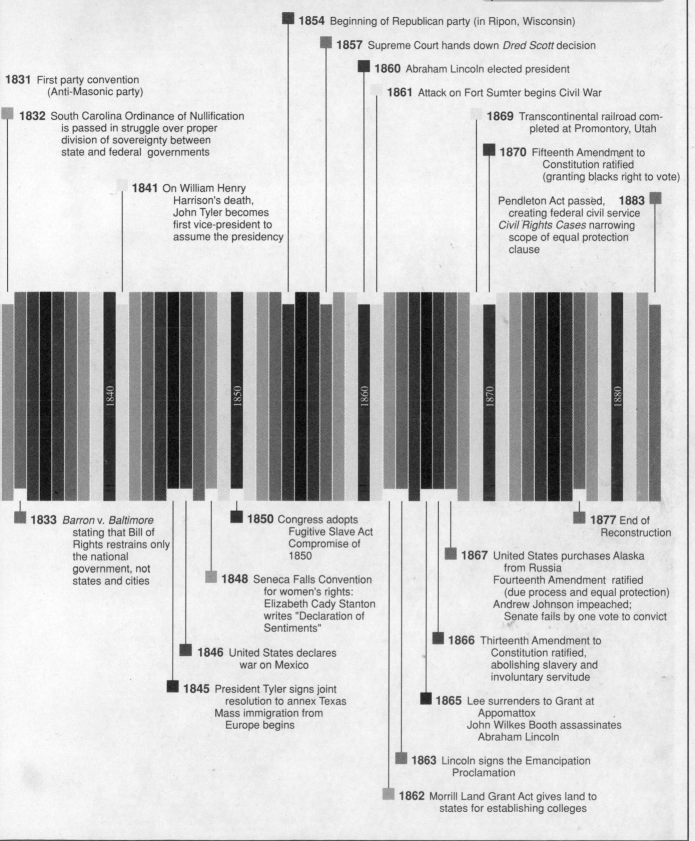

1854 Beginning of Republican party (in Ripon, Wisconsin)

1857 Supreme Court hands down *Dred Scott* decision

1860 Abraham Lincoln elected president

1861 Attack on Fort Sumter begins Civil War

1831 First party convention
(Anti-Masonic party)

1832 South Carolina Ordinance of Nullification
is passed in struggle over proper
division of sovereignty between
state and federal governments

1869 Transcontinental railroad completed at Promontory, Utah

1870 Fifteenth Amendment to
Constitution ratified
(granting blacks right to vote)

1841 On William Henry
Harrison's death,
John Tyler becomes
first vice-president to
assume the presidency

Pendleton Act passed, **1883**
creating federal civil service
Civil Rights Cases narrowing
scope of equal protection
clause

1840

1850

1860

1870

1880

1833 *Barron* v. *Baltimore*
stating that Bill of
Rights restrains only
the national
government, not
states and cities

1850 Congress adopts
Fugitive Slave Act
Compromise of
1850

1877 End of
Reconstruction

1848 Seneca Falls Convention
for women's rights:
Elizabeth Cady Stanton
writes "Declaration of
Sentiments"

1867 United States purchases Alaska
from Russia
Fourteenth Amendment ratified
(due process and equal protection)
Andrew Johnson impeached;
Senate fails by one vote to convict

1846 United States declares
war on Mexico

1866 Thirteenth Amendment to
Constitution ratified,
abolishing slavery and
involuntary servitude

1845 President Tyler signs joint
resolution to annex Texas
Mass immigration from
Europe begins

1865 Lee surrenders to Grant at
Appomattox
John Wilkes Booth assassinates
Abraham Lincoln

1863 Lincoln signs the Emancipation
Proclamation

1862 Morrill Land Grant Act gives land to
states for establishing colleges

GOVERNMENT IN AMERICA

Student:

To help you make the most of your study time and improve your grades, we have developed the following supplement designed to accompany Lineberry/ Edwards/Wattenberg, *Government in America,* Fifth Edition:

Study Guide 0-67-352136-2
by David Billeaux

You can order a copy at your local bookstore or call HarperCollins Publishers directly at 1-800-782-2665.

GOVERNMENT IN AMERICA

People, Politics, and Policy
Fifth Edition

Robert L. Lineberry
University of Houston

George C. Edwards III
Texas A&M University

Martin P. Wattenberg
University of California, Irvine

HarperCollins*Publishers*

Sponsoring Editor: Lauren Silverman
Development Editor: Deborah Samyn
Project Coordination: Proof Positive/Farrowlyne Associates, Inc.
Text Design: Matthew Doherty Design
Cover Design: Paula Meyers and Proof Positive/Farrowlyne Associates, Inc.
Cover Photo: Robert Llewellyn
Photo Research: Kelly Mountain
Production: Michael Weinstein
Compositor: Graphic World, Inc.
Printer and Binder: R. R. Donnelley & Sons, Inc.
Cover Printer: The Lehigh Press, Inc.

Government in America
People, Politics, and Policy
Fifth Edition

Copyright © 1991 by HarperCollins Publishers Inc.

Library of Congress Cataloging-in-Publication Data

Lineberry, Robert L.
    Government in America : people, politics, and policy/Robert L.
Lineberry, George C. Edwards III. Martin P. Wattenberg.—5th ed.
        p.   cm.
    Includes bibliographical references and index.
    ISBN 0-673-52111-7
    1. United States—Politics and government.   I. Edwards, George C.
II. Wattenberg, Martin P. III. Title.
JK274.L573   1990
320.973—dc20   90-42295
                                                                    CIP

90 91 92 93 9 8 7 6 5 4 3 2 1

Acknowledgments

Acknowledgments for the copyrighted materials not credited on the page
where they appear are listed in the Acknowledgments section beginning
on page C-1. This section is considered an extension of the copyright
page.

BRIEF CONTENTS

CONTENTS

PART THREE   The Policymakers   398

12   CONGRESS   406

LIST OF SELECTED FEATURES

Photo Essays

A Question of Ethics

You Are the Policymaker

You Are the Judge

America in Perspective

In Focus

The People Speak

PREFACE

Since 1980 *Government in America* has been one of the most widely used introductory-level texts in its field. In this fifth edition we have maintained the qualities that have proven themselves in the classroom.

The job of a text is to help the instructor teach well. It should, first, attract the interest of students. Second, it should convey ideas and evidence to support those ideas, to provide a basic structure for the subject on which a good teacher can base a course of instruction. We, the authors, have over a half century of experience teaching American government among us, and we have learned to present this complex subject in an engaging and understandable fashion.

Continuity and Change

Perhaps the most notable change in the fifth edition is the addition of coauthors George C. Edwards III of Texas A&M University and Martin P. Wattenberg of the University of California at Irvine, two leading scholars of American politics and government. Their participation has created the opportunity for a thorough revision. The fifth edition is completely up to date and incorporates the best recent scholarship on American government.

Focus   *Government in America* continues to adopt a "policy approach" to American government. We feel that the principal reason for studying politics is to understand the policies governments produce, and our discussion of politics is tied to the central question, "What difference does it make?" This focus engages students' interest and stimulates consideration of the most important aspects of governing. This approach was fairly unusual when introduced in the early editions, but today many other texts follow our lead.

Themes   In addition to a policy focus, two important themes run throughout the book: democracy, and the size of government. Each chapter has specific sections relating these themes to the chapter's topic.

The first theme, democracy, deals with the initial great question central to governing—*How should we be governed?*—and evaluates how well the American system lives up to citizens' expectations of democratic government. As with previous editions, we continue to incorporate theoretical issues in our discussions of different models of American government. We try to encourage students to think analytically about the theories and develop independent assessments of the American government's politics and policy.

Our second theme, the size of government, focuses on another great question of governing: *What should government do?* Here we discuss alternative views concerning the proper role and size for American government and the influence that the workings of government and politics have on the size of government. The government's size is the core question around which politics revolves in contemporary America, and this question pervades many crucial issues, from equality to budgeting.

Features   Five features appear throughout *Government in America*. Each chapter (after the first) opens with a box entitled **"Government in Action,"** which illustrates the significance of the material in the chapter with a recent example or story from American politics. This feature is designed to draw students into the chapter and preview the major themes.

It is important that students recognize and think critically about the difficult choices faced by citizens and policymakers. A second feature in each chapter is entitled **"A Question of Ethics"** and focuses on questions of personal or policy ethics, asking the student to evaluate an ethical dilemma—for example, how much money should the government spend to prolong the life of a dying hospital patient? Another feature, **"You Are the Policymaker,"** is also interactive. It asks students to make a policy decision on a question, such as whether the Supreme Court should follow the original intentions of the Constitution's framers or interpret the Constitution according to present-day standards.

Complementing our theme of democracy, each chapter contains one or more boxes, entitled **"The People Speak,"** that provide *up-to-date* opinion poll data regarding a question discussed in the chapter—whether the American people favor abortion or whether they feel that those who contribute large amounts of money to congressional candidates exercise too much power, as examples. Finally, **"America in Perspective"** boxes look at an aspect of each chapter from the perspective of how the United States compares to other countries, focusing on the tax rates in other nations, for example, or the uniqueness of the American two-party system.

We have retained and substantially updated some well-received features of the first four editions. Each chapter contains extensive material in boxes, either to highlight a case study, to present some specific research on a question, or to provide figures and tables that illustrate important points.

These boxes provide invaluable learning aids for students. Each chapter ends with a contemporary bibliography and a listing of key terms. Additional study aids appear at the back of the book: a glossary of key terms, the Declaration of Independence, the Constitution, and tables on presidents and presidential elections, party control of the presidency and Congress in the twentieth century, and Supreme Court justices serving in this century.

New to this edition are four photo essays on the development of Washington, D.C., and its political institutions. These essays provide historical background about the Washington community and introduce each of the four parts of *Government in America*.

Supplements to the Text

A comprehensive selection of teaching and learning resources has been developed to supplement the fifth edition of *Government in America*.

Laser Disc   *American Government: Issues and Images* is an original laser disc, also available on videotape. This two-sided videodisc, developed in consultation with American government professors and a multimedia courseware developer, contains nearly one hundred excerpts from newsreel collections, network news and cable TV archives, and state historical societies. The videodisc has been specifically designed for classroom use and includes pedagogically useful clips from campaign commercials and convention debates, as well as historic and recent footage about domestic and foreign policy issues. An accompanying user's guide links each excerpt to *Government in America*.

Study Guide   This comprehensive study guide, written by David Billeaux of Corpus Christi State University, helps students not only to remember the essential text material but also to examine and discover further perspectives on American government. Each chapter of the study guide contains learning objectives, a chapter synopsis/overview, a pretest, "reading for content" guides designed to focus students' reading of the text chapter, a glossary, posttest (review) questions, discussion questions, classroom exercises, and a section on research and resources.

Instructor's Manual   Professor Billeaux has also written a complete resource manual for the instructor. Each chapter of the instructor's manual includes learning objectives, a synopsis, glossary terms, highlight boxes, tables, profiles, lecture outlines, and sources for other lecture material. The manual offers two special features: complete mini-lectures, which augment the text material, and suggested projects and activities. The instructor's manual also provides a sample course syllabus and a guide to films that can enhance lectures and discussions.

Test Bank   The test item file, also prepared by Professor Billeaux, consists of two thousand multiple choice, true/false, and completion test questions. Each question is coded with the correct response and referenced to the page in *Government in America* on which the correct answer is indicated. The test bank is provided free of charge to instructors.

Test Master   In addition to the traditional printed format, the complete test bank is also available free of charge on *Test Master,* HarperCollins' computerized test-generating system. *Test Master* is flexible and easy to use. It may be obtained for use with the IBM-PC and most compatibles and with the Apple IIe and IIc.

State and Local Government   Rickert R. Althaus of South Missouri State has devised a state and local government supplement to be used exclusively with this edition of *Government in America*.

Writing a Research Paper in Political Science   This hands-on supplement, authored by Daniel E. Farlow of Southwest Texas State, is available to all adopters of the text.

The 1988 Elections in America   Larry J. Sabato of the University of Virginia provides a thorough analysis of the most recent elections in this thought-provoking ancillary.

***Super Shell* Student Tutorial Software**   *Super Shell,* a computerized student tutorial guide written by David Billeaux, is also provided free of charge to instructors. *Super Shell* was developed to help students retain the key concepts and ideas they have read. This versatile drill-and-practice software contains multiple-choice, true/false, and short answer questions for each chapter in the text. Diagnostic graphics provide immediate student reinforcement and make recommendations about areas in which further study might prove beneficial. Students can print out narrative chapter outlines or consult an easy-to-use tutorial guide. In addition, a flash card program is included to drill students on the terms in the text's glossary.

Harper Data-Analysis Package   William Parle of Oklahoma State University has prepared a student data-analysis package for the IBM-PC. The program performs several basic statistical functions, including univariate frequency distributions, bivariate frequency distributions, and bivariate frequency distributions controlling for the effects of a third variable. Free to instructors, the package comes with a "real world" data set that allows for a realistic program demonstration, a complete Help menu and Help files, a data dictionary feature, a set of screen instructions, and a user's manual.

Transparencies   Transparency acetates of figures in the text are available free to instructors who want to help students interpret visual data. These transparencies facilitate the integration of student reading with classroom lectures.

Media Program   A complete media program includes a wide selection of well-regarded films and videos for classroom use. *The Media Handbook,* designed to help instructors integrate the films and videos with their text and teaching plans, outlines various audiovisual options and suggests follow-up discussion questions.

Instructors may choose from among many excellent productions. *The Power Game,* Hedrick Smith's popular four-part PBS documentary on the elected— and unelected—government in Washington, and *Eyes on the Prize,* the award-winning six-part series on the civil rights movement, are both available through the HarperCollins media program. Also available is "The Thirty-Second President," Bill Moyers's examination of the presidency in an age of soundbites, from his PBS series *A Walk Through the Twentieth Century. The Challenge of the Presidency,* a one-hour videotape, combines David Frost's thoughtful interviews of former presidents. Adopters of *Government in America* may also receive a unique newsreel video, a selection of authentic newsreel footage that captures the key American political events of the past six decades.

***Grades* Grade-keeping and Class-management Software**   Free to instructors, *Grades* maintains data sets for up to two hundred students. It is suitable for the IBM-PC and most compatibles.

Acknowledgments

Many, many colleagues have kindly given us counsel on the drafts of this edition. They include the following:

James E. Anderson, *Texas A&M University*
Judith A. Baer, *Texas A&M University*
David M. Billeaux, *Corpus Christi State University*
Janet K. Boles, *Marquette University*
James M. Carlson, *Providence College*
Richard A. Champagne, *University of Wisconsin-Madison*

Anne N. Costain, *University of Colorado*
Patricia Crotty, *East Stroudsberg University*
Joel Diemond, *Dutchess Community College*
Bernard J. Firestone, *Hofstra University*
Elizabeth N. Flores, *Del Mar Community College*
Charles D. Hadley, *University of New Orleans*
Larry N. Gerston, *San Jose State University*
John R. Kayser, *University of New Hampshire*
Kenneth D. Kennedy, *College of San Mateo*
Laurel A. Mayer, *Sinclair Community College*
Wendell L. Mott, *Ferris State University*
Kevin V. Mulcahy, *Louisiana State University*
David J. Olson, *University of Washington*
Richard H. Payne, *Sam Houston State University*
William M. Pearson, *Lamar University*
B. Guy Peters, *University of Pittsburgh*
John K. Price, *Louisiana Tech University*
Harold W. Stanley, *University of Rochester*
Glenn Stockwell, *College of the Redwoods*
Danny G. Sutton, *Iowa State University*
John C. Syer, *California State University, Sacramento*
Robert K. Toburen, *Louisiana Tech University*
John K. White, *Catholic University of America*
Peter Woll, *Brandeis University*

A number of editors provided valuable assistance in the production of this edition of *Government in America*. Most indispensable was the contribution made by Deborah Samyn, who steadfastly supervised every aspect of the project and especially helped develop the themes and special features. Bob Olander and Dale Beda of Proof Positive/Farrowlyne Associates, Inc., expertly handled project coordination and the text and cover design. Political Science editors Lauren Silverman, Karen Bednarski, and Bruce Nichols provided important guidance, helping keep the project on course and on schedule.

We owe a special debt of gratitude to three of Professor Edwards's colleagues at Texas A&M University—Judith Baer, Frank Baumgartner, and Arnold Vedlitz—all of whom made major substantive contributions to this edition. Russell Gardner assisted in tracking down various odds and ends, and Timothy Lelesi provided valuable research assistance for the photo essays. Frances and Leonard Wattenberg each contributed a lifetime of memories about Washington, thereby helping to outline the photo essays.

Robert L. Lineberry
George C. Edwards III
Martin P. Wattenberg

ABOUT THE AUTHORS

Robert L. Lineberry currently serves as Senior Vice President at the University of Houston. He served from 1981–88 as Dean of the College of Liberal Arts and Sciences at the University of Kansas in Lawrence.

A native of Oklahoma City, Oklahoma, he received a B.A. degree from the University of Oklahoma in 1964 and a Ph.D. in political science from the University of North Carolina in 1968. He taught for seven years at Northwestern University in Evanston, Illinois.

Dr. Lineberry is currently President, Policy Studies Section, of the American Political Science Association. He is the author or coauthor of five books in political science. Dr. Lineberry has also authored or coauthored eighteen articles in professional journals in his discipline. In addition, he has taught regularly, including twenty years of instruction of freshman American government.

He has been married to Nita Lineberry for twenty-four years. They have two children, Nikki, who works in Kansas City, and Keith, a student at the University of Texas.

George C. Edwards III is Distinguished Professor of Political Science at Texas A&M University. From 1985–88 he was Visiting Professor of Social Sciences at the U.S. Military Academy at West Point. One of the country's leading scholars of the presidency, he has written over a dozen books on American politics and policy-making, including *At the Margins: Presidential Leadership of Congress, Presidential Approval, Implementing Public Policy,* and *National Security and the U.S. Constitution.*

Professor Edwards has served as President of the Presidency Research Section of the American Political Science Association and on many editorial boards. In 1988 he went to Brasília to advise those writing the new constitution for Brazil. Professor Edwards was also an issue leader for the National Academy of Public Administration's project on the 1988 Presidential Transition, providing advice to the new president.

When not writing, speaking, or advising, he prefers to spend his time skiing, watching baseball, or attending art auctions.

Martin P. Wattenberg is Associate Professor of Political Science at the University of California, Irvine. His first regular paying job was with the Washington Redskins in 1977, from which he moved on to receive a Ph.D. at the University of Michigan in 1982.

While at Michigan, Professor Wattenberg authored *The Decline of American Political Parties* (Harvard University Press), currently in its third edition. Most recently, he has written *The Rise of Candidate-Centered Politics: Presidential Elections of the 1980s,* also published by Harvard. In addition, he has contributed many professional articles to such journals as the *American Political Science*

Review, American Journal of Political Science, American Politics Quarterly, Public Opinion Quarterly, and *Public Opinion.*

Professor Wattenberg has also lectured abroad about American politics in Germany, France, Spain, and Canada. Presently, he is working with a colleague in Berlin on a project comparing American and German electoral behavior.

When not writing or lecturing, he can most often be found on the beach at Newport or at the local tennis courts.

1

INTRODUCING GOVERNMENT IN AMERICA

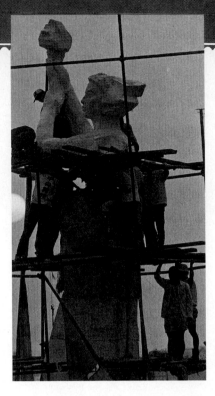

*T*he twenty-first century is fast approaching, bringing with it unimagined challenges. We want to be able to respond to these challenges individually, as citizens, and collectively, as a nation. *Government in America* will help you become a well-informed citizen, a citizen better able to lead our country into the next century.

Chapter 1 starts this process by introducing you to three important concepts: government, politics, and public policy. It also raises two fundamental questions about governing that will serve as themes for this book:

1. *How should we be governed?* Americans take great pride in calling their government democratic. Today there is a rush to establish democracy in many countries, but not everyone agrees on what democracy means. This chapter will examine the workings of democratic government. The chapters that follow will evaluate the way American government actually works against the standard of an "ideal" democracy. We will continually ask who holds **power** (the capacity to get people to do something they otherwise would not do) and who influences the policies adopted by government.

2. *What should government do?* This text will explore the consequences of the way American government works on what the government does. In other words, "Does our government do what we want it to do?" The second theme is closely linked to the first—the process of government is tied to the substance of public policy.

(Above) In today's interdependent world, one nation's actions affect all others; we are not just American citizens, but world citizens. From left: the Berlin Wall; environmental demonstrators; Tiananmen Square.

What government should do can be examined in terms of "the size of government." Debates about the size of government, including its functions, its budget, and the number of its employees, are among the most important in American political life. These debates are at the core of disputes between the major political parties and between liberals and conservatives.

Ethics is another issue that arises for all governments. Some people feel that the phrase *political ethics* is a contradiction in terms. This chapter will also examine different questions surrounding political ethics as part of an ongoing discussion of ethical questions throughout the text.

The purpose of Chapter 1 is to lay a foundation for understanding government in America. This foundation begins with the notion of government itself.

GOVERNMENT, POLITICS, AND PUBLIC POLICY

Government, politics, and public policy are interrelated. Government is important because of what it does for us—and to us. It can protect us, feed us, educate us, send us to war, tax us, and touch us in just about every aspect of our lives. All of these actions involve setting public policies. The way government makes decisions about public policies is through politics. This chapter will first examine government itself to see how it works and what implications this has for the policies it produces.

Government

Whether or not you have been interested in government, your life has been, and will be, greatly shaped by it. Few things have more to do with your standard of living, your freedoms, and your opportunities than government. Clearly, it is a topic that bears close examination.

What Is Government?   Those institutions that make public policy for a society are collectively known as **government.** In our national government, these are Congress, the president, courts, and federal administrative agencies (often called "the bureaucracy"). We also have thousands of state and local governments in the United States, and they make policies that affect us as well.

Occasionally a society's form of government undergoes radical change. This occurred in America with the rebellion against British colonial rule in 1776 and with the transfer of power from the government under the Articles of Confederation to that under the Constitution. Ever since, we have had the chance to change officeholders in our government at election time. There are nearly 500,000 elected officials in the United States; that means that somewhere, on almost every day of the year, someone is running for office.

Every government has a means of changing its leaders. Some changes, like those in American government, are orderly and peaceful. The transition between the out-going Democratic administration of Jimmy Carter and the in-coming Republican administration of Ronald Reagan, in 1981, was more dramatic than usual because of last-minute negotiations regarding the release of American hostages in Iran (embassy personnel taken prisoner by Iranian students who seized the American embassy in Tehran). Turned out by the voters, the Carter people had packed their belongings. Bookshelves were bare. White House carpenters were screwing in the appropriate nameplates for the new president and his staff; the guard was changing. Even as the inaugural ceremony was beginning, Carter's aides kept working, trying to ensure the safety of the hostages. Some had special phones at home, connected directly to the White House. At exactly

Contrasting

Explaining

noon, however, as Ronald Reagan completed his oath of office, their phones went dead.[1] A new team had taken its place and was ready to run the government.

Not all governments change so peacefully. The twentieth century has been a time of revolutionary upheaval. Iran's revolution, which overthrew the Shah, eventually led to the seizing of American hostages. The Russians in 1917 and the Chinese in 1949 changed their governments through violent revolution in order to adopt communist governments. Sometimes a change in government is less orderly than in America, but less bloody than a revolution. Massive protests disrupted the government of Philippine president Ferdinand Marcos until he left office—and the country—to be replaced by the government of Corazon Aquino. Regardless of how they assumed power, however, all governments have some functions in common.

What Governments Do   Big or small, democratic or not, governments in the modern world are similar in the following ways:

1. *Governments maintain national defense.* In the nuclear age, some governments possess awesome power to make war, maintaining large armies and deploying highly sophisticated weapons. The United States spends about $300 billion a year on national defense. Some politicians think the United States spends too much on defense; others think this amount of money provides only the barest defensive capabilities. On both sides there are those who think that military expenditures are not made efficiently.

[1]Hedrick Smith, *The Power Game: How Washington Works* (New York: Ballantine, 1988), 395.

Corazon Aquino and her running mate, Salvador Laurel, on their way to election victory in the Philippines. Although Aquino enjoyed wide popular support and a relatively peaceful transfer of power in the country's first fair election in decades, her government has had to fight off numerous—and bloody—coup attempts.

2. *Governments provide public goods.* **Public goods** are things that everyone can share. Contrast a loaf of bread, a private good, with clean air, a public good. You can buy a loaf of bread and easily consume it by yourself. Clean air, however, is available to everyone. A public good, unlike a loaf of bread, is indivisible and nonexclusive. Everyone can use a public good; no one can be denied its use.

A central principle of modern political science and economics is that *individuals have little incentive to provide public goods because no one can make a profit from them.* For instance, many businesses seem unconcerned with cleaning the air, since they do not make a profit from providing clean air. Thus governments are usually left to provide things like public parks and pollution control.

3. *Governments have police powers to provide order.* Every government has some means of maintaining order. When people protest en masse, governments may resort to extreme measures to restore order. Chinese security forces occupied streets around Tiananmen Square in June of 1989 to crush the student protest. Even in the United States, governments consider the power to maintain order one of their most important jobs. Americans today are generally supportive of an increase in the government's police powers to control high crime rates and drug abuse.

4. *Governments provide public services.* Hospitals and other public services do not build themselves. Governments in our country spend billions of dollars on schools, libraries, weather forecasting, halfway houses, and dozens of other public services.

5. *Governments socialize the young into the political culture.* Most modern governments do not trust education to chance. Almost everyone runs a school system whose curriculum consists, in part, of courses on the philosophy and practice of government in that particular system. In the United States, the government says that in public schools you cannot say a prayer at the beginning of the school day, but you may have to recite the Pledge of Allegiance.

6. *Governments collect taxes to pay for the services they provide.* In 1990 one of every three dollars earned by an American citizen was used to pay national, state, and local taxes. Although Americans often complain about the high cost of government, our tax burden is actually much lower than that of citizens in most other democratic nations.

Providing national defense, public goods, and public services; controlling order; socializing young people; and collecting taxes are not small tasks. Many important and difficult decisions must be made regarding what government should do. For example, how much should we spend on national defense? How high should taxes for Social Security be? The way we answer such questions is through politics.

Politics

Presidential candidate George Bush claimed during the 1988 campaign that Boston Harbor was one of the dirtiest in the country. Tons of effluent (the technical term for raw waste water) poured into the harbor every day. At the Boston Aquarium, kids could see a computer model of the sludge moved around

Many American public schools begin each day with the Pledge of Allegiance. Like most governments around the world, the American government uses the public schools to socialize its children. Required civics courses and governmental approval of curriculum and textbooks help ensure that the young understand and support the American system of government.

Michael Dukakis and Lloyd Bentsen, with their wives Kitty and Beryl Ann, wave to the crowd at the 1988 Democratic National Convention. Presidential campaigns are the most visible (and, some say, most sordid) form of American politics, but it is often what happens outside the media spotlight that determines the winners and losers in the political process.

Boston Harbor by the tides.[2] During the campaign candidate Bush used this murky harbor against his opponent, Massachusetts Governor Michael Dukakis, who, he claimed, was not dealing effectively with environmental problems. Some people were persuaded by Bush's claim, but others wrote it off as "just politics." We are used to one candidate attacking another—sometimes in very ugly language—for one failure or another. "Politics" has come to mean something different (and often negative) to the average voter, as opposed to a political scientist. Politics, however, is a lot more than merely what candidates do to win elections.

What Politics Is   Politics also has to do with what policies a government produces. Political scientists often cite a famous definition of **politics** by Harold D. Lasswell: "*Who gets what, when, and how.*"[3] It is one of the briefest and most useful definitions of politics ever penned. Admittedly, this broad definition covers a lot of ground (office politics, sorority politics, and so on) in which political scientists are not interested. They are interested primarily in politics related to governmental decision making.

The media usually focuses on the *who* of politics. At a minimum this includes voters, candidates, and political leaders, groups, and parties. *How* people play politics is important, too. They do it through bargaining, supporting, compromising, lobbying, and so forth. *What* refers to the substance of politics and government—the public policies that come from government. Governments

[2]*Newsweek,* July 24, 1989, 35.
[3]Harold D. Lasswell, *Politics: Who Gets What, When, and How* (New York: McGraw Hill, 1938).

distribute benefits, such as new roads; and burdens, such as new taxes. In this sense, government and politics involve winners and losers.

Politics is an important way in which society conducts its business; it is neither good nor bad. Americans often focus on the seamy side of politics. The word itself has negative connotations. Nevertheless, it is important to remember that politics can be conducted in either an ethical or an unethical way, an issue we will engage throughout *Government in America.*

Political Involvement   People get involved in politics for many reasons. Some of these reasons, no doubt, are noble, and others are not. The ways in which people get involved in politics—whether as candidates for office or simply by voting for the local school board—make up their **political participation.** Many people judge the health of a government, especially a democratic government, according to how widespread political participation is. When judged by voter turnout America does quite poorly, with one of the lowest turnout rates in the world. Low voter turnout has an effect on who holds political power. As Wolfinger and Rosenstone have shown in their study of turnout, "voters are not a microcosm of the entire body of citizens, but a distorted sample that exaggerates the size of some groups and minimizes that of others."[4]

Voting is only one way of participating. For a few Americans—a very few—politics is a vocation, rather than an avocation. They run for office, and some even earn their livelihood from holding political office.

There are thousands of Americans who treat politics not as a casual civic duty, but as something critical to them and their interests. Many of these people are members of interest groups or single-issue groups, which have recently come to prominence in American politics. One of the most important factors in modern politics is the **single-issue groups**—interest groups so single-minded that their members will vote on only one issue, ignoring a politician's stand on everything else.[5]

[4]Raymond E. Wolfinger and Steven J. Rosenstone, *Who Votes?* (New Haven, Conn.: Yale University Press, 1980), 198.

[5]On the growth of interest groups, see Jack L. Walker, "The Origins and Maintenance of Interest Groups in America," *American Political Sciences Review* 77 (June 1983): 390–406.

Permission granted by the *Detroit News.*

Elaborating

When the Supreme Court handed down its decision in a case called *Webster* v. *Reproductive Health Services* in 1989, it narrowed a woman's right to an abortion by allowing states to decide whether or not to provide funds to women who want abortions but cannot afford them. People on the *pro-choice* and the *pro-life* sides—and note the loaded term each uses for itself—turned to state politics to achieve their goals. Pro-lifers attempted to convince their legislators to restrict abortion funding by picketing abortion clinics and lobbying legislatures in many states. Pro-choicers worked on legislators to keep the right to abortion as broad as possible. Neither group considered a compromise. For this reason many politicians feel that single-issue groups such as these get in the way of policy-making. Single-issue groups have little sympathy for compromising, an approach that most politicians take as the heart and soul of their job. The influence that single-issue groups have on voters and elected officials complicates efforts to seek the middle ground on various issues.

Individual citizens and organized groups get involved in politics because they understand that the public policy choices made by governments affect them in significant ways. Will they have access to medical care? Will they be taken care of in their old age? Is the water they drink pure? These and other questions tie politics to public policy.

Public Policy

Explaining—Policy Agenda

More and more, Americans expect government to do something about their problems. The president and members of Congress are expected to keep the economy humming along; voters will penalize them at the polls if they do not (see Chapter 17). When people confront government officials with problems they expect them to solve, they are trying to influence the government's **policy agenda.** John Kingdon defined a policy agenda as "the list of subjects or problems to which government officials, and people outside of government closely associated with those officials, are paying serious attention at any given time."[6] Like individuals, governments have priorities. Some issues will be considered, and others will not. One of the key elements of democratic government is that officials, if they want to get elected, must pay attention to the problems people want them to pay attention to. When you vote, you are partly looking at whether a candidate shares your agenda or not. If you are worried about abortion, medical insurance, and Central American dictatorships, and a certain candidate talks only about schools, nuclear power, and solid waste disposal, you should find another candidate.

A government's policy agenda changes regularly. Almost no one thought about flag-burning until the Supreme Court ruled in 1989 that the First Amendment protected flag-burning as free expression. When jobs are plentiful and inflation is low, economic problems occupy a low position on the government's agenda. Nothing works better than a crisis to elevate an issue on a policy agenda. An oil spill, an airline crash, or a brutal murder will almost insure that ecology, air safety, or gun control will rise to near the top of a government's agenda.

Public policy is a choice that government makes in response to some issue on its agenda (see Table 1.1). For instance, a university's governing body

Pro-life and pro-choice groups are single-minded and uncompromising. Recent victories by pro-choice gubernatorial candidates in Virginia and New Jersey suggest that pro-choice forces remain strong despite Webster v. Reproductive Health Services.

Definition

---

[6]John Kingdon, *Agendas, Alternatives, and Public Policies* (Boston: Little, Brown, 1984), 3.

Types of Public Policies

There are many types of public policies. Every decision that government makes—a law it passes, a budget it establishes, and even a decision not to act on an issue—is public policy. Here are the most important types of public policies:

TYPE	DEFINITION	EXAMPLE
Congressional statute	Law passed by Congress	Social Security Act
Presidential action	Decision by president	American troops sent to Panama
Court decision	Opinion by Supreme Court or other court	Supreme Court ruling that school segregation is unconstitutional
Budgetary choices	Legislative enactment of taxes and expenditures	The federal budget
Regulation	Agency adoption of regulation	Food and Drug Administration approval of a new drug

could decide, in response to faculty complaints about parking problems, that student cars will be towed from faculty parking lots.

Of course, policymakers can establish a policy by doing nothing as well as by doing something. Doing nothing—or doing nothing different—is a choice. Often a debate about public policy centers on whether government should do something rather than nothing. Reporter Randy Shilts's book about the American government's response to the AIDS crisis tells a sad tale of inaction, even when the AIDS epidemic reached crisis levels.[7] Shilts traces the staggering growth in the number of AIDS victims and reveals how governments in Washington and elsewhere did little or debated quietly about what to do. Shilts claims that, since politicians viewed AIDS as a gay person's disease, they were reluctant to support measures to deal with it, fearful of losing the votes of anti-gay constituents. The issue thus remained a low priority on the government's policy agenda.

Government in America will constantly ask you to sharpen your ability to make policy choices. The "You Are the Policymaker" sections throughout the text present actual policy questions that have confronted Congress, the president, the Supreme Court, or a governmental bureaucracy. The sections challenge you to exercise your best judgment as a citizen, to analyze each issue and make a policy choice.

THE POLITICAL SYSTEM

A **political system** is a set of institutions and activities that link together government, politics, and public policy.[8] Most systems, political or not, can be diagrammed on paper. We can create simple renderings of how a nuclear power

---

[7]Randy Shilts, *And the Band Played On: Politics, People, and the AIDS Epidemic* (New York: Penguin Books, 1987).

[8]All models of political systems are indebted to David Easton, "An Approach to the Analysis of Political Systems," *World Politics* 9 (April 1957): 379–89.

Should Government Permit Gene Cloning?

These days, almost every well-educated American has heard of DNA. It is deoxyribonucleic acid, and biologists have known about it since 1869. Not until 1944, however, did they know that it is the genetic substance. In 1953 Watson and Crick demonstrated that DNA is actually made up of two strings (together called a double helix) in which all the genetic information making humans—or toads or field mice or whatever—is encoded. Today, many workaday biologists can be "gene-splicers," and it is very likely that one or more is on your campus. These biologists can take a set of genes found in DNA and essentially rework them into something else. New genes can then be "cloned," that is, reproduced. This is simple enough if what is being reproduced is a trivial scientific microbe. But when it can be extended to new life forms, public policy concerns arise.

Ananda Chakrabarty, a biologist working with General Electric (for which Ronald Reagan was once the national spokesperson) in the 1970s, developed a new form of bacteria, a microbe that could "eat" oil, thereby making it easier to clean up oil spills and pollution. If GE could patent the microbe and market it commercially, the company would profit. But could new microbes—basically new life forms—be patented like any new invention? The Supreme Court (in *Diamond* v. *Chakrabarty* [1980]), by a close vote of 5 to 4, said yes. GE could have its patent.

It was a short step from new microbes to new mammals. By the mid-1980s, researchers at the University of California at Davis had crossed a goat and a sheep (getting a "geep") and scientists at the Maryland Agricultural Experiment Station had produced a cross-eyed, arthritic pig that was much larger than normal and might revolutionize the meat market. The "experts"—the scientific community of gene-cloners, as Ira Carmen found out in a survey—were in nearly unanimous agreement that gene cloning was a vital scientific breakthrough. Carmen argued that scientific research is protected by the First Amendment guaranteeing free speech, and that "one day, the courts will have to develop some link between the Bill of Rights and contriving these new life forms."

A geep, genetically engineered by combining genes from a goat and a sheep.

Some interest groups disagreed. Jeremy Rifkin, a Washington antibiotechnology crusader, argued that Frankenstein-like experimentation could come to no good. In Washington, a House subcommittee chaired by Wisconsin Representative Robert W. Kastenmeier heard testimony from farming groups that the patenting of animals could result in fewer animal breeds and the payment of expensive royalties to patent-holders. The scientific director of the Humane Society called it "very frightening" to treat animals as "simple assemblies of genes."

Put on your citizen-as-policymaker hat. Consider the issue of whether public policy should permit cloning. Ask, too, some further questions about the issue:

1. In a democracy, who should decide questions such as this? Should the courts have the final say? What should be the role of Congress, the elected representatives of the people?

2. When there is uncertainty about a policy's impact (which is almost always the case), what should be done? Should the policy be delayed (even if other countries make advances upon us)? Should it be encouraged?

3. What should be done to balance the scientists' right of inquiry against the economic costs and benefits of a policy?

Sources: For more information on the cloning controversy, see Ira Carmen, *Cloning and the Constitution* (Madison: University of Wisconsin Press, 1985). The quotation from Carmen is from page 171. The discussion of the congressional inquiry is from the *New York Times*, June 9, 1987, 17. On Rifkin's views, see his *Algeny* (New York: Viking Press, 1983), especially part 6.

plant or an automobile works. Figure 1.1 is a model of how a political system works. The rest of this book will flesh out this skeletal version of our political system, but for now the model will help you to identify several key elements.

Political Issues and Linkage Institutions

Politics begins, of course, with people, and people do not always agree on the best course of action. A **political issue** arises when people disagree about a problem or about public policy choices made to combat a problem. There is never a shortage of political issues in this country; government, however, will not act upon an issue until it is high on the agenda.

In a democratic society, parties, elections, interest groups, and the media are key **linkage institutions** between the preferences of citizens and the government's policy agenda. Parties and interest groups both exert much effort to get the issues they feel are important to the top of the government's agenda. Elections and the media are two major forums through which potential agenda items receive public attention.

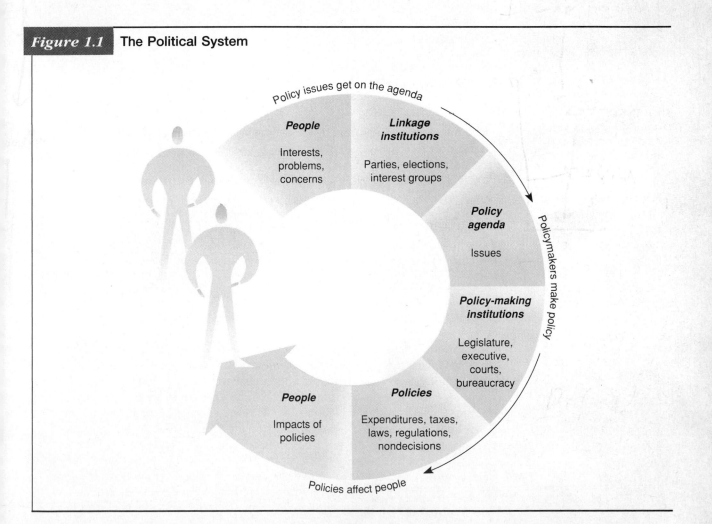

Figure 1.1 The Political System

Making Public Policy: The Policy-making Institutions

Explaining

Policymakers stand at the core of the political system. Working within the government's institutions, they scan the issues on the policy agenda, select some for attention, and make policies concerning them. The U.S. Constitution establishes three policy-making institutions: Congress, the presidency, and the courts. Today the power of the bureaucracy is so great that most political scientists consider it a fourth policy-making institution.

Very few policies are made by a single policy-making institution. (Part Three discusses these institutions separately, but they do not operate independently.) Environmental policy is a good example. Some presidents have used their influence with Congress to urge clean-air and clean-water policies. When Congress responds by passing legislation to clean up the environment, bureaucracies have to implement the new policies. Rules and regulations issued by the bureaucratic agencies fill fat volumes. In addition, every law passed and every rule made can be challenged in the courts. Courts make decisions about what the policies mean and whether they conflict with the Constitution. In policy-making, every political institution gets into the act.

Policies Have Impacts

Policy impacts are the effects policy has on people and society's problems. People who raise a policy issue usually want more than just a new law, a fancy proclamation, a bureaucratic rule, or a court judgment. They want a policy that works. Environmentalists want a policy that not only claims to prevent air pollution, but does so. Consumers want a policy that actually reduces inflation. Minority groups want a policy that not only promises them more equal treatment, but ensures it.

Having a policy implies a goal. Whether we want to reduce poverty, cut crime, clean the water, or hold down inflation, we have a goal in mind. Analysts of policy impacts ask how well the policy achieves it goal—and at what cost.

The analysis of policy impacts carries the political system back to its point of origin: people's interests, problems, and concerns. Translating people's desires into public policy is crucial to the workings of democracy.

George Bush addresses the nation during his 1989 inauguration. However influential, the president alone cannot create and implement public policy—all other branches of government play a role.

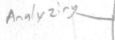
Analyzing

DEMOCRATIC GOVERNMENT

In 1848 the intellectual founders of modern communism, Karl Marx and Friedrich Engels, wrote *The Communist Manifesto,* one of the most famous political documents ever written. It began with these words: "A specter is haunting Europe. It is the specter of communism." Today one could write: "A specter is haunting Europe (and everywhere else). It is the specter of democracy."

In 1989 the Soviet Union held an election for the Supreme Soviet, its highest law-making body. It was the first free election in the USSR since the 1917 Russian Revolution, which first brought the Communists to power. Opposition candidates did not fare as well as candidates named by the Communist party, but hundreds of non-Communists were elected. To further ensure more competition in politics as part of his campaign for *glasnost* (openness), President Gorbachev, in 1990, recommended that the Communist party's right to govern be eliminated from the Soviet constitution.

These changes followed a series of stunning developments in Eastern Europe during 1989. After World War II the nations of Eastern Europe had Communist governments imposed on them by Soviet troops. Czechoslovakia, Poland, East Germany, Romania, Bulgaria, and Hungary were thus called the "Soviet Bloc."[9] Like falling dominoes, these Communist governments toppled, one after the other, in the fall of 1989. First, Solidarity, the Polish trade union that had struggled for democracy for a decade, was legally elected to power. Then the most dramatic event took place in East Germany, when the Berlin Wall was torn down. Since its construction in 1961, the wall had symbolized the division between Communist Eastern Europe and democratic Western Europe. Armed East German soldiers watched vigilantly from the guard towers, ready to shoot anyone who might try to defect to West Germany. Then, in 1989, Hungary and Czechoslovakia opened up their borders and a flood of East Germans made known their opinion of communism by taking a circular route through these neighboring countries to freedom in West Germany. Finally, the East German government realized that the only way to stem the tide was to open their border as well—including the Berlin Wall. In celebration, people from both sides danced on and around the wall; the day before they would have been shot for such actions. Only in Romania, the last of the dominoes to fall, was there violence. Communist dictator Nicolae Ceausescu ordered his security forces to fire on crowds of demonstrators, killing thousands. This did not stop the move toward democracy. Ceauşescu was forced to flee from the capital. He was captured soon afterwards, put on trial, and summarily executed.

Not just in Eastern Europe were the resounding demands for democracy heard. In May and June of 1989, a quarter-of-a-million Chinese students staged one of the world's largest protest demonstrations. They occupied Tiananmen Square in the heart of Beijing, China's capital. Under the watchful eye of a gigantic poster of Mao Tse-tung the students gathered, waited, and talked with hundreds of foreign reporters about the need for democracy in China. The Chinese government, however, sent soldiers and tanks into the square and crushed the protest. Governments around the world condemned the action.

In Mexico, Nicaragua, and other Latin-American countries, one-party or military regimes gave way to competitive party systems and civilian governments. Despite this global move towards democracy, not everyone defines democracy the way Americans do—or think they do.

Defining Democracy

The word *democracy* is overused. It takes its place among terms like *freedom, justice,* and *peace* as a word that has, seemingly, only positive connotations.

Democracy is now the sort of loaded word Humpty Dumpty spoke of in *Through the Looking Glass:* "When I make a word do a lot of work like that, I pay it extra." Today, says political scientist Giovanni Sartori, almost any political activity can be justified if done in the name of democracy.[10]

A statue of Vladimir Lenin, leader of Russia's Communist revolution, is hauled away in Bucharest, Romania, after the Communist government there was toppled. Like Romania's Communist regime, Lenin did not go down without a fight—it took two days to remove the statue. Communists remain strong in Romania and Bulgaria, where parties composed of former Communists were voted back into power in 1990.

[9]See, for example, Zbigniew Brzezinski, *The Grand Failure* (New York: Scribner's, 1989).

[10]Giovanni Sartori, *Theory of Democracy Revisited,* vol. 1 (Chatham, N.J.: Chatham House, 1987), 3.

Democracy was not always so popular. The writers of the U.S. Constitution had no fondness for democracy. Elbridge Gerry of Massachusetts, a delegate to the Constitutional Convention, said that "the evils we experience flow from the excesses of democracy." Another delegate, Roger Sherman, said that the people "should have as little to do as may be with the government." Only much later did Americans come to cherish democracy.

Today most Americans would probably say that democracy is "government by the people." This phase, of course, is part of Abraham Lincoln's famous definition of democracy from his Gettysburg Address: "government of the people, by the people, and for the people." The best that can be said of this definition is that it is brief; it is not, however, very informative. The late E.E. Schattschneider claimed that "We ought to get rid of confusing language such as 'government by the people.' To say that 230 [now 250] million Americans 'govern' does not shed much light on the role of people in the American political system."[11]

Schattschneider further remarked that

> no one has ever seen the American people because the human eye is not able to take in the view of four million square miles over which they are scattered. What would they look like if (ignoring all logistical difficulties) they could be brought together in one place? Standing shoulder to shoulder in military formation, they would occupy an area of about sixty-six square miles.
>
> The logistical problems of bringing 230 million bodies together is trivial, however, compared with the task of bringing about a meeting of 230 million minds. Merely to shake hands with that many people would take a century. How much discussion would it take to form a common opinion? A single round of five-minute speeches would require five thousand years. If only one percent of those present spoke, the assembly would be forced to listen to two million speeches. People would be born, grow old, and die while they waited for the assembly to make one decision.
>
> In other words, an all-American town meeting would be the largest, longest, and most boring and frustrating meeting imaginable. What could such a meeting produce? Total paralysis. What could it do? Nothing.[12]

If democracy means *government by the people,* Sartori asks, "Which people?" There are six ways, he says, to interpret *people*:

1. People meaning literally *everybody*
2. People meaning an undetermined large part, *a great many*
3. People meaning the *lower class* as opposed to some elite
4. People meaning an indivisible entity as an *organic whole*
5. People meaning an *absolute majority* (the majority has absolute power)
6. People meaning a *limited majority* (the majority has limited power)[13]

These are very different interpretations of *people.* No democracy permits government by literally everybody—infants, felons, and noncitizens residing in the country, for instance, have no voice in American government. What, then, do we mean when we say that democracy is *government by the people?* Here

[11]E.E. Schattschneider, *Two Hundred Million Americans in Search of a Government* (New York: Holt, Rinehart and Winston, 1969), 63.

[12]*Ibid.,* 60–61.

[13]Sartori, *Theory of Democracy Revisited,* vol. 1, 22.

Lech Walesa (third from left) presides over a Solidarity meeting. In 1989 the Polish people voiced their appreciation of the union's efforts on behalf of democracy by electing Solidarity-supported candidates to power in the country's first elections after decades of Communist rule. Greater democracy has brought a price, however; the new government has had to respond to increasing criticism as the country moves from a socialist to a market economy, bringing high inflation and unemployment.

is a basic definition, used throughout this book: **Democracy** *is a means of selecting policymakers and of organizing government so that policy represents and responds to the people's preferences.*

Traditional Democratic Theory

What we call **traditional democratic theory** rests upon several principles.[14] These principles specify how a democratic government makes its decisions. One contemporary democratic theorist, Robert Dahl, suggests that "an ideal democratic process would satisfy five criteria."[15] Here are his five cornerstones of an ideal democracy:

1. *Equality in voting.* The principle of one person, one vote is basic to democracy. When citizens have different preferences about policies or leaders, they need an equal chance to express their views.

2. *Effective participation.* Citizens must act on their opinions by participating in political institutions. Political participation need not be universal, but it must be representative. If high-income people vote at higher rates, the result is the same as if the wealthy had literally been given extra votes.

3. *Enlightened understanding.* A democratic society must be a marketplace of ideas. A free press and free speech are essential to civic understanding. When

[14]This conception of traditional democratic theory is derived from Robert A. Dahl, *Preface to Democratic Theory* (Chicago: University of Chicago Press, 1956), chaps. 2, 3; Joseph A. Schumpter, *Capitalism, Socialism, and Democracy* (New York: Harper & Row, 1942), chap. 21; Anthony Downs, *An Economic Theory of Democracy* (New York: Harper & Row, 1957), 22–24; and Carl Cohen, *Democracy* (Athens, Ga.: University of Georgia Press, 1971).

[15]Robert A. Dahl, *Dilemmas of Pluralist Democracy* (New Haven, Conn.: Yale University Press, 1983), 6.

Voting is a key prerequisite of democracy. Americans pride themselves on their democratic political system, but the Constitution's writers originally intended only wealthy white males to vote. The past two hundred years have seen a gradual move toward greater democracy in America.

one group monopolizes or distorts information, citizens cannot truly understand issues.

4. *Citizen control of the agenda.* Citizens should have the collective right to control government's policy agenda. If wealthy or powerful individuals or groups distort the agenda, then citizens cannot make government address the issues they feel are most important.

5. *Inclusion.* The government must include, and extend rights to, all those subject to its laws. Citizenship must be open to all within a nation if the nation is to call itself democratic.

Only by following these principles can a political system be called "democratic." In addition, democracies must practice **majority rule** and preserve **minority rights.** In a democracy, choosing among alternatives (whether policies or officeholders) means weighing the desires of the majority. Nothing is more fundamental to democratic theory than majority rule. Alexis de Tocqueville, the great French intellectual who traveled through American in the 1830s, wrote that "the very essence of democratic government consists in the absolute sovereignty of the majority. The power of the majority in America [is] not only preponderant, but irresistible."[16] Tocqueville, interestingly, was only describing, not approving. In fact, his observations about majority rule in America concluded with this harsh judgment: "This state of things is harmful in itself, and dangerous for the future." Today most Americans would disagree with Tocqueville. In addition, although Americans believe in majority rule, most also feel it is vital to protect minority rights such as freedom of speech in order that minorities might sometime become majorities through persuasion and reasoned argument.

In a society too large to make its decisions in open meetings, a few will have to carry on the affairs of the many. The relationship between the few leaders and the many followers is one of **representation.** The closer the correspondence between representatives and their electoral majority, the closer the approximation to democracy. Three contemporary theories presenting different views on how the representation process works are discussed in the following section.

Three Contemporary Theories of American Democracy

All bodies of knowledge use theories to simplify and explain a mass of detail. In physics, there are Newtonian theories, atomic theories, and theories of relativity. One way that the history of science can be written is in terms of the conflict of different theories over the centuries.

Theories of American politics are also plentiful. There are elite theories, rational-choice theories, cultural theories, and psychological theories, among others. Each focuses on a key element of politics, and each reaches a somewhat different conclusion. Theories of American democracy are essentially theories about who has power and influence. All, in one way or another, ask the question "Who really governs in our nation?"

[16]Alexis de Tocqueville, *Democracy in America* (New York: Mentor Books, 1956), 112–13.

Pluralism   One important theory of American democracy, **pluralist theory,** contends that many centers of influence vie for power and control. Groups compete with one another for control over public policy, with no one group or set of groups dominating. Pluralists' views of American government are thus generally positive. There are, they say, multiple access points to our government. Because power is dispersed among the various branches and levels of government, groups that lose in one arena can take their case to another. According to pluralists, bargaining and compromise are essential ingredients in our democracy. The result is a rough approximation of the public interest in public policy.

Elite and Class Theory   Critics of pluralism believe that this view paints too rosy a picture of American political life. By arguing that almost every group can get a piece of the pie, they say, pluralists miss the larger question of who owns the pie. **Elite and class theory** contends that our society—like all societies— is divided along class lines, and that an upper-class elite rules regardless of the formal niceties of governmental organization. Wealth—the holding of assets such as property, stocks, and bonds—is the basis of this power. In the United States about a quarter of the nation's wealth is held by just 1 percent of the population. Elite and class theorists believe that this 1 percent of Americans control most policy decisions because they can afford to finance election campaigns and control key institutions, such as large corporations. According to elite and class theory, a few powerful Americans do not merely influence policymakers, but *are* the policymakers.

Hyperpluralism   A third theory, **hyperpluralism,** offers a different critique of pluralism. Hyperpluralism is pluralism gone sour. Just as it is said that too many cooks spoil the broth, hyperpluralists claim that too many competing groups cripple government's ability to govern. Hyperpluralism states that many groups—not just the elite ones—are so strong that government is unable to act. These powerful groups divide the government and its authority. Hyperpluralist theory holds that government caves in to every conceivable interest and single-issue group. When politicians try to placate every group, the result is confusing, contradictory, and muddled policy—if politicians manage to make policy at all. As with elite and class theories, hyperpluralist theory suggests that the public interest is rarely translated into public policy.

Challenges to Democracy

Regardless of whether one accepts pluralism, elitism, or hyperpluralism, there are a number of continuing challenges to democracy. These challenges apply to American democracy as well as to the fledgling democracies around the world.

How Can the People Confront Complex Issues?   Traditional democratic theory holds that ordinary citizens have the good sense to reach political judgments and that government has the capacity to act upon those judgments. Today, however, we live in a society of experts, whose technical knowledge overshadows the knowledge of most people. What, after all, does the average citizen— however conscientious—know about chemical dumps, oil spills, Japanese com-

Actress Elizabeth Taylor speaks at an Artists Against AIDS rally in Washington, D.C. Interest groups often enlist well-known people to encourage average Americans to understand and act upon complex issues.

petition, fighting AIDS, fixing the savings and loan industry, and the thousands of other issues that government is faced with each year?

Alexander Hamilton, the architect of the American economic system and George Washington's secretary of the treasury, once said that every society is divided into *the few* and *the many*. He argued the few will rule; the many will be ruled. Years ago the power of the few—the elite—might have been based on property holdings. Today the elite are likely to be those who command knowledge, the experts. Even the most rigorous democratic theory does not demand that citizens be experts on everything, but as human knowledge has expanded it has become increasingly difficult to make knowledgeable decisions.

Are the People Doing Their Job?   When citizens do not seem to take their citizenship seriously, democracy's defenders worry. There is plenty of evidence that Americans know very little about who their leaders are, much less about their policy decisions. Patricia Hurley and Kim Hill found that only 17 percent of the population knew how their representative in the House of Representatives voted on *any* issue.[17] People in the United States do not take full advantage of their opportunities to shape government or select its leaders. Barely half of all eligible adults come out to the polls for presidential elections. These facts worry many democratic thinkers today.

Is American Democracy Too Dependent on Money?   Many political observers worry about the close connection between money and politics, especially in congressional elections. Political scientist Benjamin Ginsberg studied the effects of election campaign donations to members of Congress on their voting

[17]Patricia Hurley and Kim Q. Hill, "The Prospects for Issue Voting in Contemporary Congressional Elections," *American Politics Quarterly* 8 (October 1980): 446.

behavior on major bills. He concluded that "the greater the amounts of contribution received from an interest group by congressional representatives, the more representatives' roll call support for that interest tends to change."[18] When democracy confronts the might of money, the gap between democratic theory and reality widens further. Free elections are a cornerstone of democracy. When elections are bought, manipulated, sold, or sullied, democracy suffers.

Some Key Questions about Democracy

Throughout *Government in America* you will be asked to assess American democracy. The chapters that follow will acquaint you with the history of American democracy and ask important questions about the current state of democracy in the United States.

For example, the next chapter will show that the U.S. Constitution was not originally designed to promote democracy, but has slowly evolved to its current form. Much of America's move toward greater democracy has centered around the extension of civil liberties and civil rights (which Chapters 4 and 5 will review). Probably the most important civil right is the right to vote. Upcoming chapters will examine voting behavior and elections and ask the following questions about how people's opinions are formed and to what extent they are expressed via elections:

- Are people knowledgeable about matters of public policy?
- Do they apply what knowledge they have to their voting choices?
- Are American elections designed to facilitate public participation?

These are the sorts of questions you will need to ask about the people's input into government.

Linkage institutions, such as interest groups, political parties, and the media, help translate input from the public into output from the policymakers. When you explore these institutions you will consider the extent to which they either help or hinder democracy.

- Does the interest group system allow for all points of view to be heard, or are there significant biases that advantage particular groups?
- Do political parties provide voters with clear choices, or do they obscure their stands on issues in order to get as many votes as possible?
- If there are choices, does the media help citizens understand them?

It is up to public officials to actually make the policy choices, since American government is a *representative* rather than a pure democracy. For democracy to work well, elected officials should be responsive to public opinion.

- Is the Congress representative of American society, and is it well organized to react to changing times?
- Does the president look after the general welfare, or has the office become too powerful in recent years?

[18]Benjamin Ginsberg, *The Consequences of Consent: Elections, Citizen Control, and Popular Acquiescence* (Reading, Mass.: Addison-Wesley, 1981), 232.

These are some of the crucial questions you will address in discussing the executive and legislative branches of government. In addition, the way our nonelected institutions—the bureaucracy and the courts—function is also crucial to evaluating how well American democracy works. These institutions are designed to implement and interpret the law, but bureaucrats and judges often cannot avoid making public policy as well. When they do so, are they violating democratic principles, as neither institution can be held accountable, at the ballot box, for policy decisions?

All of these questions concerning democracy in America have more than one answer. A goal of *Government in America* is to familiarize you with the different ways to approach, and answer, these questions. One way to approach all of the preceding questions is to address one of the most important questions facing modern American democracy: Is government too big, too small, or just about the right size?

THE SIZE OF GOVERNMENT IN AMERICA

Some political leaders and voters think that American government is so large, so intrusive into the affairs of individual citizens and businesses, and so costly that it does more harm than good. Former President Ronald Reagan was one of the staunchest proponents of a small government. He did much to make the size of government an important issue.

Others are defenders of a large and active government, arguing that it is the only means of achieving important goals in American society. How else, they ask, can we ensure that everyone has enough to eat, clean water to drink, adequate health care, and affordable housing? How else can we ensure that the disadvantaged are given opportunities for education and jobs, and are not discriminated against?

To understand the dimensions of this debate, it is important to first get some sense of just how big American government is.

How Big Is American Government?

In terms of dollars spent, government in America is vast. Altogether, our governments—national, state, and local—spend about one out of every three dollars of our **gross national product,** the total value of all goods and services produced annually by the United States. In 1990 expenditures for all American governments amounted to about two *trillion* dollars.

Government not only spends large sums of money, but also employs large numbers of people. About eighteen million Americans work for one of our governments, mostly at the state and local level—teachers to teach America's children, police officers to deal with growing crime problems, university professors to teach college students, and so on.

Consider some facts about the size of our national government:

- It spends more than $1.2 trillion annually (printed as a number, that's $1,200,000,000,000 a year).
- It employs 5 million people.
- It owns one-third of the land in the United States.
- It occupies 2.6 billion square feet of office space, more than four times the office space located in the nation's ten largest cities.
- It owns and operates 437,000 nonmilitary vehicles.[19]

These figures are from the national government alone. They do not include some staggering figures from our state and local governments, which employ, for example, almost three times as many people as the national government. There are, at latest count, 83,237 governments in America.

If the American national government spends almost $1.2 trillion a year, how does it spend it? Most of the money goes to payments to individuals or to state and local governments. National defense takes about one quarter of the federal budget, a much smaller percentage than it did three decades ago. Social Security consumes more than one-fifth of the budget. Medicare is another a big-ticket item, requiring nearly $100 billion a year. State and local governments also get important parts of the federal government's budget. The federal government helps fund highway construction, airport construction, police departments, school districts, and other state and local functions. Americans often complain about the high cost of government, but most Americans approve of what government does with its money. There is little support to cut spending on most government programs.

[19] E.S. Savas, *Privatization: The Key to Better Government* (Chatham, N.J.: Chatham House, 1987), 13.

When expenditures grow, tax revenues must grow to pay the additional costs. When taxes do not grow as fast as spending, a budget deficit results. Budget deficits have occurred for decades in the United States. In the past few years, the national government has typically fallen short of paying its bills by $100–150 billion a year—about 10 percent of federal expenditures (these figures, critics charge, are based on some fiddling with the budget books; the actual deficit is much larger). Each year's deficit is piled onto the previous deficits, and the entire sum equals the national debt, all the money owed by the national government. Today, the national debt is about $3 trillion.

The federal government is more active than ever before in peacetime. Whatever the national problem—pollution, AIDS, earthquake relief, homelessness, hunger, sexism—many people expect Congress to solve the problem with legislation.

Thus American government certainly is large in terms of dollars spent, persons employed, and laws passed. Our concern, however, is less about the absolute size of government and more about whether government is the size we want it to be.

How Big Is Too Big? The Great Debate

On February 18, 1981, Ronald Reagan went before a joint session of Congress for the first time to announce what he called a "Program for Economic Recovery." President Reagan's speech outlined his most important goals. Government, he said, was too fat. Reagan promised to trim the government (except in the area of national defense) every day of his presidency.[20]

Abroad, Britain's Prime Minister Margaret Thatcher shared Reagan's view of government. Both she and President Reagan spoke fondly of the *free market.* If the market worked the way it should, Reagan and Thatcher maintained, economic growth would result, with ample jobs for workers and large profits for owners. Government, they claimed, stifled growth with high taxes and countless regulations. People had less incentive to work or invest, they said, because government taxed too much of their profits and incomes. Both the president and the prime minister called for more *privatization,* turning over government functions to the private sector.[21] Even behind the Iron Curtain, people were talking about the virtues of the market. President Gorbachev experimented with marketlike mechanisms to encourage economic growth in the Soviet Union. Rigid production quotas set in far-away Moscow were replaced by locally determined production goals. In almost every country, it seemed, the free market was favored while *big government* was on the run.

In principle, the majority of the American public agreed with Reagan that government was too big. In practice, however, they continued to favor more spending for virtually every domestic program (such as health care, education, and aid to big cities). A study by political scientists Thomas Ferguson and Joel Rogers found that Americans favored, if anything, an increase in governmental activity during the 1980s. Although some critics complained that government

Like Ronald Reagan and George Bush, British Prime Minister Margaret Thatcher is a strong advocate of limited government.

[20]On Reagan's efforts to revolutionize the American government and its budgets, see David Stockman, *The Triumph of Politics* (New York: Harper & Row, 1986); and Donald T. Regan, *For the Record* (San Diego: Harcourt Brace Jovanovich, 1988).

[21]See Savas, *Privatization.*

overregulated the American economy, most Americans believed there was too little, rather than too much governmental regulation.[22] It should not be surprising to learn that, measured by expenditures, annual deficits, and number of employees, the size of the national government actually grew during the Reagan years.

Liberals and Conservatives   Of all the issues that divide liberals and conservatives, probably the most important is their differing views on the appropriate size of government. In the United States, **liberals** support a more active role for government (in most spheres), together with higher spending and more regulation. In general, liberals favor

- More governmental regulation of the economy to promote such goals as worker safety, consumer protection, and a pollution-free environment.
- More policies to help disadvantaged groups, including policies to ensure and expand opportunities for poor people, minorities, and women.
- More policies to redistribute income, through taxation, from those with more to those with less.

Conservatives on the other hand, favor

- Fewer governmental regulations and a greater reliance on the market to provide such things as jobs, consumer protection, and pollution control.
- Fewer governmental policies in the name of disadvantaged groups, who conservatives believe will benefit most from a strong economy free from governmental intervention.
- Fewer tax laws that discourage business growth by establishing high rates for capital investment.

Liberals do not always favor governmental action, and conservatives do not always oppose it, however. Conservatives, for example, typically favor using the power of government to restrict or prohibit abortions and to organize prayers in public schools, while liberals generally oppose such policies. Conservatives are less likely to support restrictions on individual freedom in the economic sphere, while liberals usually oppose governmental interference with individual freedom in noneconomic matters.

A Comparative Perspective   A useful way to think about political issues, such as the size of government, is to compare the United States with other countries, especially other democracies with developed economies. Throughout *Government in America,* features entitled "America in Perspective" provide an opportunity to understand our country's government better by comparing the United States with other nations.

For example, it is possible to compare the size of the national defense sector in various countries (see "America in Perspective: The Defense Sectors of Democratic Nations with Developed Economies"). Compared with other countries, the United States devotes a large percentage of its people and resources to national defense. Only a few democratic nations have a higher share of the

[22]Thomas Ferguson and Joel Rogers, *Right Turn* (New York: Hill & Wang, 1986).

The Defense Sectors of Democratic Nations with Developed Economies

The United States commits a larger share of its resources to national defense than do most other democracies with developed economies. Only a few such nations have a larger share of their population in uniform, and only Israel and Greece devote a larger share of their economic resources to defense.

COUNTRY	MILITARY PERSONNEL (per 1,000 citizens)	MILITARY SPENDING (% of GNP[a])
Israel	47.6	13.9
Greece	20.8	7.2
United States	**9.6**	**6.6**
United Kingdom	5.9	5.3
France	10.2	4.1
Portugal	9.9	3.3
Norway	9.9	3.2
West Germany	8.1	3.2
Netherlands	7.1	3.1
Sweden	8.2	3.0
Belgium	10.9	3.0
Australia	4.5	2.9
Canada	3.3	2.3
Denmark	5.7	2.3
Switzerland	3.8	2.2
Spain	10.6	2.1
New Zealand	3.9	2.0
Austria	5.3	1.3
Japan	2.0	1.0

[a]Gross National Product.

Source: Thomas R. Dye and Harmon Ziegler, "Socialism and Militarism," *PS* 22 (December 1989), 803–806.

population in uniform, and only Israel and Greece devote more of their economic resources to the military.

Does this comparatively large defense sector mean that the American government is large in general? Many would argue that it is not, that the United States, when compared with other democracies, actually has a small government. Chapter 14 will show that the tax burden on Americans is small compared to other democratic nations, as is the percentage of the gross national product spent by all levels of government.

Further, most Western nations (Europe and North America) have a system of national health insurance, which provides most health care; the United States does not. The airlines in virtually every nation except America are owned by the national government, as are the telephone companies and most television stations. Governments have built much of the housing in most Western nations, compared to only a small fraction of the housing in America. Thus, outside the sphere of national defense, the government of the United States actually does less—is small—compared to the governments of similar countries.

Questions about the Size of Government

Debate over the role and size of government is central to contemporary American politics, and it is a theme this text will examine in each chapter that follows. The goal is not to determine for you whether the national government is too large or too small. Instead, you will explore the implications of the way politics, institutions, and policy work in America for the size of government. By raising questions such as those in the next few paragraphs, you can come up with your own conclusions about the appropriate role of government in America.

Part One of *Government in America* examines the consitutional foundations of American government. A concern with the proper size of government leads to a series of questions regarding the consitutional structure of American politics, including

- What role did Constitution's authors foresee for the federal government?
- Does the Constitution favor big government, or is it neutral on this issue?
- Why did the functions of government increase, and why did they increase most at the national rather than at the state level?
- Has bigger, more active government constrained freedom—as some feared?
- Or, does the increased role of government serve to protect civil liberties and civil rights?

Part Two focuses on those making demands upon government, including the public, political parties, interest groups, and the media. Here you will seek answers to questions such as

- Does the public favor a large government?
- Do competing political parties predispose the government to provide more public services?
- Do elections help control the size of government, or do they legitimize an increasing role for the public sector?
- Are pressures from interest groups necessarily translated into more governmental regulations, bigger budgets, and the like?
- Has media coverage of government enhanced government's status and growth, or has the media been an instrument for controlling government?

Governmental institutions themselves, obviously, deserve close examination. Part Three discusses these institutions and asks

- Has the presidency been a driving force behind increasing the size and power of government (and thus of the president)?
- Can the president control a government the size of ours?
  Is Congress, because subject to constant elections, predisposed toward big government?
- Is Congress too responsive to the demands of the public and organized interests?

The nonelected branches of government, which are also discussed in Part Three, are especially interesting when considering the issue of the size of government. For instance:

- Are the federal courts too active in policy making, intruding on the authority and responsibility of other branches and levels of government?
- Is the bureaucracy too acquisitive, constantly seeking to expand its size, budgets, and authority, or is it simply a reflection of the desires of elected officials?
- Is the bureaucracy too large, and thus a wasteful menace to efficient and fair implementation of public policies, or is it too small to carry out the responsibilities assigned to it?

The next nineteen chapters will search for answers to these and many other questions regarding the size of government. You will, undoubtedly, add a few questions of your own as you seek to resolve the issue of the proper size of government.

ETHICS AND POLITICS:
A CONTRADICTION IN TERMS?

Government is important because it deals with our deepest values. Here are a few ways governmental decisions touch some of our most profound concerns:

- Government is the only arm of our society that can legally take a life through the death penalty.
- Government, through its courts or, more recently, its hospital regulatory policies, is increasingly asked to settle questions about when life begins and ends.
- Government certifies, or declines to approve, the drugs used to fight AIDS and other diseases.
- Government regulates surrogate motherhood—when a woman, in effect, contracts with someone else to bear a child—through many state legislatures.

Government tells us whether we can have an abortion, whether we have to wear a motorcycle helmet, and even when it is acceptable to "pull the plug" on a dying patient in a hospital. Government touches our most fundamental beliefs and morals.

Perhaps more than any other country, politics in America have been shaped by ethical debates. It was the moral impropriety of taxation without representation that, in part, led the colonists to rebel against the King of England and form the United States. The greatest crisis in the nation's history—the Civil War—was spurred by fundamental ethical issues posed by the practice of slavery. Thus Americans have long been accustomed to thinking about politics not solely in terms of "who gets what, when, and how," but also in terms of right and wrong. **Political ethics** are matters of right and wrong with respect to government. Discussions of political ethics involve questions about what is the right policy to pursue, as well as about who has the integrity to be entrusted with

An AIDS patient receives care in a hospice. The government's role in AIDS education and prevention is one of today's most volatile ethical issues. The Federal Food and Drug Administration, for example, has been roundly criticized for not moving quickly to test and approve drugs used to treat AIDS.

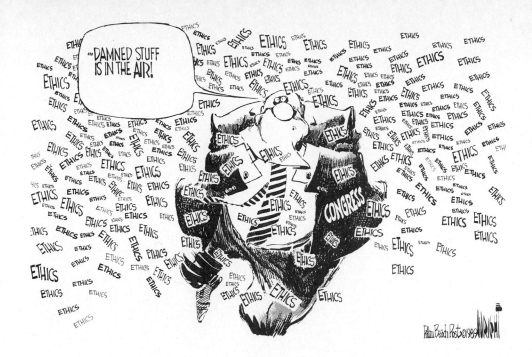

governmental power. Indeed, recent years have seen a number of prominent politicians fall from power not for what they stood for, but for how they conducted their personal affairs.

These days, staggering proportions of Americans believe that most or all politicians are corrupt, that government serves the interest of the few, and that "fat cats"—the wealthy and powerful—dominate our government. *Politician* is a word that often provokes strongly negative feelings. In "The People Speak: Rating Ethical Standards" ("The People Speak" is another regular feature of *Government in America*) you can see that politicians are not rated highly by the public in terms of honesty and ethical standards.

Given the rash of politicians whose careers have recently been ended by ethical scandals, such survey findings should not be surprising. Thomas Jefferson once said that "when a man assumes a public trust, he should consider himself public property."[23] During the 1988 presidential election campaign, a series of candidates fell victim to "the character issue." In May of 1987 former Senator Gary Hart was well in the lead for the Democratic nomination. Then he self-destructed. Chased by rumors of womanizing, Hart dared reporters to follow him around for a weekend. "You'll find it very dull," he said. Reporters from the *Miami Herald* took up the challenge by staking out his townhouse, and they landed the story of the year. They observed Hart, a married man, staying overnight with a Miami model, Donna Rice. Revelation after revelation, confession after confession followed. Next, Senator Joseph Biden dropped out of the race when one of his speeches was discovered to be a copy of someone else's. Fundamentalist preacher Pat Robertson, a Republican candidate, was haunted by charges that the birth of his first child occurred just four months after his

---

[23]Cited in Ronald D. Elving, "Candidates, the Need to Know and the Press," *PS* 21 (Spring 1988): 257.

How would you rate the honesty and ethical standards of people in these different fields—very high, high, average, low, or very low?

	Very high or high	Average	Low, or very low
Druggists, pharmacists	66%	29%	3%
Clergy	60	28	8
College teachers	54	35	6
Medical doctors	53	38	7
Dentists	51	39	7
Engineers	48	41	4
Police officers	47	39	11
Bankers	26	55	15
Funeral directors	24	50	18
Journalists	23	49	22
TV reporters, commentators	22	53	22
Newspaper reporters	22	53	22
Building contractors	22	53	20
U.S. senators	19	52	24
Lawyers	18	45	33
Business executives	16	54	25
Representatives to U.S. House	16	52	27
Local officeholders	14	50	31
Labor union leaders	14	35	45
Real estate agents	13	47	34
Stockbrokers	13	50	24
State officeholders	11	53	31
Insurance salespeople	10	41	45
Advertising practitioners	7	40	46
Car salespeople	6	29	63

Americans do not have much confidence in the ethical standards of elected officials. Only 19 percent rate United States senators as having "very high" or "high" ethical standards, and only 16 percent feel that way about members of the House. People in many other occupations, from druggists and clergy to funeral directors and building contractors, are seen as being more ethical.

Source: The question as worded is taken directly from *The Gallup Report,* December 1988, 3 (Poll date: September 1988).

marriage. The 1988 election campaign became, one political scientist remarked, a "sin-of-the-week" exposé by aggressive journalists.[24]

By 1989 the drama shifted to Congress. The Speaker of the House of Representatives, Jim Wright of Texas, became the first Speaker to resign in the face of a scandal. Wright's problems centered on his use of extraordinarily high book royalties to get around a congressional limit on outside income through speeches. Tony Coelho, the Democratic majority whip (the third most important majority-party post in the House of Representatives), resigned from Congress after his shady financial dealings with a junk bond dealer became known. Congressman Barney Frank from Massachusetts, an acknowledged homosexual, con-

[24]Bruce Buchanan, "Sizing Up the Candidates," *PS* 21 (Spring 1988): 251.

BY MEYER FOR THE SAN FRANCISCO CHRONICLE

fessed to paying a young man from an "escort service" out of his personal funds, to work for him. A Republican member of Congress, Donald Lukens, was convicted of having sex with a minor. All told, forty-seven members of Congress had some sort of ethics charges brought against them in 1989.[25]

It is often said that all is fair in love and war, but what about in political campaigning? Every campaign has charges of mudslinging, but the 1988 presidential campaign was widely considered one of the dirtiest in years. Lee Atwater, George Bush's campaign manager, said at the outset that he would make Willie Horton a household name, and he succeeded. Horton was an inmate in the Massachusetts state prison when Michael Dukakis was the state's governor. Despite being ineligible for parole, Horton was released one weekend on a prison furlough, a short leave of absence. When he was out on furlough, Horton raped a woman and beat her fiancé. Bush, in commercials and speeches, attacked Dukakis for permitting a program that would give Willie Horton freedom, even for a weekend. Apparently, said Bush's critics, it didn't matter to Atwater that the program was not sponsored by Dukakis; that Dukakis personally had nothing to do with the case; and that the issue stirred up feelings of racism because Horton was black and he had raped a white woman.

In every campaign political candidates have to ask themselves "What is fair?" Equally important, voters have to ask themselves whether a candidate's campaign

[25]William Schneider, "From an Icon to a Sleaze: Life and Death in the Polls," *Los Angeles Times,* December 21, 1989, M1.

goes so far beyond the realm of fairness that it disqualifies the candidate from office. Once in office, a politician is constantly confronted with ethical issues and dilemmas surrounding public policy. Setting policy involves not only issues of how much a policy costs, whether it will work, and whether it will solve the problem—it also involves fundamental questions of right and wrong.

Take medical care as an example. The United States now spends 12 percent of its gross national product on health care, and the cost of medical technology is skyrocketing. Because medical care is universally desirable, Americans do not believe that it is something that should be rationed. Nonetheless, California's Alameda County, which includes Oakland, and the State of Oregon have tried to do so. Seeing that federal and state money would not be enough to help pay increasing health care costs, Alameda County hired a professional ethicist to advise a committee on what services should be provided, in what priority, to the poor. Oregon decided in 1987 that it would not pay for organ transplants for the poor. More and more, policy analysts and philosophers are warning that our society will need to ration medical care.[26] Eventually local governments across the country may have to decide how much to spend to save a life. (See "A Question of Ethics: How Much Should Government Do to Prolong a Life?") Throughout *Government in America,* features entitled "A Question of Ethics" will challenge you to weigh the pros and cons of a significant ethical problem and decide how you would resolve the issue.

[26]Robert Blank, *Rationing Medicine* (New York: Columbia University, 1988).

The government's response to rising health care costs is another sensitive ethical issue. Because the government pays for a large portion of Americans' medical expenses, governmental decisions have a profound effect on the health care system. Many hospitals, especially those in rural or poor areas, were forced to close during the 1980s when the government limited Medicare funding.

How Much Should Government Do to Prolong a Life?

Former Governor Richard Lamm of Colorado once argued that people have a "duty to die." Many thought this a callous opinion. At the same time, almost everyone believes that there is some point beyond which expenditures to prolong life are not worth the cost. Medical ethicist Daniel Callahan has argued that there is a "natural life span" and that it is unwise ethically and legally to pour money into keeping people alive beyond this time. Because most of us die within the orbit of public policy (that is, in a governmentally regulated institution), in a nation in which more than 40 percent of all medical costs are public, the issue of prolonging life cannot avoid the public policy agenda.

Medicine today is dependent on and driven by technology; that is one reason medical costs are increasing so rapidly. A question that some ask, though, is this: "Can we as a nation afford to pay increasingly higher prices for each new technology that promises to extend the life of a dying patient by a few months or years?"

Take, for example, the issue of heart transplants. Roger W. Evans, a medical sociologist, argues that we should extend protection of Medicare to include heart transplants. Each year, an estimated 14,100 persons between the ages of 10 and 54 who might be helped by a heart transplant die. On the one hand, the costs of such a procedure are high; about $100,000 per operation. On the other hand, dying is also expensive—more than three-quarters of funds spent on Medicare patients who die are spent in their last six months of life.

Consider these questions:

1. Should the federal government include heart transplants in normal Medicare expenditures?
2. If not, what should public policy be toward people needing or wanting heart transplants?
3. If you think heart transplants should be covered by Medicare, how should those expenditures be allocated? On a first come, first served basis? Or should some formula be worked out to give priorities? If so, what would such a formula be like?

Sources: On the problem of death and dying as matters of social and public policy, see Daniel Callahan, *Setting Limits: Medical Goals in an Aging Society* (New York: Simon & Schuster, 1987); and Roger W. Evans, "The Heart Transplant Dilemma," *Issues in Science and Technology* (Spring 1986): 91–101. The quotation on "Can we as a nation . . . " is from the prologue to Evans's article, page 91.

SUMMARY

This first chapter serves several important purposes. First, it introduces you to the meaning of *government* itself. Government is those institutions that make authoritative public policies for society as a whole. In the United States there are four key institutions that make policy at the national level: Congress, the president, the courts, and the bureaucracy. *Politics* is, very simply, *who gets what, when, and how.* People engage in politics for a variety of reasons, and all their activities in politics are collectively called *political participation.* The end product of government and politics is *public policy.* Public policy includes all of the decisions and nondecisions by government.

The first question central to governing is *How should we be governed?* Americans are fond of calling their government democratic. Democratic government includes, above all else, a commitment to *majority rule* and *minority rights.* This text will help you evaluate the way American government works

A sight that most Americans take for granted—the peaceful exchange of power between elected officials—is a rarity in many countries. Here, Republican Ronald Reagan is sworn in by Chief Justice Warren Burger while Democrat Jimmy Carter watches.

against the standards of democracy and continually inquire as to who holds power and who influences the policies adopted by government.

The second fundamental question regarding governing is *What should government do?* One of the most important issues about government in America has to do with the size of government. One recent president, Ronald Reagan, talked often about the evils of big government. Others see the national government as rather small in comparison to the functions it performs and the size of governments in other democratic nations. *Government in America* will explore the effects of the workings of American government upon what government ends up doing.

Government deals with many of our deepest values. Ethical issues are among the most controversial in American political life. This text will constantly ask questions about ethics, regarding both personal conduct and public policy, on the premise that *political ethics* is not—or should not be—a contradiction in terms.

KEY TERMS

power
government
public goods
politics
political participation
single-issue groups
policy agenda
public policy
political system

political issue
linkage institutions
policy impacts
democracy
traditional democratic
   theory
majority rule
minority rights
representation

pluralist theory
elite and class theory
hyperpluralism
gross national product
liberals
conservatives
political ethics

FOR FURTHER READING

Blank, Robert. *Rationing Medicine*. New York: Columbia University, 1988. Blank discusses some sensitive ethical issues about health policy.

Bowman, James S., and Frederick A. Elliston, eds. *Ethics, Government, and Public Policy*. New York: Greenwood Press, 1988. A reference guide to issues of ethics and government.

Brzezinski, Zbigniew. *The Grand Failure*. New York: Scribner's, 1989. An explanation for the decline of the Soviet empire.

Dahl, Robert. *Democracy and Its Critics*. New Haven: Yale University Press, 1989. Dahl is one of the world's most articulate thinkers about democracy.

Kingdon, John. *Agendas, Alternatives, and Public Policies*. Boston: Little, Brown, 1984. One of the first efforts by a political scientist to examine the political agenda.

Savas, E.S. *Privatization: The Key to Better Government*. Chatham, N.J.: Chatham House, 1987. His subtitle calls privatization the key to better government; liberals might not agree.

Shilts, Randy. *And the Band Played On: Politics, People, and the AIDS Epidemic*. New York: Penguin Books, 1987. A sad but eye-opening study of the politics surrounding the AIDS epidemic.

Smith, Hedrick. *The Power Game: How Washington Works*. New York: Ballantine, 1988. A good introduction to the political life of our nation's capital.

Stanley, Harold W., and Richard G. Niemi. *Vital Statistics on American Politics,* 2nd ed. Washington, D.C.: Congressional Quarterly, 1990. Useful data on government, politics, and policy in the United States.

PART ONE

CONSTITUTIONAL FOUNDATIONS

The Making of a Capital City

Unlike other great national capitals such as London, Paris, Rome, or Tokyo, Washington was designed to be a capital city. The new nation had a novel idea for its capital: Why not build one from scratch to suit the specific needs of the new government? Washington was to be unlike any other capital the world had ever known. As James Sterling Young writes, it was designed to be "the company town of the national government—owned by the government, occupied by the government, conceived and created by the government to serve exclusively the purposes of government, and good for nothing else but government."[1] In its early years the new capital's unimpressive appearance matched that of the relatively modest federal government that it housed. As the size and scope of the government have grown, though, so has the capital city. This essay—the first of four in this book about Washington—traces its development from an architect's drawing board to the world's most politically important city.

The U.S. Constitution empowered the Congress to acquire a seat for the new federal government. Many sites were considered, but ultimately President Washington's preference for the rolling hills around the Potomac River prevailed. The states of Maryland and Virginia ceded a total of ten square miles along the river (including the existing port cities of

[1]James Sterling Young, *The Washington Community, 1800–1828* (New York: Harcourt Brace Jovanovich, 1966), xi–xii.

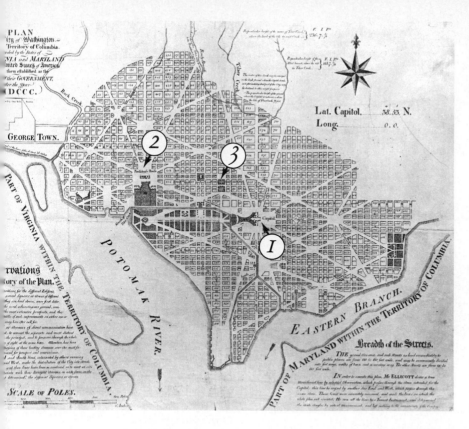

L'Enfant's original plan of Washington clearly shows the city's wide diagonal avenues crisscrossing a rectangular street pattern. Note also how L'Enfant planned to connect the Capitol (1) to the President's House (2) by Pennsylvania Avenue, while the Supreme Court building (3) was to be located between, but unconnected to, the others.

Georgetown and Alexandria), which was then titled the District of Columbia (D.C.). Within this area was to be created the new capital city later named after George Washington; hence, the official title of Washington, D.C.

President Washington personally supervised many aspects of the building of the new capital, including such mundane details as the nature of the street railings. Perhaps his most important decision was choosing a chief architect for the project—Pierre-Charles L'Enfant, a French architect who had served as an officer in the American Revolutionary War. L'Enfant's plan stressed impressive wide diagonal avenues along a rectangular network of streets. Congress, thought to be at the heart of the new government, was placed at the city's central point. Reflecting the constitutional separation of powers, the President's house was placed at some considerable distance from the Congress. However, to signify the interdependence of the two branches, these two structures were to be directly connected by Pennsylvania Avenue. The third branch of American government, the Supreme Court, was placed between the other two branches, unconnected and presumably uninfluenced by either.

The plan was a splendid and ambitious one—too much so for the tastes of some who thought it overly majestic for a nation that had rejected monarchial rule. But Washington backed up L'Enfant and the plan went forward. L'Enfant's arrogance offended many, though. City Commissioner Daniel Carroll was particularly upset when his cousin's house was demolished because it obstructed the site of one of L'Enfant's grandiose vistas. This was the last straw. Washington reluctantly dismissed the brilliant architect after just ten months on the job. Without L'Enfant's brief contribution, though, many feel that the capital would not possess its current splendor and spaciousness.

In the early years of Washington, the city was considered anything but splendid and its spaciousness was the butt of constant jokes. It was said that the wide avenues led from nowhere to nowhere else. Compared to today's sprawling metropolis, early Washington was wild in a rural sense. Cattle grazed on the Mall, snakes slithered through unfinished houses, and hogs scavanged through trash heaps. Amenities were few—the roads were unpaved, lacking both sidewalks and street lamps. When it rained, Washington became a quagmire; when the weather was dry, it became a dust bowl. In 1800 the government arrived to find a collection of four hundred shanties clustered around the unfinished congressional building and

This 1801 engraving of Georgetown and the Federal City suggests why George Washington chose these rolling hills as a site for the new capital.

the President's house, which were separated by a vast uncleared swamp. Thus, while many were willing to come to the new capital, most soon found themselves anxious to leave. The natural beauty of the area was small consolation to the well-heeled gentlemen politicians of the day.

Because of the lack of skilled labor, progress in building the city was slow even after the federal government arrived. It wasn't until 1810 that the Capitol's two wings were completed and joined by a wooden passageway. By then the exterior of the White House still hadn't been finished, but at least a stairway to the second floor had finally been built—eight years after John Adams moved into the "mansion." Then, just as Washington was beginning to show some promise, the War of 1812 brought ruin upon the city. On the night of August 24, 1814, a British

military unit entered the city and set fire to virtually all government buildings—including the Capitol and the White House. Fortunately, total de-

struction was averted when a thunderstorm quenched the fires later that night.

After the British burned the Capitol, Congress met for one session in Blodget's Hotel at Seventh and E Streets, NW. During this time the House of Representatives came within nine votes of moving out of Washington to Philadelphia, which many believed to be a safer location. Others, as much as they longed for a more cosmopolitan capital, were determined not to let it be said that the British had driven them out. They were aided by the city's bankers, who offered to finance the reconstruction. Barely five years after the British had marched through town, Washington was restored to its prewar state.

Of course the building did not stop with the reconstruction work. Within the next thirty years, Washington grew tremendously. So rapid was the growth that the older cities within the District of Columbia—Alexandria and Georgetown—felt threatened by the federal establish-

The British invasion of 1814 left Washington in ruins. The Patent Office was the only government building spared.

This painting of Washington in 1852 reveals the rapid growth of the capital city after the 1814 British invasion.

ment and sought to be returned to the control of Virginia and Maryland, respectively. Alexandria was successful because the physical barrier of the Potomac River made it seem less useful to Congress. The official act of Congress in 1846 retroceding the land stated that "experience hath shown that the portion of the District of Columbia ceded to the United States by the State of Virginia has not been, nor is ever likely to be useful."[2] It is hard to imagine how they could have been more shortsighted. With the onset of three great wars (the Civil War, World War I, and World War II) over the next hundred years, the federal government would expand to the point where it deeply regretted giving up this territory.

First, the war between the states transformed the sleepy capital from an unkempt country town into a true nineteenth-century city. When Lincoln was inaugurated in 1861, census figures showed there were eighteen hundred slaves in Washington. One slave pen, an infamous yellow house on Seventh Street, stood in full view of the Capitol building. Not surpris-

ingly, one of the first acts of the new Republican majority in Congress elected on Lincoln's coattails was to abolish slavery in the District of Columbia.

In the White House, President Lincoln, fearful of the proximity of southern military forces, ordered massive numbers of federal troops to protect the capital. Temporary barracks were set up in the Mall and at Observatory Hill, areas which L'Enfant had specifically planned for this purpose. To feed the soldiers, the basement of the Capitol building became an army bakery while the

Washington Monument grounds served as a cattle pasture providing meat for slaughter. At first, the presence of the soldiers gave the capital a dose of excitement as they drilled and paraded through the city. Twenty thousand soldiers, led by the exotic Zouaves dressed in Algerian fashion, marched the length of Pennsylvania Avenue on July 4th, 1861. It was the first grand army that Washington had ever seen, but it was not to be the last.

By late 1862, as war casualties rose, Washington was turned into an immense hospital for the Army of the Potomac. Churches, schools, hotels, warehouses, and government buildings alike were used by the military to care for the wounded. Even the Capitol building became an infirmary—two thousand cots were

At Lincoln's first inauguration in 1861, the federal government's authority was still unproven; the Civil War established its power.

[2]Howard B. Furer, ed., *Washington: A Chronological and Documentary History* (Dobbs Ferry, N.Y.: Oceana, 1975), 79.

placed in the halls and corridors of the House and Senate as well as in the Rotunda.

The war also provided the impetus necessaray to bring about municipal improvement in Washington. The paving and lighting of city streets and the addition of sewers can be largely attributed to the government's concern with meeting the needs of the military. As the need for buildings increased during the war, Washington attracted many investors interested in public services and real estate. Even after the military personnel departed, the population of Washington was still 50 percent above the prewar level. Most importantly, the triumph of the Union over states' rights strengthened the national government, and hence its capital. No longer was Washington just the seat where representatives from a loose confederation of states met—it was the power center for a full-fledged national government with clear authority.

The next great expansion of the city and the federal government oc-

This splendid 1861 march down Pennsylvania Avenue soon gave way to the realities of war, as Washington became a vast army hospital.

curred during World War I. To fight this war the government utilized the corporate form of organization for the first time on a large scale, establishing many agencies independent of the cabinet departments. In particular, the War Industries Board consolidated factory production as it standardized products, fixed prices, determined what would be produced, and developed new industries. Perhaps most importantly in terms of the war effort, the Food Administration headed by Herbert Hoover stimulated grain production to assure adequate food for American troops overseas. Washington of course became the home of these new agencies and commissions. Federal employment in the capital city exploded, jumping from 48,000 in 1917 to 121,000 in 1918. Many of these new federal workers stayed on after the troops re-

turned from France and marched victoriously down Pennsylvania Avenue under a mock-up of Paris's famous Arc de Triomphe.

The "ratchet effect" that usually follows wartime expansion, when the federal establishment retains much of its growth despite postwar layoffs, was never so true, or so consequential, as after World War II.[3] Washington during World War II was more active than ever, growing by leaps and bounds. During the first year of the war, federal employment in the capital leapt from 191,000 to 276,000. Hundreds of new government agencies needed all sorts of help to shuffle through the paper work—clerks, secretaries, typists, messengers, and more. The federal government created more records during World War II than it had in its one hundred fifty previous years combined. The trains coming into

[3]See Bruce D. Porter, "Parkinson's Law Revisited: War and the Growth of Government," *The Public Interest* 60 (1980): 50–68.

Returning World War I troops, led by General John Pershing, marched past the Treasury Annex and under a mock Arc de Triomphe.

Washington's Union Station were full of people anxious to help with this massive effort. Where to put them all proved to be the biggest problem.

In the never-ending quest for more office space, the government built as fast as possible wherever it could find vacant land. It also adapted whatever big buildings it could lay its hands on, such as skating rinks, basketball arenas, and old theaters. The military used the war as a pretext to seize almost any property it wanted. One interesting case involved the Mount Vernon Seminary, a Catholic girls' school. After surveying the property, the Navy moved in over the Christmas holidays and simply took over the entire campus—classrooms, dormitories, chapel, and all. When the students returned, their school, the new Office of Naval Intelligence, had a chain-link fence around it. The school administration, stunned over the confiscation of their campus, was left to find new facilities with $1.1 million compensation from the Navy (roughly one-fifth of the property's market value). Actions like this led many to say that if the military could seize and occupy enemy territory as

From its humble beginnings, Washington has become one of the world's most beautiful cities.

Antiaircraft guns were placed atop the main post office during World War II, which established Washington as the world's power center.

quickly as it grabbed space in Washington, the war would be won in no time flat.[4] Fortunately, it never had to defend any of this Washington real estate from the enemy. Although the army placed antiaircraft guns on the roofs of government buildings, the ammunition stacked beside them was the wrong size.

Just as the Civil War had transformed Washington into the capital of a united nation, so World War II thrust it into the role of capital of the free world. As David Brinkley writes, "A languid Southern town with a pace so slow that much of it simply closed down for the summer grew almost overnight into a crowded, harried, almost frantic metropolis struggling desperately to assume the mantle of global power."[5] Two generations later, Washington seems comfortable with this role. Whereas members of Congress once were all too anxious to get out of the capital, now they stay on even after they leave office.

[4]David Brinkley, *Washington Goes to War* (New York: Alfred A. Knopf, 1988), 117–18.

[5]*Ibid.*, xiv.

For diplomats, Washington is no longer classified as a "hardship post," but is rather the ultimate assignment.

America's capital, however, continues to be a city of stunning contrasts. Its grand government buildings, majestic avenues, and marble monuments would be the envy of any empire the world has ever known, yet within close proximity of the major tourist attractions are slums where many Washington residents live in abject poverty. While the Kennedy Center, the Smithsonian, and the National Gallery of Art have made Washington one of the world's top cultural centers, it is the city's drug culture that makes the most headlines today. Finally, it is most interesting to note, from the perspective of *Government in America*'s focus on democracy, that the city where citizens come to pressure their representatives on the issues has no congressional representatives of its own. The next historical essay on Washington (pages 194–199) reviews some of the most notable cases of citizens journeying to the nation's capital to make their political views heard. ▾▾▾

2

THE CONSTITUTION

During the 1984 Republican National Convention in Dallas, a group of about one hundred protestors marched and staged "die-ins" to dramatize the threat of nuclear war. To obtain even more attention for the cause, Gregory Lee Johnson, one of the demonstrators, burned an American flag in front of city hall. He was convicted of "desecration of a venerated object" and, under Texas law, sentenced to one year in prison and fined two thousand dollars.

Johnson appealed his conviction, arguing that the Constitution protected his right to burn the flag under its guarantee of freedom of speech. The case worked its way through the courts, and in 1989 the Supreme Court of the United States, in the case of *Texas* v. *Gregory Lee Johnson,* agreed with Johnson and found that the law under which he was prosecuted—and similar laws across the country—were unconstitutional because they violated freedom of speech.

Johnson was pleased, but he was nearly alone. The public howled its opposition to the decision and bought record numbers of flags. President Bush was outraged—he had just won election with a campaign in which he had made pledging allegiance to the flag a major issue. He immediately called for a constitutional amendment authorizing punishment of flag desecraters. Most members of Congress and many state legislatures vowed to support the amendment.

Understanding the reason that this one protestor could win against the combined forces of the public and its elected officials is central to understanding the American system of government. The Constitution su-persedes ordinary law; it is a higher law than any policy or legislation enacted by an elected official, even when such a policy or legislation represents the wishes of a majority of citizens. Thus the Constitution is often called the "supreme law of the land."

Johnson not only went unpunished, but the president's proposed amendment to the Constitution did not pass either. Its first stop was Congress, which engaged in extensive debate and posturing. Republicans wanted to support their president, while Democrats were reluctant to tamper with the Bill of Rights. Democrats had to cover themselves, however; they did not want to be accused of supporting desecration of the flag. So instead of amending the Constitution, Congress passed a law outlawing flag burning. The entire process began anew after the Supreme Court also voided this law in 1990.

The Constitution not only guarantees individual rights, but it also establishes the rules of the political game. These rules decentralize power. Even the president, "the leader of the free world," cannot force Congress to act, as Bush could not force Congress to amend the Constitution. The American government would run more efficiently if power were concentrated in someone's hands, such as the president's. Instead, there are numerous checks on the exercise of power and many obstacles to change. Some complain that this system produces stalemate while others praise the way it protects minority views. Both positions are correct, as this chapter will show.

A **constitution** is a nation's basic law. It creates political institutions, assigns or divides powers in government, and often provides certain guarantees to citizens. A constitution is more than a set of written rules. It is also an unwritten accumulation of traditions and precedents that have established acceptable styles of behavior and policy outcomes.

A constitution sets the broad rules of the game of politics, allowing certain types of competition among certain players. The rules governing the interaction among the participants in politics are not neutral. Instead, they give some participants advantages over others in the policy-making process, which is why understanding them is so important to understanding government.

Americans have a special reverence for the **U.S. Constitution.** They view it as the foundation of their freedom and prosperity. Where did the Constitution come from? Why did it take the form it did? What was it designed to accomplish? This chapter will address these questions; it will examine the background of the Constitution, and show that the ultimate source of the Constitution was a concern for limited government and self-determination.

THE ORIGINS OF THE CONSTITUTION

In 1776 a small group of men met in Philadelphia and passed a resolution that began an armed rebellion against the government of the most powerful nation on earth. The resolution was, of course, the Declaration of Independence, and the armed rebellion was the American Revolution.

The forcible overthrow of a government is a serious and unusual act. It is considered treasonous everywhere, including in the United States. Typically it is punishable by death. A set of compelling ideas drove our forefathers to take such drastic (and risky) action. It is important to understand these ideas in order to understand the Constitution.

The Road to Revolution

Life was not bad for most people in eighteenth-century America (slaves being an obvious exception). In fact, Americans "were probably freer and less burdened with cumbersome feudal and hierarchical restraints than any part of mankind."[1] Although the colonies were part of the British empire, the King and Parliament generally confined themselves to governing America's foreign policy and trade. Almost everything else was left to the discretion of individual colonial governments. Although commercial regulations irritated colonial shippers, planters, land speculators, and merchants, these rules had little influence on the vast bulk of the population who were self-employed farmers or artisans.

Britain obtained an enormous new territory in North America after the French and Indian War ended in 1763. The cost of defending this territory against foreign adversaries was large, and Parliament reasoned that it was only fair that those who were the primary beneficiaries, the colonists, should contribute to their own defense. Thus, in order to raise revenue for colonial administration and defense, the British legislature passed a series of taxes on official documents, newspapers, paper, glass, paint, and, of course, tea. Britain also began tightening up enforcement of its trade regulations, which were designed to benefit the mother country, not the colonists.

Americans resented these taxes, especially since they were imposed on them without their having direct representation in Parliament. They protested, boycotted the taxed goods, and even threw 342 chests of tea into Boston Harbor. Britain reacted by applying economic pressure through a naval blockade of the harbor, further fueling the colonists' anger. The colonists responded by forming the First Continental Congress in September 1774, sending delegates from each colony to Philadelphia in order to discuss the future of relations with Britain.

[1]Gordon Wood, *The Creation of the American Republic, 1776–1787* (Chapel Hill, N.C.: University of North Carolina Press, 1969), 3.

Declaring Independence

As colonial discontent with the English festered, the Continental Congress was in almost continuous session during 1775 and 1776. Talk of independence was common among the delegates. Virginia, as it often did in those days, played a leading role at the Philadelphia meeting of the Congress. It sent seven delegates to join the serious discussion of repudiating the rule of King George III. They were joined subsequently by a last-minute substitute for Peyton Randolph, who was needed back in Williamsburg to preside over Virginia's House of Burgesses.

The substitute, Thomas Jefferson, was a young, well-educated Virginia lawmaker who had just written a resolution in the Virginia legislature objecting to new British policies. He traveled to Philadelphia attended by his slaves Richard and Jesse, and being in no great hurry to get there, stopped along the way to purchase some books and a new stallion.[2] Jefferson brought to the Continental Congress his talent as an author and the knowledge of a careful student of political philosophy. Jefferson was not a rabble-rousing pamphleteer like Thomas Paine, whose fiery tract *Common Sense* had appeared in January 1776 and fueled the already hot flames of revolution. Jefferson was steeped in the philosophical writings of European moral philosophers, and his rhetoric matched his reading.

In May and June of 1776 the Continental Congress began debating resolutions about independence. On June 7, Richard Henry Lee of Virginia moved "that these United States are and of rights ought to be free and independent states." A committee composed of Thomas Jefferson, John Adams of Massachusetts, Benjamin Franklin, Roger Sherman of Connecticut, and Robert Livingston of New York was busily drafting a document to justify the inevitable declaration. On July 2, Lee's motion to declare independence from England was formally approved. The famous **Declaration of Independence,** primarily written by Jefferson, was adopted two days later on July 4.

The Declaration of Independence quickly became one of the most widely quoted and revered documents in America. Filled with fine principles and bold language, it can be read as both a political tract and a philosophical treatise (it is reprinted in the appendix).

Politically, the Declaration was a polemic, announcing and justifying a revolution. Most of the document—twenty-seven of thirty-two total paragraphs—listed the ways in which the King had abused the colonies. George III was accused of all sorts of evil deeds, even though he personally had little to do with Parliament's colonial policies. King George was even blamed for inciting the "merciless Indian savages" to war on the colonists. The King took the blame because the Convention delegates held that Parliament lacked authority over the colonies.

The Declaration's polemical aspects were important because the colonists needed foreign assistance to take on the most powerful nation in the world. France, which was engaged in a war with Britain, was a prime target of the delegates' diplomacy, and eventually provided aid that was critical to the success of the Revolution.

---

[2]Garry Wills, *Inventing America: Jefferson's Declaration of Independence* (New York: Doubleday, 1978), 13, 77.

John Adams (from left), Roger Sherman, Robert R. Livingston, Thomas Jefferson, and Benjamin Franklin submit the Declaration of Independence to Continental Congress President John Hancock. Legend has it that Hancock remarked, "We must be unanimous; there must be no pulling different ways; we must hang together," to which Franklin replied, "We must indeed all hang together, or, most assuredly, we shall all hang separately."

Today the Declaration of Independence is studied more as a statement of philosophy than as a political polemic. In just a few sentences, Jefferson set forth the American democratic creed, the most important and succinct statement of the philosophy underlying American government—as applicable in the 1990s as it was in 1776.

The English Heritage: The Power of Ideas

Philosophically, the Jeffersonian pen put ideas on paper that were by then common knowledge on both sides of the Atlantic, especially among those people who wished to challenge the power of kings. Franklin, Jefferson, Madison, Morris, Hamilton, and other intellectual leaders in the colonies were learned and widely read men, familiar with the words of English, French, and Scottish political philosophers. They corresponded about the ideas they were reading, they quoted the philosophers in their debates over the Revolution, and they applied those ideas to the new government they formed in the framework of the Constitution.

John Locke was one of the most influential of the philosophers read by the colonists. His writings, especially *The Second Treatise of Civil Government* (1689), profoundly influenced American political leaders. His work was "the dominant political faith of the American colonies in the second quarter of the

John Locke, 1637–1704, was an English physician, philosopher, diplomat, and civil servant. Locke wrote the Treatise of Civil Government *(1689), an important source of ideas reflected in both the Declaration of Independence and the Constitution.*

eighteenth century. A thousand pulpits thundered with its benevolent principles; a hundred editors filled their pages with its famous slogans."[3]

The foundation upon which Locke built his powerful philosophy was a belief in **natural rights.** Before governments arise, Locke held, people exist in a state of nature, where they are governed only by the laws of nature. Natural law brings natural rights, including life, liberty, and property. Because natural law is superior to human law, it can even justify a challenge to the rule of a tyrannical king. Government, Locke argued, must be built on the **consent of the governed;** in other words, the people must agree on who their rulers will be. It should also be a **limited government**—there must be clear restrictions on what rulers could do. Indeed, the sole purpose of government, according to Locke, was to protect natural rights. The idea that certain things were out-of-bounds for government influence contrasted sharply with the old notion that kings had divinely granted, absolute rights over subjects.

Two limits on government were particularly important to Locke. First, governments must provide standing laws so that people know in advance whether or not their acts will be acceptable. Second, and Locke was very forceful on this point, "the supreme power cannot take from any man any part of his property without his consent." To Locke, "the preservation of property [was] the end of government." This idea of the sanctity of property was one of the few ideas with no direct parallel in Jefferson's draft of the Declaration of Independence. Even though Jefferson borrowed from and even paraphrased Lockean ideas, he altered Locke's phrase "life, liberty, and property" to "life, liberty, and the pursuit of happiness." We shall soon see, though, how the Lockean idea of the sanctity of property figured prominently at the Constitutional Convention. James Madison, the most influential member of that body, directly echoed Locke's line about the preservation of property being the object of government.

In an extreme case, said Locke, people have a right to revolt against a government that no longer has their consent. Locke anticipated critics' charges that this right would lead to constant civil disturbances. He stressed that people should not revolt until injustices become deeply felt. The Declaration of Independence stressed the same point, emphasizing that "governments long established should not be changed for light and transient causes." But when matters went beyond "patient sufferance," severance of old ties was not only inevitable but necessary.

Jefferson's Handiwork: The American Creed

There are some remarkable parallels between Locke's thought and Jefferson's language in the Declaration of Independence (see Table 2.1). Jefferson, like Locke, finessed his way past the issue of how the rebels *knew* men had rights. He simply declared that it was "self-evident" that men were equally "endowed by their Creator with certain unalienable rights," including "life, liberty, and the pursuit of happiness." Since it was the purpose of government to "secure" these rights, if a government failed to do so, the people could form a new government.[4]

---

[3]Clinton Rossiter, *1787: The Grand Convention* (New York: Macmillan, 1966), 60.

[4]On the Lockean influence on the Declaration of Independence, see Carl L. Becker, *The Declaration of Independence: A Study in the History of Political Ideas* (New York: Random House, 1942).

Table 2.1	Locke and the Declaration of Independence: Some Parallels

LOCKE	DECLARATION OF INDEPENDENCE
Natural Rights	
"The state of nature has a law to govern it, which obliges everyone." "life, liberty, and property"	"Laws of Nature and Nature's God" "life, liberty, and the pursuit of happiness"
Purpose of Government	
"to preserve himself, his liberty, and property"	"to secure these rights"
Equality	
"men being by nature all free, equal and independent"	"all men are created equal"
Consent of the Governed	
"for when any number of men have, by the consent of every individual, made a community, with a power to act as one body, which is only by the will and determination of the majority"	"Governments are instituted among men, deriving their just powers from the consent of the governed."
Limited Government	
"Absolute arbitrary power, or governing without settled laws, can neither of them consist with the ends of society and government." "As usurpation is the exercise of power which another has a right to, so tyranny is the exercise of power beyond right, which nobody can have a right to."	"The history of the present King of Great Britain is a history of repeated injuries and usurpations."
Right to Revolt	
"The people shall be the judge. . . . Oppression raises ferments and makes men struggle to cast off an uneasy and tyrannical yoke."	"Prudence, indeed, will dictate that Governments long established should not be changed for light and transient causes; and accordingly all experience hath shewn, that mankind are most disposed to suffer, while evils are sufferable, than to right themselves by abolishing the forms to which they are accustomed. But when a long train of abuses and usurpations, pursuing invariably the same Object evinces a design to reduce them under absolute Despotism, it is their right, it is their duty, to throw off such Government."

It was in the American colonies that the powerful ideas of European political thinkers took root and grew into what Seymour Martin Lipset has termed the "first new nation."[5] With these revolutionary ideas in mind, Jefferson claimed in the Declaration of Independence people should have primacy over governments, that they should rule instead of being ruled. Moreover, each person was important as an individual, "created equal" and endowed with "unalienable

[5]Seymour Martin Lipset, *The First New Nation* (New York: Basic Books, 1963).

rights." Consent of the governed made the exercise of political power legitimate, not divine rights or tradition.

No government had ever been based on these principles. Ever since 1776, American government has tried to fulfill the high aspirations of the Declaration of Independence.

Winning Independence

The pen may be mightier than the sword, but declaring independence did not win the Revolution—it merely announced that it had begun. John Adams wrote his wife Abigail: "You will think me transported with enthusiasm, but I am not. I am well aware of the toil, blood, and treasure that it will cost us to maintain this Declaration, and support and defend these states." Adams was right. The colonials seemed little match for the finest army in the world, whose size was nearly quadrupled by hired guns from the German state of Hesse and elsewhere. In 1775 the British had 8,500 men stationed in the colonies and had hired nearly 30,000 mercenaries. At the beginning the colonists had only 5,000 men in uniform, and their number waxed and waned as the war went on. How they eventually won is a story best left to history books. How they formed a new government, however, will be explored in the following sections.

The "Conservative" Revolution

Revolutions such as the 1789 French Revolution, the 1917 Russian Revolution, and the 1978–1979 Iranian Revolution produced great societal change—as well as plenty of bloodshed. The American revolution was different. Although many people lost their lives during the Revolutionary War, the revolution itself was essentially a conservative movement that did not drastically alter the colonists' way of life. Its primary goal was to restore rights the colonists felt were already theirs as British subjects.

American colonists did not feel the need for great social, economic, or political upheavals. They "were not oppressed people; they had no crushing imperial shackles to throw off."[6] As a result, the revolution did not create class conflicts that would split society for generations to come. The colonial leaders' belief that they needed the consent of the governed blessed the new nation with a crucial element of stability—a stability the nation would need.

The Government that Failed: 1776–1787

The Continental Congress that adopted the Declaration of Independence was only a voluntary association of the states. In 1776 the Congress appointed a committee to draw up a plan for a permanent union of the states. That plan, our first constitution, was the **Articles of Confederation.**[7]

The Articles of Confederation   The Articles established a government dominated by the states. The United States, it said, was a "league of friendship and

[6] Wood, *The Creation of the American Republic, 1776–1787,* 3.

[7] On the Articles of Confederation, see Merrill Jensen, *The Articles of Confederation* (Madison: University of Wisconsin Press, 1940).

perpetual union" among thirteen states that were themselves sovereign. The Articles established a national legislature with one house; states could send as many as seven delegates or as few as two, but each state had only one vote. There was no president and no national court, and the powers of the national legislature, the Continental Congress, were strictly limited. Most authority rested with the state legislatures because the new nation's leaders feared a strong central government would become as tyrannical as British rule.

Because unanimous consent of the states was needed to put them into operation, the Articles adopted by Congress in 1777 did not go into effect until 1781, when laggard Maryland finally ratified them. In the meantime, the Continental Congress barely survived, lurching from crisis to crisis (as when some of Washington's troops threatened to create a monarchy with him as king unless Congress paid their overdue wages).

Once the Articles were ratified, all sorts of problems, logistical as well as political, plagued the Continental Congress. State delegations attended haphazardly. Thomas Jefferson, a Virginia delegate to an Annapolis meeting of the Congress, complained to his friend and fellow Virginian James Madison on February 20, 1784:

> We cannot make up a congress at all. There are eight states in town, six of which are represented by two members only. Of these, two members of different states are confined by gout, so that we cannot make a house [i.e., a quorum]. We have not sat above three days, I believe, in as many weeks. Admonition after admonition has been sent to the states to no effect. We have sent one today. If it fails, it seems as well we should all retire.[8]

The Continental Congress had few powers outside of maintaining an army and navy, and little money to do even that. Because it had no power to tax, it had to requisition money from the states. If states refused to send money (which they often did), Congress did without. In desperation, Congress sold off western lands to speculators, issued securities that sold for less than their face value, or used its own presses to print money that was virtually worthless. Congress had to disband the army, despite continued threats from the British and Spanish. The Congress also lacked the power to regulate commerce, which inhibited foreign trade and the development of a strong national economy. It did, however, manage to develop sound policies for the management of the western frontiers, passing the Northwest Ordinance of 1787 that encouraged the development of the Great Lakes region once the British and the Indians were cleared out.

In general, the weak and ineffective national government could take little independent action. All the power rested in the states. The national government could not compel the states to do anything, and it had no power to deal directly with individual citizens. The weakness of the national government prevented it from dealing with the hard times that soon faced the new nation. There was one benefit of the Articles: when the nation's leaders began to write a new Constitution, they could look at the provisions of the Articles of Confederation and know what to avoid.

---

[8]Letter from Jefferson to Madison, reprinted in George Bancroft, *The History of the Formation of the Constitution of the United States of America* (New York: Appleton, 1900), 342–43.

Changes in the States   What was happening in the states was more important than what was happening in the Continental Congress. The most important change was a dramatic increase in democracy and liberty, at least for white males. Many states adopted bills of rights to protect freedoms, abolished religious qualifications for holding office, and liberalized requirements for voting. Expanded political participation brought a new middle class to power.

It was a middle class of farmers who owned small homesteads rather than of manorial landholders, of artisans instead of lawyers. Before the revolution almost all members of New York's Assembly were either urban merchants or wealthy landowners. In the 1769 Assembly, for example, 57 percent of the legislators were nonfarmers even though nearly 95 percent of New Yorkers were farmers. But *after* the revolution a major power shift occurred. With expanded voting privileges, farmers and craftworkers became a decisive majority, and the old elite saw its power shrink. The same change happened in other states as power shifted from a handful of wealthy individuals to a more broad-based group (see Table 2.2). After a careful examination of the economic backgrounds of pre- and post-revolutionary legislators, Jackson Turner Main concluded: "The voters had ceased to confine themselves to an elite, but were selecting instead men like themselves. The tendency to do so had started during the colonial period, especially in the North, and had now increased so dramatically as almost to revolutionize the legislatures."[9] Members of the old colonial elite found this new turn of affairs quite troublesome.

[9] Jackson Turner Main, "Government by the People: The American Revolution and the Democratization of the Legislatures," *The William and Mary Quarterly,* 3rd ser. 23 (July 1966): 405. Main's article is also the source of the data on New York.

Table 2.2   **Power Shift: Economic Status of State Legislators before and after the Revolutionary War**

After the Revolution, power in the state legislatures shifted from the hands of wealthy to those with more moderate incomes, and from merchants and lawyers to farmers. This trend was especially evident in the northern states.

Status of Legislators	THREE NORTHERN STATES[a]		THREE SOUTHERN STATES[b]	
	Prewar	Postwar	Prewar	Postwar
Wealthy	36%	12%	52%	28%
Well-to-do	47%	26%	36%	42%
Moderate	17%	62%	12%	30%
Merchants and lawyers	43%	18%	23%	17%
Farmers	23%	55%	12%	26%

[a]New York, New Jersey, and New Hampshire.
[b]Maryland, Virginia, and South Carolina.
Source: Jackson Turner Main, "Government by the People: The American Revolution and the Democratization of the Legislatures," *The William and Mary Quarterly,* 3rd. ser. 23 (July 1966): Table 1. Reprinted by permission.

The structure of government in the states also became more responsive to the people. Because legislators were considered to be closer to the voters than governors or judges, power was concentrated in the legislatures. Governors were often selected by the legislatures and were kept on a short leash, with brief tenures and limited veto and appointment powers. Legislatures overruled court decisions and criticized judges for unpopular decisions.

Economic Turmoil After the Revolution, James Madison observed that "the most common and durable source of faction has been the various and unequal division of property."[10] The postrevolutionary legislatures epitomized Madison's argument that economic inequality played an important role in shaping public policy. At the top of the political agenda were economic issues. A postwar depression had left many small farmers unable to pay their debts and threatened them with mortgage foreclosures. Now under control of people more sympathetic to debtors, the state legislatures listened to the demands of small farmers. A few states, notably Rhode Island, demonstrated their support by passing policies to help debtors, favoring them over creditors. Some printed tons of paper money and passed "force acts" requiring reluctant creditors to accept the almost worthless money. Debtors could thus pay big debts with cheap currency.

Shays' Rebellion spurred the birth of the Constitution. News of the small rebellion—what we would now call a protest demonstration—quickly spread around the country, and some of the Philadelphia delegates thought a full-fledged revolution would result. The event reaffirmed their belief that the new federal government needed to be a strong one.

Shays' Rebellion Policies favoring debtors over creditors did not please the economic elite who had once controlled nearly all the state legislatures. They were further shaken when, in 1786, a small band of farmers in western Massachusetts rebelled at losing their land to creditors. Led by Revolutionary War Captain Daniel Shays, this rebellion, called **Shays' Rebellion,** was a series of armed attacks on courthouses to prevent judges from foreclosing on farms. Farmers in other states—though never in large numbers—were also unruly. Jefferson called the attack a "little rebellion," but it remained much on the minds of the economic elite. They were scared at the thought of people taking the law into their own hands and violating the property rights of others.

The Aborted Annapolis Meeting In September 1786 a handful of continental leaders assembled at Annapolis, Maryland, to discuss the problems with the Articles of Confederation and what could be done about them. It was an abortive attempt at reform. Only five states—New York, New Jersey, Delaware, Pennsylvania, and Virginia—were represented at the meeting, and the twelve delegates were few enough in number to meet around a dinner table. Called to consider commercial conflicts that had arisen among the states under the Articles of Confederation, the Annapolis delegates decided that a larger meeting and a broader proposal were needed to organize the states. This small and unofficial band of reformers (who held most of their meetings in a local tavern) issued a call for a full-scale meeting of the states in Philadelphia the following May—in retrospect, a rather bold move to be made by so small a group. Their move worked, however; the Continental Congress called for a meeting of all the states, and in May 1787 what we now call the Constitutional Convention got down to business in Philadelphia.

---

[10] In Alexander Hamilton, James Madison, and John Jay, *The Federalist Papers,* 2nd ed. Roy F. Fairfield (Baltimore: Johns Hopkins University Press, 1981).

MAKING A CONSTITUTION: THE PHILADELPHIA CONVENTION

Representatives from twelve states came to Philadelphia to heed the Continental Congress's call to "take into consideration the situation in the United States." Only Rhode Island, a stronghold of paper-money interests, refused to send delegates. Virginia's Patrick Henry, fearing a centralization of power, also "smelled a rat" in the developments in Philadelphia.

The delegates were ordered to meet "for the sole and express purpose of revising the Articles of Confederation." The Philadelphia delegates did not pay much attention to this order, however, because amending the Articles required the unanimous consent of the states, which they knew would be impossible. Thus the fifty-five delegates ignored their instructions and began writing a new constitution.

A New York delegate to the Convention, Alexander Hamilton favored a strong central government; in fact, he favored an elected king. He was less influential at the Convention than he would be later as architect of the nation's economic policy.

Gentlemen in Philadelphia

Who were these fifty-five men? They may not have been demigods, as Jefferson, perhaps sarcastically, called them, but they were certainly a select group of economic and political notables. They were mostly wealthy planters, successful (or once-successful) lawyers and merchants, and men of independent wealth. Many were college graduates, mostly from Princeton (nine alumni), Yale, William and Mary, Harvard, Columbia (then called King's College), and the University of Pennsylvania. Most were coastal residents, rather than residents of the expanding western frontiers, and a significant number were urbanites, rather than part of the primarily rural American population.

Philosophy into Action

Both philosophy and politics were prevalent at the Constitutional Convention. The delegates at Philadelphia were an uncommon combination of philosophers and shrewd political architects. The debates moved from high principles on the big issues to self-interest on the small ones.[11] The first two weeks were mainly devoted to general debates about the nature of republican government. After that, very practical, and very divisive, issues sometimes threatened to dissolve the meeting.

Obviously, fifty-five men did not share the same political philosophy. Democratic Benjamin Franklin held very different views from aristocratic Alexander Hamilton, who hardly hid his disgust for democracy. Yet at the core of their ideas, even those of Franklin and Hamilton, existed a common center. The group agreed on questions of human nature, the causes of political conflict, and the object and nature of a republican government.

Views of Human Nature   Common to the times, delegates held a cynical view of human nature. People, they thought, were self-interested. Franklin and Hamilton, poles apart philosophically, both reflected this sentiment. Said Frank-

[11]Calvin C. Jillson and Cecil L. Eubanks, "The Political Structure of Constitution-Making: The Federal Convention of 1787," *American Journal of Political Science* 28 (August 1984): 435–58. See also Calvin C. Jillson, *Constitution Making: Conflict and Consensus in the Federal Convention of 1787* (New York: Agathon, 1988).

lin: "There are two passions which have a powerful influence on the affairs of men: the love of power and the love of money." Hamilton agreed in his characteristically blunt manner: "Men love power." The men at Philadelphia believed that government should play a key role in checking and containing the natural self-interest of people.[12]

Views of Political Conflict   Of all the words written by and about the delegates, none have been more widely quoted than these by James Madison: "The most common and durable source of factions has been the various and unequal distribution of property." *The distribution of wealth* (property was the main form of wealth in those days) *is the source of political conflict.* "Those who hold and those who are without property," Madison went on, "have ever formed distinct interests in society."

These are strong and plain words. Arising from the unequal distribution of wealth are **factions,** as Madison called them (we might call them parties or interest groups). One faction is the majority, composed of the many who have little or no property. The other is the minority, composed of the few who hold much wealth. If unchecked, the delegates thought, one of these factions will eventually tyrannize the other. The majority will try to seize the government to reduce the wealth of the minority; the minority will try to seize the government to secure its own gains. Governments run by factions, the founders believed, are prone to instability, tyranny, and even violence. The effects of factions had to be checked.

Views of the Objects of Government   To Gouverneur Morris of Pennsylvania, the preservation of property was the "principal object of government." Morris was outspoken and plainly overlooked some other objects of government, including security from invasion, domestic tranquility, and promotion of the general welfare. Morris's remark typifies many of the delegates' philosophy. John Locke (who was, remember, the intellectual patron saint of many of the delegates) had said a century before that "The preservation of property [is] the end of government," and few of these men would have disagreed. Propertyholders themselves, they could not imagine a government that did not make its principal objective an economic one: the preservation of individual rights to acquire and hold wealth. A few (like Morris) were intent on shutting out the propertyless altogether. "Give the votes to people who have no property," he claimed, "and they will sell them to the rich who will be able to buy them."

Views of Government   Human nature, the delegates believed, is avaricious and self-interested. The principal cause of political conflict is economic inequality. Either a majority or a minority faction will be tyrannical if it has too much power. Property must be protected against the tyrannical tendencies of faction. Given this set of beliefs, what sort of government did the delegates believe would work? The men at Philadelphia answered in different ways, but the message was always the same. "Ambition must be made to counteract ambition," said Madison. Power should be set against power, so that no one faction would overwhelm the others. The secret of good government is "balanced"

Pennsylvania delegate Gouverneur Morris was a man of considerable means and, like Hamilton, an extreme antidemocrat, primarily concerned with protecting property holders. He was responsible for the style and wording of the Constitution.

[12]See Arthur Lovejoy, *Reflections on Human Nature* (Baltimore: Johns Hopkins University Press, 1961), 57–63.

James Madison, a Virginia lawyer and officeholder, was perhaps the most influential member of the Convention in translating political philosophy into governmental architecture. He is often called "the father of the Constitution."

government. A limited government would have to contain checks on its own power. So long as no faction could seize the whole of government at once, tyranny could be avoided. A complex network of checks, balances, and separation of powers would be required for a balanced government.

THE AGENDA IN PHILADELPHIA

The gentlemen in Philadelphia could not merely construct a government from ideas. They wanted to design a government that was consistent with their political philosophy, but they also had to meet head-on some of the thorniest issues confronting the United States of their times—issues of equality, the economy, and individual rights.

The Equality Issues

The Declaration of Independence states that all men are created equal; the Constitution is silent on equality. Some of the most important issues on the policy agenda at Philadelphia, however, concerned equality. Three issues occupied more attention than almost any others: whether or not the states were to be equally represented, what to do about slavery, and whether or not to ensure political equality.

Equality and Representation of the States   One crucial policy issue was how the new Congress would be consititued. One scheme put before the delegates by William Paterson of New Jersey is usually called the **New Jersey Plan.** It called for each state to be equally represented in the new Congress. The opposing strategy was suggested by Edmund Randolph of Virginia and is usually called the **Virginia Plan.** It called for giving each state a share of Congress that matched the state's share of the American population.

The delegates resolved this conflict with a compromise. Devised by Roger Sherman and William Johnson of Connecticut, it has been immortalized as the **Connecticut Compromise.** The compromise solution was to create two houses in Congress. One body, the Senate, would have two members from each state, and the second body, the House of Representatives, would have representation based on population. The United States Congress is still organized in exactly the same way. Each state has two senators, but its representation in the House is determined by its population.

Although the Connecticut Compromise was intended to maximize equality between the states, it actually gives more power to people who live in states with small populations than to those who live in more heavily populated states. To take the most extreme case, Wyoming has the same number of votes in the Senate—two—as California, although it has less than 2 percent of California's population. Thus a citizen of Wyoming has more than fifty times the representation in the Senate as a citizen of California.

Since it is the Senate, not the House, that ratifies treaties, confirms presidential nominations, and hears trials of impeachment, citizens in less populated states have a greater say in these key tasks. In addition, the electoral college (which is the body that actually elects the president—discussed in Chapter 9) gives small states greater weight. If no presidential candidate receives a majority in the electoral college, the final decision is made by the House of Representatives—with each state having one vote. In such as case (which has not occurred since 1824), the votes of citizens of Wyoming would carry over fifty times the weight as those of Californians.

Whether representation in the Senate is "fair" is a matter of debate. What is not open to question is that the delegates to the 1787 convention had to accommodate various interests and viewpoints in order to convince all the states to join an untested union.

Sometimes historians and political scientists describe the conflict as between big and small states (meaning states with large or small populations), each presumably looking for a plan that would maximize its representation. The votes in Philadelphia do not support this interpretation. Eight states voted on the New Jersey Plan (Georgia's delegation was split and did not vote), which supposedly favored the small states. In fact, three big states (New York, Maryland, and Connecticut) lined up with two small states (Delaware and, of course, New Jersey) to support equal representation of the states. The two Carolinas, small states at the time, voted against the New Jersey Plan.[13] It was not a sharp cleavage of small versus large. Rather, the vote depended on different views about how to achieve equality of representation, one side favoring equal representation of the states and the other favoring equal representation of people.

South Carolina planter and aristocrat Charles Cotesworth Pinckney was an articulate spokesman for the South and for slavery.

Slavery   The second equality issue was slavery. Slavery was legal in every state except Massachusetts, but it was concentrated in the South. Some delegates, like Gouverneur Morris, denounced slavery in no uncertain terms. Morris's position could not carry the day in the face of powerful southern opposition led by Charles C. Pinckney of South Carolina. The delegates did agree that Congress

[13]Paul Eidelberg, *The Philosophy of the American Constitution* (New York: Free Press, 1968), 82.

When the Constitution was written, many northern and southern delegates assumed that slavery, being relatively unprofitable, would soon die out. A single invention—Eli Whitney's cotton gin—made it profitable again. Although Congress did act to control the growth of slavery, the slave economy became entrenched in the South.

could limit future *importing* of slaves (they outlawed it after 1808), but nowhere did they forbid slavery itself. The Constitution, in fact, tilted toward recognizing slavery; it stated that slaves fleeing to free states had to be returned to their owners.

Another sticky question about slavery arose. How should slaves be counted in determining representation in Congress? Southerners were happy to see slaves counted toward determining their representation in the House of Representatives (though reluctant to count them to apportion taxation). Here the result was the famous **three-fifths compromise.** Representation and taxation were to be based upon the "number of free persons," plus three-fifths of the number of "all other persons." Everyone, of course, knew who those "other persons" were.

Political Equality   The delegates dodged one other issue on equality. A handful of delegates, led by Franklin, suggested that national elections should require universal manhood suffrage (that is, a vote for all free, adult males). This democratic thinking did not appeal to those still smarting from Shays' Rebellion. Many delegates wanted to put property qualifications on the right to vote. Ultimately, as the debate wound down, they decided to leave the issue to the states. People qualified to vote in state elections could also vote in national elections (see Table 2.3).

The Economic Issues

The Philadelphia delegates were deeply concerned about the state of the American economy. Economic issues were high on the Constitution writers' policy

Table 2.3	How Three Issues of Equality Were Resolved: A Summary

PROBLEM	SOLUTION
Slavery	
How should slaves be counted for representation in the House of Representatives?	Count each slave as three-fifths of a person.
What should be done about slavery? .	Basically, nothing. Although Congress was permitted to stop the importing of slaves after 1808, the Constitution is mostly silent on the issue of slavery.
Equality of the States	
Should states be represented equally (the New Jersey Plan) or in proportion to their population (the Virginia Plan)?	Both, according to the Connecticut Compromise. States have equal representation in the Senate, but representation in the House is proportionate to population.
Political Equality	
Should the right to vote be based on universal manhood suffrage, or should it be very restricted?	Finesse the issue. Let the states decide qualifications for voting.

agenda. People disagreed (in fact, historians still disagree) as to whether the postcolonial economy was in shambles or not. Advocates of the Constitution, called Federalists, stressed the economy's "weaknesses, especially in the commercial sector, and Antifederalists, [those opposed to a strong national government, and thus opposed to a new constitution] countered with charges of exaggeration."[14] The writers of the Constitution, already committed to a strong national government, charged that the economy was indeed in disarray. Specifically, they claimed that the following problems had to be addressed:

- States put up tariffs against products from other states.
- Paper money was virtually worthless in some states, but many state governments, which were controlled by debtor classes, forced it on creditors anyway.
- The Continental Congress was having trouble raising money as the economy went through a recession.

Understanding something about the delegates and their economic interests gives us insight into their views on political economy (see "A Question of Ethics: Self-interest in the Constitutional Convention"). They were, by all accounts, the nation's postcolonial economic elite. Some were budding capitalists. Others were creditors whose loans were being wiped out by cheap paper money. Many were merchants who could not even carry on trade with a neighboring state. Virtually all of them thought a strong national government was needed to bring economic stability to the chaotic union of states that existed under the Articles of Confederation.[15]

It is not surprising, then, that the framers of the Constitution would seek to strengthen the economic powers of the new national government. The del-

[14]Cecelia M. Kenyon, ed., *The Antifederalists* (Indianapolis, Ind.: Bobbs-Merrill, 1966), xxxv.
[15]Rossiter, *1787.*

Self-interest in the Constitutional Convention

One of the cardinal principles of law is that no one should be able to make laws or judge a case in which they are personally involved. If a legislator or judge has a personal interest in the outcome of a decision, especially if they are likely to gain economically, they are supposed to excuse themselves from the decision-making process. Who, then, can make decisions regarding a constitution, which affects every citizen?

In one of the most famous analyses of the Constitutional Convention, historian Charles Beard argued that the founders were highly self-interested in the outcome of their deliberations. Most of the delegates, he said, had bonds and investments whose value would go up if the Constitution was adopted. His was not merely an argument that the framers were propertied upper-class men protecting their interests; Beard also argued that these men would become far wealthier if the Constitution was approved. After all, he suggested, Madison himself spoke of the powerful economic motive in political affairs. Beard concluded that the members of the Philadelphia convention, with a few exceptions, stood to gain personally from the adoption of the Constitution.

Beard's charges were leveled at men that most Americans have come to revere. The notion of the founders feathering their own nests suggested that the Constitution was a *political* document in the crudest sense of the word. Were Beard's charges true?

Most historians today would say that Beard's arguments were much exaggerated. In one painstaking review, historian Robert Brown tracked down information about the economic holdings of each member of the Convention. Only a minority, he concluded, could have been said to benefit from the new government, and a few of these members ended up opposing the document. Moreover, several of the most influential delegates, including Madison, Hamilton, and Wilson, were not wealthy.

No one would dispute, however, that most of the men at Philadelphia were far wealthier than the average American at the time, and few dispute that economic turmoil in the states was much on the delegates' minds. The framers were concerned about protecting property rights, but more in the broad sense of building a strong economy than in the narrow sense of increasing their personal wealth.

Source: Charles A. Beard, *An Economic Interpretation of the Constitution of the United States* (New York: Macmillan, 1913); Robert E. Brown, *Charles Beard and the Constitution* (Princeton, N.J.: Princeton University Press, 1956); Forest B. McDonald, *We the People: The Economic Origins of the Constitution* (Chicago: University of Chicago Press, 1958); and Forest B. McDonald, *Novus Ordum Seclorum: The Intellectual Origins of the Constitution* (Lawrence: University Press of Kansas, 1986).

egates made sure that the Constitution clearly spelled out the economic powers of Congress (see Table 2.4). Consistent with the general allocation of power in the Constitution, Congress was to be the chief economic policymaker.

Congress, the new Constitution said, could obtain revenues through taxing and borrowing. These tools, along with the power to appropriate funds, became crucial instruments for influencing the economy (as Chapter 17 will discuss). By maintaining sound money and guaranteeing payment for the national debt, Congress was to encourage economic enterprise and investment in the United States. Congress was also given power to build the nation's infrastructure by constructing post offices and roads, and to establish standard weights and measures. To protect property rights, Congress was charged with punishing counterfeiters and pirates, ensuring patents and copyrights, and legislating rules for bankruptcy. Equally important (and now a key congressional power, with a wide range of implications for the economy) was Congress's new ability to regulate interstate and foreign commerce.

Table 2.4   Economics in the Constitution

POWERS OF CONGRESS

1. Levy taxes.
2. Pay debts.
3. Borrow money.
4. Coin money and regulate its value.
5. Regulate interstate and foreign commerce.
6. Establish uniform laws of bankruptcy.
7. Create standard weights and measures.
8. Punish counterfeiting.
9. Punish piracy.
10. Establish post offices and post roads.
11. Protect copyrights and patents.

PROHIBITIONS ON THE STATES

1. States cannot pass laws impairing the obligations of contract.
2. States cannot coin money or issue paper money.
3. States cannot require payment of debts in paper money.
4. States cannot tax imports or exports from abroad or other states.
5. States cannot free runaway slaves from other states *(now defunct)*.

OTHER KEY PROVISIONS

1. The new government assumes the national debt contracted under the Articles of Confederation.
2. The Constitution guarantees a republican form of government.
3. The states must respect civil court judgments and contracts made in other states.

In addition, the framers prohibited practices in the states that they viewed as inhibiting economic development, such as printing the hated paper money, placing duties on imports from other states, and interfering with lawfully contracted debts. Moreover, the states were to respect civil judgments and contracts made in other states, and they were to return runaway slaves to their owners. (This last protection of "property" rights is now, of course, defunct as a result of the Thirteenth Amendment, which outlawed slavery.) To help the states, the national government guaranteed them "a republican form of government" to prevent a recurrence of Shays' Rebellion, in which violence, instead of legislation and the courts, was used to resolve commercial disputes.

The Constitution also obligated the new government to repay all the public debts incurred under the Continental Congress and the Articles of Confederation, totaling fifty-four million dollars. Although this requirement may seem odd, there was a sound economic reason for it. Paying off the debts would ensure from the outset that money would flow into the American economy and would also restore the confidence of investors in the young nation.

Alexander Hamilton, the first secretary of the treasury, stressed the link between a national debt and the emergence of capitalism. "It is a well-known fact," he said, "that in countries in which the national debt is properly funded, and an object of established confidence, it answers most of the purposes of money. Transfers of stock or public debt are the equivalent to payment in [money]."[16] When shares of the public debt—such as the U.S. savings bonds

[16]Alexander Hamilton, "A National Debt Is a Blessing," in *Free Government in the Making,* ed. Alpheas Thomas Mason (New York: Oxford University Press, 1949), 313.

you may own—can be bought and sold, they constitute a form of capital for investment. Even today, people trade in government debt (in the form of bonds) just as they do in the stocks of corporations. Thus did the Constitution help spur a capitalist economy.

The Individual Rights Issues

There was another major item on the Constitutional Convention agenda; the delegates had to design a system that would preserve individual rights. They felt this would be relatively easy, since they were constructing a limited government that, by design, could not threaten personal freedoms. In addition, they dispersed power among the branches of the national government and between the national and state governments so that each branch or level could control the other. Also, most of the delegates believed that the various states were already doing a sufficient job of protecting individual rights.

As a result, the Constitution says little about personal freedoms. The protections it does offer are as follows:

- It prohibits suspension of the **writ of habeas corpus** (except during invasion or rebellion). Such a writ enables persons detained by authorities to secure an immediate inquiry into the causes of their detention, and, if no proper explanation is offered, a judge may order their release.
- It prohibits Congress or the states from passing bills of attainder (which punish people without a judicial trial).
- It prohibits Congress or the states from passing *ex post facto* laws (which punish people or increase the penalties for acts that were not illegal or not as punishable when committed).
- It prohibits the imposition of religious qualifications for holding office in the national government.
- It narrowly defines and outlines strict rules of evidence for conviction of treason. To be convicted, one must levy war against the United States or adhere to and aid its enemies during war. Conviction requires confession in open court or the testimony of *two* witnesses to the *same* act. The framers of the Constitution would have been executed as traitors if the revolution had failed, and they were therefore sensitive to treason laws.
- It upholds the right to trial by jury in criminal cases.

The delegates were content with their document. When it came time to obtain ratification of the Constitution, however, there was widespread criticism of the absence of specific protections of individual rights.

THE MADISONIAN MODEL

The framers believed that human nature was self-interested and that inequalities of wealth were the principal source of political conflict. Regardless, they had no desire to remove the divisions in society by converting private property to common ownership; they also believed that protecting private property was a key purpose of government. Their experience with state governments under the Articles of Confederation reinforced their view that democracy was a threat to property. Many of them felt that the unwealthy majority—an unruly mob—would tyrannize the wealthy minority if given political power. Thus the delegates to the Constitutional Convention were faced with the dilemma of reconciling economic inequality with political freedom.

Separation of Powers and Checks and Balances

James Madison was the principal architect of the government's final structure, and his work still shapes our policy-making process.[17] He and his colleagues feared both majority and minority factions. Either could take control of the government and use it to their own advantage. Factions of the minority, however, were easy to deal with; they could simply be outvoted by the majority. Factions of the majority were harder to handle. If the majority united around some policy issue, such as the redistribution of wealth, it could ride roughshod over the minority, violating their basic rights.

As Madison would later explain in the Federalist Papers,

"When my distinguished colleague refers to the will of the 'people,' does he mean his people or my 'people'?"

Drawing by Richter; © 1976 The New Yorker Magazine, Inc.

Ambition must be made to counteract ambition. . . . If men were angels, no government would be necessary. If angels were to govern men, neither external nor internal controls would be necessary. In framing a government which is to be administered by men over men, the great difficulty lies in this: you must first enable the government to control the governed; and then in the next place oblige it to control itself.[18]

To prevent the possibility of a tyranny of the majority, Madison's plan was as follows:

1. Place as much of the government as possible beyond the direct control of the majority

2. Separate the powers of different institutions

3. Construct a system of checks and balances

To thwart tyranny of the majority, first it was essential to keep most of the government beyond their power. Madison's plan placed only one element of government, the House of Representatives, within direct control of the votes of the majority. In contrast, senators were to be elected by the state legislatures and the president by special electors—in other words, they would be elected by the wealthy minority, not by the people themselves. Judges were to be appointed by the president (see Figure 2.1). Even if the majority seized control of the House of Representatives, they still could not enact policies without the concurrence of the Senate and the president. To further insulate governmental officials from public opinion, judges were given lifetime tenure and senators terms of six years, with only one-third elected at a time, as opposed to the two-year terms given to representatives to the House.

The Madisonian scheme also required a **separation of powers.** Each of the three branches of government—executive, legislative, and judicial—would be relatively independent of one another so that neither could control the others.

[17]A brilliant exposition of the Madisonian model is found in Robert A. Dahl, *A Preface to Democratic Theory* (Chicago: University of Chicago Press, 1956).

[18]Hamilton, Madison, and Jay, *The Federalist Papers,* No. 51.

The Constitution and the Electoral Process: The Original Plan

Under Madison's plan, incorporated in the Constitution, voters' electoral influence was limited and mostly indirect. Only the House of Representatives was directly elected. Senators and presidents were indirectly elected, and judges were appointed. Over the years, Madison's original model has been substantially democratized.

The Seventeenth Amendment (1913) made senators directly elected by popular majorities. Today, the electoral college has become largely a rubber stamp, voting the way the popular majority in each state votes.

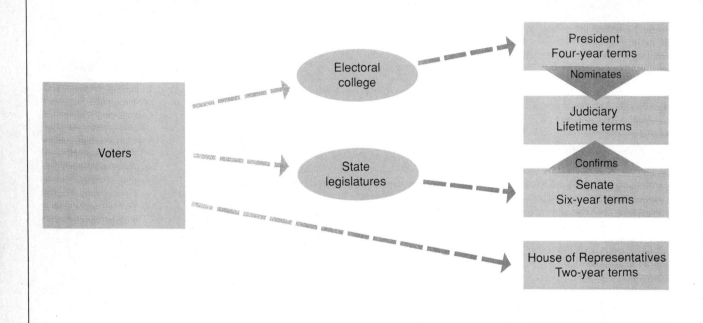

The president, Congress, and the courts were all given different pieces of the power pie. Power was not separated absolutely, however, but rather shared among the three institutions.

Since power was not completely separate, each branch required the consent of the others for many of its actions. This created a system of **checks and balances** that reflected Madison's goal of setting power against power to constrain government actions. If one institution was seized by a faction, it still could not damage the whole system, he reasoned. The system of checks and balances was as elaborate and delicate as a spider's web. The president checks Congress by holding veto power; Congress holds the purse strings of government and must approve presidential appointments.

The courts also figured into the system of checks and balances. Presidents could nominate judges, but they required confirmation by the Senate. The Supreme Court itself, in *Marbury* v. *Madison* (1803), asserted its power to check the other branches through judicial review: the right to hold actions of the other two branches unconstitutional. This right, not specifically outlined in the Constitution, considerably strengthened the Court's ability to control the other branches of government. (For a summary of separation of powers and the checks and balances system, see Figure 2.2.)

The diagram shows how Madison and his fellow Constitution writers used the doctrine of separation of powers to allow the three institutions of government to check and balance one another. Judicial review, the power of courts to hold executive and congressional policies unconstitutional, was not explicit in the Constitution but was asserted by the Supreme Court under John Marshall in *Marbury* v. *Madison*.

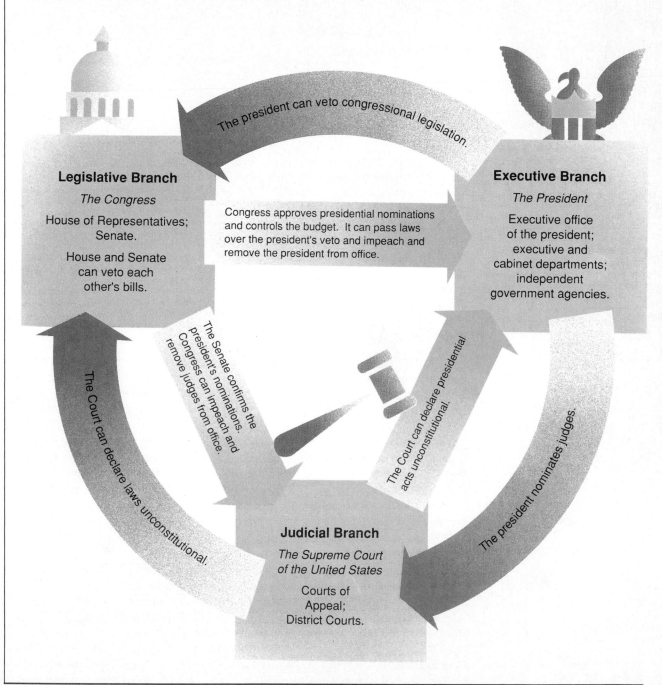

The president can veto congressional legislation.

Legislative Branch

The Congress

House of Representatives; Senate.

House and Senate can veto each other's bills.

Congress approves presidential nominations and controls the budget. It can pass laws over the president's veto and impeach and remove the president from office.

Executive Branch

The President

Executive office of the president; executive and cabinet departments; independent government agencies.

The Senate confirms the president's nominations. Congress can impeach and remove judges from office.

The Court can declare presidential acts unconstitutional.

The Court can declare laws unconstitutional.

The president nominates judges.

Judicial Branch

The Supreme Court of the United States

Courts of Appeal; District Courts.

The Constitutional Republic

When asked what kind of government the delegates had produced, Benjamin Franklin is said to have replied, "A republic. . .if you can keep it." Franklin, as usual, was correct. Since the founders did not wish to have the people directly make all decisions (as in a town meeting where everyone has one vote), and since the country was far too large for such a proposal to be feasible, they did not choose to create a direct democracy. Their solution was to establish a **republic:** a system based on the consent of the governed in which power is exercised by *representatives* of the public. This deliberative democracy required and encouraged reflection and refinement of the public's views through an elaborate decision-making process.

The system of checks and balances and separation of powers has a conservative bias that favors the *status quo*. People desiring change must usually have a sizable majority, not just a simple majority of 51 percent. Those opposed to change need only win at one point in the policy-making process, say in obtaining a presidential veto, while those who favor change must win every battle along the way. Change usually comes slowly, if at all. As a result, the Madisonian system encourages moderation and compromise. It is difficult for either a minority or a majority to tyrannize, and both property rights and personal freedoms have survived.

Franklin was also correct that such a system is not easy to maintain. It requires careful nurturing and balancing of diverse interests. Some critics argue that the policy-making process lacks efficiency, preventing quick action on pressing matters. You will examine this issue closely throughout *Government in America*.

The End of the Beginning

On the 109th day of the meetings, in stifling heat (the windows of the Pennsylvania statehouse were closed to ensure secrecy), the final version of the Constitution was read aloud. Then Dr. Franklin rose with a speech he had written, but the enfeebled Franklin had to ask James Wilson to deliver it. In it, Franklin noted that "there are several parts of this Constitution of which I do not at present approve, but I am not sure that I shall never approve them." He then offered a few political witticisms, defended the handiwork, and concluded by saying, "On the whole, Sir, I cannot help expressing a wish that every member of the Convention who may still have an objection to it, would with me on this occasion, doubt a little of his own infallibility—and make manifest our unanimity, put his name to this instrument." Nonetheless, Edmund Randolph of Virginia rose to announce apologetically that he did not intend to sign. Gouverneur Morris of Pennsylvania announced his reservations about the compromises but called the document the "best that was to be attained" and said he would "take it with all its faults." Alexander Hamilton of New York again made a plea for unity, but Elbridge Gerry of Massachusetts was adamant in opposition. Taking Franklin's remarks personally, he "could not but view them as levelled against himself and the other gentlemen who meant not to sign." He bluntly predicted that a "civil war may result from the present crisis of the United States."

On Franklin's motion, a vote was taken. Ten states voted yes, none voted no, but South Carolina's delegates were divided. As the records so quaintly put

George Washington presides over the signing of the Constitution. "The business being closed," he wrote, "the members adjourned to the City Tavern, dined together and took cordial leave of each other."

it, "The Members then proceeded to sign the instrument." Randolph, Gerry, and George Mason of Virginia, however, refused to sign. Franklin then made another short speech, saying that the sun pictured on the back of convention President George Washington's chair was a rising, not a setting, sun. Then (quoting the records again) "the Constitution being signed. . . the convention dissolved itself by Adjournment." The members themselves adjourned to a tavern. The experience of the last few hours, when conflict intermingled with consensus, reminded them that implementing this new document would be no small feat.

RATIFYING THE CONSTITUTION

The Constitution did not go into effect once the Constitutional Convention in Philadelphia was over. It had to be ratified by the states. The Constitution itself required that nine states approve the document before it could be implemented. Our awe of the founders sometimes blinds us to the bitter politics of the day. There is no way of gauging the public's feelings about the new document, but as future Chief Justice John Marshall suggests, "It is scarcely to be doubted that *in some of the adopting states, a majority of the people were in opposition.*"[19]

[19]Quoted in Charles A. Beard, *An Economic Interpretation of the Constitution of the United States* (New York: Macmillan, 1913), 299. Italics ours.

Federalists and Anti-Federalists

Throughout the states, a fierce battle erupted between the **Federalists,** who supported the Constitution, and the **Anti-Federalists,** who opposed it. Newspapers were filled with letters and articles, many written under pseudonyms, praising or condemning the document. In praise of the Constitution, three men—James Madison, Alexander Hamilton, and John Jay—wrote a series of articles under the name Publius. These articles, known as the **Federalist Papers,** are second only to the Constitution itself in characterizing the framers.

Beginning on October 27, 1787, barely a month after the convention ended, the Federalist Papers began to appear in New York newspapers. Eighty-five of them would eventually appear. They not only defended the Constitution detail by detail but also represented an important statement of political philosophy. (The essays influenced few of the New York delegates, however, who only voted to ratify the Constitution after New York City threatened to secede from the state if they did not.)

Far from being unpatriotic or un-American, the Anti-Federalists sincerely believed that the new government was an enemy of freedom, the very freedom they had just fought a war to ensure. Adopting names like Aggrippa, Cornelius, and Monteczuma, the Anti-Federalists launched bitter, biting, even brilliant attacks on the Philadelphia document. They frankly questioned the motives of the Constitution writers.

One objection was central to the Anti-Federalist's attacks: the new Constitution was a class-based document, intended to ensure that a particular economic

As an explication and defense of the Constitution, the Federalist Papers were often discussed at dinner parties and debated at countinghouses. Despite today's high literacy rates, it is doubtful that a similar set of documents, so rich in political philosophy, would be so widely read in modern America.

elite controlled the public policies of the national government. The following quotations are from three critics of the Constitution:

> This government will commence in a moderate aristocracy; it is at present impossible to foresee whether it will, in its operation, produce a monarchy, or a corrupt, oppressive aristocracy. (George Mason)

> Thus, I conceive, a foundation is laid for throwing the whole power of the federal government into the hands of those who are in the mercantile interest; and for the landed, which is the great interest of this country to lie unrepresented, forlorn and without hope. ("Cornelius")

> These lawyers, men of learning, and moneyed men. . . expect to get into Congress themselves. . . [so they can] get all the power and all the money into their own hands. (Amos Singletary of Massachusetts)[20]

Remember that these charges of conspiracy and elitism were being hurled at the likes of Washington, Madison, Franklin, and Hamilton.

The Anti-Federalists had other fears. Not only would the new government be run by a few, but it would erode fundamental liberties. James Lincoln was quoted in the records of the South Carolina ratifying convention as saying that he "would be glad to know why, in this Constitution, there is a total silence with regard to the liberty of the press. Was it forgotten? Impossible! Then it must have been purposely omitted; and with what design, good or bad, [I leave] the world to judge."

These arguments were persuasive. To allay fears that the Constitution would restrict personal freedoms, the Federalists promised to add amendments to the document specifically protecting individual liberties. (They kept their word; James Madison introduced twelve constitutional amendments during the First Congress in 1789. Ten were ratified by the states and took effect in 1791. These first ten amendments to the Constitution, which restrain the national government from limiting personal freedoms, have come to be known as the **Bill of Rights** [see Table 2.5].)

Further, opponents said that the Constitution would weaken the power of the states (which it did). Patrick Henry railed against strengthening the federal government at the expense of the states. "We are come hither," he told his fellow delegates to the Virginia ratifying convention, "to preserve the poor commonwealth of Virginia."[21] Many state political leaders feared that their own power would be diminished as well.

Finally, not everyone wanted the economy to be placed on a sounder foundation. The inflation that characterized the period under the Articles of Confederation was a problem for creditors because it made the money they received as payment on their loans decline in value. This same inflation benefitted debtors, however. Their debts (such as the mortgages on their farms) remained constant, but money became more plentiful. This made it easier for them to pay off their debts.

---

[20] The three quotations are from Kenyon, *The Antifederalists,* 195, liv, and 1, respectively.

[21] Jackson Turner Main, *The Antifederalists* (Chapel Hill: University of North Carolina Press, 1961). For more on the Anti-Federalists, see Herbert J. Storing, *What the Anti-Federalists Were For* (Chicago: University of Chicago Press, 1981).

Table 2.5	The Bill of Rights (Arranged by Function)

PROTECTION OF FREE EXPRESSION

Amendment 1:   Freedom of speech, press, and assembly
                Freedom to petition government

PROTECTION OF PERSONAL BELIEFS

Amendment 1:   No government establishment of religion
                Freedom to exercise religion

PROTECTION OF PRIVACY

Amendment 3:   No forced quartering of troops in homes during peacetime
Amendment 4:   No unreasonable searches and seizures

PROTECTION OF DEFENDANTS' RIGHTS

Amendment 5:   Grand-jury indictment required for prosecution of serious crime
                No second prosecution for the same offense
                No compulsion to testify against oneself
                No loss of life, liberty, or property without due process of law
                No taking of private property for public use without just
                    compensation
Amendment 6:   Right to a speedy and public trial by a local, impartial jury
                Right to be informed of charges
                Right to legal counsel, to compel the attendance of favorable
                    witnesses, and to cross-examine witnesses
Amendment 7:   Right to jury trial in civil suit where the value of controversy
                    exceeds $20
Amendment 8:   No excessive bail or fines
                No cruel and unusual punishments

PROTECTION OF OTHER RIGHTS

Amendment 2:   Right to bear arms
Amendment 9:   Unlisted rights are not necessarily denied
Amendment 10:   Powers not delegated to the national government or denied to
                    the states reserved for the states or the people

Ratification

Federalists may not have had the support of the majority, but they made up for it in shrewd politicking. For instance, they knew the legislatures of some states were skeptical of the Constitution, and they knew that state legislatures were populated with political leaders who would lose power under the Constitution. The Federalists thus specified that the Constitution be ratified by special conventions in each of the states—not by state legislatures.

Delaware's approval was the first, on December 7, 1787. Only six months passed before New Hampshire's approval, the ninth, made the Constitution official. Virginia and New York then voted to join the new union. Two states were holdouts; North Carolina and Rhode Island made the promise of the Bill of Rights their price for joining the other states, and they finally joined the United States in 1789.

George Washington, commander in chief of the revolutionary army and leader of the Constitutional Convention (as well as one of America's wealthiest men), became the nation's first president on April 30, 1789. The inauguration took place on the balcony of New York City's Federal Hall.

With the Constitution ratified, it was time to select officeholders. The framers of the Constitution assumed that George Washington would become the first president of the new government—even giving him the convention's papers for safekeeping—and they were right. The general was the unanimous choice of the electoral college for president. He took office on April 30, 1789, in New York City, the first national capital. New Englander John Adams became "His Superfluous Excellence," as Franklin called the vice-president.

CONSTITUTIONAL CHANGE

"The Constitution," said Jefferson, "belongs to the living and not to the dead." The U.S. Constitution is frequently—and rightly—referred to as a living document. It is constantly being tested and altered.

Generally, constitutional changes are made either by formal amendments or by a number of informal processes. Formal amendments change the letter of the Constitution. There is also an unwritten body of tradition, practice, and procedure—what political scientists sometimes call the **unwritten constitution**—that, when altered, may change the spirit of the Constitution. For instance, political parties and national conventions are not part of our written Constitution, but they are important parts of the unwritten constitution. Informal processes, such as political party platforms and current political practice, alter this unwritten constitution and thus have a profound impact on the interpretation of the Constitution. In fact, not all nations, even those that we call democratic, have written constitutions (see "America in Perspective: Democracy Without a Constitution").

The Formal Amending Process

The most explicit means of changing the Constitution is through the formal process of amendment. Article v of the Constitution outlines procedures for formal amendment. There are two stages to the amendment process—proposal and ratification—and each stage has two possible avenues (see Figure 2.3). An amendment may be proposed either by a two-thirds vote in each house of Congress or by a national convention called by Congress at the request of two-thirds of the state legislatures. An amendment may be ratified either by the legislatures of three-fourths of the states or by special state conventions called in three-fourths of the states. The president has no formal role in amending the Constitution, although the chief executive may influence the success of proposed amendments.

All but one of the successful amendments to the Constitution have been proposed by Congress and ratified by the state legislatures. The exception was the Twenty-first Amendment, which repealed the short-lived Eighteenth Amendment, the Prohibition Amendment that outlawed the sale and consumption of alcohol. The amendment was ratified by special state conventions rather than by state legislatures—proponents of repeal doubted that they could win in Bible-Belt legislatures, and so they persuaded Congress to require that state conventions be called. Today a potential amendment is being proposed by state legislatures instead of by Congress, calling for a national convention to amend the Constitution to require a balanced national budget every year. By 1990, thirty-two of the required thirty-four states had formally requested such an

America in Perspective

Democracy *without* a Constitution?

Sometimes it is difficult for Americans to understand that constitutions can be both *written* and *unwritten*. They may be surprised to learn that Great Britain—often called "the cradle of democracy"—has no written constitution at all. The unwritten constitution of Britain is a mixture of acts of Parliament, judicial pronouncements, customs, and conventions about the rules of the political game. A number of documents are British constitutional landmarks, including the Magna Carta (the Great Charter), which King John accepted at Runnymeade in 1215 and which limited the power of the monarch. None of these documents, however, outline Britian's entire governmental system, as does the U.S. Constitution.

Although in theory the British monarch has the power to overrule laws passed by Parliament (the British legislature), the last time the monarch did so was in 1707, when Queen Anne vetoed the Scottish Militia bill. Today, it is unthinkable that the British monarch would veto an act of Parliament. Thus in Great Britain, there is no way to argue that an act of Parliament is

unconstitutional, since there is no written constitution to which one can appeal. If Parliament passes a law, it remains a law.

Nevertheless, Britain is undeniably a democracy. The political system allows free speech, open and free elections, vigorously competing political parties, and all the other characteristics generally associated with democracy. British politicians simply have not had a need to produce a single constitutional document.

At no time in the past has Britain experienced a sharp break with tradition, as in the American Revolution, forcing politicians to think about the basis of authority and the allocation of power, and then to write down how the country should be governed. As long as there is a basic consensus on how governing should take place, the British system works fine. When such a consensus is lacking, no government, whether it has a written or unwritten constitution, can last.

Figure 2.3 How the Constitution Can Be Amended

The Constitution sets up two alternative routes for proposing amendments and two for ratifying them. One of the four possible combinations has been used in every case but one, but there are persistent calls for a constitutional convention to propose some new amendment or another. (Amendments to permit school prayers, to make abortion unconsitutional, and to require a balanced national budget are recent examples.)

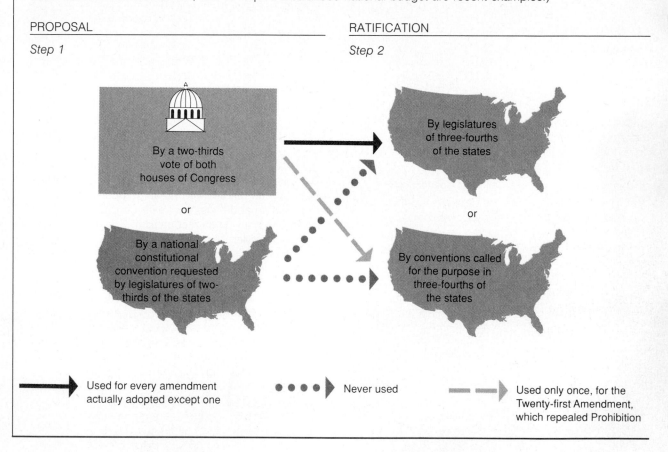

PROPOSAL

Step 1

By a two-thirds vote of both houses of Congress

or

By a national constitutional convention requested by legislatures of two-thirds of the states

RATIFICATION

Step 2

By legislatures of three-fourths of the states

or

By conventions called for the purpose in three-fourths of the states

→ Used for every amendment actually adopted except one

●●●● ▶ Never used

- - - ▶ Used only once, for the Twenty-first Amendment, which repealed Prohibition

---

amending convention (see "You Are the Policymaker: Should Congress Call a New Constitutional Convention?").

Unquestionably, formal amendments have made the Constitution more egalitarian and democratic. The emphasis on economic issues in the original document is now balanced by amendments that stress equality and increase the ability of a popular majority to affect government. The amendments are headed by the Bill of Rights (see Table 2.5), which Chapter 4 will discuss in detail. Later amendments have forbidden various political and social inequalities based on race, sex, and age (these will be discussed in Chapter 5). Of all the amendments, few are as important—or as brief—as the Thirteenth Amendment abolishing slavery. Other amendments, discussed later in this chapter, have democratized the political system, making it easier for voters to influence the government. Only one existing amendment specifically addresses the economy—the Six-

Should Congress Call a New Constitutional Convention?

Since the 1787 Constitutional Convention, Congress has received more than four hundred petitions from states requesting constitutional conventions. Most of these have been submitted since 1900. No new constitutional convention has ever been called, because no movement for a convention has obtained applications on a single subject from the required two-thirds of the states.

Calling a constitutional convention would not be an easy task. There are a number of legal questions that would have to be answered before a convention could be held, such as:

- What constitutes a valid call for a convention?
- In what time period must the required two-thirds of the states submit their resolutions? Can a state rescind its own call for a convention?
- Is Congress obligated to call a convention if requested to do so by two-thirds of the states?
- How would delegates be selected and apportioned among the states?
- Would members of Congress be eligible to run for delegate positions?

The biggest issue, however, is what would happen once the convention began. It is not clear that Congress can limit the scope and authority of a constitutional convention to the single amendment for which the convention is called to debate.

Convention opponents fear that a new constitutional convention would go well beyond its ostensible purpose and attempt to rewrite the entire Constitution, undoing the delicate balance of the Madisonian model. The thought of numerous special interest groups, clamoring for action on their favorite issues at such a convention, dampens the enthusiasm of even those who favor specific changes to the Constitution. Perhaps remembering that the delegates to the 1787 Convention were only supposed to modify the Articles of Confederation, constitutional historian Forest McDonald predicts that a new constitutional convention "would go berserk."

Proponents of a constitutional convention see things differently. They feel that the only way that certain constitutional amendments—such as requiring a balanced budget, allowing prayers in public schools, or prohibiting abortions—will ever be passed is through the convention mechanism. Congress, they argue, is unwilling or unable to propose such amendments and send them to the states for ratification. Delegates to a new constitutional convention, they believe, would act responsibly and address only the issue for which the convention was called.

As is true for most political and public policy questions, no one knows for sure what would happen. To reach a conclusion requires applying an understanding of both our constitutional system and contemporary American politics. If you favor a constitutional amendment that would require a balanced budget, for example, could you be confident that the convention would not also limit abortion rights, an action you might not support? Would you favor such a convention, despite the risks? What would *you* do?

Source: McDonald quote is from *Time,* July 6, 1987, 55.

teenth, or "income tax," Amendment. Overall, it is plain that the most important effect of these constitutional amendments has been to expand liberty and equality in America.

One of the most well-known, controversial, but failed amendments in recent years is the **Equal Rights Amendment,** or ERA. First proposed in 1923 by the nephew of suffragist Susan B. Anthony, the ERA had to wait fifty years—until 1978—before Congress passed it and sent it to the states for ratification. The proposed amendment states that "Equality of rights under the law shall not be denied or abridged by the United States or by any State on account of sex."

Feminist leaders Betty Friedan (right) and Gloria Steinem sign giant telegrams asking President Carter to influence voting on the ratification of the ERA. Despite the support of the president, Congress, and a majority of Americans, the ERA was not approved by the requisite three-fourths of the states—demonstrating the power one portion of the government can wield in the Madisonian system of checks and balances.

This seemingly innocuous amendment—who, after all, could truly oppose equal rights for women and men in this day and age?—sailed through Congress and the first few state legislatures. The Hawaiian legislature, in fact, arranged for Senator Daniel Inouye's office to signal when the Senate passed the ERA, so that Hawaii could be the first state to ratify.[22] Public opinion polls showed substantial support for the ERA. Surveys revealed that even people taking traditional views of women's roles still supported the ERA.[23]

Nevertheless, the ERA was not ratified. It failed in part because of the system of checks and balances. The ERA had to be approved not by a national majority but by three-fourths of the states. Many southern states opposed it, thus exercising their veto power despite approval by a majority of Americans (see "The People Speak: Is It Too Difficult to Amend the Constitution?").

The Informal Process of Constitutional Change

The written document called the Constitution was preserved by the members of the Constitutional Convention. They hired Jacob Shallus, a German immigrant in Philadelphia, to write out the Constitution and paid him the handsome sum of thirty dollars to do so. The convention was disbanding, having finished its

[22]The early attempts at ratification of the ERA are recounted in Janet Boles, *The Politics of the Equal Rights Amendment* (New York: Longman, 1978).

[23]Jane J. Mansbridge, *Why We Lost the ERA* (Chicago: University of Chicago Press, 1986).

work, and needed a rush job. On September 15, 1787, the conventioneers gave Shallus only forty hours to copy the Constitution itself. Prepared on four pieces of parchment made from lamb or calf skin and written with a quill pen in Shallus's elegant script, the actual document bounced from capital to capital during the early days of the Republic. Today it sits at the National Archives, bathed in helium and under the watchful eye of an electronic camera.

Of course, the written Constitution itself is never changed, even when we pass a constitutional amendment. We do not haul out Shallus's old parchment and then pen in some lines abolishing slavery or creating an income tax; the amendments, too, are deposited in the National Archives. Think for a moment of all the changes in American government that have taken place without altering a word or letter of Shallus's document; in fact, there is not a word in the Constitution that would lead one to suspect any of the following developments:

- The United States has the world's oldest two-party system, wherein not one member of Congress and no president since Washington has failed to say, "I'm a Democrat (or a Republican, or Federalist, or Whig, or whatever)."

- Abortions through the first trimester of pregnancy, and even longer under some state laws, are legal in the United States.

- Members of the electoral college consider themselves honor bound (and in some places even legally bound) to follow the preference of their state's electorate.

- Both the Senate and the House are now on TV; TV has come to set our political agenda and guide our assessments of candidates and issues.

- Government now taxes and spends about a third of our gross national product, an amount the Convention delegates might have found gargantuan.

None of these things are "unconstitutional." The parties emerged, television came to prominence in American life, first technology and then the law permitted abortions—all without having to tinker with the founders' handiwork. This is because the Constitution changes *informally* as well as *formally*. There are several ways the Constitution changes informally: through judicial interpretation and through political practice, and as a result of changes in technology and in the demands on policymakers.

Judicial Interpretation   Disputes often arise about the meaning of the Constitution. If it is the "supreme law of the land," someone has to decide how to interpret the Constitution when disputes arise. In 1803, in the famous case of **Marbury v. Madison,** the Supreme Court decided it would be the one to resolve differences of opinion (Chapter 16 discusses this case in detail). It claimed for itself the power of **judicial review.** Implied but never explicitly stated in the Constitution, this power gives courts the right to decide whether the actions of the legislative and executive branches of state and national governments are in accord with the Constitution.

Because most of the time the Constitution means what the Supreme Court says that it means, judicial interpretation can profoundly affect how the Constitution is understood. For example, in 1896 the Supreme Court decided that the Constitution allowed racial discrimination, despite the presence of the Fourteenth Amendment. Sixty years later it overruled itself and concluded that segregation by law violated the Constitution. In 1973 the Supreme Court decided that the Constitution protected a woman's right to an abortion in the first trimester of pregnancy, something the founders never addressed (these cases will be discussed in Chapters 4 and 5).

Changing Political Practice   Current political practices also change the Constitution, stretching it, shaping it, and giving it new meaning. Probably no changes are more important than those related to parties and presidential elections.

Political parties did not exist when the Constitution was written. In fact, its authors would have disliked parties, which encourage factions. Regardless, by 1800 a party system had developed and it plays a key role in making policy today. American government would be radically different if there were no political parties, even though the Constitution is silent about them.

Changing political practice has also altered the role of the electoral college, which has been reduced to a trivial role in selecting the president. The writers of the Constitution (to avoid giving too much power to the uneducated majority) intended there to be no popular vote for the president; instead, the people would vote to select wise electors who would then choose a "distinguished character of continental reputation" (as the Federalist Papers put it) to be president. These electors formed the electoral college. Each state would have the same number of electors to vote for the president as it had senators and representatives in Congress.

In 1796, the first election in which George Washington was not a candidate, electors scattered their votes among thirteen candidates. By the election of 1800 domestic and foreign policy issues had divided the country into two political parties. To avoid dissipating their support, the parties required electors to pledge in advance to vote for the candidate that won their state's popular vote, leaving electors with a largely clerical function.

Although electors are now rubber stamps for the popular vote, nothing in the Constitution prohibits an elector from voting for any candidate. Every so often, electors have decided to cast a vote for their own favorites; some state laws require electors to vote for the candidate chosen by a majority of their state's citizens, but such laws have never been enforced. The idea that the electoral college would exercise wisdom independent of the majority of people is now a constitutional anachronism, changed not by formal amendment but by political practice.

Technology   The Constitution has also been greatly changed by technology. The mass media now plays a role unimaginable in the eighteenth century, questioning governmental policies, supporting candidates, and helping shape citizens' opinions. The bureaucracy has grown in importance as the result of the development of computers, which create new potential for bureaucrats to serve the public (such as writing over thirty million Social Security checks each month)—and, at times, create mischief. Electronic communications and the development of atomic weapons have given the president's role as commander in chief added significance, increasing the power of the president in the constitutional system.

Increasing Demands on Policymakers   The significance of the presidency has also grown as a result of increased demands for new policies. The United States's evolution in the realm of international affairs, from an insignificant country that kept to itself to a superpower with an extraordinary range of international obligations, has located additional power in the hands of the chief executive, who is designated to take the lead in foreign affairs. Similarly, the increased demands of domestic policy have resulted in the president taking a more prominent role in preparing the federal budget and a legislative program.

The Importance of Flexibility It is easy to see that the document the framers produced over two hundred years ago was not meant to be static, written in stone. Instead, the Constitution's authors created a flexible system of government, one that could adapt to the needs of the times without sacrificing personal freedom. This flexibility has helped ensure the Constitution's—and nation's—survival. Although the United States is young compared to other Western nations, it has the oldest functioning Constitution. France, which experienced a revolution in 1789, the same year the Constitution was ratified, has had twelve constitutions over the past two centuries. Despite the great diversity of the American population, the enormous size of the country, and the extraordinary changes that have taken place over the nation's history, the Constitution is still going strong.

The Elaboration of the Constitution

The Constitution, even with all twenty-six amendments, is a very short document, containing fewer than eight thousand words. It does not prescribe the structure and functioning of the national government in detail. Regarding the judiciary, Congress is told simply to create a court system as it sees fit. The Supreme Court is the only court required by the Constitution, and even here the number of justices and their qualifications is left up to Congress. Similarly, many of the governing units we have today, such as the executive departments, the various

MIKE LUCKOVICH
Courtesy Times-Picayune (New Orleans)

offices in the White House, the independent regulatory commissions, and the committees of Congress, to name only a few examples, are not mentioned at all in the Constitution. The framers allowed future generations to determine their needs. As muscle grows on the constitutional skeleton, it inevitably gives new shape and purpose to the government.

UNDERSTANDING THE CONSTITUTION

Our theme of the role of government runs throughout this chapter, which focuses, of course, on just what it is that the national government can and cannot do. This section will examine the Constitution in terms of our theme of democracy and also look at the impact of the Constitution on the policy-making.

The Constitution and Democracy

Despite the fact that America is often said to be one of the most democratic societies in the world, the Constitution itself is rarely described as democratic. This is hardly surprising, considering the political philosophies of the men who wrote it. Among eighteenth-century upper-class society, democratic government was roundly despised. If democracy was a way of permitting the majority's preference to become policy, the Constitution writers wanted no part of it. The American government was to be a government of the "rich, well-born, and able," as Hamilton said, where John Jay's wish that "the people who own the country ought to govern it" would be a reality. Few people today would consider these thoughts democratic.

The Constitution did not, however, create a monarchy or a feudal aristocracy. It created a republic, a representative form of democracy modeled after the Lockean tradition of limited government. Thus the undemocratic—even anti-democratic—Constitution established a government that permitted substantial movement toward democracy.

One of the central themes of American history is the gradual democratization of the Constitution. What began as a document characterized by numerous restrictions on direct voter participation has slowly become much more democratic. Today few people share the founders' fear of democracy.

The Constitution itself offered no guidelines on voter eligibility, leaving it to each state to decide. As a result, only a small percentage of adults could vote; women and slaves were excluded entirely. Five of the sixteen constitutional amendments passed since the Bill of Rights have focused on the expansion of the electorate. The Fifteenth Amendment (1870) prohibited discrimination on the basis of race in determining voter eligibility (although it took the Voting Rights Act of 1965, discussed in Chapter 5, to make the amendment effective). The Nineteenth Amendment (1920) gave women the right to vote (some states had already done so). The Twenty-third Amendment (1961) accorded the residents of Washington, D.C., the right to vote in presidential elections. Three years later the Twenty-fourth Amendment prohibited poll taxes (which discriminated against the poor of all races). Finally, the Twenty-sixth Amendment (1971) lowered the voter eligibility age to eighteen.

Another amendment, the Seventeenth (1913), provided for direct election of senators. Presidential elections have been fundamentally altered by the development of political parties. By placing the same candidate on the ballot in all the states and requiring members of the electoral college to support the candidate receiving the most votes, parties have increased the probability that the candidate for whom most Americans vote will also receive a majority of the electoral college vote. Although it is possible for the candidate who receives the most popular votes to lose the election, this has not happened since 1888. According to the Constitution the United States selects its president through an electoral college, but in practice American citizens now directly elect the president. (For more on the electoral college, see Chapter 9.)

Technology has also diminished the separation of the people from those who exercise power. Officeholders communicate directly with the public through television, radio, and targeted mailings. Air travel makes it easy for members of Congress to commute regularly between Washington and their districts. Similarly, public opinion polls and the telephone make it possible for officials to regularly learn of citizens' opinions on important issues. Even though the American population has grown from fewer than 4 million to about 250 million people since the first census was taken in 1790, the national government has never been closer to those it serves.

The Constitution and Policy-making

The separation of powers and the checks and balances established by the Constitution allow almost all groups some place in the political system where their demands for public policy can be heard. Because many institutions share power, a group can usually find at least one sympathetic ear. Even if the president opposes the policies a particular group favors, then Congress, the courts, or some other institution can help the group achieve its policy goals.

In the early days of the civil rights movement, for example, African Americans found Congress and the president unsympathetic, so they turned to the Supreme Court. They would have had a more difficult time getting their interests on the political agenda if the Court had not had important constitutional power. Groups advocating greater equality for women had better luck getting Congress on their side to *propose* an equal rights amendment than they had convincing the state legislatures to *ratify* it.

The separation of powers and the system of checks and balances promote the politics of bargaining, compromise, and playing one institution against another. The system of checks and balances implies that one institution is checking another. *Thwarting, blocking,* and *impeding* are synonyms for *checking*. But if I block you, you block him, and he blocks me, none of us is going to accomplish anything. Some scholars suggest that so much checking was built into the American political system that effective government is almost impossible. The historian and political scientist James MacGregor Burns has argued:

> We have been too much entranced by the Madisonian model of government. . . . The system of checks and balances and interlocked gears of government . . . requires the consensus of many groups and leaders before the nation can act; . . . we underestimate the extent to which our system was designed for deadlock and inaction.[24]

---

[24]James MacGregor Burns, *The Deadlock of Democracy* (Englewood Cliffs, N.J.: Prentice-Hall, 1963), 6.

If the president, the Congress, and the courts all pull in different directions on policy, the result may be either no policy at all or a makeshift and inadequate one. The outcome may be nondecisions when hard decisions are needed. If government cannot respond effectively because its policy-making processes are too fragmented, its performance will be inadequate. Perhaps the Madisonian model has reduced the ability of government to reach effective policy decisions. (See "The People Speak: The Constitution and Public Policy".)

SUMMARY

The year 1787 was crucial in American nation-building. The fifty-five men who met in Philadelphia created a policy-making system that responded to a complex policy agenda. There were critical conflicts over equality, which led to key compromises in the New Jersey and Virginia Plans, the three-fifths compromise on slavery, and the decision to toss the issue of voting rights into the hands of the states. There was more consensus, however, about the economy. These merchants, lawyers, and large landowners felt that the American economy was in a shambles, and they intended to make the national government an economic stabilizer. The specificity of the powers assigned to Congress left no doubt that it was to forge national economic policy. The delegates knew, too, that the global

Members of the Second Continental Congress prepare to vote on the Declaration of Independence, July 2, 1776. After two days of debate on the wording of the Declaration, it was adopted on July 4. This vote was a key step in American nation-building, leading ultimately to the Constitutional Convention of 1787.

How good a job has the system of government established by the Constitution done in

	Good Job	Bad Job
Providing for the national defense?	76%	16%
Establishing a fair system of justice?	53%	37%
Treating all people equally?	41%	51%
Keeping life in America peaceful?	66%	27%

Source: The questions as worded are taken directly from a *CBS News/New York Times* Poll, May 1987.

posture of the fledgling nation was pitifully weak. A strong national government would be better able to ensure its own security.

Madison and his colleagues were less clear about the protection of individual rights. They felt that the limited government they had constructed would protect freedom, so they said little about individual rights in the Constitution. The ratification struggle revealed that protection of personal freedoms was much on the public's mind, however, so the Bill of Rights was proposed. These first ten amendments to the Constitution, along with the Thirteenth and Fourteenth Amendments, provide Americans with protection from governmental restraints on individual freedoms.

It is important to remember that 1787 was not the only year of nation-building. The nation's colonial and revolutionary heritage shaped the meetings in Philadelphia. Budding industrialism in a basically agrarian nation put economic issues on the Philadelphia agenda. What Madison was to call an "unequal division of property" made equality an issue, particularly after Shays' Rebellion. The greatest inequality of all, that between slave and free, was so contentious an issue that it was simply finessed at Philadelphia.

Nor did ratification of the Constitution end the nation-building process. Constitutional change—both formal and informal—continues to shape and alter the letter and the spirit of the Madisonian system.

That system includes a separation of powers and many checks and balances. Today Americans still debate whether the result is a government too fragmented to be controlled by anyone. In Chapter 3 we will look at yet another way that the Constitution divides the government's power: between the national and the state governments.

KEY TERMS

constitution
U.S. Constitution
Declaration of Independence
natural rights
consent of the governed
limited government
Articles of Confederation
Shays' Rebellion

factions
New Jersey Plan
Virginia Plan
Connecticut Compromise
three-fifths compromise
writ of habeas corpus
separation of powers
checks and balances
republic

Federalists
Anti-Federalists
Federalist Papers
Bill of Rights
unwritten constitution
Equal Rights Amendment
Marbury v. *Madison*
judicial review

FOR FURTHER READING

Becker, Carl L. *The Declaration of Independence: A Study in the History of Political Ideas.* New York: Random House, 1942. Classic work on the meaning of the Declaration.

Hamilton, Alexander, James Madison, and John Jay. *The Federalist Papers,* 2nd ed. Edited by Roy P. Fairfield. Baltimore: Johns Hopkins University Press, 1981. Key tracts in the campaign for the Constitution and cornerstones of American political thought.

Jensen, Merrill. *The Articles of Confederation.* Madison: University of Wisconsin Press, 1940. Definitive treatment of the Articles.

Jillson, Calvin C. *Constitution Making: Conflict and Consensus in the Federal Convention of 1787.* New York: Agathon, 1988. Sophisticated analysis of the drafting of the Constitution.

Lipset, Seymour Martin. *The First New Nation.* New York: Basic Books, 1963. Political sociologist Lipset sees the early American experience as one of nation-building.

McDonald, Forrest B. *Novus Ordo Seclorum: The Intellectual Origins of the Constitution.* Lawrence: University Press of Kansas, 1986.

Morris, Richard B. *The Forging of the Union, 1781-1789.* New York: Harper & Row, 1987. Written to coincide with the bicentennial of the Constitution, this is an excellent history of the document's making.

Rossiter, Clinton. *1787: The Great Convention.* New York: Macmillan, 1966. A well-written study of the making of the Constitution.

Storing, Herbert J. *What the Anti-Federalists Were For.* Chicago: University of Chicago Press, 1981. Analysis of the political views of those opposed to the ratification of the Constitution.

Wood, Gordon S. *The Creation of the American Republic.* Chapel Hill: University of North Carolina Press, 1969. In-depth study of American political thought prior to the Constitutional Convention.

3

*F*EDERALISM

On June 30, 1986, the Supreme Court was called into session with the usual "Oyez, Oyez, God Save This Honorable Court." The Court that day had a controversial and extremely sensitive case to decide. It involved Michael Hardwick of Atlanta, Georgia. Four years earlier, in August 1982, Atlanta police had gone to Hardwick's apartment to serve him a warrant for failing to pay a fine. Admitted to a house by one of his friends, the officers found Hardwick in bed, having sex with another man. Since homosexual activity violated the Georgia antisodomy law, the officers hauled Hardwick in. If convicted, he faced a twenty-year prison sentence.

Even though he was not formally charged by the state of Georgia, Hardwick decided to challenge the law in federal court. Believing that sexual activity among consenting adults was none of the state's business, Hardwick argued that his constitutional right to privacy forbade Georgia from arresting and prosecuting him for sodomy. A federal court dismissed Hardwick's claim on a technicality, but a federal appeals court held that the Georgia statute violated the U.S. Constitution. (Remember the discussion of *judicial review* in Chapter 2; courts have the power to hold that laws of the states or the national government violate the Constitution.)

The state of Georgia then appealed the case, called *Hardwick v. Georgia,* to the Supreme Court. The bitterly divided Court, in a five to four decision, upheld the Georgia law. The Court maintained that any state legislature could pass a law forbidding homosexual relations among adults, consenting or otherwise, if it wanted to. Relying heavily on the concept of *original intent* (the attempt to determine the original intent of the Constitution writers), the majority noted that each of the original thirteen colonies had laws against sodomy, and that until 1961 all fifty states had such laws. In his dissenting opinion, Justice Harry Blackmun called the decision "revolting." Revolting or not, it set back the efforts of homosexual groups to win legal standing under the Constitution's guarantees of privacy and equal protection.

Headlines across the country blared that the Supreme Court had ruled that homosexuality was illegal. The Supreme Court had done no such thing. The headlines reflected a grave misunderstanding of the American federal system as well as the Supreme Court. The Court had not held that homosexuality was illegal, but that *a state had the constitutional power to regulate homosexual behavior.* The issue was about the power of the states in the federal system—an issue on which America has fought a civil war—indicating just how important it is to understand American federalism.

*T*he relationship between governments at the local, state, and national levels often confuses many Americans. Governmental institutions, it seems, must be able to serve many masters. Neighborhood schools are run by locally elected school boards but also receive state and national funds, and with those funds come state and national rules and regulations. Local airports, sewage systems, pollution control systems, and police departments also receive a mix of local, state, and national funds, and hence operate under a complex web of rules and regulations imposed by each level of government.

Sometimes this complex system is almost impossible to understand. Even the national government has difficulty keeping track of the approximately $125 billion of federal aid distributed each year to states and cities.[1] In 1972, when the U.S. Treasury Department first sent revenue-sharing checks to fifty states

---

[1]Thomas Anton, *Moving Money* (New York: Oxford University Press, 1982).

and thirty-eight thousand local governments, some five thousand checks were returned, marked "addressee unknown," by the Postal Service. If the Postal Service has trouble keeping up with all the governments in America, pity the poor citizen.

This chapter will explore *American federalism,* the complex relationships between different levels of government in the United States. It will show the ways that the federal system has changed over two centuries of American government and why American federalism is at the center of important battles over policy.

WHAT FEDERALISM IS AND WHY IT IS SO IMPORTANT

Federalism is not the typical way nations organize their governments. It is a rather unusual system for governing, with particular consequences for those who live within it. This section explains what a federal system is and what difference having one makes to Americans.

What Federalism Is

A way of organizing a nation so that two or more levels of government have formal authority over the same area and people is called **federalism;** it is a system of shared power between units of government. For example, the state of Georgia has formal authority over its inhabitants (like Michael Hardwick—see this chapter's "Government in Action" box), but the national government can also pass laws and establish policies that affect Georgians. Michael Hardwick's house in Atlanta was subject to the formal authority of both the state and the national governments.

Although federalism is not unique to the United States, it is not a very common method of governing. Only 13 of the 170 or so nations of the world have federal systems. Countries with federal systems, including West Germany, Mexico, Argentina, the Soviet Union, Canada, Australia, India, and the United States, share little in common besides having federal systems (see "America in Perspective: Why Federalism?").

Most governments in the world today are not federal but **unitary governments,** in which all power resides in the central government. If the British parliament, for instance, wants to redraw the boundaries of local governments or change their forms, it can (and has). By contrast, if the U.S. Congress wants to abolish Alabama or Oregon, it cannot.

American states are unitary governments with respect to their local governments. Local governments get their authority from the states; they can be created or abolished by the states. States also have the power to make rules for their own local governments. They tell them what their speed limits can be, the way in which they should be organized, how they can tax people, what they can spend money on, and so forth. States, however, do not receive their authority from the national government but *directly* from the Constitution.

There is a third form of governmental structure, a *confederation*. The United States began as such, under the Articles of Confederation. In a confederation the national government is weak and most or all the power is in the hands of its components, for example, the individual states. Today confederations are rare except in international organizations such as the United Nations (see Chapter 20).

The workings of the federal system are sometimes called **intergovernmental relations.**[2] This term refers to the entire set of interactions among national, state, and local governments.

[2]One useful introduction to federalism and intergovernmental relations is Deil S. Wright, *Understanding Intergovernmental Relations*, 3rd ed. (Belmont, Calif.: Brooks/Cole, 1988).

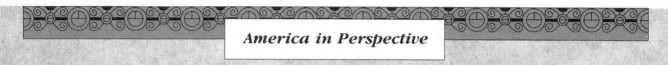

America in Perspective

Why Federalism?

There are only thirteen countries with federal systems. Trying to determine why these particular nations chose a federal system is an interesting but difficult task. The accompanying table shows that all three North American nations have federal systems, but the trend does not continue in South America, where only two nations have federal systems. Countries large in size, such as Canada and Australia, or large in both size and population, such as India, the Soviet Union, the United States, Brazil, and Mexico, tend to have federal systems, which decentralize the administration of governmental services. Nevertheless, China and Indonesia, two large countries, have unitary governments, and tiny Malaysia and Switzerland have federal systems.

A nation's diversity may also play a role in the development of a federal system. Brazil, Canada, India,

Malaysia, Switzerland, the Soviet Union, the United States, and Yugoslavia have large minority ethnic groups that often speak separate languages and practice separate religions. Many nations with unitary systems, however, ranging from Belgium to most African countries, are also replete with ethnic diversity.

Most federal systems are democracies, although most democracies are not federal systems. Authoritarian regimes generally do not wish to disperse power away from the central government, yet both the Soviet Union and Yugoslavia, perhaps reflecting the extraordinary diversity of their populations, have federal systems—of a sort. In both countries, the central government, until recently, retained ultimate power. As democracy sweeps through these countries, perhaps their national governments will give more power—and thus more freedom—to local governments.

NATION	POPULATION (millions)	AREA (million square miles)	DIVERSITY (ethnic, linguistic, and religious)
Argentina	32,697	1,072	Low
Australia	16,640	2,966	Low
Austria	7,571	32	Low
Brazil	149,362	3,286	Medium
Canada	25,907	3,852	High
Federal Republic of Germany	61,352	96	Low
India	828,934	1,222	High
Malaysia	16,754	127	High
Mexico	84,460	762	Low
Switzerland	6,632	16	Medium
Union of Soviet Socialist Republics	286,717	8,649	High
United States	247,732	3,615	Medium
Yugoslavia	23,732	99	High

Source: Arthur S. Banks, ed., *Political Handbook of the World, 1989* (Binghamton, N.Y.: CSA Publications, 1989).

Why Federalism Is So Important

The federal system in America *decentralizes our politics.* Senators are elected as representatives of individual states, not the entire nation. Likewise, presidents are elected not by a national election but by statewide elections. It is the states that run primaries to nominate presidential candidates. On election day in November, there are actually fifty-one presidential elections, one for each state plus Washington, D.C. It is even possible—as last happened in 1888—that a candidate receiving the most popular votes in the country can lose the election because of the way the electoral votes are distributed by state.

The federal system decentralizes our politics in more fundamental ways. With more layers of government, there are more opportunities for political participation. With more people wielding power, there are more points of access in government and more opportunities for interests to have their demands for public policies satisfied. With more decisions made in the states, there are fewer sources of conflict at the national level.

The federal system not only decentralizes our politics, but *decentralizes our policies,* too. The history of the federal system demonstrates the tension between the states and the national government about policy—who controls it and what it should be. In the past, people debated about whether the states or the national government should regulate the railroads, pass child labor laws, or adopt minimum wage legislation. Today people debate about whether the states or the national government should regulate abortions, enforce school desegregation, determine speed limits on highways, or tell eighteen-year-olds they cannot drink.

Policies about equality, the economy, the environment, and other matters are subject to both the centripetal force of the national government and the centrifugal force of the states. Because of the overlapping powers of the two levels of government, most of our public policy debates are also debates about federalism.

The People Speak | **One Policy or Many?**

Should there be one national policy set by the federal government or should the fifty states make their own rules on the following issues?

	One national policy	Separate state policies
Controlling pollution	49%	46%
Setting penalties for murder	62%	34%
Voting and registration of voters	64%	31%
Selecting textbooks in public schools	35%	61%
Setting minimum wages	51%	45%
Establishing safety standards in factories	65%	31%
Setting highway speed limits	42%	56%

Opinion is divided over whether there should be one national policy or separate state policies on a wide range of issues. In the absence of consensus, the central question of federalism— "Who has the power to make policy on this issue?"—remains a principal source of conflict in American politics.

Source: The questions as worded are taken directly from a *CBS News/New York Times* Poll, May 1987.

States are responsible for most public policies dealing with social, family, and moral issues. The national government does not (and constitutionally cannot) pass laws that *directly* regulate abortion, drinking ages, marriage and divorce, or sexual preferences. These policy prerogatives belong to the states. They become national issues, however, when aggrieved or angry groups take their cases to Congress or the federal courts, in an attempt to use the power of the national government to *influence* states or to get federal courts to find a state's policy unconstitutional.

Candy Lightner, for example, a New Jersey mother whose child was killed by a teenage drunken driver, formed MADD (Mothers Against Drunk Driving). This group was the seed from which sprouted hundreds of local MADD chapters, as well as offshoots like SADD (Students Against Drunk Driving). Lightner's lobbyists inundated state capitals to get the drinking age raised. Between 1976 and 1983, nineteen states raised their drinking age, typically to age twenty-one.

MADD supporters realized, however, that it was much easier to get a national law passed once than to lobby each of fifty state legislatures separately. Therefore, in 1983, at a press conference on the steps of the Capitol, Lightner and Secretary of Transportation Elizabeth Dole, Senator John Danforth (D-Mo.), Senator Richard Luger ((R-Ind.), and Senator Frank Lautenberg (D-N.J., from Lightner's home state) announced their intentions to support a nationally standard drinking age. They could not pass a bill directly setting the drinking age in the states, so they proposed using federal highway funds as an incentive for the states to pass their own bills. (See "You Are the Policymaker: Raising the Drinking Age" for more on this case).

The American states have always been policy innovators.[3] The states overflow with reforms, new ideas, and new policies. From clean air legislation to welfare

[3]On the states as innovators see Jack L. Walker, "The Diffusion of Innovations in the American States," *American Political Science Review* 63 (September 1969): 880–99.

At a 1983 press conference Transportation Secretary Elizabeth Dole announces her support of MADD and of congressional legislation to raise minimum drinking ages. Small groups such as MADD, without the resources to change policy in fifty states, often attempt to move traditionally local issues onto the national government's policy agenda.

Raising the Drinking Age

Contrary to widespread impressions, American highways are safer than ever. In the 1940s, twenty-two out of every one hundred thousand Americans died in car accidents; in the 1980s, only nineteen did, even though Americans now drive far more miles per year. Despite these statistics, the agony associated with children's deaths caused by drunk drivers is very real. When the drunken driver is a teenager, inexperienced at both driving and drinking, passions heat further. Candy Lightner's MADD had no trouble rousing sentiments against this carnage. No politician wants to be accused of supporting drunks on the road aiming two-ton vehicles at defenseless children.

The most important question about public policy, though, is not whether the problem is real but whether the solution is appropriate. The legislation stemming from the Lightner-Dole-Danforth-Lautenberg press conference was an amendment to the Surface Transportation Act of 1982. Because the federal government couldn't legislate drinking ages, it relied on a carrot-and-stick strategy: Congress would withhold 10 percent of all federal highway aid from states that did not raise their legal drinking age to twenty-one by 1988. The legislation sailed through Congress (the Senate passed it by a vote of eighty-one to sixteen, few Senators presumably wanting their votes construed as tolerating teenage drunken driving). President Reagan—remember him, the staunch opponent of federal regulations?—signed the legislation in October 1984. By the end of 1989, every state had a drinking age of twenty-one.

Popular policies may or may not be wise policies; they may or may not work. Evidence on the impact of state laws that have raised the minimum drinking age is, at best, mixed. Wagenaar studied what happened when Michigan raised its drinking age in the 1970s. He estimated that there were 1,650 fewer accidents in Michigan after it adopted a stiffer drinking-age law. A study by the Wharton School of Economics, though, reached opposite conclusions. It found that changes in the drinking age were not associated with significant changes in either fatalities or accidents.

The citizen policy analyst has to weigh both values and evidence. If a policy analyst is not just a citizen but also a political officeholder, he or she is going to have to weigh something else, too: is this going to help or hurt my chances for reelection?

Think about these questions as a policymaker:

1. How could problems with the implementation of higher drinking-age laws affect the possible impact of the policy? (For example, what would happen if the policy were enforced unevenly or not at all?)
2. How do you weigh the rights of eighteen- to twenty-year-olds to drink against the harm done by teenage drunken driving?
3. Is a national policy encouraging the states to discourage teenage drinking a good policy? Is it likely to be an effective policy? What kinds of evidence would you want to have to be confident it would be effective?
4. Would any policies in this area be best left to the states individually?

Sources: For background information on this issue, see the articles in H. Weschsler, ed., *Minimum Drinking Age Laws* (Lexington, Mass.: D. C. Heath, 1980). The studies cited are A. C. Wagenaar, *Alcohol, Young Drivers, and Traffic Accidents* (Lexington, Mass.: D. C. Heath, 1983), and Wharton School of Economics, "The Relationship Between Increases in Minimum Purchase Age for Alcoholic Beverages and the Number of Traffic Fatalities," Social Science Working Papers, the Wharton School, University of Pennsylvania, 1985.

reform, the states constitute a national laboratory to develop and test public policies and share the results with other states and the national government. Almost every policy the national government has adopted had its beginnings in the states. One or more states pioneered child labor laws, minimum wage legislation, unemployment compensation, antipollution legislation, civil rights protections, and the income tax.

Federalism is an important key to unlocking the secrets of the American political system. Which president is elected, which policy innovations are developed, at what age young men and women can legally drink, and many other issues are profoundly affected by the workings of the federal system.

THE CONSTITUTIONAL BASIS OF FEDERALISM

The word *federalism* is absent from the Constitution, and not much was said about it at the Constitutional Convention. Eighteenth-century Americans had little experience in thinking of themselves as Americans first and state citizens second. On the contrary, loyalty to state governments was so strong that the Constitution would have been resoundingly defeated had it tried to abolish them. In addition, a central government, working alone, would have had difficulty trying to govern eighteenth-century Americans.

Thus there was no other practical choice in 1787 but to create a federal system of government. As the last chapter explained, the delegates did, however, ensure that the new national government would be stronger, and the state governments weaker, than under the Articles of Confederation.

The Division of Power

The Constitution's writers carefully defined the powers of state and national governments (see Table 3.1). Although favoring a stronger national government, the framers still made states vital cogs in the machinery of government. The Constitution guaranteed states equal representation in the Senate (and even made this provision unamendable). It also made states responsible for both state and national elections, an important power. Further, the Constitution re-

National campaigns for the presidency actually take place in the states; candidates must talk about oil prices in Texas, Social Security benefits in Florida, and federal aid to cities in New York. In this photo Michael Dukakis appeals to Iowa farmers during the 1988 Democratic primary campaign.

Table 3.1 The Constitution's Distribution of Powers

SOME POWERS SPECIFICALLY GRANTED BY THE CONSTITUTION

To the National Government	To Both the National and State Governments	To the State Governments
To coin money	To tax	To establish local governments
To conduct foreign relations	To borrow money	To regulate commerce within a state
To regulate commerce with foreign nations and among states	To establish courts	To conduct elections
To provide an army and a navy	To make and enforce laws	To ratify amendments to the federal Constitution
To declare war	To charter banks and corporations	To take measure for public health, safety, and morals
To establish courts inferior to the Supreme Court	To spend money for the general welfare	To exert powers the Constitution does not delegate to the national government or prohibit the states from using
To establish post offices	To take private property for public purposes, with just compensation	
To make laws necessary and proper to carry out the foregoing powers		

SOME POWERS SPECIFICALLY DENIED BY THE CONSTITUTION

To the National Government	To Both the National and State Governments	To the State Governments
To tax articles exported from one state to another	To grant titles of nobility	To tax imports or exports
To violate the Bill of Rights	To permit slavery (Thirteenth Amendment)	To coin money
To change state boundaries	To deny citizens the right to vote because of race, color, or previous servitude (Fifteenth Amendment)	To enter into treaties
	To deny citizens the right to vote because of sex (nineteenth Amendment)	To impair obligations of contracts
		To abridge the privileges or immunities of citizens or deny due process and equal protection of the laws (Fourteenth Amendment)

quired the national government to protect states against violence and invasion. It also virtually guaranteed the continuation of each state; Congress is forbidden to create new states by chopping up old ones, unless a state's legislature approves—an unlikely event.

In Article VI of the Constitution the framers dealt with what remains a touchy question: In a dispute between the states and the national government, which prevails? The answer that the delegates provided, often referred to as the **supremacy clause,** seems clear enough. They stated that the following three items were the supreme law of the land:

1. The Constitution

2. Laws of the national government (when consistent with the Constitution)

3. Treaties (which can only be made by the national government)

Judges in every state were specifically told to obey the Constitution, even if their state constitutions or state laws directly contradicted the U.S. Constitution. Today all state executives, legislators, and judges are bound by oath to support the Constitution.

The national government, however, can only operate within its appropriate sphere. It cannot unsurp the states' powers. The question, then, is over the boundaries of the national government's powers. According to some people, the **Tenth Amendment** gives part of the answer. It states that the "powers not delegated to the United States by the Constitution, nor prohibited by it to the states, are reserved to the states respectively, or to the people." To those advocating states' rights, the amendment clearly means that the national government has only those powers specifically assigned by the Constitution. The states or people have supreme power over any activity not mentioned there. Despite this interpretation, in 1941 the Supreme Court (in *United States* v. *Darby*) called the Tenth Amendment a constitutional truism, a mere assertion that the states have independent powers of their own—not that their powers are supreme to the national government's.

The Court seemed to backtrack on this ruling in favor of national government supremacy in a 1976 case, *National League of Cities* v. *Usery*, in which it held that extending national minimum wage and maximum hours standards to employees of state and local governments was an unconstitutional intrusion of the national government into the domain of the states. In 1985, however, (in *Garcia* v. *San Antonio Metro*) the Court overturned the *National League of Cities* decision. The Court held, in essence, that it was up to Congress, not the courts, to decide which actions of the states should be regulated by the national government. Once again the Court ruled that the Tenth Amendment did not give states power supreme to the national government's for activities not mentioned in the Constitution.

Occasionally an issue arises in which states challenge the authority of the national government, such as in the late 1980s when the governors of several states refused to allow their state National Guards to engage in training exercises in Central America. National Guards are state militias, but the Constitution provides that they can be nationalized by the president. In 1990 the Supreme Court reiterated the power of the national government by siding with the president. South Dakota sued the federal government over its efforts to raise states' drinking-age laws and over its efforts to mandate a fifty-five mile-per-hour speed limit on highways. The state lost both cases.

Establishing National Supremacy

Why is it that the federal government has gained so much power at the expense of the states? Three key events have largely settled the issue of how national and state powers are related: the *McCulloch* v. *Maryland* court case, the Civil War, and the civil rights movement.

McCulloch* v. *Maryland   As early as 1819, the issue of state versus national power came before the Supreme Court in the case of ***McCulloch* v. *Maryland*.** Here are the facts of the case and the principles decided by it.

The new American government moved quickly on many economic policies. In 1791, it created a national bank. It was not a private bank like today's "First National Bank of Such and Such," but a government agency empowered to print money, make loans, and engage in many other banking tasks. A darling of such

Citing

Federalists as Alexander Hamilton, the bank was hated by those opposed to strengthening the national government's control of the economy (such as Jefferson), by farmers, and by state legislatures, who saw it as a tool of the elite.

Railing against the "Monster Bank," the state of Maryland in 1818 passed a law taxing the national bank's Baltimore branch $15,000 a year. The Baltimore branch refused to pay, whereupon the state of Maryland sued the cashier, one James McCulloch, for payment. When the state courts upheld Maryland's law and its tax, the bank appealed to the U.S. Supreme Court. John Marshall was chief justice when two of the country's ablest lawyers argued the case before the Court.

Daniel Webster argued for the national bank and Luther Martin, a signer of the Declaration of Independence, for Maryland. Martin argued that the Constitution was very clear about the powers Congress had (as outlined in Article I of the Constitution). The power to create a national bank was *not* among them. Thus, Martin argued, Congress had exceeded its powers and Maryland had a right to tax the bank. On behalf of the bank, Webster argued for a broader interpretation of the powers of the national government. The Constitution was not meant to stifle congressional powers, he said, but rather permit Congress to use all means "necessary and proper" to fulfill its responsibilities.

Marshall, never one to pussyfoot about a big decision, had his decision in favor of the bank written before the arguments ended— some said before they even began. He and his colleagues set forth two great constitutional principles in their decision. The first was *the supremacy of the national government* over the states. Said Marshall in his decision, "If any one proposition could command the universal assent of mankind, we might expect it to be this—that the government of the United States, though limited in its power, is supreme within

Pictured here is the Bank of the United States in Philadelphia. The federal government's power to establish a national bank is not mentioned in the Constitution, but in McCulloch v. Maryland *the Supreme Court ruled that Congress has certain implied powers and that national policies take precedence over state policies. These two principles have been used to expand the national government's sphere of influence.*

its sphere of action." (Notice the rhetorical flourish and exaggeration; of course national supremacy did not command the "universal assent of mankind." Marshall's rhetoric calls to mind the old story about the preacher who wrote in the margin of his sermon, "Weak point—pound the pulpit.") As long as the national government behaved in accordance with the Constitution, said the Court, its policies took precedence over state policies.

The Court also held that Congress *was* behaving consistently with the Constitution when it created the national bank. It was true, Marshall admitted, that Congress had certain **enumerated powers,** powers specifically listed in Article I, Section 8 of the Constitution. Congress could coin money, regulate its value, impose taxes, and so forth. Creating a bank was not enumerated. But the Constitution added that Congress has the power to "make all laws necessary and proper for carrying into execution the foregoing powers." That, said Marshall, gave Congress certain **implied powers.** It could make economic policy in a number of ways consistent with the Constitution. The other key principle of *McCulloch,* therefore, was that the *national government has certain implied powers that go beyond its enumerated powers.*

Today the notion of implied powers has become like a rubber band that can be stretched without breaking—the "necessary and proper" clause of the Constitution is often referred to as the **elastic clause.** Especially in the domain of economic policy, hundreds of congressional policies involve powers not specifically mentioned in the Constitution. Federal policies to regulate food and drugs, build interstate highways, protect consumers, try to clean up dirty air and water, and do many other things are all justified as implied powers of Congress.

The Constitution gives Congress the power to regulate interstate and international commerce. American courts have spent many years trying to define *commerce.* In 1824 the Supreme Court, in deciding the case of **Gibbons v. Ogden** defined commerce very broadly, encompassing virtually every form of commercial activity. Today it covers not only the movement of goods, but also radio signals, electricity, telephone messages, insurance transactions, and much more. In 1964 Congress even relied on the interstate commerce power to prohibit racial discrimination in places of public accommodation such as restaurants, hotels, and movie theaters.

Federalism as the Battleground of the Struggle for Equality   What *McCulloch* pronounced constitutionally, the Civil War (1861–65) settled militarily. The Civil War is often thought of as mainly a struggle over slavery. It was that, of course, but it was also, and perhaps more importantly, a struggle between states and the national government. In fact, Abraham Lincoln announced in his 1861 inaugural address that he would willingly support a constitutional amendment guaranteeing slavery if it would save the Union. Instead, it took a bloody civil war for the national government to assert its power over the Southern states' claim of sovereignty.

A century later, conflict between the states and the national government again erupted over states' rights and national power. Again the policy issue was equality. In 1954 the Supreme Court held that school segregation was unconstitutional. Southern politicians responded with what they called "massive resistance" to the decision. When a federal judge ordered the admission of two black students to the University of Alabama in 1963, Governor George Wallace literally "stood in the schoolhouse door" to prevent federal marshals and the

In 1963 Alabama Governor George Wallace made a dramatic stand at the University of Alabama to resist integration of the all-white school. Federal marshals won this confrontation, and since then the federal government in general has been able to impose national standards of racial equality on the states.

students from entering the Admissions Office. (In fact, the confrontation had been elaborately staged by representatives of Deputy attorney General Nicholas Katzenbach and Wallace; chalk marks were drawn on the sidewalk to show everyone where to stand during the showdown between states' rights and federal power.) Despite Wallace's efforts, the students were admitted, and throughout the 1960s the federal government enacted law after law and policy after policy to end segregation in schools, housing, public accommodations, voting, and jobs. In 1979 (after blacks began voting in large numbers in Alabama) George Wallace himself said of his stand in the schoolhouse door: "I was wrong. Those days are over and they ought to be over." The conflict between states and the national government over equality issues was decided in favor of the national government; national standards of racial equality prevailed.

States' Obligations to Each Other

Federalism involves more than relationships between the national government and state and local governments. The states must deal with each other as well, and the Constitution outlines certain obligations that each state has to every other state.

Full Faith and Credit Suppose that, like millions of other Americans, a person divorces and then remarries. For each marriage, this person purchases a marriage license, registering the marriage with a state. On the honeymoon for the second marriage, the person travels across the country. Is this person married in each state passed through, even though the marriage license is with only one state? Can the person be arrested for bigamy because the divorce occurred in only one state?

The answer, of course, is that a marriage license and a divorce, like a driver's license and a birth certificate, are valid in all states. Article IV of the Constitution requires that states give **full faith and credit** to the public acts, records, and civil judicial proceedings of every other state. This reciprocity is essential to the functioning of society and the economy. Without the full faith and credit clause, people could avoid their obligations to, say, make payments on automobile loans simply be crossing a state boundary. In addition, contracts between business firms can be enforced across state boundaries, allowing firms incorporated in one state to do business in another.

Extradition What about criminal penalties? Almost all criminal law is state law. If someone robs a store, steals a car, or commits a murder, the chances are that this person is breaking a state, not a federal, law. The Constitution says that states are required to return a person charged with a crime in another state to that state for trial or imprisonment. This practice is called **extradition.** Although there is no way to force states to comply, they usually are only too happy to do so, not wishing to harbor criminals and hoping that other states will reciprocate. This is why a lawbreaker cannot avoid punishment by simply escaping to another state.

Due to the full faith and credit clause of the Constitution, these babies' birth certificates are valid in each state. They are also entitled to most of the benefits—and subject to most of the obligations—of citizenship in any state they happen to visit, thanks to the privileges and immunities clause.

Privileges and Immunities   The most complicated obligation among the states is the requirement that citizens of each state receive all the **privileges and immunities** of any other state in which they happen to be. The goal of this constitutional provision is to prohibit states from discriminating against citizens of other states. If, for example, a Texan visits California, the Texan will pay the same sales tax and receive the same police protection as residents of California.

The states allow many exceptions to the privileges and immunities clause, however. Many readers of this book attend public universities. If you are such a student, and you also reside in the same state as your university, you usually pay a substantially lower tuition than do your fellow students from out-of-state. Similarly, only residents of a state can vote in state elections. States often attempt to pass the burdens of financing the state government to those outside the state (see "A Question of Ethics: Should Wyoming Tax the Rest of the Country for its Coal?").

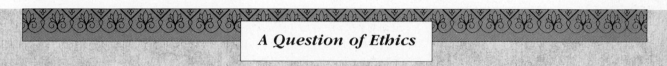

A Question of Ethics

Should Wyoming Tax the Rest of the Country for Its Coal?

If Wyoming were a nation, it would be the world's fourth largest coal producer. Richly veined with the less-polluting, low-sulphur coal, Wyoming ships ten mile-long trainloads of coal each day from Rock Springs to the coal-consuming regions of the country.

To capitalize on this wealth of natural resources, Wyoming imposed a severance tax on its coal. A severance tax is an exit cost imposed on raw materials such as oil, coal, or natural gas. For every ton of Wyoming coal shipped to Illinois, an Illinois utility—and ultimately, the consumers of that utility's electricity—had to pay the state of Wyoming $1.12 in severance taxes. In 1980 one utility company, Chicago-based Commonwealth Edison Company, paid Wyoming $13.5 million in severance taxes. In fact, the funds reaped from the severance tax were just enough to meet the needs of the entire Wyoming state budget. Wyoming could do without a state income tax and a state sales tax and still have more than $1 billion in the state treasury.

Wyoming is not the only state with a severance tax. Many oil- and coal-rich states have it. None has outdone Alaska, which imposes a 12.25 percent severance tax on oil produced from its North Slope. By the year 2010, Alaska could be collecting an annual take of $10 billion in severance taxes. Texas, Colorado, Oklahoma, Montana, West Virginia, Kentucky, and Louisiana—all blessed by nature with energy resources—charge energy-poor states a severance tax.

When Montana imposed a 30 percent severance tax on coal exported from its borders, Commonwealth Edison took Montana to court to test the constitutionality of this practice. The utility argued that Article I, Section 9 of the Constitution specifically stated that "no tax or duty shall be laid on articles exported from any State." Thus, it contended, Montana's severance tax was an unconstitutional and unreasonable burden on interstate commerce. The U.S. Supreme Court, however, did not agree. On July 2, 1981, in the case of *Commonwealth Edison* v. *Montana*, it held that Montana was within its rights to impose its severance tax.

Legality is one thing, ethics is another. Wyoming has the constitutional right to impose a severance tax, but is it ethical? If a state is fortunate enough to have coal or oil or some other valuable mineral located within its borders, is it proper to capitalize on its good fortune at the expense of citizens in other states? What do *you* think?

Source: For more information on the Wyoming case, see James Coates, "It's Economic War Among These United States," *Chicago Tribune*, June 27, 1981, 4.

The Supreme Court has never clarified just which privileges a state must make available to all Americans, and which privileges can be limited to its own citizens. In general, the more fundamental the right, such as owning property or receiving police protection, the less likely it is that a state can discriminate against citizens of another state.

INTERGOVERNMENTAL RELATIONS TODAY

American federalism has changed quite a bit over the past two centuries. This section focuses first on the federal system's gradual change from a dual federalism to a cooperative federalism.[4] It then looks at the cornerstone of the relationship between the national government and state governments: federal grants-in-aid. Later, the chapter will explore the relative growth of the national government and state governments.

From Dual to Cooperative Federalism

One way to understand the changes in American federalism over the past two hundred years is to contrast two types of federalism. The first type is called **dual federalism.** In this kind of federalism, states and the national government each remain supreme within their own spheres. The states are responsible for some policies, the national government for others. For example, the national government has exclusive control over foreign and military policy, the postal system, and monetary policy. States are exclusively responsible for schools, law enforcement, and road building. In dual federalism, the powers and policy assignments of the layers of government are distinct, as in a layer cake, and proponents of dual federalism believe that the powers of the national government should be interpreted narrowly.

Most politicians and political scientists today argue that dual federalism is outdated. They are more likely to describe the current American federal system as one of **cooperative federalism.** Instead of a layer cake, they see American federalism as more like a marble cake, with mingled responsibilities and blurred distinctions between the levels of government. In cooperative federalism powers and policy assignments are shared between states and the national government. Costs may be shared, with the national government and the states each paying a part. Administration may also be shared, with state and local officials working within federal guidelines. Sometimes even blame is shared when programs do not work well.

Before the national government began to assert its dominance over state governments, the American federal system leaned toward dual federalism. The American system, however, was never neatly separated into purely state and purely national responsibilites. For example, education was usually thought of as being mainly a state and local responsibility, yet, even under the Articles of Confederation, Congress set aside land in the Northwest Territory to be used for schools. During the Civil War, the national government adopted a policy to

---

[4]The transformation from dual to cooperative federalism is described in David B. Walker, *Toward a Functioning Federalism* (Cambridge, Mass.: Winthrop, 1981), chap. 3.

Cooperative federalism began in earnest during the Great Depression of the 1930s. In this photo Works Progress Administration Workers, paid by the federal government, build a local road in Tennessee. In subsequent decades the entire interstate highway system was constructed with a combination of national and state dollars.

create land grant colleges. Important American universities like Wisconsin, Texas A&M, Illinois, Ohio State, North Carolina State, and Iowa State owed their origins to this national policy.

In the 1950s and 1960s the national government began supporting public elementary and secondary education. In 1958 Congress passed the National Defense Education Act (largely in response to Soviet dominance in the space race). The act provided federal grants and loans for college students and financial support for elementary and secondary education in science and foreign language. In 1965 Congress passed the Elementary and Secondary Education Act, which provided federal aid to numerous schools. Although these policies expanded the national government's role in education, they were not a sharp break with the past.

Today the federal government's presence is felt in even the tiniest little red schoolhouse. Almost all school districts receive some federal assistance. To do so, they must comply with numerous federal rules and regulations. They must, for example, maintain desegregated and nondiscriminatory programs.

Highways are another example of the movement toward cooperative federalism. In an earlier era, states and cities were mostly responsible for building roads, although the Constitution does authorize Congress to support "post roads." In 1956 Congress passed an act creating an interstate highway system. Hundreds of red, white, and blue signs were planted at the beginnings of interstate construction projects. The signs announced that the interstate highway program was a joint federal-state project and specified the cost and sharing of funds. In this as in other areas, the federal system has promoted a partnership between the national and state governments.

Cooperative federalism today rests on several standard operating procedures. For hundreds of programs, cooperative federalism involves

- *Shared costs.* Washington foots part of the bill, but states or cities that want to get their share must pay part of a program's costs. Cities and states can get federal money for airport construction, sewage treatment plants, youth programs, and many other programs, but only if they pay some of the costs.

- *Federal guidelines.* Most federal grants to states and cities come with strings attached. Congress spends billions to support state highway construction, for example, but to get their share states must adopt and enforce particular speed limits.
- *Shared administration.* State and local officials implement federal policies, but they have administrative powers of their own. The U.S. Department of Labor, for example, gives billions of dollars to states for job retraining, but states have considerable latitude in spending the money.

The cooperation between the national government and state governments is such an established feature of American federalism that it takes place even when the two levels of government are in conflict on certain matters. For example, in the 1950s and 1960s southern states cooperated well with Washington in building the interstate highway system while clashing with the national government over racial integration.

In his first inaugural address Ronald Reagan argued that the states had primary responsibility for governing in most policy areas and promised to "restore the balance between levels of government." Although few officials at either the state or national levels agreed with him about ending the national government's role in domestic programs, Reagan's opposition to the national government's spending on domestic policies and the huge federal deficits of the 1980s forced a reduction in federal funds for state and local governments and shifted some responsibility for policy back to the states. Despite Reagan's move toward a more dual federalism, most Americans adopt a pragmatic view of governmental responsibilities, seeing the national government as more capable of—and thus responsible for—handling some issues, while state and local governments are better at managing others (see "The People Speak: Confidence in Government").

The People Speak   **Confidence in Government**

In which level of government do you have the most trust and confidence to handle each of the following problems most effectively?

	Federal	State	Local
Control air pollution	47%	30%	9%
Fight drugs	39%	18%	21%
Help the homeless	28%	26%	27%
Manage urban development	17%	37%	29%
Improve schools	12%	42%	32%
Recycle trash	9%	28%	50%

The American public feels that different levels of government have different strengths. Although it views air pollution and illicit drugs as national problems, it looks to state and local governments to improve schools and recycle trash.

Source: The questions as worded are taken directly from a Gallup Poll for the Advisory Commission on Intergovernmental Relations, June 1989.

Fiscal Federalism

The cornerstone of the national government's relations with state and local governments is **fiscal federalism,** the pattern of spending, taxing, and providing grants in the federal system. Subnational governments can influence the national government through local elections for national officials, but the national government has a powerful source of influence over the states—money. Grants-in-aid are the main instrument the national government uses for both aiding and influencing states and localities.

Despite the constant efforts of the Reagan administration to whittle away aid to states and cities, state and local aid from Washington still amounts to over $120 billion each year. Figure 3.1 illustrates the growth in the amount of money spent on federal grants. Federal aid, covering a wide range of policy areas (see Figure 3.2), accounts for over 18 percent of all the funds spent by state and local governments and for about 10 percent of all federal government expenditures.

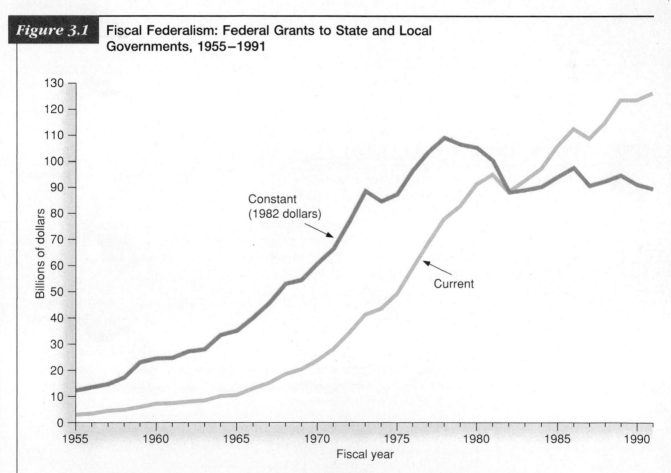

Figure 3.1 Fiscal Federalism: Federal Grants to State and Local Governments, 1955–1991

For 1955–76, years ending June 30; 1977–88, years ending September 30; 1989–91, OMB estimate.

Source: Advisory Commission on Intergovernmental Relations, *Significant Features of Fiscal Federalism, 1989 Edition,* vol. 2 (Washington, D.C.: Government Printing Office, 1989). The 1989–1991 data are estimated.

Functions of Federal Grants

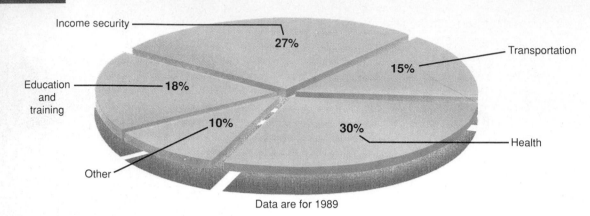

Income security — 27%

Transportation — 15%

Education and training — 18%

10%

30%

Other

Health

Data are for 1989

Source: *Budget of the United States, Fiscal Year 1990, Special Analyses* (Washington, D.C.: U.S. Government Printing Office, 1989), Table H-4.

The Federal Grant System: Distributing the Federal Pie The national government regularly publishes the *Catalogue of Federal Domestic Assistance,* a massive volume listing the host of federal aid programs available to states, cities, and other local governments. The book lists federal programs that support energy assistance for the aged poor, housing allowances for the poor, drug-abuse services, urban rat-control efforts, community arts programs, state disaster-preparedness programs, and many more.

There are two major types of federal aid for states and localities. **Categorical grants,** accounting for 80 percent of all federal aid to state and local governments, are the main source of federal aid. These grants can be used only for 1 of 422 specific purposes, or *categories,* of state and local spending. They also come with strings attached; virtually every categorical grant is enshrouded in rules and requirements about its use. One string commonly attached to categorical and other federal grants is a nondiscrimination provision, stating that aid may not be used for purposes that discriminate against minorities, women, or any other group. Another such string, a favorite of labor unions, is that federal funds may not support construction projects that pay below the local union wage.

Much federal regulation is accomplished in this indirect manner. Instead of issuing stern edicts that tell citizens or states what they can and cannot do, Congress often attaches a *rider,* a short bill, onto other legislation. Sometimes these riders accomplish serious policy goals—requiring affirmative action, forbidding discrimination, and so forth. MADD's successful campaign to get a drinking-age rider attached to federal highway aid is an excellent example of Congress indirectly imposing its will on the states (see "You Are the Policymaker," page 91). Sometimes, though, this "legislation by rider" is simply silly. Once a coalition of conservative members of Congress, led by Senator Orrin Hatch (R-Utah), got Congress to tack on to some school aid funds a rider forbidding the teaching of "secular humanism," a long-standing right-wing bugaboo referring loosely, and inaccurately, to "godless communism." No one knew exactly what secular humanism was—the bill studiously avoided defining it—but whatever it was, you would not be eligible for federal funds if you taught it.

There are two types of categorical grants. The most common type of categorical grant is a **project grant** (288 of the 422 categorical grants are project grants). A project grant is awarded on the basis of competitive applications. Grants obtained from the National Science Foundation by university professors are examples of project grants.

Formula grants are distributed, as their name implies, according to a formula (there are 134 formula grant programs). These formulas vary from grant to grant and may be computed on the basis of population, per capita income, percentage of rural population, or some other factor. A state or local government does not apply for a formula grant; a grant's formula determines how much money it will receive. As a result, Congress is the site of vigorous political battles over the formulas themselves. The most common formula grants are those for Medicaid, Aid for Families with Dependent Children, child nutrition programs, sewage treatment plant construction, public housing, community development programs, and training and employment programs.

Applications for categorical grants typically arrive in Washington in boxes, not envelopes. Complaints about the cumbersome paperwork and the many strings attached to categorical grants led to the adoption of the other major type of federal aid, **block grants.** These grants are given more or less automatically to states or communities, which have discretion in deciding how to spend the money. Block grants, first adopted in 1966, are used to support broad programs in areas like community development and social service (see Table 3.2). About 11 percent of all federal aid to state and community governments is in the form of block grants.

Another response to state and local governmental unhappiness with categorical grants was *revenue sharing*. First proposed by economists in the Johnson administration, revenue sharing became a favorite of the Nixon administration. In the revenue sharing program, virtually no strings were attached to federal aid payments—they could be used in almost any policy area. Revenue sharing was a help to many poor states and localities but never amounted to more than 2 percent of all state and local revenues. In 1987 the program fell victim to the Reagan administration's budgetary axes.

The Scramble for Federal Dollars   Hustling for federal dollars is an important task for states and communities as well as for businesses, universities, and other organizations. State and local agencies can obtain categorical grants only by applying for them, and then by meeting certain qualifications. Full-time intergovernmental relations staffs in city halls and state capitols investigate grant programs and make applications; more and more cities and states now have their own lobbyists in Washington, D.C.[5]

With so much grant money available from the federal government, most states and many cities have even set up full-time staffs in Washington, D.C. Their task is to keep track of what grants are available, and to help their states and cities be "first-est with the most-est." States and cities have even organized

The federal government often uses grants-in-aid as a carrot and stick for the states. For example, federal revenue sharing aid has been withheld from some cities until police departments have been racially and sexually integrated.

[5]On intergovernmental lobbying, see Donald H. Haider, *When Governments Go to Washington* (New York: Free Press, 1974).

Table 3.2 The Federal Block Grants

In response to complaints from state and local governments about the cumbersome paperwork and federal requirements attached to categorical grants, Congress has established thirteen block grants to support broad programs in areas like community development and social services. The grants are given more or less automatically to states or communities, which have discretion in deciding how to spend the money. About 11 percent of all federal aid to state and community governments is in the form of block grants.

HEALTH

Alcohol and Drug Abuse Treatment and Rehabilitation
Alcohol and Drug Abuse, and Mental Health Services
Maternal and Child Health Services
Preventive Health and Health Services

ELEMENTARY, SECONDARY, AND VOCATIONAL EDUCATION

Improving School Programs

CRIMINAL JUSTICE

Criminal Justice Improvements

TRANSPORTATION

Urban Mass Transportation

COMMUNITY DEVELOPMENT

Community Development for State Governments
Community Development for Local Governments

SOCIAL SERVICES

Community Services
Social Services for the Elderly and the Poor

TRAINING AND EMPLOYMENT

Job Training for Disadvantaged Adults and Youths

INCOME SECURITY

Low-Income, Home-Energy Assistance

Source: Advisory Commission on Intergovernmental Relations, *A Catalog of Federal Grant-in-Aid Programs to State and Local Governments* (ACIR: U.S. Government Printing Office, 1987), 14.

themselves into groups that act like other interest groups, including, for example, the National League of Cities, the U.S. Conference of Mayors, and the Council of State Governments.

All this hard work may pay off; airport renovation, a new water pollution program, or a new university center for the handicapped could be completed with the help of federal money. Often, however, it seems that having friends in high places is just as important as hustle. Senators and representatives regularly go to the voters with assurances that they will help secure federal grants for their home state or locality. They need continued support at the voting booth, they say, to get seniority in Congress and positions on key committees so that they can help the folks back home. In political parlance, helping obtain grants for constituents is called "bringing home the bacon."

A general rule of federalism is that the more money is at stake, the more people will argue about its distribution. As Figure 3.3 shows, there are some variations in the amount of money that states give to, and get back from, the

Source: Tax Foundation, Washington, D.C., "Memorandum on the Allocation of the Federal Tax Burden and Federal Grants-In-Aid by State, Fiscal Year 1987" (April 1988).

Figure 3.3   How Your State Fares in the Federal-Aid Game

The Tax Foundation, an independent institution specializing in tax patterns, provides an annual analysis of tax-benefit ratios by state. It compares the amount of federal income tax and other taxes contributed to the federal treasury with the amount of federal aid coming back to each state. The map shows how much each state paid to get back $1 in federal aid. Some states put in more than they got back. Florida, despite its Sunbelt status, fared the worst, putting in $1.60 for each $1 in federal aid. Other states got back more than they put in. Among the fifty States, Alaska fared best, getting back $1 after contributing only 49¢ to the federal treasury. On balance, though, Sunbelt states fared better than Frostbelt states.

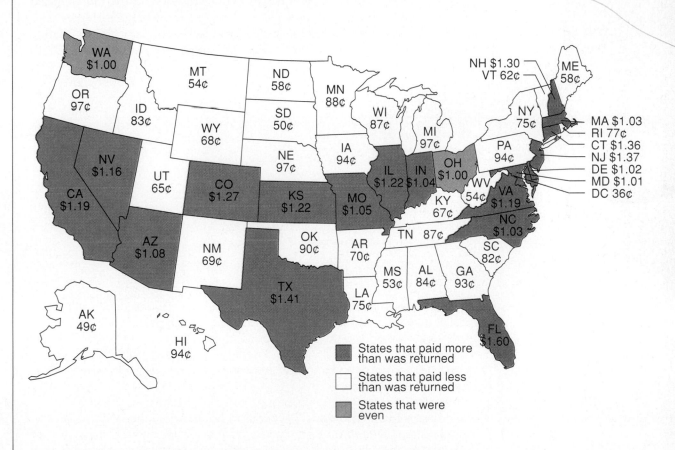

national government. On the whole, though, federal grant distribution follows the principle of *universalism*—something for everybody. The vigilance of senators and representatives keeps federal aid reasonably well spread among the states. There are not many things in America—not income, access to education, or taxes—more equitably distributed than federal aid to states and cities.

The Mandate Blues States and localities are usually pleased to receive aid from the national government, but there are times when they would just as soon not have it. For example, say Congress decides to extend a program administered by the states and funded, in part, by the national government. It passes a law requiring the states to extend the program if they want to keep receiving aid—which most states do. Congress usually (but not always) appropriates some funds to help pay for the new policy, but either way the states suddenly have to budget more funds for the project just to receive federal grant money.

Medicaid, which provides health care for poor people, is a prime example of a federal grant program that puts states in a difficult situation. Administered by the states, Medicaid receives wide support from both political parties. The national government pays 55 percent of the bill, and the states pick up the other 45 percent. Since 1984 Congress has moved aggressively to expand Medicaid to specific populations, requiring the states to extend coverage to certain children, pregnant women, and elderly poor. Congress has also increased its funding for the program a whopping 146 percent in the 1980s. Increased federal spending for Medicaid means increased spending for the states as well. In 1989, troubled by the drain on their states' budgets, forty-nine of the fifty governors called for a two-year moratorium on mandated expansions of Medicaid. In effect, they told Washington to keep its money and leave them alone for awhile.

UNDERSTANDING FEDERALISM

The federal system is central to politics, government, and policy in America. This book's themes of democracy and the size of government are especially helpful to increase an understanding of federalism. Federalism has an especially profound effect on democracy.

Federalism and Democracy

The founders established a federal system for several reasons, one of which was to allay the fears of those who believed that a powerful and distant central government would tyrannize the states and limit their voice in government. By decentralizing the political system, federalism was designed to contribute to democracy—or at least to the limited form of democracy supported by the founders. Has it done so?

Advantages for Democracy Federalism has many implications for democracy. The more levels of government, the more opportunities there are for participation in politics. Having state governments adds thousands of elected offices for which citizens may vote or run.

Adding additional levels of government also contributes to democracy by increasing access to government. Since different citizens and interest groups will have better access to either state-level governments or the national government, the two levels increase the opportunities for government to be responsive to demands for policies. For example, in the 1950s and 1960s advocates of civil rights found themselves stymied in southern states, so they turned to the national level for help in achieving racial equality. Business interests, on the other hand, have traditionally found state governments to be more responsive to their demands. Organized labor is not well established in some states, but it can usually depend on some sympathetic officials at the national level who will champion its proposals.

Different economic interests are concentrated in different states: oil in Texas, tobacco farming in Virginia, and copper mining in Montana, for example. The federal system ensures that each state can establish a power base to promote its interests. James Madison, among others, valued this pluralism of interests within a large republic.

Because the federal system assigns states important responsibilities for public policies, it is possible for the diversity of opinion within the country to be reflected in different public policies among the states. If the citizens of Texas wish to have a death penalty, for example, they can vote for politicians who support it, while those in Wisconsin can vote to abolish the death penalty altogether (see Table 3.3).

By handling most disputes over policy at the state and local level, federalism also reduces decision making and conflict at the national level. If every issue had to be resolved in Washington, the national government would be overwhelmed.

Disadvantages for Democracy On the other hand, relying on the states to supply public services has some drawbacks. States differ in the resources they

The federal system is so tangled it is sometimes difficult to see the relationship among different levels of government. The Jobs Training Partnership Act, for example, is a federal program implemented on the local level.

Table 3.3 **Diversity in Public Policy: State Death-Penalty Laws**

Because the American federal system allocates major responsibilities for public policy to the states, policies often vary with the different views of the population in different locations. The figure shows that for an issue as emotionally charged as the death penalty, different states have adopted quite different policies.

STATE	DEATH PENALTY	MINIMUM AGE	METHOD OF EXECUTION
Alabama	Yes	None	Electrocution
Alaska	No		
Arizona	Yes	None	Lethal Gas
Arkansas	Yes	15	Electrocution or Lethal Injection
California	Yes	18	Lethal Gas
Colorado	Yes	18	Lethal Gas
Connecticut	Yes	18	Electrocution
Delaware	Yes	None	Lethal Injection or Hanging
District of Columbia	No		
Florida	Yes	None	Electrocution
Georgia	Yes	17	Electrocution
Hawaii	No		
Idaho	Yes	18	Lethal Injection or Firing Squad
Illinois	Yes	18	Lethal Injection
Indiana	Yes	18	Electrocution
Iowa	No		
Kansas	No		
Kentucky	Yes	16	Electrocution
Louisiana	Yes	15	Electrocution
Maine	No		
Maryland	Yes	14	Lethal Gas
Massachusetts	No		
Michigan	No		
Minnesota	No		
Mississippi	Yes	13	Lethal Injection or Lethal Gas
Missouri	Yes	14	Lethal Gas

can devote to services like public education. Thus the quality of education a child receives is heavily dependent on the state in which the child's parents happen to reside. In 1988 Alaskan state and local governments spent an average of $7,038 for each child in the public schools, while in Arkansas the figure was only $2,410 (see Table 3.4).

Diversity in policy can also discourage states from providing services that would otherwise be available. Political scientists have found that generous welfare benefits can strain a state's treasury by attracting poor people from states with lower benefits. As a result, states are deterred from providing generous benefits to those in need. A national program with uniform welfare benefits, however, would provide no incentive for welfare recipients to move to another state in search of higher benefits.[6]

[6]Paul E. Peterson and Mark Rom, "American Federalism, Welfare Policy, and Residential Choices," *American Political Science Review* 83 (September 1989): 711–28.

Diversity in Public Policy: State Death-Penalty Laws (continued)

STATE	DEATH PENALTY	MINIMUM AGE	METHOD OF EXECUTION
Montana	Yes	None	Lethal Injection or Hanging
Nebraska	Yes	18	Electrocution
Nevada	Yes	18	Lethal Injection
New Hampshire	Yes	17	Hanging
New Jersey	Yes	18	Lethal Injection
New Mexico	Yes	18	Lethal Injection
New York	No		
North Carolina	Yes	14	Lethal Injection or Lethal Gas
North Dakota	No		
Ohio	Yes	18	Electrocution
Oklahoma	Yes	None	Lethal Injection
Oregon	Yes	16	Lethal Injection
Pennsylvania	Yes	None	Electrocution
Rhode Island	No		
South Carolina	Yes	None	Electrocution
South Dakota	Yes	None	Lethal Injection
Tennessee	Yes	None	Electrocution
Texas	Yes	17	Lethal Injection
Utah	Yes	None	Lethal Injection or Firing Squad
Vermont	Yes	None	Electrocution
Virginia	Yes	15	Electrocution
Washington	Yes	None	Lethal Injection or Hanging
West Virginia	No		
Wisconsin	No		
Wyoming	Yes	None	Lethal Injection or Lethal Gas

Source: Council of State Governments, *The Book of the States 1988–1989* (Lexington, Ky.: Council of State Governments, 1988), 404–5.

Federalism may also have a negative effect on democracy insofar as local interests are able to thwart national majority support of certain policies. As discussed earlier in this chapter, in the 1960s the states, especially those in the South, became battlegrounds when the national government tried to enforce national civil rights laws and court decisions. Because state and local governments were responsible for public education and voting eligibility, for example, and because they had passed most of the laws supporting racial segregation, federalism itself complicated and delayed efforts to end racial discrimination.

Finally, the sheer number of governments in the United States is, at times, as much a burden as a boon to democracy. Program vendors say at baseball games that "you can't tell the players without a scorecard"; unfortunately, scorecards are not available for local governments, where the players are numerous and sometimes seem to be involved in different games. The U.S. Bureau of the Census counts not only people but also governments. Its latest count revealed an astonishing 83,237 American governments (see Table 3.5).

Table 3.4 The Downside of Diversity: Spending on Public Education

The downside of the public-policy diversity fostered by federalism is that states are largely dependent on their own resources for providing public services; these resources vary widely from state to state. This table shows the wide variation among the states in the money spent on each child in the public schools.

STATE	DOLLARS PER PUPIL	STATE	DOLLARS PER PUPIL
Alabama	2,752	Montana	4,061
Alaska	7,038	Nebraska	3,641
Arizona	3,265	Nevada	3,829
Arkansas	2,410	New Hampshire	3,990
California	3,994	New Jersey	6,910
Colorado	4,359	New Mexico	3,880
Connecticut	6,141	New York	6,864
Delaware	4,994	North Carolina	3,911
District of Columbia	5,643	North Dakota	3,353
Florida	4,389	Ohio	4,019
Georgia	2,939	Oklahoma	3,051
Hawaii	3,894	Oregon	4,574
Idaho	2,814	Pennsylvania	5,063
Illinois	4,217	Rhode Island	5,456
Indiana	3,616	South Carolina	3,075
Iowa	3,846	South Dakota	3,159
Kansas	4,262	Tennessee	3,189
Kentucky	3,355	Texas	3,462
Louisiana	3,211	Utah	2,658
Maine	4,276	Vermont	4,949
Maryland	4,871	Virginia	4,145
Massachusetts	5,396	Washington	4,083
Michigan	4,122	West Virginia	3,895
Minnesota	4,513	Wisconsin	4,991
Mississippi	2,760	Wyoming	6,885
Missouri	3,566		

Source: U.S. Department of Commerce, *Statistical Abstract of the United States, 1989* (Washington, D.C.: U.S. Government Printing Office, 1989), 140.

You are now sitting within the jurisdiction of a national government, a state government, and perhaps *ten* to *twenty* local governments. The state of Illinois holds the current record for the largest number of individual governments—6,626 at the latest count. Chicago alone has about 1,200 governments.

Local governments come in four major types. *Municipalities* (or *townships*) are city governments such as Pittsburgh, Peoria, Pensacola, Phoenix, or Portland. Each municipality or township is located in 1 of 3,042 counties. *Counties* are the least numerous local governments, but they provide important services, especially for rural areas. Usually separate from both city and county governments are nearly 15,000 *school districts* responsible for elementary and secondary education. Most numerous but also most obscure are *special districts*; these nearly invisible governments handle services such as airport operation, mosquito abatement, and health care for a certain area.

National government	1
State governments	50
Local governments	83,186
Counties	3,042
Municipalities	19,200
Townships	16,691
School districts	14,721
Special districts	29,532
Total	**83,237**

Source: U.S. Bureau of the Census, *1987 Census of Governments,* vol. 1, no. 1 (Washington, D.C.: U.S. Government Printing Office, 1987).

Certainly more than 83,200 governments ought to be enough for any country. Are there too many? Americans speak eloquently about their state and local governments as grass-roots governments, close to the people (see "The People Speak: Is Closer Better?"), yet having so many governments makes it difficult to know which governments are doing what. Exercising democratic control over them is even more difficult; Americans participate in local elections at about half the already low rate in which they participate in presidential elections.

Federalism and the Growth of the National Government

President Ronald Reagan negotiated quotas on imports of Japanese cars in order to give advantages to the American auto industry, raising the price of all automobiles in the process. At the behest of steel companies, President George Bush

---

The People Speak   **Is Closer Better?**

Which level of government do you feel

	Federal	State	Local
Gives you the most for your money?	33%	23%	29%
Spends your tax dollars most wisely?	11%	20%	36%
Responds best to your needs?	18%	21%	40%
Has the most honest officials?	13%	11%	35%

In general, the closer to home government is, the more confidence people have in it. This is not necessarily the result of greater respect for local government, however. Local tax dollars are spent on policies such as roads, parks, and schools, tangible facilities that are easily understood and of immediate benefit to people, and local officials are easier to contact and observe. It is interesting that it is the federal government that is viewed as giving the most value for the tax dollar.

Source: The questions as worded are taken directly from a Gallup Poll for the Advisory Commission on Intergovernmental Relations, June 1989.

exercised his authority to continue Reagan's quotas on the amount of steel that could be imported into the country (thereby making steel products more expensive). The first major piece of legislation the Bush administration sent to Congress was a bail-out plan for the savings and loan industry, which had gotten itself into financial trouble through a combination of imprudent loans, incompetence, and corruption.

In each of these cases and dozens of others, the national government has involved itself (some might say interfered) in the economic marketplace with quotas and subsidies intended to help American businesses. As Chapter 2 explained, the national government took a direct interest in economic affairs from the very founding of the republic. As the United States changed from an agricultural to an industrial nation, new problems arose and with them new demands for governmental action. The national government responded with a national banking system, subsidies for railroads and airlines, and a host of other policies that dramatically increased its role in the economy.

The industrialization of the country raised other issues as well. With the formation of large corporations—Cornelius Vanderbilt's New York Central Railroad or John D. Rockefeller's Standard Oil Company, for example—came the potential for such abuses as monopoly pricing. If there is only one railroad in town, it can charge farmers inflated prices to ship their grain to market; if a single company distributes most of the gasoline in the country, it can set the price at which gasoline sells. Thus many interests asked the national government to restrain monopolies and encourage open competition.

There were additional demands on the national government for new public policies. Farming interests sought services such as agricultural research, rural electrification, and price supports. Labor interests wanted the national government to protect their rights to organize and bargain collectively and help provide safer working conditions, a minimum wage, and pension protection. Along with others, labor unions supported a wide range of social welfare policies, from education to health care. As the country became more urbanized, new problems arose in the areas of housing, welfare, the environment, and transportation. In each case, the relevant interest turned to the national government for help.

Why not turn to the state governments instead? In most cases, the answer is simple: a problem or policy requires the authority and resources of the national government. The Constitution forbids states from having independent defense policies, but even if it did not, would states want to take on a responsibility that represents about 60 percent of the federal work force and about 30 percent of federal expenditures?

It is constitutionally permissible but not sensible for the states to handle a wide range of other issues. It makes little sense for Louisiana to pass strict controls on polluting the Mississippi River if most of the river's pollution occurs upstream, where Louisiana has no jurisdiction. Rhode Island has no incentive to create an energy policy, since there are no energy reserves located in the state. Similarly, how effectively can a state regulate an international conglomerate such as General Motors? How can each state, acting individually, manage the nation's money supply?

Each state could have its own space program, but it is much more efficient if the states combine their efforts in one national program. The largest category of federal expenditures is for economic security, including the Social Security program. Although each state could have its own retirement program, how could state governments determine which state should pay for retirees who move to Florida or Arizona? A national program is the only feasible method of insuring the incomes of the mobile elderly of today's society.

The national government's growth is illustrated in Figure 3.4. The figure shows that the national government's share of American governmental expenditures has grown rapidly since 1929. Then, the national government spent only 2.5 percent of our gross national product; today it spends more than 20 percent of our GNP. The proportion of our GNP spent by state and local governments has grown less rapidly than the national government's share. States and localities spent 7.4 percent of our GNP in 1929, while they spend 13 percent today.

Figure 3.4 demonstrates that the states have not been supplanted by the national government; indeed, they carry out virtually all the functions they always

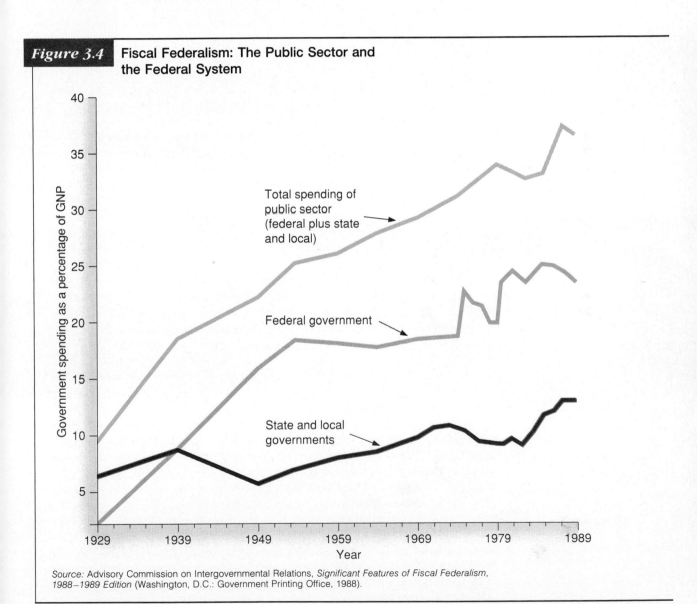

Figure 3.4 Fiscal Federalism: The Public Sector and the Federal System

Source: Advisory Commission on Intergovernmental Relations, *Significant Features of Fiscal Federalism, 1988–1989 Edition* (Washington, D.C.: Government Printing Office, 1988).

have. Instead, with the support of the American people, new responsibilities have been taken on by the national government (see "The People Speak: National Government Responsibilities"). In addition, the national government has added programs to help the states carry out their own responsibilities.

SUMMARY

Federalism is a governmental system in which power is shared between a central government and other governments. Federalism is much less common than the unitary governments typical of most parliamentary democracies. American federalism consists of fifty state governments joined in an "indestructible union," (as the Supreme Court once called it) under one national government. Today, federal power over the states is indisputable; the Supreme Court case *McCulloch* v. *Maryland* helped determine national supremacy. The federal government has recently used its fiscal leverage to impose speed limits of fifty-five miles per hour and discourage teenage drinking in the states.

The United States has moved from a system of dual federalism to one of cooperative federalism, in which the national and state governments share responsibility for public policies. Fiscal federalism is of great help to states; even after the Reagan administration reductions, the federal government distributes about $125 billion in federal funds to states and cities each year.

Federalism was instituted largely to enhance democracy in America, and it strengthens democratic government in many ways. At the same time, diverse state policies and the sheer number of local governments cause some problems as well. Demands for new policies and the necessity for national policy on certain issues have contributed to the growth of national government relative to the state governments, but the state governments continue to play a central role in the lives of Americans.

Although American federalism is about state power and national power, it is not a concept removed from most Americans' lives—just ask Michael Hardwick of Georgia. Federalism affects a vast range of social and economic policies. Slavery, school desegregation, abortion, teenage drinking, and even "secular humanism" have all been debated in terms of federalism.

KEY TERMS

federalism	implied powers	cooperative federalism
unitary governments	elastic clause	fiscal federalism
intergovernmental relations	*Gibbons* v. *Ogden*	categorical grants
supremacy clause	full faith and credit	project grants
Tenth Amendment	extradition	formula grants
McCulloch v. *Maryland*	privileges and immunities	block grants
enumerated powers	dual federalism	

FOR FURTHER READING

Anton, Thomas. *American Federalism and Public Policy.* Philadelphia: Temple University Press, 1989. An overview of how the national, state, and local governments share responsibility for policies.

Browning, Rufus P., Dale Rogers Marshall, and David H. Tabb. *Protest Is Not Enough.* Berkeley, Calif.: University of California Press, 1984. A study of ten California cities and the role played by federal programs in enhancing minority political power.

Conlan, Timothy J. *New Federalism: Intergovernmental Reform from Nixon to Reagan.* Washington, D.C.: Brookings Institution, 1988. An analysis of the efforts of Presidents Nixon and Reagan to restructure intergovernmental relations.

Elazar, Daniel J. *American Federalism: A View from the States*, 3rd ed. New York, Harper & Row, 1984. A well-known work surveying federalism from the standpoint of state governments.

Kettl, Donald F. *The Regulation of American Federalism.* Baltimore: Johns Hopkins University Press, 1987. Examines the regulations that national government imposes on state and local governments.

Riker, William. *Federalism.* Boston: Little, Brown, 1964. A highly critical account of American federalism.

Walker, David B. *Toward a Functioning Federalism.* Cambridge, Mass.: Winthrop, 1981. A concise history of American federalism, with some blueprints for improvement.

Wright, Deil S. *Understanding Intergovernmental Relations*, 3rd ed. Belmont, Calif.: Brooks/Cole, 1988. A review of the relations between the local, state, and national levels of government.

4

CIVIL LIBERTIES AND PUBLIC POLICY

From 1981 to 1989 William Von Raab was the commissioner of the U.S. Customs Service, an agency of the Treasury Department. Von Raab had a reputation in Washington as one of the most aggressive antagonists in the "war on drugs." He went so far as to impose mandatory random testing for customs employees who intercepted drugs, carried firearms, or had access to classified material. Any employee could be forced to submit to a urine test with five days' notice.

This rule was not popular with many customs employees. They regarded mandatory testing as an invasion of their privacy that was not justified by any need to protect the public (as might be the case for pilots or railroad workers, for example). The workers were also concerned about the possibility of false-positive results, since no error-free method of drug testing existed. Their anger grew when they learned that only five of the three thousand workers tested had turned out to be drug users. By that time, they had filed suit in federal court asking that the rule be declared unconstitutional. The Supreme Court heard *National Treasury Employees* v. *Von Raab,* combining it with a similar suit filed by railroad workers.

March 22, 1989, was a better day for the government than for its employees. On that day the railroad workers lost their case by a vote of seven to two. The result was closer for the customs workers. The justices voted five to four to uphold the testing requirement for employees who intercepted drugs or used firearms. The Court sent back the case involving employees with access to classified material on the grounds that not enough information existed to permit a ruling.

Justice Anthony Kennedy wrote that the government's interest in public safety and safeguarding borders was so "compelling" that it overrode the privacy interests of the workers. Two vehement dissents were written by justices who were rarely on the same side. Thurgood Marshall, a liberal, surprised no one with his statement that "there is no drug exception to the Constitution." Antonin Scalia, a Reagan appointee, broke with his usual conservative allies, including Kennedy and Chief Justice William Rehnquist. He called the testing program "an immolation of privacy and human dignity in symbolic opposition to drug use."

As this case suggests, Americans today live in a time of intense conflict about rights and liberties. Debates about the right to abortion, the right to bear arms, the rights of criminal defendants, and other similar issues are constantly in the news. Some of these conflicts come from incompatible interests. The need to protect society against crime is often in conflict with society's need to protect the rights of people accused of crime. When an accused criminal robs the local supermarket, Americans are usually willing to let constitutional guarantees run their course. Patience with constitutional technicalities often wears thin, however, when children have been sexually molested or a brutal murder has occurred.

Other conflicts arise from strong differences of opinion about what is ethical, moral, or right. To some Americans, abortion is murder, the taking of a human life. To others, a woman's right to choose whether or not to bear a child, free of governmental intrusion, is a fundamental value. Sometimes, the text of the Constitution serves as a guide in these areas; sometimes it does not. The wisdom of the Bill of Rights is constantly struggling with modern technology. If abortion is a difficult issue, for example, what happens if RU-486, a drug that enables a woman to give herself a safe abortion, becomes available? If people have the right to become parents, does a woman have the right to agree to bear a child who someone else will parent? What happens if the surrogate mother changes her mind?

Some of these issues present conflicts between an individual and the government; others, like surrogate motherhood, involve conflicts between individuals that the government is expected to resolve. The importance of these controversies reaches far beyond the few people directly involved in them. Whoever resolves the conflicts makes decisions that affect the entire society, including future generations.

Civil liberties are legal and constitutional protections against the government. Disputes about civil liberties often end up in court. Americans' civil liberties are set down in the Bill of Rights, but the courts are the arbiters of these liberties because they determine what the Constitution means in the cases that they decide. The Supreme Court of the United States is the final interpreter of the content and scope of our liberties; this ultimate power to define the Constitution accounts for the ferocious debate over presidential appointments to the Supreme Court.

Cases end up in court as *Somebody* v. *Somebody Else*. They can involve rare or commonplace events, from executions to daily recitations of the Pledge of Allegiance in public schools. Someone could file a case alleging that a high school principal has no right to refuse to publish a school paper, or that a Christmas nativity scene outside city hall breaches the constitutional separation of church and state, or that the Oklahoma law allowing a man to be executed for a crime he committed when he was fifteen constitutes cruel and unusual punishment. In fact, someone *has* made all these claims in court; all these cases will be examined in the following sections.

This chapter will also introduce you to some ordinary people who got involved in the legal process. For example, Gregory Johnson felt that burning an American flag was the best way to express his opinions about the government; the government did not agree. Jennifer Johnson (no relation) was accused of delivering drugs to a child—her own child, through an umbilical cord. Some famous people like Larry Flynt and Jerry Falwell also end up in court, where they promote their views of civil liberties.

You will meet some unsavory characters in this chapter. A convicted killer and rapist named Ernesto Miranda gave his name to one of the most famous cases in American history. As a result of *Miranda* v. *Arizona,* police now de-

Artist "Dred" Scott Tyler's exhibit at Chicago's School of the Art Institute—"What Is the Proper Way to Display the U.S. Flag?"—allowed viewers to walk on a flag displayed on the floor, thus sparking a fierce debate over freedom of expression. As with many civil liberties battles, the legal system ultimately decided the extent of Tyler's rights—a local court ruled that the exhibit could remain in place.

liver *Miranda warnings* to suspects before they question them ("You have the right to remain silent . . . "). Justice Felix Frankfurter had people like Ernesto Miranda in mind when he said that "it is a fair summary of constitutional history that the landmarks of our liberties have often been forged in cases involving not very nice people."[1]

At first glance, many questions about civil liberties look easy. The Bill of Rights's guarantee of a free press seems straightforward; either Americans can write what they choose, or they cannot. In the real world of American law, however, these issues are subtle and complex.

Throughout this chapter you will find special features entitled "You Are the Judge." Each feature describes an actual case brought before the courts and asks you to evaluate the case and render a judgment about it. Although you certainly do not know as much about the law as a judge, your sense of fairness and your ethical standards are as reliable as a judge's. Try your hand at deciding these cases. The actual court decisions are collected at the end of the chapter in a feature entitled "The Court Decides" (p.158).

An understanding of American civil liberties begins with the Bill of Rights.

THE BILL OF RIGHTS—THEN AND NOW

By the time of the 1787 convention all the state constitutions had bills of rights, some of which survive, intact, to this day. Although the new U.S. Constitution had no bill of rights, the states made it clear that adding one was a condition of ratification. The first ten amendments to the Constitution comprise the **Bill of Rights.** They were passed as a group by the First Congress in 1789 and sent to the states for ratification. In 1791 these amendments became part of the Constitution.

The Bill of Rights ensures Americans basic liberties: freedom of speech and religion, protection against arbitrary searches and being held for long periods without trial, and so forth. Because the rest of this chapter will discuss the Bill of Rights, this is a good time for you to read it carefully (see "In Focus: The Bill of Rights"). Pay particular attention to the **First Amendment,** the source of Americans' freedom of religion, speech, press, and assembly.

The Bill of Rights was passed when British abuses of the colonists' civil liberties were still a fresh and bitter memory. Newspaper editors had been jailed and citizens had been arrested without cause, detained, and forced to confess at gunpoint or worse. Thus the first ten amendments enjoyed great popular support. Today Americans still believe in the Bill of Rights and its commitment to freedom—up to a point. Mark Twain wrote that God gave the American people "the three precious gifts of freedom of speech, freedom of religion, and the prudence never to exercise either of them." Likewise, you have probably heard remarks like "Freedom of the press demands responsibility of the press," "You shouldn't criticize something unless you suggest an alternative," or "Criminals are not entitled to human dignity." These statements reflect the belief that civil liberties sometimes have to yield to other individual or societal values.

Political scientists have discovered that people are devotees of rights in theory, but their support waivers when it comes time to put those rights into

[1]U.S. v. Rabinowitz, 339 U.S. 56, 69 (1950). (Dissenting opinion of Justic Felix Frankfurter.)

The Bill of Rights

(These amendments were passed by Congress on September 25, 1789, and ratified by the states on December 15, 1791.)

Amendment I—Religion, Speech, Assembly, Petition
Congress shall make no law respecting an establishment of religion, or prohibiting the free exercise thereof; or abridging the freedom of speech, or of the press; or the right of the people peaceably to assemble, and to petition the Government for a redress of grievances.

Amendment II—Right to Bear Arms
A well regulated militia, being necessary to the security of a free State, the right of the people to keep and bear arms, shall not be infringed.

Amendment III—Quartering of Soldiers
No Soldier shall, in time of peace be quartered in any house, without the consent of the owner, nor in time of war, but in a manner to be prescribed by law.

Amendment IV—Searches and Seizures
The right of the people to be secure in their persons, houses, papers, and effects, against unreasonable searches and seizures, shall not be violated, and no warrants shall issue, but upon probable cause, supported by oath or affirmation, and particularly describing the place to be searched, and the persons or things to be seized.

Amendment V—Grand Juries, Double Jeopardy, Self-Incrimination, Due Process, Eminent Domain
No person shall be held to answer for a capital, or otherwise infamous crime, unless on a presentment or indictment of a Grand Jury, except in cases arising in the land or naval forces, or in the militia, when in actual service in time of war or public danger; nor shall any person be subject for the same offence to be twice put in jeopardy of life or limb; nor shall be compelled in any criminal case to be a witness against himself, nor be deprived of life, liberty, or property, without due process of law; nor shall private property be taken for public use, without just compensation.

Amendment VI—Criminal Court Procedures
In all criminal prosecutions, the accused shall enjoy the right to a speedy and public trial, by an impartial jury of the State and district wherein the crime shall have been committed, which district shall have been previously ascertained by law, and to be informed of the nature and cause of the accusation; to be confronted with the witnesses against him; to have compulsory process for obtaining witnesses in his favor, and to have the assistance of counsel for his defense.

Amendment VII—Trial by Jury in Common-Law Cases
In Suits at common law, where the value in controversy shall exceed twenty dollars, the right of trial by jury shall be preserved, and no fact tried by a jury, shall be otherwise reexamined in any Court of the United States, than according to the rules of the common law.

Amendment VIII—Bails, Fines and Punishment
Excessive bail shall not be required, nor excessive fines imposed, nor cruel and unusual punishments inflicted.

Amendment IX—Rights Retained by the People
The enumeration in the Constitution, of certain rights, shall not be construed to deny or disparage others retained by the people.

Amendment X—Rights Reserved to the States
The powers not delegated to the United States by the Constitution, nor prohibited by it to the States, are reserved to the States respectively, or to the people.

practice.[2] For example, Americans in general believe in freedom of speech, but many citizens would not let the Ku Klux Klan speak in their neighborhood or allow their public schools to teach about atheism or homosexuality.

contradiction 1st Amendment

[2] James W. Prothro and Charles M. Grigg, "Fundamental Principles of Democracy: Bases of Agreement and Disagreement," *Journal of Politics* 22 (1960): 276–94; John L. Sullivan et al., "The Sources of Political Tolerance: A Multivariate Analysis," *American Political Science Review* 75 (1981): 100–15.

exaggerated
example
violation
civil
rights

Real
examples

①

②

Violation by a
State of Bill of Rights

Rights in Conflict: The Tough Cases

Some cases involving civil liberties are easy to decide. Say that a police officer, looking for a neighborhood burglar, finds you jogging late one night. The officer grabs you, searches you, hauls you into the police station, bloodies your head when you refuse to confess, refuses to let you call a lawyer, and then puts you in a cell for weeks with no prospect of bail or even a hearing. Once you were able to make a phone call, a lawyer would have no trouble proving that many of your civil rights had been violated. (You might want to look at the Bill of Rights again to see how many of your rights were abused in this scenario.)

The preceding example is, obviously, an exaggeration, but such scenarios are not as unlikely as you might think. Edward Lawson, known as the "California Walkman," won a suit against the San Diego police after they had arrested him, without cause, fifteen times. Lawson liked to take walks late at night, long walks that took him far from his home. The fact that he was a young black man with long hair made him look suspicious to the police. The repeated arrests of a person who had done nothing wrong, however, were easily recognizable as violations of his rights. Usually, though, cases involving civil liberties are much more ambiguous.

The *Soldier of Fortune* lawsuit is an example of an ambiguous case. *Soldier of Fortune* magazine is read by mercenaries, adventurers, and others who live, or imagine living, in the shadowy world of jungle combat, espionage, and murder for hire. A Texas man named Robert Black found an advertisement in *Soldier of Fortune* that read, "Ex-Marines, '67-'69 Nam Vets, weapons specialist—jungle warfare. Pilot. ME. High-risk assignments. U.S. or overseas." Black made contact with the man who placed the ad, John Wayne Hearn of Atlanta, and hired Hearn to murder his wife, Sandra Black. Hearn shot and killed her on February 21, 1985. Both Robert Black and John Wayne Hearn were arrested, tried, and sentenced to life imprisonment.

Sandra Black's family sued *Soldier of Fortune,* arguing that the advertisement had contributed to her death. The magazine insisted that it could not possibly screen every ad it published, and that the First Amendment gave it the right to publish anything it wanted. A federal district court jury ruled in favor of the family and ordered the magazine to pay $1.5 million, but an appeals court reversed this judgment. The higher court found that the magazine had no duty to refrain from publishing ambiguous advertisements that might contribute to some later violation of law. This case is the sort of complex controversy that shapes American civil liberties.

The Bill of Rights and the States

Take another look at the First Amendment. Note the first words: "Congress shall make no law . . . ." A literal reading of these words suggests that a state government could make a law prohibiting the free exercise of religion, free speech, freedom of the press, and so on. The Bill of Rights was written to restrict the powers of the new central government. In 1791 Americans were comfortable with their state governments; after all, every state constitution had its own bill of rights.

What happens, though, if a state government violates the federal Bill of Rights? In 1833 the answer to that question was "nothing." A man named Barron brought his legal troubles with the city of Baltimore to the Supreme Court.

Complaining that the city had ruined his dry dock business by constructing a wharf, Barron argued that the Fifth Amendment forbade Baltimore from taking his property without just compensation. John Marshall's Court refused to consider Barron's claim. The Bill of Rights, said the Court in **Barron v. Baltimore,** restrained only the national government, not states and cities.

Almost a century later, however, the Court ruled that a state government must respect some First Amendment rights. The 1925 case **Gitlow v. New York** relied not on the First Amendment but on the Fourteenth, the second of three "Civil War Amendments" that ended slavery, gave former slaves legal protection, and ensured their voting rights. Ratified in 1868, the **Fourteenth Amendment** declared the following:

> No state shall make or enforce any law which shall abridge the privileges or immunities of citizens of the United States nor shall any state deprive any person of life, liberty, or property, without due process of law; nor deny to any person within its jurisdiction the equal protection of the laws.

In *Gitlow,* the Court announced that freedoms of speech and press "were fundamental personal rights and liberties protected by the due process clause of the Fourteenth Amendment from impairment by the states." In effect, the Court interpreted the Fourteenth Amendment to say that states could not abridge the freedoms of expression protected by the First Amendment. Not everyone agreed that the Fourteenth Amendment **incorporated** parts of the Bill of Rights into state laws. As recently as 1985, Edwin Meese, who was then attorney general, strongly criticized *Gitlow* and called for "disincorporation" of the Bill of Rights.

After the 1925 *Gitlow* case, only parts of the First Amendment were held binding on the states. Gradually, especially during the 1960s when Earl Warren was chief justice, the Supreme Court has applied most of the Bill of Rights to the states (see Table 4.1). "One by one," wrote constitutional scholar Samuel Krislov, "the provisions of the Bill of Rights have been held to apply to the states, not in their own right, but as implicit in the Fourteenth Amendment."[3] Many of the court decisions that empowered the Bill of Rights were controversial, but today, for all practical purposes, the Bill of Rights guarantees individual freedoms against infringement by state and local governments as well as by the national government. Only the Second, Third, and Seventh Amendments have not been applied specifically to the states.

FREEDOM OF RELIGION

The First Amendment makes not one but two statements about religion and government. These are commonly referred to as the establishment clause and the free exercise clause. The **establishment clause** states that "Congress shall make no law respecting an establishment of religion." The **free exercise clause** prohibits the abridgement of the citizens' freedom to worship, or not to worship, as they please. Sometimes, these freedoms conflict. The government's practice of providing chaplains on military bases is one example of this conflict; some accuse the government of establishing religion in order to ensure that members

---

[3]Samuel Krislov, *The Supreme Court and Political Freedom* (New York: Free Press, 1968), 81.

Table 4.1 The Nationalization of the Bill of Rights

DATE	RIGHT	CASE
1925	Freedom of Speech	*Gitlow* v. *New York*
1931	Freedom of the Press	*Near* v. *Minnesota*
1932	Right to Counsel in Capital Cases	*Powell* v. *Alabama*
1937	Freedom of Assembly	*De Jonge* v. *Oregon*
1940	Free Exercise of Religion	*Cantwell* v. *Connecticut*
1947	Separation of Church and State	*Everson* v. *Board of Education*
1948	Right to Public Trial	*In re Oliver*
1949	Right Against Unreasonable Searches and Seizures	*Wolf* v. *Colorado*
1958	Freedom of Association	*NAACP* v. *Alabama*
1961	Exclusionary Rule	*Mapp* v. *Ohio*
1962	Right against Cruel and Unusual Punishment	*Robinson* v. *California*
1963	Right to Counsel in Felony Cases	*Gideon* v. *Wainwright*
1964	Immunity from Self-incrimination	*Mallory* v. *Hogan*
1965	Right of Privacy	*Griswold* v. *Connecticut*
1965	Right to Confrontation of Witnesses	*Pointer* v. *Texas*
1966	Right to Impartial Jury	*Parker* v. *Gladden*
1967	Right to Speedy Trial	*Klopfer* v. *North Carolina*
1967	Right to Compulsory Process for Obtaining Witnesses	*Washington* v. *Texas*
1968	Right to Jury Trial for Serious Crimes	*Duncan* v. *Louisiana*
1969	Immunity from Double Jeopardy	*Benton* v. *Maryland*
1972	Right to Counsel for All Crimes Involving Jail Terms	*Argersinger* v. *Hamlin*

of the Armed Forces can freely practice their religion. Establishment clause and free exercise clause cases usually, however, raise different kinds of conflicts.

The Establishment Clause

Some nations, like Great Britain, have an established church that is officially supported by the government and recognized as a national institution. A few American colonies had official churches, but the religious persecutions that had brought many American citizen's ancestors to America discouraged any desire for the First Congress to establish a national church in the United States; thus the First Amendment prohibits one.

It is much less clear what else the First Congress intended by the establishment clause. Some people argued that it meant only that the government could not favor one religion over another. In contrast, Thomas Jefferson argued that the First Amendment created a "wall of separation" between church and state, forbidding not just favoritism but any support for religion at all. These interpretations continue to provoke argument, especially when religion is mixed with education.

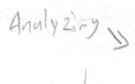

Debate is especially intense over aid to church-related schools and prayers in the public schools. Proponents of *parochiaid* (short for "aid to parochial schools"), which has existed in various forms since the 1960s, argue that it does not favor any particular religion. Opponents claim that, since the Roman Catholic Church has by far the largest religious school system in the country, it gets most of the aid. In *Lemon* v. *Kurtzman* (1971) the Supreme Court declared that aid to church-related schools must have a secular legislative purpose, not be used to advance or inhibit religion, and avoid excessive government "entanglement" with religion. There is a fine line between aid that is permissible and aid that is not. For instance, the Court has allowed parochial schools to use federal funds to buy textbooks and to subsidize off-campus testing services, but not to pay for teachers' salaries, tape recorders, or field trips.

School prayer is more controversial than just about any other religious issue. In 1962 and 1963 the Court aroused the wrath of many Americans by ruling that voluntary recitations of prayers or Bible passages, when done as part of classroom exercises in public schools, violated the establishment clause. ***Engel* v. *Vitale*** and ***School District of Abington Township, Pennsylvania* v. *Schempp*** observed that "the place of religion in our society is an exalted one, but in the relationship between man and religion, the State is firmly committed to a position of neutrality."

Some religious groups pushed for a constitutional amendment permitting school prayer, while many school districts simply ignored the decision. (In periodic surveys of public schools, political scientists continue to discover that many schools still allow prayers in their classrooms.) President Reagan pushed for an amendment twenty years after the 1962 and 1963 rulings, but the best school-prayer advocates could muster was a 1984 law requiring schools that receive federal funds to open their doors to student groups promoting religion. This law was upheld by the Supreme Court in 1990.

The Free Exercise Clause

The First Amendment also guarantees the free exercise of religion. This guarantee seems simple enough at first glance; whether people hold no religious

The People Speak	School Prayers	
	By law, prayers should not be allowed in public schools.	11%
	The law should allow public schools to schedule time when children can pray silently if they want to.	52%
	The law should allow public schools to schedule time when children, as a group, can say a general prayer not tied to a particular religious faith.	25%
	By law, public schools should schedule a time when all children would say a chosen Christian prayer.	10%

Although the Supreme Court has prohibited organized prayers of any kind in the public schools, Americans disagree. A majority favor voluntary silent prayer, while others favor spoken prayers. The results of this study demonstrate the Court's important role in protecting minority rights in the face of majority opinion.

Source: The statements as worded are taken directly from the 1988 National Election Study.

The free exercise of religious beliefs sometimes clashes with society's other values or laws, as when the Amish—who prefer to lead simple, traditional lives—refused to send their children to public schools. The Supreme Court eventually held in favor of the Amish, arguing that Amish children, living in such a close-knit community, were unlikely to become dependent on the state.

beliefs, go to church or temple, or practice voodoo, they should have the right to practice religion as they choose. The matter is, of course, more complicated than that. Religions sometimes forbid action that society thinks are necessary, or, conversely, require actions that society finds disruptive. For example, what if somebody's religion justifies multiple marriages or using illegal drugs? Muhammad Ali, the boxing champion, refused induction into the armed services during the Vietnam War because, he said, military service would violate his Muslim faith. Amish parents often refuse to send their children to public schools. Jehovah's Witnesses and Christian Scientists may refuse to accept certain kinds of medical treatment for themselves or their children.

The Supreme Court has never permitted religious freedom to be an excuse for any and all behaviors; what if, the Court once asked, a person "believed that human sacrifices were a necessary part of religious worship"? Consistently maintaining that people have an inviolable right to *believe* what they want, the courts have been more cautious about the right to *practice* a belief. For instance, Congress ruled and courts upheld that people could become conscientious objectors to war on religious grounds, but the Court did not support a Mormon who justified polygamy on religious grounds. The Court did, however, allow Amish parents to take their children out of school after the eighth grade. Reasoning that the Amish community was well established and that its children would not burden the state, *Wisconsin* v. *Yoder* (1972) held that religious freedom took precedence over compulsory education laws. You can see what happened in another case involving religious practice in "You Are the Judge: Can the Air Force Make Captain Goldman Remove His Yarmulke?"

The Rise of the Fundamentalists

Political scientist Kenneth D. Wald observes that "the last few years have been marked by great ferment in the relationship between religion and American political life . . . . [R]eligious issues and controversies have assumed much greater importance in political debate than they had commanded previously."[4] Much of this new importance is due to fundamentalist religious groups that have spurred their members to political action.

In the 1970s the Reverend Jerry Falwell, minister of the Thomas Road Baptist Church in Lynchburg, Virginia, formed an organization called the Moral Majority. (You may have seen bumper stickers proclaiming "The Moral Majority is Neither.") Falwell and others tried to make their conservative agenda the nation's political agenda.

Conservative religious groups (with the support of the Reagan administration in the 1980s), devoted much of their time and energies to three issues: abortion, school prayer, and *creation science.* No fewer than three Alabama laws, passed in 1978, 1981, and 1982, sought to legalize school prayer by making it voluntary. You can see how the case was presented in "You Are the Judge: The

[4]Kenneth D. Wald, *Religion and Politics in the United States* (Chatham, N.J.: Chatham House, 1987), 220.

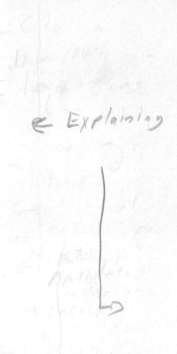

You Are the Judge

Can the Air Force Make Captain Goldman Remove His Yarmulke?

Captain S. Simcha Goldman was an orthodox Jewish rabbi and an Air Force captain. He served as a clinical psychologist for the Air Force. Being an orthodox Jew, it was Goldman's custom to wear a yarmulke, a small skullcap traditionally worn by orthodox Jewish males. The Air Force had a problem; an Air Force regulation (A.F.R. 35-10) required that "Air Force members will wear the Air Force uniform while performing their military duties" and stipulated that "headgear [may] not be worn . . . [indoors] except by armed security police in the performance of their duties." In 1981 therefore, Captain Goldman's superiors ordered him to cease wearing his yarmulke on duty indoors (even though he had never been ordered to comply with this rule in his years of service prior to 1981). When he refused to comply, he was reprimanded and threatened with discipline. His commanding officer, for example, withdrew a recommendation that Goldman's application for an extension of his Air Force service be approved, and wrote a negative reference instead.

The issue is this: Does the First Amendment, which guarantees the free exercise of religion, prohibit the Air Force from interfering with Captain Goldman's religious practice? For the Court's answer, see "The Court Decides" on page 158.

Case of Voluntary Prayer in Alabama." Fundamentalist groups have also pressed state legislatures to mandate the teaching of creation science, their alternative to Darwinian theories of evolution, in public schools. Louisiana, for example, passed a Balanced Treatment Act requiring schools that taught Darwinian theory to teach creation science, too. Regardless, the Supreme Court ruled in *Edwards* v. *Aguillard* (1987) that this law violated the establishment clause.

The year 1988 included both the ascent and the decline of the religious right. On the one hand, one of their number, Pat Robertson, made a small but respectable showing in the Republican presidential primaries. On the other hand, sex and financial scandals discredited television evangelists Jim Bakker and Jimmy Swaggart, and the antics of Oral Roberts, who said he needed donations to support his medical school or God would take him, further detracted from the movement's credibility. Falwell disbanded the Moral Majority itself in 1989 and promised to devote himself more to God's work and less to human politics.

Despite these setbacks to the religious right, the movement has made an impact. Some recent Supreme Court rulings have lowered, brick by brick, the high wall between church and state that was constructed two decades ago in cases like *Engel* and *Schempp*. *Lynch* v. *Donelly* (1984) held that Pawtucket, Rhode Island, could set up a Christmas nativity scene on public property. Five years later, *County of Allegheny* v. *American Civil Liberties Union* extended the principle to a Hanukkah menorah.

Jimmy Swaggart's well-publicized fall from grace epitomized the recent trouble of the religious right. Despite the problems of Swaggart and other fundamentalist leaders, the movement still has a powerful voice in such political issues as abortion and school prayer.

FREEDOM OF EXPRESSION

A democracy depends on the free expression of ideas. Thoughts that are muffled, speech that is forbidden, and meetings that cannot be held are the enemies of the democratic process. Totalitarian governments know this, which is the reason that they go to enormous trouble to limit expression.

Americans pride themselves on their free and open society. Freedom of conscience is absolute; Americans can *believe* whatever they want to believe. The First Amendment plainly forbids the national government from limiting freedom of *expression,* that is, the right to say or publish what one believes. Is freedom of expression, then, like freedom of conscience, also *absolute?* Supreme Court Justice Hugo Black thought so—he was fond of pointing out that the First Amendment said Congress shall make *no* law. "I read no law abridging to mean *no law abridging.*" Black was in a minority during his tenure on the Court (from 1937–1971), often paired only with Justice William O. Douglas.

Most experts interpret the First Amendment less literally, especially when it conflicts with other rights. Courts have often ruled that there are instances when speech needs to be controlled. A classic example of impermissible speech was offered in 1919 by Justice Oliver Wendell Holmes: "The most stringent protection of free speech would not protect a man in falsely shouting 'fire' in a theater and causing a panic." The courts have been called upon to decide where to draw the line separating permissible from impermissible speech. In performing this task, judges have had to balance freedom of expression against competing values like public order, national security, and the right to a fair trial.

The courts have also had to decide what kinds of activities do and do not constitute *speech* (or *press*) within the meaning of the First Amendment. Holding

Elaborating

Outlining

The Case of Voluntary Prayer in Alabama

One Alabama law authorized teachers to lead "willing students" in a prescribed prayer to "Almighty God .... the Creator and Supreme Judge of the World." Recognizing that required prayers would run afoul of *Engel* v. *Vitale,* the Alabama legislature, bowing to pressure from religious groups, had decided to try this means of permitting voluntary meditation.

Ishmael Jaffree, a Mobile County parent who had three children in Montgomery public schools, found that the idea of prayers written by the state offended his own religious beliefs, and he sued teachers, administrators, and state officials over the law. Testi-

mony from State Senator Donald G. Holmes, who sponsored the bill, conceded that the legislation was purely and simply "an effort to return voluntary prayer to our public schools." It served, he admitted, "no other purpose." Lawyers for the state of Alabama argued that the prayer was strictly voluntary and should not, therefore, offend anyone.

You be the judge: Did the Alabama legislature have the right to require that a voluntary prayer to Almighty God be uttered by "willing students"? For the Supreme Court's answer, see "The Court Decides" on page 158.

---

a political rally to attack an opposition candidate's stand on important issues gets First Amendment protection. Obscenity and libel, which look similar, do not. To make things still more complicated, certain forms of nonverbal speech, like picketing, are considered symbolic speech and receive First Amendment protection. Other forms of expression are considered *action* rather than speech. Government can limit action more easily than it can limit expression.

The one thing all freedom of expression cases have in common is the question of whether a certain expression receives the protection of the Constitution. The pages that follow examine some of the most important issues that arise in the courts as judges determine the meaning of freedom of speech.

Prior Restraint

One principle stands out clearly in the complicated history of freedom of speech laws: time and time again, the Supreme Court has struck down prior restraint on speech and the press. **Prior restraint** refers to a government's actions that prevent material from being published; in a word, prior restraint is *censorship.* In the United States, the First Amendment ensures that even if the government frowns on some material, a person's right to publish it is all but inviolable. A typical prior restraint case is ***Near* v. *Minnesota*** (1931). A blunt newspaper editor called local officials a string of names including "grafters" and "Jewish gangsters." The state closed down his business, but the Supreme Court ordered the paper reopened.[5] Of course, the newspaper editor—or anyone else—could be punished for violating a law or someone's rights *after* publication.

The extent of an individual or group's freedom from prior restraint does depend in part, however, on who that individual or group is. In 1988 the Supreme

---

[5]See Fred W. Friendly, *Minnesota Rag* (New York: Random House, 1981).

Court ruled in *Hazelwood School District* v. *Kuhlmeier* that a high school newspaper was not a public forum and could be regulated in "any reasonable manner" by school officials.

Even the strongest champion of free speech and free press would agree that *sometimes* government should limit individual behavior on the grounds of national security. Almost no one would find it odd or unconstitutional if a newspaper, for example, were hauled into court for publishing troop movement plans during a war. The national government demanded and secured the censorship of a book by former CIA agent Victor Marchetti, and it sued former CIA agent Frank Snepp for failing to have his book about Vietnam, *A Decent Interval,* submitted to the agency for censorship, even though the book revealed no classified information (in 1980 the Supreme Court upheld the government's suit in *U.S.* v. *Snepp).*

Even in the area of national security the courts are reluctant to issue injunctions prohibiting the publication of material. The most famous recent case involving prior restraint and national security was over the publication of stolen Pentagon papers. You can learn more about it in "You Are the Judge: The Case of the Purloined Pentagon Papers."

Obscenity

In *The Brethren,* a gossipy portrayal of the Supreme Court, Bob Woodward and Scott Armstrong recount the tale of Justice Thurgood Marshall's lunch with some

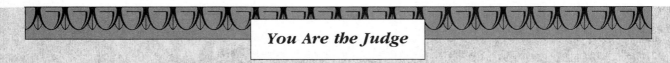

You Are the Judge

The Case of the Purloined Pentagon Papers

During the Johnson administration, the Department of Defense had amassed an elaborate secret history of American involvement in the Vietnam War. Hundreds of documents, many of them secret cables, memos, and war plans, were included. Many documented American ineptitude and South Vietnamese duplicity. One former Pentagon official, Daniel Ellsberg, who had become disillusioned with the Vietnam War, managed to retain access to a copy of these Pentagon papers. Hoping that revelations of the Vietnam quagmire would help end American involvement, he decided to leak the Pentagon papers to the *New York Times*.

The Nixon administration pulled out all the stops in its effort to embarrass Ellsberg and prevent publication of the Pentagon papers. Nixon's chief domestic affairs advisor, John Ehrlichman, approved a burglary

of Ellsberg's psychiatrist's office, hoping to find damaging information on Ellsberg. (The burglary was bungled, and it eventually led to Ehrlichman's conviction and imprisonment.) In the courts, Nixon administration lawyers sought an injunction against the *Times* that would have ordered it to cease publication of the secret documents. Government lawyers argued that national security was being breeched and that the documents had been stolen from the government by Ellsberg. The *Times* argued that its freedom to publish would be violated if an injunction were granted.

In 1971 the case of *New York Times* v. *United States* was decided by the Supreme Court. You be the judge: Did the *Times* have a right to publish secret, stolen Department of Defense documents? For the Supreme Court's answer, see "The Court Decides", on page 158.

law clerks. Glancing at his watch at about 1:50 P.M., the story goes, Marshall exclaimed, "My God, I almost forgot. It's movie day, we've got to get back."[6] Movie day at the Court was an annual event when movies brought before the Court on obscenity charges were shown in a basement storeroom.

Several justices have boycotted these showings, arguing that obscenity should never be banned—thus how "dirty" a movie is has no relevance. In 1957, however, the majority held that "obscenity is not within the area of constitutionally protected speech or press" *(Roth v. United States).* The doctrine set forth in this case still prevails. Deciding what is obscene, though, has never been an easy matter. In a line that would haunt him for the rest of his life, Justice Potter Stewart once remarked that, although he could not define obscenity, "I know it when I see it." During the Supreme Court's movie day, law clerks echoed Stewart's line, punctuating particularly racy scenes with cries of "That's it? That's it? I know it when I see it." Marshall often led the banter at the screenings. "Well, Harry," he once remarked to Justice Blackmun after a film, "I didn't learn anything. How about you?"

Efforts to define obscenity have perplexed the courts for years. Obviously, public standards vary from time to time, place to place, and person to person. Much of today's MTV would have been banned a decade or so ago. What might be acceptable on Manhattan's Upper West Side would shock residents of the Bible Belt. Even though courts have consistently ruled that states may protect children from obscenity, adults often have access to the same material. Works that some people call obscene might be good entertainment or even great art to others. At one time or another, the works of Aristophanes, Mark Twain, and even the "Tarzan" stories of Edgar Rice Burroughs were banned. The state of Georgia banned the acclaimed film *Carnal Knowledge,* a ban the Supreme Court struck down in *Jenkins* v. *Georgia* (1974).

In 1973 the Court tried to clarify its doctrine by spelling out what could be classified as obscene and thus outside First Amendment protection. The case was *Miller v. California.* Chief Justice Warren Burger wrote that materials were obscene if the work, taken as a whole, appealed to a prurient interest in sex; *and* if it showed "patently offensive sexual contact"; *and* if it "lacked serious artistic, literary, political, or scientific merit." Decisions whether or not any material was obscene, said the Court, should be made by local, not national, communities, in other words, by juries.

The Court did provide "a few plain examples" of what sort of material might fall within this definition of obscenity. Among these examples were "patently offensive representations of ultimate sexual acts, . . . actual or simulated," "patently offensive representations of masturbation or excretory functions," or "lewd exhibition of the genitals." Cities throughout the country duplicated the language of *Miller* in their obscenity ordinances, which they soon redrafted. The difficulty remains, not with deciding what sexual acts or genitals are, but in determining what is *lewd* or *offensive.* Laws must have those qualifying adjectives to prevent communities from banning anatomy texts, for example, as obscene.

Another reason that obscenity convictions can be difficult to obtain is that no nationwide consensus exists that offensive material should be banned, at least not when it is restricted to adults. In many communities the laws are lenient regarding pornography and prosecutors know that they may not get a jury to

[6]Bob Woodward and Scott Armstrong, *The Brethren* (New York: Avon, 1979), 233.

(Case)

Citing Examples

Analyzing

convict, even when the disputed material is obscene as defined by *Miller.* Thus obscene material is widely available in adult book stores, video stores, and movie theaters. Regulations aimed at keeping obscene material away from the young, who are considered to be more vulnerable to its bad influences, are more popular. The rating scheme of the Motion Picture Association of America *(G, PG, PG-13, R,* and *X)* is one example.

Despite the Court's best efforts to define obscenity and determine when it can be banned, debate continues. In one famous case a small New Jersey town with a Biblical name tried to get rid of a nude dancing parlor by using its zoning power to ban all live entertainment. The Court held in *Schad* v. *Mount Ephraim* (1981) that the measure was too broad and thus unlawful. The ruling continued, "Nor may an entertainment program be prohibited simply because it displays a nude human figure." Jacksonville, Florida, tried to ban drive-in movies containing nudity. You can see the Court's reaction in "You Are the Judge: When Can Obscenity Be Banned? The Case of the Drive-in Theater."

The newest issue in the obscenity controversy involves the claim of some women's groups that pornography degrades and dehumanizes women, thereby consigning them to inferior status. Legal scholar Catherine MacKinnon claims that "pornography is an eight-billion-dollar-a-year industry of rape and battery and sexual harassment."[7] Some cities have passed antipornography ordinances

---

[7]Catherine MacKinnon, *Feminism Unmodified* (Cambridge, M.A.: Harvard University Press, 1987), 198.

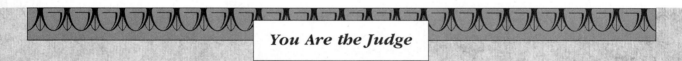

You Are the Judge

When Can Obscenity Be Banned? The Case of the Drive-in Theater

Almost everyone concedes that *sometimes* obscenity should be banned by public authorities. One instance might be when a person's right to show pornographic movies clashes with another's right to privacy. Presumably, no one wants hard-core pornography shown in public places where schoolchildren might be passersby. Showing dirty movies in an enclosed theater or in the privacy of your own living room is one thing. Showing them in public is something else. Or is it?

The city of Jacksonville, Florida, wanted to limit the showing of certain kinds of movies at drive-in theaters. Its city council reasoned that drive-ins were public places and that drivers passing by would be involuntarily exposed to movies they might prefer not to see. (Some members of the council argued that drivers distracted by steamy scenes might even cause accidents.) So the council passed a local

ordinance forbidding movies showing nudity (defined in the ordinance as "bare buttocks . . . female bare breasts, or human bare pubic areas") at drive-in theaters. Arrested for violating the ordinance, a Mr. Erznoznik challenged the constitutionality of the ordinance. He claimed that the law was overly broad and banned nudity, not obscenity. The lawyers for the city insisted that the law could be squared with the First Amendment. The government, they claimed, had a responsibility to forbid a "public nuisance," especially one that might cause a traffic hazard.

You be the judge. The issue is whether Jacksonville's ban on nudity in movies at drive-ins went too far or whether it was a constitutional limit on free speech. For the Court's answer, see "The Court Decides" on page 158.

Although the Supreme Court has ruled, in Roth v. United States, *that obscenity is not protected by the First Amendment, determining just what is obscene has proved difficult. Recognizing that different communities have different standards, the Court held in* Miller v. California *that juries on a local level have some discretion in defining obscenity.*

on the grounds that pornography harms women, but, so far, courts have struck them down on First Amendment grounds. No such case has gotten as far as the Supreme Court.

Defamation: Libel and Slander

Another type of utterance not protected by the First Amendment is **libel,** the publication of statements known to be false that are malicious and tend to damage a person's reputation. *Slander* refers to spoken defamation. Of course, if politicians could collect damages for every untrue thing someone said about them, the right to criticize the government—which the Supreme Court termed "the central meaning of the First Amendment"—would be stifled. No one would dare be critical for fear of making a factual error.

To encourage public debate, the Supreme Court has held, in cases such as **New York Times v. Sullivan** (1964), that statements about public figures are libelous only if made with malice and reckless disregard for the truth. Public figures have to prove to a jury, in effect, that whoever wrote or said untrue statements about them knew that the statements were untrue and intended to harm them. This standard makes libel cases very difficult for public figures to win, since it is very difficult to prove that a publication was intentionally malicious in reporting on a public figure.

Libel is another freedom of expression issue that involves competing values. If public debate is not free, there can be no democracy. On the other hand, some reputations will be unfairly damaged, or at least bruised, in the process. In one widely publicized case General William Westmoreland, once the commander of American troops in South Vietnam, sued CBS. On January 23, 1982, the network broadcast a documentary called "The Uncounted Enemy." It claimed that American military leaders in Vietnam, including Westmoreland, systemati-

General William Westmoreland's aborted lawsuit against CBS demonstrates the difficulty public figures have winning libel convictions. Even though Westmoreland (left, in Vietnam, and right, leaving the 1984 trial) could show that CBS had knowingly made factual errors, he realized that it would be impossible to prove that the network had been intentionally malicious, so he dropped the suit in return for a statement from CBS calling him "patriotic."

cally lied to Washington about their success there to make it appear that the United States was winning the war. All the evidence, including CBS's own internal memoranda, showed that the documentary made errors of fact. Westmoreland sued CBS for libel. Ultimately, the power of the press—in this case, a sloppy, arrogant press—prevailed. Fearing defeat at the trial, Westmoreland settled for a mild apology.[8]

In 1988 the wacky case of *Hustler Magazine* v. *Falwell* joined the ranks of unusual libel and obscenity trials. *Hustler* editor Larry Flynt had printed a parody of a Campari Liquor ad about various celebrities called "First Time" (in which celebrities related the first time they drank Campari, but with an intentional double entendre). When *Hustler* depicted the Reverend Jerry Falwell having had his "first time" in an outhouse with his mother, Falwell sued. He alleged that the ad subjected him to great emotional distress and mental anguish. The case tested the limits to which a publication can go to parody or lampoon a public figure. The Supreme Court ruled that they can go pretty far—all nine justices ruled in favor of the magazine.

As lenient as American libel laws are, they probably do inhibit the press to some extent. Libel cases are expensive to fight. There is evidence that some newspapers stifle opinion in order to be on the safe side. For example, in the spring of 1986 the *Los Angeles Times* refused to publish several episodes of the

[8]Renata Adler, *Reckless Disregard* (New York: Knopf, 1986).

syndicated cartoon strip *Doonesbury* on the grounds that they were "overblown and unfair" to members of the Reagan administration. The "Sleaze on Parade" episodes in question, however, contained only verifiable (if occasionally misleading) statements about various officials' troubles with the law.

Symbolic Speech

Freedom of speech is, more broadly interpreted, a guarantee of freedom of expression. In 1965 Mary Beth Tinker and her brother John were suspended from school in Des Moines, Iowa, when they wore black arm bands to protest the Vietnam War. The Supreme Court held in *Tinker* v. *Des Moines Independent School District* (1969) that the suspension violated the Tinkers' First Amendment rights. The right to freedom of speech, said the Court, went beyond the spoken word. When Gregory Johnson set a flag on fire to protest nuclear arms buildup during the 1984 Republican National Convention in Dallas, the Supreme Court decided that Texas's law prohibiting flag desecration violated the First Amendment (***Texas* v. *Johnson*** [1989]).

Both wearing an arm band and burning a flag are examples of **symbolic speech,** that is, actions that do not consist of speaking or writing but that express an opinion. Court decisions have classified these activities somewhere between pure speech and pure action. The doctrine of symbolic speech is not precise; for example, while burning a flag is protected speech, burning a draft card is

[Handwritten margin notes: Comparing to Freedom of speech ← / Example (symbolism) / (case) / (case 2) / Definition / Analyzing]

Drawing By Miller: © 1989 The New Yorker Magazine, Inc.

not (*U.S.* v. *O'Brien* [1968]). The cases do make it clear that First Amendment rights are not limited by a rigid definition of what constitutes speech.

Commercial Speech

Not all forms of communication receive the full protection of the First Amendment. As **commercial speech,** advertising is restricted far more extensively than expressions of opinion on religious, political, or other matters. The Federal Trade Commission (FTC) decides what kinds of goods may be advertised on radio and television and regulates the content of such advertising. The rules have changed as social mores and priorities have changed. Thirty years ago, for example, tampons could not be advertised on TV, while cigarette commercials were everywhere. Today the situation is just the reverse. The FTC attempts to make sure that advertisers do not make false claims for their products, but "truth" in advertising does not prevent misleading promises; for example, many ads imply that the right mouthwash or deodorant will improve one's love life. This dubious message is perfectly legal.

Although commercial speech does not receive the same privileges as other types of speech, the courts have been broadening its protection under the Constitution. For years many states had laws that prohibited advertising for professional services, such as those of lawyers and engineers, and for certain products ranging from eyeglasses and prescription drugs to condoms and abortions. Advocates of these laws claimed that they were designed to protect consumers against misleading claims, while critics charged that the laws prevented price competition. In recent years the courts have struck down many such restrictions as violations of freedom of speech.

Regulation of the Public Airwaves

The Federal Communications Commission (FCC) regulates the content, nature, and very existence of radio and television broadcasting. Although newspapers do not need licenses, radio and television stations do. Once a station gets a license, it must comply with regulations that may require a certain percentage of broadcast time be devoted to public service, news, and children's programming, or that require a station to make broadcast time available to political candidates or views other than those its owners support. (The rules are more relaxed for cable channels, which can specialize in a particular type of broadcasting, since consumers pay for, and thus have more choice about, the service.)

This sort of governmental interference would clearly violate the First Amendment if it were imposed on the print media. For example, the state of Florida passed a law requiring newspapers in the state to provide space for political candidates to reply to newspaper criticisms. The Supreme Court, without hesitation, voided this law (***Miami Herald Publishing Company* v. *Tornillo*** [1974]). In ***Red Lion Broadcasting Company* v. *Federal Communications Commission*** (1969) the Court upheld similar restrictions on radio and television stations, reasoning that such laws were justified by the fact that only a limited number of broadcast frequencies were available.

One FCC rule regulating the content of programs restricts the use of obscene words. Comedian George Carlin has a famous routine called, "Seven Words You Can Never Say on Television." A New York City radio station tested Carlin's assertion by airing his routine. The ensuing events proved Carlin right. In *FCC* v. *Pacifica Foundation* (1978), the Supreme Court upheld the Commission's policy of barring these words from radio or television when children might hear them.

Free Speech and Public Order

Not suprisingly, government has sometimes been a zealous opponent of speech that opposes its policies. War often brings about efforts at censorship. In one notable case during World War I, Charles T. Schenck, the secretary of the American Socialist Party, distributed thousands of leaflets that urged young men to resist the draft. Schenck was charged with impeding the war effort. The Supreme Court upheld his conviction in 1919 **(Schenck v. United States).** Justice Holmes declared that government can limit speech if it provokes a clear and present danger of substantive evils. Only when such danger exists can government restrain speech. It is hard to say, of course, when speech becomes dangerous, or whether the "evils" brought about by such speech can truly damage society or simply make it more difficult for government to do as it pleases.

The courts confronted the issue of free speech and public order during the 1950s. American anticommunism was a powerful force. Senator Joseph McCarthy and others in Congress were persecuting people they thought subversive. The national government was determined to jail the leaders of the Communist party. The vehicle was the Smith Act of 1940, which forbid the advocacy of violent overthrow of the American government. In **Dennis v. United States** (1951) the Supreme Court upheld prison sentences for several Communist party leaders. Although the activities of this tiny, unpopular group resembled yelling "fire!" in an empty theater rather than a crowded one, the Court ruled that a Communist takeover was so grave a danger that government could squelch their threat. Free speech advocates did little to stem the relentless persecution of the 1950s; the Supreme Court was not willing to protect First Amendment rights at the time. By the 1960s, however, as the political climate changed, the Court narrowed the interpretation of the Smith Act so that the government could no longer use it to prosecute dissenters.

The 1960s brought waves of protest that strained and expanded the constitutional meaning of free speech. Among the unrest over political, economic, racial, and social issues, the Vietnam War was the source of the most bitter controversy. Many people saw military service as a duty and war as an issue the government should decide. Others felt that citizens should not be asked to die or pay for conflicts that they felt were unjust. Organized protests on college and university campuses became common. People burned draft cards, seized university buildings, marched, and demonstrated against the Southeast Asian conflict.

Americans today live in less turbulent times, yet many people still want to engage in public demonstrations. Courts have been quite supportive of the right to protest, pass out leaflets, or gather signatures on petitions—so long as it is done in public places. Constitutional protections diminish once a person steps on private property, like most shopping centers. *Hudgens* v. *National Labor Relations Board* (1976) held that federal free speech guarantees did not apply when a person was on private property. *Pruneyard Shopping Center* v. *Robins* (1980), however, upheld a state's power to include shopping center politics

The prevailing political climate often determines what limits the government will place on free speech. During the early 1950s Senator Joseph McCarthy's persuasive—if unproven—accusations that many public officials were Communists created an atmosphere in which the courts placed restrictions on freedom of expression—restrictions that would be unacceptable today.

Civil Liberties in Britain

As discussed earlier, Great Britain has an unwritten constitution, a set of understood principles that limits governmental power—most of the time. For example, it would be "unconstitutional" to punish someone for an act that is not forbidden by law or for the prime minister to restrict the sovereign's access to government documents (this happened during the brief reign of Edward VIII in the 1930s, before he abdicated to marry the woman he loved). There is no equivalent, however, to the First Amendment to the U.S. Constitution that provides grounds for a lawsuit if someone disapproves of a restriction on freedom of expression. No court in Britain would overturn an act of Parliament for violating someone's freedom of speech.

Freedom of expression is generous in Great Britain, but there are some restrictions there that are unknown, or negligible, in the United States. British libel laws, for instance, are stricter than ours. In November, 1988, the government of Prime Minister Margaret Thatcher imposed a restriction that was too much for many British subjects. It forbade the broadcasting of any radio or television interviews with members of the Irish Republican Army or its legal political organization in Northern Ireland. A group of two hundred British

journalists, judges, and academics issued a plea for an act of Parliament that would guarantee freedom of expression. No such guarantee has been enacted, however. Of course, the Parliament to which they appealed was led by the same government that had imposed the restrictions.

What would happen if the administration tried something similar in the United States? The Pentagon papers case in 1971 has some similarities to Prime Minister Thatcher's gag rule; the U.S. Supreme Court refused to stop the publication of these classified documents, even though the president stated it would harm national security.

The United States has not always been ahead of Britain in permitting free speech and press, however; remember the imprisonment of American Communists like Dennis and his associates in the 1950s. When they used the First Amendment to challenge the Smith Act, the Court ruled in favor of the government. Even where written constitutions exist, judges may rely on their own views of political necessity, often shared with the legislative and executive branches that developed the civil liberties policies in the first place, to determine the scope of individual rights.

---

within its own free speech guarantee. (Activities such as public demonstrations are often included in debates about freedom of assembly, which will be discussed shortly.)

Free Press versus Fair Trial

The Bill of Rights is an inexhaustible source of potential conflicts between different types of freedoms. Clearly, the Constitution meant to guarantee the right to a fair trial as well as the right to a free press, but a trial may not be fair if press coverage inflames public opinion so much that an impartial jury cannot be found. In one famous trial, Sam Sheppard, an Ohio physician, was accused of murdering his wife. The quantity of press coverage given the trial rivaled that given the Super Bowl, and little of it was sympathetic to Sheppard. Found guilty and sent to prison, Sheppard appealed his conviction to the Supreme Court. He argued that the press coverage had interfered with his ability to get a fair trial. The Court reversed his conviction, maintaining that the press had prejudiced the jurors against Sheppard.

Journalists seek full freedom to cover all trials. They argue that the public has a right to know—although some less credible journalists want to capitalize on the fact that lurid crime stories sell newspapers and attract advertising. When a Nebraska judge issued a gag order forbidding the press to report any details of a particularly gory murder (or even to report the gag order itself), the outraged Nebraska Press Association took the case to the Supreme Court. In *Nebraska Press Association* v. *Stuart* (1972) the Court sided with the editors and revoked the gag order. In 1978 the Court reversed a Virginia judge's order to close a murder trial to the public and the press. "The trial of a criminal case," said the Court in *Richmond Newspapers* v. *Virginia,* "must be open to the public." A pretrial hearing, though, is a different matter. A 1979 case permitted a closed hearing on the grounds that pretrial publicity might compromise the defendant's right to fairness.

Although reporters want trials to be open to them, they do not always like to open their own files to the courts. Once in a while, a reporter has some information that the prosecution or defense insists is crucial evidence in a trial, although the reporter wants to protect a confidential source. More than one reporter has gone to jail when he or she refused to supply evidence. Reporters argue that freedom of the press guarantees them certain rights that other potential witnesses cannot claim.

Some states have passed **shield laws** to protect reporters in these situations. In most states, though, reporters have no more rights than other citizens once a case has come to trial. Courts, too, have ruled that in the absence of shield laws, the right of a fair trial preempts the reporter's right to protect sources. This issue came to a head in one celebrated case involving the student newspaper at Stanford University. After a violent confrontation with student protesters, the police got a search warrant and marched off to the *Stanford Daily,* which they believed to have pictures of the scene from which they could make arrests. The paper argued that its files were protected by the First Amendment, but the decision in **Zurcher v. Stanford Daily** (1976) sided with the police, not the paper.

Freedom of Assembly

The fourth freedom guaranteed by the First Amendment is the freedom to "peaceably assemble." This freedom is often neglected alongside the more trumpeted freedoms of speech, press, and religion, yet it is the basis for forming interest groups and political parties as well as for picketing and protesting in groups.

Right to Assemble   There are two facets of the freedom of assembly. First is the literal right to assemble, that is, to gather together in order to make a statement. This freedom can conflict with other societal values when it disrupts public order, traffic flow, peace and quiet, or bystanders' freedom to go about their business without interference. Within reasonable limits, called *time, place, and manner* restrictions, freedom of assembly includes the rights to parade, picket, and protest. Whatever a group's cause, they have the right to demonstrate, but no group can simply hold a spontaneous demonstration anytime, anywhere, and anyhow it chooses. Usually, a group must apply to the local city government for a permit and post a bond of a few hundred dollars—a little like making a

Nazis and anti-Nazi demonstrators square off in Chicago. The Supreme Court has generally upheld the right of any group, no matter how controversial or offensive, to peaceably assemble, as long as the group's demonstrations remain on public property.

security deposit on an apartment. The governing body must grant a permit as long as the group pledges to hold its demonstration at a time and place that allows the police to prevent major disruptions. There are virtually no limitations on the content of a group's message. In one important case the American Nazi Party applied to march in the streets of Skokie, Illinois, a Chicago suburb where many survivors of Hitler's death camps lived. You can see the Court's decision in "You Are the Judge: The Case of Nazis Applying to March in Skokie."

The balance between freedom and order is tested when protest verges on harassment. Abortion protesters lined up outside abortion clinics are now a common sight. Members of groups like "Operation Rescue" try to shame clients into staying away, and may harass them if they do come to a clinic. Courts have drawn stringent limits on the rights of these protesters. Pro-life demonstrators in a Milwaukee suburb paraded outside the home of a physician who was reported to perform abortions. The town board forbade future picketing in residential neighborhoods. In *Frisby* v. *Schultz* (1988) the Supreme Court agreed that the right of residential privacy was a legitimate local concern and upheld the ordinance.

Right to Associate   The second facet of freedom of assembly is the right to associate with people who share a common interest, including an interest in political change. In a famous case at the height of the civil rights movement, Alabama tried to harass the state chapter of the National Association for the

The Case of the Nazis Applying to March in Skokie

Hitler's Nazis, it is widely estimated, slaughtered six million Jews in death camps like Bergen-Belsen, Auschwitz, and Dachau. Many of the survivors migrated to the United States, and many settled in Skokie, Illinois. Skokie, with eighty thousand people, is a suburb just north of Chicago. In its heavily Jewish population are thousands of survivors of German concentration camps.

The American Nazi party was a ragtag group of perhaps twenty-five to thirty members. Their headquarters was a storefront building on the West Side of Chicago, near an area of expanding black population. Denied a permit to march in a black neighborhood of Chicago, the American Nazis announced their intention to march in Skokie in 1977. Skokie's city govern-ment required that they post a three hundred thousand dollar bond to get a parade permit. The Nazis claimed that the high bond was set in order to prevent their march and that it infringed on their freedoms of speech and assembly. The American Civil Liberties Union (ACLU), despite its loathing of the Nazis, defended the Nazis' claim and their right to march. (The ACLU lost half its Illinois membership because it took this position.)

You be the judge: Do Nazis have the right to parade, preach anti-Jewish propaganda, and perhaps provoke violence in a community peopled with survivors of the Holocaust? What rights or obligations does a community have to maintain order? For the Court's response, see "The Court Decides" on page 158.

Advancement of Colored People by requiring it to turn over its membership list. The Court found this demand an unconstitutional restriction on freedom of association (*NAACP v. Alabama* [1958]).

The four freedoms guaranteed by the First Amendment—religion, speech, press, and assembly—are one key part of Americans' civil liberties. When people confront the American legal system as criminal suspects, they also have certain rights under the Constitution. Even convicted criminals are guaranteed some rights, as the following section will discuss.

DEFENDANTS' RIGHTS

The Bill of Rights contains only forty-four words that guarantee the freedoms of religion, speech, press, and assembly. Most of the remaining words concern the rights of people accused of crimes. These rights were originally intended to protect the accused in *political* arrests and trials; British abuse of colonial political leaders was still fresh in the memory of American citizens. Today the protections in the Fourth, Fifth, Sixth, Seventh, and Eighth Amendments are mostly applied in criminal justice cases.

It is useful to think of the stages of the criminal justice system as a series of funnels decreasing in size. Generally speaking, a *crime* is (sometimes) followed by an *arrest*, which is (sometimes) followed by a *prosecution*, which is (sometimes) followed by a *trial*, which (usually) results in a verdict of innocence or guilt. The funnels get smaller and smaller, each dripping into the next. Many more crimes occur than are reported; many more crimes occur than arrests are made (only about one in five crimes results in an arrest); many more arrests are made than prosecutors prosecute; and many more prosecutions occur than trials. In the next few pages you will move through the criminal justice system, pausing at each stage to see how the Constitution protects the rights of the accused (see Table 4.2).

Interpreting Defendants' Rights

The Bill of Rights sets out a number of civil liberties that American citizens enjoy if they are arrested or brought to court. The Bill of Rights covers every stage of the criminal justice system; at every step, police, prosecutors, and judges must behave in accordance with the Bill of Rights. Any misstep may invalidate a conviction.

The language of the Bill of Rights comes, of course, from the late 1700s. It is often quaint, and, frankly, vague as well. One might rightly ask: Just how speedy is a "speedy trial"? How cruel and unusual does a punishment have to be in order to be constitutionally "cruel and unusual"? The courts continually have to rule on the constitutionality of actions by police, prosecutors, judges,

---

Table 4.2   **The Bill of Rights and the Stages of the Criminal Justice System**

Although our criminal justice system is complex, it can be broken down into stages. The Bill of Rights protects the rights of the accused at every stage. Here are some key constitutional guarantees at various stages of the criminal justice system.

STAGE	PROTECTIONS
1. Evidence gathered	"unreasonable search and seizure" forbidden (Fourth Amendment)
2. Suspicion cast	guarantee that "writ of habeas corpus" will not be suspended, forbidding imprisonment without evidence (Article I, Section 9)
3. Arrest made	self-incrimination forbidden (Fifth Amendment) right to have the "assistance of counsel" (Sixth Amendment)
4. Interrogation held	"excessive bail" forbidden (Eighth Amendment)
5. Trial held	"speedy and public trial" by an impartial jury required (Sixth Amendment) "double jeopardy" (being tried twice for the same crime) forbidden (Fifth Amendment) trial by jury required (Article III, Section 2) right to confront witnesses required (Sixth Amendment)
6. Punishment imposed	"cruel and unusual punishment" forbidden (Eighth Amendment)

and legislatures, actions that a citizen or group claims has violated their rights. Defendant's rights, just as those rights protected by the First Amendment, are not well defined in the Bill of Rights.

One thing that is clear, however, is that Supreme Court decisions have extended specific provisions of the Bill of Rights, one by one, to the states. Virtually all of the rights discussed in the following sections affect the actions of both the national and state authorities. Just what rights, then, do Americans enjoy in the criminal justice system?

Searches and Seizures

Police cannot arrest a citizen on a whim. Police need evidence to arrest, and courts need it to convict. Before making an arrest, police need what the courts call **probable cause** to believe that someone is guilty of a crime. Often police need to get physical evidence—a car thief's fingerprints, a purse snatched—to use in court. The Fourth Amendment is quite specific in forbidding **unreasonable searches and seizures.** To prevent abuse of police power, the Constitution requires that no court may issue a **search warrant** unless probable cause exists to believe that a crime has occurred or is about to occur. Warrants must specify the area to be searched and what the police are looking for.

There is no constitutional requirement that a warrant is necessary for a reasonable police search, however. Most searches in this country take place without warrants. Such searches are valid if probable cause exists, if the search is necessary to protect an officer's safety, or if the search is limited to material relevant to the suspected crime or within the suspect's immediate control.

In Cleveland a woman named Dollree Mapp was under suspicion for illegal gambling activities. The police broke into her home looking for a suspect, and while there, they searched the house and found a cache of obscene materials. Mapp was convicted of possessing them, but she appealed her case to the federal courts, claiming that the Fourth Amendment should be applied to state and local governments. In an important decision (**Mapp v. Ohio** [1961]), the Supreme Court ruled that the evidence had been seized illegally and reversed Mapp's conviction. Since then the Fourth Amendment has been incorporated within the rights that restrict the states as well as the federal government.

In two cases involving Fourth Amendment issues, Dow Chemical Company and a man named Ciraolo ran afoul of authorities; both cases involved aerial searches. Ciraolo was a marijuana grower. When police, responding to a tip, went to look at his place, it was surrounded by ten-foot fences. The police then rented a private plane, took pictures, and secured a conviction. Environmental Protection Agency officials took a similar aerial photo of Dow Chemical's Midland, Michigan, plant and located environmental violations. Both Ciraolo and Dow sued, claiming they were the victims of unconstitutional search and seizure. Both, however, lost when their cases came before the Supreme Court.

Ever since 1914 the courts have used an **exclusionary rule** to prevent illegally seized evidence from being introduced in the courtroom. No matter how incriminating a piece of evidence—even a shirt stained with the victim's blood—it cannot be introduced into a trial if it is not constitutionally obtained. Dollree Mapp, for example, was exonerated because the Supreme Court held that the exclusionary rule applied to state as well as national authorities. The logic of the exclusionary rule is this: if police officers are forced to gather

evidence properly, their competence will be rewarded in a conviction; if they are slapdash or ignore the rights of a suspect, they will not win a conviction. Critics of the exclusionary rule—and some of them sit on the Supreme Court—argue that its strict application may permit guilty persons to go free because of police carelessness or innocent errors. You can examine one contemporary search-and-seizure case in "You Are the Judge: The Case of Ms. Montoya."

The Burger Court made some exceptions to the exclusionary rule. *Nix* v. *Williams* (1984) allowed the use of illegally obtained evidence when this evidence led police to a discovery that they eventually would have made without it. *United States* v. *Lean,* decided in the same year, established the good-faith exception to the rule; evidence could be used if the police who seized it mistakenly thought they were operating under a constitutionally valid warrant. The Court even allowed evidence illegally obtained from a banker to be used to convict one of his customers (*United States* v. *Payner,* [1980]). The Rehnquist Court, with its conservative orientation (discussed in Chapter 5), may make even more exceptions in the future or even abolish the rule entirely.

Self-incrimination

Suppose that evidence has been gathered and suspicion directed toward a particular person, and the police are ready to make an arrest. In the American

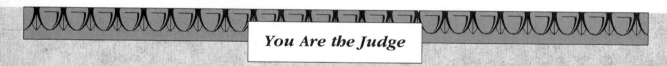

You Are the Judge

The Case of Ms. Montoya

On March 5, 1983, Rose Elviro Montoya de Hernandez arrived at the Los Angeles International Airport on Avianca Flight 080 from Bogatá, Colombia. Her first official encounter was with U.S. Customs Inspector Talamantes, who noticed that she spoke no English. Interestingly, Montoya's passport indicated eight recent quick trips from Bogatá to Los Angeles. She had five thousand dollars in bills but no billfold or credit cards.

Talamantes and his fellow customs officers were suspicious. Stationed in Los Angeles, they were hardly unaware of the fact that Colombia was a major drug supplier. They questioned Montoya, who explained that her husband had a store in Bogatá and that she planned to spend the five thousand dollars at K mart and J.C. Penney, stocking up on items for the store.

The inspector, growing warier and warier, handed Montoya over to female customs inspectors for a search. These agents noticed what the Supreme Court later referred to delicately as a "firm fullness" in Montoya's abdomen. Suspicions, already high, grew higher. The agents applied for a court order to conduct pregnancy tests, X rays, and other examinations, and eventually they found eighty-eight balloons containing 80 percent pure cocaine in Montoya's alimentary canal.

Montoya's lawyer argued that this constituted unreasonable search and seizure and that her arrest and conviction should be set aside. There was, he said, no direct evidence that would have led the officials to suspect cocaine smuggling. The government argued that the arrest had followed from a set of odd facts leading to reasonable suspicion that something was amiss.

You be the judge: Was Montoya's arrest based on a search-and-seizure incident that violated the Fourth Amendment? For the Supreme Court's answer, see "The Court Decides" on p. 158.

explaining

system the burden of proof rests on the police and the prosecutors. Suspects cannot be forced to help with their own conviction by, say, blurting out a confession in the stationhouse. The **Fifth Amendment** forbids forced **self-incrimination,** stating that no person "shall be compelled to be a witness against himself." Whether in a congressional hearing, a courtroom, or a police station, suspects need not provide evidence that can then be used against them. (Under law, though, the government may guarantee suspects *immunity*—exemption from prosecution. In return, suspects must testify regarding their own and others' misdeeds.)

analyzing + giving Miranda rights

Protection against self-incrimination begins at arrest. You have probably seen television shows in which an arrest is made and the arresting officers recite, often from memory, a set of rights to the arrestee. These rights are authentic and originated from a famous decision—perhaps the most important modern decision in criminal law—involving an Arizona man named Ernesto Miranda.[9]

Miranda was picked up as a prime suspect in the ugly rape-kidnapping of an eighteen-year-old girl. Selected by the girl from a police lineup, Miranda was questioned for two hours. During this time, he was told of neither his constitutional right against self-incrimination nor his right to counsel. In fact, it seems highly unlikely that Miranda had even heard of the Fifth Amendment. He said enough to eventually lead to a conviction. The Supreme Court reversed his conviction on appeal (***Miranda v. Arizona*** [1966]) and also set the following guidelines for police questioning of suspects:

Ernesto Miranda's overturned conviction compelled law enforcement officials to carefully inform suspects of their constitutional rights.

outline

- Suspects must be told that they have a constitutional right to remain silent and may stop answering questions at any time.
- They must be warned that what they say can be used against them in a court of law.
- They must be told that they have a right to have a lawyer present during questioning and that a public defender is available.

effects

Police departments throughout the country were disgruntled by *Miranda*. Officers felt that interrogation was crucial to any investigation. Warning suspects of their rights and letting them call a lawyer were almost certain to silence them.

[9]On the Miranda case, see Liva Baker, *Miranda: The Crime, the Law, the Politics* (New York: Atheneum, 1983).

THE WIZARD OF ID

When Neal Milner researched the effects of this decision, his data suggested that police departments often tended initially to ignore *Miranda,* partly because they did not understand it.[10] Most departments today, however, seem to take *Miranda* seriously. The usually read a *Miranda card* advising suspects of their rights. Ironically, when Ernesto Miranda himself was murdered, the suspect was read his rights from a Miranda card.

The more conservative Supreme Court majority under Chief Justice Burger did not weaken the *Miranda* rulings, as some civil libertarians feared it might. The Burger court remained strongly committed to a defendant's right to counsel, although the Rehnquist court may rule to make some exceptions to *Miranda.*

The Right to Counsel

One of the most important of the *Miranda* rights is the right to secure counsel. Even lawyers taken to court hire another lawyer to represent them. (There is an old saying in the legal profession that a lawyer who defends himself has a fool for a client.) Although in federal courts the **Sixth Amendment** has always ensured the right to counsel, not until recently did people who were tried in state courts have this right. Winning this right for poor defendants was a long fight. Until the 1930s, individuals were tried and sometimes convicted for capital offenses (those in which the death penalty could be imposed) without a lawyer. In 1932 the Supreme Court ordered the states to provide an attorney for indigent (poor) defendants accused of a capital crime *(Powell* v. *Alabama).*

Not until 1963 did the Supreme Court extend that right to everyone accused of a felony. In the Florida state prison was a man named Clarence Earl Gideon, convicted of robbing a pool hall.[11] This nickel-and-dime burglary (mostly change from a vending machine) had netted Gideon a five-year jail term. Because Gideon was too poor to hire a lawyer, he had never been represented by one. Using the prison's law books, he wrote a *pauper's petition* and sent it to the Supreme Court, which reviewed the petition and held in Gideon's favor (**Gideon v. Wainwright** [1963]). Gideon was released, retried (this time with a public defender handling his case), and acquitted. More than a thousand of Gideon's fellow Florida prisoners, plus thousands more who in other states had been convicted without benefit of counsel, were also released. Subsequently, the Court went a step further than *Gideon* and held that whenever imprisonment could be imposed, a lawyer must be provided for the accused *(Argersinger* v. *Hamlin* [1972]). Thanks to the efforts of Clarence Gideon and others, the Supreme Court has universalized this Sixth Amendment right so that today every court is required to appoint a lawyer to represent anyone who does not have the money to hire one.

Clarence Gideon (shown here reading law books in a Florida state prison) fought to obtain a lawyer for himself. His case helped ensure that the Sixth Amendment's guarantee of legal counsel would be incorporated into state law.

Trial by Jury

TV's image of courts and trials is almost as dramatic as its image of detectives and police officers, but myth and reality do not blend well. Highly publicized trials are dramatic, but rare. The death of a wealthy diet doctor, the attempted

---

[10]Neal Milner, *The Court and Local Law Enforcement* (Beverly Hills, Calif.: Sage, 1971).

[11]The story of Gideon is eloquently told by Anthony Lewis, *Gideon's Trumpet* (New York: Random House, 1964).

murder of a Rhode Island socialite, the dramatic recantation of a rape accusation in Chicago, and the multiple rapes in a New Bedford, Massachusetts barroom made headlines for weeks. (Cable News Network even carried live the trial of the barroom rapists.) In reality, most cases, even ones in which the evidence is solid, do not get to trial.

If you ever go to a typical American criminal courtroom, you will rarely see a trial complete with judge and jury. In American courts, 90 percent of all cases begin and end with a guilty plea.[12] Most cases are settled through a process called **plea bargaining.** A plea bargain results from an actual bargain struck between a defendant's lawyer and a prosecutor to the effect that a defendant will plead guilty to a lesser crime in exchange for a state's not prosecuting that defendant for a more serious one.

Critics of the plea-bargaining system believe that it permits many criminals to avoid facing the music—or as much music as they could face if tried for a more serious offense. The process, however, works to the advantage of both sides; it saves time and money that would otherwise be spent on a trial, and it permits defendants who think they might be convicted of a serious charge to plead guilty to a lesser one.

Whether plea bargaining serves the ends of justice is much debated. To its critics, plea bargaining benefits defendants. David Brereton and Jonathan Casper, studying sentencing patterns in three California counties, discovered that a larger proportion of defendants who went to trial (rather than plea-bargained) ended up going to prison, compared with those who pleaded guilty and had no trial. In answer to their question "Does it pay to plead guilty?" these authors give a qualified yes.[13] Good or bad, plea bargaining is here to stay. Only a vast increase in resources devoted to the court system could cope with a trial for every defendant.

For those 300,000 cases per year that actually go to trial, there are many rights available to defendants. The Sixth Amendment ensures the right to a speedy trial by an impartial jury. These days, defendants—those who can afford it, at least—do not leave jury selection to chance. A sophisticated technology of jury selection has developed. Jury consultants—often psychologists or other social scientists putting some of their statistical training to use—develop profiles of jurors likely to be sympathetic or hostile to a defendant. Lawyers for both sides spend hours questioning prospective jurors in a major case. One Chicago prosecutor reports that he would challenge "anyone who had one psychology or one sociology course in college," fearing, presumably, that psychology and sociology courses make people more sympathetic to defendants (no hard evidence suggests they do).

The Constitution does not specify the size of a jury; in principle, it could be anywhere from one or two people to hundreds or thousands. Tradition in England and America has set jury size at twelve, although in petty cases, six jurors are sometimes used. Whereas traditionally a jury had to be unanimous in order to convict, the Burger Court eroded those traditions, permitting states to use fewer than twelve jurors or even to convict with a less than unanimous vote.

[12]Herbert Jacob, *Urban Justice* (Englewood Cliffs, N.J.: Prentice-Hall, 1973), 98.

[13]David Brereton and Jonathan D. Casper, "Does it Pay to Plead Guilty? Differential Sentencing and the Function of the Criminal Courts," *Law and Society Review* 16(1981–1982): 45–70.

Although the Supreme Court held in Gregg *v.* Georgia *that the death penalty, whether carried out by electrocution or other means, was not cruel and unusual punishment, it is rarely implemented.*

Cruel and Unusual Punishment

Citizens convicted of a crime can expect some punishment ranging from mild to severe, with the mildest being some form of probation and the most severe, of course, being the death penalty. The **Eighth Amendment** forbids **cruel and unusual punishment,** although it does not define the phrase. Through the Fourteenth Amendment, this provision of the Bill of Rights applies to the states.

Almost all of the constitutional debate over cruel and unusual punishment has centered on the death penalty. Today some two thousand people are on death row; about a quarter of them are in two states, Florida and Texas. Very little evidence shows that the death penalty deters crime. States that do not permit it have crime rates similar to those in states that do permit the death penalty. Historically, the death penalty has been disproportionately applied to blacks. Of those persons executed between the 1930s and the 1970s, more than half were black.[14] Even today, almost half of the people on death row are members of minority groups.

For years the Supreme Court has been divided on the issue of the death penalty, and the division has shown in its decisions. In 1968 the Court overturned a death sentence because opponents of the death penalty had been excluded from the jury at sentencing *(Witherspoon* v. *Illinois),* a factor that stacked the cards, said the Court, in favor of the extreme penalty. In ***Furman* v. *Georgia*** (1972) the Court first confronted the question of whether the death penalty is inherently cruel and unusual punishment. Although *Furman* had a message, it was a confusing one; four justices said that the death penalty was not cruel and unusual punishment, yet the Court overturned Georgia's death penalty law because its imposition was "freakish" and "random."

Warned by *Furman,* thirty-five states passed new laws permitting the death penalty. Some states, to prevent arbitrariness, went to the other extreme, mandating death penalties for some crimes. In *Woodson* v. *North Carolina,* the Supreme Court ruled against mandatory death penalties.

The closest thing to a definitive word on the death penalty was ***Gregg* v. *Georgia*** (1976). Troy Gregg had murdered two hitchhikers and was awaiting execution in Georgia's state prison. Gregg's attorney made the argument that the death penalty was cruel and unusual punishment. The Court disagreed. "Capital punishment," it said, "is an expression of society's outrage at particularly offensive conduct. . . . It is an extreme sanction, suitable to the most extreme of crimes."

A divided Court rebuffed the last major challenge to the death penalty in ***McCleskey* v. *Kemp*** (1987). Five justices refused to rule that the penalty violated the equal protection of the law guaranteed by the Fourteenth Amendment. Although social scientists testified that minority defendants and murderers whose victims were white were disproportionately likely to receive death sentences, the Court insisted that this fact did not violate the Fourteenth Amendment, because there was no evidence that juries intended to discriminate on the basis of race.

Even today the death penalty remains a rarity. Painstaking legal delays and appeals stave off a death row inmate's appointed day; new arguments are made

---

[14]Abe Fortas, "The Case against Capital Punishment," in *Contemporary Debates on Civil Liberties,* ed. Glenn Phelps and Robert A. Poirier (Lexington, Mass.: Heath, 1985), 148.

or new methods of delay are found. Despite decades of legal debate, the death penalty is still, as Justice Potter Stewart once said, freakish in the way lightning is freakish. As rare as the death penalty is, however, it is an accepted part of the American criminal justice system.

THE RIGHT TO PRIVACY

The members of the First Congress who drafted the Bill of Rights and enshrined American civil liberties would never have imagined that Americans would go to court to argue about wiretapping, surrogate motherhood, or pornography. New technologies have raised ethical issues unimaginable in the eighteenth century. Today one of the greatest debates concerning Americans' civil liberties lies in the emerging area of privacy rights.

Is There a Right to Privacy?

Nowhere does the Bill of Rights say that Americans have a **right to privacy.** Clearly, though, the First Congress had the concept of privacy in mind when they crafted the first ten amendments. Freedom of religion implies the right to exercise private beliefs; protections against "unreasonable searches and seizures" make persons secure in their homes; private property cannot be seized without "due process of law." In 1928 Justice Brandeis hailed privacy as "the right to be left alone—the most comprehensive of the rights and the most valued by civilized men."

The idea that the Constitution guarantees a right to privacy was first enunciated in a 1965 case involving a Connecticut law that forbid contraceptives. It was a little-used law, but a doctor and family-planning specialist were arrested for disseminating birth control devices. The state reluctantly brought them to court, and they were convicted. The Supreme Court, in the case of *Griswold* v. *Connecticut,* wrestled with the case. Seven justices finally decided that various portions of the Bill of Rights cast "penumbras"—unstated liberties on the fringes of the more explicitly stated rights—protecting a right to privacy, including a right to family planning between husband and wife. Reasonable enough, supporters of privacy rights argued, for what could be the purpose of, for example, the Fourth Amendment if not to protect privacy? Critics of the ruling, and there were many of them, claimed that the Supreme Court was inventing protections not specified by the Constitution.

The most important application of privacy rights, though, came not in the area of birth control, but in the area of abortion. The Supreme Court unleashed a constitutional firestorm in 1973 that has never abated.

Firestorms over Abortion

In the summer of 1972 Supreme Court Justice Harry Blackmun returned to Minnesota's famous Mayo Clinic, where he had once served as general counsel. The Clinic lent him a tiny desk in the corner of a librarian's office, where he worked quietly for two weeks. His research during this short summer vacation focused on the medical aspects of abortion. Blackmun had been assigned the task of writing the majority opinion in one of the most controversial cases ever to come before the Court. The judge was chronically tardy in his opinion writing, and this decision was no exception. Later, back in Washington, Blackmun finished his draft opinion and sent it to his impatient colleagues.

The opinion, in **Roe v. Wade** (1973), has been called both radical and temperate. "Jane Roe" was the pseudonym of a Texas woman, Norma McCorvey, who had sought an abortion. She argued that the state law allowing the procedure only to save the life of a mother was unconstitutional. (In fact, McCorvey gave birth to a daughter and relinquished her for adoption.) Texas argued that states had the power to regulate moral behavior, including abortions.

Blackmun's decision followed medical authorities in dividing pregnancy into three equal *trimesters. Roe* forbade any state control of abortions during the first trimester; permitted states to allow regulated abortions, but only to protect the mother's health, in the second trimester; and allowed the states to ban abortion during the third trimester, except when the mother's life was in danger. This decision unleashed a storm of protest. The Court's staff needed extra mailboxes to handle the correspondence, some of which contained death threats.[15] By and large, though, states adjusted to the new decision, doctors and hospitals cooperated, and, however awkward the reasoning or controversial the result, the decision governed public policy. Since *Roe* v. *Wade,* about a million and a half abortions have been performed annually.

The furor has never subsided. Representative Henry Hyde (R-Ill.) persuaded Congress to tack onto Medicaid legislation a provision called the Hyde Amendment, which forbade the use of federal funds for abortions. Many states passed similar restrictions. Missouri went as far as any other state, forbidding the use of state funds or state employees to perform abortions. A clinic, Reproductive Health Services of St. Louis, challenged the law as unconstitutional. The case did not come before the Court until 1989, with a conservative majority in place. Both proponents and opponents of *Roe* v. *Wade* anxiously awaited the decision. Would the Court take this opportunity to overrule *Roe?*

It did not. **Webster v. Reproductive Health Services** upheld the law, but did not give the states license to recriminalize abortion. The decision unleashed a second storm of protest. State legislatures prepared for the deluge, but by the end of 1989 only Pennsylvania had enacted new restrictions. In Florida, Governor Bob Martinez called a special session of the legislature to consider strong antiabortion measures. "It's going to be nasty," said Janis Compton-Carr of the Florida Abortion Rights Action League, but it was not; Martinez's bill never got out of committee. Some people claimed that the pro-life movement lost much of its momentum when this bill died in committee. In the 1989 election Virginia and New Jersey elected pro-choice governors. In addition, Illinois withdrew a case, scheduled to be heard in late 1989, that would have given the Supreme Court another opportunity to reverse *Roe.* The law in question would have regulated clinics, where the vast majority of abortions are performed, out of existence. Neil Hartigan, the Illinois attorney general defending the law, wanted to run for governor—but he was finding it difficult to get campaign contributions. The state and clinics worked out a last-minute compromise, and the clinics stayed open.

Americans are deeply divided on abortion. Proponents of choice believe that access to abortion is essential if women are to be fully autonomous human

[15] Woodward and Armstrong, *The Brethren,* 271–84.

beings. Opponents call themselves pro-life because they believe that the fetus is fully human; therefore, an abortion deprives a fetus of the right to life. These positions are irreconcilable, making abortion a politician's nightmare. Wherever a politician stands, a large number of voters will be enraged.

A Time to Live and a Time to Die

The idea of rights to live, die, or have children were all but meaningless before the twentieth-century revolution in medicine and biotechnology. Today medical science can continue certain life functions, especially respiration and blood circulation, in the absence of other vital signs, like brain activity. State laws struggle to define death. At the same time, in-vitro fertilization, frozen embryos, and artificial insemination complicate efforts to define birth by separating reproduction from sexual intercourse and the parent-child relationship. Do people have rights to use these new technologies—or refuse to use them? May people make these decisions for their parents or children?

Many of the issues surrounding birth and death were crystallized in two "Baby Doe" cases. Baby Doe was born in Indiana in 1982 with Down's syndrome, a genetic defect causing mental retardation. Baby Jane Doe was born in New York in 1983 with spina bifida, a condition in which the spine fails to close

---

The People Speak **The Abortion Debate**

In few areas of public opinion research do scholars find more divided opinions than on abortion. A few people seem to feel very, very strongly about the matter, enough so that they are even "single-issue voters." A *Time* poll found that 24 percent of the people were so opposed to abortion that they would never support a candidate who would favor it regardless of their positions on other issues. On the other side, 32 percent feel strongly enough that they would not consider voting for a candidate who would vote to restrict abortion rights, whatever else that candidate believed in. About two-thirds of the population said that even in cases where they might think abortion is wrong, the government has no business preventing a woman from having an abortion. This poll suggested that most Americans are pro-choice. In another poll, a similar number—65 percent—opposed permitting an abortion "at the discretion of the mother regardless of her reasons." These two surveys (see below) thus demonstrated that Americans are gravely divided—often in their own minds—about the pro-choice and pro-life positions. One thing, though, on which decisive majorities agree is that they do not want government interfering in abortion decisions.

Do you think abortion is justified

	Yes	No	Don't know
To protect the mother from serious health risks?	78%	17%	5%
At the discretion of the mother?	26%	65%	9%
Under no circumstances?	22%	69%	9%

	Percent who agree
I would never vote for any candidate who favors abortion.	24%
I would never vote for any candidate who would restrict women's right to have an abortion.	32%

Sources: The top poll is from Gallup and appears in *Hippocrates* (May/June 1988); the bottom one is by Yankelovich and is reported in *Time*, July 17, 1989. The questions are worded exactly as they were in the polls.

properly and that can cause serious mental and physical defects. Doctors for both babies told the parents that they would die without surgery. The Indiana parents decided against surgery, at which point the hospital went to court to get permission for it. These efforts were unsuccessful, and the baby died.

In Baby Jane Doe's case, the parents and the doctors together decided against surgery. Along came Lawrence Washburn, an Albany attorney who has frequently intervened in lawsuits to prevent abortions. Washburn sued the hospital and parents, claiming that their decision constituted discrimination against a disabled person in violation of federal law. New York courts upheld the decision of the parents and the hospital. The Justice Department then filed suit, threatening to cut off the twenty to twenty-five million dollars that the hospital received each year in federal funds if it refused to release its records. Eventually, the Supreme Court affirmed parents' rights to make medical decisions for their children.[16] Baby Jane Doe did survive. You can consider another case involving parental responsibility in "You Are the Judge: The Case of the Cocaine-using Mother".

Mary Sue Davis and Junior Davis had another kind of conflict over the beginnings of life. At their divorce hearing in Tennessee, they argued about seven fertilized embryos. These had been produced through a new technique known as in-vitro fertilization, in which sperm and an ovum are joined outside a woman's body and frozen for later implantation in the uterus. Mary Sue argued that the embryos were alive, and should be released to her. Junior's lawyer argued that life begins at birth; therefore, the embryos were not living things and should be destroyed. The judge gave Mary Sue custody of the embryos.

Experts estimate that one in every six American couples who want children will experience difficulty in having them. In-vitro fertilization is a technique that can compensate for several kinds of fertility problems. Similar difficulties led

[16]Bowen v. American Hospital Association, 476 U.S. 610 (1985).

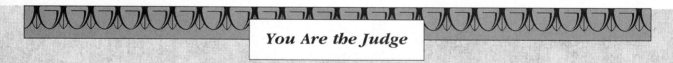

You Are the Judge

The Case of the Cocaine-using Mother

Jennifer C. Johnson was a twenty-three-year-old cocaine addict from Sanford, Florida, not far from Disney World. She gave birth to a son in 1987 and a daughter in 1989. Both were born with a cocaine derivative in their systems. Jeff Deen, the assistant state's attorney for Brevard and Seminole counties, took an unusual step; he charged Ms. Johnson with two counts of delivering drugs to minors, a violation that carried in Florida a maximum term of thirty years in prison. This statute was normally used for drug dealers charged with selling drugs to youths. In the case of Jennifer Johnson, the "delivery" of drugs took place in her uterus, through the umbilical cords of her two chil-

dren. Prosecutor Deen argued that convicting Ms. Johnson would open up a new avenue for prosecuting cocaine users and would be a victory for children. The American Civil Liberties Union, which defended Ms. Johnson, argued that frightful consequences could come from the precedent of convicting her. Pregnant addicts, for example, would be deterred from seeking help if they knew that they could be prosecuted. Poor and minority mothers would—as so often is the case—suffer the most.

You be the judge: Should Ms. Johnson be convicted? For the Court's answer, see "The Court Decides" on page 158.

Mary Beth Whitehead and Jeremy Rifkin, who cochair the National Coalition against Surrogacy, display a copy of Whitehead's surrogacy contract to a House Energy and Commerce subcommittee. Modern technology challenges the government and courts to make life and death decisions that the Constitution's writers could not have imagined.

to the famous "Baby M" case in New Jersey. When Elizabeth Stern, a physician, developed health problems that made pregnancy risky, she and her husband, William, sought help from an agency. Mary Beth Whitehead agreed to become what the press has labeled a "surrogate mother"; she was artificially inseminated with William's sperm in order to bear a child for the Sterns. In March of 1986 Whitehead gave birth to a girl, called Baby M in court records. Whitehead soon decided that she did not want to give up her baby. In 1988 the state Supreme Court gave parental rights to both natural parents. The Lewis and Whitehead cases are a foretaste of more legal quandaries to come.

Courts face questions about the right to die as well as the right to life. Modern medicine can keep people alive, though barely functioning, for months and even years. You can confront some of the ethical dilemmas involved with the right to die in "A Question of Ethics: The Right to Die."

UNDERSTANDING CIVIL LIBERTIES AND THE CONSTITUTION

American government is both democratic and constitutional. America is democratic because it is governed by officials elected by the people and answerable to them. The American government is constitutional because it has a fundamental organic law, the Constitution, that limits the things government can do. By limiting the government, the Constitution puts limits on what the people can empower the government to do. The democratic and constitutional components of government can produce conflicts, but they also reinforce one another.

Civil Liberties and Democracy

Individual rights enhance democracy. The rights ensured by the First Amendment—the freedoms of speech, press, and assembly—are essential to a democracy. If people are to govern themselves, they need access to all available information and opinions in order to make intelligent, responsible, and accountable decisions. If everyone is to have the right to participate in public life, all Americans must have the right to express any opinions that they have.

Individual participation and the expression of ideas are crucial components of democracy, but so is majority rule, which can conflict with individual rights. The majority does not have the freedom to decide that there are some ideas it

The Right to Die

When she stopped breathing, twenty-one-year-old Karen Quinlan became a national celebrity in a macabre way. Injured in an automobile accident, she lapsed into a deep coma with only faint brain waves. Quinlan's family asked the hospital to take her off her respirator and let her die. The hospital, fearing legal charges, refused. The family went to court. The Supreme Court of New Jersey, in 1976, sided with the family. It held that a patient's right to refuse treatment is a part of the right to privacy. When a patient was no longer able to speak, families or a guardian could exercise the patient's right. Quinlan was removed from her respirator, but in fact continued breathing for nearly a decade.

Today 95 percent of deaths in this country occur in a hospital or nursing home. Almost all the rest happen in accidents. Thus almost every American whose death is anticipated or predictable dies in a publicly regulated institution, a hospital or a nursing home. The government, therefore, plays a very different role than it did when death took place mostly in the quiet of a home, under the eye of a family or a physician. Just as people have strong feelings about abortions, they often have strong feelings about dying. Where feelings run high, courts and legislatures are likely to be involved.

The U.S. Supreme Court has never issued a definitive ruling on the right to die. Other courts, though, have been wrestling with the issue for more than a decade. The following are some of their decisions:

The *Barber* Case. Clarence Herbert, a fifty-five-year-old California man, suffered a massive heart attack after surgery and went into a coma. At the family's request, his doctors discontinued his life support systems and his intravenous feeding. His nurses, though, reported the action to the district attorney, who indicted Drs. Barber and Nejdl. They were convicted of murder. On appeal, the California Court of Appeals in 1983 reversed the conviction, holding that the action was an omission and not an active commission of a murder. Nonetheless, the case sent shock waves through the medical industry, which feared that medical decisions could result in murder convictions.

The *Bouviar* Case. In 1986 Elizabeth Bouviar, a young quadriplegic with cerebral palsy, was in constant pain. She garnered headlines by checking herself into a Los Angeles hospital, wishing to end her life. The hospital staff, perhaps still worried about the *Barber* case, force fed her to keep her alive. She sought a court order asking that the feeding be stopped, thus asking for permission to commit suicide under a hospital's care. The trial court rejected her request, but the California Court of Appeals held that a patient need not be comatose or near death to make a decision about treatment. The right to privacy, the court said, permitted a patient to decide on the nature of treatment. The tubes removed, Bouviar survived on a liquid diet.

The *Jefferson* case. Jessie Mae Jefferson was told that she could deliver her baby only by caesarian section. She refused, citing her religious beliefs. The hospital went to court. The Georgia Supreme Court in 1981 ordered the caesarian section performed because the unborn child's right to live outweighed the mother's right to practice her religion.

With advancing medical technology, Americans will surely see more issues related to the right to die and the right to live. American ethical values are strained by the collision of medical capacities and human choices. Thus far, most court decisions have supported a right to die, at least for people who are rational or had families capable of making their decisions. What, though, should be our policy posture toward the right to die? Easy cases are those with agreement among family and doctors, sometimes even the patient. What if there are differences of opinion? Is litigation the only, or the best, way of rendering these wrenching decisions? What criteria should the courts, hospital administrators, and public officials use to make these decisions?

Source: The preceding cases are discussed in "When the Law Plays Doctor: Ten Critical Cases," *Hippocrates* May/June, 1988, 58-59.

would rather not hear, although, at times, it tries to enforce its will upon the minority. The conflict is even sharper in relation to the rights guaranteed by the Fourth, Fifth, Sixth, Seventh, and Eighth Amendments. These rights protect all Americans, but they also make it harder to punish criminals. It is easy, though misleading, for the majority to view these guarantees as benefits for criminals at the expense of society.

Ultimately the courts decide what constitutional guarantees mean in practice. The federal courts are the branch of government least subject to majority rule. Judges, appointed for life, are not directly accountable to popular will (though, as Chapter 16 on the judiciary will show, there is indirect accountability). The courts enhance democracy by protecting liberty and equality from the excesses of majority rule.

Civil Liberties and the Size of Government

When the Constitution was adopted in the 1780s, no government on earth was anywhere near as large or as efficient as the American government is today. European countries had known more than a few despotic monarchs, but no king or emperor had an army powerful enough to repress all free thought. England had persecuted Quakers, dissident Puritans, and Roman Catholics, but members of each of these groups had escaped to North America. A European in disfavor with a king could find protection from a powerful prince.

Today's government is huge and commands vast, powerful technologies. American's Social Security numbers, credit cards, drivers' licenses, and school records are all on giant computers to which the government has immediate access. It is virtually impossible to hide from the police, the FBI, the Internal Revenue Service, or any governmental agency. Since Americans can no longer avoid the attention of government, strict limitations on governmental power are essential. The Bill of Rights provides these vital limitations.

SUMMARY

The Bill of Rights is fundamental to Americans' freedom. Civil liberties are an individual's protection against the government. Disputes about civil liberties are frequent because the issues involved are complex and divisive. Legislatures and courts are constantly defining in practice what the Bill of Rights guarantees in theory.

In a way, the notion that government can protect people from government is contradictory. Thomas Jefferson wrote in the Declaration of Independence that all men "are endowed by their creator with certain *unalienable rights.*" Jefferson's next "self-evident truth" was that "to secure these rights, governments are instituted among men." People, says Jefferson here, do not get their rights from government. Instead, rights precede government, which gets its power to rule from the people. The Bill of Rights does not give Americans freedom of religion or the right to a fair trial; these amendments recognize that these rights exist. People often speak, however, as though rights are things that government gives them.

The four freedoms guaranteed by the First Amendment are freedom of religion, speech, press, and assembly. The Bill of Rights also contains protections

Captain Goldman's yarmulke. Answer: In a five to four decision the Supreme Court upheld the right of the Air Force to enforce its dress code even against religiously-based dress choices. The narrow majority reaffirmed the Court's traditional rule that things acceptable for civilians might not be acceptable in the military.

The Alabama prayer case. Answer: If you read the discussion of the *Engel* and *Scheapp* cases, you probably concluded that the Alabama law was unconstitutional. Incredibly, though, a federal district court upheld the state law. It reasoned that the states were not bound by the First Amendment. Eventually, the Supreme Court, in *Wallace* v. *Jaffree* (1985) held the law unconstitutional. (Writing the Court's majority opinion, Justice Stevens called the district court's ruling a "remarkable conclusion.")

The Pentagon papers case. Answer: In a six to three decision a majority of the justices agreed that the "no prior restraint" rule prohibited prosecution before the papers were published. The justices also made it clear that if the government brought prosecution for theft, the Court might be sympathetic. No such charges were filed.

The drive-in theatre case. Answer: In *Erznoznik* v. *Jacksonville* (1975) the Supreme Court held that Jacksonville's ordinance was unconstitutionally broad. The City Council had gone too far; it could end up banning movies that might not be obscene at all. The ordinance would, said the Court, ban a film "containing a picture of a baby's buttocks, the nude body of a war victim or scenes from a culture where nudity is indigenous." Said Justice Powell for the Court: "Clearly, all nudity cannot be deemed obscene."

The Nazis' march case. Answer: A federal district court ruled that Skokie's ordinance did restrict freedom of assembly and association. No community could use its power to grant parade permits to stifle free expression. In October 1978, in *Collins* v. *Smith* (Collins was the Nazi leader and Smith was the mayor of Skokie), the Supreme Court let this lower court decision stand. In fact, the Nazis did not march in Skokie, settling instead for some poorly attended demonstrations in Chicago.

Ms. Montoya's case. Answer: Justice Rehnquist wrote the majority opinion, holding that U.S. Customs agents were well within their constitutional authority to search Montoya. Even though collection of evidence took the better part of two days, Justice Rehnquist remarked wryly that "the rudimentary knowledge of the human body which judges possess in common with the rest of mankind tells us that alimentary canal smuggling cannot be detected in the amount of time in which other illegal activities may be investigated through brief . . . stops."

The cocaine-using mother's case. Answer: A Florida court convicted Ms. Johnson on the charge of delivering drugs to a minor. Prosecutor Deen asked the court to put Ms. Johnson on probation, but her lawyers planned to appeal.

---

that are especially important to those accused of a crime and those convicted of one. Together they provide Americans with more liberty than most other people on earth.

One task that government must perform is to resolve conflicts between rights. Often, First Amendment rights and rights at the bar of justice exist in uneasy tension; a newspaper's right to inform its readership may conflict with a person's right to a fair trial. Today, most of the rights enjoyed under the U.S. Constitution have been extended to the states.

Today's technologies raise key questions about ethics and the Constitution. Although the Constitution does not specifically mention a right to privacy, the Supreme Court found it implied by several guarantees in the Bill of Rights. The most controversial application of privacy rights has been in abortion cases. The Court has begun to chip away at the freedom of choice promised in *Roe* v.

Wade. If the right to life is a political and legal issue, so, equally, is the right to die. Modern technology also intensifies constitutional conflicts over national security and citizens' rights by making it easier for the government to use its power. The Bill of Rights makes it clear that American government is a *constitutional* democracy in which individual rights limit governmental control.

KEY TERMS

civil liberties
Bill of Rights
First Amendment
Fourteenth Amendment
incorporated
establishment clause
free exercise clause
prior restraint
libel

symbolic speech
commercial speech
shield laws
probable cause
unreasonable searches
 and seizures
search warrant
exclusionary rule
Fifth Amendment

self-incrimination
Sixth Amendment
plea bargaining
Eighth Amendment
cruel and unusual punish-
 ment
right to privacy

KEY CASES

Barron v. *Baltimore*
 (1833)
Gitlow v. *New York* (1925)
Engel v. *Vitale* (1962)
*School District of Abing-
 ton Township, Pennsyl-
 vania* v. *Schempp*
 (1963)
Near v. *Minnesota* (1931)
Roth v. *United States*
 (1957)
Miller v. *California*
 (1973)

New York Times v. *Sulli-
 van* (1964)
Texas v. *Johnson* (1989)
*Miami Herald Publishing
 Company* v. *Tornillo*
 (1974)
*Red Lion Broadcasting
 Company* v. *FCC* v.
 United States (1919)
Dennis v. *United States*
 (1951)
Zurcher v. *Stanford Daily*
 (1976)

NAACP v. *Alabama* (1958)
Mapp v. *Ohio* (1961)
Miranda v. *Arizona*
 (1966)
Gideon v. *Wainwright*
 (1963)
Furman v. *Georgia* (1972)
Gregg v. *Georgia* (1976)
McCleskey v. *Kemp* (1987)
Roe v. *Wade* (1973)
Webster v. *Reproductive
 Health Services* (1989)

FOR FURTHER READING

Adler, Renata. *Reckless Disregard*. New York: Knopf, 1986. The story of two monumental conflicts between free press and individual reputations.

Baker, Liva. *Miranda: The Crime, the Law, the Politics*. New York: Atheneum, 1983. An excellent booklength treatment of one of the major criminal cases of our time.

Levy, Leonard W. *The Emergence of a Free Press*. New York: Oxford University Press, 1985. A major work on the framers' intentions regarding freedom of expression.

Levy, Leonard W. *The Establishment Clause: Religion and the First Amendment*. New York: Macmillan, 1986. The author argues that it is unconstitutional for government to provide aid to any religion.

Lewis, Anthony. *Gideon's Trumpet*. New York: Random House, 1964. The story of how Clarence Gideon won his right-to-counsel case and one of the best case studies of a court case ever written.

Petchesky, Rosalind. *Abortion and Woman's Choice*. New York: Longman, 1983. An insightful treatment of issues of reproductive privacy.

5

CIVIL RIGHTS AND PUBLIC POLICY

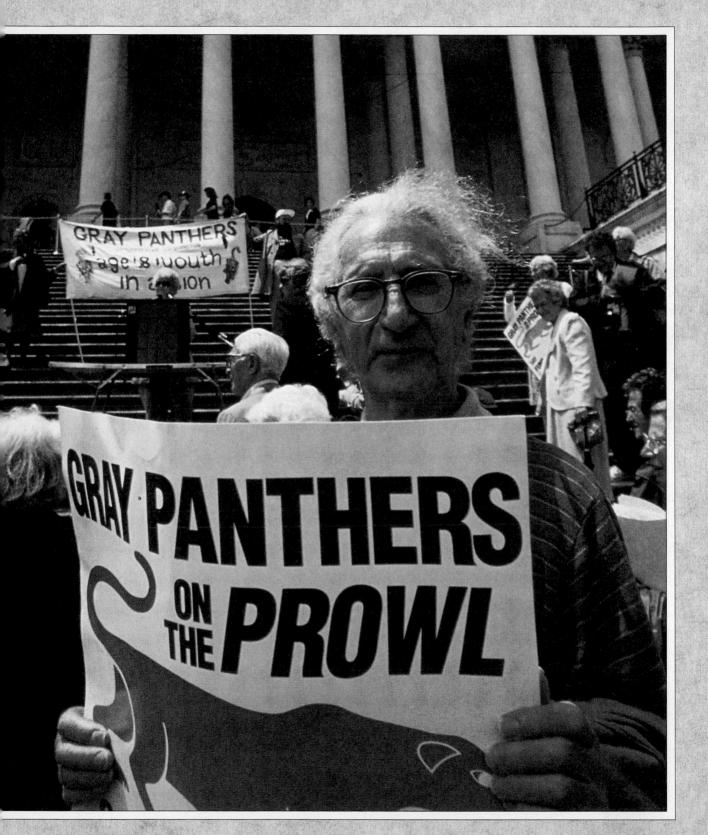

Santa Clara County, California—the home of San Jose and much of Silicon Valley, a key center of the American computer industry—is one of the nation's most rapidly growing counties. Its population has shot from 300,000 in 1950 to nearly 1.5 million today. One of the people who helped expand Santa Clara County was Diane Joyce, who repaired roads for the county. For four years Joyce patched asphalt with a road crew around San Jose and its suburbs. In 1980 she applied for a promotion, hoping to work in the less-strenuous and better-paid position of dispatcher. She knew (or soon found out) that not one of the county transportation agency's 238 skilled positions was held by a woman, even though two years earlier the county had adopted a voluntary affirmative action plan to bring more women and minorities into skilled positions. **Affirmative action,** which this chapter will examine in detail, describes policies designed to give special attention to, or compensatory treatment of, members of some disadvantaged group.

Another applicant for the job sought by Diane was Paul Johnson, a white male who had worked for the agency for thirteen years. Like Diane, Paul did well on the exam given to all applicants; in fact, the two scored among the top six applicants, Diane with a score of seventy-three, and Paul with seventy-five. Knowing that Paul's score was a shade better and his work experience longer, the supervisor decided to hire him. The county's affirmative action officers overruled the supervisor, though, and Diane got the job. Paul decided to get a lawyer.

Paul's lawyer argued that the promotion violated Title VII of the Civil Rights Act of 1964. This law, originally passed to guarantee minorities access to jobs and promotions, makes it unlawful for an employer to deprive any individual of employment opportunities because of their race, color, religion, sex, or national origin. The case worked its way up the judicial ladder to the U.S. Supreme Court.

In 1987 the Court rejected Paul's allegation that he was discriminated against on the basis of sex. Upholding earlier decisions in favor of affirmative action, the Court held that carefully constructed affirmative action plans, designed to remedy specific past discriminations, could be constitutional. In a stinging dissent, Justice Scalia complained that "The Court today completes the process of converting [the law] from a guarantee that race or sex will not be a basis for employment determinations, to a guarantee that it often will."

Equality is an issue not just for philosophers and policymakers but for ordinary people like Diane Joyce and Paul Johnson as well. Two hundred years of constitutional struggle have not ended American debate about equality. There is still disagreement over what equality is; affirmative action is just one of the many issues regarding equality on the policy agenda. Usually, it takes the courts as well as the legislatures to resolve specific questions about equality. This chapter will examine what the Constitution says about equality and how judicial and other public policies have interpreted constitutional rights to equality.

*A*mericans have never fully come to terms with equality. Most Americans favor equality in the abstract—a politician who advocated inequality would not attract many votes—yet the concrete struggle for equal rights under the Constitution has been our nation's most bitter battle.

[handwritten: Definition →] The rallying call for groups demanding more equality has been **civil rights,** which are policies that extend basic rights to groups historically subject to discrimination. The civil rights umbrella has helped protect many groups from discrimination. Throughout our history blacks, women, and other minorities have raised constitutional questions about slavery, segregation, equal pay, and a host of other issues.

The history of the struggle for equality is linked with the history of individuals. Many of them went to jail for their beliefs. Some, like Martin Luther King, Jr., and Malcolm X, even sacrificed their lives. Other heroes were everyday people who felt that constitutional guarantees of liberty and equality had not included them. The struggle for civil rights began long ago with the early abolitionists and feminists, and the fight continues. Rosa Parks, the Alabama dressmaker whose refusal to move to the back of a bus started the boycott that sparked the African-American civil rights movement, now works for a U.S. representative from Michigan. Linda Brown, the Topeka schoolgirl whose case led to the Supreme Court's 1954 school desegregation decision, is now a civic activist. Some hold public office, like Andrew Young, the former United Nations ambassador and mayor of Atlanta. Others enjoy the fruits of their victories, like Diane Joyce, a dispatcher for the transportation crews of Santa Clara County (see "Government in Action"). Each of these people pursued a vision of what they felt equality should mean in American life.

The struggle for equality pits person against person. Those who enjoy privileged positions in American society have been reluctant to give them up. The resulting controversies have been fought out in the Constitution, Congress, and the courts, but the meaning of *equality* remains as elusive as it is divisive.

Today debates about equality center on these key types of inequality in America:

- *Racial discrimination.* Two centuries of discrimination against racial minorities have produced historic Supreme Court and congressional policies that eliminate racial discrimination from the constitutional fabric. Issues such as the appropriate role of affirmative action programs have yet to be resolved, however.
- *Sexual discrimination.* The place of women in society is changing, and women's groups want their rights constitutionally guaranteed.
- *Discrimination based on age, disability, and other factors.* As America is "graying," older Americans, too, are demanding a place under the civil-rights umbrella. Handicapped people are among the newest claimants for civil rights. Also seeking constitutional protections against discrimination are groups such as gays and AIDS victims.

Two Centuries of Struggle

The struggle for equality in America is older than the government itself and continues today. Slaves sought freedom; free blacks sought the right to vote; women sought full participation in society; and poor people now use "equality" as a rallying cry in their efforts to get better treatment. The fight for equality in America affects everyone. Philosophically, the struggle involves defining the term *equality*. Constitutionally, it involves interpreting laws. Politically, it often involves power.

Conceptions of Equality

What does *equality* mean? Jefferson's statement in the Declaration of Independence that "all men are created equal" did not mean that he felt that everybody

The African-American struggle for equality paved the way for civil rights movements by women and other minorities. Here, civil rights leaders Ralph Abernathy and Martin Luther King, Jr., join President Lyndon B. Johnson, who signs the landmark Civil Rights Act of 1964, which outlawed many historic forms of discrimination.

was exactly alike, or that there were no differences among human beings. Jefferson insisted throughout his long life that blacks were genetically inferior to whites. The Declaration went on to speak, however, of "inalienable *rights*" to which all were equally entitled. A belief in equal rights has often led to a belief in *equality of opportunity;* in other words, everyone should have the same chance. What any person makes of that equal chance depends on his or her abilities and efforts.

American society does not emphasize *equal results* or *equal rewards;* few Americans argue that everyone should earn the same salary or have the same amount of property. In some other countries, such as the Scandinavian nations, for example, the government uses its taxing power to distribute resources much more equally than in the United States. These countries thus have much less poverty. On the other hand, the citizens of these more socialist countries often complain that emphasis on the equal distribution of resources stifles initiative and limits opportunity.

Early American Views of Equality

More than two hundred years ago Virginia lawyer Richard Bland proclaimed, "I am speaking of the rights of a people, rights imply equality." Bland's interpretation of the meaning of the American Revolution was not widely shared. Although few colonists were eager to defend slavery, the delegates to the

Constitutional Convention did their best to avoid facing the tension between slavery and the principles of the Declaration of Independence. Women's rights got even less attention than did slavery at the Convention. John Adams, for instance, was uncharacteristically hostile to his wife Abigail's feminist opinions. Abigail's claim that "if particular care and attention is not paid to the ladies, we are determined to foment a rebellion" prompted her husband to reply, "I cannot but laugh."[1]

Statements like Bland's were ahead of their times for America, but they were not unknown elsewhere. They linked the aspirations of people on this side of the Atlantic to those of people on the other side, like the French, who were soon to start their own revolution with cries of "liberty, equality, fraternity." Whereas in the French Revolution the king lost his head in the name of equality, in the American Revolution the king lost his colony in the name of independence.

The Constitution and Inequality

Perhaps the presence of conflicting views of equality in eighteenth-century America explains why the word *equality* does not appear in the original Constitution. In addition, 1787 America was a far different place, with different values, than contemporary America. The privileged delegates to the Constitutional Convention would have been baffled, if not appalled, at discussions of equal rights for twelve-year-old children, deaf students, gay soldiers, or female road dispatchers. The delegates came up with a plan for government, not guarantees of individual rights.

Not even the Bill of Rights mentions equality. It does, however, have implications for equality, since it does not limit the scope of its guarantees to specified groups within the society. It does not say, for example, that only whites have freedom from compulsory self-incrimination or that only men are entitled to freedom of speech. The First Amendment guarantees of freedom of expression, in particular, are important for equality because they allow the disadvantaged to work to achieve it. This kind of political activism, for instance, led to the constitutional amendment that enacted a guarantee of equality.

The first and only place in which the idea of equality appears in the Constitution is in the **Fourteenth Amendment,** one of the three amendments passed after the Civil War. (The Thirteenth abolishes slavery, and the Fifteenth extends the right to vote to blacks—black males over twenty-one, that is.) The amendment forbids the states from denying to anyone "equal protection of the laws." Those five words represent the only reference to the idea of equality in the entire Constitution, yet within them was enough force to begin assuring equal rights for all Americans. The full force of the amendment was not felt for nearly a hundred years, for it was not until the mid-twentieth century that the Fourteenth Amendment approached its full potential as an instrument for unshackling disadvantaged groups. Once dismissed as "the traditional last resort of constitutional arguments," the equal protection clause now has few rivals in generating legal business for the Supreme Court.

[1]Bland is quoted in Sidney Verba and Gary R. Orren, *Equality in America: The View from the Top* (Cambridge, Mass. Harvard University Press, 1985), 25; the Adams' quotes are from Judith A. Baer, *Equality Under the Constitution: Reclaiming the Fourteenth Amendment* (Ithaca, N.Y.: Cornell University Press, 1983), 44–47.

Analysis

Citation

"*Treat people as equals, and the first thing you know, they believe they are.*"

Drawing by Mulligan; © 1982 The New Yorker Magazine, Inc.

Giving the meaning 14th Amend.

But what does **equal protection of the laws** mean? The Fourteenth Amendment does not say that "the states must treat everybody exactly alike" or that "every state must promote equality among all its people." Presumably, it means, as one member of Congress said during the debate on the amendment, "equal protection of life, liberty and property" for all. Thus a state cannot confiscate a black person's property under the law while letting whites keep theirs, or give whites privileges denied to blacks. Some members of Congress interpreted the clause to be a much more lavish protection of rights than this, but, shortly after the amendment was ratified in 1868, the narrow interpretation won out in the courts. In *Strauder* v. *West Virginia* (1880) the Supreme Court invalidated a law barring African Americans from jury service, but the court refused to extend the amendment to more subtle kinds of discrimination.

Over the last one hundred years, however, the equal protection clause has become the vehicle for more expansive constitutional interpretations. The Court has ruled that most classifications that are *reasonable*—that bear a rational relationship to some legitimate governmental purpose—are constitutional. The person who challenges these classifications has the burden of proving that they are *arbitrary*. This is why the states can restrict the right to vote to people over the age of eighteen, for example; age is a reasonable classification, a permissible basis for determining who may vote. A classification that is arbitrary—a law singling out, say, people with red hair or blue eyes for inferior treatment—is invalid.

The Court has also ruled that racial and ethnic classifications are *inherently suspect*. These classifications are presumed to be invalid and are upheld only if there seems to be a compelling reason for them and no other way to accomplish the purpose of the law. The burden of proof is on the state. Classifications based on gender fit somewhere between these two extremes; they are presumed neither to be constitutional nor to be unconstitutional. A law that discriminates on the basis of sex must bear a *substantial* relationship to an *important* legislative purpose. If these three levels of judicial scrutiny (*reasonable, inherently suspect,* or somewhere in between) appear confusing, that appearance is reality—they are.

Today the equal protection clause is interpreted expansively enough to forbid school segregation, prohibit job discrimination, reapportion state legislatures, and permit forced busing and affirmative action. Conditions for women and minorities would be radically different if it were not for those five words.[2] The next three sections show how equal protection litigation has worked to the advantage of minorities, women, and other groups seeking protection under the civil rights umbrella.

RACE, THE CONSTITUTION, AND PUBLIC POLICY

Elaboration

Throughout American history, African Americans have been the most visible minority group in the United States. Sometime in the next generation, however,

[2]For opposing interpretations of the Fourteenth Amendment, see Baer, *Equality Under the Constitution,* and Raoul Berger, *Government by Judiciary: The Transformation of the Fourteenth Amendment* (Cambridge, Mass.: Harvard University Press, 1977).

African Americans will no longer be the largest minority group. Both Hispanic Americans and Asian Americans will comprise a greater proportion of the population. Nevertheless, African Americans have blazed the constitutional trail for securing equal rights for all Americans.

Three eras delineate African Americans' struggle for equality in America: (1) the era of slavery, from the beginnings of colonization until the end of the Civil War, (2) the era of reconstruction and resegregation, from roughly the end of the Civil War until 1954, and (3) the era of civil rights, roughly from 1954 to the present.

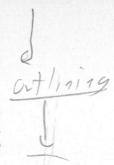

The Era of Slavery

The first African immigrants to America were kidnap victims. Most African Americans lived in slavery for the first 250 years of American settlement. Slaves were the property of their masters. They could be bought and sold and could neither vote nor own property. The southern states, whose plantations required large numbers of unpaid laborers, were the slave states.

During the slavery era, any public policy of the slave states or the federal government had to accommodate the property interests of slave owners. The Supreme Court got into the act, too, along with the legislative and executive branches (see Table 5.1). The boldest decision in defense of slavery was ***Dred Scott* v. *Sandford*** (1857), wherein Chief Justice Taney bluntly announced that a black man, slave or free, had no rights under a white man's government, and that Congress had no power to ban slavery in the western territories that were not yet states. This decision, which invalidated the hard-won Missouri Compromise (which allowed Missouri to become a slave state on the condition that northern territories would remain free of slavery), was an important milestone on the road to the Civil War.

Table 5.1	Toward Racial Equality: Milestones in the Era of Slavery

1600s–1865

Slavery takes hold in the South, comes to characterize almost all black-white relations, and is constitutionally justified.

1619	Slaves from Africa are brought to Jamestown and sold to planters.
1776	The rebels enlist African Americans in the army to fight the British, after the British offered freedom to slaves who would fight on their side against the rebels.
1787	The Constitution provides for slaves to be counted as three-fifths of a person in representation and permits Congress to forbid the importation of new slaves after 1808.
1857	The *Dred Scott* v. *Sandford* decision holds that slaves may not gain freedom by escaping to a free state or territory; it upholds the constitutionality of the slave system.
1865	The Thirteenth Amendment abolishes slavery and involuntary servitude.

The Union victory in the Civil War and the ratification of the **Thirteenth Amendment** ended slavery. The promises implicit in this amendment and the other two Civil War amendments introduced the era of reconstruction and resegregation in which these promises were first honored and then broken.

The Era of Reconstruction and Resegregation

After the Civil War ended, Congress imposed strict conditions on the former confederate states before they could be readmitted to the Union. No one who had served in secessionist state governments or the Confederate Army could hold state office; the legislatures had to ratify the new amendments; and the military would govern the states like "conquered provinces" until they could comply with the tough federal plans for reconstruction. Many African-American men held state and federal offices during the ten years following the war. To ensure his election in 1876, Rutherford Hayes promised to pull the troops out of the South and let the old slave states resume business as usual. The white Southerners lost little time reclaiming power and imposing a code of *Jim Crow laws,* or segregational laws, upon blacks. ("Jim Crow" was the name of a stereotypical Negro in a nineteenth-century minstrel song.) These laws relegated African Americans to separate public facilities, separate school systems, and even separate restrooms. What the law mandated in the South was also common practice in the North. In this era, racial segregation affected every part of life, from the cradle to the grave. African Americans were delivered by African-American physicians or midwives and buried in African-American cemeteries. Segregation was the closest that America came to the apartheid currently practiced in South Africa.

In the era of segregation, housing, schools, and jobs—as well as such lesser things as drinking fountains and rest rooms—were, in one way or another, classified "white" or "colored."

The Supreme Court provided a constitutional justification for segregation in the 1896 case of **Plessy v. Ferguson.** The Louisiana legislature required "equal but separate accommodations for the white and colored races" in railroad transportation. Although Homer Plessy was seven-eighths white, he had been arrested for refusing to leave a railway car reserved for whites. The Court upheld the law, saying that segregation was not unconstitutional as long as the facilities were substantially equal. In subsequent decisions, the Court paid more attention to the "separate" than to the "equal" part of this principle. For example, Southern states were allowed to maintain high schools and professional schools for whites even when there were no such schools for blacks. A measure of segregation in both South and North was the fact that, as late as the 1960s, nearly all the African-American physicians in the United States were graduates of two medical schools, Howard University in Washington, D.C., and Meharry Medical College in Tennessee.

Nevertheless, some progress on the long road to racial equality was made in the first half of the twentieth century. The Supreme Court and the president began to prohibit a few of the most egregious practices of segregation (see Table 5.2), paving the way for a new era of civil rights.

Table 5.2	**Toward Racial Equality: Milestones in the Era of Reconstruction and Resegregation**

1865–1954

Segregation is legally required in the South and sanctioned in the North. Lynchings of African Americans occur in the South. Beginning of civil rights policy.

1870	The Fifteenth Amendment forbids racial discrimination in voting, although many states find ways to prevent or discourage African Americans from voting.
1877	End of Reconstruction. African American gains made in the South (such as antidiscrimination laws) will be reversed as former Confederates return to power. Jim Crow laws flourish, making segregation legal.
1883	In the *Civil Rights Cases* the Supreme Court rules that the Fourteenth Amendment does *not* prohibit discrimination by private businesses and individuals.
1896	The *Plessy* v. *Ferguson* decision permits "separate but equal" public facilities, providing a constitutional justification for segregation.
1910	The National Association for the Advancement of Colored People (NAACP) is founded by blacks and whites.
1915	*Guinn* v. *United States* bans the grandfather clause that had been used to prevent African Americans from voting.
1941	Executive order forbids racial discrimination in defense industries.
1944	The *Smith* v. *Allwright* decision bans all-white primaries.
1948	President Truman orders the armed forces desegregated.
1950	*Sweatt* v. *Painter* finds the "separate but equal" formula generally unacceptable in professional schools.

The Era of Civil Rights

Legal segregation came to an end in 1954 when, in ***Brown v. Board of Education,*** the Supreme Court set aside its earlier precedent in *Plessy* v. *Ferguson.* In *Brown* v. *Board of Education,* the Court held that school segregation in Topeka, Kansas, (and several other cities) was inherently unconstitutional because it violated the Fourteenth Amendment's guarantee of equal protection (see "In Focus: *Brown* v. *Board of Education*").

In Focus

Brown v. Board of Education

After searching carefully for the perfect case to challenge legal school segregation, the National Association for the Advancement of Colored People (NAACP) selected the case of Linda Brown. An African-American student in Topeka, Kansas, Brown was required by Kansas law to attend a segregated school. In Topeka the visible signs of education—teacher quality, facilities, and so on—were substantially equal between black schools and white ones. Thus the NAACP chose the case in order to test the *Plessy* v. *Ferguson* doctrine of "separate but equal." The Court would be forced to rule directly on whether school segregation was *inherently* unequal and thereby violated the Fourteenth Amendment's requirement that states guarantee "equal protection of the laws." Decisions in several recent cases (*Sweatt* and *McLaurin,* for example) had hinted that the Supreme Court was ready to overturn the *Plessy* precedent. The NAACP's general counsel, Thurgood Marshall, argued Linda Brown's case before the Supreme Court.

Chief Justice Earl Warren had just been appointed by President Eisenhower. So important was *Brown* that the Court had already heard one round of arguments before Warren joined the Court. The justices, after hearing the oral arguments, met in the Supreme Court's Conference Room. As is traditional, the chief justice summarized the case to his colleagues briefly and then turned to the most senior associate justice to present his views. Each, from the most senior to the newest member of the Court, spoke. Believing that a unanimous decision would have the most impact, the justices agreed that Warren himself should write the opinion.

The Brown *v.* Board *lawyers (left to right): George Hayes, Thurgood Marshall (now a Supreme Court justice), and James Nabritt, Jr.*

Shortly before the decision was to be announced, President Eisenhower invited the Warrens to dinner at the White House. Pointedly seating the chief justice near John W. Davis, the lawyer arguing the southern states' case in *Brown,* the president went out of his way to tell Warren what an able man Davis was. Taking Warren by the arm on the way to after-dinner coffee and drinks, Eisenhower put in his word against school integration. After Warren announced the *Brown* decision, he was never again invited to the White House by the man who appointed him. Although Eisenhower objected strongly to the decision, he later sent federal troops to Central High School in Little Rock, Arkansas, in 1958 to enforce its desegregation.

On September 25, 1957, troops of the 101st Airborne Division escorted nine black children into Central High School in Little Rock, Arkansas. A court had ordered the school's desegregation in response to Brown v. Board of Education, *but Arkansas Governor Orville Faubus fought it. President Eisenhower used the National Guard to provide continuing protection for the students.*

Throughout the South, the reaction to *Brown* was swift and negative—a few counties threatened to close their public schools, and enrollment in private schools by whites soared. Congress, in the Civil Rights Act of 1964, responded by cutting off federal aid to schools that remained segregated. Desegregation began and proceeded slowly in the South (see Table 5.3). Some federal judges ordered the busing of students to achieve racially balanced schools, a practice upheld (but not required) by the Supreme Court in **Swann v. Charlotte-Mecklenberg County Schools** (1971).

Not all racial segregation is what is called *de jure* ("by law") segregation. *De facto* ("in reality") segregation results, for example, when children are assigned to schools near their homes, and those homes are in neighborhoods that are racially segregated. Sometimes the distinction between *de jure* and *de facto* segregation has been blurred by past official practices. As minority groups and federal lawyers demonstrated that northern schools, too, had purposely drawn district lines to promote segregation, school busing came to the North as well. Denver, Boston, and other cities instituted busing for racial balance just as southern cities did.

The **civil rights movement,** which organized both blacks and whites to end the policies and practices of segregation, began in 1955 when Rosa Parks, a black woman, refused to give up her seat in the front of a Montgomery, Alabama, bus (only whites were allowed to sit in the front seats). For her refusal, she was

Table 5.3

Percentage of Black Elementary and Secondary Students Attending School with Any Whites, in Eleven Southern States[a]

Despite the Supreme Court's decision in *Brown* v. *Board of Education* in 1954, school integration proceeded at a snail's pace in the South for a decade. Most southern black children entering the first grade in 1955 never attended school with white children. Things picked up considerably in the late 1960s, however, when the Supreme Court insisted that obstruction of implementation of its decision in *Brown* must come to an end.

SCHOOL YEAR	PERCENTAGE	SCHOOL YEAR	PERCENTAGE
1954–55	.001	1964–65	2.25
1956–57	.14	1966–67	15.9
1958–59	.13	1968–69	32.0
1960–61	.16	1970–71	85.6
1962–63	.45	1972–73	91.3

[a] Virginia, North Carolina, South Carolina, Georgia, Alabama, Mississippi, Louisiana, Texas, Arkansas, Tennessee, and Florida.
Source: Lawrence Baum, *The Supreme Court*, 3rd ed. (Washington, D.C.: Congressional Quarterly, 1989), 207.

forced off the bus. This incident prompted a bus boycott led by a local minister, Martin Luther King, Jr., who became the best-known civil rights activist until his assassination in 1968.

Sit-ins, marches, and civil disobedience were key strategies of the civil rights movement, which sought to establish equal opportunities in the political and economic sectors and to end policies that put up barriers against people because of race. The movement's trail was long and sometimes bloody. Its nonviolent marchers were set upon by police dogs in Birmingham, Alabama. Other activists were murdered in Meridian, Mississippi, and Selma, Alabama. Fortunately, the goals of the civil rights movement appealed to the national conscience, and by the 1970s overwhelming majorities of white Americans supported racial integration.[3]

It was the courts, as much as the national conscience, that put civil rights goals on the nation's policy agenda. The 1954 *Brown* v. *Board of Education* case was only the beginning of a string of Supreme Court decisions holding various forms of discrimination unconstitutional. *Brown* and these other cases gave a momentum to the civil rights movement that was to grow in the years that followed (see Table 5.4).

As a result of national conscience, the courts, the civil rights movement, and the increased importance of African-American voters, the 1950s and 1960s saw a marked increase in public policies to foster racial equality. Often passed only after filibusters in the U.S. Senate and southern representatives' attempts

---

[3]D. Garth Taylor, Paul B. Sheatsley, and Andrew M. Greeley, "Attitudes toward Racial Integration," *Scientific American* 238 (June 1978): 42–49.

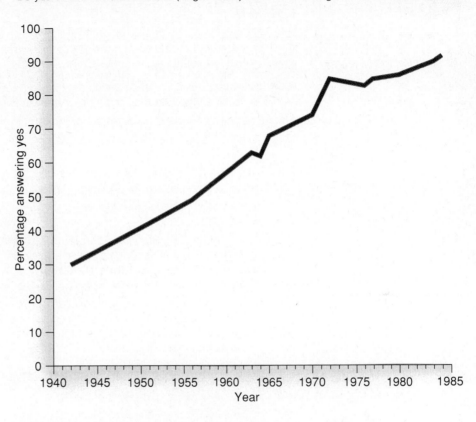

Do you think white students and (Negro/black) students should go to the same schools?

Source: The question as worded is taken directly from polls reprinted in Richard G. Niemi, John Mueller, and John W. Smith, *Trends in Public Opinion* (Westport, Conn.: Greenwood Press, 1989), 180.

at delay in the House Rules Committee, congressional innovations included policies to promote voting rights, access to public accommodations, open housing, and nondiscrimination in many other areas of social and economic life. The **Civil Rights Act of 1964** made racial discrimination illegal in hotels, motels, restaurants, and other places of public accommodation. It also forbade many forms of job discrimination. The Voting Rights Act of 1965 was the most extensive federal effort to crack century-old barriers to African-American voting in the South. The Open Housing Act of 1968 took steps to forbid discrimination in the sale or rental of housing.

So many congressional and judicial policies were instituted after 1954 that virtually every type of segregation was attacked by a legislative or judicial policy. By the 1980s, few, if any, forms of discrimination were left to legislate against. One reason for all this legislation was the fact that by the mid-1960s federal laws effectively protected the right to vote (in fact as well as on paper); members of minority groups thus had some power to hold their legislators accountable.

1954–1989

Integration becomes a widely accepted goal; the civil rights movement grows, followed by urban racial disorders in the 1960s; African-American voting increases; attention shifts to equal results and affirmative action.

1954   *Brown* v. *Board of Education* holds that segregated schools are inherently unequal and violate the Fourteenth Amendment's equal protection clause.

1955   Martin Luther King, Jr., leads a bus boycott in Montgomery, Alabama.

1957   Federal troops enforce desegregation of a Little Rock, Arkansas, high school.

1963   Civil rights demonstrators, numbering 250,000, march on Washington, D.C.

1964   Title II of the Civil Rights Act forbids discrimination in public accommodations. Title VI provides that federal grants and contracts may be withheld from violators.

Title VII of the Civil Rights Act forbids discrimination by employers and empowers the Justice Department to sue violators. The Twenth-fourth Amendment ends the poll tax in federal elections.

1965   The Voting Rights Act sends federal registrars to southern states and counties to protect African Americans' right to vote and gives registrars the power to impound ballots in order to enforce the act. Executive order requires companies with federal contracts to take affirmative action to ensure equal opportunity. Riots occur in Watts, California, and other cities and reappear every summer in various cities for the next five years.

1966   *Harper* v. *Virginia* holds that the Fourteenth Amendment forbids making a tax a condition of voting in any election.

1967   Cleveland becomes the first major city to elect a black mayor (Carl Stokes).

1968   The *Jones* v. *Mayer* decision and the Civil Rights Act of 1968 make all racial discrimination in the sale or rental of housing illegal.

1971   The *Swann* v. *Charlotte-Mecklenberg County Schools* decision approves busing as a means of combating state-enforced segregation.

1978   *California Board of Regents* v. *Bakke* forbids rigid racial quotas for medical school admissions but does not forbid considering race as a factor when deciding admissions.

1979   *Weber* v. *Kaiser Aluminum* again permits an affirmative action program to favor blacks if the program is designed to remedy past discrimination. *Dayton Board of Education* v. *Brinkman* upholds school busing to remedy northern school segregation.

1980   Jesse Jackson becomes the first serious African-American candidate for president.

1984   *Grove City College* v. *Bell* forbids the federal government from taking away all federal funds from a college that refuses to file forms saying that it does not discriminate. (Only a specific program risked its federal funds.) In 1988 Congress rewrites the Civil Rights Act to "overturn" the implications of *Grove City College.*

1989   The Supreme Court's new conservative majority issues several decisions that narrow the scope of civil rights laws.

Getting and Using the Right to Vote

When the Constitution was written, no one thought about extending the right to vote to blacks (most of whom were slaves) or to women. In the early Republic, **suffrage,** the legal right to vote, was limited to a handful of the population, mostly property-holding white males. Only after the Civil War was the right to vote extended, slowly and painfully, to African Americans.

The **Fifteenth Amendment,** adopted in 1870, guaranteed blacks the right to vote—at least in principle. It said, "The right of citizens to vote shall not be abridged by the United States or by any state on account of race, color, or previous condition of servitude." The gap between these constitutional words and their implementation, however, remained wide for a full century. States seemed to outdo one another in developing ingenious methods of circumventing the Fifteenth Amendment.

Oklahoma and other southern states used a *grandfather clause* to deny African Americans the right to vote. In this, the state required a literacy test of all prospective voters, but because such a test could disqualify illiterate whites as well as illiterate blacks, the state exempted people whose grandfathers were eligible to vote in 1860—excluding, of course, the grandchildren of slaves. The law was blatantly unfair; it was also unconstitutional, said the Supreme Court in the 1913 decision *Guinn v. Oklahoma.* To exclude African Americans from voting registers, most southern states also relied on **poll taxes,** which were small taxes levied on the right to vote that often fell due at a time of year when poor sharecroppers had the least cash on hand. To render African-American votes ineffective, most southern states also used the **white primary,** a device that permitted political parties in the heavily Democratic south to exclude blacks from primary elections, thus depriving them of a voice in the real contests and letting them vote when it mattered least. The Supreme Court declared white primaries unconstitutional in 1941.

The civil rights movement put suffrage high on its political agenda; one by one, the barriers to African-American voting fell during the 1960s. Poll taxes were declared void in the **Twenty-fourth Amendment,** passed in 1964. The **Voting Rights Act of 1965,** which sent federal election registrars to states and counties that had long histories of discrimination, resulted in hundreds of thousands of African Americans being registered in southern states and counties. The effects were swift and certain. When the act was passed in 1965 only seventy African Americans held public office in the eleven southern states; by the early 1980s more than twenty-five hundred African Americans held elected offices in those states. The greatest gains took place in states covered by the Voting Rights Act.[4] One direct result of this law was Jesse Jackson's impressive showing in the southern presidential primaries in 1988.

African Americans are not the only racial group that has suffered legally imposed disadvantages. Even before the civil rights struggle, native Americans, Asians, and Hispanics learned how powerless they could become in a society dominated by whites. The civil rights laws that African-American groups like the NAACP pushed for have benefited members of these groups as well.

The Voting Rights Act of 1965 produced a major increase in the number of African Americans registered to vote in southern states. The ability to vote gave African Americans more political clout—in the twenty years following the act more than twenty-five hundred were elected to state and local offices in that region.

[4]On the implementation of the Voting Rights Act, see Richard Scher and James Button, "Voting Rights Act: Implementation and Impact," in *Implementation of Civil Rights Policy,* ed. Charles Bullock III and Charles Lamb (Monterey, Calif.: Brooks/Cole, 1984), and Abigail M. Thernstrom, *Whose Votes Count?* (Cambridge, Mass.: Harvard University Press, 1987).

Other Minority Groups

Soon African Americans will no longer be the largest minority group in the United States. As the next chapter will discuss, America is heading toward a *minority majority,* a time when minority groups will outnumber Caucasians of European descent. Hispanic Americans—chiefly from Mexico, Puerto Rico, and Cuba but also from El Salvador, Honduras, and other countries in Central America—will soon displace African Americans as the largest minority group. Asian Americans are the fastest growing minority group; their representation in the American population rose from .5 percent to 3 percent in the three decades from 1960 to 1990.

The earliest inhabitants of the continent, the American Indians, are, of course, the oldest minority group. The history of poverty, discrimination, and exploitation experienced by native Americans is a long one. Not until 1924 were Indians made citizens of the United States, a status blacks had achieved a half-century before. Not until 1946 did Congress establish the Indian Claims Act to settle financial disputes arising from lands taken from the Indians.[5] Today native Americans benefit from the public policy gains won by African Americans, guaranteeing access to the polls, to housing, and to jobs; but huddled on reservations, American Indians know, perhaps better than any other group, the significance of the gap between public policy and private realization.

Asian Americans suffered during World War II when the U.S. government, beset by fears of a Japanese invasion of the Pacific Coast, rounded up more than one hundred thousand Americans of Japanese descent and herded them into encampments. These internment camps were, critics claimed, America's concentration camps. The Supreme Court, however, in ***Korematsu*** v. ***United States*** (1944), upheld the internment as constitutional. Congress has now provided benefits to the internees, although they have yet to be distributed.

[5]See Dee Brown, *Bury My Heart at Wounded Knee: An Indian History of the American West* (New York: Holt, Rinehart and Winston, 1970).

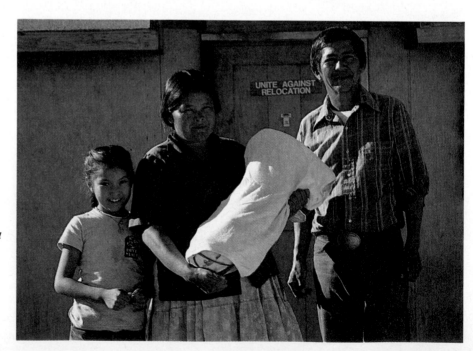

Larry Simonson, here with his family, is a leader of the Big Mountain People, a tribal group resisting displacement by the federal government. Despite being perhaps the weakest minority group politically—as well as the poorest economically—native Americans have recently become more aggressive in their struggle for civil rights.

Like native Americans and Asian Americans, Hispanic Americans benefit from the nondiscrimination policies originally passed to protect African Americans. Provisions of the Voting Rights Act of 1965 covered San Antonio, Texas, and thereby permitted Hispanic voters to lend weight to the election of Mayor Henry Cisneros. (Chapter 6 will discuss in detail these and other groups in the minority majority.)

Social movements tend to beget new social movements; this is how the African-American civil rights movement of the 1960s affected other minorities. American Indians and Hispanics began organizing and became newly active. Native American activists like Dennis Means of the American Indian Movement (AIM), Vine Deloria, and Dee Brown drew attention to the plight of the Indian tribes; twenty years later, this movement continues to struggle against the poverty, low education, and poor health of many native Americans. The United Farm Workers, led by Cesar Chavez, publicized the plight of migrant workers, a large proportion of whom are Hispanic. As for women, their political activity has been so energetic and so far-reaching that a separate section is needed to examine their struggle for equality.

WOMEN, THE CONSTITUTION, AND PUBLIC POLICY

Abigail Adams may have been practically alone in her feminist views in the 1770s, but the next century brought significant feminist activity. The first women's rights activists were products of the abolitionist movement, where they often encountered sexist opposition. Two of these women, Lucretia Mott and Elizabeth Cady Stanton, organized a meeting at Seneca Falls, in upstate New York. They had a lot to discuss. Not only were women denied the vote, but they were also subjected to a patriarchal family law and to the denial of education and career opportunities. The legal doctrine known as *coverture* deprived married women of any identity separate from that of their husbands; wives could not sign contracts or dispose of property. Divorce law was heavily biased in favor of husbands. Even abused women found it almost impossible to end their marriages, and men had the advantage in securing custody of the children.

The Battle for the Vote

On July 19, 1848, one hundred men and women signed the Seneca Falls Declaration of Sentiments and Resolutions. Patterned after the Declaration of Independence, it proclaimed: "The history of mankind is a history of repeated injuries and usurpations on the part of man toward woman, having in direct object the establishment of an absolute tyranny over her." Thus began the movement that would culminate in the ratification of the **Nineteenth Amendment** seventy-two years later, giving women the vote. Charlotte Woodward, nineteen years old in 1848, was the only signer of the Seneca Falls Declaration who lived to vote for president in 1920.

The battle for women's suffrage was fought mostly in the late nineteenth and early twentieth century. Leaders like Stanton and Susan B. Anthony were prominent in the cause, which emphasized the vote but also addressed women's other grievances. The suffragists had considerable success in the states, especially in the Pacific Northwest. Several states allowed women to vote before the constitutional amendment passed. The feminists lobbied, marched, protested, and even engaged in civil disobedience (though not to the extent that their English counterparts did).[6]

The "Doldrums": 1920–1960

Winning the right to vote did not automatically win equal status for women. In fact, the feminist movement seemed to lose rather than gain momentum after winning the vote. Perhaps everyone relaxed a bit after the big victory, but there was another reason for the decline in activism. The vote was about the only goal on which all feminists agreed. There was considerable division within the movement on other priorities.

Many suffragists accepted the traditional model of the family. Fathers were breadwinners, while mothers were bread bakers. Although most suffragists thought that women should have the opportunity to pursue any occupations they chose, many also felt that women's primary obligations centered around the roles of wife and mother. Many suffragists had defended the vote as basically an extension of the maternal role into public life, arguing that a new era of public morality would emerge when women could vote. These *social feminists* were in tune with prevailing attitudes. Public policy toward women continued to be dominated, not by the principle of equality, but by protectionism. Laws protected working women from the burdens of overtime work, long hours on the job, and heavy lifting. (The fact that these laws also protected male workers from female competition received little attention.) State laws tended to reflect—and reinforce—the traditional family roles. They concentrated on limiting women's work opportunities outside the home so they could concentrate on their duties within it. In most states, husbands were legally required to support their families, even after a divorce, and to pay child support (though divorced fathers did not always pay). When a marriage ended, mothers almost always got custody of the children (although husbands had the legal advantage in custody battles). Public policy was designed to preserve traditional motherhood and hence, supporters claimed, to protect the family and the country's moral fabric.[7]

Only a minority of feminists challenged these assumptions. Alice Paul, the author of the **Equal Rights Amendment** (ERA), was one activist who claimed that the real result of protectionist law was to perpetuate sexual inequality. Simply worded, the ERA reads, "Equality of rights under the law shall not be denied or abridged by the United States or by any state on account of sex." In the 1920s most people saw the ERA as a threat to the family. It gained little support. In fact, women were not even as likely to vote as men were.

The Second Feminist Wave

The civil rights movement of the 1950s and 1960s attracted many women activists, some of whom also joined student and antiwar movements. These women often met with the same prejudices as had women abolitionists. Betty Friedan's book

---

[6]See Eleanor Flexner, *Century of Struggle* (New York: Atheneum, 1971).

[7]See J. Stanley Lemons, *The Woman Citizen: Social Feminism in the 1920s* (Urbana: University of Illinois Press, 1973).

The Feminine Mystique, published in 1963, encouraged many women to question traditional assumptions and to assert their own rights. Groups like the National Organization for Women (NOW) and the National Women's Political Caucus were organized in the 1960s and 1970s. The Civil Rights Act of 1964 banned sex discrimination in employment. This law has been amended several times. For example, in 1972 Congress gave the Equal Employment Opportunity Commission (EEOC) the power to sue employers suspected of illegal discrimination. The Pregnancy Discrimination Act of 1978 made it illegal for employers to exclude pregnancy and childbirth from their sick-leave and health-benefits plans.

Title IX of the Education Act of 1972 forbade sex discrimination in federally subsidized education programs, including athletics. The ERA was revived. Even though it was opposed by women who defended the status quo, Congress passed it in 1972 and, six years later, extended the deadline for ratification until 1982. Nevertheless, the ERA was three states short of ratification when time ran out. Paradoxically, the defeat of the ERA had just the opposite effect that the 1920 suffrage victory had had on feminism. Far from weakening the movement, losing the ERA battle has stimulated vigorous feminist activity. Proponents have vowed to keep reintroducing the amendment in Congress (without success so far) and continue to press hard for state and federal action on women's rights. Litigation within the model developed by the African-American movement has so far achieved mixed results.

Table 5.5 includes the important court decisions on sexual equality. Before the advent of the contemporary feminist movement, the Supreme Court upheld virtually any instance of sex-based discrimination. The state and federal governments were free to discriminate against women—and, indeed, men—as they chose. In the 1970s the Court began to take a closer look at sex discrimination. In **Reed v. Reed** (1971) the Court ruled that any "arbitrary" sex-based classi-

Table 5.5 Toward Sexual Equality: Public Policy Milestones

1969–1989

1969	Executive order declares that equal opportunities for women at every level of federal service is to be national policy, and establishes a program for implementing the policy.
1971	In *Reed* v. *Reed* the Supreme Court invalidates a state law preferring men to women in court selection of an estate's administrator.
1972	Provisions of Title VII of the Civil Rights Act of 1964 are extended to cover the faculty and professional staffs of colleges and universities. The Education Act forbids sexual discrimination in public schools (with some exceptions for historically single-sex schools). The ERA is proposed by Congress and sent to the states for ratification.
1974	A woman—Ella Grasso of Connecticut—is elected governor for the first time without succeeding her husband to the office.
1976	Courts strike down an Oklahoma law setting different legal drinking ages for men and women.
1978	The deadline for ratification of the ERA is extended. Congress passes the Pregnancy Discrimination Act.
1981	The Supreme Court rules that males-only military draft registration is constitutional. Sandra Day O'Connor becomes the first woman Supreme Court Justice.
1982	The ERA ratification deadline passes without the amendment being ratified.
1984	Geraldine Ferraro is nominated as the first woman vice-presidential candidate of a major party.
1988	The Supreme Court unanimously upholds a 1984 New York City law aimed primarily at requiring the admission of women to large, private clubs that play an important role in professional life.
1989	The Supreme Court decisions discussed on page 188 apply to sex discrimination as well as to race discrimination and, therefore, make it more difficult for women to win lawsuits.

fication violated the equal protection clause of the Fourteenth Amendment. Five years later **Craig v. Boren** established a "medium scrutiny" standard: sex discrimination would be presumed to be neither valid nor invalid. The Court has used this standard to strike down laws giving husbands exclusive control over family property, laws that allow alimony payments to women only, and laws that closed a state's nursing school to men (interestingly, most of the litigants in cases raising constitutional questions about sexual discrimination have been men). A statutory rape law applying only to men and the male-only draft have been upheld, however.

Several 1989 Supreme Court rulings that make discrimination more difficult for African Americans to prove (see page 188) also apply to women. More cases are likely in the future, as Congress continues to consider new laws. Two of the most controversial issues that legislators are likely to face are wage discrimination and the role of women in the military.

Wage Discrimination and Comparable Worth

One reason that feminist activism persists has nothing to do with ideology or other social movements. The family pattern that traditionalists sought to preserve—father at work, mother at home—is becoming obsolete. In 1988 the female civilian labor force amounted to 54 million (as compared to 66.5 million males). About half of these women were married. More than half of American mothers with children below school age were in the labor force.[8] As conditions have changed, public opinion and public policy demands have changed, too. Protectionism is not dead. Women still have more duties inside the home than men do, and debates over policies like the "mommy track" (reduced work responsibilities for women workers with children) or parental leaves for women

[8]U.S. Department of Commerce, *Statistical Abstract of the United States, 1989* (Washington, D.C.: U.S. Government Printing Office, 1989), 379, 385, 386.

The People Speak   Working Women

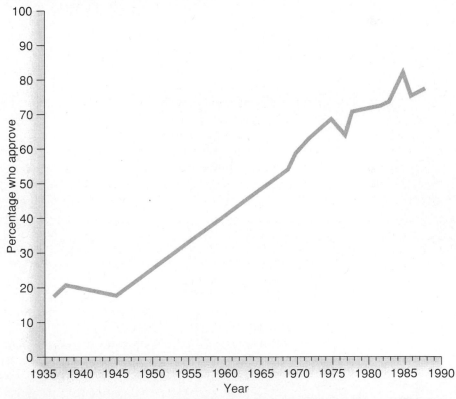

Do you approve or disapprove of a married woman earning money in business and industry if she has a husband capable of supporting her?

Attitudes toward women in the workplace have changed drastically over the past half century. Today most people believe that a woman's place is as much at the office as in the home.

Source: Richard G. Niemi, John Mueller, and John W. Smith, *Trends in Public Opinion* (Westport, Conn.: Greenwood Press, 1989), 225.

"ASHLEY IS RIGHT HENRY. SHE SHOULD BE MAKING AS MUCH AS YOU ARE ... SO I'M CUTTING YOUR SALARY IN HALF!"

only reflect this social phenomenon. Demands for equality, however, keep nudging protectionism into the background.

Traditional women's jobs often pay much less than men's jobs demanding comparable skill; a female secretary often earns far less than a male accounts clerk with the same qualifications. In 1987 the median annual earnings for full-time women workers was $17,504, compared to $26,722 for men.[9]

In 1983 the Washington Supreme Court ruled that its state government had for years discriminated against women by denying them equal pay for jobs of **"comparable worth."** The U.S. Supreme Court has remained silent so far on the merits of this issue. The executive branch under Ronald Reagan consistently opposed the idea of comparable worth. The late Clarence Pendleton, Reagan's appointee as head of the U.S. Civil Rights Commission, argued that lawsuits based on comparable worth would interfere with the free market for wages by reducing incentives for women to seek higher paying, traditionally male jobs. Pendleton called comparable worth "the craziest idea since Looney Tunes." Ridicule has not made the dispute go away.

Women in the Military

Military service is another controversial aspect of sexual equality. Women have served in every branch of the Armed Services since World War II. Originally, they served in separate units like the WACS (Women's Army Corps), WAVES (Women Accepted for Volunteer Emergency Service in the Navy), or the services' separate Nurse Corps. The military had a 2 percent quota for women (which was never filled) until the 1970s. Now women are part of the regular service. They comprise 11 percent of the armed forces, and compete directly with men

[9]*Ibid.*, 448.

for promotion. Congress opened all of the service academies to women in 1975. Women have done well, one woman cadet graduated first in her class at the U.S. Naval Academy at Annapolis, while the First Captain of the 1989–90 Corps of Cadets at West Point was a woman.

Two important differences between the treatment of men and women persist in military service. Only men must register for the draft when they turn eighteen. There is no military conscription at present (the United States has had a volunteer force since 1973), but President Jimmy Carter asked Congress to require both men and women to register after the Soviets invaded Afghanistan in 1979. Congress reinstated registration for men only, a move that was not universally popular. Federal courts ordered registration suspended while several young men brought a suit. They lost, however; the Supreme Court ruled that male-only registration bore a substantial relationship to Congress's goal of assuring combat readiness.

Statutes and regulations also prohibit women from serving in combat—the other remaining instance of sex discrimination in the military. A breach exists between policy and practice, however. Several women did participate in combat during the Amerian invasion of Panama in December 1989. By all reports, they did well. Their activities have reopened the debate over whether women should serve in combat. Many experts insist that because women, on the average, have less upper-body strength than men, they are thus inferior warriers. Critics of this view point out that some women surpass some men in upper-body strength. This debate is not only a controversy about ability; it also touches on the question of whether combat is a burden or a privilege. Clearly some women—and some who would deny them combat duty—take the latter view.

The push for sexual equality is a worldwide phenomenon (see "America in Perspective: Women's Rights under Changing Socialist Systems"). Many women are making claims for protections of their civil rights for the first time.

New Groups under the Civil Rights Umbrella

New activist groups have realized that racial minorities and women are not the only Americans who can claim civil rights; policies enacted to protect one or two groups can be applied to others. Four recent entrants into the interest-group arena are aging Americans, young Americans, the disabled, and homosexuals. All of these groups claim equal rights, as racial minorities and women have, but they represent different challenges to mainstream America.

Civil Rights and the Graying of America

America is aging rapidly. People in their eighties comprise the fastest growing age group in this country. Aging Americans, the middle-aged as well as the elderly, have claimed space under the civil rights umbrella. When the Social Security program began in the 1930s, sixty-five was the retirement age; although this age was apparently chosen arbitrarily, it soon became the mandatory retirement age for many workers. Employers routinely refused to hire people over a certain age. Graduate and professional schools often rejected applicants in their thirties on the grounds that their professions would get fewer years,

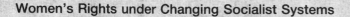

Women's Rights under Changing Socialist Systems

Although few countries have the racial and ethnic diversity of the United States, all countries have two sexes. Few, if any, societies have yet achieved full sexual equality. Since discrimination against women is a global phenomenon, feminist movements exist throughout the world. Feminists in different cultures do not all mean the same thing by *sexual equality*, but whatever the prevailing ideology, the barriers to equality that women face in industrial societies turn out to be strikingly similar.

Most American feminists accept the priorities of the capitalist system. Their idea of equal rights has emphasized equal employment and educational opportunity, full participation in public life, and freedom from sex-based discrimination. But feminists in socialist countries, where the state, rather than the private sector, controls the means of production, share the official goals of their governments; they stress economic equality and freedom from exploitation. Policies like equal pay (comparable worth) and leaves for rearing children, which many Americans perceive as incompatible with capitalist principles, are commonplace in Europe. Communist ideology maintains that sexual equality is possible only under socialism, because capitalist systems force women into unpaid domestic labor. Now that the communist governments of East-

ern Europe are dissolving, feminists confront the possibility of a more capitalist system.

Of all Eastern European countries, the German Democratic Republic (East Germany) has come the closest to full sexual equality. The nation's 1949 constitution mandates equal rights, equal pay, equal educational opportunities, and equality within marriage. The government is also committed to enabling women to fulfill their roles as both homemakers and paid workers, often at the expense of their equality. The government, for instance, provides such benefits as leaves for raising children and reduced work weeks for mothers—but not for fathers. As a result, not only has homemaking remained primarily women's responsibility, but women workers are less valuable to employers and are disproportionately represented in the lower-paying jobs. Thus East German women suffer many of the same disadvantages as women do in the capitalist United States. The socialist commitment to governmental control of the economy has not produced equality between the sexes. The likelihood of German reunification brings the danger that East German women may lose the benefits they now have, while gaining no improvements in their situation. Neither capitalism nor socialism insures sexual equality.

Source: Lynn Kamenitsa, "Feminism and the Socialist State: The Emerging East German Feminist Movement" (Paper delivered at the Annual Meeting of the Midwest Political Science Association, Chicago, 1990).

and thus less return, out of them. This policy had a severe impact on housewives and veterans who wanted to return to school.

Victims of age discrimination had a powerful champion on Capitol Hill: Representative Claude Pepper (D-Fla.), who died in 1989 at the age of eighty-eight. He sponsored and worked to pass most of the age discrimination laws that Congress has enacted. As early as 1967 Congress banned some kinds of age discrimination. In 1975 civil rights law denied federal funds to any institution discriminating against people over forty. The Age Discrimination in Employment Act was amended in 1978 to raise the general compulsory retirement age to seventy. Now compulsory retirement is being phased out altogether.

Although many workers might prefer to retire while they are still healthy and active enough to enjoy leisure, not everyone wants or can afford to do so. Social Security is not (and was never meant to be) an adequate income, and not all workers have good pension plans. Social Security itself may be in jeopardy; as the post–World War II "baby boomers" age, fewer workers will be called upon to support more retirees. (Chapter 14 will discuss this issue in more detail.) No one knows what the fate of the *gray liberation movement* will be as its members approach the status of a minority majority.

Are the Young a Disadvantaged Group, Too?

Older Americans are not the only victims of age discrimination. The young, too, have suffered from inferior treatment under the law. The *Hazelwood* case discussed in Chapter 4 provides one example of such treatment. Will there soon be an autonomous children's rights movement? There are obvious difficulties in organizing one, but that does not mean that young people are silent in asserting their rights. Walter Polovchak of Chicago is one example. In 1980, when Walter was twelve, his family emigrated from the Ukraine. His parents, quickly disillusioned, decided to return, but Walter wanted to stay in Chicago, so he ran away to live with relatives in the area. The law was on his parents' side; so were groups like the American Civil Liberties Union. Court after court ordered the boy returned to his parents. The slow movement of his case through the legal system was Walter's best ally. When he reached his eighteenth birthday, he was still in Chicago. He remains there today, an American citizen.[10]

Civil Rights and the Disabled

Disabled Americans, who comprise about 17 percent of the population, have suffered from both direct and indirect discrimination. They have often been denied rehabilitation services (a kind of affirmative action), education, and jobs. Many disabled people have been kept poor and isolated without overt discrimination. Throughout most of American history, public and private buildings have been hostile to the blind, deaf, and mobility-impaired. Stairs, buses, telephones,

[10] Walter Polovchak with Kevin Klose, *Freedom's Child* (New York: Random House, 1988).

Handicapped Americans are among the successors to the 1960s civil rights activists. Students at Gallaudet University, the nation's only university exclusively for the deaf, made national news when they fought against the appointment of a university president who was not deaf. The students won their fight: the president-elect stepped down, and a president who shared their handicap took office in October 1988.

and other necessities of modern life have been designed in ways that keep the disabled out of offices, stores, and restaurants. As one slogan said: "Once, blacks had to ride at the back of the bus. We can't even get on the bus."

The first rehabilitation laws were passed in the late 1920s, mostly to help veterans of World War I. Accessibility laws had to wait another fifty years. The Rehabilitation Act of 1973 (twice vetoed by Richard Nixon as "too costly") added handicapped people to the list of Americans protected from discrimination. Since the law defines an inaccessible environment as a form of discrimination, wheelchair ramps, grab bars on toilets, and Braille signs have become common features of the American landscape. The Education of All Handicapped Children Act of 1975 entitled all children to a free public education appropriate to their needs. The Americans with Disabilities Act of 1990 strengthened these protections, requiring employers and public facilities to make "reasonable accommodations" and prohibiting employment discrimination against the disabled.

Nobody wants to be against the disabled. After all, people like Helen Keller and Franklin Roosevelt are popular American heroes. Nevertheless, civil rights laws for the handicapped have met with vehement opposition, and, once passed, with sluggish enforcement. The source of this resistance is the same concern that troubled Nixon: cost. Budgeting for programs to help the disabled is often short-sighted, however; people often forget that changes allowing disabled people to become wage-earners, spenders, and taxpayers are a gain, rather than drain on the economy.

Are AIDS victims handicapped and thus entitled to protection? In 1987 a case that crystallized this issue came to the Supreme Court. The case was not about AIDS, but it had obvious implications for discrimination against AIDS

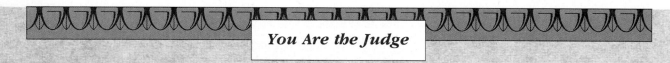

You Are the Judge

What Are the Civil Rights of the Contagious?

Gene Arline was an elementary school teacher in Nassau County, New York. When she became infected with tuberculosis—a contagious disease—the school board, citing the health of other children and teachers, dismissed her, and Arline took the school board to court. She claimed that Section 504 of the Rehabilitation Act of 1973 defines a handicapped person as "any person who has a physical or mental impairment which substantially limits one or more of such person's major life activities." The Department of Health and Human Services, which was charged by Congress with implementing the new law, defined "major life activities" to include "learning and working." Thus, said Arline's lawyers, her tuberculosis did impair a major life activity—namely, working—and

could not be used as a basis for dismissing her. The school board, joined by the Reagan administration, argued that a disease was not a handicap as the law had defined things.

You be the judge: Did the school board have a right to dismiss Arline, or was she protected against discrimination by the Rehabilitation Act of 1973?

Answer: In a seven to two decision, the Supreme Court held that Arline was covered by the protections given to the handicapped. The school board, said the majority, made no effort to determine how contagious Arline was or whether some other job could be found for her. Justice Brennan, writing the majority opinion, went out of his way in a footnote to disclaim, however, that the case had any implications for AIDS victims.

victims (see "You Are the Judge: What Are the Civil Rights of the Contagious?"). Thus far, no case dealing with AIDS victims has reached the Supreme Court. You can be sure, though, that one will.

Gay Rights

AIDS—Acquired Immune Deficiency Syndrome—has had a devastating effect on many groups, including male homosexuals in the United States. For some segments of the population, the disease has provided a convenient excuse for the kind of suspicion and outright bigotry that gay people have often encountered. Not only is homosexual activity illegal in some states (recall the discussion of *Bowers* v. *Hardwick* in Chapter 3), but homosexuals often face prejudice in hiring, education, access to public accommodations, and housing. Until the late 1960s most homosexuals concealed their sexual preference from the outside world. Many Americans still believe that they do not know any gay people, yet the best estimate is that about 10 percent of the American population is homosexual. This is a rough estimate, but it is a recurring one; about the same proportion of people in most societies have been gay. The activist slogan "We are everywhere" reflects reality.

A notorious incident in a New York City bar in 1969 stimulated the growth of the gay rights movement. The Stonewall bar, frequented by gay men, was raided by the police; violence, arrests, and injury to persons and property resulted. Both gay men and lesbians organized throughout the 1970s and 1980s, learning political skills and forming powerful interest groups. Despite setbacks like *Hardwick* and rulings permitting the Armed Forces to exclude homosexuals, gay activists have won important victories. Several cities have banned discrimination on the basis of sexual preference. Most colleges and universities now have gay rights organizations on campus. Twenty-five years ago, such public associations were unheard of.

Homosexual activists may face the toughest battle for equality. They do not enjoy even the formal, if often condescending, praise that women, older people, children, and the disabled receive. There are no positive stereotypes commonly associated with homosexuality—such as the feminine virtues attributed to women, the wisdom of the old, the innocence of children, or the courage of the disabled—that can counter the impact of the negative stereotyping that homosexuals face.

The reluctance to appear hostile to the aged or the disabled, which bridles the tongue of many potential opponents, has no apparent equivalent with respect to gay Americans. Homosexuals are safe targets. *Homophobia,* fear and hatred of homosexuals, has many causes, some very powerful. Some religions, for instance, condemn homosexuality. Such attitudes will probably continue to be characteristic of a large segment of the American public for years to come.

A NEW EQUALITY ISSUE: AFFIRMATIVE ACTION

The public policy paths for women and minorities have not been identical. They have converged, though, in the debate about affirmative action, which would extend new protections to both women and minorities. The 1960s and 1970s brought new prominence to the issue of equality for minorities and women.

New state and federal laws provided for discrimination *in favor* of these previously disadvantaged groups. Some state governments adopted affirmative action programs to increase minority enrollment, job holding, or promotion. Eventually the federal government mandated that all state and local governments, together with all institutions receiving aid from or contracting with the federal government, adopt an affirmative action program.

One such program was introduced at the University of California at Davis. Eager to produce more minority physicians for California, the medical school set aside sixteen of a total one hundred places in the entering class for "disadvantaged groups." One white applicant who did not make the freshman class was Allan Bakke, who, after receiving his rejection letter from Davis, decided to sue, claiming that he had been denied equal protection of the laws. The result was an important Supreme Court decision in Bakke's favor, ***Regents of the University of California* v. *Bakke*** (1978).[11] (For more on this case see "A Question of Ethics: *Regents of the University of California* v. *Bakke*".)

Although Bakke ended up in medical school, one Brian Weber did not get into an apprenticeship program he wanted to enter in Louisiana. In ***Weber* v. *Kaiser Aluminum Company*** (1979), the Court found that Kaiser's special training program was intended to rectify years of past employment discrimination at Kaiser. Thus, said the Court, a union-and-management-sponsored program to take more blacks than whites did not discriminate against Weber. Emphasizing strongly the "narrowness of our inquiry," Justice Brennan's majority opinion was carefully couched to avoid a blanket endorsement of affirmative action programs.

The Burger Court did not go as far as most proponents of affirmative action would have preferred. The majority of the Court insisted in case after case that judicial remedies could not be applied unless an *intent* to discriminate could be shown. Lawyers for African-American police officers in Washington, D.C., for example, argued that a civil service test for police officers seeking promotions should be held unconstitutional by the Supreme Court. The effect of the test, they argued, was discriminatory because proportionally more white officers than black officers passed the tests. The Supreme Court held, in *Washington* v. *Davis* (1976), that the intent and not the effect of a policy made it discriminatory. Of course, showing an intent to discriminate was not always easy. Affirmative action was thus constitutionally circumscribed.

In 1989 the Rehnquist Court emerged as an opponent of affirmative action, if not of civil rights in general. The Court disallowed a Richmond, Virginia, plan that reserved 30 percent of city subcontracts for minority firms; allowed white male workers to challenge affirmative action agreements reached before those workers were hired; imposed tougher standards on employees trying to prove discrimination; and ruled that current civil rights laws did not apply to on-the-job discrimination. These decisions sent a clear message to civil rights activists that they could expect little help from the Court. Increasingly activists are turning to Congress instead. The legislative branch can amend the law to negate court decisions, but there is little support from the general public for programs such as those that set aside jobs or employ quotas for members of minority groups (see "The People Speak: Affirmative Action").

The People Speak

Affirmative Action

Are you for or against preferential hiring and promotion of blacks?

For	17%
Against	65%

Should there be quotas to admit black students to college?

Yes	36%
No	64%

Most Americans oppose affirmative action or reverse discrimination programs, even though Americans in general support nondiscrimination in employment and education.

Source: The questions as worded are taken directly from the 1988 National Election Study.

[11]On the affirmative action issues raised by *Bakke* and other cases, see Allan P. Sindler, *Bakke, De Funis and Minority Admissions* (New York: Longman, 1978).

Regents of the University of California v. Bakke

Allan Bakke, a thirty-two-year-old white engineer and Vietnam veteran, applied to the medical school of the University of California at Davis. For two straight years, 1973 and 1974, he was rejected. UC-Davis, however, operated a Special Admissions Program to facilitate a larger enrollment of disadvantaged students. Sixteen of the hundred entering slots were reserved for students applying under the Special Admissions Program. The mean scores of students admitted under this program were the forty-sixth percentile on verbal tests and the thirty-fifth on science tests. (These scores were from the MCAT—Medical College Admissions Test.) Bakke's scores on the same tests were at the ninety-sixth percentile on the verbal test and at the ninety-seventh on the science test. Bakke sued UC-Davis, claiming that it denied him equal protection of the laws by discriminating against him because of his race.

The California Supreme Court agreed almost entirely with Bakke. It ordered UC-Davis to admit him to its freshman class. It also forbade UC-Davis to use race in any way as an admission standard. "No applicant," it said, "may be rejected because of his race, in favor of another who is less qualified." Losing in California's courts, UC-Davis took its case to the U.S. Supreme Court.

On June 28, 1978, the Court announced its decision. Unlike *Brown,* this case found the justices badly split. There were six separate opinions written by the justices. Justice Powell wrote the majority opinion. Joining him were Chief Justice Burger and Justices Stewart, Rehnquist, and Stevens. The Court ordered Bakke admitted, holding that the UC-Davis Special Admissions Program did discriminate against him because of his race, but it refused to order UC-Davis never to use race as a criterion for admission. A university *could,* said the Court, adopt an "admissions program where race or ethnic background is simply one element—to be weighed fairly against other elements—in the selection process." It could *not,* as UC-Davis' Special Admissions Program did, set aside a quota of spots for particular groups.

Allan Bakke, like Paul Johnson (see "Government in Action") and others whose opportunities were curtailed by reverse discrimination and affirmative action,

Allan Bakke (center, smiling) leaves class after his first day at the UC-Davis Medical School in September 1978.

insisted that these practices were unfair. Critics of reverse discrimination argue that any race or sex discrimination is wrong, even when its purpose is to rectify past injustices rather than to reinforce them. After all, Bakke and Johnson could no more help being white and male than Diane Joyce could help being a woman. Affirmative action opponents believe that merit is the only fair basis for distributing benefits. Bakke and Johnson found that the rules by which institutions operated had suddenly changed, and they suffered as a result. It is easy to sympathize with them.

On the other hand, the case for affirmative action and reverse discrimination is also strong and persuasive. Proponents of these policies argue that ideas about what constitutes merit are highly subjective, and can embody prejudices of which the decision maker may be quite unaware. Experts suggest that a man can look more like a road dispatcher, and thus get a higher rating from interviewers, than a woman might. Affirmative action supporters believe that increasing the number of women and minorities in desirable jobs is so important a social goal that it should be taken into account in determining an individual's qualifications. They claim that what white males lose from affirmative action programs are privileges to which they were never entitled in the first place; after all, nobody has the right to be a doctor or a road dispatcher.

What do *you* think? By the way, Bakke graduated from the UC-Davis Medical School in 1982 and is now a practicing physician.

UNDERSTANDING CIVIL RIGHTS AND THE CONSTITUTION

The original Constitution is silent on the issue of equality. The only direct reference is in the Fourteenth Amendment, which forbids the states from denying "equal protection of the laws." Those five words have been the basis for major civil rights statutes and scores of judicial rulings protecting the rights of minorities and women. These laws and decisions, granting people new rights, have empowered groups to seek and gain still more victories.

Civil Rights and Democracy

Equality is a basic principle of democracy. Every citizen has one vote, because democratic government presumes that each person's needs, interests, and preferences are neither any more nor any less important than the needs, interests, and preferences of each other person. Individual liberty is an equally important democratic principle, one that can conflict with equality. Democracy is often in conflict with itself.

Equality tends to favor majority rule. Since everyone's wishes rank equally, the policy outcome that most people prefer seems to be the fairest choice in cases of conflict. What happens, however, if the majority wants to deprive the minority of its rights? In situations like these, equality threatens individual liberty. Thus the principle of equality can invite the denial of minority rights, while the principle of liberty condemns such action.

Majority rule is not the only threat to liberty. Minorities have suppressed majorities. Women have long since outnumbered men in America, about 53 percent to 47 percent. In the era of segregation, many southern states had more blacks than whites. Inequality persisted because customs that reinforced it were entrenched within the society, and because inequality often served the interests of the dominant groups. When slavery and segregation existed, whites could get cheap labor. When men were breadwinners and women were homemakers, married men had a source of cheap domestic labor.

Both African Americans and women made many gains even when they lacked one essential component of democratic power: the vote. They used other rights, such as their First Amendment freedoms, to fight for equality. The democratic process is a powerful vehicle for disadvantaged groups to use in order to press their claims.

Civil Rights and the Size of Government

Civil rights laws increase the size and power of government. These laws tell individuals and institutions that there are things they must do and cannot do. Restaurant owners must serve patrons they would rather exclude. Professional schools must admit women. Employers must accommodate the disabled and make an effort to find minority workers, whether they want to or not. Libertarians and those conservatives who want to reduce the size of government are uneasy with these laws, if not downright hostile to them.

The founders might be greatly perturbed if they knew about all the civil rights laws the government has enacted. These policies do not conform to the eighteenth-century idea of limited government; but the founders would expect the national government to do whatever is necessary to hold the nation together. The Civil War showed that the original Constitution did not adequately deal with issues like slavery that could destroy the society the Constitution's writers had struggled to make secure.

Like civil liberties, civil rights is an area in which increased government activity in protecting basic rights can lead to greater checks on the government by those who benefit from such protections. The question of where to draw the line in the government's efforts to protect civil rights has received different answers at different points in American history, but few Americans desire to turn back the clock to the days of *Plessy* v. *Ferguson* and Jim Crow laws.

SUMMARY

Racial minorities have struggled for equality since the very beginning of the republic. In the era of slavery, the Supreme Court upheld the practice and denied slaves any rights. After the Civil War and Reconstruction ended, legal segregation was established. For a time the Supreme Court sanctioned the Jim Crow laws, but in 1954 the *Brown* v. *Board of Education* case held that segregation violated equal protection of the laws, which was guaranteed by the Fourteenth Amendment. The era of civil rights began. *Brown* inaugurated a movement that succeeded in ending virtually every form of legal discrimination against minorities.

Although feminists have not ignored the courts, the struggle for women's equality has emphasized legislation over litigation. Women won the right to vote in 1920, but the Equal Rights Amendment has not been ratified. This defeat did not kill the feminist movement, however. Comparable worth, women's role in

Many Americans still fear and condemn homosexuality, so, for the present, gay activists will have to fight their battles for equality without much public support.

Cesar Chavez is a powerful spokesperson for what will soon be America's largest minority group—Hispanics. As leader of the United Farm Workers Union, Chavez has worked tirelessly on behalf of poor Hispanic farm workers. Here he accepts bread from Ethel Kennedy, ending a 1988 hunger strike protesting the use of pesticides that, he claimed, are dangerous to migrant workers.

the military, and the balance between work and family are among the many controversial women's issues that are still being debated today.

The interests of women and minorities have converged on the issue of affirmative action, that is, policies requiring special efforts on behalf of disadvantaged groups. In the *Bakke* case and in decisions like *Johnson* v. *Santa Clara,* the Court ruled that affirmative action plans were both legal and constitutional, but the emerging conservative majority on the Court has recently narrowed the application of civil rights laws. Activists now look to Congress for strengthening amendments.

The civil rights umbrella is a large one. Increasing numbers of groups seek protection for their rights. Older and younger Americans, the disabled, and homosexuals have used the laws to ensure their equality. AIDS victims and other chronically ill people represent battles yet to be fought in the political arena. It is difficult to predict what controversies the twenty-first century will bring, when minority groups will outnumber the current majority.

KEY TERMS

affirmative action
civil rights
Fourteenth Amendment
equal protection of the laws
Dred Scott v. *Sandford*
Thirteenth Amendment
Plessy v. *Ferguson*
Brown v. *Board of Education*
Swann v. *Charlotte-Mecklenberg County Schools*

civil rights movement
Civil Rights Act of 1964
suffrage
Fifteenth Amendment
poll taxes
white primary
Twenty-fourth Amendment
Voting Rights Act of 1965
Korematsu v. *United States*
Nineteenth Amendment

Equal Rights Amendment
Reed v. *Reed*
Craig v. *Boren*
comparable worth
Regents of the University of California v. *Bakke*
Weber v. *Kaiser Aluminum Company*

FOR FURTHER READING

Baer, Judith A. *Equality Under the Constitution: Reclaiming the Fourteenth Amendment.* Ithaca, N.Y.: Cornell University Press, 1983. A liberal interpretation of the amendment.

Berger, Raoul. *Government by Judiciary: The Transformation of the Fourteenth Amendment.* Cambridge, Mass.: Harvard University Press, 1977. Berger is not one who favors use of the Fourteenth Amendment to expand equality.

Berry, Mary F. *Why ERA Failed.* Bloomington: Indiana University Press, 1986. An excellent account of public policies for women, with particular attention to the demise of the Equal Rights Amendment.

Brown, Dee. *Bury My Heart at Wounded Knee: An Indian History of the American West.* New York: Holt, Rinehart and Winston, 1970. History from a native American perspective.

Bullock, Charles S., III, and Charles M. Lamb. *Implementation of Civil Rights Policy.* Monterey, Calif.: Brooks/Cole, 1984. Focuses on the difficulty of turning the goals of civil rights policies into reality.

Kluger, Richard. *Simple Justice.* New York: Knopf, 1976. The story of the *Brown* case.

Mansbridge, Jane. *Why We Lost the ERA.* Chicago, University of Chicago Press, 1986. The politics of women's rights.

McGlen, Nancy, and Karen O'Connor. *Women's Rights: The Struggle for Equality in the Nineteenth and Twentieth Centuries.* New York: Praeger, 1983. A good account of the struggle for equal rights for women.

Rae, Douglas. *Equality.* Cambridge, Mass.: Harvard University Press, 1981. Some relevant political theory regarding equality.

Verba, Sidney, and Gary R. Orren. *Equality in America: The View from the Top.* Cambridge, Mass.: Harvard University Press, 1985. Verba and Orren examine the views of the American elite on equality.

Wilkinson, J. Harvie, III. *From Brown to Bakke.* New York: Oxford University Press, 1979. The political and legal history of civil rights policies between *Brown* and *Bakke*.

PART TWO

PEOPLE AND POLITICS

Taking to the Streets of Washington

In its early years getting to the city of Washington was hard enough for elected officials, much less for ordinary citizens. Access to the capital was limited and difficult, with few roads linking it to the outside world. On her way back to Washington from Baltimore, First Lady Abigail Adams once wandered aimlessly lost in the woods for two hours before a vagabond pointed her in the right direction.

Throughout the nineteenth century, continuing improvement in transportation—canals, railroads, and turnpikes—eased the city's isolation. By Lincoln's time, it had become a ritual for the wealthy and powerful to descend on Washington at the outset of a new administration to lobby for government positions and favors. It was not until the twentieth century, however, with the invention of the automobile, that it became possible for masses of average citizens to make their way to Washington to apply pressure on the government. A review of some of the major twentieth century demonstrations in our nation's capital provides a good introduction to this section of *Government in America* on people and politics.

Some of the earliest protest marches in the history of Washington were for the enfranchisement of America's largest interest group—women. When Woodrow Wilson was elected president, women came to Washington in droves to push the new, progressively minded, president to their cause. Parading on the day before Wilson's 1913 inauguration, the women carried banners reading,

The long struggle for women's suffrage—highlighted by this 1913 march in Washington—ended in 1920 when the Nineteenth Amendment granted women the right to vote.

"Tell your troubles to Woodrow." So great was the attention attracted by the parade that Wilson wondered aloud where everyone was when he arrived at the train station. Floats throughout the procession illustrated the progress the women's suffrage movement had made in the last twenty-five years, including the right to vote in nine states and territories. It was to be another seven years of struggling, though, before an amendment to the constitution granted women everywhere the right to vote.

The sight of thousands of women marching down Pennsylvania Avenue (some on horseback) was certainly strange in 1913, but imagine the shock many Washingtonians must have felt a dozen years later when forty thousand members of the Ku Klux Klan converged on the capital. In white robes and conical caps, they marched down Pennsylvania Avenue waving American flags. Their hoods, usually worn to conceal their identities, were tucked in under their caps to comply with a local ordinance against wearing masks. Resplendent in his royal purple robe with gold trimmings, the Imperial Wizard, Hiram Evans, a former dentist from Dallas,

led the parade. Occasionally, the crowd of over two hundred thousand people applauded him, but there was neither cheering nor booing. At the end of the march, as rain started to fall, few stuck around to listen to speeches extolling white supremacy, and the scheduled burning of an eighty-foot cross was cancelled. Emotions throughout the day were kept cool due to the fact that Washington's black population (then numbering one-third of the city) stayed out of sight of the Klansmen—as their pastors had urged them to do. Overall, police reported that the march was one of the most quiet and peaceful they had handled in the capital to date.

One of the least peaceful Washington demonstrations occurred seven years later in 1932 during the so-called Bonus March. Unemployed World War I veterans came to town to demand their war service bonuses be paid immediately, rather than in 1945 as Congress had provided. They had been there for their country when it needed them, said the marchers; now, during the height of the Great Depression, the government should return the favor. By the

Some two hundred thousand people watched the Ku Klux Klan parade down Pennsylvania Avenue in 1925.

sheer force of their presence—camping out on federal property—they hoped to shame the government into action. The government's response was hardly what they bargained for, however. After two months President Hoover ordered fifteen hundred federal troops under the command of General Douglas MacArthur to forcibly remove the bonus marchers from government land. Detachments of infantry and cavalry, supported by tanks commanded by Dwight Eisenhower, laid down an effective barrage of tear gas. After the camp's population of ten thousand people had been dispersed, the troops set fire to the veterans' shacks and tents. While many leaders condemned the brutality with which the eviction had been handled, President Hoover pointed to the presence of known communists among the protestors and stated that "government cannot be coerced by

mob rule." Soon Hoover joined the veterans in being out of a job, and the servicemen were given their bonuses early, after all, during the Roosevelt administration.

During the Roosevelt years the balance of opinion in Washington shifted notably away from toleration of groups like the Klan to support for civil rights. In 1939 the world-renowned singer Marian Anderson was denied the opportunity to sing at D.C.'s Constitution Hall because she was black. First Lady Eleanor Roosevelt was outraged by this action and persuaded the secretary of interior to arrange an outdoor concert for Anderson on the mall. With the giant statue of Abraham Lincoln behind her and some seventy-five thousand people before her, Anderson performed before a mixed racial audience in the still largely segregated nation's capital. Though many people came to

In 1939 Marian Anderson performed in front of the Lincoln Memorial after she was barred from Constitution Hall because of her skin color.

hear the singing rather than to support equality, it was an important symbolic step for the fledgling civil rights movement.

Almost a quarter of a century later Martin Luther King, Jr, stood in exactly the same spot to deliver his famous "I Have a Dream" speech, as the climax of the 1963 March on Washington. Frustrated by the inability of the Congress to pass civil rights legislation, the themes of the march were "unity, racial harmony, and, especially a cry to 'Pass the Bill.'"[1] More than thirty special trains and two thousand chartered buses delivered people to Washington from all across the country. The majority were black, but many whites marched right alongside, led by such celebrities as

The Great Depression led these bonus marchers to Washington, where President Hoover denied—violently—their demands for early bonus payments.

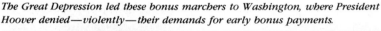

[1]Juan Williams, *Eyes on the Prize, America's Civil Rights Years, 1954–1965* (New York: Viking, 1987), 198.

Charlton Heston, Jackie Robinson, Marlon Brando, James Garner, and Diahann Carroll. At the end of the day King described his vision of the future of race relations in the United States. Dr. King told the huge crowd, and the millions watching at home on television, that he had "a dream that one day this nation will rise up and live out the true meaning of its creed: 'We hold these truths to be self-evident, that all men are created equal.'" As the crowd cheered each refrain of "I have a dream," King described a land where whites and blacks would be brothers and sisters, and where his people would be "free at last, free at last, thank God Almighty, free at last."

Toward the end of his life, King turned his attention from equality of opportunity to equality in living standards. Before his death he had planned another big march on Washington to protest the abject poverty of many minorities in America. In the

Martin Luther King, Jr.'s "I Have a Dream" speech during the 1963 March on Washington gave a distinctive voice to the civil rights movement.

Resurrection City, built as part of the 1968 Poor People's March, drew attention to inequalities in American living standards.

spring of 1968 the Poor People's March began in Memphis, where King had been assassinated, and gradually made its way to Washington. The poor people who marched into town reminded many of the unfortunate Bonus Army of 1932, and like the Bonus Army they settled in for an extended stay on federal land. The marchers quickly constructed a "Resurrection City" of plywood huts along the length of the Lincoln Memorial's reflecting pool. For six weeks they organized a series of demonstrations and listened to politicans who came to talk with them. Unfortunately, though, Resurrection City proved to be almost too faithful a replica of ghetto life, complete with drunks, junkies, gangs, hoodlums, and crime. Because of this, federal and city officials agreed to close it down after the six-week permit ended. Many in town breathed a sigh of relief when workers from the General Services Administration came to cart off the lumber and refuse from the "city." Unlike the

Bonus March, there was no violence when the encampment was demolished, though the Reverend Ralph Abernathy protested and was taken off to jail when he refused to move out of the way.

By the late 1960s massive demonstrations had become relatively common in the nation's capital as the Vietnam War spurred protest after protest. Young people played a key role in President Johnson's decision to not seek reelection by their regular chanting outside the White House of "Hey, hey, LBJ! How many kids did you kill today?" This chant could not only be heard inside the White House but on the nightly news as well, as television carried the expressions of discontent throughout the nation. It is said that Johnson was haunted for the rest of his life by what he called "that horrible song."[2]

The antiwar protests escalated as the war continued to drag on under Johnson's successor, Richard Nixon. On November 15, 1969, the biggest antiwar rally was held when 250,000 people gathered in Washington to demand a moratorium (that is, a suspension) of the war. With LBJ gone, the new chant taken up was John Lennon's "All we are saying is give peace a chance." During one part of the protest tens of thousands walked silently in a "March against Death" from Arlington National Cemetery to Capitol Hill, with each person wear-

[2]Robert A. Caro, *The Years of Lyndon Johnson: Means of Ascent* (New York: Knopf, 1990), xxiii.

197

ing a cardboard placard displaying the name of an American soldier killed in Vietnam. Some bore the placards of their own lost sons, brothers, husbands, or fathers. For hours upon hours they arrived on Capitol Hill in single file, moving past TV cameras and funeral music, to deposit a name in one of twelve coffins and then snuff out a candle. For his part, President Nixon made it known that he had ignored the demonstration, choosing to spend the afternoon watching a football game on TV.

Nixon could hardly ignore the May 3, 1971, plan by the antiwar movement to literally close down the government for a day by putting up barricades at major Washington intersections and laying down in front of cars. In response, the president gave Attorney General John Mitchell virtual carte blanche to do what was necessary to stop the protestors, short of killing them. Local police, the army, marines, and the national guard were all called out to arrest

anyone who made the slightest move to impede traffic. Suspending the usual arrest procedures as too time-consuming in this emergency situation, they began a dragnet to clear the streets of Washington. In the process they swept up not only disorderly demonstrators but also law-abiding demonstrators, and sometimes even youths who were not even demonstrators at all. By the end of the day more than seven thousand people had been herded into the city jail, the National Armory, and Robert F. Kennedy stadium. Years later the demonstrators won a class action suit and were awarded monetary compensation for various violations of their constitutional rights during the mass arrests.

Antiwar activists tried to push down a fence at RFK stadium, where police confined them during the May 3, 1971, protests.

Soon it was President Nixon himself who was under suspicion of violating the law. After Nixon decided to fire the Watergate special prosecutor rather than turn over tape recordings of his White House conversations, calls for impeachment reverberated throughout Washington. When a federal appeals court overturned the four-year-old ban on large protests in front of the White House, the Committee to Impeach the President immediately took advantage of the opportunity. On October 27, 1973, hundreds of demonstrators lined the sidewalks in front of the White House, holding signs that asked passing motorists to "Honk to Impeach." The response along Pennsylvania Avenue came in loud blasts from cars, trucks, and even city buses. The noise got so bad that the city's police started giving out tickets for disturbing the peace to those who continually circled the block just to honk. At one point a U-Haul moving

Demonstrators at the White House denounced the president's involvement in the Watergate scandal.

van with a large "Impeach Nixon" banner parked in front of the White House for a minute. About eight months later onlookers who saw a half dozen moving vans being let through the White House gates were among the first to know that Nixon was about to resign from office.

Today's demonstrations in Washington do not involve such great political dramas as civil rights, Vietnam, or Watergate, but they involve deeply felt concerns nonetheless. The state of the environment is one widely shared concern. In 1970 Senator Gaylord Nelson, one of America's most prominent liberals at the time, had the idea of a nationwide teach-in to promote environmental protection. Just as the anti–Vietnam War movement had organized rallies to educate people about what was happening in Southeast Asia, so Senator Nelson thought it would be useful to teach people about the nation's environmental problems. The result was the first Earth Day, held on April 22, 1970. Like the antiwar teach-ins it was modeled after, the Earth Day gatherings in Washington and elsewhere primarily drew the counterculture and supporters of left-wing causes. The mood of 1970's Earth Day was one of protest, and the

speakers stressed various proposals for the government to take stronger action to protect the environment. In contrast, when the second Earth Day was held in 1990, the tone had changed from protest to celebration, and the crowd from hippie to yuppie. In 1990 the speakers focused on what each individual could do to help the environment, reflecting the political consensus on the issue that had evolved since the first Earth Day.

Today the issue that draws the biggest and most frequent demonstrations in the nation's capital is one of the least consensual of modern times—abortion. Ever since the *Roe* v. *Wade* decision of 1973 legalized abortion throughout the United

States, antiabortionists have organized an annual "March for Life" on January 22 (the anniversary of the decision) in Washington to protest the Supreme Court ruling. More recently the threat that *Roe* v. *Wade* might be overturned has mobilized proabortion forces to hold their own mass rallies in Washington. Indeed, when the country waited for the decision in the *Webster* v. *Reproductive Health Services* case to be announced, both sides on the abortion issue had many demonstrators on the scene, as well as leaders to issue instant commentary on the decision for the benefit of the press.

As long as important decisions emanate from Washington, people will continue to organize mass demonstrations to make the force of their views felt by policymakers. The power centers in Washington, and how they developed, is the focus of the photo essay in Part Three.

Large crowds at the Earth Day 1990 celebrations reflected widespread support for environmental protection.

6

*P*UBLIC OPINION AND POLITICAL ACTION

Public opinion polling has become a major growth industry in recent years. Each of the three networks and almost every major newspaper now commissions its own regular poll. Polls are great investments for the media because they provide a timely story which can be billed as an exclusive. If there is nothing new in their findings, journalists can always fall back upon one sure pattern: the astounding lack of public knowledge about politics. No matter what the event or the issue, one can be virtually sure that a substantial percentage of the population will know nothing about it.

The results are often amusing, and to those who are politically aware the level of ignorance never ceases to amaze. As Richard Morin, the director of polling for the *Washington Post,* writes, "Measuring public ignorance has become a favorite parlor trick of America's pollsters. Not only is it great fun, but we also learn a lot looking up the answers to the questions we expect our random samplings of American adults to know." Here are a few of Morin's favorite examples from national opinion polls in the 1980s:

- When asked whether the United States and the Soviet Union fought on the same side in World War II, 44 percent did not know or incorrectly said they were enemies. Similarly, only 33 percent knew that our government was supporting the rebels in Nicaragua.
- Half of the population believed that "it is up to the person who is accused of the crime to prove his or her innocence."
- When asked whether Japan was a part of the Asian continent or a separate island country, 34 percent placed it on the mainland and another 9 percent were not sure.
- A national sample of adults was asked if Alaska was a territory, state, or a country. One out of six got it wrong or didn't know. Believe it or not, 5 percent said it was a country.

If you wonder how such well-known figures as Manuel Noriega and Oliver North can receive a fair trial, the answer is that it is actually not that difficult to find people who know little about them. If you wonder how the American political system can function as well as it does with such low levels of public information, read on in this chapter.

Source: Richard Morin, "Margaret Thatcher? Wasn't She Gary Hart's Girlfriend?" *Washington Post National Weekly Edition,* December 18, 1989, 38.

Elaborating

How many times have you heard a politician or a columnist intone the words "the American people..." and then claim his or her view as theirs? Because American society is so complex, it would be hard to find a statement about the American people—who they are and what they believe—that is either 100 percent right or wrong. The American people are wondrously diverse. There are about 250 million Americans, forming a mosaic of racial, ethnic, and cultural groups. America was founded on the principle of tolerating diversity and it remains one of the most diverse in the world today. Most Americans view this as one of the most appealing aspects of their society.

Such diversity makes the study of American public opinion especially complex, for there are many groups with a great variety of opinions. This is not to say that public opinion would be easy to study even if America were a more homogeneous society; as you will see, the measurement of public opinion involves careful interviewing procedures and question wording. Further complicating the task is the fact that people are often not well informed about the issues or have contradictory attitudes. Those who are least informed also are the least likely to participate in the political process, thereby leading to inequalities in who takes part in political action.

For American government to work efficiently and effectively, the diversity of the American public and its opinions must be faithfully channeled through the political process. This chapter reveals just how difficult a task this is.

THE AMERICAN PEOPLE

One way of looking at the American public is through **demography,** the science of human populations. The most valuable tool for understanding demographic changes in America is the **census.** The U.S. constitution requires that the government conduct an "actual enumeration" of the population every ten years; the first such census was conducted in 1790, the most recent in 1990. Getting a question included on the census form is a highly competitive enterprise, as groups of all different kinds seek to be counted.[1] Once a group can establish its numbers, it can then ask for federal aid in proportion to its size. In 1990 advocates for the disabled came out as one winner when the census added a question designed to count people who have difficulty taking care of themselves or getting where they need to go. The census also responded to complaints that the homeless were being left out of the count by sending out fifteen thousand workers one night to count them.

Incidentally, it was this taking of the census that led to one of the greatest inventions of modern times—the computer. Herman Hollerith, a man who

[1]See Margo Anderson, *The American Census: A Social History* (New Haven, Conn.: Yale University Press, 1988).

worked with the 1890 census, devised a way of storing massive amounts of information on punched cards, modeled after cards to guide weavers. So promising was Hollerith's idea that he left the Census Bureau to form a company known today as International Business Machines, or IBM for short.

The next few sections will examine the ways the American culture and political system are changing as a result of population changes.

The Immigrant Society

The United States has always been a nation of immigrants. As Lyndon Johnson said, America is "not merely a nation but a nation of nations." All Americans except for American Indians are either descended from immigrants or are immigrants themselves. Today federal law allows up to 630,000 new immigrants to be legally admitted every year. This is equivalent to adding a city with the population of Washington, D.C., every year.

There have been three great waves of immigration to the United States.

- Before the Civil War, northwestern Europeans (English, Irish, Germans, and Scandinavians) constituted the first wave of immigration.
- After the Civil War, southern and eastern Europeans (Italians, Jews, Poles, Russians, and others) made up the second wave.
- After World War II, Hispanics (from Cuba, Puerto Rico, Central America, and Mexico) and Asians (from Vietnam, Korea, the Philippines, and elsewhere) made up the third wave. The 1980s saw the largest number of immigrants of any decade in American history.

Immigrants bring with them their aspirations as well as their own political beliefs. Cubans in Miami, the near-majority of the city's population, typically

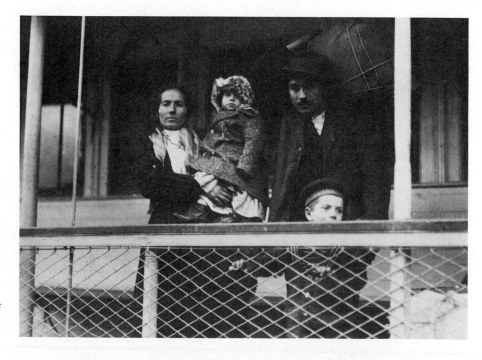

The American mosaic includes immigrants from almost every nation on earth. Many have arrived at New York's Ellis Island, as did this turn-of-the-century Italian family. More immigrants come to America now than ever before—some 600,000 a year.

have fled Castro's Marxist regime and brought their anticommunist sentiments with them.[2] Similarly, the Vietnamese came to America after the United States failed to prevent a communist takeover there. Many Mexican Americans, by contrast, have come to the United States to escape poverty; every day Mexicans cross the Rio Grande in search of economic opportunity. Because the children of these immigrants are often poor and speak little English, many Mexican-American leaders have advocated a system of bilingual education in American public schools (see "You Are the Policymaker: Bilingual Education"). The push for bilingual education is just one of the many examples of how immigration has shifted the policy agenda over the years.

Explaining

The American Mosaic

With its long history of immigration, the United States has often been called a **melting pot.** This phrase refers to a mixture of cultures, ideas, and peoples. As the third wave of immigration continues, policymakers have come to speak of a new **minority majority,** a clever phrase meaning that America will soon

[2]On Miami, see Joan Didion, *Miami* (New York: Simon & Schuster, 1987).

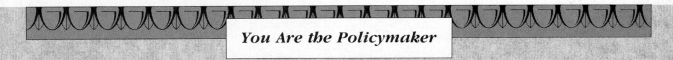

You Are the Policymaker

Bilingual Education

Bilingual education is the attempt to teach students in two languages. In 1967 Congress mandated bilingual education for school districts with substantial non-English-speaking populations. There are several ways such a policy can be implemented. First, there is *maintenance,* in which students are taught in both languages, say by teaching half in English and half in Spanish. Second is *transitional,* in which students are at first taught in both languages, with the non-English language gradually phased out as English skills improve. Third is *English as a second language,* in which instruction is primarily in English but with concentrated instruction given to non-English speakers.

Each of these three kinds of bilingual education has significant implications for policy. The first assumes that America can be a multilingual country and that it is good to preserve a multicultural heritage. The second and third assume (as some state laws have tried to pronounce) that America is a society in which everyone's primary language should be English.

The issue of bilingual education provokes strong public disagreements. Opponents argue that time spent educating students bilingually is time taken away from working on such subjects as mathematics and history. Proponents contend that being placed into English-only classes is a guarantee of failure or slow progress for the children of immigrants. Charges of racism are often dragged into the fray, a frequent occurrence when political issues involving ethnic groups are on the policy agenda.

Think about the policy issues involving bilingual education. Other immigrant groups who have come to the United States (such as Chinese, Poles, and Germans) did not, of course, have bilingual education, but they came at a time when the link between literacy and livelihood was not so direct. This is not a time, supporters of bilingual education argue, when we can pretend that an incomplete understanding of English will enable advancement to a responsible career and citizenship.

Put yourself in the role of policymaker and consider these issues:

- Would you encourage your local or state government to support bilingual education?
- If you support bilingual education, do you favor, the *maintenance, transitional,* or *English as a second language* version?

Virginia's Douglas Wilder celebrates his victory as the nation's first elected African-American governor. Wilder's election demonstrates the growing political power of minorities in general, and African Americans in particular.

cease to have a white, generally Anglo-Saxon majority. California will change first, with its large concentration of Hispanics, African Americans, and Asians. According to one projection, Hispanics alone will make up the majority of California's population by the year 2010.[3] Figure 6.1 shows the shifting population of greater Los Angeles from 1970 to projections for the year 2010. By the time you finish this book, a minority majority may be realized in the Los Angeles metropolitan area. If the current trends continue nationwide, by the middle of the twenty-first century nonwhites will be in the majority in the United States. (Of course, should birth and immigration rates change, so will these estimates.)

The largest component of the minority majority currently is the African-American population—one in eight Americans. These are the descendents of reluctant immigrants, namely Africans who were brought to America by force as slaves. A legacy of racism and discrimination has left our African-American population economically and politically disadvantaged. Nearly 33 percent of blacks currently live under the poverty line compared to about 10 percent of whites.

Despite being near the bottom of the economic spectrum, African Americans have recently been exercising a good deal of political power. The number of black elected officials has increased from 1,479 in 1970 to 6,384 in 1987.[4] In 1989 two more electoral milestones were reached. Douglas Wilder of Virginia became the nation's first elected African-American governor, and David Dinkins became the first African-American mayor of New York City.

The familiar problems of African Americans sometimes obscure the problems of other minority groups, such as Hispanics (composed largely of Puerto Ricans, Cubans, Mexicans, and Haitians). By the year 2000, however, the Hispanic

[3]Bruce Cain and Roderick Kieweit, "California's Minority Majority," *Public Opinion* (February/March 1986): 16.

[4]Richard Morin and Dan Balz, "There's Still Room for Improvement in Racial Relations," *Washington Post Weekly,* October 30, 1989, 37.

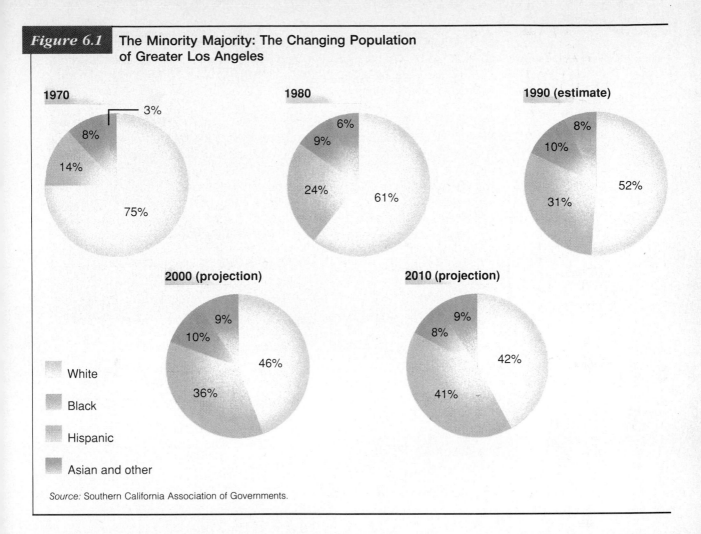

Figure 6.1 The Minority Majority: The Changing Population of Greater Los Angeles

1970
3%
8%
14%
75%

1980
6%
9%
24%
61%

1990 (estimate)
8%
10%
31%
52%

2000 (projection)
9%
10%
36%
46%

2010 (projection)
9%
8%
41%
42%

White
Black
Hispanic
Asian and other

Source: Southern California Association of Governments.

population should outnumber the black population. Like African Americans, Hispanics are concentrated in cities (contrary to the myth that most Hispanics are migrant farm workers). Hispanics are rapidly gaining power in the Southwest, and cities like San Antonio and Denver have elected mayors of Hispanic heritage.

An issue of particular concern to the Hispanic community is what to do about the problem of illegal immigration. A new immigration law, called the **Simpson-Mazzoli Act** after its congressional sponsors, required that as of June 1987 employers document the citizenship of their employees. Whether people are born in Canton, Ohio, or Canton, China, they now have to show that they are either citizens or legal immigrants in order to work. Civil and criminal penalties can now be assessed against employers who knowingly employ illegal immigrants. This law causes much concern among leaders of immigrant groups, who worry that employers might simply decline to hire members of such groups rather than take any chances.

In return for getting tougher on illegal immigrants in the work force, though, the Simpson-Mazzoli Act granted amnesty to illegal aliens who had resided in the United States since January 1982. If they could demonstrate this to the

Immigration and Naturalization Service—the agency that for years had tried to deport them—they were granted legal status. All told, three million applied and took the first step toward becoming American citizens. No longer having to worry about sneaking over the border, Christmas 1988 saw many Mexican immigrants returning home to visit for the first time since they came to the United States.

By far the worst off among American ethnic groups is the one indigenous minority, known today as native Americans. Before Europeans arrived in America, 12 to 15 million American Indians lived here. War and disease reduced their numbers to a mere 210,000 by 1910. Today about 1 million descendants of the original Americans are left. Statistics show that they are the least-healthy, the poorest, and the least-educated group in the American mosaic. Only a handful of American Indians have found wealth; fewer still, power. Some Indian tribes have discovered oil or other minerals on their land and exploited these resources successfully. Most native Americans, though, remain economically and politically disadvantaged in American society.

Americans live in a multicultural and multilingual society. America is becoming a more diverse nation all the time, yet, despite this diversity, there is much agreement among ethnic groups about what truly makes an American. (See "The People Speak: What Makes Someone an American?") Minority groups have assimilated many basic American values, such as the principle of treating all equally.

The emergence of the minority majority is just one of several major demographic changes that have altered the face of American politics. In addition, the population has also been moving and aging.

The Regional Shift

Between the 1970 and 1980 censuses, growth in the Sunbelt surged while growth in the Frostbelt sagged. Florida's population increased by 43 percent over the

---

| *The People Speak* | **What Makes Someone an American?** |

People have different ideas about what is really important in making someone a true American. I'm going to read a list of things that have been mentioned. For each one, please tell me how important it is in making a person a true American. (The figures below represent the percentage of those answering "very important.")

Characteristic	Anglos	Blacks	Hispanics	Asians
Treating all equally	89	94	81	93
Trying to get ahead	77	69	67	56
Speaking English	77	85	67	70
Voting	78	71	69	70
Speaking up for the country	51	63	54	43
Believing in God	36	65	48	35

Source: The question as worded is taken directly from a 1988 Field Poll of California, as reported in Jack Citrin, Beth A. Reingold, and Donald P. Green, "American Identity and the Politics of Ethnic Change" (Working paper 89-1 available from the Institute of Governmental Studies, University of California, Berkeley).

decade, Arizona's by 53 percent, and Nevada's by 64 percent. In contrast, New York, Rhode Island, and the District of Columbia actually lost people over the decade. Other states, Ohio, Massachusetts, and Pennsylvania for example, had virtually no population growth. In the 1980s America's population growth continued to be centered in the Sunbelt. The Census Bureau estimates that 87 percent of all the nation's population growth from 1980 to 1988 took place in the South and West.[5]

Demographic changes are associated with political changes. Because states gain or lose congressional representation as their population changes, power shifts as well. This process is called **reapportionment,** and occurs after every census. For a look at which states will gain seats and which will lose seats as of 1992, see Figure 6.2. California, Texas, and Florida continue to be the big gainers. After the reapportionment, these three states will have one-fourth of the seats in the House of Representatives.

Explaining: reapportionment

[5]Felicity Barringer, "Northeast Gains Some Population," *New York Times,* September 16, 1989.

Figure 6.2   **Winners and Losers in the 1990 Reapportionment**

After each census, seats in the House of Representatives are reallocated to the states based on population changes. Thus, as California has grown throughout this century its representation in the House has increased from just seven in 1900 to a projected fifty in 1992. As you can see from the map below, California will again be the biggest winner in the 1990 reapportionment. The biggest losers should be New York and Pennsylvania, each of which has lost about one-third of its delegation over the last forty years.

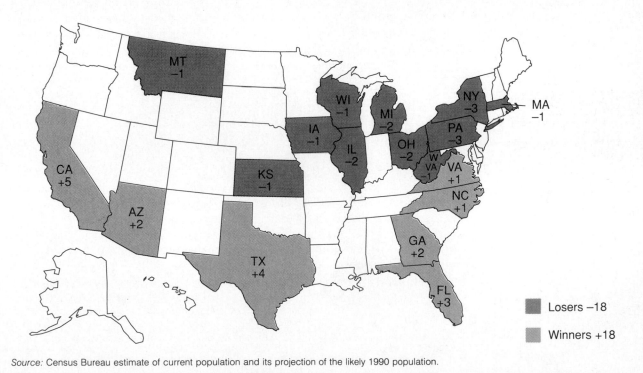

Source: Census Bureau estimate of current population and its projection of the likely 1990 population.

The Graying of America

One of the three megastates, Florida, has grown in large part as a result of its attractiveness to senior citizens. Nationwide, the fastest growing age group in America is composed of citizens over sixty-five. Not only are people living longer as a result of medical advances, but the birth rate has dropped substantially. About 60 percent of adult Americans living today grew up in families of four or more children. If the current baby bust continues, this figure will eventually be cut to 30 percent.[6]

By the year 2020, as the post–World War II baby boom generation reaches senior citizen status, there will be just two working Americans for every person over the age of sixty-five. If you think Social Security is being stretched to the limit now, just wait until 2020. The Social Security system, begun under the New Deal, is exceeded only by national defense as America's most costly public policy. The current group of older Americans and those soon to follow can lay claim to nearly five trillion dollars guaranteed by Social Security. They also hold title to nearly one trillion dollars in public and private pension plans. There is a political message in these numbers: people who have been promised benefits expect to collect them, especially benefits for which they have made monthly contributions. Thus, even Ronald Reagan's budget-cutting policies treated Social Security benefits as sacrosanct.

As the population has aged, new political interests have been mobilized. Once tossed aside as no longer productive, the aged now claim "gray power."[7] In Florida, the state's senior citizens vote against nearly every referendum for school taxes, much to the dismay of younger parents. They have managed to secure tax breaks and service benefits for older people from the Florida legislature. Senior citizens have thus discovered an old political dictum: there is strength in numbers. A growing and potent group, the aged have one advantage that no other group has—most Americans anticipate reaching senior citizen status. The growing demands to care for the elderly will almost certainly become more acute in the decades ahead.

WHAT AMERICANS LEARN ABOUT POLITICS: POLITICAL SOCIALIZATION

As the most experienced segment of the population, the elderly have undergone the most political socialization. **Political socialization** is "the process through which an individual acquires his [or her] particular political orientations—his [or her] knowledge, feelings, and evaluations regarding his [or her] political world."[8] As one becomes more socialized with age, one's political orientations grow firmer. Thus it should not be surprising that governments largely aim their socialization efforts at the young, not the old.

Authoritarian regimes are particularly concerned with indoctrinating their citizens at an early age. For example, youth groups in the Soviet Union are

---

[6]Judith Blake, *Family Size and Achievement* (Berkeley, Calif.: University of California Press, 1989).

[7]See Henry J. Pratt, *The Gray Lobby* (Chicago: University of Chicago Press, 1977).

[8]Richard Dawson et al., *Political Socialization*. 2nd ed. (Boston: Little, Brown, 1977), 33.

These children—the faces of the coming minority majority population—suggest the unique problem of American political socialization: transforming people of diverse cultural backgrounds and beliefs into American citizens.

tightly organized into the Komsomols, the Young Communist League. Membership in these groups is helpful in gaining admission to college and even to certain occupations. In the Komsomols Soviet youths learn their government's view of the advantages of communism. In contrast, socialization is a much more subtle process in the United States.

How Americans Learn: The Process of Political Socialization

Only a small portion of Americans' political learning is formal. Some Americans may take civics or government classes in high school or political science classes in college. In such formal settings, citizens learn some of the nuts and bolts of government—how many senators each state has, what presidents do, and so on. But formal socialization is only the tip of the iceberg. Americans do most of their political learning without teachers or classes. In fact, there is little evidence that formal learning about politics is long lasting; although millions of American teenagers are required to take a high school civics course, for the vast majority of white teenagers studied, taking civics made virtually no difference in their political attitudes and beliefs.[9]

Informal learning is really much more important than formal, in-class learning about politics. Most informal socialization is almost accidental. Few parents sit down with their offspring and say, "Johnny, let us tell you why we're Republicans." Words like *pick up, absorb,* and *acquire* perhaps best describe the informal side of socialization.

The agents of socialization are numerous. Among them are the family, the media, and the schools.

[9]For African-American students, civics education is somewhat more significant. See Kenneth P. Langton and M. Kent Jennings, "Political Socialization and the High School Civics Curriculum in the United States," *American Political Science Review* 62 (September 1968): 852–67.

Analyzing
Family in
Pol. Social

The Family   Parents worry endlessly about the moral, religious, and sexual values of their offspring; politics is usually the least of their worries. If their kids manage to avoid trouble with the law, stay off drugs, and get a good education, most parents consider their job well done, and could care less whether their children end up as Democrats or Republicans.

The family's role is central because of its monopoly on two crucial resources in the early years: time and emotional commitment. The powerful influence of the family is not easily broken. Most students in an American government class like to think of themselves as independent thinkers, especially when it comes to politics, yet one can predict how the majority of young people will vote simply by knowing the political leanings of their parents. In Table 6.1 you can see how well high school seniors and their parents matched up on party affiliation in a classic 1965 study by M. Kent Jennings and Richard Niemi.

As children approach adult status, though, some degree of adolescent rebellion against parents and their beliefs often takes place. Witnessing the outpouring of youthful rebellion in the 1960s, many people thought a generation gap was opening up. Radical youth supposedly condemned their backwards-thinking parents. Though such a gap did exist in a few families, the overall evidence for it was slim. When Jennings and Niemi reinterviewed their sample of young adults and their parents eight years later in 1973, they still found far more agreement than disagreement across the generational divide. Moving out of the family nest and into adulthood did result in the offspring becoming somewhat less like their parents politically, however.[10] Other socialization agents had apparently exerted influence in the intervening years.

[10]See M. Kent Jennings and Richard G. Niemi, *Generations and Politics: A Panel Study of Young Adults and Their Parents* (Princeton, N.J.: Princeton University Press, 1981).

Table 6.1	**Parent-Child Agreement on Party Identification**

In 1965 Jennings and Niemi selected a sample of high-school seniors throughout the country and interviewed them as well as one of their parents. Below you will find how closely the two generations matched on party affiliation. The numbers represent the percentage of parent-child pairs that fell into each category. (For example, the 32.6 figure indicates how often the parent and the child both said they were Democrats.)

CHILDREN	PARENTS		
	Democrat	**Independent**	**Republican**
Democrat	32.6	7.0	3.4
Independent	13.2	12.7	9.7
Republican	3.6	4.1	13.6

Agreement = 58.9%   Disagreement = 7.0%

Source: Adapted from M. Kent Jennings and Richard G. Niemi, *The Political Character of Adolescence* (Princeton, N.J.: Princeton University Press, 1973), 39.

The Mass Media   The mass media is "the new parent" according to many observers. As James Beniger and Susan Herbst write, "broadcasting enables centralized sources—for the first time in human history—to speak over the heads of traditional institutional gatekeepers like parents directly to family members in their home."[11] The average grade-school youngster spends more time each week watching television than he or she spends at school. Contrary to popular impression, heavy TV watching by children does not seem to reduce, but rather increases, knowledge about politics and government. Television now displaces parents as the chief source of information as children get older.

School   Political socialization is as important to a government as it is to an individual. This is one reason governments (including America's) often use the schools to promote loyalty to the country and support for its basic values. In most American schools, the day begins with the Pledge of Allegiance. During the 1988 presidential campaign, George Bush argued that by law teachers should have to lead students in the Pledge. His opponent, Michael Dukakis, had vetoed a bill to require this in Massachussetts, claiming that it was unconstitutional. Underlying Bush's argument was the assumption that proper socialization in the schools was crucial to the American political system—a position that Dukakis disagreed with more in terms of means than in ends.

Governments throughout the world use the schools to attempt to raise children committed to the basic values of the system. For years, American children have been successfully educated about the virtues of capitalism and democracy. In the hands of an unscrupulous government, though, educational socialization can sometimes be a dangerous tool. For example, in Nazi Germany textbooks were used to justify its murderous policies. Consider the following example from a Nazi-era math book:

> If a mental patient costs 4 Reichsmarks a day in maintenance, a cripple 5.50, and a criminal 3.50, and about 50,000 of these people are in our institutions, how much does it cost our state at a daily rate of 4 Reichsmarks—and how many marriage loans of 1,000 Reichsmarks per couple could have been given out instead?[12]

One can only imagine how the constant exposure in schools to this kind of thinking warped the minds of some young people growing up in Nazi Germany.

Both authoritarian and democratic governments care that students learn positive features about their political system because it helps ensure that youth will grow up to be supportive citizens. David Easton and Jack Dennis have argued that "those children who begin to develop positive feelings toward the political authorities will grow into adults who will be less easily disenchanted with the system than those children who early acquire negative, hostile sentiments."[13] Of course, this is not always the case; well-socialized youths of the 1960s led the opposition to the American regime and the war in Vietnam. One could argue that even these protestors had been positively shaped by the so-

[11]James R. Beniger and Susan Herbst, "Mass Media and Public Opinion: Emergence of an Institution" (Unpublished paper, 1990).

[12]Quoted in Sabine Reichel, *What Did You Do in the War Daddy? Growing Up German* (New York: Hill & Wang, 1989), 113.

[13]David Easton and Jack Dennis, *Children in the Political System* (New York: McGraw-Hill, 1969), 106–7.

cialization process, for the goal of most activists was to make the system more democratically responsive rather than to radically change American government.

Today, American educational policy consumes more than $170 billion annually. Most American schools are public schools, financed by the government; their textbooks are chosen by the local and state boards, and teachers are certified by the state government. Schooling is perhaps the most obvious intrusion of the government into Americans' socialization. Education exerts a profound influence on a variety of political attitudes and behavior. For example, better-educated men and women are more likely to vote in elections; show more knowledge about politics and public policy; and are more tolerant of opposing (even radical) opinions.

School counts. It pays off not only economically, but also in citizens who more closely approximate the democratic model. A formal civics course may not make much difference, but the whole context of education does. As Einstein once said, "Schools need not preach political doctrine to defend democracy. If they shape men [and women] capable of critical thought and trained in social attitudes, that is all that is necessary."

Political Learning over a Lifetime

Political learning does not, of course, end when one reaches eighteen, or even graduates from college. Politics is a lifelong activity. Because America is an aging society, it is important to consider the effects of growing older on political learning and behavior.

One might assume, for example, that political knowledge increases with age; if age brings wisdom, perhaps it brings information too. This, however, appears not to be the case. In one survey, Sigelman and Yanarella asked people some simple questions about economics and the environment (such as, "What is acid rain?") and found that age was a poor predictor of such knowledge.[14] Getting older may make people wiser, but it does not seem to make them more knowledgeable about politics.

Aging does increase one's political participation, as well as one's strength of party attachment. Young people (those eighteen through twenty-five) lack experience with politics, as they do with other things. Because political behavior is to some degree learned behavior, they have some learning yet to do. Political participation rises steadily with age until the infirmities of old age make it harder to participate.[15] Like other attachments, such as religion, party identification grows not so much with "age per se, but rather as a function of the length of time that the individual has felt some generalized preference for a particular party and repetitively voted for it."[16]

Politics, like most other things, is thus a learned behavior. Americans learn to vote, to pick a party, and to evaluate political events in the world around them. One of the products of all this learning is what is known as public opinion.

---

[14]Lee Sigelman and Ernest Yanarella, "Public Information on Public Issues," *Social Science Quarterly* 67 (June 1986): 402–10.

[15]See Raymond E. Wolfinger and Steven J. Rosenstone, *Who Votes* (New Haven, Conn.: Yale University Press, 1980), chap. 3.

[16]Philip E. Converse, *The Dynamics of Party Support* (Beverly Hills: Sage Publications, 1976), 12–13.

WHAT AMERICANS BELIEVE: PUBLIC OPINION AND POLICY

The public holds opinions about many topics. Premarital sex, whether flying saucers exist, the virtues of jogging, and the lengths of women's skirts are all subjects about which people can hold opinions—sometimes strong ones. In the following sections you will explore a particular kind of **public opinion:** the distribution of the population's beliefs about politics and policy issues. Saying that opinions are distributed among the population implies that there is rarely a single public opinion; in other words, so many people, so many opinions. If everyone were of one mind about some question, it would not be much of a political issue. Public opinion on policy issues becomes important when some people favor and others oppose abortion, a constitutional amendment to ban burning the flag, or raising the minimum wage. Understanding the content and dynamics of public opinion on such issues is important to political scientists and politicians alike.

Measuring Public Opinion

Although public opinion polling is a relatively new science, very sophisticated technology is now available for measuring public opinion. Public opinion polling was first developed by a young man named George Gallup, who did some polling for his mother-in-law, a longshot candidate for secretary of state in Iowa in 1932. With the Democratic landslide of that year, Gallup's mother-in-law won a stunning victory, thereby further stimulating his interest in politics. From that little acorn the mighty oak of public opinion polling has grown. The firm that Gallup founded spread throughout the democratic world, and in some languages, a *Gallup* is actually the word used for an opinion poll.[17]

It would be prohibitively expensive to ask every citizen his or her opinion on a whole range of issues. Instead, polls rely on a **sample** of the population—a relatively small proportion of people who are chosen as representative of the whole. Herbert Asher draws an analogy to a doctor's blood test to illustrate the principle of sampling.[18] Your doctor doesn't need to drain a gallon of blood from you to determine whether you have mononucleosis, AIDS, or any other disease. Rather, a small sample of blood will reveal its properties.

In public opinion polling a sample of about fifteen hundred to two thousand people can faithfully represent the "universe" of potential voters. The key to the accuracy of opinion polls is the technique of **random sampling,** which operates on the principle that everyone should have an equal probability of being selected. Your chance of being asked to be in the poll should therefore be as good as that of anyone else—rich or poor, black or white, young or old, male or female. If the sample is randomly drawn, about 12 percent of those interviewed will be black, slightly over 50 percent female, and so forth, matching the population as a whole.

Throughout the world, George Gallup's name is synonymous with public opinion polling.

---

[17]Jean M. Converse, *Survey Research in the United States: Roots and Emergence, 1890–1960* (Berkeley, Calif.: University of California Press, 1987), 116. Converse's work is the definitive study on the origins of public-opinion sampling.

[18]Herbert Asher, *Polling and the Public: What Every Citizen Should Know* (Washington, D.C.: Congressional Quarterly, 1988), 59.

"A feeling of rejection and exclusion from the affairs of the day is quite common among those of us never sought out by a poll taker."

It should be kept in mind that the science of polling involves estimation; a sample can only represent the population with a certain degree of confidence. The level of confidence is known as the **sampling error,** which depends on the size of the sample. The more people interviewed in a poll, the more confident one can be of the results. A typical poll of about fifteen hundred to two thousand respondents has a sampling error of ± 3 percent. What this means is that 95 percent of the time the poll results are within 3 percent of what the entire population thinks. If 60 percent of the sample say they approve of the job the president is doing, one can be virtually certain that the true figure is between 57 and 63 percent. There is always a certain amount of risk involved. About 5 percent of the time, a sample will produce results far off the mark, but the odds are definitely in favor of the pollsters.

In order to be within the margin of error, proper sampling techniques must be followed. In perhaps the most infamous survey ever, a 1936 *Literary Digest* poll underestimated the vote for President Franklin Roosevelt by 19 percent, erroneously predicting a big victory for Republican Alf Landon. The well-established magazine suddenly became a laughingstock and soon went out of business. While the number of responses the magazine obtained for its poll was a staggering 2,376,000, their methods were badly flawed. Trying to reach as many people as possible, they drew names from the biggest lists they could find—telephone books and motor-vehicle records. In the midst of the Great Depression the people on these lists were above the average income level (only 40 percent had telephones then; fewer still owned cars), and thus more likely to vote Republican. The moral of the story is this: Accurate representation, not the number of responses, is the most important feature of a public opinion survey. Indeed, as techniques have advanced over the last fifty years typical sample sizes have been getting smaller, not larger. As can be seen in "The People Speak: Impressions about the Accuracies of Polls," the public's confidence in them has risen substantially.

The newest computer and telephone technology has made surveying less expensive and more commonplace. Until recently, pollsters needed a national network of interviewers to traipse door-to-door in their localities with a clipboard of questions. Now most polling is done on the telephone with samples selected through **random digit dialing.** Calls are placed to phone numbers within randomly chosen exchanges (for example, 512-471-xxxx) around the country. In this manner, both listed and unlisted numbers will be reached at a cost of about one-fifth that of person-to-person interviewing. There are a couple disadvantages, however. Seven percent of the population does not have a phone, and people are somewhat less willing to participate over the telephone than in person—it is easier to hang up than to slam the door in someone's face. These are small tradeoffs for political candidates running for minor offices, for whom telephone polls are the only method they can afford.

From its modest beginning with George Gallup's 1932 polls for his mother-in-law in Iowa, polling has become a big business worldwide. Public opinion polling is one of those American innovations, like soft drinks and fast-food restaurants, that has spread throughout the world—even to the Soviet Union. From Manhattan to Moscow, from Tulsa to Tokyo, people apparently want to know what other people think.

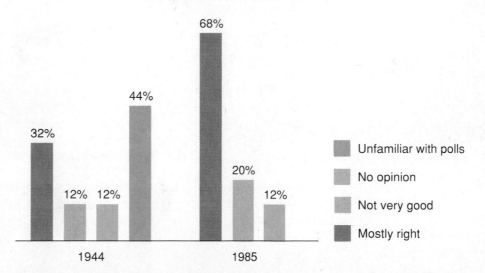

The People Speak | Impressions about the Accuracy of Polls

What is your general impression of how well [the public opinion polls] do?

- 1944: Unfamiliar with polls 32%, No opinion 12%, Not very good 12%, Mostly right 44%
- 1985: No opinion 20%, Not very good 12%, Mostly right 68%

Legend:
- Unfamiliar with polls
- No opinion
- Not very good
- Mostly right

Polls ask people about virtually everything, even about how well polls themselves work. Comparing data from the 1940s to the 1980s, one can see that Americans have become more familiar with, as well as more convinced by, public opinion polling.

Source: The question as worded is taken directly from Gallup Poll data, as reported in Barry Sussman, *What Americans Really Think* (New York: Pantheon, 1988), 99.

The Role of Polls in American Democracy

Polls help political candidates distinguish which way people are leaning. Supporters of polling insist that it is a tool for democracy. With it, they say, policymakers can keep in touch with changing opinions on the issues. No longer do politicians have to wait until the next election to see if the public approves or disapproves of the government's course. If the poll results suddenly turn, government officials can make corresponding midcourse corrections.

Critics of polling, by contrast, think it makes politicians more concerned with following than leading. Polls might have told the constitutional convention delegates that the Constitution was unpopular, or Jefferson that people did not want the Louisiana Purchase. Certainly they would have told William Seward not to buy Alaska (known widely at the time as "Seward's Folly"). Polls may thus discourage bold leadership, like that of Winston Churchill, who once said:

> Nothing is more dangerous than to live in the temperamental atmosphere of a Gallup poll, always taking one's pulse and taking one's temperature.... There is only one duty, only one safe course, and that is to try to be right and not to fear to do or say what you believe.[19]

Political scientist Benjamin Ginsberg has even argued that polls weaken democracy.[20] Polls, he says, permit government to think that it has taken public opinion into account when only passive, often ill-informed opinions have been counted. Polls substitute passive attitudes for active expression of opinion. Voting, letter writing, and other political behaviors take work. Responding to a polltaker is a lazy way indeed to claim that "my voice has been heard."

Polls can also weaken democracy by distorting the election process. They can create both "bandwagon" and "underdog" effects.[21] Although only 2 percent of people in a 1988 *New York Times* poll claimed that poll results had influenced them, 26 percent said they thought others had been influenced (showing that Americans feel "It's always the other guy who's susceptible"). Beyond this, polls play to the media's interest in the horse race, that is, who's hot and who's not. The 1988 presidential campaign saw the issues sometimes drowned out by a steady flood of poll results which technology now makes possible. In the last two months of the 1988 campaign 124 national polls were released, compared to just 44 in the same period in 1980.

Probably the most criticized type of poll is the election-day **exit poll.** For this type of poll, voting places are randomly selected from around the country. Then workers are sent out to these places and told to ask every tenth person how they voted. The results are accumulated toward the end of the day and enable the television networks to project all but very close races before the polls even close. In each of the last three presidential elections this has meant that networks have declared a winner while millions on the West Coast still had hours to vote. Critics have charged that this practice discourages many from

[19]Quoted in Norman M. Bradburn and Seymour Sudman, *Polls and Surveys: Understanding What They Tell Us* (San Francisco: Jossey-Bass, 1988), 39–40.
[20]See Benjamin Ginsberg, *The Captive Public* (New York: Basic Books, 1986).
[21]See Edouard Cloutier, Richard Nadeau and Jean Guay, "Bandwagoning and Underdoging on North-American Free Trade: A Quasi-Experimental Panel Study of Opinion Movement," *International Journal of Public Opinion Research* 1 (Autumn 1989): 242–257.

voting, and thereby affects the outcome of some state and local races. While most voters in western states have been outraged by this practice, careful analysis of survey data shows that few voters have been influenced by exit-poll results.[22]

Finally, perhaps the most pervasive criticism of polling is that by altering the wording of a question pollsters can get pretty much the results they want. Sometimes even subtle changes in question wording can produce dramatic differences. For example, at one point during the Watergate scandal only about 30 percent said they wanted Nixon "impeached and removed from office" whereas this figure doubled when respondents were asked if the president "should be tried and, if found guilty, removed from office." (See "A Question of Ethics: Loaded Poll Questions.")

Because polling sounds scientific with its talk of random samples and margins of error, it is easy to take their results for solid fact. Being an informed consumer of polls requires more than just a nuts-and-bolts knowledge of how they are conducted; you should think about whether the questions are fair and unbiased before making too much of the results. Good, bad, or indifferent, polls are here to stay. The good—or the harm—that polls do depends on how well they are done and how thoughtfully they are interpreted.

What Polls Tell Americans about Political Information

Abraham Lincoln spoke stirringly of the inherent wisdom of the American people: "It is true that you may fool all of the people some of the time; and you

[22]For a good summary of the evidence see Seymour Sudman, "Do Exit Polls Influence Voting Behavior?" *Public Opinion Quarterly* 50 (Fall 1986): 331–39.

A Question of Ethics

Loaded Poll Questions

Richard Morin, polling director of the *Washington Post,* once asked his readers to send him samples of survey questions they felt were clearly biased. Here are some of the worst questions he received:

- "Do you believe that smut peddlers should be protected by the courts and the Congress so they can openly sell pornographic materials to your children?"
- "Does the government have the right to take away our children's right to pray voluntarily in school?"
- "Does America need a constitutional amendment to balance the budget so the liberal Congress won't spend more than it can afford?"
- "Should school systems that receive federal funds be forced to hire known practicing and soliciting homosexual teachers?"

These questions are obviously slanted with terms like "smut peddlers." In addition, they present an argument for only one side of the issue. In each case the question is loaded in the conservative direction, as one might expect a liberal newspaper like the *Post* to make fun of in print, yet liberal organizations often use the same type of biased questions to try to make their point with poll data.

Although the bias in such questions is easy to spot, the ethical problem is that an organization may never report how survey questions were worded. Instead, they'll just say that xx percent opposed the selling of pornography. Thus Morin counsels that, if you are asked to participate in an obviously biased survey, you should take former First Lady Nancy Reagan's advice and "Just say no."

can even fool some of the people all of the time; but you can't fool all of the people all the time." Obviously, Lincoln recognized the complexity of public opinion.

Thomas Jefferson and Alexander Hamilton had very different views about the wisdom of common folk. Jefferson trusted people's good sense and believed that education would enable them to take the tasks of citizenship ever more seriously. Toward that end, he founded the University of Virginia. Hamilton held a contrasting view. His infamous words—"Your people, sir, are a great beast"—do not reflect confidence in people's capacity for self-government.

If there had been polling data in the early days of the American republic, Hamilton would probably have delighted in throwing some of the results in Jefferson's face. If public opinion analysts are agreed about anything, it is that the level of public knowledge about politics is dismally low. For example, in the 1988 National Election Study (conducted by the University of Michigan) a random sample was asked to identify the political office held by some of the most prominent American and world leaders. The results were as follows:

71 percent knew Mikhail Gorbachev was the leader of the Soviet Union

69 percent knew Ted Kennedy was a U.S. senator

60 percent knew Margaret Thatcher was prime minister of Great Britain

39 percent knew George Shultz was secretary of state

37 percent knew Yasser Arafat was the leader of the PLO

14 percent knew Jim Wright was Speaker of the House

4 percent knew William Rehnquist was chief justice of the Supreme Court

All told, the average respondent was able to get only three out of seven right. Less than 10 percent could identify six out of seven.

No amount of Jeffersonian faith in the wisdom of the common people can erase the fact that Americans are not very well informed about politics. Just 30 percent of the public can name both their senators, much less say how these senators generally vote. Asking most people to explain their opinion on affirmative action, MX missiles, or fiscal policy often elicits blank looks. When trouble flares in a far-off country, polls regularly find that people have no idea where that country is. For example, in 1981, only 35 percent knew the location of El Salvador, despite the fact that it was constantly in the news. (Many thought it was in the Middle East, a well-known trouble spot.) Surveys show that citizens around the globe lack a basic awareness of the world around them. (See "America in Perspective: Citizens of the World Show Little Knowledge of Geography.")

As Lance Bennett points out, these findings provide "a source of almost bitter humor in light of what the polls tell us about public information on other subjects."[23] He notes that more people know their astrological sign (76 percent) than know the name of their representative in the House. Slogans from TV commercials are better recognized than famous political figures. (For example, 82 percent of the public could identify the toilet tissue that completes the slogan "Please don't squeeze the . . .," and 79 percent knew which upset-stomach remedy used the jingle "Plop, plop, fizz, fizz. Oh, what a relief it is.")

How can Americans, who live in the most information-rich society in the world, be so ill-informed about politics? Some blame the schools. E. D. Hirsch,

[23]W. Lance Bennett, *Public Opinion and American Politics* (New York: Harcourt Brace Jovanovich, 1980), 44.

Citizens of the World Show Little Knowledge of Geography

In the spring of 1988 eleven hundred people in nine nations were asked to identify sixteen places on the following world map. Later, fifteen hundred Soviets were asked the same questions. The average citizen in the United States could identify barely more than half. Believe it or not, 14 percent of Americans could not even find their own country on the map. Despite years of fighting in Vietnam, 68 percent could not locate this Southeast Asian country. Such lack of basic geographic knowledge is quite common throughout the world. Here is the average score for each of the ten countries in which the test was administered:

COUNTRY	AVERAGE SCORE
Sweden	11.6
West Germany	11.2
Japan	9.7
France	9.3
Canada	9.2

COUNTRY	AVERAGE SCORE
United States	8.6
Great Britain	8.5
Italy	7.6
Mexico	7.4
Soviet Union	7.4

How would you do? To take the test yourself, match the numbers on the map to the places listed.

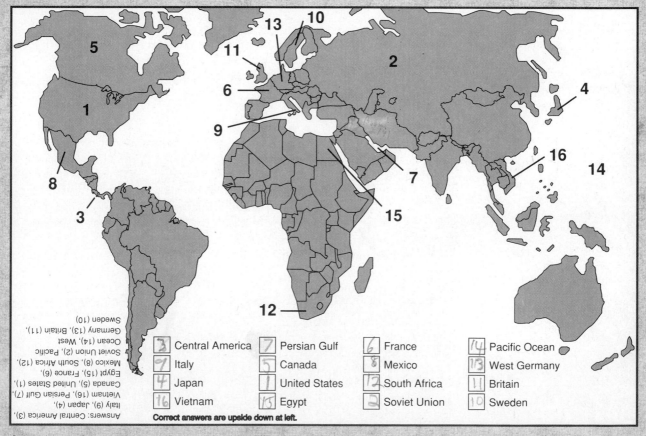

Answers: Central America (3), Italy (9), Japan (4), Vietnam (16), Persian Gulf (7), Canada (5), United States (1), Egypt (15), France (6), Mexico (8), South Africa (12), Soviet Union (2), Pacific Ocean (14), West Germany (13), Britain (11), Sweden (10)

3 Central America	7 Persian Gulf	6 France	14 Pacific Ocean
9 Italy	5 Canada	8 Mexico	13 West Germany
4 Japan	1 United States	12 South Africa	11 Britain
16 Vietnam	15 Egypt	2 Soviet Union	10 Sweden

Correct answers are upside down at left.

Source: Warren E. Leary, "Two Superpowers' Citizens Do Badly in Geography," *New York Times*, November 9, 1989, A6.

Drawing by Saxon; © 1984 The New Yorker Magazine, Inc.

"Glad you brought that up, Jim. The latest research on polls has turned up some interesting variables. It turns out, for example, that people will tell you any old thing that pops into their heads."

Jr., criticizes the schools for a failure to teach "cultural literacy."[24] People, he says, often lack the basic contextual knowledge—where Africa is, what the Vietnam War was about, and so forth—necessary to understand and use the information they receive from the news media or from listening to political candidates. Indeed, it has been found that increased levels of education over the last four decades have scarcely raised public knowledge about politics.[25] Despite the apparent glut of information provided by the media, Americans do not remember much about what they "learned" through the media. Doris Graber puts it bluntly: "By and large . . . people do not seem to gain much specific information from the media."[26] (Of course, there are many critics who say that the media fails to provide much meaningful information, a topic which will be discussed in Chapter 11.)

The "paradox of mass politics," says Russell Neuman, is that the American political system works as well as it does given the discomforting lack of public

[24]E.D. Hirsch, Jr., *Cultural Literacy* (Boston: Houghton Mifflin, 1986).

[25]Michael X. Delli Carpini and Scott Keeter, "Political Knowledge of the U.S. Public: Results from a National Survey" (Paper presented at the 1989 annual meeting of the American Association for Public Opinion Research).

[26]Doris Graber, *Mass Media and American Politics,* 2nd ed. (Washington, D.C.: Congressional Quarterly Press, 1984), 157.

knowledge about politics.[27] Part of the reason for this phenomenon is that people may not know the ins and outs of policy questions or the actors on the political stage, but they know what basic values they want upheld. When these values are violated, the sleeping giant of public opinion may be stirred to action. Examining these values is thus of great importance.

WHAT AMERICANS VALUE: POLITICAL IDEOLOGIES

A coherent set of values and beliefs about public policy is a **political ideology.**[28] An ideology is much more than a collection of "gut reactions"; it is a set of coherent and consistent policy preferences. Liberal ideology, for example, supports a strong central government that sets policies to promote equality. Conservative ideology, in contrast, supports a small, less activist government that gives freer reign to the private sector (see Table 6.2).

Do People Think in Ideological Terms?

The authors of the classic study *The American Voter* first looked carefully at the ideological sophistication of the American electorate in the 1950s.[29] They divided the public into four groups, according to ideological sophistication. Their portrait of the American electorate was not a flattering one. Only 12 percent of the people showed evidence of thinking in ideological terms, and thus were classified as *ideologues.* These people could connect their opinions and beliefs with broad policy positions taken by parties or candidates. They might say, for example, that they liked the Democrats because they were more liberal or the Republicans because they favored a smaller government. Forty-two percent of Americans were called *group benefits voters.* These people thought of politics mainly by the groups they liked or disliked (for example, "Republicans support small businessmen like me" or "Democrats are the party of the working man"). Twenty-four percent of the population were *nature of the times* voters. Their handle on politics was limited to whether the times seemed good or bad to them; they might vaguely link the party in power with the country's fortune or misfortune. Finally, 22 percent of the voters were devoid of any ideological or issue content in their political evaluations. They were called the *no issue content* group. Most of them simply voted routinely for a party or judged the candidates solely by their personalities. Overall, at least during the 1950s, Americans seemed to care little about the differences between liberal and conservative politics.

There has been much debate about whether this portrayal accurately characterizes the public today. Nie, Verba, and Petrocik took a look at the changing American voter from 1956 to 1972,[30] and argued that voters were more sophisticated in the 1970s than in the 1950s. Others, though, have concluded that

[27]W. Russell Neuman, *The Paradox of Mass Politics: Knowledge and Opinion in the American Electorate* (Cambridge, Mass.: Harvard University Press, 1986).

[28]For a more extended definition, see Robert E. Lane, *Political Ideology* (New York: Free Press, 1962), 13-16.

[29]Angus Campbell et al., *The American Voter* (New York: John Wiley, 1960), chap. 10.

[30]Norman H. Nie, Sidney Verba, and John R. Petrocik, *The Changing American Voter* (Cambridge, Mass.: Harvard University Press, 1976), chap. 7.

Table 6.2 How to Tell a Liberal from a Conservative

Liberal and *conservative*—those labels are thrown around in American politics as though everyone knows what they mean. Most Americans do know that George Bush isn't a liberal and that Edward Kennedy isn't a conservative, and no one could confuse Jesse Helms, the conservative senator from North Carolina, with Jesse Jackson. Here are some of the political beliefs likely to be preferred by liberals and conservatives. This table, to be sure, is oversimplifed. At the same time, it can serve as a rough map to distinguish between liberals and conservatives.

ON FOREIGN POLICY:	LIBERALS	CONSERVATIVES
Military spending	Believe we should probably spend less	Believe we should probably spend more
Authoritarian governments in developing nations	Support "human rights" in all nations	Think we may have to tolerate anti-Communist governments, even if they are authoritarian
The United Nations	View it as positive	View it with suspicion
ON SOCIAL POLICY:		
Abortion	Support "freedom of choice"	Support "right to life"
School prayer	Are opposed	Are supportive
Affirmative action	Favor	Oppose
ON ECONOMIC POLICY:		
Role of the government	View government as a regulator in the public interest	Favor free-market solutions
Taxes	Want to tax the rich more	Want to keep taxes low
Spending	Want to spend more on the poor	Want to keep spending low
ON CRIME:		
How to cut crime	Believe we should solve the problems that cause crime	Believe we should stop coddling criminals
Defendants' rights	Believe we should guard them carefully	Believe we should stop letting criminals hide behind the laws

people only seemed more informed and ideological because the wording of the questions had changed.[31] If the exact same methods are used to update the analysis of *The American Voter* through the 1980s, one finds some increase in the proportion of ideologues, but the overall picture looks much the same (see Table 6.3).

This does not mean that the vast majority of the population does not have a political ideology. Rather, for most people the terms liberal and conservative

[31]See, for example, John L. Sullivan, James E. Pierson, and George E. Marcus, "Ideological Constraint in the Mass Public: A Methodological Critique and Some New Findings," *American Journal of Political Science* 22 (May 1978), 233–49; and Eric R.A.N. Smith, *The Unchanging American Voter* (Berkeley, Calif.: University of California Press, 1989).

Table 6.3 — Levels of Ideological Conceptualization, 1956–1988 (in Percentage)[a]

LEVEL	1956	1960	1964	1968	1972	1976	1980	1984	1988
Ideologues	12	19	27	26	22	21	22	22	18
Group benefits	42	31	27	24	27	26	30	27	36
Nature of the times	24	26	20	29	34	30	31	34	25
No issue content	22	23	26	21	17	24	17	17	21

[a] Tables do not always add up to 100% due to rounding.

Sources: 1952–1984: Herbert B. Asher, *Presidential Elections and American Politics,* 3rd ed. (Chicago: Dorsey, 1988), 111; 1988 data supplied by Kathleen Knight of the University of Houston.

are just not as important as they are for the political elite such as politicians, activists, and the like. Relatively few people have ideologies which organize their political beliefs as clearly as shown in Table 6.2. Thus, the authors of *The American Voter* concluded that to speak of election results as indicating a movement of the public either left (to more liberal policies) or right (to more conservative policies) is a misnomer because most voters do not think in such terms. Furthermore, those that do are actually the least likely to shift from one election to the next.

The American Voter argued persuasively that Eisenhower's two election victories did not represent a shift in the conservative direction during the 1950s. In the 1980s the issue of whether public opinion had undergone a major rightward change was once again raised with the victories of Ronald Reagan—who campaigned vigorously against big government.

Public Attitudes on the Size of Government

An FDR liberal in the 1930s and 1940s, Reagan led what he proclaimed to be a conservative revolution in the 1980s. Central to his ideology was that government had gotten too large over the years. According to Reagan, government was not the solution to society's problems—it was the problem. He called for the government to "get off the backs of the American people."

Reagan's rhetoric about the bloated size of government was reminscent of the 1964 presidential campaign rhetoric of Barry Goldwater, who lost to Lyndon Johnson in a landslide. Indeed, Reagan first made his mark in politics by giving a televised speech on behalf of the embattled Goldwater campaign.[32] While the rhetoric was much the same in 1980, public opinion about the size of government had changed dramatically. In 1964 only 30 percent of the population thought the government was getting too powerful; by 1980 this figure had risen to 50 percent.

For much of the population, however, questions about the size of government have consistently elicited no opinion at all. Indeed, the most recent data

[32]See Barry M. Goldwater with Jack Casserly, *Goldwater* (New York: Doubleday, 1988), 209.

from 1988 show that 47 percent of those interviewed said they had not thought about the question. The question of government power is a complex one, but as *Government in America* will continue to stress, it is one of the key controversies in American politics today. Once again it seems that the public is not nearly as concerned with political issues as would be ideal in a democratic society.

Nor do public opinions on different aspects of the same issue hold together well. Thus, while more people today think the government is too big rather than too small, a plurality has consistently called for more spending on programs like education, health care, aid to big cities, protecting the environment, and fighting crime.[33] Many political scientists have looked at these contradictory findings and concluded that *Americans are ideological conservatives but operational liberals*—meaning that they oppose the idea of big government in principle but favor it in practice.

[33]See the data presented in Richard G. Niemi, John Mueller, and Tom W. Smith, *Trends in Public Opinion: A Compendium of Survey Data* (New York: Greenwood Press, 1989), 77–91.

The People Speak | Public Opinion on the Size of Government

Some people are afraid the government in Washington is getting too powerful for the good of the country and the individual person. Others feel that the government in Washington is not getting too strong. Do you have an opinion on this or not? (If yes) What is your feeling, do you think the government is getting too powerful or do you think the government is not getting too strong?

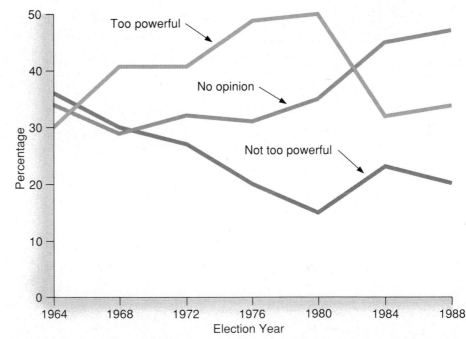

Source: The questions as worded are taken directly from 1964–1988 National Election Studies conducted by the University of Michigan.

Ronald Reagan first became known as an outspoken opponent of big government at the 1964 Republican National Convention. Most Americans seem to agree with Reagan in principle, but in practice support increased government spending and intervention for most domestic programs.

People Liked Reagan but Not His Policies

There was little inconsistency in the political beliefs of Ronald Reagan, however. During his eight years as president, he pressed ahead with a thoroughly conservative agenda that included the following:

- Reduced levels of government spending on programs like social welfare, education, and job training
- Increased defense spending, including funding for the "Star Wars" program to intercept nuclear weapons before they strike
- A tougher stance toward the Soviet Union, which Reagan once called the "Evil Empire"
- Stepped-up American support for groups that claimed to be fighting Communism (such as the Nicaraguan Contras)
- Policies to minimize government regulation of business and let the free market reign
- A 25 percent across-the-board reduction in federal income-tax rates
- Support for a conservative social agenda, including antiabortion legislation and support for school prayer and stronger law enforcement
- The appointment of Supreme Court justices to help achieve conservative political and social goals

With Reagan's landslide reelection victory in 1984 some political observers felt that a conservative wildfire had swept the country. Democratic leaders (such as former Democratic Party Chairman Robert Strauss) warned party members not to be left out on a liberal limb. "Don't be the party of spending and more spending," they cautioned fellow Democrats.

Despite Reagan's victories a common theme in the press throughout the 1980s was that people liked Reagan but not his policies. Indeed, the 1984 National Election Study revealed that although Reagan had the advantage of high approval ratings, on the major policy questions more people felt closer to the stand of Democratic candidate Walter Mondale. By fairly substantial margins, those with opinions disagreed with Reagan's willingness to commit military help to Central America and his desire to spend more on defense. By somewhat smaller margins, people saw Reagan as wanting to cut government services too deeply, not providing enough aid to minorities and women, and being too tough with the Soviet Union.[34]

With the exception of a rise in support for military spending during the 1980 campaign, public opinion specialists have been unable to document any shift toward conservative attitudes during the 1980s. As Ferguson and Rogers concluded, "If American public opinion drifted anywhere over Reagan's first term, it was toward the left, not the right, just the opposite of the turn in public policy."[35] Asked to assess Reagan's time in office, the 1988 electorate was evenly split on the wisdom of defense increases, and generally unaware and unsupportive of domestic cuts.[36]

If so many people disagreed with Reagan, why was he such a popular president, and why has George Bush been able to follow in his footsteps? The answer is simply that many swing voters, those which *The American Voter*

[34]Martin P. Wattenberg, "The Hollow Realignment: Partisan Change in a Candidate-Centered Era," *Public Opinion Quarterly* 51 (Spring 1987): 58–74.

[35]Thomas Ferguson and Joel Rogers, *Right Turn* (New York: Hill & Wang, 1986), 28.

[36]Martin P. Wattenberg, *The Rise of Candidate-Centered Politics: Presidential Elections of the 1980s.* (Cambridge, Mass.: Harvard University Press, forthcoming 1991).

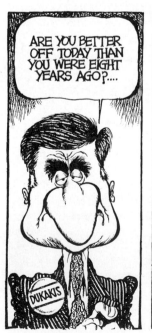

classified as *nature of the times voters,* care more about results than ideology.[37] The 1980 election was more about voting Carter out of office than voting Reagan into it. In 1984 and 1988 the Republicans had years of relative peace and prosperity on their side, and this was the key to their victories.

In sum, conservatives may have become more visible participants in the 1980s, but they did not necessarily become more numerous. Just how they—and other Americans—participate in politics is the topic of the next section.

HOW AMERICANS PARTICIPATE IN POLITICS

In politics, like many other aspects of life, the squeaky wheel gets the grease. The way citizens "squeak" in politics is to participate. Americans have many avenues of political participation open to them.

- Mrs. Jones of Iowa City goes to a neighbor's living room to attend her local precinct's presidential caucus.

- An interest group testifies before a Senate committee to express its view that warning labels should be put on record albums that contain vulgar language.

- Protestors against the massacre in Tiananmen Square gather outside the Chinese embassy in Washington to condemn the Chinese government.

- Parents in Alabama file a lawsuit to oppose textbooks that, in their opinion, promote "secular humanism."

- Mr. Smith, a Social Security recipient, writes to his senator to express his concern about a possible cut in his cost-of-living benefits.

- Ninety million people vote in a presidential election.

All of these activities are types of political participation. **Political participation** encompasses the many activities used by citizens to influence the selection of political leaders or the policies they pursue.[38] Participation can be overt or subtle. The mass protests throughout Eastern Europe in the fall of 1989 were an avalanche of political participation, yet quietly writing a letter to your congressperson is also participating. Political participation can be violent or peaceful, organized or individual, casual or consuming.

Generally, the United States has a participatory political culture. Citizens express pride in their nation: 87 percent say they are very proud to be Americans.[39] Nevertheless, barely 50 percent of adult Americans voted in the presidential election of 1988 and only about 35 percent usually turn out for congressional elections. At the local level the situation is even worse. In 1989 Mayor Bradley of Los Angeles was reelected with a turnout of just 23 percent, and in New York City a school board election drew a meager 6 percent to the polls. (For more on voter turnout and why it is so low, see Chapter 9.)

[37]This theory is carefully developed in Morris P. Fiorina, *Retrospective Voting in Presidential Elections* (New Haven, Conn.: Yale University Press, 1981).

[38]This definition is a close paraphrase of one in Sidney Verba and Norman H. Nie, *Participation in America* (New York: Harper & Row, 1972), 2.

[39]Russell J. Dalton, *Citizen Politics in Western Democracies* (Chatham, N.J.: Chatham House, 1988), 237.

Political participation can be as benign as voting or stuffing envelopes for a candidate, or as dramatic as a political protest. Here demonstrators in San Francisco erect their own "Goddess of Democracy" to show their support for the pro-democracy movement in China.

Conventional Participation

Although the line is hard to draw, political scientists generally distinguish between two broad types of participation: conventional and unconventional. Conventional participation includes many widely accepted modes of influencing government: voting, trying to persuade others, ringing doorbells, running for office, and so on. In contrast, unconventional participation includes activities that are often dramatic, such as protesting, civil disobedience, and even violence.

For a few, politics is their lifeblood; they run for office, work regularly in politics, and live for the next election. For others, it is mere drudgery, and for still others, a civic obligation. The number of Americans for whom political activity is an important part of their everyday life is miniscule, numbering at most in the tens of thousands. To these people, policy questions are as familiar as slogans on TV commercials are to the average citizen. They are the political elites, the gladiators of political conflict: the activists, the party leaders, the interest-group leaders, the judges, and the members of Congress. (Part Three will discuss the political elite in detail.)

In a classic study of American political participation conducted by Sidney Verba and Norman H. Nie, a sample of Americans was asked about their role in twelve kinds of political activities. Included were voting in presidential and local elections, contacting a government official, working in a campaign, and joining political groups. The majority of Americans participated in only one of the twelve activities—voting in presidential elections. Less than one-fifth had ever contacted a public official, given money to a candidate or party, or helped form a political group or organization.[40]

[40]Verba and Nie, *Participation in America*, 31.

Participation in politics, like other tasks, reflects specialization and division of labor. Just as people in an organization have different specialities, so do citizens in a country. Voting is a common denominator among most political activists, but other kinds of participation attract different clusters of people. In Verba and Nie's classification of American political participants, 22 percent were inactive and 11 percent were complete activists. Between these groups were people who specialized as contacters, communalists, or campaigners. (For a discussion of these participant types, see Figure 6.3.)

Protest as Participation

Unconventional forms of political participation are missing from Verba and Nie's list of activities. From the Boston Tea Party to burning draft cards, Americans have engaged in countless political protests. **Protest** is a form of political participation designed to achieve policy change through dramatic and unconventional tactics.[41] The media's willingness to cover the unusual can make protest worthwhile, drawing attention to a point of view that many Americans might never encounter. Indeed, protests today are often orchestrated to provide television cameras with vivid images. Demonstration coordinators steer participants to prearranged staging areas and provide facilities for press coverage.

[41]See a more extended definition in Michael Lipsky, *Protest in City Politics* (Chicago: Rand McNally, 1970), 2.

Figure 6.3 Participators in American Politics: Six Types

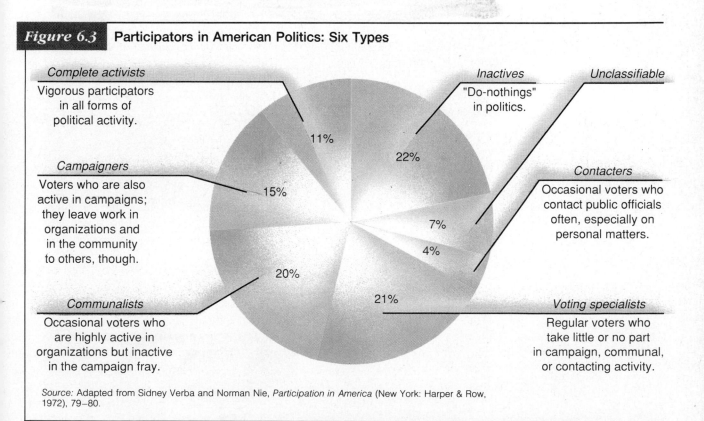

Complete activists
Vigorous participators in all forms of political activity. — 11%

Campaigners
Voters who are also active in campaigns; they leave work in organizations and in the community to others, though. — 15%

Communalists
Occasional voters who are highly active in organizations but inactive in the campaign fray. — 20%

Inactives
"Do-nothings" in politics. — 22%

Unclassifiable — 7%

Contacters
Occasional voters who contact public officials often, especially on personal matters. — 4%

Voting specialists
Regular voters who take little or no part in campaign, communal, or contacting activity. — 21%

Source: Adapted from Sidney Verba and Norman Nie, *Participation in America* (New York: Harper & Row, 1972), 79–80.

Throughout American history, individuals and groups have sometimes used **civil disobedience,** that is, they have consciously broken a law that they thought was unjust. In the 1840s Henry David Thoreau refused to pay his taxes, in order to protest against the Mexican War, and went to jail (he stayed overnight because his friend Ralph Waldo Emerson paid the taxes). Influenced by India's Mahatma Gandhi, the Reverend Martin Luther King, Jr., won a Nobel Peace Prize for his civil disobedience against segregationist law in the 1950s and 1960s. His "Letter from a Birmingham Jail" is a classic defense of civil disobedience.[42]

Sometimes political participation can be violent. The history of violence in American politics is a long one—not surprising, perhaps, for a nation born in rebellion. The turbulent 1960s included many outbreaks of violence. African-American neighborhoods in American cities were torn by riots.[43] College campuses were sometimes turned into battle zones as protestors against the Vietnam War fought police and national guard units. At Kent State, Jackson State, Cornell, Columbia, and elsewhere, peaceful demonstrations turned violent, and many were hurt (or, at Kent State and Jackson State, killed). Although supported by few people, throughout American history violence has been a means of pressuring the government to change its policies.

Class, Inequality, and Participation

Participation is very unequal in American political life. Virtually every study of political participation ever conducted has come to the conclusion that "citizens of higher social economic status participate more in politics. This generalization . . . holds true whether one uses level of education, income, or occupation

[42]This letter can be found in Juan Williams, *Eyes on the Prize: America's Civil Rights Years, 1954–1965* (New York: Viking, 1987), 187–89.

[43]On the violence of the 1960s, see James Button, *Black Violence* (Princeton, N.J.: Princeton University Press, 1978).

Perhaps the most well-known image of American political violence from the late-1960s-early-1970s period: a student lies dead on the Kent State campus, one of four killed when members of the Ohio National Guard opened fire on anti-Vietnam War demonstrators.

as the measure of social status."[44] Theorists who believe that America is ruled by a small, wealthy elite make much of this fact to support their point of view.

As one might expect from their generally poor education and income levels, minority groups like Hispanics and African Americans are also below average in terms of political participation. The differences are no longer enormous, however. For African Americans the participation gap in 1988 was a mere 5 percent below the national average; for Hispanics it was 11 percent.[45] One reason for this smaller-than-expected participation gap is that minorities feel a group consciousness that gives them an extra incentive to vote. In fact, when blacks, Hispanics, and whites of equal incomes and educations are compared, it is the minorities that participate more in politics.[46] In other words, a poor Hispanic or African American is more likely to participate than a poor white. The reason the political participation rate of these minority groups is below average is because they are so much worse off in terms of socioeconomic status.

People who believe in democracy should be concerned not only about inequalities in participation, but also about the low numbers of participants. Those who participate are easy to listen to; nonparticipants are easy to ignore. In a democracy, citizenship carries the promise—and the responsibility—of self-government.

DEMOCRACY, PUBLIC OPINION, AND POLITICAL ACTION

Throughout much of the communist world in 1989 people protested for democracy. Many said they wanted their political system to be just like America's, even though they had only a vague idea of how American democracy works. As this chapter has shown, there are many limits on the role Americans play in their political system. The average person, here and elsewhere, is not very well informed about political issues. Expecting the public to make decisions on intricate questions of public policy is clearly asking too much.

American democracy is representative rather than direct. As *The American Voter* stated many years ago, "The public's explicit task is to decide not what government shall do but rather *who shall decide* what government shall do."[47] When those under communist rule protested for democracy, what they most wanted was the right to have a say in choosing their leaders. Americans can— and often do—take for granted the opportunity to replace our leaders at the next election. Protest is thus directed at making the government listen to specific demands, not overthrowing it. In this sense it can be said that American citizens have become well socialized to democracy.

If the public's task in democracy is to choose who is to lead, it must still be asked whether it can do so wisely. If people in fact know little about where the candidates stand on the issues, how can they make rational choices? Many people voted for Reagan even though they disagreed with his policies. In doing

[44]Verba and Nie, *Participation in America,* 125.

[45]"Voting and Registration in the Election of November 1988," Series P-20, No. 435 (Washington, D.C.: Government Printing Office, advance report).

[46]On African-Americans, see Verba and Nie, *Participation in America,* chap. 10; on Hispanics, see Wolfinger and Rosenstone, *Who Votes?,* 92.

[47]Campbell et al., *The American Voter,* 541.

so, most were choosing performance criteria over policy criteria. As Morris Fiorina has written, citizens typically have one hard bit of data to go on: "They know what life has been like during the incumbent's administration. They need *not* know the precise economic or foreign policies of the incumbent administration in order to see or feel the results of those policies."[48] Thus, even if they are only voting according to the nature of the times, their voices are clearly being heard—holding presidents accountable for their actions.

SUMMARY

American society is ethnically varied. The ethnic makeup of America is changing to a minority majority, and Americans are moving towards warmer parts of the country and growing older as a society. All of these changes have policy consequences. One way of knowing the American people is through demography, the science of population changes. 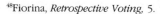 Demography, it is often said, is destiny.

Another way to know the American people is through examination of public opinion in the United States. What Americans believe—and believe they know—is public opinion, the distribution of people's beliefs about politics and policy issues. Polling is one important way to study public opinion; polls give us a fairly accurate gauge of public opinion on issues, products, and personalities. On the positive side for democracy, polls help keep political leaders in touch with the feelings of their constituents. On the minus side, though, they help politicians "play to the crowds" instead of providing leadership.

Polls have revealed again and again that the average American has a low level of political knowledge. Far more Americans know their astrological sign

[48]Fiorina, *Retrospective Voting,* 5.

Most Americans participate in the political process in a limited way. But faced with inequality or injustice, whether in the coal fields of Pennsylvania or at segregated lunch counters in the South, Americans have often responded with strong and effective protest.

than know the names of their representatives in Congress. Ideological thinking is not widespread in the American public, nor are people necessarily consistent in their attitudes. Often they are conservative in principle but liberal in practice—that is, they are against big government but in favor of more spending on a wide variety of programs. Indeed, many people apparently voted for Reagan even though they disliked his policies.

Acting on one's opinions is political participation. While Americans live in a participatory culture, their actual level of participation is unspectacular. In this country participation is a class-biased activity, with certain groups participating more than others. Those who suffer the most inequality sometimes resort to protest as a form of participation. Perhaps the best indicator of how well-socialized Americans are to democracy is that protest typically is aimed at getting the attention of the government, not overthrowing it.

KEY TERMS

demography	political socialization	exit poll
census	public opinion	political ideology
melting pot	sample	political participation
minority majority	random sampling	protest
Simpson-Mazzoli Act	sampling error	civil disobedience
reapportionment	random digit dialing	

FOR FURTHER READING

Asher, Herbert. *Polling and the Public: What Every Citizen Should Know.* Washington, D.C.: Congressional Quarterly Press, 1988. A highly readable introduction to the perils and possibilities of polling and surveys.

Campbell, Angus et al. *The American Voter.* New York: John Wiley, 1960. The classic study of the American voter, based upon data from the 1950s.

Conway, M. Margaret. *Political Participation,* 2nd ed. Washington, D.C.: Congressional Quarterly Press, 1990. An excellent text on political participation.

Ferguson, Thomas, and Joel Rogers. *Right Turn.* New York: Hill and Wang, 1986. Contrary to the conservatives' dreams, America is not becoming more conservative in its political thinking, claim Ferguson and Rogers.

Ginsberg, Benjamin. *The Captive Public.* New York: Basic Books, 1986. A critical view of the rise of polling in America.

Jennings, M. Kent and Richard G. Niemi. *Generations and Politics: A Panel Study of Young Adults and Their Parents.* Princeton, N.J.: Princeton University Press, 1981. A highly influential study of the class of 1965, their parents, and how both generations changed over the course of eight years.

Niemi, Richard G., John Mueller, and Tom W. Smith. *Trends in Public Opinion: A Compendium of Survey Data.* New York: Greenwood Press, 1989. An excellent source of data over time on a wide range of public opinion questions.

Neuman, W. Russell. *The Paradox of Mass Politics: Knowledge and Opinion in the American Electorate.* Cambridge, Mass.: Harvard University Press, 1986. Neuman addresses the question of how the system works as well as it does given the low level of public information about politics.

Verba, Sidney, and Norman H. Nie. *Participation in America.* New York: Harper & Row, 1972. An important study of American political participation.

7

*P*OLITICAL PARTIES

An anonymous wit once drew up the following list detailing the main differences between Democrats and Republicans:

Democrats buy most of the books that have been banned somewhere. Republicans form censorship committees and read them as a group.

Republicans consume three-fourths of all the rutabaga produced in this country. The remainder is thrown out.

Republicans usually wear hats and almost always clean their paint brushes.

Democrats give their worn-out clothes to those less fortunate. Republicans wear theirs.

Democrats name their children after currently popular sports figures, politicians, and entertainers. Republican children are named after their parents or grandparents, according to where the most money is.

Democrats keep trying to cut down on smoking but are not successful. Neither are Republicans.

Republicans tend to keep their shades drawn, although there is seldom any reason why they should. Democrats ought to, but don't.

Republicans study the financial pages of the newspaper. Democrats put them in the bottom of the bird cage.

Most of the stuff you see alongside the road has been thrown out of car windows by Democrats.

Republicans raise dahlias, Dalmations, and eyebrows. Democrats raise Airedales, kids, and taxes.

Democrats eat the fish they catch. Republicans hang them on the wall.

Republican boys date Democratic girls. They plan to marry Republican girls but feel they're entitled to a little fun first.

Democrats make up plans and then do something else. Republicans follow the plans their grandfathers made.

Republicans sleep in twin beds—some even in separate rooms. That is why there are more Democrats.

While offered only in jest, the list illuminates a couple of the major differences between the parties that have existed for over half a century—Democrats tend to have lower incomes than Republicans and are more likely to support social welfare spending. It is not always so easy to distinguish between the parties, however, given that each rationally chooses to stay near the center of public opinion. As this chapter will explore, the choice that does exist between the two parties is crucial to the workings of government in America.

*D*espite the fact that the framers of the U.S. Constitution did not approve of political parties, parties have contributed greatly to American democracy. In one of the most frequently—and rightly—quoted observations about American politics, E. E. Schattschneider said that "political parties created democracy . . . and democracy is unthinkable save in terms of the parties."[1] Political scientists and politicians alike believe that a strong party system is desirable and bemoan the weakening of the parties in recent decades. As President Bush recently told a meeting of college interns in Washington, "as the strength of our parties erodes, so does the strength of our political system."[2]

[1]E. E. Schattschneider, *Party Government* (New York: Farrar and Rinehart, 1942), 1.
[2]James Gerstenzang, "Bush Campaign Reforms Seek Curbs on PACs," *Los Angeles Times,* June 30, 1989, 23.

The ups and downs of the two major parties are one of the most important elements in American politics. **Party competition** is the battle between Democrats and Republicans for the control of public offices. Without this competition there would be no choice, and without choice there would be no democracy. Americans have had a choice between two major political parties since the early 1800s, and this two-party system remains intact almost two centuries later.

THE MEANING OF PARTY

William N. Chambers once remarked that "if the beginning of wisdom is to call things by their right name, some attention is due to what we mean by a political party."[3] Almost all definitions of political parties have one thing in common: Parties try to win elections. This is their core function and the key to their definition. Interest groups do not nominate candidates for office though they may try to influence elections. For example, no one has ever been elected to Congress as the nominee of the National Rifle Association, though many have received the NRA's endorsement. Thus, Anthony Downs defined a **political party** as a "team of men [and women] seeking to control the governing apparatus by gaining office in a duly constituted election."[4]

The word *team* is the slippery part of this definition. Party teams may not be so well disciplined and single-minded as teams fielded by fine football coaches. Party teams are often running every which way (sometimes toward the opposition's goal line) and are difficult to lead. In football, it is sometimes hard to tell the players without a scorecard; in American politics, it is sometimes hard to tell the players even *with* a scorecard. Party leaders often disagree about policy, and between elections the parties seem to all but disappear. So who are the members of these teams? A widely adopted way of thinking about parties in political science is as "three-headed political giants." The three heads are (1) the party-in-the-electorate, (2) the party as an organization, and (3) the party-in-government.[5]

By far the largest component of an American party is the *party-in-the-electorate*. Unlike many European political parties, American parties do not require dues or membership cards to distinguish members from nonmembers. Americans may register as Democrats, Republicans, or whatever, but registration is not legally binding and is easily changed. To be a member of a party, you need only claim to be a member. If you call yourself a Democrat, you are one—even if you never talk to a party official, never work in a campaign, and often vote for Republicans.

The *party as an organization* has a national office, a full-time staff, rules and bylaws, and budgets. In addition to a national office, each party maintains state and local headquarters. The party organization includes precinct leaders, county chairpersons, state chairpersons, state delegates to the national committee, and officials in the party's Washington office. These are the people who

[3]William N. Chambers, "Party Development and the American Mainstream," in William N. Chambers and Walter Dean Burnham, *The American Party Systems,* 2nd ed. (New York: Oxford University Press, 1967), 5.

[4]Anthony Downs, *An Economic Theory of Democracy* (New York: Harper & Row, 1957).

[5]Frank J. Sorauf and Paul Allen Beck, *Party Politics in America,* 6th ed. (Boston: Scott, Foresman/Little, Brown, 1988), 10.

Parties serve as key linkage institutions, translating citizens' preferences into governmental policy by choosing policymakers and developing policy platforms. To translate preferences into policy, parties must win elections—this is their main task and goal.

keep the party running between elections and make its rules. From the party's national chairperson to its lowliest precinct captain, the party organization pursues electoral victory.

The *party-in-government* consists of elected officials who label themselves as members of the party. Although presidents, members of Congress, governors, and lesser officeholders almost always run for election as Democrats or Republicans, they do not always agree on policy. Presidents and governors may have to wheedle and cajole their own party members into voting for their policies. In the United States it is not uncommon to put personal principle—or ambition—above loyalty to the party's leaders. These leaders are the main spokespersons for the party, however; their words and actions personify the party to millions of Americans. If the party is to translate its promises into policy, the job must be done by the party-in-government.

Because parties are everywhere in American politics—present in the electorate's mind, as an organization, and in government offices—one of their major tasks is to link the people of the United States to their government and its policies.

Tasks of the Parties

The road from public opinion to public policy is long and winding. Masses of people cannot raise their voices to government and indicate their policy preferences in unison. If all 250 million Americans spoke at once, all that would be heard is a roar of demands on government that could not possibly be dealt with. In a large democracy, **linkage institutions** translate inputs from the public into outputs from the policymakers.[6] Linkage institutions sift through all

[6]The term *linkage* is introduced in V. O. Key's classic book, *Public Opinion and American Democracy* (New York: Knopf, 1963), chap. 16.

the issues, identify the most pressing concerns, and put these onto the governmental agenda. In other words, linkage institutions help ensure that public preferences are heard loud and clear. In the United States there are four main linkage institutions: parties, elections, interest groups, and the media.

Kay Lawson writes that "parties are seen, both by the members and by others, as agencies for forging links between citizens and policymakers."[7] Here is a checklist of the tasks parties perform, or should perform, if they are to serve as effective linkage institutions:

1. *Parties pick policymakers*. No one above the local level (and often not even there) gets elected to a public office without winning a party's endorsement. A party's endorsement is called a *nomination*. (The next chapter examines nominations more closely.)

2. *Parties run campaigns*. Through their national, state, and local organizations, parties coordinate political campaigns. However, recent technology has made it easier for candidates to campaign on their own, without the help of the party organization.

3. *Parties give cues to voters*. Most voters have a **party image** of each party, that is, they know (or think they know) what the Republicans and Democrats stand for. Liberal, conservative, probusiness, antiminorities—these are some of the elements of each party's image. Even in the present era of weakened parties, many voters still rely on a party to give them cues for voting (see Figure 7.1).

4. *Parties articulate policies*. Within the electorate and in the government, each political party advocates specific policy alternatives. The Democratic party has been a fervent backer of the Equal Rights Amendment; the Republican party has not. Republicans, on the other hand, are more likely than Democrats to favor increased military spending.

5. *Parties coordinate policy-making*. In America's fragmented government, parties are essential for coordination among the branches of government. Each president, cabinet official, and member of Congress is also a member of one or the other party. When they need support to get something done, the first place they look is to their fellow partisans.

The importance of these tasks makes it easy to see why most political scientists accept Schattschneider's famous assertion that modern democracy is unthinkable without competition between political parties.

Parties, Voters, and Policy: The Downs Model

The parties compete—at least in theory—as in a marketplace. A party is in the market for voters; its products are its candidates and policies. Anthony Downs has provided a working model of the relationship among citizens, parties, and policy employing a rational-choice perspective.[8] **Rational-choice theory** "seeks to explain political processes and outcomes as consequences of purposive behavior. Political actors are assumed to have goals and to pursue those goals

[7] Kay Lawson, ed., *Political Parties and Linkage: A Comparative Perspective* (New Haven, Conn: Yale University Press, 1980), 3.

[8] Downs, *Economic Theory*.

Figure 7.1   Party-line Voting for the President, Senate, and House: 1952–1988

Even though Americans have weakened their ties to parties, parties still function as important cue-givers to many voters. Look at the percentage of voters casting a party-line vote (in other words, self-proclaimed Democrats voting for a Democratic candidate or self-proclaimed Republicans voting for a Republican candidate):

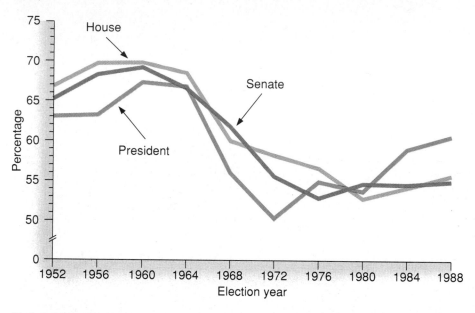

Martin P. Wattenberg, *The Decline of American Political Parties, 1952–1988* (Cambridge, Mass.: Harvard University Press, 1990), 165.

sensibly and efficiently."[9] Downs argues that voters want to maximize the chance that policies they favor will be adopted by government, and that parties want to win office. Thus, in order to win office, the wise party selects policies that are widely favored. Parties and candidates may do all sorts of things to win— kiss babies, call opponents ugly names, even lie and cheat—but in a democracy they will primarily use their accomplishments and policy positions to attract votes. If Party A more accurately figures out what the voters want than Party B, then it should be more successful.

In the American electorate a few voters are extremely liberal, a few are extremely conservative, but the majority are in the middle (see Figure 7.2). If Downs is right, centrist parties will win, and extremist parties will be condemned to a footnote in the history books. Indeed, the long history of the American party system has shown that successful parties rarely stray far from the midpoint of public opinion. Occasionally a party may misperceive voters' desires or take a risky stand on principle, hoping to persuade voters during the campaign, but

[9] Morris P. Fiorina, *Congress: Keystone of the Washington Establishment,* 2nd ed. (New Haven, Conn.: Yale University Press, 1989), 101.

Figure 7.2 The Downs Model: How Rational Parties Match Voters' Policy Preferences

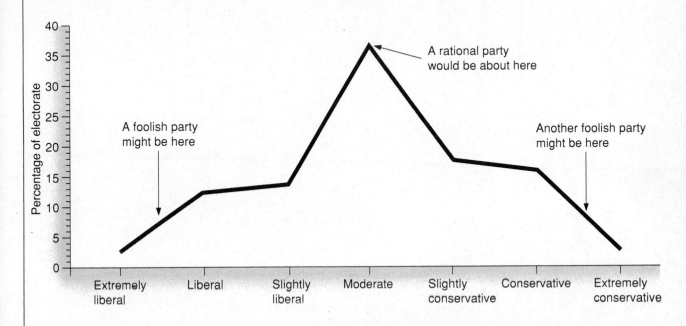

In 1988, the National Opinion Research Center asked a sample of the American electorate to classify themselves on a scale from extremely liberal to extremely conservative. The graph shows how the people located themselves and how rational (and foolish) parties would portray their stands.

A rational party would be about here

A foolish party might be here

Another foolish party might be here

Percentage of electorate

Extremely liberal · Liberal · Slightly liberal · Moderate · Slightly conservative · Conservative · Extremely conservative

Source: 1988 General Social Survey conducted by the University of Chicago's National Opinion Research Center.

in order to survive in a system where the majority opinion is middle-of-the-road, they must stay near the center.

We frequently hear criticism that there is not much difference between the Democrats and Republicans. Given the nature of the American political market, however, they have little choice. One would not expect two competing department stores to locate at opposite ends of town when most people live on Main Street. Downs also notes, though, that from a rational-choice perspective one should expect the parties to differentiate themselves at least somewhat. Just as Chrysler tries to offer something different—and better—than General Motors in order to build buyer loyalty, so Democrats and Republicans have to forge different identities to build voter loyalty. More than half of the population currently feels that important differences do exist between the parties.

Contrast Party

PARTY ERAS IN AMERICAN HISTORY

While studying political parties, remember the following: *America's is a two-party system and always has been.* Of course, there are many minor parties

Do you think there are any important differences in what the Republicans and Democrats stand for?

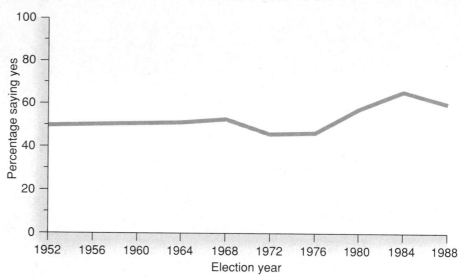

Source: The question as worded is taken directly from the National Election Studies conducted by the University of Michigan.

around—Libertarians, Communists, Vegetarians—but they almost never have a chance to win major office. In contrast, most democratic nations have more than two parties represented in their national legislature.

Throughout American history, one party has been the dominant majority party for long periods of time. A majority of voters cling to the party in power, which thus tends to win a majority of the elections. Political scientists call these periods **party eras.** The majority party does not, of course, win every election; sometimes it suffers from intraparty squabbles (as the Republicans did in 1912) and loses power. Sometimes it nominates a weak candidate, and the opposition cashes in on the majority party's misfortune.

What punctuates these party eras is a **critical election.**[10] A critical election is an electoral earthquake: the ground shakes beneath the parties; fissures appear in each party's coalition and they begin to fracture; new issues appear, dividing the electorate. A new coalition is formed for each party—one that endures for years. A critical election period may require more than one election before change is apparent, but in the end, the party system will be transformed.

This process is called **party realignment,** a rare event in American political life akin to a political revolution. Realignments are typically associated with a major crisis or trauma in the nation's history. One of the major realignments, when the Republican party emerged, was connected to the Civil War. Another was linked to the Great Depression of the 1930s, when the majority Republicans

[10] The term is from V. O. Key. The standard source on critical elections is Walter Dean Burnham, *Critical Elections and the Mainsprings of American Politics* (New York: Norton, 1975).

were displaced by the Democrats. The following sections look more closely at the various party eras in American history.

1796–1824: The First Party System

In the Federalist Papers, Madison warned strongly against the dangers of "factions," or parties. Even though New York's Alexander Hamilton was one of the coauthors of the Federalist Papers, Hamilton did as much as anyone to inaugurate our party system.[11] Hamilton was the nation's first secretary of the treasury, for which service his picture appears on today's ten dollar bill. To garner congressional support for his pet policies (particularly a national bank), he needed votes. From this politicking and coalition building came the rudiments of the Federalist party, America's first political party. The Federalists, though, were also America's shortest-lived major party. After Federalist candidate John Adams was defeated in his reelection bid in 1800, the party faded quickly. The Federalists were poorly organized and by 1820 they no longer even bothered to offer up a candidate for president. In this early period of American history, most party leaders did not regard themselves as professional politicians. Those who lost often withdrew completely from the political arena. The ideas of a loyal opposition and rotation of power in government had not yet taken hold.[12] Each party wanted to destroy the other party—not just defeat it—and such was the fate of the Federalists.

The party that crushed the Federalists was led by Virginians Jefferson, Madison, and Monroe—all of whom were elected president for two terms each in succession. They were known as the Democratic-Republicans, or sometimes as

[11]On the origins of the American party system, see William N. Chambers, *Political Parties in a New Nation* (New York: Oxford University Press, 1963).

[12]See Richard Hofstader, *The Idea of a Party System: The Rise of Legitimate Opposition in the United States, 1780–1840* (Berkeley, Calif.: University of California Press, 1969).

Aaron Burr dealt a near death-blow to the Federalist party when he killed its leader, Alexander Hamilton, in this 1804 duel. Burr, then vice-president, challenged Hamilton to the duel after the former treasury secretary publicly called him a traitor.

the Jeffersonians. Every political party depends upon a **coalition,** a set of individuals or groups supporting it. The Democratic-Republican party derived its coalition from agrarian interests rather than from the growing number of capitalists, who supported the Federalists. This made the party particularly popular in the largely rural South. As the Federalists disappeared, however, the old Jeffersonian coalition was torn apart by factionalism as it tried to be all things to all people.

1828–1860: Jackson and the Democrats versus the Whigs

More than anyone else, it was General Andrew Jackson who founded the modern American political party. In the election of 1828 he forged a new coalition that included westerners as well as southerners, new immigrants as well as settled Americans. Like most successful politicians of his day Jackson was initially a Democratic-Republican, but soon after his ascension to the presidency his party became known as simply the Democratic party, which continues to this day. (The nickname of the Republican party is the GOP, for Grand Old Party, but the Democrats are actually the older of the two parties.) The *Democratic* label was particularly appropriate for Jackson's supporters because their cause was to broaden political opportunity, eliminating many vestiges of elitism and mobilizing the masses.

While Jackson was the charismatic leader, the Democrats' behind-the-scenes architect was Martin Van Buren, who succeeded Jackson as president. Van Buren's one term in office was relatively undistinguished, but his view of party competition left a lasting mark. He "sought to make Democrats see that their only hope for maintaining the purity of their own principles was to admit the existence of an opposing party."[13] A realist, Van Buren argued that a party could not aspire to pleasing all the people all the time. He argued that a governing party needed a loyal opposition to represent parts of society that it could not. This opposition was provided by the Whigs. The Whig party included notables like Henry Clay and Daniel Webster but was only able to win the presidency when it nominated aging but popular military heroes, such as William Henry Harrison (1840) and Zachary Taylor (1848). The Whigs had two distinct wings—northern industrialists and southern planters—who were brought together more by Democratic policies they opposed than by issues on which they agreed.

1860–1932: The Republican Era

In the 1850s the issue of slavery dominated American politics and split both the Whigs and the Democrats. Slavery, said Senator Sumner, an ardent abolitionist, "is the only subject within the field of national politics which excites any real interest."[14] Congress battled over the extension of slavery to the new states and territories. In *Dred Scott* v. *Sandford* the Supreme Court of 1857 held that slaves could not be citizens and that former slaves could not be protected by the

[13]James W. Ceaser, *Presidential Selection: Theory and Development* (Princeton, N.J.: Princeton University Press, 1979), 130.

[14]Quoted in James L. Sundquist, *Dynamics of the Party System,* rev. ed. (Washington, D.C.: Brookings, 1983), 88. Sundquist's book is an excellent account of realignments in American party history.

Constitution. This decision further sharpened the divisions in public opinion, making civil war increasingly likely.

The Republicans rose in the late 1850s as *the* antislavery party. Folding in the remnants of several minor parties, the Republicans in 1860 forged a coalition strong enough to elect former Illinois Congressman Abraham Lincoln and ignite the Civil War. The "War Between the States" was one of those political earthquakes that realigned the parties. Afterward, the Republican party was in ascendency for more than sixty years. The Democrats controlled the South, though, as the Republican label remained a dirty word in the old Confederacy.

During this generally Republican era, the election of 1896 was a watershed, perhaps the most bitter battle in American electoral history. The Democrats nominated William Jennings Bryan, populist proponent of "free silver" (linking money with silver, which was more plentiful than gold, thus devaluing money to help debtors). The Republican party made clear its positions in favor of the gold standard, industrialization, the banks, high tariffs, and the industrial working classes against the "radical" western farmers and silverites. "Bryan and his program were greeted by the country's conservatives with something akin to terror."[15] The *New York Tribune* howled that Bryan's Democrats were "in league with the Devil." A staggeringly high turnout put William McKinley in the White House and brought the new working classes and moneyed interests into the Republican fold. Political scientists call the 1896 election a realigning one, because it shifted the party coalitions and entrenched the Republicans for another generation. (For more on the election of 1896, see Chapter 9.)

For three decades more, until the stock market crash of 1929 and the ensuing Great Depression, the Republicans continued as the nation's majority party. The Depression brought about another fissure in the crust of the American party system.

1932–1968: The New Deal Coalition

President Herbert Hoover's handling of the Depression turned out to be disastrous for the Republicans. He solemnly pronounced that "economic depression cannot be cured by legislative action." Hoover proved to be "no man on horseback to rescue his suffering people from the storm that enshrouded them in 1929. Salvation—of sorts—came instead from a man in a wheelchair, New York's Governor Franklin D. Roosevelt."[16] Roosevelt handily defeated Hoover in 1932, promising a *New Deal*. In his first hundred days as president, Roosevelt prodded Congress into passing scores of anti-Depression measures. Party realignment began in earnest after the Roosevelt administration got the country moving again. First-time voters flocked into the electorate, pumping new blood into the Democratic ranks and providing much of the margin for Roosevelt's four presidential victories. Immigrant groups in Boston and other cities had been initially attracted to the Democratic presidential candidacy of New York Governor Al Smith, a Catholic, in 1928.[17] Roosevelt reinforced the partisanship of these groups, and the Democrats forged the **New Deal coalition.**

[15]*Ibid.,* 1955.

[16]David M. Kennedy, "The Changing Image of the New Deal," *Atlantic Monthly,* January 1985, 90.

[17]On Boston see Gerald H. Gamm, *The Making of New Deal Democrats: Voting Behavior and Realignment in Boston, 1920–1940* (Chicago: University of Chicago Press, 1989).

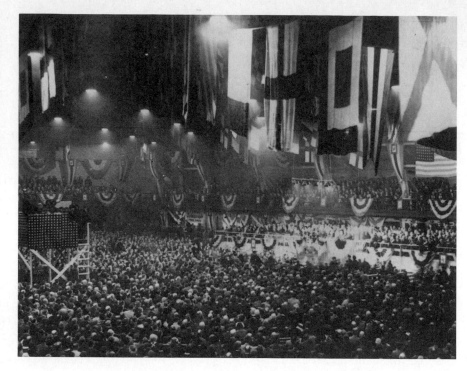

Franklin D. Roosevelt, here at the 1932 Democratic National Convention in Baltimore, engineered the New Deal coalition composed primarily of union members, southerners, intellectuals, liberals, the poor, and African Americans. Although the Democrats have been the majority party ever since Roosevelt's time, the coalition has steadily weakened since the mid-1960s.

The basic elements of the New Deal coalition were as follows:

- *Urban dwellers*. Big cities like Chicago and Philadelphia were staunchly Republican before the New Deal realignment; afterward, they were Democratic bastions.
- *Labor unions*. FDR became the first president to enthusiastically support unions, and they returned the favor.
- *Catholics and Jews*. During and after the Roosevelt period, Catholics and Jews were strongly Democratic.
- *The poor*. Though the poor had low turnout rates, their votes went overwhelmingly to the party of Roosevelt and his successors.
- *Southerners*. Ever since the pre–Civil War days, white southerners were Democratic loyalists. This continued unabated during the New Deal.
- *African Americans*. The Republicans freed the slaves, but under FDR the Democrats attracted the majority of African Americans.
- *Intellectuals*. Small in number, prominent intellectuals provided a wealth of new ideas which fueled the New Deal.

As you can see in Figure 7.3, many aspects of FDR's support continue to shape the party coalitions today.

The New Deal coalition made the Democratic Party the clear majority party for decades. Harry S Truman, who succeeded Roosevelt in 1945, promised a *Fair Deal*. World War II hero and Republican Dwight D. Eisenhower broke the Democrats' grip on power by being elected president twice during the 1950s, but the Democrats regained the presidency in 1960 with the election of John F. Kennedy. His *New Frontier* was in the New Deal tradition, with platforms and

Figure 7.3 Party Coalitions in 1988

The two parties continue to draw support from very different social groups, many of which have existed since the New Deal era. The following figure shows the percentage of Democrats and Republicans with various characteristics:

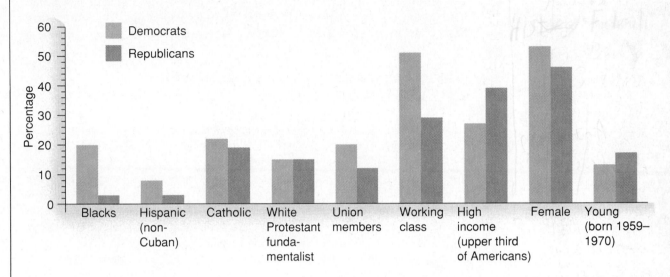

Source: Harold W. Stanley and Richard G. Niemi, "Partisanship and Group Support, 1952–1988" (Paper presented at the 1989 annual meeting of the American Political Science Association).

policies designed to help labor, the working classes, and minorities. Lyndon B. Johnson, picked as Kennedy's vice-president because he could help win southern votes, became president upon Kennedy's assassination and was overwhelmingly elected to a term of his own in 1964. Johnson's *Great Society* programs included a major expansion of government programs to help the poor, the dispossessed, and minorities. His *War on Poverty* was reminiscent of Roosevelt's activism in dealing with the Depression. Johnson's Vietnam War policies, however, tore the Democratic party apart in 1968, leaving the door to the presidency wide open for Republican candidate Richard M. Nixon.

1968–Present: The Era of Divided Government

Since 1968 the Republicans have won five out of six presidential elections. At the same time, they have consistently been the minority party in the House of Representatives. From 1981 to 1986 they managed to control the Senate, but otherwise they have been in the minority there as well. This extended period of divided government is unprecedented in American history. In the past, newly elected presidents routinely swept a wave of their fellow partisans into office with them. For example, the Democrats gained sixty-two seats in the House when Wilson was elected in 1912 and ninety-seven when FDR was elected in 1932. As a result, Wilson and FDR began their terms with a majority in the House, many of whom owed their election to the president. Nixon, Reagan, and Bush, however, were unable to bring many Republican candidates into office with them. The Republican party even lost seats in both the House and Senate while Bush won a forty-state victory in 1988. Because of this, Bush is faced with the difficult task of governing with a Congress solidly controlled by the opposition party.

Not only is this divided government the case at the federal level, but at the state level as well. By 1989 a twentieth-century low of only eighteen states had unified control of the governorship and the state legislature. Divided government, once an occasional oddity, has now become commonplace.

THE PARTIES TODAY: DEALIGNMENT AND RENEWAL

Because of the recent pattern of divided government, many political scientists believe that the party system has dealigned rather than realigned. Whereas realignment involves people changing from one party to another, **party dealignment** means that people are gradually moving away from both. When your car is realigned, it is adjusted in one direction or another to improve how it steers. Imagine if your mechanic were to remove the steering mechanism instead of adjusting it—your car would be useless and ineffective. This is what many scholars fear has been happening to the parties.

There is plenty of evidence that parties have fallen on hard times—the decline of party loyalty, for example, in the electorate. There are also signs of renewal, such as the increase in the regular Washington staff of the national party organizations (see Figure 7.4). Because political parties permeate so many

Analyzing Party structures

Figure 7.4 Democratic and Republican National Committee Staff, 1972–1988

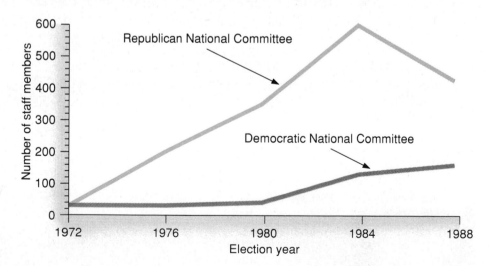

Source: 1972–1984: Paul S. Herrnson, *Party Campaigning in the 1980s* (Cambridge, Mass.: Harvard University Press, 1988), 39; 1988: Paul S. Herrnson, "Re-emerging National Party Organizations," in L. Sandy Maisel, ed., *American Parties: Changing Patterns at the Century's End* (Boulder, Colo.: Westview, 1990).

aspects of American politics, there is no simple answer as to whether they are undergoing decay or revitalization. Whatever the future of the party system (a later section of this chapter will discuss some differing opinions on this topic), political scientists generally agree that three major changes have occurred to the party system since Roosevelt's New Deal.

First, *party loyalty has declined*. In the parties' heydey it was said that people would vote for a yellow dog or a wooden Indian if their party nominated one. Now more than 90 percent of all Americans insist that "I always vote for the person whom I think is best, regardless of what party they belong to."[18] Rather than reflecting negative attitudes toward the parties, the recent dealignment has been characterized by a growing **party neutrality**.[19] In the 1980s an average of 32 percent of the electorate responded as follows to a set of open-ended questions about the parties:

Q. Is there anything in particular that you like about the Democratic party?
A. No.
Q. Is there anything in particular that you don't like about the Democratic party?
A. No.
Q. Is there anything in particular that you like about the Republican party?
A. No.
Q. Is there anything in particular that you don't like about the Republican party?
A. No.

When these questions were first asked in the 1950s, only about 10 percent of respondents answered in this neutral way, generally indicating that they were not very politically knowledgeable. Now, many of those who say nothing about the parties are quite aware of the candidates. Lacking any party anchoring, though, they are easily swayed one way or the other. It is for this reason that they are often referred to as "the floating voters."

Second, *those who do identify with a party are more likely to belong to the party that matches their ideology*. For generations after the Civil War, southern liberals and conservatives alike allied with the Democrats rather than with the hated party of Lincoln. At the same time, there was a strong liberal wing of the Republican party centered in the Northeast. Today, however, conservative southerners no longer shy away from the Republican label, and liberals hardly feel welcome in the Republican party. For the most part, people who call themselves conservatives are in the Republican party, while liberals are concentrated in the Democratic party (see Figure 7.5). The parties, as political scientists like to say, have become ideologically differentiated. Now that Southern conservatives feel comfortable in the Republican column, the Democrats' "Solid South" is a thing of the past. Indeed, both Reagan in 1984 and Bush in 1988 did about 5 percent better in the South than in the rest of the country.

Third, *even while party loyalty has lagged, party organizations have become more energetic and effective*. This has been especially true of the Republicans, but even the Democratic National Committee has found new energy. One reason for this reinvigoration of party leadership has been the computerization of

[18]Larry Sabato, *The Party's Just Begun: Shaping Political Parties for America's Future* (Glenview, Ill.: Scott, Foresman/Little, Brown, 1988), 133.

[19]Martin P. Wattenberg, *The Decline of American Political Parties, 1952–1988* (Cambridge, Mass.: Harvard University Press, 1990).

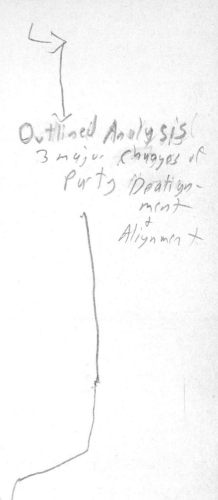

THE RETURN TO TARA

from *Herblock at Large* (Pantheon Books, 1987)

Figure 7.5 Party Identification and Ideology: 1988

Although there is a general tendency for the two parties to converge toward the center of the ideological spectrum, the parties need to differentiate themselves somewhat in order to give people incentive to identify with them. As you can see, there is a distinct difference in the ideology of the parties' members. Republicans are about three times more likely to say they are conservatives than Democrats, and Democrats are about three times as likely as Republicans to say they are liberals.

As noted in Chapter 6, however, the terms liberal and conservative are not very meaningful for a large percentage of the American public. Notice that for both Democrats and Independents the most common response to the ideology question is "haven't thought about it."

Democrats
Liberal
Moderate
Conservative
Haven't thought about it

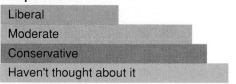

Independents
Liberal
Moderate
Conservative
Haven't thought about it

Republicans
Liberal
Moderate
Conservative
Haven't thought about it

0   10   20   30   40   50   60
Percentage identifying themselves in each group

Source: 1988 National Election Study conducted by the University of Michigan.

campaigns and fund-raising. First the Republicans and then the Democrats learned the secrets of high-tech fund-raising. The Republican party could, for example, write a direct-mail letter to every voter forty-five years of age or older who is registered in a California precinct that voted more than 60 percent for Reagan, and who lives in a house costing more than one hundred thousand dollars.[20] As Paul Herrnson documents, "The parties' national, congressional,

[20]Xandra Kayden and Eddie Mahe, Jr., *The Party Goes On: The Persistence of the Two-Party System in the United States* (New York: Basic Books, 1985), 80.

and senatorial campaign committees are now wealthier, more stable, better organized, and better staffed than ever before."[21]

In sum, the past few years have seen the emergence of what has been called the **split-level party**—a party with a strong, vigorous organization but a weak following on the mass level.[22] Each party, though, has changed in distinctive ways. The following sections give a capsule view of each.

The Democrats: Party of Representation

The most recent restructuring of the Democratic Party began in 1968, the year of the rowdiest national convention ever. As the war in Southeast Asia raged, another war of sorts took place in the streets of Chicago, the Democratic convention city. Demonstrators against the war battled Mayor Richard Daley's Chicago police in what an official report later called a "police riot." Beaten up in the streets and defeated in the convention hall, the antiwar faction won one concession from the party regulars: a special committee to review the party's structure and delegate selection procedures, which they felt had discriminated against them. Minorities, women, youth, and other groups traditionally poorly

[21]Paul S. Herrnson, *Party Campaigning in the 1980s* (Cambridge, Mass.: Harvard University Press, 1988), 121.

[22]Denise Baer and David Bositis, "Party Resurgence or Party Decline: A Crisis in Party or Party Theory?" (Paper presented at the annual meeting of the Midwest Political Science Association, Chicago, April 8–11, 1987.)

Explaining Democrats + Party Representation

Riots at the 1968 Democratic National Convention led to the creation of the McGovern-Fraser Commission, which established open procedures and affirmative action guidelines for delegate selection. These reforms have made Democratic conventions more representative than Republican conventions, but the resulting disunity seems to have hurt the Democrats in recent presidential elections.

represented in the party leadership also demanded a more open process of convention delegate selection. The result was a committee of inquiry, which was chaired first by Senator George McGovern and later by Representative Donald Fraser, who took over when McGovern left the committee to run for president.

The **McGovern-Fraser Commission** brought great changes in the Democratic party. The commission tried to make future conventions more representative; it adopted guidelines requiring that state party organizations use affirmative action to increase the representation and participation of minorities and women. No longer could party leaders handpick the convention delegates in virtual secret. All delegate selection procedures were required to be open, giving party leaders no more clout than college students or anyone else who wanted to participate. By 1972 these rules were in effect. Suddenly, the days of smoke-filled rooms were over; some of those who were protesting on the outside of the convention hall in 1968 were now on the inside. Most notably, Mayor Daley's 1972 Chicago delegation was unseated in favor of a more socially representative slate led by the young Jesse Jackson.

Since the McGovern-Fraser Commission, the party has relaxed its affirmative action requirements, although it has maintained a firm rule that each delegation must be half male and half female. The Democrats have also tried to restore a role for its party leaders. Many thought the reforms went too far, cutting out state and national leaders whose support was needed to win elections. In 1982 another commission chaired by North Carolina's Governor Hunt recommended that a portion of the delegate slots be automatically set aside for party leaders and elected officials. In both 1984 and 1988 about 15 percent of the Democratic delegates were these so-called **superdelegates.** They provided a key source of support for Walter Mondale in 1984 and voted overwhelmingly for Michael Dukakis over Jesse Jackson in 1988. As one might expect, Jackson felt that the allocation of superdelegates was unfair to his candidacy in both 1984 and 1988. He has proposed that superdelegates be allocated in proportion to a candidate's primary vote rather than going to the convention uncommitted. This would make the Democratic convention even more representative of the rank and file.

In the 1990s the Democrats have an even bigger problem than questions of procedural fairness, though: translating their broad representation into presidential election victories. In the five elections since the McGovern-Fraser reforms, the Democrats have won only one of them. Furthermore, the one recent Democratic victory—1976—was a close election whereas the four Republican victories have all been landslides in the electoral college. Many believe that the divisiveness of the Democrats' new open procedures has hurt their ability to unite for the fall campaign against the Republicans.

The Republicans: Party of Efficiency

In 1968, as the Democratic party was coming apart at the seams, the Republicans were uniting around former Vice-President Richard M. Nixon as their nominee. Six years later, in 1974, the Republicans faced a political catastrophe when Nixon, who had been resoundingly reelected in 1972, resigned the presidency in the wake of the Watergate scandal (see Chapter 13 for more on Watergate). As often happens when a party is beset by a crisis, friends of the party—in this case, the Republicans—feared for its survival, and the survival of the two-party system.

The Democratic National Committee meets to consider a new party symbol.

The Republican National Committee meets to consider a new party symbol.

They need not have worried. The Republicans went through very few of the intraparty reforms that so absorbed the Democrats. William Crotty remarks that "there was little support for reform within the Republican party. . . . Despite their problems, Republicans are well satisfied with their party, whom it represents, and the way in which it operates."[23] Democrats, much more than Republicans, considered themselves the party of pluralism, committed to policies intended to bring minorities, women, the poor, and others into the American mainstream. There were few minorities and feminists in the Republican party to demand affirmative action and a fair share of the delegates.

The Republicans had other work to do—mainly to regenerate their party. They were more concerned with winning elections than being balanced by race, sex, age, and ethnicity. After the embarrassment of Watergate, the Republicans turned to former Tennessee Senator Bill Brock to lead them in 1976. Brock wanted the Republican National Committee to provide service to state parties, not be their watchdog. While the Democrats were making their party more representative, Brock was making the Republican organization more effective and efficient.[24] He pushed for the use of computer technology to adapt the party to the modern age. Computerized lists of potential donors—large and small—gave the Republican party a great advantage in fund-raising, which they still hold

[23]William Crotty, *American Parties in Decline,* 2nd ed. (Boston: Little, Brown, 1984), 193.

[24]On the Republican reforms, see John Bibby, "Party Renewal in the National Republican Party," in Gerald M. Pomper, ed., *Party Renewal in America* (New York: Praeger, 1980), 102–15.

today. To help their candidates know what is and is not working, the Republicans have also made far more use of polling technology than have the Democrats. Democrats are trying to catch up with the Republicans' technological sophistication, but in the meantime the Republicans have the advantage in terms of organization.

Third Parties: Their Impact on American Politics

The story of American party struggle is primarily the story of two major parties, yet **third parties** pop up every year and occasionally attract the public's attention. American history is strewn with small and now forgotten minor parties: the Free Soil party (a forerunner of the Republican party); the American party (called the "Know Nothings") in 1856; the Jobless party of 1932; the Poor Man's party of 1952; and many others (see Table 7.1).

Explaining 3rd Parties

Table 7.1   The "Major" Minor Parties

ELECTION	PARTY	ITS CLAIM TO FAME
1832	Anti-Masonic party	As the name implies, this party was opposed to the Masons; it held the first national convention in 1831.
1860	Constitutional Union; Secessionist Democrats	Two of the four parties (together with the Democrats and the Republicans) who ran in the 1860 election.
1892	Populist	Agrarian opponents of banks and railroads; favored "free silver."
1912	Progressive	The "Bull Moose" party, Teddy Roosevelt's splinter from the Republican party; it got eighty-eight electoral votes and cost the Republicans the election.
1924	Progressive	Another Republican splinter party, led by Robert La Follette of Wisconsin.
1948	Progressive	Yet another Progressive Party, this one led by Democratic liberal and former Vice-President Henry A. Wallace.
1948	States' Rights	A walkout by southerners at the Democratic convention led to this Dixiecrat party, whose candidate was Strom Thurmond (S.C.).
1968	American Independent	The party of segregationist Governor George Wallace of Alabama.
1980	Independent Party	Variously named, this party represented Republican congressman John Anderson's effort to win the presidency.

Third parties come in two basic varieties. First are parties that promote certain causes—either a controversial single issue (prohibition of alcoholic beverages, for example) or an extreme ideological position like socialism or libertarianism. Second are *splinter* parties, which are offshoots of a major party. Teddy Roosevelt's Progressives in 1912, Strom Thurmond's States' Righters in 1948, and George Wallace's American Independents in 1968 all claimed they did not get a fair hearing from Republicans or Democrats and thus formed their own new parties.

Although third parties almost never win office in the United States, scholars believe they are often quite important.[25] Third parties have controlled enough votes in one-third of the last thirty-six presidential elections to have decisively tipped the electoral college vote. They have brought new groups into the electorate and have served as "safety valves" for popular discontent. George Wallace, for example, told his supporters in 1968 that they had the chance to "send a message" to Washington—one of support for tougher law-and-order measures, which is still being felt to this day.

Third parties are often the unsung heroes of American politics, bringing new issues to the political agenda. The Free Soilers of the 1850s were the first true antislavery party; the Progressives and the Populists put many social reforms on the political agenda. Many of these reforms were incorporated into the major parties' platforms and later into governmental policy. Despite the regular appearance of third parties, the two-party system is firmly entrenched in American politics. Would it make a difference if America had a multiparty system, as so many European countries have? The answer is clearly yes.

Two Parties: So What?

The most obvious consequence of two-party governance is the moderation of political conflict. If America had many parties, each would have to make a special appeal in order to stand out from the crowd. With just two parties, both will cling to a centrist position in order to maximize their appeal to voters. The parties have often been criticized for this moderation. Their sternest critics think of them as a choice between "Tweedledum and Tweedledee." Third-party candidate George Wallace in 1968 used to say that "there's not a dime's worth of difference between the parties."

The result is often political ambiguity. Why should parties risk taking a strong stand on a controversial policy if doing so will only antagonize many voters? Ambiguity is a safe strategy,[26] as extremist candidates Barry Goldwater in 1964 and George McGovern in 1972 found out the hard way. The two-party system thus throttles extreme or unconventional views.

It is not hard to imagine what a multiparty system might look like in the United States. Quite possibly, African-American groups would form their own party, pressing vigorously for more civil rights legislation. Environmentalists could constitute another party, vowing to clean up the rivers, oppose nuclear

[25]Steven J. Rosenstone, Roy L. Behr, and Edward H. Lazarus, *Third Parties in America* (Princeton, N.J.: Princeton University Press, 1984).

[26]For discussion of political ambiguity as a strategy, see Kenneth A. Shepsle, "The Strategy of Ambiguity: Uncertainty and Electoral Competition," *American Political Science Review* 66 (June 1972): 555–68; and Benjamin I. Page, *Choices and Echoes in Presidential Elections* (Chicago: University of Chicago Press, 1978), chap. 6.

America's two-party system encourages moderate politics. The presidential candidacies of Democrat George McGovern (left) and Republican Barry Goldwater (far right, with vice-presidential candidate William Miller) demonstrated the perils of controversy. McGovern, an extreme liberal, lost to Richard Nixon by a landslide in 1972; Goldwater, an ultraconservative, was crushed by Lyndon Johnson in 1964.

power, and save the wilderness. America could have religious parties, union-based parties, farmers' parties, and all sorts of others. As in some European countries, there could be half a dozen or so parties represented in Congress (see "America in Perspective: Multiparty Systems in Other Countries").

THE PARTY IN THE ELECTORATE

In most European nations being a party member means formally joining a political party. You get a membership card to carry around in your wallet or purse, you pay dues, and you vote to pick your local party leaders. In America being a party member takes far less work. There is no formal "membership" in the parties at all. If you believe that you are a Democrat or a Republican, then you *are* a Democrat or a Republican. Thus the party-in-the-electorate consists largely of symbolic images and ideas. For most people the party is a *psychological* label. They may never go to a party meeting, but they have images of the parties' stances on issues and of which groups the parties generally favor or oppose. Party images give citizens a picture of which party is probusiness or prolabor, which is the party of peace, or which is the better manager of the economy.

Party images help shape people's **party identification,** the self-proclaimed preference for one or the other party. Since 1952 the National Election Studies

Multiparty Systems in Other Countries

One of the major reasons the United States has only two parties represented in government is structural. America has a **winner-take-all system,** in which whoever gets the most votes wins the election. There are no prizes awarded for second or third place. Suppose there are three parties: one receives 45 percent of the vote, another 40 percent, and the third 15 percent. Though it got less than a majority, the party that finished first is declared the winner. The others are out in the cold. In this way, the American system discourages small parties. Unless a party wins, there is no reward for the votes it gets. Thus it makes more sense for a small party to form an alliance with one of the major parties than to struggle on its own with little hope. In the example used above, the second- and third-place parties might merge (if they can reach an agreement on policy) to challenge the governing party in the next election.

In a system which employs **proportional representation,** however, such a merger would not be necessary. Under this system, used in most European countries, legislative seats are allocated according to each party's percentage of the nationwide vote. If a party wins 15 percent of the vote, it then receives 15 percent of the seats. Even a small party can use its voice in Parliament to be a thorn in the side of the government, standing up strongly for its principles. Such is the role of the Greens in West Germany, who are ardent environmentalists. In contrast, West Ger-

many's other small party, the Free Democrats, typically uses its seats to combine with one of the larger parties to form a **coalition government** that together controls over half the seats. Coalition governments are common in Europe. Italy has regularly been ruled by a coalition since the end of World War II, for example.

Even with proportional representation, not every party gets represented in the legislature. To be awarded seats, a party must always achieve a certain percentage of votes, which varies from country to country. Israel has one of the lowest thresholds at 1 percent. This explains why there are so many parties represented in the Israeli Knesset—fifteen as of the 1988 election. The founders of Israel's system wanted to make sure that all points of view were represented, but in recent years this has turned into a nightmare, with small extremist parties holding the balance of power.

Parties have to develop their own unique identities to appeal to voters in a multiparty system. This requires strong stands on the issues—yet, after the election, compromises must be made to form a coalition government. If an agreement cannot be reached on the major issues, the coalition is in trouble. Sometimes a new coalition can be formed; other times the result is the calling of a new election. In either case, one can see that proportional representation systems are more fluid than the two-party system in the United States.

of the University of Michigan have asked a sample of citizens the question, "Generally speaking, do you usually think of yourself as a Republican, a Democrat, or an Independent?" The repeated asking of this question permits political scientists to trace party identification for over three decades of modern American politics (see Table 7.2). The clearest trend has been *the decline of both parties and resultant upsurge of independence* (mostly at the expense of the Democrats). In 1988, for the first time, Independents outnumbered both Democrats and Republicans.

Virtually every major social group—Catholics, Jews, poor whites, southerners, and so on—has moved toward a position of increased independence. The major exception has been African-American voters. A decade of Democratic civil rights policy in the 1960s moved African Americans even more solidly into the

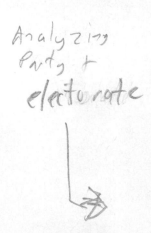

Analyzing
Party +
electorate

Table 7.2 **Party Identification in the United States, 1952–1988**[a]

YEAR	DEMOCRATS	INDEPENDENTS	REPUBLICANS
1952	48.6	23.3	28.1
1956	45.3	24.4	30.3
1960	46.4	23.4	30.2
1964	52.2	23.0	24.8
1968	46.0	29.5	24.5
1972	41.0	35.2	23.8
1976	40.2	36.8	23.0
1980	41.7	35.3	23.0
1984	37.7	34.8	27.6
1988	35.7	36.3	28.0

[a]In percentage of people; the small percentage who identify with a minor party, or who cannot answer the question, are excluded.
Source: 1952–1988 National Election Studies conducted by the University of Michigan.

Democratic party. As of 1988 only 7 percent of blacks identified themselves as Republicans. In his movement to broaden the Republican party, George Bush is hoping to bring the Republican percentage of the African-American vote up to 20 percent. If this should happen, or even if blacks should just become more independent, the Democratic party will be severely weakened.

For many white Americans, though, the abandonment of either party for a nonpartisan stance is well advanced. This abandonment occurred at all age levels in the electorate, but it was most pronounced for younger voters, who have always had the weakest party ties to start with.[27] Because of the baby boom and the lowering of the voting age to eighteen, these young voters swelled the tide of independence during the 1970s.

Not only are there more Independents now, but those who still identify with a party are no longer as loyal in the voting booth as used to be the case. For example, 42 percent of Democrats in 1972 voted for Richard Nixon rather than for their party's nominee, George McGovern. The Republicans highest defection rate ever was in 1964, when 28 percent abandoned Barry Goldwater's candidacy for that of Lyndon Johnson. Yet, party identification remains strongly linked to the voter's choice. The last two presidential elections have shown a rebounding link between party identification and voting, at least on the presidential level (see Figure 7.1 on page 242). At the same time, **ticket-splitting**—voting with one party for one office and another for other offices—is near an all-time high.[28] Because voters prefer not to make a straight choice between one party or the other, divided government has become the norm.

[27]See Helmut Norpoth and Jerrold G. Rusk, "Partisan Dealignment in the American Electorate: Itemizing the Deductions since 1964," *American Political Science Review* 76 (September 1982): 522–37.

[28]Wattenberg, *The Decline,* chap. 9.

The Party Organizations: From the Grass Roots to Washington

An organization chart is usually shaped like a pyramid, with those who give orders at the top and those who carry them out at the bottom. In drawing an organization chart of an American political party, you could put the national committee and national convention of the party at the apex of your pyramid, the state party organizations in the middle, and the thousands of local party organizations at the bottom (see Figure 7.6). When you finished with this chart, however, you would have a very incomplete picture of an American political party. The president of General Motors is at the top of GM in fact as well as on paper. By contrast, the chairperson of the Democratic or Republican national committee is on top on paper but not in fact.

Analysis – Organization chart

Figure 7.6   **An Organization Chart of the American Political Party**

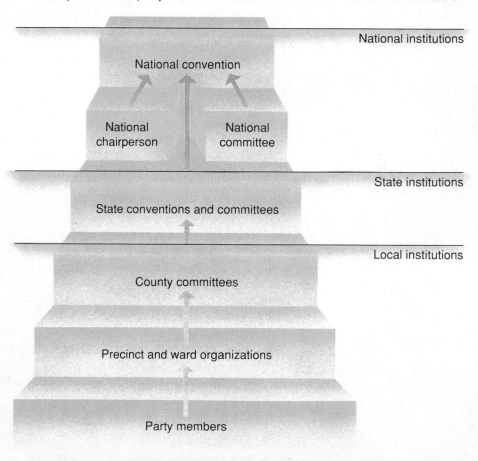

Here is the way an American political party looks on paper, but remember that real power in the party does not coincide with this neat hierarchical structure.

National institutions

National convention

National chairperson

National committee

State institutions

State conventions and committees

Local institutions

County committees

Precinct and ward organizations

Party members

As organizations, American political parties are decentralized and fragmented. As Sorauf and Beck write, party organizations

> lack the hierarchical control and efficiency, the unified setting of priorities and strategy, and the central responsibility we associate with large contemporary organizations. . . . Instead of a continuity of relationships and of operations, the American party organizations feature only improvisatory, elusive, and sporadic structure and activities.[29]

It is no accident that a leading study of national party organizations is called *Politics Without Power*.[30] One can imagine a system in which the national office of a party resolves conflicts among its state and local branches, states the party's position on the issues and then passes orders down through the hierarchy. One can even imagine a system in which the party leaders have the power to enforce their decisions by offering rewards—campaign funds, advice, appointments— to officeholders who follow the party line and punishing those who do not. Many European parties work just that way, but in America the formal party organizations have little such power. Candidates in the United States can get elected on their own. They do not need the help of the party most of the time, and hence the party organization is relegated to a relatively limited role.

Local Parties: The Dying Urban Machines

Urban party organizations are no longer very active either, except in a few places. County and city organizations may be the grass roots of the party, but grass-roots party volunteers are hard to find, especially if a local party is always in the minority. Finding people to serve as unpaid party chairs is even more difficult in this case. One Republican candidate for Congress, running in a district in Texas where a Democrat had held the office since the 1940s, had trouble tracking down the Republican county chairs in his district. When he found some of them, he encountered "what I call the Hereford look. You contact a person and ask them to do something and they agree, and you go back and ask if they've done it, and they just stand there and look at you."[31] In such places parties are disorganized and demoralized after years of being the "out party." It takes real perseverance to track down the Republican committeeperson in Chicago, where Democrats win almost every election. Trying to find the Republican headquarters in the eleventh ward—the residence of every Democratic mayor of Chicago for four decades—one industrious researcher reported, "The outside doors to the headquarters are boarded up. . . . There are two alternative entrances, however, if one is persistent enough to discover them; one behind the pin-setting machine in the bowling alley, and another through a tavern."[32]

Obviously, things are not always that bad, even for the minority party. In some cases both parties have well-oiled precinct, city, and county organizations.

---

[29]Sorauf and Beck, *Party Politics in America,* 6th ed., 152.

[30]Cornelius Cotter and Bernard C. Hennessey, *Politics Without Power* (New York: Atherton, 1964).

[31]Robert L. Lineberry, John E. Sinclair, Lawrence C. Dodd, and Alan M. Sager, "The Case of the Wrangling Professors," in Alan Clem, ed., *The Making of Congressmen* (North Scituate, Mass.: Duxbury, 1976), 188.

[32]Milton Rakove, *Don't Make No Waves, Don't Back No Losers* (Bloomington: Indiana University Press, 1975), 167.

They get out the vote, conduct grass-roots campaigns, and help state and local candidates. In some states, such as California, independent reform organizations of amateur politicians are more active than the major parties' organizations. As a rule, however, local politics is no longer a hotbed of party organization.

It was not always this way. Once, the urban political party was *the* political party organization in America. From the late nineteenth century through the New Deal of the 1930s, scores of cities were dominated by **party machines.** A machine is a particular kind of party organization, different from the typical fragmented and disorganized political party in America. It can be defined as a "party organization that depends crucially on inducements that are both specific and material."[33] A specific inducement is one that can be given to someone and withheld from someone else; if you get a job as reward for your party work, for instance, someone else cannot have it. For it to be material, it must be monetary or convertible into money, such as a building contract.

Patronage is one of the key inducements used by machines. A patronage job is one that is given for political reasons rather than for merit or competence alone. Jobs are not the only form of patronage. In return for handsome campaign contributions, machines have been known to give out government contracts (see "A Question of Ethics: The Price the Parties Paid for Nineteenth-Century Corruption").

At one time, urban machines in Albany, Chicago, Philadelphia, Kansas City, and elsewhere depended heavily on ethnic group support. Some of the most fabled machine leaders were Irish politicians, including New York's George Washington Plunkett, Boston's James Michael Curley, and Chicago's Richard J. Daley. Daley's Chicago machine was the last surviving one, steamrolling its opposition amid charges of racism and corruption.

[33]Edward C. Banfield and James Q. Wilson, *City Politics* (Cambridge, Mass.: Harvard University Press and the MIT Press, 1963), 115.

The last of the urban machine bosses—Richard J. Daley of Chicago. Daley's son, Richard M. Daley, is now Chicago's mayor, although the patronage system that kept his father in power for over twenty years has been largely dismantled by laws restricting political appointments and government contracts.

The Price the Parties Paid for Nineteenth-Century Corruption

Political parties have never had a reputation for high ethical standards. Most of America's founders believed that parties were corrupting influences on government. Jefferson spoke for many of the founders when he said, "If I could not go to heaven but with a party, I would not go there at all." Like most other politicians of his age, he viewed joining a political party as a necessary evil.

By the late nineteenth century many of the worst fears about political parties were plain for all to see. In what historians call "the Gilded Age," corruption and graft reached new heights. Important issues like slavery and the national bank had been settled. By 1880 the parties scarcely differed in their attitudes toward the issues; they competed against each other mainly to win the spoils of political office. Whereas the parties were formed to promote principles, in the late nineteenth century they existed primarily for the purpose of greed. Appointments to high office were routinely sold to the highest bidder. Party leaders made no secret of their corruption. Washington newspapers ran ads from wealthy office-seekers offering as much as one thousand dollars (a substantial sum in those days) for government posts. The parties used some of the money they made selling governmental positions to buy votes. Much of it, though, went to line the pockets of the politicians themselves. The most notable case was that of Boss Tweed of New York, whose ring reportedly made between forty and two hundred million dollars from tax receipts, payoffs, and kickbacks. This was going too far even in the Gilded Age, and Boss Tweed eventually went to jail.

In the spirit of cleaning up government, a number of reforms were instituted, many of which had the effect of permanently weakening the parties. In the 1880s the civil service was created, which established a merit criteria for most government jobs. This reform deprived the parties of the appointment power they had used to reward their friends and financial backers.

Next, ballot reform weakened the hold of the parties on the electorate. Prior to 1900, the parties printed a ticket on colored paper that listed all their candidates. People would simply take the ticket from the local party leader and drop it in the ballot box. Around the turn of the century a ballot procedure first used in Australia, and thus known as the Australian ballot, was introduced to discourage the buying of votes. This involved having the state print alternative tickets which the voter could check off in secret. The change to a secret ballot made it much more difficult for party leaders to pay voters for their vote. Perhaps more important in the long run, voters could now pick and choose from the two tickets, voting for the Republicans for some offices and the Democrats for others. Today's divided government would not have been possible without this reform.

Finally, to remove political control from corrupt party bosses, the party's ultimate power—that of nomination—was taken away. As Boss Tweed said, "I don't care who does the electing, just as long as I do the nominating." Progressive reformers countered with the idea that the cure for the ills of democracy is more democracy. Governor Robert La Follette of Wisconsin led the charge for primary elections, in which citizens would have the power to choose nominees for office. He argued that "with primary elections nominations will not be the result of compromise, or evil design, but be candidates of the majority, honestly and fairly nominated." Primary elections spread rapidly in the early twentieth century, making our party organizations the first—and still the only—in the world to have the nominating function taken away from them.

All of these reforms happened long ago, but they explain many of the reasons that political parties in America are so weak today. There is no doubt that the reforms were well intentioned and promoted higher ethical standards, but American political parties paid a high price—one they are still paying today.

Even today there are remnants of the Chicago machine, particularly in white and ethnic neighborhoods.[34] After two of Mayor Richard Daley's protégés served as mayor, former congressman Harold Washington became the first black mayor of Chicago in 1983. His battle with the city council dominated by white legislators was long and marked by racial animosity. Washington died of a heart attack in 1987, and another bitter battle for control of the city commenced. In 1989 Daley's son won a racially divided Democratic primary contest and followed his father's footsteps into the mayor's office.

The Fifty State Party Systems

American national parties are a loose aggregation of state parties, which are themselves a fluid association of individuals, groups, and local organizations. There are fifty state party systems, no two exactly alike. In a few states the parties are well organized, have sizable staffs, and spend a lot of money. Pennsylvania is one such state. In other states, however, parties are weak. It has been said of the California party system that to describe the parties' "function as minimal overstates the case. . . . The fact is that California has a political party system on paper, and that's about it."[35] California, says Kay Lawson, "has political parties so weak as to be almost nonexistent; it is the birthplace of campaigning by 'hired guns'; and it has been run by special interests for so long that Californians have forgotten what is special about that."[36] Former Governor Jerry Brown is hoping to change this state of affairs, however. In his political comeback attempt, Brown ran hard to become chair of the California Democratic party. Whether he can make anything of this usually minor position will be interesting to see.

As recently as the 1960s, most state party organizations did not even maintain a permanent headquarters office; when the state party elected a new chairperson, the party organization simply shifted its office to his or her hometown.[37] In contrast, almost all state parties today have a physical headquarters, typically in the capital city or the largest city. State party budgets have also increased. In the early 1960s, more than half the parties had a budget of less than $50,000 (in 1967 constant dollars). By the end of the 1970s, the average state party had a budget ranging from $50,000 to $150,000.

Clearly, in terms of headquarters and budgets, state parties are better organized than they used to be—yet almost any national interest group in Washington will have a richer budget, plusher headquarters, and a bigger staff than even the best state party organization.

State Parties as Legal Organizations

The states, not the federal government, regulate the parties. State statutes define a party and specify how it is to be organized. Political scientist turned congress-

---

[34]See the articles in Samuel Gove and Louis Masotti, eds., *Chicago Politics After Daley* (Urbana, Ill.: University of Illinois Press, 1981).

[35]Terry Christensen and Larry N. Gerston, *The California Connection* (Boston: Little, Brown, 1984), 37.

[36]Kay Lawson, "California: The Uncertainties of Reform," in *Party Renewal in America,* chap. 8.

[37]John Bibby et al., "Parties in State Politics," in Virginia Gray, Herbert Jacob, and Kenneth Vines, eds., *Politics in the American States,* 4th ed. (Boston: Little, Brown 1983), 76–79.

man David Price (D-N.C.) notes that "in no western democracy are parties regulated as closely as in the United States."[38] Price points out that California, where "laws covering party organization and campaign practices cover several hundred pages, is a good example of the lengths to which such regulations can go."[39] California has traditionally been an antiparty state; its complex laws hamstring the parties. One of these laws prevented the parties from making endorsements prior to primary elections, which led to a recent notable Supreme Court case. (See "You Are the Policymaker: Should State Parties Make Preprimary Endorsements?") Other states have less complex regulations than California, but all set down party law in their statutes.

Sometimes state legislation regarding the parties conflicts with national policy. In 1940 the Supreme Court held that a state could not turn its primary

[38]David Price, *Bringing Back the Parties* (Washington, D.C.: Congressional Quarterly Press, 1984), 124.
[39]*Ibid.*, 124.

You Are the Policymaker

Should State Parties Make Preprimary Endorsements?

In the 1989 Supreme Court case of *Eu* v. *San Francisco County Democratic Central Committee*, the law banning official party endorsements during primary elections in California was challenged. The state of California acknowledged that its ban deprived the parties of the right to speak out; however, it argued that it had a compelling interest to do so in order to protect voters from undue influence by party bosses. According to the state, this minor infringement of free speech was necessary to enhance unfettered competition in the primaries.

In its ruling the court acknowledged that "a state may regulate the flow of information between political associations and their members when necessary to prevent fraud and corruption." The key to its decision was that it was not convinced that voters were unduly influenced by party endorsements. Indeed, it relied in part on the declaration of Professor Malcolm Jewell, a political scientist at the University of Kentucky, whose study concluded that "the party endorsement has little, if any, effect on the way voters cast their vote." The Court also pointed out that the ban on primary endorsements sometimes enabled candidates with views antithetical to those of the party to win nominations. The Grand Dragon of the Ku Klux Klan, for example, was able to win the Democrats' nomination for the House from a San Diego district in 1980. In sum,

the Court declared that California's ban on primary endorsements "directly hampers the ability of a party to spread its message and hamstrings voters seeking to inform themselves about the candidates and the campaign issues." Thus it invalidated the law.

Now that the California parties have the right to make endorsements prior to primary elections, they are faced with the question of whether it is wise to do so. Some argue that parties can make candidates pay more attention to the platform by rewarding those who follow it closely with an official endorsement. The very fact that candidates could hope to get an endorsement might lead to greater party unity, even if most voters paid little attention to endorsements. On the other hand, some argue that party endorsements often have a way of backfiring. Many voters prefer a candidate who promises independence of action rather than loyalty to a party. Thus in some cases it is possible that the party endorsement might end up being a liability rather than an asset. In addition, some argue that the struggle to get the endorsement would add further to factional conflict within a party.

Consider these possible consequences and take on the role of policymaker for the state parties. Would you favor regular use of official endorsements prior to primary elections, or would you save this power for special circumstances only?

Source: Eu v. *San Francisco County Democratic Central Committee*, 109 Supreme Court 1013 (1989).

elections over to a party (as a "private organization") in order to prevent African-Americans from voting (*United States* v. *Classic*). More recently the federal courts have upheld the national parties when national party policy has conflicted with state law. In cases involving Illinois and Wisconsin, the Supreme Court held that the national party convention's rules took precedence over state law governing how delegates to the convention were to be picked.

The National Party Organizations

The supreme power within each of the parties is its **national convention.** It meets every four years, and its main task is to write the party's platform and then nominate its candidates for president and vice-president. (Chapter 8 will discuss conventions in detail.) Keeping the party operating between conventions is the job of the **national committee,** composed of representatives from the states and territories. Typically each state will have a *national committeeman* and a *national committeewoman* as delegates to the party's national committee. (The Democratic committee also includes assorted governors, members of congress, and other party officials.)

Day-to-day activities of the national party are the responsibility of the **national chairperson** of the party. The national party chairperson hires the staff, raises the money, pays the bills, and attends to the daily duties of the party. This person is usually handpicked by the presidential nominee of the party. In the early 1970s President Nixon asked George Bush to chair the Republican party, which he did for a year before moving back to government work. Upon becoming president, Bush picked his old friend and campaign manager, Lee Atwater of South Carolina, to take over the Republican National Committee. After their 1988 defeat, the Democrats elected Ron Brown to chair the Democratic National Committee, making him the first African American ever chosen for this position. Until recently, a southerner heading the Republicans and an African American heading the Democrats would have been unthinkable.

Recent changes in the parties are reflected in their national chairpersons. Ron Brown (left) is the first African American elected to the position, suggesting the growing strength of African Americans in the Democratic party; Lee Atwater, from South Carolina, epitomizes the move of southern conservatives into the Republican party.

THE PARTY IN GOVERNMENT: PROMISES AND POLICY

Government is a simple word used to describe a complex operation. American government includes the presidency, the Congress, the federal agencies, the governors and legislatures in the state capitals, and the courts. The winning party does not take over the entire government and get rid of government employees who support the opposition party (although Washington real estate agents practically salivate when a new president is elected), but party control does matter because each party and the elected officials who represent it generally try to turn campaign promises into action. As a result, the party that has control will ultimately determine who gets what, where, when, and how.

Voters and coalitions of voters are attracted to different parties largely (though not entirely) by their performance and policies. What parties have done in office and what they promise to do greatly influences who will join their coalition. Sometimes voters suspect that political promises are made to be broken. To be sure, there are notable instances of politicians turning—sometimes 180 degrees—from their policy promises. Lyndon Johnson repeatedly promised in the 1964 presidential campaign that he would not "send American boys to do an Asian boy's job" and involve the United States in the Vietnam War, but he did. In the 1980 campaign Ronald Reagan asserted that he would balance the budget by 1984, yet his administration quickly ran up the largest deficits in American history.

It is all too easy to forget how often parties and presidents do exactly what they say they will do. For every broken promise, many more are kept. Ronald Reagan promised to step up defense spending and cut back on social welfare expenditures, and within his first year in office he did just that. He promised a major tax cut and provided one. He promised less government regulation and quickly set about deregulating natural gas prices and occupational safety and environmental policies. Reagan knew that to go back on his campaign promises to lower taxes and reduce government regulation would not have been taken lightly. The impression that politicians and parties never produce policy out of promises is largely erroneous.

In fact, the parties have done a fairly good job over the years of translating their platform promises into public policy. Gerald Pomper has shown that party platforms are excellent predictors of a party's actual policy performance in office. He tabulated specific pledges in the major parties' platforms from 1944 to 1978. Over that period, the parties made exactly 3,194 specific policy pronouncements. Pomper then looked to see whether the winning party's policy promises were actually fulfilled. Nearly three-fourths of all promises resulted in policy actions. Others were tried but floundered for one reason or another. Only 10 percent were ignored altogether.[40]

If parties generally do what they say they will, then the party platforms adopted at the national conventions represent blueprints, however vague, for action. Consider what the two major parties promised the voters in 1988 (see Table 7.3). There is little doubt that the course taken by Bush follows the Republican platform closely.

[40]Gerald M. Pomper, *Elections in America* (New York: Longman, 1980), 161. A recent study of presidential promises from Kennedy through Reagan also reaches the conclusion that campaign pledges are taken seriously. See Jeff Fishel, *Presidents and Promises* (Washington, D.C: Congressional Quarterly Press, 1985).

Table 7.3 Party Platforms, 1988

In 1988 the party platforms contrasted dramatically in length. The Democrats' four thousand words were deliberately scant, with few promises that Republicans could attack, and more generalized to appeal to a broader spectrum of the electorate. The Republicans, expansive after eight years of rule, weighed in with forty thousand words. In 1984 the Republican platform was shorter, at thirty thousand words, but still no match for the Democrat's whopping forty-five thousand words. Amidst the sometimes vague or euphemistic rhetoric on both sides, however, there were clear differences. Here's how the 1988 platforms compared on some key issues:

REPUBLICANS	DEMOCRATS
Equality	
A free economy helps defeat discrimination by fostering opportunity for all. . . . So we will remove disincentives that keep the less fortunate out of the productive economy.	[W]e honor our multicultural heritage by assuring equal access to government services, employment, housing, business enterprise and education to every citizen. . . .
Health Care and Family	
[W]e believe in reduced government control of health care. . . . We seek to minimize the financial burdens imposed by government upon families, ensure their options and preserve the role of our traditional voluntary institutions. . . .	All Americans should enjoy access to affordable, comprehensive health services [and] a national health program providing federal coordination and leadership is necessary. . . . [We support] major increases in assistance making child care more available and affordable. . . .
Abortion	
[T]he unborn child has a fundamental right to life which cannot be infringed.	[T]he fundamental right of reproductive choice should be guaranteed regardless of ability to pay.
Energy	
We must preserve nuclear power as a safe and economic option to meet future electricity needs. . . .	We believe that . . . the country could reduce its reliance on nuclear power. . . .
Governmental Spending	
We categorically reject the notion that Congress knows how to spend money better than the American people do. Tax hikes are like addictive drugs. Every shot makes Congress want to spend more.	If we are seriously to pursue our commitments to build a secure economic future for all Americans we must provide the resources to care for our newborns . . . house the homeless . . . wage total war on drugs and protect the environment.
Central America	
[T]he United States will respond to requests from our Central American neighbors for security assistance to protect their emerging democracies against insurgencies sponsored by the Soviets, Cuba, or others.	Instead of the current emphasis on military solutions we will use negotiations and incentives to encourage free and fair elections and security for all nations in [Central America].
Defense Policy	
Even as we engage in dialogue with our adversaries to reduce the risks of war, we must continue to rely on nuclear weapons as our chief form of deterrence. This reliance will, however, move toward non-nuclear defensive weapon systems as we deploy the Strategic Defense Initiative.	[We should] ban chemical and space weapons in their entirety; promptly initiate a mutual moratorium on missile flight testing and halt all nuclear weapons testing while strengthening our efforts to prevent the spread of these weapons to other nations before the nightmare of nuclear terrorism engulfs us all.

Source: Excerpts from party platforms reprinted in *Congressional Quarterly Weekly Reports,* July 16, July 23, and August 20, 1988.

UNDERSTANDING POLITICAL PARTIES

Political parties are considered essential elements of democratic government. Indeed, one of the first steps taken toward democracy in Eastern Europe has been the formation of competing political parties to contest elections. After years of one-party totalitarian rule, Eastern Europeans were ecstatic to be able to adopt a multiparty system like those that had proved successful in the West. In contrast, the founding of the world's first party system in the United States was seen as a risky adventure in the then uncharted waters of democracy. Wary of having parties at all, the founders designed a system which has greatly restrained their political role to this day. Whether American parties should continue to be so loosely organized is at the heart of today's debate concerning their role in American democracy.

Democracy and Responsible Party Government

Ideally, in a democracy candidates should say what they mean to do if elected and be able to do what they promised once they are elected. Critics of the American party system lament that this is all too often not the case, and have called for a "more responsible two-party system."[41] Advocates of the **responsible party model** believe the parties should meet the following conditions:

1. Parties must present distinct, comprehensive programs for governing the nation.
2. Each party's candidates must be committed to its program and have the internal cohesion and discipline to carry out its program.
3. The majority party must implement its programs and the minority party must state what it would do if it were in power.
4. The majority party must accept responsibility for the performance of the government.

A two-party system operating under these conditions would make it easier for party promises to be turned into governmental policy. Because a party's office-holders would have control of the government, they would be collectively (rather than individually) responsible for their actions. Voters would therefore know whom to blame for what the government does and does not accomplish.

As this chapter has shown, American political parties fall far short of these conditions. They are too decentralized to take a single national position and then enforce it. Most candidates are self-selected, gaining their nomination by their own efforts and not the party's. Because virtually anyone can vote in party primaries, parties do not have control over those who run under their labels. For example, in 1989 the former grand wizard of the Ku Klux Klan, David Duke, won a Republican primary contest for a state House seat in Louisiana despite denunciations from President Bush and Republican National Chairman Lee Atwater. Duke not only won the primary but also the general election, and the party has been powerless to control his actions in office. In America's loosely

---

[41]The classic statement on responsible parties can be found in "Toward a More Responsible Two-Party System: A Report of the Committee on Political Parties, American Political Science Association," *American Political Science Review* 44 (1950): supplement, number 3, part 2.

organized party system, there simply is no mechanism for a party to discipline officeholders and thereby ensure cohesion in policy-making. Thus it is rare to find congressional votes in which over 90 percent of Democrats vote in opposition to over 90 percent Republicans. In 1988 this occurred on a mere 7 percent of all House votes and 3 percent of all Senate votes.

Not everyone thinks that American's decentralized parties are a problem, however. Critics of the responsible party model argue that the complexity and diversity of American society is too great to be captured by such a simple black and white model of party politics. Local differences need an outlet for expression, they say. One cannot expect Texas Democrats to always want to vote in line with New York Democrats. In the view of those opposed to the responsible party model, America's decentralized parties are appropriate for the type of limited government the founders sought to create and most Americans wish to maintain.[42]

Big Government and Weak Parties

Paradoxically, it can be argued that weak parties have not limited government, but have actually fostered big government. Because no single party in the United States can ever be said to have firm control over the government, the hard choices necessary to limit the growth of government are rarely addressed. A disciplined and cohesive governing party would have the power to say no to various demands on the government. In contrast, American's weak party structure makes it possible for politicians to focus their efforts on getting more from the government for their own constituents.

The lack of a strong party structure makes it easier for politicians to pass the buck than bite the bullet. In particular, the divided government of the Reagan-Bush era allowed Republican leaders to blame budget deficits on congressional spending for social programs, while Democratic leaders put the blame on the president's military buildup. With neither party really in charge and each pointing the finger at the other, it is no wonder that little was done to resolve the budget deficit.

Is the Party Over?

The key problem of the parties today is this: the parties are low-tech institutions in a high-tech political era. Political columnist David Broder once that that "a growing danger to the prospects for responsible party government is the technological revolution that has affected campaigning in the past decade."[43] The party, through its door-to-door canvassers, still makes house calls, yet more and more political communication is not face-to-face but rather through the mass media.[44] The technology of campaigning—television, polls, computers, political consultants, media specialists, and the like—is available for hire to candidates

America's decentralized political parties have little control over candidates, as shown by the nomination and election victories of David Duke (above, as Ku Klux Klan grand wizard, and, below, as Louisiana state representative).

[42]See Evron M. Kirkpatrick, "Toward a More Responsible Party System: Political Science, Policy Science, or Pseudo-Science?" *American Political Science Review* 65 (1971): 965–90.

[43]David S. Broder, *The Party's Over* (New York: Harper & Row, 1972), 236.

[44]Banfield and Wilson were among the first to note the impact of technology on parties when they ascribed to television the weakening of the importance of a precinct captain's visits: "The precinct captain who visits in the evening interrupts a television program and must either stay and watch in silence of else excuse himself quickly and move on." See their *City Politics,* 122.

who can afford it. Why should candidates rely on the parties for what they can buy for themselves?

No longer are parties the main source of political information, attention, and affection. The party of today has rivals that appeal to voters and politicians alike. The biggest rival is the media. With the advent of television, voters no longer need the party to find out what the candidates are like and what they stand for. The interest group is another party rival. As Chapter 10 will discuss, interest groups' power has grown enormously in recent years. They—not the parties—pioneered much of the technology of modern politics, including mass mailings and sophisticated fund-raising.

The parties have clearly been having a tough time of late, but there are indications that they are beginning to adapt to the high-tech age. Although the old city machines are largely extinct, state and national party organizations have become more visible and active than ever. More people are calling themselves Independents and splitting their tickets, but the majority still identifies with a party, and this percentage seems to have stabilized.

For a time, some political scientists were concerned that parties were on the verge of disappearing from the political scene. A more realistic view is that parties will continue to play an important—but significantly diminished— role in American politics. Leon Epstein sees the situation as one in which the parties have become "frayed." He concludes that the parties will "survive and even moderately prosper in a society evidently unreceptive to strong parties and yet unready, and probably unable, to abandon parties altogether."[45]

SUMMARY

American political life revolves around the parties. Even though political parties are one of Americans' least beloved institutions, political scientists see them as a key linkage between policymakers and the people. Parties are ubiquitous; for each party there is a *party-in-the-electorate,* a *party organization,* and a *party-in-government.* Political parties affect policy through their platforms. Despite much cynicism about party platforms, they are taken seriously when their candidates are elected.

America's is a two-party system. This fact is of fundamental importance in understanding American politics. The ups and downs of the two parties constitute party competition. In the past, one party or the other has dominated the government for long periods of time. These periods were punctuated by critical elections, in which party coalitions underwent realignment. Since 1968, however, American government has experienced a unique period of party dealignment and divided government. While parties are currently weaker at the mass level, they are stronger (and richer) than ever in terms of national and state organization. Some would have them be far more centralized and cohesive, following the *responsible party model.* American parties' loose structure allows politicians to avoid collective responsibility—a state of affairs that facilitates big government. While the party system is certainly not about to disappear, it remains to be seen whether it can fully adapt itself to the high-tech age.

[45]Leon Epstein, *Political Parties in the American Mold* (Madison: University of Wisconsin Press, 1986), 346.

KEY TERMS

party competition
political party
linkage institutions
party image
rational-choice theory
party eras
critical election
party realignment
coalition
New Deal coalition

party dealignment
party neutrality
split-level party
McGovern-Fraser
  Commission
superdelegates
third parties
winner-take-all system
proportional representa-
  tion

coalition government
party identification
ticket-splitting
party machines
patronage
national convention
national committee
national chairperson
responsible party model

FOR FURTHER READING

Black, Earl and Merle Black. *Politics and Society in the South.* Cambridge, Mass.: Harvard University Press, 1987. An excellent examination of the transformation of party politics in the South.

Downs, Anthony. *An Economic Theory of Democracy.* New York: Harper & Row, 1957. An extremely influential theoretical work which applies rational-choice theory to party politics.

Epstein, Leon. *Political Parties in the American Mold.* Madison: University of Wisconsin Press, 1986. Epstein demonstrates the remarkable persistence of both parties during a century of profound social change.

Herrnson, Paul S. *Party Campaigning in the 1980s.* Cambridge, Mass.: Harvard University Press, 1988. An analysis of the role parties play in congressional elections, arguing that they are in the process of making a comeback.

Kayden, Xandra and Eddie Mahe, Jr. *The Party Goes On: The Persistence of the Two-Party System in the United States.* New York: Basic Books, 1985. Two political consultants show how the party organizations are regenerating themselves.

Rosenstone, Steven, Roy Behr, and Edward Lazarus. *Third Parties in America.* Princeton, N.J.: Princeton University Press, 1984. An analytical study of why third parties appear when they do and what effect they have.

Sabato, Larry. *The Party's Just Begun: Shaping Political Parties for America's Future.* Glenview, Ill.: Scott, Foresman/Little, Brown, 1988. A spirited prescription for strengthening the parties.

Sorauf, Frank and Paul Allen Beck. *Party Politics in America,* 6th ed. Boston: Scott, Foresman/Little, Brown, 1988. The standard textbook on political parties.

Sundquist, James L. *Dynamics of the Party System,* rev. ed. Washington, D.C.: Brookings, 1983. One of the best books ever on the major realignments in American history.

Wattenberg, Martin P. *The Decline of American Political Parties, 1952–1988.* Cambridge, Mass.: Harvard University Press, 1990. An account of the decline of parties in the electorate.

8

NOMINATIONS AND CAMPAIGNS

It is often said that the presidency is the most difficult job in the world, but getting elected to it may well be tougher. It is quite arguable that the long campaign for the presidency puts candidates under more continuous stress than they could ever face in the White House. Some believe it is important that candidates go through this trial by fire. Others, however, worry that the system makes it difficult for politicians with other responsibilities—such as sitting governors or senior senators—to take a run at the White House.

One 1988 candidate who did not let his official responsibilities keep him from running for president was Massachusetts Governor Michael Dukakis. In an extraordinary apology to the state in January 1990, Dukakis said he underestimated the demands of running for the presidency and managing the state simultaneously. "Trying to do two jobs at the same time was more difficult and more grueling than I expected," he said. "And I underestimated the toll it would take on my family, too" referring to Kitty Dukakis's alcohol abuse problems.

Recognizing his sinking popularity in the state (only 14 percent approval in one opinion poll), Governor Dukakis said: "I know that many of you are angry with me, feel betrayed, feel that I put myself before you and the commonwealth." He noted that he was "swept up by the excitement and euphoria" when he ran for the Democratic nomination. "But a funny thing happened on the road to the White House," he said. "I ran a great campaign for the nomination, and a lousy one for the final. I lost, and in the process Massachusetts took an unfair beating. And I feel terrible about it."

As you read through this chapter, the Dukakis story is a good one to keep in mind. Campaigning for any major office has become a massive undertaking in today's political world, as you will see.

Source: "Dukakis Says Campaign Damage a Surprise," *New York Times*, January 18, 1990, A15.

With about *one half-million* elected officials in this country, someone, somewhere, is always running for office. One of the campaigns is for the world's most powerful office—the presidency of the United States. This chapter will focus mainly on this election, although it will explore some other campaigns as well. Chapter 12 will specifically discuss the congressional election process.

There are really two types of campaigns in American politics: campaigns for party nominations and campaigns between the two nominees. These are called *nomination campaigns* and *election campaigns*. The prize for the first is garnering a party's nod as its candidate; the prize for the second is winning an office. Campaigning today is an art and a science, heavily dependent, like much else in American politics, on technology.

THE HIGH-TECH CAMPAIGN

The new machines of politics have changed the way campaigns are run. During the first half of the twentieth century, candidates and their entourage piled onto a campaign train and tried to speak to as many people as time, energy, and

money would allow. Voters journeyed from miles around to see a presidential
whistle-stop tour go by and to hear a few words in person from the candidate.
Today, television is the most prevalent means used by candidates to reach voters.
Thomas Patterson stresses that "today's presidential campaign is essentially a
mass media campaign. . . . It is no exaggeration to say that, for the majority of
voters, the campaign has little reality apart from its media version."[1] Most of the
money spent on presidential campaigns these days is spent on the media, and
little of consequence occurs outside the media's ever-present gaze. Technology
has made it possible for candidates to speak directly to the American people in
the comfort of their living rooms.

In this high-tech age, times have changed since President Dwight Eisenhower
first used a TelePrompTer (a machine used to magnify a speech so that the
speaker does not have to look down at his or her text) and found it totally
confusing. He grumbled in front of a national television audience, "How does
this damned thing work, anyway?" The computer revolution has now overtaken
political campaigns. Between 15 and 25 percent of presidential campaign expenses now goes to computer services and their related tool, direct mail.[2] One
innovator in applying computer technology to politics has been Jeff Carter, son
of the former president. He designed a software program called *Statmap,* which
graphically depicts the demographics of states, congressional districts, counties,

[1]Thomas E. Patterson, *The Mass Media Election* (New York: Praeger, 1980), 3.
[2]Elizabeth Tucker, "The Computer Revolution Has Overtaken the Campaigns," *Washington Post National Weekly Edition,* March 28, 1988, 13.

"IN THE BAD OLD DAYS, THERE USED TO BE POLITICAL MACHINES"

©1984 HERBLOCK

from *Herblock through the Looking Glass* (W. W. Norton, 1984)

[handwritten note: Explaining Campaign + "use of how to"]

[handwritten note: Explaining "Why not turun"]

and so forth. Ironically, Ronald Reagan's 1984 campaign was one of Jeff Carter's first buyers. Said young Carter, "Computers are the biggest thing to hit politics since television."[3]

One of the most important uses for computer technology is to target mailings to prospective supporters. Conservative fund-raiser Richard Viguerie pioneered the mass-mailing list, including in his computerized listing the names and addresses of hundreds of thousands of contributors to conservative causes. If you are a conservative, you can use Viguerie's list—for a fee of course.

The high-tech campaign for the presidential nomination is no longer a luxury. Candidates must use the media and computer technology just to be competitive.

THE NOMINATION GAME

A **nomination** is a party's official endorsement of a candidacy for office. Anyone can play the nomination game, but few have any serious chance of victory. Generally, success in the nomination game requires money, media attention, and momentum. **Campaign strategy** is the way in which candidates attempt to manipulate each of these elements to achieve the nomination.

A campaign, whether for a nomination or the election, is often unpredictable. Even with name recognition, money, and political savvy, a major blunder can change the political complexion virtually overnight, especially when the press pounces on it. In 1968 George Romney's promising campaign for the Republican nomination fell apart soon after he arrived back from a trip to Vietnam and said that he had been "brainwashed" about the war. After all, who would want a president who admitted to having been brainwashed? Four years later Edmund Muskie decided to attack a harsh newspaper report about his wife. When he broke down emotionally during his denunciation of the newspaper's publisher, his front-running campaign for the Democratic nomination soon collapsed.

Conscious choices and slips of the tongue help determine outcomes of the nomination and election games. One thing, though, is certain: a candidate must first win a nomination to get a chance at election.

Deciding to Run

Believe it or not, not every politician wants to run for president. In 1988 many strong, perhaps even electable, candidates sat out the race. Prominent Democrats like New York Governor Mario Cuomo, Massachusetts Senator Edward Kennedy, Georgia Senator Sam Nunn, and others held their hats out of the ring.

One reason is that campaigns have become more taxing than ever. As Speaker of the House Thomas Foley says, "I know of any number of people who I think would make good presidents, even great presidents, who are deterred from running by the torture candidates are obliged to put themselves through."[4] To run for president, a person needs what Walter Mondale once called a "fire in the belly." Remarking on his 1984 bid for the presidency, Mondale

[3]Jonathan Littman, "The New Political Machine," *PC World,* August 1984, 301.

[4]R. W. Apple, Jr., "Foley Assesses Presidential Elections and Tells Why He Wouldn't Run," *New York Times*, November 4, 1988, A12.

Most Americans feel that presidential campaigns are far too long—candidates often begin their quest for votes more than a year before the Iowa caucuses. Here Richard Gephardt stumps for support in Iowa during his 1988 nomination campaign.

said, "For four years, that's all I did. I mean, all I did. That's all you think about. That's all you talk about. . . . That's your leisure. That's your luxury. . . . I told someone, 'The question is not whether I can get elected. The question is whether I can be elected and not be nuts when I get there.' "[5]

Strategies for the long campaign trail are often beneath the dignity of the office to which the candidate aspires. The *Washington Post* told the story of Democratic candidate (now House majority leader) Richard Gephardt as he campaigned in New Hampshire nearly a year before any primary votes were cast.[6] In a Nashua gift shop, Gephardt spotted a small statue of a German shepherd, bought it, and the next day took it to Cedar Rapids, Iowa, on a campaign swing through the nation's first caucus state. There Gephardt gave the statue to Connie Clark, a local Democratic activist who collected dog statues, and then spent four hours making pancakes for the breakfast assemblage at her house. By this point, Gephardt had seen Clark no less than six times, and she was not even planning to commit to a candidate for another few months. All told, Gephardt spent a whopping 144 days campaigning in Iowa.[7] Though Gephardt won in Iowa, many feel that by concentrating so exclusively on the first caucus his organization was not prepared to mount a strong campaign in later states.

In Britain campaigns are limited by law to five weeks (see "America in Perspective: Choosing Party Leaders in Great Britain"). In contrast, American campaigns seem endless; a presidential candidacy needs to be either announced or an "open secret" eighteen months before the convention. Not only do the candidates find this a long and arduous process—so does the public. In a poll

[5] Paul Taylor, "Is This Any Way to Pick a President?" *Washington Post National Weekly Edition,* April 13, 1987, 6.
[6] *Ibid.*
[7] *USA Today,* February 9, 1988, 4a.

taken in late May 1984, 69 percent of the public agreed that "the entire presidential campaign is too long and should be shortened," and 76 percent agreed that "voters lose interest in the campaign because candidates have to say the same things over and over."[8]

Still, in 1988 seven Democrats and six Republicans were serious about the presidency. Political scientists David Rohde and John Aldrich emphasize that presidential candidates need to be risk takers[9] (though many people considered Gary Hart too much of a risk taker to be taken seriously as presidential material in 1988). Presidential candidates need sufficient self-confidence to put everything on the line in hopes of reaching America's highest political office.

Those who aspire to the presidency need an electoral base from which to begin. Rarely in American history has a major party's candidate sought the presidency without first holding a key political office; most of the exceptions have been famous generals, like Dwight Eisenhower in 1952. Three offices—U.S. senator, U.S. representative, and state governor—have provided the electoral base for 78 percent of the major candidates since 1972.[10]

[8]Louis Peck, "Voters Say Campaign Lasts Too Long," *USA Today,* June 6, 1984, 1.

[9]The Rohde theory is in his "Risk-Bearing and Progressive Ambition: The Case of the U.S. House of Representatives," *American Journal of Political Science* 23 (February 1979): 1–26. The Aldrich adaptation of the theory to the presidency is in his *Before the Convention* (Chicago: University of Chicago Press, 1980), chap. 2.

[10]Paul R. Abramson, John H. Aldrich, and David W. Rohde, *Change and Continuity in the 1988 Elections* (Washington, D.C.: Congressional Quarterly Press, 1990), 16.

America in Perspective

Choosing Party Leaders in Great Britain

The short length of campaigns in Britain is only one of many major differences between the way in which British prime ministers and American presidents are chosen. The process of selecting each party's candidate for the top slot is particularly different. Anthony King, one of Britain's foremost political scientists, offers the following general observations about how British candidates for prime minister were chosen prior to the 1979 campaign, the year that Margaret Thatcher first came to power:

1. "The winners had entered politics at an early age and had served for a considerable number of years in Parliament before becoming their party's leader." Each had "served in a number of different national-level offices."

2. "The candidates were assessed and voted upon exclusively by their fellow politicians." The process of electing the leader was "entirely a party process."

3. "The leadership campaigns involved very little wear and tear on the part of the candidates and their families."

4. "The leadership campaigns cost next to nothing" (less than the equivalent of ten thousand dollars all told).

Compared to other countries around the world, the British process for selecting party leaders is typical; it is the American system that is unique.

Source: Anthony King, "How Not to Select Presidential Candidates: A View from Europe," in Robert E. DiClerico, ed., *Analyzing the Presidency,* 2nd ed. (Guilford, Conn.: Dushkin, 1990), 9–10.

"WELL, PERSONALLY, I LIKE ALL THESE CANDIDATES COMING THROUGH IOWA.... HECK, I HAVEN'T HAD TO DO THE CHORES IN MONTHS!!"

Having an electoral base is a first step, but the road to the convention is long and full of stumbling blocks. From the convention, held in the summer of election years, only one candidate will emerge as each party's standard-bearer.

Competing for Delegates

In some ways, the nomination game is tougher than the general election game; it whittles a very large number of players down to two. The goal of the nomination game is to win the majority of delegates' support at the **national party convention.**

There are fifty different roads to the national convention, one through each state. From February through June of the election year, the individual state parties busily choose their delegates to the national convention via either caucuses or primaries. Candidates hustle to try to ensure that delegates committed to them are chosen.

The Caucus Road   Before primaries existed, all state parties selected their delegates to the national convention in a meeting of state party leaders called a **caucus.** Sometimes one or two party "bosses" ran the caucus show—often the governor of the state or the mayor of its largest city. Such state party leaders could control who went to the convention and how the state's delegates voted once they got there. They were the kingmakers of presidential politics who met in smoke-filled rooms at the convention to cut deals and form coalitions.

Today's caucuses are different. In the minority of states which still have them, party rules mandate openness and strict adherence to complex rules of representation. The caucuses can sometimes be very important, as when Jesse Jackson leaped to the front of the Democratic pack with a surprise victory in the 1988 Michigan caucuses. Iowa traditionally holds the earliest caucus, and an obscure former Georgia governor named Jimmy Carter took his first big presidential step by winning it in 1976. Ever since then, candidates have jostled every four years to try to get off to a big start in Iowa.

Caucuses usually are organized like a pyramid. Small, neighborhood, precinct-level caucuses are held initially—often meeting in a church, an American Legion hall, or even someone's home. At this level delegates are chosen (based on their preference for a certain candidate) to attend county caucuses and then congressional district caucuses where delegates are again chosen to go to a higher level—this time to a state convention. It is at the state convention (months after the precinct caucuses) that delegates are finally chosen to go to the national convention. Thus the precinct caucuses we hear so much about every four years in Iowa are only the first step in a long process for selecting the state's delegates. Nevertheless, it is the first test of the candidates' vote-getting ability, and hence it has become a full-blown media extravaganza.[11]

Explaining Primaries

The Presidential Primary Road   Today most of the delegates to the Democratic and Republican conventions are selected in **presidential primaries,** in which voters in a state go to the polls and vote for a candidate (or delegates pledged to one). The presidential primary was promoted around the turn of the century by reformers who wanted to take nominations out of the hands of the party bosses (see "A Question of Ethics" in Chapter 7, page 264). Their idea was to let the people vote for the candidate of their choice and then bind the

---

[11]See Hugh Winebrenner, *The Iowa Precinct Caususes: The Making of a Media Event* (Ames, Iowa: Iowa State University Press, 1987).

Precinct-level caucuses (here in an Iowa fire station) are the first step in the nomination process. Citizens participate directly at these meetings, electing delegates to support certain candidates. These delegates then represent the people's preferences at further caucuses, leading ultimately to the state and national conventions.

delegates to vote for that candidate at the convention. In 1910 Oregon passed the first presidential primary law that required delegates to vote according to the primary results. A majority of the states now use presidential primaries.

Few developments have transformed American politics as much as the proliferation of presidential primaries. Presidential election watcher Theodore White calls the primaries the "classic example of the triumph of goodwill over common sense." Says White:

> An entirely new breed of professionals has grown up, voyaging like Gauleiters from state to state, specializing in get-out-the-vote techniques, cross sectionings, media, ethnic breakdowns, and other specialties. . . . Most of all, delegates, who were supposed to be free to vote their own common sense and conscience, have become for the most part anonymous faces, collected as background for the television cameras, sacks of potatoes packaged in primaries, divorced from party roots, and from the officials who rule states and nation.[12]

The primary season begins during the winter in New Hampshire, where license plates boldly state, "Live free or die." (One can only guess what the prison inmates of New Hampshire must think while making these plates.) If Virginia was the "mother of presidents" in the early days of the Republic, New Hampshire is today's midwife. No one has been elected President since 1952 without first having won the state's presidential primary. Fulfilling a promise made in February 1988, George Bush concluded his victory statement the night of his general election triumph over Michael Dukakis by saying, "Thank you, New Hampshire."

Like the Iowa caucuses, the importance of New Hampshire is not the amount of delegates, nor how typical the state is (if there is a typical American state, New Hampshire is certainly not it), but rather that it is always first. At this early stage the campaign is not for delegates, but for images—candidates want the rest of the country to immediately see them as frontrunners. The frenzy of political activity in this small state is given lavish attention in the national press (see "In Focus: The Frenzy of the New Hampshire Primary").

Other state primaries follow New Hampshire's. The laws determining the way in which the primaries are set up and the delegates are allocated are made by state legislatures and state parties. Even the experts are often confused by the variety of different procedures used from state to state. One thing is certain, though—week after week the primaries serve as elimination contests. Politicians, press, and public all love a winner. Candidates who fail to win in the early primaries get labeled as losers and typically drop out of the race. Usually they have little choice, as losing quickly inhibits a candidate's ability to raise the money necessary to win in other states. As Carter's former Press Secretary Jody Powell has said, "You don't so much beat candidates anymore as you bankrupt them."

In the 1980 delegate chase, one memorable term was coined. After George Bush scored a surprise victory over Ronald Reagan in the Iowa caucuses, he proudly claimed to possess "the big mo"—momentum. (Actually, Bush had only a little "mo" and quickly fell victim to a decisive Reagan victory in New Hamp-

[12]Theodore White, *America in Search of Itself: The Making of the President 1956– 1980* (New York: Harper & Row, 1982), 285.

The Frenzy of the New Hampshire Primary

New Hampshire in the winter of a presidential election year is a political junkie's dream. If you like watching hours of political debate on C-SPAN, New Hampshire during the week of the nation's first primary is for you. Nowhere else can one find as much political activity per square mile as in tiny Manchester, New Hampshire (population ninety-one thousand), during primary week.

Half the portable satellite dishes in the country are there to beam back every piece of news to the rest of the country. As with other momentous events, like a summit meeting or an inauguration, all three networks move their anchors and top reporters to the scene to broadcast the nightly news. In 1988 NBC set up shop in the Holiday Inn along Manchester's only downtown shopping street. CBS took over the Sheraton Wayfarer near the city's suburban shopping mall. ABC, taking advantage of having the only local affiliate in New Hampshire, used its studios for their national news broadcast.

All the candidates are there too, of course. Thus New Hampshire voters get an unmatched chance to see the candidates up close and personal. If a person has the inclination to see a candidate all they have to do is look up that candidate's schedule for the day in any of the New Hampshire or Boston newspapers. Chances are good that all of the candidates will be within easy driving distance of their home sometime during the final week. And if a person does not have the time or interest to seek out a candidate, chances are their path will cross that of several of the candidates anyway. Ask an interested voter how he or she likes a candidate and you may get the answer of "I don't know. I've only met that one twice."

Whether a Manchester resident goes out on an errand or just stays at home to watch TV, it's hard to avoid the politicking. Everywhere a person goes candidates' signs abound—in people's yards, on street corners, and planted in snow banks. The sidewalks of the city's main streets are full of activists holding up signs and passing out literature, buttons, and assorted political paraphernalia (in 1988 the Bush people even gave out copies of Barbara Bush's favorite recipes for quiche and oatmeal lace cookies). A per-

Activists gather outside a suburban Manchester mall for the final rally of the 1988 primary campaign.

son can make an activist's day be letting him or her put a candidate's bumper sticker on their car.

When New Hampshirites turn on their TVs they find that product commercials on all their favorite shows have been supplanted by hard-hitting candidate commercials. The candidates take great advantage of the fact that money spent on Boston television does not count toward the spending limit in New Hampshire, and thus flood the market from across the state border. If a person misses the latest commercials that evening, they can just stay up till eleven o'clock to see them all on the local news.

Finally, election day arrives and the activists move indoors to work the phones to get the vote out. As the returns come in, the candidates make the rounds among the major media centers to make their statements. Reporters make their instant analysis and tell the world of the stunning results (New Hampshire is well known for providing unexpected finishes).

The next day the state looks like Cinderella after the ball. The satellite trucks are on their way out, and once busy streetcorners are suddenly empty. Life in Manchester once again looks no different than in most small towns in America. Its' citizens, however, can relish the fact that for a short time they were at the center of the political universe—and that it is only four more years till the next primary.

shire.) The term neatly describes what candidates for the nomination are after. Primaries and caucuses are more than an endurance contest, though they are certainly that—they are also proving grounds. Week after week, the challenge is to do *better than expected.* To get "mo" going, candidates have to beat people they were not expected to beat, collect margins above predictions, and never, above all else, lose to people they were expected to trounce. Momentum is good to have, but it is no guarantee of victory, as candidates with a strong base sometimes bounce back. Political scientist Larry Bartels found that "substantive political appeal may overwhelm the impact of momentum, as it did for Reagan against Bush and for Mondale against Hart."[13]

Evaluating the Primary and Caucus System   The primaries and the caucuses are here to stay. That does not mean, however, that political scientists or commentators are particularly happy with the system. Criticisms of this marathon campaign are numerous; here are a few of the most important:

- *Disproportionate attention goes to the early caucuses and primaries.* Take a look at Figure 8.1, which shows how critics think America's media-dominated campaigns are distorted by early primaries and caucuses. Neither New Hampshire nor Iowa is particularly representative of the national electorate. Both are rural; both have only small minority populations; and neither is at the center of the political mainstream. Whereas Iowa is more liberal than the nation as a whole, New Hampshire is the reverse. Thus, while Iowa and New Hampshire are not always "make or break" contests, they play a key—and a disproportionate—role in building momentum, money, and media attention.

[13]Larry M. Bartels, *Presidential Primaries and the Dynamics of Public Choice* (Princeton, N.J.: Princeton University Press, 1988), 269.

- *Money plays too big a role in the caucuses and primaries.* Momentum means money—getting more of it than your opponents. Many people think that money plays too large a role in American presidential elections. (This topic will be discussed in detail shortly.) Candidates who drop out early in the process often lament that their inability to raise money left them without a chance to really compete.

- *Participation in primaries and caucuses is low and unrepresentative.* Although about 50 percent of the population votes in the November presidential election, only about 25 percent cast ballots in presidential primaries. Participation in caucus states is much smaller, as a person must usually devote several hours to attending a caucus. Except for Iowa, where media attention boosts the turnout to about 20 percent, only about 5 percent of registered voters typically show up for caucuses. Moreover, voters in pri-

---

Figure 8.1 **The Inflated Importance of Iowa and New Hampshire in the Presidential Nomination Process**

In 1984, 34 percent of all TV news stories about the nomination campaigns were about Iowa and New Hampshire, in spite of the fact that these two small states selected only about 2 percent of the convention delegates. Here, according to an analysis of coverage by the *New York Times,* are the fifty states drawn to scale according to the media attention their primaries and caucuses received in 1984:

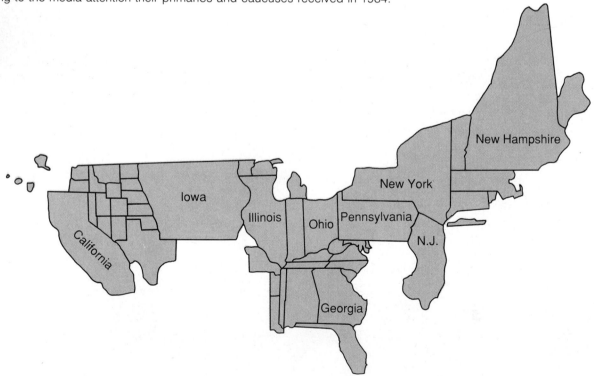

Source: William C. Adams, "As New Hampshire Goes . . . ," in Gary R. Orren and Nelson W. Polsby, eds., *Media and Momentum* (Chatham, N.J.: Chatham House, 1987), 43.

maries and caucuses are hardly representative of voters at large, tending to be better educated and more affluent.

- *Primaries and caucuses exaggerate regional factors in decision making.* In 1988, southern states, feeling that northern states like New Hampshire and Iowa had disproportionate influence in the choice of the Democratic nominee, created **Super Tuesday** by moving all their primaries to the same day in early March. No longer could conservative Democrats be ignored, said southern democratic leaders. Although the hope of southern Democrats did not materialize (Bush was the only conservative to score a big triumph on Super Tuesday), efforts to play to regional advantage often lead to the manipulation of the primary calendar. California, whose primary has come too late to play a decisive role in the nomination process since 1972, is the latest to enter the fray, moving its primary date for 1992 to just after New Hampshire's.

- *The system gives too much power to the media.* Critics contend that the media have replaced the party bosses as the new kingmakers. Deciding who has momentum at any given moment, the press readily labels candidates as winners and losers.

Is this, critics ask, the best way to pick a president? Critics answer their own question with a strong no, and have come up with a number of reform proposals (see "You Are the Policymaker: National and Regional Presidential Primary Proposals").

Nevertheless, the current system has powerful defenders—most notably the candidates themselves. For example, George Bush writes in his 1987 autobiography, *Looking Forward,* that

> our presidential selection process may be pressurized, chaotic, sometimes even unfair; but I disagree with critics who think that it needs a massive overhaul—especially those who argue that television, because it can reach millions, makes it unnecessary for a candidate to travel the country "retailing" his campaign message.
>
> For all its flaws, the virtue of the present system is that it brings presidential candidates—as well as Presidents—out of the insulated politics of television and electronic computers into contact with the flesh-and-blood world.[14]

Even candidates who finish well back in the pack usually support the process. Senator Paul Simon, who barely lost in Iowa and carried only his native Illinois, argues that it is best to start the race in small states where people can meet the candidates face-to-face and where "a candidate of limited means has a chance."[15] He adds that the people of Iowa and New Hampshire, recognizing their important role in the process, "make their commitments with considerably more caution and care than do most citizens in other states."[16] Former Arizona Governor Bruce Babbitt, who got great press coverage but few votes in 1988, defends the length of the nomination race. He argues that "it has to be long, to allow us to surface national leadership outside of a parliamentary system. Congress

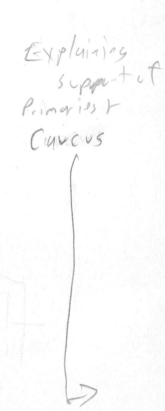

Explaining support of Primaries & Caucus

[14]George Bush, *Looking Forward* (New York: Doubleday, 1987).

[15]Paul Simon, *Winners and Losers: The 1988 Race for the Presidency—One Candidate's Perspective* (New York: Continuum, 1989), 112.

[16]*Ibid.,* 113.

National and Regional Presidential Primary Proposals

The idea of holding a **national primary** to select party nominees has been discussed virtually ever since state primaries were introduced. In 1913 President Woodrow Wilson proposed it in his first message to Congress. Since then over two hundred fifty proposals for a national presidential primary have been introduced in Congress. These proposals do not lack for public support, as opinion polls have consistently shown that a substantial majority of Democrats, Republicans, and Independents alike favor such a reform.

According to its proponents, a national primary would bring directness and simplicity to the process for the voters as well as the candidates. The length of the campaign would be shortened and no longer would votes in one state have more political impact than votes in another. The concentration of media coverage on this one event, say its advocates, would increase not only political interest in the nomination decision, but also public understanding of the issues involved.

A national primary would not be so simple, respond the critics. Since Americans would not want a candidate nominated with 25 percent of the vote from among a field of six candidates, in most primaries a runoff election between the top two finishers in each party would have to be held. So much for making the campaign simpler, national primary critics note. Each voter would have to vote three times for president—twice in the primaries and once in November.

Another common criticism of a national primary is that only well-established politicians would have a shot of breaking through in such a system. Big money

and big attention from the national media would become more crucial than ever. Obscure candidates, like Jimmy Carter in 1976, would never have a chance. Do Americans, however, really want politicians without an established reputation to become president?

Perhaps more feasible than a national primary is holding a series of **regional primaries,** in which, say, states in the eastern time zone would vote one week, central time zone the next, and so on. This would impose a more rational structure and cut down on candidate travel. No longer would candidates be faced with campaigning simultaneously in primaries at opposite ends of the country. (In 1984 Gary Hart complained that his wife got to campaign in California while he was stuck in New Jersey; he won California but was trounced in New Jersey for this remark.)

The major problem with the regional primary proposal, however, is the advantage gained by whichever region goes first. For example, if the western states were the first to vote, any candidate from California would have a clear edge in building momentum. Although most of the proposed plans call for the order of the regions to be determined by lottery, this would not erase the fact that regional advantages would surely be created from year to year.

Put yourself in the role of policymaker. Do the advantages of either the national primary or regional primary proposals outweigh the disadvantages? Would they represent an improvement over the current system? Keep in mind that there are almost always unintended consequences associated with reforms.

does not automatically produce national leadership."[17] It is important to enable new national leaders to emerge, says Babbitt, and the current American system facilitates this.

Obviously, some of the candidates would like to see some changes, but as long as most candidates and citizens support the process in general, major reform is unlikely. For the forseeable future, states will continue to select del-

[17] Bruce Babbitt, "Bruce Babbitt's View from the Wayside," *Washington Post National Weekly Edition,* February 29, 1988, 24.

egates in primaries and caucuses to attend the national conventions, where the nominees are formally chosen.

The Convention Send-off

Once, party conventions provided great drama. Great speeches were given, dark-horse candidates suddenly appeared, and ballot after ballot was held as candidates jockeyed to win the nomination. It took the Democrats 46 ballots in 1912, 44 in 1920, and a record 103 in 1924 to nominate their presidential standard-bearer. Multiballot conventions died out in 1952, however, with the advent of television.

Nevertheless, television did not immediately put an end to drama at the conventions. In fact, for a while it helped to create it. In 1964 NBC's John Chancellor was arrested for standing in the aisles while reporting from the floor of the Republican Convention. His producers promised him bail, and as he was escorted off the floor he signed off saying, "This is John Chancellor reporting under custody and now returning you to the anchor booth." Four years later it was protestors in the streets of Chicago that were being arrested at the Democratic Convention. The networks shifted back and forth from scenes of violence in the streets to the bitter debate and occasional scuffles inside the convention hall. In 1972 the Democrats were at it again, this time extending their debates late into the night, causing nominee George McGovern to give his acceptance speech at three in the morning. Some delegates took pity on the overworked TV anchors, holding up signs like "Free Walter Cronkite" (who then anchored CBS's coverage).

Today, though, the drama has largely been drained from the conventions, as the winner is a foregone conclusion. No longer can a powerful governor shift a whole block of votes at the last minute. Delegates selected in primaries and open caucuses have known preferences. The last time there was any doubt as

Despite a strong effort by his supporters at the 1924 Democratic National Convention, Alfred E. Smith eventually withdrew after 95 ballots, and John W. Davis received the nomination after a record 103 ballots. Davis subsequently lost the presidential election to Republican Calvin Coolidge. Today's conventions have little such drama, as the parties strictly control the proceedings to present a unified image.

to who would win at the convention was in 1976, when Ford barely edged Reagan for the Republican nomination. The parties have also learned that it is not in their best interest to provide high drama. The raucous conventions held by the Republicans in 1964 and the Democrats in 1968 and 1972 captured the public's attention, but they also exposed such divisiveness that the parties were unable to unite for the fall campaign.

Without such drama, the networks have scaled back their coverage substantially and the Nielsen ratings have fallen to new lows.[18] Most people would prefer watching taped highlights rather than live coverage (see "The People Speak: Should the Conventions Be Televised Live?"). Indeed, the highest rating any network garnered during the 1988 conventions was 8.7 for NBC the night of Jesse Jackson's speech. By comparison, the next week CBS obtained a rating of 15.1 for its coverage of the Miss Teen USA Pageant.

One can hardly blame people for tuning out the conventions, though, when little news is made at them. Today's conventions are carefully scripted to present the party in its best light. Delegates are no longer there to argue for their causes, but rather to merely support their candidate. The parties carefully orchestrate a massive send-off for the presidential and vice-presidential candidates. The party's leaders are there in force, as are many of its most important followers— people whose input will be key during the campaign. Thus, although conventions are no longer very interesting, they are a significant rallying point for the parties.

The conventions are also important in developing the party's policy positions and in promoting political representation. In the past, conventions were essentially an assembly of state- and local-party leaders, gathered together to bargain over the selection of the party's ticket. Almost all delegates were white, male, and over forty. Lately, party reformers, especially among the Democrats, have worked hard to make the conventions far more demographically representative.

Meeting in an oversized, overstuffed convention hall in a major city, a national convention is a short-lived affair. The highlight of the first day is usually the keynote speech, in which a dynamic speaker recalls party heroes, condemns the opposition party, and touts the nominee-apparent.

The second day centers on the party platform—the party's statement of its goals and policies for the next four years. The platform is drafted prior to the convention by a committee whose members are chosen in rough proportion to each candidate's strength. Any time over a quarter of the delegates to the platform committee disagree with the majority, they can bring an alternative *minority plank* to the convention floor for debate. In former times, contests over the platform were key tests of candidates' strength prior to the actual nomination. Now they serve mostly as a way for the minority factions in the party to make sure that their voices are heard. Concessions on the party platform, such as those by the Dukakis camp to the Jackson camp in 1988, are sometimes crucial to maintaining party unity on the second day.

The third day is devoted to choosing a presidential candidate. One of each candidate's eminent supporters will give a speech extolling the candidate's virtues; a string of seconding speeches will then follow. Demonstrations erupt

[18]See Martin P. Wattenberg, "When You Can't Beat Them, Join Them: Shaping the Presidential Nominating Process to the Television Age." *Polity* 21 (Spring 1989): 587–97.

Explain minority plank

as if spontaneous, though in reality they are carefully planned. Toward the end of the evening balloting begins as states announce their votes ("Florida, the sunshine state, casts all its votes for . . . "). After all the votes are counted, the evening's last demonstration celebrates the long-anticipated nomination.

On the final day of the convention, the vice-presidential nominee is chosen by roll call vote. The nominee then comes to the podium to make a brief acceptance speech. This is followed by the grand finale—the presidential accceptance speech, in which the battle lines for the coming campaign are drawn. Afterward all the party leaders come out to congratulate the party's ticket, raise their hands, and bid the delegates farewell.

THE CAMPAIGN GAME

Once nominated, candidates concentrate on campaigning for the general election. These days, the word *campaign* is part of American political vocabulary, but it was not always so. The term was originally a military one: generals mounted campaigns, using their scarce resources to achieve strategic objectives. Political campaigns are like that, too—resources are scarce, expenditures in the presidential race are limited by federal law, and both have to be timed and targeted. A candidate's time and energy are also finite. Choices must be made concerning where to go and how long to spend at each stop.

More than organization and leadership are involved in campaigns. Artistry also enters the picture, for campaigns deal in images. The campaign is the canvas on which political strategists try to paint portraits of leadership, competence, caring, and other images Americans value in presidents. To project the right image to the voters, three ingredients are needed: a campaign organization, money, and media attention.

Organizing the Campaign

In every campaign, there is too much to do and too little time to do it. Every candidate must prepare for nightly banquets and endless handshaking. More importantly, to effectively organize their campaigns candidates must do the following:

- *Line up a campaign manager.* Some candidates try to run their own campaign, but they usually end up regretting it. A professional campaign manager can keep the candidate from getting bogged down in organizational details. This person also bears the day-to-day responsibility for maintaining ethics in the organization (see "A Question of Ethics: Is All Fair in Love and Campaigning?").

- *Get a fund-raiser.* Money, as this chapter will soon discuss in detail, is an important key to election victory.

- *Get a campaign counsel.* With all the current federal regulation of campaign financing, legal assistance is essential to ensure compliance with the laws.

- *Hire media and campaign consultants.* Candidates have more important things to do with their time than plan ad campaigns, contract for buttons and bumper stickers, and buy TV time and newspaper space. Professionals can get them the most exposure for their money.

A Question of Ethics

Is All Fair in Love and Campaigning?

According to legend, the late Claude Pepper's opponent in a 1950 Florida Senate race was quoted extensively as having told rural voters:

> Are you aware that Claude Pepper is known all over Washington as a shameless extrovert? Not only that, but this man is reliably reported to practice nepotism with his sister-in-law and he has a sister who was once a thespian in wicked New York. Worst of all, it is an established fact Mr. Pepper before his marriage habitually practiced celibacy.

Obviously, such rhetoric would not comport with the Code of Ethics of the American Association of Political Consultants, which pledges its members "to appeal to the good and commendable ideals in the American voters," and to refrain from "irrational appeals" or disseminating "false or misleading information."

That Democratic and Republican consultants could agree on such a code indicates that campaign professionals do not believe that all is fair in campaigning. This is not to say that they think punches must be pulled, but rather that when one is thrown it should be thrown properly. It is not always so easy, however, to determine what is proper and what is not.

The 1988 prison furlough issue, discussed briefly in Chapter 1, is a perfect case in point. Was the Bush campaign's infamous "revolving door" TV ad unfair and misleading? It showed a long line of prisoners passing through a prison turnstile, while the announcer says that even murderers not eligible for parole were furloughed through a Massachusetts program during Michael Dukakis's governorship. Many escaped and are still at large, the announcer states. The Dukakis camp immediately screamed foul. The ad was intentionally vague, they said, falsely implying that hordes of convicted murderers were running wild as a result of the furlough policy. Bush's campaign managers did not see it that way, though, responding that nothing untrue was said and that their lawyers had cleared the ad.

To dramatize and personalize the issue, Bush used the case of Willie Horton—a murderer who raped a Maryland woman one weekend during a furlough from a Massachusetts prison. Although Bush never mentioned the fact that Horton was black in his speeches and never showed his picture in his ads, others did. For example, a committee separate from the Bush campaign produced a TV ad which showed a scary mug shot of Horton and an interview with his rape victim, who happened to be white. Democrats charged that this was playing on racial fears. How could Bush bring up the Horton case without expecting to inject racial issues into the campaign, they asked? The Bush campaign responded that they had never mentioned race at all. Should they take the blame for what others had done?

Ultimately, it is up to the voters to be the arbiters. If people felt that the Bush campaign had been unethical, they could have voted against his candidacy in protest. Unlike in Claude Pepper's case, at least the charges were out in the open and each side had the opportunity to make their views widely known via television. In this sense, there may be more controversy about the ethics of campaigns these days, but the ability of the voters to enforce their own sense of fairness has probably increased.

- *Assemble a campaign staff.* It is desirable to hire as many professionals as the campaign budget allows, but it is also important to get a coordinator of volunteers to see to it that envelopes are licked, doorbells rung, and other small but vital tasks are addressed.

- *Plan the logistics.* A modern presidential campaign involves jetting around the country at an incredible pace. Good advance people handle the complicated details of candidate scheduling and see to it that events are well publicized and attended.

- *Get a research staff and policy advisors.* Candidates have little time to master the complex issues reporters will ask about. Policy advisors—often distinguished academics—feed them information they need to keep up with events.
- *Hire a pollster.* There are dozens of professional polling firms that do opinion research to tell candidates how they are going over with the voters and what is on the voters' minds.
- *Get a good press secretary.* Candidates running for major office have reporters dogging them every step of the way. The reporters need news, and a good press secretary can help them make their deadlines with stories that the campaign would like to see reported.

Most of these tasks cost money. Campaigns are not cheap, and the role of money in campaigns is a controversial one.

Money and Campaigning

There is no doubt that campaigns are expensive and, in America's high-tech political arena, growing more so (see Table 8.1). As California Treasurer Jesse Unruh used to say, "Money is the mother's milk of politics." Candidates need money to build a campaign organization and to get their message out. Many people and groups who want certain things from the government are all too willing to give it—thus there is the common perception that money buys votes and influence. The following sections take a close look at the role of money in campaigns.

The Maze of Campaign Finance Reforms   As the costs of campaigning skyrocketed with the growth of television, and as the Watergate scandal exposed large, illegal campaign contributions, momentum developed in the early 1970s

| Table 8.1 | Increasing Campaign Costs |

Here are some comparisons between the 1984 and 1988 campaign price tags:

ITEM	PERCENTAGE INCREASE	1984	1988
Thirty-second commercial during a prime-time show in Des Moines, Iowa	63.6%	$1,100	$1,800
One night's stay in a double room at the Marriott Hotel in Des Moines, Iowa	11.7%	$ 85	$ 95
One telephone interview by a poll taker	40%	$ 25	$ 35
One campaign button, bought in lots of one thousand	66.6%	15¢	25¢
One ream of photocopier paper	8.2%	$ 3.39	$ 3.67

Source: New York Times, February 6, 1988, 9.

Partly in response to disclosures that individuals like W. Clement Stone had contributed more than one million dollars to the Nixon reelection campaign, the 1974 Federal Election Campaign Act placed strict limits on the amount a person can contribute to candidates for national office. The act also provides government funding for presidential candidates and limits their spending.

for campaign financing reform. Several public interest lobbies (see Chapter 11), notably Common Cause and the National Committee for an Effective Congress, led the drive. In 1974 the Congress passed the **Federal Election Campaign Act.** It had two main goals: tightening reporting requirements for contributions and limiting overall expenditures. In essence, here is what the act, with subsequent amendments did:

- *It created the **Federal Election Commission (FEC).*** A bipartisan body, the six-member FEC administers the campaign finance laws and enforces compliance with their requirements.
- *It provided public financing for presidential primaries and general elections.* Presidential candidates who raise five thousand dollars on their own in at least twenty states can get individual contributions of up to two hundred fifty dollars matched by the federal treasury. For the general election, the party nominees each get a fixed amount of money to cover all their campaign expenses.
- *It limited presidential campaign spending.* If presidential candidates accept federal support at any stage, they agree to limit their campaign expenditures to an amount prescribed by federal law.
- *It required disclosure.* Regardless of whether they accept any federal funding, all candidates must file periodic reports with the FEC, listing who contributed and how the money was spent.
- *It limited contributions.* Scandalized to find out that wealthy individuals like J. Willard Marriott had contributed one million dollars to the 1972 Nixon campaign, Congress limited individual contributions to one thousand dollars. This limit has yet to be adjusted for inflation, and many feel such an adjustment is long overdue.

While the campaign reforms were generally welcomed by both parties, the constitutionality of the act was challenged in the 1976 case of *Buckley* v. *Valeo.* In this case the Supreme Court struck down the portion of the act that had limited the amount individuals could contribute to their own campaigns as a violation of free speech.

Overall, there is little doubt that campaign spending reforms have made campaigns more open and honest. Small donors are encouraged and the rich are restricted. A campaign's financial records are now open for all to examine, and FEC auditors try to make sure that the regulations are enforced.

The Proliferation of PACS The campaign reforms also encouraged the spread of **Political Action Committees,** generally known as **PACs.** Before the 1974 reforms, corporations were technically forbidden from donating money to political campaigns, but many wrote big checks anyway. Unions could make indirect contributions, although limits were set on how they could aid candidates and political parties. The 1974 reforms created a new, more open, way for interest groups like business and labor to contribute to campaigns. Any interest group, large or small, can now get into the act by forming their own PAC to directly channel contributions of up to five thousand dollars per candidate. Because *Buckley* v. *Valeo* extended the right of free speech to PACs, they can spend unlimited amounts indirectly, that is, if such activities are not coordinated with the campaign.

PACs have proliferated in recent years. The FEC counted 9,100 PACs in 1988. Independent PAC outlays in that year amounted to about $120 million. Many believe that this has led to a system of open graft.[19] Few developments since the Watergate crisis have generated so much cynicism about government as the explosive growth of PACs over the last fifteen years.

A PAC is formed when a business association, or some other interest group, decides to contribute to candidates they believe will be favorable toward their goals. The group registers as a PAC with the FEC, and then puts money into the PAC coffers. The PAC can collect money from stockholders, members, and other interested parties. It then donates the money to candidates, often after careful research on their issue stands and past voting records. One very important ground rule prevails: All expenditures must be meticulously accounted for to the FEC. Thus if PACs are corrupting democracy, at least they are doing so openly.

Candidates need PACs because high-tech campaigning is expensive. Tightly contested races for the House of Representatives can sometimes cost one million dollars; senate races can easily cost one million dollars for television alone. PACs play a major role in paying for expensive campaigns. Thus there emerges a symbiotic relationship between the PACs and the candidates: candidates need money, which they insist can be used without compromising their integrity; PACs want access to officeholders, which they insist can be gained without buying votes. Justin Dart of Dart Industries, a close friend of former President Reagan, remarks of his PAC that "talking to politicians is fine, but with a little money, they hear you better."[20]

An abundance of PACs are around to help out the candidates. There are big ones, such as the Realtors Political Action Committee and the American Medical Association Political Action Committee. There are little ones, too, representing smaller industries or business associations: EggPAC, FishPAC, FurPAC, LardPAC, and—for the beer distributors, of course—SixPAC.[21] You can see in Table 8.2 some of the biggest PACs in terms of contributions.

Critics of the PAC system worry that all this money leads to PAC control over what the winners do once in office. Archibald Cox and Fred Wertheimer of Common Cause write that the role of PACs in campaign finance "is robbing our nation of its democratic ideals and giving us a government of leaders beholden to the monied interests who make their election possible."[22] On some issues, it seems clear that PAC money has made a difference. The Federal Trade Commission, for example, once passed a regulation requiring that car dealers list known mechanical defects on the window sticker of used cars. The National Association of Automobile Dealers quickly became the fourth largest donor in the 1980 congressional elections, contributing just over one million dollars to candidates of both parties. Soon afterwards, 216 representatives cosponsored a

[19]See, for example, Brooks Jackson, *Honest Graft: Big Money and the American Political Process* (New York: Alfred A. Knopf, 1988).

[20]Quoted in Jeffrey Berry, *The Interest Group Society* (Boston: Little, Brown, 1984), 162.

[21]*Ibid.,* 162–63.

[22]Archibald Cox and Fred Wertheimer, "The Choice is Clear: It's People vs. the PACs," in Peter Woll, ed., *Debating American Government,* 2nd ed. (Glenview, Ill.: Scott, Foresman, 1988), 125.

According to the Federal Election Commission, which monitors Political Action Committee (PAC) spending carefully, here are the twenty largest PAC contributors to federal candidates for the 1987–88 election cycle:

1. Realtors PAC	$3,040,969
2. Democratic Republican Independent Voter Education Committee	$2,856,724
3. American Medical Association PAC	$2,316,496
4. National Education Association PAC	$2,104,689
5. National Association of Retired Federal Employees PAC	$1,979,850
6. United Auto Workers Voluntary Community Action Program	$1,953,099
7. Association of Trial Lawyers of American PAC	$1,913,558
8. Letter Carriers Political Action Fund	$1,737,982
9. American Federation of State, County, and Municipal Employees	$1,663,386
10. Machinists Nonpartisan Political League	$1,490,780
11. National Association of Home Builders PAC	$1,448,560
12. Carpenters' Legislative Improvement Committee	$1,363,498
13. National Association of Life Underwriters PAC	$1,329,150
14. AT&T PAC	$1,305,112
15. Airline Pilots Association PAC	$1,217,000
16. National Automobile Dealers Association PAC	$1,202,420
17. International Brotherhood of Electrical Workers	$1,197,190
18. Auto Dealers and Drivers for Free Trade PAC	$1,158,700
19. United Food and Commerical Workers International Union	$1,152,110
20. American Bankers Association BANKPAC	$1,151,050

Source: Federal Election Commission.

House resolution nullifying the FTC regulation. Of these, 186 had been aided by the auto dealers' PAC.[23]

It is questionable, however, whether such examples are the exception or the rule. Most PACs give money to candidates who agree with them in the first place. For instance, the antiabortion PACs will not waste their money supporting outspokenly pro-choice candidates. Frank Sorauf's careful review of the subject concludes that "there simply are no data in the systematic studies that would support the popular assertions about the 'buying' of the Congress or about any other massive influence of money on the legislative process."[24] (For more on the link between PACs and Congress see "A Question of Ethics" in Chapter 12, page 424.)

[23]This is discussed in Berry, *The Interest Group Society,* 172.
[24]Frank J. Sorauf, *Money in American Elections* (Glenview, Ill.: Scott, Foresman, 1988), 312.

The impact of PAC money on presidents is even more doubtful. Presidential campaigns are, of course, partly subsidized by the public and so are less dependent upon PACs. Moreover, presidents have well-articulated positions on most important issues. A small contribution from any one PAC is not likely to turn a presidential candidate's head.

To summarize, money matters in campaigns. Because it matters during campaigns, it sometimes also matters during legislative votes. Although scare stories about the proliferation of PACs may be exaggerated, campaign finance is an old issue that is not likely to go away as long as campaigns continue to be so expensive.

Are Campaigns Too Expensive?   Every four years Americans spend over one billion dollars on national, state, and local elections. This seems like a tremendous amount of money, yet, compared with the amount of money Americans spend on items of far less importance, campaigns actually are relatively inexpensive (see Table 8.3). For example, each year a typical soap company will spend twice the cost of a presidential campaign to advertise its products.

Table 8.3 | **The Costs of American Elections: Comparatively, a Bargain**

Journalists often portray the costs of American elections as a national scandal, yet those costs are low in comparison with other nations. (In Israel, for example, the cost is more than $20 per vote.) American elections cost, per voter, about as much as a dinner at a fast-food restaurant. In 1988 the estimated total cost of the presidential election was about $.5 billion. This was a sizable amount of money to be sure, but Americans spent more on a number of consumer goods, such as the following:

ITEM	COST (billions of $)
Color televisions	7.9
Videocassette recorders	4.8
Refrigerators	4.6
Microwave ovens	3.5
Personal computers	3.3
Clothes washers	2.5
Prerecorded videotapes	2.4
Air conditioners	1.5
Camcorders	1.4
Radios	.8
Calculators	.8
Blank floppy disks	.8
FAX machines	.7

Source: U.S. Department of Commerce, *Statistical Abstract of the United States 1989* (Washington, D.C.: Government Printing Office, 1989), 748. Data are for 1987.

What bothers politicians most about the rising costs of high-tech campaigning is that fund-raising has come to take up so much of their precious time. In 1988 former Florida Governor Reuben Askew pulled out of a Senate race he was favored to win for this very reason. "Something is seriously wrong with our system when many candidates for the Senate need to spend 75 percent of their time raising money," Askew said.[25] Many officeholders feel that the need for continuous fund-raising distracts them from their jobs as legislators.

Public financing of campaigns would take care of this problem. Some lawmakers support some sort of public financing reform; however, it will be very difficult to get Congress to agree on equal financing for the people who will challenge them for their seats. Incumbents will not readily give up the advantage they have in raising money.

Does Money Buy Victory?   Money is, of course, absolutely crucial to electoral victory; important offices are rarely won these days by candidates who spend virtually nothing. One of the last of this nonspending breed was Senator William Proxmire of Wisconsin, who recently retired. In 1988 he was succeeded by wealthy businessman Herbert Kohl, who funded his multimillion dollar campaign entirely out of his own pocket. (As Kohl said, he was so rich that at least no one had to worry about him being bought by special interests.) In this era of high-tech politics, pollsters, public relations people, direct-mail consultants, and many other specialists are crucial to a campaign, and they cost money.

Perhaps the most basic complaint about money and politics is that there may be a direct link between dollars spent and votes received. Few have done more to dispel this charge than political scientist Gary Jacobson. His research

[25]Dexter Filkins, "The Only Issue Is Money," *Washington Post National Weekly Edition,* June 13, 1988, 28.

Today's high-tech campaigns demand money. Senator Herbert Kohl spent millions of his own personal fortune to ensure the name recognition that William Proxmire, who Kohl replaced, had gained through years of service.

has shown that "the more incumbents spend, the worse they do."[26] This fact is not as odd as it at first sounds. It simply means that incumbents who face a tough opponent must raise more money to meet the challenge. When a challenger is not a serious threat (as they all too often are not), incumbents can afford to campaign cheaply. More important than having "more" money is having "enough" money. Once candidates have sufficient exposure for the voters to really know them, additional funds make relatively little difference. All the money in the world will not convince voters to elect someone they know to be a scoundrel.

The Media and the Campaign

Money matters, and so does media attention. Media coverage is determined by two factors: (1) how candidates use their advertising budget, and (2) the "free" attention they get as newsmakers. The first, obviously, is relatively easy to control; the second, harder but not impossible. Most every logistical decision in a campaign—where to eat breakfast, whom to include on the rostrum, when to announce a major policy proposal—is calculated according to its intended media impact. Years ago, say, in the election of 1896, the biggest item in a campaign budget might have been renting a railroad train. Today the major item is unquestionably television advertising. About half the total budget for a presidential or senatorial campaign will be used for television advertising.

No major candidate these days can do without what political scientist Dan Nimmo calls "the political persuaders."[27] A new profession of political consultants has emerged, and for the right price, they can turn a disorganized campaign into a well-run, high-tech operation. They can do it all—polling or hiring the pollster, molding a candidate's image, advising a candidate on his or her spouse's role, handling campaign logistics, managing payrolls, and so forth. Incumbents as well as challengers turn to professional consultants for such help.

All this concern with public relations worries some observers of American politics. They fear a new era of politics in which the slick slogan and the image salesperson will dominate, an era when Madison Avenue will be more influential than Main Street. Most political scientists, however, are coming to the conclusion that such fears are overblown. Research has shown that campaign advertising can be a source of information about issues as well as about images. Thomas Patterson and Robert McClure examined the information contained in TV advertising and found it impressive. In fact, they concluded, viewers could learn more about candidates' stands on the issues from watching their ads than from watching the nightly TV news. Most news coverage stresses where the candidates went, how big their crowds were, and other campaign details. Only rarely do the networks delve into where the candidates stand on the issues. In contrast, political ads typically address issues.[28] Perhaps there is less conflict between

[26]Gary C. Jacobson, "The Effects of Campaign Spending in Congressional Elections," *American Political Science Review* 72 (June 1978): 469. Chapter 12 will examine congressional elections further.

[27]Dan Nimmo, *The Political Persuaders: The Techniques of Modern Campaigning* (Englewood Cliffs, N.J.: Prentice-Hall, 1970).

[28]Thomas E. Patterson and Robert D. McClure, *The Unseeing Eye* (New York: Putnam, 1976).

Modern campaigns also demand media savvy. Roger Ailes, George Bush's media advisor, is one of a new breed of political consultants who help shape a candidate's image as presented by the media.

issues and *images* than appears on the surface. The candidates' positions are a crucial part of their images. Getting those positions across to voters is as important as persuading them that a candidate is honest, competent, and a leader.

Candidates attempt to manipulate their images through advertising and image building, but they have less control over the other aspect of the media—coverage of the news. To be sure, most campaigns have press aides who feed "canned" news releases to reporters. Still, the media largely determine for themselves what is happening in a campaign. Campaign coverage seems to be a constant interplay between hard news about what candidates say and do and the human-interest angle, which most journalists think sells newspapers or interests television viewers.

Apparently, news organizations believe that policy issues are of less interest to voters than the campaign itself. The result is that news coverage is disproportionately devoted to campaign strategies, speculation about what will happen next, poll results, and other aspects of the campaign game. Patterson tabulated the amount of media attention to the campaign itself and the amount of attention to such substantive issues as the economy in the 1976 presidential race. Examining several newspapers and news magazines as well as television network news, he found that attention to the "game" far exceeded attention to substance.[29] Once a candidate has taken a policy position and it has been reported on, it becomes old news. The latest poll showing Smith ahead of Jones is thus more newsworthy in the eyes of the media. Bush's media consultant, Roger Ailes, calls this his "orchestra pit" theory of American politics: "If you have two guys on stage and one guy says, 'I have a solution to the Middle East problem,' and the other guy falls in the orchestra pit, who do you think is going to be on the evening news?"[30]

The Impact of Campaigns

Politicians are great believers in campaigns. Almost all of them figure that a good campaign is the key to victory. Many political scientists, however, question their importance. Reviewing the evidence, Dan Nimmo concluded, "Political campaigns are less crucial in elections than most politicians believe."[31] For years, researchers studying campaigns have stressed that campaigns have three effects on voters: **reinforcement, activation,** and **conversion.** Campaigns can reinforce voters' preferences for candidates; they can activate voters, getting them to contribute money or ring doorbells as opposed to merely voting; and they can convert, changing voters' minds.

Four decades of research on political campaigns lead to a single message: campaigns mostly reinforce and activate; only rarely do they convert. The evidence on the impact of campaigns points clearly to the conclusion that the best-laid plans of campaign managers change very few votes. Given the millions of dollars spent on political campaigns, it may be surprising to find that they do not have a great effect, but several factors tend to weaken campaigns' impact on voters:

[29]Patterson, *Mass Media Election,* 22–25.

[30]David R. Runkel, ed., *Campaign for President: The Managers Look at '88* (Dover, Mass.: Auburn, 1989), 136.

[31]Nimmo, *The Political Persuaders,* 5.

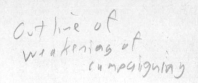
Outline of weakening of campaigning

- Most people pay relatively little attention to campaigns in the first place.
- People have a remarkable capacity for **selective perception:** paying most attention to things they already agree with and interpreting events according to their own predispositions.
- Factors such as party identification, though less important than they used to be, still influence voting behavior regardless of what happens in the campaign.
- Incumbents start with a substantial advantage in terms of name recognition and an established track record.

This does not mean, of course, that campaigns never change voters' minds, or that converting a small percentage is unimportant. In tight races, a good campaign can make the difference between winning and losing.

UNDERSTANDING NOMINATIONS AND CAMPAIGNS

Throughout the history of American politics, election campaigns have become longer and longer as the system has become increasingly open to public participation. Reformers in both the nineteenth and twentieth centuries held that the solution to democratic problems was more democracy—or as John Lennon sang, "Power to the people." In principle, more democracy always sounds better than less, but it is not such a simple issue in practice.

Are Nominations and Campaigns Too Democratic?

If one judges American campaigns solely by how open they are, then certainly the American system must be viewed favorably. In other countries the process of leadership nomination occurs within a relatively small circle of party elites. Thus politicians must work their way up through an apprenticeship system. In contrast, America has an entrepreneurial system in which the people play a crucial role at every stage from nomination to election. In this way, party outsiders can get elected in a way virtually unknown outside the United States. By appealing directly to the people, a candidate can emerge from nowhere to win the White House, as did Jimmy Carter. In this sense, the chance to win high office is open to almost everyone.

There is a price to be paid for all this openness, however. The process of selecting American leaders is a convoluted one, which has little downtime before it revs up all over again. Some have even called the American electoral process "the permanent campaign."[32] Many analysts wonder if people would pay more attention to politics if it did not ask so much of them. Given so much democratic opportunity, many citizens are simply overwhelmed by the process and stay on the sidelines. Similarly, the burdens of the modern campaign can discourage good candidates from throwing their hats into the ring. One of the most worrisome burdens candidates must face is amassing a sufficient campaign war

[32]Sidney Blumenthal, *The Permanent Campaign* (New York: Simon & Schuster, 1982).

The American political system allows citizens a voice at almost every point of the election process, unlike many countries where a political elite controls nominations and elections. Jimmy Carter, for example, here with his wife Rosalynn, won the 1976 presidential election by appealing directly to the people, rather than coming up through the party ranks.

chest. The system may be open, but it requires a lot of fund-raising to be able to take one's case to the people.

Do Big Campaigns Stimulate Big Government?

Today's big campaigns involve much more communication between candidates and voters than America's founders ever could have imagined. In their view, the presidency was to be an office responsible for seeing to the public interest as a whole. They wished to avoid "a contest in which the candidates would have to pose as 'friends' of the people or make specific policy commitments."[33] Thus the founders would probably be horrified by the modern practice of political candidates making numerous promises during nomination and election campaigns.

Because states are the key battlegrounds of presidential campaigns, candidates must tailor their appeals to the particular interests of each major state. In Iowa, for instance, promises are typically made to keep agricultural subsidies high, federal programs to help big cities are usually announced in New York, and in Texas, oil industry tax breaks are promised. To secure votes from each region of the country, candidates end up supporting a variety of local interests. Promises mount as the campaign goes on, and these promises usually add up to new government programs and money. The way modern campaigns are conducted is thus one of many reasons why politicians always find it easier to expand the size of American government than to limit it.

SUMMARY

In this age of high-tech politics, campaigns have become more media-oriented and far more expensive. There are really two campaigns of importance in presidential (and other) contests: the campaign for nomination and the campaign for election.

There are two ways by which delegates are selected to the national party conventions—state caucuses and primaries. The first caucus is traditionally held in Iowa, the first primary in New Hampshire. These two small, atypical American states have disproportionate power in determining who will be nominated and thus become president. This influence stems from the massive media attention devoted to these early contests and the momentum generated by winning them.

Money matters in political campaigns. As the costs of campaigning have increased, it has become all the more essential to raise large campaign war chests. While federal campaign finance reform in the 1970s lessened the impact of big contributors, it also allowed the proliferation of PACs. Some believe that PACs have created a system of legal graft in campaigning; others feel that the evidence for this view is relatively weak.

In general, politicians tend to overestimate the impact of campaigns; political scientists have found that campaigning serves primarily to reinforce citizens' views as opposed to converting them. American election campaigns are easily the most open and democratic in the world—some say too open. They are also

[33]James W. Ceaser, *Presidential Selection: Theory and Development* (Princeton, N.J.: Princeton University Press, 1979), 83.

extraordinarily long, leading politicans to make many promises along the way that contribute to big government.

KEY TERMS

nomination	national primary	Political Action Committees (PACs)
campaign strategy	regional primaries	reinforcement
national party convention	Federal Election Campaign Act	activation
caucus	Federal Election Commission (FEC)	conversion
presidential primaries		selective perception
Super Tuesday		

FOR FURTHER READING

Asher, Herbert B. *Presidential Elections and American Politics,* 4th ed. Chicago: Dorsey, 1988. A standard text on the electoral process.

Bartels, Larry M. *Presidential Primaries and the Dynamics of Public Choice.* Princeton, N.J.: Princeton University Press, 1988. The best recent book on voters' choices in the nominating season.

Fenno, Richard F. *The Presidential Odyssey of John Glenn.* Washington, D.C.: Congressional Quarterly Press, 1990. A marvelous case study of a failed presidential campaign.

Orren, Gary R. and Nelson W. Polsby, eds. *Media and Momentum.* Chatham, N.J.: Chatham House, 1987. The story of the exaggerated impact of New Hampshire on our presidential selection process.

Patterson, Thomas E. *The Mass Media Election.* New York: Praeger, 1980. A good review of the role of the media in elections, particularly the 1976 election.

Runkel, David R., ed. *Campaign for President: The Managers Look at '88.* Dover, Mass.: Auburn, 1989. The managers of seventeen presidential campaigns gather at Harvard to discuss their experiences in the 1988 primaries and general election.

Sabato, Larry J., ed. *Campaigns and Elections: A Reader in Modern Politics.* Glenview, Ill.: Scott, Foresman, 1989. A good set of readings on the nuts and bolts of running a campaign.

Shafer, Byron E. *Bifurcated Politics: Evolution and Reform in the National Party Convention.* Cambridge, Mass.: Harvard University Press, 1988. The story of how conventions have been transformed from important decision-making bodies to TV sideshows.

Sorauf, Frank J. *Money in American Elections.* Glenview, Ill.: Scott, Foresman, 1988. A definitive work on the impact of money on elections, an impact that Sorauf thinks is often exaggerated.

Winebrenner, Hugh. *The Iowa Precinct Caucuses: The Making of a Media Event.* Ames, Iowa: Iowa State University Press, 1987. A highly critical view of the Iowa caucuses from one of the state's leading political analysts.

9

*E*LECTIONS AND VOTING BEHAVIOR

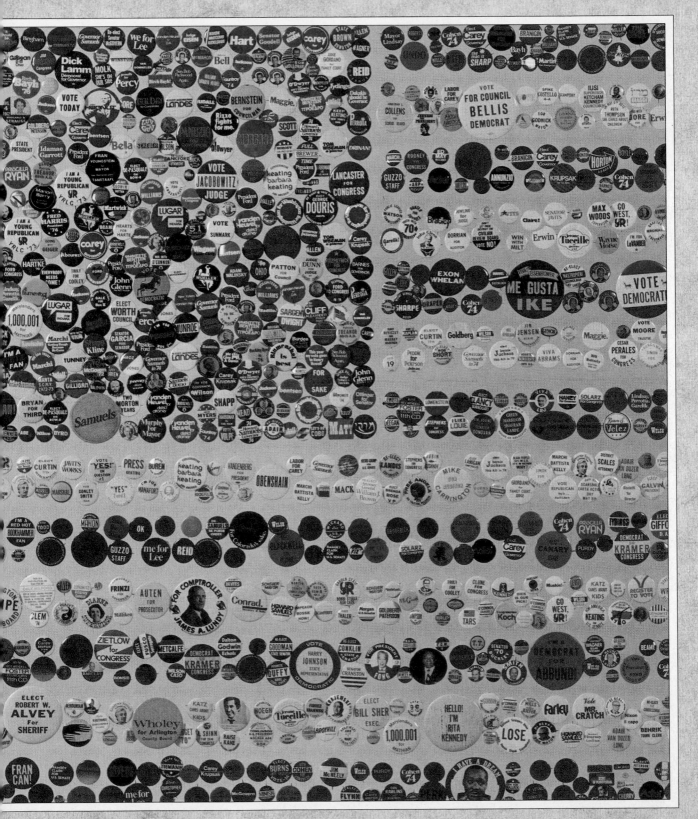

305

In February of 1990 the House of Representatives voted 289 to 132 for a bill that would make it easier than ever before to register to vote. Traditionally, voter registration procedures have been left to the state governments. The so-called motor-voter bill would be a major expansion of federal election law, establishing national standards for voter registration for the first time. Effective in 1993, the House bill would

- Provide for automatic registration of eligible citizens when they fill out an application, renewal, or change of address on a driver's license.

- Require that forms to register by mail be made available at unemployment and public assistance offices, schools, libraries, and hunting and fishing license offices.

- Bar the purging of people from voter rolls merely because they did not vote in the last election.

- Require that states periodically review their voter lists for accuracy, and purge voters who have moved out of their district.

- Authorize fifty million dollars to help cover the cost of new procedures—primarily the expense of computerizing the voting rolls in some states.

Proponents of the bill hailed the measure as the most important expansion of voting rights since racial barriers to voting were barred by the 1965 Voting Rights Act. Majority Whip William Gray of Pennsylvania noted that "each generation has widened the circle of participation. . . with this bill sixty to seventy million unregistered voters will have an easier time getting inside that circle." Opponents of the bill, on the other hand, worried about the increased possibilities for fraud. Minority Leader Robert Michel of Illinois maintained that the new process would virtually invite those who wanted to vote under several names to do so. Michel, a Republican, cited reports that up to one hundred thousand fraudulent votes had been cast over the last decade in his own state's biggest city, the Democratic stronghold of Chicago. If the bill becomes law, he said, "We'll really be taken to the cleaners." Others replied that the concern should not be with the possibility that some people might vote more than once, but that so many are not voting at all.

Regardless of whether one favors this bill or not, it will clearly have a major effect should it pass the Senate and be signed into law by the president. As this chapter will discuss, the bureaucratic hurdle of registration is one of the primary reasons for America's low voter turnout. Should the motor-voter bill become law, we may have to substantially rewrite parts of this chapter for the next edition of *Government in America*.

Source: "Democrats Drive Voter Bill, but Big Potholes Remain," *Congressional Quarterly Weekly Report,* February 10, 1990, 410–11.

 rdinary citizens—not just pollsters, pundits, and political scientists— search for meaning in elections. One of the most astute observers of American politics, journalist Walter Lippman, once remarked:

We call an election an expression of the popular will. But is it? We go into a polling booth and mark a cross on a piece of paper for one of two, or perhaps three or four names. Have we expressed our thoughts on the public policy of the United States? Presumably we have a number of thoughts on this and that with many buts and ifs and ors. Surely the cross on a piece of paper does not express them.[1]

This chapter will give you a perspective on how elections function in the American system, as well as how voters generally behave. The focus here is primarily

[1]Quoted in Stanley G. Kelley, Jr., *Interpreting Elections* (Princeton, N.J.: Princeton University Press, 1983), 3–4.

on presidential elections; Chapter 12 will examine congressional elections in detail.

HOW AMERICAN ELECTIONS WORK

Elections serve many important functions in American society. They *socialize* and *institutionalize* political activity, making it possible for most political participation to be channeled through the electoral process rather than bubbling up through demonstrations, riots, or revolutions. Because elections provide *regular access to political power,* leaders can be replaced without being overthrown. As you will see shortly, the presidential election of 1800 was the first transition of power between parties accomplished by voters' ballots in the history of the world. One set of leaders left office and another set assumed control peacefully—all because of an election. They were able to do so because the election had **legitimacy** in the eyes of the American people; that is, the election was almost universally accepted as a fair and free method to select political leaders.

As you can see in the following comparison between the Mexican and American presidential elections of 1988, the legitimacy of elections is not something to be taken lightly.

The Importance of Electoral Legitimacy

In mid-July 1988 nearly a quarter of a million Mexican citizens marched on their nation's capital to protest what appeared to be widespread fraud in the presidential election. With Mexico's foreign debt topping $100 billion, the government had responded with a deliberate austerity program. In the midst of these

Cuauhtemoc Cardenas's supporters demand "no alfraude"—no fraud—after the 1988 Mexican presidential election. American voters rarely question the fairness of election results, allowing officeholders to govern with a legitimacy they can take for granted.

hard times the 1988 Mexican presidential election sorely tested the country's fragile democracy. Critics charged that the government had deliberately delayed reporting the results for days until it could manipulate its candidate's victory. The long-dominant Party of the Institutionalized Revolution (PRI) had nominated Harvard-educated economist Carlos Salinas de Gortari, who reportedly received 50.4 percent of the vote. Opposition-party candidate Cuauhtemoc Cardenas, son of one of Mexico's most popular presidents, spoke to the protestors, urging them to "exercise moral and political pressure on the government" to report new and accurate election results.[2] What Cardenas really wanted, of course, was for the government to bend to pressure and call new elections.

Nevertheless, Salinas de Gortari was inaugurated as president soon afterward, taking office under a cloud of scandal and deepening political crisis. A year later a poll asked Mexicans whether they thought Salinas really won or not. Twenty-four percent said he did, 33 percent said he may not have, 35 percent said he definitely did not, and 5 percent were unsure.[3] These continuing doubts about the legitimacy of the Mexican election have clearly hampered the effectiveness of the Salinas government.

Four months after the Mexican election the United States also held a presidential election, its results broadcast on television that very evening. Michael Dukakis telephoned George Bush to concede the election shortly after all the polls had closed. He then appeared on television to thank his supporters and wish the president-elect the very best. Millions of Dukakis supporters grumbled about the results, but protest was unthinkable. The next day they went about their business as normal. Such is the importance of electoral legitimacy; even if it means giving up power and long-cherished policy dreams, the losers accept the results calmly without calling their supporters to the streets.

Some Unique American Electoral Features

As democracy continues to spread throughout the world, the legitimacy of American elections no longer seems to be as unique as it once was. There are, however, a number of features of the American electoral system that are quite unique. Unlike most other democracies, the United States has three kinds of elections: those which *select party nominees,* those which *select officeholders from among the nominees,* and those in which voters engage in *making or ratifying legislation.* Typically, elections in other countries perform only one of these three functions—selecting officeholders.

Elections held for the purpose of picking party nominees are called **primaries.** Although Americans are most familiar with presidential primaries (as discussed in Chapter 8), most states also use primaries to select party nominees for congressional and state offices. These state primaries are called **direct primaries** because party nominees are chosen directly by the people. (In contrast, presidential primaries are indirect because they choose only delegates to go to a national convention.)

Also virtually unique to the United States is a system of state-level elections that permit voters to enact legislation directly. The **initiative petition** enables

[2] This protest was reported in the *New York Times,* July 17, 1988, 4.

[3] "Presidential Politics: The View from Mexico," *Los Angeles Times,* August 20, 1989, sec. 1, p. 6.

Referendums give American citizens a direct voice in the legislative process. Here activists work to win approval of California's Proposition 103, which proposed legislation requiring reduced auto insurance rates. The referendum passed in 1988, but state officials and insurance industry representatives continue to haggle over the new law's implementation.

voters in twenty-three states to put proposed legislation on the ballot. All that is usually required is for signatures to be gathered in numbers equaling 10 percent of the voters in the previous election. In this way citizens can force a decision on an issue upon which state legislatures have failed to act. The most famous example is California's Proposition 13, which in 1978 put a limit on the rise in property taxes in California. Another example of a provision for direct legislation is the **referendum,** whereby voters are given the chance to approve or disapprove some legislative act or constitutional amendment.

Primaries, initiative petitions, and referendums have all been reforms of the American election system. Today America has an election system that permits all adult citizens to play a role in the electoral drama, but some political scientists believe that the American system could broaden participation if it used technology more effectively (see "You Are the Policymaker: Should America Use Electronic Voting?"). Indeed, the history of American elections has been a history of their increasing technological sophistication and their increasing democracy.

A TALE OF THREE ELECTIONS

Times change, and so do elections. Modern campaigns are slick, high-tech affairs. Imagine John Adams and Thomas Jefferson standing under bright TV lights, adjusting their wigs, and waiting for the "Presidential Debate of 1800" to begin. Or think of Abraham Lincoln securing the nomination and then lining up an ad agency and a professional pollster. Early twentieth-century candidates like Woodrow Wilson and Franklin Roosevelt did not have network exit polls to report their victories before the polls even closed in the West; they had to wait for the returns to come in slowly. A glance at three American elections should give you a good idea of how they have changed over nearly two centuries.

Should America Use Electronic Voting?

Although modern technology is widely available, Americans have not harnessed much of it to improve democracy. Though most precincts now use either voting machines or computer punch cards to record votes, the high-tech age has not yet made much of an impact on the American democratic process.

North Carolina, though, is experimenting with what is known as *teledemocracy*. A program called *OPEN/net* is broadcast live from Raleigh via cable to two million homes in one hundred cities. A taped government meeting is shown during the first hour, followed by a second hour of relevant panel discussion involving government officials and experts. Citizens are given the opportunity to interact directly with the panel through a call-in format—democracy is on the air during prime time.

Political scientist Benjamin Barber proposes that such experiments go even further, maintaining that in a strong democracy people are supposed to govern themselves, not merely pull a lever on a voting machine. He posits a plan to convene a set of local assemblies, each with one thousand to five thousand citizen-members who, through technology, could have "on-line" access to information about major legislative bills. Through use of a telephone, these citizens would have the opportunity to vote on bills they saw debated on cable TV. Voters would simply call up after the discussion was finished and punch in a *one* if they favored the proposal and a *two* if they opposed it. The results could be known in a manner of minutes.

Assume the role of the policymaker. Would it be wise if the United States brought elections into the twenty-first century by teledemocracy? Should Americans be able to vote through teledemocracy on key local issues like sex education in schools?

Sources: On the North Carolina experiment, see *Government Technology*, February 1988, 1. Barber's proposal is in his *Strong Democracy* (Berkeley: University of California Press, 1985).

1800: The First Electoral Transition of Power

By current standards, the 1800 election was not much of an election at all: no primaries, no nominating conventions, no candidate speeches, and no entourage of reporters. Both incumbent President John Adams and challenger Thomas Jefferson were nominated by their parties' elected representatives in Congress—Federalists for Adams and Democratic-Republicans for Jefferson. Once nominated, the candidates sat back and let their state and local organizations promote their cause. Communication and travel were too slow for candidates to get their message across themselves. Besides, campaigning was considered below the dignity of the presidential office.

Newspapers of the time, however, were little concerned with dignity, or for that matter honesty. Most were rabidly partisan and did all they could to run down the opposition's candidate. Jefferson was regularly denounced as a bible-burning atheist, the father of mulatto children, and a mad scientist. Adams, on the other hand, was said to be a monarchist "whose grand object was to destroy every man who differed from his opinions."[4]

[4]Morton Grodzins, "Political Parties and the Crisis of Succession in the United States: The Case of 1800." In Joseph LaPalombara and Myron Weiner, eds., *Political Parties and Political Development* (Princeton, N.J.: Princeton University Press, 1966), 319.

The focus of the campaign was not on voters, but rather on the state legislatures, on which the responsibility for choosing members of the electoral college rested. When the dust settled the Jeffersonians had won a slim victory in terms of electoral votes; however, they also had committed a troubling error. In the original constitutional system each elector cast two ballots, and the top vote-getter was named president and the runner-up became vice-president.[5] In 1796 Jefferson had become Adams's vice-president by virtue of finishing second. Not wanting Adams to be his vice-president, Jefferson made sure that all his electors also voted for his vice-presidential choice—Aaron Burr of New York. The problem was that when each and every one of them did so, Jefferson and Burr ended up tied for first. This meant that the Federalist-controlled House of Representatives would have to decide between the two Democratic-Republican candidates. Burr saw the chance to steal the presidency from Jefferson by cutting a deal with the Federalists, but his efforts failed. After thirty-five indecisive ballots in the House, the Federalists finally threw their support to Jefferson. On March 4, 1801, the transition from Adams to Jefferson marked the first peaceful transfer of power between parties via the electoral process in the history of the world.

1896: A Bitter Fight over Economic Interests

Nearly a century later the election of 1896 was largely fought over economics. By then national nominating conventions had become well established, and Republicans, meeting in St. Louis for their convention, had a clear front-runner, former Congressman William McKinley. The Republicans' major issues were support for the gold standard and high tariffs. The gold standard linked money to gold, which was scarce; thus debtors never got a break from inflation. Tariffs protected capitalists and their workers from foreign competition. After piling

[5]In 1804 the Twelfth Amendment to the Constitution changed the procedure to the one we know today, in which each elector votes separately for president and vice-president.

William Jennings Bryan was the Democratic party's standard bearer at the turn of the century. Eastern industrialists, fearing Bryan's powerful speeches and populist politics, used their financial clout to help William McKinley defeat "The Boy Orator of the Platte" (thus named after a river in his native Nebraska) in the 1896 and 1900 presidential elections.

up a commanding majority on the first ballot at St. Louis, McKinley sat back to see what the upcoming Democratic convention would do.

The Democrats met in Chicago's sticky July heat. They had an issue—unlimited coinage of silver—but no clear front-runner. Their incumbent president, Grover Cleveland, was blamed for the 1893 depression and a resolution praising the Cleveland administration was hooted down. The high point of the Chicago convention was a speech by young William Jennings Bryan of Nebraska, whose "Cross of Gold" speech proclaimed the virtues of the silver rather than the gold standard. "You shall not crucify mankind on a cross of gold," he concluded, and went on to win the nomination on the fifth ballot.

The flamboyant Bryan broke with tradition and took to the stump in person. He gave six hundred speeches as his campaign train traveled through twenty-six states, logging eighteen thousand miles. Debtors and silver miners were especially attracted to Bryan's pitch for cheap silver money. In contrast, the serene McKinley was advised to sit home in Ohio and run a front-porch campaign. He did, and managed to label the Democrats as the party of depression ("In God We Trust, with Bryan We Bust").

Bryan won the oratory, but McKinley won the election. Eastern manufacturers contributed a small fortune—perhaps as much as fifteen million dollars—to the Republicans. (Not until 1964 did any party spend as much to win the presidency.) A few manufacturers even told their workers not to report back to work if Bryan won. Only white southerners, westerners in the silver producing states, and rural debtors lined up behind the Democrats. The Republicans won overwhelmingly in the industrial northeast and midwest, and became firmly entrenched as the nation's majority party for the next several decades. As Walter Dean Burnham writes, Bryan's

effort to create a coalition of the dispossessed created instead the most enduringly sectional political alignment in American history—an alignment which eventually separated the Southern and Western agrarians and transformed the most industrially advanced region of the country into a bulwark of industrialist Republicanism.[6]

McKinley triumphed by a margin of 271 to 176 in the electoral college. Nearly 80 percent of the eligible electorate voted in one of the highest turnouts ever.

1988: Bush Wins One for the Gipper

The 1988 election marked the first time since 1960 that an election was held to choose a successor to a retiring two-term president. Like 1960, the Republicans nominated their incumbent vice-president and the Democrats nominated a relatively unknown candidate from Massachusetts to try to lead them back to the White House. Unlike 1960, though, this time the vice-president won, becoming the first sitting vice-president to win a presidential election since Martin Van Buren in 1836.

By 1988 the convention procedure developed by Van Buren (see Chapter 7) was usually only a formality to ratify the decisions of presidential primaries.

[6]Walter Dean Burnham, *The Current Crisis in American Politics* (New York: Oxford University Press, 1982), 48.

With a crowded field of Republican and Democratic candidates early in the year, journalists salivated at the prospect of an *open convention* in which no candidate would have a majority on the first ballot and bargaining would have to take place to determine a candidate. That speculation proved to be erroneous, however. One by one the contenders dropped out, losing early primaries, running out of cash, or, in two cases, getting involved in personal scandals. (Gary Hart dropped out after his tryst with model Donna Rice; Joseph Biden quit the race after being accused of plagiarizing a speech.) Only the Democrats managed to keep much of a race going until their convention. Reverend Jesse Jackson, the first major African-American candidate for the presidency, continued to challenge Michael Dukakis through the last primaries in June, even though he trailed by a large margin. Using his big chunk of delegates as leverage, Jackson stated that he deserved "serious consideration" for the vice-presidential nomination. Dukakis, however, felt that he needed a southerner on the ticket in order to win and instead picked Texas Senator Lloyd Bentsen as his running mate. Plans to call Reverend Jackson with the news were garbled, and Jackson heard about Dukakis's choice from the press first—a slight that rubbed salt into the wound. It was the first mistake in what had been touted as a model of efficient campaigning, and it would not be the last.

While Dukakis was still dealing with Jackson, George Bush was focusing all his energies on gearing up for the election campaign. Bush had run into a land mine at the first caucus in Iowa, finishing third behind Senate Republican leader Robert Dole and evangelist Pat Robertson, but after his dramatic comeback in New Hampshire and sweep of the South on Super Tuesday the nomination was his. From March until the Republican Convention in August the only suspense for the Republicans was who Bush would choose for his vice-president. Many experts felt that Bush needed to choose a staunch conservative to appease the right wing of the party, but virtually no one expected that he would attempt to

Many Americans felt that the 1988 campaign was the most negative and superficial in recent memory. Michael Dukakis sought to toughen his image with this ride in a General Dynamics tank; the campaign stunt backfired when the Bush campaign used footage of the ride in advertisments ridiculing Dukakis's defense policy positions.

do so by choosing the largely unknown Dan Quayle, junior senator from Indiana. Stunned journalists scurried to tell the nation whatever they could find out about the young senator. The process by which he joined the National Guard—and thereby avoided fighting in Vietnam—was closely scrutinized, as was his lackluster academic record. Later, in the vice-presidential debates, Quayle would leave himself an opening any opponent would die for. Debating Senator Bentsen, Quayle compared his brief experience in office with that of John F. Kennedy before he became president. In front of millions of TV viewers, Senator Bensten responded indignantly that "I knew John F. Kennedy. I worked with Jack Kennedy. And senator you're no Jack Kennedy." In journalist language, it was the best *sound-bite* of the campaign.

Political commentators and voters alike complained that the 1988 campaign was far too negative (see "The People Speak: Voters Rate the 1988 Campaign"), though it was certainly less so than the bitter campaigns of 1800 or 1896. Unlike these nineteenth-century campaigns, however, in 1988 it was the candidates themselves and not their supporters who were hurling the charges back and forth. As late as 1940 Franklin D. Roosevelt had gone through the entire campaign without once mentioning the name of his opponent, Wendell Willkie. In contrast, Bush's major campaign strategy was to convince the voters that Dukakis was a Massachusetts liberal far out of the mainstream. Again and again, he hammered at the issues of the furlough of murderer Willie Horton and Dukakis's veto of a bill requiring teachers to lead students in the Pledge of Allegiance. It was, said campaign chroniclers Jack Germond and Jules Witcover, the "trivial pursuit of the presidency."[7] Despite this criticism, Bush's campaign was successful; it brought out issues of patriotism and law and order on which Bush clearly had an edge.

[7]Jack Germond and Jules Witcover, *Whose Broad Stripes and Stars? The Trivial Pursuit of the Presidency, 1988* (New York: Warner, 1989).

The People Speak **Voters Rate the 1988 Campaign**

Never in recent memory was a campaign so widely criticized for being overly bitter and lacking in substantive issues than in 1988. The *Washington Post* spoke for many in the media when it editorialized that "This has been a terrible campaign, a national disappointment." By and large, voters agreed. A postelection *New York Times/CBS News* poll yielded the following distribution of opinion:

Compared with past presidential campaigns, do you think the campaign has been more positive this year, more negative this year, or about the same?

More positive	5%	About the same	29%
More negative	63%	Don't know	3%

Compared with past presidential campaigns, do you think there has been more discussion of the issues in this campaign, less discussion of the issues, or about the same amount of discussion?

More discussion	9%	About the same	27%
Less discussion	60%	Don't know	4%

Source: The questions as worded are taken directly from a *New York Times/CBS News* Poll, November 1988.

Ultimately most political scientists concluded that Bush won not because of his negative campaigning, but rather because of the performance of the economy during the Reagan administration.[8] With low unemployment and inflation, as well as steady economic growth, conditions were ideal for Bush to go out and "win one for the Gipper" (referring to Reagan's past acting role as Notre Dame football star George Gipp). The popular vote was 54 percent for Bush and 46 percent for Dukakis. Forty states were carried by the Bush-Quayle ticket, thus giving them a wide margin in the electoral college. What the Democrats used to depend on as the "Solid South" was instead solid for the Republicans. In fact, the South (including Texas, Lloyd Bentsen's home state) formed the core of Republican support, voting at 5 percent above the national average for Bush (see Figure 9.1). Until the Democrats can break this new Republican lock on the South, it will be very difficult for them to win back the presidency.

In House and Senate races, however, the Republicans continued to trail the Democrats. In the House the Democrats actually gained three seats in 1988, and they picked up one in the Senate as well, thereby leaving Bush with the lowest

[8]Robert S. Erickson, "Economic Conditions and the Presidential Vote." *American Political Science Review* 83 (1989): 567–73.

Figure 9.1   **The 1988 Vote**

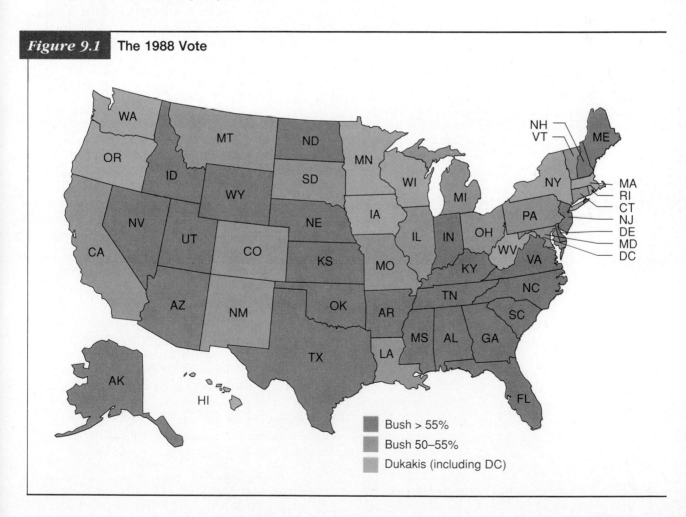

Bush > 55%

Bush 50–55%

Dukakis (including DC)

level of party support in Congress of any newly elected twentieth-century president. If you wonder why President Bush did not immediately embark on new initiatives in 1989, the answer has much to do with his party's weak position in the Congress.

In 1988, as in all election years, voters faced two key choices: whether to vote and, if they chose to, how to vote. The following sections will investigate the ways that voters make these choices.

WHETHER TO VOTE: A CITIZEN'S FIRST CHOICE

The nearly two centuries of American electoral history have witnessed greatly expanded **suffrage,** the right to vote. In the election of 1800 only property-owning white males over the age of twenty-one were typically allowed to vote. Now the right to vote is guaranteed to all over the age of eighteen—male or female, white or nonwhite, homeowner or homeless. (For these developments, particularly as they affect women and minorities, see Chapter 5.)

Interestingly, as the right to vote has been extended, proportionately fewer of those eligible have chosen to exercise that right. In the past hundred years, the 80 percent turnout in the 1896 election was the high point of electoral participation. In 1988 only 50 percent of the adult population voted for president—the lowest figure since 1924 (see Figure 9.2).

Who Votes and Who Stays Home?

When only half the population votes, the necessity of studying nonvoters takes on added importance. The most useful study of nonvoting in American elections was done by Raymond Wolfinger and Steven Rosenstone.[9] Several conclusions are apparent from their research:

- *Voting is a class-biased activity.* People with higher than average educational and income levels vote more than people with lower educational and income levels. Among all factors affecting turnout, this one is the most important.

- *Young people have the lowest turnout rate.* As people age their likelihood of voting increases, until the infirmities of old age make it difficult for them to get to the polls.

- *Whites vote with greater frequency than members of minority groups.* African Americans, Puerto Ricans, and Chicanos are all underrepresented among the ranks of voters, but this can be explained by their generally low level of education and income. Blacks and other minority groups with high levels of income and education vote more than whites with comparable socioeconomic status.

- *Southerners do less voting than northerners.* Although the 1965 Voting Rights Act forced the South to make it easier for its citizens (particularly African Americans) to vote, the historical legacy of low participation remains.

[9]Raymond E. Wolfinger and Steven J. Rosenstone, *Who Votes?* (New Haven, Conn.: Yale University Press, 1980).

Figure 9.2 The Decline of Turnout: 1896–1988

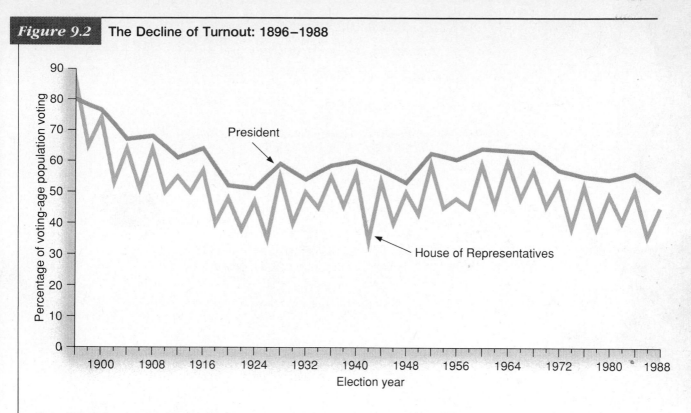

Sources: For data up to 1930, *Historical Statistics of the United States* (Washington, D.C.: Government Printing Office, 1975), part 2, 1071, 1078–79, 1084. For 1930 to 1980, see U.S. Bureau of the Census, *Statistical Abstract of the United States, 1980* (Washington, D.C.: Government Printing Office, 1981) 248. For post-1980 data, see *Congressional Quarterly Election 1988* (Washington, D.C.: Congressional Quarterly, 1988).

- *Government employees are heavy participators in the electoral process.* Having something at stake (their jobs and the future of the programs they work on) and being in a position to know more about government impels government workers to high levels of participation.

- *Voting is not very strongly related to gender.* In an earlier period many women were discouraged from voting, but today women vote just about as frequently as men do.

These differences in turnout rates are often cumulative. Possessing several of these traits (say, being well educated, middle-aged, and a government worker) adds significantly to one's likelihood of voting. Conversely, being young, poorly educated, and southern is likely to add up to a very low probability of voting.

As Wolfinger and Rosenstone point out, the best predictor of whether a person will vote is whether that person is registered. America's unique registration system is in part to blame for why Americans are significantly less likely to go to the polls than citizens of other democratic nations (see "America in Perspective: Why Turnout in the United States Is So Low Compared to Other Countries").

America in Perspective

Why Turnout in the United States Is So Low Compared to Other Countries

Despite living in a culture that encourages participation, Americans have a woefully low turnout rate compared to other democracies. Here are some figures on voting rates in the United States and other industrial nations:

East Germany, 1990	93%	Israel, 1988	79%
Australia, 1987	89%	Denmark, 1988	75%
New Zealand, 1987	87%	Great Britain, 1987	75%
Belgium, 1987	87%	Canada, 1988	75%
Austria, 1986	87%	Japan, 1990	73%
Netherlands, 1986	86%	Ireland, 1987	72%
Sweden, 1988	85%	Finland, 1987	72%
Italy, 1987	85%	Portugal, 1987	71%
Norway, 1985	84%	Iceland, 1988	71%
West Germany, 1987	84%	Spain, 1986	69%
Greece, 1985	83%	Hungary, 1990	64%
Luxemborg, 1984	83%	**United States**, 1988	50%
France, 1988	81%	Switzerland, 1987	46%

There are several reasons given for this phenomenon. Probably the most often cited reason is the unique American requirement of voter registration. The governments of other democracies take the responsibility of seeing to it that all of their eligible citizens are on the voting lists. In America the responsibility for registration lies solely with the individual.

A second difference between the United States and other countries is that the American government asks citizens to vote far more often. While the typical European voter may be called upon to cast two or three ballots in a four-year period, many Americans are faced with a dozen or more separate elections in the space of four years. Furthermore, Americans are expected to vote for a much wider range of political offices. With 1 elected official for every 442 citizens and elections held somewhere virtually every week, it is no wonder that it is so difficult to get Americans to the polls. It is probably no coincidence that the one European country that has a comparable turnout rate—Switzerland—has also overwhelmed its citizens with voting opportunities, calling eighty-nine national elections in the period between 1947 and 1975.

Finally, the stimulus to vote is not as high in the United States because the choice offered Americans is not as great as in other countries. This is because the United States stands virtually alone in the democratic world in lacking a major left-wing socialist party. When European voters go to the polls they are deciding on whether or not their country will be run by parties with socialist goals or alternatively by conservative, and in some cases religious parties. The consequences of their vote for redistribution of income and the size of government are far greater than the ordinary American voter can conceive of.

Sources: For turnout figures around the world: annual reports by T. Mackie in the November issue of the *European Journal of Political Research*, 1985–1989; 1990 figures from various news reports.

The Registration System

A century ago politicans used to say, "Vote early and often." Cases such as West Virginia's 159,000 votes being cast by 147,000 eligible voters in 1888 were not unusual. Largely to prevent corruption associated with stuffing ballot boxes, states adopted **voter registration** around the turn of the century. By requiring citizens to register in advance of election day, elections were made much more ethical. Today Americans worry much more about people stealing elections through computer fraud than by casting multiple ballots (see "A Question of Ethics: Computer Fraud in Vote Counting").

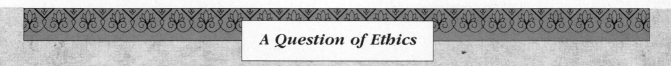

A Question of Ethics

Computer Fraud in Vote Counting

In 1962 Joseph P. Harris, a political science professor at Berkeley, came up with the idea of having people cast their ballots by making punches on a standard IBM card. The cards could then be run through a computer to tabulate the vote—faster and more reliably than possible with paper ballots, and without the expense of bulky lever machinery.

The result was *Votomatic*, which today is the most widely used electronic vote-counting system in the nation. Slightly more than half of voters in 1988 voted via computerized vote-counting systems. In California this figure is now 97 percent.

Compared to paper ballots, there is no question that computerized tabulation of votes offers many advantages. Computers rarely skip over ballots or make mistakes in arithmetic. One does not have to be a computer science major, though, to know that a computer program is only as good as the person who does the programming. While it might take an organized effort of many people to alter a paper-ballot count, a single programmer could place a command in a computer which could drastically alter the results. For instance, a programmer could write the code so that every time a particular candidate received a vote it would be counted twice.

Such flagrant computer fraud has probably never occurred; however, a number of other problems have cropped up with computerized tallying. In 1968 a programming error in Missoula, Montana, led to votes for Richard Nixon being counted for Hubert Humphrey

and vice versa. In Orange County, California, faulty programming caused fifteen thousand votes for Jimmy Carter and Edward Kennedy in the 1990 primary to be counted instead for Lyndon LaRouche and Jerry Brown. In Carroll County, Maryland, sloppy testing allowed an incorrect computer program to miss about thirteen thousand votes. When these votes were tallied later, the outcome of the election was changed.

Nor is computerized vote-counting immune from ballot-box stuffing. In Chicago, a city famous for voting chicanery, Democratic ward bosses in 1982 punched out false ballots for voters who had died, and in one instance ran the same straight-Democratic-party ticket through the card-reading machine 198 times. Fifty-eight people were ultimately convicted of federal election crimes.

In California, election officials now manually recount a random sample of 1 percent of the vote to check for any sign of fraud. In a number of states—including Texas, New York, and California—laws require election officials to place their computer programs in escrow so they can be examined by independent experts in cases of disputed results. Despite these safeguards many experts remain worried about the prospect of a major scandal in computerized vote tallying. As Willis H. Ware, a senior scientist at the RAND Corporation writes, "There is probably a Chernobyl or a Three Mile Island waiting to happen in some election, just as a Richter-8 earthquake is waiting to happen in California."

Source: William Trombley, "Computers: Bugs in the Ballot Box." A three part series in the *Los Angeles Times*, July 2–4, 1989.

Registration procedures differ greatly from state to state, though this may change if the congressional proposal discussed in this chapter's "Government in Action" feature is ever enacted. Presently, states in the upper Great Plains and the Northwest make it easiest to register: voters can sign up at many everyday locations such as supermarkets, and no elaborate procedures are used. In sparsely populated North Dakota there is no registration at all, and in Minnesota, Wisconsin, and Maine voters can register just prior to voting on election day. It is probably no coincidence that these four states were among the top five in turnout during the 1988 election (see Table 9.1). By contrast, states in the South

Table 9.1	**Turnout in 1988: State by State**				

RANK	STATE	VOTERS (in percentage)	RANK	STATE	VOTERS (in percentage)
1	Minnesota	66.3	27	Louisiana	51.3
2	Montana	62.4	28	Delaware	51.0
3	Maine	62.2	29	Wyoming	50.3
4	Wisconsin	62.0	30	Pennsylvania	50.1
5	North Dakota	61.5	31	Mississippi	49.9
6	South Dakota	61.5	32	Maryland	49.1
7	Utah	60.0	33	Oklahoma	48.7
8	Iowa	59.3	34	Kentucky	48.2
9	Vermont	59.1		Virginia	48.2
10	Oregon	58.6	36	New York	48.1
11	Idaho	58.3	37	California	47.4
12	Massachusetts	58.1	38	New Mexico	47.3
13	Connecticut	57.9	39	Arkansas	47.0
14	Nebraska	56.8	40	West Virginia	46.7
15	Colorado	55.1	41	Alabama	45.8
	Ohio	55.1	42	Arizona	45.0
17	Missouri	54.8	43	Nevada	44.9
18	New Hampshire	54.7	44	Florida	44.7
19	Washington	54.6		Tennessee	44.7
20	Kansas	54.3	46	Texas	44.2
21	Michigan	54.0	47	North Carolina	43.4
22	Illinois	53.3	48	Hawaii	43.0
	Indiana	53.3	49	District of Columbia	39.4
24	Rhode Island	53.0	50	South Carolina	38.9
25	New Jersey	52.1	51	Georgia	38.8
26	Alaska	51.7			

Source: Congressional Quarterly, Inc.

still have the most difficult hurdles to clear when it comes to registering to vote. For example, in Travis County, Texas (which includes Austin), registration is handled by the county tax collector, a fact not widely advertised to county residents.[10] Thus Southern states continue to have the nation's lowest turnout rates—below 40 percent in Georgia and South Carolina in 1988.

Although such variations in voter turnout cannot be blamed entirely on the registration system, Wolfinger and Rosenstone estimate that if all the states adapted their registration requirements along the lines of those in which registration is easiest, America's national turnout rate would probably increase by about 9 percent.[11] This would still leave the American turnout rate below that of every Western European country.

Other analysts, however, are not so sure that registration is at the heart of the problem. They point to the fact that turnout has steadily declined in the United States since 1960 even though registration procedures have actually been made easier. For example, many states have enacted postal registration and permitted deputy registrars to go out and register people rather than have the people come to them. Curtis Gans, director of the Committee for the Study of the American Electorate, is disheartened by data showing that states which have liberalized election laws now have lower turnouts than before they instituted reforms. He concludes that "the will to vote is what is eroding in our society."[12]

A Policy Approach to Deciding Whether to Vote

Realistically, when ninety million people vote in a presidential election (as they did in 1988) the chance of one vote affecting the outcome is very, very slight. Once in a while, of course, an election is decided by a handful of votes. In 1948 Lyndon Johnson won a race for the U.S. Senate by a total of 87—very suspicious—votes, earning him the nickname "Landslide Lyndon."[13] In 1960 John Kennedy carried the state of Hawaii by a mere 115 votes. It is more likely, however, that you will be struck by lightning during your lifetime than participate in an election decided by a single vote.

Not only does your vote probably not make much difference to the outcome, but voting is somewhat costly. You have to spend some of your valuable time becoming informed, making up your mind, and getting to the polls. If you carefully calculate your time and energy, you might rationally decide that the costs of voting outweigh the benefits.

Economist Anthony Downs, in his model of democracy, tries to explain why a rational person would ever bother to vote. He argues that rational people vote if they believe that the policies of one party will bring more benefits than the policies of the other party.[14] Thus people who see **policy differences** between

[10]Frances Fox Piven and Richard A. Cloward, *Why Americans Don't Vote* (New York: Pantheon, 1988), 178.

[11]Wolfinger and Rosenstone, *Who Votes?*, 73.

[12]Richard L. Berke, "Experts Say Low 1988 Turnout May Be Repeated," *New York Times,* November 13, 1988, 17.

[13]For a gripping account of Johnson's manipulations to win this election see Robert A. Caro, *The Years of Lyndon Johnson: Means of Ascent* (New York: Knopf, 1990).

[14]Anthony Downs, *An Economic Theory of Democracy* (New York: Harper & Row, 1957), chap. 14.

the parties are more likely to join the ranks of voters. If you are an environmentalist and you expect the Democrats to pass more environmental legislation than the Republicans, then you have an additional incentive to go to the polls. On the other hand, if you are truly indifferent—that is, if you see no difference whatsoever between the two parties—you may rationally decide to abstain. You may also abstain if you believe that the Democrats' proenvironmental platform is balanced by Republican policies, such as those to control inflation. Even if you are indifferent about the outcome, you may decide to vote anyway, simply to support democratic government. In that case, you are impelled to vote by a sense of **civic duty.**

Why, then, is there so much inequality in voting, with the rich and the well-educated participating more than the poor and the less-educated? First, in nearly every election, on nearly every issue, the upper classes are more likely to recognize and understand policy differences than the lower classes. In particular, higher education trains a person to see the impact of policy decisions and the nuances of party platforms. Second, upper-class people score higher on **political efficacy,** the belief that ordinary people *can* influence the government. In other words people low in socioeconomic status turn out less because they are more likely to think their votes do not really matter. Third, the poor and less-educated find the bureaucratic hurdles of the registration process especially difficult. It might not seem much of a chore for you to register to vote after having gone through course registration at your school, but for those not fortunate enough to go to college it does not seem so easy (see Figure 9.3).

Until some of these factors which inhibit voting—such as registration and low efficacy levels—change dramatically, it is likely that American elections will continue to be decided by only about half the eligible voters. How these voters make their decisions will be discussed in the following sections.

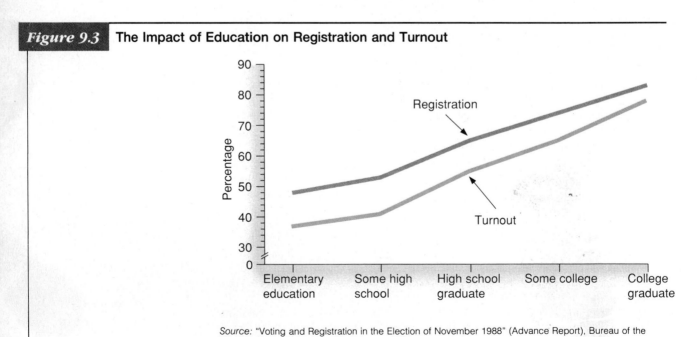

Figure 9.3 **The Impact of Education on Registration and Turnout**

Source: "Voting and Registration in the Election of November 1988" (Advance Report), Bureau of the Census, Series P-20, No. 435, February 1989.

HOW AMERICANS VOTE: EXPLAINING CITIZENS' DECISIONS

Here is a common explanation of how Americans vote, one favored by journalists and politicians: Americans vote because they agree more with the policy views of Candidate A than of Candidate B. Of course, Candidate A has gone to a lot of time and trouble—as did George Bush in 1988—to get those views implanted in the public mind. Because citizens vote for the candidate whose policy promises they favor, say many journalists and politicians, the election winner has a mandate from the people to carry out the promised policies. This idea is sometimes called the **mandate theory of elections.**

Politicians, of course, are attracted to the mandate theory. It lets them justify what they want to do by claiming public support for their policies. As President Bush stated shortly before his inauguration, "When the American people vote, they have a right to expect their substantive decision will be heard."[15]

Political scientists, however, think very little of the mandate theory of elections.[16] Whereas victorious politicians are eager to proclaim "the people have spoken," political scientists know that the people rarely vote a certain way for the same reasons. Instead, political scientists focus on three major elements of voters' decisions: (1) voters' party identification; (2) voters' evaluation of the candidates; and (3) the match between voters' policy positions and those of the candidates and parties—a factor termed *policy voting*.

Party Identification

Party identifications are crucial for many voters in that they provide a regular perspective through which they can view the political world. "Presumably," say Niemi and Weisberg, "people choose to identify with a party with which they generally agree. . . . As a result they need not concern themselves with every issue that comes along, but can generally rely on their party identification to guide them."[17] Parties tend to rely on groups that lean heavily in their favor to form their basic coalition. Even before an election campaign begins, Republicans usually assume they will not receive much support from African Americans, Jews, Mexican Americans, and most intellectuals. Democrats have an uphill struggle attracting groups that are staunchly Republican in their leanings, such as conservative evangelical Christians or upper-income voters.

With the emergence of television and candidate-centered politics, the hold of the party on the voter eroded substantially during the 1960s and 1970s, and then stabilized at a new and lower level during the 1980s.[18] In the 1950s scholars singled out party affiliation as the best single predictor of a voter's decision. It was said that many voters would vote for a yellow dog or a wooden Indian if

[15]Cathleen Decker, "Bush Asserts He Won Clear Mandate in Vote," *Los Angeles Times,* January 10, 1989, 4.

[16]See George C. Edwards III, *At the Margins* (New Haven, Conn.: Yale University Press, 1989), chap. 8.

[17]Richard G. Niemi and Herbert F. Weisberg, eds., *Controversies in Voting Behavior,* 2nd ed. (Washington, D.C.: Congressional Quarterly Press, 1984), 164–65.

[18]See Martin P. Wattenberg, *The Decline of American Political Parties, 1952–1988* (Cambridge, Mass.: Harvard University Press, 1990).

their party nominated one. "My party—right or wrong" was the motto that typified strong party identifiers. Voting along party lines is no longer common, particularly in elections for the House of Representatives, where incumbency is now paramount (see Chapter 12). Many voters have come to feel that they no longer need the parties to guide their choices, given that modern technology makes it possible for them to evaluate and make their own decisions about the candidates.

Candidate Evaluations: How Americans See the Candidates

All candidates try to present a favorable personal image. Using laboratory experiments, political psychologists Shawn Rosenberg and Patrick McCafferty show that it is possible to manipulate a candidate's appearance in a way that affects voters' choices. Holding a candidate's issue stands and party identification constant, they find that when good pictures are substituted for bad ones, a candidate's vote-getting ability is significantly increased. Although a laboratory setting may not be representative of the real world, Rosenberg and McCafferty conclude that "with appropriate pretesting and adequate control over a candidate's public appearance, a campaign consultant should be able to significantly manipulate the image projected to the voting public."[19]

To do so a consultant would need to know what sort of candidate images voters are most attuned to. Research by Miller, Wattenberg, and Malanchuk shows that the three most important dimensions of candidate image are integrity,

[19]Shawn W. Rosenberg with Patrick McCafferty, "Image and Voter Preference," *Public Opinion Quarterly* 51 (Spring 1987): 44.

Personal integrity does not always translate into electoral victory. Jimmy Carter was greatly respected for his willingness to speak plainly and honestly to the American people, as he did during this 1980 campaign visit. Nevertheless, Carter lost his bid for reelection because many voters felt that Ronald Reagan would be a stronger and more reliable leader.

reliability, and competence.[20] In 1976 Jimmy Carter told Americans, "I will never lie to you." Even going down to defeat in 1980, Carter was still seen as a man with great integrity. Therefore it obviously takes more than honesty to win. A candidate must also be seen as being dependable, strong, and decisive—traits which Miller, Wattenberg, and Malanchuk label as "reliability." On this dimension Reagan had the clear edge over Carter in 1980 and Mondale in 1984. The personal traits most often mentioned by voters, though, involve competence. In 1988 Michael Dukakis proudly proclaimed that the major election issue was not ideology but competence. Ironically, the majority of voters were more impressed with Bush's wide experience in office than with Dukakis's lawyer-like precision.

Such evaluations of candidate personality are sometimes seen as superficial and irrational judgments. Miller and his colleagues disagree with this interpretation, arguing that "candidate assessments actually concentrate on instrumental concerns about the manner in which a candidate would conduct governmental affairs."[21] If a candidate is too incompetent to carry out policy promises, or too dishonest for those promises to be trusted, it makes perfect sense for a voter to pay more attention to personality than policies. Interestingly, Miller and his colleagues find that college-educated voters are actually the most likely to view the candidates in terms of their personal attributes (see Figure 9-4).

Policy Voting

Policy voting occurs when people base their choices in an election on their own issue preferences. True policy voting can only take place when several conditions are met. First, voters must have a clear view of their own policy positions. Second, voters must know where the candidates stand on policy issues. Third, they must actually cast a vote for the candidate whose policy positions coincide with their own.

Given these conditions, policy voting is not always easy—even for the educated voter. In 1988 Bush made it clear where he stood on the tax issue with his famous line, "Read my lips. No new taxes!" More often, however, candidates decide that the best way to handle an issue is to cloud their positions in rhetoric. For example, in 1968 both major party candidates—Nixon and Humphrey—were deliberately ambiguous about what they would do to end the Vietnam War. This made it extremely difficult for voters to cast their ballots according to how they felt about the war. The media may not be of much help, either, as they typically focus more on the "horse race" aspects of the campaign than on the policy stands of the candidates. Voters thus often have to work very hard to engage in policy voting.

In the early days of voting research, the evidence seemed clear—voters rarely voted on policies, preferring to rely on party identification or candidate evaluations to make up their minds. In the 1950s the authors of *The American Voter* stressed that only a small percentage of the American electorate relied on issues to decide their votes.[22] *The Changing American Voter* challenged this

[20]Arthur H. Miller, Martin P. Wattenberg, and Oksana Malanchuk, "Schematic Assessments of Presidential Candidates, "*American Political Science Review* 80 (1986): 521–40.

[21]*Ibid.,* 536.

[22]Angus Campbell et al., *The American Voter* (New York: Wiley, 1960), chap. 6.

Miller, Wattenberg, and Malanchuk analyzed people's responses to open-ended questions asking survey respondents what they liked and disliked about the two presidential nominees. The responses were divided into those about personality attributes, issue stands, and links to the parties and interest groups. Interestingly, it was the college-educated respondents who made the most references to candidate personality, as you can see in the following graph:

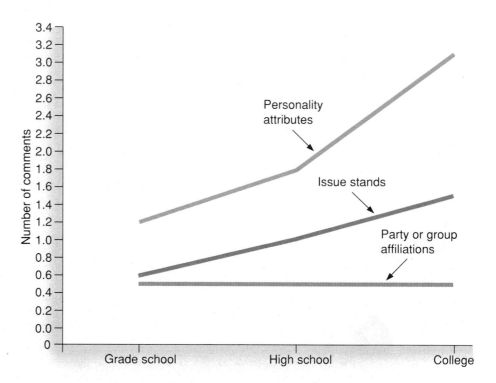

The Figure entries are averages based on all nine presidential surveys for the period from 1952 to 1984. There was little variation in the year-to-year figures, thus justifying collapsing the years together.

Source: Arthur H. Miller, Martin P. Wattenberg, and Oksana Malanchuk, "Schematic Assessments of Presidential Candidates," *American Political Science Review 80 (1986):526.*

claim, however, arguing that voters in more recent years had become more sophisticated about issues and better able to use policy positions to gauge candidates.[23]

While it is questionable whether voters are really much more sophisticated now about issues (see Chapter 6), policy voting has become somewhat easier

[23]Norman H. Nie, Sidney Verba, and John R. Petrocik, *The Changing American Voter* (Cambridge, Mass.: Harvard University Press, 1976).

than in the past. This is due to the fact that today's candidates are regularly forced to take some clear stands in order to appeal to their own party's primary voters. As late as 1968 it was still possible to win a nomination by dealing with the party bosses, but now it is the issue-oriented activists in the primaries that candidates must appeal to first. No longer can a candidate get a party's nomination without taking stands on the major issues of the day, as both Humphrey and Nixon did concerning the Vietnam War in 1968. Thus what has changed is not the voters, but the electoral process which once discouraged policy voting by greatly blurring differences between the candidates.

Party voting, candidate evaluation, and policy voting all play a role in elections. Their impact is not equal from one election to another, but they are the main factors affecting voter decisions. In presidential elections, once voters make their decision it is not just a simple matter of counting the ballots to see who has won the most support nationwide. Rather, the complicated process of determining electoral college votes begins.

THE LAST BATTLE: THE ELECTORAL COLLEGE

It is the **electoral college,** not the popular vote, which actually determines the president of the United States. The electoral college is a unique American institution, created by the Constitution. The American Bar Association once called it "archaic, undemocratic, complex, ambiguous, indirect, and dangerous."[24] Many (but certainly not all) political scientists oppose its continued use, as do most voters (see "The People Speak: Should the Electoral College Be Abolished?").

Because the founders wanted the president to be selected by the nation's elite, not directly by the people, they created the electoral college, a body of electors who are charged solely with the task of voting for the president and vice-president. Fortunately, political practice since 1828 has made the vote of members of the electoral college responsive to popular majorities. Today the electors almost always vote for the candidate who won their state's popular vote. Occasionally, though, electors will exercise the right to vote their conscience, as did one West Virginia elector in 1988 who voted for Bentsen for president and Dukakis for vice-president.

The following list outlines the way in which the electoral college system works today:

- Each state, according to the Constitution, has as many electoral votes as it has U.S. senators and representatives.[25] The state parties select slates of electors, which they use as a reward for faithful service to the party.

- Aside from Maine, each state has a winner-take-all system.[26] Electors vote as a bloc for the winner, whether the winner got 35 percent or 95 percent of the popular vote.

[24]American Bar Association, *Electing the President* (Chicago: ABA, 1967), 3.

[25]The Twenty-third Amendment (1961) permits the District of Columbia to have three electors, even though it has no representatives in Congress.

[26]In Maine an elector is allocated for every congressional district won, and whoever wins the state as a whole wins the two electors allotted to the state for its senators.

"WE'RE TAKING AN EXIT POLL—HOW WOULD YOU LIKE TO MAKE AN EXIT?"

from *Herblock through the Looking Glass* (W. W. Norton, 1984)

■ Electors meet in their states in December, following the November election, and then mail their votes to the vice-president (who is also president of the Senate). The vote is counted when the new congressional session opens in January, and reported by the vice-president. Thus George Bush had the duty of announcing his own election in early 1989.

■ If no candidate receives an electoral college majority, then the election is thrown into the House of Representatives, which must choose from among the top three electoral vote winners. An interesting quirk in the House voting is that each state delegation has one vote, thus giving the one representative from Wyoming an equal say with the forty-five representatives from California.

The electoral college is important to the presidential election for two reasons. First, it introduces a bias into the campaign and electoral process. Providing the election is not thrown into the House, it gives extra clout to big states. The winner-take-all rule means that winning big states like California, New York, Texas, and Ohio is more important than piling up big leads in small states (see Figure 9-5). Politicians would rather get New York's thirty-six votes than North Dakota's three. Furthermore, big states are likely to have big cities (New York has New York City, Texas has Houston, California has Los Angeles, Illinois has Chicago, and so on). Thus the big-state bias produces an urban bias in the electoral college.

The electoral college attracts special attention when the prospect looms that either the election will be thrown into the House or that the electoral college result may not reflect the popular vote. Only twice has the election been decided by the House—in 1800, as discussed earlier, and in 1824. Not since 1888 has the popular-vote winner lost in the electoral college. In almost every close election, however, a few changes here and there have the potential to produce an incompatible result. In 1976 a shift of just six thousand votes in Ohio and four thousand votes in Hawaii would have given Ford the election even though Carter would still have led by a substantial margin in the popular vote.

Until either a popular-vote winner is denied election or a decision is again thrown into the House, reform of the electoral college is unlikely. On this issue most politicians abide by the old adage, "If it ain't broke, don't fix it."

Whether the American electoral system as a whole is compatible with democratic theory is a broader question to which this chapter now turns.

DEMOCRACY AND ELECTIONS

Elections accomplish two tasks according to democratic theory. First, and most obviously, they *select the policymakers*. Second, elections are supposed to help *shape public policy*. Whether elections in fact make the government pay attention to what the people think is at the center of debate concerning how well democracy works in America (see "The People Speak: Do Elections Make Government Listen?"). In the hypothetical world of rational choice theory and the Downs model (see Chapter 7), elections do in fact guide public policy; however, over a generation of social-science research on this question has produced mixed findings. It is more accurate to describe the connection between elections and public policy as a two-way street: elections—to some degree—affect public policy, and public-policy decisions partly affect electoral outcomes.

Figure 9.5 The Electoral College Map for the 1990s

Based on current estimates from the Census Bureau, the following map shows approximately how many delegates each state will have in the electoral college of the 1990s:

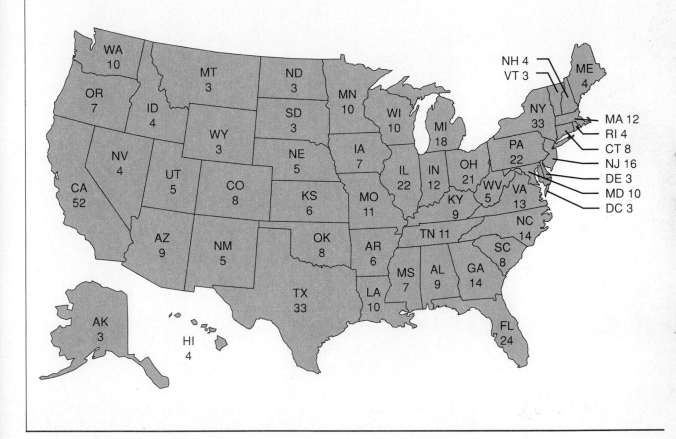

Elections Affect Public Policy

There will probably never be a definitive answer to the question of how much elections affect public policy, for it is a somewhat subjective matter. The broad contours of the answer, however, seem reasonably clear: *The greater the policy differences between the candidates, the more likely voters will be able to steer government policies by their choices.*

Of course, the candidates do not always do their best to clarify the issues. One result is that the policy stands are often shaped by what Benjamin Page once called "the art of ambiguity," in which "presidential candidates are skilled at appearing to say much while actually saying little."[27] Learning how to sidestep controversial questions and hedge answers is indeed part of becoming a professional politician, as you can observe at most every presidential press conference.

[27]Benjamin Page, *Choices and Echoes in American Presidential Elections* (Chicago: University of Chicago Press, 1978), 153.

"And here with us this evening, to skirt the issues, are Senator Tom Kirkland and Congressman Alan Sullivan."

So long as politicians can take refuge in ambiguity (and the skimpy coverage of issues in the media does little to make them clarify their policy stands), the possibility of democratic control of policy is lessened. As with policy voting, if citizens cannot see the policy differences between candidates then they can hardly express their own beliefs by voting for one over the other.

When individual candidates do offer a plain choice to the voters (what 1964 Republican nominee Barry Goldwater once called "a choice, not an echo"), voters are more able to guide the government's policy direction. Ronald Reagan followed in Goldwater's footsteps in the 1980s by making clear his intention to cut the growth of domestic spending, reduce taxes, and build up American military capability. Once elected, he proceeded to do just what he said he would—demonstrating that elections can sometimes dramatically affect public policy.

Public Policy Affects Election Outcomes

If elections affect policies, then policies can also affect elections. Most policies have consequences for the well-being of certain groups or the society as a whole. Those who feel better off as a result of certain policies are likely to support candidates who pledge to continue those policies, whereas those who feel worse off are inclined to support opposition candidates. This is known as the theory of **retrospective voting,**[28] in which voters essentially ask the simple question "What have you done for me lately?" Incumbents who provide desired results are rewarded; those who fail to do so are not reelected.

Nothing makes incumbent politicians more nervous than the state of the economy. When the economy takes a downturn, the call to "throw the rascals out" usually sweeps the nation. In presidential elections, people unhappy with the state of the economy tend to blame the incumbent. Republican Herbert Hoover was in office when the stock market crash of 1929 sparked the Great Depression. Hoover became so unpopular that the shantytowns occupied by unemployed people were called "Hoovervilles" and the apples they sold were called "Hoover apples." Hoover and his fellow Republicans were crushed by Franklin Roosevelt in the 1932 elections. Nearly half a century later in 1980 Democrat Jimmy Carter was swept out of office by Ronald Reagan in the midst of high inflation, unemployment, and interest rates. Just as Democrats brought up the specter of Hoover's failed administration for decades after the Great Depression, so Republicans now remind Americans each election of the economic troubles under the last Democratic president.

Clearly, elections affect policy, but public policy—especially the perception of economic policy impacts—can affect elections. Politicians, once in office, use fiscal policy to keep the American economy running on an even keel. (How they try to do this is considered in Chapter 17.) If economic troubles mount, voters point their fingers at incumbent policymakers, and those fingers are more likely to pull the lever for the challengers on election day. As V. O. Key once wrote, "The only really effective weapon of popular control in a democratic regime is the capacity of the electorate to throw a party from power."[29]

Elections and the Size of Government

While the threat of electoral punishment constrains policymakers, it also helps to increase generalized support for government and its powers. Because voters know that the government can be replaced at the next election, they are much more likely to feel that it will be responsive to their needs. Furthermore, when people have the power to dole out electoral reward and punishment, they are more likely to see government as their servant instead of their master. As Benjamin Ginsberg writes, "Democratic elections help to persuade citizens that expansion of the state's powers represents an increase in the state's capacity to serve them."[30]

Therefore, rather than wishing to be protected from the state, citizens in a democracy often seek to benefit from it. It is no coincidence that "individuals who believe they can influence the government's actions are also more likely to believe, in turn, that the government should have more power."[31] Voters like

Economic conditions can have a profound effect on election outcomes. In 1932 voters expressed their despair over the Great Depression by electing Franklin Roosevelt in a landslide over Herbert Hoover. Here an unemployed man sells "Hoover apples" in front of the capitol.

---

[28]See Morris P. Fiorina, *Retrospective Voting in American National Elections* (New Haven, Conn.: Yale University Press, 1981).

[29]V. O. Key, *The Responsible Electorate* (New York: Random House, 1966), 76.

[30]Benjamin Ginsberg, *Consequences of Consent* (Reading, Mass.: Addison-Wesley, 1982), 194.

[31]*Ibid.,* 198.

to feel that they are sending a message to the government to accomplish something. It should thus be no surprise that as democracy has spread government has come to do more and more, and its size has grown.

SUMMARY

This chapter has examined the final act in the electoral drama. Once the parties have made their nominations and the campaign has concluded, voters take center stage. Elections have changed dramatically since 1800 when Adams ran against Jefferson. By 1896 it was acceptable to campaign, and William Jennings Bryan did so with a vengeance. At that time suffrage—the right to vote—was still limited mostly to white males. Now the democratization of elections has made suffrage available to all American citizens over the age of eighteen.

Voters make two basic decisions at election time. The first is whether to vote. Americans' right to vote is well established, but in order to do so citizens must go through the registration process. America's unique registration system is one major reason why turnout in American elections is much lower than in most other democracies. The 1988 election between George Bush and Michael Dukakis was another in a long string of low-turnout elections.

Second, those who choose to vote must decide for whom to cast their ballots. Over a generation of research on voting behavior has helped political scientists to understand the dominant role played by three factors in voter's choices: party identification, candidate evaluations, and policy positions.

Elections are the centerpiece of democracy. Few questions are more important in understanding American government than this: Do elections matter? Under the right conditions, elections can influence public policy, and policy outcomes can influence elections. Elections also legitimize the power of the state, thereby making it easier to expand the size of the government.

Victorious candidates like to claim a mandate for their policy agenda, but political scientists argue that few citizens base their votes solely on a candidate's position on various issues. Party identification and candidate evaluation also play key roles in voting decisions.

Key terms

legitimacy
primaries
direct primaries
initiative petition
referendum

suffrage
voter registration
policy differences
civic duty
political efficacy

mandate theory of
  elections
policy voting
electoral college
retrospective voting

For further reading

Campbell, Angus, et al. *The American Voter*. New York: Wiley, 1960. The classic study of the American electorate in the 1950s, which has shaped scholarly approaches to the subject ever since.

Ginsberg, Benjamin. *Consequences of Consent*. Reading, Mass.: Addison-Wesley, 1982. Emphasizes that elections are a means both for the people to control the government and for the government to control the people.

Kelley, Stanley G., Jr. *Interpreting Elections*. Princeton, N.J.: Princeton University Press, 1983. Presents a theory of "the simple act of voting."

McCormick, Richard P. *The Presidential Game*. New York: Oxford University Press, 1982. An interesting historical look at the origins of presidential politics.

Nie, Norman H., Sidney Verba, and John R. Petrocik. *The Changing American Voter*. Cambridge, Mass.: Harvard University Press, 1976. Challenges some of the assumptions of Campbell et al.'s *The American Voter*.

Niemi, Richard G. and Herbert F. Weisberg, eds. *Controversies in Voting Behavior,* 2nd ed. Washington, D.C.: Congressional Quarterly Press, 1984. An excellent set of readings on some of the most hotly debated facets of voting.

Piven, Frances Fox and Richard A. Cloward. *Why Americans Don't Vote*. New York: Pantheon, 1988. A distinctly left-wing approach to the question of low American turnout.

Polsby, Nelson W. and Aaron Wildavsky. *Presidential Elections,* 7th ed. New York: Free Press, 1988. The classic text on the subject.

Wolfinger, Raymond E., and Steven J. Rosenstone. *Who Votes?* New Haven, Conn.: Yale University Press, 1980. The best quantitative study of who turns out and why.

10

INTEREST GROUPS

One of the most successful lobbies in Washington during the 1980s was that of the savings and loan industry. The industry wanted more freedom from federal regulators to run their business and make investments as they saw fit. In the deregulatory climate of the Reagan years, they were quite successful in this goal. The result was that while some S&Ls profited, many others undertook risky investments that lost money. The government had to take over many failed savings and loans and use taxpayer dollars to pay back depositers.

Probably the most famous case is that of Lincoln Savings and Loan, headed by Charles Keating. When federal regulators threatened to take over Lincoln, Keating turned to five U.S. senators to intervene on his behalf. Not surprisingly, the five he called upon for help (Alan Cranston, Donald Riegle, Dennis DeConcini, John McCain, and John Glenn) had all been the recipients of very large political contributions from Keating. The five senators met twice as a group for over two hours with the head of the Federal Home Loan Bank Board, pressuring him to drop his plan to shut down the financially ailing business. When five senators get together, bureaucrats listen. Lincoln was allowed to stay in business for two more years, accumulating more and more debt until it was finally closed in 1989 with a staggering $2.5 billion deficit.

When the story of the senators' involvement broke, all five contended that whatever they did on Keating's behalf was no different from any inquiry a member of Congress routinely makes on behalf of a constituent. Senator McCain, for example, compared it to helping a little old lady who did not get her Social Security check. Others noted that they were concerned by the possibility that thousands of their constituents could lose their jobs if Lincoln were closed.

Many critics took a more cynical view of the senators' actions, however, calling the case a prime example of how special interests' campaign contributions taint congressional action. They argued that Keating's situation was a regulatory matter in which the goal should have been the integrity of the savings and loan system, not the protection of constituents. They viewed the fact that Keating had made such large contributions to the senators as clear evidence that influence had been bought and sold. It is doubtful that the senators would have gone to such lengths for Keating—perhaps even given him the time of day—without the contributions.

The worst and oldest stereotype of a lobbyist is of someone who bribes a lawmaker to get a favorable policy decision. In contrast, Charles Keating's leverage with the five senators was obtained by open and legal means. Indeed, as this chapter will show, the problems of honest lobbying now appear to outweigh the traditional problems of dishonest lobbying.

O ur nation's capital has become a hub of interest group activity. On any given day it is possible to observe pressure groups in action in many forums. In the morning you could attend congressional hearings in which you are sure to see interest groups testifying for and against proposed legislation. At the Supreme Court you might stop in to watch a public interest lawyer arguing for strict enforcement of environmental regulations. Take a break for lunch at a nice Washington restaurant and you may well see a lobbyist entertaining a member of Congress.

The afternoon could be spent in any department of the executive branch (such as commerce, defense, or the interior), where you might catch bureaucrats working out rules and regulations with friendly—or sometimes unfriendly—representatives of the interests they are charged with overseeing. To get a sense of some of the major lobbying organizations' size, you could stroll past the impressive headquarters of the National Rifle Association, the AFL-CIO, or the National Association of Manufacturers. To see some lobbying done on college students' behalf, you might drop by One Dupont Circle, where all the higher education groups have their offices. They lobby for student loans and scholarships, as well as aid to educational institutions. At dinner time, if you were able to wangle an invitation to a Georgetown cocktail party, you may well see lobbyists trying to get the ear of government officials—both elected and unelected.

All of this lobbying activity poses an interesting paradox: Although turnout in elections has declined since 1960, participation in interest groups has mushroomed. According to Jack Walker, "the American public is more extensively organized for political action today than ever before, and there is no reason to believe that the process will soon be reversed."[1] This chapter will explore the factors behind the interest group explosion, how these groups enter the policy-making process, and what they get out of it.

THE ROLE AND REPUTATION OF INTEREST GROUPS

All Americans have some interests they want represented. Organizing to promote these interests is an essential part of democracy. The right to organize groups is protected by the Constitution, which guarantees people the right "peaceably to assemble, and to petition the Government for a redress of grievances." This important First Amendment right has been carefully defended by the Supreme Court. The freedom to organize is as fundamental to democratic government as freedom of speech or of the press.

Defining Interest Groups

The term *interest group* seems simple enough to define. *Interest* refers to a policy goal; a *group* is a combination of people. An **interest group,** therefore, is an organization of people with similar policy goals entering the political process to try to achieve those aims. Whatever their goals—outlawing abortion or ensuring the right to one, regulating tax loopholes or creating new ones—interest groups pursue them in many arenas. Every branch of government is fair game; every level of government, local to federal, is a possible target. A policy battle lost in Congress may be turned around when it comes to bureaucratic implementation or the judicial process.

This multiplicity of policy arenas helps distinguish interest groups from political parties. Parties fight their battles through the electoral process—they run candidates for public office. Interest groups may support candidates for office, but American interest groups do not run their own slate of candidates, as in some other countries (see "America in Perspective: Interest Groups as Parties in Other Democracies"). In other words, no one is ever listed on the ballot as a candidate of the National Rifle Association or Common Cause. It may be well known that a candidate is actively supported by a particular group, but that candidate faces the voters as a Democrat or a Republican.

Politicians need to keep many interest groups happy. During the 1988 presidential campaign, George Bush appealed to veterans at a convention of the Veterans of Foreign Wars—one of the nation's oldest, largest, and most powerful interest groups—by emphasizing his views on a strong national defense.

[1]Jack L. Walker, "The Mobilization of Political Interests" (Paper presented at the annual meeting of the American Political Science Association, Chicago, Ill., September 1–4, 1983), 35.

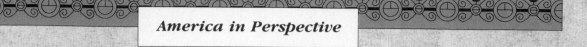

Interest Groups as Parties in Other Democracies

In many countries with multiparty systems, interest groups form their own political parties to push for their demands. With proportional representation systems (see Chapter 7), all it takes is between 1 and 5 percent of the vote, depending on the country, for a narrowly based party to win seats in the national legislature. While special interest groups usually cannot win very many seats, their impact can be large if their votes are crucial in obtaining a majority in the Parliament.

In many of the Scandinavian countries, for example, farmers' parties have long been in existence. Typically, the farmers' party has received between 10 and 20 percent of the vote in nations such as Sweden and Finland. For a conservative, nonsocialist government to be formed, their support is often critical. Therefore any conservative government in these countries will be quite responsive to agrarian inter-

ests. If you are troubled by the fact that American agricultural policy is heavily influenced by congressional representatives from farm states, imagine a situation where key officeholders owe their election exclusively to this single economic interest.

Many new interest groups in Europe have formed parties not on the basis of shared economic interests, like labor or agriculture, but rather on shared values. In particular, Green parties have sprung up throughout Western Europe to represent the concerns of environmentalists. Imagine having two dozen members of the American Congress insist on discussing the environmental impact of every decision. While these members might not often win, they would certainly bring more attention to the issue of environmental protection. This is the situation in countries where the Greens have won enough votes to enter the national legislature, such as in West Germany.

Another key difference between parties and interest groups is that *interest groups are often policy specialists, whereas parties are policy generalists*. Most interest groups have a handful of key policies to push: a farm group cares little about the status of urban transit; an environmental group has its hands full bringing polluters into court without worrying about the minimum wage. Unlike political parties, these groups do not face the constraint imposed by trying to appeal to everyone.

Why Interest Groups Get Bad Press

Despite their importance to democratic government, interest groups traditionally have received bad press in America. The authors of the Federalist Papers thought they were no better than political parties, which they also disliked. Madison's derogatory term *faction* was general enough to include both parties and groups. Today Americans' image of interest groups is no more favorable. On a slow news day editorial cartoonists can always depict lobbyists skulking around in the congressional hallways, their pockets stuffed with money, just waiting to funnel it to a legislator's wallet (see "A Question of Ethics: Some Examples of Dishonest Lobbying").

Defenders of the interest group system counter that for every Watergate and HUD scandal, hundreds of basically honest transactions between Congress and interest groups take place. There is little doubt that honest lobbying outpaces dishonest lobbying by a wide margin; however, many political scientists now believe that honest lobbying (such as the Lincoln Savings case) poses greater problems for democracy than dishonest lobbying.

THEORIES OF INTEREST GROUP POLITICS

Understanding the debate over whether honest lobbying—and interest groups generally—create problems for government in America requires an examination of three important theories, which were introduced in Chapter 1. **Pluralist theory** argues that interest group activity brings representation to all. According to pluralists, groups compete and counterbalance one another in the political marketplace. In contrast, **elite theory** argues that just a few groups have most of the power—primarily the wealthy. Finally, **hyperpluralist theory** asserts that too many groups are getting too much of what they want, resulting in a government policy that is often contradictory and lacking in direction. The following sections will examine each of these three theories more closely.

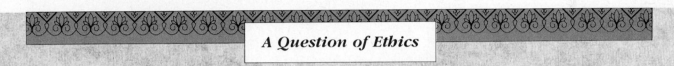

A Question of Ethics

Some Examples of Dishonest Lobbying

For as long as the republic has existed, stories of interest groups bribing public officials have regularly surfaced. In the nineteenth and early twentieth century such behavior was quite commonplace. Even one of the Senate's greatest figures, Daniel Webster of Massachusetts, demanded money in return for his support for chartering the Bank of the United States. Once when the money did not arrive on time, Webster complained to the president of the Bank: "My retainer has not been renewed or refreshed as usual. If it is wished that my relation to the Bank should be continued, it may be well to send me the usual retainers."

In the early twentieth century one of the most celebrated cases of bribery involved the powerful National Association of Manufacturers (NAM). A lobbyist for NAM stated publicly in 1913 that he had bribed numerous members of Congress for legislative favors. He had even gone so far as to pay the chief House page a sizeable sum every month for inside information obtained by eavesdropping on members' cloakroom discussions.

Most recently, in 1980 the FBI conducted a sting operation in which agents posed as wealthy Arabs seeking to bribe members of Congress to help their relatives obtain U.S. residency. In what came to be known as *Abscam,* the FBI filmed seven members of Congress taking cash in return for their promise to help. (One actually stuffed wads of money into every conceivable pocket of his suit.) All seven were convicted of charges ranging from bribery to conspiracy.

The principal method of controlling dishonest lobbying has been through disclosure laws, which have been tightened substantially over the past two decades. Lobbyists are required to identify themselves, who they represent, and their legislative interests. PACs must keep complete records of where they get their money and how they spend it. Members of Congress are required to file regular, detailed financial statements, making it difficult to hide ill-gotten income. Thus the relationship between public officials and lobbyists is probably more free of out-and-out bribery than ever before in American history.

Source: "The Washington Lobby," in *CQ Guide to Current American Government: Spring 1990 Guide* (Washington, D.C.: Congressional Quarterly Press, 1990), 34–38.

"YOU'LL LIKE THEM ... THEIR SPECIAL INTEREST IS GIVING AWAY MORE MONEY THAN OTHER SPECIAL INTEREST GROUPS!"

Pluralism and Group Theory

Pluralist theory rests its case on the many centers of power in the American political system. The extensive organization of competing groups is seen as evidence that influence is widely dispersed among them. Pluralists believe that groups win some and lose some, but no group wins or loses all the time. A considerable body of writings by pluralist theorists offers a *group theory of politics,*[2] which contains several essential arguments.

- *Groups provide a key linkage between people and government.* All legitimate interests in the political system can get a hearing from government once they are organized.

- *Groups compete.* Labor, business, farmers, consumers, environmentalists, and other interests constantly make claims on one another.

- *No one group is likely to become too dominant.* When one group throws its weight around too much, its opponents are likely to intensify their organization and thus restore balance to the system. For every action, there is a reaction.

- *Groups usually play by the "rules of the game."* In the United States group politics is a fair fight, with few groups lying, cheating, stealing, or engaging in violence to get their way.

- *Groups weak in one resource can use another.* Big business may have money on its side, but labor has numbers. All legitimate groups are able to affect public policy by one means or another.

[2]The classic work is David B. Truman, *The Governmental Process,* 2nd ed. (New York: Alfred A. Knopf, 1971).

Pluralists would never deny that some groups are stronger than others, or that competing interests do not always get an equal hearing. Still, they can point to many cases in which a potential group organized itself and then got action. African Americans, women, and consumers are all groups who were long-ignored by government officials, but once organized, redirected the course of public policy. In sum, pluralists argue that lobbying is open to all and is therefore not to be regarded as a problem.

Elites and the Denial of Pluralism

Whereas pluralists are impressed by the vast number of organized interests, elitists are impressed by how insignificant most of them are. *Real* power, elitists say, is held by relatively few people, key groups, and institutions. They maintain that the government is run by a few big interests looking out for themselves—a view that the majority of the public has agreed with for the last two decades (see "The People Speak: Perceptions of the Dominance of Big Interests").

Elitists critique pluralist theory by pointing to the concentration of power in a few hands. Where pluralists find dispersion of power, elitists find inter-locking and concentrated power centers. About one-third of top institutional

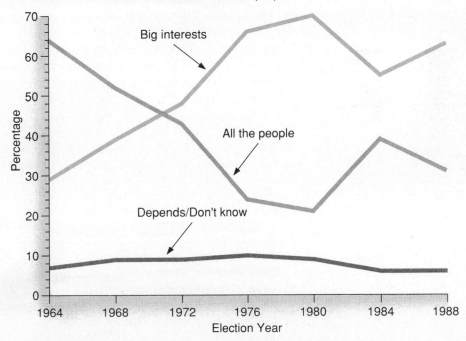

The People Speak | **Perceptions of the Dominance of Big Interests**

Would you say the government is pretty much run by a few big interests looking out for themselves or that it is run for the benefit of all the people?

Big interests

All the people

Depends/Don't know

Percentage

1964 1968 1972 1976 1980 1984 1988

Election Year

Source: The question as worded is taken directly from National Election Studies conducted by the University of Michigan.

positions—corporate boards, foundation boards, university trusteeships, and so on—are occupied by people who hold more than one such position.[3] Elitists see the rise of mighty multinational corporations as further tightening the control of corporate elites. A prime example is America's giant oil companies. Robert Engler has tried to show that government has always bent over backwards to maintain high profits for the oil industry.[4] When confronted with the power of these multinational corporations, consumer interests are readily pushed aside, according to elitists.

In sum, the elitist view of the interest group system makes the following points:

- The fact that there are numerous groups proves nothing, because groups are extremely unequal in power.
- Awesome power is controlled by the largest corporations.
- The power of a few is fortified by an extensive system of interlocking directorates.
- Other groups may win many minor policy battles, but the corporate elites prevail when it comes to the big decisions.

Thus honest lobbying is a problem, say elite theorists, because it benefits the few at the expense of the many.

Hyperpluralism and Interest Group Liberalism

Hyperpluralism, also critical of pluralism, argues that the pluralist system is out of control. Theodore Lowi coined the phrase *interest group liberalism* to refer to the government's excessive deference to groups. Interest group liberalism holds that virtually all pressure group demands are legitimate and that the job of the government is to advance them all.[5]

In an effort to please and appease every interest, agencies proliferate, conflicting regulations expand, programs multiply, and, of course, the budget skyrockets. If environmentalists want clean air, government imposes clean-air rules; if businesses complain that cleaning up pollution is expensive, government gives them a tax write-off for pollution-control equipment. If the direct-mail industry wants cheap rates, government gives it to them; if people complain about junk mail, the Postal Service gives them a way to take their name off mailing lists. If cancer researchers convince the government to launch an antismoking campaign, tobacco sales may drop; if they do, government will subsidize tobacco farmers to ease their loss.

Interest group liberalism is promoted by the network of **subgovernments** in the American political system. These subgovernments (which are also known as iron triangles, and will be discussed in greater detail in Chapter 14) are composed of key interest group leaders interested in policy *X;* the government agency in charge of administering policy *X;* and the members of congressional committees and subcommittees handling policy *X.*

[3]Thomas R. Dye, *Who's Running America? The Bush Era,* 5th ed. (Englewood Cliffs, N.J.: Prentice-Hall, 1990), 170.

[4]Robert Engler, *The Brotherhood of Oil* (Chicago: University of Chicago Press, 1977).

[5]Theodore J. Lowi, *The End of Liberalism,* 2nd ed. (New York: Norton, 1979).

All the elements composing subgovernments have a similar goal: protecting their self-interest. The network of subgovernments in the agricultural policy area of tobacco is an excellent example. Tobacco interest groups include the Tobacco Institute, the Retail Tobacco Distributors of America, and the tobacco growers. Various agencies in the Department of Agriculture administer tobacco programs, and they depend on the tobacco industry's clout in Congress to help keep their agency budgets safe from cuts. Finally, most of the members of the House Tobacco Subcommittee are from tobacco growing regions. All of these elements thus have a common desire in protecting the interests of tobacco farmers. Similar subgovernments of group-agency-committee ties exist in scores of other policy areas.

Hyperpluralists' major criticism of the interest group system is that relations between groups and the government become too cozy. Hard choices about national policy rarely get made. Instead of making choices between *X* or *Y,* the government pretends there is no need at all to choose and tries to favor them both. It is a perfect script for policy paralysis. In short, the hyperpluralist position on group politics is that

- Groups have become too powerful in the political process as government tries to aid every conceivable interest.
- Interest group liberalism is aggravated by numerous subgovernments—comfortable relationships among a government agency, the interest group it deals with, and congressional subcommittees.
- Trying to please every group results in contradictory and confusing policy.

Ironically, the recent interest group explosion is seen by some as weakening the power of subgovernments. As Morris Fiorina writes, "A world of active public interest groups, jealous business competitors, and packs of budding investigative reporters is less hospitable to subgovernment politics than a world lacking in them."[6] With so many more interest groups to satisfy, and with many of them competing against one another, a cozy relationship between groups and the government is plainly more difficult to sustain.

THE INTEREST GROUP EXPLOSION

The number of interest groups in the United States is indeed increasing rapidly. Although no one has ever compiled a *Who's Who* of interest groups, the closest thing is the annual *Encyclopedia of Associations*.[7] Although not an exhaustive inventory, the *Encyclopedia* shows the variety of groups in the United States. You can see a sampling of its entries in Table 10.1. This table makes several

[6]Morris P. Fiorina, *Congress: Keystone of the Washington Establishment,* 2nd ed. (New Haven, Conn.: Yale University Press, 1989), 122.

[7]Karin E. Koek, Susan B. Martin, and Annette Novallo, eds. *Encyclopedia of Associations, 1989* (Detroit: Gale Research Company, 1988).

Table 10.1   Sampling of Groups

NAME (date of founding)[a]	HEADQUARTERS	MEMBERSHIP	STAFF	PUBLICATIONS
Groups Interested in Economic Policy				
National Electrical Manufacturers Association (1926)	Washington, D.C.	600	100	*News Bulletin*
National Association of Manufacturers (1895)	Washington, D.C.	13,250	200	*Enterprise*
Underwear-Negligee Associates (1946)	New York	100	—[b]	—[b]
Pharmaceutical Manufacturers Association (1958)	Washington, D.C.	105	90	*Newsletter, Trademark Bulletin; State Capitol Reports; Science and Technology Notes*
Air Line Pilots Association, Int'l. (1931)	Washington, D.C.	40,000	280	*Air Line Pilot Newsletter*
AFL-CIO (1955)	Washington, D.C.	13,200,000	500	*News*
Glycerine and Oleochemicals Association (1983)	New York	18	—[b]	—[b]
National Consumers League (1899)	Washington, D.C.	5,000	5	*Bulletin*
National Peanut Council (1941)	Washington, D.C.	250	9	*Peanut News*
American Farm Bureau Federation (1919)	Park Ridge, Ill.	3,300,000	102	*Farm Bureau News*
American Mushroom Institute (1955)	Kennet Square, Pa.	450	4	*Mushroom News; Mushroom Newswire*
National Potato Council (1948)	Denver, Colo.	14,000	3	*Spudletter*

[a]All data based on reports from individual groups.   [b]No data reported.
Source: Denise Akey, ed, *Encyclopedia of Associations, 1989,* 23rd ed. (Detroit: Gale Research Company, 1990).

---

important points about interest groups. (1) The majority of groups now have their headquarters in Washington, D.C. (2) There are an enormous number of highly specialized and seemingly trivial groups such as the National Potato Council. (3) Almost every group—large or small—has a staff and publications.

Many groups' interests are primarily economic. The trade, commercial, and business section of the *Encyclopedia* lists 3,806 groups, beginning with organizations of accountants and ending with those of wholesale distributors. Between these two types one can find such groups as the American Cricket Growers Association and the Glycerine and Oleochemicals (Fatty Acids) Association.

It seems that there is now an organized group for every conceivable interest. Indeed, the growth rate of interest groups has been astounding. Jack Walker studied 564 groups listed in the *Washington Information Directory* and tried to trace their origins and expansion.[8] He found that 80 percent of the groups

[8]Jack L. Walker, "The Origins and Maintenance of Interest Groups in America," *American Political Science Review* 77 (June 1983), 390–406.

Sampling of Groups (continued)

NAME (date of founding)[a]	HEADQUARTERS	MEMBERSHIP	STAFF	PUBLICATIONS
Groups Interested in Equality Policy				
National Organization for Women (1966)	Washington, D.C.	260,000	—[b]	*National NOW Times*
National Association for the Advancement of Colored People (1909)	Washington, D.C.	400,000	132	*Crisis; Report*
National Urban League (1910)	New York	50,000	2,000	*The Urban League Review; State of Black America*
National Women's Political Caucus (1971)	Washington, D.C.	75,000	15	*Women's Political Times*
Groups Interested in Energy/Environmental Policy				
American Petroleum Institute (1919)	Washington, D.C.	52,000	400	Publishes statistical information manuals, etc.
American Mining Congress (1897)	Washington, D.C.	450	50	*Journal; Coal and Noncoal Mining Technology*
Sierra Club (1892)	San Francisco, Ca.	416,000	250	*Sierra; National News*
Water Pollution Control Federation (1928)	Washington, D.C.	32,000	62	*Highlights*
Some Other Interest Groups				
Veterans of Foreign Wars (1899)	Kansas City, Mo.	2,053,270	275	*VFW Magazine; Washington Action*
Common Cause (1970)	Washington, D.C.	280,000	152	*Common Cause*
American Medical Association (1847)	Chicago, Ill	271,000	—[b]	*Journal; American Medical News*

originated from occupational, industrial, or professional memberships. Interestingly, half of the groups he studied were established after World War II. Walker also found a gravitation of groups to Washington, D.C. In 1960 only 66 percent of the groups in his study were headquartered in the nation's capital; today about 90 percent are. Very few occupations or industries now go without an organized group to represent them in Washington.

There are many reasons for this explosion in the number of groups. Certainly one of the major factors has been the development of sophisticated technology. Andrew McFarland observes that

> technological innovations have made the coordination of constituents' activities and efforts of lobbyists much easier. Many lobbyists, for example, have available computerized lists of names and phone numbers of group members that can be easily arranged by congressional district or state. Address labels can be printed automatically or members can be called by WATS line from a group's headquarters.[9]

Technology did not create interest group politics, but it surely eased the job.

How Groups Try to Shape Policy

Small or large, no interest group has enough staff, money, or time to do everything possible to achieve their policy goals. Interest groups must choose from a variety of tactics. Table 10.2 illustrates the range and frequency of tactics employed by a sample of interest groups. The three traditional strategies are lobbying, electioneering, and litigation. In addition, groups have lately developed a variety of sophisticated techniques to appeal to the public for widespread support. These four general strategies are the topic of the next four sections.

Lobbying

The term **lobbying** comes from the place where petitioners used to collar legislators. In the early years of politics in Washington, members of Congress had no offices and typically stayed in boarding houses or hotels while Congress was in session. A person could not call them up on the phone or make an appointment with their secretary; the only sure way of getting in touch with them was to wait in the lobby where they were staying, so as to catch them either coming in or going out. Because these people spent so much of their time waiting in lobbies they were dubbed *lobbyists*.

Of course, merely loitering in a lobby does not make one a lobbyist—there must be a particular reason for such action. Lester Milbrath has offered a more precise definition of the practice. He writes that *lobbying* is a "communication, by someone other than a citizen acting on his [or her] own behalf, directed to a governmental decision-maker with the hope of influencing his [or her] decision."[10] Lobbyists, in other words, are political persuaders. They are the representatives of organized groups, normally work in Washington, and handle groups' legislative business (see "In Focus: The Lobbyists").

---

[9]Andrew S. McFarland, *Common Cause: Lobbying in the Public Interest* (Chatham, N.J.: Chatham House, 1984), 1.

[10]Lester W. Milbrath, *The Washington Lobbyists* (Chicago: Rand McNally, 1963), 8.

Table 10.2 Percentage of Groups Using Various Lobbying Techniques

TECHNIQUE	PERCENTAGE
Testifying at hearings	99
Contacting government officials directly to present a point of view	98
Engaging in informal contacts with officials—at conventions, over lunch, etc.	95
Presenting research results or technical information	92
Sending letters to members of an organization to inform them about its activities	92
Entering into coalitions with other organizations	90
Attempting to shape the implementation of policies	89
Talking with people from the press and the media	86
Consulting with government officials to plan legislative strategy	85
Helping to draft legislation	85
Inspiring letter-writing or telegram campaigns	84
Shaping the government's agenda by raising new issues and calling attention to previously ignored problems	84
Mounting grassroots lobbying efforts	80
Having influential constituents contact their congressperson's office	80
Helping to draft regulations, rules, or guidelines	78
Serving on advisory commissions and boards	76
Alerting members of Congress to the effects of a bill on their districts	75
Filing suit or otherwise engaging in litigation	72
Making financial contributions to electoral campaigns	58
Doing favors for officials who need assistance	56
Attempting to influence appointments to public office	53
Publicizing candidates' voting records	44
Engaging in direct-mail fund-raising	44
Running advertisements in the media about issues	31
Contributing work or personnel to electoral campaigns	24
Making public endorsements of candidates for office	22
Engaging in protests or demonstrations	20

Source: Kay L. Schlotzman and John T. Tierney, *Organized Interests and American Democracy* (New York: Harper & Row, 1986).

Although lobbyists are primarily out to influence members of Congress, it is important to remember that they can be of help to them as well. Ornstein and Elder list five ways lobbyists can help a member of Congress.

- They are an important source of information. Members of Congress have to concern themselves with many policy areas; lobbyists can confine themselves to only one, and thus can provide specialized expertise.
- They can help a member with political strategy. Lobbyists are politically savvy people, and they are free consultants.
- They can help formulate campaign strategy and get the group's members behind a politician's reelection campaign.
- They are a source of ideas and innovations. Lobbyists cannot introduce bills, but they can peddle their ideas to politicians eager to attach their name to an idea that will bring them political credit.

In Focus

The Lobbyists

Washington lobbyists have a bad reputation. They are depicted by cartoonists as people with too much ready cash to channel into too many corrupting purposes. Yet they see themselves as people accomplishing an important representative mission.

Lobbying is a high-pressure job. Turnover is heavy; the average Washington lobbyist lasts less than five years. Most are extremely well educated, and a lobbyist for a major group will be paid well in excess of ninety thousand dollars a year. Although women are increasingly seen in the public interest lobbying role, 94 percent of the representatives of business and professional associations are men.

Basically, lobbyists are of two types. First are regular, paid employees of a corporation, union, or association. They may hold a title such as vice-president for government relations, but everyone knows that their office is in Washington for a reason, even if the company headquarters are in Milwaukee. Second are lobbyists available for hire on a temporary basis. One group may be too small to afford a full-time lobbyist;

another may have a unique, but temporary, need for access to Congress or the executive branch. Several thousand Washingtonians are available as "lobbyists for hire."

A handful of individuals, some of them former officeholders or government officials, are what Jeffrey Berry calls the "superstars of lobbying." They may charge five hundred dollars per hour for lobbying services. Among the most successful is Charls E. Walker, who was Richard Nixon's deputy secretary of the treasury. His specialty is tax law. Eastern Airlines, Ford, Procter and Gamble, and other corporate giants pay him handsomely to watch and work for minuscule changes in tax laws that could gain (or cost) them millions of dollars. Walker rarely prowls the halls of the Capitol, but works mostly by phone and over lunches. Contacts are important to him, much more so than any electoral threat he poses. Few voters would know or care what Charls Walker wanted them to do, but a great many powerful people think of him as a conduit to power.

Source: For more information on the Washington lobbyists, from which this overview is taken, see Jeffrey Berry, *The Interest Group Society,* 2nd ed. (Glenview, Ill.: Scott, Foresman, 1989), chap. 4.

- They provide friendship. It is a rare member of Congress who could not say, "Some of my best friends are lobbyists."[11]

Like anything else, lobbying can be done crudely or gracefully. Lobbyists can sometimes be heavy-handed. They can threaten or cajole a legislator, implying that electoral defeat is a certain result of not "going along." They can even make it clear that money flows to the reelection coffers of those who cooperate. It is often difficult to tell the difference between lobbying as a shady business and as a strictly professional representation of legitimate interests.

Political scientists are not in agreement about the effectiveness of lobbying. Much evidence suggests that lobbyists' power over policy is often much exaggerated. A classic 1950s study of the influence of groups on foreign-trade policy started with the hypothesis that when major business lobbies spoke, Congress listened—and acted accordingly.[12] Instead, the study found groups involved in

[11]Norman Ornstein and Shirley Elder, *Interest Groups, Lobbying, and Policymaking* (Washington, D.C.: Congressional Quarterly Press, 1978), 59–60.

[12]Raymond A. Bauer, Ithiel de Sola Pool, and Lewis A. Dexter, *American Business and Public Policy* (New York: Atherton, 1963).

trade policy to be ineffective, understaffed, and underfinanced. Usually the lobbyists were too disorganized to be effective. Members of Congress often had to pressure the interest groups to actively support legislation which would be in their own interest. Similarly, Milbrath concluded his own analysis of lobbying by arguing that "there is relatively little influence or power in lobbying per se."[13] Lobbyists are most effective, he claims, as information sources and are relatively ineffectual in winning over legislators.

There is plenty of contrary evidence to suggest that sometimes lobbying can persuade legislators to support a certain policy. The National Rifle Association, which has for years kept major gun control policies off the congressional

[13]Milbrath, *The Washington Lobbyists,* 354.

NOMA McCOLLOUGH: Wife, mother and High Power Shooting Champion. Two-time National Women's Champion and the first woman to ever win the 1000 yard Wimbledon Championship. Member of the National Rifle Association.

"Most people are surprised when I tell them I still shoot for fun. But it's true. I find competitive shooting very relaxing and personally satisfying.

"Ever since I started winning some big matches and competing equally with men, I hear many women say 'You only weigh 100 pounds! If you can do it, so can I.'

"And I tell them they don't have to be champions to win at shooting. A person can win at trying. Practicing, getting better and enjoying yourself are the rewards.

"I'm a member of the NRA and so is my husband. They do so much to support competition and protect shooting programs. And thanks to the NRA, I'll continue to compete and my children will grow up with the same opportunity to enjoy the sport."

I'm the NRA.

Last year, the NRA sanctioned over 6,000 tournaments in 24 shooting disciplines involving more than 100,000 men and women. If you would like to join the NRA and want more information about our programs and benefits, write Harlon Carter, Executive Vice President, P.O. Box 37484, Dept. NM- 28 , Washington, D.C. 20013. *Paid for by the members of the National Rifle Association of America.*

For years the National Rifle Association has successfully lobbied against gun control policies, arguing that the Constitution guarantees all citizens the right to bear arms. In addition to intense lobbying and electioneering, the NRA uses advertisements such as this one to build popular support with which to pressure policymakers.

agenda, is one of Washington's prime examples of a successful lobby. In a more specific example, intensive lobbying by the nation's most wealthy senior citizens—enraged by the tax burden imposed upon them by the 1988 Catastrophic Health Care Act—led Congress to repeal the act only a year after it was passed.

Nailing down the specific effects of lobbying is difficult, partly because it is hard to isolate its effects from other influences. Lobbying clearly works best on people already committed to the lobbyist's policy position. Thus, like campaigning, lobbying is directed primarily toward activating and reinforcing one's supporters. For example, antiabortion lobbyists would not think of approaching Colorado's Patricia Schroeder to attempt to convert her to their position. If Congresswoman Schroeder is lobbied by anyone on the abortion issue, it will be by the pro-choice faction—urging her not to compromise with the opposition.

Electioneering

Because lobbying works best with those already on the same side, getting the right people into office or keeping them there is also a key strategy of interest groups. Many groups therefore get involved in **electioneering,** aiding candidates financially and getting their members out to support them. Pressure group involvement in campaigns is nothing new. In the election of 1896 (see Chapter 9) silver-mining interests poured millions into the presidential campaign of William Jennings Bryan, who advocated unlimited coinage of silver.

Recently, **Political Action Committees** (PACs) have provided a means for groups to participate in electioneering more than ever before. The number of PACs has mushroomed from 608 in 1974 to 4,268 in 1988.[14] (See Figure 10.1.)

[14]Harold W. Stanley and Richard G. Niemi, *Vital Statistics on American Politics,* 2nd ed. (Washington: Congressional Quarterly Press, 1990), 160.

Figure 10.1 The PAC Explosion: 1974–1988

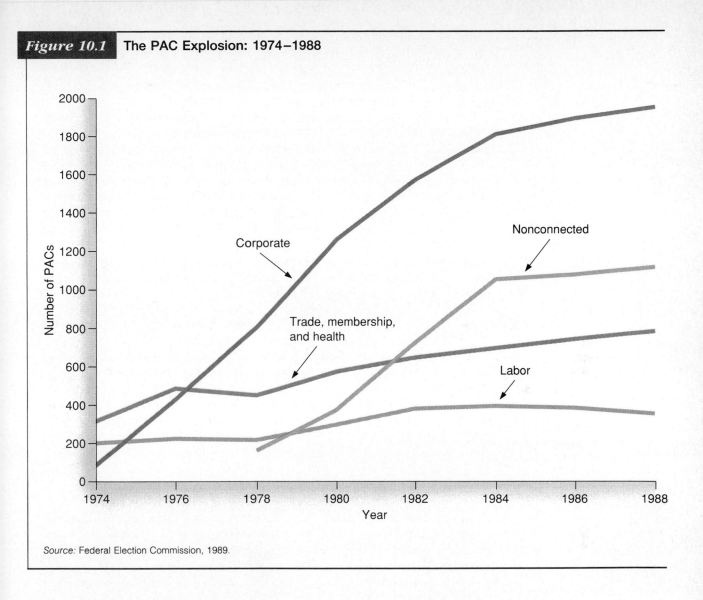

Source: Federal Election Commission, 1989.

No major interest group seeking to exert influence on the electoral process these days can pass up the opportunity to honestly and openly funnel money into the campaign coffers of their supporters. As campaign costs have risen in recent years, PACs have come along to help pay the bill. Nearly half of the members of the House (210 out of 435) elected in 1988 received the majority of their campaign funds from PACs, according to a Common Cause study. Furthermore, this advantage was not enjoyed by their challengers. PACs gave a whopping eighty-two million dollars to House incumbents during the 1987–88 election cycle compared to a mere nine million dollars to the challengers.[15]

Why does the PAC money go so overwhelmingly to incumbents? The answer is that PAC contributions basically are investments for the future, and incumbents

[15]"No Contest," *Common Cause News,* March 28, 1989.

are the most likely to be able to return the investment. Sometimes PACs like to play it safe, however; an examination of seven hotly contested Senate races in 1988 showed that 274 PACs guaranteed that their investments were risk free by contributing to both the Democratic and Republican candidates for the same seat.[16]

Only a handful of candidates have resisted the lure of PAC money in recent years. One candidate described his experiences trying to get on the PAC band-wagon. When Democrat Steve Sovern ran for the House from Iowa's Second District in 1980, he made the now common pilgrimage to Washington to meet with potential contributors. "I found myself in line with candidates from all over," he reported. Each PAC had eager candidates fill out a multiple-choice questionnaire on issues important to it. Candidates who answered right and who looked like winners got the money. Sovern later reported that "the process made me sick." After his defeat he organized his own PAC called LASTPAC (for Let the American System Triumph), which urged candidates to shun PAC campaign contributions.[17] The grandfather of public interest lobbies, Common Cause, is also waging a public campaign against PACs.

Litigation

If one fails in Congress or gets only a vague piece of legislation, the next step is to go to court in the hope of getting specific rulings. Karen Orren has linked much of the success of environmental interest groups to their use of lawsuits. "Frustrated in Congress," she wrote, "[they] have made an end run to the courts, where they have skillfully exploited and magnified limited legislative gains."[18] Environmental legislation, such as the Clean Air Act, typically includes written provisions allowing ordinary citizens to sue for enforcement. As a result every federal agency involved in environmental regulation now has hundreds of suits pending against it at any given time. These suits may not halt environmentally troublesome practices, but the constant threat of a lawsuit increases the likeli-hood that businesses will consider the environmental impact of what they do.

Perhaps the most famous interest group victories in court were by civil rights groups in the 1950s. While civil rights bills remained stalled in Congress, these groups won major victories in court cases concerning school desegre-gation, equal housing, and labor market equality. More recently, consumer groups have used suits against businesses and federal agencies as a means of enforcing consumer regulations. As long as law schools keep producing lawyers, groups will fight for their interests in court. Indeed, the increase in the pro-portion of lawyers licensed to practice in Washington has been phenomenal throughout the 1970s and 1980s (see Figure 10.2).

One tactic that lawyers employ to make the views of interest groups heard by the judiciary is the filing of **amicus curiae** ("friend of the court") **briefs.** *Amicus* briefs consist of written arguments submitted to the courts in support of one side of a case. Through these written depositions, a group states its collective position as well as how its own welfare will be affected by the outcome

---

[16]"No Risk Investments," *Common Cause News,* May 9, 1989.

[17]The Sovern story is told in "Taking an Ax to PACs," *Time,* August 20, 1984, 27.

[18]Karen Orren, "Standing to Sue: Interest Group Conflict in Federal Courts," *American Political Science Review* 70 (September 1976): 724.

Figure 10.2 Washington Lawyers

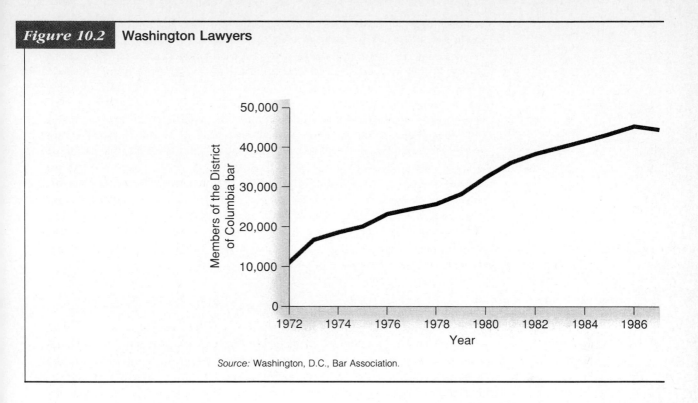

Source: Washington, D.C., Bar Association.

of the case. Numerous groups may file friend of the court briefs in highly publicized and emotionally charged cases. For example, in the case of *Regents of the University of California* v. *Bakke* (see Chapter 5), which challenged affirmative action programs as reverse discrimination, over a hundred different groups filed *amicus* briefs.

A more direct judicial strategy employed by interest groups is the filing of **class action lawsuits,** which enables a group of similarly situated plaintiffs to combine similar grievances into a single suit. For instance, flight attendants won a class action suit against the airline industry's regulation that all stewardesses had to be unmarried. As one lawyer who specializes in such cases states, "The class action is the greatest, most effective legal engine to remedy mass wrongs."[19]

Going Public

Groups are also interested in the opinions of the public. Public opinion ultimately makes its way to policymakers, and so interest groups carefully cultivate their public image. Interest groups market not only their stand on issues but their reputations as well. Business interests want people to see them as what made America great (not as wealthy Americans trying to ensure large profits). The Teamsters Union likes to be known as a united organization of hard-working men and women (not as an organization often influenced by organized crime). Farmers cultivate the image of a sturdy family working to put bread on the table

[19]Ronald J. Hrebenar and Ruth K. Scott, *Interest Group Politics in America,* 2nd ed. (Englewood Cliffs, N.J.: Prentice-Hall, 1990), 201.

(not the huge agribusinesses that have largely replaced family farms). In this way, many groups try to create a reservoir of goodwill with the public at large.

Lately, more and more organizations have launched expensive public relations (PR) efforts. Soft sell and reasoned analysis—even presenting both sides of the issues—are the hallmark of this new era of public relations. Caterpillar, the manufacturer of massive earth-moving and strip-mining machinery, inundated *National Geographic* and other magazines with balanced ads presenting both sides of environmental issues such as strip-mining. Mobil Oil runs the most visible corporate PR effort to influence the public with its op-ed style ads in the *New York Times* and other major publications every week. These ads typically address issues affecting the oil industry and big business in general. One time it even ran an ad entitled "Why Do We Buy This Space?" which answered "that business needs voices in the media, the same way labor unions, consumers, and other groups in our society do."[20] No one knows just how effective these image-molding efforts are, but many groups seem to firmly believe what businesses learned long ago—advertising pays off.

TYPES OF INTEREST GROUPS

Whether they are lobbying, electioneering, litigating, or appealing to the public, interest groups are omnipresent in the American political system. As with other aspects of American politics and policy-making, political scientists loosely categorize interest groups into clusters. Some deal mainly with economic issues, others with issues of energy and the environment, and still others with equality issues.

Of course, not all groups are easily molded into these three policy arenas. Public interest groups like Common Cause and ideological groups like the now disbanded Moral Majority involve themselves in a whole range of issues. Even groups that have a prevailing interest in one policy area do not always confine their activities to that alone. The American Petroleum Institute and the American Mining Conference, for example, have a great influence on economic as well as energy issues. Still, the Pharmaceutical Manufacturers are not likely to spend their valuable resources lobbying for or against environmental bills or school-busing policies. The classifications discussed in the following sections are made on the assumption that most groups concern themselves with a limited range of issues.

Economic Interests

All economic interests are ultimately concerned with wages, prices, and profits. In the American economy, government does not determine these directly. Only on rare occasions has the government imposed wage and price controls. This has usually been during wartime, although the Nixon administration briefly used wage and price controls to combat inflation. More commonly, public policy in America has economic effects through regulations, tax advantages, subsidies and contracts, and international trade policy.

[20]Quoted in Jeffrey M. Berry, *The Interest Group Society,* 2nd ed. (Glenview, Ill.: Scott, Foresman, 1989), 103.

Business, labor, and farmers all fret over the impact of government regulations. Even a minor change in government regulatory policy can cost industries a great deal or bring increased profits. Tax policies also affect the livelihood of individuals and firms. How the tax code is written determines whether people and producers pay a lot or a little of their incomes to the government. Because government often provides subsidies (to farmers, small businesses, railroads, minority businesses, and others), every economic group wants to get its share of direct aid and government contracts. In this era of economic global interdependence, all groups worry about import quotas, tariffs (fees placed on imports), and the soundness of the American dollar. In short, business executives, factory workers, and farmers seek to influence government because regulations, taxes, subsidies, and international economic policy all affect their economic livelihoods. The following sections discuss the impact of some of the major organized interests in the economic policy arena.

Labor Numerically, labor has more affiliated members than any other interest group. Nearly thirteen million workers are members of unions belonging to the AFL-CIO, itself a union of unions. Several million others are members of non-AFL-CIO unions, especially the International Brotherhood of Teamsters, which represents truck drivers, among others.

Like labor unions everywhere, American unions press for policies to ensure better working conditions and higher wages. Recognizing that many workers would like to enjoy union benefits without actually joining a union and thus paying dues, unions have fought hard to establish the **union shop,** which requires new employees to join the union representing them. In contrast, business groups have supported **right-to-work laws,** which outlaw union membership as a condition of employment. They argue that such laws deny basic freedoms—namely the right not to belong to a group. In 1947 the biggest blow ever to the American labor movement occurred when Congress passed the Taft-Hartley Act, permitting states to adopt right-to-work laws (known as "slave labor laws" within the AFL-CIO). Most of the states that have right-to-work laws are in the South, which traditionally has had the lowest percentage of unionized workers.

The American labor movement reached its peak in 1970, when 25 percent of the work force belonged to a union; since then the percentage has declined to about 16 percent. One factor behind this decline is that low wages in other countries have diminished the American job market in a number of key manufacturing areas. Steel once made by American workers is now made more cheaply in Korea and imported to the United States. The United Auto Workers have found their clout greatly reduced as Detroit has faced heavy competition from Japanese automakers. Thus in the 1990s unions are more concerned with international economic policy than ever before.

Agriculture Once the occupation of the majority of Americans, only 3 percent now make their living as farmers. The family farm has given way to massive agribusinesses, often heavily involved with exports. To the vast majority who have never lived on a farm, the tangled policies of acreage controls, price supports, and import quotas are mysterious and confusing. To agribusinesses and the few family farmers still around, however, government policies are often more important than the whims of nature.

Collectively, labor unions remain America's largest interest group, despite declining memberships in recent decades. Strikes are unions' most powerful weapons. This recent strike by Greyhound bus drivers, which has been marred by violence, forced Greyhound to shut down many of its least traveled routes between rural areas.

There are several broad-based agricultural groups (the American Farm Bureau Federation, the National Farmers' Organization), but equally important are the commodity associations formed of peanut farmers, potato growers, dairy farmers, and other producers. The U.S. Department of Agriculture and the agricultural subcommittees in Congress are organized along commodity lines. As mentioned earlier in this chapter, this organizational system leads to very cordial relations between the policymakers, the bureaucrats, and the interest groups—promoting classic examples of what hyperpluralists call subgovernments.

Business   If the elite theorists are correct, however, and there is an American power elite, certainly it would be dominated by leaders of the biggest banks, insurance companies, and multinational corporations. Elitists' views may or may not be exaggerated, but business is certainly well organized for political action. Business PACs have increased more dramatically than any other category of PACs, as shown in Figure 10.1. Most large firms, such as AT&T and Ford, now have offices in Washington that monitor legislative activity. Two umbrella organizations, the National Association of Manufacturers (NAM) and the Chamber of Commerce, include most corporations and businesses and speak for them when general business interests are at stake.

Different business interests compete on many specific issues, however. Trucking and construction companies want more highways, but railroads do not. An increase in international trade will help some businesses expand their markets, but others may be hurt by foreign competition. Business interests are generally unified when it comes to promoting greater profits, but often fragmented when policy choices have to be made.

The hundreds of trade and product associations are far less visible than the NAM and the Chamber of Commerce, but they are at least as important in pursuing policy goals for their members. They fight regulations that would reduce their profits and seek preferential tax treatment as well as government subsidies and contracts. America's complex schedule of tariffs are monuments to the activities of the trade associations. Although they are the least visible of Washington lobbies, their successes are measured in amendments won, regulations rewritten, and exceptions made (see "You Are the Policymaker: Trade Deficits, the 1988 Election, and Special Interests").

Consumers and Public Interest Lobbies   Pluralist theory holds that for virtually every interest in society there is an organized group, but what about the interests of all of us—the buying public? Today over two thousand organized groups are championing various causes or ideas "in the public interest."[21] These **public interest lobbies** can be defined as organizations that seek "a collective good, the achievement of which will not selectively and materially benefit the membership or activists of the organization."[22] If products are made safer by the lobbying of consumer protection groups, it is not the members of such groups alone that will benefit. Rather, everyone should be better off—regardless of whether they joined in the lobbying or not.

---

[21]H.R. Mahood, *Interest Group Politics in America: A New Intensity* (Englewood Cliffs, N.J.: Prentice-Hall, 1990), 162.

[22]Jeffrey M. Berry, *Lobbying for the People* (Princeton, N.J.: Princeton University Press, 1977), 7.

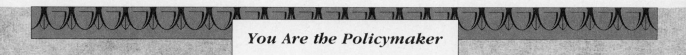

Trade Deficits, the 1988 Election, and Special Interests

Driven by a prickly trade deficit in an election year, President Reagan signed a one-thousand page trade bill into law in August of 1988. He had earlier vetoed the first version, which required companies to give workers advance notice of plant closings. (This controversial provision later passed as a separate bill to calm labor interests, defuse Democrats, and further bolster George Bush's election chances.)

Below are highlights of this mildly protectionist bill, coauthored by Senator Lloyd Bentsen of Texas, the 1988 Democratic candidate for vice-president. It does not represent a major shift in trade policy, it contains no significant tariff increases or new quotas, and it erects no major new trade barriers. Why this bill, then? It does include a few policy measures that may eventually help open certain foreign markets, shore up some domestic industries and give a future president a stronger hand in ongoing international trade negotiations, plus it has a popular medley of accounting changes, symbolic amendments, and special favors.

In fact, the bill is a feast for a wide range of special interests that together successfully laid claim to representing the national interest in an election year. The major winners here were high-tech companies, the oil industry, agriculture, and export businesses in general. No wonder that both chambers of Congress approved it overwhelmingly earlier in the summer as Campaign '88 began in earnest. Do you think this omnibus bill will help to lower the trade deficit? Would you have urged your congressperson to pass it? See for yourself which powerful groups are well served by the bill's passage, which

- Repeals the "windfall profits tax" for oil and gas companies.
- Strengthens the ability of American firms to protect their patents and copyrights from "international thievery."
- Directs the president to seek reciprocity in trade relations—for example, the bill bars foreign companies from being primary dealers of U.S. government securities unless American firms have the same opportunity in such a company's homeland (Japanese firms are targets here).
- Authorizes spending as much as one billion dollars a year for retraining workers displaced by imports (financed by a "painless" import fee; most of the money goes to the states).
- Bans for three years sales to the United States by Japan's Toshiba Corporation (following illegal sales to the Soviet Union, by one of Toshiba's subsidiaries, of sophisticated machine tools that could be used to make submarines quieter).
- Permits the United States to unilaterally identify nations engaged in "pervasive" unfair trade. The list of practices to be weighed in considering retaliation includes violations of workers' rights, a provision supported by unions. Also, the United States can work for antidumping agreements of goods like computer chips.
- Provides for subsidies for agricultural exports (grains and oilseeds).
- Grants Warner-Lambert Company permission to extend the patent on Lopid, its anticholesterol drug, if the FDA approves it for use in fighting heart disease.
- Amends the Foreign Corrupt Practices Act and reduces the potential liability of American corporate officers for actions by their foreign employees.

If ever a lobbying effort was spurred by a single person, it was the consumer movement. At first Ralph Nader took on American business almost single-handedly in the name of consumerism. He was propelled to national prominence by a book, *Unsafe at Any Speed,* which attacked General Motors' Corvair as a mechanically deficient and dangerous automobile. General Motors made the mistake of hiring a private detective to dig into his background and to follow him around, hoping that there might be some dirt they could uncover that

Public interest groups devote their time and energy to causes from which they will not benefit directly. Common Cause, for example, works to ensure a government that is responsive to all citizens, not a select few. Its members are now leading the fight to control PAC contributions to election campaigns.

would discredit him. No one who knew the ascetic lawyer would have ever expected to find anything of the kind. Ultimately Nader learned about the investigation, sued General Motors for invasion of privacy, and won a hefty damage settlement in court. He used the proceeds to launch the first major consumer group in Washington, D.C.

Consumer groups have won many legislative victories in recent years. In 1973 Congress responded to consumer advocacy by creating the Consumer Product Safety Commission. Congress authorized it to regulate all consumer products and even gave it the power to ban particularly dangerous ones—bearing in mind that household products are responsible for thirty thousand deaths annually. Among the products the commission has investigated are children's sleepwear (some of which contained a carcinogen), hot tubs, and lawn mowers.

Consumer groups are not the only ones claiming to be public interest groups. Groups speaking for those who cannot speak for themselves seek to protect children, animals, and the mentally ill; good-government groups such as Common Cause push for openness and fairness in government; religious groups like the now-disbanded Moral Majority crusade for the protection of ethical and moral standards in American society; and environmental groups seek to preserve ecological balance.

Energy and Environmental Interests

Among the newest political interest groups are the environmentalists. A handful, like the Sierra Club and the Audubon Society, have been around since the nineteenth century, but many others trace their origins to the first Earth Day, April 22, 1970. On that day ecology-minded people marched on Washington and other places to symbolize their support for environmental protection. Recently the twentieth anniversary of Earth Day was celebrated with another round of rallies calling for continued attention to the state of the environment.

Environmental groups have promoted pollution-control policies, wilderness protection, and population control. Perhaps more significant, however, is what they have opposed. Their hit list has included strip-mining, supersonic aircraft, the Alaskan oil pipeline, offshore oil drilling, and nuclear power plants. On these and other issues environmentalists have exerted a great deal of influence on Congress and state legislatures.

The concerns of environmentalists often come into direct conflict with energy goals. Environmentalists insist that, in the long run, energy supplies can be ensured without harming the environment or risking radiation exposure from nuclear power plants. On the issue of nuclear power plants their arguments have had a profound impact on public policy. No new nuclear power plants have been approved since 1977, and many which had been in the works were cancelled.[23] Short-term energy needs, however, have won out over environmental concerns in many other cases. Energy producers argue that environmentalists oppose nearly every new energy project. Given that there is no sign of a major drop in energy demands, they argue that some limited risks have to be taken. What is worse, they ask—an occasional oil spill off the shore of Alaska or long lines every day at the gas pumps? Thus, despite environmentalist oppositions, Congress subsidized the massive trans-Alaskan pipeline, which a consortium of companies use to transport oil from Alaska's North Slope. Similarly, the strip-mining of coal continues despite the constant objections from environmentalists. Group politics intensifies when two public interests clash, such as environmental protection and an ensured supply of energy.

Environmental activist Jeremy Rifkin heads the Foundation for Economic Alternatives, which campaigns against genetic engineering. A lawyer, Rifkin has used the courts effectively to expose what he believes are the serious risks involved with genetic experimentation involving people, plants, and animals.

Equality Interests

The Fourteenth Amendment guarantees equal protection under the law. American history, though, shows that this is easier said than done. Two sets of interest groups, representing women and minorities, have made equal rights their main policy goal. Chapter 5 reviewed the long history of the civil rights movement; this section is concerned with its policy goals and organizational base.

Equality at the polls, in housing, on the job, in education, and in all other facets of American life has long been the dominant goal of African-American groups. The oldest and largest of these groups is the National Association for the Advancement of Colored People (NAACP). It argued and won the monumental *Brown* v. *Board of Education* case in 1954. In that decision the Supreme Court held that segregated schools were unconstitutional. The NAACP and other civil rights groups have also lobbied and pressed court cases to forbid discrimination in voting, employment, and housing. Although they have won many victories in principle, equality in practice has been much slower in coming. Today civil rights groups continue to push for more effective affirmative action programs to ensure that minority groups are given educational and employment opportunities. The NAACP's main vehicle in recent years has been the Fair Share

[23]For an interesting analysis of how changes in the regulatory environment, congressional oversight, and public opinion altered the debate on nuclear power, see Frank R. Baumgartner and Bryan D. Jones, "Shifting Images and Venues of a Public Issue: Explaining the Demise of Nuclear Power in the United States" (Paper presented at the 1989 annual meeting of the American Political Science Association).

program, which negotiates agreements with national and regional businesses to increase minority hiring and the use of minority contractors. Affirmative action is not as emotionally charged an issue as desegregation, but it too has been controversial.

When the NAACP was just starting up, suffragists were in the streets and legislative lobbies demanding women's right to vote. The Nineteenth Amendment, ratified in 1920, guaranteed women the vote, but other guarantees of equal protection remained absent from the Constitution. More recently, women's rights groups, such as the National Organization for Women (NOW), have lobbied for an end to sexual discrimination. Their primary goal has been the passage of the Equal Rights Amendment (ERA), which states that "equality of rights under the law shall not be abridged on account of sex."

Within a month after the ERA was approved by the Congress in 1972, it had been overwhelmingly ratified by fifteen states. Even Texas and Kansas, fairly conservative states, voted decisively for the ERA in the first year. The quiet consensual politics of the ERA ratification process soon came to a boisterous end when Phyllis Schlafly, a conservative activist from Alton, Illinois, started up a highly visible STOP ERA movement. She and her followers argued the ERA would destroy the integrity of the family, require communal bathrooms, lead to women in combat, and eliminate legal protections that women already had. Their emotional appeal was just enough to stop the ERA three states short of the thirty-eight necessary for ratification. In 1979 Congress extended the customary seven-year deadline for ratification for another three years, but to little avail. Not a single additional state approved the ERA in spite of the heavy lobbying from NOW and other like-minded groups. In 1982 the amendment whose time seemed to have come in 1972 simply passed away.

Interest groups often clash on issues, as when Phyllis Schlafly's Eagle Forum battled NOW and other women's groups over ratification of the ERA. Here Schlafly addresses a STOP ERA rally in the rotunda of the Illinois state capitol; her well-publicized efforts helped defeat pro-ERA forces in her home state.

Though the ERA seems dead for the moment, NOW remains committed to enacting the protection it would have constitutionally guaranteed by advocating the enactment of many individual statutes. As is often the case with interest group politics, issues are rarely settled once and for all; rather, they shift to different policy arenas.

WHAT MAKES AN INTEREST GROUP SUCCESSFUL?

There are many factors that affect how successful an interest group is. Among them are the size of the group (the smaller the better), its intensity, and its financial resources. It is somewhat counterintuitive to learn that small groups are actually more likely to get their way than large groups. Thus considerable space will be devoted here to explaining this surprising finding. The discussion will then turn to some of the other more readily apparent factors.

The Surprising Ineffectiveness of Large Groups

In one of the most oft-quoted statements concerning interest groups, E.E. Schattschneider wrote that "pressure politics is essentially the politics of small groups. . . . Pressure tactics are not remarkably successful in mobilizing general interests."[24] There are perfectly good reasons why consumer groups are less effective than producer groups, patients are less effective than doctors, and energy conservationists are less effective than oil companies—small groups have organizational advantages over large groups.

To shed light on this point it is important to distinguish between a potential and an actual group. A **potential group** is composed of all people who might be group members because they share some common interest.[25] In contrast, an **actual group** is composed of whatever portion of the potential group chooses to join. The examples in Table 10.3 show that groups vary enormously in the degree to which they enroll their potential membership. Consumer organizations are minuscule when compared with the total number of consumers, which is almost every American. Some organizations, however, do very well in organizing virtually all of their potential members. The U.S. Savings and Loan League, the Tobacco Institute, and the Air Transport Association include a good portion of their potential members. Compared with consumers, these groups are tightly organized.

Economist Mancur Olson explains this phenomenon in his book, *The Logic of Collective Action.*[26] Olson points out that all groups, as opposed to individuals, are in the business of providing collective goods. A **collective good** is something of value, such as clean air, that cannot be withheld from a potential group member. When the AFL-CIO wins a higher minimum wage, all low-paid workers benefit—regardless of whether or not they are a member of the union. In other

[24]E.E. Schattschneider, *The Semisovereign People* (New York: Holt, Rinehart & Winston, 1960), 35.

[25]Truman, *The Governmental Process,* 2nd ed., 511.

[26]Mancur Olson, *The Logic of Collective Action* (Cambridge, Mass.: Harvard University Press, 1965), especially 9–36.

Table 10.3 Potential versus Actual Groups

Some groups organize most of their potential membership. Others suffer an enormous shortfall between their actual membership and the group they claim to speak for. Obviously, estimating the true potential membership of a group is difficult, but if you will tolerate some very rough approximations, we can compare groups' actual to potential membership. In the following table, the first four groups have a tiny fraction of their potential membership; the last four have a very high proportion of their potential members.

GROUP	ORGANIZATION	MEMBERSHIP
Consumers	National Consumers League, a Washington-based consumer action group	Potential: 250,000,000 (Every American) Actual: 8,000
African Americans	National Association for the Advancement of Colored People, the largest civil rights organization	Potential: 29,700,000 (Every African American) Actual: 400,000
Women	National Organization for Women, a leading women's rights organization	Potential: 130,000,000 (Every woman)[a] Actual: 160,000
Taxpayers	National Taxpayers Union, a "taxpayers' rights" group advocating tax and government spending cuts	Potential: 180,000,000 (Every adult 18 and over) Actual: 150,000
Physicians	American Medical Association, a professional organization of medical doctors	Potential: 594,000 (All M.D.s) Actual: 271,000
Savings and Loan Associations	U.S. League of Savings Institutions, an organization of local savings and loan associations	Potential: 3,892 (All S&Ls) Actual: 3,400
Tobacco	Tobacco Institute, the organization of tobacco manufacturers	Potential: 14 (All cigarette manufacturers) Actual: 11
Airlines	Air Transport Association of America, the organization of U.S. airlines	Potential: 93 (All U.S. air carriers) Actual: 29

[a]NOW membership is open to both women and men, but the interests it espouses are women's interests, so, practically speaking, its potential membership is all women, and most all of its actual members are women.
Sources: For data on actual organizational memberships, see Denise Akey, ed. *Encyclopedia of Associations, 1990* (Detroit: Gale Research Company, 1989); for data on potential organizational memberships, see U.S. Bureau of the Census, *Statistical Abstract of the United States: 1989* (Washington, D.C.: Government Printing Office, 1989).

words, members of the potential group share in benefits that members of the actual group work to secure. If this is the case, an obvious and difficult problem results: why should potential members work for something if they can get it for free? Why join the group, pay dues, and work hard for a goal when a person can benefit from the group's activity without doing anything at all? A perfectly rational response is thus to sit back and let other people do the work. This is commonly known as the **free-rider problem.**

The bigger the group, the more serious the free-rider problem. That is the gist of **Olson's law of large groups:** "The larger the group, the further it will fall short of providing an optimal amount of a collective good."[27] Small groups thus have an organizational advantage over large ones. In a small group a given member's share of the collective good may be great enough that he or she will try to secure it. The old saying that "everyone can make a difference" is much more credible in the case of a small group. In the largest groups, however, each member can only expect to get a tiny share of the policy gains. Weighing the costs of participation against the relatively small benefits, the temptation is always to "let George do it." Therefore, as Olson argues, the larger the potential group, the less likely potential members are to contribute.

This distinct advantage of small groups helps explain why public interest groups have a hard time making ends meet. Consumer groups and environmentalists claim to seek "public interest" goals, but the gains they win are usually spread thin over millions of people. In contrast, the lobbying costs and benefits for business are concentrated. Suppose, for example, that consumer advocates take the airlines to court over charges of price fixing and force the airlines to return ten million dollars to consumers in the form of lower prices. This ten million dollar settlement is spread over 250 million Americans—about four cents per person (actually, the benefit is a little higher if one divides only by the number of people who use airlines). The ten million dollar airline loss is shared by ninety carriers at over one hundred thousand dollars apiece. One can quickly see which side will be better organized in such a struggle.

In sum, Olson's law of large groups explains why small interest groups are generally more effective. The power of business in the American political system is thus due to more than just money, as proponents of elite theory would have us believe. Besides their financial strength, large corporations also enjoy an inherent size advantage. Small potential groups like business have an easier time organizing themselves for political action than large potential groups, such as consumers. Once well organized, large groups may be quite effective, but it is much harder for them to get together in the first place.

Intensity

One way a large potential group may be mobilized is through an issue that people feel intensely about, such as abortion. Intensity is a psychological advantage that can be enjoyed by small and large groups alike. When a group shows that it cares deeply about an issue, politicians are more likely to listen—many votes may well be won or lost on a single issue. Because of this, the rise of single-issue groups has been one of the most dramatic political developments in recent years.

A **single-issue group** can be defined as a group that has a narrow interest, dislikes compromise, and single-mindedly pursues its goal. Anti-Vietnam War activists may have formed the first modern single-issue groups. Opponents of nuclear power plants, gun control, and abortion are just some of the many such groups that exist today. All these groups deal with issues that evoke the strong emotions characteristic of single-interest groups.

Perhaps the most emotional issue of all has been that of abortion. The 1973 Supreme Court ruling in *Roe* v. *Wade,* upholding the right of a woman to secure an abortion during the first trimester of pregnancy, spurred a wave of group

[27]*Ibid.,* 35.

formation. Opponents quickly labeled this court decision as legalized murder and formed such organizations as the National Right to Life Committee. Organizing at the state level, antiabortion groups aimed their sights on candidates for state and local offices. In 1978 they were thought to be crucial in dislodging proabortion incumbents in Minnesota and Iowa.[28] Throughout the 1980s they adamantly supported the campaigns of Presidents Reagan and Bush and hounded pro-choice candidates like Geraldine Ferraro and Michael Dukakis. Befitting the intensity of the issue, their activities have not been limited to electioneering and lobbying. Protesting—often in the form of blocking entrances to abortion clinics—has now become a common practice for antiabortion activists.

Pro-choice activists have organized as well, forming groups like the National Abortion Rights Action League. Since the 1989 *Webster* v. *Reproductive Health Services* case allowed states greater freedom to restrict abortions, the pro-choice side has become better mobilized than ever before. When the law was on their side, pro-choice advocates could not match the antiabortionists in terms of intensity. Now that the legal tide has turned against them, their intensity level has risen. In 1989 proabortion groups were widely credited with the victories of gubernatorial candidates in Virginia and New Jersey. Like the antiabortionists, their position is crystal clear, not subject to compromise, and influences their vote. Regardless of which side candidates for political office are on, they will be taking heat on the abortion issue for years to come.

Financial Resources

One of the major indictments of the American interest group system is that it is biased toward the wealthy. Senate Minority Leader Robert Dole once remarked that he had never been approached by a Poor People's PAC. There is no doubt that money talks in the American political system, and those who have it get

[28]Marjorie Randon Hershey, "Direct Action and the Abortion Issue: The Political Participation of Single-issue Groups" in Allan J. Cigler and Burdett A. Loomis, eds., *Interest Group Politics,* 2nd ed. (Washington, D.C.: Congressional Quarterly Press, 1986), 35.

LITMUS TEST

heard. A big campaign contribution may ensure a phone call, a meeting, or even a direct *quid pro quo*. When Lincoln Savings and Loan Chairman Charles Keating was asked whether the $1.3 million he had funnelled into the campaigns of five U.S. Senators had anything to do with these Senators later meeting with federal regulators on his behalf, he candidly responded, "I certainly hope so."

Critics charge that PACs, the source of so much money in today's expensive high-tech campaigns, distort the governmental process in favor of those that can raise the most money. Moderate Republican Representative Jim Leach of Iowa believes that "it's a myth to think they [the PACs] don't want something in return."[29] They may only want to be remembered on one or two crucial votes or with an occasional intervention with government agencies, but multiply this by the thousands of special interests that are organized today and the worst fears of the hyperpluralists could be realized—a government that constantly yields to every organized special interest.

It is important to emphasize, however, that even on some of the most important issues the big interests do *not* always win. The best example of this in recent years is the Tax Reform Act of 1986. In *Showdown at Gucci Gulch,* two reporters from the *Wall Street Journal* chronicle the improbable victory of sweeping tax reform.[30] In this case a large group of well-organized, highly paid (and thus Gucci-clad) lobbyists were unable to preserve many of their most prized tax loopholes. One of the heroes of the book, Senator Packwood of Oregon, was Congress's top PAC recipient during the tax reform struggle— raking in $992,000 for his reelection campaign. As Chair of the Senate Finance Committee, however, Packwood ultimately turned against the hordes of lobbyists trying to get his ear on behalf of various loopholes. The only way to deal with the tax loophole problem, he concluded, was to go virtually cold turkey by eliminating all but a very few. "There is special interest after special interest that is hit in this bill" Packwood gloated, pointing out that many of them contributed to his campaign. In the end, passage of the reform bill offered "encouraging proof that moneyed interests could not always buy their way to success in Congress."[31]

UNDERSTANDING INTEREST GROUPS

The problem of interest groups in America today remains much the same as Madison defined it over two hundred years ago. A free society must allow for the representation of all groups that seek to influence political decision making; yet, because groups are usually more concerned with their own self-interest rather than with the needs of society as a whole, for democracy to work well it is important that they not be allowed to assume a dominant position.

Interest Groups and Democracy

James Madison's solution to the problems posed by interest groups was to create a wide-open system in which many groups would be able to participate. By

[29]"Taking an Ax to the PACs," p. 27.

[30]Jeffrey H. Birnbaum and Alan S. Murray, *Showdown at Gucci Gulch: Lawmakers, Lobbyists, and the Unlikely Triumph of Tax Reform* (New York: Vintage, 1987).

[31]*Ibid.,* 235.

extending the sphere of influence, according to Madison, groups with opposing interests would counterbalance one another. Pluralist theorists believe that a rough approximation of the public interest emerges from this competition.

With the tremendous growth of interest group politics in recent years, some observers feel that Madison may at last have gotten his wish. For every group with an interest there now seems to be a competing group to watch over them— not to mention public interest lobbies to keep a watch over them all. Robert Salisbury argues that "the growth in the number, variety, and sophistication of interest groups represented in Washington" has transformed policy-making such that it "is not dominated so often by a relatively small number of powerful interest groups as it may once have been."[32] Paradoxically, Salisbury concludes that the increase in lobbying activity has resulted in less clout overall for interest groups—and better democracy.

Elite theorists clearly disagree with this conclusion and point to the prolif-eration of business PACs as evidence that the interest group system is corrupting American politics more than ever. A democratic process requires a free and open exchange of ideas in which candidates and voters should be able to hear one another out, but PACs, the source of so much money in elections, distort the process. Elite theorists particularly note that wealthier interests are greatly advantaged by the PAC system. Business PACs have become the dominant force in the fund-raising game. Furthermore, out of 2,000 corporate PACs, the top 135 accounted for half of the campaign contributions from such groups in 1988.

PACs can sometimes link money to politics at the highest levels. The old party machines may have bought votes in the voting booth; the new PACs are accused of buying votes in the legislative chambers. Technology—especially television—makes American elections expensive; candidates need much money to pay for high-tech campaigns, and PACs are able to supply that money. In return, they ask only to be remembered when their interests are clearly at stake.

Interest Groups and the Size of Government

The power of special interest groups through PACs and other means also has implications for the size of government. America's two most recent presidents both remarked at the end of their time in office that their attempts to cut waste in federal spending had been frustrated by interest groups. In his farewell address Carter "suggested that the reason he had so much difficulty in dealing with Congress was the fragmentation of power and decision making that was exploited by interest groups."[33] Similarly, Reagan remarked in December 1988 that "special interest groups, bolstered by campaign contributions, pressure lawmakers into creating and defending spending programs."[34] Above all else, most special interest groups strive to maintain established programs which benefit them—and thus promote larger government.

However, one can also make the argument that the growth in the size of government in recent decades accounts for a good portion of the proliferation

[32]Robert H. Salisbury, "The Paradox of Interest Groups in Washington—More Groups, Less Clout" in Anthony King, ed., *The New American Political System,* 2nd version. (Washington, D.C.: American Enterprise Institute, 1990), 204.

[33]Hrebenar and Scott, *Interest Group Politics in America,* 2nd ed., 234.

[34]Steven V. Roberts, "Angered President Blames Others for the Huge Deficit," *New York Times,* December 14, 1988, A16.

of interest groups. The more areas the federal government has become involved in, the more interest groups have arisen to attempt to influence policy. As William Lunch notes, "a great part of the increase was occasioned by the new government responsibility for civil rights, environmental protection, and greater public health and safety."[35] For example, once the government got seriously into the business of protecting the environment, many groups sprung up to lobby for strong standards and enforcement. Given the tremendous effects of environmental regulations on many industries, it should come as no surprise that they also organized to see to it that their interests were taken into account. As Salisbury writes, many groups have "come to Washington out of need and dependence rather than because they have influence."[36]

SUMMARY

This chapter's discussion of group politics has familiarized you with the vast array of interest groups in American politics, all vying for policies they prefer. Pluralists see groups as the most important way people can have their policy preferences represented in government. Hyperpluralists, though, fear that too many groups are getting too much of what they want, skillfully working the many subgovernments in the American system. Elitists believe that a few wealthy individuals and multinational corporations exert control over the major decisions regarding distribution of goods and services.

[35]William M. Lunch, *The Nationalization of American Politics* (Berkeley: University of California Press, 1987), 206.
[36]Salisbury, "The Paradox of Interest Groups," 229.

Like other public interest groups, the Children's Defense Fund works against Olson's law of large groups; that is, it is easier to organize a small group with clear economic goals than it is to organize a large group with broader goals. Nevertheless, Marian Wright Edelman is a tireless worker for children's rights to education, nutrition, and protection from abuse.

Interest groups can choose from among four basic strategies to maximize their effectiveness. Lobbying is one well-known group strategy. Although the evidence on its influence is mixed, it is clear that lobbyists are most effective with those legislators already sympathetic to their side. Thus electioneering becomes critical because it helps put supportive people in office. Often today, groups operate in the judicial as well as the legislative process, using litigation when lobbying fails or is not enough. Many also find it important to shape a good image, employing public relations techniques to present themselves in the most favorable light.

This chapter also examined some of the major kinds of interest groups, particularly those concerned with economic, equality, and energy and environmental policy. Public interest lobbies claim to be different from other interest groups, representing, they say, an important aspect of the public interest. Recently there has been a rapid growth of single-interest groups, which focus narrowly on one issue and are not inclined to compromise.

A number of factors influence a group's success in achieving its policy goals. Most surprising is that small groups have an organizational advantage over large groups. Large groups often fall victim to the free-rider problem, which we called Olson's law of large groups. An asset which can be enjoyed by groups both large and small is intensity. Money always helps lubricate the wheels of power, though it is hardly a sure-fire guarantee of success.

The problem of controlling interest groups remains as crucial to democracy today as it was in Madison's time. Some believe that the growth of interest groups has worked to divide political influence just as Madison hoped it would. Others point to the PAC system as the new way in which special interests corrupt American democracy.

KEY TERMS

interest group	Political Action Committees	actual group
pluralist theory	*amicus curiae* briefs	collective good
elite theory	class action lawsuits	free-rider problem
hyperpluralist theory	union shop	Olson's law of large
subgovernments	right-to-work laws	groups
lobbying	public interest lobbies	single-issue group
electioneering	potential group	

FOR FURTHER READING

Berry, Jeffrey M. *The Interest Group Society,* 2nd ed. Glenview, Ill.: Scott, Foresman, 1989. One of the best contemporary textbooks on interest groups.

————. *Lobbying for the People.* Princeton, N.J.: Princeton University Press, 1977. The major study of public interest lobbies.

Birnbaum, Jeffrey H. and Alan S. Murray. *Showdown at Gucci Gulch: Lawmakers, Lobbyists, and the Unlikely Triumph of Tax Reform.* New York: Vintage, 1987. A fascinating account of how the 1986 tax reform bill passed over the objections of the gucci-clad lobbyists.

Boles, Janet K. *The Politics of the Equal Rights Amendment.* New York: Longman, 1978. The trials and tribulations of the ERA in its quest for ratification.

Cigler, Allan J. and Burdett A. Loomis, eds. *Interest Group Politics,* 2nd ed. Washington, D.C.: Congressional Quarterly Press, 1986. An excellent collection of original articles on the modern interest group system.

Dye, Thomas R. *Who's Running America? The Bush Era,* 5th ed. Englewood Cliffs, N.J.: Prentice-Hall, 1990. A good summary of the elitist view of interest groups.

Godwin, R. Kenneth. *One Billion Dollars of Influence.* Chatham, N.J.: Chatham House, 1988. An interesting look at the direct marketing of politics via direct mail.

Lowi, Theodore J. *The End of Liberalism,* 2nd ed. New York: Norton, 1979. A critique of the role of subgovernments and the excessive deference to interest groups in the American political system.

McFarland, Andrew S. *Common Cause: Lobbying in the Public Interest.* Chatham, N.J.: Chatham House, 1984. A study of the major public interest lobby.

Olson, Mancur. *The Logic of Collective Action.* Cambridge, Mass.: Harvard University Press, 1965. Develops an economic theory of groups, showing how the cards are stacked against larger groups.

Schlozman, Kay L. and John T. Tierney. *Organized Interests and American Democracy.* New York: Harper & Row, 1986. Survey results from a sample of Washington lobbyists are used to draw a portrait of the interest group system.

11

THE MASS MEDIA AND THE POLITICAL AGENDA

When the Iowa caucuses officially marked the opening of the 1988 presidential nomination campaign, twenty-five hundred journalists showed up to cover the event—one for every local precinct in the whole state. Later in the year, when President Reagan traveled to Moscow for a summit with Mikhail Gorbachev, more media people than presidential staff went along.

In both cases there were few surprises and thus little news to report, yet because the media was there in such numbers, each story nevertheless dominated the news for a week. As something important might have happened, the press had to be there. Having committed massive resources to being on the scene, the press felt compelled to report on every detail. Bombarded with stories about such events, it would be astonishing if the public failed to see them as important.

Such is the power of the media in this high-tech age. The media has the power to direct what Americans think about. The press plays a crucial role in shaping the American political and policy agenda—what's hot and what's not in politics and government. It can make and break candidates, and sometimes even presidents. With the new adversarial journalism, reporters see politicians as their natural prey and politicians see the press as a tiger that must be tamed for them to succeed. A politician who fails to control the agenda via the media is one whose campaign or cause is lost from the start.

*I*n today's technological world, the media—just like computers, atomic power, aircraft, and automobiles—is everywhere. The American political system has entered a new period of **high-tech politics,** a politics in which the behavior of citizens and policymakers, as well as the political agenda itself, is increasingly shaped by technology. The **mass media** is a key part of that technology. Television, radio, newspapers, magazines, and other means of popular communication are called *mass media* because they reach and profoundly influence not only the elites but the masses.

This chapter examines media politics, focusing on the following topics:

- The rise of the modern media in America's advanced technological society
- How news gets made and presented through the media
- The biases in the news
- The impact of the media on policymakers and the public

This chapter also reintroduces the concept of the *policy agenda,* in which the media plays an important role.

THE MASS MEDIA TODAY

These days, the news media often makes the news as well as reports it. Television news anchors are paid Hollywood-style salaries and sometimes behave in Hollywood style (as Dan Rather did when he stalked off the set of the evening news one night, and as Diane Sawyer did when she modeled for *Vanity Fair*). At the 1988 summit Tom Brokaw got to visit with Mikhail Gorbachev before Ronald Reagan did. Secure in their jobs as long as their ratings remain high, TV anchors have taken their place beside presidents, senators, and others who shape public opinion and policy.

Few media encounters made as much news as the so-called Am-Bush of then Vice-President George Bush by CBS anchorman Dan Rather in January of 1988. Doing a profile of all the presidential candidates, CBS saved Bush until last and then wrote him that "Dan Rather is very interested in your profile and has decided to do it himself." Bush's aides were wary; many Americans were still asking questions—"What did he know and when did he know it?"—about Bush's involvement in the Iran-Contra affair. Bush prepared for a Rather attack and volunteered to appear live in order to prevent any possible editing of his remarks by CBS. Pressed (some would say badgered) by Dan Rather about his role in the Iranian arms deal, the typically placid Bush attacked Rather head on. The Bush campaign could not have been more pleased; here was their candidate, often characterized as a "wimp," battling on live TV with a prominent anchorman. A public opinion poll for *Time* gave the advantage to Bush over Rather by a margin of 42 to 27 percent.[1]

This was just one example of how the Bush campaign masterminded an effective media strategy. It far outshone the Dukakis campaign in influencing what issues were discussed by the media and what was reported about their candidate. Events were scrupulously planned to make one simple point, and press access to Bush was strictly controlled. In contrast, the Dukakis media

[1]Michael J. Robinson and Margaret Petrella, "Who Won the George Bush-Dan Rather Debate?" *Public Opinion* 10 (March/April 1988), 44.

Modern political success depends upon control of the mass media. When Dan Rather confronted George Bush on live television about his role in the Iran-Contra affair, Bush used the exchange to his advantage. By reacting in anger, he managed to dodge questions about his role in the scandal as well as to shed his image as a political "wimp."

events often lacked a clear theme. An even worse mistake at the outset was allowing the press to question Governor Dukakis every day. The more questions a candidate answers, the more choice the press has on what to report, and therefore, the less likely it is to focus on what the candidate wants them to concentrate on.

Candidates have learned that the secret to controlling the media's focus is limiting what they can report on to carefully scripted events. These are known as **media events.** A media event is staged primarily for the purpose of being covered. If the media is not there, the event would probably not happen or would have no significance. Take the early morning scene of George Bush shaking hands at a factory gate the week of the crucial 1988 New Hampshire primary. The couple dozen hands he shook could scarcely have made a difference, but Bush was not really there to win votes by personal contact. Rather, the point was to show him reaching out to the average working person.

Getting the right image on TV news for just thirty seconds can easily have a greater payoff than a whole day's worth of handshaking. In addition, a large part of today's so-called thirty-second presidency is the slickly produced TV commercial. In recent years negative commercials have come to dominate many campaigns. Many people are worried that the tirade of accusations, innuendos, and countercharges in political commercials is poisoning the American political process. Some would even use the government's regulatory power over television to curb negative advertising (see "You Are the Policymaker: Should Negative Political Ads Be Curbed?").

Yet image making doesn't stop with the campaign—it's also a critical element in day-to-day governing. Politicians' images in the press are seen as good indicators of their clout. This is especially true of presidents, who in recent

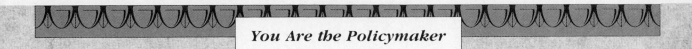

Should Negative Political Ads Be Curbed?

Democratic Senator Ernest Hollings of South Carolina and Republican Senator John Danforth of Missouri are both fed up with negative TV commercials. Together they have introduced a bill in the Senate to use the government's regulatory power over the public airwaves to discourage such commercials. Their proposal, known as the "Clean Campaign Act of 1989" (S. 999), is aimed at making candidates either voice their charges against an opponent in person, or not at all.

Under provisions of the legislation, candidates are not forbidden to run negative advertisements. Everyone agrees that this would be an infringement of freedom of speech. Thus the ability of a candidate to run advertisements speaking out personally against one's opponent is unaffected by the bill. However, if charges are made not by the candidate, but by an ominous sounding announcer, Danforth and Hollings believe that the government should step in. Their bill requires stations airing such ads to give the opponent free response time.

While this simple provision does not necessarily preclude negative advertising, most agree that it would probably cut it down to a minimum. No one wants to give away free response time to the opposition, and most candidates are likely to be reluctant to attack an opponent in person.

Critics of the bill offer both constitutional and practical political objections. Senator Mitch McConnell (R-Ky.) states that "its clear purpose is to inhibit political speech. It's not likely to withstand a court test." Senator John McCain (R-Ariz.) views the bill as a way to make it easier for incumbents to get reelected. By making it more difficult to attack an incumbent's record, challengers may find it even harder to win voters' support, argues Senator McCain.

What do you think? Would you support the proposal? To what extent do you believe it would clean up campaigns, limit free speech, or protect incumbents? In short, what are the various trade-offs involved?

Source: "Senators Divide on Proposals To Tame Negative TV Ads," Congressional Quarterly Weekly Report, July 22, 1989, 1890.

years have devoted major attention to maintaining a well-honed public image. As President Nixon wrote in an internal White House memo in 1969:

> When I think of the millions of dollars that go into one lousy 30-second television spot advertising a deodorant, it seems to me unbelievable that we don't do a better job in seeing that Presidential appearances always have the very best professional advice whenever they are to be covered on TV. . . .
>
> The President should never be without the very best professional advice for making a television appearance.[2]

Few, if any, administrations devoted so much concern and energy to the president's media appearances than did Ronald Reagan's. It has often been said that Reagan played to the media as he had played to the cameras in Hollywood. According to Mark Hertsgaard, news management in the Reagan White House operated on the following seven principles: (1) plan ahead, (2) stay on the offensive, (3) control the flow of information, (4) limit reporters' access to the

[2]December 1, 1969, memo from Nixon to H.R. Haldeman in Bruce Oudes, ed., From: The President—Richard Nixon's Secret Files (New York: Harper & Row, 1988), 76–77.

president, (5) talk about the issues *you* want to talk about, (6) speak in one voice, and (7) repeat the same message many times.[3]

The task of applying these principles initially fell to Michael Deaver, who occupied the office right outside the Oval Office. Deaver was responsible for advising the president on image making

> and image was what he talked about nearly all of the time. It was Deaver who identified the [news] story of the day at the eight o'clock staff meeting, and coordinated plans for dealing with it, Deaver who created and approved photo opportunities. . . . He saw—designed—each presidential action as a one-minute or two-minute spot on the evening network news, or a picture on page one of the *Washington Post* or the *New York Times* and conceived every Presidential appearance in terms of camera angles.[4]

To Ronald Reagan, the presidency was often a performance, and aides like Deaver helped to choreograph his public appearances. Perhaps there will never again be a president so concerned with public relations as Reagan, but for a president to ignore the power of image and the media would be perilous. In today's high-tech age, presidents can hardly lead the country if they cannot effectively communicate with it.

Indeed, more and more of American government and politics hinge upon the media. In the American political system, the media is the manipulator and the manipulated, the hunter and the hunted. Critics inside and outside of the media fear that the media can determine the American political agenda, aiding one candidate while ruining another. In 1987 reporters literally stalked Gary Hart after stories emerged concerning his alleged womanizing. In 1989, when

---

[3]Mark Hertsgaard, *On Bended Knee: The Press and the Reagan Presidency* (New York: Farrar, Straus & Giroux, 1988), 34.

[4]Donald T. Regan, *For the Record* (New York: Harcourt Brace Jovanovich, 1988), 247–48.

The Reagan administration carefully—and masterfully—controlled the president's image as presented by the media. To avoid having Reagan give unrehearsed answers, for example, a favorite tactic of his advisors was to place the media at a distance and rev a helicopter engine so that the president could not hear reporters' questions.

John Tower was nominated for secretary of defense, the media all but examined Senator Tower's liver in investigating his drinking habits (see "A Question of Ethics: Has Media Intrusiveness Gone Too Far?").

The media has helped create what Elinor Fuchs calls the "theatricalization of American politics." "In America," she says, "most of us go to the theatre for entertainment, or at best to collect a moving or exciting experience."[5] These

[5]Elinor Fuchs, "Theatricalization of American Politics," *American Theatre,* January 1987, 18.

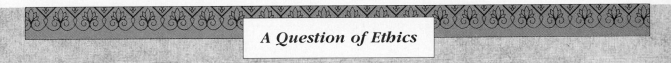

A Question of Ethics

Has Media Intrusiveness Gone Too Far?

As the press has come to scrutinize the ethics of public officials more and more, their own practices have come into question. Is every detail of a politician's private life fair game for the press? To what lengths should journalists go to get information? How sure of the facts should they be before printing potentially damaging stories?

Just before Roosevelt announced his candidacy for a fourth term in 1944, his doctor found that he had a badly enlarged heart and was suffering from hypertensive heart disease and acute bronchitis. The prognosis for him living another four years was bleak, yet the public knew nothing of his doctor's findings. Today presidential candidates are expected to release all their medical records. If the president has an operation of any type, the media will cover every aspect of it. Are the president's bowels functioning well? Stay tuned for details at eleven.

When John F. Kennedy ran for president reporters observed him in a compromising situation with a woman other than his wife. Again, the public learned nothing of this. In contrast to the accidental observations of Kennedy's shenanigans, reporters from the *Miami Herald* actually staked out Gary Hart's townhouse to investigate his behavior. Soon afterwards, still photographs and home movies of Hart and Donna Rice together became hot items in the news.

Most people thought that the question of Hart's fidelity was a relevant question for the media to look into, but many questioned the reporters' methods in this case and others like it. Are politicians to be stalked like common criminals? Should reporters leaf through politicians' garbage in search of interesting

tidbits—as they once did outside Henry Kissinger's home? How about publishing a list of the movies a person has rented—as was done in the case of Supreme Court nominee Robert Bork? In short, how much is the public entitled to know, and should the media have to respect certain privacy rights?

If sensitive personal topics are to be covered, the standards of evidence required should be fairly high. Unfortunately, this is not always the case. When Carl Bernstein and Bob Woodward were investigating the Watergate scandal, their rule of thumb was that nothing could be printed unless it was confirmed by two authoritative sources. This ideal standard is hard to meet, though, and often rumors become stories in the media without any hard confirmation. John Tower was reported to have dated a Russian ballerina who was on the KGB payroll; Michael Dukakis was rumored to have seen a psychiatrist after his brother's death; Kitty Dukakis was said to have burned an American flag during a Vietnam War protest. All these stories made the news; each turned out to be based on nothing more than hearsay. While they were eventually dismissed as groundless, damage was done to the individuals involved.

A 1989 Times-Mirror poll summarizes both sides of the issue of media intrusiveness. On the positive side, 60 percent of the public believes that press coverage of the personal and ethical behavior of politicians helps weed out the kind of people who should not be in office. On the negative side, though, 73 percent feel news organizations often invade people's privacy. What do you think? Is this an inevitable tradeoff, and one that is worth the price?

Source: Poll information is from "The People and the Press, Part 5" (Report issued by the Times-Mirror Center for the People and the Press, November 1989).

days, politics and government are national theater. Colonel Oliver North outscored the soap operas in his televised Iran-Contra testimony. The trials and tribulations of Gary Hart *were* a political soap opera. The villains (the Ayatollah, Noriega, the "Evil Empire"), the victims (the Iranian hostages, the starving African children, the AIDS sufferers), the heroes (Lech Walesa, American soldiers in Panama), the scripts (Watergate, the Iran-Contra hearings, the Gary Hart saga)—all these combine to make politics theater. With the media, as Shakespeare said, "All the world's a stage, and all the men and women merely players."

THE DEVELOPMENT OF THE MASS MEDIA

Lyndon Johnson was one of two recent American presidents (the other was Richard Nixon) to feel that he was hounded out of office by the press.[6] Back in his hometown of Johnson City, Texas, the retired president agreed—for a handsome fee—to a CBS televised memoir. One day, getting ready for a filming session, Johnson was asked what had been the biggest change in politics during his long career. "You guys," said Johnson. "All you guys in the media. All of politics has changed because of you. You've broken all the machines and the ties between us in Congress and the city machines. You guys have given us a new kind of people."[7] True or exaggerated (and Johnson was well known for exaggeration), Johnson's view is a common one: we live in the mass media age.

It was not always this way, of course. There was virtually no daily press at all when the First Amendment was written during Washington's presidency. The daily newspaper is largely a product of the late nineteenth century; radio and television have been around only since the first half of the twentieth. As recently as the presidency of Herbert Hoover (1929–33), reporters submitted their questions to the president in writing, and he responded in writing—if at all. As he put it, "The President of the United States will not stand and be questioned like a chicken thief by men whose names he does not even know."[8]

Hoover's successor, Franklin D. Roosevelt (1933–45), practically invented media politics. To Roosevelt, the media was a potential ally. Power radiated from Washington under him—and so did news. Roosevelt promised reporters two **press conferences**—presidential meetings with reporters—a week, and he delivered them. He held 337 press conferences in his first term, 374 in his second, and 279 in his third. Roosevelt was *the* newsmaker. Stories and leads flowed from the White House like a flood; the United Press news syndicate carried four times as much Washington news under FDR as it had under Hoover.[9] FDR was also the first president to use radio, broadcasting a series of reassuring "fireside chats" to the Depression-ridden nation. Roosevelt's crafty use of radio helped him win four presidential elections. Theodore White tells the story of the time in 1944 when FDR found out that his opponent, Thomas E. Dewey,

[6]On Lyndon Johnson's stormy relations with the press, especially during the Vietnam War, see Kathleen J. Turner, *Lyndon Johnson's Dual War: Vietnam and the Press* (Chicago: University of Chicago Press, 1985).

[7]The Johnson interview is recounted in David Halberstam, *The Powers That Be* (New York: Dell Books, 1979), 15–16.

[8]Quoted in David Brinkley, *Washington Goes to War* (New York: Alfred A. Knopf, 1988), 171.

[9]Halberstam, *The Powers That Be,* 19.

Franklin D. Roosevelt was the first president to use the media effectively. A great favorite of reporters, FDR held some one thousand press conferences during more than twelve years in office. He was also the first president to use radio as a political tool, giving "fireside chats" to reassure the nation during the Great Depression.

had purchased fifteen minutes of air time on NBC immediately following his own address. Roosevelt spoke for fourteen minutes and then left one minute silent. Thinking that the network had experienced technical difficulties, many changed their dials before Dewey came on the air.[10]

Another Roosevelt talent was knowing how to feed the right story to the right reporter. He used presidential wrath to warn reporters off material he did not want covered, and chastised news reports he deemed inaccurate. His wrath was rarely invoked, however, and the press revered him, never even reporting to the American public that the President was confined to a wheelchair. The idea that a political leader's private life might be public business was alien to journalists in FDR's day.

This relatively cozy relationship betwen politicians and the press lasted through the early 1960s. As ABC's Sam Donaldson writes, when he first came to Washington in 1961, "many reporters saw themselves as an extension of the government, accepting, with very little skepticism, what government officials told them."[11] The events of the Vietnam War and the Watergate scandal, though, soured the press on government. Today's newspeople work in an environment of cynicism. To them, politicians rarely tell the whole story; the press sees ferreting out the truth as their job. No one epitomized this attitude in the 1980s better than Donaldson, who earned a hard-nosed reputation by regularly shouting unwanted questions at President Reagan. In his book, *Hold On, Mr. President!,* Donaldson says,

> If you send me to cover a pie-baking contest on Mother's Day, I'm going to ask dear old Mom whether she used artificial sweetener in violations of the rules, and while

---

[10] Theodore H. White, *The Making of the President, 1972* (New York: Atheneum, 1973), 250.
[11] Sam Donaldson, *Hold On, Mr. President!* (New York: Random House, 1987), 54.

she's at it, could I see the receipt for the apples to prove she didn't steal them. I maintain that if Mom has nothing to hide, no harm will have been done. But the questions should be asked.[12]

Many political scientists disagree that no harm comes from such reporting. **Investigative journalism,** the use of detectivelike reporting methods to unearth scandals, pits reporters against political leaders. Guaranteed freedom of speech by the First Amendment, the American media has a unique ability to display the government's dirty linen (see "America in Perspective: The Media Elsewhere"). There is evidence that TV's fondness for investigative journalism has contributed to greater public cynicism and negativism about politics.[13]

[12]*Ibid.,* 20.

[13]See the classic report by Michael J. Robinson, "Public Affairs Television and the Growth of Political Malaise: The Case of 'The Selling of the Pentagon'," *American Political Science Review* 70 (June 1976): 409–32.

America in Perspective

The Media Elsewhere

The American media is the freest in the world. It is constitutionally protected by the First Amendment, which gives legal protection available in few other countries.

Even in democratic nations like Great Britain the media does not enjoy the independence of its American counterpart. There is more **censorship**—governmental regulation of media content—permitted in the United Kingdom than in the United States. In Britain the Official Secrets Act prohibits the media from covering anything the British government wants to stamp secret, and jail terms can be imposed for violating the act. One particularly silly episode involved the publication of *Spycatcher,* a book by Peter Wright, during the 1980s. Wright, a longtime employee of the British Secret Service, claimed that a top official of Her Majesty's Secret Service was in fact a double agent. Prime Minister Thatcher's government banned publication of the book and newspaper coverage of it (even of the banning itself) in Great Britain. Because *Spycatcher* had already been published in the United States, Canada, Australia, and elsewhere, Thatcher's critics thought it particularly ludicrous to attempt to ban the book in Britain.

British newspapers, like most in Europe, are much more partisan than American newspapers. Whereas American journalists pride themselves on their objec-

tivity, the British papers are fierce partisans of the Conservative or Labour party. By American standards, many British papers are gritty and salacious, some resembling the *National Enquirer.* On the other hand, the British Broadcasting Company (BBC) is a publicly owned corporation with a reputation for highbrow news coverage and programming. Ratings are only one factor taken into account in determining the content of what is shown on the BBC—quality is highly valued as well. Although the British government appoints the BBC's Board of Governors, it is rarely able to exert any control over the network's independent-minded executives.

Political control of television and newspapers in the communist world, on the other hand, is pervasive. The national newspaper of the Soviet Communist party, *Pravda* (Russian for "truth"), gives the party's views on everything from American life to government policy. When Soviet leadership or policy changes, it is *Pravda's* task to mirror those changes faithfully. Sometimes *Pravda* is the source of outright disinformation; it has, for example, accused the United States of masterminding the attempted assassination of Pope John Paul II and of intentionally spreading AIDS in Africa. *Glasnost,* however, has brought changes even to *Pravda,* which now regularly criticizes official corruption and inefficiency.

Scholars distinguish between two kinds of media: the **print media,** which includes newspapers and magazines, and the **broadcast media,** which consists of television and radio. Each has reshaped political communication at different points in American history. The following sections look at their development and role in the political system.

The Print Media

The first newspaper, which appeared some fifteen hundred years before the printing press, was the Roman gazette *Acta Diurna* ("Action Journal"), a kind of house organ for the regime of Julius Caesar in 59 B.C. Like its modern counterparts, the *Acta Diurna* reported on sports in the Colosseum, details of trials and executions, political news, and social events. The Roman gazette was posted in prominent places so that passersby could read it, like newspapers today in many developing countries, such as China. Like news in communist countries, it was strictly censored by the authorities.[14]

The first American daily newspaper was printed in Philadelphia in 1783, but such papers did not proliferate until the technological advances of the mid-nineteenth century (see Figure 11.1). Rapid printing and cheap paper made possible the "penny press," which could be bought for a penny and read at home. In 1841 Horace Greeley's *New York Tribune* was founded, and in 1851 the *New York Times* started up. By the 1840s the telegraph permitted a primitive "wire service," which relayed news stories from city to city faster than ever before. The Associated Press, founded in 1849, depended heavily on this new technology.

Two newspaper magnates, Joseph Pulitzer and William Randolph Hearst, enlivened journalism around the turn of the century. Between them—Pulitzer operating in New York and Hearst in burgeoning San Francisco—they published stories about hijinks in high places. This was the era of *yellow journalism,* wherein violence, corruption, wars, and gossip were the main topics. Hearst even sent an artist to cover the Spanish-American conflict in Cuba, telling him, "You furnish the pictures and I'll furnish the war" by arousing American opinion against Spain. On a visit to the United States at that time, young Winston Churchill said that "the essence of American journalism is vulgarity divested of truth."[15]

Newspapers consolidated into **chains** during the early part of the twentieth century. Today's massive media conglomerates (Gannett, Knight-Ridder, and Newhouse are the largest) control newspapers with 78 percent of the nation's daily circulation.[16] Thus three of four Americans now read a newspaper owned not by a fearless local editor but by a corporation headquartered elsewhere. Often these chains control television and radio stations as well.

Among the press there is, of course, a pecking order. Almost from the beginning the *New York Times* was a cut above most newspapers in its influence and impact; it is the nation's "newspaper of record" and now publishes a national edition available most everywhere in the United States. Its clearest rival today

[14]The story of the first newspapers comes from Charles Panati, *Browser's Book of Beginnings* (Boston: Houghton Mifflin, 1984), 144–45.

[15]William Manchester, *The Last Lion: Winston Churchill, Visions of Glory, 1874–1932* (Boston: Little, Brown, 1984), 225.

[16]Doris A. Graber, *Mass Media and American Politics,* 3rd ed. (Washington, D.C.: Congressional Quarterly Press, 1989), 45.

Figure 11.1 Media Milestones

NEWSPAPERS

1690	First newspaper published in the colonies; suppressed after first issue
1783	First daily newspaper in the U.S.—*Pennsylvania Evening Post*
1851	*New York Times* founded

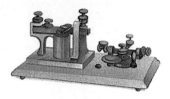

TELEGRAPH

1844	First telegraph message sent
1849	Associated Press (AP) founded to distribute telegraphic news to the daily press
1963	"Hot Line" established between the White House and the Kremlin

TELEPHONE

| 1876 | Telephone invented |
| 1878 | The first telephone in the White House was installed in the Oval Office—the telephone number was "1" |

RADIO

1903	Radio invented
1920	First commercial radio station (KDKA in Pittsburgh)
1924	First live radio coverage of a nominating convention
1930s	President Franklin D. Roosevelt uses radio for "fireside chats" with the American people
1941–45	Radio news covers World War II

TELEVISION

1923	Television invented
1948	First televised nominating conventions
1952	First presidential campaign commercials; Richard Nixon makes his famous "Checkers Speech"
1960	Candidates Kennedy and Nixon hold the first televised presidential debates
1961	President Kennedy holds the first live televised presidential press conference
1963	Network news expands to thirty minutes
1960s	Television brings the Vietnam War to American living rooms
1973	Senate Watergate committee holds televised hearings on the Watergate scandal
1989	Revolutions televised as they happened in Eastern Europe

is the *Washington Post,* offering perhaps the best coverage inside Washington and a sprightlier alternative to the stodgier *Times.* It now prints a national weekly edition which compiles its most important news analysis and commentary articles of the week. Papers such as the *Chicago Tribune* and the *Los Angeles Times,* as well as those in Atlanta, Des Moines, and other big cities are also major national institutions. For most newspapers in medium-sized and small towns, though, the main source of national and world news is the Associated Press. About 80 percent of the non-Communist world's news comes from just four sources: the Associated Press, United Press International (now struggling with bankruptcy), the *New York Times* news service, and the *Los Angeles Times/Washington Post* news service.

Magazines—the other component of the print media—are read avidly by Americans, although the political content of leading magazines is pretty slender. The so-called newsweeklies—mainly *Time, Newsweek,* and *U.S. News and World Report*—rank well behind such popular favorites as the *Reader's Digest, TV Guide,* and *Family Circle* (see Figure 11.2). While *Time*'s circulation is a bit better than that of the *National Enquirer* (for "people with enquiring minds," its ads tell us), the *Star* and *Playboy* edge out *Newsweek* in sales competition. Serious magazines of political news and opinion are basically reserved for the educated elite in America; magazines such as the *New Republic,* the *National*

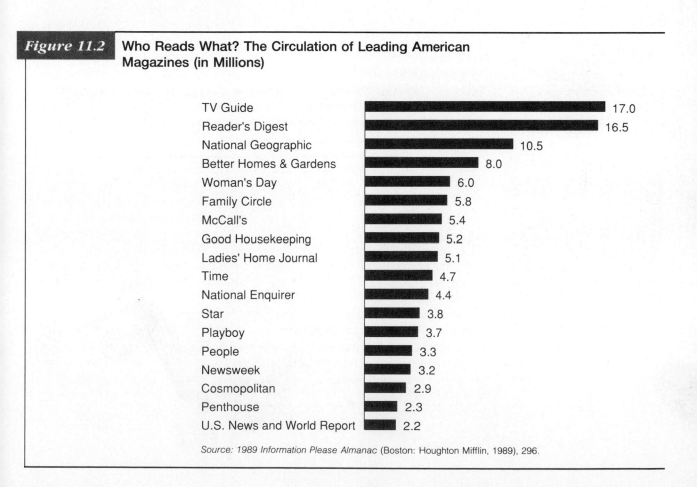

Figure 11.2 **Who Reads What? The Circulation of Leading American Magazines (in Millions)**

TV Guide	17.0
Reader's Digest	16.5
National Geographic	10.5
Better Homes & Gardens	8.0
Woman's Day	6.0
Family Circle	5.8
McCall's	5.4
Good Housekeeping	5.2
Ladies' Home Journal	5.1
Time	4.7
National Enquirer	4.4
Star	3.8
Playboy	3.7
People	3.3
Newsweek	3.2
Cosmopolitan	2.9
Penthouse	2.3
U.S. News and World Report	2.2

Source: 1989 Information Please Almanac (Boston: Houghton Mifflin, 1989), 296.

Review, and *Commentary* are greatly outsold by such American favorites as *Hot Rod, Weightwatchers Magazine,* and *Organic Gardening.*

The Broadcast Media

Gradually, the broadcast media has displaced the print media as Americans' principal source of news and information. The radio was invented in 1903, the same year as the Wright brothers' famous flight. The first modern commercial radio station was Pittsburgh's KDKA, whose maiden broadcast was of the 1920 Harding-Cox presidential election returns. By the middle of the 1930s radio ownership had become almost universal in America, and during World War II radio went into the news business in earnest. CBS took an early lead in broadcasting news, partly because it had a lot of unsponsored airtime to fill and news was cheap to produce.

Whereas CBS pioneered radio news, NBC pioneered television news. As a form of technology, television is almost as old as radio; the first television station actually appeared in 1931, barely a decade after the first radio station. By the beginning of World War II there were already twenty-three television stations in the United States. By 1949 there were a million TV sets in American homes, and just two years later there were ten million.

The 1950s and early 1960s were the adolescent years for American television. During those years the political career of Richard Nixon was made and unmade by television. In 1952, while running as Dwight Eisenhower's vice-presidential candidate, Nixon made a famous speech denying that he took under-the-table gifts and payments. Claiming that his wife, Pat, wore only a "Republican cloth coat," he did admit that one gift he had taken was his dog Checkers. Noting that his daughters loved the dog, Nixon said that regardless of his political future they would keep it. His homey appeal brought a flood of sympathetic telegrams to the Republican National Committee, and party leaders had little choice but to leave him on the ticket.

In 1960 Nixon was again on television's center stage, this time in the first televised **presidential debate** against Senator John F. Kennedy. Nixon blamed his poor appearance in the first of the four debates for his narrow defeat in the election. Haggard from a week in the hospital and with his five o'clock shadow and perspiration clearly visible, Nixon looked awful compared to the crisp, clean, attractive Kennedy. The poll results from this debate illustrate the visual power of television in American politics; whereas people listening on the radio gave the edge to Nixon, those who saw it on television thought Kennedy won. Russell Baker, who covered the event for the *New York Times,* writes in his memoirs that "television replaced newspapers as the most important communications medium in American politics" that very night.[17]

Just as radio had taken the nation to the war in Europe and the Pacific during the 1940s, television took it to the war in Vietnam during the 1960s. TV exposed governmental naïveté (some said it was outright lying) about the progress of the war. Napoléon once said that "four hostile newspapers are more to be feared than a thousand bayonets." Lyndon Johnson learned the hard way that three television networks could be even more consequential. Every night, in living color, Americans were seeing the horrors of war through television.

Edward R. Murrow gained fame during World War II as a CBS radio journalist. He then made the transition to television, where he pioneered in-depth reporting, paving the way for modern investigative journalists.

[17]Russell Baker, *The Good Times* (New York: William Morrow, 1989), 326.

President Johnson soon had two wars on his hands, one in faraway Vietnam and the other at home with antiwar protesters, both covered in detail by the media. In 1968 CBS anchorman Walter Cronkite journeyed to Vietnam for a firsthand look at the state of the war. In an extraordinary TV special Cronkite reported that the war was not being won, nor was it likely to be. Watching from the White House, Johnson sadly remarked that if he had lost Cronkite then he had lost the support of the American people.

With the growth of cable TV, particularly the Cable News Network (CNN), television has recently entered a new era of bringing the news to people—and political leaders—as it happens. President Bush regularly watches CNN when an international crisis occurs, as do other world leaders such as Margaret Thatcher of Britain, King Hussein of Jordan, and King Fahd of Saudi Arabia. Marlin Fitzwater, Bush's press secretary, states that "CNN has opened up a whole new communications system between governments in terms of immediacy and directness. In many cases it's the first communication we have."[18]

Since 1963, surveys have consistently shown that more people rely on TV for the news than any other medium (see "The People Speak: Where Citizens Get Their News and What They Trust"). Furthermore, by a regular two to one margin, people think television reports are more believable than newspaper stories. (Consider the old sayings "Don't believe everything you read" and "I'll

[18]Maureen Dowd, "Where Bush Turns for the Latest," *New York Times,* August 11, 1989, All.

Where do you usually get most of your news about what's going on in the world today—from the newspapers or radio or television or magazines or talking to people? (More than one answer permitted.)

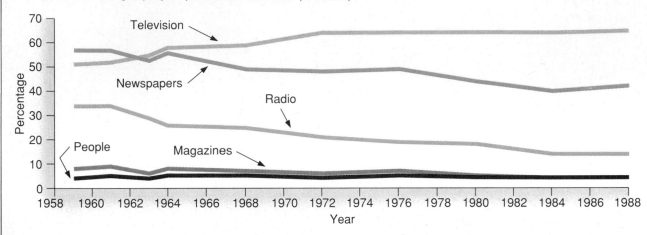

If you got conflicting or different reports of the same news story from radio, television, the magazines, and the newspapers, which of the four versions would you be most inclined to believe?

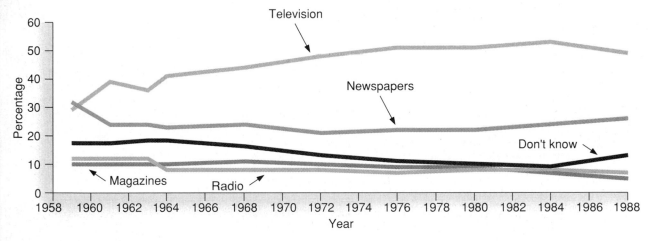

Source: The questions as worded are taken directly from Harold W. Stanley and Richard G. Niemi, *Vital Statistics on American Politics,* 2nd ed. (Washington, D.C.: Congressional Quarterly Press, 1990), 69.

believe it when I see it.") While people are predisposed to be skeptical about what they read in a newspaper, with television seeing is believing.

REPORTING THE NEWS

Regardless of the medium, it cannot be emphasized enough that news reporting is a business in America. Striving for the bottom line—profits—shapes how journalists define the news, where they get the news, and how they present it.

Because some news stories attract more viewers or readers than others, there are certain inherent biases in what the American public sees and reads about.

Defining News

As every journalism student will quickly tell you, *news* is what is timely and different. It is when a man bites a dog as opposed to when a dog bites a man. An oft-repeated speech on foreign policy or a well-worn statement on fighting drug abuse is less newsworthy than an odd episode. Getting into a presidential helicopter is not news; bumping your head as you board the helicopter—as President Ford once did—is different, and thus news. In its search for the unusual, the news media can give its audience a very peculiar view of events and policymakers.

Millions of new and different events happen every day; journalists must decide which of them are newsworthy. No one has taken a more careful look at the definition and production of news than Edward J. Epstein, who, given a unique opportunity to observe NBC's news department for a year, wrote *News from Nowhere*, an inside account of the TV news business.[19] Epstein found that some important characteristics of the TV news business result from the nature of the viewing audience. In their pursuit of high ratings, news shows are tailored to a fairly low level of audience sophistication. To a large extent, TV networks define news as what is entertaining to the average viewer.

Finding the News

Epstein called his book *News from Nowhere* to make the point that the organizational process shapes the news. Of course, news does come from somewhere. Americans' popular image of correspondents or reporters somehow ferreting out the news is accurate in some cases, yet a surprising amount of news comes from well-established sources. Much comes tailor-made in press releases or in **trial balloons,** information leaked to the media to see what the political reaction will be. Interestingly, however, most TV news stories originate from other news media. Epstein tracked down the sources of 440 major stories during his time at NBC and found that the correspondents—those attractive men and women who read news stories so smoothly—accounted for exactly 1 percent of news stories. The AP and UPI wire services accounted for 70 percent of TV news stories.[20] Similarly, print reporters read the wires and other newspapers and rely almost exclusively on established sources to get their stories (see Table 11.1).

Despite this reliance on familiar sources, an enterprising reporter occasionally has an opportunity to live up to the image of the crusading truth-seeker. Local reporters Carl Bernstein and Bob Woodward of the *Washington Post* uncovered important evidence in the Watergate case. Columnists like Jack Anderson regularly expose the uglier side of government corruption and inefficiency. Such reporting is highly valued among the media. Pulitzer prizes typically go to reporters who get exclusive stories through painstaking legwork.

Bob Woodward (left) and Carl Bernstein, two obscure local reporters for the Washington Post, *painstakingly uncovered the first details of the Watergate scandal. Watergate signaled a new era in the relationship between journalists and politicians; journalists assumed that politicians had something to hide, and politicians assumed that reporters were out to embarrass them.*

[19] Edward J. Epstein, *News from Nowhere: Television and the News* (New York: Random House, 1973). Many of this text's observations on TV news come from Epstein.

[20] *Ibid.,* 142.

Table 11.1 Sources for Newspaper Stories

Very little of the news is generated by spontaneous events or a reporter's own analysis. Rather, most stories are drawn from situations over which newsmakers have substantial control. Leon Sigal examined the sources for news stories in the *New York Times* and the *Washington Post,* the nation's two most prestigious newspapers. Listed here are the percentage of news stories drawn from the following soures:

SOURCE	PERCENT
Interviews	24.7
Press conferences	24.5
Press releases	17.5
Official proceedings	7.9
Other nonspontaneous events	4.5
News commentary and editorials	2.3
Leaks	1.5
Nongovernmental proceedings	1.5
Spontaneous events	1.2
Reporter's own analysis	0.9

Source: Leon V. Sigal, *Reporters and Officials: The Organization and Politics of News Reporting* (Lexington, Mass.: Heath, 1973), 122.

Presenting the News

Once the news has been "found," it has to be neatly compressed into a thirty-second news segment or fit in among the advertisements in a newspaper. If you had to pick a single word to describe news coverage by the print and broadcast media, it would be *superficial.* "The name of the game," says former White House press secretary Jody Powell, "is skimming off the cream, seizing on the most interesting, controversial, and unusual aspects of an issue."[21] TV news, in particular, is little more than a headline service. Except for the little-watched but highly regarded *MacNeil-Lehrer Newshour* on PBS and ABC's late-night *Nightline,* analysis of news events rarely lasts more than a minute. Patterson's careful study of campaign coverage (see Chapter 8) found only skimpy attention to the issues during a presidential campaign. Clearly, if coverage of political events during the height of an election campaign is thin, coverage of day-to-day policy questions is even thinner. Issues such as nuclear power, money supply, and pollution control are complex, and complex issues are difficult to treat in a short news clip.

Strangely enough, as technology has enabled the media to pass along information with greater speed, news coverage has become less complete.[22]

[21]Jody Powell, "White House Flackery," in Peter Woll, ed., *Debating American Government,* 2nd ed. (Glenview, Ill.: Scott, Foresman, 1988), 180.

[22]This point is well-argued in Kathleen Hall Jamieson, *Eloquence in an Electronic Age* (New York: Oxford University Press, 1988).

Whereas newspapers once routinely reprinted the entire text of important political speeches, now the *New York Times* is virtually the only paper that does—and even they have cut back sharply on this practice. In place of speeches, Americans now hear **sound bites** of fifteen seconds or less on TV. A speech can be uninspiring and unconvincing, but if it contains one snappy sound bite, that is all that matters—for only this portion will appear on TV. Even successful politicians often feel frustrated by this process. A year after his 1976 election victory Jimmy Carter told a reporter that

> it's a strange thing that you can go through your campaign for president, and you have a basic theme that you express in a 15- or 20-minute standard speech, . . . [but] the traveling press—sometimes exceeding 100 people—will never report that speech to the public. The peripheral aspects become the headlines, but the basic essence of what you stand for and what you hope to accomplish is never reported.[23]

Rather than presenting their audience with the whole chicken, the media typically gives just a McNugget. Why then should a politician work to build a carefully crafted case for his or her point of view when a catchy line will do just as well?

Bias in the News

Many people believe that the news is biased in favor of one point of view or another. The vast majority of social science studies have found, however, that the media is not systematically biased toward a particular ideology or party. A number of factors help to explain why the news is typically characterized by

[23]Quoted in Austin Ranney, *Channels of Power* (New York: Basic Books, 1983), 116.

political neutrality. Most reporters strongly believe in journalistic objectivity, and few are rabid partisans deeply concerned with expressing one party's views on issues. The rotation of assignments and rewards for objective news-gathering also work against the introduction of any political biases. Media outlets have a direct financial stake in attracting viewers and subscribers and do not want to lose their audience by appearing biased—especially when there are multiple versions of the same story readily available. It seems paradoxical to say that competition produces uniformity, but this often happens in the news business.

However, to conclude that the news contains little explicit partisan or ideological bias is not to argue that it does not distort reality in its coverage. Ideally the news should mirror reality; in practice there are far too many possible stories for this to be the case. Journalists must select which stories to cover and to what degree. Because news reporting is a business, the overriding bias is toward stories which will draw the largest audience. Surveys show that people are most fascinated by stories with conflict, violence, disaster, or scandal (see "The People Speak: Stories Citizens Have Tuned In and Out"). Good news is unexciting; bad news has the drama that brings in big audiences.

Television is particularly biased toward stories that generate good pictures. Seeing a **talking head** (a shot of a person's face talking directly to the camera)

The People Speak   Stories Citizens Have Tuned In and Out

Since 1986 the monthly survey of the Times Mirror Center for the People and the Press has asked Americans how closely they have followed major news stories. As one would expect, stories involving disaster or human drama have drawn more attention than complicated issues of public policy. A representative selection of their findings is presented below. The percentage in each case is the proportion who reported following the story "very closely."

The explosion of the space shuttle *Challenger*	80%
1989 San Francisco earthquake	73%
Rescue of baby Jessica McClure from a well	69%
Oil spill in Alaska	52%
Supreme Court decision on flag burning	51%
Opening of the Berlin Wall	50%
Murder of Lt. Col. Higgins in Lebanon	49%
Nuclear accident at Chernobyl	46%
Iran-Contra hearings	33%
1988 Democratic convention	30%
1988 Republican convention	27%
Passage of Savings and Loan bailout bill	26%
Congressional repeal of catastrophic health insurance	19%
Nomination of Robert Bork to the Supreme Court	17%
Education summit held by Bush and the nation's governors	15%
House approval of a capital gains tax cut	14%

Source: "Public Interest and Awareness of the News" (Report Issued by the Times Mirror Center for the People and the Press, December 1989).

is boring; viewers will switch channels in search of more interesting visual stimulation. For example, during the Bush-Rather debate discussed earlier, CBS's ratings actually went down as people tired of watching two talking heads argue for an extended period of time.[24] A shot of ambassadors squaring off in a fistfight at the United Nations, on the other hand, will up the ratings. Such a scene was shown three times in one day on CBS in 1973. Not once, though, was the cause of the fight discussed.[25] Network practices like these have led observers such as Lance Bennett to write that "the public is exposed to a world driven into chaos by seemingly arbitrary and mysterious forces."[26]

THE NEWS AND PUBLIC OPINION

How does the threatening, hostile, and corrupt world often depicted by the news media shape what people believe about the American political system? This question is, frankly, difficult to answer. Studying the effects of the news media on people's opinions and behaviors is a difficult task. One reason is that it is hard to separate the media from other influences. When presidents, legislators, and interest groups, as well as news organizations, are all discussing an issue, it is not easy to isolate those opinion changes which come from political leadership from those which come from the news. Moreover, the effect of one news story on public opinion may be trivial; the cumulative effect of dozens of news stories may be quite important.

For many years students of the subject tended to doubt that the media had more than a marginal effect on public opinion. The "minimal effects hypothesis" stemmed from the fact that early scholars were looking for direct impacts—for example, whether or not the media affected how people voted.[27] When the focus turned to how the media affects *what Americans think about,* more positive results were uncovered. In a series of controlled laboratory experiments Shanto Iyengar and Donald Kinder subtly manipulated the stories participants saw on TV news.[28] They found they could significantly affect the importance people attached to a given problem by splicing a few stories about it into the news over the course of a week. Iynegar and Kinder do not maintain that the networks can make something out of nothing, nor conceal problems that actually exist. They conclude that "what television news does, instead, is alter the priorities Americans attach to a circumscribed set of problems, all of which are plausible contenders for public concern."[29] This effect is of no small consequence. By increasing public attention to specific problems, television news can influence the criteria by which the public evaluates political leaders. When unemployment goes up but inflation goes down, does public support for the president increase or decrease? The answer could depend in large part on which story is emphasized in the media.

The media's choice to cover—or ignore—certain issues can affect public opinion. Nuclear power advocates, for example, including many scientists, claim that constant media coverage of anti-nuclear protests, such as this demonstration against a nuclear power plant in Seabrook, New Hampshire, has biased the public against nuclear power.

[24]Robinson and Petrella, "Who Won the Bush-Rather Debate," 43.

[25]Robinson, "Public Affairs Television," 428.

[26]W. Lance Bennett, *News: The Politics of Illusion,* 2nd ed. (New York: Longman, 1988), 46.

[27]See Paul F. Lazarsfeld et al., *The People's Choice* (New York: Columbia University Press, 1944).

[28]Shanto Iyengar and Donald R. Kinder, *News That Matters* (Chicago: University of Chicago Press, 1987).

[29]*Ibid.,* 118–19.

In another study, Page, Shapiro, and Dempsey examined changes in public attitudes about issues over time. They examined public opinion polls on the same issues at two points in time, carefully coding the news coverage of these issues on the networks and in print during the interim. People's opinions did indeed shift with the tone of the news coverage. The impact of news commentators—such as John Chancellor and David Brinkley—seemed particularly significant in affecting opinion change. Another source of opinion change was presidential statements, though this varied by the popularity of the president. Not surprisingly, popular presidents were much more effective in changing people's opinions than unpopular ones. In contrast, interest groups seemed to have a negative impact on opinion change, suggesting that interest groups' overt activities on behalf of a certain policy position may in fact discourage support for that position. Of all the influences on opinion change these researchers examined, the impact of news commentators was the strongest. If Page and his colleagues are correct, the news media today is one of the most potent—perhaps the most potent—engines of public opinion change in America.[30]

Much remains unknown about the effects of the media and the news on American political behavior. Enough is known, however, to conclude that the media is a key political institution. The media controls much of the technology that in turn controls much of what Americans believe about politics and government. For this reason, it is important to look at the American policy agenda and the media's role in shaping it.

THE POLICY AGENDA AND THE SPECIAL ROLE OF THE MEDIA

When someone asks you, "What's your agenda?" he or she wants to know something about your priorities. As discussed in Chapter 1, governments also have agendas. John Kingdon defines **policy agenda** as "the list of subjects or problems to which government officials, and people outside of government closely associated with those officials, are paying some serious attention at any given time."[31] Interest groups, political parties, individual politicians, public relations firms, bureaucratic agencies—and, of course, the president and Congress—are all pushing for their priorities to take precedence over others. Education, AIDS research, Star Wars, aid to the homeless, inflation—these and scores of other issues compete for attention from the government.

Political activists depend heavily upon the media to get their ideas placed high on the governmental agenda. Political activists are often called **policy entrepreneurs**—people who invest their political "capital" in an issue (as an economic entrepreneur invests capital into an idea for making money). Kingdon says that policy entrepreneurs can "be in or out of government, in elected or appointed positions, in interest groups or research organizations."[32] Policy entrepreneurs' arsenal of weapons includes press releases, press conferences, and

---

[30]See their report in "What Moves Public Opinion?" *American Political Science Review* 81 (March 1987): 23–44.

[31]John W. Kingdon, *Agendas, Alternatives, and Public Policies.* (Boston: Little, Brown, 1984), 3.

[32]*Ibid.,* 129.

letter writing; buttonholing reporters and columnists; trading on personal contacts; and in cases of desperation, resorting to the dramatic. In addition, people in power can use a **leak,** a carefully placed bit of inside information given to a friendly reporter. Leaks benefit both the leaker and the recipient: leakers win points with the press for sharing "secret" information, and reporters can print or broadcast exclusive information.

Because so much of politics is theater, the staging of political events to attract media attention is a political art form. Dictators, revolutionaries, prime ministers, and presidents alike all play to the cameras. When Henry Kissinger, Nixon's top foreign policy advisor, arranged Nixon's famous trip to China, he was reminded that domestic appearances were as important as foreign policy gains. Meeting with Kissinger and Nixon, White House Chief of Staff Bob Haldeman "saw no sense in making history if television were not there to broadcast it."[33] The three men then had a lengthy discussion regarding how to obtain plentiful, favorable media coverage. Orchestrated minute by minute, Nixon's 1972 trip to China was perhaps the biggest media event of all time. The Chinese government was cooperative, knowing that good press coverage would aid it in establishing relations with the United States. They even bought the satellite transmitter needed by the networks to broadcast the visit live to America. In the end, Nixon's trip to China was presented to the American public as a TV mini-series. Befitting the art form that it was, years later it became the subject of a successful opera production.

The media is not always monopolized by political elites; the poor and downtrodden can use it, too. Civil rights groups in the 1960s relied heavily on the media to tell their stories of unjust treatment. Many believe that the introduction of television helped to accelerate the movement by showing Americans—in the North and South alike—just what the situation was.[34] Protest groups have learned that if they can stage an interesting event that attracts the media's interest, at least their point of view will be heard. Radical activist Saul Alinsky once dramatized the plight of one neighborhood by having its residents collect rats and dump them on the mayor's front lawn. The story was one local reporters could hardly resist.

More important, though, than a few dramatic events is conveying a long-term, positive image via the media. Policy entrepreneurs—individuals or groups, in or out of government—depend on good will and good images. Sometimes it helps to hire a public relations firm, one which specializes in getting a specific message across. Groups, individuals, and even countries have hired public relations firms to improve their image and their ability to peddle their issue positions (see "In Focus: Hiring a PR Firm Can Even Help a Nation's Image").

After her husband died of cancer, policy entrepreneur Mary Lasker spearheaded efforts to increase the federal government's support of cancer research. She deserves much of the credit for the billions of dollars the government now invests in such research.

UNDERSTANDING THE MASS MEDIA

The media is so crucial in today's society that it is often referred to as the "fourth branch of government." The media acts as a key linkage institution between the people and the policymakers, having a profound impact on the political policy

[33]Henry A. Kissinger, *White House Years* (Boston: Little, Brown, 1979), 757.

[34]See the interview with Richard Valeriani in Juan Williams, *Eyes on the Prize* (New York: Viking, 1987), 270–71.

Hiring a PR Firm Can Even Help a Nation's Image

Major corporations have long maintained public relations units. Today more and more interest groups spend money on PR firms to present a desired public image. Even nations have gotten into the act, hiring public relations firms to improve their image in the United States. Much is at stake for these nations; the United States is the world's largest source of aid and trade.

In an innovative study Jarol Manheim and Robert Albritton examined six nations (the Republic of Korea, the Philippines, Yugoslavia, Argentina, Indonesia, and Zimbabwe) that hired American public relations firms to improve their image problems in the United States.

In addition, they selected one country, Mexico, which had considered hiring a PR firm, but had decided not to. The authors then systematically compared coverage of these nations in the *New York Times* both before and after signing on their PR consultants. The result: for the six nations that hired PR firms, positive images presented in the *Times* increased; Mexico's image was unchanged.

If this evidence can be generalized, it appears that even foreign countries, as well as American corporations or politicians, can alter their public image through carefully orchestrated public relations activities.

Source: Jarol B. Manheim and Robert B. Albritton, "Changing National Images: International Public Relations and Media Agenda Setting," *American Political Science Review* 78 (September 1984): 641–57.

agenda. Bernard Cohen goes so far as to state that "no major act of the American Congress, no foreign adventure, no act of diplomacy, no great social reform can succeed unless the press prepares the public mind."[35] If Cohen is right, then the growth in the size of government in America would not have been possible without the need for it being established through the media. The following sections will consider the extent to which the media has paved the way for big government and will also look at how it has helped, as well as hindered, democracy.

The Media and the Size of Government

The watchdog function of the media helps to keep government small. Many observers feel that the press is biased against whoever holds office at the moment and that reporters want to expose them in the media. Reporters, they argue, hold disparaging views of most public officials, believing that they are self-serving, hypocritical, lacking in integrity, and preoccupied with reelection. Thus it is not surprising that journalists see a need to debunk public officials—and their policy proposals. With every new proposal being met with such skepticism, regular constraints are placed on the growth of government.

The watchdog orientation of the press can be characterized as neither liberal nor conservative, but reformist. Reporters often see their job as crusading against foul play and unfairness in government and society. It is when they focus on injustice in society that they inevitably encourage the growth of government.

[35]Bernard Cohen, *The Press and Foreign Policy* (Princeton, N.J.: Princeton University Press, 1963), 13.

Once the media identifies a problem in society—such as poverty, inadequate medical care for the aged, or poor education for certain children—reporters usually begin to ask what the government is doing about the problem. Could it be acting more effectively to solve the problem? What do people in the White House and the Congress have to say about it? In this way the media portrays government as responsible for handling almost every major problem. Though skeptical of what politicians say and do, the media reports on America's social problems in a manner that encourages government to take on more and more tasks.

Democracy and the Mass Media

As Ronald Berkman and Laura Kitch remark, "Information is the fuel of democracy."[36] Widespread access to information could be the greatest boon to democracy since the secret ballot, yet most observers think it has fallen way short of this potential. Noting the vast increase in information available through the news media, Berkman and Kitch state that "if the sheer quantity of news produced greater competency in the citizenry, then we would have a society of political masters. Yet, just the opposite is happening."[37] The rise of the "information society" has not brought about the rise of the "informed society." For one thing, thorny issues like the economy, nuclear power, and biotechnology

[36]Ronald W. Berkman and Laura W. Kitch, *Politics in the Media Age* (New York: McGraw-Hill, 1986), 311.
[37]*Ibid.,* 313.

"What'll it be—entertainment news or entertainment?"

are not well covered in the media. The media does a much better job of covering the "horse race" aspects of politics than it does of covering substantive issues.

Whenever the media is criticized for being superficial, its defense is to say that this is what people want. Network executives remark that if people suddenly started to watch shows such as the *MacNeil-Lehrer Newshour,* then they would gladly imitate them. If the American people want serious coverage of the issues, they will be happy to give it to them. Network executives claim that they are in business to make a profit, and to do so they have to appeal to the maximum number of people. It is not their fault if the resulting news coverage is superficial, they argue; blame capitalism, or blame the people—most of whom like news to be more entertaining than educational. Thus if people are not more informed in the high-tech age, it is largely because they do not care to hear about complex political issues. In this sense one can say that the people really do rule through the media.

SUMMARY

Plenty of evidence points to the power of the media in American politics. The media is ubiquitous. There is evidence that the news and its presentation are an important—perhaps the most important—shaper of public opinion on political issues. The media is an important ingredient in shaping the policy agenda, and political entrepreneurs carefully use the media for this purpose.

The media can be categorized as the print and the broadcast media. Gradually, the broadcast media has replaced the print media as the principal source of news. The media largely defines "news" as people and events out of the ordinary. Due to economic pressures, the media is biased in favor of stories with high drama that will attract people's interest, instead of extended analyses

The media's power to shape public opinion was demonstrated during the Vietnam War. Journalists brought the horrors of war—and, often, the hypocrisy of the government's policies—directly into American living rooms. When news anchor Walter Cronkite reported that, in his view, the war was unwinnable, President Johnson said that he had lost the war for public support.

of complex issues. With the media's superficial treatment of important policy issues, it should be no surprise that the incredible amount of information available to Americans today has not visibly increased their political awareness or participation.

KEY TERMS

high-tech politics	print media	talking head
mass media	broadcast media	policy agenda
media events	chains	policy entrepreneurs
press conferences	presidential debate	leak
investigative journalism	trial balloons	
censorship	sound bites	

FOR FURTHER READING

Bennett, W. Lance. *News: The Politics of Illusion,* 2nd ed. New York: Longman, 1988. A critical look at how the media distorts our view of the world.

Epstein, Edward J. *News From Nowhere: Television and the News.* New York: Random House, 1973. Although somewhat dated, this account still provides an excellent view of network news.

Graber, Doris A. *Mass Media and American Politics,* 3rd ed. Washington, D.C.: Congressional Quarterly Press, 1989. The standard textbook on the subject.

Halberstam, David. *The Powers That Be.* New York: Dell Books, 1979. A massive inquiry into the origins and influence of the *Washington Post, Los Angeles Times,* CBS, and *Time.*

Hertsgaard, Mark. *On Bended Knee: The Press and the Reagan Presidency.* New York: Farrar, Straus & Giroux, 1988. An in-depth look at how the press treated Reagan, and vice versa.

Hess, Stephen. *The Washington Reporters.* Washington, D.C.: Brookings Institution, 1981. An excellent examination of the working conditions of the Washington press corps.

Iyengar, Shanto and Donald R. Kinder. *News That Matters.* Chicago: University of Chicago Press, 1987. Two political psychologists show how the media can affect the public agenda.

Jamieson, Kathleen Hall. *Eloquence in an Electronic Age.* New York: Oxford University Press, 1988. A noted communications scholar takes a look at how television has altered political discourse.

Kingdon, John W. *Agendas, Alternatives, and Public Policy.* Boston: Little, Brown, 1984. The best overall study of the formation of the policy agenda.

Turner, Kathleen J. *Lyndon Johnson's Dual War: Vietnam and the Press.* Chicago: University of Chicago Press, 1985. The struggle between Lyndon Johnson and the press over the Vietnam War.

PART THREE

THE
POLICYMAKERS

The Development of Washington Power Centers: The White House, the Capitol, and the Supreme Court

Probably the most recognized center of political power in the world today is the White House. The oldest public building in Washington sits amid 18 acres of greenery. Its 132 rooms, 28 working fireplaces, and 20 bathrooms (all totalling 86,184 square feet) provide both an office and a home for the president. As President Coolidge once remarked, however, "Nobody lives in the White House, they just come and go."

The cornerstone for the President's House (as it was first called) was laid by George Washington on October 13, 1792—the three hundredth anniversary of Christopher Columbus's discovery of America. In the spirit of democracy, the architectural design was left up to a contest established and run by the commissioners of the new federal city. The winner was James Hoban, an Irish-born architect then living in South Carolina, who modeled his plan after the Duke of Leinster's House in Dublin. For his effort Hoban received a prize of five hundred dollars (about what a member of Congress made per year in those days). Interestingly, one of the rejected designs in the competition was signed anonymously as "A.Z." It was later revealed that A.Z. was Thomas Jefferson.

The first president to take up residence in the White House was John Adams, who moved in on November 1, 1800, from his mansion in Philadelphia. The following evening he wrote a letter to his wife, Abigail, that included the prayer Franklin Roosevelt later had carved on the mantel of the State Dining Room: "I pray heaven to bestow the best of blessing on this house and all that shall hereafter inhabit it. May none but honest and wise men ever rule under this roof." While the men who occupied the house during its early years were certainly wise and honorable, the roof leaked terribly—causing regular damage to the ceilings and furniture.

Of course, it was the British who did the most damage to the President's House, setting it afire in 1814. Legend has it that after the marks from the flames were covered up with glistening white paint the mansion first came to be known as the "White House." This is doubtful, however, as

Andrew Jackson opened the "people's house" to thousands of citizens during his 1829 inaugural party.

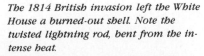

The 1814 British invasion left the White House a burned-out shell. Note the twisted lightning rod, bent from the intense heat.

reference was made to it by this name (one often used in those days for Southern plantation houses) in accounts of the fire. In any case, when President Madison issued invitations for the first New Year's Reception in the repaired structure in 1818, he referred to it as the "Executive Mansion." It was formally known by this name until 1902, when Theodore Roosevelt convinced Congress to elevate and dignify the name by which the people commonly called it.

Many presidents have remarked that the house at 1600 Pennsylvania Avenue is really the people's house. Andrew Jackson took this notion literally when he first assumed office, throwing open his new home to everyone in town. Thousands crowded into the Executive Mansion, where they partied, brawled, broke glassware, and pressed around the president until he fled by a back door. When the party ended, the house was smeared all over with the remains of

a fourteen-hundred-pound wheel of cheese that had been brought in for the occasion.

The wild party at Jackson's inauguration is one of many examples of the relatively light security in and around the White House during the nineteenth century. Even during the Civil War the front door to the mansion was open all day and late into the evening. As Margaret Leech wrote, "There was no watchman on duty in the parlors, and costly furnishings were stolen and defaced by the sightseers who roamed at will on the first floor."[1] The *Washington Star* reported that "ladies and gentlemen of high standing had been caught in the act of collecting souvenirs, and that one lady had fainted when discovered."[2] Occasionally, people wan-

[1] Margaret Leech, *Reveille in Washington, 1860–1865* (New York: Harper & Row, 1941), 331.
[2] *Ibid.*, 393.

dered aimlessly about upstairs when the attendant at the staircase was absent from his post.

When the Secret Service was given the job of protecting the president, the president's family, and the White House after the assassination of President McKinley in 1901, security improved markedly. Still, the lush White House lawn continued to be available as a picnic lunch spot for government employees. Interestingly, during World War I, the lawn was kept trim by sheep that President Wilson brought in to take the place of the White House gardeners, whom he sent off to fight. David Brinkley notes that, as late as 1941, it was still possible "to walk through the White House gate and into the grounds without showing a pass or answering any questions."[3] Anyone could even drive right up to the president's front door in the 1930s. Brinkley tells the story of a Ford convertible caught in one of Washington's sudden rainstorms during this period. The driver turned into the White House driveway, pulled up under the famous portico for shelter, put his top up, and then moved on.[4]

After World War II the White House underwent its most radical changes since the British burned it in 1814. President Harry Truman, who was accustomed to sitting out on the porch at his home in Independence, Missouri, built a balcony outside his second-floor White House study. Critics charged that Truman was meddling with the historic appearance of the building in which he was just a temporary tenant. Indeed, the back of the twenty dollar bill had to be redesigned to include the balcony in the engraving of the White House. So controversial was the new balcony that it became an issue in the 1948 presidential campaign between Truman and Thomas Dewey. A favorite Republican slogan in 1948 was that "Truman was screwy to build a porch for Dewey."

Despite his unexpected reelection victory, Truman was not able to enjoy his balcony as much as he would have liked. Eleanor Roosevelt had warned the Trumans they would have trouble with rats scurrying around the White House, but no one had any idea of just how bad a condition the house was in until structural engineers were called in to see why one of the legs on the Trumans' piano had fallen through the floor. The engineers reported that the mansion was unsafe to live in. In order to install modern plumbing and electricity, beams had been cut through without any thought as to the load they were supporting; the third floor, built in 1927, was too heavy for the walls to support, and the clay footings of the old mansion were compressing, causing the building to sink. Three alternative plans were proposed to meet the situation, two of which called for the demolition of the historic structure. Truman decided on the third and most expensive alternative, which involved completely gutting the interior and building a new steel frame within the preserved White House exterior. The paneling and interior details were

[3]David Brinkley, *Washington Goes to War* (New York: Knopf, 1988), 84.

[4]*Ibid.*

While the White House gardeners were off fighting World War I, these sheep tended to the lawn.

carefully numbered, stored, and later replaced. To defray a small portion of the renovation costs, bits and pieces of the original White House material that could not be reused were sold to souvenir collectors. (About thirty thousand bricks were purchased for a dollar each, plus shipping charges.) All told, the reconstruction took nearly four years, during which time the Trumans lived across the street in Blair House.

By the time the Trumans moved back into the White House in 1952, the eighteenth century mansion had been transformed into a twentieth century command post for nuclear war. A new and deeper basement had been dug, in which the president and his military advisors could live for an extended period of time while conducting a war. Nothing could be more telling of the president's awesome powers in the nuclear age than the situation room in the basement of the White House. It is said that President Johnson sometimes personally selected bombing targets from this room during the Vietnam War. But Johnson, like every president, was acutely aware that the fortress-like White House was not the only power center in Washington. In particular, LBJ noted that he had "never seen a Congress that didn't eventually take the measure of the President it was dealing with."[5]

The legislative power of the U.S. government is exercised sixteen blocks down Pennsylvania Avenue on Capitol Hill. Originally known as Jenkins Hill, the site for the Congress was referred to by the city's archi-

President Johnson and his key advisors struggled over Vietnam War strategy in the White House's situation room.

tect, Pierre L'Enfant, as a "pedestal waiting for a monument." Like the White House, the design for the Capitol was decided by a contest. None of the drawings submitted by the deadline proved satisfactory, however. Some were impractical and others were clearly ludicrous—such as one design which called for the dome to be topped with a monstrous weathercock with its wings spread wide. When William Thornton, a physician, inventor, and amateur architect asked for permission to submit a late entry the frustrated contest officials were therefore receptive. Thornton's design immediately "captivated the eyes and judgment of all" according to Thomas Jefferson. President Washington personally recommended Thornton's plan, writing that he was impressed by its "grandeur, simplicity and convenience." After Thornton's plan was officially approved, Washington laid the cornerstone of the Capitol on September 18, 1793,

reportedly wearing a masonic apron embroidered by Madame Lafayette. Interestingly, the plans for the Capitol called for Washington's tomb to be in the basement, but his heirs refused to have the body moved from Mount Vernon after his death.

In 1800 both Houses of Congress moved into the only building of the Capitol which was yet completed, in what is now known as the Senate wing. On November 22, 1800, President John Adams came to the new building to address the first ever joint session of Congress. Said Adams, "I congratulate you, gentlemen, on the prospect of a residence not to be changed. . . . May this territory be the residence of virtue and happiness." (It would not be until the presidency of Woodrow Wilson that a president would again come in person to address the Congress.)

A year later in 1801 the House of Representatives moved into its own separate structure. The failure to

[5]Doris Kearns, *Lyndon Johnson and the American Dream* (New York: Harper & Row, 1976), 216.

401

erect the central portion of the Capitol, connecting the Senate and House wings, made it "an architectural monstrosity—twin boxes of white stone on a shrubless heath of hard-packed stone dust, the void between them bridged by a covered boardwalk resembling the construction sheds that dotted the grounds."[6] It was not until 1827 that the link between the two

[6]James Sterling Young, *The Washington Community, 1800–1828* (New York: Harcourt Brace Jovanovich, 1966), 44.

wings was completed and crowned with a low wooden dome that Thornton had planned.

The first Senate and House chambers in the Capitol also had their problems. Part of the Senate ceiling fell in 1803, narrowly missing the vice-president, and again in 1808, killing the Senate clerk. Hot-air furnaces installed directly under the floor of the House of Representatives emanated so much heat that the lower chamber became popularly known as "the Oven." Furthermore, the demo-

cratic process was hampered by the poor acoustics in both chambers. One Representative declared from the floor of the House that it "was perfectly unfit for the purpose of legislation, and that it was impossible in its present state, either to hear or be heard."[7] The Senate chamber echoed. At the desk where Henry Clay sat, whispering could be clearly heard from a number of feet away, leading some to speculate that the "Great Compromiser" was able to work out his deals after overhearing what various key Senators were saying in private.

After Clay's intricate compromise of 1850 kept the union precariously together for ten more years, plans were begun for a magnificent new cast-iron dome for the Capitol. This impressive dome was inspired by the world's first iron dome at St. Isaac's Cathedral in St. Petersburg (now Leningrad). Its height was set at 285 feet above the eastern plaza as this was as high as the local fire department's equipment could then reach. The basic design has since been copied by many state capitols, but only the dome in Austin, Texas is higher—by a margin of seven feet.

[7]*Ibid.,* 45.

What George Washington had earlier described as the "grandeur, simplicity and convenience" of the original Capitol is evident in this 1846 photograph.

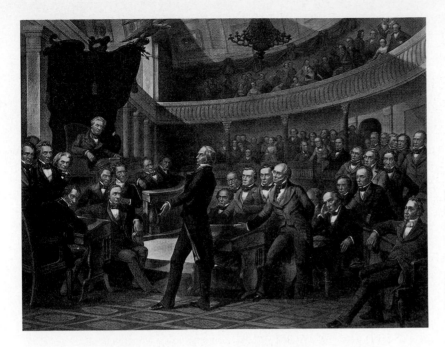

When President Lincoln was inaugurated the Capitol dome was roughly half completed. In spite of the Civil War Lincoln ordered that the construction continue. "If people see the Capitol going on," Lincoln said, "it is a sign we intend the Union shall go on." On December 2, 1863, the last of five sections of a nineteen-foot-tall, seven-ton statue entitled *Freedom* was hoisted up to crown the dome. The bronze statue depicts a woman in flowing garments with one hand on a shield and the other on a sheathed sword. Originally, the headpiece of the statue was to be a liberty cap modeled after those worn by the emancipated slaves of Rome. Mississippi's Jefferson Davis, then U.S. secretary of war but soon to become president of the Confederacy, objected to this symbolism. Thus a helmet with an eagle head and feathers was used instead, which to this day is often mistaken for an Indian warrior.

In the twentieth century the expansion of congressional powers and activities can be seen not so much in the continuing additions to the Capitol itself but rather in the construction of supporting office buildings all around it. In 1908 the first House office building opened, followed by the first Senate office building in 1909. As the number of employees of the legislative branch increased from a mere six thousand in 1908 to approximately forty thousand today, Capitol Hill grew as well. Four more office buildings were built to house the rapidly increasing staff, along with a massive underground network of support services. In what some refer to as the

The Capitol's new cast iron dome was completed during the Civil War.

"congressional catacombs" one can now find such amenities as a private subway system, exercise rooms, barber shops, restaurants, post offices, banks, airline ticket offices, print shops, and many others. Gradually, a whole miniature city has been built to support the Congress. When the Congress met in joint session on March 2, 1989, to mark the two hundredth anniversary of its first meeting, it had surely come a long way.

The Supreme Court, by contrast, has never had any desire for a fortress like the White House or a city unto itself like Capitol Hill. All it ever wanted for the first century and a half of its existence was a place of its own. A separate home for the Court, as proposed by L'Enfant, was not to come about until the twentieth century. Raising the funds to build the Executive Mansion and the Capitol had strained the limits of the new federal city's budget. Clearing the swamp area that L'Enfant had planned to use for the judicial branch did not

seem fiscally prudent given the small volume of business then handled by the Court. In its first two terms, for example, there were no cases at all on the docket. Selection of officers, the framing of rules, and admission of members to its bar were all the Court had to keep itself occupied in its early years. Thus at the time it seemed quite reasonable to simply allocate a portion of the Capitol for the Court to do its work.

The Congress, however, was far from generous with its space. The Court was relegated to such a small corner in the basement of the Capitol that the justices were compelled to put on their robes in the presence of spectators. The ultimate indignity, though, came after the British burned the Capitol, when the Supreme Court had to meet for one term in a local tavern. In an 1850 report on the extension of the Capitol, it was noted that "the members had suffered much from the inconvenience of the Courtroom, and from its cold, damp loca-

The Supreme Court found a home in the former Senate chamber from 1860 to 1935.

tion which had proved injurious to health."[8] Once the extension was completed, the Court was treated to a hand-me-down: the old Senate chamber and offices. There it resided from 1860 to 1935.

When former President Taft took over as chief justice in 1921 (the only person ever to have served in both positions), he found the Supreme Court's quarters untenable. With the expanding administrative workload of the Court, the twelve rooms it had for offices were hardly adequate. As Taft complained, the shelves in the Court's conference room were stacked so high that it would take an airplane to reach the top ones. Using his considerable political skills and experience, the ex-president lobbied intensely for the Court to have a building of its own.

This March 2, 1989, joint session of Congress met in the House chamber to mark the beginning of its third century of work.

[8]Catherine Hetos Skefos, "The Supreme Court Gets a Home," in *Yearbook 1976* (Washington, D.C.: Supreme Court Historical Society, 1977), 26.

In 1929 he at last succeeded in gaining an appropriation of about ten million dollars to build on the site of the old Capital Prison, roughly halfway between the House and Senate office buildings.

Designed by architect Cass Gilbert, the Supreme Court building reflects a dignified grandeur: 24,700 pieces of marble were required for the exterior walls alone. Within the building, two self-supporting cantilevered marble spiral staircases ascend five stories. (The only other places in the world with such staircases are the Paris Opera House and the Vatican.) So intent was Gilbert on getting the finest marble possible that he journeyed to Rome to meet with fascist dictator Benito Mussolini to ask his assistance in dealing with the best Italian quarries.

Inside the building the courtroom itself is surprisingly small, allowing for the seating of just 355 people. Rich velvet curtains behind the justices' bench and the colonnade provide an imposing background, however. Elaborately carved chairs

The solemn dignity of this courtroom offers an appropriate—as well as imposing—setting for the Supreme Court to hear its cases.

were designed for the nine justices, but they preferred to retain the old leather chairs they had traditionally used. Today visitors to the Court are still struck by the somewhat disorderly look of the varying heights of the justices' chairs.

While the Court is no longer a poor orphan seeking shelter within the confines of the Capitol, it, like the executive, remains dependent on congressional appropriations. Soon after moving into their pristine new building, the justices became upset by starlings regularly soiling the majestic columns. Proposing to drive the birds away by installing electric wires, the Court asked Congress for special funds for this purpose. The chair of the House Appropriations Committee refused, however, stating: "If they drive the starlings off the Court they'll just fly across the street to the Capitol and roost on us."[9]

As the above story illustrates, power in Washington is carefully guarded, but also decentralized. Today power is increasingly being spread out beyond the White House, Capitol, and the Supreme Court as the size and scope of government continues to grow. The last photo essay, in Part Four, will examine the proliferation of Washington policy-making centers. ►►►►

The modern Supreme Court building is often called the "Marble Palace."

[9]Brinkley, *Washington Goes to War*, 8.

405

12

Congress

In January 1989 Ronald Reagan submitted his last budget to Congress. The budget included a 51 percent pay increase for members of Congress, raising their annual salaries to $135,000. The pay raise had been planned for months. The Quadrennial Commission, a blue-ribbon panel that meets every four years to make recommendations to the president about pay levels for approximately twenty-five hundred federal officials including members of Congress, cabinet officers, and federal judges, had endorsed the large pay raise to compensate for two decades of inflation and to provide incentives for Congress to abandon honoraria, the large sums members may receive for speaking to organized interests.

When President Bush took office shortly after Reagan submitted his budget, he also endorsed the pay raise. In addition, almost every member of Congress who chose to run for election in the 1988 elections had won, and most had won by comfortable margins. Things looked good for the pay raise.

Yet congressional leaders still feared a voter backlash to raising their salaries, so they devised a plan in which the pay raise would take effect automatically unless both the House and the Senate passed and the president signed a resolution blocking the raise. The use of this arcane procedure was to shield what was happening from the public eye. The pay raise proposal was also coupled with a provision prohibiting the acceptance of honoraria. This provision provided political justification for the increase in pay.

Then things started to unravel. Editorial writers pummeled Congress for both the size of the hike and for skirting a vote. Mail from angry constituents, who knew little about honoraria but a lot about salaries, flooded Capitol Hill. Many members, privately hoping for a pay raise, responded to their constituents and started to publicly criticize the pay raise. Consumer activist Ralph Nader, Common Cause, and others began organizing protests to the raise.

In a fund-raising newsletter Lee Atwater, chairman of the Republican National Committee, lambasted Democrats for supporting the pay raise. Although he later admitted that he had made a mistake, his actions made Democrats nervous about criticism in the next election.

In a setback to the House Democratic leadership, pay raise opponents—many of them Democrats— won a procedural vote that forced the Speaker of the House, the most powerful member of Congress, to schedule a vote to block the raise. The House eventually voted 380 to 48 to kill the pay raise, and the Senate followed suit by a 94 to 6 margin.

This is the world of Congress: the prominent role of the president in the passage of legislation; leaders that cannot control followers; constituents that continue to reelect their representatives and senators but know little about them and dislike Congress as a whole; partisan politics; a mass media anxious to raise issues of congressional ethics; constant concerns for responsiveness to constituents and reelection, even at the *beginning* of a term; active, organized interest groups; and the constant potential for a firestorm of criticism. Clearly, Congress is at the center of American politics; this chapter examines its important position.

T he framers of the Constitution conceived of Congress as the center of policy-making in America. The great disputes over public policy were to be resolved there—not in the White House or the Supreme Court. Although the prominence of Congress has ebbed and flowed over the course of American history, in recent years Congress has been the true center of power in Washington.

Congress's tasks become more difficult each year. It passes the budget of the national government and declares American wars (if the president has not

beaten Congress to it) as it always has, but the rush of legislation through the congressional labyrinth has never been more complicated. On any day a representative or senator can be required to make a sensible judgment about nuclear missiles, nuclear waste dumps, abortion, trade competition with Japan, the enormous federal deficit, the soaring costs of Social Security and Medicare, and countless other issues.

Just finding time to debate these issues has become increasingly difficult. For one thing, most important congressional activity is done in individual offices and in committee rooms, not in the House and Senate chambers. The Senate ("the world's greatest deliberative body," it likes to call itself) has little time for deliberation. Former Senate Majority Leader Howard Baker said that moving the Senate is like "trying to push a wet noodle." Much the same story is true in the House.

Many within and outside Congress are frustrated. Oklahoma Representative Mike Synar swears that while visiting a Cub Scout pack in Grove, Oklahoma, he asked if any of the boys could tell him the difference between Congress and the Cub Scouts. One boy replied: "We have adult supervision."[1]

Why do such frustrations exist in a body that each member puts blood, sweat, tears, and a great deal of money into joining? Some are frustrated with the tremendous, disjointed agenda of Congress. Said one perceptive midwestern senator:

> We are losing control of what we are doing here. . . . There isn't enough time in a day to keep abreast of everything we should know to legislate responsibly, dealing with so many bills, having to attend so many committee and subcommittee meetings,

---

[1]Gregg Easterbrook, "What's Wrong with Congress?" *Atlantic Monthly,* December 1984, 57.

listening to lobbyists, having to worry about problems of constituents, and, of course, keeping a close watch on politics back home. You know, one *has* to get reelected.[2]

Other frustrations concern the lobbying explosion, which was discussed in Chapter 10. On key votes, as senators and representatives stream into the chambers from all over Capitol Hill, lobbyists stand near the doorways buttonholing waverers or slashing a thumbs-up or thumbs-down sign to their supporters. Thousands of dollars in campaign contributions ride on the outcome. Still others are frustrated with the fragmentation of power in the Congress itself. Members of Congress can be, and often are, fiercely independent. (Senate Minority Leader Robert Dole once dryly observed that "we have a lot of self-starters here. The last time I counted, there were one hundred." The Senate, said his predecessor as Republican leader, Howard Baker, was as unwieldy as "hogs on ice.")

To complicate matters further, nowhere is the issue of ethics in government raised as often or in as titillating a manner as in regard to Congress. Nineteen eighty-nine was an especially notable year for ethical questions. Speaker of the House Jim Wright of Texas and House Majority Whip Tony Coelho of California both resigned amid charges of financial improprieties. Wright's Republican accuser, House Minority Whip Newt Gingrich of Georgia, was himself under investigation for financial misdeeds. Ethical violations seemed so common that comedian Jay Leno cracked, "The Home Shopping Network announced it's going to merge with C-SPAN, for those of you who want the convenience of buying a politician in the privacy of your own home."

Frustrating or not, there is no shortage of men and women running for congressional office. The following sections will introduce you to these people.

Former Speaker of the House Jim Wright announces his resignation in June of 1989. Wright's fall from power was the most dramatic in a series of finance- and sex-related scandals that have recently rocked Congress.

THE REPRESENTATIVES AND SENATORS

Being a member of Congress is a difficult and unusual job. A person must be willing to spend considerable time, trouble, and money to obtain a crowded office on Capitol Hill. To nineteenth-century humorist Artemus Ward, such a quest was inexplicable: "It's easy to see why a man goes to the poorhouse or the penitentiary. It's because he can't help it. But why he should voluntarily go live in Washington is beyond my comprehension."

The Job

Perhaps the most prominent characteristic of a member of Congress's job is hard work. Representatives and senators deeply resent popular beliefs that they are overpaid, underworked, corrupt, and ineffective. Members have even commissioned their own time-and-motion studies of their efficiency to demonstrate that they do work hard (see Table 12.1). For example, the typical representative is a member of about six committees and subcommittees; a senator is a member of about ten.[3] Contrary to the laws of physics, members are often scheduled to be in two places at the same time.

---

[2]Quoted in Tad Szulc, "Is Congress Obsolete?" *Saturday Review,* March 3, 1979, 20.

[3]Steven S. Smith and Christopher J. Deering, *Committees in Congress* (Washington, D.C.: Congressional Quarterly Press, 1984), 53.

Table 12.1 A Representative's "Average Day"

ACTIVITY	AVERAGE TIME
In the House chamber	Total 2:53 hours
In committee/subcommittee work	
Hearings	26 minutes
Business	9 minutes
Markups	42 minutes
Other	7 minutes
	Total 1:24 hours
In his or her office	
With constituents	17 minutes
With organized groups	9 minutes
With others	20 minutes
With staff aides	53 minutes
With other representatives	5 minutes
Answering mail	46 minutes
Preparing legislation, speeches	12 minutes
Reading	11 minutes
On the telephone	26 minutes
	Total 3:19 hours
In other Washington locations	
With constituents at the Capitol	9 minutes
At events	33 minutes
With leadership	3 minutes
With other representatives	11 minutes
With informal groups	8 minutes
In party meetings	5 minutes
Personal time	28 minutes
Other	25 minutes
	Total 2:02 hours
Other	Total 1:40 hours
Total average representative's day	11:18 hours

Source: U.S. House of Representatives, Commission on Administrative Review, *Administrative Reorganization and Legislative Management* (95th Congress, 1st session, 1977, H. Doc. 95–232): 18–19.

There are attractions to the job, however. First and foremost is power. Members of Congress make key decisions about important matters of public policy. In addition, the salary and the perks that go with it make the job tolerable. Members of Congress receive the following:

- A salary of $124,400 for representatives and $101,400 for senators (who also may accept $23,568 of "honoraria" for making speeches), high by most Americans' standards, but well below that of four hundred corporation presidents who earn more than $250,000 annually
- Free office space in Washington and in their constituency, usually cramped with staffers who practically sit on top of one another

- A staff allowance of almost $407,000 for each member of the House and anywhere from about $970,000 to about $1,683,000 for each senator, depending on the size of the state

- Handsome travel allowances to see their constituents each year, plus opportunities to travel at low fares or even free to foreign nations on congressional inquiries (what critics call "junkets")

- Virtually unlimited franking privileges—the free use of the mails to communicate with constituents—costing Congress almost $150 million a year, on top of the $4 million to $5 million it spends on machines that duplicate a member's signature in real ink (it will even smear if a constituent should test its authenticity)

- Generous retirement benefits

- Plenty of small privileges like free flowers from the National Botanical Gardens, research services from the Library of Congress, exercise rooms and pools, and cut-rate meals and haircuts

Despite the salaries, the perquisites, and the twenty-five thousand staff members, Congress is relatively inexpensive. Per citizen, Americans spend annually about the equivalent of the cost of a hamburger, fries, and cola at a favorite fast-food franchise on running the nation's legislature.

The People

There are 535 members of Congress. An even hundred, two from each state, are members of the Senate. The other 435 are members of the House of Representatives. The Constitution specifies only that members of the House must

Members of Congress who do not share their constituents' economic and social backgrounds can nonetheless represent their concerns. Senator Edward Kennedy, for example, born into one of America's wealthiest families, has championed the poor and underprivileged throughout his career. Here Kennedy speaks to flood victims in West Virginia.

be at least twenty-five years old and have been American citizens for seven years, that senators must be at least thirty and have been American citizens for nine years, and that all must be residents of the states from which they are elected.

By no stretch of the imagination could anyone call the members of Congress typical or average Americans. Elite theorists are quick to point out that members come mostly from occupations with high status and usually have substantial incomes. Although calling the Senate a "rich man's club" is an exaggeration, the proportion of millionaires and near-millionaires in Congress is much higher than in an average crowd of 535 people. If one looks at a collective portrait of the Congress, as in Table 12.2, one quickly discovers what an atypical collection of Americans it is. Law is the dominant occupation, with other elite occupations— business and academia—also well represented.

Only a handful (twenty-four) of representatives are African American (compared with about 12 percent of the total population), and almost all of those

Table 12.2 **A Portrait of the 101st Congress: Some Statistics**

CHARACTERISTIC	HOUSE (435 total)	SENATE (100 total)
Party		
Democrat	260	55
Republican	175	45
Sex		
Men	410	98
Women	25	2
Race		
Black	24	0
Hispanic	12	0
White and other	399	100
Average Age		
	52 years	56 years
Religion		
Protestant	274	72
Roman Catholic	120	19
Jewish	31	8
Other and unspecified	10	1
Prior Occupation[a]		
Law	184	63
Business and banking	138	28
Education	42	11
Public service/politics	94	20
Agriculture	19	4
Journalism	17	8

[a]Some members specify more than one occupation
Source: *Congressional Quarterly Weekly Report*, November 12, 1988.

representatives are elected from overwhelmingly black constituencies. No state is mostly black, and there are now no African Americans in the Senate. There are twelve Hispanics in the House. In terms of numbers, though, women are the most underrepresented group: half the population is female, but only two senators and twenty-five representatives are female.

How important are the personal characteristics of members of Congress? Since power in Congress is highly decentralized, the backgrounds of representatives and senators could be important if they influence how those officials vote on issues. Can a group of predominantly white, upper-middle-class, middle-aged Protestant males adequately represent a much more diverse population? On the other hand, how effective would a group of demographically average people be in making major policy decisions?

Obviously, members of Congress cannot claim *descriptive* representation, that is, representing constituents through mirroring their personal, politically relevant characteristics. They may engage in *substantive* representation, representing the interests of groups. For example, members of Congress with a background of wealth and privilege, such as Senator Edward Kennedy, can be champions of the interests of the poor.[4] Moreover, most members of Congress have lived for many years in the constituencies they represent and share the beliefs and attitudes of at least a large proportion of their constituents. If they do not share such perspectives, they may find it difficult to keep their seats. The next sections will examine just how members of Congress obtain their positions in the first place.

CONGRESSIONAL ELECTIONS

Congressional elections are wearing, expensive,[5] and, as you will see, generally foregone conclusions—yet the role of politician is the most universal one in Congress. Men and women may run for Congress to forge new policy initiatives, but they also run because they are politicians, because they enjoy politics, and because a position in Congress is near the top of their chosen profession. Even if they dislike politics, without reelection they will not be around long enough to shape policy.

Who Wins?

Everyone in Congress is a politician, and every politician has his or her eye on the next election. The players in the congressional election game are the incumbents and the challengers.

Incumbents are those already holding office. Sometime during each term, the incumbent has to decide whether to run again or to retire voluntarily. Most will decide to have another go at it and will enter their party's primary, almost always emerge victorious (only two members of Congress lost in 1986 and only one in 1988), and typically win in the November general election, too. Indeed,

[4]On various views of representation, see Hanna Pitkin, *The Concept of Representation* (Berkeley, Calif.: University of California Press, 1967).

[5]An excellent review of the costs of congressional campaigns and the uses to which money is put in them is Edie N. Goldenberg and Michael W. Traugott, *Campaigning for Congress* (Washington, D.C.: Congressional Quarterly Press, 1984).

the most important fact about congressional elections is this: *Incumbents usually win.*

Thus, the most important resource to ensure an opponent's defeat is *not* having more money than an opponent, although that helps. It is *not* being more photogenic, though that helps, too. The best thing a candidate can have going for him or her is simply to be the incumbent (see Figure 12.1).

Gary Jacobson's study of congressional elections puts it like this: for House elections "the picture seems clear enough.... On the average, fewer than 2 percent...are defeated in primary elections and fewer than 7 percent lose general elections."[6] Not only do more than 90 percent of the incumbents seeking reelection win (99 percent won in 1988), but they tend to win with big electoral margins. In 1988 more than 87 percent of the House incumbents won with more than 60 percent of the vote. Perhaps most astonishing of all, the evidence is that even when challengers' positions on the issues are closer to the voters' positions, incumbents still tend to win.[7]

[6]Gary C. Jacobson, *The Politics of Congressional Elections,* 2nd ed. (Boston: Little, Brown, 1987), 26.

[7]John L. Sullivan and Eric Uslaner, "Congressional Behavior and Electoral Marginality," *American Journal of Political Science* 22 (August 1978): 536–53.

Figure 12.1   The Incumbency Factor in Congressional Elections

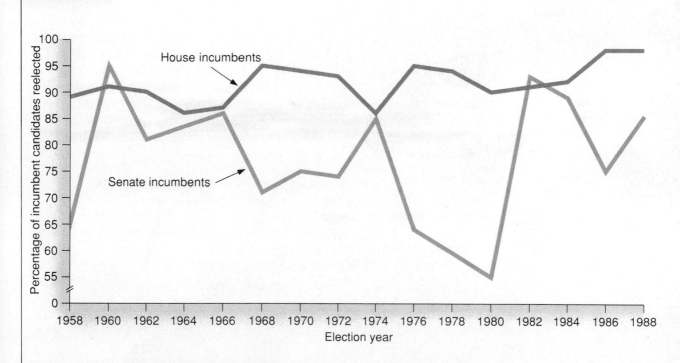

Source: Norman J. Ornstein, Thomas E. Mann, and Michael J. Malbin, *Vital Statistics on Congress, 1987–1988* (Washington D.C.: American Enterprise Institute, 1987), and *Congressional Quarterly Weekly Report* November 2, 1988. Figures reflect incumbents running in both primary and general elections.

The picture for the Senate is a little different. Even though senators still have a better-than-even chance of beating back a challenge, the odds are hardly as handsome as for House incumbents, and senators win by narrower margins (only 62 percent of the incumbent senators seeking reelection in 1988 won with more than 60 percent of the vote). One reason is that an entire state is almost always more diverse than a congressional district and thus provides more of a base for opposition to an incumbent. At the same time, senators have less personal contact with their constituencies, which on average are nearly ten times larger than those of members of the House of Representatives. Senators also receive more coverage in the media than representatives do and are more likely to be held accountable on controversial issues. Moreover, senators tend to draw more visible challengers, such as governors or members of the House, who are already known to voters and who have substantial financial backing—a factor that lessens the advantages of incumbency. Many of these challengers, as one might expect, know that the Senate is a stepping-stone to national prominence and sometimes even the presidency.

Despite their success at reelection, incumbents have a strong feeling of vulnerability. As Thomas Mann put it, members of Congress perceive themselves as "unsafe at any margin."[8] Thus they have been raising and spending more campaign funds, sending more mail to their constituents, traveling more to their states and districts, and staffing more local offices than ever before.[9] They realize that with the decline of partisan loyalty in the electorate, they bear more of the burden of obtaining votes.

The Advantages of Incumbents

There are several possible explanations for the success of incumbents. One is that voters know how their elected representatives vote on important policy issues and agree with their stands, sending them back to Washington to keep up the good work. This, however, is not the case. In fact, voters are rather oblivious to how their senators and representatives actually vote.[10] As one expert put it, "Mass public knowledge of congressional candidates declines precipitously once we move beyond simple recognition, generalized feelings, and incumbent job ratings."[11]

Another possibility is that voter assessments of presidential candidates influence their voting for Congress. Stories of presidential "coattails" (so called because other candidates were said to ride into office by clinging to presidential coattails) seem to be just stories.[12] (More than half the Democrats elected to the

[8]Thomas Mann, *Unsafe at Any Margin* (Washington, D.C.: American Enterprise Institute, 1978).

[9]Glenn R. Parker, *Homeward Bound* (Pittsburgh: University of Pittsburgh Press, 1986); and John R. Johannes, *To Serve the People* (Lincoln, Neb.: University of Nebraska Press, 1984).

[10]Actually, only about 17 percent of the population can make an accurate guess about how their representatives have voted on *any* issue in Congress. Patricia Hurley and Kim Q. Hill, "The Prospects for Issue Voting in Contemporary Congressional Elections," *American Politics Quarterly* 8 (October 1980): 446.

[11]Mann, *Unsafe at Any Margin,* 37.

[12]That presidential elections and congressional elections are not closely related is an argument made in Lyn Ragsdale, "The Fiction of Congressional Elections as Presidential Events," *American Politics Quarterly* 8 (October 1980): 375–98.

House in 1988 won their seats in districts carried by Republican George Bush.) Nor do members of Congress gain or lose very much from the ups and downs of the economy.[13] So if voters know little about how their representatives and senators vote, if presidential effects are unconnected with congressional races, and if economic conditions do not have much impact, what accounts for the success of congressional incumbents?

Members of Congress engage in three primary activities that increase the probability of their reelections: advertising, credit claiming, and position taking.[14]

Advertising   For members of Congress, *advertising* means much more than placing ads in the newspapers and on television. Most congressional advertising takes place between elections and takes the form of contact with constituents. The goal is *visibility.*

Members of Congress work hard to get themselves known in their constituencies. As Table 12.3 demonstrates, they usually succeed. Not surprisingly, members concentrate on staying visible. Trips home are frequent. The average member will make about thirty-five trips back to their home district every year.[15]

---

[13]John R. Owens and Edward C. Olson, "Economic Fluctuations and Congressional Elections," *American Journal of Political Science* 24 (August 1980): 469–93; and Benjamin Radcliff, "Solving a Puzzle: Aggregate Analysis and Economic Voting Revisited," *Journal of Politics* 50 (May 1988): 440–58.

[14]David R. Mayhew, *Congress: The Electoral Connection* (New Haven, Conn.: Yale University Press, 1974).

[15]Richard F. Fenno, Jr., *Home Style* (Boston: Little, Brown, 1978), 32.

Table 12.3   **Contact with Members of Congress (Percentage of Constituents Having Contact)**

Members of Congress have very high levels of contact with their constituents. This contact is not simply a product of advertisements during an ongoing election campaign. Note that the percentages of constituents who have had contact with senators running and not running for reelection are almost identical; it is continuous attention to constituents that brings visibility.

TYPE OF CONTACT	REPRE-SENTATIVES	SENATORS (running for reelection)	SENATORS (not running for reelection)
Received mail from	73	77	72
Saw on television	60	90	84
Read something about	65	86	84
Heard on radio	30	55	54
Attended meeting	13	20	19
Met personally	16	18	16
Met with staff	9	16	15

Source: A 1988 National Election Study (conducted by the University of Michigan) and a 1988 Senate Election Study.

Credit Claiming   Congresspersons also engage in credit claiming, which involves personal and district service. One member told Richard Fenno about the image he tried to cultivate in his constituency:

> [I have] a very high recognition factor. And of all the things said about me, none of them said, "He's a conservative or a liberal," or "He votes this way on such and such an issue." None of that at all. There were two things said. One, "He works hard." Two, "He works for us." Nothing more than that. So we made it our theme, "O'Connor gets things done"; and we emphasized the dams, the highways, the buildings, the casework.[16]

Like most members of Congress, this representative quickly discovered that service can help spell success. His campaign literature stressed fourteen thousand individuals "helped with problems involving the federal government," twenty-five thousand "incidental requests" met, twenty thousand letters on "national issues" answered, seven hundred "community projects" assisted, and the candidate's 93 percent attendance record in Congress. Not how members vote but how many folks know them and how these people size up their service to them are what counts for reelection.

Morris Fiorina has stressed this close link between service and success.[17] Members of Congress, he says, *can* go to the voters and stress their policy–making record. They *can* make promises about their stands on new policy issues on the agenda. The problem with facing the voters on one's record— past, present, and future—is that policy positions make enemies as well as friends. A member of Congress's vote for reducing government spending may win some friends, but it will make enemies of voters who happen to connect that vote with service cutbacks. Besides, a congressperson can almost never show that he or she alone was responsible for a major policy. Being only one of 435 members of the House or of 100 senators, a person can hardly promise to end inflation, cut taxes, or achieve equal rights for women single-handedly.

One thing, though, always wins friends and almost never makes enemies: *servicing the constituency.* There are two ways members of Congress can service their constituencies: through casework and through the pork barrel. **Casework** is helping constituents as individuals, cutting through some bureaucratic red tape to get people what they think they have a right to get. The **pork barrel** is the mighty list of federal projects, grants, and contracts available to cities, businesses, colleges, and institutions.

Do you have trouble getting your check from the Social Security Administration on time? Call your congressperson, who can cut red tape. Do you have trouble getting federal bureaucrats to respond to Pottsville's request for federal construction money? Call your congressperson. Representatives and senators can single-handedly take credit for each of these favors. Fiorina put it like this:

> Even committee chairmen have a difficult time claiming credit for a piece of major legislation, let alone a rank-and-file congressman. Ah, but casework, and the pork barrel. In dealing with the bureaucracy, the congressman is not merely one vote in

---

[16]*Ibid.,* 106–7.

[17]The "service spells success" argument is made in Morris P. Fiorina, *Congress: Keystone of the Washington Establishment,* 2nd ed. (New Haven, Conn.: Yale University Press, 1989), and, with a slightly different emphasis, in Glenn R. Parker, "The Advantages of Incumbency in Congressional Elections," *American Politics Quarterly* 8 (October 1980): 449–61.

435. Rather he is a nonpartisan power, someone whose phone calls snap an office to attention. He is not kept on hold. The constituent who receives aid believes that his congressman and his congressman alone got results. Similarly, congressman find it easy to claim credit for federal projects awarded in their districts. The congressman may have instigated the project in the first place, issued regular progress reports, and ultimately announced the award through his office. Maybe he can't claim credit for the 1965 Voting Rights Act, but he can take credit for Littletown's spanking new sewage treatment plant.[18]

Getting things done for the folks back home often gets an incumbent the chance to serve them again.

Critics often raise the question of whether pork barrel expenditures for particular constituencies really serve the national interest, especially in times of large budget deficits. Members of Congress are inclined to agree with Representive Jamie Whitten of Mississippi, the powerful chairman of the House Appropriations Committee, that pork barrel is "what [is done] in the other fella's district"—getting money for one's own constituents, in other words, is simply being a good representative. Silvio Conte of Massachusetts, the senior Republican on the committee, often complained loudly about other members seeking pork barrel projects for their constituencies, even appearing on the House floor wearing a pig's mask. But in the best tradition of congressional double-talk, in 1989 he made a blunt appeal to his colleagues for a two-million dollar science research project for Smith College, which is located in his district. When it comes to federal expenditures, members of Congress rarely see a conflict between the national interest and the interests of their constituencies.

Because pork barrel incentives are so great, Congress often has a difficult time containing itself, as is the case with military bases, which provide jobs and money for a local economy. The Pentagon has traditionally found it almost impossible to close unnecessary military bases because of opposition from members of Congress. The budget crises of the 1980s and 1990s, however, have provided incentives to tame congressional avarice, and Congress has empowered an independent commission to recommend bases to be closed or scaled back. If approved by the secretary of defense, the entire list takes effect automatically unless Congress passes a law rejecting it as a whole. In 1989 eighty-six military bases were targeted for closure, and Congress upheld the commission's recommendations. Dozens more were earmarked for closure in 1990.

As a result of the advantages of incumbency in advertising and credit claiming, incumbents, especially in the House, are usually much better known and have a more favorable public image than their opponents.[19] Shrewd use of the resources available to incumbents may give them an advantage (see "You Are the Policymaker: Should Incumbents Advertise at Taxpayer Expense?"), but congressional elections are not determined solely by casework and pork barrel.[20] Other factors play a role as well.

Representative Silvio Conte used a pig nose and ears to protest pork barrel spending—until he wanted multimillion dollar federal grants for his Massachusetts district. Because credit claiming is so important to reelection, members of Congress rarely pass up the opportunity to increase federal spending in their state or district.

[18]Fiorina, *Congress: Keystone of the Washington Establishment,* 2nd ed., 43.

[19]Jacobson, *The Politics of Congressional Elections,* 108–22.

[20]See, for example, Paul Feldman and James Jondrow, "Congressional Elections and Local Federal Spending," *American Journal of Political Science* 28 (February 1984): 147–63; Glenn R. Parker and Suzanne L. Parker, "The Correlates and Effects of Attention to District by U.S. House Members," *Legislative Studies Quarterly* 10 (May 1985): 223–42; and John C. McAdams and John R. Johannes, "Congressmen, Perquisites, and Elections," *Journal of Politics* 50 (May 1988): 412–39.

Should Incumbents Advertise at Taxpayer Expense?

Perhaps the most effective means of engaging in advertising, credit claiming, and position taking at the same time is the congressional newsletter. It is simple to use, reaches virtually all voters, and best of all (for incumbents)—it is free.

The *franking privilege* (free use of the mail for members of Congress) was originally provided to allow members to answer constituents' mail. Only about 5 percent of the over one billion pieces of congressional mail sent each year is used for this purpose, however. Most of the rest is devoted to mailing newsletters. Until 1990 each member of Congress could make up to six mass mailings a year. Now they are limited to three.

To send out a newsletter, members of Congress need only to have their staff write one, have it printed (at taxpayer expense, of course), and address it to "postal patron." It is then the job of the Postal Service to deliver one to *every* dwelling in their constituency.

As you might expect, this kind of mail is sent out in ever increasing quantities as election day approaches. For a while it peaked in October right before election day. October mailings are now banned, so the mailings peak in September. In 1987, a non-election year, the House spent forty-four million dollars on mail. In 1988 it jumped to seventy-eight million dollars. The increase of thirty-four million dollars in the election year can be said to be the amount of public money House members spent on their reelections through the frank. This comes to about seventy-eight thousand dollars per representative.

A typical newsletter, such as Texas representative Joe Barton's, is not used to raise controversial issues. The cover boldly proclaims Barton the taxpayers' friend (certainly a courageous position given the amount spent on the newsletter). Inside are pictures and stories showing him taking a firm stand against child pornography, touring a law enforcement center (his contribution in the fight against illegal drugs), visiting with a group of sixth graders from his constituency, and announcing several routine grants received in his district. In general, the stories are designed to appeal to everyone and reflect well upon his legislative and leadership abilities.

Proponents of the newsletter argue that it is an essential link between members of Congress and their

constituents. It is an opportunity, they say, to inform citizens who otherwise pay little attention to what occurs in Washington.

Others suggest the newsletters are simply another means of incumbents assuring their reelections and that they should be eliminated altogether, saving the taxpayers' money. Congress seems to have little inclination to approve such a proposal. If you were in Congress, what would *you* do? Would you vote to spend tax dollars on newsletters for incumbents? Or would you insist that members of Congress communicate with their constituents in less costly (and less politically effective) ways?

Position Taking Members of Congress must also engage in *position taking* on matters of public policy when they vote on issues and when they respond to constituents' questions about where they stand on issues. You have seen that in establishing their public images, members of Congress emphasize their personal qualities as experienced, hardworking, trustworthy representatives who have served their constituencies, an image often devoid of partisan or programmatic content. Nevertheless, all members must take policy stands, and the positions they take may make a difference in the outcome of an election, especially if the issues are on matters salient to voters and their stands are out of line with those of a majority of their constituents. This is especially the case in elections for the Senate, in which issues are likely to play a greater role than in House elections.

Weak Opponents Another advantage for incumbents is that they are likely to face weak opponents. Seeing the advantages of incumbency, potentially effective opponents are often unlikely to risk challenging members of the House.[21] Those who do run are usually not well known or well qualified and lack experience as well as organizational and financial backing.[22] The lack of adequate campaign funds is a special burden, because challengers need money to become as well known to voters as incumbents are from their advertising and claim taking.[23]

The Role of Party Identification

At the base of every electoral coalition are the members of the candidate's *party* in the constituency. Although party loyalty at the voting booth is not as strong as it was a generation ago, it is still a good predictor of voting behavior. In the 1988 congressional elections, for example, about three-fourths of voters who identified with a party voted for Senate or House candidates of their party.[24] Most members of Congress represent constituencies in which their party is in the majority.

Defeating Incumbents

In light of the advantages of incumbents, it is reasonable to reflect with Jacobson that "since most incumbents do work hard to remain in office and are therefore extremely difficult to defeat, it is not absurd to ask why . . . anyone challenges them at all."[25] One of the main reasons, Jacobson suggests, is simply that chal-

---

[21]On strategies of challengers, see Gary C. Jacobson and Samuel Kernell, *Strategy and Choice in Congressional Elections,* 2nd ed. (New Haven, Conn.: Yale University Press, 1983); and Gary Jacobson, "Strategic Politicians and the Dynamics of U.S. House Elections, 1946–1986," *American Political Science Review* 83 (September 1989); 773–94.

[22]See Gary Jacobson, *Money in Congressional Elections* (New Haven, Conn.: Yale University Press, 1980).

[23]On the importance of challenger quality and financing, see Alan I. Abramowitz, "Explaining Senate Election Outcomes," *American Political Science Review* 82 (June 1988): 385–403; Donald Philip Green and Jonathan S. Krasno, "Salvation for the Spendthrift Incumbent," *American Journal of Political Science* 32 (November 1988): 884–907.

[24]Norman J. Ornstein, Thomas E. Mann, and Michael J. Malbin, *Vital Statistics on Congress, 1989–1990* (Washington, D.C.: American Enterprise Institute, 1989), 65.

[25]Jacobson, *The Politics of Congressional Elections,* 56.

lengers are often naive about their chances of winning. Not blessed with money for expensive polls, they rely on friends and local party leaders, who often tell them what they want to hear. Sometimes they do get some unexpected help: incumbents almost have to beat themselves, and some do.

An incumbent tarnished by scandal or corruption becomes instantly vulnerable. Clearly, voters *do* take out their anger at the polls. For example, Representative Pat Swindall of Georgia faced election while under indictment for involvement in a scheme for laundering funds obtained from the sale of illicit drugs. To make matters worse, the FBI had his deal making on tape, which was played repeatedly on television. Swindall lost in a landslide. In a close election, negative publicity can turn easy victory into defeat.[26]

Incumbents may also be redistricted out of their familiar turfs. After each federal census, Congress reapportions its membership. States that have gained in population will be given more seats; states that have lost population will lose one or more of their seats. The state legislatures then have to redraw their states' district lines; one incumbent may be moved into another's district, where the two must battle for one seat. A state party majority is more likely to move two of the opposition party's representatives into the same district than two of its own.

Money in Congressional Elections

When an incumbent is not running for reelection and the seat is open, there is a greater likelihood of competition. If the party balance in a constituency is such that either party has a chance of winning, there may be strong candidates running for each side, each with enough money to establish name recognition among the voters. Most of the turnover in the membership of Congress is the result of vacated seats, particularly in the House.

It costs a great deal more money to elect a Congress than to elect a president. Each of the two presidential candidates in 1988 received about $46 million from the federal treasury, which covered nearly the entire cost of each presidential campaign. The $250 million mark for congressional elections was passed in 1982. The 1988 Senate races alone cost $190 million; House candidates spent another $222 million. Thus the cost of congressional elections in the 1987–88 election cycle was $410 million. In 1986 the candidates for the Senate seat in California alone spent almost $23 million; those for the seat in Florida, about $13 million. One hundred and forty candidates for the House spent at least $.5 million in 1988.[27] A look at spending in congressional elections can be found in Table 12.4.

Aside from the fact that candidates spend enormous sums on campaigns for Congress, it is important to ask where this money comes from and what it buys. Although most of the money spent in congressional elections comes from individuals, 33 percent (about $148 million) of the funds raised by candidates for Congress in 1988 came from the more than four thousand Political Action Committees (PACs) (see Chapter 10). Critics of PACs offer plenty of complaints about the present system of campaign finance. Why, they ask, is money spent

---

[26]John G. Peters and Susan Welch, "The Effects of Corruption on Voting Behavior in Congressional Elections," *American Political Science Review* 74 (September 1980): 697–708.

[27]Ornstein et al., *Vital Statistics on Congress, 1989–1990,* chap. 3.

Table 12.4   Spending in Congressional Elections, 1988

A typical candidate for a House seat spends more than a quarter of a million dollars on the campaign; Senate candidates spend about ten times as much. Incumbents, especially in House elections, have a considerable advantage over their opponents, which, of course, is one reason incumbents do so well. The real spending contest, though, is in districts where the seat is open. When there is no incumbent and each party feels it has a chance to win, the spending is greatest.

CANDIDATE	AVERAGE EXPENDITURE
House	
All candidates	$ 273,811
Incumbent	$ 378,316
Challenger	$ 118,877
Open seat	$ 480,685
Senate	
All candidates	$2,802,118
Incumbent	$3,898,821
Challenger	$1,816,113
Open seat	$2,886,383

Source: Norman J. Omstein, Thomas E. Mann, and Michael J. Malbin, *Vital Statistics on Congress, 1989–1990* (Washington, D.C.: American Enterprise Institute, 1989), 71–79.

to pay the campaign costs of a candidate already heavily favored to win? In 1988 incumbents in both houses got $118 million from PACs, challengers received $14 million, and the rest went to candidates for open seats. In 1986 Jim Wright, the House majority leader at the time, got $595,827, and House Minority Leader Robert Michel received $455,111—in both cases, for running in safe seats. Even more interesting is that PACs often make contributions *after* the election. The thirteen freshman senators elected in 1986, for example, received $1.6 million from PACs following the election, even though those senators would not be running again for six years. Much of this money came from groups that had supported the senators' opponents during the election.[28]

What PACs are seeking is *access* to policymakers. Thus they give most of their money to incumbents, who are likely to win anyway, and when they support someone who loses they quickly make amends and contribute to the winner. PACs want to keep the lines of communication open and create a receptive atmosphere in which to be heard. Since each PAC is limited to an expenditure of five thousand dollars per candidate (most give less), a single PAC can at most account for only a small percentage of a winner's total spending. If one PAC does not contribute to a candidate, there are plenty more PACs from which to seek funds.

Some organized interests circumvent the limitations on contributions, however, and create or contribute to several PACs. This may increase their leverage

[28]Congressional Quarterly, *Current American Government, Spring 1988* (Washington, D.C.: Congressional Quarterly Press, 1988), 89.

The People Speak

Do Contributors Have Too Much Power?

Do individuals, groups, and corporations that contribute to political campaigns end up having too much influence over public officials?

Yes	81%
No	16%

Source: The question as worded is taken directly from a Harris Poll, April 1989.

with those to whom they contribute. In the late 1980s one tycoon, Charles Keating, managed to contribute *$1.3 million* to the campaigns of five senators. These senators then interceded with the Federal Home Loan Bank Board to avoid (for a while, at least) enforcement of banking regulations on Keating's savings and loan, as discussed in Chapter 10, "Government in Action." Many people saw a connection between the campaign contributions and the senators' actions (see "A Question of Ethics: Do PACs Buy Votes?").

Aside from the question of money buying influence, what does it buy the candidates who spend it? In 1986 Republican Senate candidates outspent their Democratic opponents in twenty-three of the thirty-four states having Senate races—a total advantage of $28 million—but lost twenty of the thirty-four elections. Californian Ed Zschau spent $11.8 million, $1 million more than his rival,

---

A Question of Ethics

Do PACs Buy Votes?

The effect of PAC campaign contributions is one of the hottest ethical issues on Capitol Hill today. Critics of PACs, including Common Cause, are convinced that PACs are not trying to elect but to influence. Critics are fond of suggesting links between donations and congressional votes. For example, in November 1983 the 250 House members who voted to retain dairy price supports had received $1.7 million—about $6,800 each—from a dairy PAC. Most critics fear the worst; Gregg Easterbrook summarizes his argument this way: "Money can . . . buy individual congressmen's votes on a bill, or distort congressmen's thinking on an issue—normally all an interest group needs to achieve its ends."

Connection is not causation, however. Most senators and representatives are firm in their conviction that their decisions are not affected by PAC contributions. Political scientists are also skeptical of the influence of PACs. There is little systematic evidence that contributions affect outcomes on voting in Congress.

PACs usually contribute to those who already agree with them or to those who are likely to win (or who have already won). In addition, because national organizations are dependent on local units for raising money, Washington lobbyists must be resposive to the desires of local contributors. Thus funds often go to candidates that the lobbyists feel are undeserving, which weakens their bargaining power. Moreover, PACs are not "outside" interests—they usually contribute to or lobby members of Congress from districts or states to which they have geographic ties.

Of course, PACs may influence voting in Congress by reinforcing members in their views and perhaps activating some to work on behalf of the interests PACs represent, rather than by converting ("buying") those opposed to the interests' goals. Such influence is less dramatic than conversion, but it can be crucial to legislative success.

President Bush called for banning business, labor, and trade association PACs—the source of 87 percent of the $156 million PACs gave congressional candidates during 1987 and 1988. Less concerned about selling their votes than losing their seats, members of Congress did not support the president.

Whatever *your* conclusion about PACs, keep Bo Pilgrim in mind. In July 1989 Lonnie (Bo) Pilgrim, a millionaire chicken farmer with interests in legislation, visited the chamber of the Texas state Senate and handed several senators checks for ten thousand dollars—with a blank for them to fill in their names.

Sources: Easterbrook's quote is from his "What's Wrong with Congress?" *Atlantic Monthly,* December 1984, 70; Other information is from John R. Wright, "PACs, Contributions, and Roll Calls," *American Political Science Review* 79 (June 1985): 400–14; Janet M. Grenzke, "PACs and the Congressional Supermarket: The Currency Is Complex," *American Journal of Political Science* 33 (February 1989): 1–24; and John R. Wright, "PAC Contributions, Lobbying, and Representation," *Journal of Politics* 51 (August 1989): 713–29.

Senator Alan Cranston, and still lost. Obviously, spending a lot of money in a campaign is no guarantee of success.

Money is important, however, for challengers. The more they spend, the more votes they receive. Money buys them name recognition and a chance to be heard. Incumbents, by contrast, already have high levels of recognition among their constituents and receive little benefit from campaign spending; what matters is how much their opponents spend. Challengers have to raise a lot of money if they hope to succeed in defeating an incumbent, but, as Table 12.4 shows, they usually are substantially outspent by incumbents.[29] In open seats, the candidate who spends the most usually wins.

Stability and Change

You have seen that incumbents usually win reelection. As a result, there is stability in the membership of Congress. In the 101st Congress the average senator had served for ten years and the average member of the House for eight years. This length of time provides the opportunity for representatives to gain some expertise in dealing with complex questions of public policy. At the same time, it also insulates them from the winds of political change. Safe seats make it more difficult for citizens to "send a message to Washington" with their votes. Especially for the House, it takes a large shift in votes to affect the outcomes of most elections. Nevertheless, the American people seem comfortable with this situation and reelect their representatives and senators again and again.

HOW CONGRESS IS ORGANIZED TO MAKE POLICY

The Constitution assumes, indeed requires, that policy-making be the primary role of Congress and its members. Considering bills, voting intelligently for policy in the national interest, and doing one's legislative homework means making policy. Of all the senators' and representatives' roles, this one is toughest. One reason is the enormous amount of work required in a short period of time. Little time is available for even the most conscientious member to examine policy alternatives. Instead, when ringing bells announce a roll-call vote, representatives or senators rush into the chamber from their offices or from a hearing, often unsure of what is being voted on. Often, "uncertain of [their] position, [members of Congress] will seek out one or two [people] who serve on the committee which considered and reported the bill, in whose judgment [they have] confidence."[30] Congressional policy-making is so varied and confusing that members frequently resort to these "cue givers"—other, more knowledgeable members who can help them make up their minds.[31]

Congress is a collection of generalists trying to make policy on specialized topics. Members are short of time, and of expertise as well. Amateurs in almost

Spending enormous sums of money can help a challenger offset the incumbent's advantage in a congressional election, but incumbents still win most of the time. For example, Democratic Senator Alan Cranston (above) fought off Republican Ed Zshau's $11.8 million campaign challenge in 1986. Cranston spent almost $11 million himself.

[29]Jacobson, *The Politics of Congressional Elections,* 49–53, 122–25.

[30]So says former House Speaker Jim Wright, in *You and Your Congressman* (New York: Putnam, 1976), 190.

[31]Donald R. Matthews and James Stimson, *Yeas and Nays: Normal Decision-Making in the House of Representatives* (New York: Wiley, 1975).

every subject, they are surrounded by people who know (or claim to know) more than they do—lobbyists, agency administrators, even their own staffs. Even if they had time to study all the issues thoroughly, making wise national policy would be difficult. If economists disagree about policies to fight unemployment, how are legislators to know which ones may work better than others? Congress's constitutional organization gave it just a hint of specialization, when it was split into the House and the Senate. The complexity of today's issues require much more specialization. Congress tries to cope with these demands through its elaborate committee system, as will be discussed in the following sections.

American Bicameralism

A **bicameral legislature** is one divided into two houses. The U.S. Congress and every American state legislature except Nebraska's are bicameral. As discussed in Chapter 2, the Connecticut Compromise at the Constitutional Convention created a bicameral Congress. Each state is guaranteed two senators, and its number of representatives is determined by the population of the state (California has forty-five representatives; Alaska, Delaware, North Dakota, South Dakota, Vermont, and Wyoming have just one each). By creating a bicameral Congress, the Constitution set up yet another check and balance. No bill can be passed unless both House and Senate agree on it; each body can thus veto the policies of the other.

Although Americans sometimes blur the distinction between senators and representatives, the members of Congress see sharp differences between the two bodies. These differences are shown in Table 12.5. Members even hold stereotypes of "the other body": senators are seen by their House counterparts as grandstanders, eyeing the White House instead of tending to legislative business, and the House, seen through Senate eyes, is a bit unimaginative and even parochial.

Table 12.5 House versus Senate: Some Key Differences

CHARACTERISTIC	HOUSE OF REPRESENTATIVES	SENATE
Constitutional powers	Must initiate all revenue bills; must pass all articles of impeachment	Must give "advice and consent" to many presidential appointments; must approve treaties; tries impeached officials
Membership	435 members	100 members
Term of office	2 years	6 years
Centralization of power	More centralized; stronger leadership	Less centralized; weaker leadership
Political prestige	Less prestige	More prestige
Role in policy	More influential on budget; more specialized	More influential on foreign affairs; less specialized
Turnover	Small	Moderate
Role of seniority	More important in determining power	Less important in determining power

---

The House   More than four times larger than the Senate, the House is also more institutionalized, that is, more centralized, more hierarchical, and less anarchic. Party loyalty to leadership and party-line voting are more common than in the Senate.[32] Partly because there are more members, leaders in the House do more leading than leaders in the Senate. First-term House members, however, are still more likely to be seen and not heard, and have less power than senior representatives have.

Both the House and the Senate set their own agendas. Both use committees, which will be examined shortly, to winnow down the thousands of bills introduced. One institution unique to the House, though, plays a key role in agenda setting: the **House Rules Committee.** This committee reviews most bills coming from a House committee before they go to the full House. Performing a traffic-cop function, it then gives each bill a "rule," which schedules the bill on the calendar, allots time for debate, and sometimes even specifies what kind of amendments may be offered.

For years the Rules Committee was dominated by southern representatives who strongly opposed policies promoting equality for blacks. These conservative members had an easy solution to the problem of civil rights legislation: deny it a rule, thus burying it. But the power of the Rules Committee was decreased in the 1960s, and as conservative members have died, retired, or been defeated, the conservative majority has gradually been replaced by a majority more responsive to the House leadership. The Speaker of the House now directly appoints the members of the Rules Committee.

The Senate   The Constitution's framers thought the Senate would protect elite interests against the tendencies of the House to protect the masses. Thus to the House they gave the power of initiating all revenue bills and of impeaching officials; to the Senate they gave responsibility for ratifying all treaties, for confirming important presidential nominations (including nominations to the Supreme Court), and for trying impeached officials. Experience has shown that when the same party controls each chamber, the Senate is just as liberal as (some say more liberal than) the House. The real differences between the bodies lie in the Senate's organization and decentralized power.

Smaller than the House, the Senate is also less disciplined and less centralized. Today's senators are more equal in power than representatives are. They are also more equal than senators have been in the past. Some years ago Donald Matthews described the insignificance of freshman senators, even calling the first term an "apprenticeship." Freshmen senators confided to Matthews that senior members advised them thus: "You may think you are smarter than the older fellows, but after a time you find that this is not true," and "Keep on asking for advice, boy, that's the way to get ahead around here."[33] In 1981, though, the Senate had sixteen newcomers, none of them eager to take a back seat to old-timers. Even very new senators got top committee assignments; some even became chairs of key subcommittees. One of them, Dan Quayle of Indiana, made his mark chairing a subcommittee handling a key bill on job training.

[32]Nelson W. Polsby et al., "Institutionalization of the House of Representatives," *American Political Science Review* 62 (1968): 144–68.

[33]Donald R. Matthews, *U.S. Senators and Their World* (Chapel Hill: University of North Carolina Press, 1960), 93.

Committees and the party leadership are important in determining the Senate's legislative agenda, just as they are in the House. Party leaders do for Senate scheduling what the Rules Committee does in the House. One item unique to the Senate is the **filibuster.** In the House, debate can be ended by a simple majority vote. Priding itself on freedom of discussion, the Senate in the past permitted unlimited debate on a bill. But if debate is unlimited, opponents of a bill may try to talk it to death; Strom Thurmond (R-S.C.) once held forth for a full twenty-four hours. Yielding at times to a fresh voice, filibusterers can tie up the legislative agenda until proponents decide to give up their battle. Filibusters were a favorite device of southern senators to prevent civil rights legislation. In 1959, 1975, and again in 1979, the senate adopted rules to make it easier to close off debate. Today sixty members present and voting can halt a filibuster.

Congressional Leadership

Leading 100 or 435 men and women in Congress, each jealous of his or her own power and responsible to no higher power than the constituency, is no easy task. "Few members of the House, fewer still in the Senate," Robert Peabody once wrote, "consider themselves followers."[34] Chapter 7 discussed the party-in-government. Much of the leadership in Congress is really party leadership. There are a few formal posts, whose occupants are chosen by nonparty procedures, but those who have the real power in the congressional hierarchy are those whose party put them there (see Table 12.6).

The House   Chief among these in the House of Representatives is the **Speaker of the House.** This office is mandated by the Constitution. ("The House of Representatives," it says, "shall choose their Speaker and other Officers.") In practice the majority party does the choosing. Before each Congress begins, the majority party puts forward its candidate for Speaker, who turns out—because this person attracts the unanimous support of the majority party—to be a shoo-in. Typically, the Speaker is a very senior member of the party. Thomas Foley of Washington state, elected Speaker in 1989, had been in Congress since 1964. Today the Speaker is two heartbeats away from the presidency, being second in line (after the vice-president) to succeed a president who resigns or dies in office.

[34]Robert L. Peabody, *Leadership in Congress* (Boston: Little, Brown, 1976), 4.

Table 12.6   **Party Leaders in the 101st Congress**

HOUSE	SENATE
Speaker: Thomas Foley (D-Wash.)	Majority Leader: George Mitchell (D-Maine)
Majority Leader: Richard Gephardt (D-Mo.)	Majority Whip: Alan Cranston (D-Calif.)
Majority Whip: William Gray (D-Pa.)	
	Minority Leader: Robert Dole (R-Kans.)
Minority Leader: Robert Michel (R-Ill.)	Minority Whip: Alan Simpson (R-Wyo.)
Minority Whip: Newt Gingrich (R-Ga.)	

Years ago, the Speaker was king of the congressional mountain. Autocrats like "Uncle Joe Cannon" and "Czar Reed" ran the House like a fiefdom. A great revolt in 1910 whittled down the Speaker's powers and gave some of them to committees, but six decades later members of the House restored some of the Speaker's powers. Today the Speaker of the House has some important formal powers. The Speaker

- Presides over the House when it is in session.
- Plays a major role in making committee assignments, coveted by all members to ensure their electoral advantage. The speaker appoints, for example, eight members of the Democratic Steering and Policy Committee, which functions as the "Committee on Committees" for House Democrats.
- Appoints or plays a key role in appointing the party's legislative leaders and the party leadership staff.
- Exercises substantial control over which bills get assigned to which committees.

In addition, the Speaker has a great deal of informal clout inside and outside Congress. When the Speaker's party is different from the president's party, he or she is often a national spokesperson for the party. The bank of microphones in front of the Speaker of the House is a commonplace feature of the evening news. A good Speaker also knows the members well, including past improprieties, what ambitions they harbor, and what pressures they are under at the current time.

Leadership in the House, though, is not a one-person show. The Speaker's principal partisan ally is the **majority leader,** a job that has been the main stepping-stone to the Speaker's role. The majority leader is responsible for scheduling bills in the House. More importantly, the majority leader is responsible for rounding up votes in behalf of the party's position on legislation. Working with the majority leader are the party's **whips,** who carry the word to party troops, counting votes beforehand and leaning on waverers whose votes are crucial to a bill.

The minority party is also organized, ever poised to take over the Speakership and other key posts if it should win a majority in the House. The Republicans have been the minority party in the House since 1955, although they have had a president to look to for leadership for most of the past three decades. Lately a group of younger, more conservative Republicans has made life for the Republican **minority leader** difficult. One of their ringleaders has been Representative Newt Gingrich of Georgia, a proponent of a "Conservative Opportunity Society."[35] In 1984 he began using the House's television coverage to make stirring speeches (to empty chambers) condemning the Democrats. In 1985, when the Democratic majority in the House refused to seat a Republican from a close race in Indiana, the so-called Young Turk Republicans went into open revolt. Using parliamentary obstreperousness to block legislation, they made life difficult for both the Democratic majority and their own minority leader, Robert Michel of Illinois. In 1989 Gingrich was elected House Republican whip.

Thomas Foley of Washington state is the current Speaker of the House. Foley has served in the House for more than twenty-five years.

House Minority Whip Newt Gingrich of Georgia is known for his conservative politics and confrontational style.

[35]On Gingrich, see Nicholas Lemann, " 'Conservative Opportunity Society,' " *Atlantic Monthly,* May 1985, 22–36.

Senate Majority Leader George Mitchell's abilities as a public spokesperson for his party are suited to the decentralized power structure in today's Congress, where even leaders must stump for support.

The Senate   The Constitution makes the vice-president of the United States the president of the Senate; this is the vice-president's only constitutional job. But even the mighty Lyndon Johnson, who had been the Senate majority leader before becoming vice-president, found himself an outsider when he returned as the Senate's president. Vice-presidents usually ignore their senatorial chores, leaving power in the Senate up to party leaders. Senators typically return the favor, ignoring vice-presidents except in the rare case when their vote can break a tie.

Thus the Senate majority leader, aided by the majority whips, is a party's wheelhorse, corralling votes, scheduling the floor action, and influencing committee assignments. No majority leader left quite the imprint that Lyndon Johnson did. He got the job in 1955 during his second term. Johnson was a small-town Texas boy who thrived on power. He was almost mesmerizing in his mixture of tall tales, crude talk, boundless energy, and attention to legislative detail. In the lobbies and offices, the Capitol cloakrooms and the Washington bars, the "Johnson treatment" was legendary. He combined wheedling, needling, charm, flattery, pressure, promises, near physical abuse, obscenities, bear hugs, and stories to cajole members of Congress into compromise.

In 1989 the Democrats selected the current Senate majority leader, George Mitchell of Maine. His differences with Johnson reflect the changes that have occurred in Congress since the 1950s. Both senators were capable men, but where Johnson was the master at quiet deals and one-on-one persuasion, Mitchell's greatest asset is his polished style in speaking on behalf of the party in public, especially on television. This skill is important in today's political climate, since power is no longer in the hands of a few key members of Congress who are insulated from the public. Instead, power is widely dispersed, requiring leaders to appeal broadly for support.

Congressional Leadership in Perspective   Despite their stature and power, congressional leaders are not in strong positions to move their troops. Both houses of Congress are highly decentralized and have shown no inclination for major changes in the way they operate. Leaders are elected by their fellow party members and must remain responsive to them. Except in the most egregious cases (which rarely arise), leaders cannot punish those who do not support the party's stand, and no one expects members to vote against their constituents' interests. Senator Robert Dole nicely summed up the leader's situation when he once dubbed himself the "Majority Pleader."

The Committees and Subcommittees

Will Rogers, the famous Oklahoma humorist, once remarked that "outside of traffic, there is nothing that has held this country back as much as committees."[36] Members of the Senate and the House would apparently disagree. Most of the real work of Congress goes on in committees. In fact, South Carolina's Senator Ernest Hollings once remarked that so little is done on the Senate floor that a senator could run naked through the chamber and no one would notice. Most senators would be handling committee business. Committees dominate congressional policy-making in all its stages, although they usually attract little attention.

[36]Quoted in Smith and Deering, *Committees in Congress,* 1.

Committees regularly hold hearings to investigate problems and possible wrongdoings and to oversee the executive branch. Most of all, *they control the congressional agenda and guide legislation* from its introduction to its send-off for the president's signature. Committees can be grouped into four types, of which the first is by far the most important.

1. **Standing committees** are formed to handle bills in different policy areas (see Table 12.7). Each house of Congress has its own standing committees; members do not belong to a committee in the other house. In the One Hundreth Congress, the Senate's 16 standing committees had 85 subcommittees, while the House's 22 standing committees had 140 subcommittees. The typical representative served on 1.7 committees and 3.8 subcommittees, while the smaller number of senators averaged 2.9 committees and 7.0 subcommittees each.

2. **Joint committees** exist in a few policy areas; their membership is drawn from both the Senate and the House.

3. **Conference committees** are formed when the Senate and the House pass a particular bill in different forms. Appointed by the party leadership, a conference committee consists of members of each house chosen to iron out Senate and House differences and report back a compromise bill.

4. **Select committees** are appointed for a specific purpose. The Senate select committee that looked into Watergate is a well-known example.

Table 12.7	Standing Committees in the Senate and in the House

SENATE COMMITTEES	HOUSE COMMITTEES
Agriculture, Nutrition, and Forestry	Agriculture
Appropriations	Appropriations
Armed Services	Armed Services
Banking, Housing, and Urban Affairs	Banking, Finance, and Urban Affairs
Budget	Budget
Commerce, Science, and Transportation	District of Columbia
Energy and Natural Resources	Education and Labor
Environment and Public Works	Energy and Commerce
Finance	Foreign Affairs
Foreign Relations	Government Operations
Governmental Affairs	House Administration
Judiciary	Interior and Insular Affairs
Labor and Human Resources	Judiciary
Rules and Administration	Merchant Marine and Fisheries
Small Business	Post Office and Civil Service
Veterans' Affairs	Public Works and Transportation
	Rules
	Science and Technology
	Small Business
	Standards of Official Conduct
	Veterans' Affairs
	Ways and Means

The Committees at Work: Legislation and Oversight   With more than eleven thousand bills submitted by members every two years, some winnowing is essential. Every bill goes to a committee, which then has virtually the power of life and death over it. Usually only bills getting a favorable committee report are considered by the whole House or Senate.

New bills sent to a committee typically go directly to a subcommittee, which can hold hearings on the bill. Sizable committee and subcommittee staffs conduct research, line up witnesses for hearings, and write and rewrite bills. One output of the committees and their subcommittees is their report on proposed legislation, typically bound in beige or green covers and available from the Government Printing Office. Their most important output, though, is the "marked up" (rewritten) bill itself, submitted to the full House or Senate for debate and voting.

The work of committees does not stop when the bill leaves the committee room. Members of the committee will usually serve as "floor managers" of the bill, helping party leaders hustle votes for it. They will also be the cue-givers to whom other members turn for advice. When the Senate and House pass different versions of the same bill, some committee members will be on the conference committee.

The committees and subcommittees do not leave the scene even after legislation is passed. They stay busy in legislative **oversight,** the process of monitoring the bureaucracy and its administration of policy. Oversight is handled mainly through hearings. When an agency wants a bigger budget, the use of its present budget is reviewed. Even if no budgetary issues are involved, members of committees constantly monitor how a law is being implemented. Agency heads and even cabinet secretaries testify, bringing graphs, charts, and data on the progress they have made and the problems they face. Committee staffs and

Most of Congress's work takes place—and most of its members' power is wielded—in the standing committees and their numerous subcommittees. Here members of the Senate's Foreign Relations Committee prepare for a hearing on arms reduction.

committee members grill agency heads about particular problems. For example, a member may ask a Small Business Administration official why constituents who are applying for loans get a runaround. On another committee, officials charged with listing endangered species may defend the grey wolf against a member of Congress whose sheep-ranching constituents are not fond of wolves. Oversight, one of the checks Congress can exercise on the executive branch, gives Congress the power to pressure agencies and, in the extreme, to cut their budgets in order to secure compliance with congressional wishes, even congressional whims.[37]

Occasionally congressional oversight rivets the nation's attention. One such example occurred in 1973 when the Senate established the Select Committee on Campaign Activities to investigate the misdeeds and duplicity of the 1972 presidential campaign, otherwise known as the Watergate scandal. This was followed the next year by the House Judiciary Committee's hearings on the impeachment of President Nixon for his conduct in attempting to cover up the scandal. Shortly after that committee recommended three articles of impeachment, the president resigned.

More recently, a special joint committee was established in 1987 to investigate what became known as the Iran-Contra affair, referring to the secret sale of arms to Iran (for which the president hoped to obtain the release of American hostages held in the Middle East) and the diversion of some of the funds from these sales to the contras fighting the Sandinista government in Nicaragua (in the face of congressional prohibition of such aid). Many thought the hearings, especially the testimony of Lieutenant Colonel Oliver North, made for great spy-novel-like entertainment, but did little to illuminate the issues involved in the matter.

Congress keeps tabs on more routine activities of the executive branch through its committee staff members, who have expertise in the specialized fields of the agencies that their committees oversee and who maintain an extensive network of formal and informal contacts with the bureaucracy. Through reading the voluminous reports Congress requires of the executive and receiving information from agency sources, complaining citizens, members of Congress and their personal staff, state and local officials, interest groups, and professional organizations, staff members can keep track of the implementation of public policy.[38]

Members of Congress have many competing responsibilities, and there are few political payoffs for carefully watching a government agency if it is implementing policy properly. It is difficult to go to voters and say, "Vote for me. I oversaw the routine handling of road building." Because of this lack of incentives, problems may be missed until it is too late to do much about them. A major scandal involving the Department of Housing and Urban Development's administration of housing programs during the Reagan presidency was not uncovered until 1989, after Reagan had left office. Taxpayers could have saved well over one hundred billion dollars if Congress had insisted that the agencies regulating the savings and loan industry enforced their regulations more rigorously (see Chapter 17).

[37]For more on congressional oversight, see Christopher H. Foreman, Jr., *Signals From the Hill* (New Haven, Conn.: Yale University Press, 1988).

[38]Joel D. Aberbach, *Keeping a Watchful Eye: The Politics of Congressional Oversight* (Washington, D.C.: Brookings Institution, 1990).

"*No, no. When I say this new secret weapon can slip past their defenses undetected, I'm not referring to the Russians, I'm referring to Congress.*"

Nevertheless, Congress *did* substantially increase its oversight activities in the 1970s and 1980s. As the size and complexity of the national government grew in the 1960s, and after numerous charges that the executive branch had become too powerful (especially in response to the widespread belief that Presidents Johnson and Nixon had abused their power), Congress responded with more oversight. The tight budgets of recent years have provided additional incentives for oversight as members of Congress have sought to protect programs they favor from budget cuts and to get more value for the tax dollars spent on them. As the publicity value of receiving credit for controlling governmental spending has increased, so has the number of representatives and senators interested in oversight.[39]

Getting on a Committee   One of the first worries for an incoming freshman member of Congress (after paying off campaign debts) is getting on the right committee. Although it is not always easy to know what the right committee is, it is fairly easy to figure out some wrong committees. The Iowa newcomer does not want to get stuck on the Merchant Marine and Fisheries committee; the Brooklyn freshman would like to avoid Agriculture. Members seek committees that will help them achieve three goals: reelection, influence in Congress, and the opportunity to make policy in areas they think are important.[40]

[39]Aberbach, *Keeping a Watchful Eye.*
[40]Richard Fenno, *Congressmen in Committees* (Boston: Little Brown, 1973), 1.

Just after their election, new members write to the party's congressional leaders and members of their state delegation, indicating their committee preferences. Every committee includes members from both parties, but a majority of each committee's members as well as its chair come from the majority party. Each party in each house has a slightly different way of picking its committee members. Party leaders almost always play a key role. The parties try to grant member's requests for committee assignments whenever possible. They want their members to please their constituents (being on the right committee should help them play their role of constituency representative more effectively) and develop expertise in an area of policy. The parties also try to apportion among the state delegations the influence that comes with committee membership, in order to accord representation to diverse components of the party.[41]

Getting Ahead on the Committee: Chairs and the Seniority System   If committees are the most important influencers of the congressional agenda, **committee chairs** are the most important influencers of the committee agenda. They play dominant—though no longer monopolistic—roles in scheduling hearings, hiring staff, appointing subcommittees, and managing committee bills when they are brought before the full house.

Until the 1970s there was a simple rule for picking committee chairs, the **seniority system.** It worked like this: If committee members had served on their committee longest and their party controlled the chamber, they got to be chairs—whatever their party loyalty, mental state, or competence.

This system gave a decisive edge to members from "safe" districts. They were least likely to be challenged for reelection and most likely to achieve seniority. In the Democratic party, most safe districts were in the South; as a result, southern politicians had power beyond their numbers. They chaired many committees, often dominating them. For years it seemed to some that southerners may have lost the Civil War but won the Congress as a consolation prize. James O. Eastland of Mississippi chaired the Senate Judiciary Committee, which handled civil rights legislation, a policy arena that Eastland did not favor. L. Mendel Rivers of South Carolina chaired the House Armed Services Committee, engineering military bases, shipyards, and defense contracts for his district. Today, although the South may be rising again, its hold on congressional committee chair positions is dwindling. The South is becoming a two-party region, and electoral losses, aging, and mortality have taken their toll on southern committee chairs.

Woodrow Wilson, a political scientist before he became a politician, once said that the government of the United States was really the government by the chairs of the standing committees of Congress. So powerful were the chairs for most of the twentieth century that they could bully members or bottle up legislation at any time—and with almost certain knowledge that they would be chairs for the rest of their electoral life. But in the 1970s the Congress faced a revolt of its younger members. Both parties in both branches permitted members to vote on committee chairs; in 1975 the House Democrats dumped four chairs with 154 years of seniority among them. Today seniority remains the *general rule* for selecting chairs, but there are exceptions. (You can look at the overthrow

---

[41]A good study of committee assignments is Kenneth Shepsle, *The Giant Jigsaw Puzzle* (Chicago: University of Chicago Press, 1978).

of one key committee chair in 1985 in "In Focus: Armed Services Gets a New Chair.")

These and other reforms have somewhat reduced the clout of the chairs. Today, two authorities on congressional committees could actually write: "Chairs are far less able to mold the decisionmaking processes of their committees. Indeed, the most common complaint we heard about committee leadership from committee members and staff was that chairs are no longer responsible for their committees' actions."[42] Such an observation would have been unthinkable two decades ago.

The Mushrooming Caucuses: The Informal Organization of Congress

Although the formal organization of Congress consists of its party leadership and its committee structures, equally important is the informal organization of the House and Senate. The informal networks of trust and mutual interest can

[42]Smith and Deering, *Committees in Congress,* 177.

In Focus

Armed Services Gets a New Chair

On January 4, 1985, House Democrats convened to vote on their organization for the upcoming congressional session. Attention focused on a potential revolt against Representative Melvin Price, the eighty-year-old chairman of the House Armed Services Committee. The party caucus voted 121 to 118 to remove Price. Ironically, Price had succeeded to the chair during the first revolt of the members in 1975, when he replaced the unpopular Edward Hebert of Louisiana. Old and frail, Price himself had allowed that, if he were reelected, this term would be his last. Members decided not to wait.

The surprise came with the selection of Price's successor. House Democratic leaders nominated the second-ranking member of the Armed Services Committee, Charles Bennett of Florida. From the floor, however, members nominated Les Aspin, the seventh most senior member on the panel. Aspin defeated Bennett on a vote of 125 to 103. Aspin and his supporters had waged a vigorous campaign for the post.

Two years later it was Aspin's turn to be on the firing line. Upset at his support for the MX missile and aid to the contras in Nicaragua, a majority of Demo-

Les Aspin's rise and near-fall illustrates the reduced power of committee chairs.

crats voted to remove him from the chair. They could not agree on a successor, however, and so two weeks later, after Aspin had circulated a letter of contrition, they voted to reinstate him. Chastened by the experience, Aspin promised to deal more effectively and openly with his fellow party members.

spring from numerous sources. Friendship, ideology, and geography are long-standing sources of informal organization.

Lately these traditional informal groupings have been dominated by a growing number of caucuses. A **caucus** is a grouping of members of Congress sharing some interest or characteristic. In the 101st Congress there were more than seventy of these caucuses, most of them containing members from both parties and some from both the House and the Senate. The goal of all caucuses is to shape the agenda of Congress. They do this by elevating their particular issues or interests to a prominent place in the day-to-day workings of Congress. They are rather like interest groups, but with a difference: their members are members of Congress, not petitioners to Congress on the outside looking in. The caucuses—interest groups within Congress—are nicely situated to pack more punch than interest groups outside Congress.

Some, such as the Black Caucus, the Congresswomen's Caucus, and the Hispanic Caucus, are based on characteristics of the members. Others, such as the Sunbelt Caucus and the Northeast-Midwest Congressional Coalition, are based on regional groupings. Still others, such as the Moderate/Conservative Democrats, are ideological groupings. And still others, such as the Steel, Travel and Tourism, Coal, and Mushroom caucuses, are based on some economic interest important to a set of constituencies. (Yes, there is a Mushroom Caucus, composed of members interested in protecting the interests of mushroom growers).

The activities of these caucuses are directed toward their fellow members of Congress and toward administrative agencies. Within Congress they press for committees to hold hearings, they push particular legislation, and they pull together votes on bills they favor. The Steel Caucus, for example, contains 160 members whose districts include major steelproducing enterprises (nearly one in five Pennsylvanians is employed in the steel industry). It pushed the House Ways and Means Committee to hold hearings on the plight of the steel industry. The Mushroom Caucus successfully pressured the executive branch to ban the importing of canned mushrooms, hoping to help domestic mushroom producers.

This explosion of informal groups in Congress has made the representation of interests in Congress a more direct process, cutting out the middleman, the lobbyist. The caucuses proceed on the assumption that no one is a more effective lobbyist than a senator or representative.

As with other interest groups, the caucuses seek to influence the legislative process—the way bills become law. The following sections will discuss this process, which is often termed "labyrinthine," in that getting a bill through Congress is very much like completing a difficult, intricate maze.

The proliferation of congressional caucuses gives members of Congress an informal, yet powerful, means of shaping the policy agenda. Composed of legislative insiders who share similar concerns, the caucuses—like the Hispanic Caucus pictured here—exert a much greater influence on policy-making than most citizen-based interest groups can.

THE CONGRESSIONAL PROCESS

The last chapter described the government's agenda. Congress' agenda is, of course, a crowded one: about fifty-five hundred bills are introduced annually. A **bill** is a proposed law, drafted in precise, legal language. Anyone—even you or I—can draft a bill. The White House and interest groups are common sources of polished bills. However, only members of the House or the Senate can formally submit a bill for consideration. What happens to a bill as it works its way through the legislative labyrinth is depicted in Figure 12.2. Most bills are quietly killed off early in the process. Some are introduced mostly as a favor to a group or a constituent; others are private bills, granting citizenship to a constituent or paying a settlement to a person whose car was demolished by a Postal Service truck; still other bills may alter the course of the nation.

Basically, Congress is a reactive and cumbersome decision-making body. Rules are piled upon rules and procedures upon procedures.[43] Some congressional strategists are masters of the art of the *rider,* an amendment, typically unrelated to the bill itself, intended to be carried along on the back of another bill. Legislators often use riders to pass a bill that on its own does not have enough support to pass. A bill must pass one procedure after another to get through the system. Indeed, so complex is the system that President John F. Kennedy once remarked that "it is very easy to defeat a bill in Congress. It is much more difficult to pass one."[44] As you will shortly see, even presidents find it hard to influence Congress.

There are, of course, countless influences on this legislative process. Presidents, parties, constituents, groups, the congressional and committee leadership structure—these and more offer members cues for their decision making. A few of the major influences will now be examined, starting with the president.

Presidents and Congress: Partners and Protagonists

In late March 1985, President Reagan rode by motorcade to Capitol Hill. He went for lunch just five hours before the Senate was to vote on appropriating $1.5 billion for the MX missile. At lunch he met with Republican senators and emphasized how essential the MX was to successful arms negotiations with the Soviet Union. (He won the vote in the Senate, fifty-five to forty-five.) He had started his intensive lobbying effort three weeks before, hosting 8:00 A.M. breakfasts for small groups of twenty-five to thirty-five senators and representatives at the White House. Each included the secretary of state, the secretary of defense, and the national security advisor. The president personally called dozens of other members of Congress. (The White House switchboard tracked down New York Senator Alphonse D'Amato in Manhattan's Little Italy section, eating dinner at a favorite restaurant. Thinking it was a practical joke by his old friend Congressman Guy Molinari, D'Amato shouted into the phone: "Molinari, you creep, cut out this crap.") There were promises, too. No one made them public, of course, but one White House aide insisted that there was nothing "illegal or expensive" about the commitments President Reagan gave those who supported his position.[45]

It seems a wonder that presidents—even with all their power and influence—can push and wheedle anything through the cavernous congressional process. Paul Light remarks that

> the President must usually win at least ten times to hope for final passage: (1) in one House subcommittee, (2) in the full House committee, (3) in the House Rules

---

[43]For a thorough discussion of recent rule changes and the impact of procedures, see Steven S. Smith, *Call to Order: Floor Politics in the House and Senate* (Washington, D.C.: Brookings Institution, 1989).

[44]Paul Light, *Artful Work: The Politics of Social Security Reform* (New York: Random House, 1985), 13.

[45]The MX lobbying story is told in *Time,* April 1, 1985, 20–21.

Figure 12.2 **How a Bill Becomes a Law**

Many bills travel, in effect, full circle, coming first from the White House as part of the presidential agenda, then returning to the president at the end of the process. In the interim, there are two parallel processes in the Senate and House, starting with committee action. If a committee gives a bill a favorable report, the whole chamber considers it. When it is passed in different versions by the two chambers, a conference committee drafts a single compromise bill.

	HOUSE	**SENATE**
Bill introduction	Bill is put into the legislative "hopper" by a member and assigned to a committee.	Bill is put into the legislative "hopper" by a member and assigned to a committee.
Committee action	The bill is usually referred by the committee to a subcommittee for study, hearings, revisions, and approval. ▼ The bill goes back to the full committee, which may amend or rewrite the bill. ▼ The committee decides whether to send the bill to the House floor, recommending its approval, or to kill it.	The bill is usually referred by the committee to a subcommittee for study, hearings, revisions, and approval. ▼ The bill goes back to the full committee, which may amend or rewrite the bill. ▼ The committee decides whether to send the bill to the Senate floor, recommending its approval, or to kill it.
Floor action	Usually the bill goes to the Rules Committee to grant a rule governing debate. The leadership schedules the bill. ▼ The bill is debated, amendments are offered, and a vote is taken.	The leadership of the Senate schedules the bill. ▼ The bill is debated, amendments are offered, and a vote is taken.
Conference action	If the bill is passed in different versions by the Senate and the House, a conference committee composed of members of each house irons out differences. ▼ The conference committee bill is returned to each house for a vote.	
Presidential decision	The president signs or vetoes the bill.	

Committee to move to the floor, (4) on the House floor, (5) in one Senate subcommittee, (6) in the full Senate subcommittee, (7) on the Senate floor, (8) in the House-Senate conference committee to work out the differences between the two bills, (9) back to the House floor for final passage, and (10) back to the Senate floor for final passage.[46]

Presidents are partners with Congress in the legislative process, but all presidents are also Congress' antagonists, struggling with Congress to control legislative outcomes.

Presidents have their own legislative agenda, based in part on their party's platform and their electoral coalition. Their task is to persuade Congress that their agenda should also be Congress's agenda. Lyndon Johnson once claimed (with perhaps a touch of that famous Johnsonian overstatement), "If an issue is not included on the presidential agenda, it is almost impossible—short of crisis—to get the Congress to focus on it."[47] Political scientists sometimes call the president the *chief legislator,* a phrase that might have appalled the Constitution writers, with their insistence on separation of powers. Presidents do, however, help create the congressional agenda. They are also their own best lobbyists.

Presidents have many resources with which to influence Congress. (Presidential leadership will be studied in Chapter 13.) They may try to influence members directly—calling up wavering members and telling them that the country's future hinges on this one vote, for example—but not often. If presidents picked just one key bill and spent ten minutes on the telephone with each of the 535 members of Congress, they would spend eighty-nine hours chatting with them. Instead, presidents wisely leave most White House lobbying to the congressional liaison office and work mainly through regular meetings with the party's leaders in the House and Senate.

It is hard to measure one person's power over another's, and especially hard to measure presidential power over congressional power. The *Congressional Quarterly* regularly calculates a "presidential success score" (see Figure 12.3), which is based on the proportion of congressional votes in which the president's position won. Nevertheless, supporting a winning position does not prove that the president caused the victory.

As one scholar puts it, presidential leadership of Congress is *at the margins.*[48] In general, successful presidential leadership of Congress has not been the result of the dominant chief executive of political folklore who reshapes the contours of the political landscape to pave the way for change. Rather than creating the conditions for important shifts in public policy, the effective American leader is the less heroic *facilitator* who works at the margins of coalition building to recognize and exploit opportunities presented by a favorable configuration of political forces.

Presidents are only one of many claimants for the attention of Congress, especially on domestic policy. As the next chapter will show, popular presidents or ones with a large majority of their party in each house of Congress have a

[46]Light, *Artful Work,* 13.

[47]Doris Kearns, *Lyndon Johnson and the American Dream* (New York: New American Library, 1976), 146.

[48]George C. Edwards III, *At the Margins* (New Haven, Conn.: Yale University Press, 1989).

Figure 12.3   Presidential Success on Votes in Congress

Presidential success rates for influencing congressional votes varies widely among presidents and within a president's tenure in office. Presidents are usually most successful early in their tenures and when their party has a majority in one or both houses of Congress. Regardless, in almost any year the president will lose on many issues. Congress considers the president's views when it makes decisions, but when it disagrees with the White House, which it often does, it does not hesitate to go in its own direction.

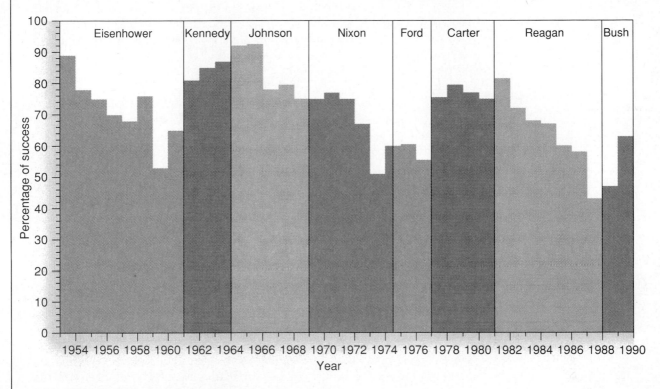

Source: Independent calculation of Congressional Quarterly data. See George C. Edwards, III, *At the Margins: Presidential Leadership of Congress* (New Haven, Conn.: Yale University Press, 1989), Table 2.1.

good chance of getting their way. Yet as Figure 12.3 shows, presidents often lose. Although Ronald Reagan began with a strong record of victories, after the Democrats won control of the Senate in the 1986 elections and Reagan's approval ratings plummeted in the wake of the Iran-Contra affair, he was successful only 44 percent of the time in 1987. Moreover, the outcome of many of the favorable votes could not be attributed to his influence.

Presidents remain an important influence on Congress, but they rarely dominate it. Ronald Reagan was considered a strong chief executive, and budgeting was one of his principal tools for affecting public policy. Yet the budgets he proposed to Congress were typically pronounced DOA, dead on arrival. Members of Congress truly compose an independent branch.

Party, Constituency, and Ideology

Presidents come and go; the parties linger on. Presidents do not determine a congressional member's electoral fortunes; constituents do. Where presidents are less influential, on domestic policies especially, party and constituency are more important.

Party Influence   On some issues, members of the parties stick together like a marching band. They are most cohesive when Congress is electing its official leaders. A vote for Speaker of the House is a straight party-line vote, with every Democrat on one side and every Republican on the other. On other issues, however, the party coalition may come unglued. Votes on civil rights policies, for example, have shown deep divisions within each party. Figure 12.4 shows the percentage of times a majority of Democrats were opposed by a majority of Republicans.

Differences between the parties are sharpest on questions of social welfare and economic policy.[49] When voting on labor issues, traditionally Democrats cling together, leaning toward the side of the unions, whereas Republicans almost always vote with business. On social welfare issues—poverty, unemployment aid, help to the cities—Democrats are more generous than Republicans. That the parties split this way should not be too surprising if you recall the party coalitions described in Chapter 7. Once in office, party members favor their electoral coalitions.

Party leaders in Congress help "whip" their members into line. Their power to do so is limited, of course. They cannot drum a recalcitrant member out of the party (as party leaders in Britain can). Leaders have plenty of influence, however, including some say about committee posts, the power to boost a member's pet projects, and the subtle but significant influence of information to which a member is not privy.

Recently the parties, especially the Republicans, have been a growing source of money for congressional campaigns. In the past the Democratic and Republican congressional campaign committees were informal organizations that did little, and collected little, for party campaigners in the constituencies. Lately, though, the congressional campaign committees have energized both parties, helping to recruit candidates, running seminars in campaign skills, and conducting polls. Equally important, the congressional campaign committees today have money to hand out to promising candidates. The parties can thus make an impact on the kinds of people who sit in Congress on either side of the aisle.

Constituency versus Ideology   Members of Congress are representatives, expected by their constituents to represent their interests in Washington. In 1714 Anthony Henry, a member of the British Parliament, received a letter from some of his constituents asking him to vote against an excise tax. He is reputed to have replied in part:

> Gentleman: I have received your letter about the excise, and I am surprised at your insolence in writing to me at all. . . .
> . . . may God's curse light upon you all, and may it make your homes as open

[49]Aage Clausen, *How Congressmen Decide: A Policy Focus* (New York: St. Martin's, 1973).

In democracies with parliamentary systems such as Great Britain, almost all votes are party-line votes. Parties, as Chapter 7 showed, are considerably weaker in the United States. Party affiliation is a rallying point for representatives and senators and does influence their votes, yet in a typical year a majority of Democrats and Republicans oppose each other less than half the time. Members of both parties often end up deserting their colleagues and voting against the party line. In recent years partisanship has been stronger in the House than in the Senate.

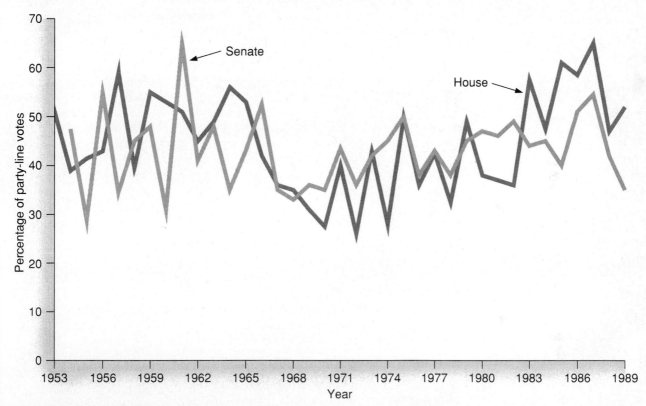

[a]Data indicate the percentage of all recorded votes on which a majority of voting Democrats opposed a majority of voting Republicans.
Source: Normal J. Ornstein, Thomas E. Mann, and Michael J. Malbin, *Vital Statistics on Congress, 1989–1990* (Washington, D.C.: American Enterprise Institute, 1987), 208; *Congressional Quarterly Weekly Report,* January 6, 1989, 55–57; and *Congressional Quarterly Weekly Report,* December 30, 1989, 3546–50.

and as free to the excise officers as your wives and daughters have always been to me while I have represented your rascally constituency.[50]

Needless to say, notions of representation have changed since Henry's time.

Sometimes representation requires a balancing act, however. If some representatives favor more defense spending but suspect that their constituents do

[50]Quoted in Peter G. Richards, *Honourable Members* (London: Faber and Faber, 1959), 157.

not, what are they to do? The English politician and philosopher Edmund Burke favored the concept of legislators as *trustees,* using their best judgment to make policy in the interests of the people. Others prefer the concept of representatives as *instructed delegates,* mirroring the preferences of their constituents. Actually, members of Congress are *politicos,* adopting both the trustee and instructed delegate roles as they strive to be both representatives and policymakers.[51]

The best way constituents can influence congressional voting is simple: elect a representative or senator who agrees with their views. John Sullivan and Robert O'Connor discovered that congressional candidates tend to take policy positions different from each other's. Moreover, the winners tend to vote on roll calls pretty much as they said they would.[52] If voters use their good sense to elect candidates who match their policy positions, then constituents *can* influence congressional policy.

If voters miss their chance and elect someone out of step with their thinking, it may be difficult to influence that person's votes. It is hard even for well-intentioned legislators to know what people want. Some pay careful attention to their mail, but the mail is a notoriously unreliable indicator of people's thinking; individuals with extreme opinions on an issue are more likely to write than those with moderate views. Some members send questionnaires to constituents, but the answers they receive are unreliable because few people respond. Some try public opinion polling, but it is expensive if professionally done and unreliable if not.

Defeating an incumbent is no easy task. Even legislators whose votes are out of step with the views of their constituents tend to be reelected. Most citizens have trouble recalling the names of their congressional representatives, let alone keeping up with their representatives' voting records. According to one expert, "Probably less than a third of all constituents can recognize who their representatives are and what policy positions they have generally taken—and even that third tends not to evaluate incumbents on the basis of policy."[53] A National Election Study found that only 11 percent of the people even claimed to remember a particular vote of their representative.

On some controversial issues, however, legislators ignore constituent opinion at great peril. For years southern members of Congress would not have dared to vote for a civil rights law. Lately representatives and senators have been concerned about the many new "single-issue groups." Such groups care little about a member's overall record; to them, a vote on one issue—gun control, abortion, the ERA, or whatever—is all that counts. Ready to pounce on one wrong vote and pour money into an opponent's campaign, these new forces in constituency politics make every legislator nervous.

Nevertheless, most issues are obscure. On such issues legislators can safely ignore constituency opinion. On a typical issue the prime determinant of a

---

[51]See Roger H. Davidson, *The Role of the Congressman* (New York: Pegasus, 1969); and Thomas E. Cavanaugh, "Role Orientations of House Members: The Process of Representation" (Paper delivered at the annual meeting of the American Political Science Association, Washington, D.C., August 1979).

[52]John L. Sullivan and Robert E. O'Connor, "Electoral Choice and Popular Control of Public Policy: The Case of the 1966 House Elections," *American Political Science Review* 66 (December 1972): 1256–68.

[53]Robert A. Bernstein, *Elections, Representation, and Congressional Voting Behavior* (Englewood Cliffs, N.J.: Prentice-Hall, 1989), 99.

congressional member's vote is personal ideology. On issues where ideological divisions are sharp and constituency preferences and knowledge are likely to be weak, such as defense and foreign policy, ideology is virtually the only determinant of voting. As ideological divisions weaken and constituency preferences strengthen, members are more likely to deviate from their own position and adopt those of their constituencies. Thus when they have differences of opinion with their constituencies, members of Congress take account of constituency preferences but are not controlled by them.[54]

Lobbyists and Interest Groups

Lobbyists have a dismal image, one worsened by periodic scandals in which someone seeking to influence Congress presents huge amounts of cash to senators and representatives. No one knows how much lobbyists spend to influence legislation, but it undoubtedly runs into the billions—recall the $1.3 million Charles Keating alone gave to five senators to encourage them to intercede with the Federal Home Loan Bank Board.

Such stories give lobbyists a bad name, no doubt often deserved. But lobbyists have a job to do—namely, to represent the interests of their organization. Lobbyists, some of them former members of Congress, can provide legislators with crucial information and often with assurances of financial aid in the next campaign.

Lobbying groups have an estimated eleven thousand representatives in Washington.[55] Forty groups alone are concerned with the single issue of protecting Alaska's environment; the bigger the issue, the more lobbyists are involved in it. Any group interested in influencing national policy-making, and that includes almost everyone, either hires Washington lobbyists or sends its own. Washington lobbyists can be a formidable group.

Lobbyists do not hold all the high cards in their dealings with Congress; congressional representatives hold some trump cards of their own. The easiest way to frustrate lobbyists is to ignore them. Lobbyists usually make little headway with their opponents anyway: the lobbyist for General Motors arguing against automobile pollution controls would not have much influence with a legislator concerned about air pollution. Members of Congress can make life uncomfortable for lobbyists, too. They can embarrass them, expose heavy-handed tactics, and spread the word among an organization's members that it is being poorly represented in Washington. Last but not least, Congress *can* regulate lobbyists, although it has never done so very strictly.

For more than forty years lobbyists have been regulated mainly by the 1946 Federal Regulation of Lobbying Act. Paid lobbyists whose principal purpose is to influence or defeat legislation must register and file reports with the secretary of the Senate and the clerk of the House. In theory, by forcing lobbyists to report who they are, who finances them, and what bills they are trying to pass or defeat, the law would not only prevent shady deals between lobbyists and Congress but also curb the influence of special interests. In fact, however, the law has been largely unenforceable; only four cases have been prosecuted under

[54]On the importance of ideology, see Bernstein, *Elections, Representation, and Congressional Voting Behavior*.

[55]Arthur C. Close, ed., *Washington Representatives 1984* (Washington: Columbia Books, 1989).

it. Moreover, few organizations are even required to register as lobbyists, inasmuch as the law covers only direct contacts with Congress and only those organizations whose principal activity is lobbying. Special interest groups are thriving; indirect, grass-roots lobbying—such as computerized mailings to encourage citizens to pressure their representatives on an issue—has grown also.

There are many forces that affect senators and representatives as they decide how to vote on a bill. After his exhaustive study of influences on congressional decision making, John Kingdon concluded that none was important enough so as to determine that congresspeople vote as they do because of that one influence.[56] The process is as complex for individual legislators as it is for those who want to influence their votes.

UNDERSTANDING CONGRESS

Congress is a complex institution. Its members want to make sound national policy, but they also want to be there after the next election. How do these sometimes conflicting desires affect American democracy and the size of American government?

Congress and Democracy

In a large nation, the success of democratic government depends on the quality of representation. In a tiny decision-making body, people can cast their own votes, but Americans could hardly hold a national referendum on every policy issue on the government agenda. Instead, Americans delegate decision-making power to representatives. If Congress is a successful democratic institution, it will have to be a successful representative institution.

Certainly some aspects of Congress make it very *un*representative. Its members are an American elite (see "America in Perspective: The House of Lords"). Its leadership is chosen by its own members, not by any vote of the American people. Voters have little direct influence over the men and women who chair key committees or lead congressional parties. Voters in just a single constituency control the fate of committee chairs and party leaders; voters in the other 434 House districts and the other 49 states have no real say, for example, about who chairs a committee considering new forms of energy, a committee considering defense buildups, or a committee making economic policy.

Nevertheless, the evidence in this chapter demonstrates that Congress does try to listen to the American people. Who voters elect makes a difference in how votes turn out; which party is in power affects policies. Linkage institutions *do* link voters to policymakers. No doubt Congress could do a better job at representation than it does. Legislators find it hard to know what constituents want. Groups may keep important issues off the legislative agenda. Members may spend so much time servicing their constituencies that they have little time left to represent those constituencies in the policy-making process.

Members of Congress are responsive to the people, if the people make it clear what they want. In response to popular demands Congress established a program in 1988 to shield the elderly against the catastrophic costs associated

---

[56]John W. Kingdon, *Congressmen's Voting Decisions,* 3rd ed. (Ann Arbor: University of Michigan Press, 1989), 242.

The House of Lords: Elitist Anachronism?

Although Americans may complain about the elitist nature of Congress, the British Parliament (one of the world's oldest), has an upper house of the legislature composed entirely of unelected members—1,195 of them. The House of Lords, as the body is called, meets in ornate splendor and is able to trace its roots back a full millennium.

As the name of the chamber implies, the members are all nobles. Two-thirds have hereditary titles, passed down through the generations and presumably unreleated to merit or ability. There are also twenty-six bishops of the Church of England, the Lord Chancellor (head of the judiciary) and eighteen senior judges (Britain does not have a separation of powers system), and life peers, those selected by the prime minister to reward party service, honor individuals who have achieved distinction in or out of government, ease awkward colleagues into gilded exile, and console party nominees defeated at the polls. Life peers cannot pass their titles down to their offspring.

Most of the lords rarely, if ever, attend a session of Parliament. In fact there are only 250 seats. Free from the restrictions of party discipline, nagging constituents, or government pressure, those who do participate debate, amend, and perfect legislation passed in the House of Commons, Britain's democratically elected legislative body. Some waggishly refer to the House of Lords as the House of Correction. The lords cannot affect tax and appropriations bills, but they can delay the passage of other bills for one session of Parliament (no more than a year), although the exercise of this power is unusual.

It is difficult to reconcile such a body with democratic values, and Americans, living in a country founded on egalitarian principles and without a tradition of nobility, typically find the House of Lords an anachronism. The British, however, seem to make this ancient institution work for them.

with acute illness. In 1989, in response to complaints about higher Medicare premiums, Congress abolished most of what it had created the previous year.

Reforming Congress

Reformers have tried to promote a more open, democratic Congress. To a large degree, they have succeeded. Looking at Congress in the 1950s, one could say that it was like a stepladder. The members advanced one rung at a time toward the heights of power with each reelection. At the top was real power in Congress. Committee chairs were automatically selected by seniority. Their power on the committee was unquestioned. Bills disappeared forever into chairs' "vest pockets" if they did not like them. They alone created subcommittees, picked their members, and routed bills to them. If committees controlled bills from the cradle to the grave, the chairs were both midwives and undertakers. At the bottom of the ladder, the norm of apprenticeship—"be seen and not heard"—prevailed. The standing Washington line about seniority was this: "Son, the longer you're here, the more you'll come to appreciate the seniority system." The system was democratic—one person, one vote—when the roll call came, but it was not democratic when the bill itself was shaped, shelved, or sunk.

Democratization   The waves of congressional reform in the 1960s and especially the 1970s changed all this. Lyndon Johnson had started the reform ball rolling during his majority leadership with the "Johnson rule," which gave each

Cable television's live coverage of Congress has further democratized the legislative process by letting Americans see their representatives at work. As one can guess, members of Congress occasionally try to manipulate the broadcasts. When conservative House Republicans were staging long speeches denouncing the Democrats, for example, Democratic Speaker Tip O'Neill ordered the cameras to pan the audience, revealing an empty chamber.

senator a seat on at least one key committee. This reform allowed junior members more room at the top.

By the 1970s the reform movement, bent on democratizing Congress, picked up speed.[57] It tried to create more democracy by spreading power around. First to go was the automatic and often autocratic dominance of the most senior members as committee chairs. Instead, chairs were elected by the majority party, and some of the most objectionable chairs were dropped. The chairs' power was also cut by the proliferation of subcommittees, which "widened the distribution of authority, visibility, and resources in both chambers."[58]

Subcommittees became the new centers of power in Congress. Freshman senators and representatives came to chair major subcommittees. In the House five separate subcommittees now focus on consumer legislation, a dozen on welfare policy, and six on energy. Legislative hurdles are harder to overcome because of the proliferation of subcommittees.

Not only the formal reforms of Congress but also the proliferation of informal caucuses have tended to decentralize power in Congress. Burdett Loomis remarks that "the proliferation of caucuses illustrates the shoring up of particularistic forces in Congress. . . . And while members decry the increase in single-issue politics, they have only to consider their own behavior."[59]

All these recent changes in Congress—seniority reform, the subcommittee explosion, and the burgeoning caucuses—have fragmented the power of Congress. Richard Fenno, a veteran congressional observer, once remarked that the "performance of Congress as an institution is very largely the performance of its committees" but that the committee system is the "epitome of fragmentation and decentralization."[60]

Interest groups grow on committees and subcommittees like barnacles on a boat. After a while, these groups develop intimacy and influence with "their" committee. Committee decisions usually carry the day on the roll call vote. Thus the committee system links congressional policy-making to the multiplicity of interests, rather than to a majority's preferences.

Representativeness versus Effectiveness   The central legislative dilemma for Congress is combining the faithful representation of constituents with the making of effective public policy. Supporters see Congress as a forum in which many interests compete for a spot on the policy agenda and over the form of a particular policy—just as the founders intended it to be.

Critics wonder if Congress is so responsive to so many interests that policy is as uncoordinated, fragmented, and decentralized as Congress itself. The agricultural committees busily tend to the interests of tobacco farmers while committees on health and welfare spend millions for lung cancer research. One committee wrestles with domestic unemployment while another makes tax policy that encourages businesses to open new plants out of the country.

[57]For more on congressional reform, see Leroy N. Rieselbach, *Congressional Reform* (Washington, D.C.: Congressional Quarterly Press, 1986).

[58]David E. Price, "Congressional Committees and the Policy Process" in *Congress Reconsidered,* 3rd ed., ed. Laurence C. Dodd and Bruce I. Oppenheimer (Washington, D.C.: Congressional Quarterly Press, 1985), 179.

[59]Burdett Loomis, "Congressional Caucuses and the Politics of Representation," in *Congress Reconsidered,* 2nd ed., ed. Dodd and Oppenheimer.

[60]Richard Fenno, "If, as Ralph Nader Says, Congress Is the 'Broken Branch,' How Come We Love Our Congressmen So Much?" in *Congress in Change,* ed. Norman Ornstein (New York: Praeger, 1975), 282.

In addition, some observers feel Congress is too representative—so much so that it is incapable of taking decisive action to deal with difficult problems. One reason government cannot balance the budget, they say, is that Congress is protecting the interests of too many people. With each interest trying to preserve the status quo, bold reforms cannot be enacted. On the other hand, defenders of Congress point out that, being decentralized, there is no oligarchy in control to prevent the legislature from taking comprehensive action. In fact Congress has enacted the huge tax cut of 1981, the comprehensive (and complicated) tax reform of 1986, and the various versions of the Gramm-Rudman-Hollings bill to balance the budget (see Chapter 14).[61]

There is no simple solution to Congress's dilemma. It tries to be both a representative and objective policy-making institution. As long as this is true, it is unlikely to please all its critics.

Congress and the Size of Government

If Congress is responsive to a multitude of interests and those interests desire government policies to aid them in some way, does the nature of Congress predispose it to continually increase the size of the public sector?

In addition, do the benefits of servicing constituents provide an incentive for members of Congress to tolerate, even to expand, an already big government? The more policies there are, the more potential ways members could help their constituencies. The more bureaucracies there are, the more red tape members can help cut. Big government helps members of Congress get reelected and even gives them good reason to support making it bigger.

Members of Congress vigorously protect the interests of their constituents. At the same time, there are many members who agree with Ronald Reagan that government is not the answer to problems, but *is* the problem. They make careers out of fighting against government programs (although these same senators and representatives typically support programs aimed at their constituents).

Americans have contradictory preferences regarding public policy. As discussed in previous chapters, they want to balance the budget and pay low taxes, but they also support most government programs. Congress does not impose programs upon a reluctant public; instead, it responds to demands for them.

Perhaps these contradictory preferences help explain the pervasive ticket splitting in national elections in which Republicans are elected to the presidency and Democrats to Congress. While the president can watch out for the large issues—taxes, defense, and the overall budget—Congress can protect favorite domestic policy programs.

SUMMARY

According to the Constitution, members of Congress are the government's policymakers, but legislative policymaker is only one of the roles of a member of Congress. They are also politicians, and politicians always have their eye on the next election. Success in congressional elections may be determined as much by constituency service—casework and the pork barrel—as by policy-making.

[61]See M. Darrell West, *Congress and Economic Policymaking* (Pittsburgh: University of Pittsburgh Press, 1987).

Senators and representatives have become so skilled at constituency service that incumbents have a big edge over challengers. Not only do incumbents tend to win, but they tend to win by big margins.

The structure of Congress is so complex that it seems remarkable that legislation gets passed at all. Its bicameral division means that bills have two sets of committee hurdles to clear. Recent reforms have decentralized power, and so the job of leading Congress is more difficult than ever.

Presidents try hard to influence Congress, and parties and elections can also shape legislators' choices. The impact of these factors clearly differs from one policy area to another. Party impacts are clearest on issues for which the party's coalitions are clearest—social welfare and economic issues, in particular. Constituencies influence policy mostly by the initial choice of a representative. Members of Congress do pay attention to voters, especially on visible issues, but most issues do not interest voters. On these less visible issues other factors, such as lobbyists and member's individual ideologies, influence policy decisions.

Congress clearly has some undemocratic and unrepresentative features. Its members are hardly average Americans. Even so, they pay attention to popular preferences, when they can figure out what they are. People inside and outside the institution, however, think that Congress is ineffective. Its objective policy-making decisions and representative functions sometimes conflict, yet from time

"Listen, pal! I didn't spend seven million bucks to get here so I could yield the floor to you."

to time Congress does show that it can deal with major issues in a comprehensive fashion. Many members of Congress have incentives to increase the size of the federal government, but these incentives are provided by the people who put them in office.

KEY TERMS

incumbents	majority leader	oversight
casework	whips	committee chairs
pork barrel	minority leader	seniority system
bicameral legislature	standing committees	caucus
House Rules Committee	joint committees	bill
filibuster	conference committees	
Speaker of the House	select committees	

FOR FURTHER READING

Bernstein, Robert A. *Elections, Representation, and Congressional Voting Behavior.* Englewood Cliffs, N.J.: Prentice-Hall, 1989. Examines the issue of constituency control over members of Congress.

Dodd, Lawrence C., and Bruce I. Oppenheimer, eds. *Congress Reconsidered,* 4th ed. Washington, D.C.: Congressional Quarterly Press, 1989. Excellent essays on the problems of Congress in the 1980s.

Fenno, Richard F., Jr. *Home Style.* Boston: Little, Brown, 1978. How members of Congress mend fences and stay in political touch with the folks back home.

Fiorina, Morris P. *Congress: Keystone of the Washington Establishment,* 2nd ed. New Haven, Conn.: Yale University Press, 1989. Argues that members of Congress are self-serving in serving their constituents, ensuring their reelection but harming the national interest.

Goldenberg, Edie N., and Michael W. Traugott. *Campaigning for Congress.* Washington, D.C.: Congressional Quarterly Press, 1984. A good book on congressional campaigns.

Jacobson, Gary C. *The Politics of Congressional Elections,* 2nd ed. Boston: Little, Brown, 1987. An excellent review of congressional elections.

Kingdon, John W. *Congressmen's Voting Decisions,* 3rd ed. Ann Arbor: University of Michigan Press, 1989. A thorough and insightful study of voting decisions.

Malbin, Michael. *Unelected Representatives.* New York: Basic Books, 1980. A study of congressional staffs.

Mayhew, David R. *Congress: The Electoral Connection.* New Haven, Conn.: Yale University Press, 1974. An analysis of Congress based on the premise that the principal motivation of congressional behavior is reelection.

Ornstein, Norman, and Shirley Elder. *Interest Groups, Lobbying, and Policymaking.* Washington, D.C.: Congressional Quarterly Press, 1978. A good examination of lobbying, with several informative case studies.

Sinclair, Barbara. *Majority Leadership in the U.S. House.* Baltimore: Johns Hopkins University Press, 1983. Examines how leaders go about building coalitions.

Smith, Steven, S., and Christopher J. Deering. *Committees in Congress.* Washington, D.C.: Congressional Quarterly Press, 1984. A thorough overview of the complex committee structure in the House and Senate.

Sorauf, Frank J. *Money in American Elections.* Boston: Little, Brown, 1988. A clear, careful overview of campaign finance.

13

THE PRESIDENCY

In June of 1989 George Bush proposed a wide-ranging antipollution measure designed to clean up the nation's air. In doing so he transformed a twelve-year stalemate in Congress into an atmosphere in which the passage of a clean-air bill seemed inevitable. The president's action brought myriad geographical and economic interests to the bargaining table and forced the most obstructionist and dogmatic players to sit down and deal.

The last amendments to clean-air laws had occurred in 1977. Since that time there had been deadlock as environmentalists failed repeatedly to update the legislation. The chief reason was the opposition of President Reagan, who consistently blocked clean-air initiatives on the grounds that the science on which they were based was shaky, the need for them was unproven, or that business and industry had done enough already.

Reagan's resistance strengthened powerful congressional Democrats who opposed further amendments to the clean-air laws. John Dingell of Michigan, the chair of the Energy and Commerce Committee in the House, controlled the avenue through which clean-air legislation had to travel. His concern was protecting the auto companies (Ford Motor Company's headquarters is in his district). Senate Majority Leader Robert Byrd of West Virginia feared acid rain proposals would destroy the market for high-sulphur coal from his state and throw thousands of miners out of work.

After introducing his bill, Bush confined his public participation in the clean-air debate largely to news conference complaints that Congress was dawdling on his legislation. His aides said the president was saving his strength for a time he could make a major difference, such as in the final negotiations over the bill.

In the meantime Bush's top aides sent contradictory signals to Capitol Hill. Environmental Protection Agency Administrator William K. Reilly was lobbying for a stronger bill while White House Chief of Staff John H. Sununu was pressing for a weaker one. The president's chief allies in the House felt free to jettison key parts of his bill for provisions they liked better. To obtain a needed endorsement from a major environmental group, the president was forced to give the Environmental Defense Fund bargaining power in the negotiations over his proposal.

Other forces were at work in the arena of environmental policy-making as well. In December of 1987 Congress had blocked a Dingell-backed amendment to extend the deadlines for achieving clean air. In 1989 Democrat George Mitchell of Maine (from a state that suffers from acid rain) became the new Senate majority leader. Environmental protection was one of his highest priorities. In addition, polls showed widespread and growing concern in the public about the environment as well as broad support for more controls on pollution and a willingness to pay for them.

Thus a clean-air bill was passed in 1990. President Bush's sponsorship had changed the dynamics of the issue in Congress, yet the administration could not force Congress to act, and the president's role during most of the legislative process was a modest one. In the absence of congressional inclination to support stronger environmental protection laws, changes in congressional leadership, or supportive public opinion, the president would have had a difficult time obtaining passage of his bill. Even under these auspicious conditions, the president had to bargain with Congress and interest groups and settle disputes within his own administration.

No one can facilitate change like the president, yet presidents do not dominate the policy-making process. First and foremost, presidents are politicians, usually confined to trying to persuade others to support their policies. This chapter will take a close look at how presidents exercise leadership in the American political system.

Powerful, strong, leader of the free world, commander in chief—these are common images of the American president. The president epitomizes American government. The only place in the world where television networks assign a permanent camera crew is the White House. The presidency is power—at least according to popular myth.

In this presidency-as-powerhouse myth, presidents are the government's command center. Problems are brought to their desk; they decide the right courses of action, issue orders, and an army of aides and bureaucrats carry out their commands. Nothing could be further from the truth, as presidents themselves soon discover. As one presidential aide put it, "Every time you turn around people resist you."[1]

All modern presidents have complained that moving even their own administrations into action was tough. Although presidents have vast powers, sometimes these vast powers do not work very well. As Harry Truman was getting ready to turn over the Oval Office to Dwight Eisenhower, a former general, he mused: "He'll sit here and he'll say, 'Do this! Do that!' *And nothing will happen*. Poor Ike—it won't be a bit like the army. He'll find it very frustrating."[2]

The main reason presidents have trouble getting things done is that other policymakers with whom they deal have their own agendas, their own interests, and their own sources of power. Congress is beholden not to the president but to the individual constituencies of its members. Cabinet members often push their departmental interests and their constituencies (the Department of Agriculture has farmers as its constituency, the Department of Labor has unions, and so on). Presidents operate in an environment filled with checks and balances and competing centers of power. As Richard Neustadt has argued, presidential power is the power to *persuade*, not to command.[3]

Since not everyone bends easily to even the most persuasive president, the president must be a *leader*. To accomplish policy goals, the president must get other people, important people, to do things they otherwise would not do. To be effective, the president must have highly developed *political skills* to mobilize influence, manage conflict, negotiate, and fashion compromises. This chapter will examine presidential leadership, but first, you will meet some of the presidents themselves.

THE PRESIDENTS

The presidency is an institution composed of the roles presidents must play, the powers at their disposal, and the large bureaucracy at their command. It is also a highly personal office. The personality of the individual who serves as president makes a difference.

---

[1]Quoted in Thomas E. Cronin, *The State of the Presidency*, 2nd ed. (Boston: Little, Brown, 1980), 223.

[2]Quoted in Richard E. Neustadt, *Presidential Power* (New York: Wiley, 1980), 9.

[3]Neustadt, *Presidential Power*.

Great Expectations

When President Bush took the oath of office on January 20, 1989, he faced many daunting tasks. Perhaps the most difficult of these was living up to the expectations of the American people. Americans expect the chief executive to ensure peace, prosperity, and security.[4] As President Carter remarked, "The President is . . . held to be responsible for the state of the economy . . . [and] for the inconveniences, or disappointments, or the concerns of the American people."[5] Americans want the good life, and they look to the president to provide it.

In addition to expecting successful policies from the White House, Americans expect their presidents to be extraordinary individuals (which, of course, buttresses the public's policy expectations). The public expects presidents to be intelligent, cool in a crisis, competent, and highly ethical. Citizens also demand that their public and private lives be exemplary.

Americans are of two minds about the presidency. On the one hand, they badly want to believe in a powerful president, one who can do good. They look back longingly on the great presidents of the first American century—Washington, Jefferson, Lincoln—and some in the second century as well, especially Franklin D. Roosevelt and John F. Kennedy.

On the other hand, Americans do not like a concentration of power. Although there has been a substantial enlargement of presidential responsibilities in the past few decades, there has been no corresponding increase in presidential power to meet these new expectations. Americans are basically individualistic and skeptical of authority. According to Samuel Huntington, "The distinctive aspect of the American Creed is its antigovernment character. Opposition to

[4]On the public's expectations of the president, see George C. Edwards III, *The Public Presidency* (New York: St. Martin's Press, 1983), chap. 5.

[5]Office of the White House Press Secretary, *Remarks of the President at a Meeting with Non-Washington Editors and Broadcasters*, September 21, 1979, 12.

'Okay, bring in the new guy . . .'

power, and suspicion of government as the most dangerous embodiment of power, are the central themes of American political thought."[6] Throughout *Government in America*, you have seen the American political culture's strong belief in limited government, liberty, individualism, equality, and democracy. These values generate a distrust of strong leadership, authority, and the public sector in general.

It is in this environment of contradictory views and limited power that the president must attempt to lead. For years, a famous presidential motto was captured in the sign that President Harry S Truman had on his desk: "The Buck Stops Here." (Jimmy Carter put the same sign on his desk, too.) If American's expectations (in part fielded by unrealistic campaign promises) exceed the president's leadership resources or resourcefulness, future presidents may find a new motto for the office: "Dashed Hopes Begin Here."

Because Americans' expectations of the presidency are so high, it is doubly important who serves as president. Just who are the people who have occupied the Oval Office?

Who They Are

When Warren G. Harding, one of the least illustrious American presidents, was in office, Clarence Darrow remarked, "When I was a boy, I was told that anybody could become president. Now I'm beginning to believe it." The Constitution simply states that the president must be a natural-born citizen at least thirty-five years old and have resided in the United States for at least fourteen years. In fact, all American presidents have been white, male, and, except for John Kennedy, Protestant. In other ways, however, the recent collection of presidents suggests considerable variety. Since World War II, there has been a Missouri haberdasher; a war hero; a Boston Irish politician; a small-town Texas boy who grew up to become the biggest wheeler-dealer in the Senate; a California lawyer described by his enemies as "Tricky Dick" and by his friends as a misunderstood master of national leadership; a former Rose Bowl player who had spent his entire political career in the House; a former governor who had been a Georgia peanut wholesaler; an actor who was also a former governor of California; and a former CIA Chief and ambassador who was the son of a U.S. senator (see "In Focus: Recent Presidents").

All manner of men have occupied the Oval Office. Thomas Jefferson was a scientist and scholar who assembled dinosaur bones when presidential business was slack. Woodrow Wilson, the only political scientist ever to become president, combined a Presbyterian moral fervor and righteousness with a professor's intimidating style of leadership and speech making. His successor, Warren G. Harding, became president because Republican leaders thought he looked like one. Poker was his pastime. Out of his element in the job, Harding is almost everyone's choice as the worst American president. His speech making, said opponent William G. McAdoo, sounded "like an army of pompous phrases marching across the landscape in search of an idea." Harding's friends stole the government blind, prompting his brief assessment of the presidency: "God, what a job!"

[6]Samuel P. Huntington, *American Politics: The Promise of Disharmony* (Cambridge, Mass.: Belknap, 1981), 33.

Recent Presidents

Harry S Truman (1945–53) was a Democrat from Missouri. A haberdasher by trade, Truman worked his way up through the political machine in Kansas City to become U.S. senator from Missouri. Tapped by Roosevelt to be his vice-presidential running mate in 1944, Truman had barely taken office when FDR died. Truman had to decide whether to drop atomic bombs on Japan (he ordered them dropped) and then presided over the trying times of postwar recovery and the beginning of the Cold War. A man of strong opinions, Truman often shot from the lip. Never popular while in office (partly because FDR was a hard act to follow), his stature seemed to grow once he retired to Independence, Missouri.

Dwight D. Eisenhower (1953–61), a Republican, was born in Texas and reared in Kansas. Although "Ike" had been the commander of Allied Forces in Europe during World War II, he never voted until he became the Republican nominee in 1952. He presided over the relatively tranquil 1950s, offering to the public a grandfatherly image of dependable conservatism and cool crisis management. His public standing remained high, and he crushed the Democratic nominee, Adlai Stevenson, in the 1952 and 1956 presidential elections. Ike made Richard Nixon his vice-president but never his friend; he even declined to invite Nixon inside his house at Gettysburg, Pennsylvania.

John F. Kennedy (1961–63) was a Democrat from Massachusetts. JFK is remembered most for his leadership style; his elegant wife, Jackie; and his tragic assassination in Dallas, Texas, on November 22, 1963. Kennedy was a senator before he ran for president in 1960. Handsome, virile, and graceful, he touted culture and made *charisma* a household word. Kennedy's legislative record was not enviable, but his popularity with the public was impressive. His presidency began in the 1960s era of liberal domestic policies and staunchly anti-Communist foreign policies.

Lyndon B. Johnson (1963–69) was a Democrat from Texas. As Senate majority leader, Lyndon Johnson was one of the most skilled politicians ever to walk the Capitol corridors. In private he was simultaneously charming, cunning, and coercive. After the culture and charisma of the Kennedy years, LBJ's public image seemed coarse and he was easily ridiculed. Johnson was frustrated that he, unlike Kennedy, somehow lacked the "right background" to mix with Harvard-educated elites. Nonetheless, he tackled the presidency with energy, launching the War on Poverty at home and escalating the Vietnam War abroad. The latter caused the unmaking of his presidency. In March 1968 he announced that he would neither seek nor accept renomination.

Richard M. Nixon (1969–74), a Republican, was from California and later New York. Eisenhower's vice-president, Nixon was a natural candidate for the Republicans in 1960 but lost that presidential race to John F. Kennedy. Trying again in 1968, Nixon edged out Democrat Hubert Humphrey and the American

In this potpourri of personalities, James David Barber has looked for some patterns in order to understand how presidents perform. He suggests that one examine presidents by looking at their *presidential character*.[7] Presidents, he claims, vary in their *activity* or *passivity* toward the job. Some, like Lyndon Johnson, throw themselves into the job with great vigor and work furiously at being president; others, like Calvin Coolidge (who sometimes slept eleven hours at night), do not. Presidents also vary in their *positive* or *negative* response to

James David Barber, *The Presidential Character*, 3rd ed. (Englewood Cliffs, N.J.: Prentice-Hall, 1985).

Independent party's George Wallace. Most interested in foreign policy, Nixon wound down the Vietnam War and established American links with China. Running for reelection in 1972, he crushed George McGovern. During that campaign, though, the Watergate break-in started the beginning of the end of the Nixon presidency. After the House Judiciary Committee voted to recommend his impeachment for high crimes and misdemeanors, Nixon resigned on August 9, 1974.

Gerald R. Ford (1974–1977) was a Republican from Michigan. Ford spent his political career in the House of Representatives before becoming president. He was "the accidental president," becoming vice-president when Spiro T. Agnew left office under a cloud of scandal and later becoming president when the same thing happened to Nixon. Though cartoonists depicted Ford as physically clumsy and none too intelligent (Lyndon Johnson said nasty things about his intelligence), Ford reestablished respect for a Watergate-tainted presidency. Ford's pardon of Nixon caused him to slip in the polls and, he maintained, cost him reelection.

Jimmy Carter (1977–81) was a Democrat from Georgia. Carter, who had been a naval officer, a peanut warehouser, and a governor, surprised the nation by first winning the Democratic nomination in 1976 and then defeating the incumbent president, Gerald Ford. "If I had to choose one politician to sit at the Pearly Gates and pass judgment on my soul," wrote Carter's ex-speech writer James Fallows in the *Atlan-*

tic, "Jimmy Carter would be the one." But Carter also, claimed Fallows, lacked the sophistication, the ability to communicate his goals, and the passion necessary to be an effective leader. Once in office, Carter demonstrated that being a Washington outsider may help get one elected but makes it hard to influence the Washington community. Carter was defeated in his bid for reelection by Ronald Reagan.

Ronald W. Reagan (1981–89) was a Republican from California. Born in Illinois, Reagan moved to California and pursued a show-business career, becoming an actor of middling stature. His presidency of the Screen Actors' Guild brought him into politics. As governor of California, he was ideologically conservative but more liberal in his policies than opponents had feared. As president, he managed to convey genial affability, using power with poise. Resoundingly reelected in 1984, his principal goals were to pare domestic spending and boost defense spending while coping with massive deficits.

George H. W. Bush (1989–present) is a Republican from Texas. The son of a prominent New England family, Bush moved to Texas and made his fortune in the oil business. After a short tenure in Congress, he held a series of prominent jobs, including head of the Central Intelligence Agency, ambassador to the United Nations, ambassador to China, and vice-president for eight years under Ronald Reagan.

politics. Some, like Franklin Roosevelt or John Kennedy, claim to love politics and enjoy the job of being president; others, like Richard Nixon, feel that duty impels their performance and have a grim, self-sacrificial attitude toward the job.

Barber argues that those presidents who are both active and negative, presidents like Lyndon Johnson and Richard Nixon (see Table 13.1), are prone to tragedy. When such presidents experience certain kinds of stress, he says, their psychological needs will cause them to persist in failed policies.

Not all presidential scholars agree with Barber's typology of presidential character. Garry Wills describes Barber's analysis as an example of the "games academics play."[8] Some criticize the categories in which presidents are placed. There is good reason to believe, for example, that Eisenhower was not "passive" at all.[9] Others feel that one cannot learn much from such categories. Kennedy, Carter, Ford, and Bush all fall into the "active-positive" category, but there were great differences in their performances as president. There are many opinions, but no single answer to the question of what makes a successful president.

How They Got There

Regardless of their background or character, all presidents must come to the job through one of two basic routes. No one is born to be the future president in the way that someone is born to be the future king or queen of England.

Elections: The Normal Road to the White House   Most presidents take a familiar journey to 1600 Pennsylvania Avenue: they run for president through the electoral process, which is described in Chapters 8 and 9. Once in office, presidents are guaranteed a four-year term by the Constitution, but the **Twenty-second Amendment**, passed in 1951, limits them to two terms.

Only nine of the thirty-four presidents before George Bush have actually served two or more full terms in the White House: Washington, Jefferson, Madison, Jackson, Grant, Wilson, Franklin Roosevelt, Eisenhower, and Reagan. A few decided against a second term ("Silent Cal" Coolidge said simply, "I do not choose to run"). Four other presidents (Polk, Pierce, Buchanan, and Hayes) also threw in the towel at the end of one full term. Six others (both of the Adamses, Van Buren, Taft, Hoover, and Carter) thought the voters owed them a second term, but the voters disagreed.

The Vice-Presidency: Another Road to the White House   For better than 10 percent of American history, the presidency has actually been occupied by an individual not elected to the office. About one in five presidents got the job not through the normal road of elections but because they were vice-president

Each president has shaped the office in his own image. Lyndon Johnson's presidency was characterized by a willingness to attack a broad range of issues, from communism in Vietnam to poverty in America—and by exhaustion from grappling with so many complex problems.

[8]Garry Wills, *The Kennedy Imprisonment* (Boston: Atlantic-Little, Brown, 1982), 186. See also Alexander George, "Assessing Presidential Character," *World Politics* 26 (January 1974): 10–30.

[9]On Eisenhower as a leader, see Fred I. Greenstein, *The Hidden-Hand Presidency* (New York: Basic Books, 1982).

Table 13.1	Barber's Classification of Recent Presidents' Character			
	ACTIVE-POSITIVE	**ACTIVE-NEGATIVE**	**PASSIVE-POSITIVE**	**PASSIVE-NEGATIVE**
	Kennedy	Johnson	Reagan	Eisenhower
	Ford	Nixon		
	Carter			
	Bush			

Source: James David Barber, *The Presidential Character,* 3rd ed. (Englewood Cliffs, N.J.: Prentice-Hall, 1985).

Table 13.2   Incomplete Presidential Terms

PRESIDENT	TERM	SUCCEEDED BY
William Henry Harrison	March 4, 1841–April 4, 1841	John Tyler
Zachary Taylor	March 5, 1849–July 9, 1850	Millard Fillmore
Abraham Lincoln	March 4, 1865–April 15, 1865[a]	Andrew Johnson
James A. Garfield	March 4, 1881–September 19, 1881	Chester A. Arthur
William McKinley	March 4, 1901–September 14, 1901[a]	Theodore Roosevelt
Warren G. Harding	March 4, 1921–August 2, 1923	Calvin Coolidge
Franklin D. Roosevelt	January 20, 1945–April 12, 1945[b]	Harry S Truman
John F. Kennedy	January 20, 1961–November 22, 1963	Lyndon B. Johnson
Richard M. Nixon	January 20, 1969–August 9, 1974[a]	Gerald R. Ford

[a] Second term.
[b] Fourth term.

when the incumbent president either died or (in Nixon's case) resigned (see Table 13.2). In the twentieth century almost one-third (five of sixteen) of those who occupied the office were "accidental presidents." The most accidental of all was Gerald Ford, who did not run for either the vice-presidency or the presidency before taking office. Ford was nominated vice-president by President Nixon when Vice-President Spiro Agnew resigned; he then assumed the presidency when Nixon himself resigned.

Neither politicians nor political scientists have paid much attention to the vice-presidency. Once the choice of a party's "second team" was an afterthought; now it is mostly an effort to placate some important symbolic constituency. The occupants have rarely enjoyed the job. John Nance Garner, one of Franklin D. Roosevelt's vice-presidents, said the job was "not worth a warm bucket of spit." Some have performed so poorly as to have been an embarrassment to the president. After Woodrow Wilson's debilitating stroke, almost everyone agreed that Vice-President Thomas Marshall—a man who shirked all responsibility, including cabinet meetings—would be a disaster as acting president. Spiro Agnew, Richard Nixon's first vice-president, had to resign and was convicted of evading taxes on bribes he had accepted.

Once in office, vice-presidents find that their main job is waiting. Constitutionally, they are assigned the minor task of presiding over the Senate and voting in case of a tie. As George Bush said when he was vice-president, "The buck *doesn't* stop here." Recent presidents, though, have taken their vice-presidents more seriously, involving them in policy discussions and important diplomacy.[10]

Jimmy Carter and Ronald Reagan, both Washington outsiders, chose vice-presidents who had substantial Washington experience: Walter Mondale and George Bush. To become intimates of the president, both had to be completely loyal, losing their political independence in the process. Vice-President Bush for example, was implicated in the Iran-Contra affair, but he steadfastly refused to reveal his discussions with President Reagan on the matter.

---

[10] See Paul C. Light, *Vice Presidential Power* (Baltimore: John Hopkins University Press, 1984).

When his turn came to choose a vice-president, Bush selected Senator Dan Quayle of Indiana. Considered by many a political lightweight, Quayle has kept a relatively low profile while meeting regularly with the president and representing him in discussions with the leaders of numerous countries.

Impeachment and Succession   Getting rid of a discredited president before the end of a term is no easy task. The Constitution prescribes how to do it through **impeachment,** which is roughly the political equivalent of an indictment in criminal law. The House of Representatives may, by majority vote, impeach the president for "Treason, Bribery, or other high Crimes and Misdemeanors." Once the House votes for impeachment, the case goes to the Senate, which tries the accused president, with the chief justice presiding. By a two-thirds vote, the Senate may convict and remove the president from office.[11]

Only once has a president been impeached: Andrew Johnson, Lincoln's successor, was impeached by the House in 1868 on charges stemming from his disagreement with radical Republicans. He escaped conviction in the Senate by one vote. Richard Nixon came as close to impeachment as any president since. On July 31, 1974, the House Judiciary Committee voted to recommend his impeachment to the full House as a result of the **Watergate** scandal. Nixon escaped a certain vote for impeachment by resigning (see "A Question of Ethics: Watergate").

[11]On the impeachment process, see a book that, remarkably, was published exactly a year before Nixon's impeachment became an issue: Raoul Berger, *Impeachment: The Constitutional Problems* (Cambridge, Mass.: Harvard University Press, 1973).

Richard Nixon was the only American president ever to resign his office. Nixon decided to resign rather than face impeachment for his role in the Watergate scandal, a series of illegal wiretaps, break-ins, and cover-ups.

Constitutional amendments cover one other important problem concerning the presidential term: presidential disability and succession. Several times a president has lain disabled, incapable of carrying out the job for weeks or even months at a time. After Woodrow Wilson suffered a stroke, his wife became virtual acting president. The **Twenty-fifth Amendment** (1967) clarified some of the Constitution's vagueness about disability. It permits the vice-president to become acting president if the vice-president and the president's cabinet determine that the president is disabled, and it outlines how a recuperated president can reclaim the Oval Office. Other laws specify the order of presidential succession—from the vice-president, to the Speaker of the House, to the president pro tempore of the Senate, and down through the cabinet.

The Twenty-fifth Amendment also created a means for selecting a new vice-president when the office becomes vacant—a not-infrequent occurrence. The president nominates a new vice-president, who assumes the office when both houses of Congress approve the nomination.

PRESIDENTIAL POWERS

The contemporary presidency hardly resembles the one the Constitution framers designed in 1787. The executive office they conceived had more limited authority, fewer responsibilities, and much less organizational structure than today's presidency. The founders feared both anarchy and monarchy. They wanted an independent executive but disagreed on both the form it should take and the powers it should exercise. In the end they created an executive unlike any the world had ever seen[12] (see "America in Perspective: What a Difference a Border Makes" on page 466).

At first some delegates proposed a plural executive, dividing responsibility for various areas of power or functioning as a committee. Others felt that governing a large nation required a single president with significant powers. James Wilson, a delegate from Pennsylvania, argued that only a single individual could combine the necessary characteristics of "energy, dispatch, and responsibility." Critics immediately responded that such an executive would be dangerous— "the fetus of monarchy," claimed Edmund Randolph. Wilson carried the day, aided by the fact that virtually everyone assumed that the first president would be George Washington, the person the delegates most trusted not to abuse power.

Constitutional Powers

When it came to detailing the executive's power, the delegates to the Constitutional Convention turned for inspiration to the constitutions of New York and New Jersey, states with strong governors. Couching the description of presidential powers in the language of two state constitutions made it more palatable to the delegates, who adopted most of it with little debate.

The Constitution says remarkably little about presidential power. The discussion of the presidency begins with these general words: "The executive power

[12]On the creation of the presidency see Donald L. Robinson, *"To the Best of My Ability"* (New York: Norton, 1987); Thomas E. Cronin, ed., *Inventing the American Presidency* (Lawrence, Kan.: University Press of Kansas, 1989).

A Question of Ethics

Watergate

If a novelist had invented Watergate, it would have made a fascinating but not very believable story. As reality, it caused the resignation of the president who was elected by what was then the largest popular majority in American history—Richard M. Nixon.

Dozens of events and decisions produced the Watergate affair. Many centered on Nixon's 1972 reelection campaign. His campaign manager, former Attorney General John Mitchell, hired a man named G. Gordon Liddy as counsel to the Committee to Re-elect the President (CREEP). Liddy did little lawyering at CREEP, but he did develop an expensive "counter-intelligence" program.

On January 2, 1972, Liddy presented his multimillion-dollar plan to Mitchell, who later described the plan as including "mugging squads, kidnapping teams, prostitutes to compromise the opposition, and electronic surveillance." He ordered Liddy to scale down the program.

One offshoot of Liddy's plan was the planting of a wiretap at the headquarters of the Democratic National Committee (DNC) in Washington's Watergate complex. On June 17, 1972, five men were caught inside the DNC headquarters with burglary tools, bugging devices, and a stack of one hundred dollar bills.

Their links to CREEP soon became known, and Liddy himself was arrested. Nixon's press secretary, Ron Ziegler, dismissed the incident as a "third-rate burglary," and Nixon assured the press that the White House had no involvement whatsoever in the bungled break-in.

To this day, no one has demonstrated that Nixon had prior knowledge of the break-in. But within hours after the arrests, paper shredders at the White House and CREEP were destroying documents that might link the burglars to the White House. CREEP and White House officials pressured Nixon's personal lawyer, Herbert Kalmbach, to collect funds quietly to "support the families" of the accused. Anthony Ulasewicz, a former New York policeman working for the White House, later regaled the Watergate Committee with stories of leaving money in paper bags to be picked up and delivered to the accused burglars. *Washington Post* reporters Robert Woodward and Carl Bernstein began an investigation that eventually tracked the Watergate break-in and its cover-up to the very door of the Oval Office.

As the trail got closer, Nixon's aides resigned one by one. Chief of Staff Bob Haldeman, domestic-policy advisor John Ehrlichman, and others were writing their

shall be vested in a president of the United States of America." It goes on to list just a few powers (see Table 13.3). The framers' invention fit nicely within the Madisonian system of shared power and checks and balances. There is little that presidents can do on their own, and they share executive, legislative, and judicial power with the other branches of government.

Institutional balance was essential to the convention delegates, who had in mind the abuses of past executives combined with the excesses of state legislatures (discussed in Chapter 2). The problem was how to preserve the balance without jeopardizing the independence of the separate branches or impeding the lawful exercise of their authority. In the end the framers resolved this problem by checking those powers that they believed to be most dangerous, the ones that historically had been subject to the greatest abuse (for example, they gave Congress the power to declare war and approve treaties and presidential appointments), while protecting the general spheres of authority from encroachment (the executive, for instance, was given a qualified veto).

resignations and ringing up their lawyers simultaneously. On May 17, 1973, hearings of the Senate Select Committee on Campaign Activities opened, chaired by Senator Sam Ervin (D–N.C.). Nixon's former White House counsel, John Dean, claimed that Nixon had known more than he was admitting and had played fast and loose with the truth about White House involvement. Haldeman and Ehrlichman defended the president.

One White House functionary, Alexander Butterfield, broke the news that Nixon had a secret taping system that recorded every conversation in the Oval Office. The battle for control of the tapes began. The Ervin committee demanded them. Courts trying the Watergate defendants subpoenaed them. Nixon asserted that executive privilege permitted him to refuse to disclose them. Finally, the Supreme Court, in *United States* v. *Nixon* (1974), ruled that Nixon had to hand over the tapes to courts trying the Watergate burglars. The tapes confirmed that Nixon *had* been involved in the cover-up (a felony) and had been lying to the American people.

As the Watergate cover-up unraveled, more became known about what John Mitchell called "the White House horrors." Nixon's White House aides and CREEP officials had sponsored the burglary of the office of a psychiatrist treating Daniel Ellsberg, an opponent of the Vietnam War who had leaked classified documents to the press; they had had the administration's opponents' income tax records audited, had tapped phones illegally, had collected campaign contributions (preferably cash) in return for specific favors, and had manipulated Nixon's own tax returns.

The House launched impeachment hearings in 1974. On July 31, 1974, the Judiciary Committee recommended Nixon's impeachment. Facing almost certain impeachment by the House and probable conviction by the Senate, Nixon resigned ten days later. Shortly after assuming the presidency, Gerald Ford pardoned Nixon, arguing that years of trials and appeals would aggravate bitterness over Watergate. Most of Nixon's aides were not so lucky—many were convicted and served prison sentences.

Nevertheless, to this day there are some, perhaps many, who believe that Richard Nixon was unfairly hounded from office. They claim he and his aides really did nothing that was uncommon in American politics. His only problem, they contend, is that he got caught. Should Nixon have lost his presidency? What do *you* think?

Presidential responsibility was also encouraged by provisions for reelection and a short term of office. For those executives who flagrantly abused their authority, impeachment was the ultimate recourse.

The Expansion of Power

Today there is more to presidential power than the Constitution alone suggests, and that power is derived from many sources. Chapter 3 showed that the role of the president has changed as America increased in prominence on the world stage and that technology has also reshaped the presidency. George Washington's ragtag militias (mostly disbanded by the time the first commander in chief took command) are of a different order than the mighty nuclear arsenal that today's president commands.

Presidents themselves have taken the initiative in developing new roles for the office. Thomas Jefferson was the first leader of a mass political party. Andrew

Jackson presented himself as the direct representative of the people. Lincoln mobilized the country for war, while Theodore Roosevelt mobilized the public behind his policies. He and Woodrow Wilson set precedents for presidents serving as world leaders, while Wilson and Franklin D. Roosevelt developed the role of the president as manager of the economy. These presidents enlarged the power of the presidency by expanding the president's responsibilities and political resources. The following sections will explore the relationship between these responsibilities and resources by examining how contemporary presidents try to lead the nation.

RUNNING THE GOVERNMENT: THE CHIEF EXECUTIVE

Despite the fact that the president is often called the "chief executive," it is easy to forget that one of the president's most important roles is presiding over the administration of government. This role does not receive the same publicity as appealing to the public for support of policy initiatives, dealing with Congress, or negotiating with the Soviet Union, but it is of great importance nevertheless.

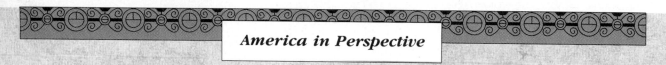

America in Perspective

What a Difference a Border Makes

Mexico's constitution resembles the American Constitution in many important ways. It provides for the separation of power among three branches of government, legal opposition parties, and independent, organized interest groups. Under such a system one might anticipate that Mexican presidents would face a necessity to persuade similar to that of chief executives in the United States. Such an assumption would be incorrect, however, because the Mexican government is characterized by a strong centralization of power in the hands of presidents and their parties, a structure that might make American presidents envious indeed.

Mexican presidents enjoy a wide range of constitutionally invested and de facto authority. Neither the judicial nor the legislative branches are independent of their control. The decisions of the highest court in Mexico generally follow the policy of the executive, and the legislative branch is even more compliant. The two houses of the legislature are often regarded

as a rubber stamp for presidential policy. In addition, presidents can appoint or dismiss all but a few public officeholders, including the governors of the states.

Immunity from criticism in the press has eroded in recent years, but criticism is still discouraged by a state monopoly on the supply of newsprint paper. Moreover, there are regular payoffs to reporters covering government agencies—the Christmas season is made especially merry for journalists by the arrival on their doorsteps of huge baskets of liquor and gourmet foods sent by government and party officials. The government also controls the bulk of paid advertisements in many publications, and it uses its discretion to discourage critics.

It is easy to imagine American presidents wishing they were south of the border in Mexico. Things may be changing, however. The 1988 presidential election in Mexico was the most divisive in history. One will have to wait to see if this lessens the deference to the chief executive.

Sources: Judith Adler Hellman, *Mexico in Crisis*, 2nd ed. (New York: Holmes and Meier, 1983), 127–28, 160; Wayne A. Cornelius and Ann L. Craig, "Politics in Mexico," in Gabriel A. Almond and G. Bingham Powell, eds., *Comparative Politics Today: A World View* (Boston: Little, Brown, 1988), 442–44.

Table 13.3	Constitutional Powers of the President

NATIONAL SECURITY POWERS

Commander in chief of the armed forces

Make treaties with other nations, subject to the agreement of two-thirds of the Senate

Nominate ambassadors, with the agreement of a majority of the Senate

Receive ambassadors of other nations, thereby conferring diplomatic recognition on other governments

LEGISLATIVE POWERS

Present information on the state of the union to Congress

Recommend legislation to Congress

Convene both houses of Congress on extraordinary occasions

Adjourn Congress if the House and Senate cannot agree on adjournment

Veto legislation (Congress may overrule with two-thirds vote of each house)

ADMINISTRATIVE POWERS

"Take care that the laws be faithfully executed"

Appoint officials as provided for by Congress and with the agreement of a majority of the Senate

Request written opinions of administrative officials

Fill administrative vacancies during congressional recesses

JUDICIAL POWERS

Grant reprieves and pardons for federal offenses (except impeachment)

Appoint federal judges, with the agreement of a majority of the Senate

You can see in Table 13.3 that the Constitution tells the president to "take care that the laws be faithfully executed." In the early days of the republic, this clerical-sounding function was fairly easy. Today the sprawling federal bureaucracy spends more than one trillion dollars a year and numbers five million civilian and military employees. Running such a large organization would be a full-time job for even the most talented of executives, yet it is only one of the president's many jobs.

One of the resources for controlling this bureaucracy is the presidential power to appoint top-level administrators. New presidents have about three hundred of these high-level positions available for appointment—cabinet and subcabinet jobs, agency heads, and other non-civil-service posts—plus two thousand lesser jobs. Since passage of the Budgeting and Accounting Act of 1921, presidents have had one other important executive tool, the power to recommend agency budgets to Congress.

The vastness of the executive branch, the complexity of public policy, and the desire to accomplish their policy goals has led presidents in recent years to pay even closer attention to appointing officials who will be responsive to their policies. Presidents have also taken more interest in the regulations issued by agencies. This trend toward centralizing decision making in the White House pleases those who feel the bureaucracy should be more responsive to elected officials. On the other hand, it dismays those who believe that increased politicalization of policy-making and implementation will undermine the "neutral competence" of professional bureaucrats and may encourage them to follow the policy preferences of the president rather than the intent of laws as passed by Congress.

Chapter 15 on the bureaucracy will explore the president's role as chief executive more fully. This chapter will focus on how presidents go about organizing and using the part of the executive branch most under their control: the cabinet, the Executive Office of the President, and the White House staff.

The Cabinet

Although the group of presidential advisors known as the **cabinet** is not mentioned in the Constitution, every president has had one. The cabinet is too large, too diverse, and its members too concerned with representing the interests of their departments for it to serve as a collective board of directors. The major decisions remain in the president's hands. Legend has it that Abraham Lincoln asked his cabinet to vote on an issue, and the result was unanimity in opposition to his view. He announced the decision as "seven nays and one aye, the ayes have it."

George Washington's cabinet was small, consisting of just three secretaries (state, treasury, and war) and the attorney general. Presidents since Washington have increased the size of the cabinet by requesting that new executive departments be established. These requests must be approved by Congress, which creates the department. Today thirteen secretaries and the attorney general head executive departments and constitute the cabinet (see Table 13.4). In addition, presidents may designate other officials (the ambassador to the United Nations is a common choice) as cabinet members.

George Bush placed a number of his closest associates in his cabinet.[13] James Baker, his campaign manager, became secretary of state, and Robert Mosbacher, his chief fund-raiser, became secretary of commerce. He also named an African American, two Hispanics, and two women to the cabinet (one, Elizabeth Dole, is the wife of Senator Robert Dole, his chief rival for the Republican nomination). Another rival, Jack Kemp, ended up as secretary of the scandal-plagued Department of Housing and Urban Development.

Even in his "official family," the president is subject to the constitutional system of checks and balances, however. President Bush met resistance when he nominated John Tower, a former senator, to be secretary of defense. After a bitter debate, he was rejected by the Senate, handing the president a serious defeat. Tower's critics charged that his drinking and womanizing and his consulting for defense contractors disqualified him from serving in such an important post.

Bush's cabinet meets every three or four weeks, essentially for briefing sessions. He uses cabinet councils on domestic or economic policy composed of relevant agencies to hammer out policy on contentious issues in which several departments have a stake.

[13]For a study of the backgrounds of cabinet members see Jeffrey E. Cohen, *The Politics of the U.S. Cabinet* (Pittsburgh: University of Pittsburgh Press, 1988).

Table 13.4 The Cabinet Departments

DEPARTMENT	FUNCTION
The Department of State	Founded in 1789, responsible for making foreign policy, including treaty negotiations
The Department of Treasury	The government's banker, founded in 1789
The Department of Defense (DOD)	Created in 1947 by consolidating the former Departments of the Army, the Navy, and the Air Force
The Department of Justice	Created in 1870 to serve as the government's attorney, headed by the attorney general
The Department of the Interior	Created in 1849, manages the nation's natural resources, including wildlife and public lands
The Department of Agriculture	Created in 1862, administers farm and food stamp programs and aids farmers
The Department of Commerce	Created in 1903 as the Department of Commerce and Labor, aids businesses and conducts the U.S. census
The Department of Labor	Separated from the Department of Commerce in 1913, runs programs and aids labor in various ways
The Department of Health and Human Services	Runs health, welfare, and social security programs; Created as the Department of Health, Education, and Welfare in 1953, it lost its education function in 1979
The Department of Housing and Urban Development	Created in 1966, responsible for urban and housing programs
The Department of Transportation	Created in 1966, responsible for mass transportation and highway programs
The Department of Energy	Created in 1977, responsible for energy policy and research, including atomic energy
The Department of Education	Created in 1979, responsible for the federal government's education programs
The Department of Veterans Affairs	Created in 1988, responsible for programs aiding veterans

The Executive Office

Next to the White House sits an ornate (some would say unsightly) building called the EOB, or Executive Office Building. It houses a collection of offices and organizations loosely grouped into the Executive Office of the President. Some of these offices (such as the Council of Economic Advisors) are created by legislation, and some are organized essentially by the president. Starting small in 1939, when it was established by President Roosevelt, the Executive Office has grown with the rest of government. In the Executive Office are housed three major policy-making bodies—the National Security Council, the Council of Economic Advisors, and the Office of Management and Budget—plus several other units serving the president (see Figure 13.1).

The **National Security Council (NSC)** is the committee that links the president's key foreign and military policy advisors. The president, vice-president, and secretaries of state and defense are its members, but its informal membership is broader. The president's special assistant for national security affairs plays a major role in the NSC. The occupant of this post has responsibility

Figure 13.1 Executive Office of the President

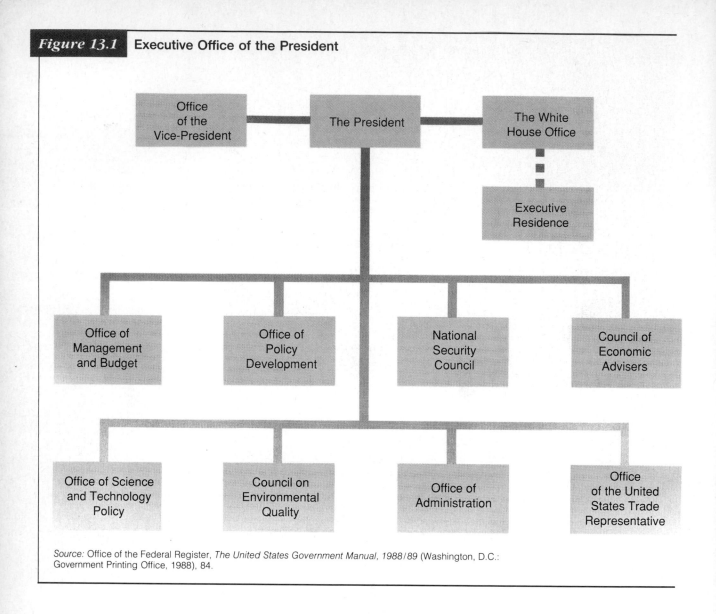

Source: Office of the Federal Register, *The United States Government Manual, 1988/89* (Washington, D.C.: Government Printing Office, 1988), 84.

for running the council's staff, coordinating options and information, and personally advising the president.

The **Council of Economic Advisors (CEA)** has three members, each appointed by the president, who advise him on economic policy. They prepare the *Annual Report of the Council of Economic Advisors* and help the president make policy on inflation, unemployment, and other economic matters.

The **Office of Management and Budget (OMB)** grew out of the Bureau of the Budget (BOB) created in 1921. It is composed of a handful of political appointees and more than six hundred career officials, many of whom are highly skilled professionals. Its major responsibility is to prepare the president's budget (discussed in Chapter 14). President Nixon revamped the BOB in 1970 in an attempt to make it a managerial as well as a budgetary agency, changing its name in the process to stress its managerial functions.

The president's special assistant for national security heads the staff of the National Security Council and typically plays a central role in foreign and defense policy-making. No occupant of this post has been more influential than Henry Kissinger, shown here advising President Nixon on the Vietnam War.

Because each presidential appointee and department will have its own agenda, presidents need a clearinghouse—the OMB. Presidents use the OMB to review legislative proposals from the cabinet and other executive agencies so they can determine whether or not they want an agency to propose them to Congress. The OMB assesses the proposals' budgetary implications and advises presidents on the proposals' consistency with their overall program.

Though presidents find that the Executive Office is smaller and less unwieldy than the cabinet departments, it is still filled with people performing jobs required by law. There is, however, one part of the presidential system that presidents can truly call their own—the White House staff.

The White House Staff

The White House staff consists of the key aides the president sees daily—the chief of staff, congressional liaison people, press secretary, national security advisor, and a few other administrative and political assistants. Actually, there are about six hundred people at work on the White House staff—many of whom the president rarely sees—providing the chief executive with a wide variety of services ranging from advance travel preparations to answering the thousands of letters received each year (see Figure 13.2).

The top aides in the White House hierarchy are people who owe almost total loyalty to the president, and the president turns to them for advice on the most serious and mundane matters of governance. Good staff people are self-effacing, working only for the boss and hiding from the limelight. The 1939 report of the Brownlow Committee, which served as the basis for the development of the modern White House staff, argued that presidential assistants

Figure 13.2   Principal Offices in the White House

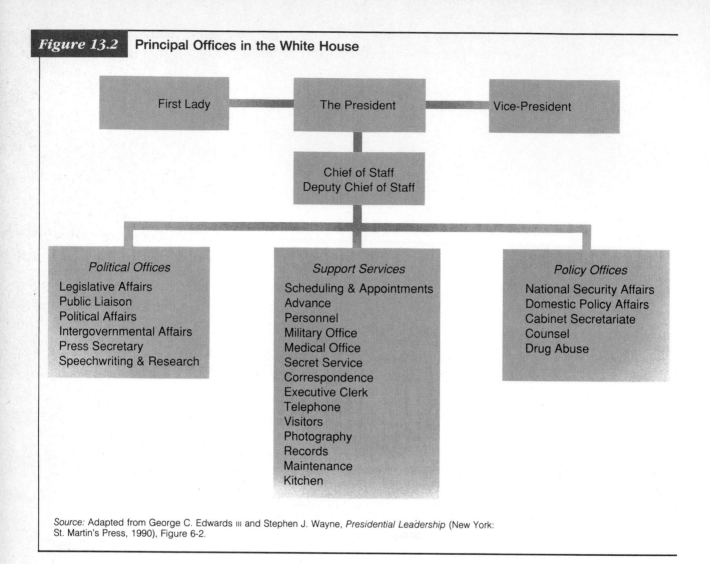

Political Offices	Support Services	Policy Offices
Legislative Affairs	Scheduling & Appointments	National Security Affairs
Public Liaison	Advance	Domestic Policy Affairs
Political Affairs	Personnel	Cabinet Secretariate
Intergovernmental Affairs	Military Office	Counsel
Press Secretary	Medical Office	Drug Abuse
Speechwriting & Research	Secret Service	
	Correspondence	
	Executive Clerk	
	Telephone	
	Visitors	
	Photography	
	Records	
	Maintenance	
	Kitchen	

Source: Adapted from George C. Edwards III and Stephen J. Wayne, *Presidential Leadership* (New York: St. Martin's Press, 1990), Figure 6-2.

should have a "passion for anonymity." So important are their roles, though, that the names of top White House aides quickly become known. Woodrow Wilson's Colonel Edward M. House, Franklin D. Roosevelt's Harry Hopkins, Dwight Eisenhower's Sherman Adams, John Kennedy's Theodore Sorensen, Richard Nixon's Henry Kissinger, Jimmy Carter's Hamilton Jordon and Jody Powell, and Ronald Reagan's James Baker and Edwin Meese, for example, did much to shape the contours of domestic and global policy.

Presidents rely heavily on their staffs for information, policy options, and analysis. Different presidents have different relationships with their staffs. They each organize the White House to serve their own political and policy needs and their own decision-making style. Most presidents end up choosing some form of *hierarchical* organization with a chief of staff at the top, one whose job it is to see that everyone else is doing his or her job and that the president's time and interests are protected. A few, such as John Kennedy, have employed a *wheel-and-spokes* system of White House management in which many aides have equal status and are balanced against one another in the process of decision making.[14] In all systems, White House aides are central in the policy-making process, fashioning options, negotiating agreements, writing presidential statements, controlling paperwork, molding legislative details, and generally giving the president their opinions on most matters.

No presidential management styles contrasted more sharply than those of Presidents Carter and Reagan. Carter was a detail man, pouring endlessly over memoranda and facts. (He was, said presidential observer Hugh Sidey, "not a leader but a decision maker.") President Reagan was the consummate delegator. So adept at dispersing authority was Reagan that his advisors—the news media often called them "his handlers"—felt it periodically necessary to have the president insist that "I am the boss" in media interviews.

George Bush's operating style falls between the extremes of his two immediate predecessors. He consults widely both within and outside of government, and he insists on letting others' views reach him unfiltered by his staff. He is considerably more accessible than Reagan and devotes more energy to decision making. At the same time, he likes to delegate responsibility to his subordinates and has respect for the expertise of others.

Despite the reliance of presidents on their staffs, it is the president who sets the tone for the White House. Although it is common to blame presidential advisors for mistakes made in the White House, it is the president's responsibility to demand that staff members analyze a full range of options and their likely consequences before they offer the president their advice. If the chief executive does not demand quality staff work, it is less likely to be done and disaster or embarrassment may follow (see "You Are the Policymaker: Is This Any Way to Make Decisions?").

Presidents not only have responsibility for running the executive branch. They must also deal intensively with the legislative branch—these dealings are the topic of the following sections.

White House staff members play a key role in presidential decision making, often becoming as well known as the president. George Bush's top aide, John Sununu (left), for example, has developed a reputation as a tough but fair chief of staff, strictly controlling the president's time but generally allowing him to hear multiple points of view.

PRESIDENTIAL LEADERSHIP OF CONGRESS: THE POLITICS OF SHARED POWERS

Near the top of any presidential job description would be "working with Congress." Since the American system of separation of powers is actually one of *shared* powers, presidents can rarely operate independently of Congress. If they are to succeed in leaving their stamp on public policy, much of their time in office will be devoted to trying to lead the legislature to support their initiatives.

Chief Legislator

Nowhere does the Constitution use the phrase *chief legislator*; it is strictly a phrase invented by textbook writers to emphasize the executive's importance in the legislative process. The Constitution does require that the president give a State of the Union address to Congress and instructs the president to bring

[14]Two useful books on the history and functions of the White House staff are John Hart, *The Presidential Branch* (New York; Pergamon, 1987), and Bradley H. Patterson, Jr., *The Ring of Power* (New York: Basic Books, 1988).

Is This Any Way to Make Decisions?

On January 17, 1986, President Ronald Reagan signed a document, technically called a "finding," that paved the way for the United States to secretly sell arms directly to Iran in the hope of obtaining the release of American hostages held in the Middle East. The arrangement also created the opportunity to generate profits on the arms sales that could be, and were, diverted covertly to the contras fighting the Nicaraguan government.

The finding was presented to the president by his national security advisor, Vice Admiral John Poindexter. It had a cover memo, prepared by Lieutenant Colonel Oliver North, but the president did not read it. Although the memo pointed out that the plan was opposed by the secretaries of state and defense, their views were not included, nor were justifications for the assertions of success contained in the memo. Eleven days earlier, not realizing that it was only a proposal for discussion and *before* the National Security Council meeting he called to discuss it had been held, the president signed a similar finding that had not been fully analyzed by his staff.

The policy was a failure and undermined America's strongly asserted policy of not trading arms, or anything else, for hostages. When details of this policy decision began to emerge that November, there was a broad public outcry and the president's popularity fell substantially in the polls, his political clout lost. Things got even worse when the diversion of funds to the contras came to light. At this point the president fired North, accepted the resignation of Poindexter, and had to face a year of congressional hearings and a highly critical report by a special commission he appointed to examine his handling of the matter.

A spate of books written by top officials in the Reagan administration (detractors call them "kiss and tell" books) revealed what others had long suspected: Ronald Reagan was a peculiarly detached decision maker. Having strong views on the basic goals of public policy, he left it to others to implement his broad vision. Aides prepared detailed scripts on index cards for his use in meetings, and he even followed the advice of astrologers on scheduling matters.

If presidents focus too closely on the details of policy, they may not be able to project a clear vision of policy to their administration or the public. Yet if they do not grasp the specifics of policy alternatives, they are in danger of being unable to adequately evaluate likely consequences. Presidents then become prisoners of their premises. If you were president, what would *you* do?

Sources: Report of the Congressional Committees Investigating the Iran-Contra Affair (Washington, D.C.: Government Printing Office, 1987), and *The Tower Commission Report* (New York: Bantam, 1987).

other matters to Congress's attention "from time to time." In fact, as Chapter 12 discussed, the president is a major shaper of the congressional agenda.

The Constitution also gives the president power to **veto** congressional legislation. Once Congress passes a bill, the president may (1) sign it, making it law; (2) veto it, sending it back to Congress with the reasons for rejecting it; or (3) let it become law after ten working days by not doing anything. Congress can pass a vetoed law, however, if two-thirds of each house vote to override the president. At one point in the lawmaking process the president has the last word, however: if Congress adjourns within ten days after submitting a bill, the president can simply let it die by neither signing nor vetoing it. This process is called a **pocket veto.** You can see how frequently recent presidents used the veto in Table 13.5.

Table 13.5 Presidential Vetoes

PRESIDENT	REGULAR VETOES	VETOES OVERRIDDEN	PERCENTAGE OF VETOES OVERRIDDEN	POCKET VETOES	TOTAL VETOES
Eisenhower	73	2	3	108	181
Kennedy	12	0	0	9	21
Johnson	16	0	0	14	30
Nixon	26	7	27	17	43
Ford	48	12	25	18	66
Carter	13	2	15	18	31
Reagan	39	9	23	39	78
Bush[a]	13	0	0	0	13

[a] As of July 1990.

The presidential veto is usually effective; only about 4 percent of all vetoed bills have been overridden by Congress since the nation's founding. Thus even the threat of a presidential veto can be an effective tool for persuading Congress to give more weight to presidents' views. On the other hand, the veto is a blunt instrument. Presidents must accept or reject bills in their entirety; they cannot veto only the parts they do not like. As a result, the White House often must accept provisions of a bill it opposes in order to obtain others that it desires. In 1987 Congress passed the entire discretionary budget of the federal government in one omnibus bill (discussed in Chapter 14). President Reagan had to accept the whole package or lose appropriations for the entire government.

The presidential veto is an inherently negative resource. It is most useful for preventing legislation. Much of the time, however, presidents are more interested in passing their own legislation. Here they must marshall their political resources to obtain positive support for their programs. Presidents' three most useful resources are their party leadership, public support, and their own legislative skills.

Party Leadership

No matter what other resources presidents may have at their disposal, they remain highly dependent upon their party to move their legislative programs. Representatives and senators of the president's party almost always form the nucleus of coalitions supporting presidential proposals and provide, year in and year out, considerably more support than do members of the opposition party. Thus party leadership in Congress is every president's principal task when seeking to counter the natural tendencies toward conflict between the executive and legislative branches inherent in the American government's system of checks and balances.[15]

[15] For a discussion of presidential party leadership in Congress, see George C. Edwards III, *At the Margins: Presidential Leadership of Congress* (New Haven, Conn.: Yale University Press, 1989), 3–5.

The Bonds of Party   For most senators and representatives, being in the same political party as the president creates a psychological bond—based on personal loyalties or emotional commitments to their party and their party leader, a desire to avoid embarrassing "their" administration and thus hurting their chances for reelection, and a basic distrust of the opposition party—that produces an inclination to support the White House. Members of the same party also agree on many matters of public policy, and they are often supported by similar electoral coalitions, reinforcing the pull of party ties.

If presidents could rely on their fellow party members to vote for whatever the White House sent up to Capitol Hill, presidential leadership of Congress would be rather easy. All presidents would have to do is to make sure members of their party showed up to vote. If their party had the majority, presidents would always win. If their party was in the minority, presidents would only have to concentrate on converting a few members of the other party to their side.

Slippage in Party Support   Things are not so simple, however. Despite the pull of party ties, all presidents experience substantial slippage in the support of their party in Congress. Presidents can count on their own party members for support no more than two-thirds of the time, even on key votes. Thus presidents are forced to be active in party leadership and to devote their efforts to conversion as much as to mobilization of members of their party.

The primary obstacle to party unity is the lack of consensus among party members on policies, especially in the Democratic party. Jimmy Carter, the last Democratic president, remarked, "I learned the hard way that there was no party loyalty or discipline when a complicated or controversial issue was at stake—none."[16]

[16]Jimmy Carter, *Keeping Faith* (New York: Bantam, 1982), 80.

Although members of a president's party are inclined to support presidential initiatives, party support in Congress is not a given. All presidents must work hard to receive such support, especially by courting the favor of the party's congressional leaders. Here President Bush meets with Senate Minority Leader Robert Dole.

This diversity of views often reflects the diversity of constituencies represented by party members. The frequent defection from support of Democratic presidents by the Southern Democrats (such defectors are called "boll weevils") is one of the most prominent features of American politics. When constituency opinion and the president's proposals conflict, members of Congress are more likely to vote with their constituents, to whom they must return for reelection. If the president is not popular in their constituencies, congressional party members may avoid identifying too closely with the White House.

Leading the Party　　The president has some assets as party leader, including congressional party leaders, services and amenities for party members, and campaign aid. Each asset is of limited utility, however.

The president's relationship with party leaders in Congress is a delicate one. Although the leaders are predisposed to support presidential policies and typically work closely with the White House, they are free to oppose the president or lend only symbolic support, and they may be ineffective. Moreover, party leaders are not in a position to reward or discipline members of Congress on the basis of presidential support.

To create goodwill with congressional party members, the White House provides them with many amenities, ranging from photographs with the president to rides on Air Force One. Although this arrangement is to the president's advantage and may earn the benefit of the doubt on some policy initiatives, party members consider it their right to receive benefits from the White House and are unlikely to be especially responsive to the president as a result.

Just as the president can offer a carrot, so, too, can the president wield a stick in the form of withholding favors. Such withholding is rarely done. Despite the resources available to the president, if party members wish to oppose the White House, there is little the president can do to stop them. The parties are highly decentralized, as you have seen in Chapter 7. National party leaders do not control those aspects of politics that are of vital concern to members of Congress: nominations and elections. Members of Congress are largely self-recruited, gain their party's nomination by their own efforts and not the party's, and provide most of the money and organizational support needed for their elections. The presidents can do little to influence the results of these activities.

One way for the president to improve the chances of obtaining support in Congress is to increase the number of fellow party members in the legislature. The term **presidential coattails** refers to voters casting their ballots for congressional candidates of the president's party because those candidates support the president. Most recent studies show a diminishing connection between presidential and congressional voting, however, and few races are determined by presidential coattails.[17] The small change in party balance that usually occurs when the electoral dust has settled is striking. In the ten presidential elections between 1952 and 1988, the party of the winning presidential candidate gained an average of 10 seats (out of 435) per election in the House. In the Senate the opposition party gained seats in only half of the elections (1956, 1960, 1972, 1984, and 1988), and there was no change in 1976. The net gain for the president's party in the Senate averaged only 1 seat per election (see Table 13.6).

[17]For a review of these studies and an analysis showing the limited impact of presidential coattails on congressional election outcomes, see Edwards, *The Public Presidency*, 83–93.

Table 13.6 **Congressional Gains or Losses for the President's Party in Presidential Election Years**

Presidents cannot rely on their coattails to carry into office senators and representatives of their party to help pass presidential legislative programs. The president's party typically gains few, if any, seats when the president wins election. For instance, the Republicans lost seats in both houses when President Bush was elected in 1988.

YEAR	PRESIDENT	HOUSE	SENATE
1952	Eisenhower	+22	+1
1956	Eisenhower	−2	−1
1960	Kennedy	−22	−2
1964	Johnson	+37	+1
1968	Nixon	+5	+6
1972	Nixon	+12	−2
1976	Carter	+1	0
1980	Reagan	+34	+12
1984	Reagan	+14	−2
1988	Bush	−3	−1

What about midterm elections, held between presidential elections? Can the president depend on increasing the number of fellow party members in Congress then? Actually the picture is even more bleak than during presidential elections. As you can see in Table 13.7, the president's party typically *loses* seats in these elections. In 1986 the Republicans lost eight seats in the Senate, depriving President Reagan of a majority.

To add to these party leadership burdens, the president's party often lacks a majority in one or both houses of Congress. Between 1953 and 1988 there were twenty-two years in which Republican presidents faced a Democratic House of Representatives and sixteen years in which they encountered a Democratic Senate. President Bush currently faces both a House and a Senate with large Democratic majorities.

As a result of election returns and the lack of dependable party support, the president usually has to solicit help from the opposition party. The opposition is generally not fertile ground for seeking support. Nevertheless, even a few votes may be enough to bring the president the required majority.

Public Support

One of the president's most important resources for leading Congress is public support. Presidents with the backing of the public have an easier time influencing Congress. Said one top aide to Ronald Reagan, "Everything here is built on the idea that the president's success depends on grassroots support."[18] Presidents

[18]Quoted in Sidney Blumenthal, "Marketing the President," *New York Times Magazine*, September 13, 1981, 110.

with low approval ratings in the polls find the going tougher. As one of President Carter's aides put it, "No president whose popularity is as low as this president's has much clout on the Hill."[19] Members of Congress and others in Washington closely watch two indicators of public support for the president: approval in the polls and mandates in presidential elections.

Public Approval Members of Congress anticipate the public's reactions to their support for or opposition to presidents and their policies. They may choose to be close to or independent from the White House—depending on the president's standing with the public—to increase their chances for reelection. Representatives and senators may also use the president's standing in the polls as an indicator of the ability to mobilize public opinion against presidential opponents.

Public approval also makes other leadership resources more efficacious. If the president is high in the public's esteem, the president's party is more likely to be responsive, the public is more easily moved, and legislative skills become more effective. Thus public approval is the political resource that has the most potential to turn a situation of stalemate between the president and Congress into one supportive of the president's legislative proposals.

Public approval operates mostly in the background and sets the limits of what Congress will do for or to the president. Widespread support gives the president leeway and weakens resistance to presidential policies. It provides a cover for members of Congress to cast votes to which their constituents might otherwise object. They can defend their votes as support for the president rather than support for a certain policy alone.

Lack of public support strengthens the resolve of those inclined to oppose the president and narrows the range in which presidential policies receive the

---

[19]Quoted in "Slings and Arrows," *Newsweek*, July 31, 1978, 20.

Table 13.7	Congressional Gains or Losses for the President's Party in Midterm Election Years

The president's party typically *loses* seats in midterm elections. Thus presidents cannot rely on helping elect members of their party once in office.

YEAR	PRESIDENT	HOUSE	SENATE
1954	Eisenhower	−18	−1
1958	Eisenhower	−47	−13
1962	Kennedy	−4	+3
1966	Johnson	−47	−4
1970	Nixon	−12	+2
1974	Ford	−47	−5
1978	Carter	−15	−3
1982	Reagan	−26	0
1986	Reagan	−5	−8

benefit of the doubt. In addition, low ratings in the polls may create incentives to attack the president, further eroding an already weakened position. For example, after the arms sales to Iran and the diversion of funds to the contras became a *cause célèbre* in late 1986, it became more acceptable in Congress and in the press to raise questions about Ronald Reagan's capacities as president. Disillusionment is a difficult force for the White House to combat.

The impact of public approval or disapproval on the support the president receives in Congress is important, but it occurs at the margins of the effort to build coalitions behind proposed policies. No matter how low presidential standing dips, the president still receives support from a substantial number of senators and representatives. Similarly, no matter how high approval levels climb, a significant portion of the Congress will still oppose certain presidential policies. Members of Congress are unlikely to vote against the clear interests of their constituencies or the firm tenets of their ideology out of deference to a widely supported chief executive. Public approval gives the president leverage, not control.[20]

In addition, presidents cannot depend on having the approval of the public and it is not a resource over which they have much control, as you will see later. Once again it is clear that presidents' leadership resources do not allow them to dominate Congress.

Mandates   The results of presidential elections are another indicator of public opinion regarding presidents. An electoral mandate, the perception that the voters strongly support the president's character *and* policies, can be a powerful symbol in American politics. It accords added legitimacy and credibility to the newly elected president's proposals. Moreover, concerns for both representation and political survival encourage members of Congress to support new presidents if they feel the people have spoken.

More importantly, mandates change the premises of decision. Following the 1932 election the essential question became how government should act to fight the Depression rather than whether it should act. Similarly, following the 1964 election the dominant question in Congress was not whether to pass new social programs, but how many social programs to pass and how much to increase spending. In 1981 the tables were turned; Ronald Reagan's victory placed a stigma on big government and exalted the unregulated marketplace and large defense efforts. Reagan had won a major victory even before the first congressional vote.

Although presidential elections can structure choices for Congress, merely winning an election does not provide presidents with a mandate. Every election produces a winner, but mandates are much less common. Even large electoral victories, such as Richard Nixon's in 1972 and Ronald Reagan's in 1984, carry no guarantee that Congress will interpret the results as mandates from the people to support the president's programs, especially if the voters also elect majorities in Congress from the other party (of course, the winner may claim a mandate anyway).[21]

[20]Edwards, *At the Margins*, chaps. 6–7.

[21]For an analysis of the factors that affect perceptions of mandates, see Edwards, *At the Margins*, chap. 8.

Legislative Skills

Presidential legislative skills come in a variety of forms, including bargaining, making personal appeals, consulting with Congress, setting priorities, exploiting "honeymoon" periods, and structuring congressional votes. Of these skills, bargaining receives perhaps the most attention from commentators on the presidency, and by examining it one can learn much about the role that a president's legislative skills play in leading Congress.

There is no question that many bargains occur and that they take a variety of forms. Reagan's Budget Director David Stockman recalled that "the last 10 or 20 percent of the votes needed for a majority of both houses [on the 1981 tax cut] had to be bought, period." The concessions for members of Congress included special breaks for oil-lease holders, real estate tax shelters, and generous loopholes that virtually eliminated the corporate income tax. "The hogs were really feeding" declared Stockman. "The greed level, the level of opportunism, just got out of control."[22]

Nevertheless, bargaining in the form of trading support on two or more policies or providing specific benefits for representatives and senators occurs less often and plays a less critical role in the creation of presidential coalitions in Congress than one might think. For obvious reasons, the White House does not want to encourage the type of bargaining Stockman describes, and there is a scarcity of resources with which to bargain, especially in an era of large budget deficits (discussed in Chapter 14).

Moreover, the president does not have to bargain with every member of Congress to receive support. On controversial issues on which bargaining may be useful, the president almost always starts with a sizable core of party supporters and may add to this group those of the opposition party who provide support on ideological or policy grounds. Others may support the president because of relevant constituency interests or strong public approval. Thus the president needs to bargain only if this coalition does not provide a majority (two-thirds on treaties and veto overrides), or, if this is not the case, the president needs to bargain only with enough people to provide that majority.

Presidents may improve their chances of success in Congress by making certain strategic moves. It is wise, for example, for a new president to be ready to send legislation to the Hill early during the first year in office in order to exploit the "honeymoon" atmosphere that typically characterizes this period. Obviously, this is a one-shot opportunity.

An important aspect of presidential legislative strategy can be establishing priorities among legislative proposals. The goal of this effort is to set Congress's agenda, for if presidents are unable to focus Congress' attention on their priority programs, these programs may become lost in the complex and overloaded legislative process. Setting priorities is also important because presidents and their staffs can lobby effectively for only a few bills at a time. Moreover, each president's political capital is inevitably limited, and it is sensible to focus it on a limited range of personally important issues. Otherwise this precious resource might be wasted.

Presidents influence the legislative agenda more than any other political figure. One of Ronald Reagan's chief legislative skills was the ability to effectively communicate his policy priorities to Congress and the public, as he did in this 1988 State of the Union address. No matter what a president's skills are, however, the "chief legislator," as the president is often called, can rarely exercise complete control over the agenda.

[22]David Stockman, *The Triumph of Politics* (New York: Harper & Row, 1986), 251, 253, 260–61, 264–65; and William Greider, "The Education of David Stockman," *Atlantic*, December 1981, 51.

In 1981 Ronald Reagan followed both these strategies of moving fast and setting priorities and met with great success, obtaining passage of a large tax cut, a substantial increase in defense expenditures, and sizable decreases in spending for domestic policies. George Bush, in contrast, did not enter the White House geared for legislative action and did little to articulate his priorities. With a large budget deficit, few legislative goals, and the opposition in the majority in both the House and Senate, he did not feel it necessary or useful to focus his energies on Congress. From the outset Bush seemed destined to make his mark on foreign policy—where the president has more latitude to maneuver.

The president is the nation's key agenda builder; what the administration wants strongly influences the parameters of Washington debate. John Kingdon's careful study of the Washington agenda found that "no other single actor in the political system has quite the capability of the president to set agendas."[23] There are limits to what the president can do, however.

By his second year in office, Ronald Reagan's honeymoon with Congress was over, and he had lost control of the legislative agenda. Although the White House can put off dealing with many national issues at the beginning of a new president's term in order to focus on its highest priority legislation, it cannot do so indefinitely. Eventually it must make decisions about a wide range of matters. Soon the legislative agenda is full and more policies are in the pipeline, as the administration attempts to satisfy its constituents and responds to unanticipated or simply overlooked problems. Moreover, Congress is quite capable of setting its own agenda, providing competition for the president's proposals.

In general, presidential legislative skills must compete, as presidential public support does, with other, more stable factors that affect voting in Congress: party, ideology, personal views and commitments on specific policies, constituency interests, and so on. By the time a president tries to exercise influence on a vote, most members of Congress have made up their minds on the basis of these other factors.

Systematic studies have found that, once one takes into account the status of their party in Congress and their standing with the public, presidents renowned for their legislative skills (such as Lyndon Johnson) are no more successful in winning votes, even close ones, or obtaining congressional support than those considered less adept at dealing with Congress (such as Jimmy Carter).[24] The president's legislative skills are not at the core of presidential leadership of Congress. Even skilled presidents cannot reshape the contours of the political landscape and *create* opportunities for change. They can, however, recognize favorable configurations of political forces, such as existed in 1933, 1965, and 1981, and effectively exploit them to embark on major shifts in public policy.

Perhaps presidents' most important role and their heaviest burden is their responsibility for national security. Dealing with Congress is only one of the many challenges presidents face in the realm of defense and foreign policy.

[23]John Kingdon, *Agendas, Alternatives, and Public Policies* (Boston: Little, Brown, 1984), 25. On presidential agenda setting see Paul C. Light, *The President's Agenda* (Baltimore: Johns Hopkins University Press, 1983).

[24]Edwards, *At the Margins*, chaps. 9–10; and Richard Fleisher and Jon Bond, "Presidential Leadership Skill and Success in Congress" (Paper presented at the annual meeting of the Southern Political Science Association, Atlanta, Georgia, November 1986).

THE PRESIDENT AND NATIONAL SECURITY POLICY

Constitutionally, the president has the leading role in American defense and foreign policy (often termed *national security* policy). Such matters are of obvious importance to the country—involving issues ranging from foreign trade to war and peace—and occupy much of the president's time. There are several dimensions to the president's national security responsibilities, including negotiating with other nations, commanding the armed forces, managing crises, waging war, and obtaining the necessary support in Congress.

Chief Diplomat

The Constitution allocates certain powers in the realm of national security exclusively to the executive. The president alone extends diplomatic recognition to foreign governments, as Jimmy Carter did on December 14, 1978, when he announced the exchange of ambassadors with the People's Republic of China and the downgrading of the U.S. Embassy of Taiwan. The president also can terminate relations with other nations, as Carter did with Iran after Americans were taken hostage in Tehran.

The president also has the sole power to negotiate treaties with other nations, although the Constitution requires the Senate to approve them by a two-thirds vote. Sometimes presidents win and sometimes they lose when presenting a treaty to the Senate. Woodrow Wilson lost his effort to persuade the Senate to approve the League of Nations treaty in 1920. After extensive lobbying, Jimmy Carter persuaded the Senate to approve a treaty returning the Panama Canal to Panama (over such objections as those of one senator who declared,

Presidents usually conduct diplomatic relations through envoys, but occasionally they engage in personal diplomacy. Here President Carter celebrates with Egyptian President Anwar Sadat and Israeli Prime Minister Menachem Begin following the signing of the Camp David Accords, a peace treaty between the two nations that was mediated by Carter.

"We stole it fair and square"). Carter was not so lucky when he presented the SALT II treaty on arms control; it never even made it to a vote on the Senate floor.

Occasionally presidential diplomacy involves more than negotiating on behalf of the United States. Theodore Roosevelt won the Nobel Peace Prize for his role in settling the war between Japan and Russia. One of Jimmy Carter's greatest achievements was in forging a peace treaty between Egypt and Israel. For thirteen days he mediated negotiations between the leaders of both countries at his presidential retreat, Camp David.

As the leader of the Western world, the president must try to lead America's allies on matters of both economics and defense. This is not an easy task, given the natural independence of sovereign nations; the reduced status of the United States as an economic power relative to other countries, such as Japan and West Germany; and the many competing influences on policy-making in other nations. As in domestic policy-making, the president must rely principally on persuasion to lead. Chapter 20 will examine the president's global role in more detail.

Commander in Chief

Because the Constitution's framers wanted civilian control of the military, they made the president the commander in chief of the armed forces. President George Washington actually led troops to crush the Whiskey Rebellion in 1794. Today presidents do not take the task quite so literally, but their military decisions have changed the course of history. Once he became president, Harry Truman was told about a major new weapon, the atomic bomb. Truman weighed the consequences of using this frightful weapon to defeat the Japanese and end

In 1950 President Harry Truman fulfilled his role as commander in chief by pinning a distinguished service medal on the shirt of General Douglas MacArthur, who was commanding American troops in Korea. The following year Truman exercised his powers by dismissing MacArthur for disobeying orders— an unpopular decision given MacArthur's fame as a World War II hero.

World War II. "The final decision," he said, "on where and when to use the atomic bomb was up to me. Let there be no mistake about it."[25] He personally selected the target and the date. Two decades later, Lyndon Johnson personally selected targets for bombing missions in North Vietnam. Richard Nixon made the decision to invade Cambodia in 1970. Ronald Reagan joined the ranks of presidents exerting their prerogatives as commander in chief when he sent American troops to invade the Caribbean island of Grenada, to serve as peacekeepers in fractious Lebanon, and to bomb Libya. George Bush ordered the invasion of Panama in 1989.

When the Constitution was written, the United States did not have—nor did anyone expect it to have—a large standing or permanent army. Today the president is commander in chief of two million uniformed men and women. In his farewell address George Washington warned against "entangling alliances," but today America has commitments to defend nations across the globe. Even more importantly, the president commands a vast nuclear arsenal. Never more than a few steps from the president is "the football," a macabre briefcase with all the codes needed to unleash nuclear war. The Constitution, of course, states that only Congress has the power to declare war, but it is unreasonable to believe that Congress can convene, debate, and vote on a declaration of war in the case of a nuclear attack. The House and Senate chambers would be gone—*literally* gone—before the conclusion of a debate.

War Powers

Perhaps no issue of executive-legislative relations generates more controversy than the continuing dispute over war powers. Though charged by the Constitution with declaring war and voting on the military budget, Congress long ago became accustomed to presidents making short-term military commitments of troops or naval vessels. In recent decades, though, presidents have paid even less attention to constitutional details; for example, Congress never declared war during the conflicts in either Korea or Vietnam (see "The People Speak: The Power to Declare War").

In 1973 Congress passed (over President Nixon's veto) the **War Powers Resolution**. A reaction to disillusionment about American fighting in Vietnam and Cambodia, the law was intended to give Congress a greater voice in the

[25]Harry S Truman, *Year of Decision* (New York: New American Library, 1955), 462.

The People Speak **The Power to Declare War**

Who should have the power to declare war—the president or Congress?

President	33%
Congress	57%

There has been much controversy over the issue of who should be able to commit the United States to war, but the public overwhelmingly wants Congress to make the decision.

CBS News/New York Times Poll, May 1987.

Although the Constitution grants to Congress the power to declare war, presidents usually initiate military actions. Here Franklin Roosevelt asks a joint session of Congress to declare war on Japan, one day after the December 7, 1941, Japanese bombing of Pearl Harbor. Presidents since Roosevelt have not bothered with such constitutional niceties— wars in Korea and Vietnam (and military interventions in Grenada and Panama) have been conducted without a congressional declaration.

introduction of American troops into hostilities. It required presidents to consult with Congress, whenever possible, prior to using military force, and it mandated the withdrawal of forces after sixty days unless Congress declared war or granted an extension. Congress could at any time pass a concurrent resolution (which could not be vetoed) ending American participation in hostilities.

The War Powers Resolution cannot be regarded as a success for Congress, however. All presidents serving since 1973 have deemed the law an unconstitutional infringement on their powers, and there is reason to believe the Supreme Court would consider the law's use of the **legislative veto** to end American involvement in fighting a violation of the doctrine of separation of powers. As in the case of the 1989 invasion of Panama, presidents have largely ignored the law and sent troops into hostilities, sometimes with heavy loss of life, without effectually consulting with Congress. The legislature has found it difficult to challenge the president, especially when American troops were endangered, and the courts have been reluctant to hear a congressional challenge on what would be construed as a political, rather than legal, issue.[26]

Questions continue to be raised about the relevance of American's two-hundred-year-old constitutional mechanisms for engaging in war. Some observers are concerned that modern technology allows the president to engage in hostilities so quickly that opposing points of view do not receive proper consideration, thereby undermining the separation of powers. Others stress the importance of the commander in chief having the flexibility to meet America's global responsibilities and combat international terrorism without the hindrance of congressional checks and balances. All agree that the change in the nature of warfare brought about by nuclear weapons inevitably delegates to the president the ultimate decision to use them.

Crisis Manager

The president's roles as chief diplomat and commander in chief are related to another presidential responsibility, crisis management. A **crisis** is a sudden, unpredictable, and potentially dangerous event. Most occur in the realm of foreign policy. Crises often involve hot tempers and high risks, and quick judgments are needed despite sketchy information. Whether it is American hostages held in Iran or the discovery of Soviet missiles in Cuba, a crisis challenges the president to make difficult decisions. Crises are rarely the president's doing, but badly handled, they can be the president's undoing.

Early in American history there were fewer immediate crises. By the time officials knew of a problem, it often had resolved itself. Communications could take weeks or even months to reach Washington. Similarly, officials' decisions often took weeks or months to reach those who were to implement them. The most famous land battle of the War of 1812, the Battle of New Orleans, was fought *after* the United States had signed a peace treaty with Great Britain. Word of the treaty did not reach the battlefield, and so General Andrew Jackson won a victory for the United States that contributed nothing toward ending the war, although it did help put him in the White House as the seventh president.

[26]For an analysis of war powers and other issues related to separation of powers, see Louis Fisher, *Constitutional Conflicts Between Congress and the President* (Princeton, N.J.: Princeton University Press, 1985).

With modern communications, however, the president can instantly monitor events almost anywhere. Moreover, because situations develop more rapidly today, there is a premium on rapid action, secrecy, constant management, consistent judgment, and expert advice. Congress usually moves slowly (one might say deliberatively), is large (making it difficult to keep secrets), decentralized (requiring continual compromising), and composed of generalists. As a result, the president—who can come to quick and consistent decisions, confine information to a small group, carefully oversee developments, and call upon experts in the executive branch—has become more prominent in handling crises.

Working with Congress

As America begins it third century under the Constitution, presidents might wish the framers had been less concerned with checks and balances in the area of national security. In recent years Congress has challenged presidents on all fronts including foreign aid, arms sales, the development, procurement, and deployment of weapon systems, the negotiation and interpretation of treaties, the selection of diplomats, and the continuation of nuclear testing.

Congress has a central constitutional role in making national security policy, although this role is often misunderstood. The allocation of responsibilities for such matters is based upon the founders' apprehensions about the concentration and subsequent potential for abuse of power. They divided the powers of supply and command, for example, in order to thwart adventurism in national security affairs. Congress can thus refuse to provide the necessary authorizations and appropriations for presidential actions, while the chief executive can refuse to act (for example, by not sending troops into battle at the behest of the legislature).

Despite the constitutional role of Congress, the president is the driving force behind national security policy, providing energy and direction. Although Congress is well organized to openly deliberate on the discrete components of policy, it is not well designed to take the lead on national security matters. Its role has typically been oversight of the executive rather than initiation of policy. Congress frequently originates proposals for domestic policy, but for national security policy, information is less readily available and the president has a more prominent role as the country's sole representative in dealing with other nations and as commander in chief of the armed forces (functions that effectively preclude a wide range of congressional diplomatic and military initiatives). In addition, the nature of national security issues may make the failure to integrate the elements of policy more costly than in domestic policy. Thus members of Congress typically prefer to encourage, criticize, or support the president rather than initiate their own national security policy. If leadership occurs, it will usually be centered in the White House.

Commentators on the presidency often refer to the "two presidencies"—one for domestic policy and the other for national security policy.[27] By this they mean that the president has more success in leading Congress on matters of national security than on matters of domestic policy. The typical member of

---

[27]The phrase was originated by Aaron Wildavsky in "The Two Presidencies," *TransAction* 4 (December 1966): 7–14.

Congress, however, supports the president on national security roll call votes only slightly more than half the time. There is a significant gap between what the president requests and what members of Congress are willing to give. Certainly the legislature does not accord the president overwhelming support on national security policy.[28]

Nevertheless, presidents do end up obtaining much, often most, of what they request from Congress on national security issues. Some of the support they receive is the result of agreement on policy, but presidential leadership also plays an important role. That role is not one in which presidents simply bend the legislature to their will, however; rather, they lead by persuasion.

Presidents require resources in order to persuade others to support their policies. As noted earlier, an important presidential asset can be the support of the American people. The following sections will take a closer look at how the White House tries to increase and use public support.

POWER FROM THE PEOPLE: THE PUBLIC PRESIDENCY

"Public sentiment is everything. With public sentiment nothing can fail; without it nothing can succeed." These words, spoken by Abraham Lincoln, pose what is perhaps the greatest challenge to any president: to obtain and maintain the public's support. Because presidents are rarely in a position to command others to comply with their wishes, they must rely on persuasion. *Public support is perhaps the greatest source of influence a president has,* for it is difficult for other power holders in a democracy to deny the legitimate demands of a president who has popular backing.

Going Public

John Kennedy was the first president to regularly use public appearances to seek popular backing for his policies. Despite his popularity and skills as a communicator, Kennedy was often frustrated in his attempts to win widespread support for his administration's "New Frontier" policies.

Presidents are not passive followers of public opinion. John Kennedy's closest aide, Theodore Sorensen, recalled that "no problem of the Presidency concerned him [Kennedy] more than that of public communication—educating, persuading and mobilizing that opinion."[29]

The White House is a virtual whirlwind of public relations activity.[30] You can get a sense of the level of presidential public activity from examining Table 13.8. John Kennedy, the first "television president," considerably increased the rate of public appearances held by his predecessor. Kennedy's successors, with the notable exception of Richard Nixon, have been even more active in making public appearances. Indeed, they have averaged more than one appearance every weekday of the year.

Often the president's appearances are staged purely to obtain the public's attention. When George Bush introduced his clean-air bill, he flew to Idaho to use the eye-catching Grand Tetons as a backdrop. He announced his support

[28]Edwards, *At the Margins*, chap. 4.

[29]Theodore C. Sorensen, *Kennedy* (New York: Bantam, 1966), 346.

[30]See William W. Lammers, "Presidential Attention-Focusing Activities," in *The President and the Public*, ed. Doris A. Graber (Philadelphia: ISHI, 1982), 145–71, and Samuel Kernell, *Going Public* (Washington, D.C.: Congressional Quarterly Press, 1986), chap. 4.

Table 13.8 Level of Presidents' Public Activities[a]

PRESIDENT	TOTAL ACTIVITIES	YEARLY AVERAGE	MONTHLY AVERAGE
Eisenhower	901	113	9
Kennedy	784	277	23
Johnson	1,649	319	27
Nixon	1,084	195	16
Ford	1,228	503	42
Carter	1,350	338	28
Reagan[b]	1,482	371	31

[a] All domestic and foreign appearances by a president.
[b] 1981–84.

Source: Gary King and Lyn Ragsdale, *The Elusive Executive* (Washington, D.C.: Congressional Quarterly Press, 1988), 270, 274–75.

for a constitutional amendment to prohibit flag burning in front of the Iwo Jima Memorial in Arlington National Cemetery. In cases such as these the president could have simply made an announcement, but the necessity of public support drives the White House to employ public relations techniques similar to those used to publicize products.

In many democracies, the jobs of head of state and head of government are occupied by different people. For example, the queen is head of state in England, but she holds little power in government and politics. In America, these roles are fused. As head of state, the president is America's ceremonial leader and symbol of government. Trivial but time-consuming activities—tossing out the first baseball of the season, lighting the White House Christmas tree, meeting some extraordinary Boy Scout—are part of the ceremonial function of the presidency. Meeting foreign heads of state, receiving ambassador's credentials, and making global goodwill tours represent the international side of this role. Presidents rarely shirk these duties, even when they are not inherently important. Ceremonial activities give them an important symbolic aura and a great deal of favorable press coverage, contributing to their efforts to build public support.

Presidential Approval

Much of the energy the White House devotes to public relations is aimed at increasing the president's public approval. The reason is simple: the higher the president stands in the polls, the easier it is to persuade others to support presidential initiatives.

Because of the connection between public support and presidential influence, the president's standing in the polls is monitored closely by the press, members of Congress, and others in the Washington political community. "President watching" is a favorite American pastime. For years the Gallup Poll has asked Americans this question: "Do you approve or disapprove of the way [John Kennedy, George Bush, or whoever] is handling his job as president?" You can see the results in Figure 13.3.

Presidents frequently do not have widespread public support, often failing to win even majority approval. In Figure 13.4 you can see the average approval

For years the Gallup Poll has asked Americans, "Do you approve or disapprove of the way _____ is handling his job as president?" Here you can track the percentage approving presidential performance from Truman to Reagan. Notice that all presidents seem to be most popular when they first enter office; later on, their popularity often erodes.

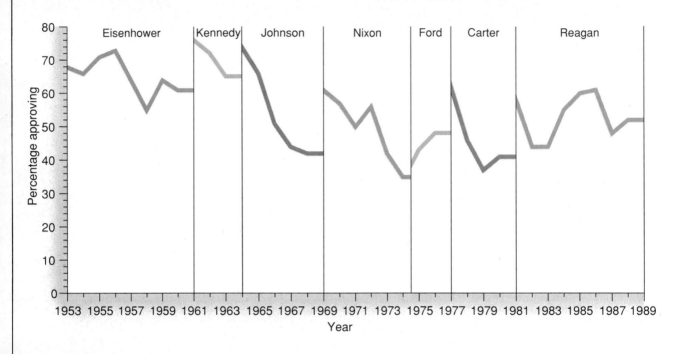

Source: George C. Edwards III, *Presidential Approval* (Baltimore: Johns Hopkins University Press, 1990).

levels of recent presidents. Nixon, Ford, and Carter did not even receive approval from 50 percent of the public on the average. Ronald Reagan, a "popular" president, had only a 52 percent approval level. George Bush has enjoyed much higher levels of approval than his predecessors. Whether he can maintain them throughout his term remains to be seen.

Presidential approval is the product of many factors.[31] At the base of presidential evaluations is the predisposition of many people to support the president. Political party identification provides the basic underpinning of approval or disapproval and mediates the impact of other factors. On average, those who identify with the president's party give 39 percentage points higher approval than those who identify with the opposition party. In other words, Democrats love Democratic presidents while Republicans are equally fond of GOP chief executives. Moreover, partisans are not prone to approving presidents of the other party. Presidents also usually benefit from a "honeymoon" with the Amer-

[31]Edwards, *The Public Presidency*, chap. 6, and George C. Edwards III, *Presidential Approval* (Baltimore: Johns Hopkins University Press, 1990).

ican people after taking office. Predispositions provide the foundations of presidential approval and furnish it with a basic stability.

Some observers believe that "honeymoons" are fleeting phenomena in which new occupants of the White House receive only a short breathing period from the public before beginning their inevitable descent in the polls. You can see in Figure 13.3 that declines certainly do take place, but they are neither inevitable nor swift. Throughout his two terms in office, Ronald Reagan experienced considerable volatility in his relations with the public, but his record certainly does not indicate that the loss of public support is inexorable or that it cannot be revived and maintained.

Changes in approval levels appear to be due primarily to the public's evaluation of how the president is handling policy areas such as the economy, war, energy, and foreign affairs. Contrary to the conventional wisdom, citizens seem to focus on the president's efforts and stands on issues rather than on personality ("popularity") or simply how presidential policies affect them (the "pocketbook"). Job-related personal characteristics of the president, such as integrity and leadership skills, also play an important role in influencing presidential approval.

Sometimes public approval of the president takes sudden jumps. One popular explanation for these surges of support are "rally events," which John Mueller defined as events that relate to international relations, directly involve the United States and particularly the president, and are specific, dramatic, and sharply focused.[32] A classic example is the 20 percent rise in President Carter's approval ratings in the period after Americans were taken hostage by Iranian militants in November 1979. Such occurrences are rare and isolated events, however; they have little enduring impact on a president's public approval. (In fact, Carter's approval ratings plummeted when the hostages were not released.)

---

[32]Mueller also included the inaugural period of a president's term as a rally event. John E. Mueller, *War, Presidents and Public Opinion* (New York: Wiley, 1973), 208–213.

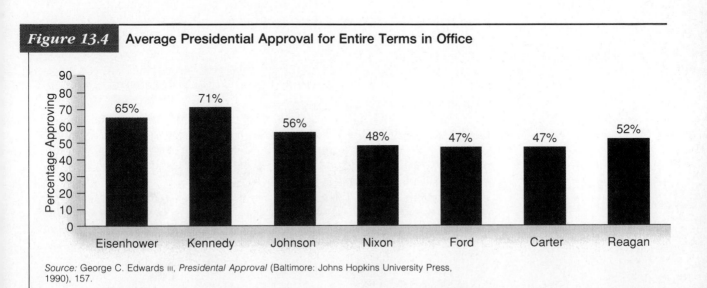

Figure 13.4 Average Presidential Approval for Entire Terms in Office

Source: George C. Edwards III, *Presidental Approval* (Baltimore: Johns Hopkins University Press, 1990), 157.

The criteria on which the public evaluates presidents, such as the way they are handling the economy, where they stand on complex issues, and whether or not they are "strong" leaders, are open to many interpretations. The modern White House makes extraordinary efforts to control the context in which presidents appear in public and the way they are portrayed by the press, in order to try to influence how the public views them. The fact that presidents are frequently low in the polls anyway is persuasive testimony to the limits of presidential leadership of the public. As one student of the public presidency put it, "The supply of popular support rests on opinion dynamics over which the president may exert little direct control."[33]

Policy Support

Commentators on the presidency often refer to it as a "bully pulpit," implying that presidents can persuade or even mobilize the public to support their policies if only they are skilled enough communicators. Certainly presidents frequently do attempt to obtain public support for their policies with speeches over television or radio or to large groups.[34] All presidents since Truman have had media advice from experts on lighting, makeup, stage settings, camera angles, clothing, pacing of delivery, and other facets of making speeches.

Despite this aid and despite the experience that politicians have in speaking, presidential speeches aimed at directly leading public opinion have typically been rather unimpressive. In the modern era only Franklin D. Roosevelt, John Kennedy, and Ronald Reagan could be considered effective speakers. The rest

[33]Kernell, *Going Places*, 137.

[34]See Jeffrey K. Tulis, *The Rhetorical Presidency* (Princeton, N.J.: Princeton University Press, 1987), on presidents' efforts to build policy support.

were not, and typically did not look good under the glare of hot lights and the unflattering gaze of television cameras. Partly because of his limitations as a public speaker, President Bush waited until he had been in office for over seven months before making his first nationally televised address.

Moreover, the public is not always receptive to the president's message. Chapter 6 showed that Americans are not especially interested in politics and government, and so it is not easy to get their attention. Citizens also have predispositions about public policy (however ill-informed) that act as screens for presidential messages. In the absence of national crises—which, fortunately, are rare—most people are unreceptive to political appeals.[35]

The public may misperceive or ignore even the most basic facts regarding a presidential policy. As late as 1986, 62 percent of Americans did not know which side the United States supported in Nicaragua, despite extensive, sustained coverage of the president's policy in virtually all components of the media for many years.[36] Similarly, in June 1986 only 40 percent of the public had heard or read at least "some" about the tax reform bill before the Senate,[37] President Reagan's highest domestic priority.

Ronald Reagan, sometimes called the "Great Communicator," was certainly interested in policy change and went to unprecedented lengths to influence public opinion on behalf of such policies as deregulation, decreases in spending on domestic policy, increases in the defense budget, and aid for the contras. Nevertheless, support for regulatory programs and spending on health care, welfare, urban problems, education, environmental protection, and aid to minorities *increased*, not decreased, during Reagan's tenure.[38] Support for increased defense expenditures was decidedly lower when he left office than when he was inaugurated.[39] In the foreign policy realm, near the end of 1986 only 25 percent of the public favored the president's cherished aid to the contras in Nicaragua.[40]

Presidents often use commercial public relations techniques to win support for their policy initiatives. President Bush, for example, used the heroic backdrop of the Iwo Jima Memorial— which celebrates U.S. Marines raising a flag on the Pacific island during World War II—to gain public approval for a constitutional amendment banning flag burning.

Mobilizing the Public

Sometimes merely changing public opinion is not sufficient, and the president wants the public to communicate its views directly to Congress. Mobilization of

[35]For a recent discussion of the social flow of information, see Robert Huckfeldt and John Sprague, "Networks in Context: The Social Flow of Political Information," *American Political Science Review* 81 (December 1987): 1197–216.

[36]*CBS News/New York Times* Poll (News release, April 15, 1986, Table 16).

[37]*CBS News/New York Times* Poll (News release, June 24, 1986, Table 9).

[38]William Schneider, "The Voters' Mood 1986: The Six-Year Itch," *National Journal*, December 7, 1985, 2758; "Supporting a Greater Federal Role," *National Journal*, April 18, 1987, 924; "Opinion Outlook," *National Journal*, April 18, 1987, 964; Seymour Martin Lipset, "Beyond 1984: The Anomalies of American Politics," *PS* 19 (Spring 1986): 223; and "Federal Budget Deficit," *Gallup Report*, August 1987, 25, 27. See also *CBS News/New York Times* Poll (News release, October 27, 1987, Tables 16, 20).

[39]Lipset, "Beyond 1984"; "Supporting a Greater Federal Role," 924; "Defense," *Gallup Report*, May 1987, 2–3. See also "Opinion Outlook," *National Journal*, June 13, 1987, 1550; and *CBS News/ New York Times* Poll (News release, October 27, 1987, Table 15).

[40]*CBS News/New York Times* Poll (News release, December 1, 1986, Table 5). See also *CBS News/New York Times* Poll (New release, October 27, 1987, Table 17); and "Americans on Contra Aid: Broad Opposition," *New York Times*, January 31, 1988, sec. 4, p. 1. For a broader comparison of public opinion and the Reagan administration's policies, see John E. Reilly, ed., *American Public Opinion and U.S. Foreign Policy 1987* (Chicago: Chicago Council on Foreign Relations, 1987), chaps. 5–6.

the public may be the ultimate weapon in the president's arsenal of resources with which to influence Congress. When the people speak, especially when they speak clearly, Congress listens attentively.

Mobilizing the public involves overcoming formidable barriers and accepting substantial risks. It entails the double burden of obtaining both opinion *support* and political *action* from a generally inattentive and apathetic public. If the president tries to mobilize the public and fails, the lack of response speaks clearly to members of Congress.

Perhaps the most notable recent example of the president mobilizing public opinion to pressure Congress is Ronald Reagan's effort to obtain passage of his tax-cut bill in 1981. Shortly before the crucial vote in the House, the president made a televised plea for support of his tax-cut proposals and asked the people to let their representatives in Congress know how they felt. Evidently Reagan's plea worked, as thousands of phone calls, letters, and telegrams poured into congressional offices. On the morning of the vote, Speaker Tip O'Neill declared, "We are experiencing a telephone blitz like this nation has never seen. It's had a devastating effect."[41] The president easily carried the day.

The Reagan administration's effort at mobilizing the public on behalf of the 1981 tax cut is significant not only because of the success of presidential leadership but also because it appears to be a deviant case—even for Ronald Reagan. In the remainder of his tenure, the president went repeatedly to the people regarding a wide range of policies, including the budget, aid to the contras in Nicaragua, and defense expenditures. Despite high levels of approval for much of that time, Reagan was never again able to arouse many in his audience to communicate their support of his policies to Congress. Most issues hold less appeal to the public than substantial tax cuts.

THE PRESIDENT AND THE PRESS

Despite all their efforts to lead public opinion, presidents do not directly reach the American people on a day-to-day basis. It is the mass media that provides people with most of what they know about chief executives and their policies. The media also interprets and analyzes presidential activities, even the president's direct appeals to the public. The press is thus the principal intermediary between the president and the public, and relations with the press are an important aspect of the president's efforts to lead public opinion.

No matter who is in the White House or who reports on presidential activities, presidents and the press tend to be in conflict. George Washington complained that the "calumnies" against his administration were "outrages of common decency." Thomas Jefferson once declared that "nothing in a newspaper is to be believed." Presidents are inherently policy advocates. Presidents want to control the amount and timing of information about their administration, whereas the press wants all the information that exists without delay. As long as their goals are different, presidents and the media are likely to be adversaries.

Because of the importance of the press to the president, the White House monitors the media closely. President Johnson installed a special television in

---

[41]Quoted in "Tax Cut Passed by Solid Margin in House, Senate," *Congressional Quarterly Weekly Report*, August 1, 1981, 1374.

Although often at odds with one another, the president and the press both benefit from their relationship: the president needs the press to reach the public, and the press relies on the president as a prime source of news. Here President Dwight Eisenhower holds his first press conference. Eisenhower was the first president to allow reporters to make transcripts of his press conferences, putting his words " on the record."

the Oval Office so that he could watch the news on all three networks at once; near the oversized set stood news tickers from AP, UPI, and Reuters. The White House also goes to great lengths to encourage the media to project a positive image of the president's activities and policies. About one-third of the high-level White House staff members are directly involved in media relations and policy of one type or another, and most staff members are involved at some time in trying to influence the media's portrayal of the president.

The person who most often deals directly with the press is the president's **press secretary**, who serves as a conduit of information from the White House to the press. Press secretaries conduct daily press briefings, giving prepared announcements and answering questions. They and their staff also arrange private interviews with White House officials (often done on a background basis, in which the reporter may not attribute remarks to the person being interviewed), photo opportunities, and travel arrangements for reporters when the president leaves Washington.

The best-known direct interaction between the president and the press is the presidential press conference. Presidents since Eisenhower have typically met with the press about twice a month (the exceptions were Nixon and Reagan, who averaged a press conference only about every two months). George Bush often meets with the press in informal sessions, but rarely holds a prime-time, televised press conference. Despite their visibility, press conferences are not very useful means of eliciting information. Presidents and their staffs can anticipate most of the questions that will be asked and prepare answers to them ahead of time, reducing the spontaneity of the sessions. Moreover, the large size and public nature of press conferences reduce the candor with which the president can respond to questions.

The president has a retreat in the Maryland mountains called Camp David. Reporters are not allowed there, with one exception. About twenty minutes before the president's helicopter lands, two reporters are allowed to sit in something akin to a duck blind about 150 yards from where the helicopter lands and observe the landing. They leave immediately after, without ever speaking to the president. They are there for one reason: to be on hand in case the president's helicopter crashes.

Most of the news coverage of the White House comes under the heading "body watch." In other words, reporters focus on the most visible layer of presidents' personal and official activities and provide the public with step-by-step accounts. They are interested in what presidents are going to do, how their actions will affect others, how they view policies and individuals, and how they present themselves, rather than in the substance of policies or the fundamental processes operating in the executive branch. Former ABC White House correspondent Sam Donaldson tells the story of covering a meeting of Western leaders on the island of Guadeloupe. It was a slow news day, and so Donaldson did a story on the roasting of the pig the leaders would be eating that night, including "an exclusive look at the oven in which the pig would be roasted."[42] Since there are daily deadlines to meet and television reporters must squeeze their stories into sound bites measured in seconds, not minutes, there is little time for reflection, analysis, or comprehensive coverage.

Bias is the most politically charged issue in relations between the president and the press. A large number of studies have concluded that the news media, including the television networks and major newspapers, is not biased *systematically* toward a particular person, party, or ideology, as measured in the amount of favorability of coverage. The bias found in such studies is inconsistent; the news is typically characterized by careful neutrality.[43]

Some observers believe that news coverage of the presidency often tends to emphasize the negative (although the negative stories are typically presented in a neutral manner). Stories on brewing scandals involving presidential appointees are one example. Another is reflected in an excerpt from President Carter's diary, regarding a visit to an army base in Panama in 1978:

> I told the Army troops that I was in the Navy for 11 years, and they booed. I told them that we depended on the Army to keep the Canal open, and they cheered. Later, the news reports said that there were boos and cheers during my speech.[44]

On the other hand, one could argue that the press is inherently biased *toward* the White House. A consistent pattern of favorable coverage exists in all major media outlets, and the president is typically portrayed with an aura of dignity and treated with deference.[45] According to Sam Donaldson, generally considered the most aggressive White House reporter, "For every truly tough question I've put to officials, I've asked a dozen that were about as tough as

[42]Sam Donaldson, *Hold On, Mr. President* (New York: Random House, 1987), 196–97.

[43]Two of the leading studies are Michael J. Robinson and Margaret A. Sheehan, *Over the Wire and on TV* (New York: Russell Sage Foundation, 1983); and Daniel C. Hallin, "The Media, the War in Vietnam, and Political Support," *Journal of Politics* 46 (February 1984): 2–24.

[44]Carter, *Keeping Faith*, 179–80.

[45]Michael Baruch Grossman and Martha Joynt Kumar, *Portraying the President: The White House and the News Media* (Baltimore: Johns Hopkins University Press, 1981), chaps. 10–11.

Grandma's apple dumplings."[46] Thus, when he left after serving as President Reagan's press secretary for six years, Larry Speakes told reporters they had given the Reagan administration "a fair shake."[47]

You should also remember that the White House can largely control the environment in which the president meets the press—even going so far as to have the Marine helicopters revved as Ronald Reagan approached them so that he could not hear reporters' questions and give unrehearsed responses.

UNDERSTANDING THE AMERICAN PRESIDENCY

Because the presidency is the single most important office in American politics, there has always been concern about whether the president is a threat to democracy. There has been a similar concern for the implications of such a potentially powerful figure for the size of government in America.

The Presidency and Democracy

From the time the Constitution was written there has been a fear that the presidency would degenerate into a monarchy—or at least into a dictatorship. Even America's greatest presidents have heightened these fears at times. Despite George Washington's well-deserved reputation for peacefully relinquishing power, he also had certain regal tendencies that fanned the suspicions of the Jeffersonians (see "In Focus: The Father of the Expense Account"). Abraham Lincoln, for all his humility, exercised extraordinary powers at the outbreak of the Civil War.

During the 1950s and 1960s, on the other hand, it was fashionable for political scientists, historians, and commentators to favor a powerful presidency. Historians rated presidents from strong to weak, there being no question that "strong" meant good and "weak" meant bad. Political scientists waxed eloquent about the presidency as the epitome of democratic government.[48]

By the 1970s many felt differently. The Vietnam War was unpopular. Lyndon Johnson and the war made people reassess the role of presidential power, and Richard Nixon and the Watergate scandal redoubled their thinking. Presidential duplicity was revealed in the Pentagon papers, a series of secret documents slipped to the press by Daniel Ellsberg. Nixon's "enemies list," his avowed goal to "screw our enemies" by illegally auditing their taxes, tapping their phones, and using "surreptitious entry" (a euphemism for burglary), asserted that presidents felt above the law. Nixon's lawyers argued solemnly to the Supreme Court and Congress that the presidency has "inherent powers" permitting presidents to order acts that otherwise would be illegal. Nixon protected himself with an umbrella defense of executive privilege, claiming that he did not need to provide evidence to Congress or the courts.

[46]Donaldson, *Hold On, Mr. President*, 237–38.

[47]Quoted in Eleanor Randolph, "Speakes Aims Final Salvo at White House Practices," *Washington Post*, January 31, 1987, A3.

[48]A good example is Clinton Rossiter, *The American Presidency*, rev. ed. (New York: Harcourt Brace Jovanovich, 1960).

The Father of the Expense Account

Americans revere George Washington as the epitome of integrity and the father of their country. The presiding officer of the Constitutional Convention and the first president had a curious way of seeking remuneration for his public service, however.

After his selection as commander in chief of the Continental Army in 1775, Washington rejected a salary for his services. Instead, he merely asked that the Continental Congress reimburse him for his expenses. Thus, instead of the $48,000 he would have received for eight years of service during the War of Independence, he turned in an expense account bill of nearly $500,000. (The buying power of that sum in today's economy would be tens of millions of dollars.)

No doubt most of the expenses were perfectly legitimate, but envision a modern day congressional committee examining the last item on Washington's expense account: $27,665.30 (hundreds of thousands of dollars in today's terms) to pay the expenses of Martha Washington's visits to her husband at his winter headquarters. Obviously, the rigors of Valley Forge were not shared equally by all. Washington wrote a long footnote justifying the submission of this figure; evidently, he had wrestled with his conscience—and won. Washington was willing to make every sacrifice for liberty except to reduce his standard of living. (In fact, the general also bought up deeds to land that Congress was paying the troops in lieu of cash, thus increasing his already substantial wealth.)

Such shrewd maneuvering makes Washington's portrait on the dollar bill a fitting monument. When Washington offered the same deal—no salary, only expenses—to the country after his election as the first president under the Constitution, Congress turned him down and provided a salary of $25,000 per year instead. They knew the salary would be far less expensive.

Source: Marvin Kitman, *George Washington's Expense Account* (New York: Harper & Row, 1988).

Early defenders of a strong presidency made sharp turnabouts in their position. In his book *The Imperial Presidency*, historian Arthur Schlesinger, an aide of John Kennedy's, argued that the presidency had become too powerful for the nation's own good.[49] (Critics pointed out that Schlesinger did not seem to feel that way when he worked in the White House.) Whereas an older generation of scholars had written glowing accounts of the presidency, a newer generation wrote about "The Swelling of the Presidency" and "Making the Presidency Safe for Democracy."[50]

The Nixon era was followed by the presidencies of Gerald Ford and Jimmy Carter, who many critics saw as weak leaders and failures. Ford himself spoke out in 1980, claiming that Carter's weakness had created an "imperiled" presidency. In the 1980s Ronald Reagan experienced short periods of great influence and longer ones of frustration as the American political system settled back into its characteristic mode of stalemate and incremental policy-making. The Iran-Contra affair kept concern about a tyrannical presidency alive, while, in most instances, Reagan's inability to impose his will on Congress evoked a desire on the part of some people (mostly conservative) for a stronger presidency.

[49] Arthur Schlesinger, *The Imperial Presidency* (Boston: Houston Mifflin, 1973).
[50] The titles of chaps. 5 and 11 in Cronin, *State of the Presidency*.

Concerns over presidential power are generally closely related to policy views. Those who oppose the president's policies are the most likely to be concerned about too much presidential power. As you have seen, however, aside from acting outside the law and the Constitution, there is little prospect of the presidency being a threat to democracy. The Madisonian system of checks and balances remains intact.

The Presidency and the Size of Government

The president is the central leader in American politics and some of the most noteworthy presidents in the twentieth century (including Theodore Roosevelt, Woodrow Wilson, and Franklin Roosevelt) have successfully advocated substantial increases in the role of the national government. Supporting an increased role for government is not inherent in the presidency, however; leadership can move in many directions.

All five of the presidents since Lyndon Johnson have championed constraints on government and limits on spending, especially in domestic policy. It is often said that the American people are ideologically conservative and operationally liberal. In the past generation it has been their will to choose presidents who reflected their ideology and a Congress that represented their appetite for public service. It has been the president more often than Congress who has said "no" to government growth.

SUMMARY

This chapter has looked at the president and the presidency. Americans expect a lot from presidents—perhaps too much. The myth of the president as powerhouse clouds American's image of presidential reality. Presidents mainly have the power to persuade, not to impose their will.

Presidents do not work alone. Gone are the days when the presidency meant the president plus a few aides and advisors; the cabinet, the Executive Office of the President, and the White House staff all assist today's presidents. These services come at a price, however, and presidents must organize their subordinates effectively for decision making and policy execution.

Although presidential leadership of Congress is central to all administrations, it often proves frustrating. Presidents rely on their party, the public, and their own legislative skills to persuade Congress to support their policies, but most of the time their efforts are at the margins of coalition building. Rarely are presidents in a position to create through their own leadership opportunities for major changes in public policy. They may, however, use their skills to exploit favorable political conditions to bring about policy change.

Some of the president's most important responsibilities fall in the area of national security. As chief diplomat and commander in chief of the armed forces, the president is the country's crisis manager. Still, disputes with Congress over war powers and presidential discretion in foreign affairs demonstrate that even in regard to national security the president operates within the Madisonian system of checks and balances.

Since presidents are dependent on others to accomplish their goals, their greatest challenge is to obtain support. Public opinion can be an important

Three former presidents meet with President Ronald Reagan before travelling to Egypt for the funeral of Egyptian President Anwar Sadat, who was assassinated in 1981. From left: Richard Nixon, President Reagan, Gerald Ford, and Jimmy Carter.

resource for presidential persuasion, and the White House works hard to influence it. Public approval of presidents and their policies is often elusive, however; the public does not reliably respond to presidential leadership.

KEY TERMS

Twenty-second Amendment
impeachment
Watergate
Twenty-fifth Amendment
cabinet
National Security Council (NSC)

Council of Economic Advisors (CEA)
Office of Management and Budget (OMB)
veto
pocket veto
presidential coattails
War Powers Resolution

legislative veto
crisis
press secretary

FOR FURTHER READING

Barber, James David. *The Presidential Character*, 3rd ed. Englewood Cliffs, N.J.: Prentice-Hall, 1985. Provocative work predicting performance in the White House.

Burke, John P., and Fred I. Greenstein. *How Presidents Test Reality*. New York: Russell Sage Foundation, 1989. Excellent work on presidential decision making.

Edwards, George C., III. *At the Margins: Presidential Leadership of Congress*. New Haven, Conn.: Yale University Press, 1989. Examines the president's efforts to lead Congress and explains their limitations.

————. *The Public Presidency*. New York: St. Martin's Press, 1983. The relationship between the president and public opinion in the White House's pursuit of popular support.

Fisher, Louis. *Constitutional Conflicts Between Congress and the President*. Princeton, N.J.: Princeton University Press, 1985. Presents the constitutional dimensions of the separation of powers.

Grossman, Michael Baruch, and Martha Joynt Kumar, *Portraying the President: The White House and the News Media*. Baltimore: Johns Hopkins University Press, 1981. A comprehensive study of presidential relations with the press.

Light, Paul C. *The President's Agenda*. Baltimore: Johns Hopkins University Press, 1983. The presidential role in setting the Washington issue agenda.

Nathan, Richard P. *The Administrative Presidency*. New York: Wiley, 1983. The president's role in managing the bureaucracy.

Neustadt, Richard E. *Presidential Power*. New York: Wiley, 1980. The most influential book on the American presidency; argues that presidential power is the power to persuade.

Pfiffner, James P. *The Strategic Presidency*. Chicago: Dorsey, 1988. Organizing the presidency.

14

CONGRESS, THE PRESIDENT, AND THE BUDGET: THE POLITICS OF TAXING AND SPENDING

On January 29, 1990, President Bush submitted to Congress his proposal for the next year's budget, asking for $1.2 trillion to run the national government in 1991. It was a massive document. Richard Darman, the director of the Office of Management and Budget and the person with the responsibility for putting together the president's budget, described the budget as follows:

> The sheer size of the budget makes it seem like a monster. It contains almost 190,000 accounts. At the rate of one per minute, eight hours per day, it would take over a year to reflect upon these! The budget's annual outlays are larger than all countries' economies except those of the United States, Japan, and the Soviet Union. (The federal budget is roughly the size of the entire West German economy.)

Not only was the budget large, but more importantly, packed into its pages were decisions on thousands of public policies. At its core, however, the budgetary process revolves around two major questions: Where does government's money come from? Where does it go? In other words, who bears the burdens of paying for government, and who receives the benefits? No set of questions is more central to politics.

The president knew he would face challenges on all fronts regarding his budget proposal. In recent years presidents have typically found their budgets to be DOA (dead on arrival) on Capitol Hill. From the president's perspective this is critical, because Congress, not the White House, has the ultimate power to determine how much the government will tax and what it will spend taxes for.

President Bush hoped that the budget would be ready by the time the new fiscal year began over nine months later. He knew that the budget might not be done on time, and that in the meantime there would be a long, sometimes tortuous, and probably acrimonious fight over priorities in spending and over tax rates. Democrats would want to cut defense expenditures and increase spending on domestic programs while many Republicans would resist such changes.

The president also found himself in something of a bind. He had made a dramatic pledge—"Read my lips, no new taxes"—during his speech accepting the Republican party's nomination for president in August 1988. He also had said that he wanted to be known as the "education president," clean up the environment, end the scourge of illegal drugs, provide more day care for the children of working Americans, and care for the homeless. How would he fund the policies to make the United States a "kinder, gentler nation"? He was being criticized for running a "presidency by gesture."

Bush knew that these criticisms were just the beginning. Somehow he and Congress had to agree on a plan to lower the deficit, working in an atmosphere in which each side would be blaming the other for being irresponsible in handling the nation's affairs. It would be a difficult process. This chapter will examine what government does with its $1.2 trillion annual budget, how it raises this much money, and how it goes about making decisions to spend it.

*T*he Constitution allocates various tasks to both the president and Congress, but it generally leaves it up to each branch to decide whether or not to exercise its power to perform a certain task. There is an exception, however. Every year they *must* produce a budget. If they fail to do so, the government will come to a standstill. The army will have to be disbanded, Social Security offices will have to close, and food stamps will not be distributed to the poor.

For most of your lifetime the dominant issue at the national level has not been whether it is good for the government to spend money to feed the poor, educate the young, or clean the environment. Most people support such policies. Instead, the central political issue has been how to pay for these policies.

Resources have been scarce because each year during the 1980s (and into the 1990s) the national government has run up a large budget deficit. A budget **deficit** occurs when **expenditures** exceed **revenues.** In other words, the national government spends more money than it receives in taxes. As a result, the total national debt rose sharply during the 1980s, increasing from less than one trillion dollars to over three trillion dollars in 1990. About 14 percent of all current budget expenditures go to paying just the *interest* on this debt.

With the national government awash in red ink, the president and Congress have been caught in a budgetary squeeze: Americans want them to balance the budget, maintain or increase the level of government spending on most policies, and keep taxes low. As a result, the president and Congress are preoccupied with budgeting, trying to cope with these contradictory demands.

Budgets are also central to the policy-making process because they reflect the values of decision makers regarding public policy. Indeed, for many programs, budgeting *is* policy. The amount of money spent on a program determines how many people are served, how well they are served, or how much of something (weapons, vaccines, and so on) the government can purchase.

In this chapter you will learn how the president and Congress produce a budget, making decisions on both taxes and expenditures. In short, you will look at how government manages its money—really, of course, *your* money. The following section will begin this investigation by asking the logical first question: Why are government budgets so big?

The president makes the first move in the budgetary process— submitting a budget proposal each year in January—but Congress ultimately approves the actual budget that goes into effect each October. Compromise is thus a key element of budget making; President Bush, for example, even offered to back down from his "no new taxes" pledge to ease negotiations on the 1991 budget.

BIG GOVERNMENTS, BIG BUDGETS

One answer to the question of why budgets are so large is simple: big budgets are necessary to pay for big governments. Among the most important changes of the twentieth century is the rise of large governments.[1] Actually, among Western nations, America has one of the *smallest* public sectors relative to the size of the American GNP (see "America in Perspective: How Big Is Big?"). Nevertheless, with a budget of $1.2 trillion per year, it is difficult to characterize the national government as anything but large—some would say enormous.

As with other Western nations, the growth of government in the United States has been dramatic. Political scientist E.E. Schattschneider took a look backward at government growth:

The beginnings were almost unbelievably small. In 1792 the federal government . . . resembled the present government in about the way Henry Ford's old bicycle repair shop resembles the modern Ford Motor Company. President Washington made his budget on a single sheet of paper. Jefferson ran his Department of

---

[1]For some perspectives on the rise of government expenditures, see David Cameron, "The Expansion of the Public Economy: A Comparative Analysis," *American Political Science Review* 72 (December 1978): 1243–61; and William D. Berry and David Lowery, *Understanding United States Government Growth* (New York: Praeger, 1987).

How Big Is Big?

When one hears about trillion-dollar federal budgets and budget deficits that may run $150 billion in a single year, its easy to think of "big government." The figures in the accompanying graph, however, show that the national, state, and local governments in the United States actually spend a smaller percentage of their country's resources than those in almost all other democracies with developed economies. Only Japan spends a smaller percentage, and it, unlike the United States, has a very small defense budget. All the major Western democracies devote a considerably larger share of their wealth to government services, with Sweden spending almost two out of every three dollars in the economy on government programs. Compared with these countries, the United States has a rather modest public sector.

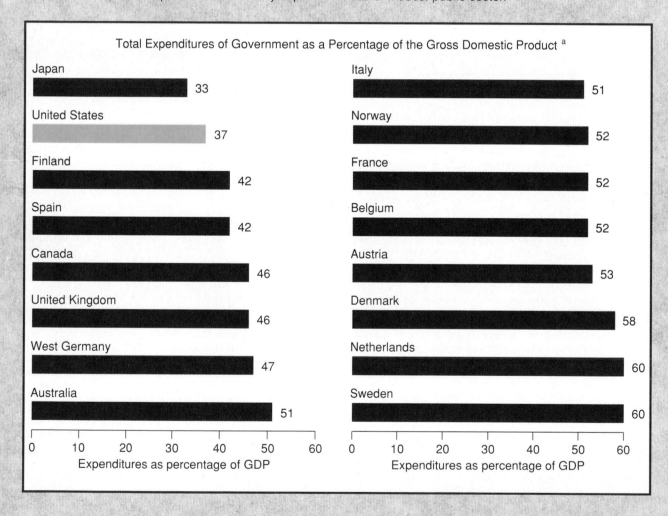

Total Expenditures of Government as a Percentage of the Gross Domestic Product [a]

Country	%	Country	%
Japan	33	Italy	51
United States	37	Norway	52
Finland	42	France	52
Spain	42	Belgium	52
Canada	46	Austria	53
United Kingdom	46	Denmark	58
West Germany	47	Netherlands	60
Australia	51	Sweden	60

Expenditures as percentage of GDP

[a]Gross Domestic Product is Gross National Product minus the value of goods and services produced outside the country.
Source: OECD Economic Outlook 44 (June 1989): 185.

Foreign Affairs with a staff of six writing clerks. The government issued three patents in 1790. As late as 1822 the government spent $1000 for the improvement of rivers and harbors and President Monroe vetoed a $9000 appropriation for the repair of the Cumberland Road.[2]

This relatively tiny government was, said Schattschneider, the "grain of mustard seed" from which today's huge government has grown. American governments—national, state, and local—spend one-third of the Gross National Product. The national government alone spends about 23 percent of the GNP.

No one, of course, knows for sure exactly why government has grown so rapidly in all the Western democracies. William Berry and David Lowery launched a major assault on the question, but their findings were mixed. On balance, however, they found the most support for the view that the public sector expands principally in response to changes in the public's preferences and in economic and social conditions that affect the public's level of demand for government activity.[3] This is why the rise of big government has been strongly resistant to reversal: citizens like government services. Even Ronald Reagan, a strong leader with an antigovernment orientation, succeeded only in slowing the *growth* of government, not in actually trimming its size. When he left office, the federal government employed more people and spent more money than when he was inaugurated.

Two conditions associated with government growth in America are the rise of the social service state and the rise of the national security state. The following sections will examine them briefly.

The Rise of the Social Service State

In 1935, during the Great Depression and the administration of President Franklin D. Roosevelt, Congress passed the **Social Security Act.** The act was intended to provide a minimal level of sustenance to older Americans and thus to save them from poverty.

In January 1940 the treasurer of the United States sent the nation's first Social Security check to Ida Fuller of Brattleboro, Vermont, in the amount of $22.54. An early entrant into the fledgling Social Security program, Fuller had contributed less than the amount of her first check to the system. By the time she died in December 1974 at the age of one hundred, she had collected $20,944.42 from the Social Security Administration. These days, more than forty million Americans receive checks from the Social Security system. Each check is mailed dutifully from Washington on the third day of each month. In the 1950s disability insurance was included in the Social Security program; thus, workers who had not retired but who were disabled could also collect benefits. In 1965, **Medicare** was added to the system, which provides both hospital and physician coverage to retirees and to some poor persons. Today barely half the Social Security checks go to retired workers; other checks go to the disabled, to Medicare patients, and to others who qualify. Social Security has become the most expensive public policy in the world.

---

[2] E.E. Schattschneider, *Two Hundred Million Americans in Search of a Government* (New York; Holt, Rinehart and Winston, 1969), 29–30.

[3] Berry and Lowery, *Understanding United States Government Growth.*

Social Security is less an insurance program than a kind of intergenerational contract (see "A Question of Ethics: Is There Justice between Generations?"). Essentially, money is taken from the working members of the population and spent on the retired members. Today, though, demographic and economic realities threaten to dilute this intergenerational bargain. In 1940 the entire Social Security system was financed with a 3 percent tax on payrolls; by 1990, the tax was in excess of 15 percent. Economist Eli Ginzberg calculated that in 1945 fifty workers paid taxes to support each Social Security beneficiary. In 1980 about three workers supported each beneficiary. By the year 2035, when today's young college students will be getting their Social Security checks, fewer than two workers will be supporting each beneficiary.[4]

Not surprisingly, the Social Security program faced a problem as the 1980s began. As Paul Light candidly described the problem: "It was going broke fast. More money was going out in benefits than was coming in . . . . At the height of the crisis, social security was spending about $3000 more per minute than it was taking in."[5] Worse, that was only the short-term problem. The aging population added more people to the Social Security rolls annually; once there, people tended to stay on the rolls because life expectancies were increasing.

[4]Eli Ginzberg, "The Social Security System," *Scientific American,* January 1982, 55. See also Alicia H. Munnell, *The Future of Social Security* (Washington, D.C.: The Brookings Institution, 1977).

[5]Paul Light, *Artful Work: The Politics of Social Security Reform* (New York: Random House, 1985), 89.

Lyndon Johnson's "Great Society" initiatives in the mid-1960s greatly expanded America's social services network, adding Medicare and Medicaid to the Social Security system and creating many new programs designed to aid the poor. Here LBJ campaigns during the 1964 presidential election.

Is There Justice between Generations?

Phillip Longman retells an old thirteenth-century folktale about justice between generations. It is called "The Tale of the Ungrateful Son." An old man has finally decided that he is unable to take care of himself and asks his adult son if he can move in with the son and his family at their country farm. Promising to hand over his modest wealth when he dies, the old man moves in. He becomes a greater and greater burden. Finally, the son decides to move his father to the barn, where he can die quietly. Too embarrassed to tell his father directly, he asks his own son to take the grandfather to the barn and wrap him in their best horse blanket. The grandson sorrowfully does as he is told but tears the blanket in half, giving the old man only one-half of it. The boy's father is angry upon hearing that the child has used only half the blanket to wrap the grandfather and curses the grandson. "But father," the child replies, "I am saving the other half for you."

What does one generation owe to another? In the United States today, the Social Security system represents Americans' major intergenerational commitment. It is a major commitment indeed. Americans spend more on older people at all levels of government than they do on persons age seventeen and younger by more than three to one. Not all of these older people, of course, are poor. Though there are poor people among the aged, older Americans' actual after-tax per capita income is higher than that of the rest of the population.

One thing that all older Americans have in common is a strong belief that they are entitled to benefits from the Social Security system, a program into which they paid during their working lives. Yet the system itself is troubled, and likely to become more so. Even the Social Security Administration's most optimistic predictions contain gloomy scenarios: by the year 2055 the cost of disability benefits, pension benefits and Medicare (Social Security's three main programs) will be the equivalent of 42 percent of *all* taxable payrolls in the United States (at present, it consumes only 14 percent of all payrolls).

Like the grandson in the old folktale, Americans must determine, as a matter of public policy, what one generation owes to another. What is *your* opinion?

Source: Phillip Longman, "Justice between Generations," *Atlantic Monthly*, June 1985, 73–81.

Said Light: "Diseases that once were life-threatening had been rendered harmless. If longevity continued to grow, most retirees could expect to live past 90 by the turn of the century."[6] Building automatic escalators for taxes became a congressional necessity.

Social Security is not, of course, the only social policy of the federal government that costs money. In health, education, job training, and scores of other areas, the rise of the social service state has contributed to America's growing budget. No brief list could do justice to the range of social programs of the government, which provides funds for the aged, businesses run by minority entrepreneurs, consumer education, drug rehabilitation, environmental education, food subsidies for the poor, guaranteed loans to college students, housing allowances for the poor, inspections of hospitals, and so on. Liberals often favor these programs to assist individuals and groups in society; conservatives see them as a drain on the federal treasury. In any event, they cost money—a lot of it (see Figure 14.1).

[6]*Ibid.*, 95.

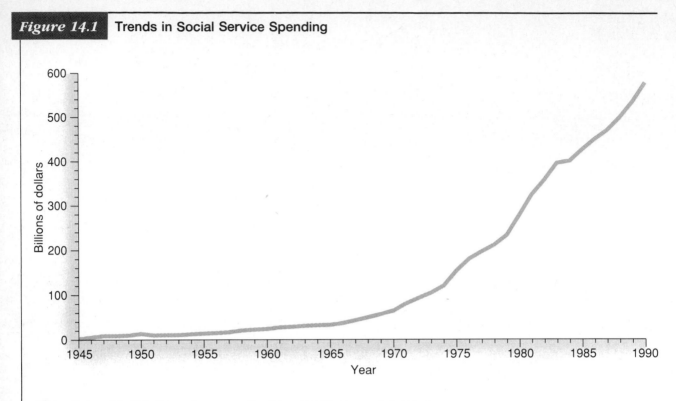

Figure 14.1 Trends in Social Service Spending

Billions of dollars

Source: *Budget of the United States Government, Fiscal Year 1991* (Washington, D.C.: U.S. Government Printing Office, 1990), A-317.

The Rise of the National Security State

A generation ago, the most expensive part of the federal budget was not its social services but its military budget. It was President Eisenhower—not some liberal antimilitary activist—who coined the phrase *military industrial complex* to characterize the close correspondence between military brass and the corporations that supply their hardware needs.

Before World War II, the United States largely disbanded its military forces at the end of a war. Since World War II, however, the "cold war" with the Soviet Union has resulted in a permanent military establishment and expensive military technology. Fueling the military machine has greatly increased the cost of government. Although President Reagan proposed scrapping scores of domestic programs in his annual budget requests, he also urged Congress to substantially increase the defense budget. Throughout his entire second term Congress balked, however, and the 1990s began with talk of a "peace dividend" from reduced defense expenditures in response to the lessening of tensions in Europe (discussed in Chapter 20). Nevertheless, the budget of the Department of Defense still constitutes about one-fourth of all federal expenditures (see Figure 14.2).

Payrolls and pensions for the 3.15 million people who work for the Pentagon, the 1.2 million reservists, and the thousands of military retirees constitute a

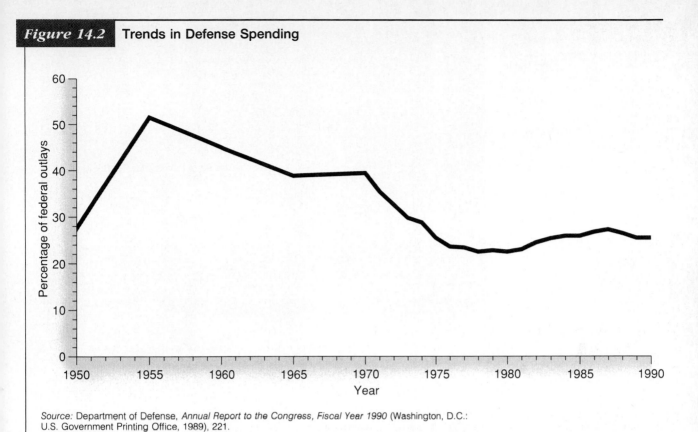

Figure 14.2 **Trends in Defense Spending**

Source: Department of Defense, *Annual Report to the Congress, Fiscal Year 1990* (Washington, D.C.: U.S. Government Printing Office, 1989), 221.

large component of the defense budget. The greatest expenditure of defense funds, however, is for the research, development, and *procurement* (purchasing) of military hardware. The costs of procurement are high, even though total military expenditures have declined as a percentage of American GNP since the end of World War II. The cost of advanced technology makes any weapon, fighter plane, or component more expensive than its predecessors. Moreover, cost overruns are common. The American fleet of 132 Stealth bombers will cost almost twice the original estimate—over one half *billion* dollars each. According to former Secretary of the Air Force Edward C. Aldridge, "Whatever it costs, it's worth it."[7] Many critics of such expensive military hardware would disagree.

Scandal has also plagued the Pentagon's procurement and provided vivid illustrations for critics of defense spending. One $436 hammer supplied by Gould, Inc., could have been duplicated at a local hardware store for $10. During the 1980s the secretary of defense launched major reforms in procurement, even going so far as to temporarily cancel contracts with mighty General Dynamics. Most observers remain skeptical about the government's ability to substantially reduce the costs of military procurement, however.

[7]Richard Halloran, "Cost Estimate of Stealth Bombers Increased 16% by the Air Force," *New York Times,* December 17, 1988, 10.

The Air Force unveiled its new Stealth bomber in 1989. The plane's unusual shape allows it to fly undetected by enemy radar, but such advanced technology costs money—over $500 million per plane. Funding for the bomber has been a source of continuing debate during recent budget negotiations.

The rise of the social service state and the national security state together are linked with much of American governmental growth since the end of World War II. Although American social services have expanded less than such services have in Western European nations, American military expenditures have expanded more rapidly. Together, these factors help explain why the budgetary process is the center of attention in American government today.

THE BUDGETARY PROCESS

Budgets are produced through a long and complex process that starts and ends with the president and has the Congress squarely in the middle. Because budgets are so important to almost all other policies, the budgetary process is the center of political battles in Washington and involves nearly everyone in government. This section examines the process and the politics through which the president and Congress produce a budget.

Everyone has a basic understanding of budgeting. Public budgets are superficially like personal budgets. Aaron Wildavsky has remarked that "a budget is a document that contains words and figures that propose expenditures for certain objects and purposes." There is more to public budgets than bookkeeping, however, because such a **budget** is a policy document allocating burdens (taxes) and benefits (expenditures). Thus, "budgeting is concerned with translating financial resources into human purposes. A budget therefore may also be characterized as a series of goals with price tags attached."[8]

[8]Aaron Wildavsky, *The New Politics of the Budgetary Process* (Boston: Little, Brown, 1988), 1–2. See also Robert D. Lee, Jr., and Ronald W. Johnson, *Public Budgeting Systems,* 2nd ed. (Baltimore: University Park Press, 1977), 11–15.

Figure 14.3 gives a quick overview of the federal budget. It offers a simplified picture of the two sides of the budgetary coin—revenues and expenditures—but the distribution of the government's $1.1 trillion budget for fiscal year 1990 is the outcome of a very complex budgetary process. Nestled inside the figure's tax and expenditures figures are thousands of policy choices, prompting plenty of politics.

Budgetary Politics

Public budgets are the supreme example of Harold Lasswell's definition of politics as "who gets what, when and how." Budget battles are fought over contending interests, ideologies, programs, and agencies.

Stakes and Strategies   Every political actor has a stake in the budget. Mayors want to keep federal grants-in-aid flowing in; defense contractors like a big defense budget; scientists like to see the National Science Foundation given a large budget. Agencies within the government also work to protect their interests. Individual members of Congress act as policy entrepreneurs for new ideas—which cost money—and support constituent benefits, which also do not come free. Presidents try to use budgets to manage the economy and leave their imprint on Congress' policy agenda.

Figure 14.3   **The Federal Government Dollar (Fiscal Year 1991 Estimate)**

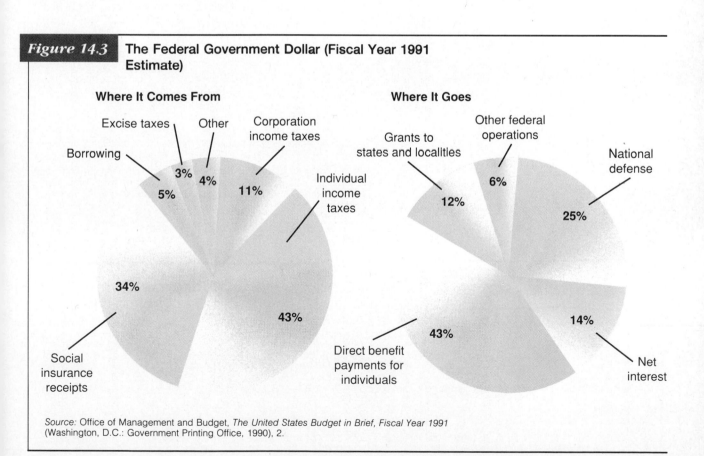

Source: Office of Management and Budget, *The United States Budget in Brief, Fiscal Year 1991* (Washington, D.C.: Government Printing Office, 1990), 2.

You can think of budgetary politics as resembling a game in which players choose among strategies.[9] Agencies pushing their budgetary needs to the president and Congress, for instance, try to link the benefits of their program to a senator's or representative's electoral needs.[10] Almost invariably, agencies pad their requests a bit, hoping that the almost inevitable cuts will be bearable. (President John Adams justified this now common budgetary gambit by saying to his cabinet, "If some superfluity not be given [Congress] to lop off, they will cut into the very flesh of the public necessities.") Interest groups try to identify their favorite programs with the national interest. Mayors tell Congress not how much they like to have federal aid flowing but how crucial cities are to national survival. Farmers stress not that they like federal aid but that feeding a hungry nation and world is the main task of American agriculture. All the players have their own strategies in the game of budgetary politics, and in the pluralistic politics of budget making, there are plenty of players.

The Players Deciding how to carve up almost a quarter of the GNP is a process likely to attract plenty of interest, from those formally required to participate in the budgeting process as well as those whose stakes are too big to ignore it. Here are the main actors in the budgetary process:

- *The interest groups.* No lobbyist worth his or her pay would ignore the budget. Lobbying for a group's needs takes place in the agencies, with presidents (if the lobbyist has access to them), and before congressional committees. A smart agency head will be sure to involve interest groups in defending the agency's budget request.
- *The agencies.* Convinced of the importance of their mission, the heads of agencies almost always push for higher budget requests. They send their requests to the Office of Management and Budget and later get a chance to present themselves before congressional committees as well.

[9]A good description of budgetary strategies is in Wildavsky, *The New Politics of the Budgetary Process,* chap. 3.

[10]For a discussion of the ways bureaucracies manipulate benefits to gain advantage with members of Congress, see Douglas Arnold, *Congress and the Bureaucracy* (New Haven, Conn.: Yale University Press, 1979), and the articles in Barry S. Rundquist, ed., *Political Benefits* (Lexington, Mass.: D. C. Heath, 1980).

Public opinion is a key element in the budgeting process, affecting all players. Occasionally, the public has a direct role in budget making, as when the citizens of Massachusetts voted on Proposition 2 1/2, a referendum proposing strict limits to local property taxes. Despite protests against the proposed legislation—many citizens argued that tax limits would restrict many important government services— the proposition was passed in 1980 and implemented in 1982.

- *The Office of Management and Budget (OMB).* The OMB is responsible to the president, its boss, but no president has the time to understand and make decisions about the billions of dollars in the budget, parceled out to hundreds of agencies, some of which the chief executive has probably never heard of. The director and staff of the OMB have considerable independence from the president, making them major actors in the annual budget process.

- *The president.* The final decisions on what to propose to Congress are the president's. In early January, after the Congress has convened, the president gives a budget address and unveils the proposed budget; the president then spends many a day trying to ensure that Congress will stick close to the recommendations.

- *The tax committees in Congress.* The government cannot spend money it does not have. The **House Ways and Means Committee** and the **Senate Finance Committee** write the tax codes, subject to the approval of Congress as a whole.

- *The Budget Committees and the Congressional Budget Office (CBO).* The CBO, which is the congressional equivalent of the OMB, and its parent committees, the Senate and House Budget Committees, set the parameters of the congressional budget process through examining revenues and expenditures in the aggregate and proposing resolutions to bind Congress within certain limits.

- *The subject-matter committees.* Committees of Congress write new laws, which require new expenditures. Committee members' may use hearings either to publicize the accomplishments of their pet agencies, thus supporting larger budgets for them, or to question agency heads about waste or overspending.

- *The Appropriations Committees and their subcommittees.* The Appropriations Committee in each house decides who gets what. These committees take new or old policies coming from the subject-matter committees and decide how much to spend. Their subcommittees hold hearings on specific agency requests.
- *The Congress as a whole.* The Constitution requires that Congress as a whole approve taxes and appropriations, and senators and representatives alike have a strong interest in delivering federal dollars to their constituents. A dam here, a military base there, a new post office somewhere else—these are the items members look for in the budget.
- *The General Accounting Office (GAO).* Congress' role does not end when it has passed the budget. The GAO works as Congress' eyes and ears, auditing, monitoring, and evaluating what agencies are doing with their budgets.

Budgeting involves a cast of thousands, but their roles are carefully scripted and their time on stage limited. This is because budget making is both repetitive—the same things must be done each year—and sequential—they must be done in the proper order and more or less on time. The budget cycle begins in the executive branch a full nineteen months before the fiscal year begins.

The President's Budget

Until 1921 the various agencies of the executive branch sent their budget requests to the secretary of the treasury, who in turn forwarded them to the Congress. Presidents played a limited role in proposing the budget, or sometimes no role at all. Agencies basically peddled their own budget requests to Congress. In 1921 Congress passed the Budget and Accounting Act, requiring presidents to propose an executive budget to Congress and creating the Bureau of the Budget to help them. In the 1970s President Nixon reorganized the Bureau of the Budget and gave it a new name—the Office of Management and Budget (OMB). The OMB, whose director is a presidential appointee requiring Senate approval, now supervises preparation of the federal budget and advises the president on budgetary matters.

It takes a long time to prepare a presidential budget.[11] By law, the president must submit a budget on the fifteenth day of the new congressional session in January. Almost a year before, the process begins (see Table 14.1) when the OMB communicates with each agency, sounding out its requests and tentatively issuing guidelines. By the summer the president has decided on overall policies and priorities and has established general targets for the budget. These are communicated to the agencies.

The budget makers now get down to details. During the fall the agencies submit formal, detailed estimates for their budgets, zealously pushing their needs to the OMB. Budget analysts at the OMB pare, investigate, weigh, and meet on agency requests. Typically, the agency heads ask for hefty increases; sometimes they threaten to go directly to the president if their priorities are not met by

[11]A good review of the formation of the executive budget is Howard E. Schuman, *Politics and the Budget,* 2nd ed. (Englewood Cliffs, N.J.: Prentice-Hall, 1988), chap. 2.

Table 14.1	**The President's Budget: An Approximate Schedule**

SPRING

Budget policy developed	The OMB presents to the president an analysis of the economic situation and they discuss the budgetary outlook and policies. The OMB then gives guidelines to the agencies, which in turn review current programs and submit to the OMB their projections of budgetary needs for the coming year. The OMB goes over these projections and prepares recommendations to the president on final policy, programs, and budget levels. The president establishes guidelines and targets.

SUMMER

Agency estimates submitted	The OMB conveys the president's decisions to the agencies and advises and assists them in preparing their budgets.

FALL

Estimates reviewed	The agencies submit to the OMB formal budget estimates for the coming fiscal year, along with projections for future years. The OMB holds hearings, reviews its assessment of the economy, and prepares budget recommendations for the president. The president reviews these recommendations and decides on the agencies' budgets and overall budgetary policy. The OMB advises the agencies of these decisions.

WINTER

President's budget determined and submitted	The agencies revise their estimates to conform with the president's decisions. The OMB once again reviews the economy and then drafts the president's budget message and prepares the budget document. The president revises and approves the budget message and transmits the budget document to Congress shortly after it convenes.

the OMB. As the Washington winter sets in, the budget document is readied for final presidential approval. There is some last-minute juggling—agencies may be asked to change their estimates to conform with the president's decisions, or cabinet members may make a last-ditch effort to bypass the OMB and convince the president to increase their funds. With only days—or hours—left before the submission deadline, the budget document is rushed to the printers. Then the president sends it to Capitol Hill. The next steps are up to Congress.

Congress and the Budget

According to the Constitution, all federal appropriations must be authorized by Congress. Thus Congress always holds one extremely powerful trump card in national policy-making: the power of the purse.[12] No money is spent and no taxes are collected in direct response to the president's budget—that is, the president proposes, but Congress disposes. By law, Congress must decide between January, when the president submits the proposed budget, and October 1, when the fiscal year begins, how to spend more than a trillion dollars.

Reforming the Process   For years Congress budgeted in a piecemeal fashion. Each agency request was handled by a subcommittee of the House and Senate Appropriations Committees; then all these appropriations were added to produce a total budget. People never quite knew what the budget's bottom line would be until all the individual bills were totaled up. What Congress spent had little to do with any overall judgment of how much it should spend.

The **Congressional Budget and Impoundment Control Act of 1974** was designed to reform the congressional budgetary process. Its supporters hoped that it would also make Congress less dependent on the president's budget and more able to set and meet its own budgetary goals. Here is what the act established:

- A *fixed budget calendar*. For each step in the budgetary process there is an established completion date. In the past Congress sometimes failed to appropriate money to agencies until after the fiscal year was over, leaving agencies drifting for months with no firm budget. Now there is a timetable mandated by law, which was amended in 1985 (see Table 14.2).
- A *Budget Committee in each house*. These two committees are supposed to recommend to Congress target figures for the *total* budget size by April 1 of each year. By April 15, Congress is to agree on the total size of the budget, which guides the Appropriations Committees in juggling figures for individual agencies.
- A *Congressional Budget Office*. The **Congressional Budget Office (CBO)** advises Congress on the likely consequences of its budget decisions, forecasts revenues, and is a counterweight to the president's OMB.

The new budgeting system was supposed to force Congress to consider the budget (both projected expenditures and projected revenues) as a whole, rather than in bits and pieces, as it had done before. An important part of the process of establishing a budget is to set limits on expenditures based on revenue projections, a step that is supposed to be done through a **budget resolution.** Thus in April of each year both houses are expected to agree upon a budget resolution, thereby binding Congress to a total expenditure level that should form the bottom line of all federal spending for all programs. Only then is Congress supposed to begin acting on the individual appropriations.

Put in terms of a family budget, Family A might decide to budget by adding up all its needs and wants and calling that its budget. Such a strategy almost guarantees overspending the family income. Family B, though, might begin by looking first at its revenue and then trying to bring its total expenditures into line with its revenue before dealing with its individual expenditure decisions.

[12]An important work on congresssional budget making is Wildavsky, *The New Politics of the Budgetary Process*. See also Allen Schick, *Congress and Money* (Washington, D.C.: The Urban Institute, 1980).

Table 14.2 The Congressional Budget Process: Targets and Timetables

DATE	ACTION TO BE COMPLETED
First Monday after January 3	Congress receives the president's budget.
February 15	The CBO submits a budget report to the House and Senate Budget Committees, including an analysis of the president's budget.
February 25	Other committees submit reports on outlays and revenues to Budget Committees in each house.
April 1	Budget Committees report concurrent resolution on the budget, which sets a total for budget outlays, an estimate of expenditures for major budget categories, and the recommended level of revenues. This resolution acts as an agenda for the remainder of the budgetary process.
April 15	Congress completes action on concurrent resolution on the budget.
May 15	Annual appropriations bills may be considered in the House.
June 10	House Appropriations Committee reports last annual appropriations bill.
June 15	Congress completes action on reconciliation legislation, bringing budget totals into conformity with established ceilings.
June 30	House completes action on annual appropriation bills.
October 1	The new fiscal year begins.

Source: Committee on the Budget, U.S. Senate, *The Congressional Budget Process* (Washington, D.C.: Government Printing Office, 1988), 26.

With its 1974 reforms, Congress was trying to force itself to behave more like Family B than Family A.

Like the president's budget proposal, the congressional budget resolution assumes that certain changes will be made in law, primarily to achieve savings incorporated into the spending totals and thus meet the budget resolution. These changes are legislated in two separate ways.

First is budget **reconciliation,** which revises program authorizations to achieve required savings; it usually also includes tax or other revenue adjustments. Usually reconciliation comes near the end of the budgetary process, but in 1981, in an attempt to strike while his political standing was high and to overcome the opposition of special interests and the parochialism and power of congressional committees, President Reagan successfully proposed using an extremely complex reconciliation bill to reduce the budget by approximately forty billion dollars. Reagan felt that he could obtain substantial cuts only if he lumped them all together in one bill in which everyone lost something. The preparation of the bill was so hurried that few members of Congress could give it serious consideration; the name and telephone number of Rita Seymour, a CBO staffer, were even inadvertently included in one amendment.

The second way that laws are changed to meet the budget resolution involves more narrowly drawn legislation. An **authorization bill** is an act of Congress that establishes a discretionary government program or an entitlement, or that continues or changes such programs. Authorizations specify program goals and, for discretionary programs, set the maximum amount that they may spend. For entitlement programs, an authorization sets or changes eligibility standards and benefits that must be provided by the program. Authorizations may be for one year, or they may run for a specified or indefinite number of years.

An additional measure, termed an **appropriations bill,** must be passed to actually fund programs established by authorization bills. The appropriations bills usually cover one year and cannot exceed the amount of money authorized for a program, but they may appropriate less than was authorized.

The Success of the 1974 Reforms　Have these reforms worked? If *worked* means that Congress has brought its spending into line with its revenues, then the reforms are almost a total failure. Congressional budgets have been in the red every year since the 1974 amendments. In fact, the red ink has grown from a puddle to an ocean (see Figure 14.4). Presidents have made matters worse, submitting budget proposals containing large deficits.

In addition, Congress has often failed to meet its own budgetary timetable. There has been too much conflict over the budget for the system to work according to design. Moreover, in many instances Congress has not been able to reach agreement and pass appropriations bills at all, and has instead resorted to **continuing resolutions,** laws that allow agencies to spend at the previous year's level. Sometimes, as in 1986 and 1987, appropriations bills have been lumped together in one enormous and complex bill (rather than in the thirteen separate appropriations bills that are supposed to pass), precluding adequate review by individual members of Congress and forcing the president to either accept unwanted provisions or veto the funding for the entire government. These omnibus bills in 1986 and 1987 also became magnets for unrelated and controversial pieces of legislation that could not pass on their own.

On the other hand, the 1974 reforms have helped Congress view the entire budget early in the process; now Congress can at least see the forest as well as the trees. The problem, as you will see, is not so much the procedure as disagreement over how scarce resources should be spent—or whether they should be spent at all.

More Reforms　By 1985 Congress was desperate. President Reagan refused to consider tax increases to pay for federal spending and continued to submit budgets that contained huge deficits. In response to growing frustration at its inability to substantially reduce annual budget deficits, Congress enacted the Balanced Budget and Emergency Deficit Control Act, better known as **Gramm-Rudman-Hollings** after its cosponsors, Senators Phil Gramm of Texas, Warren Rudman of New Hampshire, and Ernest Hollings of South Carolina.

This legislation, as it has been amended, mandates maximum allowable deficit levels for each year until 1993, when the budget is to be in balance. If Congress fails to meet the deficit goals, automatic across-the-board spending cuts must be ordered by the president (a number of programs, including Social Security and interest on the national debt, were exempt from this process). In 1989 automatic cuts went into effect for several weeks at the end of the year until Congress and the president could agree on a budget.

Gramm-Rudman-Hollings is clearly an indelicate, unthinking approach to budgeting; no one likes the arbitrary nature of the automatic budget cuts, half of which come from defense and half from domestic programs. Even Senator

Figure 14.4 | Annual Federal Deficits, 1970–1995

Yearly deficits mushroomed during the Reagan administration (1981–1988), despite the president's oft-repeated commitment to a balanced budget. Notice the OMB's optimistic figures for the estimates of deficits in the early 1990s.

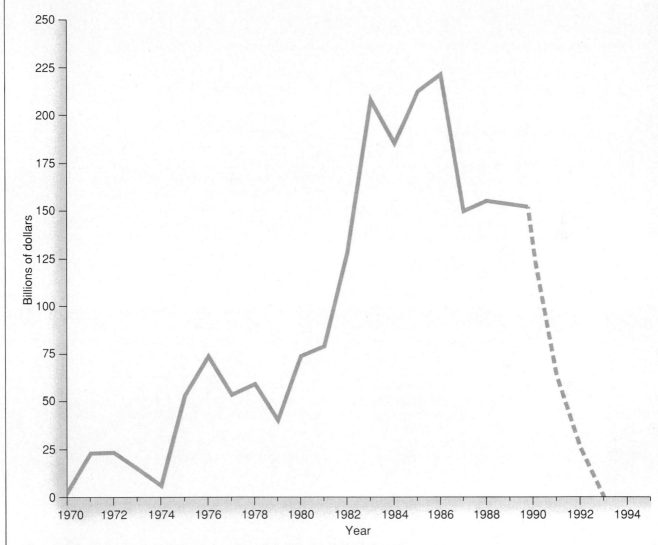

Source: *Budget of the United States Government, Fiscal Year 1991* (Washington, D.C.: Government Printing Office, 1990), A-281.

Rudman describe it as "a bad idea whose time has come." In the absence of consensus on spending priorities, Congress felt it had no other way to force itself to reduce the deficit. Success has been elusive, however, as you can see in both Figure 14.4 and "In Focus: Calculating the Deficit: Houdini Would Be Proud."

Calculating the Deficit: Houdini Would Be Proud

In each year since the passage of the Gramm-Rudman-Hollings deficit-reduction law, the president and Congress have claimed compliance with the statute's steadily declining annual deficit limits. Figure 14.4 shows, however, that the deficit has not been declining in the past few years. In fact, the deficit remained stuck at about $150 billion a year from 1987 to 1989.

How can this happen when the law requires reductions in deficit spending? The answer is that Congress, with the White House's complicity, has frequently resorted to rearranging or changing budgetary figures in order to appear to comply with Gramm-Rudman-Hollings while actually missing the mark. In 1987 Congress readjusted the deficit objectives upward and gave itself more time to balance the budget.

The deficit target for the 1990 budget was $100 billion, with a $10 billion margin of error. The president and Congress were ultimately able to "meet" the target only by engaging in a great deal of fiscal gimmickry. The official estimates of the deficit are made by the president's Office of Management and Budget (OMB). The OMB accommodates Congress with rosy projections of both the expenditures (low) and the revenues (high) that will occur in the next year.

This is only the beginning of the budgetary slight of hand, however. At the urging of President Bush, Congress decided not to count most of the enormous cost of bailing out the savings and loan industry toward the budget deficit. The money still had to be spent, just like any other expenditure, but Congress and the president simply pretended that it was not there for purposes of calculating the deficit. Of the bail-out funds that did count against the deficit, Congress decided to allocate them to the previous year's budget. (Once the Office of Management and Budget has certified that Congress has met the deficit target for a given year, Congress can spend as much as it likes later in that year—not the best system for promoting disciplined spending.)

Perhaps the biggest gimmick of all involves the Social Security trust fund, which has been running a huge surplus. This money is set aside and can only be used to pay for future Social Security recipients. Nevertheless, both the White House and Congress subtract it from the deficit, making the deficit seem smaller than it really is. In 1989 the official deficit was $152 billion. Without counting the $52 billion Social Security surplus, the deficit would have been $204 billion.

In addition, the Postal Service was running almost $2 billion in the red, so Congress simply removed it from the budget. The Pentagon moved up the payday for members of the military by one day so that this 1990 expenditure actually counted toward the 1989 budget. The same technique was followed for some agricultural programs' payments.

Thus Congress and the president have found ways to "meet" deficit targets and engage in huge deficit spending at the same time. This budgetary sleight of hand got so bad that Senator Ernest Hollings, one of the original sponsors of Gramm-Rudman-Hollings, declared, "I want a divorce."

THE BUDGET: WHERE IT COMES FROM AND WHERE IT GOES

Two questions are central to politics: Who bears the burdens of paying for government? Who receives the benefits? Most of the political struggles you read about in the newspapers are focused on determining policies about revenues and expenditures. This section will look at the substance of the budget to see how the American government raises money and where that money is spent.

Where It Comes From

"Taxes," said the late Supreme Court Justice Oliver Wendell Holmes, Jr., "are what we pay for civilization." Despite his assertion that "I like to pay taxes," most taxpayers throughout history would not have agreed. The art of taxation, said Jean-Baptiste Colbert, Louis XIV's finance minister, is in "so plucking the goose as to procure the largest quantity of feathers with the least possible amount of squealing."[13] You can see in Figure 14.5 where the federal government has been getting its feathers. Only a small share comes from excise taxes (for example, those on gasoline) and other sources; the three major sources of federal revenues are the personal and corporate income tax, social insurance taxes, and borrowing and deficit spending.

Income Tax: The Government's Golden Egg? Bleary-eyed, millions of American taxpayers struggle to the post office before midnight every April 15 to mail their income tax forms. **Income taxes** take a share of money earned. Although the government briefly adopted an income tax during the Civil War, the first peacetime income tax was enacted in 1894. Though the tax was only 2 percent of income earned beyond the then-magnificent sum of $4,000, a lawyer opposing it called the tax the first step of a "communist march." The Supreme Court wasted little time in declaring the tax unconstitutional in *Pollock* v. *Farmer's Loan and Trust Co*. (1895).

In 1915, the **Sixteenth Amendment** was added to the Constitution, explicitly permitting Congress to levy an income tax. Congress had already started one before the amendment was ratified, and the **Internal Revenue Service** was established to collect it. Today the IRS receives about 135 million tax returns each year, subjecting each one to some scrutiny by people or computers. It audits in greater detail more than 2 million tax returns, investigates thousands of suspected criminal violations of the tax laws, and annually prosecutes and secures the conviction of thousands of errant taxpayers or nonpayers.[14]

Corporations, like individuals, pay income taxes. Although corporate taxes once yielded more revenues than individual income taxes, that is no longer the case. Today corporate taxes yield about eleven cents of every federal revenue dollar, compared with forty-three cents coming from individual income taxes.

Social Insurance Taxes Social Security taxes come from both employers and employees. Money is deducted from employee's paychecks and matched by their employers. Unlike other taxes, these payments do not go into the government's general money fund but are earmarked for a specific purpose: the Social Security Fund, to pay benefits to the old, the disabled, and the widowed.

Social Security taxes have grown faster than any other source of federal revenue, and they will surely grow even more. In 1957 there were a mere 12 percent of federal revenues; today they are about one-third. In 1990 the gov-

"You know, the idea of taxation with representation doesn't appeal to me very much either."

Drawing by Handelsman; © 1970 The New Yorker Magazine, Inc.

---

[13]Quoted in Gerald Carson, *The Golden Egg: The Personal Income Tax, Where It Came From, How It Grew* (Boston: Houghton Mifflin, 1977), 12.

[14]Statistics on the number of returns and audits come from the U.S. Department of Commerce, *Statistical Abstract of the United States, 1988* (Washington, D.C.: Government Printing Office, 1988), 302.

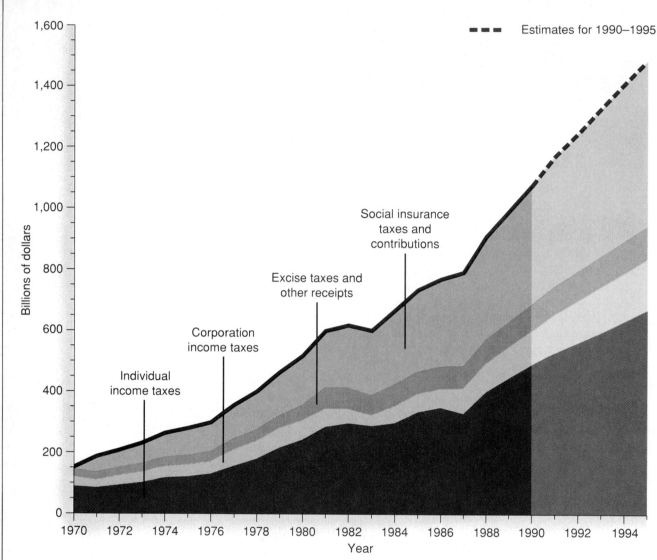

Figure 14.5 Federal Revenues, 1970–1995

- - - Estimates for 1990–1995

1,600

1,400

1,200

1,000

Billions of dollars

800

Social insurance
taxes and
contributions

Excise taxes and
other receipts

600

Corporation
income taxes

400

Individual
income taxes

200

0

1970 1972 1974 1976 1978 1980 1982 1984 1986 1988 1990 1992 1994

Year

Source: The United States Budget in Brief, Fiscal Year 1991 (Washington, D.C.: Government Printing Office, 1990), A-28.

ernment in Washington estimated that it would collect $385 billion in Social Security taxes out of nearly $1.1 trillion it collected in taxes altogether. To keep the Social Security system solvent, Congress scheduled a series of increases in Social Security taxes throughout the 1980s.

Borrowing   Like families and firms, the federal government may borrow money to make ends meet. When families and firms need money, they go to their neighborhood bank, savings and loan association, or moneylender. When the federal government wants to borrow money, the Treasury Department sells bonds, guaranteeing to pay interest to the bondholder. Citizens, corporations, mutual funds, and other financial institutions can all purchase these bonds; there is always a lively market in government bonds.

Today the **federal debt**—all of the money borrowed over the years and still outstanding—exceeds $3.1 trillion (see Figure 14.6). When President Reagan took office in 1981, the debt was about 34 percent of the GNP; when he left the White House in early 1989, it had risen to 56 percent of the GNP. Although the president and Congress worked to pare billions from the budget, much of what they saved had to be allocated to paying the interest on the government's borrowed money—about $176 billion in 1990 alone—instead of being allocated for current policies. Yesterday's consumption of public policies is at the expense of tomorrow's taxpayers, because borrowing money shifts the burden of repayment to future taxpayers who will have to service the debt.

Government borrowing also crowds out private borrowers, both individuals and businesses, from the loan marketplace. (For instance, your local bank may know that you are a fine credit risk, but it thinks the federal government is an even better one.) In 1988 about half of all the net private savings in the country went to the federal government. The American government is also dependent on foreign investors, including other governments, to fund its debt—not a favorable position for a superpower. Most economists believe that this competition to borrow money increases interest rates and make it more difficult for businesses to invest in capital expenditures (such as new plants and equipment) that produce economic growth.

Aside from its impact on private borrowing, the federal debt raises additional concerns. Given current interest rates, every dollar that the government borrows today will cost taxpayers twenty-four dollars in interest over the next thirty years. Government is borrowing not so much for its capital needs (as individuals and firms do when they buy a house or build a factory) as for its day-to-day expenses. Most families wisely do not borrow money for their food and clothing, yet the government is largely borrowing money for its farm subsidies, its military pensions, and its aid to states and cities.

Not everyone is concerned about the federal debt, however. Robert Eisner, an economist at Northwestern University, argues that several considerations should temper the view that the national government is getting too far into debt. First, as a share of American GNP, the federal debt is much smaller than it was after World War II, when it was 120 percent of the GNP. Second, taking inflation into account often turns deficit years into surplus years. Third, if the government counted its debt as families and business firms do—that is, by balancing assets against liabilities—the government would be in pretty good shape.[15]

Despite Eisner's optimistic view, most observers are concerned about the national debt. The perceived perils of gigantic deficits have led to calls for a **balanced budget amendment.** Now passed in somewhat varied forms by the legislatures of nearly two-thirds of the states, the proposed amendment to the Constitution would require Congress to balance peacetime federal budgets. Only

---

[15]Robert Eisner, *How Real Is the Federal Deficit?* (New York: Free Press, 1986).

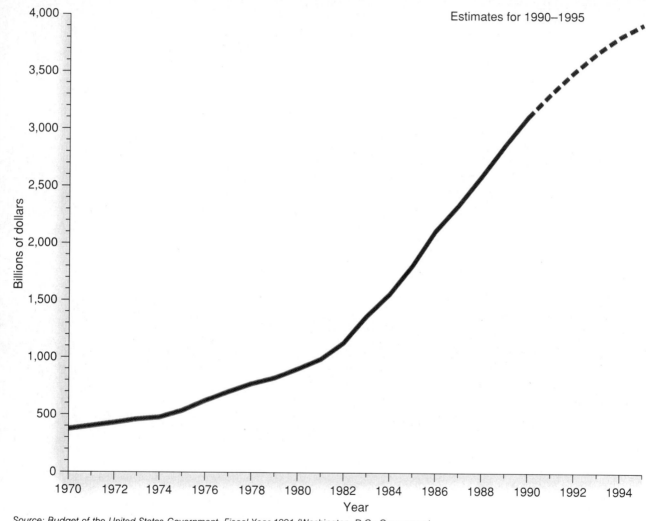

Figure 14.6 Total Federal Debt, 1990–1995

The national debt mushroomed in the 1980s. A principal reason was the loss of revenue resulting from the huge tax cut proposed by President Reagan in 1981. The large increase in defense expenditures in the early years of the Reagan administration was another contributing factor.

Estimates for 1990–1995

Source: Budget of the United States Government, Fiscal Year 1991 (Washington, D.C.: Government Printing Office, 1990) A-304.

a three-fifths vote in both houses of Congress could authorize a specific expenditure beyond the government's expected revenues.[16]

[16]On the balanced budget amendment, see Aaron Wildavsky, *How to Limit Government Spending* (Berkeley, Calif.: University of California Press, 1980), and William R. Keech, "A Theoretical Analysis of the Case for a Balanced Budget Amendment" (Paper presented at the annual meeting of the American Political Science Association, Washington, D.C., August 30–September 2, 1984).

However large government's borrowing, most of its income still comes from taxes. Few government policies provoke more heated discussion than taxation.

Taxes and Public Policy

Probably no government policy affects as many Americans as tax policy. In addition to raising revenues to finance its services, the government can use taxes to make citizens' incomes more or less equal, to encourage or discourage growth in the economy, and to promote specific interests. Whereas in Chapters 17 and 18 you will see how taxes affect economic and equality issues, the following sections will focus on how tax policies can promote the interests of particular groups or encourage specific activities.

Tax Loopholes   No discussion of taxes goes very far before the subject of tax loopholes comes up. Hard to define, a tax loophole presumably is some tax break or tax benefit. The IRS Code, which specifies what income is subject to taxation, is riddled with exemptions, deductions, and special cases. Jimmy Carter, campaigning for the presidency, called the American tax system a "national disgrace" because of its special treatment for favored taxpayers. Some taxpayers, he stressed, get advantages from the tax code that not everyone else can use. Businesspeople, he complained, can deduct as business expenses costly "three-martini lunches" while ordinary workers, carrying a sandwich and coffee in a thermos to work, cannot write off their lunch expenses.

Tax writing is done by the House Ways and Means Committee and the Senate Finance Committee. Their periodic revisions of the tax code (sometimes

"Sir, we've come to the conclusion that it's absolutely impossible to assemble a tax plan that doesn't benefit the rich."

called tax reforms) almost invariably add another layer of exemptions and special considerations. Cutting through the jargon may reveal that only a handful of individuals can benefit from a particular exemption. In November 1975 Texas computer magnate H. Ross Perot benefited from an obscure change in the tax code to the tune of some fifteen million dollars. Perot's legal advisor was a former Internal Revenue Service commissioner, and Perot was reported to be a generous contributor to the campaign chests of several members of congressional tax-writing committees.[17] A clause in the 1978 tax reform amendment was designed to benefit the heirs of Ernest and Julio Gallo, the California winemakers. Permitting them to pay inheritance taxes over a period of years instead of all at once, the bill saved the Gallo heirs a tidy sum. Despite President Carter's urging to eliminate tax loopholes, the 1978 Congress added dozens of exemptions to the already exemption-ridden tax code.

However outraged people may be by such stories, the fact is that very little federal money is lost through these and other "raids on the federal treasury." They may offend Americans' sense of fair play, but they cost the federal government very little. Loopholes are really only a type of tax expenditure that benefits few Americans.

Tax Expenditures What *does* cost the federal budget a substantial sum is the system of **tax expenditures,** defined by the 1974 Budget Act as "revenue losses attributable to provisions of the federal tax laws which allow a special exemption, exclusion, or deduction." They represent the difference between what the government actually collects in taxes and what it would have collected without special exemptions. Tax expenditures thus amount to subsidies for some activity. The following examples will help clarify this idea:

- If it wanted to, the government could send checks for billions of dollars to charities. Instead, it permits some taxpayers to deduct their contributions to charities from their income, thus encouraging charitable contributions.

- If it wanted to, the government could give cash to families wise enough or rich enough to buy a home. Instead, it permits homeowners to deduct from their income the billions of dollars they collectively pay each year in mortgage interest.

- If it wanted to, the government could write a check to all those businesses that invest in new plants and equipment. It does not, but it does allow such businesses to deduct those expenses from their taxes at a more rapid rate than they deduct other expenses. The owners of these businesses, including stockholders, in effect get a subsidy unavailable to owners of other businesses.

Tax expenditures are among the most obscure aspects of the generally obscure budgetary process, partly because they receive no regular review by Congress—a great advantage for those who benefit from a tax expenditure. Few ordinary citizens seem to realize their scope; you can see their magnitude in Table 14.3.

On the whole, tax expenditures benefit middle- and upper-income taxpayers and corporations. Poorer people, who tend not to own homes, can take little

[17]Carson, *The Golden Egg*, 181–82.

Table 14.3

Tax Subsidies: The Money Government Does Not Collect

Tax expenditures are essentially monies that government could collect but does not because they are exempted from taxation. The Office of Management and Budget estimated that the total tax expenditures in 1991 would equal $419 billion—about a third of the total federal appropriations. Individuals were expected to receive $357 billion in tax expenditures, and corporations $62 billion. Here are some of the largest tax expenditures and their cost to the treasury:

TAX EXPENDITURE	MAIN BENEFICIARY	COST
Company contributions to pension funds	Families	$47 billion
Deductions for charitable contributions	Families and Corporations	$16 billion
Mortgage interest on owner-occupied houses	Families	$47 billion
Accelerated depreciation	Corporations	$26 billion
Deductions for state and local taxes	Families	$34 billion
Company-paid benefits	Families	$33 billion
Social Security benefits	Families	$16 billion
Deductions for interest earned on state and local government bonds	Families	$11 billion

In other words, government could easily close its budget deficit by taxing things it does not now tax, such as Social Security benefits, pension fund contributions, charitable contributions, and the like. You can easily figure out, though, that these are not popular items to tax, and doing so would evoke strong opposition from powerful interest groups.

Source: Budget of the United States Government, Fiscal Year 1991 (Washington, D.C.: Government Printing Office, 1990), A-71–A-73, A-76.

advantage of provisions that permit homeowners to deduct mortgage interest payments. Likewise, poorer people in general can take less advantage of a deduction for charitable expenses.

To some, tax expenditures like business-related deductions, tuition tax credits, and capital gains tax rates are loopholes. To others, they are public policy choices supporting a social activity worth subsidizing. Either way, they amount to the same thing: revenues that the government loses because certain items are exempted from normal taxation or are taxed at lower rates.

The Never-ending Quest for Tax Reduction   The annual rite of spring— the preparation of individual tax returns—is invariably accompanied by calls for tax reform and, frequently, tax reduction. During the Carter administration, Senator William Roth (R-Del.) and Representative Jack Kemp (R-N.Y.) had written the Kemp-Roth bill, a plan to cut federal income taxes in stages. The 1980 Republican platform enthusiastically endorsed Kemp-Roth and promised tax cuts if Republicans were returned to power in Washington. They were, and Reagan and his administration set about cutting federal taxes. (See "America in Perspective: How Much Is Too Much?")

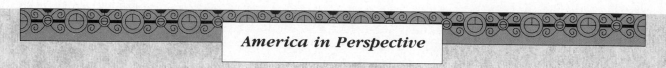

America in Perspective

How Much Is Too Much?

Hardly anyone likes to pay taxes, and it is common for Americans—and citizens all over the world—to complain that taxes are too high. The figures in the accompanying graph show that the national, state, and local governments in the United States tax a smaller percentage of the resources of the country than do those in almost all other democracies with developed economies. The Scandinavian countries of Sweden, Norway, and Denmark take half of the wealth of the country in taxes each year.

Compared with these, citizens in the United States have a rather light tax burden. Naturally, tax levels are related to the level of public services that governments provide. If you compare this graph with "America in Perspective: How Big Is Too Big" (page 506), you see that the big taxers are also the big spenders.

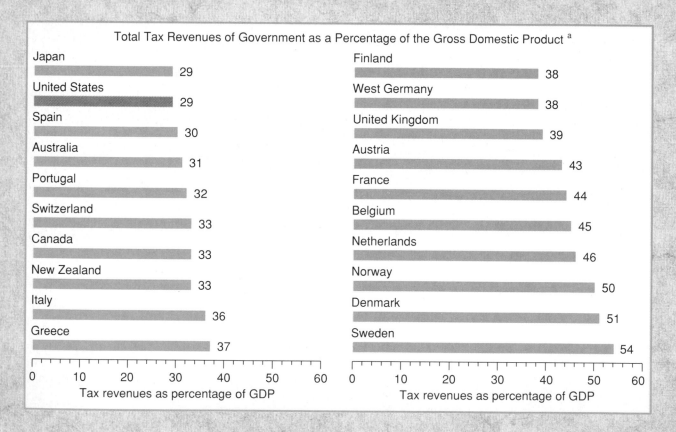

Total Tax Revenues of Government as a Percentage of the Gross Domestic Product [a]

Country	Tax revenues as percentage of GDP
Japan	29
United States	29
Spain	30
Australia	31
Portugal	32
Switzerland	33
Canada	33
New Zealand	33
Italy	36
Greece	37
Finland	38
West Germany	38
United Kingdom	39
Austria	43
France	44
Belgium	45
Netherlands	46
Norway	50
Denmark	51
Sweden	54

[a] Gross Domestic Product is Gross National Product minus the value of goods and services produced outside the country.
Source: U.S. Department of Commerce, *Statistical Abstract of the United States, 1988* (Washington, D.C.: Government Printing Office, 1989), 827.

Early in his administration, President Reagan proposed a massive tax-cut bill, essentially a slightly modified version of the original Kemp-Roth proposal. Standing in the way of tax cuts is never easy, and in July 1981 Congress passed Reagan's tax-cutting proposal. Over a three-year period, Americans would have their federal tax bills reduced 25 percent—for a total reduction of $754.4 billion. Here are some of the provisions of that tax legislation:

- Over a period of thirty-three months beginning in October 1981, individuals received tax reductions amounting to 25 percent.
- Corporate taxes were reduced.
- New tax incentives were provided for personal savings and corporate investment.
- Taxes were *indexed* to the cost of living. Beginning in 1985, government would no longer get a larger share of income when inflation pushed incomes into higher brackets while the tax rates stayed the same. (This is important because people who have high incomes also pay a higher *percentage* of their incomes in taxes.)

President Reagan and his aides celebrated the 1981 tax reductions with champagne toasts. Average American workers, generally blessed with an additional three to seven dollars in their weekly paychecks, may have done the same. Actually, what Reagan expected them to do was save and invest; he hoped people would put their savings into investments that might create jobs, rather than frittering it away on consumables.

The tax cuts did not fall evenly on all Americans. In April 1984 the Congressional Budget Office released a report on the impact of the new tax cuts. About 80 percent of tax reductions went to families earning between $20,000 and $80,000 annually, that is, families making more than the median family income; only 7 percent of tax cuts went to families earning less than $20,000. Because many social service programs were curtailed, benefits to poorer families were often lost. Thus when the net losses in benefits were figured in, families below the median income fared even more poorly. A family earning $10,000 to $20,000 came out only $30 ahead, and one earning less than $10,000 gained $20 in tax cuts but lost $410 in benefits.[18]

The Never-ending Quest for Tax Reform   Gripes about taxes are at least as old in America as the Boston Tea Party. Loopholes given to one special interest in return for its political support are hard to deny to other groups. During his 1984 campaign, President Reagan solemnly promised that he would not raise anyone's taxes. Nonetheless, the desire for tax reform had been brewing in Congress for years. Democratic members like Senator Bill Bradley of New Jersey and Representative Richard Gephardt of Missouri, as well as Republicans like Senator Bob Kasten of Wisconsin, had tossed tax reform bills into the congressional hopper.

When President Reagan first revealed his massive tax simplification plan in 1985, with its proposals to eliminate many tax deductions and tax expenditures, it was met with howls of protest. The insurance industry, for example, launched a six million dollar advertising campaign to save the tax deductions for fringe

[18]Congressional Budget Office, reported in *Time*, April 16, 1984, 23.

Representative Jack Kemp, a New York Republican, is an influential advocate of conservative budgetary reforms. His plan to reduce taxes, written with Senator William Roth, helped pave the way for congressional approval of President Reagan's 1981 tax-reduction proposal.

The People Speak

Taxes and Equity

Which do you think is the worst tax—that is, the least fair?

Federal income tax	27%
State income tax	10%
State sales tax	18%
Local property tax	32%

Source: The question as worded is taken directly from a Gallup Poll for the Advisory Commission on Intergovernmental Relations, June 1989.

President Reagan signs the Tax Reform Act of 1986, passed with the backing of congressional leaders and administration officials. The legislation—the most wide-ranging reform of federal tax policy since the Sixteenth Amendment legalized income taxes in 1915—was implemented despite the protests of numerous interest groups that did not want to lose their tax deductions.

benefits (much of which are in the form of life and health insurance) that employers set aside for employees. A pitched battle was waging between tax reformers and interest groups determined to hold onto their tax benefits.

For once, however, a tax reform plan was not derailed. For one thing, Democrats, including the powerful chairman of the House Ways and Means Committee, Dan Rostenkowski, were enthusiastic about tax reform. They also did not want the Republicans to get all the credit for reform. The president actually had more problems obtaining the support of those in his own party and had to make an unusual trip to Capitol Hill to plead with House Republicans to support the tax bill after its initial defeat when it came to the floor.

The Senate posed an even bigger problem, as the bill was loaded with special tax treatments for a wide variety of groups. While the president was on a trip abroad, the Finance Committee met behind closed doors throughout a weekend and emerged with a bill similar in spirit to that supported by the president and the House. The Tax Reform Act of 1986 was one of the most sweeping alterations in federal tax policy in history. It eliminated or reduced the value of many tax deductions and changed the system of fifteen separate tax brackets to just two generally lower rates (28 percent and 15 percent).

Where It Goes: Federal Expenditures

In 1932, when President Franklin D. Roosevelt took office in the midst of the Great Depression, the federal government was spending just over three billion dollars a year. Today that sum would get the federal government through less than a day. Program costs once measured in the millions are now measured in the billions. Comparisons over time are, of course, a little misleading, because they do not take into account changes in the value of the dollar. You can see in Figure 14.7 how the federal budget has grown in actual dollars.

Figure 14.7 Federal Expenditures, 1971–1995

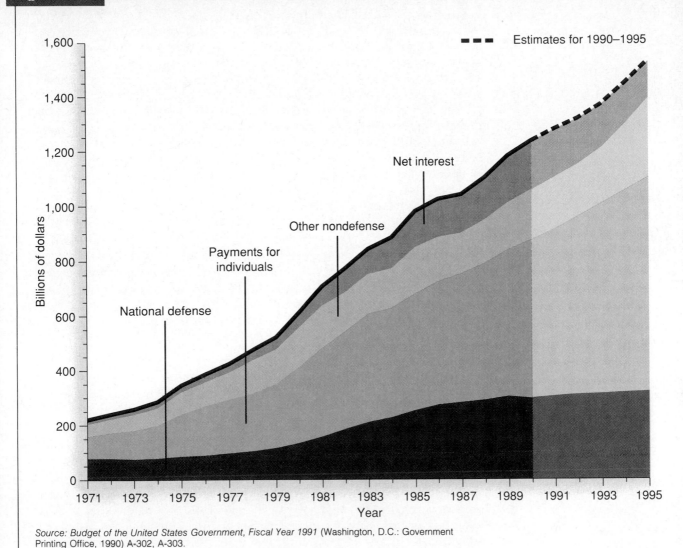

- - - Estimates for 1990–1995

Net interest

Other nondefense

Payments for individuals

National defense

Billions of dollars

Year

Source: Budget of the United States Government, Fiscal Year 1991 (Washington, D.C.: Government Printing Office, 1990) A-302, A-303.

Figure 14.7 makes two interesting points. First, what the government spends money on changes over time. Second, expenditures keep rising. Thus the following sections explore two important questions: Where does the money go? Why is it difficult to control federal expenditures?

The Big Change: Declining Defense Budgets and Growing Social Budgets   In the 1950s and early 1960s, spending for past, present, and future wars amounted to more than half the federal budget. The Department of Defense got the majority of federal dollars. Liberals complained that government was shortchanging the poor while lining the pockets of defense contractors. Things soon changed, however. Over a decade and a half, from the mid-1960s to the early 1980s, defense expenditures crept downward in real dollars while social welfare expenditures more than doubled.

The biggest slice of the budget pie, once reserved for defense, now belongs to *income security* expenditures, a bundle of policies extending direct and indirect aid to the old, the poor, and the needy. These were the expenditures whose rate of growth in the first year of the Reagan era was pared substantially. The Reagan budget also devoted a larger share to military spending (Chapter 20 will review the defense budget and the issue of defense spending.) Even so, income security expenditures continued, even in the more austere Reagan years, to make up the largest share of the federal budget.

Other social service expenditures paralleled the upward growth of income security. In the past twenty years, health expenditures have grown to support Medicaid, medical education, and research. Education aid and worker-training programs have grown, too. Together they add to the already burgeoning budget for social expenditures. Why is it so difficult to bring this increasing federal budget under control?

Incrementalism   Sometimes political scientists use the term *incrementalism* to describe the spending and appropriations process. **Incrementalism** means simply that the best predictor of this year's budget is last year's budget plus a little bit more (an increment). According to Aaron Wildavsky, "The largest determining factor of the size and content of this year's budget is last year's. Most of each budget is a product of previous decisions."[19] According to Wildavsky, incremental budgeting has several features:

- Very little attention is focused on the budgetary *base,* the amounts agencies have had over the previous couple of years. Most of the time, agencies can safely assume they will get at least what they had last year.
- Most of the debate and attention are focused on the proposed increment.
- The budget for any given agency tends to grow by a little bit every year.

This picture of the federal budget is one of constant, slow growth. Wildavsky and his colleagues devised a simple mathematical model of the incremental process; it predicted federal budgets with remarkable accuracy.[20] Other students of the budget suggest that the incremental theory leaves something to be desired. John Gist, for example, showed that although expenditures mandated by an existing law or obligation (such as Social Security) followed a neat pattern of increase, other parts of the budget did not.[21] Paul Schulman showed that budgets for the National Aeronautics and Space Administration (NASA) were hardly incremental; they first rose as fast as a NASA rocket but later plummeted to a fraction of their former size.[22] Incrementalism may be a *general* tendency of the budget, but it does not fully describe all budgetary politics.

---

[19] Wildavsky, *The New Politics of the Budgetary Process,* 78.

[20] Otto Davis, M. A. H. Dempster, and Aaron Wildavsky, "A Theory of the Budgetary Process," *American Political Science Review* 60 (September 1966): 529–47.

[21] John R. Gist, *Mandatory Expenditures and the Defense Sector* (Beverly Hills, Calif.: Sage, 1974).

[22] Paul R. Schulman, "Nonincremental Policymaking: Notes Toward an Alternative Paradigm," *American Political Science Review* 69 (December 1975): 1354–70.

Precisely because so much of the budgetary process looks incremental—as well as poorly thought out, ill-informed, and irrational—there is a never-ending call for budgetary reform. The idea is always to make it easier to compare programs so that the "most deserving" ones can be supported and the "wasteful" ones cut. Lyndon Johnson tried to impose *Program Planning-Budgeting Systems* (PPBS) on the whole government. According to this system, agencies must budget by programs and show explicitly the goals being achieved. The congressional reforms of 1974 were Congress' effort to make budgeting more rational. Jimmy Carter brought to Washington *zero-based budgeting* (ZBB) ideas that he had practiced as the governor of Georgia. ZBB requires agencies making up budget requests to pretend that their base is zero and then justify everything above zero, a very difficult task. When the Department of Agriculture experimented with ZBB, it found a big increase in its budgetary workload, with little change in the results.[23]

Incrementalism makes it hard to pare the budget. The budget is too big to review from scratch each year, even for the most systematic and conscientious members of Congress. There is another reason federal spending is hard to control: more and more of it has become uncontrollable. "The growth in federal spending," insists Lance LeLoup, "is almost completely attributable to growth in uncontrollable items."[24]

The Allowance Theory and Uncontrollable Expenditures   At first glance, it is hard to see how one could call the federal budget uncontrollable. After all, Congress has the constitutional authority to budget, to add or subtract money from an agency. Indeed, President Reagan proposed and Congress adopted some of his proposals to cut the growth of government spending. How, then, can one speak of an uncontrollable budget?

Consider for a moment what many political scientists call the "allowance theory" of the budget. In this theory, a government budget works rather like an allowance. Mom and Dad hand over to Mary Jean and Tommy a monthly allowance, say $10 each, with the stern admonition, "Make that last till the end of the month because that is all we are giving you until then." In the allowance model of the budget, Congress plays this parental role; the agencies play the roles of Mary Jean and Tommy. Congress thus allocates a lump sum—say, $5.2 billion—and instructs agencies to meet their payrolls and other expenses throughout the fiscal year. When most Americans think of the government's budget, they envision the budget as something of an allowance to the agencies.

About three-fourths of the government's budget, however, does not work this way at all. Vast expenditures are determined not by how much Congress appropriates to an agency but by *how many eligible beneficiaries* there are for some particular program. **Uncontrollable expenditures** result from policies that make some group automatically eligible for some benefit. Thus an expenditure is classified as uncontrollable "if it is mandated under current law or by a previous obligation."[25] Congress writes the eligibility rules; the number of

[23]Wildavsky, *The New Politics of the Budgetary Process,* 416–20.

[24]Lance LeLoup, *Budgetary Politics: Dollars, Deficits, Decisions* (Brunswick, Ohio: King's Court, 1977), 62.

[25]*Ibid.*

people eligible and their level of guaranteed benefits determine how much Congress must spend. The Social Security Administration, for example, does not merely provide benefits on a first come, first served basis until the money runs out. Many expenditures are uncontrollable because Congress has in effect obligated itself to pay X level of benefits to Y number of recipients. Such policies are called **entitlements.** Each year, Congress' bill is a straightforward function of the X level of benefits times the Y beneficiaries.

The biggest uncontrollable expenditure of all is, of course, the Social Security system, costing more than $265 billion in fiscal year 1991, up from $33.8 billion as recently as 1970. Men who are over sixty-five and women who are over sixty-two get automatic Social Security payments. Of course, Congress can, if it desires, cut the benefits or tighten eligibility restrictions. Doing so, however, would provoke a monumental outcry from millions of older voters. Other items—veterans aid, agricultural subsidies, military pensions, Medicare, civil service workers' retirement benefits, interest on the national debt— are uncontrollable expenditures, also. Government cannot decide this year, for example, that it will not pay the interest on the federal debt, or will chop in half the pensions earned by former military personnel.

Altogether, the federal budget document itself estimates that *fully three-fourths of the federal budget is uncontrollable*—meaning that Congress *can* control such expenditures, but only by changing a law or existing benefit levels. To control the uncontrollables, Congress can either cut benefits or cut down on beneficiaries. You can see why neither would be a popular strategy for an elected Congress (see "You Are the Policymaker: Balancing the Budget").

UNDERSTANDING BUDGETING

Citizens and politicians alike fret about whether government is too big. President Bush was elected by claiming that government has too many hands in Americans' pockets. He promised not to raise taxes to pay for more government spending. Of course, not everyone agrees that the national government is too large (even Bush had backtracked on his "no new taxes" pledge by 1990). There is agreement on the centrality of budgeting to modern government and politics, however. Exploring the themes of democracy and the size of government will help you to better understand the federal budgeting process.

Democracy and Budgeting

Almost all democracies have seen a substantial growth in government in the twentieth century. One explanation for this growth is that politicians spend money to "buy" votes. They do not buy votes in the sense that a corrupt political machine pays off voters to vote for its candidates; rather, policymakers spend public money on things voters will like—and will remember on election day. As you saw in Chapter 12, members of Congress have incentives to make government grow; they use both constituency services and pork barrel policies to deliver benefits to the folks back home and government grows as a result.

Economists Allen Meltzer and Scott Richard have argued that government grows in a democracy because of the equality of suffrage. In the private sector, they maintain, people's incomes are unequal, whereas in the political arena

Balancing the Budget

You have seen that the national government is running budget deficits of unprecedented size and that the national debt has ballooned. Moreover, public-opinion polls have found that Americans believe the deficit to be a serious problem.

You have also seen that three-fourths of the federal budget is "uncontrollable," mostly composed of expenditures that have widespread public support, such as payments to individuals under Social Security.

Thus, here is the situation you face as a budget decision maker: According to the OMB, in fiscal year 1991 the national government will have revenues (including Social Security taxes) of about $1.16 trillion. Its mandatory expenditures for domestic policy (entitlements and other prior obligations) total about $590 billion. Maintaining current national defense programs, which have experienced no real increase in spending in the preceding six years, will cost an additional $307 billion. Nondiscretionary payments on the national debt will cost another $174 billion. That leaves

you with just $45 billion to spend and still balance the budget. Continuing discretionary domestic policy programs will take $170 billion, however. If you spend this amount you will run a deficit of more than $135 billion—and you have not even had a chance to fund any new programs, nor have you taken into consideration the increased expenditures necessary to fund the bailout of insolvent savings and loan institutions.

What would *you* do? Would you drastically reduce defense expenditures? Or would you leave them alone and close down the entire rest of the government, including programs for space and science, transportation and public works, economic subsidies and development, education and social services, health research and services, and law enforcement and other core functions of government—programs that also have broad public support. Perhaps you would show great political courage and seek a tax increase to pay for these programs. What *would* you do?

power is much more equally distributed. Each voter has one vote. Parties must appeal to a majority of the voters. Hence, claim Meltzer and Richard, poorer voters will always use their votes to support public policies that redistribute benefits from the rich to the poor. Even if such voters cannot win in the marketplace, they can use the electoral process to their advantage. As Meltzer and Richard summarize, "Government continues to grow because there is a decisive difference between the political process and the market process. The market process produces a distribution of income that is less equal than the distribution of votes. Consequently, those with the lowest income use the political process to increase their income."[26] Many politicians willingly cooperate with the desire of the working class voters to expand their benefits, because voters return the favor at election time. As one would expect from this reasoning, the most rapidly growing expenditures are items like Social Security, Medicaid, Medicare, and social welfare programs, which benefit the poor more than the rich.

Often one thinks of elites, particularly corporate elites, as being opposed to big government. Recently, however, Lockheed and Chrysler Corporation have appealed to the government for large bailouts when times got rough. Corpo-

[26]Allen Meltzer and Scott F. Richard, "Why the Government Grows (and Grows) in a Democracy," *The Public Interest* 52 (Summer 1978): 117.

rations support a big government that offers them contracts, subsidies, and other benefits. A $100 billion procurement budget at the Department of Defense benefits defense contractors, their workers, and their shareholders.

Poor and rich voters alike have voted for parties and politicians who promised them benefits. When the air is foul, Americans expect government to help clean it up. When Americans get old, they expect a Social Security check. In a democracy, what people want has some link to what government does. Citizens are not unwilling victims of big government and its big taxes; they are at least coconspirators.

Government also grows by responding to groups and their demands. The parade of PACs is one example of groups asking government for assistance. From agricultural lobbies supporting loans to zoologists pressing for aid from the National Science Foundation, groups seek to expand their favorite part of the budget. They are aided by committees, and government agencies that work to fund projects favored by supportive groups (see the discussion on iron triangles in Chapter 15).

You have also seen, however, that some politicians compete for votes by promising *not* to spend money. After all, Ronald Reagan did not win election to the presidency twice by promising to raise taxes and provide more services. No country has a more open political system than the United States, but as this chapter's "America in Perspective" features demonstrate, Americans have chosen to tax less and spend less on public services than almost all other democracies. The size of government budgets varies widely among democratic nations. Thus democracy may encourage government spending, but it does not compel it.

One of the most common criticisms of government is the failure to balance the budget. Public officials are often criticized for lacking the will to deal wtih the problem, yet it is not lack of resolve that prevents a solution to enormous budget deficits. Instead, it is a lack of consensus on policy. Americans want to spend but not pay taxes and, being a democracy, that is exactly what the government does. The inevitable result is red ink.

The Budget and the Size of Government

This text's theme of the size of government has pervaded this chapter. The reason is obvious—in many ways the budget *is* the size of government. The bigger the budget, the bigger the government.

The budgetary process can limit government. One could accurately characterize policy-making in the American government since 1980 as the "politics of scarcity"—scarcity of funds, that is. Thus the budget can be a force for reining in the government as well as for expanding its role.

In 1989 George Bush called drugs the "gravest domestic threat facing our nation," but he proposed to increase spending on the war against illegal drugs by less than .001 percent of the federal budget. There was no money to fund new programs. The president was reduced to speaking loudly and carrying a small budgetary stick in other policy areas as well. Although Bush has said that he wants to be known as the "education president," he has had no available funds to make notable strides in that area. On the twentieth anniversary of the American astronauts' first moon landing, Bush announced a new goal of sending people to Mars. The president, however, did not address the question of how he would pay for such a huge project. He went to Poland to cheer the liberalizing political and economic changes occurring in Eastern Europe, but he was not able to offer substantial American aid to underwrite the transition to democracy. America's large budget deficit is as much a constraint on government as it is evidence of a burgeoning public sector.

SUMMARY

When the federal government's budget consumes nearly one-fourth of America's gross national product, it demands close attention. In all Western democracies, government budgets have grown during the twentieth century. In the United States, the rise of the social service state and the national security state have been closely linked with this growth.

Budget making is complex, with many actors playing many roles. The president sets the budgetary agenda, while Congress and its committees approve the budget itself.

The government's biggest revenue source, of course, remains the income tax, but the Social Security tax is becoming increasingly important. Lately, more and more of the government's budget has been financed through borrowing. Annual deficits of around $150 billion have boosted the federal debt to over $3 trillion.

On the spending side, the big change is from a government dominated by defense spending during the 1950s to one dominated by social services spending

Senators Warren Rudman (from left), Phil Gramm, and Ernest Hollings meet just before passage of their Balanced Budget and Emergency Deficit Control Act of 1985. Critics saw the measure as a "meat-axe" approach to budgeting, but the three senators argued that nothing else would force the president and Congress to balance the budget.

Drawing by Dana Fradon; © 1989 The New Yorker Magazine, Inc.

"I like the concept if we can do it with no new taxes."

in the 1990s. President Reagan, for one, wanted to reverse this balance by increasing military expenditures and cutting domestic ones. Nonetheless, much of the American budget consists of "uncontrollable" expenditures, which are extremely difficult to pare. Many of these are associated with Social Security payments and with grants-in-aid.

There is a view that democracy turns politics into a bidding war for votes, increasing the size of the budget in the process. In the United States, however, many candidates campaign on not spending money or increasing taxes. Although larger budgets mean larger government, the budget, at least in times of substantial deficits such as those the United States has experienced in the past decade, can also serve as a constraint on further government growth.

KEY TERMS

deficit
expenditures
revenues
Social Security Act
Medicare
budget
House Ways and Means
   Committee
Senate Finance Committee
Congressional Budget and
   Impoundment Control
   Act of 1974

Congressional Budget Office
   (CBO)
budget resolution
reconciliation
authorization bill
appropriations bill
continuing resolutions
Gramm-Rudman-Hollings
income taxes
Sixteenth Amendment
Internal Revenue Service
federal debt
balanced budget amendment

tax expenditures
incrementalism
uncontrollable expenditures
entitlements

FOR FURTHER READING

Berry, William D., and David Lowery. *Understanding United States Government Growth.* New York: Praeger, 1987. An empirical analysis of the causes of the growth of government in the period since World War II.

Light, Paul. *Artful Work: The Politics of Social Security Reform.* New York: Random House, 1985. A case study of the perennial crisis of Social Security and what has been done about it.

Pechman, Joseph A. *Federal Tax Policy,* 5th ed. Washington, D.C.: The Brookings Institution, 1987. The standard work on the substance of federal tax policy.

Piven, Francis Fox, and Richard Cloward. *Regulating the Poor.* New York: Pantheon, 1971. Argues that government budgets increase in response to the troubles the poor cause, not the troubles the poor have.

Schick, Allen. *Congress and Money.* Washington, D.C.: The Urban Institute, 1980. A readable review of Congress' role in the budgetary process.

Schuman, Howard E. *Polictics and the Budget.* Englewood Cliffs, N.J.: Prentice-Hall, 1988. An excellent primer on the entire budgetary process.

Wildavsky, Aaron. *The New Politics of the Budgetary Process.* Boston: Little, Brown, 1988. The standard work on the budgetary process.

————. *How to Limit Government Spending.* Berkeley, Calif.: University of California Press, 1980. A forceful but balanced plea for a constitutional amendment to control government spending.

15

*T*HE BUREAUCRACIES

Americans are taken hostage in the Middle East. The president orders the army to send its special Delta Force to rescue them. A new spy satellite is needed to monitor rapidly changing events in Eastern Europe. The president orders the National Aeronautical and Space Administration (NASA) to place one in orbit. Forest fires ravage Yellowstone National park. The president orders the Forest Service to put them out. An epidemic breaks out among those exposed to certain chemicals used in the Vietnam War. The president orders the Department of Veterans Affairs to treat the victims in its hospitals.

Whom does the president turn to when action is needed? The answer is simple: to bureaucrats. Yes, bureaucrats. Soldiers, scientists, forest rangers, and physicians may have little in common except that they are all bureaucrats, working in government organizations and performing specialized tasks to implement public policy.

Bureaucrats do much more than simply follow orders. They possess crucial information and expertise that make them partners with the president and Congress in decision making about public policy. Who knows more than bureaucrats about Social Security recipients or the military capabilities of the Soviet Union? Moreover, because of their expertise, bureaucrats inevitably have discretion in carrying out policy decisions.

Americans rarely congratulate someone for being a good bureaucrat. Unsung, taunted by cartoonists, maligned by columnists, bureaucrats are the scapegoats of American politics. Americans may call presidents great and reelect members of Congress, but almost no one praises bureaucrats. Those who compose the bureaucracy, however, perform most of the vital services provided by the federal government. Clearly, they bear closer examination.

Gary Miller and Terry Moe rightly observe that "public bureaucracy has never been especially popular, but in recent years its image has gone from bad to worse."[1] Recent presidents have railed against the very agencies they administer. President Reagan suggested as part of his 1985 deficit reduction package that federal workers could pitch in by taking a 5 percent pay cut.

Nothing better illustrates the complexity of modern government than its massive bureaucracies. The *Federal Register* lists all the government regulations issued annually by Washington bureaucracies; each year it exceeds fifty thousand pages. Americans are required to submit more than two billion forms and documents (mostly about taxes) to the government each year. One plant with seventy-five employees kept two people working half-time writing reports required by the federal government.[2]

Bureaucratic power extends to every corner of American economic and social life, yet bureaucracies are scarcely hinted at in the Constitution. Each bureaucratic agency is created by Congress, which sets its budget and writes the policies it administers. Most agencies are responsible to the president, whose

---

[1] Gary J. Miller and Terry M. Moe, "Bureaucrats, Legislators, and the Size of Governments," *American Political Science Review* 77 (June 1983): 297.

[2] These and other tidbits about the federal paperwork burden are described in Herbert Kaufman, *Red Tape* (Washington, D.C.: The Brookings Institution, 1977), 5–6.

constitutional responsibility to "take care that the laws shall be faithfully executed" sheds only a dim light on the problems of managing so large a government. How to manage and control bureaucracies is, in this bureaucratic age, a central problem of democratic government.

THE BUREAUCRATS

Bureaucrats are typically much less visible than the president or members of Congress. As a result, Americans usually know little about them. This section will examine some myths about bureaucrats and learn who they are, how they got their jobs, and what they do.

Some Bureaucratic Myths and Realities

Bureaucrat-baiting is a popular American pastime. George Wallace, former Alabama governor and frequent presidential hopeful, warmed up his crowds with a line about "pointy-headed Washington bureaucrats who can't even park their bicycles straight." Even successful presidential candidates climbed aboard the antibureaucracy bandwagon. Jimmy Carter complained about America's "com-

Bureaucrats are the scapegoats of American politics. Here is one image of the uncontrollable bureaucracy, made up of paperwork and red tape, let loose on Washington.

plicated and confused and overlapping and wasteful" bureaucracies; Gerald Ford complained about the "dead-weight" of bureaucracies; Ronald Reagan insisted that bureaucrats "overregulated" the American economy, causing a decline in productivity.

Any object of such unpopularity will spawn plenty of myths. The following are some of the most prevalent myths:

- *Americans dislike bureaucrats.* Despite the rhetoric about bureaucracies, Americans are generally satisfied with bureaucrats and the treatment they get from them. Daniel Katz and his associates studied the relationship between citizens and bureaucrats. Americans may dislike bureaucracies, but they like bureaucrats. Katz and his colleagues found a "relative high degree of satisfaction" with bureaucratic encounters.[3] Some 57 percent thought that the bureaucrats they dealt with did the "right amount" to help them; an additional 16 percent thought the bureaucrats did "more than they had to."

- *Most federal bureaucrats work in Washington, D.C.* Only about 11 percent of three million federal civilian employees work in Washington. California leads the nation in federal employees, with 325,000. New York and Texas have more than 150,000 each, and 120,000 more work in foreign countries and American territories. A good way to see where federal bureaucrats work is to look in your local phone book under "U.S. Government." You will probably find, among many others, listings for the local offices of the Postal Service, the Social Security Administration, the FBI, the Department of Agriculture's county agents, recruiters for the armed services, air traffic controllers, and, of course, the Internal Revenue Service.

- *Bureaucracies are growing bigger each year.* This myth is half true and half false. The number of *government* employees *has* been expanding, but not the number of *federal* employees. Almost all the growth in the number of public employees has occurred in state and local governments. The fourteen million state and local public employees far outnumber the three million civilian federal government employees (see Figure 15.1). As a percentage of America's total work force, *federal* government employment has been shrinking, not growing; it now amounts to about 3 percent of all civilian jobs. Of course, many state and local employees work on programs that are federally funded, and the federal government hires many private contractors to provide goods and services ranging from hot meals to weapons systems.

- *Bureaucracies are ineffective, inefficient, and always mired in red tape.* This image of bureaucracies dies hard. No words describing bureaucratic behavior are better known than "red tape." Bureaucracy, however, is simply a way of organizing people to perform work. General Motors, a college or university, the U.S. Army, the Department of Health and Human Services, and the Roman Catholic Church are all bureaucracies. Bureaucracies are a little like referees: When they work well, no one gives them much credit, but when they work poorly, everyone calls them unfair or incompetent or inefficient. Bureaucracies may be inefficient at times, but no one has found a substitute for them; and no one has yet demonstrated that government

[3]Daniel Katz et al., *Bureaucratic Encounters: A Pilot Study in the Evaluation of Government Services* (Ann Arbor: Survey Research Center, University of Michigan, 1975), 184. See also Charles T. Goodsell, *The Case for Bureaucracy,* 2nd ed. (Chatham, N.J.: Chatham House, 1985), chap. 2.

Figure 15.1 **Growth in Government Employees**

The number of government employees has grown rapidly since 1950. The real growth, however, has been in the state and local sector, with its millions of teachers, police officers, and other service deliverers. Many state and local employees and programs, though, are supported by federal grants-in-aid. (Note that the figures for federal employment do not include military personnel.)

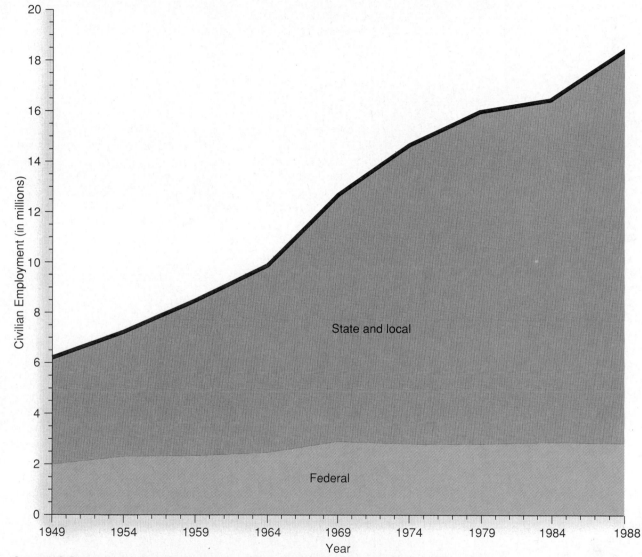

Source: U.S. Bureau of Labor Statistics, Department of Labor, *Monthly Labor Review* (Washington, D.C.: Government Printing Office, January 1980, September 1987, April 1988, and June 1989.)

| Table 15.1 | Federal Civilian Employment |

EXECUTIVE DEPARTMENTS	NUMBER OF EMPLOYEES[a]
Agriculture	109,567
Commerce	40,150
Defense	1,051,019
Education	4,424
Energy	16,535
Health and Human Services	117,495
Housing and Urban Development	13,212
Interior	71,372
Justice	76,402
Labor	18,444
State	25,491
Transportation	63,197
Treasury	154,432
Veterans Affairs	212,231

LARGER INDEPENDENT AGENCIES	
Environmental Protection Agency	14,088
General Services Administration	19,246
National Aeronautics and Space Administration	23,054
Tennessee Valley Authority	23,056
U.S. Information Agency	8,756
U.S. Postal Service	788,429

[a]Figures are for 1989.
Source: Budget of the United States Government, Fiscal Year 1991 (Washington, D.C.: Government Printing Office, 1991), A-77.

bureaucracies are more or less inefficient, ineffective, or mired in red tape than private bureaucracies.[4]

Anyone who looks with disdain on American bureaucracies should contemplate life without them. Despite all the carping about bureaucracies, the vast majority of tasks carried out by governments at all levels are noncontroversial. Bureaucrats deliver mail, test milk, clean streets, issue Social Security and student loan checks, run national parks, and perform other perfectly acceptable governmental tasks. Most of the folks who work for cities, states, and the national government are ordinary people, the sort who are likely to be your neighbors.

A plurality of all federal civilian employees work for just a few agencies (see Table 15.1). The Department of Defense employs about 36 percent of federal *civilian* workers in addition to the 2.2 million men and women in uniform. Altogether, the DOD (Washington's abbreviation for the Department of Defense) is composed of well over 3 million employees, making up about 60 percent of the federal bureaucracy. Clearly, most federal bureaucrats serve in one way or another in the area of national defense.

[4]See Goodsell, *The Case for Bureaucracy,* 48–55.

The Postal Service accounts for an additional 25 percent of federal civilian employees, and the various health professions constitute nearly 10 percent (one in three doctors, for example, works for the government). The Department of Veterans Affairs, clearly related to national defense, has almost .25 million employees. All other functions of government are handled by the remaining 5 percent of federal employees.

Who They Are and How They Got There

Because there are 3 million civilian bureaucrats (17 million if we add state and local public employees), it is hard to imagine a statistically typical bureaucrat. Bureaucrats are male and female, black and white, well paid and not so well paid. Like other institutions, the federal government has been under pressure to expand its hiring of women and minorities. Congress has ordered federal agencies to make special efforts to recruit and promote previously disadvantaged groups, but women and nonwhites still cluster at the lower ranks. (Congress has exempted itself from these rules.) As a whole, the permanent bureaucracy is more broadly representative of the American people than legislators, judges, or presidential appointees in the executive branch[5] (see Figure 15.2).

The diversity of bureaucratic jobs mirrors the diversity of private sector jobs, including occupations literally ranging from *A* to *Z*. Working for government are accountants, bakers, census analysts, defense procurement specialists, electricians, foreign service officers, guards in federal prisons, home econo-

[5]*Ibid.,* chap. 5.

Figure 15.2   **Characteristics of Federal Civilian Employees[a]**

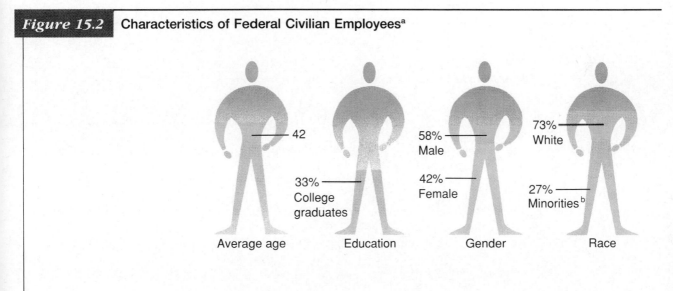

42 — Average age

33% College graduates — Education

58% Male
42% Female — Gender

73% White
27% Minorities[b] — Race

[a]Does not include postal workers.
[b]Includes blacks, Orientals, native Americans, and Hispanics.

Source: Office of Personnel Management, *Federal Civilian Workforce Statistics, Employment and Trends as of November 1988* (Washington, D.C.: U.S. Government Printing Office, 1989), 70.

mists, Indian Affairs agents, judges, kitchen workers, lawyers, missile technologists, narcotics agents, ophthalmologists, postal carriers, quarantine specialists, radiologists, stenographers, truck drivers, underwater demolition experts, virologists, wardens, X-ray technicians, youth counselors, and zoologists (see Table 15.2).

Civil Service: From Patronage to Protection   Until roughly one hundred years ago, a person got a job with the government through the patronage system. **Patronage** is a hiring and promotion system based on knowing the right people. Working in a congressional campaign, making large donations, and having the right connections helped win jobs with the government. Nineteenth-century presidents staffed the government with their friends and allies. Scores of office seekers would swarm over the White House after Inauguration Day. It is said that during a bout with malaria, Lincoln told an aide to "send in the office seekers" because he finally had something to give them all.

It was a disappointed office seeker named Charles Guiteau who helped end this "spoils system" of federal appointments in 1881. Frustrated because President James A. Garfield would not give him a job, Guiteau shot and killed Garfield.

Table 15.2   **Full-Time Civilian White-Collar Employees of the Federal Government (by Selected Occupational Categories)**

EMPLOYMENT CATEGORIES	NUMBER OF EMPLOYEES
General Administrative, Clerical, and Office Services	457,761
Engineering and Architecture	169,769
Medical, Dental, and Public Health	142,292
Accounting and Budget	142,286
Business and Industry	99,311
Legal and Kindred	73,445
Supply	57,666
Social Sciences, Psychology, and Welfare	55,139
Investigation	63,489
Biological Sciences	53,849
Personnel Management and Industrial Relations	51,090
Physical Sciences	42,909
Transportation	42,257
Education	32,825
Information and the Arts	21,503
Quality Assurance	19,704
Equipment, Facilities, and Service	18,148
Mathematics and Statistics	15,139
Library and Archives	9,712
Veterinary Medical Science	2,474
Copyright, Patent and Trademark	2,063

Source: U.S. Office of Personnel Management, *Federal Civilian Workforce Statistics Monthly Release, Employment Trends as of May 1988,* 76–81.

The so-called Prince of Patronage himself, Vice-President Chester A. Arthur, then became president. Arthur, who had been collector of the customs for New York—a patronage-rich post—surprised his critics by pushing for passage of the **Pendelton Act** (1883), which created the federal Civil Service. At first, only about 10 percent of federal employees were covered by Civil Service; today, only 15 percent are *exempt* from it, and most agencies not covered by Civil Service have developed their own merit hiring systems to prevent patronage.

The rationale for all **civil service** systems rests on the idea of merit and the desire to create a nonpartisan government service. The **merit principle**—using entrance exams and promotion ratings—is intended to produce administration by people with talent and skill. Creating a nonpartisan civil service means insulating government workers from the risk of being fired because a new party comes to power. At the same time, the **Hatch Act,** passed in 1940, prohibits those employees from active participation in partisan politics.

The **Office of Personnel Management (OPM)** is in charge of hiring for most agencies of the federal government. Its members are appointed by the president and confirmed by the Senate. The OPM has elaborate rules about hiring, promotion, working conditions, and firing. To get a Civil Service job, normally, candidates must first take a test. If they pass, they will be sent to agencies when jobs requiring their skills open up. For each position that is open, the OPM will send three names to the agency. Except under unusual circumstances, the agency must hire someone on this list of three eligibles. (This process is called the "rule of three.") Once hired, a person is assigned a **GS (General Schedule) rating,** ranging from GS 1 to GS 18. Salaries are keyed to rating and experience. At the very top of the civil service system are about eight thousand members of the *Senior Executive Service,* the "cream of the crop" of the federal employees. These executives earn high salaries and may be moved from one agency to another as leadership needs change.

Once hired, and after a probationary period, civil servants are protected—overprotected, critics claim—by the Civil Service system. Ensuring a nonpartisan Civil Service requires that workers have protection from dismissals that are politically motivated. Protecting all workers against political firings may also protect a few from dismissal for good cause. Firing incompetents is hard work. In one recent year, the government managed to fire only 236 employees for incompetence, a small fraction of the 3 million civilian federal workers. According to Civil Service regulations, the right of appeal must be exhausted before one's paycheck stops. Appeals can consume weeks, months, or even years. More than one agency has decided to tolerate incompetents, assigning them trivial or no duties, rather than invest its resources in the nearly hopeless task of discharging them. Firing female, minority, or older workers may be even more difficult than dislodging young or middle-aged white males. These groups not only have the usual Civil Service protections but also can resort to antidiscrimination statutes to appeal their firings. When one agency tried to fire a forty-eight-year-old messenger for abusive behavior, the employee sued, charging age discrimination. He lost, but the case dragged on for more than three years.

The rise of public service unions has also made it more difficult to remove federal employees. Not all federal employees are unionized, but almost all employees in the Postal Service and some other agencies are. Federal employees are forbidden by law to strike. Government unionization became a prominent issue in 1981 when the Professional Air Traffic Controllers Organization

(PATCO), the men and women who monitor and direct takeoffs and landings at airports, went on strike for higher pay and better working conditions. The strike was in violation of federal law and an oath they had signed. President Reagan responded after only two days by firing those controllers who refused to report to work. New controllers were hired, and federal unionization suffered a severe blow.

President Carter tried to make it easier to fire nonperformers. In 1978 he pushed through Congress legislation that reformed the firing system; however, procedures for firing unproductive civil servants are still elaborate. After receiving a notice of termination, an employee has thirty days to appeal to the Merit Systems Protection Board, to which the agency in question must present evidence of the employee's incompetence. If the board orders the discharge, the employee can still appeal to federal courts.

The courts have been protective of the right to keep a federal job. In 1974 the Supreme Court, in *Arnett* v. *Kennedy,* held that federal employees could not be fired without "due process of law," a provision of the Fifth Amendment that applies to property. In lay terms, the Supreme Court in effect held that federal jobs are private property, in the same way that your furniture or house is private property. Workers willing to take the federal government to court have an excellent chance of keeping their jobs.[6]

The Other Route to Federal Jobs: Recruiting from the Plum Book   As an incoming administration celebrates its victory and prepares to take control of the government, Congress publishes the **plum book,** which lists top federal jobs (that is, "plums") available for direct presidential appointment, often with Senate confirmation. Hugh Heclo has estimated that there are about three hundred of these top policy-making posts, mostly cabinet secretaries, undersecretaries, assistant secretaries, and bureau chiefs, and a few thousand lesser ones.[7] Every incoming president launches a nationwide talent search to fill them (see "You Are the Policymaker: The Rewards of Public Service"). The president's

[6]Robert M. Kaus, "How the Supreme Court Sabotaged Civil Service Reform," *Washington Monthly* 10 (December 1978): 38–44.
[7]Hugh M Heclo, *A Government of Strangers: Executive Politics in Washington* (Washington, D.C.: The Brookings Institution, 1977), 94.

Doonesbury

BY GARRY TRUDEAU

The Rewards of Public Service

In June 1988 Derek Bok, president of Harvard University, told graduating students that the increasing disparity in pay between the public and private sectors could lead to a dangerous shortage of talented people in government jobs. He was not alone in his view. Ann Banning, the director of recruitment, Office of Presidential Personnel, testified that "what we increasingly see is that men and women at the peak of their private sector careers don't even seriously consider taking senior federal jobs."

Yet Congress, which ultimately sets the compensation levels for executive-branch employees, has been very reluctant to increase their pay. This is especially true of the highest-level executive officials. After all, they ask, why should we increase the income of officials who earn far more than the average American (a cabinet member made $134,100 in 1991; an assistant secretary made $104,500) when we have to cut back on programs that serve those less fortunate? Moreover, there are few benefits at the polls for increasing the pay of bureaucrats.

As a result, top federal executives have lost much of their purchasing power in the past twenty years. In some respects, salary limitations have always been balanced by the benefits of power and position. Federal executives deal with complex issues and make difficult decisions, often with profound, long-term national and international consequences. These challenges are also burdens, however, and they are coupled with the necessity of living under constant public and media scrutiny.

Thus Americans are faced with a dilemma: Just how much *should* the government pay top bureaucrats? What would *you* do?

Source: "Bok Assails Gaps in Pay in Vital Jobs," *New York Times,* June 10, 1988, A16; Commission on Executive, Legislative, and Judicial Salaries, *Quality Leadership,* December 15, 1986.

---

aides write scholars, influential members of Congress, state officials, interest group leaders, and others, seeking advice on whom to appoint to key posts. The president seeks individuals who combine executive talent, political skills, and sympathy for similar policy positions. Often, the president tries to include men and women, blacks and whites, people from different regions, and party members representing different interests (although few recent presidents have appointed so high a percentage of middle-aged white males as did Ronald Reagan). Some positions, especially ambassadorships, go to large campaign contributors. A few of these top-flight appointees will be civil servants, temporarily elevated to a "supergrade" status on the General Schedule; most, though, will be political appointees, "in-and-outers" who stay for a while and then leave.

Once in office, these administrative policymakers constitute what Heclo has called a "government of strangers." Their most important trait is their transience. The average assistant secretary or undersecretary lasts about twenty-two months.[8] Few top officials stay long enough to know their own subordinates well, much less people in other agencies. Administrative routines, budget cycles, and legal complexities are often new to them. To these new political executives, the possibilities of power may seem endless. They soon learn, however, that senior civil servants know more, have been there longer, and will outlast them. One newly appointed political executive told of his experience as follows:

[8]*Ibid.,* 103.

I spent the first days up with [the secretary], and it was marvelous all the plans we were making—the executive suites, limousines, and all that. Then I went down to the catacombs and there were all these gray men, you know—GS 15s, 16s, and I understood what they were saying to me. "Here we are. You may try to run us around. You may even run over us and pick a few of our boys off, but we'll stay and you won't. Now what's in it for us, sonny boy?"[9]

The security of the civil servants' jobs, the transience and even ignorance of their superiors—all contribute to the bureaucracy's resistance to change. Although plum-book appointees may have the outward signs of power, most find it difficult to exercise real control over much of what their subordinates do.

What They Do: Some Theories of Bureaucracy

Bureaucracies govern modern states, but governmental bureaucracies are not the only type of bureaucracies. Perhaps the oldest is the hierarchical governance of the Roman Catholic Church. Bureaucracies run American armies, corporations, schools, and almost every other social, political, and economic institution. The following sections explain three prominent theories of bureaucracy.

The Weberian Model   Most people have confronted a bureaucracy only to be told, "Perhaps Mrs. Smith could help you; your problem is really under her jurisdiction," or "You'll have to talk to the supervisor, because I am only enforcing our rules."

The classic conception of bureaucracy was advanced by the German sociologist Max Weber, who stressed that the bureaucracy was a "rational" way for a modern society to conduct its business.[10] To Weber, a **bureaucracy** depends upon certain elements: it has a *hierarchical authority structure,* in which power flows from the top down and responsiblity from the bottom up; it uses *task specialization,* so that experts instead of amateurs perform technical jobs; and it develops extensive *rules,* which may seem nit-picking at times but which allow similar cases to be handled similarly instead of capriciously. Bureaucracies work on the *merit principle,* in which entrance and promotion are on the basis of demonstrated abilities rather than on "who you know." Bureaucracies behave with *impersonality* so that all of their clients are treated impartially. Weber's classic prototype of the bureaucratic organization depicts the bureaucracy as a well-organized machine with plenty of working, but hierarchical, parts.

The Acquisitive, Monopolistic Bureaucracy   When agency heads sit before congressional committees to discuss their budgetary needs, they rarely (unless under overwhelming pressure from the White House) testify that the agency needs a *lower* budget.

The neat, Weberian model is only one way of thinking about bureaucracies. Other, more contemporary writers have seen bureaucracies as essentially "acquisitive," busily maximizing their budgets and expanding their powers. Con-

[9]*Ibid.,* 194–95.
[10]H. H. Gerth and C. Wright Mills, *From Max Weber: Essays in Sociology* (New York: Oxford University Press, 1958), chap. 8.

servative economist William Niskanen, once a member of President Reagan's Council of Economic Advisors, believes that bureaucracies are like private corporations in seeking goals,[11] except that private corporations seek to maximize their *profits* whereas governmental bureaucracies seek to maximize their *budgets*. Bureaucratic administrators are committed to the "products" they "sell"—national security, schooling, public health, higher education, police protection—and their piece of the government's total budget pie is a good measure of how highly their product is valued. Moreover, all administrators take more professional pride in running a large, well-staffed agency than a puny one. For these reasons, insists Niskanen, bureaucracies are themselves largely responsible for the growth of modern governments.[12] Bureaucracies may even couple with Congress in an unholy alliance to expand big government (see the discussion of Fiorina's theory in Chapter 12).

Not only can bureaucracies be acquisitive; they can also be monopolistic. In the private sector, a monopoly, being the sole supplier of some key good, is free from competition. It can afford to exact high prices and behave inefficiently. Public bureaucracies are typically monopolies, too. As a general rule there is no alternative to the local fire department or water supply system; certainly, there is no alternative to the national defense system. Only well-to-do people really have an alternative to the local school system, the Social Security system, or government-run Medicare for the elderly. Some of Americans' complaints about bureaucracies are really complaints about bureaucratic monopoly. No matter how the bureaucracies behave, they will not lose their clients; there is no competitive pressure to force them to improve service. Many conservative, and even liberal, critics of bureaucracy have favored *privatizing* some bureaucratic services to cut back on their monolithic and monopolistic power.[13] Local garbage collection or fire protection, for example, could be contracted out to private companies. Governments might thus accept the best service at the lowest price.

[11] William Niskanen, *Bureaucracy and Representative Government* (Chicago: Aldine-Atherton, 1971).

[12] For critiques of the Niskanen perspective, see Miller and Moe, "Bureaucrats, Legislators, and the Size of Government"; and William D. Berry and David Lowery, *Understanding United States Government Growth* (New York: Praeger, 1987).

[13] See, for example, E. S. Savas, *Privatization: The Key to Better Government* (Chatham, N.J.: Chatham House, 1987).

The People Speak   **Bureaucracy and Governmental Waste**

Do people in the government waste a lot of the money we pay in taxes, some of it, or don't waste very much of it?

	1964	1968	1972	1984	1988
A lot	47%	59%	66%	65%	64%
Some	44%	34%	30%	29%	34%
Not very much	6%	4%	2%	4%	3%

Source: The question as worded is taken directly from National Election Studies.

Garbage Cans and Bureaucracies   One Washington official, lobbying for some policy changes in the nation's capital, told John Kingdon:

> I can trace the path of ideas. But my personal theory is that people plant seeds every day. There are a lot of ideas around. . . . The real question is, which of these ideas will catch hold? When you plant a seed, you need rain, soil, and luck.[14]

Both the Weberian model and the model of the acquisitive, monopolistic bureaucracy make bureaucracies sound calculating and purposive. Another view of bureaucracy, though, makes them sound ambling and groping, affected by chance. Cohen, March, and Olsen suggest that the typical organization is a "loose collection of ideas, [rather than] a coherent structure."[15] Likely as not, they say, organizations operate by trial and error. Far from being tightly controlled, they are typically loosely run. For most organizations, technological certainty is low. It is rarely clear that one policy will work and another fail. Lots of ideas may be floating around any organization. Faced with a particular problem, members of the organization may pull one of them from the "garbage can" of ideas and latch onto it. Organizations are not necessarily trying to find solutions to problems; *just as often, solutions are in search of problems.* The police department gets a new computer and then discovers how many tasks it has that need computerizing. Kingdon's careful study of governmental agenda building found much to recommend the "garbage can" model of policy-making.[16]

Each of these perspectives offers a different view of the American bureaucracy. None of them is completely right. Consider each of them as you examine the organization and functions of bureaucracies in modern America.

How Bureaucracies Are Organized

A complete organizational chart of the American federal government would be big enough to occupy a large wall. You could pore over this chart, trace the lines of responsibility and authority, and see how government is organized—at least on paper. You can see a very simplified organizational chart of the executive branch in Figure 15.3. A much easier way to look at how the federal executive branch is organized is to group agencies into four basic types: cabinet departments, regulatory agencies, government corporations, and independent agencies.

The Cabinet Departments

Each of the fourteen cabinet departments is headed by a secretary (with the exception of the Department of Justice, headed by the attorney general) chosen by the president and approved by the Senate. Beneath the secretary are undersecretaries, deputy undersecretaries, and assistant secretaries. Each department

---

[14]John Kingdon, *Agendas, Alternatives, and Public Policies* (Boston: Little, Brown, 1984), 81.

[15]Michael Cohen, James March, and Johan Olsen, "A Garbage Can Model of Organizational Choice," *Administrative Science Quarterly* 17 (March 1972): 1.

[16]Kingdon, *Agendas, Alternatives, and Public Policies,* 88–94.

Figure 15.3 Organization of the Executive Branch

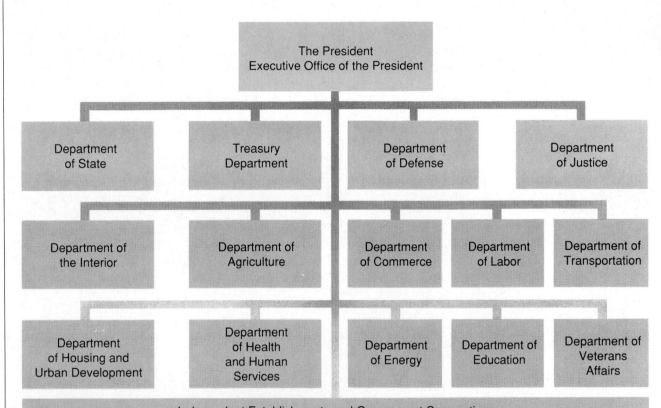

The President
Executive Office of the President

Department of State	Treasury Department	Department of Defense	Department of Justice
Department of the Interior	Department of Agriculture	Department of Commerce	Department of Labor	Department of Transportation
Department of Housing and Urban Development	Department of Health and Human Services	Department of Energy	Department of Education	Department of Veterans Affairs

Independent Establishments and Government Corporations

ACTION
Administrative Conference of the U.S.
African Development Foundation
American Battle Monuments Commission
Appalachian Regional Commission
Board for International Broadcasting
Central Intelligence Agency
Commission on the Bicentennial of the United States
Commission on Civil Rights
Commission of Fine Arts
Commodity Futures Trading Commission
Consumer Product Safety Commission
Environmental Protection Agency
Equal Employment Opportunity Commission
Export-Import Bank of the U.S.
Farm Credit Administration
Federal Communications Commission
Federal Deposit Insurance Corporation
Federal Election Commission
Federal Emergency Management Agency

Federal Home Loan Bank Board
Federal Labor Relations Authority
Federal Maritime Commission
Federal Mediation and Conciliation Service
Federal Reserve System, Board of Governors of the
Federal Retirement Thrift Investment Board
Federal Trade Commission
General Services Administration
Inter-American Foundation
Interstate Commerce Commission
Merit Systems Protection Board
National Aeronautics and Space Administration
National Archives and Records Administration
National Capital Planning Commission
National Credit Union Administration
National Foundation on the Arts and Humanities
National Labor Relations Board
National Mediation Board
National Science Foundation
National Transportation Safety Board
Nuclear Regulatory Commission

Occupational Safety and Health Review Commission
Office of Personnel Management
Panama Canal Commission
Peace Corps
Pennsylvania Avenue Development Corporation
Pension Benefit Guaranty Corporation
Postal Rate Commission
Railroad Retirement Board
Securities and Exchange Commission
Selective Service System
Small Business Administration
Tennessee Valley Authority
U.S. Arms Control and Disarmament Agency
U.S. Information Agency
U.S. International Development Cooperation Agency
U.S. International Trade Commission
U.S. Postal Service

Source: Office of the Federal Register, *United States Government Manual 1988–89* (Washington, D.C.: Government Printing Office, 1987), 21.

manages some specific policy areas (see the list on page 469), and each has its own budget and its own staff.

Each department has a different mission and is organized somewhat differently. The Department of Interior, a well-established and traditional department, is portrayed in Figure 15.4. The real work of a department is done in the bureaus (sometimes called a service, office, administration, or some other name) which divide the work into more specialized areas.

Until the 1970s the largest cabinet department was the Department of Defense. Today the Department of Health and Human Services (HHS) is the largest federal department in dollars spent (although the Department of Defense still has more employees). Spending one-third of the federal budget, HHS runs such massive programs as Social Security, Medicare, and Medicaid. In Washington, it is known as the most unwieldy government agency.

The Regulatory Agencies

Each **independent regulatory agency** has responsibility for some sector of the economy, making and enforcing rules designed to protect the public interest. These agencies also judge disputes over those rules. Their powers are so far-reaching that they are sometimes called "the fourth branch of government."[17] They are also sometimes called the alphabet soup of American government, because most such agencies are known in Washington by their initials. Here is a sampling of these independent regulatory agencies:

- *ICC (the Interstate Commerce Commission),* the oldest of the regulatory agencies, founded in 1887 to regulate railroads and, later, other interstate commerce, specifically trucking
- *FRB (the Federal Reserve Board),* charged with governing banks and, even more importantly, regulating the supply of money
- *NLRB (the National Labor Relations Board),* created to regulate labor-management relations
- *FCC (the Federal Communications Commission),* charged with licensing radio and TV stations and regulating their programming in the public interest, as well as with regulating interstate long-distance telephone rates
- *FTC (the Federal Trade Commission),* intended to regulate business practices and control monopolistic behavior, and now involved in policing the accuracy of advertising
- *SEC (the Securities and Exchange Commission),* created to police the stock market

Each of these independent regulatory agencies is governed by a small commission, usually with five to ten members appointed by the president and confirmed by the Senate for fixed terms. Unlike cabinet officers or members of the president's staff, regulatory commission members cannot be fired by the

[17]On the independent regulatory agencies, the classic work is Marver Bernstein, *Regulating Business by Independent Commission* (Princeton, N.J.: Princeton University Press, 1955). See also, on regulation, James Q. Wilson, ed., *The Politics of Regulation* (New York: Basic Books, 1980); A. Lee Fritschler and Bernard H. Ross, *Business Regulation and Government Decision-Making* (Cambridge, Mass.: Winthrop, 1980); and the February 1982 issue of *Policy Studies Review.*

Figure 15.4 Organization of the Department of the Interior

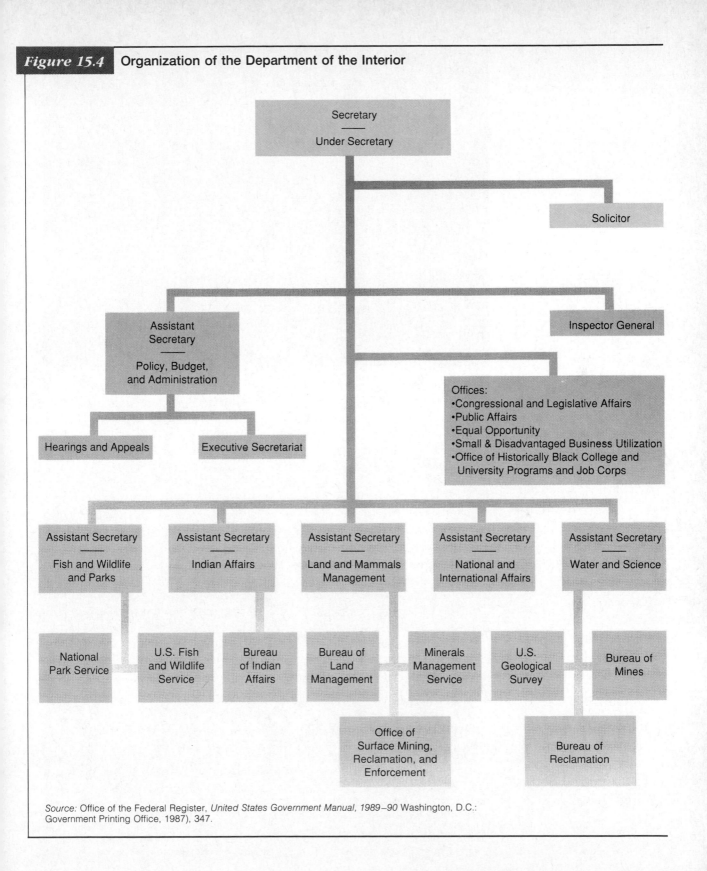

Source: Office of the Federal Register, *United States Government Manual, 1989–90* Washington, D.C.: Government Printing Office, 1987), 347.

The Environmental Protection Agency is the federal government's largest independent regulatory agency, overseeing the administration of all environmental legislation. Here an EPA official inspects plastic sheeting designed to contain oil spills.

president. The Supreme Court made this decision after President Franklin Roosevelt fired a man named Humphrey from the Federal Trade Commission. Humphrey died shortly afterward, but his angry executors sued for back pay, and the Court held that presidents could not fire members of regulatory agencies without just cause (*Humphrey's Executor* v. *United States* [1935]).

Interest groups consider the rule making by independent regulatory agencies—and, of course, their membership—very important. The FCC can deny a multimillion-dollar TV station a license renewal, a power that certainly sparks the interest of the National Association of Broadcasters. The FTC regulates business practices, a power prompting both business and consumers to pay careful attention to its activities and membership.

So interested are interest groups in regulatory bodies that critics often point to the "capture" of the regulators by the regulatees.[18] It is not uncommon for members of commissions to be drawn from the ranks of the regulated. Sometimes, too, members of commissions or staffs of these agencies move on to jobs in the very industries they were regulating. Some lawyers among them can use contacts and information gleaned at the agency later, when they represent clients before their former employers at the agency. The bureaucracy's relationship with interest groups will be discussed in more detail later in this chapter.

The Government Corporations

The federal government also has a handful of **government corporations.** These are not exactly like private corporations in which you can buy stock and

[18]Bernstein, *Regulating Business,* 90. For a partial test of the capture theory that finds the theory not altogether accurate, see John P. Plumlee and Kenneth J. Meier, "Capture and Rigidity in Regulatory Administration," in *The Policy Cycle,* ed. Judith May and Aaron Wildavsky (Bevery Hills, Calif.: Sage, 1978). Another critique of the capture theory is Paul J. Quirk, *Industry Influence in Federal Regulatory Agencies* (Princeton, N. J.: Princeton University Press, 1981).

collect dividends, but they *are* like private corporations—and different from other parts of the government—in two ways. First, they provide a service that *could be* handled by the private sector. Second, they typically charge for their services, though often at cheaper rates than the consumer would pay a private sector producer.

The granddaddy of the government corporations is the Tennessee Valley Authority (TVA), which, at least until recently, provided inexpensive electricity to millions of Americans in Tennessee, Kentucky, Alabama, and neighboring states. Through Comsat, a modern-day government corporation that sells time-sharing on NASA satellites, you can rent time on a space satellite for radio communications. Even the post office, one of the original cabinet departments (first headed by Benjamin Franklin), has become a government corporation: the U.S. Postal Service. Once in a while, the government has taken over a "sick industry" and turned it into a government corporation. Amtrak, the railroad passenger service, is one example. Congress grumbles about Amtrak's multi-billion-dollar subsidy (although some critics point out that billions of dollars in federal highway funds also constitute something of a subsidy for the auto industry), but members of Congress have only reluctantly agreed to let Amtrak shed its most unprofitable runs.

The Independent Executive Agencies

The **independent executive agencies** are essentially all the rest of the government—not cabinet departments, not regulatory commissions, and not government corporations. Their administrators are typically appointed by the president and serve at his pleasure. To list and describe these scores of bureaus would be tedious, but they are listed in the current issue of the *United States Government Manual.* The following are a few of the biggest (in size of budget):

- *General Services Administration (GSA),* the government's landlord, which handles buildings, supplies, and purchasing
- *National Science Foundation (NSF),* which supports scientific research
- *National Aeronautics and Space Administration (NASA),* the agency that brings Americans to the moon and points beyond

In an effort to make the agency financially independent as well as more responsive to consumers, Congress, in 1970, transformed the Post Office Department into the U.S. Postal Service, the government's largest corporation. The agency has improved its fiscal performance (partly due to increased postal rates), although it is now subject to direct competition from private businesses offering parcel and overnight mail services.

BUREAUCRACIES AS IMPLEMENTORS

In modern government bureaucracies are essentially *implementors* of policy. They take congressional, presidential, and sometimes even judicial pronouncements and develop procedures and rules for implementing policy goals. They also manage the routines of government, from delivering mail to collecting taxes to training troops. The following sections will focus more closely on this crucial function of governing.

What Implementation Means

Public policies are rarely self-executing. One of the few policies that administers itself is the president's decision to "recognize" a foreign government. It is entirely the chief executive's prerogative to do so, and once it is done, diplomatic relations with the country are thereby established.

Most policies, though, are not self-executing. Congress typically announces the goals of a policy in broad terms, sets up an administrative apparatus, and leaves to the bureaucracy the task of working out the details of the program—in other words, the bureaucracy is left to implement the program. Policy **implementation** is the stage of policy-making between the establishment of a policy (such as the passage of a legislative act, the issuing of an executive order, the handing down of a judicial decision, or the promulgation of a regulatory rule) and the consequences of the policy for the people whom it affects.[19] Two different authors, writing in the same year, loosely paraphrased a famous line about war from German General Karl von Clausewitz and applied it to the implementation process: "Implementation is the continuation of policymaking by other means."[20] At a minimum, implementation includes three elements:

- Creation of a new agency or assignment of responsibility to an old one
- Translation of policy goals into operational rules of thumb; development of guidelines for the program or policy
- Coordination of resources and personnel to achieve the intended goals[21]

Why the Best-Laid Plans Sometimes Flunk the Implementation Test

There is a famous line from the Scottish poet Robert Burns: "The best laid schemes o' mice and men/Gang aft a-gley [often go awry]." So, too, with the best intended public policies. Policies that people expect to work often fail. Martha Derthick told the sad tale of a "new towns in-town" program in which the government was to sell surplus property to groups that were helping to expand urban housing. In fact, little property was sold and few houses were built.[22] High expectations followed by dashed hopes is the all-too-common fate of well-intended public policies.

Program Design   Implementation can break down for several reasons. One is faulty program design. "It is impossible," said Eugene Bardach, "to implement well a policy or program that is defective in its basic theoretical conception." Consider, he suggested, the following hypothetical example:

> If Congress were to establish an agency charged with squaring the circle with compass and straight edge—a task mathematicians have long ago shown is impossible—we could envision an agency coming into being, hiring a vast number of consultants, commissioning studies, reporting that progress was being made, while at the same time urging in their appropriations request for the coming year that the Congress augment the agency's budget.[23]

[19] George C. Edwards III, *Implementing Public Policy* (Washington, D.C.: Congressional Quarterly Press, 1980), 1.

[20] Eugene Bardach, *The Implementation Game* (Cambridge, Mass.: The MIT Press, 1977), 85; and Robert L. Lineberry, *American Public Policy: What Government Does and What Difference It Makes* (New York: Harper & Row, 1977), 71. Clausewitz called war "the continuation of politics by other means."

[21] Lineberry, *American Public Policy*, 70–71.

[22] Martha Derthick, *New Towns In-Town* (Washington, D.C.: The Urban Institute Press, 1972).

[23] Bardach, *The Implementation Game*, 250–51.

Lack of Clarity   Congress is fond of stating a broad policy goal in legislation and then leaving implementation up to the bureaucracies. Members of Congress can thus escape messy details, and blame for the implementation decisions can be placed elsewhere.

One such policy was the controversial Title IX of the Education Amendments of 1972,[24] which said: "No person in the United States shall, on the basis of sex, be excluded from participation in, be denied the benefits of, or be subjected to discrimination under any education program or activity receiving federal financial assistance." Because almost every college and university receives some federal financial assistance, almost all were thereby forbidden to discriminate by sex. Interest groups supporting women's athletics had convinced Congress to include a provision about college athletics as well. So Section 844 read:

> The Secretary [of HEW then, today of Education] shall prepare and publish . . . proposed regulations implementing the provisions of Title IX . . . relating to prohibition of sex discrimination in Federally assisted education programs *which shall include with respect to intercollegiate athletic activities reasonable provisions considering the nature of the particular sports* [italics added].

Just what did this section mean? Supporters of women's athletics thought it meant that discrimination against women's sports was also prohibited. Some, with good reason, looked forward to seeing women's sports on an equal footing with men's. One member of the House-Senate Conference Committee had proposed language specifically exempting "revenue-producing athletics" (meaning men's football and basketball) from the prohibition. The committee rejected this suggestion, but to colleges and universities with big-time athletic programs, and to some alumni, the vague Section 844 called for equality in golf and swimming—not men's football and basketball programs, which could continue to have the lion's share of athletic budgets.

Joseph Califano, President Carter's secretary of HEW, was the man in the middle on this tricky problem. His staff developed a "policy interpretation" of the legislation, which he announced in December 1978. HEW's interpretation of the hundred or so words of Section 844 of Title IX took thirty pages. It recognized that football was "unique" among college sports. If football was unique, the interpretation implied (but did not directly say) that male-dominated football programs could continue to outspend women's athletic programs.

Supporters of equal budgets for male and female athletics were outraged. Charlotte West of the Association for Intercollegiate Athletics for Women called it "a multitude of imprecise and confusing explanations, exceptions, and caveats." Even the football-oriented National Collegiate Athletic Association was wary of the interpretation. One of its lawyers allowed, "They are trying to be fair. The question is how successful they are." A one-hundred-word section in a congressional statute, which prompted a thirty-page interpretation by the bureaucracy, in turn prompted scores of court suits. The courts have had to rule on such matters as whether or not Title IX requires that exactly equivalent dollar amounts be spent on women's and men's athletics.

Bureaucracies are often asked to implement unclear laws. When Congress decided to prohibit sexual discrimination in college athletics, for example, it left to bureaucrats the task of creating guidelines that would end discrimination while addressing the diverse needs of different sports. It took years—and several lawsuits—to establish the law's meaning.

---

[24] The implementation of the athletics policy is well documented in two articles by Cheryl M. Fields in the *Chronical of Higher Education,* December 11 and 18, 1978, on which this account relies.

The complex case of implementing Title IX for intercollegiate athletics contains an important lesson: policy problems that Congress cannot resolve are not likely to be resolved easily by bureaucracies.

Lack of Resources   As noted earlier, the conventional wisdom is that bureaucracies are bloated. The important issue, however, is not the size of the bureaucracy in the abstract but whether it is the appropriate size to do the job it has been assigned to do. It is often the case that, as big as a bureaucracy may seem in the aggregate, it frequently lacks the staff, along with the necessary training, funding, supplies, and equipment, to carry out the tasks it has been assigned to do. Recently, for example, the news has been filled with complaints such as the following:

- A shortage of staff was responsible for delays in the testing of new drugs to combat AIDS.
- The Air Force and Navy had too few experienced jet pilots.
- The Department of Energy lacked managers and supervisors with the technical skills to run the American bomb production system.
- The Justice Department lacked the staff to enforce the nation's antitrust laws.
- In their inspections of facilities handling and storing hazardous wastes, inadequately trained inspectors for the Environmental Protection Agency were found to be overlooking more than half of the serious violations.
- Some observers feared that the lack of financing to maintain the national parks would lead to permanent deterioration of such treasured American vacation spots as Yosemite and Yellowstone.
- Drug runners had more and faster ships and planes for smuggling drugs into the country than government agents had for trying to catch them.

Critics argue that bureaucracies are bloated, but the opposite situation is actually more common—many bureaucrats lack the resources they need to properly implement public policies. The overcrowding of national parks such as Yosemite puts a severe strain on the National Park Service's ability to maintain the natural environment, for example.

Administrative Routine   For most bureaucrats, most of the time, administration is a routine matter. They follow **standard operating procedures,** better known as SOPs, to help them make numerous everyday decisions. Such rules save time. If a Social Security caseworker had to invent a new rule for every potential client and have it cleared at higher levels, few clients would be served. Thus detailed manuals are written to cover as many particular situations as officials can anticipate. The regulations elaborating the Internal Revenue Code compose the bible of an IRS agent; similarly, a customs agent has binders filled with rules and regulations about what can and cannot be brought into the United States free of duty.

SOPs also bring uniformity to complex organizations, and justice is better served if rules are applied uniformly, as in the implementation of welfare policies that distribute benefits to the needy or in the levying of fines for underpayment of taxes. Uniformity also makes personnel interchangeable. Soldiers, for example, can be transferred to any spot in the world and still know how to do their job by referring to the appropriate manual.

Routines, then, are essential to bureaucracy. They become frustrating to citizens, who term them "red tape" when they do not appear to appropriately address a situation. SOPs then become obstacles to action. Presidents have had many a plan thwarted by SOPs; they certainly frustrated Franklin D. Roosevelt:

> The Treasury is so . . . ingrained in its practices that I find it impossible to get the action and results I want. . . . But the Treasury is not to be compared with the State Department. You should go through the experience of trying to get any changes in the thinking, policy, and action of the career diplomats. . . . But [both] put together are nothing as compared to the Na-a-vy. . . . To change anything in the Na-a-a-vy is like punching a feather bed. You punch it with your right and you punch it with your left until you are finally exhausted, and then you find the damn bed just as it was before you started punching.[25]

In an October 1983 terrorist attack on their barracks outside Beirut, Lebanon, 241 Marines were killed while they slept. A presidential commission appointed to examine the causes of the tragedy concluded that, among other factors contributing to the disaster, the Marines in the peacekeeping force were "not trained, organized, staffed or supported to deal effectively with the terrorist threat."[26] In other words, they had not altered their SOPs regarding security, basic to any military unit, to meet the unique challenges of a terrorist attack.

Administrators' Dispositions   Paradoxically, bureaucrats operate not only within the confines of routines but often with considerable discretion to behave independently. **Administrative discretion** is the authority of administrative actors to select among various responses to a given problem.[27] Discretion is greatest when rules do not fit a case, but even in agencies with elaborate rules and regulations, especially when more than one rule fits, there is still room for discretion. Although the IRS code is massive, it wields vast discretion even if it

---

[25]Quoted in M. S. Eccles, *Beckoning Frontiers* (New York: Knopf, 1951), 336.

[26]*Report of the DOD Commission on Beirut International Airport Terrorist Act, October 23, 1983,* December 20, 1983, 133.

[27]On administrative discretion, see Gary S. Bryner, *Bureaucratic Discretion* (New York: Pergamon Press, 1987).

Bureaucrats typically apply thousands of pages of rules in the performance of routine tasks, but many of them—especially street-level bureaucrats—must exercise administrative discretion as well. This border patrol officer, for example, must judge who he will search carefully and who he will let by with a quick check.

tries to follow the code to the letter. The IRS agent must be "armed against the machinations, not of the average citizen, but of the cleverest adversary the best law schools can produce."[28] Here are a few examples:

- Congress and the IRS code say that medical expenses above a certain percentage of income are deductible, but how about the expenses of a vasectomy? (The IRS said yes.)
- A girl ordered to take strenuous exercise under the supervision of a doctor was enrolled by her father in $8,436 worth of ballet lessons. Was it deductible? (The IRS said no.)
- Congress and the IRS code say that business expenses are deductible, but can an airline flight attendant deduct the cost of clothes? (The IRS said yes.)
- Are taxi expenses incurred in visiting your stockbroker a deductible expense? (The IRS said yes.)

Some administrators exercise more discretion than others. Michael Lipsky coined the phrase **street-level bureaucrats** to refer to those bureaucrats who are in constant contact with the public (often a hostile one) and have considerable discretion; they include police officers, welfare workers, and lower court judges.[29] No amount of rules, not even the thousands of pages of IRS rules, will eliminate the need for bureaucratic discretion on some policies.

Since bureaucrats will inevitably exercise discretion, it is important to understand how they use it. Ultimately, how they use it depends on their dispo-

[28]Gerald Carson, *The Golden Egg* (Boston: Houghton Mifflin, 1977), 10. The examples given in this paragraph are from Carson.

[29]Michael Lipsky, *Street-Level Bureaucracy* (New York: Russell Sage Foundation, 1980).

sitions about the policies and rules they administer. Although bureaucrats may be indifferent to the implementation of many policies, others will be in conflict with their policy views or personal or organizational interests. When people are asked to execute orders with which they do not agree, slippage is likely to occur between policy decisions and performance. A great deal of mischief may occur as well (see "A Question of Ethics: Cashing In").

On one occasion, President Nixon ordered Secretary of Defense Melvin Laird to bomb a hideaway of the Palestine Liberation Organization, a move Laird opposed. According to the secretary, "We had bad weather for forty-eight hours. The Secretary of Defense can always find a reason not to do something."[30] Thus the president's order was stalled for days and eventually rescinded.

Controlling the exercise of discretion is a difficult task. It is not easy to fire bureaucrats in the Civil Service, and removing appointed officials may be politically embarrassing to the president, especially if those officials have strong

[30]Quoted in Seymour Hersh, *The Price of Power: Kissinger in the Nixon White House* (New York: Summit, 1983), 235–36.

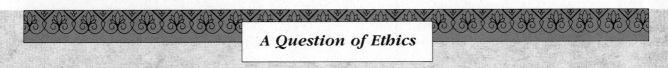

A Question of Ethics

Cashing In

Much of the multibillion dollar housing budget of the Department of Housing and Urban Development (HUD) is spent at the discretion of HUD officials. During the tenure of Samuel Pierce, the secretary of HUD during the Reagan administration (1981–1988), former department officials and prominent members of the Republican party received large fees for lobbying HUD on behalf of clients seeking government subsidies for housing projects.

Former Secretary of the Interior James Watt was paid $300,000 for making eight phone calls to HUD and one brief visit to Pierce, his friend and former cabinet colleague. Watt freely admitted that he had no prior experience in housing policy, but he saw no ethical problem with cashing in on his "credibility" with Pierce. The consulting agency that hired Watt, headed by Joseph Strauss, a former special assistant to Pierce, made no bones about Watt's lack of expertise. "The reason we hired him," Strauss declared, "was because of his access and his influence."

Watt was not alone in cashing in on the HUD gold mine in the 1980s. Many former high-level HUD officials also received large fees, typically in the six-figure range, for helping to obtain HUD financing.

Political party officials were also not hesitant to peddle their influence for large fees. For example, William Taylor, the former Republican state chairman in Florida, received over $500,000 for his efforts to lobby HUD. He testified that he saw nothing wrong in trading on political ties for private gain. He even went so far as to use Republican National Committee stationery to write Pierce—to ensure that the secretary would not forget who Taylor was.

Although Pierce became only the third current or former cabinet member to plead the Fifth Amendment before a congressional committee, most of what his former subordinates and political friends did was not illegal. The question is whether it was *ethical*. Because of the influence of high-priced, well-connected lobbyists, certain housing projects were funded while more deserving projects received no funds.

Should those with close connections to program officials cash in on their positions? Or is influence peddling an appropriate award for public service and political activity? Should program officials be responsive to their friends and former colleagues? What do *you* think?

support in Congress and among interest groups. In the private sector, leaders of organizations provide incentives such as pay raises to encourage employees to perform their tasks in a certain way. In the public sector, however, special bonuses are rare, and pay raises tend to be small and across-the-board. Moreover, there is not necessarily room at the top for those bureaucrats who are especially able. Unlike a typical private business, a government agency cannot expand just because it is performing a service effectively and efficiently.

Fragmentation   Sometimes responsibility for a policy area is dispersed among several units within the bureaucracy. In the field of welfare, for example, more than one hundred federal human services programs are administered by ten different departments and agencies. The Department of Health and Human Services has responsibility for the Aid to Families with Dependent Children program; the Department of Housing and Urban Development provides housing assistance; the Department of Agriculture runs the Food Stamp program; and the Department of Labor administers manpower-training programs and provides assistance in obtaining employment.

This diffusion of responsibility makes the coordination of policies both time-consuming and difficult. For years, efforts to control the flow of illicit drugs into the country has been hindered by lack of cooperation among the Drug Enforcement Administration in the Department of Justice, the Customs Service in the Treasury Department, the State Department, and other relevant agencies.

Sometimes those who are supposed to comply with a law receive contradictory signals from different agencies. The regulation of hazardous wastes, such as the radioactive waste produced by the nuclear power industry, is one of the major concerns of the Environmental Protection Agency and a matter of paramount concern to the public. The Department of Energy, however, has routinely paid all the fines its contractors have received for violating laws designed to protect the environment, and it has even paid the legal fees the contractors incurred while defending themselves against the fines. The Energy Department has also given generous bonuses to its contractors even while they were being fined by the EPA. Such contradictory policies obviously undermine efforts to limit pollution of the environment.

If fragmentation is a problem, why not reorganize the government? Congressional committees recognize that they would lose jurisdiction over agencies if they were merged with others. Interest groups (such as the nuclear power industry) do not want to give up the close relationships they have developed with "their" agencies. Agencies themselves do not want to be submerged within a broader bureaucratic unit. All these forces fight reorganization, and, usually, they win.[31]

A Case Study: The Voting Rights Act of 1965

Policy implementation does not always work. Even when a policy is controversial, however, implementation can be effective if goals are clear and means to achieve the goals are unambiguous.

---

[31]For a careful analysis of efforts to reorganize the federal bureaucracy, see Peri E. Arnold, *Making the Managerial Presidency* (Princeton, N.J.: Princeton University Press, 1986).

The Voting Rights Act of 1965 was successfully implemented because its goal was clear: to register African Americans to vote in southern counties where their voting rights had been denied for years. This federal registrar, like hundreds of others working for the Department of Justice, helped bring the vote to some three hundred thousand African Americans in less than a year.

In 1965, Congress, responding to generations of discrimination against prospective black voters in the South, passed the Voting Rights Act. The act singled out six states in the Deep South in which the number of African-American registrants was minuscule. Congress ordered the Justice Department to send federal registrars to each county in those states to register qualified voters. Congress outlawed literacy tests and other tests previously used to discriminate against black registrants. Stiff penalties were provided for those who interfered with the work of federal registrars.

Congress charged the attorney general with implementing the Voting Rights Act. He acted quickly, dispatching hundreds of registrars, some protected by U.S. marshals, to southern counties. Within seven and a half months after passage of the act, more than three hundred thousand new African-American voters were on the rolls. The proportion of the southern black population registered to vote increased from 43 percent in 1964 to 66 percent in 1970, partly (though certainly not entirely) because of the Voting Rights Act.[32]

The Voting Rights Act was, by any standard, a successful case of implementation, but not because it was popular with everyone. Southern representatives and senators were outraged by it, and a filibuster delayed its passage in the Senate. It was successful because its goal was clear (to register large numbers of black voters); its implementation was straightforward (sending out people to register them); and the authority of the implementors was plain (they had the

[32] On the implementation and impact of the Voting Rights Act, see Charles S. Bullock III and Harrell R. Rodgers, Jr., *Law and Social Change: Civil Rights Laws and Their Consequences* (New York: McGraw-Hill, 1972), chap. 2; Richard Scher and James Button. "Voting Rights Act: Implementation and Impact." in *Implementation of Civil Rights Policy,* ed. C. S. Bullock and C. M. Lamb (Monterey, Calif.: Brooks/Cole, 1984), chap. 2; and Abigail M. Thernstrom, *Whose Votes Count?* (Cambridge, Mass: Harvard University Press, 1987).

support of the attorney general and even U.S. marshals) and concentrated in the Justice Department, which was disposed to implementing the law vigorously.

BUREAUCRACIES AS REGULATORS

Government **regulation** is the use of governmental authority to control or change some practice in the private sector. All sorts of activities are subject to government regulation. Regulations by government pervade Americans' everyday lives and the lives of businesses, universities, hospitals, and other institutions. This is the most controversial role of the bureaucracies, yet Congress gives them broad mandates to regulate activities as diverse as interest rates, the location of nuclear power plants, and food additives.

Regulation in the Economy and in Everyday Life

The notion that the American economy is largely a "free enterprise" system, unfettered by government intervention, is about as up-to-date as a shiny new Model T Ford. You can begin to understand the sweeping scope of governmental regulation by examining how the automobile industry is regulated. Buying and selling stock in an automobile corporation are regulated by the Securities and Exchange Commission; relations between the workers and managers of the company come under the scrutiny of the National Labor Relations Board; because automakers are major government contractors, affirmative action in hiring workers is mandated and administered by the Department of Labor and the Equal Employment Opportunity Commission; pollution-control, energy-saving, and safety devices are required by the Environmental Protection Agency, the National Highway Traffic Safety Administration, and the Department of Transportation;

Most government regulation is clearly in the public interest. For example, the U.S. Department of Agriculture is charged with regulating the quality of meat products, a task it was given after novelist Upton Sinclair exposed the meat-packaging industry's unsanitary conditions at the turn of the century.

and unfair advertising and deceptive consumer practices in marketing cars come under the watchful eye of the Federal Trade Commission.

Everyday life itself is the subject of bureaucratic regulation (see "In Focus: A Full Day of Regulation"). Almost all bureaucratic agencies—not merely the ones called independent regulatory agencies—are in the regulatory business.

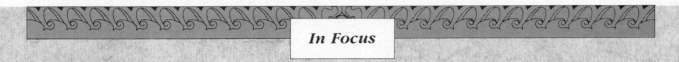

In Focus

A Full Day of Regulation

Factory worker John Glasswich (not his real name) works in the city of Chicago and lives with his wife and three young children in suburban Mount Prospect, Illinois. Both at work and at home, federal regulations impact his life. He is awakened at 5:30 A.M. by his clock radio, set to a country music station licensed to operate by the Federal Communications Commission. For breakfast he has cereal, which has passed inspection by the Food and Drug Administration, as has the lunch his wife packs for him. The processed meat in his sandwich is packed under the careful supervision of the Food Safety and Quality Service of the U.S. Department of Agriculture.

John takes the train to work, buying a quick cup of coffee before the journey. The caffeine in his coffee, the FDA has warned, has caused birth defects in laboratory animals, and there is discussion in Washington about regulating it. Paying his fare (regulated by the government), he hops aboard and shortly arrives at work, a small firm making refrigeration equipment for the food industry.

At home, Mrs. Glasswich is preparing breakfast for the children. The price of the milk she serves is affected by the dairy price supports regulated by the Agricultural Stabilization and Conservation Service. As the children play, she takes note of the toys they use, wanting to avoid any that could be dangerous. A Washington agency, the Consumer Product Safety Commission, also takes note of children's toys, regulating their manufacture and sale. The lawn mower, the appliances, the microwave oven, and numerous other items around the Glasswich house are also regulated by the Consumer Product Safety Commission. Setting out for the grocery store and the bank, Mrs. Glasswich encounters even more government regula-

tions. The car has seat belts mandated by the National Highway Traffic Safety Administration and gets gas mileage certified by the Department of Transportation. It happens that the car's pollution-control devices are now in need of service, because they do not meet the requirements of the Environmental Protection Agency. The bank at which Mrs. Glasswich deposits money and writes a check is among the most heavily regulated institutions she encounters in her daily life. Her passbook savings rate is regulated by the Depository Institutions Deregulation Committee.

Meanwhile, John Glasswich is at work assembling food-processing machinery. He and his fellow workers are members of the International Association of Machinists. Their negotiations with the firm are held under rules laid down by the National Labor Relations Board. One day not too long ago, the firm was visited by inspectors from the Occupational Safety and Health Administration, a federal agency charged with ensuring worker safety. OSHA inspectors noted several violations and forwarded a letter recommending safety changes to the head of the firm. Getting home, Glasswich has a beer before dinner. It was made in a brewery carefully supervised by the Bureau of Alcohol, Tobacco, and Firearms, and when it was sold, federal and state taxes were collected.

After dinner (almost all the food served has been transported by the heavily regulated trucking industry), the children are sent to bed. An hour or so of television, broadcast on regulated airwaves, is followed by bedtime for the Glasswiches. A switch will turn off the electric lights, whose rates are regulated by the Illinois Commerce Commission and the Federal Regulatory Commission.

Source: Based on a more elaborate account by James Worsham, "A Typical Day Is Full of Rules," *Chicago Tribune*, July 12, 1981, 1ff.

Regulation: How It Grew, How It Works

From the beginnings of the American republic until 1887, the federal government made almost no regulatory policies; the little regulation produced was handled by state and local authorities. Even the minimum regulatory powers of state and local governments were much disputed. In 1877 the Supreme Court upheld the right of government to regulate the business operations of a firm. The case, called *Munn* v. *Illinois,* involved the right of the state of Illinois to regulate the charges and services of a Chicago warehouse. During this time, farmers were seething about alleged overcharging by railroads, grain elevator companies, and other business firms. In 1887—a decade after *Munn*—Congress created the first regulatory agency, the Interstate Commerce Commission (ICC), and charged it with regulating the railroads, their prices, and their services to farmers; the ICC thus set the precedent for regulatory policy-making.

As regulators, bureaucratic agencies typically operate with a large grant of power from Congress, which may detail goals to be achieved but permits the agencies to sketch out the regulatory means. In 1935, for example, Congress created the National Labor Relations Board to control "unfair labor practices," but the NLRB had to play a major role in defining "fair" and "unfair." Most agencies charged with regulation first have to develop a set of rules, often called guidelines. The appropriate agency may specify how much food coloring it will permit in a wiener, how many contaminants it will permit an industry to dump into a stream, how much radiation from a nuclear reactor is too much, and so forth. Guidelines are developed in consultation with, and sometimes with the agreement of, the people or industries being regulated.

Next, the agency must apply and enforce its rules and guidelines, either in court or through its own administrative procedures. Sometimes it waits for complaints to come to it, as the Equal Employment Opportunity Commission does; sometimes it sends inspectors into the field, as the Occupational Safety and Health Administration does; and sometimes it requires applicants for a permit or license to demonstrate performance consistent with congressional goals and agency rules, as the Federal Communications Commission does. Often government agencies take violators to court, hoping to secure a judgment and fine against an offender. Whatever strategy Congress permits a regulating agency to use, all regulation contains these elements: (1) a *grant of power and set of directions* from Congress; (2) a *set of rules and guidelines* by the regulatory agency itself; and (3) some *means of enforcing compliance* with congressional goals and agency regulations.

Government regulation of the American economy and society has, of course, grown in recent decades. The budgets of regulatory agencies, their level of employment, and the number of rules they issue are all increasing—and did so even during the Reagan administration. As "In Focus: A Full Day of Regulation" shows, there are few niches of American society in which regulation is not a reality. Not surprisingly, this situation has led to charges that government is overdoing it.

Is There Too Much Regulation?   Almost every regulatory policy was created to achieve some desirable social goal. Who would disagree with the goal of a safer workplace, when more than ten thousand people are killed annually in industrial accidents? Who would dissent from greater highway safety, when more than fifty thousand die each year in automobile accidents? Who would disagree with policies to promote equality in hiring, when the history of opportunities for women and minorities is one of discrimination? Who would disagree with policies to reduce industrial pollution, when pollution threatens health and lives?

To be sure, regulations are rarely popular with the regulated. Automobile manufacturers do not appreciate regulations to install expensive pollution-control equipment; business managers would feel little regret if the Occupational Safety and Health Administration disappeared tomorrow. Aside from the expected opposition from the objects of regulation, though, it is still possible to pose the question, How much regulation is enough?

Critics are fond of stressing that Americans rarely evaluate the costs of regulation in relation to its benefits. Suppose, for example, that some particular condition of working in the chemical industry were associated with four deaths and several hundred injuries annually. If hundreds of millions of dollars needed to be spent to improve or eliminate that condition, the cost per life saved might be prohibitively high. John Morrall has drawn attention to the peculiar differences in the valuation of human life imposed by different regulatory agencies.[33] The Occupational Health and Safety Administration insisted that the steel industry improve the safety of its coke ovens, estimated to be responsible for twenty-seven deaths annually among steelworkers. The cost of saving lives by making the improvements (perhaps $1.3 billion) is high indeed, ranging from $9 million to $48 million per life saved. Another agency, the National Highway Traffic Safety

Opponents of government regulation contend that the rapid increase in the number and scope of environmental regulations during the past two decades has stifled economic growth. Others argue that such regulations are essential to protect the nation's air, land, and water—and the people who use it.

[33] John Morall III, "OSHA and U.S. Industry," in *Economic Effects of Government-Mandated Costs,* ed. Robert F. Lanzilotti (Gainesville: University of Florida Press, 1979), chap. 5.

Administration, proposed regulations requiring air bags in cars that could have a cost-to-life-saved ratio of less than $120,000.

Critics also point out that regulation is often confusing, contradictory, and inefficient. Sometimes regulation itself seems hazardous to one's health. One case involved children's sleepwear. In 1972 the Consumer Product Safety Commission required that children's sleepwear be treated with a flame-retardant chemical. A chemical called Tris was used, and prices jumped 20 percent. Five years later, though, the same Consumer Product Safety Commission banned Tris when it was linked to cancer. As Margorie Boyd remarked, "Parents were understandably shocked to learn that they had been paying a higher price in order to expose their children to a cancer-causing agent."[34]

Few government regulations have been as controversial as those in the area of worker safety and health. The Occupational Safety and Health Administration (OSHA) has become the favorite scapegoat of regulatory critics, but government has been in the business of regulating worker safety for a long time. The evidence on the success of such efforts is mixed.

Is There a Better Way?   Charles L. Schultze, chairman of President Carter's Council of Economic Advisors, was—like Murray L. Weidenbaum, who held the same position under President Reagan—a critic of the current state of federal regulation. Schultze reviewed the regulatory activities of the Environmental Protection Agency and the Occupational Safety and Health Administration. Neither agency's policies, he concluded, had worked very well.[35] He described the existing system as **command-and-control policy:** the government tells business how to reach certain goals, checks that these commands are followed, and punishes offenders. Schultze preferred an **incentive system.** He argued that instead of telling businesses how their ladders must be constructed, measuring the ladders, and charging a small fine for violators, it would be more efficient and effective to levy a high tax on firms with excessive worker injuries. Instead of trying to develop standards for 62,000 pollution sources, as EPA now does, it would be easier and more effective to levy a high tax on those who cause pollution. The government could even provide incentives in the form of rewards for such socially valuable behavior as developing technology to reduce pollution. Incentives, Schultze argued, use marketlike strategies to regulate industry. They are, he claimed, more effective and efficient than command-and-control regulation.

Not everyone is as keen on the use of incentives as Schultze. Defenders of the command-and-control system of regulation might compare the present system to preventive medicine; it is designed to minimize pollution or workplace accidents before they become too severe. Defenders of the system might argue, too, that penalties for excessive pollution or excessive workplace accidents would take place only after substantial damage had been done. They also might add that if taxes on pollution or unsafe work environments were merely externalized (that is, passed along to the consumer as higher prices), they would not be much of a deterrent. Moreover, it would take a large bureaucracy to carefully

[34]Margorie Boyd, "The Protection Consumers Don't Want," *Washington Monthly* 9 (September 1977): 32.

[35]Charles L. Schultze, *The Public Use of the Private Interest* (Washington, D.C.: The Brookings Institution, 1977).

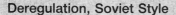

Deregulation, Soviet Style

Soviet leader Mikhail Gorbachev is trying to turn his country from an economic straggler into a front-runner. As part of his policy of *perestroika,* or restructuring, he is trying to deregulate the Soviet economy. In the Soviet Union virtually all economic production and exchange lies under government control. The marketplace has been superseded by administrative mechanisms as a means of allocating basic goods in the economy, leaving to the agencies of government tasks that private individuals and corporations perform in the United States and other capitalist economies.

This policy of strict regulation has been a failure; there has been essentially no growth in the Soviet economy for the past twenty years. Central planning has been unable to cope with the complexities of a modern economy, as can be seen in how one goes about purchasing an automobile in the USSR. For the average Muscovite, it takes nearly four years to earn enough money to afford a small automobile. Then, even if a person has the money, the waiting list for cars is so long that it takes eight years to get one. If a person gets a car, it will break down frequently, and spare parts will be in short supply.

Prices play a central role in any economy. In the Soviet Union the State Committee for Prices has set about five hundred thousand separate prices. The job is so huge that prices tend to stay unchanged for a decade or more, until the bureaucrats have time to work out a new set. Prices for some basic foods have not changed for more than twenty years. Moreover, the prices established by the government have little to do with supply and demand or the cost of production. Thus they cannot provide information about what to

make, where to buy, and which investments are profitable. Prices are so distorted that planners cannot even tell which products are profitable for export and which are not.

The leader of the Communist world is not a closet capitalist, however. Gorbachev wants a bit more private enterprise, and he wants the market to take over some tasks administrators do badly. He wants factories, for example, to obtain their own financing, customers, and suppliers. Nevertheless, the Soviet economy will remain planned and mostly publicly owned. Factories will still have to fulfill state orders, and the government will remain in control of foreign trade. The State Committee for Prices will continue to exist, fixing some prices and monitoring and setting guidelines for others. Gosplan, the state planning committee, and the bureaus and ministries are to concentrate on grand strategy and avoid meddling in details. The massive apparatus of central command is being trimmed, not abolished.

Moreover, there is likely to be resistance to change. The bureaucracy stands to lose perks and power in the economic restructuring and is unlikely to give them up without a fight. The foreign trade ministry, for example, has been restructured, renamed, and its powers reduced, but the new State Commission for Foreign Economic Relations still keeps an eye on the entire foreign trade system. Furthermore, despite the ministry's "restructuring," Western businesspersons often find they are dealing with the same people sitting at the same desks and with the same telephone numbers.

Source: "The Soviet Economy: Russian Roulette," *The Economist,* April 9, 1988, 3–18.

monitor the level of pollution discharged, and it would require a complex calculation to determine the level of tax necessary to encourage businesses not to pollute.

Toward Deregulation   These days, *deregulation* is a fashionable term in Washington and elsewhere[36] (see "America in Perspective: Deregulation, Soviet

[36]See Martha Derthick and Paul J. Quirk, *The Politics of Deregulation* (Washington, D.C.: The Brookings Institution, 1985).

Style"). The idea behind deregulation is that the number and complexity of regulatory policies have made regulation too complex and burdensome. To critics, the problem with regulation is that it raises prices, distorts market forces and—worst of all—does not work. Specifically, here are some of the accusations against the regulatory system:

- It raises prices. If the producer is faced with expensive regulations, cost will inevitably be borne by the consumer in the form of higher prices.
- It hurts America's competitive position abroad. Other nations may have fewer regulations on pollution, worker safety, and other business practices than the United States. Thus American products may cost more in the international marketplace, hurting sales in other countries.
- It does not always work well. Tales of failed regulatory policies are numerous. Regulations may be difficult or cumbersome to enforce. Critics charge that regulations sometimes do not achieve the results that Congress intended—and that they simply create massive regulatory bureaucracies.

President Reagan's conservative political philosophy was opposed to much government regulation, but even before the Reagan administration, sentiment toward deregulation was building in the Washington community. Even liberals sometimes joined the antiregulation chorus. Among them was Senator Edward Kennedy of Massachusetts, who pushed for airline deregulation. Indeed, deregulation was pressed by the airline industry, too, and in 1978 the Civil Aeronautics Board (CAB) began to deregulate airline prices and airline routes. Today, competitive airline fares, including inexpensive "no frills" flights, are the result of Congress's and the bureaucracy's decisions to dismantle the regulation of airlines. In 1984, the CAB formally disbanded, even bringing in a military bugler to play taps at its last meeting. Not everyone, though, believes that deregulation is in the nation's best interest (see "In Focus: Deregulation: A Dissenting View").

UNDERSTANDING BUREAUCRACIES

You have looked at bureaucracies as implementors and regulators. In carrying out each of these functions, bureaucracies are making public policy—not just administering someone else's decisions. The fact that bureaucrats are not elected yet compose most of the government raises fundamental issues regarding who controls governing and what the bureaucracy's role should be.

Bureaucracy and Democracy

Bureaucracies constitute one of America's two unelected policy-making institutions (courts being the other). In democratic theory, popular control of government depends on elections, but we could not possibly elect the five million federal civilian and military employees, or even the few thousand top men and women, though they spend more than a trillion dollars of the American GNP. Nevertheless, the fact that voters do not elect civil servants does not mean that bureaucracies cannot respond to and represent the public's interests. (Figure 15.2 showed that bureaucrats are actually more representative of the public than

Deregulation: A Dissenting View

Surveys about deregulation are pretty clear on one point: most Americans favor less government regulation in general, although they approve of almost every specific area of regulation, such as worker safety, pollution, and consumer product controls. These days, most conservatives and many liberals believe that government regulation has simply gone too far. It is time, they insist, to start deregulating the economy, permitting the market to work in its own way.

Of course, every regulation was once put into effect for some specific purpose or in response to a specific demand. Two dissenters to the whole idea of deregulation are Susan J. Tolchin and Martin Tolchin. In their book *Dismantling America,* they make a case that the rush to deregulate is a poor idea. "Regulatory reform," they say, "has turned out to be an exercise in national self-deception because of the singularity of its dominant goal: short-term relief for business." Far

from costing money, they argue, government regulation has saved lives and money. Crib safety standards have reduced infant injuries by 44 percent since 1964; air pollution regulations may have saved between $5 billion and $58 billion a year in health and other costs; automobile safety standards have probably saved more than twenty-eight thousand lives in an eight-year period, with seat belt requirements alone responsible for a 20 percent reduction in automobile deaths.

Businesses, say Tolchin and Tolchin, favor deregulation because it saves them money. Pesky pollution controls, bothersome worker safety regulations, and obnoxious noise abatements may cost corporations billions, but they may save lives and money, too. There is, at least, some support for the idea that regulation is not too much of a good thing.

Source: Susan J. Tolchin and Martin Tolchin, *Dismantling America: The Rush to Deregulate* (New York: Oxford University Press, 1983).

presidents or members of Congress.) Much depends on whether bureaucracies are effectively controlled by the policymakers that citizens do elect—the president and Congress.

Presidents Try to Control the Bureaucracy   Chapter 13 took a look at some of the frustrations presidents endure in trying to control the government they are elected to run. Presidents try hard—not always with success—to impose their policy preferences on agencies. The following are some of their methods:

- *Appoint the right people to head the agency.* Normally, presidents control the appointments of agency heads and subheads. Putting their people in charge is one good way for presidents to influence agency policy,[37] yet even this has its problems. President Reagan's efforts to whittle the powers of the Environmental Protection Agency led to his appointment of controversial Anne Gorsuch to head the agency. Gorsuch had previously supported policies opposite to the goals of the EPA. When Gorsuch attempted to implement her policies, legal squabbles with Congress and political controversy ensued, which ultimately led to her resignation. To patch up the damage

[37]A good work on this point is Richard P. Nathan, *The Administrative Presidency* (New York: Wiley, 1983).

Gorsuch had done to his reputation, Reagan named a moderate and seasoned administrator, William Ruckelshaus, to run the agency. Ironically, Ruckelshaus demanded, and got, more freedom from the White House than Gorsuch had sought.

- *Issue orders.* Presidents can issue **executive orders** to agencies. More typically, presidential aides pass the word that "the President was wondering if. . . ." That usually suffices, although agency heads are reluctant to run afoul of Congress or the press on the basis of a broad presidential hint.

- *Tinker with an agency's budget.* The Office of Management and Budget is the president's own final authority on any agency's budget. The OMB's threats to cut here or add there will usually get an agency's attention. Each agency, however, has its constituents within and outside of Congress, and Congress, not the president, does the appropriating.

- *Reorganize an agency.* Although President Reagan promised, proposed, and pressured to abolish the Department of Energy and the Department of Education, he never succeeded, largely because each was in the hands of an entrenched bureaucracy, backed by elements in Congress and strong constituent groups. Reorganizing an agency is hard to do if it is a large and strong one, and often not worth the trouble if it is a small and weak one.

Congress Tries to Control the Bureaucracy Congress exhibits a paradoxical relationship with the bureaucracies. On the one hand (as Morris Fiorina has shown), members of Congress often find a big bureaucracy congenial.[38] Big government provides services to constituents. Moreover, when Congress lacks the answers to policy problems, it hopes the bureaucracies will find them. Unable itself, for example, to resolve the touchy issue of equality in intercollegiate athletics, Congress passed the ball to HEW. Unable to decide how to make workplaces safer, Congress produced OSHA. As you saw in Chapter 12, Congress is increasingly the problem-identifying branch of government, setting the bureaucratic agenda but letting the agencies decide how to implement the goals it sets.

On the other hand, Congress has found it hard to control the government it helped create. There are several measures Congress can take to oversee the bureaucracy, such as the following:

- *Influence the appointment of agency heads.* Even when senatorial approval of a presidential appointment is not required, members of Congress are not shy in putting forward their ideas about who should and should not be running the agencies. When congressional approval is required, members are doubly influential. Committee hearings on proposed appointments are almost guaranteed to produce lively debates if some members find the nominee's likely orientations unpalatable. University of Chicago Law School Dean Norval Morris, nominated by President Carter to head the Law Enforcement Assistance Administration, was shot down by anti-gun-control senators who found his writings about gun control objectionable.

- *Tinker with an agency's budget.* With the congressional power of the purse comes a mighty weapon for controlling bureaucratic behavior. At the same

[38]Morris Fiorina, *Congress: Keystone of the Washington Establishment,* 2nd ed. (New Haven, Conn.: Yale University Press, 1989).

Former FBI Director J. Edgar Hoover is an example of a powerful bureaucrat who worked outside the law. Hoover took over the new agency in 1924, and, after consolidating his power following World War II, began collecting information on presidents, members of Congress, and, later, liberal groups and civil rights leaders. Partly because they were afraid of what he might have in his files, elected officials were unwilling to control Hoover, who did not relinquish power until his death in 1972.

time, Congress knows that agencies perform services that its constituents demand. Too much budget cutting may make an agency more responsive, at the price of losing an interest group's support for a reelection campaign.

- *Hold hearings.* Committees and subcommittees can hold periodic hearings as part of their oversight job. Flagrant agency abuses of congressional intent can be paraded in front of the press, but responsibility for oversight typically goes to the very committee that created a program; the committee thus has some stake in showing the agency in a favorable light.

- *Rewrite the legislation or make it more detailed.* Every statute is filled with instructions to its administrators. To limit bureaucratic discretion and make its instructions clearer, Congress can write new or more detailed legislation. Still, even voluminous detail (as you saw in the case of the IRS) can never eliminate discretion.

Through these and other devices, Congress tries to keep bureaucracies under its control. Never entirely successful, Congress faces a constant battle to limit and channel the vast powers that it delegated to the bureaucracy in the first place.

Iron Triangles and Issue Networks   There is one other crucial explanation for the difficulty presidents and Congress face in controlling bureaucracies: agencies have strong ties to interest groups on the one hand and to congressional committees and subcommittees on the other. You learned in Chapter 10 that bureaucracies often enjoy cozy relationships with interest groups and with committees or subcommittees of Congress. When agencies, groups, and committees all depend on one another and are in close, frequent contact, they form what are sometimes called *iron triangles* or *subgovernments.*[39] These triads have advantages on all sides (see Figure 15.5).

There are plenty of examples of subgovernments at work. A subcommittee on aging, senior citizens' interest groups, and the Social Security Administration are likely to agree on the need for more Social Security benefits. Robert Rettig has recounted how an alliance slowly jelled around the issue of fighting cancer. It rested on three pillars: cancer researchers, agencies within the National Institutes of Health, and members of congressional health subcommittees.[40]

When these iron triangles shape policies for senior citizens or cancer or tobacco or any other interest, each policy is made independently of the others, sometimes even in contradiction to other policies. Moreover, their decisions tend to bind larger institutions, like Congress and the White House. Congress willingly lets its committees and subcommittees make decisions. The White House may be too busy wrestling with global concerns to fret over agricultural issues, older Americans, or cancer. If so, these subgovernments add a strong decentralizing and fragmenting element to the policy-making process.

Hugh Heclo points out that the system of subgovernments is now overlayed with an amorphous system of *issue networks*. There is now more widespread participation in bureaucratic policy-making, and many of the participants have technical policy expertise and are interested in issues because of intellectual or emotional commitments rather than material interests. Those interested in environmental protection, for example, have challenged formerly closed subgovernments on numerous fronts (see Chapter 19). This opening of the policy-making process complicates the calculations and decreases the predictability of those involved in the stable and relatively narrow relationships of subgovernments.[41]

The explosion of legislative subcommittees has greatly increased Congress' oversight activities. Numerous subcommittees may review the actions of a single agency. A half-dozen or more subcommittees may review the activities of the Department of Energy, the Department of Agriculture, or the Department of Commerce. Different committees may send different signals to the same agency. One may press for sterner enforcement, another for more exemptions. As the oversight process has become more vigorous, it has also become more fragmented, thus limiting the effectiveness of the bureaucracies.

Bureaucracy and the Size of Government

To many, the huge American bureaucracy is the prime example of a federal government growing out of control. As mentioned earlier in this chapter, some observers view the bureaucracy as acquisitive, constantly seeking to expand its size, budgets, and authority. Much of the political rhetoric against big government also adopts this line of argument, along with complaints about red tape, senseless

---

[39]On the role of subgovernments and iron triangles, see Randall Ripley and Grace Franklin, *Congress, Bureaucracy and Public Policy,* 4th ed. (Homewood, Ill.: Dorsey Press, 1984), 8–10.

[40]Robert Richard, *Cancer Crusade* (Princeton, N.J.: Princeton University Press, 1977).

[41]Hugh Heclo, "Issue Networks and the Executive Establishment," in *The New American Political System,* ed. Anthony King (Washington, D.C.: American Enterprise Institute, 1978), 87–124.

Figure 15.5 Iron Triangles: One Example

Iron triangles—composed of bureaucratic agencies, interest groups, and a congressional committee or sub-committee—dominate much domestic policy-making by combining internal consensus with a virtual monopoly on information in their area. The tobacco triangle is one example; there are dozens more. Iron triangles are characterized by mutual dependency, in which each element provides key services, information, or policy for the others. The arrows indicate some of these mutually helpful relationships.

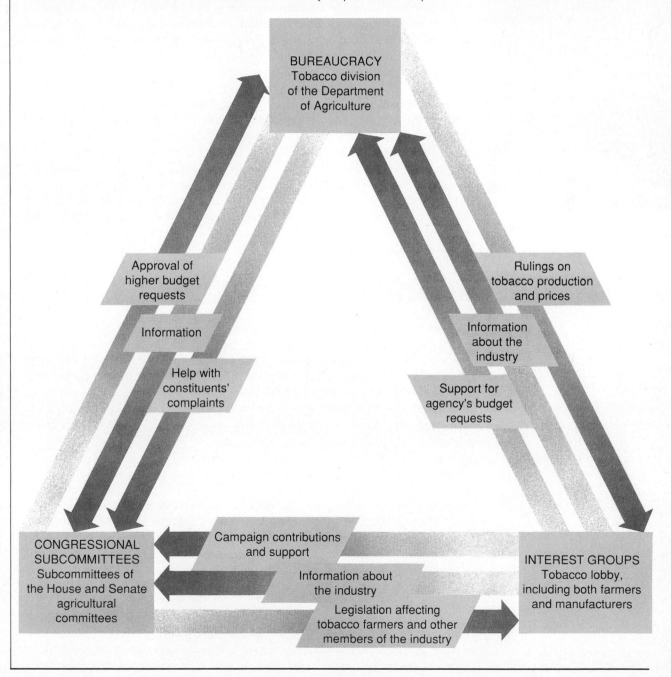

Bureaucrats are often ridiculed, but they perform vital, sometimes heroic, services. Here police and firefighters join forces to search for survivors after a department store roof collapsed in Brownsville, Texas.

regulations, and the like. It is easy to take pot shots at a faceless bureaucracy that usually cannot answer back.

One should keep in mind, however, that the federal bureaucracy, as Figure 15.1 illustrates, has not grown over the past two generations. Indeed, considering the fact that the population of the country has grown significantly over this period, the federal bureaucracy has actually *shrunk* in size relative to the population it serves.

Originally, the federal bureaucracy had a modest role of promoting the economy, defending the country, managing foreign affairs, providing justice, and delivering the mail. Its role gradually expanded to provide services to farmers, business, and workers. The discussion of federalism in Chapter 3 showed that as the economy and the society of the United States changed, additional demands were made on government. Government—and the bureaucracy—is now expected to play an active role in dealing with social and economic problems. Thus, as stated earlier in this chapter, a good case can be made that the bureaucracy is actually too *small* for many of the tasks currently assigned to it, tasks ranging from the control of illicit drugs to the protection of the environment.

In addition, it is important to keep in mind that when the president and Congress chose to deregulate certain areas of the economy or cut taxes, the bureaucracy could not and did not prevent it from doing so. The question of what and how much the federal government should do—and thus how big the bureaucracy should be—is answered primarily at the polls and in Congress, the White House, and the courts—not by "faceless bureaucrats."

SUMMARY

Bureaucracies shape policy as administrators, as implementors, and as regulators. In this chapter you examined who bureaucrats are, how they got there, and what they do. Today most bureaucrats working for the federal government got their jobs through the Civil Service system, although a few at the very top are appointed by the president.

In general, there are four types of bureaucracies: the cabinet departments, the regulatory agencies, the government corporations, and the independent executive agencies.

As policy makers, bureaucrats play three key roles. First, they are policy implementors, translating legislative policy goals into programs. Policy implementation does not always work well, and when it does not, bureaucrats usually take the blame, whether they deserve it or not. Second, bureaucrats administer public policy. Much of administration involves a routine, but almost all bureaucrats still have some discretion. Third, bureaucrats are regulators. Congress increasingly delegates large amounts of power to bureaucratic agencies and expects them to develop rules and regulations. Scarcely a nook or cranny of American society or the American economy escapes the long reach of bureaucratic regulation.

Although bureaucrats are not elected, bureaucracies are not necessarily undemocratic. It is essential that bureaucracies be controlled by elected decision makers, but presidential or congressional control over bureaucracies is difficult. One reason is that bureaus have strong support from interest groups, a factor that contributes to pluralism because interest groups try to forge common links with bureaucracies and congressional committees. These iron triangles tend to decentralize policy-making, thereby contributing to hyperpluralism.

KEY TERMS

patronage	plum book	street-level bureaucrats
Pendleton Act	bureaucracy	regulation
civil service	independent regulatory agency	command-and-control
merit principle	government corporations	policy
Hatch Act	independent executive agen-	incentive system
Office of Personnel	cies	executive orders
Management (OPM)	implementation	
GS (General Schedule)	standard operating procedures	
rating	administrative discretion	

FOR FURTHER READING

Arnold, Peri E. *Making the Managerial Presidency.* Princeton, N.J.: Princeton University Press, 1986. A careful examination of efforts to reorganize the Federal bureaucracy.

Edwards, George C., III. *Implementing Public Policy.* Washington, D.C.: Congressional Quarterly Press, 1980. A good review of the issues involved in implementation.

Derthick, Martha, and Paul J. Quirk. *The Politics of Deregulation.* Washington, D.C.: Brookings Institution, 1985. Explains why advocates of deregulation prevailed over the special interests that benefited from regulation.

Goodsell, Charles T. *The Case for Bureaucracy.* Chatham, N.J.: Chatham House, 1985. A strong case on behalf of the effectiveness of bureaucracy.

Gormley, William T., Jr. *Taming the Bureaucracy.* Princeton, N.J.: Princeton University Press, 1989. Examines remedies for controlling bureaucracies.

Heclo, Hugh. *A Government of Strangers: Executive Powers in Washington.* Washington, D.C.: The Brookings Institution, 1977. A study of the top executives of the federal government, who constitute (says the author) a "government of strangers."

Peterson, Paul, Barry G. Rabe, and Kenneth K. Wong. *When Federalism Works.* Washington, D.C.: The Brookings Institution, 1986. Examines federal grant-in-aid programs and explains why they are implemented better in some areas than in others.

Pressman, Jeffrey, and Aaron Wildavsky. *Implementation,* 3rd ed. Berkeley, Calif.: University of California Press, 1984. The classic—and often witty—study of implementation.

Rourke, Francis E. *Bureaucratic Power in National Policymaking, 4th ed.* Boston: Little, Brown, 1986. Classic work on bureaucratic politics.

Rourke, Francis E. *Bureaucracy, Politics, and Public Policy,* 3rd ed. Boston: Little, Brown, 1984. An excellent introduction to the role of bureaucracy in policy-making.

Savas, E. S. *Privatization: The Key to Better Government.* Chatham, N.J.: Chatham House, 1987. A conservative economist's argument that many public services performed by bureaucracies would be better handled by the private sector.

Tolchin, Susan J., and Martin Tolchin. *Dismantling America.* Boston: Houghton Mifflin, 1983. A powerful critique of deregulation philosophy, politics, and practice.

Wilson, James Q., ed. *The Politics of Regulation.* New York: Basic Books, 1980. Excellent essays on regulation and deregulation.

16

THE COURTS

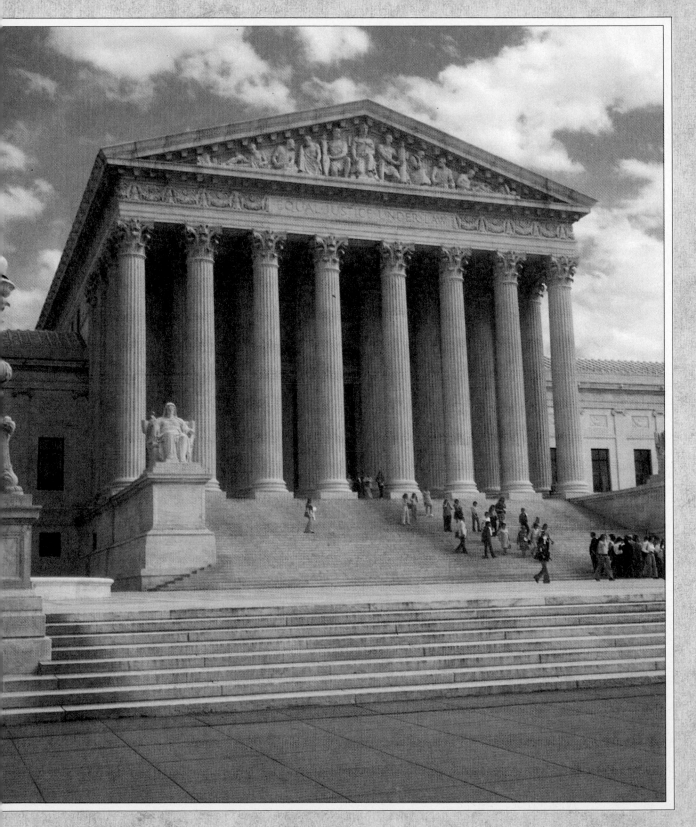

In 1986 the legislature of the state of Missouri passed a law prohibiting the use of state money to fund abortions. On April 26, 1989, the state's attorney general, William Webster, found himself defending the constitutionality of the law before the U.S. Supreme Court in the case of *Webster* v. *Reproductive Health Services*. He was not alone. Also speaking on behalf of the law was Charles Fried, a Harvard University law professor and former solicitor general of the United States, who was aiding Webster on behalf of the Bush administration. For years Fried had argued that the Constitution provided no one a right to an abortion, much less an abortion at public expense.

Frank Susman, an attorney from St. Louis, defended abortion rights and argued that the Missouri law was unconstitutional. He had been involved in representing abortion rights organizations for nearly two decades. The *Webster* case was his fifth appearance before the Supreme Court.

The attorneys for both sides had engaged in extensive preparation, but their supporters were not content to rely solely on arguments in the courtroom. On April 9, three hundred thousand abortion rights advocates organized by the National Organization of Women, the American Civil Liberties Association, and Planned Parenthood marched in support of the *Roe* v. *Wade* decision protecting abortion rights and made sure their parade route passed directly in front of the Supreme Court building. The National Abortion Rights League organized a drive to send a million postcards to the Court, took out ads in *Time* and other magazines, and even hired polling firms and media consultants to aid its cause. Those opposed to abortion engaged in similar efforts, including spending $150,000 for a four-page insert in *USA Today* the day before the case was heard in the Supreme Court. In addition, the two sides in the debate bombarded the Court with legal briefs from advocacy organizations on both sides, as well as from public officials, scientists, historians, and physicians.

Inside the Supreme Court building, often referred to as the "Marble Palace," attention was focused on Justice Sandra Day O'Connor, who was widely perceived as holding the balance of power on the abortion issue. Webster, Fried, and Susman all shaped their arguments to win her vote. She had also been the target of a massive lobbying campaign that had

deluged her office with letters. The mail was so heavy at times that some of her professional correspondence was lost in the avalanche of communications on abortions.

On July 3 the Court handed down its decision. As you learned in Chapter 4, the decision upheld the Missouri law but did not overturn the basic right to an abortion. Justice O'Connor was indeed the swing vote, supporting both abortion rights and limitations.

Reaction from both sides was swift, with antiabortion activists praising the Court and advocates of abortion rights criticizing it. The latter were energized to become more active in the electoral arena, however, and achieved several notable successes in elections in 1989, including the election of Douglas Wilder (an abortion rights supporter) as governor of Virginia.

The close connection between law and politics in the *Webster* case characterizes the American judicial system. Of all the nations in the world, the United States has the most powerful courts. Many significant issues of public policy come before them in one form or another. With so much at stake in judicial decisions, it is important to understand how the courts work within the American political system.

*I*f you happen to visit the Supreme Court, you will first be impressed by the marble Supreme Court building, with the motto "Equal Justice under Law" engraved over its imposing columns. The Court's surroundings and procedures suggest the nineteenth century. The justices, clothed in black robes, take their seats at the bench in front of a red velvet curtain. Behind the bench there are still spitoons, one for each justice. (Today the spitoons are used as wastebaskets.) The few cases the Court selects for oral arguments are scheduled for about an hour each. Lawyers arguing before the Court often wear frock coats and striped trousers. They find a goose quill pen on their desk, bought by the Court from a Virginia supplier. (They may take it with them as a memento of their day in court.) Each side is normally allotted thirty minutes to present its case. The justices may, and do, interrupt the lawyers with questions. When the time is up, a discreet red light goes on at the lawyer's lectern.

However impressive the Supreme Court may be, only the tiniest fraction of American judicial policy is made there. To be sure, the Court decides a handful of key issues each year. Some will shape people's lives, even deciding issues of life and death. In recent years the Court has authorized abortion, upheld busing to end school segregation, vacillated about capital punishment, upheld some forms of affirmative action programs while rejecting others, and ordered President Nixon to release secret White House tapes during the Watergate affair. In addition to the Supreme Court, there are twelve federal courts of appeal, ninety-one federal district courts, and thousands of state and local courts. It is in these less noticed courts that the great bulk of American legal business is transacted.

The American court system is complex, just as the federal system itself is complex. There are state court systems and a federal court system. Most cases begin and end in one or the other system, usually the former. Sometimes judges' and juries' decisions are appealed to a higher court, but no one has any constitutional right to take a case to the Supreme Court. The Supreme Court hears only a very small percentage of all cases brought to court in America. This chapter will discuss all sorts of courts, both state and federal, as well as all sorts of judges—the men and women in black robes who are important judicial policymakers.

THE NATURE OF THE JUDICIAL SYSTEM

The judicial system in the United States is, at least in principle, an adversarial one in which the courts provide an arena for two parties to bring their conflict before an impartial arbiter (a judge). The system is based on the theory that justice will emerge out of the struggle between two contending points of view. In reality, most cases never reach trial because they are settled by agreements reached out of court.

Federal judges are restricted by the Constitution to deciding "cases or controversies," that is, actual disputes rather than hypothetical ones. They do not issue advisory opinions on what they think, in the abstract, may be the meaning or constitutionality of a law. Two parties must bring a case to them. This arrangement also illustrates that the judiciary is essentially passive, dependent on others to take the initiative.

Another constraint on the courts is that they may decide only **justiciable disputes.** Conflicts must not only arise from actual cases but also be capable of being settled by legal methods. Thus one would not go to court to determine whether or not Congress should fund the Strategic Defense Initiative (SDI), for the matter could not be resolved through legal methods or knowledge.

The Courts at Work

To better understand the judicial system, take a look at a typical day in the courts of a major American city, San Antonio, Texas. It was a hot day in September, and both state and federal courts were in session in the Bexar County Courthouse. Two full floors of courtrooms were busy. There, as in all American courts, the task of the judges is to apply and interpret the law in a particular **case.** Every case is a dispute between a **plaintiff** and a **defendant,** the former bringing some charge against the latter. Sometimes the plaintiff is the government itself, which may bring a charge against an individual or a corporation. The government may charge the defendant with the brutal murder of Jones, or the XYZ Corporation with illegal trade practices. All cases are identified with the name of the plaintiff first and of the defendant second, for example, *State* v. *Smith* or *Anderson* v. *Baker*. The task of the judge or judges is to apply the law to the case, determining whether the plaintiff or the defendant is legally correct. In many (but not all) cases, a **jury,** a group of citizens (usually twelve), is responsible for the determination of guilt.

Two kinds of cases were being heard in the Bexar County Courthouse: *criminal law* and *civil law.* In **criminal law** cases an individual is charged with violating a specific law. The offense may be harmful to an individual or to society as a whole, but in either case it warrants punishment, such as imprisonment or a fine. In San Antonio, as in other urban courts, one often sees criminal defendants brought from the county jail to court in groups, chained together, awaiting their time before the court.

In Judge Raymond Wietzel's court, a Mr. Hernandez was unchained from his fellow prisoners. A deputy sheriff escorted Hernandez to where his lawyer stood, in front of the judge's bench. Judge Wietzel asked if Hernandez understood his rights and the bargain he was about to make, and a district attorney announced the plea bargain (see Chapter 4) in which Hernandez agreed to plead guilty to a reduced charge to avoid a trial. The judge accepted the plea and formally handed Hernandez over to the custody of state corrections officers. Down the hall, Judge Rickhoff was presiding over a jury trial. Four beefy defendants were accused of knifing and beating up two men at Big J's Lounge.

Civil law involves no charge of criminality, no charge that a law has been violated. It concerns a dispute between two parties (one of whom, of course, may be the government itself) and defines relationships between them. It consists of both statutes and common law (the accumulation of judicial decisions). In the 225th District Court, for example, Judge Chapa was hearing the case of *Chavez* v. *Edgewood School District*. Ms. Chavez was suing the school district over a worker's compensation issue. An employee of the district, she had lifted a box and claimed to have injured herself.

Across town in Hemisfair Plaza, the U.S. District Court for the Western District of Texas was in session that afternoon. A Mr. Gonzales was suing the San Antonio Police Department. His rights under federal civil rights laws had been violated, he claimed, because police used excessive force to subdue him when he was arrested. A police officer was testifying that ample force had been required to arrest Gonzales, who had even bitten one officer.

Just as it is important not to confuse criminal and civil law, it is important not to confuse state and federal courts. The vast majority of all civil and criminal cases involve state law and are tried in state courts. Civil cases such as divorce and criminal cases such as burglary normally begin and end in the state, not the federal, courts.

The American court system is complex. The august serenity and majesty of the U.S. Supreme Court is a far cry from the grimy urban court where strings of defendants are bused from the local jail for their day—often only a few minutes— in court (see "In Focus: Justice at the Local Level"). One important distinction among American courts comes in the matter of jurisdiction. Courts with **original jurisdiction** are those in which a case is heard first, usually in

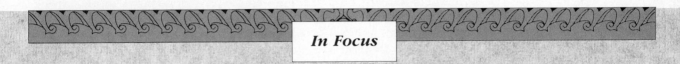

In Focus

Justice at the Local Level

Americans' impressions of the judicial system is often shaped by their perceptions of the Supreme Court or by television coverage of some major trial. Citizens expect the judicial system to be fair, impartial, consistent, and evenhanded. Most judicial business is handled by local courts, however, and many studies have indicated that great differences in procedure and punishment exist from place to place at the local level.

Political scientists James Eisenstein, Roy Flemming, and Peter Nardulli looked carefully at nine local courts in Pennsylvania, Michigan, and Illinois. The courts they studied handled felony cases, that is, such serious crimes as armed robbery, burglary, larceny, and selling hard drugs. They found some similarities but also many basic differences.

Despite the seriousness of the felony crimes, jury trials were rare. Most defendants pleaded guilty. The courts followed different routes to arrive at this common outcome, however. In some courts, defendants routinely pleaded guilty to the charge originally brought against them by the prosecutor. In other

courts defendants pleaded guilty to less serious or fewer charges than they were first accused of committing. These divergent prosecutor policies resulted from how carefully or leniently the prosecutor's office charged felony defendants and how much discretion the courtroom prosecutors had.

Sentences and the speed of justice also varied. In one Illinois court only 25 percent of the burglary defendants were given prison sentences, but in a Michigan court over 70 percent of these defendants were sent to state prisons. Overall, prison sentences were longer in Michigan courts than in Illinois or Pennsylvania courts. Justice was slow in Michigan, however. The fastest Michigan court took nearly twice as long to conclude its cases as the courts in the other two states.

American federalism virtually guarantees such diversity in allocating justice. Since most justice is and always has been handled at the local level, the concept of "equal justice under law" is not an accurate portrayal of a major part of the American judicial system.

Source: James Eisenstein, Roy B. Flemming, and Peter F. Nardulli, *The Contours of Justice: Communities and Their Courts* (Boston: Little, Brown, 1988).

a trial. These are the courts that determine the facts about a case. The great majority of judicial business is transacted in courts of original jurisdiction—the county or municipal courts first hear a traffic charge, a divorce case, or a criminal charge. Most judicial business also ends in these courts. More than 90 percent of court cases begin and end in the court of original jurisdiction.

Lawyers can sometimes appeal an adverse decision to a higher court for another decision. Courts with **appellate jurisdiction** hear cases brought to them on appeal from a lower court. Appellate courts do not review the factual record, only the legal issues involved. At the state level the appellate process normally ends with the state's highest court of appeal, usually called the state supreme court. Appeals from a state high court can be taken only to the U.S. Supreme Court.

Participants in the Judicial System

Although judges are the policymakers of the American judicial system, they are not the only participants. In judicial policy-making, only a small part of the action takes place in the courtroom, and only a few persons participate: the judge; the **litigants** (the plaintiff and the defendant), nervously watching a process they do not always understand; the ever-present lawyers; and sometimes a jury, paying close attention to the proceedings.

Litigants end up in court for a variety of reasons. Some are reluctant participants—the defendant in a criminal case, for example. Others are eager for their day in court. For some, the courts can be a potent weapon in the search for a preferred policy. Atheist Madlyn Murray O'Hair was an enthusiastic litigant, always ready to take the government to court for (as she saw it) promoting religion.

Not everyone can challenge a law, however. Litigants must have what is called **standing to sue.** Essentially this phrase means that litigants must have serious interest in a case, which is typically determined by whether or not they have sustained or are in immediate danger of sustaining a direct and substantial injury from another party or an action of government. Except in cases pertaining to governmental support for religion, merely being a taxpayer and being opposed to a law do not provide the standing necessary to challenge that law in court. Nevertheless, Congress and the Supreme Court have liberalized the rules for standing, making it somewhat easier for citizens to challenge governmental or corporate actions in court.

In recent years there has been some broadening of the concept of standing to sue. **Class action suits** permit a small number of people to sue on behalf of all other people similarly situated. These suits may be useful in cases as varied as civil rights, in which a few persons seek an end to discriminatory practices on behalf of all who might be discriminated against, and environmental protection, in which a few persons may sue a polluting industry on behalf of all who are affected by the air or water it pollutes. Following an explosion of such cases, the Supreme Court in 1974 began making it more difficult to file these suits.

Because they know well the power of the courts to shape policy, interest groups often seek out litigants whose cases seem particularly strong. Few groups have been more successful in finding good cases and good litigants than the National Association for the Advancement of Colored People, which selected the school board of Topeka, Kansas, and a young schoolgirl named Linda Brown as one of the litigants in *Brown* v. *Board of Education.* NAACP legal counsel Thurgood Marshall (later a Supreme Court justice) believed that Topeka presented a stronger case than other school districts in the United States. The American Civil Liberties Union, an ardent defender of individual liberties, is another interest group that is always seeking good cases and good litigants. One ACLU attorney, stressing that principle took priority over a particular client, even admitted that the ACLU's clients are often "pretty scurvy little creatures. . . . It's the principle that we're going to be able to use these people for that's important."[1] (For an example, see Chapter 4 about the case of the Nazis who tried to march in Skokie, Illinois.)

Lawyers have become another indispensable actor in the judicial system. Law is the nation's fastest growing profession.[2] The United States counted about one hundred thousand lawyers in 1960 but about seven hundred thousand in 1990, one for every thirty-six Americans. Lawyers busily translate policies into legal language and then enforce them or challenge them. Jimmy Carter's secretary of labor, Ray Marshall—a mere economics professor by trade—told of his problems with his department's lawyers when he was trying to understand one regulation:

Sometimes ordinary people find themselves involved in extraordinary court decisions. Linda Brown was a plaintiff in Brown v. Board of Education, *a key civil rights case in which the Supreme Court overturned its earlier* Plessy v. Ferguson *ruling that had legalized segregation.*

> I remember that I called in one of our lawyers—and I've since learned that we have 400 of them—and asked him to bring me the law and let me read it.
>
> He said, "It wouldn't do you any good. You couldn't understand it." I said, "Well, I'm not illiterate, why can't I understand it?" He just said flatly, "Well, you just can't." So I said, "Well, do you understand it?" And he replied, "Yes, but I'm a lawyer."
>
> That stopped me for a moment. So I tried another tack. "Well, can you write it so that I can understand it?" He agreed that he could write it so I could understand it. But, he said, "We wouldn't be able to enforce it, then."[3]

Lawyers create the need for more lawyers.

Once lawyers were mostly available for the rich. Today public interest law firms can sometimes handle legal problems of the poor and middle classes. The federally funded Legal Service Corporation employs lawyers to serve the legal needs of the poor, though the Reagan administration made drastic cuts in legal aid. Some employers and unions now provide legal insurance, which works like medical insurance. Members with legal needs—for a divorce, a consumer complaint, or whatever—can secure legal aid through prepaid plans. As a result, more people than ever before can take their problems to the courts.

The audience for this judicial drama is a large and attentive one that includes interest groups, the press (a close observer of the judicial process, especially of its more sensational aspects), and the public, who often have very strong opinions about how the process works. All these participants—plaintiffs, defendants, lawyers, interest groups, and others—play a role in the judicial drama, even though many of their activities take place outside the courtroom. How

[1]Quoted in Lawrence C. Baum, *The Supreme Court,* 2nd. ed. (Washington, D.C.: Congressional Quarterly Press, 1985), 72.

[2]Barbara Curran, *Supplement to the Lawyers' Statistical Report: The U.S. Legal Profession in 1985* (Chicago: American Bar Foundation, 1986).

[3]Quoted in *Current Public Policy Research* (May 1977): 8.

they arrive in the courtroom and which court they go to reflect the structure of the court system.

The central participants in the judicial system are, of course, the judges. Once on the bench they must draw upon their backgrounds and beliefs to guide their decision making. Some, for example, will be more supportive of abortion or of prayer in the public schools than others will. Because presidents and others involved in the appointment process know perfectly well that judges are not neutral automatons who methodically and literally interpret the law, they work diligently to place candidates of their choice on the bench. Who are the men and women who serve as federal judges and justices (only members of the Supreme Court are called justices; all others are called judges), and how did they obtain their positions?

THE POLITICS OF JUDICIAL SELECTION

Appointing a federal judge or a Supreme Court justice is a president's chance to leave an enduring mark on the American legal system. Guaranteed by the Constitution the right to serve "during good behavior," federal judges and justices enjoy, for all practical purposes, lifetime positions. They may be removed only by conviction of impeachment, which has occurred only seven times in the two centuries under the Constitution. No Supreme Court justice has ever been removed from office, although one, Samuel Chase, was tried but not convicted by the Senate in 1805. Nor can members of the federal judiciary have their salaries reduced, a stipulation that further insulates them from political pressures.

Although the president nominates persons to fill judicial slots, the Senate must confirm each nomination by majority vote. Since the judiciary is a coequal branch, the upper house of the legislature sees no reason to be especially deferential to the executive's recommendations. Thus the president's discretion, because of the Senate's role, ends up being less than it appears.

The Lower Courts

The customary manner in which the Senate disposes of state-level federal judicial nominations is through **senatorial courtesy.** Under this unwritten tradition (which began under George Washington in 1789), nominations for these positions are not confirmed when opposed by a senator from the state in which the nominee is to serve (all states have at least one federal district court). In the case of courts of appeal judges nominees are not confirmed if opposed by a senator from the state of the nominee's residence, if the senator is of the same party as the president.

To invoke the right of senatorial courtesy, the relevant senator usually simply states a general reason for opposition. Other senators then honor their colleague's views and oppose the nomination, regardless of their personal evaluations or the candidate's merits.

Because of the strength of this informal practice, presidents usually check carefully with the relevant senator or senators ahead of time so that they will avoid making a nomination that will fail to be confirmed. In many instances this is tantamount to giving the power of nomination to these senators. Typically, when there is a vacancy for a federal district judgeship, the one or two senators of the president's party from the state where the judge will serve suggest one or more names to the attorney general and the president. If neither senator is of the president's party, the party's state congresspersons or other state party leaders may make suggestions.

The Department of Justice and the Federal Bureau of Investigation then conduct competency and background checks on these persons, and the president usually selects a nominee from those who survive the screening process. It is difficult for the president to reject in favor of someone else the recommendation of the party's senator if the person recommended clears the hurdles of professional standing and integrity. In one celebrated case, President Kennedy had to agree to the appointment of Mississippi Senator James O. Eastland's old college roommate—and a racial reactionary—to the federal bench there. Thus the Constitution is turned on its head, and the Senate ends up making nominations, which the president then approves.

Others have input in judicial selection as well. The Department of Justice may ask sitting judges, usually federal judges, to evaluate prospective nominees. Sitting judges may also initiate recommendations to advance or retard someone's chances of being nominated. In addition, candidates for the nomination are often active on their own behalf. They have to alert the relevant parties that they desire the position and orchestrate a campaign of support. As one appellate judge observed, "People don't just get judgeships without seeking them. Anybody who thinks judicial office seeks the man is mistaken. There's not a man on the court who didn't do what he thought needed to be done."[4]

The president usually has more influence in the selection of judges to the federal courts of appeal than to federal district courts. Since the decisions of appellate courts are generally more significant than those of lower courts, the president naturally takes a greater interest in appointing people to these courts. At the same time, individual senators are in a weaker position to determine who the nominee will be because the jurisdiction of an appeals court encompasses several states. Although custom and pragmatic politics require that these judgeships be apportioned among the states in a circuit, the president has some discretion in doing this and therefore has a greater role in recruiting appellate judges than district court judges. Even here, however, senators from the state in which the candidate resides may be able to veto a nomination.

Jimmy Carter attempted to alter the role of senators in the judicial selection process by seeking more leeway in the selection of appellate court judges and by establishing the U.S. Circuit Judge Nominating Commission to identify the best qualified persons for these courts. He also urged senators to employ merit panels in reaching their recommendations on district court judges. These efforts were abandoned, however, when Ronald Reagan entered the White House.

The Supreme Court

The president is vitally interested in the Supreme Court because of the importance of its work, and will generally be intimately involved in the recruitment

[4]Quoted in J. Woodford Howard, Jr., *Courts of Appeals in the Federal Judicial System: A Study of the Second, Fifth, and District of Columbia Circuits* (Princeton, N.J.: Princeton University Press, 1981), 101.

process. Nominations to the Court may be a president's most important legacy to the nation.

A president cannot have much impact on the Court unless there are vacancies to fill. Although on the average there has been an opening on the Supreme Court every two years, there is a substantial variance around this mean. Franklin D. Roosevelt had to wait five years before he could nominate a justice. All the while he was faced with a Court that found much of his New Deal legislation unconstitutional. In more recent years, Jimmy Carter was never able to nominate a justice. Indeed, between 1972 and 1984 there were only two vacancies on the Court. Nevertheless, Richard Nixon was able to nominate four justices in his first three years in office, and Ronald Reagan had the opportunity to add three new members.

When the chief justice's position is vacant, the president may nominate either someone already on the Court or someone from outside it to fill the position. Usually presidents choose the latter course to widen their range of options, but if they decide to elevate a sitting associate justice—as President Reagan did with William Rehnquist in 1986—he or she must go through a new confirmation hearing by the Senate Judiciary Committee.

The president operates under fewer constraints in nominating members to the Supreme Court than to the lower courts. Although many of the same actors are present in the case of Supreme Court nominations, their influence is typically quite different. The president usually relies on the attorney general and the Department of Justice to identify and screen candidates for the Court. Sitting justices often try to influence the nominations of their future colleagues, but presidents feel no obligation to follow their advice.

Senators play a much less prominent role in the recruitment of Supreme Court justices than in the selection of lower court judges. No senator can claim that the jurisdiction of the Court falls within the realm of his or her special expertise, interest, or sphere of influence. Thus presidents typically consult with senators from the state of residence of a nominee after they have decided whom to select. At this point senators are unlikely to oppose a nomination, because they like having their state receive the honor and are well aware that the president can simply select someone from another state.

Candidates for nomination usually keep a low profile. Little can be accomplished through aggressive politicking, and because of the Court's standing, it might offend those who play important roles in selecting nominees. The ABA's Standing Committee on the Federal Judiciary has played a varied but typically modest role at the Supreme Court level. Presidents have not generally been willing to allow the committee to prescreen candidates before their nominations are announced.

Through 1990, 104 persons have served on the Supreme Court. Of the 143 nominees, 3 were nominated and confirmed twice, 8 were confirmed but never served, and 28 failed to secure Senate confirmation. Presidents, then, have failed 20 percent of the time to appoint the nominees of their choice to the Court, a percentage much higher than that for any other federal position.

Thus, although home-state senators do not play prominent roles in the selection process for the Court, the Senate as a whole does. Through its Judiciary Committee it may probe a nominee's judicial philosophy in great detail.

Six nominees have failed to receive Senate confirmation in this century (see Table 16.1). The last two of these occurred in 1987. On June 26, 1987, Justice

Table 16.1 Twentieth-Century Senate Rejections of Supreme Court Nominees

NOMINEE	YEAR	PRESIDENT
John J. Parker	1930	Hoover
Abe Fortas[a]	1968	Johnson
Clement F. Haynsworth, Jr.	1969	Nixon
G. Harrold Carswell	1970	Nixon
Robert H. Bork	1987	Reagan
Douglas H. Ginsburg[a]	1987	Reagan

[a]Nominations withdrawn. Fortas was serving on the Court as an associate justice and was nominated to be chief justice.

Lewis Powell announced his retirement from the Supreme Court. President Reagan had already been able to elevate Justice William Rehnquist to the position of chief justice and had also nominated Sandra Day O'Connor and Antonin Scalia. With yet another appointee, he would have a solid bloc of conservative votes on the Court for years to come.

Reagan nominated Judge Robert Bork to fill the vacancy. Everyone agreed that Bork was highly intelligent and a distinguished legal scholar; he had also served in the Justice Department (he was the one who had fired special Watergate prosecutor Archibald Cox). At this point, however, agreement ended.

Bork testified before the Senate Judiciary Committee for twenty-three hours. At the end, his supporters portrayed him as a distinguished, scholarly man who would practice *judicial restraint,* deferring to Congress and state legislatures and adhering to the **precedents** of the Supreme Court—the way similar cases had been decided in the past. Conversely, his opponents saw him as an extreme judicial activist who would use the Supreme Court to achieve conservative political ends, reversing decades of court decisions. A wide range of interest groups entered the fray, mostly in opposition to the nominee, and in the end, following a bitter floor debate, the Senate rejected the president's nomination by a vote of forty-two to fifty-eight.

Six days after the Senate vote on Bork, the president nominated Judge Douglas H. Ginsburg to the high court. Just nine days later, however, Ginsburg withdrew his nomination after disclosures that he had used marijuana while a law professor at Harvard. It was not until the spring of 1988 that Reagan was finally successful in filling the vacancy with Judge Anthony Kennedy.

Nominations are most likely to run into trouble under certain conditions. Presidents whose parties are in the minority in the Senate or who make a nomination at the end of their terms face a greatly increased probability of substantial opposition. Equally important, opponents of a nomination usually must be able to question a nominee's competence or ethics in order to defeat a nomination. Ideological opposition is generally not enough, as the case of Chief Justice William Rehnquist, who was strongly opposed by liberals, illustrates. Questions of competence and ethics provide a rationale for opposition that can attract moderates and make ideological protests seem less partisan.

THE BACKGROUNDS OF JUDGES AND JUSTICES

What is the result of this complex process of judicial recruitment? What kind of people are selected? The Constitution sets no special requirements for judges, but most observers conclude that the federal judiciary is composed of a distinguished group of men and women. Competence and ethical behavior are important to presidents for reasons beyond merely obtaining Senate confirmation of their judicial nominees. Skilled and honorable judges and justices reflect well on the president and will likely do so for many years. Moreover, they are more effective representatives of the president's views.

Although the criteria of competence and character screen out some possible candidates, they still leave a wide field from which to choose. Other characteristics then play prominent roles.

The judges serving on the federal district and circuit courts are not a representative sample of American people (see Table 16.2). They are all lawyers (although this is not a constitutional requirement), and they are overwhelmingly white males. Jimmy Carter appointed forty women, thirty-seven African Americans, and sixteen Hispanics to the federal bench, more than all previous presidents combined. Ronald Reagan did not continue this trend, although he was the first to appoint a woman to the Supreme Court. His administration placed a higher priority on screening candidates on the basis of ideology than on screening them in terms of ascriptive characteristics.

Federal judges have typically held office as a judge or prosecutor, and often they have been involved in partisan politics. This involvement is generally what brings them to the attention of senators and the Department of Justice when

Table 16.2	Backgrounds of Recent Federal District and Appeals Court Judges

CHARACTERISTIC	APPEALS COURT		DISTRICT COURT	
	Reagan	Carter	Reagan	Carter
Total number of nominees	78	56	290	202
Occupation (%)				
Politics/government	6.4	5.4	12.8	4.4
Judiciary	55.1	46.6	37.2	40.3
Large law firm	12.9	10.8	17.7	14.0
Moderate size firm	10.3	16.1	19.3	19.8
Solo or small firm	1.3	5.4	10.4	13.9
Professor of law	12.8	14.3	2.1	3.0
Other	1.3	1.8	0.7	0.5
Experience (%)				
Judicial	60.3	53.6	46.6	54.5
Prosecutorial	28.2	32.1	44.1	38.6
Neither one	34.6	37.5	28.3	28.2
Party (%)				
Democrat	—	82.1	4.8	92.6
Republican	97.4	7.1	93.4	4.4
Independent	1.3	10.7	1.7	2.9
Past party activism (%)	69.2	73.2	58.6	60.9
Religious origin or affiliation (%)				
Protestant	55.1	60.7	60.0	60.4
Catholic	30.8	23.2	30.4	27.7
Jewish	14.1	16.1	9.3	11.9
Ethnicity or race (%)				
White	97.4	78.6	92.4	78.7
Black	1.3	16.1	2.1	13.9
Hispanic	1.3	3.6	4.8	6.9
Asian	—	1.8	0.7	0.5
Sex (%)				
Male	94.9	80.4	91.7	85.6
Female	5.1	19.6	8.3	14.4
Average Age	50.0	51.9	48.7	49.7

Source: Sheldon Goldman, "Reagan's Judicial Legacy," *Judicature* 72 (April-May 1989): 318–30.

they seek nominees for judgeships. As former U.S. Attorney General and Circuit Court Judge Griffin Bell once remarked, "For me, becoming a federal judge wasn't very difficult. I managed John F. Kennedy's presidential campaign in Georgia. Two of my oldest and closest friends were senators from Georgia. And I was campaign manager and special unpaid counsel for the governor."[5]

Like their colleagues on the lower federal courts, Supreme Court justices share characteristics that are quite unlike those of the typical American and that

[5]Quoted in Nina Totenberg, "Will Judges Be Chosen Rationally?" *Judicature* 60 (August/September 1976): 93.

Most members of the federal judiciary have had backgrounds quite unlike those of typical Americans. Thurgood Marshall is the only African American ever to sit on the Supreme Court, and Sandra Day O'Connor is the only woman. All other members of the Court have been white males, most of them from the upper-middle and upper classes.

qualify them as an elite group. All have been lawyers, and all but two (Thurgood Marshall, nominated in 1967, and Sandra Day O'Connor, nominated in 1981) have been white males. Most have been in their fifties and sixties when they took office, from the upper-middle to upper class, and Protestants.[6]

Race and sex have become more salient criteria in recent years. In the 1980 presidential campaign Ronald Reagan even promised to appoint a woman to the first vacancy on the Court if he were elected. Women and minorities may serve on all federal courts more frequently in the future because of increased opportunity for legal education and decreased prejudice against their judicial activity, as well as because of their increasing political clout.

Geography was once a prominent criterion for selection to the Court, but it is no longer very important. Presidents do like to spread the slots around, however, as was the case when Richard Nixon decided that he wanted to nominate a southerner. At various times there have been what some have termed a "Jewish seat" and a "Catholic seat" on the Court, but these guidelines are not binding on the president. For example, after a half-century of having a Jewish justice, the Court has not had one since 1969.

Typically justices have held high administrative or judicial positions before moving to the Supreme Court (see Table 16.3). Most have had some experience as a judge, often at the appellate level, and many have worked for the Department of Justice. Some have held elective office, and a few have had no government service but have been distinguished attorneys. The fact that many justices, including some of the most distinguished ones, have not had previous judicial

[6]See John Schmidhauser, *Judges and Justices: The Federal Appellate Judiciary* (Boston: Little, Brown, 1978).

experience may seem surprising, but the unique work of the Court renders this background much less important than it might be for other appellate courts.

Partisanship is an important influence on the selection of judges and justices. Only 13 of 104 members of the Supreme Court have been nominated by presidents of a different party. Moreover, many of the thirteen exceptions were actually close to the president in ideology, as was the case in Richard Nixon's appointment of Lewis Powell. Herbert Hoover's nomination of Benjamin Cardozo seems to be one of the few cases in which partisanship was completely dominated by merit as a criterion for selection. Usually more than 90 percent of presidents' judicial nominations are of members of their own parties.

The role of partisanship is not really surprising. Most of a president's acquaintances are made through the party, and there is usually a certain congruity between party and political views. Most judges and justices have at one time been active partisans, an experience that gave them visibility and helped them obtain the positions from which they moved to the courts.

Judgeships are also considered very prestigious patronage plums. Indeed, the decisions of Congress to create new judgeships, and thus new positions for party members, are closely related to whether or not the majority party in Congress is the same as the party of the president. Members of the majority party in the legislature want to avoid providing an opposition party president with new positions to fill with their opponents.

Ideology is equally important as party. Presidents want to appoint to the federal bench people who share their views. In effect, all presidents try to "pack" the courts. They want more than "justice"; they want policies with which they agree. Presidential aides survey candidates' decisions (if they have served on a lower court), speeches, political stands, writings, and other expressions of opinion. They also turn for information to people who know the candidates well. Although it is considered improper to question judicial candidates about upcoming court cases, it is appropriate to discuss broader questions of political

---

Table 16.3   Supreme Court Justices, 1990

NAME	YEAR OF BIRTH	PREVIOUS POSITION	NOMINATING PRESIDENT	YEAR OF APPOINTMENT
Byron R. White	1917	Deputy U.S. Attorney General	Kennedy	1962
Thurgood Marshall	1908	U.S. Court of Appeals	Johnson	1967
Harry Blackmun	1908	U.S. Court of Appeals	Nixon	1970
William H. Rehnquist[a]	1924	Assistant U.S. Attorney General	Nixon	1971
John Paul Stevens	1920	U.S. Court of Appeals	Ford	1975
Sandra Day O'Connor	1930	State Court of Appeals	Reagan	1981
Antonin Scalia	1936	U.S. Court of Appeals	Reagan	1986
Anthony M. Kennedy	1936	U.S. Court of Appeals	Reagan	1988
David H. Souter	1939	U.S. Court of Appeals	Bush	1990[b]

[a]William Rehnquist was promoted from associate justice to chief justice by President Reagan in 1986.
[b]David Souter was nominated to replace William Brennan on July 23, 1990. At the time this text went to press, Souter's nomination had not yet been approved.

and judicial philosophy. The Reagan administration was especially concerned about such matters and had each potential nominee fill out a lengthy questionnaire and be interviewed by a special committee in the Department of Justice.

Members of the federal bench also play the game of politics, of course, and may try to time their retirements so that a president with compatible views will choose their successors. This is one reason justices remain on the Supreme Court for so long, even when they are clearly infirm. William Howard Taft, a rigid conservative, even feared a successor being named by Herbert Hoover, a more moderate conservative.

Such tactics do not always succeed. In 1968 Chief Justice Earl Warren submitted his resignation to President Johnson, who he felt would select an acceptable successor. When Johnson's choice of Abe Fortas failed to win confirmation, however, the opportunity to nominate the new chief justice passed to Warren's old California political rival, the newly elected president, Richard Nixon, who nominated a conservative, Warren Burger, as chief justice.

Presidents are typically pleased with their nominees to the Supreme Court and through them have slowed or reversed trends in the Court's decisions. Franklin D. Roosevelt's nominees substantially liberalized the Court, whereas Richard Nixon's turned it in a basically conservative direction.

Nevertheless, it is not always easy to predict the policy inclinations of candidates, and presidents have been disappointed in their nominees about a fourth of the time. President Eisenhower, for example, was displeased with the liberal decisions of both Earl Warren and William Brennan. Once when asked whether he had made any mistakes as president, he replied, "Yes, two, and they are both sitting on the Supreme Court."[7] Richard Nixon was certainly disappointed when Warren Burger, whom he had nominated as chief justice, wrote the Court's decision calling for immediate desegregation of the nation's schools shortly after his confirmation. This turn of events did little for the president's "southern strategy." Burger also wrote the Court's opinion in *U.S. v. Nixon,* which forced the president to release the Watergate tapes. Nixon's resignation soon followed.

Thus presidents influence policy through the values of their judicial nominations, but this impact is limited by numerous legal and extra-legal factors beyond the chief executive's control. As Harry Truman put it, "Packing the Supreme Court can't be done. . . . I've tried it and it won't work. . . . Whenever you put a man on the Supreme Court, he ceases to be your friend. I'm sure of that."[8]

There is no doubt that various women's, racial, ethnic, and religious groups desire to have as many of their members as possible appointed to the federal bench. At the very least, judgeships have symbolic importance for them. Thus presidents face many of the same pressures for representativeness in selecting judges that they experience in naming their cabinet.

What is less clear is what policy differences result when presidents nominate persons with different backgrounds to the bench. The number of female and minority group judges is too few and their service too recent to serve as a sound basis for generalizations about their decisions. Many members of each party have been appointed, of course, and it appears that Republican judges in general

[7]Quoted in Henry J. Abraham, *Justices and Presidents: A Political History of Appointments to the Supreme Court,* 2nd ed. (New York: Oxford University Press, 1985), 263.

[8]*Ibid.,* 70.

are somewhat more conservative than Democratic judges. Former prosecutors serving on the Supreme Court have tended to be less sympathetic toward defendants' rights than other justices have. Thus background does make some difference,[9] yet for reasons you will examine in the following sections, on many issues party affiliation and other characteristics bring no more predictability to the courts than they do to Congress.

THE STRUCTURE OF THE FEDERAL JUDICIAL SYSTEM

The Constitution is vague about the federal court system. Aside from specifying that there will be a Supreme Court, the Constitution left it to Congress' discretion to establish lower federal courts of general jurisdiction. In the Judiciary Act of 1789, Congress saw fit to create these *constitutional courts,* and although the system has been altered over the years, America has never been without them. The current organization of the federal court system is displayed in Figure 16.1.

Congress has also established *legislative courts* for specialized purposes. These courts include the Court of Military Appeals, the Court of Claims, the Court of International Trade, and the Tax Court. They are staffed by judges who have fixed terms of office and who lack the protections of judges on constitutional

[9]On the impact of the background of members of the judiciary, see Robert A. Carp and C. K. Rowland, *Policymaking and Politics in the Federal District Courts* (Knoxville, Tenn.: University of Tennessee Press, 1983); Thomas G. Walker and Deborah J. Barrow, "The Diversification of the Federal Bench: Policy and Process Ramifications," *Journal of Politics* 47 (May 1985): 596–617; and C. Neal Tate, "Personal Attribute Models of the Voting Behavior of United States Supreme Court Justices: Liberalism in Civil Liberties and Economics Decisioins, 1946–1978," *American Political Science Review* 75 (June 1981): 355–67.

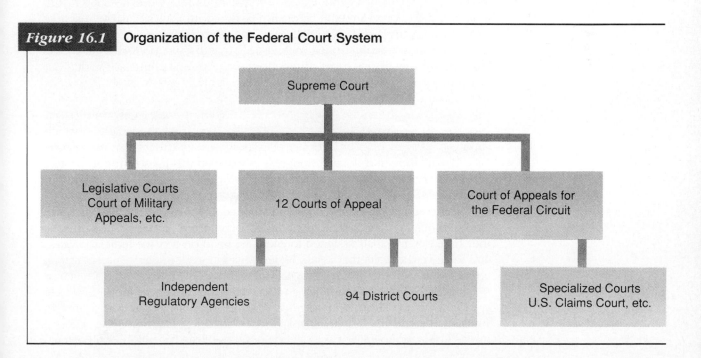

Figure 16.1 **Organization of the Federal Court System**

Supreme Court

Legislative Courts Court of Military Appeals, etc.

12 Courts of Appeal

Court of Appeals for the Federal Circuit

Independent Regulatory Agencies

94 District Courts

Specialized Courts U.S. Claims Court, etc.

courts against removal or salary reductions. The following sections, however, will focus on the courts of general jurisdiction.

District Courts

The entry point for most litigation in the federal courts is one of the ninety-one **district courts,** at least one of which is located in each state, plus one in Washington, D.C., and one in Puerto Rico (there are also three somewhat different territorial courts for Guam, the Virgin Islands, and the Northern Mariana Islands). The district courts are courts of original jurisdiction; they hear no appeals. They are the only federal courts in which trials are held and in which juries may be empaneled. The 576 district court judges usually preside over cases alone, but certain rare cases require that three judges constitute the court. Each district court has between two and twenty-seven judges, depending on the amount of judicial work within its territory.

The jurisdiction of the district courts extends to the following:

- Federal crimes
- Civil suits under federal law
- Civil suits between citizens of different states where the amount exceeds fifty thousand dollars
- Supervision of bankruptcy proceedings
- Review of the actions of some federal administrative agencies
- Admiralty and maritime law cases
- Supervision of the naturalization of aliens

It is important to note that about 98 percent of all the criminal cases in the United States are heard in state and local court systems, not in the federal courts. Moreover, 83 percent of the 44,585 criminal cases that were decided in the federal district courts in 1988 were disposed of without trial, as the result of guilty pleas or the withdrawal of charges by the prosecution.

Most civil suits in the United States are also handled in state and local courts. The vast majority of civil cases commenced in the federal courts are settled out of court. In 1988, only 5 percent of the 239,634 civil cases in which decisions were made were decided by trial.

Diversity of citizenship cases involve civil suits between citizens of different states (such as a citizen of California suing a citizen of Texas) or suits in which one of the parties is a citizen of a foreign nation and the matter in question exceeds fifty thousand dollars. Congress established this jurisdiction to protect against the possible bias of a state court in favor of a citizen from that state. In these cases federal judges have to apply the appropriate state laws.

District judges are assisted by an elaborate supporting cast. In addition to clerks, bailiffs, law clerks, stenographers, court reporters, and probation officers, they have U.S. marshals assigned to each district to protect the judicial process and to serve the writs they issue. Federal magistrates, appointed to eight-year terms, issue warrants for arrest, determine whether or not to hold arrested persons for action by a grand jury, and set bail; they also hear motions subject to review by their district judge and, with the consent of both parties in civil cases and defendants in petty criminal cases, preside over some trials. Federal magistrates are becoming essential components of the federal judicial system.

Although most cases at the district court level are routine, U.S. attorneys sometimes make a name for themselves by vigorously prosecuting federal laws. Rudolph Guliani gained fame by pursuing and convicting Mafia leaders and white collar criminals such as stock market manipulator Ivan Boesky.

Another important player at the district court level is the U.S. attorney. Each district has one, nominated by the president and confirmed by the Senate, and he or she serves at the pleasure of the president (U.S. attorneys do not have lifetime appointments). These attorneys and their staffs prosecute violations of federal law and represent the U.S. government in civil cases.

Most of the cases handled in the district courts are routine, and few result in policy innovations. Usually district court judges do not even publish their decisions. Although most federal litigation ends at this level, a large percentage of those cases that district court judges actually decide (as opposed to those settled out of court or by guilty pleas in criminal matters) are appealed by the losers. A distinguishing feature of the American legal system is the relative ease of appeals and the long time it may take to reach final resolution on an issue.

Courts of Appeal

The U.S. **courts of appeal** are appellate courts empowered to review all final decisions of district courts except in the rare instances in which the law provides for direct review by the Supreme Court (injunctive orders of special three-judge district courts and certain decisions holding acts of Congress unconstitutional). They also have authority to review and enforce orders of many federal regulatory agencies, such as the Securities and Exchange Commission and the National Labor Relations Board. In 1988, 37,524 cases were heard in the courts of appeal, most of them coming from the district courts.

The United States is divided into twelve judicial circuits, including one for the District of Columbia (see Figure 16.2). Each circuit includes at least two states and has between 6 and 28 permanent circuit judgeships (156 in all), depending on the amount of judicial work in the circuit. Each court of appeals normally hears cases in panels consisting of three judges, but each may sit *en*

Figure 16.2 The Federal Judicial Circuits

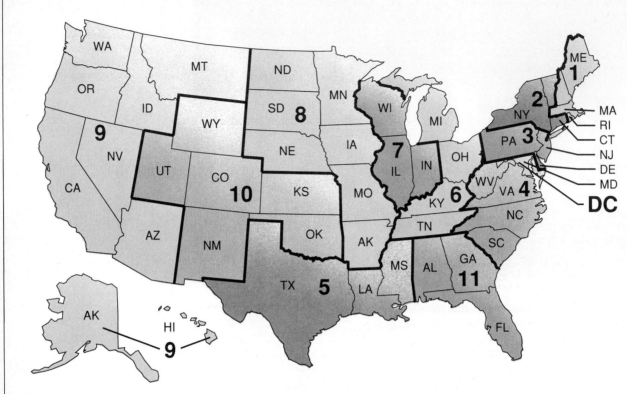

Not shown are Puerto Rico (First Circuit), Virgin Islands (Third Circuit), and Guam and the Northern Mariana Islands (Ninth Circuit).

banc (with all judges present) in particularly important cases. Decisions in either arrangement are made by majority vote of the participating judges.

There is also a special appeals court called the U.S. Court of Appeals for the Federal Circuit. Composed of twelve judges, it was established by Congress in 1982 to hear appeals in specialized cases, such as those regarding patents, copyrights, and trademarks, claims against the United States, and international trade.

The focus of cases in the courts of appeal is on correcting errors of procedure and law that occurred in the original proceedings of the cases. The courts of appeal hold no trials and hear no testimony. Their decisions set precedent for all the courts and agencies within their jurisdictions.

The Supreme Court

Sitting at the pinnacle of the American judicial system is the U.S. **Supreme Court.** The Court does much more for the American political system than deciding discrete cases. Among its most important functions are resolving conflicts among the states and maintaining national supremacy in the law. It also plays an important role in ensuring uniformity in the interpretation of national laws. For example, in 1984 Congress created a federal sentencing commission to write guidelines aimed at reducing the wide disparities that existed in punishment for similar crimes tried in federal courts. By 1989 more than 150 federal district judges had declared the law unconstitutional, while another 115 had ruled it was valid. Only the Supreme Court could resolve this inconsistency in the administration of justice, which it did when it upheld the law.

There are nine justices on the Supreme Court: eight associates and one chief justice (see Table 16.4). The Constitution does not require that number, however, and there have been as few as six justices and as many as ten. The size of the Supreme Court was altered many times between 1801 and 1869. In 1866 Congress reduced the size of the Court from ten to eight members so that President Andrew Johnson could not nominate new justices to fill two vacancies. When Ulysses S. Grant took office, Congress increased the number of justices to nine, since it had confidence he would nominate members to its liking. Since that time the number of justices has remained stable.

All nine justices sit together to hear cases and make decisions. The first decision is which cases to decide. A familiar battle cry for losers in litigation in lower courts is "I'll appeal this all the way to the Supreme Court!" In reality this is highly unlikely to happen. Unlike other federal courts, the Supreme Court controls its own agenda.

You can see in Figure 16.3 that the court does have an original jurisdiction, yet very few cases arise under it, as Table 16.5 illustrates. Almost all the business of the Court comes from the appellate process, and cases may be appealed from both federal and state courts. In the latter instance, however, a "substantial federal

---

Table 16.4 | Chief Justices of the U.S. Supreme Court

CHIEF JUSTICE	NOMINATING PRESIDENT	YEARS OF SERVICE
John Jay	Washington	1789–1795
John Rutledge	Washington	1795[a]
Oliver Ellsworth	Washington	1796–1800
John Marshall	Adams	1801–1835
Roger B. Taney	Jackson	1836–1864
Salmon P. Chase	Lincoln	1864–1873
Morrison R. Waite	Grant	1874–1888
Melville W. Fuller	Cleveland	1888–1910
Edward D. White	Taft	1910–1921
William Howard Taft	Harding	1921–1930
Charles Evans Hughes	Hoover	1930–1941
Harlan Fiske Stone	F. Roosevelt	1941–1946
Fred M. Vinson	Truman	1946–1953
Earl Warren	Eisenhower	1953–1969
Warren E. Burger	Nixon	1969–1986
William H. Rehnquist	Reagan	1986–present

[a]Not confirmed by the Senate.

Figure 16.3 The Organization and Jurisdiction of the Courts

UNITED STATES SUPREME COURT

Original jurisdiction of the Supreme Court	Appellate jurisdiction of the Supreme Court (federal route)	Appellate jurisdiction of the Supreme Court (state route)
Cases involving foreign diplomats Cases involving a state: •Between the United States and a state •Between two or more states •Between one state and citizens of another state •Between a state and a foreign country	U.S. Courts of Appeal Court of Appeals for the Federal Circuit Legislative Courts	State Courts of Last Resort

question" must be involved. In deference to the states, cases from state courts involving federal questions are heard only in the Supreme Court and then only after the petitioner has exhausted all the potential remedies in the state court system.

The Court will not try to settle matters of state law or determine guilt or innocence in state criminal proceedings. To obtain a hearing in the Supreme Court, a defendant convicted in a state court might demonstrate, for example, that his or her trial was not fair as required by the Bill of Rights, which was extended to cover state court proceedings by the due process clause of the Fourteenth Amendment. The great majority of cases heard by the Supreme Court come from the lower federal courts.

THE COURTS AS POLICYMAKERS

"Judicial decision making," a former Supreme Court law clerk wrote in the *Harvard Law Review,* "involves, at bottom, a choice between competing values by fallible, pragmatic, and at times nonrational men [and women] in a highly

Table 16.5 | Full Opinions in the Supreme Court's 1988–1989 Term

TYPE OF CASE	NUMBER OF CASES
Original jurisdiction	0
Civil actions from lower federal courts	88
Federal criminal and habeas corpus cases	18
Civil actions from state courts	21
State criminal cases	16
TOTAL	143

Source: "The Supreme Court, 1986 Term: The Statistics," Harvard Law Review 103 (November 1989): 398–401.

complex process in a very human setting."[10] This is an apt description of policy-making on the Supreme Court and on other courts, too. The next sections will look at how courts make policy, paying particular attention to the role of the U.S. Supreme Court; although it is not the only court involved in policy-making and policy interpretation, its decisions have the widest implications for policy.

Accepting Cases

Deciding what to decide about is the first step in all policy-making. Courts of original jurisdiction cannot very easily decide not to consider a case; appeals courts, including the U.S. Supreme Court, have much more control over their agendas. The approximately 5,000 cases submitted annually to the U.S. Supreme Court must be read, culled, and sifted. Every Wednesday afternoon and every Friday morning the nine justices meet in conference. Alongside them in the conference room sit some twenty-five carts, each wheeled in from the office of one of the nine justices, and each filled with petitions, briefs, memoranda, and every item the justices are likely to need during their discussions. These meetings operate under the strictest secrecy; only the justices themselves attend.

At these weekly conferences two important matters are hammered out. First is an agenda: the justices consider the chief justice's "discuss list" and decide which cases they want to discuss. Few of the justices can take the time to read materials on every case coming to the Court; most rely heavily on their law clerks (each justice now has four) to screen them. If four justices agree to take on a case, it can be scheduled for oral argument or decided on the basis of the written record already on file with the Court.

The most common way for the Court to put a case on its docket is by issuing to a lower federal or state court a **writ of certiorari,** a formal document that calls up a case. Some cases—principally those in which federal laws have been found unconstitutional, in which federal courts have concluded that state laws violate the federal Constitution, or in which state laws have been upheld in state courts despite claims that they violate federal law or the Constitution—are

[10]Quoted in Nina Totenberg, "Behind the Marble, Beneath the Robes," *New York Times Magazine,* March 16, 1975, 37.

Twice each week the Supreme Court justices meet in this conference room to choose, discuss, or dismiss cases. The Court rules on only about 5 percent of the cases on its docket each year, and it issues written opinions on an even smaller percentage of them.

technically supposed to be heard by the Court "on appeal." In reality, though, the Court exercises broad discretion over hearing these cases.

Cases that involve major issues—especially civil liberties, conflict between different lower courts on the interpretation of federal law, or disagreement between a majority of the Supreme Court and lower court decisions—are principal reasons for the Court's choosing to hear a case.[11]

Since getting into the Supreme Court is half the battle, it is important to remember this chapter's earlier discussion of standing to sue, a criterion the Court often uses to decide whether to hear a case. In addition, the Court has used other means to avoid deciding cases that are too politically "hot" to handle or that divide the Court too sharply.[12]

Another important influence on the Supreme Court is the **solicitor general.** As a presidential appointee and the third-ranking official in the Department of Justice, the solicitor general is in charge of the appellate court litigation of the federal government. The solicitor general and a staff of about two dozen experienced attorneys (1) decide whether or not to appeal cases the government has lost in the lower courts, (2) review and modify the briefs presented in

[11]Doris Marie Provine, *Case Selection in the United States Supreme Court* (Chicago: University of Chicago Press, 1980); and Stuart H. Teger and Douglas Kosinski, "The Cue Theory of Supreme Court Certiorari Jurisdiction: A Reconsideration," *Journal of Politics* 42 (August 1980): 834–46.

[12]Sidney Ulmer, "The Supreme Court's Certiorari Decisions: Conflict as a Predictive Variable," *American Political Science Review* (December 1984): 901–11.

government appeals, and (3) represent the government before the Supreme Court. Unlike attorneys for private parties, the solicitors general are careful to seek Court review only of important cases. By avoiding frivolous appeals and displaying a high degree of competence, they typically have the confidence of the Court, which in turn grants review of a large percentage of the cases for which they seek it.

In the end, the Supreme Court decides very few cases. In its 1988–89 term, of the 4,806 cases on its docket the Court made decisions in only 229 of them. Moreover, in only 143 of those cases did the Court issue formal written opinions that could serve as precedent and thus as the basis of guidance for lower courts (a few of the opinions were for several cases consolidated into one). In 86 cases the Court simply reached a **per curiam decision,** that is, a decision without explanation. It dismissed appeals or denied petitions for writs of certiorari, habeas corpus, or mandamus in more than 4,000 other cases. A few appeals were also withdrawn.[13]

Making Decisions

The second task of the weekly conferences is to discuss cases actually accepted and argued before the Court. Beginning the first Monday in October and lasting until June, the Court hears oral arguments in two-week cycles—two weeks of courtroom arguments followed by two weeks of reflecting on cases and writing opinions about them.

Before the justices enter the courtroom to hear the lawyers for each side present their arguments, they have received elaborately prepared written briefs from each party to the case. They probably also have received several other briefs from parties (often groups) who are interested in the outcome of the case but are not formal litigants. These **amicus curiae** ("friend of the court") **briefs** may, in an attempt to influence the Court's decision, raise additional points of view and present information not contained in the briefs of the attorneys for the official parties to the case. In controversial cases there may be many such briefs submitted to the Court; fifty-eight were presented in the landmark *Bakke* case on affirmative action (discussed in Chapter 5).

Amicus curiae briefs have another important role: the government, under the direction of the solicitor general, may submit them in cases in which it has an interest. For instance, a case between two parties may involve the question of the constitutionality of a federal law. The federal government naturally wants to have its voice heard on such matters, even if it is not formally a party to the case. These briefs are also a means, frequently used by the Reagan administration, to urge the Court to change established doctrine, such as the law dealing with defendants' rights.

In most instances the attorneys for each side have only a half-hour to address the Court. During this time they summarize their briefs, emphasizing their most compelling points. The justices may listen attentively, interrupt with penetrating or helpful questions, request information, talk to one another, read (presumably briefs), or simply gaze at the ceiling. After twenty-five minutes a white light

---

[13]"The Supreme Court, 1988 Term: The Statistics," *Harvard Law Review* 103 (November 1987): 398.

Here Chief Justice William Rehnquist prepares an opinion in his office. The Court's written opinions play a key role in judicial policy-making, helping to establish precedents for future cases.

comes on at the lectern from which the lawyer is speaking, and five minutes later a red light signals the end of that lawyer's presentation, even if he or she is in midsentence. Oral argument is over.

Back in the conference room, the chief justice, who presides, raises a particular case and invites discussion, turning first to the senior associate justice. Discussion can range from perfunctory to profound and from brotherly to bitter. If the votes are not clear from the individual discussions, the chief justice may ask each justice to vote. Once a tentative vote has been reached, it is necessary to write an **opinion,** a statement of the legal reasoning behind the decision.

Opinion writing is no mere formality. In fact, the content of an opinion may be as important as the decision itself. Broad and bold opinions have far-reaching implications for future cases; narrowly drawn opinions may have little impact beyond the case being decided. Tradition in the Supreme Court requires that the chief justice, if in the majority, either write the opinion or assign it to some other justice in the majority. If the chief justice is part of the minority, the opinion is assigned by the senior associate justice in the majority. (Opponents of former Chief Justice Burger have charged that he manipulated this assigning role, sometimes unilaterally assigning the writing of the majority opinion even when he was in the minority.) Drafts are then circulated among the majority, suggestions are made, and negotiations take place among the justices. Votes can be gained or lost by the content of the opinion. An opinion that proves unacceptable to a clear majority is reworked and redrafted.

Justices are free to write their own opinions, to join in other opinions, or to associate themselves with part of one opinion and part of another. *Dissenting opinions* are those written by justices opposed to all or part of the majority's decision. *Concurring opinions* are those written not only to support a majority decision but also to stress a different constitutional or legal basis for the judgment. When the opinions are written and the final vote taken, the decision is announced. At least six justices must participate in a case, and decisions are made by majority vote. If there is a tie (because of a vacancy on the Court or because a justice chooses not to participate), the decision of the lower court from which the case came is sustained. Five votes in agreement on the reasoning underlying an opinion are necessary for the logic to serve as precedent for judges of lower courts.

The vast majority of cases reaching the courts are settled on the principle of **stare decisis** ("let the decision stand"), meaning that an earlier decision should hold for the case being considered. All courts rely heavily upon precedent—the way similar cases were handled in the past—as a guide to current decisions. Lower courts, of course, are expected to follow the precedents of higher courts in their decision making. If the Supreme Court, for example, rules in favor of the right to abortion under certain conditions, it has established a precedent and lower courts are expected to follow that precedent.

The Supreme Court is in a position to overrule its own precedents, and it has done so dozens of times.[14] One of the most famous such instances occurred with *Brown* v. *Board of Education* (1954) (see Chapter 5), in which the court overruled *Plessy* v. *Ferguson* (1896) and found that segregation in the public schools violated the Constitution.

[14]A.P. Blaustein and A.H. Field, "Overruling Opinions in the Supreme Court," *Michigan Law Review* 57, no. 2 (1957): 151.

What happens when precedents are not clear? This is especially a problem for the Supreme Court, which is more likely than other courts to handle cases at the forefront of the law. Precedent is typically less firmly established on these matters. Moreover, the justices are often asked to apply the vague phrases of the Constitution ("due process of law," "equal protection," "unreasonable searches and seizures") or vague statutes passed by Congress to concrete situations. This provides leeway for the justices to disagree (only about one-fourth of the cases in which full opinions are handed down are decided unanimously) and for their values to influence their judgment.

As a result, it is often easy to identify consistent patterns in the decisions of justices. For example, if there is division on the Court (indicating that precedent is not clear) and you can identify a conservative side to the issue at hand, there is a high probability that William Rehnquist and Sandra Day O'Connor will be on that side. Thurgood Marshall and William Brennan, by contrast, will very probably be voting on the other side of the issue. Liberalism and conservatism have several dimensions, including freedom, equality, and economic regulation. The point is that policy preferences do matter in judicial decision making, especially on the nation's highest court[15] (see "You Are the Policymaker: The Debate over Original Intentions").

Once announced, copies of a decision are conveyed to the press as it is being formally announced in open court. Media coverage of the court remains primitive. Doris Graber reports that "much court reporting, even at the Supreme

[15]See, for example, David W. Rohde and Harold J. Spaeth, *Supreme Court Decision Making* (San Francisco: W.H. Freeman, 1976), and Jeffrey A. Segal and Albert O. Cover, "Ideological Values and the Votes of U.S. Supreme Court Justices," *American Political Science Review* 83 (June 1989): 557–66.

"Do you ever have one of those days when everything seems un-Constitutional?"

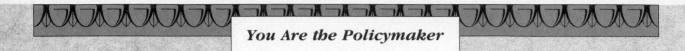
The Debate over Original Intentions

The most contentious issue involving the courts is the role of judicial discretion. According to Christopher Wolfe, the difficulty is this: "The Constitution itself nowhere specifies a particular set of rules by which it is to be interpreted. Where does one go, then, in order to discover the proper way to interpret the Constitution?"

Some have argued for a jurisprudence of **original intent** (sometimes referred to as *strict constructionism*). This view holds that judges and justices should determine the intent of the framers of the Constitution regarding a particular matter and decide cases in line with that intent. Such a view is popular with conservatives, such as Ronald Reagan's close advisor and attorney general, Edwin Meese. Advocates of strict constructionism view it as a means of constraining the exercise of judicial discretion, which they see as the foundation of the liberal decisions of the past four decades, especially on matters of civil liberties, civil rights, and defendants' rights (discussed in Chapters 4 and 5).

They also see following original intent as the only basis of interpretation consistent with democracy. Judges, they argue, should not dress up constitutional interpretations with *their* views on "contemporary needs," "today's conditions," or "what is right." It is the job of legislators, not judges, to make such judgments.

Other jurists, such as former Justice William Brennan, disagree. They maintain that what appears to be deference to the intentions of the framers is simply a cover for making conservative decisions. They assert that the Constitution is subject to multiple meanings by thoughtful people in different ages. Judges will differ in time and place about what they think the Constitution means. Thus basing decisions on original intent is not likely to have much affect on judicial discretion.

In addition, Brennan and his supporters contend that the Constitution is not like a paint-by-numbers kit. Trying to reconstruct or guess the framers' intentions is very difficult. Recent key cases before the Supreme Court have concerned issues, such as school busing, abortions, and wire tapping, that the framers could not have imagined; there were no public schools or buses, no contraceptives or modern abortion techniques, and certainly no electronic surveillance equipment or telephones in 1787. Not long ago the Supreme Court was asked to rule on the case of a female tourist from Colombia whose stomach, filled with more than eighty small balloons of cocaine, had been pumped by the authorities. She claimed it was an "unreasonable search and seizure," but was it a violation of the intent of the framers, who never heard of "coke" and could not imagine a stomach pump?

As you have seen, the founders embraced general principles, not specific solutions, when they wrote the

Court level, is imprecise and sometimes wrong."[16] More importantly in the legal community, the decisions are bound weekly and made available to every law library and lawyer in the United States. There is, of course, an air of finality to the public announcement of a decision, but, in fact, even Supreme Court decisions are not self-implementing; they are actually "remands" to lower courts, instructing them to act in accordance with the Court's decisions.

Implementing Court Decisions

Reacting bitterly to one of Chief Justice Marshall's decisions, President Jackson is said to have grumbled: "John Marshall has made his decision; now let him

[16]Doris Graber, *Mass Media and American Politics,* 2nd ed. (Washington, D.C.: Congressional Quarterly Press, 1984), 249.

Constitution. They frequently lacked discrete, discoverable intent. Moreover, there is often no record of their intentions, nor is it clear whose intentions should count—those of the writers of the Constitution, those of the more than sixteen hundred members who attended the ratifying conventions, or those of the voters who sent them there. This problem grows more complex when you consider the amendments to the Constitution, which involve thousands of additional "framers."

Others point out that it is not even clear that the framers expected that their "original intent" should guide others' interpretation of their document. Historian Jack N. Rakove points out that there is little historical evidence that the framers believed their intentions should guide later interpretations of the Constitution. In fact, there is some evidence for believing that Madison—the key delegate—left the Constitutional Convention bitterly disappointed with the results, and wrote as much to his friend Jefferson. What if Madison had one set of intentions but—like anyone working in a committee—got a different set of results?

Thus the lines are drawn. On one side is the argument that any deviation from following the original intentions of the Constitution framers is a deviation from principle, leaving unelected judges to impose their views on the American people. If judges do not follow original intentions, then on what do they base their decisions?

On the other side are those who believe that it is often impossible to discern the views of the framers, and that there is no good reason to be constrained by the views of the eighteenth century, which reflect a more limited conception of constitutional rights. In order to cope with current needs, they argue, it is necessary to adapt the principles in the Constitution to the demands of each era.

The choice here is at the very heart of the judicial process. If you were a justice sitting on the Supreme Court and were asked to interpret the meaning of the Constitution, what would *you* do?

Sources: Christoper Wolfe, *The Rise of Modern Judicial Review* (New York: Basic Books, 1986), 17. Wolfe is a strong critic of the rise of judicial activism and the lack of adherence to the original intent of criteria of judicial review. For further arguments in favor of original intent see Raoul Berger, *Government by Judiciary: The Transformation of the Fourteenth Amendment* (Cambridge, Mass.: Harvard University Press, 1977). For views in favor of judicial activism see Traciel V. Reid, "A Critique of Interpretivism and Its Claimed Influence upon Judicial Decision Making," *American Politics Quarterly* 16 (July 1988):329–56, and Jack N. Rakove, "Mr. Meese, Meet Mr. Madison," *Atlantic Monthly,* December 1986, 79.

enforce it." Court decisions carry legal, even moral, authority, but courts do not possess a staff of police officers to enforce their decisions. They must rely upon other units of government to carry out their enforcement. **Judicial implementation** refers to how and whether court decisions are translated into actual policy, affecting the behavior of others.

You should think of any judicial decision as the end of one process—the litigation process—and the beginning of another process—the process of judicial implementation. Sometimes delay and foot-dragging follow upon even decisive court decisions. There is, for example, the story of the tortured efforts of a young black man named Virgil Hawkins to get himself admitted to the University of Florida Law School.[17] Hawkins's efforts began in 1949, when he first applied for admission, and ended unsuccessfully in 1958, after a decade of

[17]Baum, *The Supreme Court,* 181–82.

Virgil Hawkins's unsuccessful struggle to attend the all-white University of Florida Law School illustrates how judicial implementation can affect the impact of court decisions. The Supreme Court ordered the school to admit Hawkins in 1956, but the school and state refused to implement the ruling, continuing to appeal the case. Two years later a Florida district court again denied admission to Hawkins, although it did order the school's desegregation.

court decisions. Despite a 1956 order from the U.S. Supreme Court to admit Hawkins, continued legal skirmishing produced a 1958 decision by the U.S. District Court in Florida ordering the admission of nonwhites but upholding the denial of admission to Hawkins himself. Other courts and other institutions of government can be roadblocks in the way of judicial implementation.

Charles Johnson and Bradley Canon suggest that implementation of court decisions involves several elements.[18] First, there is an *interpreting population,* heavily composed of lawyers and other judges. They must correctly sense the intent of the original decision in their subsequent actions. Second, there is an *implementing population.* Say that the Supreme Court held (as it did) that prayers in the public schools are unconstitutional. Then the implementing population (school boards and school administrators) must actually abandon prayers. Police departments, hospitals, corporations, government agencies—all may be part of the implementing population. Judicial decisions are more likely to be smoothly implemented if implementation is concentrated in the hands of a few highly visible officials, such as the president or state legislators. Third, every decision involves a *consumer population.* The potential "consumers" of an abortion decision are those who want abortions (and those who oppose them); the consumers of the *Miranda* decision (see Chapter 4) are criminal defendants and their attorneys. The consumer population must be aware of its newfound rights and stand up for them.

Congress and presidents can also help or hinder judicial implementation. In 1954 the Supreme Court held that segregated schools were "inherently unconstitutional" and ordered public schools desegregated with "all deliberate speed." President Eisenhower refused to state clearly that Americans should comply with this famous decision in *Brown* v. *Board of Education.* Congress was not much more helpful; only a decade later did it pass legislation denying federal aid to segregated schools. Different presidents have different commitments to a particular judicial policy. After years of court and presidential decisions supporting busing to end racial segregation, the Reagan administration in December 1984 went before the Supreme Court and argued against a school-busing case in Norfolk, Virginia.

Implementing a Court Decision: The Case of Abortion   In 1971 the Supreme Court heard oral arguments on a thorny constitutional question: Does a woman have a right to an abortion, or does a state have the constitutional power to regulate, limit, or even forbid abortion? The case involved a plaintiff from Texas who remained technically anonymous (hence the name Jane Roe in the case *Roe* v. *Wade*). Texas lawyer Sarah Weddington urged the Court to declare unconstitutional a Texas statute limiting the right of abortion. Weddington argued that numerous constitutional provisions forbade state intervention in an abortion decision. Justice Byron White pressed her on the difficult subject of when during the course of a pregnancy a state law might limit abortion. Weddington insisted that "the Constitution, as I see it, gives protection to people only after birth." In defense of the Texas statute, the state's Assistant Attorney General Jay Floyd faced spirited questioning by Justice Thurgood Marshall. If

---

[18]Charles Johnson and Bradley C. Canon, *Judicial Policies: Implementation and Impact* (Washington, D.C.: Congressional Quarterly Press, 1984), chap. 1.

Texas contended that an unborn fetus had constitutional rights, Marshall wanted to know, then when did those rights begin? "There is life," Floyd contended, "from the moment of impregnation." Pressed by Justice Marshall on the constitutional protection of a newly conceived embryo, Floyd finally admitted that "there are unanswerable questions in this field."[19]

Announced in 1973, the Court's opinion turned on its insistence that the right of privacy "is broad enough to encompass a woman's decision whether or not to terminate her pregnancy." At the same time, the Court held, this right was not absolute. During the first three months of pregnancy a state could not regulate abortion; during the second trimester a state could regulate abortion to ensure the health of the mother; and during the third trimester a state could regulate and even forbid abortion to protect the life of the fetus.

Response to the Court's decision was sharply divided. While some felt it was a wise compromise, the decision was strongly opposed by antiabortion groups, chief among them the National Right to Life Committee and the Ad Hoc Committee in Defense of Life. These and other groups took their case to Congress, where they unsuccessfully pressed for an amendment to the Constitution that would forbid abortions altogether. They had more success in promoting legislation sponsored by Representative Henry Hyde (R-Ill.) that forbade the use of federal Medicaid funds to pay for poor women's abortions. Also active in the states, antiabortion groups urged state legislatures to restrict the use of public funds for abortion. A few radical antiabortionists picketed and even bombed abortion clinics.

Nearly a generation of spirited, often bitter public debate has followed the *Roe* v. *Wade* decision. Abortion has been an annual issue in Congress and the state legislatures; courts have considered hundreds of additional cases after *Roe;* and presidential campaigns and nominating conventions have included heated abortion debates. What, then, has been the impact of the Supreme Court's decision? The number of abortions *did* increase after the 1973 decision. An estimated 740,000 legal abortions were performed in 1973. Gradually increasing each year, by 1985 an estimated 1.6 million legal abortions were performed. Susan Hansen, though, concluded that *Roe* v. *Wade* was only one of many factors associated with the increase in abortions after 1973, and perhaps a minor one at that. Abortions had been increasing at a faster rate before the 1973 decision, and many factors, including the growing public acceptance of abortion, were associated with the increase.[20]

As the abortion case suggests, the fate and effect of a Supreme Court decision are complex and unpredictable. The implementation of any court decision involves many actors besides the justices, and the justices have no way of ensuring that their decisions and policies will be implemented. Courts have made major changes in public policies not because their decisions are automatically implemented but because the courts both reflect and help to determine the national policy agenda.

[19]The account of the oral argument before the Court relies on Bob Woodward and Scott Armstrong, *The Brethren* (New York: Avon, 1979), 193–96. On the implementation of *Roe* v. *Wade,* see also Johnson and Canon, *Judicial Policies,* chap. 1.

[20]Susan B. Hansen, "State Implementation of Supreme Court Decisions: Abortion Rates Since 'Roe' v. *Wade, Journal of Politics* 42 (1980): 372–95.

THE COURTS AND THE POLICY AGENDA

Even though American courts and judges work largely alone and in isolation from daily contact with other political institutions, you have seen that they do play a key role in shaping policy agenda. Like all policymakers, however, the courts are choice-takers. Confronted with controversial policies, they make controversial decisions that leave some people winners and others losers. They have made policy about slavery and segregation, about corporate power and capital punishment, and about dozens of other controversial matters.

A Historical Review

Until the Civil War, the dominant questions before the Court regarded the strength and legitimacy of the federal government and slavery. These issues of nation-building were resolved in favor of the supremacy of the national government. From the Civil War until 1937, questions of the relationship between the federal government and the economy predominated. During this period the Court restricted the power of the federal government to regulate the economy. From 1938 to the present, the paramount issues before the Court have concerned personal liberty and social and political equality. In this era the Court has enlarged the scope of personal freedom and civil rights and has removed many of the constitutional restraints on the regulation of the economy.

Few played a more important role in making the Court a significant national agenda-setter than John Marshall, chief justice from 1801 to 1835. His successors have continued not only to respond to the political agenda but also to shape discussion and debate about it.

John Marshall and the Growth of Judicial Review   Scarcely was the government housed in its new capital when Federalists and Democrats clashed over the courts. In the election of 1800 Democrat Thomas Jefferson had beaten Federalist John Adams. Determined to leave at least the judiciary in trusted hands, Adams tried to fill it with Federalists. He allegedly stayed at his desk until nine o'clock signing commissions on his last night in the White House (March 3, 1801).

In the midst of this flurry, Adams appointed William Marbury to the minor post of justice of the peace in the District of Columbia. In the rush of last-minute business, however, Secretary of State John Marshall failed to deliver commissions to Marbury and sixteen others. He left the commissions to be delivered by the incoming secretary of state, James Madison.

When the omission was discovered, Madison and Jefferson, furious at Adams's actions, refused to deliver the commissions. Marbury and three others in the same situation sued Madison, asking the Supreme Court to issue a **writ of mandamus** ordering Madison to give them their commissions. They took their case directly to the Supreme Court under the Judiciary Act of 1789, which gave the Court original jurisdiction in such matters.

The new chief justice was none other than Adam's secretary of state and arch-Federalist John Marshall, himself one of Adams's "midnight appointments" (he took his seat on the Court barely three weeks before Adams's term ended). Marshall and his Federalist colleagues were in a spot. Threats of impeachment

John Marshall, chief justice from 1801 to 1835, established the Supreme Court's power of judicial review in the 1803 case Marbury v. Madison. In their ruling on the case, Marshall and his associates declared that the Court had the power to determine the constitutionality of congressional actions.

came from Jeffersonians fearful that the Court would vote for Marbury. Moreover, if the Court ordered Madison to deliver the commissions, he was likely to ignore it, thereby risking ridicule for the nation's highest court over a minor issue. Marshall had no means of compelling Madison to act.

The Court could also deny Marbury's claim. Taking that option, however, would concede the issue to the Jeffersonians and give the appearance of retreat in the face of opposition, thereby reducing the power of the Court.

Marshall devised a shrewd solution to the case of **Marbury v. Madison**. In February 1803 he delivered the unanimous opinion of the Court. First, Marshall and his colleagues argued that Madison was wrong to withhold Marbury's commission. The Court also found, however, that the Judiciary Act of 1789, under which Marbury had brought suit, contradicted the plain words of the Constitution about the Court's original jurisdiction. Thus Marshall dismissed Marbury's claim, saying that the Court, according to the Constitution, had no power to require that the commission be delivered.

Conceding a small battle over Marbury's commission (he did not get it), Marshall won a much larger war, asserting for the courts the power to determine what is and is not constitutional. As Marshall wrote, "An act of the legislature repugnant to the Constitution is void," and "it is emphatically the province of the judicial department to say what the law is." Thus the chief justice established the power of **judicial review,** the power of the courts to hold acts of Congress, and by implication the executive, in violation of the Constitution.

Marbury v. *Madison* was part of a skirmish between the Federalists on the Court and the Democratically controlled Congress. Partly, for example, to rein in the Supreme Court, the Jeffersonian Congress in 1801 abolished the lower federal appeals courts and made the Supreme Court justices return to the unpleasant task of "riding circuit"—serving as lower court justices around the country. This was a bit of studied harassment of the Court by its enemies. After *Marbury,* angry members of Congress, together with other Jeffersonians, claimed that Marshall was a "usurper of power," setting himself above Congress and the president. This view, however, was unfair. State courts, before and after the Constitution, had declared acts of their legislatures unconstitutional. In the Federalist Papers, Alexander Hamilton had expressly assumed the power of the federal courts to review legislation, and the federal courts had actually done so. *Marbury* was not even the first case of striking down an act of Congress; a lower federal court had done so in 1792, and the Supreme Court itself had approved a law after a constitutional review in 1796. Marshall was neither inventing nor imagining his right to review laws for their constitutionality.

The case also illustrates that the courts must be politically astute in exercising their power over the other branches. By in effect reducing its *own* power—the authority to hear cases such as Marbury's under its original jurisdiction—the Court was able to assert the right of judicial review in a fashion that the other branches could not easily rebuke.

More than any other power of the courts, judicial review has embroiled them in policy controversy. Before the Civil War the Supreme Court, headed by Chief Justice Roger Taney, held the Missouri Compromise unconstitutional because it restricted slavery in the territories. The decision was one of many steps along the road to the Civil War. After the Civil War, the Court was again active, this time using judicial review to strike down dozens of state and federal laws curbing the growing might of business corporations.

The "Nine Old Men"   Never was the Court so controversial as during the New Deal. At President Roosevelt's urging, Congress passed dozens of laws designed to end the Depression. The Court, though, was dominated by conservatives, most nominated by Republican presidents, who viewed federal intervention in the economy as unconstitutional and tantamount to socialism.

The Supreme Court began to dismantle New Deal policies one by one. One of the string of anti-Depression measures was the National Recovery Act. Although it was never particularly popular, the Court sealed its doom in *Schechter Poultry Corporation* v. *United States* (1935), declaring the act unconstitutional because it regulated purely local business that did not affect interstate commerce. Incensed, Roosevelt in 1937 proposed what critics called a "court-packing plan." Noting that the average age of the Court was over seventy, Roosevelt railed against those "nine old men." Since Congress can set the number of justices, he proposed that Congress expand the size of the Court, a move that would have allowed him to appoint additional justices sympathetic to the New Deal. Congress objected and never passed the plan. Indeed, it became irrelevant when two justices, Chief Justice Charles Evans Hughes and Associate Justice Owen Roberts, began switching their votes in favor of New Deal legislation. (One wit called it the "switch in time that saved nine.") Shortly thereafter Associate Justice William Van Devanter retired, and Roosevelt got to make the first of his many appointments to the Court.

The Warren Court   Few eras of the Supreme Court have been as active in shaping public policy as that of the Warren Court (1953-69), presided over by Chief Justice Earl Warren. Scarcely had President Eisenhower appointed Warren when the Court faced the issue of school segregation. In 1954 it held that laws requiring segregation of the public schools were unconstitutional. Later it expanded the rights of criminal defendants, extending the right to counsel and protections against unreasonable search and seizure and self-incrimination (see Chapter 4 and "A Question of Ethics: The Rule of Law versus Individual Justice"). It ordered states to reapportion their legislatures according to the principle of one person, one vote. So active was the Warren Court that right-wing groups, fearing that it was remaking the country, posted billboards all over the United States urging Congress to "Impeach Earl Warren."[21]

The Burger Court   Warren's retirement in 1969 gave President Richard Nixon his hoped-for opportunity to appoint a "strict constructionist"—that is, one who interprets the Constitution narrowly—as chief justice. He chose Minnesotan Warren E. Burger, then a conservative judge on the District of Columbia Court of Appeals. As Nixon hoped, the Burger Court turned out to be more conservative than the liberal Warren Court. It narrowed defendants' rights, though it did not overturn the fundamental contours of the *Miranda* decision. The conservative Burger Court, however, also wrote the abortion decision in *Roe* v. *Wade*, required school busing in certain cases to eliminate historic segregation, and upheld affirmative action programs in the *Weber* case (see Chapter 5). One of the most notable decisions of the Burger Court weighed against Burger's ap-

The Warren Court's controversial decisions on desegregation, criminal defendants' rights, and voting reapportionment led to calls for Chief Justice Earl Warren's impeachment. Critics argued that the unelected justices were making policy decisions that were the responsibility of elected officials. Here demonstrators protest Court rulings that expanded defendants' rights.

[21]An excellent overview of the Warren period is by former Watergate special prosecutor and Harvard law professor Archibald Cox, *The Warren Court* (Cambridge, Mass.: Harvard University Press, 1968).

A Question of Ethics

The Rule of Law versus Individual Justice

Ernesto Miranda, a twenty-three-year old eighth grade dropout and ex-convict who had a police record extending back ten years and a dishonorable discharge from the army, was arrested in Phoenix and identified by two women as the man who robbed one at knifepoint and kidnapped and raped the other. He made a confession in his own handwriting, noting that he was doing so voluntarily and with full knowledge of his legal rights.

At his trial the police officers who obtained Miranda's confession testified that they had not informed him of his right to counsel and that no counsel was present during the confession. Over the objections of Miranda's lawyer, the judge admitted the confession into evidence, and Miranda was found guilty of kidnapping and rape. In a separate trial he was found guilty of armed robbery.

Following an unsuccessful appeal to the Arizona Supreme Court, the U.S. Supreme Court agreed to review Miranda's case in 1966. The issue before the justices was whether the confession of a poorly educated, mentally abnormal, indigent defendant who had not been told of his right to counsel, and who had confessed in police custody without a lawyer present to represent him, was admissible as evidence in court.

The dilemma was a difficult one to resolve. There was every reason to believe that Miranda was guilty, and if the Court ruled that his confession was not admissible, it was possible that he might not be convicted in a new trial and would thus go free. Such a result was hard to reconcile with the concept of justice in a criminal trial. On the other hand, there was a question of the rule of law, in which accused persons—any persons—have rights, including that of counsel and against self-incrimination. What should the Court do in such a case?

As you learned in Chapter 4, the Supreme Court decided not to allow Miranda's confession as evidence and specified procedures the police must use when questioning persons accused of crimes. Miranda was retried and convicted once again. He was later killed in a barroom fight. The Supreme Court was criticized severely for its decision, and it became an issue in the 1968 presidential election when Richard Nixon promised to nominate justices who would weigh the trade-offs involved in such cases differently, giving more weight to concerns for punishing the guilty.

pointor, Richard Nixon. At the height of the Watergate scandal (see Chapter 13), the Supreme Court was called upon to rule on whether Nixon's White House tapes had to be turned over to the courts. It unanimously ordered him to do so, in ***United States v. Nixon*** (1974) and thus hastened his resignation.

The Rehnquist Court   By the late 1980s Ford, Nixon, and Reagan appointees composed a clear Supreme Court majority, now led by Chief Justice William Rehnquist. Its two most liberal members, Marshall and Brennan, were two of the oldest justices. One justice, Harry A. Blackmun, even took the extraordinary step of speaking out publicly at the Cosmos Club in Washington. The Supreme Court, he said, "was moving to the right . . . where it wants to go, by hook or by crook." It had become, he remarked sadly, "a rotten way to earn a living."[22]

The Rehnquist Court has not created a revolution in constitutional law. Instead, as discussed in Chapters 4 and 5, it has been slowly chipping away at liberal decisions such as those regarding defendants' rights, abortion, and affir-

---

[22]*Washington Post Weekly Review,* October 1, 1984, 33.

mative action. Many professional Supreme Court watchers expect this trend to continue as the conservative majority consolidates its hold on the Court.

UNDERSTANDING THE COURTS

Powerful courts are unusual; few nations have them. The power of American judges raises questions about the compatibility of unelected courts with a democracy and about the appropriate role for the judiciary in policy-making.

The Courts and Democracy

Announcing his retirement in 1981, Justice Potter Stewart made a few remarks to the handful of reporters present. Embedded in his brief statement was this observation: "It seems to me that there's nothing more antithetical to the idea of what a good judge should be than to think it has something to do with representative democracy." He meant that judges should not be subject to the whims of popular majorities. In a nation that insists so strongly that it is democratic, where do the courts fit in?

In some ways the courts are not a very democratic institution. Federal judges are not elected and are almost impossible to remove. Indeed, their social backgrounds probably make the courts the most elite-dominated policy-making institution. If democracy requires that key policymakers always be elected or be continually responsible to those who are, then the courts diverge sharply from the requirements of democratic government. As you saw in Chapter 2, the Constitution's framers wanted it that way. Chief Justice Rehnquist, a judicial conservative, put the case as follows: "A mere change in public opinion since the adoption of the Constitution, unaccompanied by a constitutional amendment, should not change the meaning of the Constitution. A merely temporary majoritarian groundswell should not abrogate some individual liberty protected by the Constitution."[23]

The courts are not entirely independent of popular preferences, however. Turn-of-the-century Chicago humorist Finley Peter Dunne had his Irish saloon-keeper character "Mr. Dooley" quip that "th' Supreme Court follows th' iliction returns." Many years later, political scientist Richard Funston analyzed the Supreme Court decisions in critical election periods. He found that "the Court is normally in line with popular . . . majorities."[24] Even when the Court seems out of step with other policymakers, it eventually swings around to join the policy consensus, as it did in the New Deal. A study of the period from 1937 to 1980 found that only on the issue of prayers in the public schools was the Court clearly out of line with public opinion.[25]

[23]William Rehnquist, "The Notion of a Living Constitution," in *Views from the Bench*, ed. Mark W. Cannon and David M. O'Brien (Chatham, N.J.: Chatham House, 1985), 129.

[24]Richard Funston, "The Supreme Court and Critical Elections," *American Political Science Review* 69 (1975): 810.

[25]David G. Barnum, "The Supreme Court and Public Opinion: Judicial Decision Making in the Post–New Deal Period," *Journal of Politics* 47 (May 1985): 652–62. See also John B. Gates, "Partisan Realignment, Unconstitutional State Policies, and the U.S. Supreme Court, 1837–1964," *American Journal of Political Science* 31 (May 1987): 259–80, and Thomas R. Marshall, "Public Opinion, Representation, and the Modern Supreme Court," *American Politics Quarterly* 16 (July 1988): 296–316.

The People Speak

Life Tenure for Justices

Do you think Supreme Court justices should serve for life, or should they serve for a specific number of years?

For life	16%
Limited term	80%

Source: The question as worded is taken directly from a *CBS News/The New York Times* Poll, May 1987.

Interest groups often use the judicial system to pursue their policy goals, forcing the courts to rule on important social issues. Some Hispanic parents, for example, have successfully sued local school districts to compel bilingual education.

Despite the fact that the Supreme Court sits in a "marble palace," it is not as insulated from the normal forms of politics as one might think. The two sides in the abortion debate flooded the Court with mail, encompassed it in advertisements and protests, and bombarded it with seventy-eight amicus curiae briefs in the *Webster* v. *Reproductive Health Services* case. It is unlikely that members of the Supreme Court cave in to interest group pressures, but they are aware of the public's concern about issues and this becomes part of their consciousness as they decide cases. Political scientists have found that the Court is more likely to hear the cases for which interest groups have filed amicus curiae briefs.[26]

Courts can also promote pluralism. When groups go to court, they use litigation to achieve their policy objectives.[27] Both civil rights groups and environmentalists, for example, have blazed a path to show how interest groups can effectively use the courts to achieve their policy goals. The legal wizard of the NAACP's litigation strategy, Thurgood Marshall, not only won most of his cases but also won for himself a seat on the Supreme Court. Almost every major policy decision these days ends up in court. Chances are good that some judge can be found who will rule in an interest group's favor. On the other hand, agencies and businesses commonly find themselves ordered by different courts to do opposite things. The habit of always turning to the courts as a last resort can add to policy delay, deadlock, and inconsistency (see "America in Perspective: Courts and Culture").

[26]Gregory A. Caldeira and John R. Wright, "Organized Interests and Agenda Setting in the U.S. Supreme Court," *American Political Science Review* 82 (December 1988): 1109–28.

[27]On group use of the litigation process, see Karen Orren, "Standing to Sue: Interest Group Conflict in the Federal Courts," *American Political Science Review* 70 (September 1976): 723–42, and Karen O'Connor and Lee Epstein, "The Rise of Conservative Interest Group Litigation," *Journal of Politics* 45 (May 1983): 479–89.

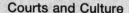

Courts and Culture

The Japanese and Americans have many things in common. Both live in nations that are modern industrial giants with robust economies and complex societies. The role of the law and the judiciary in the daily life of the people of Japan is quite different from that of citizens in the United States, however.

The role of the courts in Japan is influenced by the prevailing attitude toward law and the court system. The Japanese typically find adversary proceedings distasteful and will resort to going to court only when all the preferred traditional forms of informal mediation and negotiation have failed. Most people prefer to settle disputes through a compromise agreement arrived at with the mediation of friends, relatives, or influential persons, rather than engage in litigation in courts.

The Japanese have traditionally preferred amicable and harmonious social relations, relations that would be jeopardized by clear-cut court decisions based on the assertion of individuals' legal rights and on the assignment of moral fault. They prefer to de-emphasize conflict and the existence of disputes and to seek compromise solutions. The Japanese are also less prone to desire the application by others of the universalistic standards that characterize the law. Instead, they favor participating in the settlement of disputes, applying their personal criteria for reconciling differences.

This attitude toward litigation is reflected in the small number of practicing lawyers in Japan. There are far fewer (about one-twenty-fifth) lawyers per capita in Japan than in the United States, and only about one-fourth as many civil suits per capita come to court in Japan as compared with the United States.

All is not well in the land of the rising sun, however. Some of the functions performed by American lawyers are handled in Japan by legal specialists and by graduates of law faculties who have knowledge of the law but who are not professionally trained as lawyers. Moreover, the increased tempo of life in modern Japan has brought greater use of courts and legal procedures, especially in commercial matters.

There is also more involved here than just the cultural preferences of potential litigants. The Japanese government has deliberately restricted access to the courts through a formidable system of procedural barriers. In addition, the number of courts and lawyers is purposely kept small to encourage Japanese citizens to resolve their differences in other forums.

Sources: Bradley M. Richardson and Scott C. Flanagan, *Politics in Japan* (Boston: Little, Brown, 1984), 59–60; Marc Galanter, "Reading the Landscape of Disputes: What We Know and Don't Know (and Think We Know) About Our Allegedly Contentious and Litigious Society," *UCLA Law Review* 31 (October 1983): 51–59.

What Courts Should Do: The Issue of Judicial Power

The courts, Alexander Hamilton wrote in the Federalist Papers, "will be least in capacity to annoy or injure" the people and their liberties. Throughout American history, critics of judicial power have disagreed. They see the courts as too powerful for their own—or the nation's—good. Yesterday's critics focused on John Marshall's "usurpations" of power, on the proslavery decision in *Dred Scott,* or on the efforts of the "nine old men" to kill off Franklin Roosevelt's New Deal legislation. Today's critics are never short of ammunition to show that courts go too far in making policy.

Courts make policy on both large and small issues. In recent years courts have made policies on major issues involving school busing, abortion, affirmative action, nuclear power, and other key issues. In other cases around the country, courts have done the following:

- Ordered the city of Mobile, Alabama, to change its form of government because it allegedly discriminated against minorities (the Supreme Court overturned this decision)
- Closed some prisons and ordered other states to expand their prison size
- Eliminated high school diplomas as a requirement for a fire fighter's job
- Decided that Mexican-American children have a constitutional right to a bilingual education[28]

There are strong disagreements concerning the appropriateness of allowing the courts to have a policy-making role. Many scholars and judges favor a policy of **judicial restraint,** in which judges play minimal policy-making roles, leaving policy decisions strictly to the legislatures. These observers stress that the federal courts, composed of unelected judges, are the least democratic branch of government and question the qualifications of judges for making policy decisions and balancing interests. Advocates of judicial restraint believe that decisions such as those on abortion and school prayer go well beyond the "referee" role they feel is appropriate for courts in a democracy.

On the other side are proponents of **judicial activism,** in which judges make bolder policy decisions, even charting new constitutional ground with a particular decision. Advocates of judicial activism emphasize that the courts may alleviate pressing needs, especially of those who are weak politically or economically, left unmet by the majoritarian political process.

It is important not to confuse judicial activism or restraint with liberalism or conservatism. In Table 16.6 you can see the varying levels of the Supreme Court's use of judicial review to void laws passed by Congress in different eras. The table shows that in the early years of the New Deal judicial activists were conservatives. During the tenure of Earl Warren as chief justice (1953–69), activists made liberal decisions. It is interesting to note that the tenure of the conservative Chief Justice Warren Burger (1969–86) and several conservative nominees of Republican presidents marked the most active use of judicial review in the nation's history.

The problem remains of reconciling the American democratic heritage with an active policy-making role for the judiciary. The federal courts have developed a doctrine of **political questions** as a means to avoid deciding some cases, principally those regarding conflicts between the president and Congress. The courts have shown no willingness, for example, to settle disputes regarding the War Powers Resolution (see Chapter 13).

Similarly, judges typically exercise discretion to attempt, whenever possible, to avoid deciding a case on the basis of the Constitution, preferring less contentious "technical" grounds. They also employ issues of jurisdiction, mootness (whether a case presents an issue of contention), standing, ripeness (whether the issues of a case are clear enough and evolved enough to serve as the basis of a decision), and other conditions to avoid adjudication of some politically

The late Justice William O. Douglas, who served on the Court from 1939–1975, was a leading proponent of judicial activism. Along with Justices Hugo Black and William J. Brennan, Jr., he led the Warren Court's prominent role in the social reforms of the 1950s and 1960s.

---

[28]These and other examples of judicial activism are reported in a critical assessment of judicial intervention by Donald Horowitz, *The Courts and Social Policy* (Washington, D.C.: The Brookings Institution, 1977).

Table 16.6 | Supreme Court Rulings in Which Federal Statutes Have Been Found Unconstitutional

PERIOD	STATUTES VOIDED[a]
1798–1864	2
1864–1910	33 (34)[b]
1910–1930	24
1930–1936	14
1936–1953	3
1953–1969	25
1969–1986	34
1986–present	4
	TOTAL 139

[a]In whole or in part.
[b]An 1883 decision in the *Civil Rights Cases* consolidated five different cases into one opinion declaring one act of Congress void. In 1895 *Pollock* v. *Farmers Loan and Trust Co.* was heard twice, with the same result each time.

Source: Adapted from Henry J. Abraham, *The Judicial Process,* 5th ed. (New York: Oxford University Press, 1986), 294.

charged cases. The Supreme Court refused to decide, for example, whether it was legal to carry out the war in Vietnam without an explicit declaration of war from Congress.

Thus, as you saw in the discussion of *Marbury* v. *Madison,* from the earliest days of the Republic federal judges have been politically astute in their efforts to maintain the legitimacy of the judiciary and to husband their resources. (Remember, judges are typically recruited from political backgrounds.) They have tried not to take on too many politically controversial issues at one time. They have also been much more likely to find state laws (more than 1,000) rather than federal laws (approximately 139, as shown in Table 16.6) unconstitutional.

Another factor that increases the acceptability of activist courts is the ability to overturn their decisions. First, the president and the Senate determine who sits on the federal bench. Second, Congress, with or without the president's urging, can begin the process of amending the Constitution to overcome a constitutional decision of the Supreme Court. Although this process does not occur rapidly, it is a safety valve. The Sixteenth Amendment, providing for a federal income tax, was passed in response to a decision of the Supreme Court nullifying the existing income tax. When the Supreme Court voided state laws prohibiting flag burning, President Bush immediately proposed a constitutional amendment that would permit such laws.

Even more drastic options are available. In 1807 the Federalists, just before leaving office, created a tier of circuit courts and populated them with Federalist judges; the Jeffersonian Democrats took over the reins of power and promptly abolished the entire level of courts. In 1869 the Radical Republicans in Congress altered the appellate jurisdiction of the Supreme Court to prevent it from hearing a case that concerned the Reconstruction Acts (*Ex parte McCardle*). This kind of alteration has never recurred, although Congress did threaten to employ the method in the 1950s regarding some matters of civil liberties.

Finally, if the issue is one of **statutory construction,** in which a court interprets an act of Congress, the legislature routinely passes legislation that clarifies existing laws and, in effect, overturns the courts. In 1984, for example, the Supreme Court ruled, in *Grove City College* v. *Bell,* that when an institution receives federal aid, only the program or activity that actually gets the aid, not the entire institution, is covered by four federal civil rights laws. In 1988 Congress passed a new law specifying that the entire institution is affected. Thus the description of the judiciary as the "ultimate arbiter of the Constitution" is hyperbolic; all the branches of government help define and shape the Constitution.

SUMMARY

The American judicial system is complex. Sitting at the pinnacle of the judicial system is the Supreme Court, but its importance is often exaggerated. Most judicial policy-making and norm enforcement take place in the state courts and the lower federal courts.

Today's Supreme Court is headed by Chief Justice William Rehnquist. William J. Brennan, Jr., announced his resignation on July 21, 1990, and President Bush nominated David H. Souter to replace him. Front row, from left: Thurgood Marshall, former Justice Brennan, Chief Justice Rehnquist, Byron R. White, and Harry Blackmun. Back row, from left: Antonin Scalia, John Paul Stevens, Sandra Day O'Connor, and Anthony M. Kennedy.

Throughout American political history courts have shaped public policy about the economy, liberty, equality, and, most recently, ecology. In the economic arena, until the time of Franklin D. Roosevelt courts traditionally favored corporations, especially when government tried to regulate them. Since the New Deal, though, the courts have been more tolerant of government regulation of business, shifting much of their policy-making attention to issues of liberty and equality. From *Dred Scott* to *Plessy* to *Brown,* the Court has moved from a role of reinforcing discriminatory policy toward racial minorities to a role of shaping new policies for protecting civil rights. Most recently, environmental groups have used the courts to achieve their policy goals.

A critical view of the courts claims that they are too powerful for the nation's own good and are rather ineffective policymakers besides. Throughout American history, however, judges have been important agenda-setters in the political system. Many of the most important political questions make their way into the courts at one time or another. The judiciary is an alternative point of access for those seeking to obtain public policy decisions to their liking, especially those who are not advantaged in the majoritarian political process.

Once in court, litigants face judges whose discretion in decision making is typically limited by precedent. Nevertheless, on questions that raise novel issues, as do many of the most important questions that reach the Supreme Court, the law is less firmly established. Here there is more leeway and judges become more purely political players, balancing different interests and linked to the rest of the political system by their own policy preferences and the politics of their selection.

KEY TERMS

justiciable disputes	class action suits	stare decisis
case	senatorial courtesy	original intent
plaintiff	precedents	judicial implementation
defendant	district courts	writ of mandamus
jury	courts of appeal	*Marbury* v. *Madison*
criminal law	Supreme Court	judicial review
civil law	writ of certiorari	*United States* v. *Nixon*
original jurisdiction	solicitor general	judicial restraint
appellate jurisdiction	per curiam decision	judicial activism
litigants	amicus curiae briefs	political questions
standing to sue	opinion	statutory construction

FOR FURTHER READING

Abraham, Henry J. *Justices and Presidents: A Political History of Appointments to the Supreme Court,* 2nd ed. New York: Oxford University Press, 1985. A readable history of the relationships between presidents and the justices they appointed.

Baum, Lawrence. *The Supreme Court,* 3rd ed. Washington, D.C.: Congressional Quarterly Press, 1989. An excellent work on the operations and impact of the Court.

Carp, Robert A., and C. K. Rowland. *Policymaking and Politics in the Federal District Courts.* Knoxville: University of Tennessee Press, 1983. The best work on the operations of the lower federal courts.

Ely, John Hart. *Democracy and Distrust.* Cambridge, Mass.: Harvard University Press, 1980. An appraisal of judicial review and an effort to create a balanced justification for the role of the courts in policy-making.

Horowitz, Donald. *The Courts and Social Policy.* Washington, D.C.: The Brookings Institution, 1977. A critical assessment of the courts' role in social issues.

Howard, J. Woodford, Jr. *Courts of Appeals in the Federal Judicial System.* Princeton, N.J.: Princeton University Press, 1981. A leading work on the federal courts of appeal.

Jacob, Herbert. *Law and Politics in the United States* Boston: Little, Brown, 1986. An introduction to the American legal system with an emphasis on linkages to the political arena.

Johnson, Charles A., and Bradley C. Cannon. *Judicial Policies: Implementation and Impact.* Washington, D.C.: Congressional Quarterly Press, 1984. One of the best overviews of judicial policy implementation.

O'Brien, David M. *Storm Center,* 2nd ed. New York: Norton, 1990. An overview of the Supreme Court's role in American politics.

Posner, Richard A. *The Federal Courts: Crisis and Reform.* Cambridge, Mass.: Harvard University Press, 1985. A provocative analysis of the institutional problems besetting the federal courts.

Woodward, Bob, and Scott Armstrong. *The Brethren.* New York: Simon & Schuster, 1979. A gossipy "insider's" portrayal of the Supreme Court.

PART FOUR

POLICIES

The Development of Administrative Policy Centers in Washington

Today one cannot go far in Washington—or even the Maryland and Virginia suburbs—without encountering some department, agency, or bureau of the federal government. It was not always this way, of course. When the government moved to Washington in 1800 only the departments of State, Treasury, War, and Navy existed. There was an attorney general (now the head of the Department of Justice), but throughout the early nineteenth century he worked out of his home without the aid of even a single clerk. All told, the federal government arrived in the new city created for it with a mere 130 administrative employees. Nearly two hundred years later, this figure has swelled to about 350,000. Still more federal employees work just outside Washington in buildings such as the Pentagon, for which space could not be found in the city. How this massive expansion has taken place is the subject of this essay. Because the story is such a large and complex one, this short photo essay can only scratch the surface, focusing on just a few of its important and interesting aspects.

Virtually all of today's administrative centers evolved in order to implement legislation passed over the course of American history. If you read the Constitution carefully, you will find few instances in which it specifically establishes statutory authority for administrative units. One exception is the U.S. Patent Office. The Constitution empowers the Con-

This 1846 photo shows the Patent Office building (background) as part of its Washington neighborhood. The building now serves as the National Portrait Gallery.

gress to promote the progress of science by securing for inventors the exclusive right to their discoveries. Precedent for government responsibility for granting patents had long been established in the colonies. Indeed, just twenty-six years after the landing at Plymouth Rock the first American patent was issued in Massachusetts for a water mill device. Establishing an office to award patents was thus high on the agenda of the new federal government. Along with the Post Office it became one of the first administrative centers in Washington.

In 1814 the Patent Office had the distinction of being the only government building not burned during the British invasion. Superintendent of Patents William Thornton—who is best remembered for designing the Capitol building—appealed to a Brit-

ish officer during the attack to save the building. "Are you Englishmen or Goths and Vandals?" he asked. "This is the Patent Office, the depository of the inventive genius of America, in which the whole civilized world is concerned. Would you destroy it?" Spared by the British, the original Patent Office was destroyed by an accidental fire in 1836. Rebuilt soon thereafter in the Greek revival style, it remains today as one of Washington's landmark buildings. Besides housing the Patent Office for nearly a century, it has also served as a Civil War hospital, the site of an inaugural ball for Lincoln (who himself once applied for a patent for his method of getting boats over shallow waters), and most recently as the National Portrait Gallery.

As technology has progressed, the work of the Patent Office has

changed tremendously. Until recently, for example, it would have been unthinkable that patents could be awarded for the invention of new life forms. One thing remains constant however: frustrating delays for inventors. As early as 1848 Congress investigated this problem, which led to the hiring of additional patent examiners. By the early twentieth century the situation had further deteriorated. In 1916 Patent Number 1,203,190 was granted—over thirty-six years after its initial filing. Today the Patent Office receives more than 150,000 applications a year, with the average wait for a decision being eighteen months. The demands of awarding patents for breakthroughs in biotechnology have particularly overburdened the office during the last few years. Keeping up with the inventive genius of Americans remains as difficult as ever as the twenty-first century approaches.

While inventions have spurred American economic growth, it has been the Treasury Department that has monitored and guided it. Like the Patent Office, the original Treasury building was destroyed by fire in the 1830s. A new site was chosen close to the White House during the presidency of Andrew Jackson. Unfortunately, the placement of the building prevented the carrying out of L'Enfant's plan for Pennsylvania Avenue to directly connect the Capitol and the White House. (To this day, traffic down the avenue has to detour right

ment's subunits is the Bureau of Engraving and Printing, which prints fifty-nine billion dollars in paper currency and treasury bonds each year. In addition, over thirty billion postage stamps are printed by the bureau each year. The existence of the bureau dates back to 1862, when its six employees worked in the attic of the Treasury building. Their job was to emboss the official seal on bills that had been printed under government contract by private companies.

Since 1880 the Bureau of Engraving and Printing has had its own building south of the Mall, in which all production operations involving national currency are centered. Today it is one of the most popular sight-seeing attractions in Washington, with about five thousand people

and then left around the Treasury building.) Some believe that Jackson made this choice intentionally so that he would no longer have to look out at the branch with which he so often quarreled. Another legendary version has it that one day while surveying the possible sites Jackson impatiently stuck his cane into the ground, ordering that "here, right here, is where I want its cornerstone laid." Neither story is true, however. Befitting the department for which it was constructed, the major factor in the site selection was an economic one: it was chosen because it lay on affordable government land.

The Department of Treasury has a number of enforcement agencies under its jurisdiction, including the

IRS, the U.S. Customs Service, and the Secret Service (originally created in 1860 to suppress counterfeiting, but now best known for its role in protecting the president). Perhaps most interesting of all the Treasury Depart-

A worker at the Bureau of Printing and Engraving inspects some of the billions of dollars that the government prints each year.

touring the facility each weekday. Visitors can observe the massive printing presses—which cost upwards of $500,000 each—churning out money. During the tour one can pick up various bits of trivia, such as that the average life expectancy of a dollar bill is just eighteen months, that American paper currency is actually 75 percent cotton and 25 percent linen, and that between 1912 and 1918 the bureau washed, dried, and ironed dirty bills.

While the Bureau of Engraving and Printing is responsible for producing America's currency, it is up to the Federal Reserve System to decide how much money will be put into circulation. The Fed, which has only fifteen hundred employees, administers as well as formulates policy for the credit and monetary affairs of the U.S. government. A tour of the Federal Reserve building on Constitution Avenue is also available to the public, but is far less popular than the Bureau of Engraving and Printing tour. Although the work of the Fed is as important as most any administrative center in Washington (see Chapter 17), it is relatively little known. This is in large part due to the stealthy operating procedures of its Board of Governors. No transcripts are ever taken of the board's meetings, and most of its decisions are kept secret for six weeks afterward.

The most secretive government agency is of course the Central Intelligence Agency (CIA), located just across the Potomac River from Washington in the wooded seclusion of Langley, Virginia. Until recently even the location of the CIA was classified information. It was hardly the best kept secret in town, however. In the early 1970s a *Sixty Minutes* correspondent drove up to the gate with a

The Fed's Board of Governors meets behind closed doors to discuss and establish the nation's monetary policies.

camera crew as part of an exposé on the CIA. When questioned on camera, the guard denied that the CIA was behind the gate but refused to comment about what was there. Soon afterward the agency relented and put up a road sign on the George Washington Parkway to indicate its location. (Of course, uninvited visitors are still turned back at the gate.) Other indications of the greater openness of today's CIA are that most employees are now permitted to say they work for the agency and to answer their office phones with their name rather than a four-digit extension.

The CIA's location is no longer an official secret—this road sign now lists the CIA along with the nearby FHWA (Federal Highway Works Administration).

While the CIA is the collector of Washington's most secret government information, the National Archives is the repository of America's most public documents. Among the most fa-

mous documents on display in the Archives building are the Declaration of Independence, the Constitution, and the Bill of Rights. Each is housed in a case containing special gases that protect the document from further deterioration. In the event of nuclear attack, the cases will slide into a deep underground vault. Tourists come to see these national treasures, but scholars come to the National Archives to search through its vast holdings of governmental records. All told, there are enough documents in the archives to fill 150,000 four-drawer filing cabinets.

The Archives building is appropriately located right in the middle of Washington's most concentrated area of bureaucracy: the Federal Triangle. The Triangle consists of twelve government buildings situated between Pennsylvania Avenue, Constitution Avenue, and Fifteenth Street. The intersections of these roads result in a triangular pattern that mirrors the geometric relationship of the Capitol, the Washington Monument, and the White House. Commissioned in the 1920s, each building in the Triangle

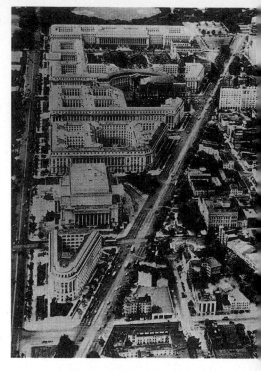

Construction on the Federal Triangle— never really "finished"—began with the Commerce building (top) and ended with the Labor Department building (at the triangle's apex).

was designed in the same overall style, built to the same height, and covered with a red tile roof. Modeling their master plan after the Louvre in Paris, the Triangle architects planned circles, gardens, and a large courtyard in the middle. Unfortunately the architects failed to plan for sufficient parking for employees who worked in the buildings. Therefore what was to have been a grand plaza in the middle was soon turned into a parking lot, and it remains one to this day.

At the base of the Federal Triangle is the Department of Commerce. When it was completed in 1932 the Commerce building was the largest office building in the world. It has 3,311 rooms, 5,200 windows, 32 elevators, and 8 miles of corridors. The building is nevertheless too small to meet the needs of the Commerce De-

partment today. Ironically, critics of the building initially doubted that Commerce would ever be able to make use of all the space—dubbing it "Hoover's Folly" after the president whose administration built it.

Similar skepticism was expressed in the early 1940s when plans were announced for the Department of Defense's massive Pentagon building. Roughly five times as large as the Commerce building, the Pentagon consists of 3.7 million square feet, with 17.5 miles of corridors. It has often been remarked that no spy would enter the Pentagon for fear that he or she would not be able to find a way out. One legendary story involves a pregnant woman in labor

Visitors crowd around the Declaration of Independence, the Constitution, and the Bill of Rights, all on permanent display at the National Archives building.

asking a guard for help in getting to the hospital. Said the guard, "Madam, you should not have come here in this condition." The woman answered, "When I came in here I wasn't."

The building, which opened in 1943 after just sixteen months of around-the-clock construction, has 7,748 windows, 4,200 clocks, 683 water fountains, and 280 rest rooms. Built on reclaimed swampland on the Virginia side of the Potomac River, the Pentagon's foundation rests on 41,492 concrete piles. For decades the Pentagon was the biggest office building in the world, but it is now second to New York's World Trade Center. Its sixty-seven-acre parking lot is still probably the largest anywhere, though. Interestingly, a 1987 survey of the cars parked there revealed that 45 percent were foreign made—the majority in Japan, whose attack on Pearl Harbor led to the Pentagon's construction.

After World War II the Pentagon was supposed to be converted into a warehouse. In fact, Franklin Roosevelt had suggested that it be built without windows so as to make it more suitable for storage. The secretary of war ruled this out, however, saying that he would never work in a building designed like a "cold-storage warehouse for bananas." Providing windows proved to be wise given that the Pentagon turned out to be too small to house the needs of the military both during and after the war.

To supplement the Pentagon, hideous "temporary" buildings were put up on both sides of the Lincoln Memorial's scenic reflecting pool during World War II. They were so placed because President Roosevelt was well aware of the difficulties in guaranteeing that such structures

The Pentagon, home to the Department of Defense, contains an astonishing 17.5 miles of corridors.

would indeed have a short life span. As assistant secretary of the Navy during World War I, Roosevelt had personally advised that temporary buildings be placed across from the White House so as to ensure their removal after the war. President Wilson, however, did not wish to be bothered by all the noise from the construction and asked for them to be moved a couple blocks away. Because they were not placed in an absolutely offensive location and were relatively solid, these buildings were still in place as World War II began.

Learning from this experience, FDR ordered that temporary World War II buildings should be such an eyesore that no one would want to keep them around for long, and so flimsy that they would fall apart in any event. Eyesores they were, and they quickly began to deteriorate as

planned. Contrary to Roosevelt's plan, however, a quarter century later many of these "temporary" buildings were still being used by the government. It took the personal intervention of President Nixon to finally have them torn down, but even then not until suitable alternative office space could be found. Clearly, it is not in the nature of the government to shrink. ►▼▼▼

These "temporary" Navy Department offices, built during World War II, were not torn down until the early 1970s.

17

*E*CONOMIC POLICY-MAKING

Americans are not great savers. According to the Office of Management and Budget, U.S. citizens save only about 4.2 percent of their income. This compares to 9.9 percent in Canada, 10.8 percent in West Germany, and a whopping 20.3 percent in Japan. Thus when the U.S. government looks to borrow money to finance the deficit, it now finds that Americans have an inadequate supply of cash on hand to lend. Foreigners, especially the Japanese, must therefore be relied upon to fund America's capital investment needs. Because of high American interest rates, they are quite willing to invest in the United States. This helps for now, but the earnings on those investments flow abroad, and there is always the fear of what would happen if, for political reasons, foreigners were to stop lending money to the United States.

It is fears such as this that have led President Bush to propose the Family Savings Account. This plan would encourage savings by letting taxpayers put away twenty-five hundred dollars a year in such ac-counts, and, after seven years, withdraw any amount with no tax on the accumulated earnings. At present, people can earn tax-free interest on Individual Retirement Accounts, but until the depositor turns sixty these funds cannot be withdrawn without penalty. If people could accumulate interest tax-free for other major expenses, such as a college education, the savings rate would improve, according to Bush. Critics of the proposal, however, point out that because couples with incomes up to $120,000 (and singles up to $60,000) would be eligible for the Family Savings Account, those who would benefit the most would be people with incomes far above the average.

Proposals such as this one are the heart of economic policy-making. As you will see, even in America's free enterprise economy the government has some limited tools to affect economic behavior, and hence who gets what. How it goes about this important task is the subject of this chapter.

*F*ew policy issues evoke stronger disagreement than those about the economy. Policymakers worry constantly about the state of the economy, and voters often judge officeholders by how well the economy performs. With their jobs on the line, policymakers depend heavily on the advice of professional economists. Yet, more often than not, their advice has been a cacaphony, not a chorus. President Truman once became so frustrated by hearing economists tell him "on the one hand . . . , but on the other hand . . . " that he asked his aides to find him a one-armed economist.

Today many descriptions of the American economy are available; being so diverse, not all of them can be correct. This chapter explores the economy and the public policies dealing with it.

POLITICS AND ECONOMICS

Americans are accustomed to seeing politics and economics as two quite different subjects. Robert Reich remarks that

> Americans tend to divide the dimensions of our national life into two broad realms. The first is the realm of government and politics. The second is the realm of business and economics. . . . The choice is falsely posed. In advanced industrial nations like

the United States, drawing such sharp distinctions between government and the market has ceased to be useful.[1]

The view that politics and economics are closely linked is neither new nor unique. Indeed, both James Madison, the architect of the Constitution, and Karl Marx, the founder of communist theory, argued that economic conflict was at the root of politics. The viewpoint taken in this chapter is that politics and economics are powerful, intertwined forces shaping public policies—and public lives, as you can see in "In Focus: Public Policy and Steel."

Government and the Economy

Economic problems create social problems. Thus the most sensitive part of a voter's anatomy is the pocketbook. When the economy goes sour, the cry of "throw the rascals out" reverberates throughout the country; too much unemployment or inflation can increase unemployment among politicians.

Measuring how many and what types of workers are unemployed is one of the major jobs of the Bureau of Labor Statistics (BLS) in the Department of Labor. To carry out this task, they conduct a random survey of the population every month. Unlike most of the surveys discussed in this book, the sample size is not a mere one or two thousand, but rather a massive fifty thousand. Therefore policymakers can be assured that any change of over one-tenth of 1 percent is more than could possibly be attributed to sampling error. No one questions using a survey to determine the **unemployment rate,** but some economists do challenge the BLS's definition of this rate: the proportion of the labor force actively seeking work but unable to find a job. Critics maintain that those who have given up looking for a job should also be included.

[1]Robert B. Reich, *The Next American Frontier* (New York: Penguin Books, 1983), 4–5.

Unemployment, the nation's most sensitive economic issue, has a devastating effect on millions of Americans. In 1982, when more than 10 percent of the population was out of work—a higher percentage than at any time since the Great Depression—jobless individuals such as these depended on their federal aid checks.

Public Policy and Steel

The steel industry, like much of older, industrial America, is in trouble. Import quotas, air pollution policies, policies to reduce gasoline consumption, labor regulation, and a host of other government policies affect the steel industry, and what affects the steel industry also affects neighborhoods and families who depend on it.

By 1985 the steel industry, once one of America's strongest, operated at only 42 percent of capacity. Some two hundred thousand jobs had disappeared in the industry since 1965. Steel companies were busy selling off even profitable plants to find capital for other, nonsteel ventures. Part of Big Steel's problems stemmed from Japanese competition; cheaper labor costs and more advanced technology permitted Japanese companies to sell their steel cheaper than American companies could sell their steel. This situation led to efforts to persuade President Reagan to cut imports from Japan. Counting Japan as a valued ally and suspecting that the Japanese would retaliate against other American products, Reagan refused. Japan, though, continued to cooperate with voluntary quotas, and Prime Minister Nakasone even urged a "buy American" program in his country.

Other government policies affect profits and jobs in the steel industry. Take the case of energy policies. Short of oil, Congress and the Department of Transportation adopted policies to reduce energy consumption in cars. Automobile manufacturers were ordered to produce cars lighter in weight to consume less fuel. Heavy steel was the loser to lighter aluminum and plastics. A 1977 Ford car contained 2,344 pounds of steel; a 1985 Ford car contained 1,520 pounds. In 1976 the steel industry sent 25 percent of its total output to the automobile industry. Five years later—after environmental and energy regulations on the auto industry—only 15 percent of Big Steel's output went to the automobile industry.

As one business journal bluntly put it:

> Congress, in legislating fuel-consumption standards for American cars, committed itself to a radically different industrial structure. You downsized American cars to save gas, and you wound up downsizing not only the U.S. auto industry itself but a substantial part of the industrial base that supported it. You saved gasoline. And you destroyed blue-collar jobs.

Sources: The story of steel, autos, and government regulation is taken from Kenneth Dolbeare, *Democracy at Risk* (Chatham, N.J.: Chatham House, 1984), 70–71. The quotation is from *Forbes*, November 22, 1982, 161.

The effects of unemployment are clear for all to see. One careful analysis found that a 1 percent increase in the unemployment rate was associated with the following:

- A 4.1 percent increase in the suicide rate
- A 3.4 percent increase in admissions to state mental hospitals
- A 5.7 percent increase in the homicide rate
- A 1.9 percent increase in deaths from cirrhosis of the liver (usually associated with alcoholism)[2]

Of course, unemployment's effects are probably more subtle than suggested by statistical analyses. It is unlikely that people who lose their jobs suddenly become

[2]M. Harvey Brenner, *Estimating the Social Costs of National Economic Policy: Implications for Mental and Physical Health, and Criminal Aggression* (Washington, D.C.: Government Printing Office, 1976).

Figure 17.1 Unemployment: Joblessness in America, 1960–1989

The United States has always experienced some joblessness. The late 1960s were a time of considerable prosperity, with unemployment falling to less than 4 percent. It rose in the less prosperous 1970s, however, and in 1982 and 1983 unemployment averaged almost 10 percent. By 1989, though, it had settled back to between 5 and 6 percent. Each 1 percent in the unemployment rate represents more than a million people out of work. Unemployment falls especially heavily upon minorities, who typically suffer unemployment rates two or three times higher than for whites.

Unemployment, like any other measure of a policy problem, is partly a matter of definition. The unemployment rate would be higher if it included what the Bureau of Labor Statistics calls "discouraged workers," people who have become so frustrated that they have stopped actively seeking employment. On the other hand, if the unemployment rate included only those who were unemployed long enough to cause them severe hardship, it would be much lower, since most people are out of work only a short time.

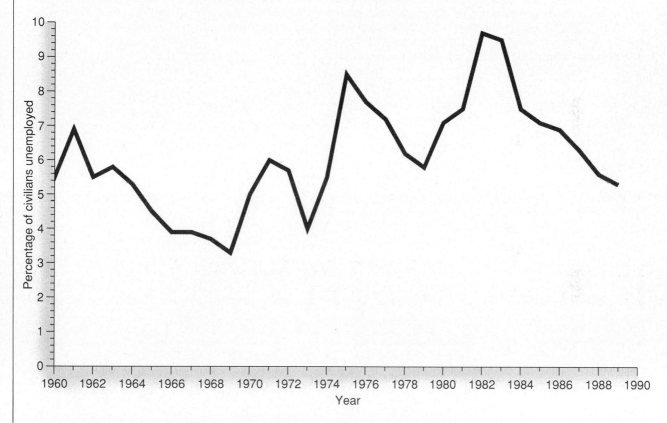

Source: Economic Report of the President, 1990 (Washington, D.C.: Government Printing Office, 1990).

suicidal or alcoholics. It is likely, however, that economic conditions are significantly associated with complex social problems.

The problem of inflation is the other half of policymakers' regular economic concern. For decades the government has also kept tabs on the **Consumer Price Index (CPI),** the key measure of inflation. Unlike unemployment, inflation hurts some but actually benefits others. Some groups are especially hard hit, such as those who live on fixed incomes—their rent and grocery costs go up, but their income does not. In contrast, people whose salary increases are tied to the CPI but whose mortgage payments are fixed may find that inflation actually increases their buying power. As David Piachaud puts it, "Inflation acts neither as Robin Hood nor as Robber Baron: neither the poor nor the rich are

---

Figure 17.2 | **Inflation: Increases in the Cost of Living, 1960–1989**

Inflation was low in the 1960s, but it began to roar in the 1970s, partly as a consequence of the huge increases in the price of energy resulting from the Arab oil embargo that began in 1973. Between 1967 and the end of 1978, the cost of living doubled. Throughout the late 1970s, the cost of medical care, housing, energy, and almost everything else was soaring. Prices were escalating so fast that the average family's real income (its income after the effects of inflation had been discounted) was actually going down. The cost of living increased 50 percent between late 1978 and early 1984. Inflation cooled, however, after the recession of 1982, permitting real wages to catch up to their former levels.

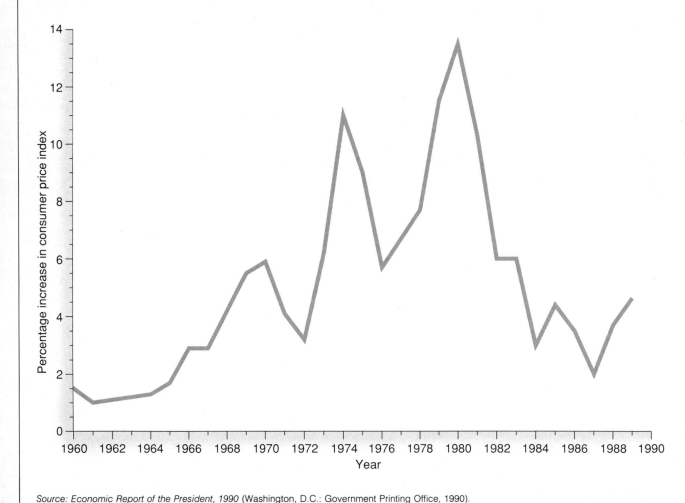

Source: Economic Report of the President, 1990 (Washington, D.C.: Government Printing Office, 1990).

affected in a uniform way."[3] In any case, there are few people who welcome the economic uncertainty generated by high inflation.

Elections and the Economy

People who are unemployed, worried about the prospect of being unemployed, or struggling with racing inflation have an outlet to express their dissatisfaction—the polling booth. Ample evidence indicates that voters pay attention to economic trends in making up their minds on election day, and that they consider not just their own financial situation, but the economic condition of the nation as well. In a careful analysis of two decades of election study data, Roderick Kiewiet finds that voters who experience unemployment in their family are more likely to support Democratic candidates.[4] It is not only a voter's personal experience with unemployment that benefits the Democrats; employed voters who feel that joblessness is a serious national problem lean strongly to the Democratic party. Concern over inflation, on the other hand, has had less impact on voter choices, according to Kiewiet. Perceptions of Nixon's forceful handling of the problem did help him win reelection in 1972, whereas spiraling inflation in 1980 certainly contributed to Carter's defeat. These cases, however, are exceptions to the general rule that most of the time people are not sufficiently affected by inflation for it to influence their vote.

Political Parties and the Economy

Because voters are sensitive to economic conditions, the parties must pay close attention to those conditions when selecting their policies. Some years ago, Nobel laureate Paul Samuelson articulated a common belief about the two parties in the United States. "We tend to get our recessions during Republican administrations," he remarked. "The Democrats," he continued, "are willing to run with some inflation; the Republicans are not."[5] This observation leads to an interesting hypothesis about party behavior: Republicans are willing to risk higher unemployment and recession, while Democrats are willing to tolerate high inflation. Douglas Hibbs investigated this hypothesis as part of his influential analysis of economic policy in twenty advanced industrialized democracies. His general conclusion was that economic policies "pursued by left-wing and right-wing governments are broadly in accordance with the objective economic interests and subjective preferences of their class-defined core political constituencies."[6]

Parties thus behave very much the way voters expect them to. In the United States, the Democratic coalition is made up heavily of groups who worry the most about unemployment—union members, minorities, and the poor. This gives the Democratic party a special incentive to pursue policies designed to

[3]David Piachaud, "Inflation and the Income Distribution," in Fred Hirsch and John H. Goldthorpe, eds., *The Political Economy of Inflation* (Cambridge, Mass.: Harvard University Press, 1978), 115.

[4]D. Roderick Kiewiet. *Macroeconomics and Micropolitics: The Electoral Effects of Economic Issues* (Chicago: University of Chicago Press, 1983).

[5]Quoted in Douglas Hibbs, "Political Parties and Macroeconomic Policy," *American Political Science Review* 71 (December 1977): 1467.

[6]*Ibid.*, 1468.

lower unemployment. On the other side, the Republican coalition rests more heavily on a base of people who are most concerned about steady prices for their goods and services—business owners, managers, and professional people. Therefore Republican administrations have taken stronger action to keep inflation down, even at the risk of greater unemployment.

Politicians and parties exert enormous effort to control the economy. The impact of government on the economic system is substantial, but also sharply limited by a basic commitment to a free enterprise system. Before examining the obstacles the American government faces in guiding the economy, the following sections will introduce you to the economic tools it does possess.

GOVERNMENT'S INSTRUMENTS FOR CONTROLLING THE ECONOMY

The time when government could ignore economic problems, confidently asserting that the private marketplace could handle them, has long passed—if it ever really existed. Especially since the Great Depression and the New Deal, government has been actively involved in steering the economy. When the stock market crash of 1929 sent unemployment soaring, President Herbert Hoover clung to the **laissez-faire** principle that government should not meddle with the economy. In the next presidential election Hoover was handed a crushing defeat by Franklin D. Roosevelt, whose New Deal experimented with dozens of new federal policies to put the economy back on track.

Since the New Deal, policymakers have made it part of their regular business to seek to control the economy. They cannot do it by magic or prayers (when George Bush was campaigning against Ronald Reagan in 1980, for instance, he called Reagan's economic policy "voodoo economics"). They need policy tools, and the American political economy offers two such tools: monetary policy and fiscal policy.

Monetary Policy and the Fed

One way the government can control the economy is through **monetary policy,** that is, the manipulation of the supply of money in private hands. An economic theory called **monetarism** holds that the supply of money is the key to the nation's economic health. Monetarists believe that having too much cash and credit in circulation generates inflation. Essentially, they advise holding the growth in money supply to the rise in the real (in other words, after inflation) gross national product. Politicians worry constantly about the money supply because it affects the rate of interest their constituents have to pay for home loans, new cars, starting up new businesses, and so on.

The main agency for making monetary policy is "the Fed," whose formal title is the Board of Governors of the Federal Reserve System. Created by Congress in 1913 to regulate the lending practices of banks and thus the money supply, the **Federal Reserve System** was intended to be formally beyond the control of the president and Congress. Its seven-member Board of Governors—appointed by the president and confirmed by the Senate—are expected to do their job without regard to partisan politics. Accordingly, members of the Fed are given fourteen-year terms designed to insulate them from political pressures.

Alan Greenspan (right), chair of the Federal Reserve Board, prepares to brief the Senate Banking Committee. The Fed controls the supply of money to individuals and businesses, thus wielding enormous influence over interest rates, inflation, and unemployment—an influence which draws the close attention of Congress and the president.

The Fed has three basic instruments for controlling the money supply. First, the Fed sets *discount rates* for the money that banks borrow from the Federal Reserve banks. If they raise this rate, banks will have to pass their increased costs along to their customers. Thus fewer people will want to take out loans and less money will be in circulation. Second, the Fed sets *reserve requirements* that determine the amount of money that banks must keep in reserve at all times. When they increase this requirement banks have less money to lend out, and therefore charge their customers more for it. And third, the Fed can exercise control over the money supply by simply creating more money to sell to the banks. Whereas raising the costs of borrowing money increases the risk of unemployment and recession, making more money available to borrow increases the risk of inflation.

In sum, the amount of money available, interest rates, inflation, and the availability of jobs are all affected either directly or indirectly by the complicated financial dealings of the Fed. The Fed can profoundly influence the state of the economy—it is no wonder then that it attracts the attention of politicians. When the Fed, under the leadership of Paul Volker, decided to tighten the money supply in late 1979 in order to control inflation, interest rates soared. President Carter, already suffering from what he termed a crisis of confidence, saw his popularity rating fall to nearly the same level as the prime rate (about 20 percent). The resulting deep recession helped Reagan win office in 1980, but also made the early years of his presidency difficult until the economic recovery took hold in 1983.

The Secretive Deliberations of the Fed

In many ways, decision making at the Fed resembles that of the Supreme Court. The Fed meets behind closed doors, keeps no transcripts of its deliberations, and does not even release many of its decisions for six weeks. Although the Fed is often well aware of the potential impact of its actions, its policy is to keep mum about it. Even in 1979, when its Board of Governors knew that their decisions would throw the economy into a downturn, they said little aside from some oblique comments on "substantial adjustments" and "necessary pain" ahead.

Like the Court, the Fed claims that secrecy is needed to keep its activities above politics; however, there is no economic constitution for the Fed to follow. They are not merely interpreting public policy but clearly making it. What, then, is the justification for all the secrecy? Allan Greenspan, chair of the Fed, believes that secrecy makes it possible for the Fed to take unpopular political stands, such as raising interest rates when necessary.

Critics in Congress and academia, on the other hand, feel that the primary purpose is for the Fed to avoid criticism. They worry that the central bank is profoundly undemocratic. Professor James David Barber is particularly skeptical of the argument that Fed governors can only act in the public interest if they meet in secret. "That," he says, " is the kind of argument King George III would make." What do *you* think?

Sources: William Greider, *Secrets of the Temple: How the Federal Reserve Runs the Country* (New York: Simon & Schuster, 1987); the quote is from David E. Rosenbaum, "Little Chance Seen for Bills on Fed Rein," *New York Times*, October 10, 1989, C1.

With so much riding on its decisions, presidents quite naturally try to persuade the Fed to pursue policies in line with their plan for the country. There is some evidence that the Fed is generally responsive to the White House, although not to the extent of trying to influence election outcomes.[7] Nevertheless, even the chief executive can be left frustrated by the politically insulted decisions of the Fed (see "A Question of Ethics: The Secretive Deliberations of the Fed").

Fiscal Policy: Bigger versus Smaller Government

How much the government runs in the red (being in the black hardly seems plausible these days) is one factor in determining the nation's economic health. **Fiscal policy** describes the impact of the federal budget—taxing, spending, and borrowing—on the economy. Unlike monetary policy, fiscal policy is shaped mostly by the Congress and the president. The use of fiscal policy to stimulate the economy is most often associated with advocates of big government, but as you will see proponents of small government also believe that fiscal policy

---

[7]See William Greider, *Secrets of the Temple: How the Federal Reserve Runs the Country* (New York: Simon & Schuster, 1988); Nathaniel Beck, "Elections and the Fed: Is There a Political Monetary Cycle?" *American Journal of Political Science* 31 (February 1987): 194–216; and Nathaniel Beck, "Presidential Influence on the Federal Reserve in the 1970s," *American Journal of Political Science* 26 (August 1982): 415–45.

should be used for this purpose. Whether bigger government or smaller government best ensures a strong economy has become the central issue in economic policy-making.

On the side of big government is **Keynesian economic theory,** named after English economist John Maynard Keynes. Soon after the 1936 publication of his landmark book, *The General Theory of Employment, Interest, and Money*, Keynesianism became the dominant economic philosophy in America. This theory emphasized that government spending could help the economy weather its normal ups and downs, even if it meant running in the red. Keynes argued that government could spend its way out of the Depression by stimulating the economy through spending. If businesses were not able to expand, it would be up to the government to pick up the slack, he claimed. If there were no jobs available for people, the government should create some—building roads, dams, houses, or whatever seems most appropriate. The key would be to get money back in the consumers' pocket, for if few have money to buy goods then little will be produced. Thus the government's job would be to increase the demand when necessary—the supply would take care of itself.

So dominant was Keynesian thinking in government policy-making that Democrats and Republicans alike adhered to its basic tenets—that is, until the Reagan administration. Reagan's economic gurus proposed a radically different theory based on the premise that the key task for government economic policy is to stimulate the supply of goods, not their demand.[8] Thus this theory has been labeled **supply-side economics.** To supply-siders, big government soaked up too much of the gross national product; by taxing too heavily, spending too freely, and regulating too tightly, government curtailed economic growth. Supply-side economists argued that incentives to invest, work harder, and save could be increased by cutting back on the scope of government—especially tax rates. Economist Arthur Laffer proposed (legend says on the back of a cocktail napkin) a curve suggesting that the more government taxed, the less people worked, and thus the smaller the government's tax revenues. Cut the taxes, Laffer reasoned, and people would work harder and thereby stimulate the economy by producing a greater supply of goods. In its most extreme form, this theory held that by taking a smaller percentage of people's income the government would actually get more total revenue as production increased.

Faced with the worst economic downturn since the Depression of the 1930s, Reagan and the supply-siders believed that cutting taxes would pull business out of its doldrums. During his first administration, Reagan fought for and won massive tax cuts, mostly for the well-to-do. One cannot emphasize enough how this approach differed from the established Keynesian model. Rather than public works programs to stimulate demand, Americans got tax cuts to stimulate supply; rather than a fiscal policy that promoted bigger government, Americans got a policy that tried, but ultimately failed, to reduce the size of government.

Whichever fiscal approach politicians favor, one formerly controversial issue is now agreed upon—it is the government's responsibility to use fiscal policy to try to control the economy. Like controlling the weather, this is much easier said than done.

John Maynard Keynes's influential economic theories encouraged the use of government spending to stimulate the economy during down periods.

[8]One supply-side theory can be found in George Gilder, *Wealth and Poverty* (New York: Basic Books, 1981).

OBSTACLES TO CONTROLLING THE ECONOMY

Some scholars argue that politicians manipulate the economy for short-run advantage to win elections. Edward Tufte writes, "When you think economics, think elections; when you think elections, think economics."[9] Tufte concluded that between World War II and 1976, real disposable income (after taxes and inflation) tended to increase more at election time than at other times. In addition, transfer payments, such as Social Security and veterans' benefits, seemed more likely to increase just prior to an election.

A neat trick if you can do it, one might say about the ability of politicians to so precisely control economic conditions to facilitate their reelection. There are some missing links in the argument, however. For starters, most of the evidence is circumstantial—no one has shown that decisions to influence the economy at election time have been made on a regular basis. Controlling unemployment and inflation with precision is like stopping on an economic dime. All the instruments for controlling the economy have one aspect in common: they are difficult to use. To begin with, politicians—and even economists—do not understand the workings of the economy sufficiently well to always choose the correct adjustments to ensure prosperity. In addition, benefits like Social Security are now *indexed* meaning that they go up automatically as the cost of living increases, a procedure that reduces politicians' ability to manipulate them for political gain. Even when politicians do have control, most policies must be decided upon a year or more before they will have their full impact on the

[9]Edward R. Tufte, *Political Control of the Economy* (Princeton, N.J.: Princeton University Press, 1978), 65.

Many factors limit the American government's ability to control the economy. The 1973 OPEC oil embargo (in response to America's support of Israel in the Yom Kippur War) and the 1979 Iranian revolution led to increased oil prices, gas lines, inflation, and economic recession. Likewise, the 1990 Iraqi invasion of Kuwait sent oil prices soaring.

economy. The president's budget, for example, is prepared many months in advance of its enactment into law. Thus it is hard to know what the economy will be like when the money is actually spent. Given the present state of knowledge, economic forecasting is as much art as it is science.[10]

The American capitalist system presents an additional restraint on controlling the economy. Because the private sector is much larger than the public sector, it dominates the economy. An increase in the price of raw materials or in the wages of union workers can offset a host of government efforts to control inflation. What's more, in the increasingly interdependent world the activities of other nations can throw a monkey wrench in the government's economic plans. This occurred twice in the 1970s when OPEC oil price increases sent shock waves throughout the American economy.

Fiscal policy is also hindered by the budgetary process. As you saw in Chapter 14, most of the budget expenditures for any given year are "uncontrollable." Given that most spending is already mandated by law, it is very difficult to make substantial cuts. Coordinating economic policy-making is equally difficult. The president and Congress both have central roles but may not see eye to eye on taxes or spending, and neither may agree with the independent-minded Fed on the money supply. As with the rest of policy-making in the United States, the power to make economic policy is decentralized.

ARENAS OF ECONOMIC POLICY-MAKING

When the government spends one-third of America's gross national product and regulates much of the other two-thirds, one can be sure that its policies will provoke much debate. Liberals tend to favor active government involvement in the economy in order to smooth out the unavoidable inequality of a capitalist system. Conservatives maintain that the most productive economy is one in which the government exercises a hands-off policy of minimal regulation.

Liberal or conservative, most interest groups seek benefits, protection from unemployment, or safeguards against harmful business practices. Agriculture, business, consumers, and labor are four of the major actors in, and objects of, government economic policy. The following sections examine the role of each in economic policy-making.

Agriculture and Public Policy: The Bitter Harvest

In February 1985 President Reagan's budget director, David Stockman, was testifying before the Senate Budget Committee. Pressed by some senators as to why to the president's budget proposed drastic cuts in aid to financially troubled farmers, Stockman candidly replied:

> For the life of me, I cannot figure out why the taxpayers of this country have the responsibility to go in and refinance bad debt that was willingly incurred by con-

---

[10]One recent promising development is a new theory currently being used by the Fed to predict inflation. See Peter T. Kilborn, "Federal Reserve Sees a Way to Gauge Long-Run Inflation," *New York Times*, June 13, 1989, 1.

senting adults who went out and bought farmland when the price was going up and thought that they could get rich, or who went out and bought machinery and production assets because they made a business judgment that they could make some money.[11]

Farm-state senators and representatives were naturally incensed with this bold challenge to federal assistance their constituents had come to rely on. Ever since the Agricultural Adjustment Act of 1933, passed in response to the ravages of the Depression, the government has subsidized farmers.

Through *price supports* the government guarantees the prices of certain commodities in order to ensure stability in agricultural production. In some cases farmers are actually paid for *not* producing more crops, so as not to flood the marketplace. The government also purchases food directly and stores it, thereby making prices higher than they would be if the entire crop were made available to consumers. The idea behind these policies is that the short-run costs of keeping prices up are less than the long-run costs that might result from falling prices. If too many farmers were forced out of business by low prices, say advocates of price supports, America's food supply might be endangered. The stakes are too high, they claim, to allow the free market to reign completely. The price to taxpayers is by no means cheap—twenty-two billion dollars in fiscal year 1989. Critics, like David Stockman, view farm subsidies as little more than a huge welfare program. One small but controversial component of farm subsidy programs is discussed in "You Are the Policymaker: Is the Honey Program Too Sweet?"

Despite government subsidies for agriculture, farmers have recently faced hard times. The technological revolution has reduced the need for labor while increasing the prices of farm machinery, such as tractors and harvesters. Small family farms have been squeezed out of business. In the decade between 1960 and 1970 the American farm population dropped by about a third, and by the late 1980s almost another third was gone. Farmers often borrowed heavily,

[11]Quoted in *Time*, February 18, 1985, 24.

Doonesbury

BY GARRY TRUDEAU

Is the Honey Program Too Sweet?

The Department of Agriculture's program of price supports and subsidized loans for beekeepers is small as such programs go, costing under $100 million annually. It reflects many of the problems of farm subsidies, however. After World War II, when sugar was no longer rationed and beeswax was not needed for waterproofing munitions, the price of honey fell. Congress, concerned that there would be too few bees for pollinating crops, came to the rescue with programs guaranteeing that beekeepers would get at least a minimum return on their investment. By the mid-1980s, larger beekeepers had relocated to such areas as the Dakotas, where they could take advantage of the more abundant floral sources to produce honey. Crops in those areas are not as dependent on bees for pollination, however—a fact that prompted complaints that the government's program did not promote pollination but just propped up honey production.

Unfortunately, in recent years there has been little demand for American honey. In the 1980s world honey supplies increased and the high value of the dollar encouraged foreign producers to dump their honey in the United States. Since beekeepers can borrow money from the federal government and repay it at whatever price they sell their honey for on the market, even if that price is below the loan price, they have no incentive to control their production. They get to keep the difference between the loan rate and the repayment rate. Because of the low demand for honey, every pound they produce costs taxpayers money.

A few very large beekeeping operations receive a greatly disproportionate share of the honey subsidies. They argue that if the honey program were eliminated, they would be put out of business. Moreover, they say that farmers cannot get along without them. Organized as the American Honey Producers Association, the major beekeepers have been spending a significant amount of time and money defending the program. Put yourself in the place of a member of Congress. What would you do?

Source: "Honey Program Much Too Sweet for Conte," *Congressional Quarterly Weekly Report*, April 30, 1988, 1149–52.

expecting that a continued rise in their property values would keep them afloat. From 1981 through 1987, however, the price of an average acre of farm property fell by 34 percent. Farm debts soared, exports decreased substantially, and bankruptcies rivaled Depression-era rates. Indeed, farm income in the 1980s was below what it had been in the 1950s.

Business and Public Policy: Subsidies amidst Regulations

In contrast, big business prospered and grew during the 1980s. The government looked the other way as big companies swallowed up smaller ones to become even larger. Many regulations were cut back, following Reagan's promise to get the government off the backs of business.

The corporation has long stood at the center of the American economy. Every year, *Fortune* magazine publishes a listing of the *Fortune 500*, the five hundred largest industrial corporations in the United States. In Table 17.1 you can see the assets of the top twenty-five. Their leaders are the giants of American business, controlling assets in the hundreds of billions of dollars. To elite theo-

Table 17.1 America's Top Twenty-five Industrial Corporations in Terms of Assets

RANK[a]	COMPANY	HOME OFFICE	ASSETS (millions of $)
1	General Motors	Detroit, Mich.	173,297
2	Ford Motor	Dearborn, Mich.	160,893
3	General Electric	Fairfield, Conn.	128,344
4	Exxon	New York, N.Y.	83,219
5	IBM	Armonk, N.Y.	77,734
6	Chrysler	Highland Park, Mich.	51,038
7	Mobil	New York, N.Y.	39,080
8	Philip Morris	New York, N.Y.	38,528
9	RJR Nabisco	New York, N.Y.	36,412
10	Du Pont Chemical	Wilmington, Del.	34,715
11	Chevron	San Francisco, Calif.	33,884
12	Amoco	Chicago, Ill.	30,430
13	Xerox	Stamford, Conn.	30,088
14	Shell Oil	Houston, Tex.	27,599
15	Texaco	White Plains, N.Y.	25,636
16	Time Warner	New York, N.Y.	24,791
17	Eastman Kodak	Rochester, N.Y.	23,652
18	Atlantic Richfield	Los Angeles, Calif.	22,261
19	Dow Chemical	Midland, Mich.	22,166
20	Occidental Petroleum	Los Angeles, Calif.	20,741
21	Westinghouse Electric	Pittsburgh, Pa.	20,314
22	USX	Pittsburgh, Pa.	17,500
23	Tenneco	Houston, Tex.	17,381
24	Procter & Gamble	Cincinnati, Ohio	16,351
25	Weyerhaeuser	Tacoma, Wash.	15,976

TOTAL 1,172,030

[a]In 1989.
Source: Fortune, April 23, 1990, 346.

rists, they represent "monopoly capital," a concentration of wealth sufficient to shape both America's and the world's economy.[12] Indeed, the concentration of resources among the top one hundred corporations has been increasing since 1950 (see Figure 17.3). Corporate giants have also internationalized in the postwar period. Some **multinational corporations**—businesses with vast holdings in many countries—are bigger than most governments.

The Changing Face of Corporate Capitalism   "A better idea." "We try harder." These are the types of slogans one would like to think describe prospering corporations. Providing innovative new products or better service is not

---

[12]The argument that the American economy is dominated by "monopoly capital" is common among Marxist economists. See, for example, James O'Connor, *The Fiscal Crisis of the State* (New York: St. Martin's, 1973).

Figure 17.3 Percentage of Industrial Assets Controlled by the Top One Hundred Corporations

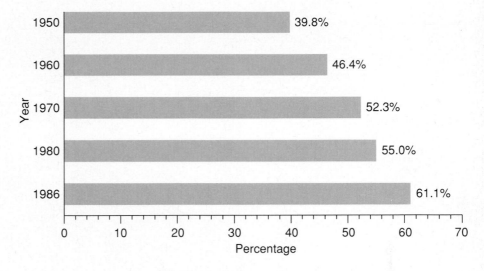

Source: Adapted from Thomas R. Dye, *Who's Running America: The Bush Era,* 5th ed. (Englewood Cliffs, N.J.: Prentice-Hall, 1990), 20.

only a way to make a good profit, but also to contribute to economic growth. No doubt it always will be.

In the 1980s, however, a new form of entrepreneurship flourished—that of merger mania. Billions were spent by conglomerates buying up and buying out other companies. Completed corporate mergers amounted to a whopping $200 billion in 1986 compared to just $30 billion six years earlier.[13] The recent history of this textbook is just one of many examples. The first three editions were published by Little, Brown. Then, Little, Brown was taken over by Scott, Foresman in time for the fourth edition. Now, as you can see, the fifth edition is being published by HarperCollins—who bought out Scott, Foresman. With each merger your authors find themselves confronted with an even bigger publishing house.

Interestingly, mergers need not even be completed for corporate raiders to make a bundle. Millions, even hundreds of millions, in profits can be made by merely threatening to buy another company. "Greenmailers," as they are called, buy a substantial proportion of stock in Corporation *X* and make public their desire to secure controlling interest in the company. As their newly acquired stock soars in value, they have the opportunity to take a windfall profit by selling out, which many of them do. This highly risky business has been labeled "paper entrepreneurialism" by Robert Reich. He and others criticize it as producing no products and no new jobs. "Paper entrepreneurs," Reich insists,

[13]Murray L. Weidenbaum, *Business, Government, and the Public*, 4th ed. (Englewood Cliffs, N.J.: Prentice-Hall, 1990), 458.

JEFF DANZIGER
Courtesy Christian Science Monitor

"provide nothing of tangible use. . . . [R]esources circulate endlessly among giant corporations, investment bankers, and their lawyers, but little new is produced."[14] Business leaders, though, respond that the fear of corporate takeovers keeps management constantly on its toes, providing better products and services.

Another popular argument in favor of the increased concentration of corporate assets is that it strengthens the American economy against foreign competition from giant Japanese and European firms. Certainly, competition from abroad has not helped American corporations. Foreign products now account for about a fifth of all American consumption, and American workers have suffered from this trend. As you can see in Table 17.2, not even technology pioneered in the United States has been safe from foreign businesses. Two decades ago virtually all of the color TVs, record players, and telephones sold in America were American-made; now one has to search hard to find "Made in the U.S.A." on any of these products.

An increasing number of Americans believe that the greatest threat to national security comes not from communist military power, but rather from the economic power of Japan and other capitalist competitors. When the Japanese buy expensive American real estate like New York's Rockefeller Center, concern about foreign domination rises throughout the country. For example, Representative Doug Applegate of Ohio said the following on the House floor in 1989:

> Mr. Speaker, the Berlin Wall is coming down, but the Bamboo Wall is getting taller, and it is getting stronger. Japan is beating us in American Monopoly. They are buying

[14]Reich, *The Next American Frontier*, 57.

Table 17.2 | **Our Idea, Their Manufacturing**

All of the technologies shown here were pioneered in the United States. Yet since 1970 you can see that foreign competitors have made major inroads in selling American technology to Americans.

TECHNOLOGY	U.S. SHARE OF DOMESTIC MARKET (%)				1987 VALUE OF U.S. MARKET
	1970	1975	1980	1987	(millions of $)
Phonographs	90	40	30	1	630
Tape recorders					
Audio	40	10	10	1	500
Video	10	10	1	1	2,895
Televisions					
Black and white	65	30	15	2	175
Color	90	80	60	10	14,050
Telephone sets	99	95	88	25	2,000
Semiconductors	89	71	65	64	19,100
Machine tools					
Horizontal numerically controlled lathes	100	92	70	40	401
Machining Centers	100	97	79	35	485

Source: Congressional Quarterly Weekly Report, May 13, 1989, 1107.

America out, they are shutting us out. . . . We should be mad as hell, and we should be getting back to what America used to be, and that is: No. 1.[15]

It is important, however, to keep in mind that while foreign investment in the United States is growing it still remains below that of most other economic powers. As of 1986, 9 percent of American manufacturing assets were owned by foreign companies compared to 14 percent in Great Britain and 17 percent in West Germany.[16] Furthermore, despite an enormous trade deficit, the United States is the world's leading exporter of merchandise (excluding oil). Although West Germany led in the mid-1980s, the United States has now regained a substantial lead and actually exports twice as much as Japan (see "America in Perspective: Still the World's Top Exporter").

Regulating Business   Government regulation of business is at least as old as the first antitrust act, the Sherman Act of 1890. The purpose of **antitrust policy** is to ensure competition and prevent monopoly (control of a market by one company). Antitrust legislation permits the Justice Department to sue in federal court to break up companies controlling too large a share of the market. It also generally prevents restraints on trade or limitations on competition.

[15]Quoted in David S. Broder, "Way Short of the Mark," *Washington Post Weekly*, December 4–10, 1989, 4.

[16]Tom Redburn, "Difference Between 'Us' and 'Them' Blurs in a Global Economy," *Los Angeles Times*, August 8, 1989, part IV, page 1.

Still the World's Top Exporter

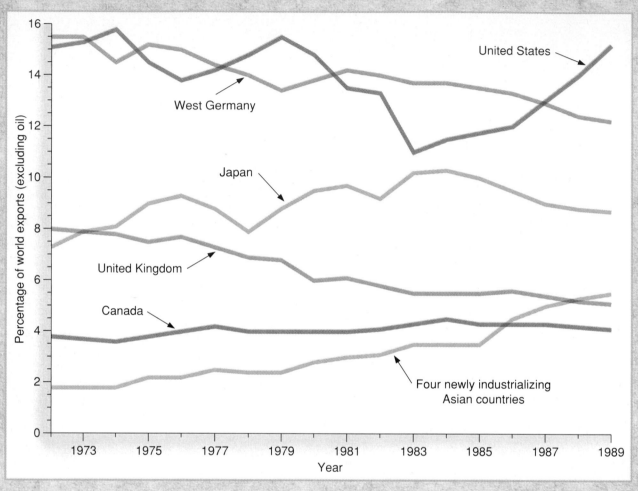

Source: International Monetary Fund.

Enforcement of antitrust legislation, however, has varied. Some presidents have prided themselves on being "trustbusters," while others, like Reagan and Bush, have made antitrust enforcement a low priority.

Antitrust suits are usually lengthy and always expensive; some last decades and cost millions of corporate and federal dollars. The recently settled suits against AT&T and IBM were no exception. Both companies were the target of Justice Department antitrust charges. After seven years, an out-of-court settlement with AT&T resulted in its agreement to sell twenty-two local operating organizations, the Bell companies. A thirteen-year effort to break up IBM was deemed

without merit by the attorney general's office, and the case was dropped. In both cases, though, due to the upheaval of the industries involved, the eventual result may be increased competition—a consequence that is consistent with the Reagan/Bush policy toward American business.

Antitrust policy is hardly the only way business is regulated; Chapter 15 reviewed a variety of regulatory policies affecting businesses. Business owners and managers, especially in small businesses, complain constantly about regulation, but before they complain too much, they should remember some of the benefits they get from government.

Benefiting Business Government has not always been just a silent partner in American business. In a few cases—namely, Chrysler, Lockheed, and the nation's railroads—government loans or buyouts have made government an actual partner or owner in corporate America. When a crucial industry falls on hard times, it usually looks to the government for help in terms of subsidies, tax breaks, or loan guarantees.

Throughout economic booms and busts, the Department of Commerce serves as a veritable storehouse of aids for business. It collects data on products and markets through the Bureau of the Census, helps businesses export their wares, and protects inventions through the Patent Office. The Small Business Administration is the government's counselor, advisor, and loan maker to small businesses. Several agencies fund research that is of value to businesses involved with natural resources, transportation, electronics and computers, and health. In fact, the federal government is the principal source of research and development funding in the United States.

Calvin Coolidge's saying that "the business of America is business" rings particularly true when Republican administrations are in office, but some would argue that it applies almost all the time. One of the reasons that official Washington is so hospitable to business interests is that industry lobbyists in Washington are well organized and well funded (see Chapter 10). Businesses organized for lobbying have been around for years; consumer groups, by contrast, are a relatively new entry onto the economic policy stage.

Consumer Policy: The Rise of the Consumer Lobby

Years ago the governing economic principle of consumerism was "let the buyer beware." With a few exceptions, public policy ignored consumers and their interests. The first major consumer protection policy in the United States was the Food and Drug Act of 1906, which prohibited the interstate transportation of dangerous or impure food and drugs. Today the **Food and Drug Administration (FDA)** has broad regulatory powers over the contents, marketing, and labeling of food and drugs. It is the FDA's responsibility to ascertain the safety and effectiveness of new drugs before approving them for marketing in America.

One recent criticism of the FDA is that cuts in its funding (starting in 1979 under Carter and continuing throughout the Reagan years) have left it overburdened and seriously understaffed. Thus, although federal laws stipulate that new drug applications be completed in six months, the average review now takes thirty-one months. For instance, the agency's inability to quickly approve experimental drugs for the treatment of AIDS has currently engulfed it in public controversy, bringing on strong protests from gay activists and AIDS patients. As the FDA's resources were stretched to the limit during the 1980s, the number

Budget cuts made during the 1980s left many independent regulatory agencies open to criticism from the consumer groups they were created to protect. Here demonstrators protest FDA delays in testing and approving experimental drugs for AIDS patients.

Table 17.3

Some Recent Consumer Product Safety Commission Investigations

PRODUCT	DEFECT OR HAZARD	ACTION TAKEN
Lawn tractor	Loss of steering control	Repaired free at customer's home
Bicycle	Handlebar may disengage	Free replacement of part to those requesting
Aluminum chair	Potential to collapse	Refund, replace, or repair at customer's option
Piano lamp	Fire hazard	Voluntary recall for replacement
Mobile home furnace	Fire hazard	Voluntary recall
Ceiling fan	Defective mounting mechanism	Refund or replacement of hanging mechanism
Wheelbarrow	Defective wheel rim	Wheels recalled and replaced
Toy helicopter	Blades may fly off	Full refund offered
Chain saw	Chain may fly off	Full refund offered
Bassinets	Leg braces could fail	Repair kits provided
Gym swing	Cross beam may fail	Repair kit offered plus allowance for welding costs
Heater-air conditioner	Fire hazard	On-site repair of all units
Oscillating fan	Fire hazard	Replaced
Stroller	Children's fingers may get caught	Media used to publicize new lock

Source: U.S. Consumer Product Safety Commission. Adapted from Murray L. Weidenbaum, *Business, Government, and the Public,* 4th ed. (Englewood Cliffs, N.J.: Prentice-Hall, 1990), 53.

of inspections of drugs and foods declined from 32,778 in 1980 to 19,876 in 1988.[17] The cutbacks at the FDA are just one example of the decline of government regulation of business during the 1980s, a stark reversal of the pattern during the 1960s and 1970s.

Consumerism was a sleeping political giant until the 1960s, when it was awakened by self-proclaimed consumer activists such as Ralph Nader. Uncovering clear cases of unsafe products and false advertising, they argued that it was the government's responsibility to be a watchdog on behalf of the consumer. With broad public support, the 1960s and 1970s saw a flood of consumer protection legislation. Created in 1972 by the Product Safety Act, the Consumer Product Safety Commission (CPSC) has broad powers to ban hazardous products from the market. Today the CPSC regulates the safety of items ranging from toys to lawn mowers. In Table 17.3 you can see some of the products the CPSC recently investigated for defects, and the action it took.

The **Federal Trade Commission (FTC),** traditionally responsible for regulating trade practices, also jumped into the business of consumer protection in the 1960s and 1970s, becoming a defender of consumer interests in truth in advertising. The FTC ordered Carter's Liver Pills to drop "liver" from its name because the pills have no medical effect on the liver. It made new rules about product labeling, exaggerated product claims, and the use of celebrities in advertising. In 1968 Congress made the FTC the administrator of the new Consumer Credit Protection Act. This act stipulates that whenever you borrow money,

[17]Philip J. Hilts, "A Guardian of U.S. Health Is Failing Under Pressures," *New York Times,* December 4, 1989, 1.

even if only by using a credit card, you must receive a form stating the exact amount of interest you must pay. Through such forms and other means, the FTC enforces truth in lending.

Labor and Government

Perhaps the biggest change in economic policy-making has been the virtual 180-degree turn in public policy toward labor unions over the past century. Throughout most of the nineteenth century and well into the twentieth, the federal government allied with business elites to squelch labor unions. The courts interpreted the antitrust laws as applying to unions as well as businesses. Until the Clayton Antitrust Act of 1914 exempted unions from antitrust laws, the mighty arm of the federal government was busier busting unions than trusts. Government lent its hand to enforcing "yellow dog contracts," contracts that forced the workers to agree not to join a union as a condition of employment.

The major turnabout in government policy toward labor took place during the New Deal. In 1935 Congress passed the **National Labor Relations Act,** often called the Wagner Act after its sponsor, Senator Robert Wagner of New York. The Wagner Act guaranteed workers the right of **collective bargaining**— the right to have representatives of their labor unions negotiate with management to determine working conditions. It also set rules to protect unions and organizers. For example, under the Wagner Act an employer cannot fire a worker who advocates the possibility of unionizing.

After World War II a series of strikes and a new Republican majority in Congress tilted federal policy somewhat back in the direction of management. The **Taft-Hartley Act** of 1947 continued to guarantee unions the right of collective bargaining, but prohibited various unfair practices by unions as well. It also gave the president power to halt major strikes by seeking a court injunction for an eighty-day "cooling off" period. Most importantly, section 14B of the law

The conflict between union and nonunion workers has often led to violence. When Greyhound bus drivers went on strike in 1989, for example, nonunion drivers, called "scabs" by union drivers, were the targets of verbal and physical abuse.

permitted states to adopt what union opponents call **right-to-work laws.** Such laws forbid requirements in labor contracts that workers must join a union to hold their jobs. The effect of right-to-work laws is to subject unions to the free-rider problem (see Chapter 10); workers can enjoy the benefits of union negotiations without contributing dues to support the union.

Later public policies focused on union corruption. Stirred by revelations of the mismanagement of funds, racketeering, and violence by some unions, Congress tried to crack down by passing the Labor-Management Reporting and Disclosure Act, called the Landrum-Griffin Act, in 1959. The act required that union members exercise more control over their leaders and forbade ex-convicts from serving as union officials for five years after their release.

Unions have had two notable successes over the years, which have become staples of the American economy. First, partly as the result of successful union lobbying, the government provides unemployment compensation—paid for by workers and employers—to cushion the blows of unemployment. Second, since the New Deal the government has guaranteed a minimum wage, setting a floor on the hourly wages earned by employees. In Figure 17.4 you can see how the minimum wage has increased since 1970. Quite clearly, the Reagan Adminis-

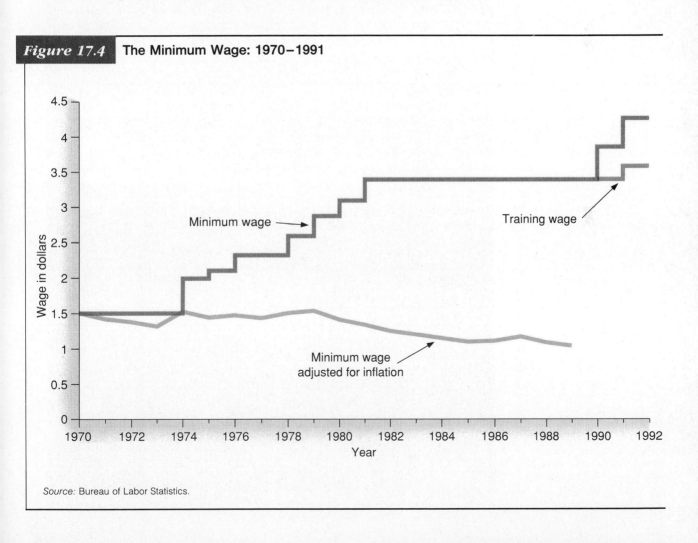

Figure 17.4 **The Minimum Wage: 1970–1991**

Source: Bureau of Labor Statistics.

tration was not sympathetic to union calls for a higher minimum wage; there was not a single increase during Reagan's entire eight years in office. Taking inflation into account, the earning power of the minimum wage declined steadily throughout the 1980s. More recently, though, President Bush approved a measure that will raise the wage to $4.25 by 1991 and establish a lower "training wage" for teenage employees. Such a training wage has been opposed by unions for years, but ultimately they accepted this as part of a compromise to increase the minimum wage for established workers.

DEMOCRACY AND ECONOMIC POLICY-MAKING

The minimum wage and unemployment compensation are just two of many economic policies that contradict Karl Marx's assumptions of how a capitalist system inevitably exploits ordinary workers. Looking at mid-nineteenth century business practices, Marx saw an economic system in which working conditions were long, hard, and miserable. Most workers barely managed to earn a subsistence living while the rich got richer off their labor. In a completely free economic system, there was no way to compel the owners of the factories to

In New York, circa 1890, this Bohemian cigar maker and his family worked seventeen hours a day, seven days a week, for thirteen cents an hour. As American workers have slowly gained more political power, they have demanded government action to improve working conditions.

treat the workers better. Exploitation would continue, and even get worse, Marx felt. His radical solution was for the state to assume all power over the economy in a revolution of the proletariat. In the communist system envisioned by Marx, all the means of production would be owned by the state—in which each citizen would be an equal shareholder.

In America, however, solutions to many of the problems of a free enterprise economy were achieved through the democratic process. As the voting power of the ordinary worker grew, so did the potential for government regulation of the worst ravages of the capitalist system. Political pressure grew for action to restrict unfair business practices and protect individual rights. Over time, the state assumed responsibility for setting the age at which one could work, determining the normal work week, establishing standards for safety on the job, protecting pension funds, and many other aspects of economic life. Just as the right of free speech is not interpreted so as to allow someone to shout "fire" in a crowded movie theater, so the right to free enterprise is no longer interpreted as giving businesses the right to employ ten-year-olds or to force employees to work in unsafe conditions. All Americans now agree that such practices, which were once common, are areas in which the government should step in. Through the ballot box, Americans essentially decided to give up certain economic freedoms for the good of society as a whole.

It would be a vast exaggeration, however, to say that democracy regularly facilitates an economic policy that looks after general rather than specific interests. As you have seen throughout this text, the decentralized American political system often works against efficiency in government. In particular, groups that may be adversely affected by an economic policy have many avenues through which they can work to block it. Therefore one of the consequences of democracy for economic policy-making is that it is difficult to make decisions that hurt particular groups or that involve short-term pain for long-term gain. Of course, this is the way most Americans presumably want it to be.

SUMMARY

In the United States the political and economic sectors are closely intermingled. Politicians feel strongly about the economy and pay close attention to it, but only scattered evidence indicates that they can successfully manipulate the economic situation at election time. The two parties do have different economic policies, particularly with respect to unemployment and inflation; Democrats try to curb unemployment more than Republicans (though they risk inflation in so doing), and Republicans are generally more concerned with controlling inflation.

Two major instruments are available to government for managing the economy: monetary and fiscal policy. Democrats lean more toward Keynesian economics, which holds the government must stimulate greater demand when necessary via bigger government (such as federal job programs). On the other hand, Republicans now advocate supply-side economics, which calls for smaller government (such as tax cuts) to increase the incentive to produce more goods.

Through public policy government also regulates various sectors of the economy. It directly subsidizes agriculture, regulates business, and offers some

The government sometimes comes to the aid of struggling businesses. When Chrysler Corporation was close to bankruptcy—a failure that would have hurt thousands of workers and many American industries—the government guaranteed private loans that saved the automaker. In 1983 Chrysler Chair Lee Iacocca, in front of a mock check for $813,487,500, announced that the company was repaying the final two-thirds of the loans ahead of schedule.

protection to consumers and labor. Through the democratic process some of the unjust aspects of a capitalist economy—which have caused revolutions in other countries—have been curbed in the United States.

KEY TERMS

unemployment rate	Keynesian economic	Federal Trade Commis-
Consumer Price Index	theory	sion (FTC)
(CPI)	supply-side economics	National Labor Relations
laissez-faire	multinational corpora-	Act
monetary policy	tions	collective bargaining
monetarism	antitrust policy	Taft-Hartley Act
Federal Reserve System	Food and Drug Adminis-	right-to-work laws
fiscal policy	tration (FDA)	

FOR FURTHER READING

Barnet, Richard J., and Ronald Muller. *Global Reach: The Power of the Multinational Corporations*. New York: Simon & Schuster, 1974. The definitive work on multinational corporations.

Dolbeare, Kenneth M. *Democracy at Risk*. Chatham, N.J.: Chatham House, 1984. A perspective from the left on the politics of economic renewal.

Gilder, George. *Wealth and Poverty*. New York: Basic Books, 1981. A supply-sider's bible.

Grieder, William. *Secrets of the Temple: How the Federal Reserve Runs the Country*. New York: Simon & Schuster, 1987. A book that demystifies the Fed.

Kiewiet, D. Roderick. *Macroeconomics and Micropolitics*. Chicago: University of Chicago Press, 1983. A good study of the electoral effects of economic issues.

Reich, Robert. *The Next American Frontier*. New York: Times Books, 1983. Argues that "paper entrepreneurs" are loose in the economy, to no good end.

Rousseas, Stephen. *The Political Economy of Reaganomics*. Armonk, N.Y.: M.E. Sharpe, 1982. A good review of Reagan's economic policies and philosophy.

Stein, Herbert. *Presidential Economics*, 2nd ed. Washington, D.C.: American Enterprise Institute, 1988. The making of economic policy from FDR to Reagan.

Tufte, Edward R. *Political Control of the Economy*. Princeton, N.J.: Princeton University Press, 1978. A bold argument that politicians manipulate the economy to their electoral advantage.

Weidenbaum, Murray L.: *Business, Government, and the Public*, 4th ed. Englewood Cliffs, N.J.: Prentice-Hall, 1990. An excellent text on how the private and public sectors interact.

18

SOCIAL WELFARE POLICY-MAKING

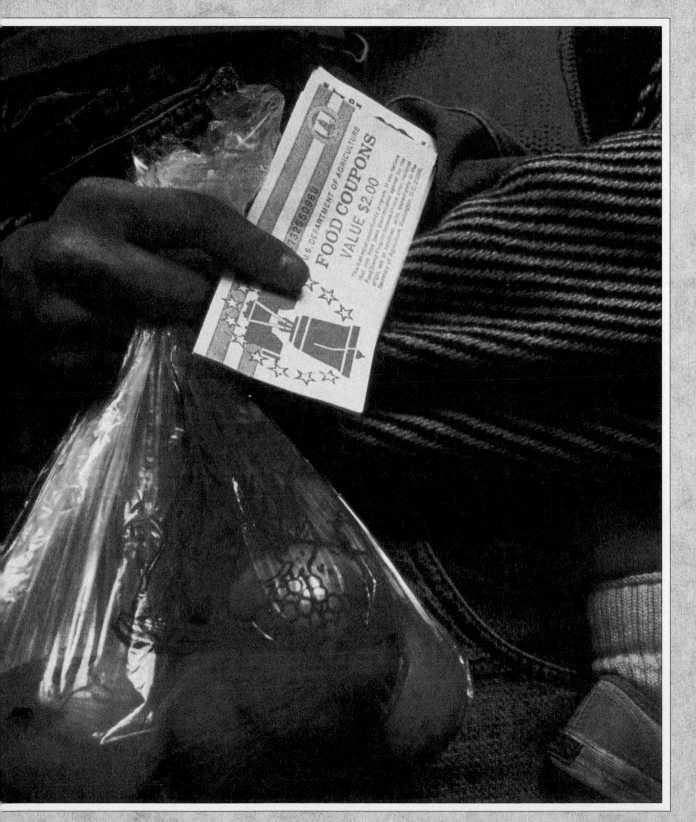

In 1968 a team of doctors traveled to poor regions in the United States and reported that hunger, malnutrition, and related health problems were widespread. Findings such as these helped fuel the growth in social welfare programs including those providing food stamps, school lunches, and maternal and infant nutrition supplements in the late 1960s and 1970s. In 1977 another team of doctors from around the country reported that much had been accomplished and that conditions were definitely improved.

In 1985, however, a follow-up study conducted by the Physician Task Force on Hunger in America reported that conditions had worsened since 1977. "We believe that today hunger and malnutrition are serious problems in every region of the nation. We have, in fact, returned from no city and no state where we did not find extensive hunger."

The task force placed much of the blame for this worsening condition on the federal government. It argued that cuts in federal nutrition and income support programs created holes in America's safety net just at the time when economic changes were having an extensive, negative impact on poverty and unemployment levels.

There is no consensus among Americans about the appropriate actions that should be taken about social problems like hunger and malnutrition. Some, agreeing with the task force, believe that government at all levels must take immediate and decisive action to alleviate this kind of suffering in America. Others believe government should take little or no action to meddle in what are essentially private sector concerns.

The problems of the poor seem to be growing. Today the infant mortality rate in America is one of the highest in the industrialized world. In Washington, D.C., the infant mortality rate approaches levels seen only in underdeveloped nations. The existence of these problems may not all be the result of governmental action or inaction, but as they have done in other major crises, many Americans look to government for solutions to these social problems. Whatever citizens decide to do, government will be a major participant.

The political process will determine what public policies will be implemented to address these social problems. Advocates of various policies, supporters of particular groups, service providers, beneficiaries, government officials, political party factions, candidates and prospective candidates, and various components of the public will struggle with and against each other to fashion these policies. Each group will bring their own goals and perspectives to the contest. Some will want government to do more, while others believe government should be less involved. The results will not be perfect, but they will reflect the dynamics of democratic politics that are the essence of the American political system.

Source: Physician Task Force on Hunger in America, *Hunger in America: The Growing Epidemic* (Boston: Harvard University School of Public Health, 1985). The quotation is from page xiv.

*A*mericans may all agree in theory with the ringing words of the Declaration of Independence that "all men are created equal," but not all Americans end up equal. Women are less well-off than men economically—especially if they head single-parent families. Blacks and other minorities are less well-off than white Americans—especially if they drop out of school.

The United States has a great variety of citizens and population groups, and these individuals and groups achieve different levels of material success. The fact that such differences exist in American democracy, however, raises important political questions: What are the economic differences among Americans? Why do they exist? Are they acceptable? Should we help those who achieve less?

Poverty in America is concentrated among a few groups. More than one-third of single-parent, female-headed families, for example, live below the poverty line. Here a single mother in Kentucky prepares her family's first meal of the day: a watered-down can of stew eaten around noon. Large percentages of African Americans, young Americans, and rural residents are also poor.

What kind of help should we provide them? What roles should the government and the private sector play in helping those who are less fortunate than others? What are the appropriate and best government policies? How should these policies be implemented? What groups in America will support and oppose these policies and why?

The answers Americans provide to these questions determine the nation's approach to **social welfare policies.** Social welfare policies are attempts to provide assistance and support to specific groups in society. Some benefits may be provided to certain groups as entitlements, such as Social Security and Medicare benefits for the elderly. Other benefits, such as food stamps and unemployment payments, may be provided selectively to those who are in particular need and who meet specific eligibility criteria.

Who gets these benefits, how they are provided, what level of support is provided, and who is eligible to receive them are issues that must be resolved by the political system. How America resolves these issues depends on how its leaders, political parties, interest groups, and citizens view the nature of poverty and wealth, the legitimate role of government, appropriate levels of taxing and spending, and the effectiveness of various social welfare programs.

There are many needy citizens in the United States. Some are young, some are aged, some are sick, some are unemployed. The government has established a number of national, state, and local programs to provide assistance to these people. Conservatives, moderates, and liberals in America often disagree about the conduct and impact of these programs, and proposed changes in these programs are on the political agenda virtually all the time.

This chapter puts all of these issues in a broader context. It explores the problems of social welfare in American society and discusses the options citizens face in attempting to deal with this very controversial—and very important—policy area.

INCOME, POVERTY, AND PUBLIC POLICY

Americans are a rich people. Once Americans had the highest per capita income on earth. Today, several oil-rich Arab shiekdoms and Western European countries have inched ahead. Even so, Americans do pretty well, especially given their relatively low cost of living and low taxes in comparison with other nations. In 1987 Americans' median family income was $30,853, almost $2,000 higher than it was in 1980 (even accounting for inflation). In this people of plenty, there is still a great deal of poverty, however. The following sections look more closely at who is getting what in America today.

Who's Getting What?

The novelist F. Scott Fitzgerald once wrote to his friend Ernest Hemingway, "The rich are different from you and me." "Yes," replied Hemingway, "they have more money." Some Americans, of course, have lots more money than others. In fact, the distribution of income across segments of the American population is quite uneven. The concept of **income distribution** describes the share of national income earned by various groups in the United States.

Thomas B. Edsall remarks that "the distribution of income and wealth in a democratic country goes to the heart of its political ethic, defining the basic contours of a nation's sense of justice and equality."[1] The range of American incomes is vast indeed. You can see in Figure 18.1 how income in America has been distributed in recent decades. Generally, there has been little change in the distribution of income in the United States since the 1950s. Beginning in 1978, though, and continuing into the 1980s, has been a period in which the old adage "the rich get richer and the poor get poorer" applies more and more to the United States.

This situation, where one group believes it is doing less well in relation to another reference group, is called **relative deprivation.** Harrison, Tilly, and Bluestone remark that "it now seems fairly clear that both family incomes and individual wages and salaries are being distributed more and more unequally among the working people of the United States . . . . The sense of relative deprivation, of frustrated expectations, of falling behind, of being badly paid—this is becoming the common experience of a growing number of Americans."[2] Between 1979 and 1986 the wealthiest one-fifth of Americans saw their incomes grow from $70,260 to $76,300 (in 1986 dollars). The poorest one-fifth saw their

[1] Thomas B. Edsall, *The New Politics of Inequality* (New York: Norton, 1984), 18.

[2] Bennet Harrison, Chris Tilly, and Barry Bluestone, "Rising Inequality" in *The Changing American Economy*, ed. David Obey and Paul Sarbanes (New York: Basil Blackwell, 1986), 123.

Figure 18.1   Who Gets What? Income Shares of American Households

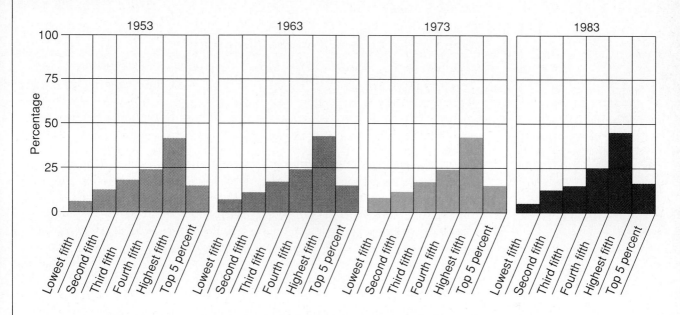

Sources: *Money Income of Households, Families, and Persons in the United States: 1982* (Washington, D.C.: Bureau of the Census, 1984), series P-60, no. 142, Table 17; and *Statistical Abstract of the United States, 1985* (Washington, D.C.: Government Printing Office, 1984).

incomes actually fall (again, adjusting for inflation) from $8,761 to $8,033. This situation has produced more inequality: $9.50 in income was added to those at the top for every $1.00 lost by those at the bottom.[3]

Although the words *income* and *wealth* might seem similar, they are not the same thing. **Income** is the amount of money collected between any two points in time (say, a week or a year); **wealth** is the amount already owned, including stocks, bonds, bank accounts, cars, houses, and so forth. Throughout most of the last generation, wealth has been much less evenly distributed than income, with the top 1 percent of the wealth-holders possessing about 25 percent of all American wealth.[4]

You can see from Figure 18.1 that many of the poor are losing ground, relatively speaking, to higher-income groups. This fact would be less painful if all groups were increasing their wealth, with the poor increasing at a slightly lower rate. The problem is that many of the poor are losing ground in absolute terms as well. With inflation, the purchasing power of the poor may in many cases actually be decreasing. Decreases like these mean much more than simple

[3] *New York Times*, May 1, 1988, F3.

[4] James D. Smith and Stephen D. Franklin, "The Concentration of Personal Wealth," *American Economic Review*, cited in U.S. Department of Commerce, *Social Indicators 1976* (Washington, D.C.: Department of Commerce, 1976), 466.

percentage or dollar comparisons can easily convey. Because of rising prices and low levels of income and wealth, many citizens find themselves in great difficulty when they seek to feed, clothe, shelter, and provide medical attention for their families.

Who's at the Bottom? Poverty in America

Counting the poor may seem easy, but it is not. First one needs to define poverty. Compared with people in India, American poor seem almost prosperous. England is a poor country by American standards, but it is not afflicted with the poverty of rural Mexico. Mexico City may look poor to the foreign visitor, but millions from Mexican farms and villages come there seeking prosperity—relatively speaking.

To count the poor, the U.S. Bureau of the Census has established the **poverty line,** which takes into account what a family would need to spend for an "austere" standard of living and a family's size. During the 1960s and early 1970s, the number of Americans living below the poverty line plummeted from a high of nearly 40 million (22.2 percent of the population) in 1960 to a low of 24.5 million (11.4 percent) in 1978.[5] Since that time, however, the number of poor has risen to around 32 million (13.1 percent) in 1989. What is most disconcerting is that many of these poor, around 13 million, are children under the age of eighteen.[6]

A careful, decade-long study of five thousand American families showed that poverty may be even more extensive than the poverty line suggests.[7] In this

[5]For an excellent discussion of the trends in American poverty over time, See Sar A. Levitan, *Programs in Aid of the Poor*, 6th ed. (Baltimore: Johns Hopkins University Press, 1990), chap. 1.

[6]*Ibid.*

[7]Greg J. Duncan and James N. Morgan, eds., *Five Thousand American Families* (Ann Arbor: University of Michigan Institute for Social Research, 1977).

Estimates vary, but most experts believe that around one million Americans—like this man across the street from the White House—are homeless. Cuts to government programs that funded low-income housing and unemployment benefits, in addition to the deinstitutionalization of the mentally ill, forced thousands of people out into the streets during the 1980s.

Table 18.1 Who Are the Poor? Characteristics of Persons below the Poverty Line

GROUP	PERCENTAGE OF ALL POOR	PERCENTAGE WHO ARE POOR
White	68.5	11.0
Black	27.8	31.1
Spanish origin	18.6	27.3
Married-couple families	44.4	6.1
Families with male head, no wife	4.1	11.4
Families with female head, no husband	51.4	34.6
Under 15	34.0	21.2
65 or older	10.7	12.4
Metropolitan residents	70.0	12.3
Nonmetropolitan residents	30.0	18.1
Northeast	16.1	10.5
South	40.5	16.1
Midwest	23.6	13.0
West	19.8	13.2

Source: U.S. Bureau of the Census, "Money, Income and Poverty Status of Families and Persons in the U.S.: 1986," *Current Population Reports,* series P-60 (1987).

representative sample of American families, almost a third were below the poverty level at least once during the decade, suggesting that as many as 70 million Americans live close enough to the poverty line that some crisis can push them into poverty.

Although the poor are a varied group, poverty is more common among some groups—African Americans, young Americans, female-headed families, and rural residents—than among others. Table 18.1 reports the characteristics of persons in America below the poverty line.

THE NATURE OF WEALTH AND POVERTY

Speculations on the nature of wealth and poverty are much more important than mere liberal and conservative ideological disagreements. Citizens' views on who are poor and why they are poor affect their approaches to solving the problems of poverty. If most Americans think people are poor because of weaknesses within themselves, they will support very different kinds of government actions than if they believe that poverty is more the result of environmental or situational factors. People's understanding of the causes of poverty will direct and limit what they believe government can and should do about it. There is no consensus in America on the causes of poverty; "The People Speak: Why Are the Poor Poor?" shows what various groups of Americans think are the causes of individual poverty.

Is There a Culture of Poverty?

Conservatives and liberals in America tend to disagree on the reasons why some people are rich and others are poor. In general, conservatives tend to believe that individual characteristics, attitudes, and values are the primary factors affecting wealth or poverty status. The poor, many conservatives argue, possess a **culture of poverty,** negative attitudes and values toward work, family, and success that condemn them to lower levels of accomplishment. The poor, the culture-of-poverty argument goes, are present-oriented, lack self-control, possess poor work habits, and have weak family structures and relationships.

Liberals (and many others) take strong exception to these assertions that the situation of the poor can be explained by their culture of poverty. Some people face more hostile environments than others, they argue. These negative environments include legal restrictions, social and cultural customs, educational limits, discrimination, and the stereotypical attitudes many employers, educators, lenders, insurers, and other powerful members of society hold toward the poor. People are poor, these critics argue, not because of particular characteristics or values they themselves possess or fail to possess—they are poor because they face external barriers to their success.[8]

Are the conservatives right? If they are, social scientists should observe the presence of long-term welfare status among America's poor, and should also see a set of values and attitudes, a culture of poverty, developing among the poor. The facts do not support either of these assertions, however. Examination of the welfare roles over time indicates that most beneficiaries are not long-term recipients. According to Sar Levitan, in recent years "nearly three of every ten AFDC [Aid to Families with Dependent Children] families had received welfare benefits for less than one year, and a majority of families had remained on the rolls for less than four years. Fewer than 8 percent of all AFDC families had received assistance without interruption for more than ten years."[9]

As for the existence of a particular set of negative attitudes that characterize a dependent, helpless poor, most researchers cannot find it. For example, in Greg Duncan's ten-year study of the economic life of American families, he

[8] For a discussion of the nature of wealth and poverty in American society, see Arnold Vedlitz, *Conservative Mythology and Public Policy in America* (New York: Praeger, 1988), chaps. 2 and 3.

[9] Sar A. Levitan, *Programs in Aid of the Poor,* 5th ed. (Baltimore: Johns Hopkins University Press, 1985), 38–9.

Crime, drugs, gangs, and poverty are a part of daily life for the urban underclass. Slogans like "just say no," which assume that addictions and other problems can be helped by a simple change in attitude, seem meaningless in the face of hostile urban environments such as this one at a Chicago-area housing project.

found no distinctive set of attitudes—no culture of poverty—distinguishing the poor from the nonpoor. Instead, it was more commonly some crisis or opportunity—losing a job, getting a divorce, working longer hours, having a new mouth to feed—that accounted for movement into or out of the poverty class.[10]

Lately much attention has focused on the *urban underclass,* the poorest of the poor in America. These are the Americans whose economic opportunities are severely limited in almost every way. They constitute a large percentage of the Americans afflicted by homelessness, crime, drugs, alcoholism, unwanted pregnancies, and other endemic social problems (see "In Focus: The Urban Underclass: What Is the Problem? What Is to Be Done?").

How Public Policy Affects Income

Incomes are affected by many ingredients. Some people work hard; others are lazy. Some find themselves living in expanding economic times, while others suffer through recessions and depressions. Some live in regions that are booming with opportunities, while others reside in areas of scarcity and decline. Although local, state, and national governments may affect some of these conditions, most of them are not readily subject to governmental control. The government does, however, spend one out of every three dollars in the American economy, and thus has a major impact on its citizens' wealth and income. In particular, there are two principal ways in which government can affect a person's income: (1) government can manipulate incomes through its taxing powers, and (2) government can affect income through its expenditure policies.

Taxation   "Nothing," said Benjamin Franklin, "is certain in life but death and taxes." In general, there are three types of taxes; each can affect citizens' incomes

[10]Duncan and Morgan, *Five Thousand American Families.*

The Urban Underclass: What Is the Problem? What Is to Be Done?

Consider some sobering facts about America's minorities:

- In 1959, 15 percent of black births were to single mothers; by 1982, 57 percent of black babies were born to an unmarried mother. In other words, in the 1980s more than half of all African-American babies were born into a single-parent family.

- The proportion of black men who are employed dropped from 80 percent in 1930 (in the early years of the Great Depression) to 56 percent in 1983.

- By the mid-1980s, 46 percent of black children were living below the poverty line.

These are significant and distressing facts about black America in general. Consider, too, who black sociologist William J. Wilson calls the "truly disadvantaged"—people in neighborhoods where the very worst of conditions exist. Wilson notes that income inequality increased during the past several decades at a greater rate among black than among white families. Thus what a famous government report said of America in general in the 1960s—"The United States is moving toward two societies, one black and one white, separate and unequal"—is true *within* black communities as well. In the poorest of the poor neighborhoods, all the problems that afflict minorities in general are exacerbated.

Wilson argues that these problems are not derived from the culture of the poorest of the poor. Rather, they are a function of the lack of jobs—good jobs or just any jobs—available to people in the inner cities. The nation's four largest northern cities (New York, Chicago, Philadelphia, and Detroit) lost a million low-skilled jobs in a single decade. From a female's point of view, there is a shortage of "marriageable," that is, employed, males. Where teenage male unemployment runs 50 percent or more, there is little to do besides drift into lawlessness, drug addiction or drug sales, and alcoholism.

Wilson advocates racially nonspecific programs—programs not advocated to "help poor minority groups"—as a partial solution to this problem. Such policies, through, do not often reach the political agenda when Republicans want to be fiscal conservatives and Democrats are afraid of being labeled "welfare liberals."

Source: William J. Wilson, *The Truly Disadvantaged: The Inner City, the Underclass, and Public Policy* (Chicago: University of Chicago Press, 1987).

in a different way. First, if the government takes a bigger bite from the income of a rich family than from the income of a poor family, it has a **progressive tax,** such as charging millionaires 50 percent of their income and the poor 5 percent of theirs. Second, if the government takes the same shares from everyone, rich and poor alike, it has a **proportional tax.** Third, if the government establishes a **regressive tax,** the poor pay a greater share of their income in taxes than do the rich.

Rarely are taxes overtly regressive. No state intentionally charges a higher rate of taxes for poor families and a lower rate for rich ones. Some taxes, however, are regressive in effect. Consider state sales taxes, for example. States typically raise more than half of their state tax revenues from their state sales tax. Poor families usually spend a larger proportion of their income on items subject to state sales tax, while rich families spend money on stocks, bonds, or tax shelters. This means that poor families pay a higher percentage of their incomes in state sales taxes than well-to-do families.

Taxes, therefore, can have an impact on the distribution of income in three ways: (1) progressive taxes can make the poor richer and the rich poorer, (2) proportional taxes can have no net effect on income, and (3) regressive taxes can make the rich richer and the poor poorer.

The best evidence indicates that the overall incidence of taxes in America is proportional, not regressive or progressive. This is because regressive state and local taxes are counterbalanced by more progressive federal taxes.[11]

It is true, however, that at the national level the wealthy are paying a good deal of the income taxes used to support many government policies, including poverty-related social welfare programs. In 1986, for example, taxpayers making over $100,000 made up about 1.5 percent of total taxpayers but paid about 30 percent of total income taxes. At the same time, taxpayers making under $11,000 made up 32 percent of taxpayers and paid less than 2 percent of total income taxes that year.[12] This is not to imply that all are paying their proper share or that the current income tax structure is completely equitable.

For example, taxes not based on income, like Social Security payroll taxes, would show a quite different distribution in payments between rich and poor citizens. This is because all workers, regardless of their total income, pay the same percentage of their wages as Social Security taxes up to the taxable salary ceiling. If the Social Security wage-tax ceiling is, say, $45,000, a worker making $45,000 and one making $145,000 would pay the same amount in Social Security payroll taxes. Different taxes, then, may place different burdens on different income groups. It is instructive, however, to know which groups in society are providing the various types of governmental income used to support certain key social welfare programs.

There is one more important way in which government can affect a person's income: through its spending and benefits.

Government Expenditures   Government can affect the income a citizen receives by a simple act: it can write you a check. Literally billions of government checks are written every year, mostly to Social Security beneficiaries and retired government employees. Government can also give an "in-kind payment," something with cash value that is not cash itself (food stamps are one example; a low-interest loan for college education is another). All these benefits from government are called **transfer payments.** Have these substantial transfer payments redistributed income in America?

It is clear that many are better off after these transfers than before, particularly the elderly, who are experiencing significantly less poverty today than they did twenty-five years ago, primarily because of Social Security payments and Medicare. Many of the poor have been raised above the poverty line by these cash and in-kind transfers. In fact, when one takes the transfer payments into account, about half those in poverty are raised above the official poverty line. In spite of these marginal improvements relative to poverty status, however, there is little evidence that transfer programs have significantly redistributed income in America or created greater income equality.

---

[11]For an excellent discussion of taxation in America, see Joseph A. Pechman and Benjamin A. Okner, *Who Bears the Tax Burden?* (Washington, D.C.: The Brookings Institution, 1974).

[12]U.S. Department of Treasury/Internal Revenue Service, *Statistics of Income Bulletin*, vol. 9, num. 1 (Summer 1989): 51.

A careful (and complicated) study of government's impact on income equality has been conducted by Morgan Reynolds and Eugene Smolensky. They estimated the effect of government expenditures in various categories (schooling, highways, defense, policing, and so on) on individual incomes. Looking at three points in time—1950, 1960, and 1970—they concluded that government spending had done little to make incomes more equal. Despite massive government commitments to social programs during this thirty-year period, income inequality had hardly been touched by public policy.[13]

Clearly, income inequality is a common feature of life in industrialized societies and one that has not been easily reversed in the United States. It needs to be pointed out that, although income inequality is recognized as a problem in America, policies of income redistribution aimed at reducing this inequality have never been generally accepted public policy. Americans tend to favor equal opportunity over equal outcomes and reject redistributional policies that would work to achieve an end to income inequality by government action.

SOCIAL WELFARE PROGRAMS

Social welfare programs have not ended poverty, significantly redistributed wealth, or substantially reduced income inequality in America. Many would argue that these programs were never intended to accomplish such goals. It is true, however, that these programs have produced substantial improvements in the day-to-day living conditions of many Americans.

Entitlement and Poverty Programs

Programs like Social Security and Medicare have substantially improved older Americans' quality of life. Medicaid, Food Stamps, and housing and family assistance programs have also kept many American families from despair and hopelessness. These programs are summarized in Table 18.2.

Entitlement programs like Social Security and Medicare, programs that do not require an income or means test for eligibility, are the largest and most expensive social welfare programs in America. In 1990 Social Security payments came to about $250 billion while payments for Medicare amounted to almost $100 billion. These programs have had quite a positive effect on the health and income of older Americans. With Medicare, the elderly are receiving more and better medical treatment, and Social Security payments are helping to lift most of the elderly out of poverty. In 1962 nearly 50 percent of America's elderly families were below the poverty line; today that figure is less than 15 percent.

Programs aimed specifically at the poor—means-tested programs that require a certain poverty level for eligibility, like Medicaid and Food Stamps—are funded at much lower levels than entitlement programs for the elderly. Medicaid, the medical assistance program for the poor, spent about $45 billion in 1991, and many of these expeditures went to the elderly poor for nursing home care and supplemental medical expenses. Current levels of spending for Food Stamps, a program that supplements a family's food budget, and Aid to

The debate over social welfare policies (the Food Stamp program, for example) is often split along party lines. Although Republicans fear being labelled the party of insensitivity, many of them believe that welfare programs only encourage dependence on government aid. Democrats generally support such programs, providing their opponents the opportunity to accuse them of being big-spenders.

[13]Morgan Reynolds and Eugene Smolensky, *Public Expenditures, Taxes, and the Distribution of Income* (New York: Academic Press, 1977).

Table 18.2	The Major Social Welfare Programs and Number of Recipients, 1989

SOCIAL INSURANCE PROGRAMS

Old Age, Survivors, and Disability Insurance (OASDI)[a]
Monthly payments to retired or disabled people and to surviving members of their families. Paid for by a payroll tax on employees and employers. Popularly called *Social Security.*
Recipients: 39.0 million

Medicare[a]
Part A: Federal government pays for part of the cost of hospital care for retired and disabled people covered by Social Security. Paid for by payroll taxes on employees and employers.
Recipients: 32.6 million

Part B: Voluntary program of medical insurance (pays physicians) for persons 65 or over and disabled Social Security beneficiaries who pay the premiums.
Enrolled: 32.1 million

Medicaid[b]
Provides medical and hospital aid to the poor through federally assisted state health programs. Need is the only criterion; if you are poor, you qualify.
Recipients: 24.0 million

PUBLIC ASSISTANCE PROGRAMS

Food Stamps[b]
Coupons that can be used to buy food. Given to people whose income is below a certain level. Paid for out of general federal revenues.
Recipients: 20.6 million

Aid to Families with Dependent Children (AFDC)[b]
Payments to families with children, either one-parent families or, in some states, two-parent families where the breadwinner is unemployed. Paid for partly by states and partly by the federal government.
Recipients: 10.9 million

Supplemental Security Income (SSI)[b]
Cash payments to aged, blind, or disabled people whose income is below a certain amount. Paid for by general federal revenues.
Recipients: 5.6 million

Unemployment Insurance (UI)[a]
Weekly payments to workers who have been laid off and cannot find work. Benefits and requirements determined by states. Paid for by taxes on employers.
Recipients: 6.8 million

[a]No means test (a means test is a required demonstration of need based on income and assets).
[b]Means test.

Families with Dependent Children (AFDC), which provides direct payments to poor families with children, are about $12 billion and $17 billion respectively.

Even though the expenditures for all these poverty programs are substantially less than those provided for entitlement programs, they have raised many of the poor above the official poverty line. For example, in 1982 cash and in-kind transfers lifted 63.3 percent of the pretransfer poor out of poverty.[14] These programs help a lot of poor Americans escape some of the ravages of poverty.

Social Welfare Policy Elsewhere

The United States is not the only nation that provides social welfare benefits to its citizens. In fact, most industrial nations not only provide such benefits, but the benefits are usually more generous than those in the United States. The comparative figures are quite striking, as you can see in "America in Perspective: Social Welfare Here and Abroad."

[14]See John L. Palmer and Isabel V. Sawhill, eds., *The Reagan Record: An Assessment of America's Changing Domestic Priorities* (Cambridge, Mass.: Ballinger Publishing, 1984), 197.

Social Welfare Here and Abroad

Americans hear a great deal about poverty and social welfare programs. The newspapers, television, and political debates and campaigns all debate the nature of the problem and of the increased costs of the programs in terms of taxes and debt. All this may lead citizens to conclude that American social welfare programs are somehow fundamentally different, particularly more expensive and intrusive, than those in other nations. The following table looks at one social welfare program, Social Security, and compares America's level of performance with that of other industrialized democracies.

As the findings in this table indicate, the level of Social Security spending in the United States is *not* greater than that in most other industrialized countries. On the contrary, American levels of spending are substantially less than that of every other nation

except Japan. It is not a fair assessment to view American social welfare efforts, like Social Security, as being excessive when compared to other nations. That does not mean that the United States ought to spend more or it ought to spend less, but knowing how America ranks compared to other nations can help citizens put their efforts and demands into a better perspective.

NATION	SOCIAL SECURITY BENEFITS (% of national income)[a]
Japan	14.0
United States	17.9
United Kingdom	25.8
Germany	31.0
France	33.3[b]
Sweden	43.3

[a]1983
[b]1980
Source: OECD Economic Surveys—Japan, 1987/88, Organization for Economic Cooperation and Development, 1988, 132.

Other national governments and their citizens often take quite a different approach to the problems of poverty and social welfare than does the United States. In Great Britain, for example, comprehensive medical services are provided through a National Health Service. In addition to traditional health and welfare services, Sweden provides its citizens public day-care services. Israel provides its citizens substantial housing subsidies.

Americans tend to see poverty and social welfare needs as individual rather than governmental concerns, while European nations tend to support greater governmental responsibility for these problems. Also, Europeans often have a more positive attitude toward government, while Americans are more likely to distrust government action in areas like social welfare policy.

Nations also differ in how universal or selective they make their social welfare payments. Some nations, like Switzerland and Australia, focus much attention on selective benefits that are targeted at specific groups with specific needs, especially needs demonstrated by means tests. Other nations, like those in Scandinavia, tend to favor universal benefits that go to large categories of the population without reference to demonstrated need. America has both types of programs; Social Security and Medicare programs are universal, while poverty programs are selective.

Taxes commensurate with the benefits of social policy are commonplace in Western European nations, often reaching more than 40 percent of personal income (see Chapter 14). In the United States, taxes are about 33 percent of personal income, and they support a much larger defense budget than do taxes in Europe. Japan is the only nation with a developed economy that spends a smaller proportion of its gross national product on social policies than does the United States, in part because in Japan the family's traditional role in supporting its generations is still commonplace. Japanese corporations also provide workers with pensions and other benefits that exceed those provided by American businesses.

THE EVOLUTION OF AMERICA'S SOCIAL WELFARE PROGRAMS

For centuries societies have considered family welfare a private, not a public concern. Children were to be nurtured by their parents and, in turn, to nurture them in their old age. When churlish children cast off their parents or when selfish parents lavished riches on themselves and let their children go hungry, significant social pressure was often enough to lead wayward parents or children to accept their proper responsibilities. Sometimes the law would be invoked to force parents to support their children in childhood and adolescence or—more rarely—to force children to support their parents in old age. There was a time, in other words, when an implied contract existed between one generation and the next. Support now would be returned in support later. Governments had little to do with this implicit intergenerational contract. Reciprocal arrangements like these may have been more workable in less technologically advanced, more homogeneous societies.

After the turn of the century, however, America and other industrialized societies recognized the breakdown in these family-based support networks. With the growth of large, depersonalized cities and the requirements of the urban workforce, the old ways of thinking about the problems of the elderly and the poor seemed inadequate. American governments on both the national and state levels were required to take a more active role in social welfare support. As with other major policy changes in America, these changes in the patterns of government support for the needy were incremental in nature, with key breakthroughs in policy direction coming at times of particular societal need or crisis. A major change in how Americans viewed government's role in providing social welfare support came during the Great Depression and the major strains this economic downturn placed on individual resources.

The New Deal and the Elderly

After the onset of the Great Depression in 1929, many nations, including the United States, began to think that governments must do more to protect their citizens against the vicissitudes of events such as a depression. Families would not always have the resources to look after themselves as they would wish. External circumstances, often far beyond the control or responsibility of individuals or their families, began to be seen as major contributors to short- and long-term poverty and need. In 1935 the American government responded to this change in attitude by passing one of the most significant pieces of social welfare legislation of all time, the Social Security Act. This act brought govern-

No event has shaped American social welfare policy more than the Great Depression. Franklin Roosevelt's administration initiated hundreds of New Deal programs in its efforts to help citizens like these jobless men. Government spending on social welfare has not declined since, even during the Reagan administration.

ment into the equation of one generation's obligations to another. Never would middle-class family choices be quite the same. Adults could put their own children, instead of their parents, first. Later, in 1965, when the federal government adopted Medicare, adults were freed even more from paying for their own parents' expenses. Thus the post-1965 generation of adults was the first to be substantially free of the ancient obligation of caring not only for its children but for its parents, too. "Substantially free" does not, of course, mean that millions of Americans did not dutifully fill in gaps left by Social Security or Medicare. The burden, though, was not theirs alone, for government benefits provided a crucial cushion at a time when money was needed for other things.

Being free of these obligations seemed, of course, easy, even cheap. Government now picked up the tab for what average citizens had been paying for. Children could be supported through college and a new home could be built without having to save for the possible catastrophic illness of a parent. The middle class had a new financial freedom.

The costs, of course, were shifted but not reduced; what citizens had paid out of their pocket they now paid for in taxes. First Social Security and then Medicare were the most rapidly increasing parts of the federal budget. In 1953, when the Social Security bill was still small (because benefits were limited and retirees were fewer), the average family paid just 8.7 percent of its income in federal income and payroll taxes. By 1980 that figure soared to 16.2 percent, and it was rising every year. Today Americans over the age of eighty make up the fastest growing age-group. Americans spend 12 percent of their nation's gross national product on medical care. Every year, a larger part of that cost goes to aiding—sometimes keeping alive—older Americans. In the 1980s, for the first time, the United States spent more of its public dollars on the aged than on the young. Whereas in the 1960s the number of aged Americans living in poverty was a national scandal, today, due in part to rapidly escalating government benefits, the proportion of poor elderly Americans is smaller than the proportion of children who live in poor families. Nationally, there has been a redistribution of government benefits from younger people to older people.

To illuminate intergenerational equality issues, economist Robert Kuttner makes the following comparison[15]: A male born in 1921, who is about to retire today, saw a very different government and very different policies than did a young woman born in 1961. The worker born in 1921 saw government help him through the Great Depression of the 1930s. Perhaps he even had a public works job to tide him through those difficult years. Chances are he fought in World War II and then returned home to find government helping him with a GI Bill loan to buy a house or get an education. He enjoyed a rise in his real income during the 1950s and 1960s and probably saw government initiate a whole raft of projects to benefit people just like him. Government built a new interstate highway system; it expanded the public schools; it expanded its protection for him on the job. If he was black, he saw the government adopt civil rights policies to protect him from discrimination. Further, the government did all these things while keeping his taxes relatively low.

Now consider the young woman born in 1961. As she enters the world of work, says Kuttner, "the role of government as provider looms much smaller, and government as taxer looms much larger."[16] Because take-home income has not kept pace with inflation since the early 1970s, her taxes are higher than her parents'. Whereas in 1944 they paid 3 percent of their earnings to support their elders through Social Security, she pays more than 15 percent of her earnings for that purpose. She grew up in a house whose mortgage was assisted by the Veterans Administration or some other federal loan program; today, although she wants to buy a house, she cannot afford one. Most federal housing subsidies are gone. In 1949 the average thirty year old could buy a house on 14 percent of his or her income; by 1985 that figure had risen to 44 percent.

Interest groups have now been formed by the middle generation, and where interest groups form, an issue will arise on the government agenda. All Americans benefit from public policy, but from the perspective of those in the principal working-age group, the government has moved resources away from them and toward other groups such as children and the aged. The issue posed by problems of **intergenerational equity** is this: Who should get what share of public policy benefits and at what costs? This is a complex, emerging debate about social policy and may, in the future, pit different age groups against one another.

The elderly have become one of the country's most articulate and effective interest groups. Although primarily concerned with protecting government benefits to older Americans, groups such as the Gray Panthers have also become involved in issues that bridge, instead of widen, generation gaps.

President Johnson and the Great Society

In the 1960s America experienced an outpouring of federal programs to help the poor and the elderly, to create economic opportunities for those at the lower rungs of the economic ladder, to make the unequal more equal, and to reduce discrimination against minorities. Many of these programs were established during the presidency of Lyndon B. Johnson (1963–69), whose administration coined the term "The Great Society" for these policy initiatives. Johnson

[15]Robert Kuttner, "Renewing Opportunity," in *The Changing American Economy*, 138–41.
[16]*Ibid.*, 138.

In 1965 President Lyndon Johnson signed Medicare legislation into law. The program, which helps older Americans with their medical expenses, was first proposed more than a decade earlier by former President Harry Truman (right), who was invited to the signing.

was a policy entrepreneur, initiating antipoverty programs, community development programs, Medicare, school-aid schemes, job-retraining programs, and a host of other public programs. During this period government revenues were still growing and budget deficits were low. Although the Vietnam War eventually drained funds from Johnson's Great Society, many of the programs Ronald Reagan later railed against were set in place during the Johnson period. Richard Nixon, Johnson's Republican successor, carried on and even expanded many of them, as did Presidents Ford and Carter.

We have already learned that these programs were primarily of two types—entitlements and poverty programs. Although both types of programs were part of the Great Society, each had a different political dynamic bringing it into being as government policy. John Kingdon has argued that problem areas reach the political agenda through a convergence of "streams." Problems get identified and brought into the open, policies get identified with problem solutions, and changes in public opinion, political leadership, and other factors in the political environment create a window of opportunity for action.[17]

The entitlement and poverty programs that made up the Great Society had quite different streams. The entitlement programs, aimed primarily at the elderly, had strong political support. The elderly were a growing political constituency, important to both political parties. Demographic trends showed an expanding elderly population, and medical advances were increasing health options and demands for care. Public opinion supported greater attention to the elderly and the nation's age-group makeup made it easier for the large youth and working-age populations to provide benefits to a relatively small elderly population without creating too much hardship on the younger groups.

[17]John Kingdon, *Agendas, Alternatives, and Public Policies* (Boston: Little, Brown, 1984).

Advocates of greater spending for poverty programs had a more difficult time. Poverty was closely tied to race issues in the minds of many people, and problems of racial discrimination and segregation were still quite fresh. In addition, the ability of the poor and their supporters to form strong political bases from which to demand government help was limited. Compared to the elderly, poverty groups were less organized, less powerful, viewed as less legitimate, and often, unlike the elderly, faced with strong counter groups.

On the positive side, minorities and the poor were becoming a more important constituency in the Democratic party, which was beginning to pay more attention to the electoral demands of these groups. The growth of the civil rights movement, the increasing media attention paid to poverty and discrimination, and the outbreak of urban violence created a climate of opinion that supported greater attention to the problems of poverty.

Perhaps the most important element for the success of both program types, however, was strong presidential leadership. Making important changes in social welfare programs usually requires strong presidential commitment, and this was provided by President Johnson. He made these programs a centerpiece of his administration and worked to rally the Congress, public opinion, and major interest groups behind him. The role of political leadership, particularly presidential leadership, cannot be underestimated in building the public and political coalitions needed to support new program initiatives in the area of social welfare policy. It was the active leadership of a subsequent president, Ronald Reagan, that helped build coalitions to move American social welfare programs in a different direction.

President Reagan and Limits to the Great Society

Unlike Presidents Nixon, Ford, and Carter, who largely accepted and even expanded some portions of the programs initiated by Johnson, President Reagan took a very different tack. Again, the streams surrounding social welfare policy in his administration had changed substantially from those present for the preceding presidents. Public opinion support for some welfare programs was eroding, particularly among members of the traditional Democratic coalition. It was possible, therefore, for Republicans to make some headway into the Democratic party's constituency by taking a more restrictive stand on social welfare programs.

In addition, the growing demands of defense spending and elderly entitlement programs had increased government deficits and threatened to raise taxes and stifle economic growth. The working class and the middle- and upper-income groups were seeing their incomes threatened and were looking for places to cut government expenditures. One thing that had not changed was the vulnerability of the poor. Their group bases of support were still smaller than those of the elderly. The poor were limited to the Democratic party, which was becoming more divided on support for poverty and social welfare programs, and the poor's interest group strength and legitimacy was still weak. The elderly still had bipartisan support and strong electoral and interest group bases.

Just as in the Johnson era, the major actor was the president. In this case, President Reagan chose to target poverty programs as the major way to cut government spending. This action would serve his own ideological beliefs of less government and more self-sufficiency, and it would also satisfy the political demands of a worried public calling for the same solution—cut government spending on poverty programs. The president set the tone, rallied public opinion, and worked to create congressional coalitions to support these efforts.

The Omnibus Budget Reconciliation Act (OBRA) of 1981 initiated many of the cuts President Reagan had sought. For example, OBRA included substantial cuts in the AFDC program, estimated to be about 14 percent. These cuts resulted in an AFDC caseload reduction of about 12 percent, with many who remained on the roles receiving lower benefits.[18]

In this and subsequent policy battles, Democratic leaders in the Congress worked to limit these cuts. Although many cuts were made—many program growth rates were reduced, many benefits were reduced, many program burdens were shifted to the states, and many previously eligible recipients were removed from the roles—the basic outlines of the original programs have persisted.

The Future of Social Welfare Policy

More and more, political campaigns and congressional debates have focused on the social welfare policy programs initiated in the Johnson period and modified or expanded during subsequent administrations. Although President Reagan was not successful in completely dismantling the Great Society programs, he was able to focus more attention on the programs and set the stage for continuing debate. The major question remains: What should government do in the area of social welfare policy?

The major point of disagreement is over the extent to which social welfare programs, like those implemented in the Great Society, work. Discussion is heated over whether these programs help or hurt the poor; whether they ameliorate or exacerbate poverty; whether they provide a much needed safety net for the truly needy; or whether they encourage dependence and failure.

In the late 1970s, Americans witnessed growing inflation, rising interest rates, burgeoning government deficits, increased unemployment, more crime, and further disintegration of the family. Many believed that the programs implemented in the Great Society had contributed to these problems. This led a number of Americans to question the appropriateness of increased government activity in the social policy arena. With the inauguration of President Reagan in 1981, many at the highest levels of government were seeking ways to reduce government spending in social welfare program areas. Such reductions often seemed justified by reports of the failure of past social policies to achieve an end to the problems of poverty.

A major study underwritten by the conservative Manhattan Institute and conducted by Charles Murray seemed to provide the budget cutters with the ammunition needed to begin dismantling the social programs of earlier years.[19] Murray's book argued that not only did the social programs of the Great Society and later administrations fail to curb the advance of poverty, they actually made the situation worse. The problem, Murray maintained, was that these public

---

[18] For a more detailed discussion of the impact of OBRA on cuts in social welfare programs, see Tom Joe and Cheryl Rogers, *By the Few for the Few: The Reagan Welfare Legacy* (Lexington, Mass.: Lexington Books, 1985), chap 7.

[19] Charles Murray, *Losing Ground: American Social Policy, 1950–1980* (New York: Basic Books, 1984).

policies discouraged the poor from solving their problems. Murray contended that the programs actually made it profitable to be poor and victimized, thus encouraging the poor to stay that way. For example, Murray argued that poor couples could obtain more benefits if they remained single rather than marrying; thus most would not marry, thereby leading to further disintegration of the family.

Agreeing with much or all of Murray's argument whether or not they were directly influenced by it, President Reagan and his advisors sought to dismantle or reduce funding for many programs and to shift program responsibilities from the federal to the state and local levels. As discussed, the Aid to Families with Dependent Children Program was particularly hard hit. Tom Joe and Cheryl Rogers reported that "the administration chose to change twenty-seven specific AFDC policies in such a way that fewer people would be eligible for benefits and many of those that were eligible would receive reduced benefits.[20]

Many scholars, however, have strongly criticized Murray's arguments and the program cuts emanating from them. In directly challenging Murray's assertions, political scientist Arnold Vedlitz has argued that "the conservatives exaggerate both the expectations and intentions of the programs and denigrate their accomplishments . . . . The reality of these programs is that they were never designed to end poverty, presidential rhetoric to the contrary."[21] Both Vedlitz and John Schwarz[22], another political scientist, have pointed out many ways in which these programs helped the poor and elderly during very tumultuous social and economic times. In a separate challenge to Murray's position, economists David Ellwood and Lawrence Summers showed that not only was spend-

[20]Joe and Rogers, *By the Few for the Few,* 23.
[21]Arnold Vedlitz, *Conservative Mythology,* chap. 6.
[22]John E. Schwarz, *America's Hidden Success,* rev. ed. (New York: W.W. Norton, 1988).

Economic changes often force middle-class Americans out of jobs. Declines in the steel and automotive industries over the past two decades, for example, have swelled the ranks of the unemployed in the nation's urban manufacturing centers.

ing for the poor relatively limited in these programs, but that macroeconomic cycles were responsible for much of the movement into and out of poverty during the post-1965 period.[23]

Scholars like Ellwood and Summers, Vedlitz, and Schwarz are much more likely to conclude that the social welfare policies begun in the Great Society, limited though they were in direct aid to the poor, contributed much to easing the shocks to the American economic and social system caused by international oil crises, a weakened dollar, deindustrialization of the American economy, increased foreign economic competition, and the vast expansion of the labor force when baby boomers entered the job market. Much was happening in the domestic and world economy to increase the problems of poverty and unemployment in America during the post-1965 period; many analysts believe that the position of the poor would have been much worse were it not for the safety net programs enacted during much of this period.

For those looking for the "right" answer, the evidence is clearly mixed. Scholars disagree on how beneficial the programs were and are. Although the preponderance of evidence does seem to support the notion that the programs were helpful in general, one can still ask if more could have been done with other programs or other approaches. What are future policymakers to do? How should they deal with the political pressures on both sides of these complex issues? What position should key leaders, like the president, take?

What is the correct path for Americans to take if they wish to help the poor? Knowing what is ethical depends on knowing what are the real causes of poverty, but a thorough and fair examination of the nature of poverty in America will show that it is a complex phenomenon, with many antecedents. Poverty presents no simple ethical certainties and presents few simple policy solutions (see "A Question of Ethics: Does Assistance Help or Hurt the Poor?" for a more detailed discussion of this issue).

UNDERSTANDING SOCIAL WELFARE POLICY

Discussing and debating social welfare policies is a very difficult task in capitalist, democratic political systems like the United States'. Americans struggle to balance individual merit and the rewards of initiative with the reality of systemic environmental inequalities and the need to provide support to many. Citizens disagree on how much government can or should do to even out the competition and protect those who are less able to compete. In short, Americans seek to retain a commitment to both competition and compassion. Sorting out the proper balance of these values is at the heart of policy disagreements about social welfare programs.

Democracy and Social Welfare

There are no easy answers to the problems social welfare policies create for a democratic society. There is evidence of people in great need and evidence

---

[23]David T. Ellwood and Lawrence H. Summers, "Is Welfare Really the Problem?" *Public Interest* 83 (Spring 1986); 57–78.

Does Assistance Help or Hurt the Poor?

Assume that a service club at your college or university is concerned about the poor in your community. A club member tells you and your friend about a poor family she knows who cannot afford to buy proper clothes for their children or purchase enough food or heat for the winter months. The club member asks if you and your friend can spare a few dollars to help this family in need.

You reply that this situation is terrible. You are glad to help with your own contribution, but you wonder how government can allow this to happen and why it does not do more to help victims of circumstances like these. Your friend takes a very different view. These people probably are lazy or wasteful, she asserts. Their poverty is their problem. If our government helps them, we are only encouraging their continued dependence.

What is the ethical thing to do? Both you and your friend want to help this family. Your desire to help them is based on your belief that poverty is transitory and often the result of external factors beyond a person's control, such as the loss of a job, illness, or discriminatory behavior toward the person's group. The situation must change for them to escape poverty, you believe. For you, helping now is the ethical thing to do.

Your friend, however, believes that personal factors, not situational ones, are the main causes of poverty. The poor have bad values that result in their poverty, she says. Their values must change for them to escape poverty. To help them now is to encourage continued dependency and long-term poverty, she argues. The only ethical thing to do, she declares, is not to give money to this family now. They must learn to help themselves.

What would you do? What will you tell your friend? Should the service club be helping poor families? What is the ethical thing to do?

that, although much has and can be accomplished, the results of social welfare programs may be limited and the costs astronomical. The demand for action by some is met by the call for restraint from others.

In a democracy these competing demands are resolved by government decision makers, but these decision makers do not act in a vacuum. They are aligned with and pay allegiance to various groups in society. These groups are members of their legislative constituencies, members of their electoral coalitions, and members of their political party. Many of these groups are terribly important to the decision makers in providing the financial assistance needed to seek and retain political office in what has become a very expensive electoral process.

In the social welfare policy arena, the competing groups are often quite uneven in the resources they bring to the struggle. For example, the elderly are relatively well organized and often have the resources needed to wield significant influence in support of their programs. In contrast, those who oppose various programs for the elderly are often relatively unorganized and unfocused. In the pressure cooker of legislative decision making, the elderly can turn up more heat. As a result, they are usually successful in protecting and expanding their programs.

For the poor, influencing political decisions is more difficult. They vote less, lack strong, focused organizations and money, and face powerful, wealthy, and well-organized opposition when they and their supporters seek to expand poverty programs. Groups supporting continuation or expansion of social welfare programs for the poor often fail to translate their concerns into specific policies. Democracies encourage competition and compromise, but in this democratic competition the contestants are not always equal and the results do not always satisfy all the parties.

Once benefits are given to citizens, the nature of democratic politics makes it difficult to withdraw them. Policy-making in the United States is very incremental in nature. Once put in place, policies develop a life of their own. They engage supporters in the public, in Congress, in the bureaucracy, and among key interest groups.

Tremendous pressures come from these supporters to keep or expand programs and to preserve them from elimination. These pressures persist even when the size and costs of programs seem to have grown beyond anything anyone might have originally envisioned.

For example, the mushrooming of the Social Security Program has become one of America's most severe budget problems: in 1960 there were 14.2 million beneficiaries receiving $11.3 billion; by 1990 more than 38 million beneficiaries were receiving over $200 billion. Despite a succession of more conservative presidents since Lyndon Johnson left office in 1969, government now spends a larger share of the gross national product on social welfare policies than it did during his administration. Although the pressures to hold down program expansion and growth are present, inertia, plus various constituencies' demands, seem to make it virtually impossible to slow down.

Social Welfare Policy and the Size of Government

Past democratic conflicts and compromises in the social welfare policy area have given Americans a huge social welfare bureaucracy at all levels of government and hundreds of billions of dollars in taxes and expenditures to support a panoply of social welfare programs. Tens of thousands of government employees at federal, state, and local levels process requests for service, evaluate eligibility, authorize payments, screen service providers, and monitor for efficiency, fraud, and abuse.

This expenditure of money and energy is not necessarily bad. These activities and these employees are, for the most part, providing useful and cost-efficient services. It is true that some portion of the social welfare dollars goes into management and oversight, thereby limiting the amount that gets directly to the recipient. At the same time, many argue that expenditures for management and oversight activities are necessary because they make sure that the correct amount is delivered to the appropriate beneficiary under the proper program guidelines.

Large government programs, be they in the area of national defense or social welfare, require large organizations to administer them. The appropriate way to evaluate these administrative systems is not to focus on their size or expense alone, but to weigh their size and expense against the conduct of their mission, the goals and accomplishments of their programs, and the extent to which private, non-governmental entities could realistically be depended on to help. "You Are the Policymaker: Helping the Homeless" asks you to consider the vast array of issues surrounding only one program area, aid for the homeless.

Helping the Homeless

During the 1980s homelessness became a serious problem in America. The number of homeless is difficult to determine precisely, but private and public estimates range from a low of three hundred thousand to over one million Americans. Even more important than the increase in the overall number of homeless is the drastic change in the types of homeless individuals one now sees in major cities. In the past most of the homeless were single, middle-aged men, often with alcohol or related problems. Today many more of the homeless are families, especially female-headed families with small children. The face of homelessness in America has changed and with it has come a new call from many to take decisive action.

You must decide what is to be done about this problem. You face both short-term and long-term concerns. You need to find some way to handle the scores of homeless now present in the nation's major cities, and you need to design plans to reduce the population of future homeless Americans. The issues you face are familiar ones noted in this chapter. You must decide what the government can do directly and what it can do indirectly through stimulation of the private sector. When you identify a proper governmental role, you must decide what level of government—federal, state, or local—will take which actions and how these actions will be coordinated.

You have many options from which to choose. You can directly implement a federal program that provides housing vouchers to poor families and individuals who meet certain eligibility standards. This program would be costly, but it would preserve private sector involvement and choice for the recipients. The vouchers, however, might raise housing costs and not provide any additional low-cost housing units in the short run. You might create tax incentives for private investors to build new low-income housing units. Again, the costs would be high and you would have to guarantee occupancy and protection from other debt and insurance risks.

Whatever you decide to do, you must recognize that there will be resource limitations. You must, therefore, decide how to raise additional revenues or how to reassign existing revenues to meet the new program's needs. You could recommend raising taxes or cutting expenditures in other social welfare programs like AFDC or Food Stamps. Either option will bring in other political forces seeking to promote their political agenda.

The proper choices are not easy or obvious. They require much thought, examination, and discussion. All this debate will take place in a political context where competing groups have different views about the nature of the problem, different perspectives on the relative importance of the problem, and different opinions on the proper role of government. Whatever you decide to do, you will also have to build political support for your proposed actions. This means garnering support in national, state, and local corridors of government—and this generally means compromising. What compromises are you prepared to make and how will they affect homeless families in America?

SUMMARY

You have seen in this chapter that government action and inaction can play a major role in affecting the social welfare status of many of America's poor and elderly citizens. Entitlement programs like Social Security and Medicare have significantly improved the lot of the elderly, but they are very costly programs that threaten to grow even larger and more expensive. Programs aimed more specifically at the poor cost less (and perhaps have accomplished less), but they seem likely to remain objects of political controversy for many years to come.

You have also learned about the nature of wealth and poverty and have discovered that ideas about the causes of poverty are closely related to decisions about what to do about it. Some believe that poverty results from problems within the individual—creating a culture of poverty—while others have shown that legal, social, and economic environments may be the most important correlates of poverty status. Individuals' ideas about the causes of poverty are closely associated with what social welfare policies they support and with what they believe society's responsibilities are to the poor.

Social welfare programs, like other government policies, evolve slowly over time. There are important watershed events and policies, like Social Security in 1935 and the Great Society in the late 1960s, but much of the growth and change in American social welfare policies is incremental in nature, building on past policies, adding a little here, taking a little there. This process of evolution brings into play all the major actors in the political process—the president, Congress, interest groups, and the public.

In the next decade Americans will have to struggle over the future directions and financial commitments for social welfare policy. The issues are already well developed and include considerations of the legitimate role of government and the effectiveness, costs, and fairness of various programs.

With limited financial resources and growing national debt, choices will be even more difficult to make in the future. Should the government continue spending for the elderly at current levels and rates of increase? As the economy continues to become more technologically sophisticated, how will Americans make use of all of their human capital to best serve the nation? Can the United States afford to have a large and essentially nonproductive underclass?

These are just some of the important social policy questions Americans will face in the coming years. How we as citizens answer them may have a great deal to do with our quality of life in the twenty-first century.

Despite increasing social welfare expenditures, the number of Americans living below the poverty line continues to grow.

KEY TERMS

social welfare policies

income distribution

relative deprivation

income

wealth

poverty line

culture of poverty

progressive tax

proportional tax

regressive tax

transfer payments

intergenerational equity

FOR FURTHER READING

Hochschild, Jennifer L. *What's Fair?* Cambridge, Mass.: Harvard University Press, 1981. A study of people's attitudes toward income distribution.

Levitan, Sar A. *Programs in Aid of the Poor.* 6th ed. Baltimore: Johns Hopkins University Press, 1990. An excellent overview of social welfare programs.

Murray, Charles. *Losing Ground: American Social Policy, 1950–1980.* New York: Basic Books, 1984. A conservative's argument that social policies have not worked, but have made things worse.

Obey, David and Paul Sarbanes, eds. *The Changing American Economy.* New York: Basil Blackwell, 1986. Cochairs of the Joint Economic Committee of Congress, Obey and Sarbanes have brought together a useful selection of articles on the economy and equality.

Page, Benjamin. *Who Gets What from Government?* Berkeley, Calif.: University of California Press, 1983. A useful assessment of the impact of government on people's incomes.

Vedlitz, Arnold. *Conservative Mythology and Public Policy in America.* New York: Praeger, 1988. A good counterweight to Murray.

Wilson, William J. *The Truly Disadvantaged: The Inner City, the Underclass, and Public Policy.* Chicago: University of Chicago Press, 1987. The story of the poorest of the poor.

19

POLICY-MAKING FOR HEALTH, ENERGY, AND THE ENVIRONMENT

New and complex problems are constantly brought up in government. More and more, these issues involve scientific controversies associated with the environment. One such example is the greenhouse effect—the gradual warming of the planet caused by the burning of fossil fuels. Oil, coal, and many other fuels that Americans use to run their cars or to generate electricity produce carbon dioxide. The accumulation of carbon dioxide in the atmosphere traps heat, gradually causing the earth's temperature to rise. Scientists have known for quite some time about the problem of global warming, but getting everyone to agree on a solution will not be easy. The costs of reducing carbon dioxide emissions by shifting to alternative energy sources are staggering: optimistic estimates are in the range of $800 billion; pessimistic (and possibly more accurate) ones are closer to $4 trillion. These costs would not be paid in a single year, of course, but they amount to almost the entire American GNP.

Financial costs would not be the only way in which solving the greenhouse effect might affect citizens. There may be increased government regulation in many areas of daily life. Americans are accustomed, for example, to driving their cars, but the freedom to do so might be severely limited in many areas of the country. Some cities, like Los Angeles, are already moving towards adopting standards of emission that would virtually rule out most current cars. Americans might all like the freedom to drive their cars whenever they want, but many citizens would also agree that governments must impose restrictions if the alternative is a worldwide catastrophe. More and more, scientists are becoming convinced that this may indeed be the choice facing governments in the future. In the past, most government antipollution standards have focused on industry; in the future, they may affect individuals much more directly.

One possible solution to the greenhouse effect is to replace coal-burning electrical plants with nuclear power plants. The United States has no repository for the waste that these plants produce, however, and no state is volunteering to build one. If there is increasing pressure to build more nuclear power plants, one can expect considerable political debate about their safety.

Many countries stand to pay a high price if global warming is not stopped. If sea levels rise, countries like Holland, Bangladesh, and India could face tremendous flooding problems, as could many areas of the United States. On the other hand, some countries in cooler climates might be able to improve their agricultural outputs. Getting all these countries to agree on solutions is not likely to be easy.

Global warming and the greenhouse effect are thus likely to affect Americans' personal lives, national policy-making, and international politics. Citizens may be affected by new regulations concerning air pollution, increasing the costs or even prohibiting some activities now taken for granted. National policy-making institutions may be forced to weigh the trade-offs between energy production and air pollution, and may face increasing pressure to enact strict and possibly unpopular regulations on business and private citizens. Finally, efforts to solve the global warming problem may require international negotiations. The costs of avoiding global warming seem high for the United States, but they are even greater for many underdeveloped countries strapped with problems of hunger, disease, and debt. They may expect the United States and other developed countries to bear a greater share of the burden, since the developed countries are the source of most air pollution. Such disagreements over who should pay the costs of preventing global warming are likely to be important questions of international relations in the future. Fostering the cooperation necessary among various nations will not be easy. Americans can expect energy and environmental issues to become increasingly important in many areas of their lives and politics.

Source: On global warming see Peter Passell, "Cure for Greenhouse Effect: The Costs Will Be Staggering," *New York Times*, November 19, 1989, 1.

T he current pace of technological change is dizzying. From the production of the first typewriter to the production of the first word processor took just over a century; from the discovery of the proton to the explosion of atomic bombs took about three decades; from the invention of the jet airplane to the first spacecraft took only fifteen years; and from the time of the first patenting of a microorganism to the first patenting of an animal took just eight years.

The increasing speed of technological advance creates special problems for government and for policymakers. New issues must be dealt with, posing both practical and moral problems for the political system. When medical researchers develop new techniques for prolonging life, everyone is of course pleased. Many of these new technologies, however, are amazingly expensive. These new medical technologies have changed the basic approach to medical care; their cost has transformed the American medical system. Doctors now complain about loss of control to insurance agencies and government regulators, but the health care industry now consumes over one-tenth of the nation's entire gross national product. As health care has become so expensive, new public policy problems have been created even as old health problems have been solved.

Health is not the only area where technological developments have had a great impact on the nature of American democracy (see Table 19.1). The rapid growth of the American economy during the twentieth century has brought energy and pollution problems to the forefront of politics. Complex issues of energy—for example, choosing from competing sources of electricity or between off-shore oil drilling and dependence on foreign sources of oil—have created political problems during the last quarter century.

More leisure time and disposable income, made possible by advancing technologies, have made Americans more sensitive to the quality of the environment. New environmental movements have transformed many areas of American politics. Those concerned with pollution and related issues are making their voices heard at every level of the federal system. As Americans have become more concerned with environmental quality, government has been called upon again and again to impose new restrictions on activities in the private sector— always a controversial topic.

Not only does technological change affect how Americans live their lives, but it also changes what they expect the government to do. This chapter examines public policy in three technologically complex areas: health, energy, and the environment.

HEALTH

One of the largest single components of America's gross national product is health. Overall, about 12 percent of the GNP goes to the health industry. This percentage has been rising over time as the technological revolution has increased standards of health care as well as the costs necessary to pay for it. Generally, one can ask three important questions concerning health care and public policy in the United States: What is the quality of health care in America?

Table 19.1

Table 19.1   Life in the Fast Lane: Technological Change in the Twentieth Century

TECHNOLOGY	1900	1945	1990
Best means of transportation	Horse, train	Automobile	Airplane, automobile
Electricity	Little or none	Nearly universal	Nearly universal
Telephones	Invented, not widespread	Widespread among middle-income families	Nearly universal
Mass communication	Word of mouth or newspapers	Radio	Television, computer
Written communication	Mail, books, some magazines	Newspapers, books, magazines	Newspapers, books, magazines, satellite, computer networks
Most powerful weapons of war	Howitzers, cannons, rifles	Atomic bombs	Hydrogen bombs
Political campaigns	By train	By radio, public rallies	By television, computers, direct mail
"Last frontier" of human exploration	North and South Poles being "discovered"	Most of world explored; some discussion of space	Genes, space
Recent advance in medicine	Asprin first marketed in 1899	Vaccinations against polio and other human scourges nearly ready	Transplants of human organs
Recent advance in biology	Darwinian theory gaining acceptance	Early ideas about DNA and human heritability discussed	Genetic engineering, animal patents
Recent advance in physics	Einstein working on his second paper on relativity	Ability to produce weapons even more destructive than the atomic bomb	Experiments in superconductivity

How is health care policy organized? Who influences health care policy in the United States?

Health Care in America

America is one of the wealthiest countries in the world, and it spends a higher proportion of its wealth on health care than any other country. Still, Americans are not the healthiest people in the world. Health care statistics show that, although Americans are generally healthy (which is to be expected given the country's wealth), they still lag behind other countries in some key health care categories (see Table 19.2).

The average American has a life expectancy of 75 years—a high number, but not the highest in the world. Despite advances in medical technology, the average American does not live as long than the average Icelander. In terms of *infant mortality rate*—the proportion of babies who do not survive their first year of life, a common indicator of a nation's health—the United States is only eighteenth among the world's nations. As Table 19.2 shows, the chances of an American baby dying the first year of life are almost double that of a baby born

Table 19.2 Comparing America's Health: Life Expectancy and Infant Mortality Rates in Selected Countries

COUNTRY	LIFE EXPECTANCY	INFANT MORTALITY RATE (deaths per 1,000 births)
Iceland	77.1	6
Japan	77.2	6
Switzerland	76.5	7
France	75.2	8
Canada	75.7	8
Britain	74.5	9
United States	**75.0**	10
East Germany	72.4	10
USSR	69.7	28

Source: World Quality of Life Indicators, 1989 (Santa Barbara, Calif.: ABC-CLIO, 1989).

in Iceland or in Japan. Overall, infant mortality rates in the United States are on a par with those in such countries as Costa Rica, Bulgaria, and Poland, and behind countries such as Jamaica and Cuba.[1]

Much of the money that Americans pay for health care goes to expensive services like organ transplants, kidney dialysis, and other treatments that are not widely available outside of the United States. The high-tech services available to Americans are far superior to those available in most other Western countries. They also cost a lot. In fact, Americans spend more and more on medical care every year. The percent of GNP spent on health care has risen steadily during the past thirty years, as indicated in Figure 19.1.

Today America spends 12 percent of its GNP on health, more than double the percentage of a generation ago.[2] The reasons for these increases are many. American health providers have overbuilt medical care facilities (25 percent of all hospital beds are vacant on any given day), and doctors and hospitals have few incentives to be more efficient. Because insurance companies pay for most health care expenses, patients have no reason to ask for cheaper care, and doctors have no reason to compete with each other to offer it. In fact, with the rise in medical malpractice suits, doctors are well advised to order extra tests, however expensive they may be, to ensure that they cannot be sued—an approach that is sometimes called "defensive medicine." These practices drive up the costs of medical care for everyone. As doctors are hit with higher and higher costs for insurance against malpractice suits, they increase their fees to pay their premiums. Because insurance companies pay the bills, patients are not upset; however, increased costs associated with medical care are making insurance rates skyrocket.

[1]See the discussion in B. Guy Peters, *American Public Policy,* 2nd ed. (Chatham, N.J.: Chatham House, 1986), 184–85.

[2]See Arnold J. Heidenheimer, Hugh Heclo, and Carolyn Teich Adams, *Comparative Public Policy,* 3rd ed. (New York: St. Martin's Press, 1990), 85.

Figure 19.1 Percent of GNP Spent on Health

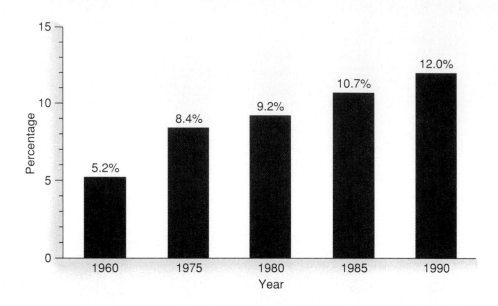

Source: Arnold J. Heidenheimer, Hugh Heclo, Carolyn Teich Adams, *Comparative Public Policy*, 3rd ed. (New York: St. Martin's Press, 1990), 85.

How can one explain the contradiction between the high costs that Americans pay for health care—the highest costs in the world—and the fact that Americans are not the world's healthiest people? One explanation can be found in the way the American health care industry organizes itself.

Health Care Policy

American health care policy is dominated by contrasts. Many citizens have access to the highest quality care in the world; others do not. When looking at health care policy, the first thing to consider is the question of access.

Access   Inequalities in health and health care are a grave problem in America. Like other issues, health is strongly related to race and income. In particular, access to health insurance is not universal in the United States, as it is in many countries. For those Americans who do not have health insurance, having the most up-to-date research and equipment available is less important than, simply, access to a family doctor or someone to administer neonatal care. Americans spend large amounts of money on health, and the world's highest-quality care is available to some citizens. Nevertheless, many poor and working Americans are relegated to an inferior health care system.

Most Americans—90 percent of the population—do, of course, have some form of health insurance (although that percentage is actually declining). Getting and keeping health insurance are often linked to having a job. In 1983 thirty-four million Americans went without health insurance for all or part of the year;

eleven million of them were in the families of workers who had lost a job.[3] In 1986 and 1987 the Census Bureau reported that over a period of twenty-eight months, sixty-three million Americans went without insurance coverage during part of that time. Often, this is associated with short periods of unemployment. Still, the Census Bureau estimates that thirty-two million Americans go without insurance in any given month.[4]

Access to health insurance is closely tied to race and income in the United States. Seventy-two percent of whites had health insurance during the entire period covered by the Census Bureau survey, as compared with 62 percent of blacks and 48 percent of Hispanics. Clearly, access to insurance is unequal.

Even among those who are covered by insurance, coverage is often incomplete. Especially for those with low-paying jobs, health insurance may not cover all their health needs. A recent poll conducted in three countries found that over 7 percent of Americans had foregone "needed medical care" because of financial concerns in the previous twelve months. In Canada and Britain the corresponding figure was less than 1 percent. Britain has a system of nationalized health care; Canada has a system of national health insurance.

The poll also revealed that Americans were not pleased with their health care system. Eighty-nine percent of the Americans polled said that the health care system was in need of fundamental change, while only 42 percent of Canadians and 67 percent of the British thought so. A majority of Americans said that they would like to have a system like the Canadian one, but only 3 percent of Canadians said that they would like to have the American system.[5]

When one looks at the life expectancy and infant mortality rates as reported in Table 19.1, the same discrepancies that are apparent for health insurance stand out again. Whites had an average life expectancy in 1988 of 75.5 years, but blacks could only expect to live 69.5 years. For black males, life expectancy was only 65.1 years—a full decade shorter than the average for whites, and lower than the averages in many Eastern European and third world countries.[6]

Similarly, infant mortality rates among those with good insurance plans and a family doctor are very low. For the poor and those without insurance, on the other hand, the statistics are disturbing. Black infant mortality in 1987—17.9 per 1,000 babies born—was over twice as high as the 8.6 figure for whites. In fact, over the past decade, the gap between the races has been getting wider.

Tremendous advances have been made in the ability to keep some premature babies alive, but many pregnant women, especially in the nation's ghettos, lack the care needed to ensure that their babies will be born healthy. Instead of having a regular doctor (few doctors practice in poor neighborhoods), many of the nation's poor go only to hospital emergency rooms. Prenatal care is an important component in reducing health risks during the first year of life, but prenatal care is not available to all.[7] Often, the availability of family doctors and

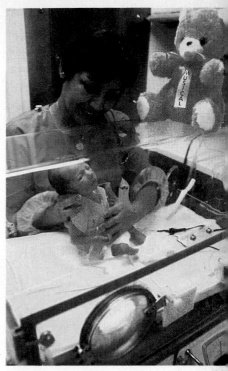

Americans pride themselves on having the world's most advanced medical technology, but many American citizens lack the resources to obtain even the most basic health care. As a result, infant mortality rates in the United States, especially among racial minorities and the poor, are much higher than in many other Western nations.

[3]Michael Harrington, *The New American Poverty* (New York: Penguin Books, 1984), 50.

[4]U.S. Department of Commerce, Bureau of the Census, Public Information Office, "More than One-Quarter of Population Had Health Insurance Gaps, Census Bureau Survey Shows," April 12, 1990.

[5]See Dennis Hevesi, "Polls Show Discontent with Health Care," *New York Times,* February 15, 1989, 8.

[6]"U.S. Health Gap Is Getting Wider," *New York Times,* March 23, 1990.

[7]See Howard W. French, "Bringing Basic Health Care to the Poor," *New York Times,* November 26, 1989, B-1.

routine hospital services are more important in determining the quality of a nation's health care than the most up-to-date medical and research equipment.

One important way in which American medical care differs from that of most other democracies is in the role that the government plays. America's is the most private medical care system in the developed world (see Figure 19.2). This fact may be a key to explaining why access to quality health care is unequal, and why Americans may not get their money's worth in the health care marketplace.

The Role of Government   Compared to other countries, American governments play a relatively small role in health care. Just over 40 percent of the country's total health bill is paid for by government sources, while the average for industrialized countries is about 77 percent. Forty percent amounts to much

---

Figure 19.2   Government Spending as a Percent of Total Health Spending in Selected Democracies

As in many other areas of the economy, the role of government is smaller in the United States than in other comparable countries. The United States lacks national health insurance or a national health service to provide health care directly to those who need it. Still, the government accounts for over 40 percent of all money spent on health care in this country—a sizeable percentage. In fact, the government is the largest single source of health care dollars, providing more funds than even private insurance companies.

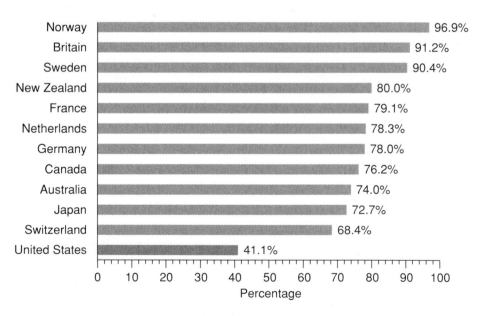

Source: Adopted from Arnold J. Heidenheimer, Hugh Heclo, and Carolyn Teich Adams, *Comparative Public Policy*, 3rd ed. (New York: St. Martin's Press, 1990), 63. Data are for 1985.

more than most Americans realize. Many hospitals are connected to public universities, and much medical research is financed through the **National Institutes of Health (NIH),** for example. Further, the federal government pays for much of the nation's medical bill through its Medicare program for the elderly and its Medicaid program for the poor. The government thus plays an important health care role in America, though less so than in other countries.

Who pays for Americans' health care? As noted earlier, government payments account for a total of 41 percent of all health care payments. This includes Medicare, Medicaid, and other payments, such as those for veterans. Private insurance companies cover 32 percent, and Americans pay 25 percent of their health care costs out of their own pockets. Americans often think that insurance companies pay most health care costs, but in fact the government is more heavily involved than the private insurance industry.

Harry S Truman was the first president to call for **national health insurance,** a compulsory insurance program to finance all Americans' medical care. The idea was strongly opposed by the American Medical Association, the physicians' interest group, which called it socialized medicine. National health insurance has never been adopted. Nonetheless, in 1965 Congress recognized the special problems of elderly Americans by adopting **Medicare.** Medicare is part of the Social Security system. Part A of Medicare provides hospitalization insurance; Part B, which is voluntary, permits older Americans to purchase inexpensive coverage for doctor fees and other expenses. Today, as the number of older Americans is growing rapidly—and as the cost of medical care is growing just as fast—the funding of health care for the elderly is one of the country's most pressing public policy issues.

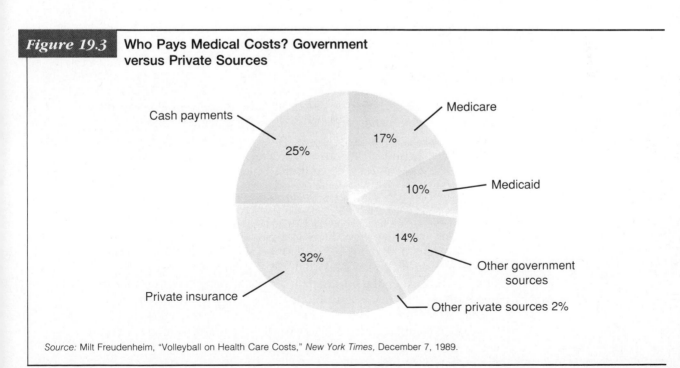

Figure 19.3   **Who Pays Medical Costs? Government versus Private Sources**

Cash payments 25%

Medicare 17%

Medicaid 10%

Other government sources 14%

Other private sources 2%

Private insurance 32%

Source: Milt Freudenheim, "Volleyball on Health Care Costs," *New York Times,* December 7, 1989.

Not to be confused with Medicare is **Medicaid,** a program designed to provide insurance coverage for the poor. Like other public assistance programs, Medicaid is funded by both the states and the national government. Unlike Medicare, which goes to all elderly Americans regardless of their income, Medicaid is a means-tested program. Only those who make less than a certain amount of money are eligible to receive it. Debates arise about the formulas for determining eligibility, since often people with low paying jobs are not eligible, while those on welfare may qualify. Thus, because of the loss of health benefits and the high cost of purchasing them privately, it may not pay to take a low-wage service job—obviously, the government does not want to encourage people *not* to work. The government also does not want to force employers to offer health insurance, which would place a great burden on them. Some compromise needs to be reached, however, to stop millions of Americans from going without health insurance.

Government in America plays an important role in health care, even if it is less than in other countries. One way to explain the uneven access to health care in the United States is to look at who participates in making health care policy.

Policy-making for Health Care

The cost of medical care in a high-tech age raises issues people do not usually like to discuss, much less debate as public policy problems. Death is one such issue—today 90 percent of all Americans die either in hospitals or in nursing homes, most of them funded and regulated by the government. Like it or not, health care is a governmental problem in the United States.

One of the reasons for America's emphasis on expensive and high-tech solutions to complicated health problems may be that there has traditionally been no single institution paying medical bills. With a mixture of government funds, private insurance, and out-of-pocket payments, no one actor has responsibility for all costs. In countries with national health care systems (or national health insurance), government policymakers have focused more on ensuring equality of care and on keeping costs down. In the United States equality of care and cost containment have taken a back seat to technological advance. Thus Americans have high-tech, expensive, and unequal care.

Comparing the costs of standard medical procedures in the United States with those in similar countries can lead to some surprises. For example, a doctor's home visit costs triple in the United States what it costs in Japan and double the average European cost. A total hysterectomy costs about $300 in Japan, $151 in Germany, and $187 in France, but about $1,754 in the United States.[8] Small wonder that America's total health care bill is so large.

Many lifesaving procedures are extremely expensive, so allocating them involves complicated questions of public policy. Each dollar spent on expensive procedures to save a few lives cannot be spent on other, equally pressing, health needs. Thus when the government allows Medicare payments for certain procedures, less money is available for rural hospitals, for health clinics in poor areas of the nation's cities, or for other problems. For example, in 1972 Congress extended Medicare protection to virtually all patients with kidney failure or end-

[8]See Heidenheimer et al, 88.

stage renal disease. Today, more than eighty thousand patients with these problems cost Medicare two billion dollars annually.[9]

One reason for uneven government and private health care policies has to do with the representation of interests. Powerful lobbying organizations representing hospitals, doctors, and the elderly want Medicare to pay for the latest techniques. Politicians hardly feel comfortable denying these lifesaving measures to those who may have voted them into office. On the other hand, many groups are unrepresented in government. Their health needs may not be met simply because no well-organized groups are insisting that the government meet them.

The elderly, for example, are now one of the most powerful voting and lobbying forces in American politics. Health care policy which favors the elderly is one of the results of this interest group activity. The American Association of Retired Persons (AARP) has grown from about 150,000 in 1959 to over 28 million in 1989, making it the largest voluntary association in the world.[10] This single group now can claim to represent one American in ten, and speaks with authority on all questions associated with the elderly. The political power of the elderly was brought home very clearly to members of Congress in 1989 when older people objected to the Social Security surtax designed to pay for new catastrophic illness coverage. Congress was forced to repeal the tax after the "gray lobby" flexed its muscles.

For workers in low-paying service jobs that do not include health insurance, or for those who are unemployed and cannot afford private health insurance, there is no organization capable of exerting such influence in government. Since many of these people do not vote, the bias in representation is even greater. The groups that enjoy good health care coverage in the United States are largely those that are well organized to influence the government.

One group that is increasingly active in health care policy-making is business. Conflict between the government, which pays many medical bills, and private employers, who pay insurance premiums for their employees, is increasing. Each side wants the other to assume more of the health care burden. For example, the government saved $1.3 billion in 1989 by forcing patients to exhaust their private insurance before allowing government programs to begin making payments.[11] As the government reduces its payments in such ways, hospitals pass on their costs to those patients with private insurance. As private insurance rates increase, employers attempt to reduce their burden by cutting out benefits that are covered by government programs. Employers and the government end up in what some have called a "volleyball game" over who pays for health costs. Business groups are increasingly calling for some greater regulation or government activity in the health care field. For example, they complain that their foreign competitors avoid the high costs of private insurance premiums because governments, rather than employers, cover health insurance costs in many other countries.

Insurance rates and medical fees will be an important public policy problem for some time to come. There are likely to be increasing calls for more gov-

Health care policy-making involves difficult ethical issues. Should limited federal funds, for example, be spent on the expensive, unproven, but potentially life-saving artificial heart technology shown above? Or should public money be devoted to less dramatic medical procedures that could help many more Americans?

[9] Roger W. Evans, "The Heart Transplant Dilemma," *Issues in Science and Technology,* Spring 1986, 92.

[10] See the *Encyclopedia of Associations,* 24th ed. (Detroit: Gale Research, Inc., 1990).

[11] On this topic, see Milt Freudenheim, "Volleyball on Health Care Costs," *New York Times,* December 7, 1989, B-1.

ernment regulation over fees, and some attempt to help those who fall through the cracks of the American health care system. Health care is one area where increasing technology has many impacts on American public policy; such impacts are also clear in the area of energy.

ENERGY

Modern American society depends on the availability of abundant sources of energy. Producing the amounts of energy necessary to retain Americans' standard of living and accustomed patterns of life is increasingly difficult, however. Government is constantly involved in battles concerning what forms of energy the country should be producing, and from what sources.

The federal government shapes energy policies in dozens of ways. For one thing, it owns much of the land from which energy comes. In California, for example, about half the land is owned by government. David Davis, a political scientist who specializes in the subject, emphasizes that energy politics is fragmented.[12] Whereas some energy sources (such as nuclear power) are tightly regulated by the government, others (such as coal) are left mostly to the free market.

America's Energy Profile

Once Americans used wood, animals, and people power for energy. Today 95 percent of the nation's energy comes from coal, oil, and natural gas. Americans search continually for new and more efficient sources of energy, both to increase supplies and to reduce pollution. Much of the research on new energy sources and efficiencies comes from the government in Washington.

Oil, accounting for half the energy Americans use, is one of nature's **nonrenewable resources.** Some resources, like the wind or solar energy, are renewable; that is, using them once does not reduce the amount left to be used in the future. These things are constantly renewed by nature. Oil, coal, and other common sources of energy, however, are not renewable.

More than half of the world's recoverable reserves of oil lie in the Middle East, with Saudia Arabia alone controlling much of this resource. States like Texas, Oklahoma, Louisiana, and Alaska produce considerable amounts of oil within the United States, but not enough to meet the country's needs. America imports just over 50 percent of its annual consumption of oil from other countries, in particular the Middle East. The United States is not as dependent on foreign sources of oil as many European countries, like France or Italy, which have virtually no oil of their own, or like Japan, which also imports all of its oil. On the other hand, America's dependence on foreign oil is growing: from 1985, when imports were less than 33 percent of demand, they have increased to 54 percent in January of 1990.[13]

Oil has made its mark on political history, being by almost any measure the world's biggest business. It fuels wars in the Middle East. Oil, as much as

---

[12] David Davis, *Energy Politics,* 3rd ed. (New York: St. Martin's Press, 1982), 13.

[13] Matthew L. Wald, "U.S. Reliance on Imported Oil Is at Record High," *New York Times,* February 16, 1990.

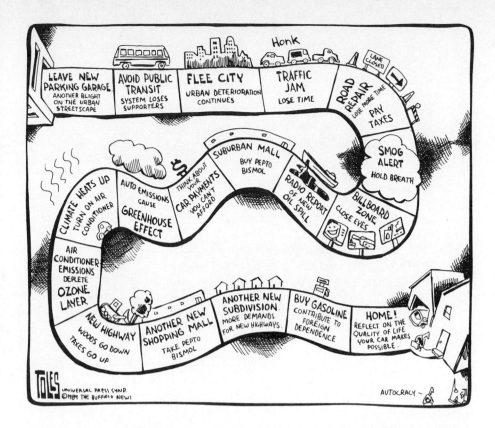

anything else, is at the root of the decades of tension between Iran and the United States.[14] Domestically, when fingers are pointed at a corporate or political elite, the names of oil companies soon come up.

Coal, not oil, is America's most abundant fuel. An estimated 90 percent of the country's energy resources are in coal deposits, enough to last for hundreds of years. Coal, however, accounts for only about 20 percent of the energy Americans use. Coal may be the nation's most abundant fuel, but unfortunately, it is also the dirtiest. It is responsible for the black lungs of coal miners and for the soot-blackened cities of the Northeast. Acid rain is traced to the burning of coal to produce electricity. Coal may be abundant, but most Americans do not want to rely on it exclusively for their energy needs.

The most controversial energy source is nuclear power, which accounts for about 14 percent of America's energy profile. Environmentalists dislike nuclear power both because of the possibility of a radiation leak at a plant and because of the enormous difficulty of nuclear waste disposal. Pronuclear activists argue that burning coal to generate electricity continues to blacken miners' lungs, cause acid rain to defoliate forests and kill lakes, increase global warming, and create other problems. The trade-offs between nuclear and other forms of energy bring into focus many of the problems of politics in a high-tech age.

Finally, despite considerable media attention to newer fuels—solar energy, windmills, geothermal power, and the like—their contribution to America's

[14]James A. Bill, *The Eagle and the Lion: The Tragedy of American-Iranian Relations* (New Haven, Conn.: Yale University Press, 1988).

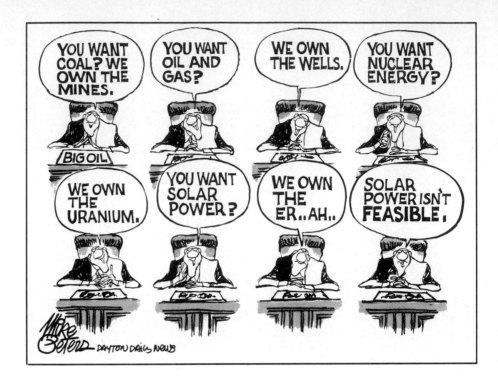

energy supply is negligible. Until the costs of fuel once again skyrocket (as oil prices did in the 1970s), there will be neither economic nor political incentives to invest heavily in new fuels.

Policy-making for Energy Issues

Energy issues involve a number of different actors, from local governments (who often own municipal power companies) to the states, the federal government, and outside interests. They often pit environmentalists against energy producers, and even different levels of government against each other. For example, many local power companies are owned by cities, but are regulated by states and the federal government. Federalism plays an important role in energy issues.

Energy issues continually present thorny problems for policymakers to resolve. For example, there are a number of ways to produce electricity. The United States generates about 44 percent of its electricity by burning coal. About 29 percent comes from either natural gas or petroleum. Nuclear power represents about 14 percent of electrical production, and hydroelectric power about 13 percent. All other forms of energy, including solar power, wind, wood, geothermal, together account for only about .5 percent of America's electrical capacity.[15]

Each source of electricity creates problems. Coal is abundant, but filthy. Its use leads to global warming, depletion of the ozone, and acid rain. Natural gas and petroleum contribute to the depletion of the ozone, and petroleum is associated with oil spills. Nuclear power produces radioactive waste, and hy-

[15]Energy Information Administration, *Inventory of Power Plants in the United States, 5.*

This dying forest on Mount Mitchell in North Carolina shows the devastating effects of acid rain, which is formed when tall smokestacks at coal-burning plants belch pollution high into the atmosphere. Much of the acid rain caused by American industries actually falls in Canada; officials there estimate that more than two thousand lakes have "died" as a result of acid rain.

droelectric power plants flood large areas of land. None of these forms of electricity generation is perfect, but Americans want their lights to come on when they flip a switch. Policymakers must decide what is the proper mix of sources of energy to use. "America in Perspective: Comparing Sources of Electricity" shows how the United States compares with a few other countries.

Opposition to nuclear power became the rallying point for a large and powerful environmental movement during the 1960s and 1970s. Some argue, however, that increasing environmental concerns about global warming and acid rain may lead to a resurgence of interest in nuclear power. They contend that new, safer designs for nuclear power plants may avoid many of the hazards of leaks, and that the former foes of nuclear power may become its supporters. Of course, disposal of the waste remains a fundamental problem to the nuclear industry, so one should not soon expect a reversal of the environmentalists' opposition to nuclear power.[16] In fact, there are strong environmental arguments against many forms of energy production. Discussing energy policy in the United States, therefore, almost automatically means a discussion of environmental policy as well.[17]

THE ENVIRONMENT

One might think that such a cherished national treasure as the natural environment would be almost above politics. After all, public opinion analyst Louis Harris reported in the early 1980s that "the American people's desire to battle

[16]See Matthew L. Wald, "The Nuclear Industry Tries Again," *New York Times,* November 26, 1989, C-1, for a discussion of new, safer reactors.

[17]See John L. Campbell, *Collapse of an Industry: Nuclear Power and the Contradictions of U.S. Policy* (Ithaca, N.Y.: Cornell University Press, 1988).

Comparing Sources of Electricity: Nuclear, Conventional, and Hydro Power

Every country must decide what mix of energy sources to use to meet its electricity needs. These decisions are based on the availability of natural resources and on the mobilization of political interests. Hydroelectric power is generally inexpensive and poses few environmental problems, especially when fast-flowing rivers or waterfalls already exist. Countries are limited by nature in the extent to which they can exploit this resource, however. Italy, for example, has many dams in the northern alpine regions. Most countries face a choice between conventional sources of electricity (essentially coal or oil) and nuclear power. France has virtually eliminated conventional sources, as is evident in the accompanying graph. In the near future France will reduce the use of conventional sources even further, to less than 5 percent of the total. In the United States over 70 percent of the country's electricity comes from conventional sources.

How did the French do it? In 1973 the Arab oil embargo hit France much harder than the United States, because France imported over 95 percent of its oil. National leaders decided to adopt an ambitious plan to build fifty-five new nuclear reactors. Ten years later, over 60 percent of the nation's electricity came from nuclear power. Frank Baumgartner, a political scientist who has studied this decision, says that France's nuclear program was implemented successfully because participation is strictly limited to technical experts. Opportunities for nuclear power opponents to intervene in administrative hearings, to initiate court cases, or to obstruct the process in any way are limited by law. The national legislature has not played an important role, in contrast to the active role that the American Congress has sometimes played in nuclear power regulation. Similarly, the courts have not intervened as they have in other countries. (One of Napoleon's legacies is that the executive branch is rarely subject to independent judicial review.) Local governments in France are not in a position to oppose national government decisions, either (another Napoleonic legacy). Finally, regulatory procedures are designed in such a way as to limit the opportunity for nongovernmental officials to participate; in other words, no environmental impact statements. "The most fundamental difference between French and U.S. policymaking concerning nuclear power," explains Baumgartner, "is the great authority of the high civil service to make decisions virtually in secret and without any public debate over the merits of its choices, which are always portrayed as simply the technical and neutral implementation of decisions made by the elected officials." The complicated institutional structures and open participation requirements of American policy-making would have made France's massive implementation of nuclear power impossible.

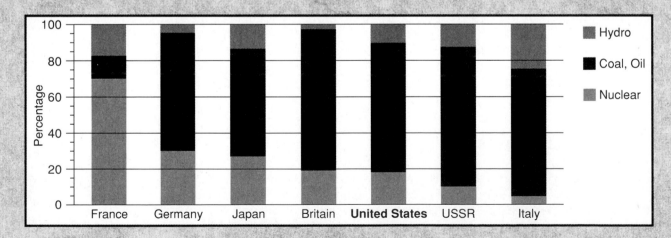

Sources: Frank R. Baumgartner, *Conflict and Rhetoric in French Policymaking* (Pittsburgh: University of Pittsburgh Press, 1989), 202. Tabular information is from *Basic Statistics of the Community* (Brussels: European Community, 1989).

pollution is one of the most overwhelming and clearest we have ever recorded in our twenty-five years of surveying public opinion."[18] As you have learned throughout this book, however, politics infuses itself into all public decisions, even measures to control air and water pollution. One way in which pollution is related to political choices is through its possible impact on business, economic growth, and jobs.

Economic Growth and the Environment

Environmental controls figure prominently in the debate about local and state economic development. As you saw in Chapter 3, the federal system puts the states in a competition for economic advantage. Millions of dollars are spent by states and cities pushing for large investments, such as a billion-dollar GM Saturn plant. New business is a boon to the local and state economies as well as to the political fortunes of their politicians. Business elites can often argue that stringent pollution control laws will drive businesses away by driving up their costs. On the other hand, those states with lax pollution enforcement may find their citizens unhappy, and those businesses that move to them may find employees unwilling to come along. Thus state competition does not always work against pollution standards. In fact, sometimes states compete with each other to enforce tighter pollution controls (see "In Focus: Nondegradation and the Sunbelt-Frostbelt Conflict").

Inevitably, business and government battle over the impact of pollution control on economic development. This is one of the trade-offs policymakers often face: will tougher pollution legislation drive away commerce and industry? No one, of course, knows for sure. Many states are betting that they will not. California, which has the most stringent antipollution laws in the country, still attracts thousands of businesses every year. It may be costly to enforce pollution legislation, but states can save money by reducing health risks to residents. In addition, many newer industries are in the service rather than the industrial sector of the economy, and these new businesses often do not want to locate in areas where environmental enforcement is lax.

Public Concern about the Environment

Whatever the facts from state to state, there will still be arguments about the impact of tough pollution legislation on state and local economic development. Politicians have not been slow to figure out that pollution regulations can have an impact on economic development. They also know that public sentiment is strongly in favor of cleaning up the environment (see "The People Speak: The Environment: A Higher Priority"), and this strong public support for environmental protection is probably a more powerful influence on politicians than a state's interest in attracting business through lax environmental laws.

Americans now are much more concerned about the environment than they were when President Reagan came to office in 1981. Steadily increasing percentages of Americans are willing to see the government spend money to clean up the environment. In the spring of 1990 polls found three-quarters of all Americans saying that "we must protect the environment, even if it means in-

---

[18]Louis Harris, *Washington Post,* January 15, 1982.

Nondegradation and the Sunbelt-Frostbelt Conflict: A Case Study of Environmental Politics

The fledgling Environmental Protection Agency (EPA), created in 1970, had to deal with industrial pollution, among other things. Congress required that the EPA set standards for "ambient air"—standards about just how clean the air had to be. States and localities were required to take policy actions to bring air cleanliness up to standards set by the EPA. Naturally, environmentalists insisted that *higher* standards be adopted for those areas with *cleaner* air. It would be silly, said environmentalists, to set standards so low in clean-air San Antonio that industries and autos might pollute it to the level of dirty-air Bethlehem, Pennsylvania.

Sure enough, in 1977 Congress wrote some amendments to the Clean Air Act, formally requiring the "nondegradation" standard. A community could not, insisted the policy, permit "degradation" of its air quality, whether it started out with pristine air or the foulest air in the country. Let us say you wanted to lo-

cate a new plant in a community that had little pollution. You could not, said the law, worsen air quality there, even if it might still be better than the air in 99 percent of the rest of the country. Thus you would have to install expensive "scrubbers" if you used coal, or other expensive pollution abatement techniques if you did not.

The results were predictable. Industries were discouraged from relocating in clean-air environments, mostly in the Sunbelt, because of the cost of doing so. Robert Crandall did a careful analysis of the supporters of this clean-air amendment. Not surprisingly, they hailed mostly from urban, industrialized areas of the Northeast—the areas likely, without a nondegradation policy, to lose industry to the Sunbelt. No doubt each vote was motivated by a sincere environmental concern. Still, environmental concern can often be mixed with an equal measure of self-interest.

Source: Robert Crandall, *Controlling Industrial Pollution* (Washington, D.C.: The Brookings Institution, 1983).

creased government spending and higher taxes."[19] Americans today are more concerned about the environment and increasingly willing to see the government enact strict regulations against polluters.

The increasing public concern with the environment is not only a phenomenon of the 1980s. Concern for the environment has increased greatly in the United States since the 1950s, when few environmental groups were around. Since then, growth in membership for many of the most important groups has been measured in the millions. Since the passage of important legislation in the early 1970s, these groups have gained important victories and many of their goals are now part of the political mainstream. In 1989 President Bush named William J. Reilly to be the head of the Environmental Protection Agency; he had previously been the head of the World Wildlife Federation.

Environmental Policies in America

The centerpiece of federal environmental policy is the **National Environmental Policy Act (NEPA)** passed in 1969.[20] It requires government agencies

[19] Richard L. Berke, "Oratory of Environmentalism Becomes the Sound of Politics," *New York Times,* April 17, 1990.

[20] For a legislative and administrative discussion and evaluation of the NEPA, see Richard A. Loroff, *A National Policy for the Environment: NEPA and Its Aftermath* (Bloomington: Indiana University Press, 1976).

Do you agree or disagree with the following statement: Protecting the environment is so important that requirements and standards cannot be too high, and continuing environmental improvements must be made regardless of cost.

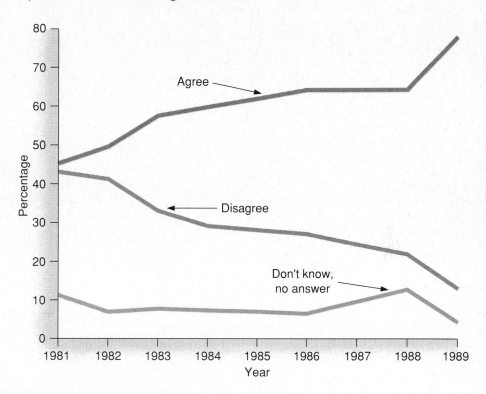

Sources: The question as worded is taken directly from a *New York Times* poll and five *CBS News/New York Times* polls. The 1982 figure represents registered voters only.

to complete an **environmental impact statement (EIS);** every time an agency proposes to undertake a policy potentially disruptive to the natural environment, it must file an EIS with the Environmental Protection Agency, specifying what effects the policy could have. Big dams and small post offices, major port construction and minor road widening—proposals for all these projects must include an EIS (see "A Question of Ethics: Snail Darters, Spotted Owls, and Jobs").

Strictly speaking, an environmental impact statement is merely a procedural requirement. "In theory," says William Ophuls, "an agency can report that a proposed activity will cause the sky to fall . . . and still proceed with the project once it has satisfied the procedural requirements of the act."[21] In practice, the filing of impact statements alerts environmentalists to proposed projects. Environmentalists can then take agencies to court for violating the act's procedural

[21]William Ophuls, *Ecology and the Politics of Scarcity* (San Francisco: Freeman, 1977), 177.

Snail Darters, Spotted Owls, and Jobs

Sometimes small creatures can disrupt large plans. The three-inch long snail darter was the subject of "the most legendary congressional clash between wildlife and the economy" when the Tennessee Valley Authority proposed construction of a dam which would have destroyed its primary breeding area. Since the fish was on the endangered species list and did not thrive elsewhere, a huge battle was waged over the fate of the dam.

Similarly, in 1989 and 1990 intense fights centered on the northern spotted owl, a bird which prospers in the large, centuries-old trees of the Pacific Northwest. Environmentalists want areas of old-growth timber declared off-limits to lumber companies in order to protect the owl. Timber industry spokesmen contend that environmentalists are not concerned so much with the owl, but want to prohibit harvesting the few remaining virgin forests the country has. They complain about "the wine and cheese and brie crowd that are trying to park-ify the national forests." Should timber companies be allowed to harvest trees that were here before the Revolution, and which are on publicly owned land? Should the fate of small fish interfere with plans to build important energy facilities? Often, public policies have unintended consequences on other species of life. Balancing economic interests against environmental impacts is complicated by the ethical questions involved.

Source: Congressional Quarterly, September 9, 1989, 2308.

requirements if the agencies file incomplete or inaccurate impact statements. Because environmental impacts are usually so complicated and difficult to predict, it is relatively easy to argue that the statements are either incomplete or inaccurate in some way. Agencies have often abandoned proposed projects to avoid prolonged court battles with environmental groups. The law does not give the environmental groups the right to stop any environmentally unsound activities, but it does give them the opportunity to delay construction so much that agencies simply give up. Chances are that many of the biggest public works projects of the past century, including the Hoover Dam, Kennedy Airport, Cape Canaveral's space facility, and most Tennessee Valley Authority projects, would not have survived the environmental scrutiny to which they would have been subject had they been undertaken after the NEPA was enacted. In any case, the NEPA has been a very effective tool in preventing much environmental despoliation.

Another landmark piece of legislation affecting the environment is the **Clean Air Act of 1970.** It charges the Department of Transportation (DOT) with the responsibility of reducing automobile emissions. For years after the act's passage, fierce battles raged between the automakers and the DOT about how stringent the requirements had to be. Automakers claimed it was impossible to meet DOT standards; the DOT claimed that automakers were deliberately dragging their feet in the hope that Congress would delay or weaken the requirements. In fact, Congress did weaken them, again and again. Still, the smaller size of American cars, the use of unleaded gasoline, and the lower gas consumption of new cars are all due in large part to DOT regulations. In 1990 Congress passed a reauthorization of the Clean Air Act, which significantly increased the controls on cars, oil refineries, chemical plants, and coal-fired utility plants. This bill was the strongest step forward in the fight to clean the air since the bill's original passage twenty years earlier (see " You Are the Policymaker: Determining Standards for Clean Air").

Congress acted to control pollution of the nation's lakes and rivers with the **Water Pollution Control Act of 1972.** This was enacted in reaction to the tremendous pollution of northeastern rivers and the Great Lakes. Since its passage, water quality has improved dramatically. The agency charged with administering these laws is the **Environmental Protection Agency (EPA).** Created in 1970, it is now the nation's largest federal regulatory agency. The EPA has a wide-ranging mission; in addition to the NEPA, the Clean Air Act, and the Water Pollution Control Act, it is also charged with administering policies dealing with toxic wastes such as dangerous chemicals.

Dealing with Toxic Wastes

Environmental concerns have been at the forefront of political action in recent decades, but what went on before the environmental movement focused public attention on the pollution of the environment? For one, polluters created problems that are going to cost taxpayers billions to solve. The government will probably be called upon to clean up the mess that was made by companies long-since out of business. Most of these cleanup problems involve the creation and handling of toxic wastes. The EPA will be at the center of this effort for decades to come.

During the 1940s and 1950s, for example, before government oversight of toxic substances was as stringent as it is now, Hooker Chemical Company

This photo shows government officials videotaping evidence of illegally stored toxic waste. The EPA has imposed strict standards for the disposal of toxic wastes, but many toxic waste dumps were created years ago by companies no longer in business. The government is thus asked to clean up the dangerous sites, at a cost of millions of dollars each year.

Determining Standards for Clean Air

As Congress considers standards for industry to clean the air of toxic substances, there are many complicated trade-offs. In the 1970 Clean Air Act Congress ordered the Environmental Protection Agency to list all air pollutants likely to cause an increase in death or serious illness. Then the EPA was to have one year to set limits on emissions in order to protect public health. Twenty years later the EPA had set standards for only 7 toxins. The Senate Environment Committee has listed 224 toxins that it thinks should be regulated. The EPA itself has provided a list of 186. Why is it so difficult to set limits on air pollution? Why has it taken decades to list only 7 out of some 200 toxic substances in air pollution?

One reason is the scope of the problem. In 1987 the EPA estimated the amount of toxins belched out by American factories to be 2.7 billion pounds. Then they reported that their estimate may be low; the actual figure may be two to five times higher. People had not realized the scope of the emissions problem until the EPA report. Once the scope became clear, pressure for quick government action increased. Environmentalists, who had claimed that the problem was worse than the government estimated, were reinforced in their perceptions, giving them greater clout in Congress.

Another reason for delay is the complicated nature of the evidence. For example, many of the toxic emissions that come from factory smoke are known to cause cancer in high doses, but there is debate about their effects in smaller doses. How much of each toxin is required to give someone cancer is not well known. Some people argue that the EPA should enforce a *zero-emissions policy*. Such a policy would allow no emissions of those toxins that are known to cause cancer in any quantity. This might be safe, but it would be likely to close down whole segments of industry, devastating local and state economies. Thus setting the precise standards is a tricky exercise in balancing economic costs with the health of the population.

Another problem for policymakers is where to put the first priority for action. There are some emissions that come from large chemical plants, automobile factories, and the like, but there are many others that come from millions of small sources such as cars, dry cleaners, wood stoves, and gas stations. The EPA estimates that such local sources cause up to three-quarters of all the cancers in some urban areas.

If you were involved in determining standards for clean air, how would you set standards for emissions of toxins? With a zero-emissions policy, or some less-strict standard? How high should the emissions levels be for each of the toxins you would have to regulate? Would you think it best to focus government enforcement activities on cleaning up the relatively small number of large industrial polluters, or towards regulating the large number of small polluters? These are a few of the questions you would be faced with as a policymaker trying to address the diverse problems in the area of clean-air legislation.

Source: George Hager, "Clean-Air Package, Part One: Toxic Air Pollutants," *Congressional Quarterly,* April 22, 1989, 888-89. Much of this example is based on his article.

dumped toxic wastes near the shores of the Love Canal in New York. Then in 1953 the company generously donated a sixteen-acre plot next to the canal to build a school. Thereafter tons of chemicals, some in rotting barrels, were discovered, and children and adults were found later to have developed liver, kidney, and other health problems. With the company out of business and the level of contamination so great that only the government could deal with it, popular outcry led to action from Washington. The federal government has since become the major source for dealing with toxins, even those generated from private sources.

In the late 1970s Congress reacted to increased pressure to meet this expensive new need by establishing a $1.6 billion **Superfund,** created by taxing chemical products. The fund was created partly in response to the Love Canal debacle, but also because of the huge number of other toxic waste dumps which have been found. Renewed in the 1980s, the Superfund nonetheless has a long way to go. Even on those projects where Superfund monies are being spent to clean up the wastes, workers find that the damage is often so serious that they may never be cleaned satisfactorily. As experience in dealing with these dumps increases, the EPA finds that each is more difficult than it hoped to clean; and as it investigates more and more sites, it finds that there are many more dangerous sites than imagined. Cleaning up wastes left by private businesses (and by some government operations, such as the production of nuclear weapons) is going to take decades and cost billions of dollars.

Making Environmental Policy

Nobody is against cleaning up the environment. It is a political question only because environmental concerns often conflict with equally legitimate concerns about foreign trade, economic growth, and jobs. For example, on federally owned land, including national parks and forests, there has long been a policy of multiple use whereby mining and lumbering leases are awarded to private companies. Often the industries supported by these arrangements are important sources of jobs to otherwise depressed areas.

Many of these industrial activities allow America to decrease its dependence on foreign sources of oil or other minerals. Massive battles pitting lumbering interests against national and local environmental groups have raged in Alaska, where exports of lumber products to Japan provide jobs, but where the Tongass National Forest has lost large parts of its most beautiful old forests. Similarly, harvesting old-growth timber on public lands has caused great concern in Washington state. In both Washington and Alaska, environmentalists have complained that some of the few remaining large tracts of virgin forest, with trees hundreds of years old, are being felled by logging companies operating under generous lease agreements with the U.S. government, which owns the lands. Oil exploration on public lands and offshore in coastal waters also brings the goals of environmental protection and economic growth into conflict. The spill of the Exxon *Valdez* off the coast of Alaska demonstrated the environmental risks of oil exploration.

Policy-making concerning the environment essentially concerns two groups: those who pollute, and those who complain about the pollution. Those who produce pollution, of course, do so in their efforts to make cars, to produce electricity, and to make the consumer products that Americans take for granted. One of the biggest changes in policy-making for environmental issues is that recent years have seen whole new sectors of society joining interest groups to complain about pollution and to press for government action. Once, only a few conservation groups were active in attempting to conserve public lands or oppose potentially damaging projects. Pollution was mostly seen as an inevitable product of economic growth; since Americans wanted jobs, they accepted the pollution that accompanied the businesses.

The 1960s and 1970s saw an explosion of environmental interest groups. The combined memberships of the five most prominent environmental groups

In March of 1989 the Exxon Valdez ran aground off the southern coast of Alaska, spilling eleven million gallons of crude oil. Despite a two-billion dollar cleanup effort, the oil killed thousands of fish and animals and ruined miles of shoreline. No single oil spill has drawn so much public attention to the environmental dangers of America's reliance on oil as an energy source.

(the Izaak Walton League, the National Audubon Society, the National Wildlife Federation, the Sierra Club, and the Wilderness Society) grew from 439,400 in 1966 to over 6.3 million members in 1990.[22] Common Cause, the consumers' organization (which is often active in environmental issues), was founded in August 1970. Within six months it had 100,000 members; by 1990 there were 275,000.[23] Obviously, American interest groups discovered much untapped interest in the early 1970s. As old groups were transformed into active political organizations and as new groups formed and grew, the nature of environmental policy-making changed. At first many politicians viewed these new lobbyists with skepticism. Over time, however, the environmental movement has made its way into the halls of government. Now politicians of both parties seek the support of environmental groups as they enter the electoral season.[24] Issues that were once considered only from the point of view of jobs and economic growth are now much more controversial. Government policies designed to clean up the environment are sure to be controversial, expensive, and debated for a long time to come.

UNDERSTANDING TECHNOLOGY AND POLICY

Technologically complex issues such as health, energy, and the environment pose many special problems in a democracy. They are difficult to understand when discussed in the terms familiar to experts, but are so important that most Americans do not want to leave them to "experts" to decide. This section discusses how democracies handle technological issues, then considers the impact of these issues on the size of government.

Democracy and Technology

Very few Americans actually understand how a nuclear power plant operates. Neither do most know how to conduct a heart operation. Does this mean that citizens should not be allowed to participate in the public policy debate concerning complex technologies? High-tech issues, more than any others, strain the limits of public participation in a democracy. Further, the issues associated with high technology are often so complex that many different levels of government—local, state and national—become heavily involved. Whether it be the new ethical issues raised by machines and devices that can keep patients alive indefinitely—respirators, artificial kidneys, and the like—or whether it be the threats to public safety inherent in a nuclear power plant accident, governments are constantly called to make decisions involving tremendously complex technologies. Maintaining the right balance between public participation and technological competence is not an easy task.

[22]*Encyclopedia of Associations,* 24th ed., vol. 1 (Detroit: Gale Research Company, 1990), 423-25, 658; Stephen Fox, *John Muir and His Legacy: The American Conservation Movement* (Boston: Little, Brown, 1981).

[23]*Encyclopedia of Associations,* 1627, 1709; Andrew S. McFarland, *Common Cause: Lobbying in the Public Interest* (Chatham, N.J.: Chatham House, 1984).

[24]See Berke, "Oratory of Environmentalism Becomes the Sound of Politics."

In the face of complex, high-tech issues such as nuclear power, many Americans rely on interest groups to provide technological expertise and to serve as advocates for the public interest. These demonstrators, however, took to the streets themselves to protest a proposed nuclear energy plant in their community— despite the fact that they probably knew little about nuclear energy.

High-technology issues make it especially difficult to include the public in a reasoned political debate. Often groups of specialists are the only ones who seem qualified to make decisions. Still, in the United States, dramatic change has occurred. Environmental groups that once focused only on dramatic statements or loud protests now have their own staffs of scientists. Because knowledge is important in a highly complex debate, they have given themselves the resources to develop that knowledge. No longer in the United States are major public issues such as environmental pollution debated in the absence of well-informed groups looking out for the public interest.

Policy-making for technological issues seems to rely heavily on group representation. Individual citizens are unlikely to have the information or the resources to participate meaningfully, because of the complexity of the debates. Interest groups—associations of professionals and citizens—play an active role in making the complicated decisions that will affect all Americans for generations to come.

Technology Issues and the Size of Government

Americans do not hesitate to call for government to play a greater role in high-technology issues. Citizens expect all levels of the government to become more and more active in protecting the environment, and in other areas as well. The increasing average age of America's population means that health issues are going to gain in importance. Because of the government's large role in health, its activities will certainly increase. For example, over forty million Americans now depend on Social Security payments of some kind, and proposals to cut the staff of the Social Security Administration have been rejected because of the impact it might have on the ability of employees to take care of all those entitled

WILLIS ©1989
THE SAN JOSE
MERCURY NEWS
COPLEY NEWS SERVICE

I RECYCLE

II DRIVE LESS

III CONSERVE ENERGY

IV BAN CHLORO-FLUOROCARBONS

V STOP BURNING FOSSIL FUELS

VI STOP BURNING RAIN FORESTS

VII STOP KILLING OFF OTHER SPECIES

VIII STOP DUMPING TOXIC WASTE

IX CLEAN UP N-PLANTS

X BE FRUITFUL BUT STOP MULTIPLYING

to assistance. President Bush personally intervened to make sure proposed cuts would not take place.[25] Few disagreed with the president's action.

The Social Security Administration is not the only federal bureaucracy that enjoys broad public support. The **Food and Drug Administration (FDA)** faces a rapidly increasing work load. Many consumer activists, health professionals, and even drug manufacturers (who are regulated by the FDA) are calling for increased funding and staffing levels for the agency. The AIDS epidemic, cancer research, new health laws, inspections of imported foods, licensing of new drugs—all these fall within the jurisdiction of the FDA. Few Americans would like to see the agency have its staff or funding cut.[26]

Just as Americans would not like to see the FDA cut, they like to think that nuclear power plants are inspected by federal officials to ensure safety. The number of inspections of nuclear reactors conducted by the staff of the Nuclear Regulatory Commission (NRC) has grown from only two hundred in 1961 to over four thousand in 1985. As the plants grow older, citizens might want more, not fewer, people working in this federal agency. When the Exxon *Valdez* spilled millions of gallons of oil into the waters off Alaska, no one complained about the use of the Coast Guard in coordinating the cleanup. Not only are government programs designed to clean up the environment likely to continue to grow in

[25]Martin Tolchin, "Bush Bars Reduction in Social Security Staff," *New York Times,* December 15, 1989, 14.

[26]See Philip J. Hilts, "A Guardian of U.S. Health Is Failing under Pressures," *New York Times,* December 4, 1989, 1.

size (with the support of the public), but the scope of government regulations is likely to grow as well. Already businesses must comply with many regulations concerning pollution emissions, as states like California and cities like Los Angeles struggle to clean up their filthy air.[27] In the future governments will be more and more active in regulating the health industry, providing funds to the elderly for their health benefits, making sure America meets its energy needs, and ensuring environmental quality. Growth, not decline, in the size of government is expected in all these areas.

SUMMARY

Americans live in an age driven by technology. As with much in human history, technology brings its blessings and its curses. Today Americans can do much to control birth, death, and the genetics of life itself. Today scientists patent mice; tomorrow they may patent strains of human genetic material. Energy researchers now look for superconductive materials to enhance the efficiency of the present energy system. In particular, there are three areas in which technology meets public policy: health, energy, the environment.

Health care already consumes 12 percent of America's GNP, and with increased technology, its costs will almost certainly continue to rise. The government has chosen to accept patents on new life-forms and to invest in these new technologies. Scientists have the ability to manipulate the genes of life itself. These tremendous advances have improved health care, but there are also tremendous problems associated with health care in America: inadequate insurance coverage (or no coverage at all) for many people, and ever-increasing costs for even routine medical attention. Health is an area of striking contrasts in America, and of monumental policy problems.

Second, America faces important energy problems. Of the different ways to produce energy, none is perfect. Coal, the country's most abundant resource, is also the dirtiest source of energy, causing many environmental and health problems. Nuclear power, once thought of as a solution to the nation's energy needs, is at a virtual standstill because of massive public fear of the technology. Oil has been at the center of many national and international crises, from the Persian Gulf to the Exxon *Valdez*.

Finally, Americans are increasingly concerned with the environment. Environmental issues will continue to cause the government to become involved in many aspects of daily life, and often pit citizens' groups against important economic interests. The government has become very active in ensuring the quality of America's air, land, and water.

In all three of these areas, government policy is, and will continue to be, at the center of public debate. Decisions made in Washington, in state capitals, and in international negotiations will affect all Americans in terms of health care, energy use, the nature of the environment, and the quality of life in general. Further, governmental activities can be expected to grow, rather than to decrease, in each of these areas. Finally, citizen participation has profoundly influenced

---

[27]Robert Reinhold, "California Stepping Up Pressure on Auto Industry to Cut Pollution," *New York Times,* December 16, 1989, 1.

Health, energy, and environmental issues are often intertwined. This coke plant in Ohio, for example, processes coal into a fuel-efficient form, but it also has a damaging effect on the surrounding environment and the health of its neighbors. Policy-makers thus must weigh the nation's energy needs against health and environmental concerns.

governmental decisions in these areas. Voting and organizing interest group campaigns will continue to be important means of influencing government decisions in all three of these areas.

KEY TERMS

National Institutes of
   Health (NIH)
national health insurance
Medicare
Medicaid
nonrenewable resources
National Environmental
   Policy Act (NEPA)

environmental impact
   statement (EIS)
Clean Air Act of 1970
Water Pollution Control
   Act of 1972
Environmental Protec-
   tion Agency (EPA)
Superfund

Food and Drug Adminis-
   tration (FDA)

FOR FURTHER READING

Frohock, Fred M. *Special Care: Medical Decisions at the Beginning of Life.* Chicago: University of Chicago Press, 1987. An analysis of the human and policy dimensions of what to do with deformed newborns.

Heidenheimer, Arnold J., Hugh Heclo, and Carolyn Teich Adams. *Comparative Public Policy,* 3rd ed. New York: St. Martin's Press, 1990. The authors present a number of interesting comparisons of the major industrialized nations.

Kash, Don E., and Robert W. Rycroft. *U.S. Energy Policy: Crisis and Complacency.* Norman: University of Oklahoma Press, 1984. A good overview of recent energy policy in the United States.

McCormick, John. *Reclaiming Paradise: The Global Environmental Movement.* Bloomington: Indiana University Press, 1989. A discussion of the origins and the explosive growth of the environmental movement worldwide.

McFarland, Andrew S. *Common Cause: Lobbying in the Public Interest.* Chatham, N.J.: Chatham House, 1984. McFarland gives a history of the rise of the consumers' organization, with a discussion of its activities.

Nelkin, Dorothy, ed. *Controversy: The Politics of Technical Decisions.* Ithaca, N.Y.: Cornell University Press, 1979. Nelkin discusses the problems of high-tech decision making, presenting a number of interesting case studies.

Ophuls, William. *Ecology and the Politics of Scarcity.* San Francisco: Freeman, 1977. A discussion of environmentalists' worst nightmare—advocating a more authoritarian regime to handle a scarcity of clean air and water.

Schrepfer, Susan R. *The Fight to Save the Redwoods.* Madison: University of Wisconsin Press, 1983. Schrepfer gives a readable history of the environmental movement during most of the current century.

Weart, Spencer. *Nuclear Fear: A History of Images.* Cambridge, Mass.: Harvard University Press, 1988. Weart traces the popular understanding of the atom over the past century; he shows how far from reality have been both the claims and the fears of this new technology.

Winner, Langdon. *The Whale and the Reactor.* Chicago: University of Chicago Press, 1986. Winner discusses the dilemmas of living in a high-tech society.

20

FOREIGN AND DEFENSE POLICY-MAKING

Contrary to popular imagery, nuclear wars are not started by pushing a button; they are started by turning a key. Sitting underneath the North Dakota wheat fields in large egg-shaped containers are numerous pairs of young Air Force officers, the lieutenants, captains, and majors whose job it would be to launch nuclear missiles toward the Soviet Union or other targets in the event of nuclear war. Each officer sits at a separate console and carries only a revolver for protection. The console contains a computer terminal, a video display screen, collections of codes, and fail-safe procedures. Consoles are so placed that one officer cannot reach two keyboards. If the order to launch came, each pair of officers would have to insert their keys and turn them almost simultaneously.

If all went according to plan, missiles would be launched from silos in the Dakotas and other plains and southern states. New B-1B and aging B-52 bombers carrying cruise missiles and gravity bombs would take off as the missiles were launched, flying only a few hundred feet above the ground (to avoid Soviet radar detection), winging their way to Moscow and other strike sites. No doubt missiles and bombers would be flying from the other direction as well. Showers of nuclear bombs would rain on the earth. Cities would disintegrate; radiation would eventually kill millions who survived the blasts; forests would be in flames. According to American war plans, Moscow would be hit with 60 nuclear warheads, Leningrad with more than 40, and the forty next largest Soviet cities with an average of 14.4 warheads each. Eighty percent of all Soviet cities with a population greater than twenty-five thousand would be hit. Each would be in flames. Presumably, American cities would suffer similar fates.

A military aide with the "football," a suitcase containing the codes necessary to order a nuclear attack, is never far from the president—even in Moscow's Red Square, which President Reagan toured in 1988.

A full-scale nuclear war is not a likely scenario. The possibility of self-destruction on a global scale, however, underlies the importance of America's foreign policy and the high priority the nation's leaders give to national security.

Source: Thomas Powers, "Nuclear Winter and Nuclear Strategy," *Atlantic Monthly,* November 1984, 63.

*E*very American community and citizen is connected with communities and citizens across the globe. The threat of nuclear war is not the only global connection. Today an interdependent economy connects all nations; there is a massive movement of goods, services, information, ideas, and people across national boundaries. However unsettled and difficult American domestic issues appear, they seem tame in comparison with global ones: terrorism, cocaine trafficking, trade imbalances, nuclear proliferation, poverty, arms races, and revolutions, to name just a few. Handled well, these problems become crises avoided; handled badly, they could escalate into war.

War and peace are serious business. Policymakers devote much energy to pursuing peace and planning for war, and such plans and pursuits have become ever more important in today's interdependent world. Military policy is the making and implementing of policies devoted to planning, preparing for, and fighting wars. It is one part of foreign policy, which involves protecting and promoting American interests abroad.

AMERICAN FOREIGN POLICY: METHODS AND ACTORS

Foreign policy is like domestic policy—it involves making choices—but the choices involved are about relations with the rest of the world. Because the president is the main force behind foreign policy, every morning the White House receives a highly confidential intelligence briefing that might cover Soviet naval movements, last night's events in some trouble spot on the globe, or Fidel Castro's health. The briefing is part of the massive informational arsenal the president uses to manage American foreign policy. In making decisions about these issues, President Bush faces a task that has some similarities to domestic policy-making. In both foreign and domestic affairs, policymakers select goals, adopt policies to achieve them, and then try to implement those policies. Moreover, like domestic policy, foreign policy is most often a political result rather than a clearly logical design for carrying out a set of national objectives. Americans may, for example, desire economic prosperity, peace, individual liberties, low taxes, favorable foreign trade, full employment, social welfare, effective deterrence, regional stability, and global prestige and influence—all worthy and important national goals, yet all influenced in different ways by particular foreign and national security policies. Various groups, parties, experts, and political leaders will disagree with great intensity as to which of these national goals should have priority. They will also disagree about the effects of any policy alternative on any of the goals.

The instruments of foreign policy are, however, different from those of domestic policy. Foreign policies depend ultimately on three types of tools: *military, economic, and diplomatic.* Among the oldest instruments of foreign policy are war and the threat of war. German General Karl von Clausewitz once called war a "continuation of politics by other means." Today, *economic* instruments are becoming weapons almost as potent as those of war. The control of oil can be as important as the control of guns. Trade regulations, tariff policies, and monetary policies are other economic instruments of foreign policy. A number of recent studies have called attention to the importance of a country's economic vitality to its long-term national security.[1] *Diplomacy* is the quietest instrument. It often evokes images of ambassadors at chic cocktail parties, but the diplomatic game is played for high stakes. Sometimes national leaders meet in summit talks. More often, less prominent negotiators work out treaties handling all kinds of national contracts, from economic relations to the dispensation of stranded tourists.

[1]See, for example, Paul Kennedy, *The Rise and Fall of the Great Powers* (New York: Random House, 1987).

Actors on the World Stage

If all the world's a stage, there are more actors on it than ever. More than one hundred nations have emerged since 1945. Once foreign relations were almost exclusively transactions between nations, using military, economic, or diplomatic methods to achieve foreign policy goals. Today's world stage is more crowded.

International organizations act as both players and stages for international conflict. Best known of these is the **United Nations (UN).** Now housed in a magnificent skyscraper in New York City, it was created in 1945. Its members agree to renounce war and respect certain human and economic freedoms. The UN General Assembly is composed of all member nations, today numbering 159. Each nation has one vote, except for the Soviet Union, which effectively has three (the Byelorussian and Ukranian soviet socialist republics are counted as separate members). Although not legally binding, General Assembly resolutions can achieve a measure of collective legitimization when a broad international consensus is formed on some matter concerning relations among states. The Security Council, though, is the seat of real power in the UN. Five of its eleven members (the United States, Great Britain, China, France, and the Soviet Union) are permanent members; the others are chosen from session to session by the General Assembly. Each permanent member has a veto over Security Council decisions, including any decisions that would commit the UN to a military peacekeeping operation. The Secretariat directs the administration of UN programs; its head, the secretary general, usually comes from a neutral or nonaligned nation. In addition to its peacekeeping function the UN runs a number of programs focused on economic development and health, education, and welfare concerns. The UN has drawn heavy criticism in recent years among American conservatives, who complain that the General Assembly has become a forum for "America bashing" by Communist and third world states. Nonetheless, the United States continues to be the UN's largest benefactor.

The UN is only one of many international organizations. The International Monetary Fund, for example, helps regulate the chaotic world of international finance; the World Bank finances development projects in new nations; and the International Postal Union helps get the mail from one country to another.

Regional organizations have proliferated in the post–World War II era. These are organizations of several nations bound by a treaty, often for military reasons. **The North Atlantic Treaty Organization (NATO)** was created in 1949. Its members—the United States, Canada, most Western European nations, and Turkey—agreed to combine military forces and to treat a war against one as a war against all. Today more than one million NATO troops (including about 325,000 Americans) are spread from West Germany to Portugal. They face more than one million troops from the **Warsaw Pact,** the regional security community of the Soviet Union and its Eastern European allies (see Figure 20.1). The figures for both alliances are changing dramatically as the cold war thaws.

Regional organizations can be economic rather than military. The **European Economic Community (EEC),** often called the Common Market, is an economic alliance of the major Western European nations. The EEC coordinates monetary, trade, immigration, and labor policies so that its members have become one economic unit, just as the fifty United States are an economic unit. Other economic federations exist in Latin America and Africa, but none are as unified as the EEC.

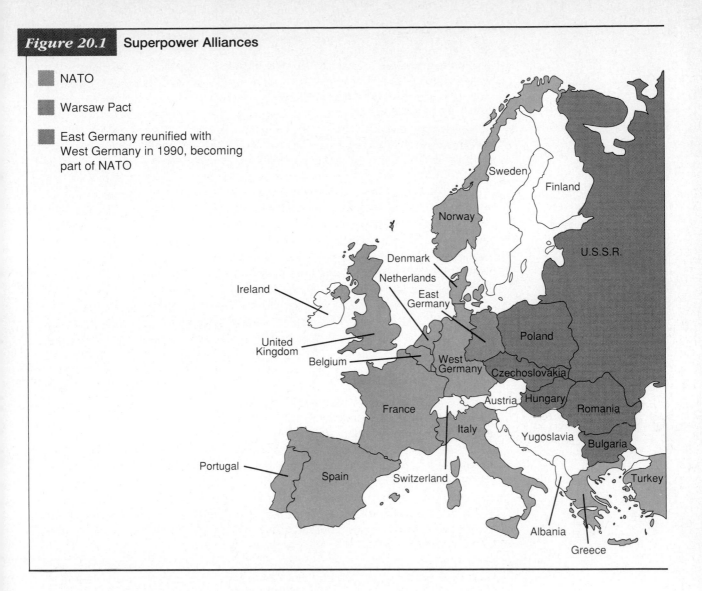

Figure 20.1 Superpower Alliances

- NATO
- Warsaw Pact
- East Germany reunified with West Germany in 1990, becoming part of NATO

Chapter 17 discussed the newest entrants on the world stage, the potent *multinational corporations,* or MNCs. Today one-third of the world's industrial output comes from these corporations.[2] Sometimes more powerful (and often much wealthier) than the government under which they operate, MNCs have voiced strong opinions about governments, taxes, and business regulations. They have even linked forces with agencies like the CIA to overturn governments they disliked. In the 1970s, for example, several of these corporations worked with the CIA to "destabilize" the Marxist government in Chile; Chile's military overthrew the government in 1973. Even when they are not so heavy-handed, MNCs are forces to be reckoned with in almost all nations.

[2] Raymond Vernon, *Storm over the Multinationals: The Real Issues* (Cambridge, Mass.: Harvard University Press, 1977), 15.

Groups are also actors on the global stage. Churches and labor unions have long had international interests and activities. Today, environmental and wildlife groups such as Greenpeace have also proliferated. Ecological interests are active in international as well as national politics. Groups interested in protecting human rights, such as Amnesty International, have also grown. Not all groups, however, are committed to saving whales or oceans. Some are committed to the overthrow of particular governments and operate as terrorists around the world. Airplane hijacking, assassinations, bombings, and similar terrorist attacks have made the world a more unsettled place. Conflicts within a nation or region thus spill over into world politics.

Finally, *individuals* are international actors. The recent explosion of tourism sends Americans everywhere and brings floods of Japanese, European, and third world tourists to America. Tourism creates its own costs and benefits and thus always affects the international economic system. Although tourism may enhance friendship and understanding among nations, if more of *us* go to see *them* than the other way around, it can also worsen problems with a country's balance of payments. In addition to tourists are the growing numbers of students going to and coming from other nations; they are carriers of ideas and ideologies.

Just as there are more actors on the global stage than in the past, there are also more American decision makers involved in foreign policy problems.

The Policymakers

The president, as you saw in Chapter 13, is the main force behind foreign policy. As chief diplomat, the president makes treaties; as commander in chief of our armed forces, the president deploys American troops abroad.

Presidents do not act alone in foreign policy; they are aided (and sometimes thwarted) by a huge national security bureaucracy. They must also contend with the views and desires of Congress, which also wields considerable clout in the foreign policy arena, sometimes doing so in opposition to a president. The following sections look at the diplomatic and defense sides of the vast foreign policy and national security bureaucracy and at the role of Congress in foreign and defense policy.

The Diplomats   The Department of State is the foreign policy arm of the U.S. government. Its chief, the **secretary of state** (Thomas Jefferson was the first), has traditionally been the key advisor to the president on foreign policy matters. The State Department now staffs more than 250 overseas posts and employs 24,000 people, of whom 8,000 are foreign service officers. The department itself is organized into area specialties—a section on Middle Eastern affairs, one on European affairs, and so on, with each country handled by a "country desk." American ambassadors represent the nation in 132 embassies and 9 international organizations. Once mostly a dignified and genteel profession, diplomacy is increasingly a dangerous job. The November 1979 seizure of the American embassy in Tehran is an extreme example of the hostilities that diplomats can face.

Many recent presidents have found the State Department overbureaucratized and intransigent. Even its colloquial name, "Foggy Bottom," taken from the part of Washington where it is located, conjures up a less than cooperative image. Many recent presidents have bypassed institutional arrangements for

The secretary of state is the nation's chief foreign policy advisor, presiding over a global bureaucracy of diplomats. Henry Kissinger (right) was the most active and charismatic secretary of state in recent years, smoothing relations with China and negotiating settlements between Israel and its Middle Eastern neighbors.

foreign policy decision making and have instead established more personal systems for receiving policy advice. Presidents Nixon and Carter, for example, relied more heavily on their special assistants for national security affairs (Henry Kissinger and Zbigniew Brzezinski, respectively) than on their secretaries of state. Foreign policy was thus centered in the White House and was often disconnected from what was occurring in the State Department. Critics, though, charged that this situation led to split-level government and chronic discontinuity in foreign policy.[3] President Reagan, by contrast, relied less on his assistants for national security affairs (six different men filled the job in eight years), while Secretary of State George Schultz was a powerful player. George Bush continued this pattern, appointing his closest friend, James Baker, as secretary of state.

The National Security Establishment   These days foreign policy and military policy are closely linked. Thus the Department of Defense is a key foreign policy actor. Often called the Pentagon after the five-sided building in which it is located, the Defense Department was created after World War II. The Army, Navy, and Air Force were collected into one giant department, although they have never been thoroughly integrated and continue to plan and operate largely independent of one another. Recent reforms, made law under the Goldwater-Nichols Defense Reorganization Act of 1986, were designed to increase interservice cooperation and centralization of the military hierarchy. The **secretary of defense** manages a budget larger than that of most nations and is the president's main military advisor.

[3]I.M. Destler, "National Security Management: What Presidents Have Wrought,"*Political Science Quarterly* 95 (Winter 1980–81): 573–88.

The State Department, the Defense Department, and the CIA work together—not always smoothly—with the president and Congress to form national security policy. Here President Lyndon Johnson meets with (from left) Secretary of State Dean Rusk, Secretary of Defense Robert McNamara, and CIA Director John McCone.

The commanding officers of each of the services, plus a chair, constitute the **Joint Chiefs of Staff.** American military leaders are sometimes portrayed as gung-ho hawks in policy-making, presumably eager to crush some small nation with a show of American force. Richard Betts carefully examined the advice given to the president by the joint chiefs in many crises, and found the joint chiefs no more likely than civilian advisors to push an aggressive military policy. (The most hawkish advice, incidentally, came from the admirals. The most dovish advice came from the Army generals and the Marine Corps.[4]) During the Reagan administration, on several occasions the president's uniformed advisors cautioned against aggressive actions, including the use of military force, favored by the State Department. Steeped in the mythology of generals like George Patton and Curtis Lemay, many Americans would be surprised at the cautious attitudes of America's top military leaders.

American foreign policy and military policy are supposed to be coordinated. To do this, an organization called the National Security Council (NSC) was formed in 1947. The NSC is composed of the president, the vice-president, the secretary of defense, and the secretary of state; the NSC staff is managed by the president's national security advisor. This position first gained public prominence when it was occupied by the flamboyant, globe-trotting Henry Kissinger during President Nixon's first term.

Despite the coordinating role assigned to the NSC, conflict within the foreign policy establishment remains common. The NSC staff has sometimes competed with, rather than integrated, policy advice from cabinet departments, particularly State and Defense. It has also become involved in covert operations. A scandal erupted in November 1986 when it became known that the NSC staff was involved

[4]Richard Betts, *Soldiers, Statesmen, and Cold War Crises* (Cambridge, Mass.: Harvard University Press, 1977), 216, table A.

in a secret operation to sell antitank missiles to Iran in return for Iranian help in gaining the release of hostages held by Iranian-backed terrorists in Lebanon. Some of the money from the sale was funneled secretly to anti-Communist rebels (called contras) fighting the Nicaraguan government, despite a congressional ban on such aid. The scandal resulted in the resignation of the president's assistant for national security affairs, Vice Admiral John Poindexter, and the sacking of a number of lower-level NSC officials, including Lieutenant Colonel Oliver North. North went from obscurity to national prominence virtually overnight as he described his involvement in the affair before a televised congressional inquiry in 1987. Both Poindexter and North were subsequently convicted of felony charges related to the diversion of funds and misleading Congress.

No discussion of the institutional structures of foreign policy would be complete without mentioning the **Central Intelligence Agency (CIA).** Although it was created after World War II to coordinate American intelligence activities abroad, the CIA quickly became involved in intrigue, conspiracy, and meddling, as well as intelligence gathering. Technically, its budget and staff are secret; estimates put them at several billion dollars and twenty thousand people. The CIA plays a vital role in providing information and analyses necessary for effective development and implementation of national security policy.

The CIA has a long history of involvement in other nations' internal affairs. After the end of World War II, when Eastern European nations had fallen under Moscow's shadow and Western European nations were teetering, the CIA provided aid to anti-Communist parties in Italy and West Germany. It was no less busy in the third world, where, for example, it nurtured coups in Iran in 1953 and in Guatemala in 1954. The CIA has also trained and supported armies— the most notable, of course, in Vietnam. It has subsidized Communist defectors, often in an extravagant style. The most recent worries about CIA activity have been in Central America, where a group called the Sandinistas overthrew Nicaraguan dictator Anastasio Somoza in 1979. The new Marxist regime developed close ties with the Soviet Union and Cuba and embarked on a massive military buildup. Determined to undermine the regime, the Reagan administration aggressively supported assistance to anti-Sandinista rebels. Congressional inquiries suggested that the CIA, under Director William Casey, was quietly involved in covert operations to assist the contra rebels. Director Casey died in 1987, while his agency and the NSC staff were under intense congressional and public scrutiny for involvement in the Iran-Contra affair.

The years after World War II saw a steady growth of all these military and foreign policy institutions. As the American role on the world stage grew, so did the importance of these institutions as foreign policy instruments.

Congress   The U.S. Congress shares with the president constitutional authority over foreign and defense policy. Congress has sole authority, for example, to declare war, to raise and organize the armed forces, and to appropriate funds for national security activities. The Senate determines whether treaties will be ratified and ambassadorial and cabinet nominations confirmed. The "power of the purse" gives Congress considerable clout, and each year senators and representatives examine defense budget authorizations carefully.[5]

[5]A good short study of the role of Congress in the defense budget process is James Lindsay, "Congress and Defense Policy: 1961–1986," *Armed Forces and Society* 13 (Spring 1987): 371–401.

Congress' important constitutional role in foreign and defense policy is sometimes misunderstood. It is a common mistake among some journalists, executive officials, and even some members of Congress to believe that the Constitution vests foreign policy solely in the president. Sometimes this erroneous view leads to perverse results, as in the Iran-Contra affair that dominated the news in late 1986 and much of 1987. Officials at high levels in the executive branch "sought to protect the president's 'exclusive' prerogative by lying to Congress, to allies, to the public, and to one another." Louis Fisher suggests that such actions undermined the "mutual trust and close coordination by the [two branches that] are essential attributes in building a foreign policy that ensures continuity and stability."[6]

BEYOND THE COLD WAR? AMERICAN FOREIGN POLICY AFTER WORLD WAR II

Throughout most of its history, the United States followed a foreign policy course called **isolationism;** it tried to stay out of other nations' conflicts, particularly European wars. The famous Monroe Doctrine, enunciated by President James Monroe, reaffirmed America's inattention to Europe's problems and warned European nations to stay out of Latin America. The United States saw Central and South America as its own political backyard and did not hesitate to send Marines, gunboats, or both to intervene in South American and Caribbean affairs. When European nations were at war, however, Americans relished their distance from the conflicts. So it was until World War I (1914–18).

In the wake of World War I, President Woodrow Wilson urged the United States to join the League of Nations. The U.S. Senate refused to ratify the League of Nations treaty, signaling that the country was not ready to abandon the longstanding American habit of isolationism. It was Pearl Harbor that dealt a deathblow to American isolationism. At a conference in San Francisco in 1945, a charter for the United Nations was signed. The United States was an original signatory and soon donated land to house the United Nations permanently in New York City.

The Cold War

At the end of World War II Germany and Japan were vanquished and much of Europe was strewn with rubble. The United States was unquestionably the dominant world power, both economically and militarily. It had not only helped to bring the war to an end but also inaugurated a new era in warfare by dropping the first atomic bombs on Japan in August 1945. Since only the United States possessed nuclear weapons, Americans looked forward to an era of peace secured by their nuclear umbrella.

After World War II the United States forged strong alliances with the nations of Western Europe. To help them rebuild their economies, it poured billions of dollars into war-ravaged European nations through the aid package known as the Marshall Plan, named after its architect, Secretary of State George C.

---

[6]Louis Fisher, "Executive-Legislative Relations in Foreign Policy" (Paper presented at the United States–Mexico Comparative Constitutional Law Conference, Mexico City, June 17, 1988), 1.

Marshall. A military alliance was also forged; the creation of NATO in 1949 affirmed the mutual military interests of the United States and Western Europe and remains a cornerstone of American foreign and defense policy today.

Containment and Korea   Although many Americans also expected cooperative relations with their wartime ally, the Soviet Union, they soon abandoned their hopes. There is still much dispute about how the cold war between the United States and the Soviet Union started.[7] Even before World War II ended, some American policymakers feared that their Soviet allies were intent on spreading communism not only to their neighbors but everywhere. All of Eastern Europe fell under Russian domination as World War II ended. Soviet support of a revolt in Greece in 1946 added to fears of Soviet aggression. In 1946 Winston Churchill warned that the Russians had sealed off Eastern Europe with an "iron curtain." Writing in *Foreign Affairs* in 1947, foreign policy strategist George F. Kennan proposed a policy of "containment."[8] His **containment doctrine** called for the United States to isolate the Soviet Union, "contain" its advances, and resist its encroachments—by peaceful means if possible, but with force if necessary. The Soviet Union had its own response—the Berlin Blockade of 1948–49.

The fall of China to Mao Zedong's Communist-led forces in 1949 seemed to confirm American fears that communism was a cancer spreading over the

[7]An excellent treatment of the origins of the cold war is Daniel Yergin, *Shattered Peace: The Origins of the Cold War and the National Security State* (Boston: Houghton Mifflin, 1977).

[8]The article was titled "Sources of Soviet Conduct" and appeared in *Foreign Affairs* (July 1947), under the pseudonym *X*.

"free world." In the same year the Soviet Union exploded its first atomic bomb. The invasion of pro-American South Korea by Communist North Korea in 1950 fueled American fears further. Believing the Korean invasion was linked with Soviet imperialism, President Truman said bluntly, "We've got to stop the Russians now," and sent American troops to Korea under United Nations auspices. The Korean War was a chance to put containment into practice. It dragged on until July 23, 1953, involving China as well as North Korea.

The 1950s were the decade of the **cold war;** never quite erupting into armed battle, the United States and the Soviet Union were often on the brink of war. John Foster Dulles, secretary of state under Eisenhower, even proclaimed a policy of "brinksmanship," in which the United States was to be prepared to use nuclear weapons in order to influence the actions of the Soviet Union and Communist China. Fear of communism affected domestic as well as foreign policy. **McCarthyism** assumed that international communism was conspiratorial, insidious, bent on world domination, and infiltrating American government and cultural institutions. Named after Senator Joseph McCarthy, who with flimsy evidence accused scores of prominent Americans of being Communists, McCarthyism flowered during the Korean War. Domestic policy in general was deeply affected by the cold war and by anti-Communist fears. A burgeoning defense budget during the Korean War and later in the 1950s was another result.

The Swelling of the Pentagon   The cold war ensured that military needs and massive national security expenditures would remain fixtures in the American economy. As early as 1947 aircraft manufacturers were noting that the decline of military procurement after World War II would injure the industry; to avert dislocation, they launched a campaign to sell planes to the Air Force.[9] Thus were forged some of the first links between policymakers' perceptions of the Soviet threat and corporations' awareness of profits to be made from military hardware. Generals and admirals felt that they needed weapons systems, and private industry was happy to supply them for a profit. Defense expenditures grew to be the largest component of the federal buget in the 1950s, consuming thirteen dollars of every one hundred dollars of the GNP by 1954. Large parts of this defense budget were spent on weapons supplied by giant companies like Westinghouse, RCA, Western Electric, and General Motors.

The interests shared by the armed services and defense contractors produced what some call a *military-industrial complex.* The phrase was coined not by a left-wing critic of the military but by President Dwight D. Eisenhower, himself a former general. Elite theorists especially pointed to this tight alliance between business and government. Economist Seymour Melman wrote about *pentagon capitalism,* linking the military's drive to expand with the profit motives of private industry.[10] As the defense budget grew, so did the profits of aircraft producers and other defense contractors.

In the 1950s an **arms race** between the Soviet Union and the United States commenced. One side's weaponry goaded the other side to procure yet more weaponry, with one missile leading to another, and so on. Later sections of this chapter will examine efforts to control this arms race.

---

[9]Yergin, *Shattered Peace,* 268.

[10]Seymour Melman, *Pentagon Capitalism: The Political Economy of War* (New York: McGraw-Hill, 1970).

The Vietnam War   Even though it reached its peak during the 1960s, American involvement in Vietnam did not begin then. The Korean War and the 1949 victory of Mao Zedong's Communist forces in China fixed the government's attention on Asian communism. In 1950, while the Korean War raged and just after the fall of Chiang Kai-shek in China, President Truman decided to aid the French effort to retain France's colonial possessions in Southeast Asia.[11]

During the early 1950s the Viet Minh—the Vietnamese Communist forces— began to receive military aid from the new Communist government in China. In 1954 the French were defeated by the Viet Minh, led by Ho Chi Minh, in a battle at Dien Bien Phu. U.S. Defense Department officials seriously considered using atomic weapons to aid the French cause at Dien Bien Phu but decided against it. On May 7, 1954, the Viet Minh raised their flag at Dien Bien Phu. The next morning, peace talks among the participants and other major powers began in Geneva, Switzerland.

Though a party to the resultant agreements, the United States never accepted the Geneva agreement to hold national elections in Vietnam in 1956. Instead, it began supporting one non-Communist leader after another in South Vietnam, each seemingly more committed than the last to defeating Ho Chi Minh's forces in the north.

Vietnam first became an election-year issue in 1964. President Lyndon B. Johnson, who had succeeded John F. Kennedy when the latter was assassinated, was seeking his first full term. His Republican opponent, Arizona Senator Barry Goldwater, was a foreign policy hard-liner. Since Truman's time, the United States had sent military "advisors" to South Vietnam, which was in the midst of

[11]Stanley Karnow, *Vietnam: A History* (New York: Penguin Books, 1983), 43. Karnow's book is one of the best of many excellent books on Vietnam. See also Frances FitzGerald, *Fire in the Lake* (Boston: Little, Brown, 1972), and David Halberstam, *The Best and the Brightest* (New York: Random House, 1972).

The Vietnam War Memorial is one of Washington, D.C.'s most moving sights. Often called "The Wall," the memorial lists the names of more than fifty-eight thousand Americans killed during the Vietnam War.

a civil war spurred by the Viet Cong (also known as the National Liberation Front), who sought reunification of South Vietnam with Communist North Vietnam. During the 1964 campaign, Johnson promised that he would not "send American boys to do an Asian boy's job" of defending the pro-American regime in South Vietnam. Goldwater advocated tough action in Vietnam; he would send American troops if necessary and even defoliate the jungles with chemicals so that the Viet Cong guerrillas would have no place to hide.

There was a standing joke after Johnson's victory in 1964: "They told me that if I voted for Goldwater, we'd have half a million American troops in Vietnam in four years. I did, and we do." Unable to contain the forces of the Viet Cong and North Vietnam with American advisors, Johnson sent in American troops— more than five hundred thousand at the peak of the undeclared war. He dropped more bombs on Communist North Vietnam than the United States had dropped on Germany in all of World War II. American troops and massive firepower failed to contain the North Vietnamese, however. At home, widespread protests against the war contributed to Johnson's decisions not to run for reelection in 1968 and to begin peace negotiations.

The new Nixon administration prosecuted the war vigorously, in Cambodia as well as in Vietnam, but also worked to negotiate a peace treaty with the Viet Cong and North Vietnam. At last a peace treaty was signed in 1973, but no one really expected it to hold. South Vietnam's capital, Saigon, finally fell to the North Vietnamese Army in 1975. South and North Vietnam were reunited into a single nation, and Saigon was renamed Ho Chi Minh City, in honor of the late leader of Communist North Vietnam.

Looking back on the Vietnam War, few Americans think it was worthwhile. It divided the nation and made citizens painfully aware of the ability of the government to lie to them—and perhaps worse, to itself. It reminded Americans that even a "great power" nation cannot prevail in a protracted military conflict against a determined enemy unless there is a clear objective and unless the national will is sufficiently committed to expend vast resources on the task.

The Era of Détente

Even while the Vietnam War was being waged, Richard Nixon—an old fighter of the cold war—supported a new policy that came to be called détente. The term was popularized by Nixon's national security advisor, later secretary of state, Henry Kissinger.

Détente represented a slow transformation from conflict thinking to co-operative thinking in foreign policy strategy. It sought a relaxation of tensions between the superpowers, coupled with firm guarantees of mutual security. The policy assumed that the United States and the Soviet Union had no long-range and irrevocable sources of conflict; that both had an interest in peace and world stability; and that a nuclear war was—and should be—unthinkable. Thus foreign policy battles between the United States and the USSR were to be waged with diplomatic, economic, and propaganda weapons; the threat of force was downplayed.

One major initiative coming out of détente was the **Strategic Arms Limitation Talks (SALT).** These talks represented an effort by the United States and the Soviet Union to agree to scale down their nuclear capabilities, with each maintaining sufficient power to deter a surprise attack by the other. The first

SALT treaty was signed by Nixon in 1972 and was followed by negotiations for a second SALT treaty. SALT II, after six years of laborious negotiations, was finally signed and sent to the Senate by President Carter in 1979. The U.S. Senate never approved the SALT II treaty, however, even though both Jimmy Carter and Ronald Reagan insisted that they would be committed to its arms limitations: no more than 2,250 strategic nuclear missile launchers and other nuclear weaponry restrictions on both sides.

The philosophy of détente was applied to the People's Republic of China as well as to the Soviet Union. After the fall of pro-American Chiang Kai-shek in 1949, the United States had refused to extend diplomatic recognition to the world's most populous nation, recognizing instead Chiang's government-in-exile on the nearby island of Taiwan. As a senator in the early 1950s, Richard Nixon had been an implacable foe of "Red China," even suggesting that the Democratic administration had traitorously "lost" China. Nevertheless, it was the same Richard Nixon who, as president two decades later, first visited the People's Republic and sent an American mission there. President Jimmy Carter extended formal diplomatic recognition in November 1978. Since then cultural and economic ties between the United States and China have increased greatly. Hardly an American state fails to claim a "sister province" relationship with one of China's provinces.

Not everyone favored détente. Few saw more threats from the "Evil Empire," as he called the Soviet Union, than Ronald Reagan. He viewed the Soviet invasion of Afghanistan in 1979 as typical Russian aggression, which, if unchecked, could only grow more common. He hailed "anti-Communist" governments everywhere and pledged to increase American defense spending.

President Richard Nixon, a staunch anti-Communist, opened the way to normal diplomatic relations between the United States and the People's Republic of China by visiting Peking in 1972. This photo shows Nixon reviewing troops with Chinese Prime Minister Chou En-lai.

Reversing the Trend: The Reagan Rearmament

From the middle 1950s to 1981 the defense budget had been declining as a percentage of both the total federal budget and the gross national product. In 1955, during the Eisenhower administration, the government was spending 61 percent of its budget for defense purposes, or about 10 percent of the GNP (the total value of all the goods and services produced in the United States that year). By the time President Reagan took office in 1981 less than 25 percent of the federal budget and 5.2 percent of the GNP were devoted to defense expenditures. This was a substantial cut indeed, though it came about more because levels of social spending had increased than because military spending had declined. Republican Richard Nixon used to boast that he was the first president in recent history who committed more of the national budget to social services than to military expenditures.

During his campaign for the presidency Reagan had argued that "we cannot negotiate arms control agreements that will slow down the Soviet military buildup as long as we let the Soviets move ahead of us in every category of armaments." By 1980 the Soviet Union was spending nearly $175 billion for defense; the United States, about $125 billion. America faced, said Reagan, a "window of vulnerability" because the Soviet Union was galloping ahead of the United States in military spending.

As president, Reagan was determined to reverse this historic diminishing of defense spending and proposed the largest peacetime defense spending increase in American history—a five-year defense buildup to cost $1.5 trillion.

The early days of the Reagan administration were the most critical in this defense spending buildup. The news came down to the Pentagon rank-and-file quickly: President Carter's last budget had proposed a large increase in defense spending, and the Reagan administration would add $32 billion on top of that. Defense officials were ordered to find places to spend more money.[12] These heady days for the Pentagon lasted only through the first term of Reagan's presidency, however. In the second term, concern over huge budget deficits brought defense spending to a standstill. After taking inflation into account, Congress appropriated no increase in defense spending at all from 1985 to 1988.

The Final Thaw in the Cold War?

On May 12, 1989, in a commencement address at Texas A&M University, President Bush announced a new era in American foreign policy. He termed it one "beyond containment." The United State's goal would be more than the negative one of containing Soviet expansionism. Bush declared that it was time to seek the integration of the Soviet Union into the community of nations.

The cold war ended as few had anticipated—spontaneously. Suddenly the elusive object of forty years of post–World War II U.S. foreign policy—freedom and self-determination for Eastern Europeans and Soviet peoples and the re- duction of the military threat from the East—appeared within reach. Forces of change sparked by Soviet leader Mikhail Gorbachev led to a staggering wave of

[12]Nicholas Lemann, "The Peacetime War," *Atlantic Monthly,* October 1984, 72.

"Miss Clark, find Joe Stalin and tell him Communism is dead."

upheaval that shattered Communist regimes and the postwar barriers between Eastern and Western Europe. The Berlin Wall, the most prominent symbol of oppression in Eastern Europe, came tumbling down, and East Germany's Communist party lay in shambles as East and West Germany moved toward a unified, democratic republic. Non-Communist governments formed in Poland, Czechoslovakia, and Hungary, and reformers overthrew the old-line Communist leaders in Bulgaria and Romania.

Events were happening so fast and in so many places at once that no one was quite sure how to deal with them. President Bush declared, "Every morning I receive an intelligence briefing, and I receive the best information available to any world leader today. And yet, the morning news is often overtaken by the news that very same evening."[13]

For all its risks and uncertainties, the cold war was characterized by a stable and predictable set of relations among the great powers. Now international relations have entered an era of improvisation as nations struggle to come up with creative responses to change in the global balance of power. The American national security establishment evidently feels that caution and prudence dictate that change on the Western side of the battered iron curtain be slower than on the other side.

Overall, there is an implicit agreement that the Soviet Union not use force to stop the forces of change in Eastern Europe. In return, the United States agrees not to seek changes in boundaries or military alliances. In other words, Eastern Europe can go about its reforms without active intervention from the two superpowers.

In 1989 reform seemed on the verge of occurring in China as well as in Eastern Europe. That spring in Tiananmen Square, the central meeting place in Beijing, thousands of students held protests on behalf of democratization. Finally, the aging Chinese leaders could tolerate challenges to their rule no longer, and forcibly—many would say brutally—evacuated the square, crushing some protestors under armored tanks. It is still not clear how many students were killed and how many others arrested, but the reform movement received a serious setback. This suppression of efforts to develop democracy returned a chill to what had been a warming relationship between the United States and the People's Republic of China (see "A Question of Ethics: In Defense of Human Rights").

Almost everyone agrees that today's more cooperative, albeit more complicated, international environment portends an overhaul of the American national security infrastructure. Armed forces and alliances, defense industries, and budgets that have been built up since World War II will all be reassessed in light of the recent cold war thaw.

THE DEFENSE OF THE REALM: THE POLITICS OF DEFENSE POLICY

The politics of national defense are played for high stakes—the nation's security. Domestic political concerns, budgetary limitations, and ideology all have a role in influencing decisions regarding the structure of defense policy and negotiations with allies and adversaries.

---

[13]Quoted in Andrew Rosenthal, "Striking a Defensive Tone, Bush Sees Virtue in Caution," *New York Times,* February 8, 1990, A10.

In Defense of Human Rights

Americans sat riveted to their television screens for several weeks in May and June of 1989 as they watched Chinese students and workers in Beijing's Tiananmen Square protest on behalf of greater democracy. This was heady stuff for the world's most populous country, apparently emerging from two generations of totalitarian rule.

For a time it looked as if China's rulers would accommodate demands for reform. On the night of June 3, however, the army violently crushed the democracy movement, killing hundreds—perhaps thousands—of protestors and beginning a wave of executions, arrests, and repression.

Westerners were shocked at the bloodshed and widely condemned the Chinese government. Regardless, in July and December 1989 President Bush sent his national security advisor, Brent Scowcroft, and Deputy Secretary of State Lawrence Eagleburger to meet secretly with Chinese leaders. Bush also lifted economic sanctions against China. The president claimed he was not normalizing relations with China, but many political leaders criticized him for moral capitulation to the hard-line Communist leaders.

The president asked, "How else should nuclear powers deal with each other?" and pointed out that the United States maintains relations with many countries that have even more egregious records of human rights violations than China's. In addition, Bush argued that keeping the lines of communication open would increase his ability to encourage the Chinese leaders to moderate their repression.

His critics responded, "How can you deal with immoral leaders who slaughter their own people for nonviolently advocating rights that Americans cherish? Is there no place for morality in international relations?"

If you were President Bush, what would *you* do?

The Structure of National Defense

All public policies include budgets, people, and equipment. In the realm of national defense these elements are especially critical because of the size of the budget and the bureaucracy as well as the destructive potential of modern weapons.

Defense Spending   You saw in Chapter 14 that defense spending composes about one-fourth of the federal budget. Critics of defense spending see excessive investment in weapons as bordering on scandalous. Vast sums of money are involved (see Figure 20.2). Two ships launched by the Navy in 1982 cost a total of $1.63 billion. *Each* Stealth bomber costs over $500 million. Both East and West have become committed to high-tech warfare. Each weapons system becomes more complex and, of course, more expensive.

Cutbacks in the Soviet presence in Eastern Europe and the democratic reforms sweeping the Warsaw Pact nations provide momentum for significant reductions in defense spending, what some call the *peace dividend.* Some scholars have argued that America faces a trade-off between defense spending and social spending. A nation, they claim, must choose between guns and butter, and more guns mean less butter. Evidence for the existence of such a trade-off is mixed, however. In general, defense and domestic policy expenditures appear

Figure 20.2 **Defense Spending**

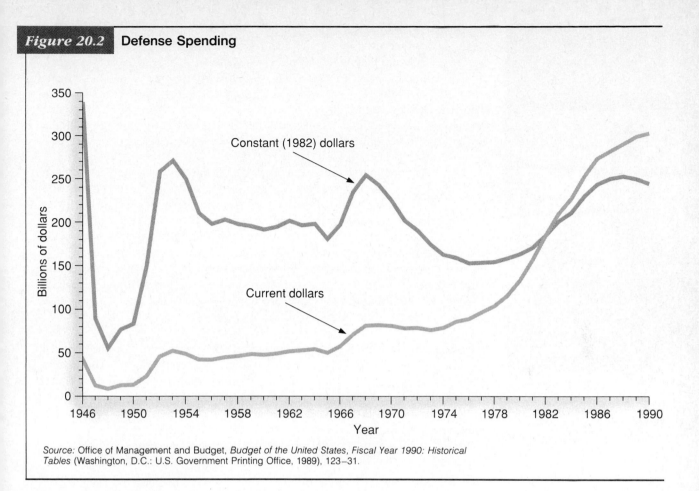

Figure 20.2 Defense Spending

Source: Office of Management and Budget, *Budget of the United States, Fiscal Year 1990: Historical Tables* (Washington, D.C.: U.S. Government Printing Office, 1989), 123–31.

to be independent of each other.[14] Ronald Reagan's efforts to increase military budgets while cutting back on domestic policy expenditures seems to have stemmed more from his own ideology than from any inevitable choice between the two.

Pressures to cut defense spending and allocate funds to decrease the budget deficit or expand domestic programs are strong. Changing spending patterns is not easy, however. For example, dozens of military hardware acorns planted during the lush years of the early 1980s are now maturing into mighty, expensive oaks. Nevertheless, defense spending will decrease as weapons systems are cancelled or procurement is slowed and as the size of the armed forces is reduced. The consequences of changes in the perception of the Soviet Union's military threat will be one of the principal budgetary issues of the early 1990s.

[14]See for example, Bruce Russett, "Defense Expenditures and National Well-Being," *American Political Science Review* 76 (December 1982): 767–77; William K. Domke, Richard C. Eichenberg, and Catherine M. Kelleher, "The Illusion of Choice: Defense and Welfare in Advanced Industrial Democracies, 1948–78," *American Political Science Review* 77 (March 1983): 19–35; and Alex Mintz, "Guns versus Butter: A Disaggregated Analysis," *American Political Science Review* 83 (December 1989): 1285–96.

The Trident submarine is one of the U.S. Navy's most sophisticated weapons. A key part of America's nuclear weapons triad, the Trident can launch missiles from the ocean's depths, where it is virtually invisible and invulnerable to enemy attack. Like most weapons systems, however, the submarines cost hundreds of millions of dollars more than planned.

Defense spending is a thorny political issue, entangled with ideological disputes. Conservatives fight deep cuts in defense spending, pointing out that the Soviet Union retains a potent military capability and insisting that America needs to maintain its readiness at a high level. In addition, they credit the reforms associated with Mikhail Gorbachev to Western toughness and the massive increase in defense spending that occurred in the early 1980s. When the Soviet Union saw that it could not outspend the United States, they argue, it finally decided not to continue to allocate so much of its scarce resources to defense and to loosen its grip on Eastern Europe.

Liberals maintain that the Pentagon wastes money and that the United States buys too many guns and too little butter. They argue that the erosion of the Communist party's authority was well under way when Gorbachev rose to power, and it accelerated as *glasnost* made the party's failures matters of public ridicule, and as democratization freed new forces to challenge the existing order. Gorbachev and his fellow reformers, they contend, were responding primarily to internal, not external pressures. Inadequacies and defects at the core of the Soviet economy—the inertia, wastefulness, and corruption inherent in the system—were the driving forces that brought change to the Soviet Union, not American defense spending.

Personnel   The structure of America's defenses has been based on a large standing military force and a triad of strategic nuclear weapons. The United States has more than 2.1 million men and women on active duty and about 2.5 million in the National Guard and Reserves (see Table 20.1). One-half million active duty troops are deployed abroad, mostly in Europe. This is a very costly enterprise and one that frequently evokes calls to bring the troops home. Many observers feel that America's allies, especially prosperous nations like Japan and West Germany, should bear a greater share of common defense costs.

Weapons   To deter an aggressor's attack, the United States relies on a triad of nuclear weapons: ground-based intercontinental ballistic missiles (ICBMs), submarine-launched ballistic missiles (SLBMs), and strategic bombers. Both the United States and the Soviet Union have massive numbers of large nuclear warheads—about twenty-five thousand between them (see "America in Perspective: The Nuclear Balance"). These weapons, like troops, are costly, and they pose obvious dangers to human survival. The rapid drive toward democracy in Eastern Europe, combined with Moscow's economic torpor and the Pentagon's budgetary squeeze, will push arms reduction inexorably onto the agenda of discussions between President Bush and President Gorbachev.

One thing is certain, however. Expensive, high-tech weapons systems will continue to play an important role in America's defense posture. One of the most expensive and controversial items in the defense budget is the MX missile.

The MX: From the Racetrack to the Bargaining Table

In June 1979 the Carter administration announced plans to build the largest missile in the American arsenal, called the MX (which stands for "experimental missile"). Every missile would be seventy feet long and weigh 192,000 pounds. Each would contain ten warheads, any one of which could be aimed at a different site. Each warhead would possess more destructive force than thirty of the original atomic bombs dropped on Hiroshima and Nagasaki and would be accurate to within six hundred feet (about a city block), even when fired from six thousand miles away.[15]

Debate ensued about where to house the MX missiles. Although they would fit in existing silos for Minuteman missiles, the problem was that if American missiles could land on a dime and knock out Soviet missiles, there was every reason to assume that Soviet missiles were equally accurate. Defense Department planners came up with the idea of creating a mobile missile system. Submarine-launched ballistic missiles (SLBMs) were already mobile and hidden beneath the sea; if the MX missiles could similarly be moved about on land and hidden in a kind of nuclear shell game, an attacker would waste missiles trying to locate and knock them out. Thus emerged a variety of plans for what Herbert Scoville, Jr., called "the classical shell game with the Soviet Union in which the MX missile was a 190,000 pound pea and heavy concrete shelters were the shells."[16] Toying with a variety of options—putting the missiles in dirigibles, building a 9,100-mile-long covered trench, placing the missiles on hovercraft—the Defense Department finally settled on the idea of housing them in silos somewhere in the American West. The plan that was finally adopted by the Carter administration was to build forty-six hundred silos to house two hundred missiles. Pentagon planners devised a scheme to build forty thousand miles of roads—a sort of racetrack around which the MXs would travel. Trucks could convey each missile from one silo to another around an area about the size of New Jersey. One version of the plan even proposed creating public parks and recreational areas along the roads. The official estimate of the cost was thirty-five billion dollars, an estimate almost everyone thought was too low. The Air Force even suggested a site, the Great Basin region of Utah and Nevada.

In those states even people strongly and ideologically committed to nuclear superiority over the Soviet Union did not want the missiles in their backyards. Utah Senator Jake Garn, a Reagan Republican, and Nevada Senator Paul Laxalt, one of Reagan's strongest legislative supporters, found the MX idea appealing

[15]Herbert Scoville, Jr., *MX* (Cambridge, Mass.: MIT Press, 1981), 12–14.
[16]*Ibid.,* 18.

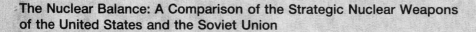

The Nuclear Balance: A Comparison of the Strategic Nuclear Weapons of the United States and the Soviet Union

Political leaders frequently brandish estimates showing that the United States and the Soviet Union are closely competitive in the arms race or, worse, that the Soviet Union is well ahead. These estimates should be viewed with considerable caution. They depend on many factors—accuracy and quality of weapons systems, for example—that are not reflected in the numbers. Here is one estimate of the strategic balance. You can see that the Soviet Union has emphasized building ICBM missiles, whereas the United States has concentrated on long-range bombers and submarine-launched missiles as delivery vehicles for nuclear weapons.

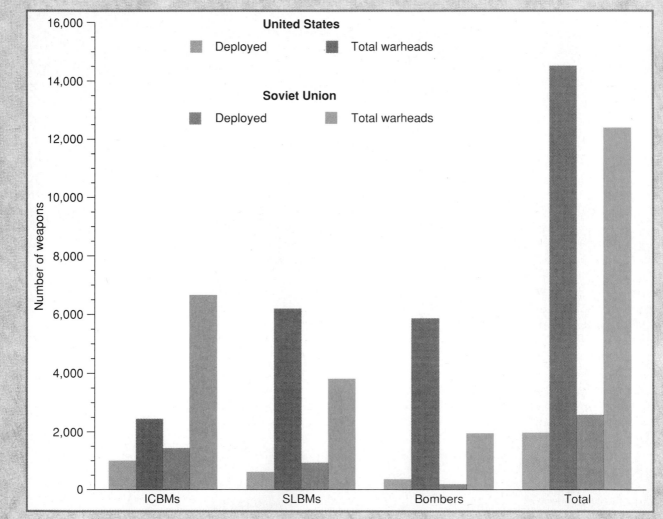

Source: International Institute for Strategic Studies, *The Military Balance, 1989–1990* (London: International Institute for Strategic Studies, 1987), 212.

but the location wanting. So did the Mormon church, not only a religious but also a political power in the region. Environmentalists were no happier. As with every other public project that would disturb nature, the MX project had to have an environmental impact statement (EIS) prepared (see Chapter 19). The EIS for the MX was massive, running nineteen hundred pages in nine volumes. MX construction, claimed the Air Force, would create sixty thousand jobs in the region, but boom times would be followed by bust times, as workers drawn to the construction would encounter joblessness after its completion. More than 160,000 acres of land would have to be cleared for the MX, and some of that land would permanently lose its native vegetation. Water for construction would have to be diverted from the Colorado River—the source of water for millions in Arizona and California. The problems, said the Air Force, were "manageable." To environmentalists, they were catastrophic.

The Reagan administration reviewed the options. Locating the missiles proved harder than building them. President Reagan appointed a commission, headed by former National Security Advisor Brent Scowcroft, to review the MX, which the president then started calling the "Peacekeeper" missile. The Scowcroft commission decided that it might not be important after all to make the MX a mobile missile; existing missile silos would do. When Congress threatened to cut funding, the president insisted that the MX would be an important bargaining chip with the Russians. How, he asked, could they believe that we meant business at the arms reduction talks if we were already throwing in the towel on the MX?

Angry over an American decision to deploy Pershing missiles in Europe, the Soviet Union walked out of arms control talks in Geneva in December 1983. On March 13, 1984, the MX again appeared as a bargaining chip in negotiations with the Soviets, as Secretary of Defense Caspar Weinberger again went to

The Reagan administration argued that the MX missile was an important bargaining chip during arms negotiations with the Soviet Union. Here Max Kampelman (left), the chief arms negotiator for the United States, meets with his Soviet counterpart Alexei Obukhov at the start of a round of arms reduction talks in 1986.

Congress to urge MX production. Linking the missile with restarting the **Strategic Arms Reduction Talks (START),** the defense secretary brought along Paul Nitze, the Reagan administration arms control advisor. Together they stressed the importance of having the MX funding as a bargaining tool to pressure the Soviet Union to return to the START talks. The next month the presidential commission recommended basing one hundred MX missiles in existing silos. Finally, in July 1984, Congress approved funds for twenty-one of the MX missiles. In 1985 there were again MX debates in the House and Senate, and again Congress approved more funding for the missiles, although this time capping the number at forty, about half of what President Reagan had requested.

In 1989 there was a new president, George Bush. He found that Congress was still unenthusiastic about the MX and that there was concern about the utility of basing them in silos. Congress decided to explore the possibility of placing some of the missiles on railroad cars that could be dispersed across great areas of countryside, and once again it capped the total number of MX missiles that could be deployed in any fashion, this time at fifty.

It had been a long, ironic story. The world's most powerful missile, pushed by the world's most powerful officeholder, had nothing but trouble finding a home. The MX finally came about because President Reagan persuaded Congress that more military hardware was needed to persuade the Soviets to reduce military hardware. Arms control negotiations often work in this contradictory way.

Restarting START, the Star Wars Gambit, and INF Reductions

In 1983 President Reagan unveiled a new plan for defense against missiles. He called it the **Strategic Defense Initiative (SDI);** critics quickly renamed it "Star Wars." Whereas the 1972 SALT talks had prohibited the development of antiballistic missiles (ABMs)—defensive weapons that would supposedly knock out missiles before they could strike—Reagan's plans for SDI proposed creating a global umbrella in space, wherein "fifth generation" computers would scan the skies and use various high-tech devices to destroy invading missiles. Because President Reagan was not very specific about the system he had in mind, all sorts of speculation flooded Washington and the scientific community. The administration proposed a research program costing twenty-six billion dollars in fiscal years 1985 through 1990. The Pentagon's Strategic Defense Initiative Organization (SDIO) had the task of sorting out science from science fiction.

All proposals for a space-based defense system had to consider certain facts. A missile's trip from the Soviet Union to a silo in Montana (or to the White House) would take about thirty minutes. The missile would go through several stages: lift-off, entry into space, midcourse, and reentry. Presumably, a missile—or thousands of missiles—could be intercepted at any point on its trajectory. Detection would be crucial. Missiles generate heat and light and radar images, but so do thousands of other items in the sky. To be effective, a system would have to distinguish among missiles and airplanes, satellites, space junk, and, of course, decoys. Chemical and X-ray lasers were proposed, each to be based in space, presumably in some sort of space station. Eventually the SDI researchers decided to settle on a "first generation" capacity that emphasized weapons that would rely upon kinetic energy. These included "smart rocks" (antimissile missiles that would respond to heat generated by warheads) and "railguns" (devices that would use electromagnets to accelerate a projectile along a rail to high speeds before launching).

Any SDI system, though, would require the perfection of computers vastly more powerful than any currently produced. Because the system would have to be fully computerized, it is unlikely that human decisions could interfere. Only seconds or minutes would be allowed for crucial decisions. Automatic decisions would have to be made. Thus computers using artificial intelligence would be expected to perform tasks that previously only the president could perform. The first of the Defense Department's studies estimated that any program for the SDI would have to be put through fifty million debugging runs before it would be battle-ready. Critics asked if even this would be enough. Computers not only make errors on their own but are dependent upon the errors humans build into their programs.[17]

A further argument put forward by critics of SDI was that even if the system were technologically and economically feasible to deploy initially, it could be easily defeated, relatively cheaply, by saturating the system with ever more targets. It would be cheaper, said these critics, for the Soviets to deploy another hundred missiles than for the United States to upgrade an SDI umbrella to defeat those new missiles.

Many proponents of SDI have reduced their expectations about the size and capabilities of any defensive shield that could be erected over the next generation. Talk of a smaller system capable of protecting against an accidental launch of a few missiles or against a threat by some third country that might develop nuclear weapons has begun to replace the dream of an impenetrable umbrella over the United States capable of defeating a massive Soviet nuclear strike. Although Congress repeatedly cut the president's budget requests for SDI, the appropriations remain considerable—more than $3.8 billion was allocated for SDI development in 1990.

The Strategic Defense Initiative remains a sticking point in U.S.-Soviet relations. The Soviet Union, partly eager to present a new face of peace under its new administration and partly concerned about the implications of SDI, returned to the START talks in Geneva in the spring of 1985. Although both sides agreed in principle to cut their long-range arsenals by about half (to six thousand weapons each), a treaty remained elusive throughout Ronald Reagan's tenure. Negotiators continued to haggle over verification measures, the treatment of cruise missiles that are capable of carrying both conventional and nuclear warheads, and, of course, SDI.

Progress was made in arms control, however, during the May 1988 Moscow summit when President Reagan and Mikhail Gorbachev exchanged ratified copies of a new treaty eliminating **intermediate-range nuclear forces (INF).** Reagan, who had built his reputation on fervid anticommunism and had denounced earlier arms control efforts (such as Jimmy Carter's SALT II agreement), became the first American president to sign a treaty to reduce current levels of nuclear weapons. Under the terms of the INF treaty, more than twenty-five hundred nuclear weapons with ranges between 300 and 3,400 miles were to be destroyed.

---

[17] The discussion of SDI relies on "Exploring the High Tech Frontier," *Time,* March 11, 1985; Johnathan Jocky, "The 'Star Wars' Defense Won't Compute," *Atlantic Monthly,* June 1985, 18–30; and Kurt Gottfried, "The Physicists Size Up SDI," *Arms Control Today,* July/August 1987, 28–32.

President Reagan and Soviet President Mikhail Gorbachev begin their 1988 summit meeting in Moscow. The two presidents later signed a treaty eliminating intermediate-range nuclear missiles from Europe. The INF treaty marked the first time an American president had agreed to reduce current levels of nuclear weapons.

Today, awesome as nuclear weapons are, more issues than nuclear weaponry inhabit the world stage. Mightly powers such as the United States and the Soviet Union are mired in smaller but intractable issues. The Soviets wrestle with dissent at home and in Eastern Europe, with declining productivity, and with corruption. Gorbachev faces resistance from a massive Communist party bureaucracy as he embarks on a sweeping program to try to revitalize the stagnant Soviet economy. The United States, too, wrestles with issues across the globe, issues that the world's strongest country often feels it should not have to face.

GULLIVER'S TROUBLES AND THE NEW GLOBAL AGENDA

By whatever standards one uses, the United States is the world's mightiest power. Its very strength seems to belie an essential weakness, however. Events on the world stage often appear to run counter to the American script. In the long and controversial Vietnam War, five hundred thousand American troops were not enough. Economic vulnerability has increased. Oil supply lines depend on a precarious Middle Eastern peace and the safe passage of huge tankers through a sliver of water called the Strait of Hormuz. In Asia, Africa, and Latin America, movements of national liberation are often opposed by the United States, but they topple pro-American (and often right-wing) governments anyway, as the Sandinistas did in Nicaragua. In Iran the United States for years supported the pro-American but brutally repressive regime of the Shah, whose vast oil riches and military power could not prevent Islamic revolutionaries from overthrowing him in 1979 and forming a new government run by mullahs and ayatollahs who seemed to blame the "American Satan" for all that was wrong in their unhappy land. At the beginning of the 1990s, Americans became increasingly frustrated as the Bush administration appeared to be losing its highly publicized "war on drugs" to an international network of wealthy drug lords called *narco-traficantes*.

Harvard political scientist Stanley Hoffman likened the United States' plight to that of Jonathan Swift's Gulliver, the traveler seized and bound by the tiny Lilliputians.[18] For Americans, as for Gulliver, merely being big and powerful is no guarantee of dominance. Time after time and place after place, so it seems, the American Gulliver loses to the Lilliputians. Nowhere does Gulliver confront more problems than in the troubled Middle East.

A Case in Point: The Middle East

The Middle East is a great triangle of civilization, roughly bounded by Iran on the east, Egypt on the south, and Turkey on the north. It has been a place of turbulence for at least a millennium. Until recently the United States could safely ignore the region because much of it, including Palestine, was under the rule of the British empire. In 1948, after World War II, the United Nations created the state of Israel, intended as a homeland for Jews surviving the scourge of fascism; however, returning the Jews to their historic homeland involved displacing Palestinians from theirs. Millions of homeless Palestinians still live in camps near Israeli borders. Spawning dozens of organizations committed to the destruction of Israel—the Palestinian Liberation Organization (PLO) is merely the best known—the Palestinians have created a major hurdle for Middle Eastern peace. Four times since its founding Israel has gone to war with its Arab neighbors. Each time the United States has been Israel's key supporter and arms supplier.

During the 1970s the American commitment to Israel, long supported by the American Jewish community, had to confront the new reality of Arab oil. Though bested repeatedly by Israeli military power, Arab nations had an economic weapon Israel could not match, one on which American dependence grew annually. An oil embargo by the Arab members of the **Organization of Petroleum Exporting Countries (OPEC)** in the winter of 1973–74 brought home to the United States the reality of economic power in world politics. If it did nothing else, the boycott persuaded Washington that peace between Israel and its Arab neighbors would have to be a primary foreign policy goal of the United States.

A spectacular peace initiative was launched by Egyptian President Anwar Sadat (who had also launched the 1973 war against Israel), the action culminating in a peace treaty between Egypt and Israel in 1979. Negotiations were facilitated by the efforts of President Carter, who arranged a week of meetings at Camp David between Sadat and Israeli Prime Minister Menachem Begin. Henry Kissinger, to whom Sadat gave the pen he had used in signing the Camp David accords, remarked, "It is a new world now." Euphoria and exuberance in Wash-

[18]Stanley Hoffman, *Gulliver's Troubles, or the Setting of American Foreign Policy* (New York: McGraw-Hill, 1968).

New Priorities on the Global Agenda

Which of these five international problems is most important right now?

Arms control	13%
Terrorism	9%
Drug traffic	48%
Palestinian unrest	4%
Central America	22%

Source: The question as worded is taken directly from a *CBS News/New York Times* Poll, March 1988.

Rock throwing, burning, and other forms of harassment are the main tactics of the Palestinian intafadeh. Many American policymakers, weary of the constant Palestinian-Israeli violence—and fearful that continuing Arab anger will jeopardize America's oil supply— have called on Israel to negotiate with the Palestinians. Hard-line elements in Israel, however, continue to block any move towards settlement, and the American deployment of troops to Saudi Arabia in 1990 further increased tensions in the Middle East.

ington, Cairo, and Jerusalem only temporarily overshadowed backlash in the Arab world, however. Sadat was praised in Washington and Jerusalem but scorned in Arab capitals. Even the more moderate Arab nations cut off diplomatic relations and aid to Egypt. OPEC quickly announced a series of staggering increases in oil prices. Significantly, President Carter, immediately after bidding farewell to Sadat and Begin, went to work on the task of finding a new energy policy. Two years after signing the treaty, Sadat was assassinated in Egypt by a band of militant Moslem fundamentalists.

Israel, in fact, was never fully supportive of the framework of the 1979 treaty. To protect its borders from the PLO, Israel invaded Lebanon in the summer of 1982, an action leading to bloody attacks on refugee camps in Beirut. The United States, Britain, and Italy agreed to send troops to Lebanon to separate the warring factions there. A year later, hundreds of American Marines were killed in a terrorist attack. President Reagan moved the remaining troops offshore and later eliminated almost completely an American presence in Lebanon. The country continues to be torn by violent clashes among a variety of religious factions.

In late 1987 Israel faced a massive uprising (termed *intafadeh*) by Palestinians in territories adjacent to and occupied by Israel: the West Bank of the Jordan River and the tiny Gaza Strip. The Israeli public and government were divided over how to deal with the continuing problem of the Palestinians. One side, led by Foreign Minister Shimon Peres, felt that Israeli security in the long run required some accommodation toward the Palestinians' demands for autonomy. The other side, led by Prime Minister Yitzak Shamir, resisted pressure from Peres (and the Reagan administration) to make any conciliatory moves that might threaten Israeli control over the territories. Today the outlook for a solution to the Arab-Israeli dilemma is not promising.

Energy and religion are the volatile ingredients of Middle Eastern politics. Both Arab and Israeli governments now confront the threat of Islamic fundamentalism, particularly in Iran. A war between Iran and Iraq drained both countries and spilled over into the Persian Gulf, where in 1987 the U.S. Navy was sent to protect shipping in that vital corridor.

Why Gulliver Has Troubles: New Issues

One explanation for America's tribulations is that the nation's supposed strong suit—military might—is no longer the primary instrument of foreign policy. Robert Keohane and Joseph Nye, in describing the minor role of military force in contemporary international politics, say that among the developed nations "the perceived margin of safety has widened: Fears of attack in general have declined, and fears of attacks by one another are virtually nonexistent."[19] Even between the United States and the Soviet Union, military might is so balanced that both have willingly entered into strategic arms reduction talks.

Today military power is virtually useless in resolving many international issues. "Force," argue Keohane and Nye, "is often not an appropriate way of achieving other goals (such as economic and ecological welfare) that are becoming more important [in world affairs]."[20] Economic conflicts do not readily

[19]Robert O. Keohane and Joseph S. Nye, *Power and Interdependence: World Politics in Transition* (Boston: Little, Brown, 1977), 77.
[20]*Ibid.,* 27–28.

yield to nuclear weapons. America cannot persuade Arab nations to sell it cheap oil by bombing them, nor can it prop up the lagging steel industry's position in world trade by resorting to military might. The American Gulliver is long on firepower at the very time firepower is no longer the major instrument of foreign policy.

Conflict among large powers, the threat of nuclear war, and the possibility of conventional war have certainly not disappeared, but grafted onto them are new issues. Former Secretary of State Henry Kissinger described the new era eloquently:

> The traditional agenda of international affairs—the balance among major powers, the security of nations—no longer defines our perils or our possibilities. Now we are entering a new era. Old international patterns are crumbling; old slogans are uninstructive. The world has become interdependent in economics, in communications, in human aspirations.[21]

Scholars such as Paul Kennedy and David Calleo envision a new world order different from the bipolar hegemony of the United States and the Soviet Union.[22] Kennedy warns both superpowers of the historical dangers of "imperial overstretch," suggesting that great empires in a stage of relative economic decline vis-à-vis emerging powers accelerate their decline by clinging to vast military commitments.

It is time to examine the new international patterns directly. They, like much of American domestic politics and policy, revolve around three issues: equality, economics, and energy and the environment.

Inequality and World Politics

A major transformation in the international system over the past two decades has been the addition of North-South conflict to the old rivalries between East and West. Whereas the cold war meant continuous conflict between the Soviet Union and the West, world politics today includes a growing conflict between rich and poor nations, the rich nations primarily being concentrated in the northern hemisphere, the poor nations in the southern hemisphere (see Table 20.2).

The old expression "the rich get richer and the poor get poorer" describes fairly accurately the inequalities among nations today. The income gap between rich, industrialized nations and poor, underdeveloped ones is widening rather than narrowing. One reason for the widening gap is suggested by a modern-day twist on the old line about rich and poor: "The rich get richer and the poor get children." While birthrates in the developed nations are leveling off, those in the poorer nations are skyrocketing, outpacing any increases in these countries' gross national products. If a nation's gross national product increases by 3 percent but its birthrate is 5 percent, the nation has to divide 3 percent more money among 5 percent more people.

---

[21]*Ibid.,* 3.

[22]Paul Kennedy, *The Rise and Fall of the Great Powers* (New York: Random House, 1987), and David Calleo, *Beyond American Hegemony: The Future of the Western Alliance* (New York: Basic Books, 1987).

Table 20.2　Rich Nations, Poor Nations

NATION	POPULATION (millions)	POPULATION GROWTH (%)	LIFE EXPECTANCY AT BIRTH (years)	GROSS NATIONAL PRODUCT (per capita $)
Low-income				
Zimbabwe	10.1	3.4	61	540
Bangladesh	114.7	2.8	54	170
Indonesia	187.7	1.9	59	880
Pakistan	110.4	2.7	55	370
China	1,112.3	1.6	69	320
Middle-income				
Algeria	24.9	3.0	65	2,645
Malaysia	16.7	2.0	68	2,092
Colombia	31.9	2.0	66	1,140
High-income				
United States	248.2	.9	76	19,800
Japan	123.2	.5	78	15,030
United Arab Emirates	2.1	6.4	70	11,900
France	56.0	.3	76	16,800

Sources: The World Bank, *World Development Report, 1987* (New York: Oxford University Press, 1987), Table 1, 202-3, and Central Intelligence Agency, *The World Factbook 89* (Washington, D.C.: U.S. Government Printing Office, 1989).

Less developed countries have responded to their poverty by borrowing money, and international banks have been willing participants in this debt dependency. Nations unable to pay the installments could simply refinance their debt, though naturally at ever-higher interest rates. Viewed from any perspective, the foreign debts of third world governments are truly staggering, often amounting to large percentages of their gross national products.

There is another complication to the issue of international inequality. Not only are there wide gaps between rich and poor nations (international inequality), but there are also big gaps between the rich and poor within developing countries (intranational inequality). Every nation has income inequality. The poorer the nation, though, the wider the gaps between rich and poor.[23] The poor in a poor country are doubly disadvantaged; not only does their economic system produce little wealth, but a handful of rich families often hoard the wealth of the country. Moreover, many people feel that the provision of economic aid by other nations serves only to further enrich the few without helping the many within a poor nation.

Much of the world's inequality is economic, dividing rich from poor between and within nations. Some of the inequality is racial, with one racial group dominating another (see "You Are the Policymaker: The Case of South Africa"). Whatever their form, inequalities are a thorny thicket for foreign policy.

[23]Michael Don Ward, *The Political Economy of Distribution: Equality Versus Inequality* (New York: Elsevier, 1978), 44.

If American policy has done little to alter income distribution at home, it would be surprising to discover that American foreign policy had attempted to eliminate international inequalities. At various conferences underdeveloped nations, claiming that the developed nations have exploited their resources, pass resolutions calling for a redistribution of the world's wealth. These requests have never gotten a sympathetic hearing in Washington.

Several American policy initiatives have, however, been directed at the problem of world poverty. Foreign aid programs have assisted with agricultural modernization, irrigation, and population control. Food for Peace programs have subsidized the sale of American agricultural products to poor countries (and simultaneously given an economic boost to American farmers). Peace Corps volunteers have fanned out over the globe to provide medical care and other services in less developed nations. Nevertheless, foreign aid has never been very popular with Americans. Lacking a constituency, foreign aid is often cut by Congress. Today the United States devotes a smaller share of its GNP to foreign economic development than any other developed nation.

In an increasingly interdependent economic system, however, it becomes harder to ignore the claims of poor nations. Nations Lilliputian in size have discovered that possessing significant economic resources adds to their stature. Natural gas in Mexico, like copper in Chile and oil in Iran, supplies American needs. So does cocaine grown in Bolivia and processed in Colombia. Inequalities become harder to ignore when the poor control resources that the rich want. Following the OPEC lead, poor countries now try to obtain higher prices for products they produce.

The International Economy

Once upon a time, nations took pains to wall themselves off from the world. They erected high tariff barriers to fend off foreign products and amassed large armies to defend their borders against intruders. Times have changed. One key word describes today's international economy: *interdependency*. When two people are independent, they can go about their business without fearing that the actions of one will affect the actions of the other. In a time of **interdependency,** actions reverberate and affect other people's economic lifelines.

A Tangled Web of Interdependency   Foreign products are not free. When citizens pay for them, they send dollars out of the country. When an oil tanker arrives in Houston, dollars travel to Saudi Arabia. If other nations do not buy as many of American products as Americans do of theirs, then the country is paying out more than it is taking in. If the United States puts military bases in Germany, the money that soldiers spend for a night on the town goes into German pockets. If American tourists spend their dollars abroad, they, too, carry American dollars away. All these instances combine to upset the **balance of payments,** the ratio of what a country pays for imports to what it earns from exports. When a country imports more than it exports, it has a balance of payments *deficit.* Year after recent year, the American balance of payments has been preceded by a minus sign.

Though not the only culprit, the excess of imports over exports decreases the dollar's buying power against marks, yens, pounds, and other currencies, making Americans pay more for goods they buy from other nations. This decline

The Case of South Africa

All nations exhibit inequalities between the rich and the poor, the powerful and the powerless. Nowhere, though, are the inequalities as visible as in the Republic of South Africa. The white-run government of South Africa is one of the last vestiges of the colonial era, which sent European colonizers to Asia, Africa, and Latin America to exploit native resources and extend Western European empires. The years after World War II witnessed quiet revolutions and bloody ones that swept away remnants of colonialism everywhere in Africa except South Africa and its neighbor, Rhodesia. White rule in Rhodesia crumbled under a worldwide economic boycott, and the country is now known as Zimbabwe.

South Africa's 18.5 million nonwhites are ruled with an iron fist by 4.2 million whites, mostly a mixture of descendants of Dutch and British settlers. The policy tool by which the white minority governs the black majority is *apartheid*, a rigid system of racial segregation that strictly confines blacks to menial jobs, the poorer countryside, and starkly subordinate social conditions. Armed with vast powers under the Suppression of Communism Act, the government can silence even white opponents of apartheid.

It is obvious that the South African regime conflicts with key American beliefs about majority rule, minority rights, civil liberties, and equality. The South African government argues that blacks living there have higher incomes and better nutrition than do blacks in African countries that have black rule. South Africa is also a storehouse of some of the world's key raw materials, many of which the United States needs.

American policy options are numerous. The United States could do one or more of the following:

- Refuse to involve itself at all in the international problems of South Africa, invoking the familiar argument that intervening in the internal affairs of other nations may not achieve any goals and may even create more problems.
- Boycott South Africa, even though South Africa is a major source of several key resources

- Support South African guerrilla movements with indirect or direct aid, even though a successful revolution in South Africa might produce a government hostile to the United States

In an attempt to force South Africa to dismantle its apartheid policies, Congress adopted—over President Reagan's veto—limited economic sanctions against it in 1986. In addition, in response to calls for "divestiture" of American investments in South Africa, about half the American firms with businesses in South Africa have left. Most observers, however, have concluded that these moves failed to bring about positive results. Political and economic conditions in fact worsened for blacks for several years after the sanctions were enacted, and some white-dominated South African companies even made windfall gains by buying out American firms that "divested."

In 1988 the South African government extended its two-year state of emergency aimed at suppressing protests against white minority rule. The U.S. Congress was in a quandary over whether or not to toughen sanctions by banning most trade with South Africa and outlawing American investment there.

Then in 1990 South African President F. W. de Klerk took the lead to open up the political process. He legalized the opposition African National Congress and released its leader, Nelson Mandela, from prison. (Mandela promptly called on the United States to maintain sanctions.) In June 1990, he ended the state of emergency in most of the country. He also entered into negotiations over the status of nonwhites—but he left untouched the basic structure of apartheid.

American policy, like South Africa itself, faces an uncertain future. Should it increase sanctions to pressure white leaders toward further change, or should the United States encourage the moderates in South Africa by assisting the economy? What would *you* do?

in the dollar, however, also makes American products cheaper abroad, thereby increasing our exports. In the late 1980s the United States experienced an export boom that helped reduce by nearly two-thirds the merchandise trade deficit with Western Europe. The U.S. trade deficit with Japan and other Asian countries has also declined, but much more slowly.

A poor balance of payments also exacerbates unemployment. Not only dollars but also jobs are flowing abroad. Labor is cheaper in Mexico, Taiwan, South Korea, and Japan, and so products made there can be priced lower than American-made products (see Figure 20.3). Sometimes American firms have shut down their domestic operations and relocated in countries where labor costs are lower. The AFL-CIO claims that one million American jobs have been lost to foreign competition. Under a special act guaranteeing compensation to American workers who lose their jobs to foreign competition, the Department of Labor has aided thousands of workers. The Labor Department, however, would be the first to note that short-term aid is no substitute for a long-term job.

Making American International Economic Policy   Coping with foreign economic issues is becoming just as difficult, and increasingly just as important, as coping with domestic ones. In a simpler time the main instrument of international economic policy was the **tariff,** a special tax added to the cost of imported goods. Tariffs are intended to raise the price of imported goods and thereby protect American businesses and workers from foreign competition. Tariff making, though, is a game everyone can play. High U.S. tariffs encourage other nations to respond with high tariffs on American products. In the twentieth century the world economy has moved from a period of high tariffs and protectionism to one of lower tariffs and freer trade. The high tariffs that the government enacted early in (and some say that helped cause) the Great Depression were the last of their kind. Growing interdependence has posed new challenges to American foreign economic policy.

Figure 20.3 The Global Connection and a Personal Computer

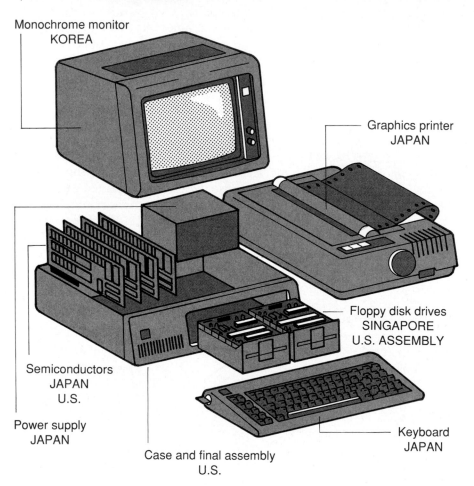

The industry standard in personal computers is the IBM PC. Here is where the parts of the PC are made around the world; note that only a small fraction of the manufactured parts are made in the U.S.A. Does this have implications for American foreign policy? You bet it does. "Foreign sourcing" costs American jobs. Foreign economic policies must try to cope with this problem by making American products more salable abroad.

Monochrome monitor
KOREA

Graphics printer
JAPAN

Floppy disk drives
SINGAPORE
U.S. ASSEMBLY

Semiconductors
JAPAN
U.S.

Power supply
JAPAN

Case and final assembly
U.S.

Keyboard
JAPAN

Source: Reprinted from the March 11, 1985, issue of *Business Week* by special permission, Copyright © 1985 by McGraw-Hill, Inc.

American international economic policies are dominated by a multiplicity of decision makers and interests; pluralism pervades the tangled politics of foreign economic policy. Stephen D. Cohen examined the system for international economic policy-making and found dozens of agencies and actors making pieces of foreign economic policy. All in all, he concluded, "The society of the United States is hopelessly pluralistic. Government in general and international economic policy in particular reflect this situation."[24] Texas Senator Lloyd Bentsen said that American foreign economic policy is shaped "almost by accident . . . a kind of guerrilla warfare among the Departments of State, Treasury, Agriculture, the Federal Reserve Board [and others]."[25] Agencies and members of Congress, as well as their constituents, each pursue their own policy goals. For example, the Treasury Department and the Federal Reserve Board worry about the negative balance of payments, while the Department of Defense spends billions in other countries to maintain American troops abroad. The Departments of Agriculture and Commerce and their constituents, farmers and businesspeople, want to peddle American products abroad. The Department of Labor and the unions worry that the nation may export not only products but jobs to other countries where labor costs are cheap. In 1988 Congress attempted to pass an omnibus trade bill aimed at protecting American industries and retaliating against "unfair" trade practices abroad.

In an interdependent world, issues of economics and trade share the foreign policy stage with military and diplomatic issues. So, too, do issues of energy and the international environment.

The Global Connection, Energy, and the Environment

Nothing symbolizes the global connection of energy and the environment as succinctly as the massive oceangoing oil tankers. In 1946 the largest oil tanker was a mere 18,000 tons. Today the biggest are 326,000 tons, and bigger ones are planned. They have made several individuals very rich; they have made it possible to import half of the oil Americans now use; and they have also despoiled fisheries and beaches when they have spilled their contents.

Growing Energy Dependency   Most, though not all, of these tankers are sailing from nations of OPEC, the organization that first made headlines in 1973 when it responded to American support of Israel in the short Yom Kippur War by embargoing oil shipments to the United States and Western European nations.

Energy transfers show convincingly that world politics is a politics of growing dependency. The less developed nations have long depended on more industrialized nations. Recently the industrialized nations have discovered the meaning of dependency, especially because of their growing need for imported energy sources. Americans are less dependent on imported oil than most nations. The European Economic Community (EEC) imports almost 100 percent of its oil. Japan does not produce a barrel of its own. Most of the less developed nations also depend on oil imports, but they have fewer resources to pay the new oil barons than the United States, the EEC, or Japan does.

With some flair, and perhaps some oversimplification as well, three University of California political scientists captured America's new worries about oil and energy dependence:

Oil is energy; energy is money; money is control; control is power. Oil in the wrong hands is money misspent and control corrupted; control corrupted is power abused;

[24]Stephen D. Cohen, *The Making of United States International Economic Policy* (New York: Praeger, 1977), 103.
[25]*Ibid.*

power abused is force misused; with oil out of control, force follows. With force out of control, so may be the world.[26]

This is a grim view. Perhaps it assumes too much about the importance of oil as a resource of control. After all, the era of scarce oil in the 1970s and early 1980s was followed by an oil *glut*. Prices sank as supplies increased, nations and businesses depending on oil income suffered a severe recession (as did oil-producing states such as Texas, Oklahoma, and Louisiana), oil millionaires went bankrupt, and discipline within the OPEC cartel crumbled. Even the deliberate attacks on oil tankers in the Persian Gulf by Iran and Iraq (a spillover from their land war) had no great effect on the vast supplies of oil available on world markets. This abundance, of course, was a great boon to users of energy. Speed limits on U.S. highways, which had been reduced in the 1970s to save energy, were raised in many states. One should not forget, however, that circumstances may again restrict the availability of oil and that the United States now imports 50 percent of the oil it uses (see Figure 20.4).

Environment and the World Commons   The oceans traveled by the supertankers are an important part of the world commons. When a supertanker cracks up and spills its oil on the beaches, it makes environmental headlines. Supertankers are hardly the only ecological problem in the world commons, however.

Almost every nation faces environmental problems at least as severe as America's. A nation's political ideology seems unrelated to its level of environmental despoliation. The Soviet Union certainly ranks among the worst offenders.[27] The explosion of a nuclear reactor at Chernobyl contaminated a vast area not only within the USSR but in other European nations as well. West Germany has poured as many chemicals into the Rhine as Americans have poured into their rivers. Underdeveloped nations almost always trade off ecological sensitivity for economic growth. Environmentalists have preached to less developed nations to think ecologically, but in places where economic development means the difference between starvation and salvation, most ecological pleas go unheard.

Global issues of environment and energy have crept slowly onto the nation's policy agenda. Recent concerns over the effects of fluorocarbons, found in many household products, on the Earth's ozone layer have generated international studies and diplomatic discussions. Americans have bargained with other nations to restrict overfishing of some of the world's fishing areas; they have pressured the Japanese to eliminate whaling; they have shown their concern about pollution in the Rhine and the deforestation of the tropical rain forests. Issues closer to home, however, are often harder to preach about. The Canadian government has become gravely concerned about acid rain, which afflicts the eastern half of its country (and America, as well). Rain containing more than ten times the normal acidity falls on lakes in the northeastern United States and Canada. On the pH scale, a measure of acidity in which seven is neutral, the Adirondack

[26]Edward Friedland, Paul Seabury, and Aaron Wildavsky, "Oil and the Decline of Western Power," *Political Science Quarterly* 90 (Fall 1975): 437.

[27]Marshall L. Goldman, *The Spoils of Progress: Environmental Pollution in the Soviet Union* (Cambridge, Mass.: MIT Press, 1972).

Dependency on imported oil decreased in the early 1980s, but by 1990 it had increased to nearly half of the oil used in the United States.

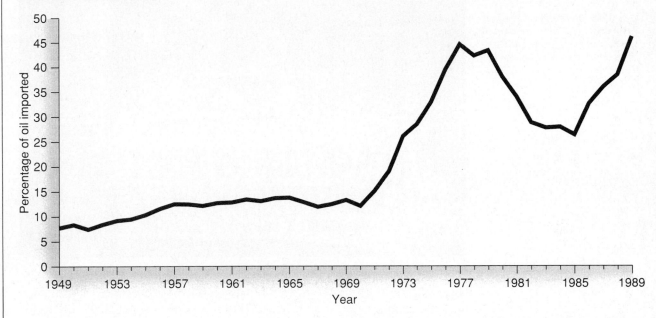

Sources: Energy Information Administration, *Annual Energy Review 1988* (Washington, D.C.: U.S. Government Printing Office, 1988), 113; and the American Petroleum Institute.

Lakes in northeastern New York consistently measure five (vinegar measures three, for example). Acid rain has soured some goodwill between Americans and their Canadian neighbors, but global issues of the world commons have yet to become a major issue of U.S. foreign policy.

UNDERSTANDING FOREIGN AND DEFENSE POLICY-MAKING

Foreign and defense policy are perhaps the most exotic arenas of public policy, dealing with issues and nations that are often far from America's shores. Nevertheless, the themes that have guided your understanding of American politics throughout *Government in America*—democracy and the size of government— can also shed some light on the topic of international relations.

Democracy and Foreign and Defense Policy-making

To some, democracy has little to do with the international relations of the United States. Because domestic issues are closer to their daily lives and easier to understand, Americans are usually more interested in domestic policy than

Public opinion plays an important part in American foreign and defense policy; as with other issues, policymakers are reluctant to make unpopular decisions. Worldwide demonstrations against the arms race are responsible, in part, for the recent willingness of American and Soviet policymakers to negotiate reductions in conventional and nuclear arms.

foreign policy. This would seem to give public officials more discretion in making foreign policy. In addition, some scholars say, those with the discretion are elites in the State Department and unelected military officers in the Pentagon.

There is little evidence, however, that policies at odds with the wishes of the American people can be sustained, and civilian control of the military is not in question. When the American people hold strong opinions regarding international relations—such as during the war in Vietnam—they find policymakers responsive to them.

In addition, the system of separation of powers discussed so often in *Government in America* plays a crucial role in foreign as well as domestic policy. You saw in Chapter 12 that Congress has a central role in matters of international relations. Whether treaties are ratified, defense budgets appropriated, weapons systems authorized, or foreign aid awarded is ultimately at the discretion of the Congress, the government's most representative policy-making body. Congressional elections are rarely determined by specific issues such as the proper funding for the Strategic Defense Initiative, but public demands for and objections to policies are likely to be heard in Washington.

Size of Government and Foreign and Defense Policy-making

America's global connections as a superpower have many implications for how active the national government is in the realm of foreign policy and national defense. Treaty obligations to defend allies around the world, the nation's economic interests in an interdependent global economy, and pressing new questions on the global agenda—ranging from illicit drugs to environmental protection—guarantee that the national government will be active in international relations.

You have seen that national defense requires an enormous budget of about three hundred billion dollars a year and a total of about three million civilian and military employees for the Department of Defense. If tensions with Eastern Europe and the Soviet Union continue to lessen, it is likely that the defense sector of government will shrink. The United States will remain a superpower and will continue to have interests to defend around the world, however. As long as this is the case, the defense budget and the defense-related bureaucracy will be sizable.

SUMMARY

The world—its politics and its economics—intrudes on Americans more each year. This chapter looked at America's global connection and the contours of its foreign policy.

The cold war began shortly after World War II, when the containment doctrine became the basis of American foreign policy. The cold war led to actual wars in Korea and Vietnam when the United States tried to contain Communist advances. With containment came a massive buildup of the military apparatus, resulting in what some people called the military-industrial complex. Gradually, containment has been balanced by détente, although America still maintains an enormous defense capability. Both foreign and defense policy are likely to be substantially altered in response to the apparent thaw in the cold war that began in 1989.

The president remains the main force behind national security policy-making. At the opening of the Nixon Library in 1990, four American presidents—Ronald Reagan (from left), Richard Nixon, George Bush, and Gerald Ford—gathered among statues of past and present world leaders.

For many years the share of the national budget spent on defense declined. Advocates of a stronger military posture argued that the Soviet Union was becoming militarily superior to the United States. Ronald Reagan was one of those advocates of expanded defense spending, and his budget priorities reflected a greater commitment to the Department of Defense. Like presidents before him, Reagan grappled with the content as well as the amount of defense spending. The tangled decision making about the MX missile, for example, has extended over the administrations of five American presidents.

Although the American Gulliver has great military power, many of the world's issues today are not military ones. Interconnected issues of equality, economics, and energy and the environment have become important. As the inequalities between rich and poor nations widen, the North-South cleavage has become more acute. The international economic system pulls the United States deeper and deeper into the world's problems as its own interdependence and vulnerability become more apparent.

In today's world, military power does not automatically bring success in foreign policy. In an era of tight global connection, problems of equality, the economy, and energy and the environment do not merely parallel their domestic manifestations; the way foreign policy confronts the international dimensions of these key issues determines the very shape of domestic policy.

KEY TERMS

foreign policy	isolationism	intermediate-range nuclear forces (INF)
United Nations (UN)	containment doctrine	Organization of Petroleum Exporting Countries (OPEC)
North Atlantic Treaty Organization (NATO)	cold war	
Warsaw Pact	McCarthyism	
European Economic Community (EEC)	arms race	interdependency
	détente	balance of payments
secretary of state	Strategic Arms Limitation Talks (SALT)	tariff
secretary of defense	Strategic Arms Reduction Talks (START)	
Joint Chiefs of Staff		
Central Intelligence Agency (CIA)	Strategic Defense Initiative (SDI)	

FOR FURTHER READING

Brzezinski, Zbigniew. *Game Plan: A Geostrategic Framework for the Conduct of the U.S.-Soviet Contest.* Boston: Atlantic Monthly Press, 1986. An analysis of superpower competition by a former national security advisor.

Calleo, David. *Beyond American Hegemony.* New York: Basic Books, 1987. An important study of America's role as a world power in an age of increasing economic interdependence and competition.

Destler, I.M. *Making Foreign Economic Policy.* Washington, D.C.: The Brookings Institution, 1980. Perhaps the most useful work on the politics of foreign economic policy.

Hilsman, Roger. *The Politics of Policymaking in Defense and Foreign Affairs.* Englewood Cliffs, N.J.: Prentice-Hall, 1987. An insightful analysis of how the American political system copes with defense and foreign policy problems.

Kennedy, Paul. *The Rise and Fall of the Great Powers.* New York: Random House, 1987. A provocative historical analysis of the interconnections between relative economic strength and military power.

Mueller, John. *Retreat from Doomsday: The Obsolescence of Major War.* New York: Basic Books, 1989. An insightful rethinking of defense policy.

Nye, Joseph S., Jr., et al., eds. *Fateful Visions: Avoiding Nuclear Catastrophe.* Cambridge, Mass.: Ballinger, 1988. Fourteen notable experts explore key national security issues for the 1990s.

Oye, Kenneth, et al., eds. *Eagle Resurgent: The Reagan Era in American Foreign Policy.* Boston: Little, Brown, 1987. An excellent collection of articles on U.S. foreign policy.

Yergin, Daniel. *Shattered Peace: The Origins of the Cold War and the National Security State.* Boston: Houghton-Mifflin, 1977. An excellent political history of the early years of the cold war and containment.

THE DECLARATION OF INDEPENDENCE*

IN CONGRESS, JULY 4, 1776

The unanimous Declaration of the thirteen united States of America

When in the Course of human events it becomes necessary for one people to dissolve the political bands which have connected them with another, and to assume among the powers of the earth, the separate and equal station to which the Laws of Nature and of Nature's God entitle them, a decent respect to the opinions of mankind requires that they should declare the causes which impel them to the separation.

We hold these truths to be self-evident, that all men are created equal, that they are endowed by their Creator with certain unalienable Rights, that among these are Life, Liberty and the pursuit of Happiness. That to secure these rights, Governments are instituted among Men, deriving their just powers from the consent of the governed, That whenever any Form of Government becomes destructive of these ends, it is the Right of the People to alter or to abolish it, and to institute new Government, laying its foundation on such principles and organizing its powers in such form, as to them shall seem most likely to effect their Safety and Happiness. Prudence, indeed, will dictate that Governments long established should not be changed for light and transient causes; and accordingly all experience hath shewn that mankind are more disposed to suffer, while evils are sufferable, than to right themselves by abolishing the forms to which they are accustomed. But when a long train of abuses and usurpations, pursuing invariably the same Object evinces a design to reduce them under absolute Despotism, it is their right, it is their duty, to throw off such Government, and to provide new Guards for their future security.—Such has been the patient sufferance of these Colonies; and such is now the necessity which constrains them to alter their former Systems of Government. The history of the present King of Great Britain is a history of repeated injuries and usurpations, all having in direct object the establishment of an absolute Tyranny over these States. To prove this, let Facts be submitted to a candid world.

He has refused his Assent to Laws, the most wholesome and necessary for the public good.

He has forbidden his Governors to pass Laws of immediate and pressing importance, unless suspended in their operation till his Assent should be obtained; and when so suspended, he has utterly neglected to attend to them.

He has refused to pass other Laws for the accommodation of large districts of people, unless those people would relinquish the right of Representation in the Legislature, a right inestimable to them and formidable to tyrants only.

He has called together legislative bodies at places unusual, uncomfortable, and distant from the depository of their Public Records, for the sole purpose of fatiguing them into compliance with his measures.

He has dissolved Representative Houses repeatedly, for opposing with manly firmness his invasions on the rights of the people.

*This text retains the spelling, capitalization, and punctuation of the original.

He has refused for a long time, after such dissolutions, to cause others to be elected; whereby the Legislative Powers, incapable of Annihilation, have returned to the People at large for their exercise; the State remaining in the mean time exposed to all the dangers of invasion from without, and convulsions within.

He has endeavored to prevent the population of these States; for that purpose obstructing the Laws for Naturalization of Foreigners; refusing to pass others to encourage their migration hither, and raising the conditions of new Appropriations of Lands.

He has obstructed the Administration of Justice, by refusing his Assent to Laws for establishing Judiciary powers.

He has made Judges dependent on his Will alone, for the tenure of their offices, and the amount and payment of their salaries.

He has erected a multitude of New Offices, and sent hither swarms of Officers to harass our people, and eat out their substance.

He has kept among us, in times of peace, Standing Armies without the Consent of our legislatures.

He has affected to render the Military independent of and superior to the Civil power.

He has combined with others to subject us to a jurisdiction foreign to our constitution, and unacknowledged by our laws; giving his Assent to their Acts of pretended Legislation:

For quartering large bodies of armed troops among us:

For protecting them, by a mock Trial, from punishment for any Murders which they should commit on the Inhabitants of these States:

For cutting off our Trade with all parts of the world:

For imposing Taxes on us without our Consent:

For depriving us in many cases, of the benefits of Trial by Jury:

For transporting us beyond Seas to be tried for pretended offences:

For abolishing the free System of English Laws in a neighboring Province, establishing therein an Arbitrary government, and enlarging its Boundaries so as to render it at once an example and fit instrument for introducing the same absolute rule into these Colonies:

For taking away our Charters, abolishing our most valuable Laws, and altering fundamentally the Forms of our Governments:

For suspending our own Legislatures, and declaring themselves invested with power to legislate for us in all cases whatsoever.

He has abdicated Government here, by declaring us out of his Protection and waging War against us.

He has plundered our seas, ravaged our Coasts, burnt out towns, and destroyed the lives of our people.

He is at this time transporting large Armies of foreign Mercenaries to compleat the works of death, desolation and tyranny, already begun with circumstances of Cruelty & perfidy scarcely paralleled in the most barbarous ages, and totally unworthy the Head of a civilized nation.

He has constrained our fellow Citizens taken Captive on the high Seas to bear Arms against their Country, to become the executioners of their friends and Brethren, or to fall themselves by their Hands.

He has excited domestic insurrections amongst us, and has endeavored to bring on the inhabitants of our frontiers, the merciless Indian Savages, whose known rule of warfare, is an undistinguished destruction of all ages, sexes and conditions.

In every stage of these Oppressions We have Petitioned for Redress in the most humble terms: Our repeated Petitions have been answered only by repeated injury. A Prince, whose character is thus marked by every act which may define a Tyrant, is unfit to be the ruler of a free people.

Nor have We been wanting in attention to our Brittish brethren. We have warned them from time to time of attempts by their legislature to extend an unwarrantable jurisdiction over us. We have reminded them of the circumstances of our emigration and settlement here. We have appealed to their native justice and magnanimity, and we have conjured them by the ties of our common kindred to disavow these usurpations, which would inevitably interrupt our connections and correspondence. They too have been deaf to the voice of justice and consanguinity. We must, therefore, acquiesce in the necessity, which denounces our Separation, and hold them, as we hold the rest of mankind, Enemies in War, in Peace Friends.

We, therefore, the Representatives of the united States of America, in General Congress, Assembled, appealing to the Supreme Judge of the world for the rectitude of our intentions, do, in the Name, and by Authority of the good People of these Colonies, solemnly publish and declare, That these United Colonies are, and of Right ought to be Free and Independent States; that they are Absolved from all Allegiance to the British Crown, and that all political connection between them and the State of Great Britain, is and ought to be totally dissolved; and that as Free and Independent States, they have full Power to levy War, conclude Peace, contract Alliances, establish Commerce, and to do all other Acts and Things which Independent States may of right do. And for the support of this Declaration, with a firm reliance on the protection of divine Providence, we mutually pledge to each other our Lives, our Fortunes and our sacred Honor.

JOHN HANCOCK

NEW HAMPSHIRE
Josiah Bartlett,
Wm. Whipple,
Matthew Thornton.

MASSACHUSETTS BAY
Saml. Adams,
John Adams,
Robt. Treat Paine,
Elbridge Gerry.

RHODE ISLAND
Step. Hopkins,
William Ellery.

CONNECTICUT
Roger Sherman,
Samuel Huntington,
Wm. Williams,
Oliver Wolcott.

NEW YORK
Wm. Floyd,
Phil. Livingston,
Frans. Lewis,
Lewis Morris.

NEW JERSEY
Richd. Stockton,
Jno. Witherspoon,
Fras. Hopkinson,
John Hart,
Abra. Clark.

PENNSYLVANIA
Robt. Morris,
Benjamin Rush,
Benjamin Franklin,
John Morton,
Geo. Clymer,
Jas. Smith,
Geo. Taylor,
James Wilson,
Geo. Ross.

DELAWARE
Caesar Rodney,
Geo. Read,
Tho. M'kean.

MARYLAND
Samuel Chase,
Wm. Paca,
Thos. Stone,
Charles Caroll
*   of Carrollton.*

VIRGINIA
George Wythe,
Richard Henry Lee,
Th. Jefferson,
Benjamin Harrison,
Thos. Nelson, jr.,
Francis Lightfoot Lee,
Carter Braxton.

NORTH CAROLINA
Wm. Hooper,
Joseph Hewes,
John Penn.

SOUTH CAROLINA
Edward Rutledge,
Thos. Heyward, Junr.,
Thomas Lynch, jnr.,
Arthur Middleton.

GEORGIA
Button Gwinnett,
Lyman Hall,
Geo. Walton.

THE CONSTITUTION OF THE UNITED STATES OF AMERICA*

(Preamble)

We the People of the United States, in Order to form a more perfect Union, establish Justice, insure domestic Tranquility, provide for the common defence, promote the general Welfare, and secure the Blessings of Liberty to ourselves and our Posterity, do ordain and establish this Constitution for the United States of America.

ARTICLE I.

(The Legislature)

SECTION 1. All legislative Powers herein granted shall be vested in a Congress of the United States, which shall consist of a Senate and House of Representatives.

SECTION 2. The House of Representatives shall be composed of Members chosen every second Year by the People of the several States, and the Electors in each State shall have the Qualifications requisite for Electors of the most numerous Branch of the State Legislature.

No person shall be a Representative who shall not have attained to the Age of twenty five Years, and been seven Years a Citizen of the United States, and who shall not, when elected, be an Inhabitant of that State in which he shall be chosen.

Representatives and direct [Taxes][1] shall be apportioned among the several States which may be included within this Union, according to their respective Numbers [which shall be determined by adding to the whole Number of free Persons, including those bound to Service for a Term of Years, and excluding Indians not taxed, three fifths of all other Persons].[2] The actual Enumeration shall be made within three Years after the first Meeting of the Congress of the United States, and within every subsequent Term of ten Years, in such Manner as they shall by Law direct. The Number of Representatives shall not exceed one for every thirty Thousand, but each State shall have at Least one Representative; and until such enumeration shall be made, the State of New Hampshire shall be entitled to chuse three, Massachusetts eight, Rhode-Island and Providence Plantations one, Connecticut five, New-York six, New Jersey four, Pennsylvania eight, Delaware one, Maryland six, Virginia ten, North Carolina five, South Carolina five, and Georgia three.

When vacancies happen in the Representation from any State, the Executive Authority thereof shall issue Writs of Election to fill such Vacancies.

---

*This text retains the spelling, capitalization, and punctuation of the original. Brackets indicate passages that have been altered by amendments.

[1]See Amendment XVI.

[2]See Amendment XIV.

The House of Representatives shall chuse their speaker and other Officers; and shall have the sole Power of Impeachment.

SECTION 3. The Senate of the United States shall be composed of two Senators from each State [chosen by the Legislature thereof],[3] for six Years; and each Senator shall have one Vote.

Immediately after they shall be assembled in Consequence of the first Election, they shall be divided as equally as may be into three Classes. The Seats of the Senators of the first Class shall be vacated at the Expiration of the second year, of the second Class at the Expiration of the fourth Year, and of the third Class at the Expiration of the sixth Year, so that one third may be chosen every second Year [and if Vacancies happen by Resignation, or otherwise, during the Recess of the Legislature of any State, the Executive thereof may make temporary Appointments until the next Meeting of the Legislature, which shall then fill such Vacancies].[4]

No Person shall be a Senator who shall not have attained to the Age of thirty Years, and been nine Years a Citizen of the United States, and who shall not, when elected, be an Inhabitant of that State for which he shall be chosen.

The Vice President of the United States shall be President of the Senate, but shall have no Vote, unless they be equally divided.

The Senate shall chuse their other Officers, and also a President pro tempore, in the Absence of the Vice President, or when he shall exercise the Office of President of the United States.

The Senate shall have the sole Power to try all Impeachments. When sitting for that Purpose, they shall be on Oath or Affirmation. When the President of the United States is tried, the Chief Justice shall preside: And no Person shall be convicted without the Concurrence of two thirds of the Members present.

Judgment in Cases of Impeachment shall not extend further than to removal from Office, and disqualification to hold and enjoy any Office of honor, Trust or Profit under the United States; but the Party convicted shall nevertheless be liable and subject to Indictment, Trial, Judgment and Punishment, according to Law.

SECTION 4. The Times, Places and Manner of holding Elections for Senators and Representatives, shall be prescribed in each State by the Legislature thereof; but the Congress may at any time by Law make or alter such Regulations, except as to the Places of chusing Senators.

[The Congress shall assemble at least once in every Year, and such Meeting shall be on the first Monday in December, unless they shall by Law appoint a different Day.][5]

SECTION 5. Each House shall be the Judge of the Elections, Returns and Qualifications of its own Members, and a Majority of each shall constitute a Quorum to do Business; but a smaller Number may adjourn from day to day, and may be authorized to compel the Attendance of absent Members, in such Manner, and under such Penalties as each House may provide.

Each House may determine the Rules of its Proceedings, punish its Members for disorderly Behaviour, and, with the Concurrence of two thirds, expel a Member.

Each House shall keep a Journal of its Proceedings, and from time to time publish the same, excepting such Parts as may in their judgment require Secrecy; and the Yeas and Nays of the Members of either House on any question shall, at the Desire of one fifth of those present, be entered on the Journal.

---

[3]See Amendment XVII.
[4]See Amendment XVII.
[5]See Amendment XX.

Neither House, during the Session of Congress, shall, without the Consent of the other, adjourn for more than three days, nor to any other Place than that in which the two Houses shall be sitting.

SECTION 6. The Senators and Representatives shall receive a Compensation for their Services, to be ascertained by Law, and paid out of the Treasury of the United States. They shall in all Cases, except Treason, Felony and Breach of the Peace, be privileged from Arrest during their Attendance at the Session of their respective Houses, and in going to and returning from the same; and for any Speech or Debate in either House, they shall not be questioned in any other Place.

No Senator or Representative shall, during the Time for which he was elected, be appointed to any civil Office under the Authority of the United States, which shall have been created, or the Emoluments whereof shall have been encreased during such time; and no Person holding any Office under the United States, shall be a Member of either House during his Continuance in Office.

SECTION 7. All Bills for raising Revenue shall originate in the House of Representatives; but the Senate may propose or concur with Amendments as on other Bills.

Every Bill which shall have passed the House of Representatives and the Senate, shall, before it become a Law, be presented to the President of the United States; If he approves he shall sign it, but if not he shall return it, with his Objections to that House in which it shall have originated, who shall enter the Objections at large on their Journal, and proceed to reconsider it. If after such Reconsideration two thirds of that House shall agree to pass the Bill, it shall be sent, together with the Objections, to the other House, by which it shall likewise be reconsidered, and if approved by two thirds of that House, it shall become a Law. But in all such Cases the Votes of both Houses shall be determined by yeas and Nays, and the Names of the Persons voting for and against the Bill shall be entered on the Journal of each House respectively. If any Bill shall not be returned by the President within ten Days (Sundays excepted) after it shall have been presented to him, the Same shall be a Law, in like Manner as if he had signed it, unless the Congress by their Adjournment prevent its Return, in which Case it shall not be a Law.

Every Order, Resolution, or Vote to which the Concurrence of the Senate and House of Representatives may be necessary (except on a question of Adjournment) shall be presented to the President of the United States; and before the Same shall take Effect, shall be approved by him, or being disapproved by him, shall be repassed by two thirds of the Senate and House of Representatives, according to the Rules and Limitations prescribed in the Case of a Bill.

SECTION 8. The Congress shall have Power To lay and collect Taxes, Duties, Imposts and Excises, to pay the Debts and provide for the common Defence and general Welfare of the United States; but all Duties, Imposts and Excises shall be uniform throughout the United States;

To borrow Money on the credit of the United States;

To regulate Commerce with foreign Nations, and among the several States, and with the Indian Tribes;

To establish a uniform Rule of Naturalization, and uniform Laws on the subject of Bankruptcies throughout the United States;

To coin Money, regulate the Value thereof, and of foreign Coin, and fix the Standard of Weights and Measures;

To provide for the Punishment of counterfeiting the Securities and current Coin of the United States;

To establish Post Offices and post Roads;

To promote the Progress of Science and useful Arts, by securing for limited Times to Authors and Inventors the exclusive Right to their respective Writings and Discoveries;

To constitute Tribunals inferior to the supreme Court;

To define and punish Piracies and Felonies committed on the high Seas, and Offences against the Law of Nations;

To declare War, grant Letters of Marque and Reprisal, and make Rules concerning Captures on Land and Water;

To raise and support Armies, but no Appropriation of Money to that Use shall be for a longer Term than two Years;

To provide and maintain a Navy;

To make Rules for the Government and Regulation of the land and naval Forces;

To provide for calling forth the Militia to execute the Laws of the Union, suppress Insurrections and repel Invasions;

To provide for organizing, arming, and disciplining, the Militia, and for governing such Part of them as may be employed in the Service of the United States, reserving to the States respectively, the Appointment of the Officers, and the Authority of training the Militia according to the discipline prescribed by Congress;

To exercise exclusive Legislation in all Cases whatsoever, over such District (not exceeding ten Miles square) as may, by Cession of particular States, and the Acceptance of Congress, become the Seat of the Government of the United States, and to exercise like Authority over all Places purchased by the Consent of the Legislature of the State in which the Same shall be, for the Erection of Forts, Magazines, Arsenals, dock-Yards, and other needful Buildings;—And

To make all Laws which shall be necessary and proper for carrying into Execution the foregoing Powers, and all other Powers vested by this Constitution in the Government of the United States, or in any Department or Officer thereof.

SECTION 9. The Migration or Importation of such Persons as any of the States now existing shall think proper to admit, shall not be prohibited by the Congress prior to the Year one thousand eight hundred and eight, but a Tax or duty may be imposed on such Importation, not exceeding ten dollars for each Person.

The Privilege of the Writ of Habeas Corpus shall not be suspended, unless when in Cases of Rebellion or Invasion the public Safety may require it.

No Bill of Attainder or ex post facto Law shall be passed.

[No Capitation, or other direct, Tax shall be laid, unless in Proportion to the Census or Enumeration herein before directed to be taken.][6]

No Tax or Duty shall be laid on Articles exported from any State.

No Preference shall be given by any Regulation of Commerce or Revenue to the Ports of one State over those of another; nor shall Vessels bound to, or from, one State, be obliged to enter, clear, or pay Duties in another.

No Money shall be drawn from the Treasury, but in Consequence of Appropriations made by Law; and a regular Statement and Account of the Receipts and Expenditures of all public Money shall be published from time to time.

No Title of Nobility shall be granted by the United States: And no Person holding any Office of Profit or Trust under them, shall, without the Consent of the Congress, accept of any present, Emolument, Office, or Title, of any kind whatever, from any King, Prince, or foreign State.

SECTION 10. No State shall enter into any Treaty, Alliance, or Confederation; grant Letters of Marque and Reprisal; coin Money; emit Bills of Credit; make any Thing but gold and silver Coin a Tender in Payment of Debts; pass any Bill of Attainder, ex post facto Law, or Law impairing the Obligation of Contracts, or grant any Title of Nobility.

No State shall, without the Consent of the Congress, lay any Imposts or Duties on Imports or Exports, except what may be absolutely necessary for executing its inspection Laws: and the net Produce of all Duties and Imposts, laid by any State on Imports or

[6]See Amendment XVI.

Exports, shall be for the Use of the Treasury of the United States; and all such Laws shall be subject to the Revision and Controul of the Congress.

No State shall, without the Consent of Congress, lay any Duty of Tonnage, keep Troops, or Ships of War in time of Peace, enter into any Agreement or Compact with another State, or with a foreign Power, or engage in War, unless actually invaded, or in such imminent Danger as will not admit of delay.

ARTICLE II.

(The Executive)

SECTION 1. The executive Power shall be vested in a President of the United States of America. He shall hold his Office during the Term of four Years, and, together with the Vice President, chosen for the same Term, be elected, as follows.

Each State shall appoint, in such Manner as the Legislature thereof may direct, a Number of Electors, equal to the whole Number of Senators and Representatives to which the State may be entitled in the Congress; but no Senator or Representative, or Person holding an Office of Trust or Profit under the United States, shall be appointed an Elector.

[The Electors shall meet in their respective States, and vote by Ballot for two Persons, of whom one at least shall not be an Inhabitant of the same State with themselves. And they shall make a List of all the Persons voted for, and of the Number of Votes for each; which List they shall sign and certify, and transmit sealed to the Seat of the Government of the United States, directed to the President of the Senate. The President of the Senate shall, in the Presence of the Senate and House of Representatives, open all the Certificates, and the Votes shall then be counted. The Person having the greatest Number of Votes shall be the President, if such Number be a Majority of the whole Number of Electors appointed; and if there be more than one who have such Majority, and have an equal Number of Votes, then the House of Representatives shall immediately chuse by Ballot one of them for President; and if no Person have a Majority, then from the five highest on the List the said House shall in like Manner chuse the President. But in chusing the President, the Votes shall be taken by States, the Representation from each State having one Vote; A quorum for this Purpose shall consist of a Member or Members from two thirds of the States, and a Majority of all the States shall be necessary to a Choice. In every Case, after the Choice of the President, the Person having the greatest Number of Votes of the Electors shall be the Vice President. But if there should remain two or more who have equal Votes, the Senate shall chuse from them by Ballot the Vice President.][7]

The Congress may determine the Time of chusing the Electors, and the Day on which they shall give their Votes; which Day shall be the same throughout the United States.

No Person except a natural born Citizen, or a Citizen of the United States, at the time of the Adoption of this Constitution, shall be eligible to the Office of President; neither shall any Person be eligible to that Office who shall not have attained to the Age of thirty five Years, and been fourteen Years a Resident within the United States.

[In Case of the Removal of the President from Office, or of his Death, Resignation, or Inability to discharge the Powers and Duties of the said Office, the Same shall devolve on the Vice President, and the Congress may by Law provide for the Case of Removal, Death, Resignation or Inability, both of the President and Vice President, declaring what Officer shall then act as President, and such Officer shall act accordingly, until the Disability be removed, or a President shall be elected.][8]

The President shall, at stated Times, receive for his Services, a Compensation, which shall neither be increased nor diminished during the Period for which he shall have

[7]See Amendment XII.
[8]See Amendment XXV.

been elected, and he shall not receive within that Period any other Emolument from the United States, or any of them.

Before he enter on the Execution of his Office, he shall take the following Oath or Affirmation:—"I do solemnly swear (or affirm) that I will faithfully execute the Office of President of the United States, and will to the best of my Ability, preserve, protect and defend the Constitution of the United States."

SECTION 2. The President shall be Commander in Chief of the Army and Navy of the United States, and of the Militia of the several States, when called into the actual Service of the United States; he may require the Opinion, in writing, of the principal Officer in each of the executive Departments, upon any Subject relating to the Duties of their respective Offices, and he shall have Power to grant Reprieves and Pardons for Offences against the United States, except in Cases of Impeachment.

He shall have Power, by and with the Advice and Consent of the Senate, to make Treaties, provided two thirds of the Senators present concur; and he shall nominate, and by and with the Advice and Consent of the Senate, shall appoint Ambassadors, other public Ministers and Consuls, Judges of the supreme Court, and all other Officers of the United States, whose Appointments are not herein otherwise provided for, and which shall be established by Law: but the Congress may by Law vest the Appointment of such inferior Officers, as they think proper, in the President alone, in the Courts of Law, or in the Heads of Departments.

The President shall have Power to fill up all Vacancies that may happen during the Recess of the Senate, by granting Commissions which shall expire at the end of their next Session.

SECTION 3. He shall from time to time give to the Congress Information of the State of the Union, and recommend to their Consideration such Measures as he shall judge necessary and expedient; he may, on extraordinary Occasions, convene both Houses, or either of them, and in Case of Disagreement between them, with Respect to the Time of Adjournment, he may adjourn them to such Time as he shall think proper; he shall receive Ambassadors and other public Ministers; he shall take Care that the Laws be faithfully executed, and shall Commission all the Officers of the United States.

SECTION 4. The President, Vice President and all civil Officers of the United States, shall be removed from Office on Impeachment for, and Conviction of, Treason, Bribery, or other high Crimes and Misdemeanors.

ARTICLE III.

(The Judiciary)

SECTION 1. The judicial Power of the United States, shall be vested in one supreme Court, and in such inferior Courts as the Congress may from time to time ordain and establish. The Judges, both of the supreme and inferior Courts, shall hold their Offices during good Behaviour, and shall, at stated Times, receive for their Services, a Compensation, which shall not be diminished during their Continuance in Office.

SECTION 2. The judicial Power shall extend to all Cases, in Law and Equity, arising under this Constitution, the Laws of the United States, and Treaties made, or which shall be made, under their Authority;—to all Cases affecting Ambassadors, other public Ministers and Consuls;—to all Cases of admiralty and maritime Jurisdiction;—to Controversies to which the United States shall be a Party;—to Controversies between two or more States;[—between a State and Citizens of another State;—][9] between Citizens of

[9]See Amendment XI.

different States,—between Citizens of the same State claiming Lands under Grants of different States, [and between a State, or the Citizens thereof, and foreign States, Citizens or Subjects.][10]

In all Cases affecting Ambassadors, other public Ministers and Consuls, and those in which a State shall be Party, the supreme Court shall have original Jurisdiction. In all the other Cases before mentioned, the supreme Court shall have appellate Jurisdiction, both as to Law and Fact, with such Exceptions, and under such Regulations as the Congress shall make.

The Trial of all Crimes, except in Cases of Impeachment, shall be by Jury; and such Trial shall be held in the State where the said Crimes shall have been committed; but when not committed within any State, the Trial shall be at such Place or Places as the Congress may by Law have directed.

SECTION 3. Treason against the United States, shall consist only in levying War against them, or in adhering to their Enemies, giving them Aid and Comfort. No Person shall be convicted of Treason unless on the Testimony of two Witnesses to the same overt Act, or on Confession in open Court.

The Congress shall have Power to declare the Punishment of Treason, but no Attainder of Treason shall work Corruption of Blood, or Forfeiture except during the Life of the Person attainted.

ARTICLE IV.

(Interstate Relations)

SECTION 1. Full Faith and Credit shall be given in each State to the public Acts, Records, and judicial Proceedings of every other State. And the Congress may by general Laws prescribe the Manner in which such Acts, Records and Proceedings shall be proved, and the Effect thereof.

SECTION 2. The Citizens of each State shall be entitled to all Privileges and Immunities of Citizens in the several States.

A Person charged in any State with Treason, Felony, or other Crime, who shall flee from Justice, and be found in another State, shall on Demand of the executive Authority of the State from which he fled, be delivered up, to be removed to the State having Jurisdiction of the Crime.

[No Person held to Service or Labour in one State under the Laws thereof, escaping into another, shall, in Consequence of any Law or Regulation therein, be discharged from such Service or Labour, but shall be delivered up on Claim of the Party to whom such Service or Labour may be due.][11]

SECTION 3. New States may be admitted by the Congress into this Union; but no new State shall be formed or erected within the Jurisdiction of any other State; nor any State be formed by the Junction of two or more States, or Parts of States, without the Consent of the Legislatures of the States concerned as well as of the Congress.

The Congress shall have Power to dispose of and make all needful Rules and Regulations respecting the Territory or other Property belonging to the United States; and nothing in this Constitution shall be so construed as to Prejudice any Claims of the United States, or of any particular State.

SECTION 4. The United States shall guarantee to every State in this Union a Republican Form of Government, and shall protect each of them against Invasion, and on Application

[10]See Amendment XI.

[11]See Amendment XIII.

of the Legislature, or of the Executive (when the Legislature cannot be convened) against domestic Violence.

ARTICLE V.

(Amending the Constitution)

The Congress, whenever two thirds of both Houses shall deem it necessary, shall propose Amendments to this Constitution, or, on the Application of the Legislatures of two thirds of the several States, shall call a Convention for proposing Amendments, which, in either Case, shall be valid to all Intents and Purposes, as Part of this Constitution, when ratified by the Legislatures of three fourths of the several States, or by Conventions in three fourths thereof, as the one or the other Mode of Ratification may be proposed by the Congress; Provided that no Amendment which may be made prior to the Year One thousand eight hundred and eight shall in any Manner affect the first and fourth Clauses in the Ninth Section of the first Article; and that no State, without its Consent, shall be deprived of its equal Suffrage in the Senate.

ARTICLE VI.

(Debts, Supremacy, Oaths)

All Debts contracted and Engagements entered into, before the Adoption of this Constitution, shall be as valid against the United States under this Constitution, as under the Confederation.

This Constitution, and the laws of the United States which shall be made in Pursuance thereof; and all Treaties made, or which shall be made, under the Authority of the United States, shall be the supreme Law of the Land; and the Judges in every State shall be bound thereby, any Thing in the Constitution or Laws of any State to the Contrary notwithstanding.

The Senators and Representatives before mentioned, and the Members of the several State Legislatures, and all executive and judicial Officers, both of the United States and of the several States, shall be bound by Oath or Affirmation, to support this Constitution; but no religious Test shall ever be required as a Qualification to any Office or public Trust under the United States.

ARTICLE VII.

(Ratifying the Constitution)

The Ratification of the Conventions of nine States, shall be sufficient for the Establishment of this Constitution between the States so ratifying the Same.

Done in Convention by the Unanimous Consent of the States present the Seventeenth Day of September in the Year of our Lord one thousand seven hundred and Eighty seven and of the Independence of the United States of America the Twelfth. IN WITNESS whereof we have hereunto subscribed our Names,

Go. WASHINGTON
Presid't. and deputy from Virginia

Attest
WILLIAM JACKSON
Secretary

DELAWARE
Geo. Read
Gunning Bedford jun
John Dickinson
Richard Basset
Jaco. Broom

MASSACHUSETTS
Nathaniel Gorham
Rufus King

CONNECTICUT
Wm. Saml. Johnson
Roger Sherman

NEW YORK
Alexander Hamilton

NEW JERSEY
Wh. Livingston
David Brearley
Wm. Paterson
Jona. Dayton

PENNSYLVANIA
B. Franklin
Thomas Mifflin
Robt. Morris
Geo. Clymer
Thos. FitzSimons
Jared Ingersoll
James Wilson
Gouv. Morris

NEW HAMPSHIRE
John Langdon
Nicholas Gilman

MARYLAND
James McHenry
Dan of St. Thos. Jenifer
Danl. Carroll

VIRGINIA
John Blair
James Madison Jr.

NORTH CAROLINA
Wm. Blount
Richd. Dobbs Spaight
Hu. Williamson

SOUTH CAROLINA
J. Rutledge
Charles Cotesworth
  Pinckney
Charles Pinckney
Pierce Butler

GEORGIA
William Few
Abr. Baldwin

Articles in addition to, and amendment of the Constitution of the United States of America, proposed by Congress and ratified by the Legislatures of the several states, pursuant to the Fifth Article of the original Constitution.

(The first ten amendments were passed by Congress on September 25, 1789, and were ratified on December 15, 1791.)

Amendment I—*Religion, Speech, Assembly, Petition*

Congress shall make no law respecting an establishment of religion, or prohibiting the free exercise thereof; or abridging the freedom of speech, or of the press; or the right of the people peaceably to assemble, and to petition the Government for a redress of grievances.

Amendment II—*Right to Bear Arms*

A well regulated Militia, being necessary to the security of a free State, the right of the people to keep and bear Arms, shall not be infringed.

Amendment III—*Quartering of Soldiers*

No Soldier shall, in time of peace be quartered in any house, without the consent of the Owner, nor in time of war, but in a manner to be prescribed by law.

Amendment IV—*Searches and Seizures*

The right of the people to be secure in their persons, houses, papers, and effects, against unreasonable searches and seizures, shall not be violated, and no warrants shall issue, but upon probable cause, supported by Oath or affirmation, and particularly describing the place to be searched, and the persons or things to be seized.

Amendment V—*Grand Juries, Double Jeopardy, Self-incrimination, Due Process, Eminent Domain*

No person shall be held to answer for a capital, or otherwise infamous crime, unless on a presentment or indictment of a Grand Jury, except in cases arising in the land or naval forces, or in the Militia, when in actual service in time of War or public danger; nor shall any person be subject for the same offence to be twice put in jeopardy of life or limb; nor shall be compelled in any criminal case to be a witness against himself, nor be deprived of life, liberty, or property, without due process of law; nor shall private property be taken for public use, without just compensation.

Amendment vi—*Criminal Court Procedures*

In all criminal prosecutions, the accused shall enjoy the right to a speedy and public trial, by an impartial jury of the State and district wherein the crime shall have been committed, which district shall have been previously ascertained by law, and to be informed of the nature and cause of the accusation; to be confronted with the witnesses against him; to have compulsory process for obtaining witnesses in his favor, and to have the assistance of counsel for his defence.

Amendment vii—*Trial by Jury in Common-law Cases*

In Suits at common law, where the value in controversy shall exceed twenty dollars, the right of trial by jury shall be preserved, and no fact tried by a jury, shall be otherwise re-examined in any Court of the United States, than according to the rules of the common law.

Amendment viii—*Bails, Fines, and Punishment*

Excessive bail shall not be required, nor excessive fines imposed, nor cruel and unusual punishments inflicted.

Amendment ix—*Rights Retained by the People*

The enumeration in the Constitution, of certain rights, shall not be construed to deny or disparage others retained by the people.

Amendment x—*Rights Reserved to the States*

The powers not delegated to the United States by the Constitution, nor prohibited by it to the States, are reserved to the States respectively, or to the people.

Amendment xi—*Suits against the States (Ratified February 7, 1795)*

The Judicial power of the United States shall not be construed to extend to any suit in law or equity, commenced or prosecuted against one of the United States by Citizens of another State, or by Citizens or Subjects of any Foreign State.

Amendment xii—*Election of the President and Vice-President (Ratified June 15, 1804)*

The Electors shall meet in their respective states, and vote by ballot for President and Vice-President, one of whom, at least, shall not be an inhabitant of the same state with themselves; they shall name in their ballots the person voted for as President, and in distinct ballots the person voted for as Vice-President, and they shall make distinct lists of all persons voted for as President, and of all persons voted for as Vice-President, and of the number of votes for each, which lists they shall sign and certify, and transmit sealed to the seat of the government of the United States, directed to the President of the Senate;—The President of the Senate shall, in the presence of the Senate and House of Representatives, open all the certificates and the votes shall then be counted;—The person having the greatest number of votes for President, shall be the President, if such number be a majority of the whole number of Electors appointed; and if no person have such majority, then from the persons having the highest numbers not exceeding three on the list of those voted for as President, the House of Representatives shall choose immediately, by ballot, the President. But in choosing the President, the votes shall be taken by states, the representation from each state having one vote; a quorum for this purpose shall consist of a member or members from two-thirds of the states, and a majority of all the states shall be necessary to a choice. [And if the House of Representatives shall not choose a President whenever the right of choice shall devolve upon them, before the fourth day of March next following, then the Vice-President shall act as President, as in the case of the death or other constitutional disability of the President.][12]—The person having the greatest number of votes as Vice-President, shall be the Vice-President, if such number be a majority of the whole number of Electors appointed, and if no person have a majority, then from the two highest numbers on the list, the Senate shall choose the Vice-President; a quorum for the purpose shall consist of two-thirds of the whole number of Senators, and a majority of the whole number shall be necessary to a choice. But no person constitutionally ineligible to the office of President shall be eligible to that of Vice-President of the United States.

Amendment XIII—*Slavery (Ratified on December 6, 1865)*

SECTION 1. Neither slavery nor involuntary servitude, except as a punishment for crime whereof the party shall have been duly convicted, shall exist within the United States, or any place subject to their jurisdiction.

SECTION 2. Congress shall have power to enforce this article by appropriate legislation.

Amendment XIV—*Citizenship, Due Process, and Equal Protection of the Laws (Ratified on July 9, 1868)*

SECTION 1. All persons born or naturalized in the United States, and subject to the jurisdiction thereof, are citizens of the United States and of the State wherein they reside. No State shall make or enforce any law which shall abridge the privileges or immunities of citizens of the United States; nor shall any State deprive any person of life, liberty, or property, without due process of law; nor deny to any person within its jurisdiction the equal protection of the laws.

SECTION 2. Representatives shall be apportioned among the several States according to their respective numbers, counting the whole number of persons in each State, excluding Indians not taxed. But when the right to vote at any election for the choice of electors for President and Vice President of the United States, Representatives in Congress, the Executive and Judicial officers of a State, or the members of the Legislature thereof, is denied to any of the male inhabitants of such State, being twenty-one years of age, and citizens of the United States, or in any way abridged, except for participation in rebellion, or other crime, the basis of representation therein shall be reduced in the proportion which the number of such male citizens shall bear to the whole number of male citizens twenty-one years of age in such State.

SECTION 3. No person shall be a Senator or Representative in Congress, or elector of President and Vice President, or hold any office, civil or military, under the United States, or under any State, who, having previously taken an oath, as a member of Congress, or as an officer of the United States, or as a member of any State legislature, or as an executive or judicial officer of any State, to support the Constitution of the United States, shall have engaged in insurrection or rebellion against the same, or given aid or comfort to the enemies thereof. But Congress may by a vote of two-thirds of each House, remove such disability.

[12]Amendment xx.

Section 4. The validity of the public debt of the United States, authorized by law, including debts incurred for payment of pensions and bounties for services in suppressing insurrection or rebellion, shall not be questioned. But neither the United States nor any State shall assume or pay any debt or obligation incurred in aid of insurrection or rebellion against the United States, or any claim for the loss or emancipation of any slave, but all such debts, obligations and claims shall be held illegal and void.

Section 5. The Congress shall have power to enforce, by appropriate legislation, the provisions of this article.

Amendment xv—*The Right to Vote (Ratified on February 3, 1870)*

Section 1. The right of citizens of the United States to vote shall not be denied or abridged by the United States or by any State on account of race, color, or previous condition of servitude.

Section 2. The Congress shall have power to enforce this article by appropriate legislation.

Amendment xvi—*Income Taxes (Ratified on February 3, 1913)*

The Congress shall have power to lay and collect taxes on incomes, from whatever source derived, without apportionment among the several States, and without regard to any census or enumeration.

Amendment xvii—*Election of Senators (Ratified on April 8, 1913)*

The Senate of the United States shall be composed of two Senators from each State, elected by the people thereof, for six years; and each Senator shall have one vote. The electors in each State shall have the qualifications requisite for electors of the most numerous branch of the State legislatures.

When vacancies happen in the representation of any State in the Senate, the executive authority of such State shall issue writs of election to fill such vacancies: *Provided,* That the legislature of any State may empower the executive thereof to make temporary appointments until the people fill the vacancies by election as the legislature may direct.

This amendment shall not be so construed as to affect the election or term of any Senator chosen before it becomes valid as part of the Constitution.

Amendment xviii—*Prohibition (Ratified on January 16, 1919)*

Section 1. After one year from the ratification of this article the manufacture, sale, or transportation of intoxicating liquors within, the importation thereof into, or the exportation thereof from the United States and all territory subject to the jurisdiction thereof for beverage purposes is hereby prohibited.

Section 2. The Congress and the several States shall have concurrent power to enforce this article by appropriate legislation.

Section 3. This article shall be inoperative unless it shall have been ratified as an amendment to the Constitution by the legislatures of the several States, as provided in the Constitution, within seven years from the date of the submission hereof to the States by the Congress.[13]

---

[13]See Amendment xxi.

Amendment XIX—*Women's Right to Vote (Ratified on August 18, 1920)*

The right of citizens of the United States to vote shall not be denied or abridged by the United States or by any State on account of sex.

Congress shall have power to enforce this article by appropriate legislation.

Amendment XX—*Terms of Office, Convening of Congress, and Succession (Ratified February 6, 1933)*

SECTION 1. The terms of the President and Vice President shall end at noon on the 20th day of January, and the terms of Senators and Representatives at noon on the 3d day of January, of the years in which such terms would have ended if this article had not been ratified; and the terms of their successors shall then begin.

SECTION 2. The Congress shall assemble at least once in every year, and such meeting shall begin at noon on the 3d day of January, unless they shall by law appoint a different day.

SECTION 3. If, at the time fixed for the beginning of the term of the President, the President elect shall have died, the Vice President elect shall become President. If a President shall not have been chosen before the time fixed for the beginning of his term, or if the President elect shall have failed to qualify, then the Vice President elect shall act as President until a President shall have qualified; and the Congress may by law provide for the case wherein neither a President elect nor a Vice President elect shall have qualified, declaring who shall then act as President, or the manner in which one who is to act shall be selected, and such person shall act accordingly until a President or Vice President shall have qualified.

SECTION 4. The Congress may by law provide for the case of the death of any of the persons from whom the House of Representatives may choose a President whenever the rights of choice shall have devolved upon them, and for the case of the death of any of the persons from whom the Senate may choose a Vice President whenever the right of choice shall have devolved upon them.

SECTION 5. Sections 1 and 2 shall take effect on the 15th day of October following the ratification of this article.

SECTION 6. This article shall be inoperative unless it shall have been ratified as an amendment to the Constitution by the legislatures of three-fourths of the several States within seven years from the date of its submission.

Amendment XXI—*Repeal of Prohibition (Ratified on December 5, 1933)*

SECTION 1. The eighteenth article of amendment to the Constitution of the United States is hereby repealed.

SECTION 2. The transportation or importation into any State, Territory, or possession of the United States for delivery or use therein of intoxicating liquors, in violation of the laws thereof, is hereby prohibited.

SECTION 3. This article shall be inoperative unless it shall have been ratified as an amendment to the Constitution by conventions in the several States, as provided in the Constitution, within seven years from the date of the submission hereof to the States by the Congress.

Amendment XXII—*Number of Presidential Terms (Ratified on February 27, 1951)*

No person shall be elected to the office of the President more than twice, and no person who has held the office of President, or acted as President, for more than two years of a term to which some other person was elected President shall be elected to the office of the President more than once. But this Article shall not apply to any person holding the office of President when this Article was proposed by the Congress, and shall not prevent any person who may be holding the office of President, or acting as President, during the term within which this Article becomes operative from holding the office of President or acting as President during the remainder of such term.

Amendment XXIII—*Presidential Electors for the District of Columbia (Ratified on March 29, 1961)*

SECTION 1. The District constituting the seat of Government of the United States shall appoint in such manner as the Congress may direct:

A number of electors of President and Vice President equal to the whole number of Senators and Representatives in Congress to which the District would be entitled if it were a State, but in no event more than the least populous State; they shall be in addition to those appointed by the States, but they shall be considered, for the purposes of the election of President and Vice President, to be electors appointed by a State; and they shall meet in the District and perform such duties as provided by the twelfth article of amendment.

SECTION 2. The Congress shall have power to enforce this article by appropriate legislation.

Amendment XXIV—*Poll Tax (Ratified on January 23, 1964)*

SECTION 1. The right of citizens of the United States to vote in any primary or other election for President or Vice President, for electors for President or Vice President, or for Senator or Representative in Congress, shall not be denied or abridged by the United States or any State by reason of failure to pay any poll tax or other tax.

SECTION 2. The Congress shall have power to enforce this article by appropriate legislation.

Amendment XXV—*Presidential Disability and Vice Presidential Vacancies (Ratified on February 10, 1967)*

SECTION 1. In case of the removal of the President from office or of his death or resignation, the Vice President shall become President.

SECTION 2. Whenever there is a vacancy in the office of the Vice President, the President shall nominate a Vice President who shall take office upon confirmation by a majority vote of both Houses of Congress.

SECTION 3. Whenever the President transmits to the President pro tempore of the Senate and the Speaker of the House of Representatives his written declaration that he is unable to discharge the powers and duties of his office, and until he transmits to them a written declaration to the contrary, such powers and duties shall be discharged by the Vice President as Acting President.

SECTION 4. Whenever the Vice President and a majority of either the principal officers of the executive departments or of such other body as Congress may by law provide, transmit to the President pro tempore of the Senate and the Speaker of the House of Representatives their written declaration that the President is unable to discharge the powers and duties of his office, the Vice President shall immediately assume the powers and duties of the office as Acting President.

Thereafter, when the President transmits to the President pro tempore of the Senate and the Speaker of the House of Representatives his written declaration that no inability exists, he shall resume the powers and duties of his office unless the Vice President and a majority of either the principal officers of the executive department or of such other body as Congress may by law provide, transmit within four days to the President pro tempore of the Senate and the Speaker of the House of Representatives their written declaration that the President is unable to discharge the powers and duties of his office. Thereupon Congress shall decide the issue, assembling within forty-eight hours for that purpose if not in session. If the Congress, within twenty-one days after receipt of the latter written declaration, or, if Congress is not in session, within twenty-one days after Congress is required to assemble, determines by two-thirds vote of both Houses that the President is unable to discharge the powers and duties of his office, the Vice President shall continue to discharge the same as Acting President; otherwise, the President shall resume the powers and duties of his office.

Amendment XXVI—*Eighteen-year-old Vote (Ratified on July 1, 1971)*

SECTION 1. The right of citizens of the United States, who are eighteen years of age or older, to vote shall not be denied or abridged by the United States or by any State on account of age.

SECTION 2. The Congress shall have power to enforce this article by appropriate legislation.

PRESIDENTS OF THE UNITED STATES

YEAR	PRESIDENTIAL CANDIDATES	POLITICAL PARTY	ELECTORAL VOTE	PERCENTAGE OF POPULAR VOTE
1789	**George Washington**	—	69	—
	John Adams		34	
	Others		35	
1792	**George Washington**	—	132	—
	John Adams		77	
	Others		55	
1796	**John Adams**	Federalist	71	—
	Thomas Jefferson	Democratic-Republican	68	
	Thomas Pinckney	Federalist	59	
	Aaron Burr	Anti-Federalist	30	
	Others		48	
1800	**Thomas Jefferson**	Democratic-Republican	73	—
	Aaron Burr	Democratic-Republican	73	
	John Adams	Federalist	65	
	C. C. Pinckney	Federalist	64	
	John Jay	Federalist	1	
1804	**Thomas Jefferson**	Democratic-Republican	162	—
	C. C. Pinckney	Federalist	14	
1808	**James Madison**	Democratic-Republican	122	—
	C. C. Pinckney	Federalist	47	
	George Clinton	Independent-Republican	6	
1812	**James Madison**	Democratic-Republican	128	—
	De Witt Clinton	Fusion	89	
1816	**James Monroe**	Democratic-Republican	183	—
	Rufus King	Federalist	34	
1820	**James Monroe**	Democratic-Republican	231	—
	John Q. Adams	Independent-Republican	1	
1824	**John Q. Adams**	National Republican	84	30.5
	Andrew Jackson	Democratic	99	
	Henry Clay	Democratic-Republican	37	
	W. H. Crawford	Democratic-Republican	41	

Note: Presidents are shown in boldface.
*Died in office, succeeding vice president shown in parentheses.
†Resigned
‡Appointed vice president
**Horace Greeley died between the popular vote and the meeting of the presidential electors.

YEAR	PRESIDENTIAL CANDIDATES	POLITICAL PARTY	ELECTORAL VOTE	PERCENTAGE OF POPULAR VOTE
1828	**Andrew Jackson**	Democratic	178	56.0
	John Q. Adams	National Republican	83	
1832	**Andrew Jackson**	Democratic	219	55.0
	Henry Clay	National Republican	49	
	William Wirt	Anti-Masonic	7	
	John Floyd	Nullifiers	11	
1836	**Martin Van Buren**	Democratic	170	50.9
	William H. Harrison	Whig	73	
	Hugh L. White	Whig	26	
	Daniel Webster	Whig	14	
1840	**William H. Harrison***	Whig	234	53.0
	Martin Van Buren	Democratic	60	
	(John Tyler, 1841)			
1844	**James K. Polk**	Democratic	170	49.6
	Henry Clay	Whig	105	
1848	**Zachary Taylor***	Whig	163	47.4
	Lewis Cass	Democratic	127	
	(Millard Fillmore, 1850)			
1852	**Franklin Pierce**	Democratic	254	50.9
	Winfield Scott	Whig	42	
1856	**James Buchanan**	Democratic	174	45.4
	John C. Fremont	Republican	114	
	Millard Fillmore	American	8	
1860	**Abraham Lincoln**	Republican	180	39.8
	J. C. Breckinridge	Democratic	72	
	Stephen A. Douglas	Democratic	12	
	John Bell	Constitutional Union	39	
1864	**Abraham Lincoln***	Republican	212	55.0
	George B. McClellan	Democratic	21	
	(Andrew Johnson, 1865)			
1868	**Ulysses S. Grant**	Republican	214	52.7
	Horatio Seymour	Democratic	80	
1872	**Ulysses S. Grant**	Republican	286	55.6
	Horace Greeley	Democratic	**	
1876	**Rutherford B. Hayes**	Republican	185	47.9
	Samuel J. Tilden	Democratic	184	
1880	**James A. Garfield***	Republican	214	48.3
	Winfield S. Hancock	Democratic	155	
	(Chester A. Arthur, 1881)			
1884	**Grover Cleveland**	Democratic	219	48.5
	James G. Blaine	Republican	182	
1888	**Benjamin Harrison**	Republican	233	47.8
	Grover Cleveland	Democratic	168	
1892	**Grover Cleveland**	Democratic	277	46.0
	Benjamin Harrison	Republican	145	
	James B. Weaver	People's	22	

YEAR	PRESIDENTIAL CANDIDATES	POLITICAL PARTY	ELECTORAL VOTE	PERCENTAGE OF POPULAR VOTE
1896	**William McKinley**	Republican	271	51.0
	William J. Bryan	Democratic	176	
1900	**William McKinley***	Republican	292	51.7
	William J. Bryan	Democratic	155	
	(**Theodore Roosevelt,** 1901)			
1904	**Theodore Roosevelt**	Republican	336	56.4
	Alton B. Parker	Democratic	140	
1908	**William H. Taft**	Republican	321	51.6
	William J. Bryan	Democratic	162	
1912	**Woodrow Wilson**	Democratic	435	41.8
	Theodore Roosevelt	Progressive	88	
	William H. Taft	Republican	8	
1916	**Woodrow Wilson**	Democratic	277	49.2
	Charles E. Hughes	Republican	254	
1920	**Warren G. Harding***	Republican	404	60.3
	James M. Cox	Democratic	127	
	(**Calvin Coolidge,** 1923)			
1924	**Calvin Coolidge**	Republican	382	54.1
	John W. Davis	Democratic	136	
	Robert M. LaFollette	Progressive	13	
1928	**Herbert C. Hoover**	Republican	444	58.2
	Alfred E. Smith	Democratic	87	
1932	**Franklin D. Roosevelt**	Democratic	472	57.4
	Herbert C. Hoover	Republican	59	
1936	**Franklin D. Roosevelt**	Democratic	523	60.8
	Alfred M. Landon	Republican	8	
1940	**Franklin D. Roosevelt**	Democratic	449	54.7
	Wendell L. Willkie	Republican	82	
1944	**Franklin D. Roosevelt***	Democratic	432	53.4
	Thomas E. Dewey	Republican	99	
	(**Harry S Truman,** 1945)			
1948	**Harry S Truman**	Democratic	303	49.5
	Thomas E. Dewey	Republican	189	
	J. Strom Thurmond	States' Rights	39	
1952	**Dwight D. Eisenhower**	Republican	442	55.1
	Adlai E. Stevenson	Democratic	89	
1956	**Dwight D. Eisenhower**	Republican	457	57.4
	Adlai E. Stevenson	Democratic	73	
1960	**John F. Kennedy***	Democratic	303	49.7
	Richard M. Nixon	Republican	219	
	(**Lyndon B. Johnson,** 1963)			
1964	**Lyndon B. Johnson**	Democratic	486	61.0
	Barry M. Goldwater	Republican	52	
1968	**Richard M. Nixon**	Republican	301	43.4
	Hubert H. Humphrey	Democratic	191	
	George C. Wallace	American Independent	46	

YEAR	PRESIDENTIAL CANDIDATES	POLITICAL PARTY	ELECTORAL VOTE	PERCENTAGE OF POPULAR VOTE
1972	**Richard M. Nixon†**	Republican	520	60.7
	George S. McGovern	Democratic	17	
	(Gerald R. Ford, 1974)‡			
1976	**Jimmy Carter**	Democratic	297	50.1
	Gerald R. Ford	Republican	240	
1980	**Ronald Reagan**	Republican	489	50.7
	Jimmy Carter	Democratic	49	
	John Anderson	Independent	—	
1984	**Ronald Reagan**	Republican	525	58.8
	Walter Mondale	Democratic	13	
1988	**George Bush**	Republican	426	53.4
	Michael Dukakis	Democratic	112	

PARTY CONTROL OF THE PRESIDENCY, SENATE, AND HOUSE OF REPRESENTATIVES IN THE TWENTIETH CENTURY

CONGRESS	YEARS	PRESIDENT	SENATE			HOUSE		
			D	R	OTHER*	D	R	OTHER*
57th	1901–03	McKinley / T. Roosevelt	29	56	3	153	198	5
58th	1903–05	T. Roosevelt	32	58	—	178	207	—
59th	1905–07	T. Roosevelt	32	58	—	136	250	—
60th	1907–09	T. Roosevelt	29	61	—	164	222	—
61st	1909–11	Taft	32	59	—	172	219	—
62d	1911–13	Taft	42	49	—	228‡	162	1
63d	1913–15	Wilson	51	44	1	290	127	18
64th	1915–17	Wilson	56	39	1	230	193	8
65th	1917–19	Wilson	53	42	1	200	216	9
66th	1919–21	Wilson	48	48‡	1	191	237‡	7
67th	1921–23	Harding	37	59	—	132	300	1
68th	1923–25	Coolidge	43	51	2	207	225	3
69th	1925–27	Coolidge	40	54	1	183	247	5
70th	1927–29	Coolidge	47	48	1	195	237	3
71st	1929–31	Hoover	39	56	1	163	267	1
72d	1931–33	Hoover	47	48	1	216‡	218	1
73d	1933–35	F. Roosevelt	59	36	1	313	117	5
74th	1935–37	F. Roosevelt	69	25	2	322	103	10
75th	1937–39	F. Roosevelt	75	17	4	333	89	13
76th	1939–41	F. Roosevelt	69	23	4	262	169	4
77th	1941–43	F. Roosevelt	66	28	2	267	162	6
78th	1943–45	F. Roosevelt	57	38	1	222	209	4
79th	1945–47	Truman	57	38	1	243	190	2
80th	1947–49	Truman	45	51‡	—	188	246‡	1

*Excludes vacancies at beginning of each session. Party balance immediately following election.
†The 437 members of the House in the 86th and 87th Congresses are attributable to the at-large representative given to both Alaska (January 3, 1959) and Hawaii (August 21, 1959) prior to redistricting in 1962.
‡Chamber controlled by party other than that of the president.
D = Democrat
R = Republican

CONGRESS	YEARS	PRESIDENT	SENATE			HOUSE		
			D	R	OTHER*	D	R	OTHER*
81st	1949–51	Truman	54	42	—	263	171	1
82d	1951–53	Truman	48	47	1	234	199	2
83d	1953–55	Eisenhower	47	48	1	213	221	1
84th	1955–57	Eisenhower	48‡	47	1	232‡	203	—
85th	1957–59	Eisenhower	49‡	47	—	234‡	201	—
86th†	1959–61	Eisenhower	64‡	34	—	283‡	154	—
87th†	1961–63	Kennedy	64	36	—	263	174	—
88th	1963–65	{ Kennedy Johnson	67	33	—	258	176	—
89th	1965–67	Johnson	68	32	—	295	140	—
90th	1967–69	Johnson	64	36	—	248	187	—
91st	1969–71	Nixon	58‡	42	—	243‡	192	—
92d	1971–73	Nixon	55‡	45	—	255‡	180	—
93d	1973–75	{ Nixon Ford	57‡	43	—	243‡	192	—
94th	1975–77	Ford	61‡	38	—	291‡	144	—
95th	1977–79	Carter	62	38	—	292	143	—
96th	1979–81	Carter	59	41	—	277	158	—
97th	1981–83	Reagan	47	53	—	243‡	192	—
98th	1983–85	Reagan	46	54	—	269‡	166	—
99th	1985–87	Reagan	47	53	—	253‡	182	—
100th	1987–89	Reagan	55‡	45	—	258‡	177	—
101st	1989–91	Bush	55‡	45	—	260‡	175	—

Supreme Court Justices serving in the Twentieth Century

NAME	NOMINATED BY	SERVICE
John M. Harlan	Hayes	1877–1911
Horace Gray	Arthur	1882–1902
Melville W. Fuller	Cleveland	1888–1910
David J. Brewer	Harrison	1890–1910
Henry B. Brown	Harrison	1890–1906
George Shiras, Jr.	Harrison	1892–1903
Edward D. White	Cleveland	1894–1910
Rufus W. Peckham	Cleveland	1895–1909
Joseph McKenna	McKinley	1898–1925
Oliver W. Holmes	T. Roosevelt	1902–1932
William R. Day	T. Roosevelt	1903–1922
William H. Moody	T. Roosevelt	1906–1910
Horace H. Lurton	Taft	1910–1914
Edward D. White	Taft	1910–1921
Charles E. Hughes	Taft	1910–1916
Willis Van Devanter	Taft	1911–1937
Joseph R. Lamar	Taft	1911–1916
Mahlon Pitney	Taft	1912–1922
James C. McReynolds	Wilson	1914–1941
Louis D. Brandeis	Wilson	1916–1939
John H. Clarke	Wilson	1916–1922
William H. Taft	Harding	1921–1930
George Sutherland	Harding	1922–1938
Pierce Butler	Harding	1922–1939
Edward T. Sanford	Harding	1923–1930
Harlan F. Stone	Coolidge	1925–1941
Charles E. Hughes	Hoover	1930–1941
Owen J. Roberts	Hoover	1930–1945
Benjamin N. Cardozo	Hoover	1932–1938
Hugo L. Black	F. Roosevelt	1937–1971
Stanley F. Reed	F. Roosevelt	1938–1957
Felix Frankfurter	F. Roosevelt	1939–1962
William O. Douglas	F. Roosevelt	1939–1975

Boldface type indicates service as chief justice.
*Nominated in 1990; not yet confirmed as of publication.

NAME	NOMINATED BY	SERVICE
Frank Murphy	F. Roosevelt	1940–1949
Harlan F. Stone	F. Roosevelt	1941–1946
James F. Byrnes	F. Roosevelt	1941–1942
Robert H. Jackson	F. Roosevelt	1941–1954
Wiley B. Rutledge	F. Roosevelt	1943–1949
Harold H. Burton	Truman	1945–1958
Fred M. Vinson	Truman	1946–1953
Tom C. Clark	Truman	1949–1967
Sherman Minton	Truman	1949–1956
Earl Warren	Eisenhower	1953–1969
John M. Harlan	Eisenhower	1955–1971
William J. Brennan, Jr.	Eisenhower	1956–1990
Charles E. Whittaker	Eisenhower	1957–1962
Potter Stewart	Eisenhower	1958–1981
Byron R. White	Kennedy	1962–
Arthur J. Goldberg	Kennedy	1962–1965
Abe Fortas	Johnson	1965–1969
Thurgood Marshall	Johnson	1967–
Warren E. Burger	Nixon	1969–1986
Harry A. Blackmun	Nixon	1970–
Lewis F. Powell, Jr.	Nixon	1971–1987
William H. Rehnquist	Nixon	1971–1986
John Paul Stevens	Ford	1975–
Sandra Day O'Connor	Reagan	1981–
William H. Rehnquist	Reagan	1986–
Antonin Scalia	Reagan	1986–
Anthony M. Kennedy	Reagan	1988–
David H. Souter	Bush	1990–*

GLOSSARY

activation. One of three key consequences of electoral campaigns for voters, meaning that the voter is activated to contribute money or ring doorbells instead of just voting. See also **reinforcement** and **conversion.**

actual group. That part of the **potential group** consisting of members who actually join. See also **interest group.**

administrative discretion. The authority of administrative actors to select among various responses to a given problem. Discretion is greatest when routines, or **standard operating procedures,** do not fit a case.

advertising. According to David Mayhew, one of three primary activities undertaken by members of Congress to increase the probability of their reelection. Advertising involves contacts between members and their constituents between elections. See also **credit claiming** and **position taking.**

affirmative action. A policy designed to give special attention to or compensatory treatment of members of some previously disadvantaged group.

agenda. See **policy agenda.**

agents of socialization. Families, schools, television, peer groups, and other influences that contribute to **political socialization** by shaping formal and especially informal learning about politics.

American Constitution. The document written in 1787 and ratified in 1788 that sets forth the institutional structure of U.S. government and the tasks these institutions perform. It replaced the **Articles of Confederation.** See also **constitution** and **unwritten constitution.**

amicus curiae briefs. Legal briefs submitted by a "friend of the court" for the purpose of raising additional points of view and presenting information not contained in the briefs of the formal parties in an attempt to influence a court's decision.

Anti-Federalists. Opponents of the **American Constitution** at the time when the states were contemplating its adoption. They argued that the Constitution was a class-based document, that it would erode fundamental liberties, and that it would weaken the power of the states. See also **Federalists.**

antitrust policy. A policy designed to ensure competition and prevent monopoly, which is the control of a market by one company.

appellate jurisdiction. The jurisdiction of courts that hear **cases** brought to them on appeal from lower courts.

These courts do not review the factual record, only the legal issues involved. Compare **original jurisdiction.**

appropriations bill. An act of Congress that actually funds programs within limits established by **authorization bills.** Appropriations usually cover one year.

arms race. A tense relationship beginning in the 1950s between the Soviet Union and the United States whereby one side's weaponry became the other side's goad to procure more weaponry, and so on.

authorization bill. An act of Congress that establishes, continues, or changes a discretionary government program or an entitlement. It specifies program goals and maximum expenditures for discretionary programs. Compare **appropriations bill.**

Articles of Confederation. The first constitution of the United States, adopted by Congress in 1777 and enacted in 1781. The Articles established a national legislature, the Continental Congress, but most authority rested with the state legislatures.

balance of payments. The ratio of what is paid for imports to what is earned from exports. When more is imported than exported, there is a balance of payments deficit.

balanced budget amendment. A proposed amendment to the Constitution that would instruct Congress to hold a national convention to propose to the states a requirement that peacetime federal budgets be balanced. It has been passed in varied forms by the legislatures of nearly two-thirds of the states.

Barron* v. *Baltimore*.** The 1833 Supreme Court decision holding that the **Bill of Rights** restrained only the national government, not the states and cities. Almost a century later, the Court first ruled in ***Gitlow* v. *New York that state governments must respect some **First Amendment** rights.

bicameral legislature. A legislature divided into two houses. The U.S. Congress and every American state legislature except Nebraska's are bicameral.

bill. A proposed law, drafted in precise, legal language. Anyone can draft a bill, but only a member of the House of Representatives or the Senate can formally submit one for consideration.

Bill of Rights. The first ten amendments to the **American Constitution,** drafted in response to some of the **Anti-Federalist** concerns. These amendments define such basic liberties as freedom of religion, speech, and press and protections against arbitrary searches by the police and being held with no chance to talk to a lawyer.

block grants. Federal grants given more or less automatically to states or communities to support broad programs in areas like community development and social services. Compare **categorical grants.**

broadcast media. Television and radio, as compared with **print media.**

***Brown* v. *Board of Education*.** The 1954 Supreme Court decision holding that school segregation in Topeka, Kansas, was inherently unconstitutional because it violated the **Fourteenth Amendment's** guarantee of **equal protection.** This case marks the end of legal segregation in the United States. See also ***Plessy* v. *Ferguson*.**

budget. A policy document allocating burdens (taxes) and benefits (expenditures). See also **balanced budget amendment.**

budget resolution. A resolution binding Congress to a total expenditure level, which is supposed to be the bottom line of all federal spending for all programs.

bureaucracy. According to Max Weber, a hierarchical authority structure that uses task specialization, works on the merit principle, and behaves with impersonality. Bureaucracies govern modern states.

cabinet. A group of presidential advisors not mentioned in the Constitution, although every president has had one. Today it is composed of twelve secretaries and the attorney general.

capitalism. An economic system in which individuals and corporations, not the government, own the principal means of production and seek profits. Pure capitalism means the strict noninterference of the government in affairs of business. Compare **mixed economy.**

case. A dispute before a court involving a **plaintiff** and a **defendant.**

casework. Helping constituents as individuals; cutting through bureaucratic red tape to get people what they think they have a right to get. See also **pork barrel.**

categorical grants. Federal grants that can be used only for specific purposes, or "categories," of state and local spending. They come with strings attached, such as nondiscrimination provisions. Compare **block grants.**

caucus (congressional). A grouping of members of Congress sharing some interest or characteristic. Most are composed of members from both parties and some from both houses.

caucus (state party). A meeting of all state party leaders for selecting delegates to the **national party convention.** Caucuses are usually organized as a pyramid.

censorship. Governmental regulations of media content. More censorship is permitted in Great Britain than in the United States.

census. A valuable tool for understanding demographic changes. The Constitution requires that the government conduct an "actual enumeration" of the population every ten years. See also **demography.**

Central Intelligence Agency (CIA). An agency created after World War II to coordinate American intelligence activities abroad. It became involved in intrigue, conspiracy, and meddling as well.

chains. See **newspaper chains.**

change. The degree that **public opinion** is shifting or stable over time. See also **consensus** and **conflict.**

checks and balances. An important part of the Madisonian model designed to limit government's power by requiring that power be balanced among the different governmental institutions that continually check one another's activities. This system reflected Madison's goal of setting power against power. See also **separation of powers.**

civic duty. The belief that, in order to support democratic government, a citizen should always vote.

civil disobedience. A form of **political participation** that reflects a conscious decision to break a law believed to be immoral and to suffer the consequences. See also **protest.**

civil law. The body of law involving **cases** without a charge of criminality. It concerns disputes between two parties and consists of both statutes and **common law.** Compare **criminal law.**

civil liberties. The legal and constitutional protections against government. Although our civil liberties are formally set down in the **Bill of Rights,** the courts, police, and legislatures define their meaning.

civil rights. The policies extending basic rights to minority groups or other groups historically subject to discrimination. Many groups, especially African Americans and more recently women, have raised constitutional questions about slavery, segregation, equal pay, and other issues. See also **Civil Rights Act of 1964.**

Civil Rights Act of 1964. The law that made racial discrimination against any group in hotels, motels, and restaurants illegal and forbade many forms of job discrimination. See also **civil rights movement** and **civil rights policies.**

civil rights movement. A movement that began in the 1950s and organized both blacks and whites to end the policies of segregation. It sought to establish equal opportunities in the political and economic sectors and to end policies that erected barriers against people because of race.

civil rights policies. Policies that extend government protection to particular disadvantaged groups. Compare **social welfare policies.**

civil service. A system of hiring and promotion based on the **merit principle** and the desire to create a non-partisan government service. Compare **patronage.**

class action lawsuits. Lawsuits permitting a small number of people to sue on behalf of all other people similarly situated.

Clean Air Act of 1970. The law that charged the Department of Transportation (DOT) with the responsibility of reducing automobile emissions.

clearance rate. The proportion of crimes resulting in an arrest. This statistic has remained stable for years.

coalition. A group of individuals with a common interest upon which every political party depends. See also **New Deal Coalition.**

coalition government. When two or more parties join together to form a majority in a national legislature. This form of government is quite common in the multiparty systems of Europe.

coattails. See **presidential coattails.**

collective bargaining. Negotiations between representatives of labor unions and management to determine acceptable working conditions.

collective good. Something of value (money, a tax write-off, prestige, clean air, and so on) that cannot be withheld from a group member.

command-and-control policy. According to Charles Schultze, the existing system of **regulation** whereby government tells business how to reach certain goals, checks that these commands are followed, and punishes offenders. Compare **incentive system.**

commercial speech. Communication in the form of advertising. It can be restricted more than many other types of speech but has been receiving increased protection from the Supreme Court.

committee chairs. The most important influencers of the congressional agenda. They play dominant roles in scheduling hearings, hiring staff, appointing subcommittees, and managing committee bills when they are brought before the full house.

committees (congressional). See **conference committees, joint committees, select committees,** and **standing committees.**

common law. The accumulation of judicial decisions applied in **civil law** disputes.

comparable worth. The issue raised when women holding traditionally female jobs are paid less than men for working at jobs of comparable skill.

conference committees. Congressional committees formed when the Senate and the House pass a particular **bill** in different forms. Party leadership appoints members from each house who iron out the differences and report back a single bill. See also **standing committees, joint committees,** and **select committees.**

conflict. A clash occurring when an issue is characterized by **public opinion** that is sharply divided. Compare **consensus** and **change.**

Congressional Budget and Impoundment Control Act of 1974. An act designed to reform the congressional budgetary process. Its supporters hoped that it would also make Congress less dependent on the president's budget and more able to set and meet its own budgetary goals.

Congressional Budget Office (CBO). A counterweight to the president's **Office of Management and Budget (OMB).** The CBO advises Congress on the likely consequences of budget decisions and forecasts revenues.

Connecticut Compromise. The compromise reached at the Constitutional Convention that established two houses of Congress: the House of Representatives, in which **representation** is based on a state's share of the U.S. population, and the Senate, in which each state has two representatives. Compare **New Jersey Plan** and **Virginia Plan.**

consensus. Agreement. Consensus is reflected by an opinion distribution in which a large majority see eye to eye. Compare **conflict** and **change.**

consent of the governed. According to John Locke, the required basis for government. The **Declaration of Independence** reflected Locke's view that governments derive their authority from the consent of the governed.

conservatism. A **political ideology** whose advocates fear the growth of government, deplore government's drag on private sector initiatives, dislike permissiveness in society, and place a priority on military needs over social needs. Compare **liberalism.**

conservatives. Those who advocate **conservatism.** Compare **liberals.**

constitution. A nation's basic law. It creates political institutions, assigns or divides powers in government, and often provides certain guarantees to citizens. Constitutions can be both written and unwritten. See also **American Constitution.**

constitutional courts. Lower federal courts of original jurisdiction created by Congress by the Judiciary Act of 1789. Compare **legislative courts.**

Consumer Price Index (CPI). The key measure of inflation that relates prices in one year to prices for a base year that are figured as one hundred.

containment doctrine. A **foreign policy** strategy advocated by George Kennan calling for the United States to isolate the Soviet Union, "contain" its advances, and resist its encroachments, by peaceful means if possible, but by force if necessary.

continuing resolutions. When Congress cannot reach agreement and pass appropriations bills, these allow agencies to spend at the level of the previous year.

convention. See **national party convention.**

conversion. One of three key consequences of electoral campaigns for voters, meaning that the voter's mind is actually changed. See also **reinforcement** and **activation.**

cooperative federalism. A system of government in which powers and policy assignments are shared between states and the national government. They may also share costs, administration, and even blame for programs that work poorly. Compare **dual federalism.**

Council of Economic Advisors (CEA). A three-member body appointed by the president to advise the president on economic policy.

courts. See **constitutional courts, legislative courts, district courts,** and **courts of appeal.**

courts of appeal. Appellate courts empowered to review all final decisions of district courts, except in rare cases. In addition, they also hear appeals to orders of many federal regulatory agencies. Compare **district courts.**

Craig v. Boren. In this 1976 Supreme Court decision the Court determined that gender classification cases would have a "heightened" or "middle level" of scrutiny. In other words, the courts were to show less deference to gender classifications than to more routine classifications, but more deference than to racial classifications.

credit claiming. According to David Mayhew, one of three primary activities undertaken by members of Congress to increase the probability of their reelection. It involves personal and district service. See also **advertising** and **position taking.**

criminal law. The body of law involving a **case** in which an individual is charged with violating a specific law. The offense may be harmful to an individual or society and in either case warrants punishment, such as imprisonment or a fine. Compare **civil law.**

crisis. A sudden, unpredictable, and potentially dangerous event requiring the president to play the role of crisis manager.

critical election. An electoral "earthquake" whereby new issues emerge, new coalitions replace old, and the majority party is often displaced by the minority party. Critical election periods are sometimes marked by a national crisis and may require more than one election to bring about a new **party era.** See also **party realignment.**

cruel and unusual punishment. Court sentences prohibited by the **Eighth Amendment.** Although the Supreme Court has ruled that mandatory death sentences for certain offenses are unconstitutional, it has not held that the death penalty itself constitutes cruel and unusual punishment. See also *Furman* **v.** *Georgia, Gregg* **v.** *Georgia,* and *McClesky* **v.** *Kemp.*

culture of poverty. Negative attitudes and values toward work, family, and success that condemn the poor to low levels of accomplishment. The view that there is a culture of poverty is most commonly held by **conservatives.**

Dartmouth College **v.** *Woodward.* The 1819 case in which the Supreme Court held that Dartmouth's charter, as well as the charter of any corporation, is a legal contract that cannot be tampered with by a government.

dealignment. See **party dealignment.**

debate. See **presidential debate.**

debt. See **federal debt.**

Declaration of Independence. The document approved by representatives of the American colonies in 1776 that stated their grievances against the British monarch and declared their independence.

defendant. The participant in a **case** who is charged by a **plaintiff.** The defendant may be an individual or a corporation.

deficit. An excess of federal **expenditures** over federal **revenues.** See also **budget.**

delegate. See **instructed delegate.**

democracy. A system of selecting policymakers and of organizing government so that policy represents and responds to the public's preferences.

democratic theory. See **traditional democratic theory.**

demography. The science of population changes. See also **census.**

Dennis **v.** *United States.* A 1951 Supreme Court decision that permitted the government to jail several American Communist party leaders under the Smith Act, a law forbidding advocacy of the violent overthrow of the U.S. government.

dependency. See **interdependency.**

détente. A slow transformation from conflict thinking to cooperative thinking in **foreign policy** strategy and policy-making. It sought a relaxation of tensions between the superpowers, coupled with firm guarantees of mutual security.

direct primaries. **Primaries** used to select party nominees for congressional and state offices.

district courts. The ninety-one federal courts of original jurisdiction. They are the only federal courts in which no trials are held and in which juries may be empaneled. Compare **courts of appeal.**

Dred Scott **v.** *Sandford.* The 1857 Supreme Court decision ruling that a slave who had escaped to a free state enjoyed no rights as a citizen and that Congress had no authority to ban slavery in the territories.

dual federalism. A system of government in which states and the national government each remain supreme within their own spheres, each responsible for some policies. Compare **cooperative federalism.**

due process clause. Part of the **Fourteenth Amendment** guaranteeing that persons cannot be deprived of life, liberty, or property by the United States or state governments without due process of law. See also *Gitlow* **v.** *New York.*

efficacy. See **political efficacy.**

Eighth Amendment. The constitutional amendment that forbids **cruel and unusual punishment,** although it does not define this phrase. Through the **Fourteenth Amendment,** this **Bill of Rights** provision applies to the states.

elastic clause. The final paragraph of Article I, Section 8, of the Constitution, which authorizes Congress to pass all laws "necessary and proper" to carry out the enumerated powers. See also **implied powers.**

electioneering. Direct group involvement in the electoral process. Groups can help fund campaigns, provide testimony, and get members to work for candidates, and some form **Political Action Committees (PACs).**

electoral college. A unique American institution, created by the Constitution, providing for the selection of the president by electors chosen by the state parties. Although the electoral college vote usually reflects a popular majority, the winner-take-all rule gives clout to big states.

electoral mandate. A concept based on the idea that "the people have spoken." It is a powerful symbol in American electoral politics, according legitimacy and credibility to a newly elected president's proposals. See also **mandate theory of politics.**

elite. The upper class in a society that utilizes wealth for political power. According to the **elite and class theory** of government and politics, elites control policies because they control key institutions.

elite and class theory. A theory of government and politics contending that societies are divided along class lines and that an upper class **elite** will rule, regardless of the formal niceties of governmental organization. Compare **hyperpluralism, pluralist theory,** and **traditional democratic theory.**

Engel* v. *Vitale*.** The 1962 Supreme Court decision holding that state officials violated the **First Amendment** when they wrote a prayer to be recited by New York's schoolchildren. Compare ***School District of Abington Township, Pennsylvania* v. *Schempp.

entitlements. Policies for which expenditures are uncontrollable because Congress has in effect obligated itself to pay X level of benefits to Y number of recipients. Each year, Congress' bill is a straightforward function of the X level of benefits times the Y beneficiaries. Social Security benefits are an example.

entrepreneur. See **political entrepreneur.**

enumerated powers. Powers of the federal government that are specifically addressed in the Constitution; for Congress, these powers are listed in Article I, Section 8, and include the power to coin money, regulate its value, and impose taxes. Compare **implied powers.**

environmental impact statement (EIS). A report filed with the **Environmental Protection Agency**

(EPA) that specifies what environmental effects a proposed policy would have. The **National Environmental Policy Act** requires that whenever a governmental agency proposes to undertake a policy potentially disruptive of the environment, it must file a statement with the EPA.

Environmental Protection Agency (EPA). An agency of the federal government created in 1970 and charged with administering all the government's environmental legislation. It also administers policies dealing with toxic wastes. The EPA is the largest federal **independent regulatory agency.**

equal opportunity. A policy statement about equality holding that the rules of the game should be the same for everyone. Most of our **civil rights** policies over the past three decades have presumed that equality of opportunity is a public policy goal. Compare **equal results.**

equal protection of the laws. Part of the **Fourteenth Amendment** emphasizing that the laws must provide equivalent "protection" to all people. As one member of Congress said during debate on the amendment, it should provide "equal protection of life, liberty and property" to all a state's citizens.

equal results. A policy statement about equality holding that government has a duty to help break down barriers to **equal opportunity. Affirmative action** is an example of a policy justified as promoting equal results rather than merely equal opportunities.

Equal Rights Amendment. A constitutional amendment, passed by Congress in 1978 and sent to the state legislatures for ratification, stating that "equality of rights under the law shall not be denied or abridged by the United States or by any state on account of sex." Despite substantial public support and an extended deadline, the amendment failed to acquire the necessary support from three-fourths of the state legislatures.

equity. See **intergenerational equity.**

establishment clause. Part of the **First Amendment** stating that "Congress shall make no law respecting an establishment of religion."

European Economic Community (EEC). An economic alliance of the major Western European nations, often called the Common Market. The EEC coordinates monetary, trade, immigration, and labor policies.

exclusionary rule. The rule that evidence, no matter how incriminating, cannot be introduced into a trial if it was not constitutionally obtained. The rule prohibits use of evidence obtained through **unreasonable search and seizure.**

executive agency. See **independent executive agency.**

executive orders. Regulations originating from the executive branch. Executive orders are one method presidents can use to control the bureaucracy; more often, though, presidents pass along their wishes through their aides.

exit polls. **Public opinion** surveys used by major media pollsters to predict electoral winners with speed and precision.

expenditures. Federal spending of **revenues.** Major areas of such spending are social services and the military.

extradition. A legal process whereby an alleged criminal offender is surrendered by the officials of one state to officials of the state in which the crime is alleged to have been committed.

facilitator. According to George Edwards, the effective leader who works at the margin of coalition building to recognize and exploit opportunities presented by a favorable configuration of political forces.

factions. Interest arising from the unequal distribution of property or wealth that James Madison attacked in the **Federalist Papers** Number 10. Today's parties or interest groups are what Madison had in mind when he warned of the instability in government caused by factions.

federal debt. All the money borrowed by the federal government over the years and still outstanding. Today the federal debt approaches three trillion dollars.

Federal Election Campaign Act. A law passed in 1974 for reforming campaign finances. It created the **Federal Election Commission (FEC),** providing public financing for presidential primaries and general elections, limited presidential campaign spending, required disclosure, and attempted to limit contributions.

Federal Election Commission (FEC). A six-member bipartisan agency created by the **Federal Election Campaign Act** of 1974. The FEC administers the campaign finance laws and enforces compliance with their requirements.

Federal Regulation of Lobbying Act. Passed in 1946, an act requiring congressional lobbyists to register and state their policy goals. According to the Supreme Court, the law applies only to groups whose "principal" purpose is **lobbying.**

Federal Reserve System. The main instrument for making **monetary policy** in the United States. It was created by Congress in 1913 to regulate the lending practices of banks and thus the money supply. The seven members of its board of governors are appointed to fourteen-year terms by the president with the consent of the Senate.

Federal Trade Commission (FTC). The **independent regulatory agency** traditionally responsible for regulating false and misleading trade practices. The FTC has recently become active in defending consumer interests through its truth-in-advertising rule and the Consumer Credit Protection Act.

federalism. A way of organizing a nation so that two levels of government have formal authority over the same land and people. It is a system of shared power between units of government. Compare **unitary government.**

Federalist Papers. A collection of eighty-five articles written by Alexander Hamilton, John Jay, and James Madison under the name "Publius" to defend the Constitution in detail. Collectively, these papers are second only to the **American Constitution** in characterizing what the framers had in mind.

Federalists. Supporters of the **American Constitution** at the time the states were contemplating its adoption. See also **Anti-Federalists** and **Federalist Papers.**

Fifteenth Amendment. The constitutional amendment adopted in 1870 to extend **suffrage** to blacks.

Fifth Amendment. The constitutional amendment designed to protect the rights of persons accused of crimes, including protection against double jeopardy, **self-incrimination,** and punishment without due process of law.

filibuster. A strategy unique to the Senate whereby opponents of a piece of legislation try to talk it to death, based on the tradition of unlimited debate. Today, sixty members present and voting can halt a filibuster.

First Amendment. The constitutional amendment that establishes the four great liberties: freedom of the press, of speech, of religion, and of assembly.

fiscal federalism. The patterns of spending, taxing, and grants between governmental units in a federal system.

fiscal policy. The policy that describes the impact of the federal budget—taxes, spending, and borrowing—on the economy. Unlike **monetary policy,** which is mostly controlled by the **Federal Reserve System,** fiscal policy is almost entirely determined by Congress and the president, who are the budget makers. See also **Keynesian economic theory.**

Food and Drug Administration (FDA). The federal agency formed in 1913 and assigned the task of approving all food products and drugs sold in the United States. All drugs, with the exception of tobacco, must have FDA authorization.

foreign policy. A policy that, like domestic policy, involves choice taking, but additionally involves choices about relations with the rest of the world. The president is the chief initiator of foreign policy in the United States.

Fourteenth Amendment. The constitutional amendment adopted after the Civil War that states, "No State shall make or enforce any law which shall abridge the privileges or immunities of citizens of the United States; nor shall any state deprive any person of life, liberty, or property, without due process of law; nor deny to any person within its jurisdiction the **equal protection of the laws.**" See also **due process clause.**

fragmentation. A situation in which responsibility for a policy area is dispersed among several units within the bureaucracy, making the coordination of policies both time-consuming and difficult.

free exercise clause. A **First Amendment** provision that prohibits government from interfering with the practice of religion.

free-rider problem. The problem faced by unions and other groups when people do not join because they do not have to join in order to benefit from the group's activities. The bigger the group, the more serious the free-rider problem. See also **interest group.**

full faith and credit clause. A clause in Article IV, Section 1, of the Constitution requiring each state to recognize the official documents and civil judgments rendered by the courts of the other states.

Furman* v. *Georgia. The 1972 Supreme Court decision that overturned Georgia's death penalty law but did not declare the death penalty itself unconstitutional. The majority of the justices found that the imposition of the death sentence was often "freakish" and "random."

General Schedule rating. See **GS (General Schedule) rating.**

Gibbons* v. *Ogden. A landmark case decided in 1824 in which the Supreme Court interpreted very broadly the clause in Article I, Section 8, of the Constitution giving Congress the power to regulate interstate commerce, encompassing virtually every form of commercial activity. The commerce clause has been the constitutional basis for much of Congress's regulation of the economy.

Gideon* v. *Wainwright. The 1963 Supreme Court decision holding that anyone accused of a felony, where imprisonment may be imposed, has a right to a lawyer, however poor he or she might be. See also **Sixth Amendment.**

Gitlow* v. *New York. The 1925 Supreme Court decision holding that freedoms of press and speech are "fundamental personal rights and liberties protected by the **due process clause** of the **Fourteenth Amendment** from impairment by the states" as well as the federal government. Compare ***Barron* v. *Baltimore.***

government. The institutions and processes through which **public policies** are made for a society.

government corporation. A government organization that, like business corporations, provides a service that could be provided by the private sector and typically charges for its services. The U.S. Postal Service is an example. Compare **independent regulatory agency** and **independent executive agency.**

Gramm-Rudman-Hollings. Named for its sponsors and also known as the Balanced Budget and Emergency Deficit Act, legislation mandating maximum allowable deficit levels each year until 1991, when the budget was to be in balance. In 1987, the balanced budget year was shifted to 1993.

grandfather clause. One of the methods used by southern states to deny blacks the right to vote. In order to exempt illiterate whites from taking a literacy test before voting, the clause exempted people whose grandfathers were eligible to vote in 1860, thereby disenfranchising the grandchildren of slaves. The grandfather clause was declared unconstitutional by the Supreme Court in 1913. See also **poll taxes** and **white primary.**

grants. See **categorical grants** and **block grants.**

Gregg* v. *Georgia. The 1976 Supreme Court decision that upheld the constitutionality of the death penalty, stating that "It is an extreme sanction, suitable to the most extreme of crimes." The court did not, therefore, believe that the death sentence constitutes **cruel and unusual punishment.**

gross national product. The sum total of the value of all the goods and services produced in a nation.

GS (General Schedule) rating. A schedule for federal employees, ranging from GS 1 to GS 18, by which salaries can be keyed to rating and experience. See **civil service.**

Hatch Act. A federal law prohibiting government employees from active participation in partisan politics.

high-tech politics. A politics in which the behavior of citizens and policymakers and the political agenda itself are increasingly shaped by technology.

House Rules Committee. An institution unique to the House of Representatives that reviews all bills (except revenue, budget, and appropriations bills) coming from a House committee before they go to the full House.

House Ways and Means Committee. The House of Representatives committee that, along with the **Senate Finance Committee,** writes the tax codes, subject to the approval of Congress as a whole.

hyperpluralism. A theory of government and politics contending that groups are so strong that government is weakened. Hyperpluralism is an extreme, exaggerated, or perverted form of **pluralism.** Compare **elite and class theory, pluralist theory,** and **traditional democratic theory.**

ideology. See **political ideology.**

impacts. See **policy impacts.**

impeachment. The political equivalent of an indictment in criminal law, prescribed by the Constitution. The House of Representatives may impeach the president by a majority vote for "Treason, Bribery, or other high Crimes and Misdemeanors."

implementation. The stage of policy making between the establishment of a policy and the consequences of the policy for the people whom it affects. Implementation involves translating the goals and objectives of a policy into an operating, ongoing program. See also **judicial implementation.**

implied powers. Powers of the federal government that go beyond those enumerated in the Constitution. The Constitution states that Congress has the power to "make all laws necessary and proper for carrying into execution" the powers enumerated in Article I. Many federal policies are justified on the basis of implied powers. See also *McCulloch* v. *Maryland,* **elastic clause,** and **enumerated powers.**

incentive system. According to Charles Shultze, a more effective and efficient policy than **command-and-control;** in the incentive system, marketlike strategies are used to manage the market.

income. The amount of funds collected between any two points in time. Compare **wealth.**

income distribution. The "shares" of the national income earned by various groups.

income taxes. Shares of individual wages and corporate revenues collected by the government. The first income tax was declared unconstitutional by the Supreme Court in 1895, but the **Sixteenth Amendment** explicitly authorized Congress to levy a tax on income. See also **Internal Revenue Service.**

incorporated. A term describing the result of the process whereby the Supreme Court has held that the protections of the Bill of Rights limit state and local governments as well as the national government.

incrementalism. The belief that the best predictor of this year's **budget** is last year's budget, plus a little bit more (an increment). According to Aaron Wildavsky, "Most of the budget is a product of previous decisions."

incumbents. Those already holding office. The most important fact about congressional elections is that incumbents usually win.

independent executive agency. The government not accounted for by **cabinet** departments, **independent regulatory agencies,** and **government corporations.** Its administrators are typically appointed by the president and serve at his pleasure. The Veterans Administration is an example.

independent regulatory agency. A government agency with responsibility for some sector of the economy, making and enforcing rules supposedly to protect the public interest. It also judges disputes over these rules. The Interstate Commerce Commission is an example. Compare **government corporation** and **independent executive agency.**

industrial policy. A conscious effort of government to channel economic investment and thus growth. Except by accident, the United States has never pursued industrial policy.

INF Treaty. The elimination of intermediate range nuclear forces (INF) through an agreement signed by President Reagan and Mikhail Gorbachev during the May 1988 Moscow summit. It was the first treaty to reduce current levels of nuclear weapons.

initiative petition. A state-level method of direct legislation used by voters in twenty-three states to put proposed legislation on the ballot. See also **referendum.**

instructed delegate. A legislator who mirrors the preferences of his or her constituents. Compare **trustee.**

interdependency. Mutual dependence, meaning that the actions of nations reverberate and affect one another's economic lifelines.

interest group. An organization of people with shared policy goals entering the policy process at several points to try to achieve those goals. Interest groups pursue their goals in many arenas.

intergenerational equity. The issue of the distribution of government benefits and burdens among the generations and over time. Affected groups include children, the working and middle classes, and the aged, all of whom are beneficiaries of public policies.

intergovernmental relations. The workings of the federal system, by which is meant the entire set of interactions among national, state, and local governments.

Internal Revenue Service. The office established to collect federal **income taxes,** investigate violations of the tax laws, and prosecute tax criminals.

investigative journalism. The use of detectivelike reporting to unearth scandals, scams, and schemes, putting reporters in adversarial relationships with political leaders.

isolationism. A **foreign policy** course followed throughout most of our nation's history, whereby the United States has tried to stay out of other nations' conflicts, particularly European wars. Isolationism was reaffirmed by the Monroe Doctrine.

issue. See **political issue.**

Joint Chiefs of Staff. The commanding officers of the armed services who advise the president on military policy.

joint committees. Congressional committees on a few subject-matter areas with membership drawn from both houses. See also **standing committees, conference committees,** and **select committees.**

judicial activism. A judicial philosophy in which judges make bold policy decisions, even charting new constitutional ground. Advocates of this approach emphasize that the courts can correct pressing needs, especially those unmet by the majoritarian political process.

judicial implementation. How and whether court decisions are translated into actual policy, affecting the behavior of others. The courts rely on other units of government to carry out enforcement.

judicial interpretation. A major informal way by which the Constitution is changed by the courts as they balance citizens' rights against those of the government. See also **judicial review.**

judicial restraint. A judicial philosophy in which judges play minimal policy-making roles, leaving that strictly to the legislatures. Compare **judicial activism.**

judicial review. The power of the courts to determine whether acts of Congress, and by implication the executive, are in accord with the **American Constitution.** Judicial review was established by John Marshall and his associates in *Marbury* v. *Madison.* See also **judicial interpretation.**

jurisdiction. See **original jurisdiction** and **appellate jurisdiction.**

jury. A panel responsible for determining guilt or innocence in a legal **case.**

justiciable disputes. A constraint on the courts meaning that a **case** must be capable of being settled by legal methods.

Keynesian economic theory. The theory emphasizing that government spending and deficits can help the economy weather its normal ups and downs. Proponents of this theory advocate using the power of government to stimulate the economy when it is lagging. See also **fiscal policy.**

***Korematsu* v. *United States*.** A 1944 Supreme Court decision that upheld as constitutional the internment of more than 100,000 Americans of Japanese descent in encampments during World War II.

laissez-faire. The principle that government should not meddle in the economy. See also **capitalism.**

leak. See **news leak.**

legislative courts. Courts established by Congress for specialized purposes, such as the Court of Military Appeals. Judges who sit there have fixed terms and lack the protections of **constitutional court** judges.

legislative veto. The ability of Congress to override a presidential decision. Although the **War Powers Resolution** asserts this authority, there is reason to believe that, if challenged, the Supreme Court would find the legislative veto in violation of the doctrine of separation of powers.

legitimacy. A characterization of elections by political scientists meaning that they are almost universally accepted as a fair and free method to select political leaders. When legitimacy is high, as in the United States, even the losers accept the results peacefully.

libel. The publication of knowingly false or malicious statements that damage someone's reputation.

liberals. Those who advocate **liberalism.** Compare **conservatives.**

liberalism. A **political ideology** whose advocates prefer an active government in dealing with human needs, support individual rights and liberties, and place a priority on social needs over military needs.

limited government. The idea that certain things are out of bounds for government because of the **natural rights** of citizens. Limited government was central to John Locke's philosophy in the seventeenth century, and it contrasted sharply with the prevailing view of the divine rights of monarchs.

linkage institutions. The channels or access points through which issues and people's policy preferences get on the government's **policy agenda.** In the United States, elections, **political parties,** and **interest groups** are the three main linkage institutions.

litigants. The **plaintiff** and the **defendant** in a **case.**

lobbying. According to Lester Milbrath, a "communication, by someone other than a citizen acting on his own behalf, directed to a governmental decisionmaker with the hope of influencing his decision."

McCarthyism. The fear, prevalent in the 1950s, that international Communism was conspiratorial, insidious, bent on world domination, and infiltrating American government and cultural institutions. It was named after Senator Joseph McCarthy and flourished after the Korean War.

***McClesky* v. *Kemp*.** The Supreme Court upheld the death penalty in this 1987 case, even in the face of evidence that minority defendants and murderers whose victims were white were more likely to receive death sentences.

***McCulloch* v. *Maryland*.** An 1819 Supreme Court decision that established the supremacy of the national government over state governments. In deciding this case, Chief Justice John Marshall and his colleagues held that Congress had certain **implied powers** in addition to the **enumerated powers** found in the Constitution.

McGovern-Fraser Commission. A commission formed at the 1968 Democratic convention in response to demands for reform by minority groups and others who sought better representation.

machine. According to Edward C. Banfield and James Q. Wilson, a "party organization that depends crucially on inducements that are both specific and material." Machines and their local leaders exchange favors for votes and personalize politics.

majority leader. The principal partisan ally of the Speaker of the House or the party's wheelhorse in the Senate. The majority leader is responsible for scheduling bills, influencing committee assignments, and rounding up votes in behalf of the party's legislative positions.

majority rule. A fundamental principle of **traditional democratic theory.** In a democracy, choosing among alternatives requires that the majority's desire be respected. See also **minority rights.**

mandate. See **electoral mandate** and **mandate theory of elections.**

mandate theory of elections. The idea that the winning candidate has a mandate from the people to carry out his or her platforms and politics. Politicians like the theory better than political scientists do.

***Mapp* v. *Ohio*.** The 1961 Supreme Court decision ruling that the Fourth Amendment's protection against **unreasonable searches and seizures** must be extended to the states as well as the federal government. See also **exclusionary rule.**

***Marbury* v. *Madison*.** The 1803 case in which Chief Justice John Marshall and his associates first asserted the right of the **Supreme Court** to determine the meaning of the **American Constitution.** The decision established the Court's power of **judicial review** over acts of Congress, in this case the Judiciary Act of 1789.

mass media. Television, radio, newspapers, magazines, and other means of popular communication that profoundly influence elites and masses. They are a key part of **high-tech politics.** See also **broadcast media** and **print media.**

media events. Purposely staged events in front of the media that nonetheless look spontaneous. In keeping with politics as theater, media events can be staged by individuals, groups, and government officials, especially presidents.

Medicaid. A public assistance program designed to provide health care for poor Americans. Medicaid is funded by both the states and the national government. Compare **Medicare.**

Medicare. A program added to the Social Security system in 1965 that provides hospitalization insurance for the elderly and permits older Americans to purchase inexpensive coverage for doctor fees and other expenses. Compare **Medicaid.**

melting pot. The mixing of cultures, ideas, and peoples that have changed the American nation. The United States, with its history of immigration, has often been called a melting pot.

merit principle. The idea that hiring should use entrance exams and promotion ratings to produce administration by people with talent and skill. See also **civil service** and compare **patronage.**

***Miami Herald Publishing Company* v. *Tornillo*.** A case decided in 1974 in which the Supreme Court held that a state could not force a newspaper to print replies from candidates it had criticized, illustrating the limited power of government to restrict the **print media.** See ***Red Lion Broadcasting Company* v. *FCC*.**

***Miller* v. *California*.** A 1973 Supreme Court decision that avoided defining obscenity by holding that community standards be used to determine whether material is obscene in terms of appealing to a "prurient interest."

minority leader. The principal leader of the minority party in the House of Representatives or in the Senate.

minority majority. The emergence of a non-Caucasian majority, as compared with a white, generally Anglo-Saxon majority. It is predicted that, by about the middle of the next century, Hispanic Americans, African Americans, and Asian Americans will outnumber white Americans.

minority rights. A principle of **traditional democratic theory** that guarantees rights to those who do not belong to majorities and allows that they might join majorities through persuasion and reasoned argument. See also **majority rule.**

***Miranda* v. *Arizona*.** The 1966 Supreme Court decision that sets guidelines for police questioning of accused persons to protect them against **self-incrimination** and to protect their right to counsel.

mixed economy. An economic system whereby the government is deeply involved in decisions that affect the economy through its role as regulator, consumer, subsidizer, taxer, employer, and borrower. The United States can be considered a mixed economy. Compare **capitalism.**

monetarism. An economic theory holding that the supply of money is the key to a nation's economic health. Monetarists believe that too much cash and credit in circulation produces inflation. See also **monetary policy.**

monetary policy. Based on **monetarism,** monetary policy is the manipulation of the supply of money in private hands by which the government can control the economy. See also the **Federal Reserve System** and compare **fiscal policy.**

multinational corporations. Large businesses with vast holdings in many countries. Many of these companies are larger than most governments.

***NAACP* v. *Alabama*.** The Supreme Court protected the right to peaceably assemble in this 1958 case when it decided the NAACP did not have to reveal its membership list and thus subject its members to harassment.

national chairperson. One of the institutions that keep the party operating between conventions. The national chairperson is responsible for the day-to-day activities of the party and is usually handpicked by the presidential nominee. See also **national committee.**

national committee. One of the institutions that keep the party operating between conventions. The national committee is composed of representatives from the states and territories. See also **national chairperson.**

National Environmental Policy Act (NEPA). The law passed in 1969 that is the centerpiece of federal environmental policy in the United States. The NEPA established the requirements for **environmental impact statements.**

national health insurance. A compulsory insurance program for all Americans that would have the government finance our medical care. First proposed by President Harry S Truman, the plan has been soundly opposed by the American Medical Association.

National Institutes of Health (NIH). Agencies of the national government that conduct research on health and medical issues—an example of how the government is involved in health policy.

National Labor Relations Act. A 1935 law, also known as the Wagner Act, that guaranteed workers the right of **collective bargaining,** set down rules to protect unions and organizers, and created the National Labor Relations Board to regulate labor-management relations.

national party convention. The supreme power within each of the parties. It meets every four years to nominate the presidential and vice-presidential candidates of the party and to write the party's platform.

national primary. A proposal by critics of the **caucuses** and **presidential primaries** who would replace those electoral methods with a nationwide primary held early in the election year.

National Security Council. An office created in 1947 to coordinate the president's foreign and military policy advisors. Its formal members are the president, vice president, **secretary of state,** and **secretary of defense,** and it is managed by the president's national security advisor.

NATO. See **North Atlantic Treaty Organization.**

natural rights. Rights held to be inherent in human beings, not dependent on governments. John Locke asserted that natural law, which is superior to human law, specifies certain rights of "life, liberty, and property," a sentiment reflected in the **Declaration of Independence.**

***Near* v. *Minnesota*.** The 1931 Supreme Court decision holding that the **First Amendment** protects newspapers from **prior restraint.**

necessary and proper clause. See **elastic clause.**

New Deal Coalition. A **coalition** forged by Franklin Roosevelt and the Democrats who dominated American politics from the 1930s to the 1960s. Its basic elements were the urban working class, ethnic groups, Catholics and Jews, the poor, southerners, blacks, and Democratic intellectuals.

New Jersey Plan. The proposal at the Constitutional Convention that called for equal **representation** of each state in Congress regardless of the state's population. Compare **Virginia Plan** and **Connecticut Compromise.**

***New York Times* v. *Sullivan*.** Decided in 1964, this case established the guidelines for determining whether public officials and public figures could win damage suits for libel. To do so, said the Court, they must prove that

the defamatory statements made about them were made with "actual malice" and reckless disregard for the truth.

news leak. A carefully placed bit of inside information given to a friendly reporter. Leaks can benefit both the leaker and the leakee.

newspaper chains. Newspapers published by massive media conglomerates that account for almost three-quarters of the nation's daily circulation. Often these chains control **broadcast media** as well.

Nineteenth Amendment. The constitutional amendment adopted in 1920 that guarantees women the right to vote. See also **suffrage.**

nomination. The official endorsement of a candidate for office by a **political party.** Generally, success in the nomination game requires momentum, money, and media attention.

nonrenewable resources. Minerals and other resources that nature does not replace when consumed. Many commonly used energy resources, such as oil and coal, are nonrenewable.

North Atlantic Treaty Organization (NATO). Created in 1949, an organization whose members are the United States, Canada, most Western European nations, and Turkey, all of whom agreed to combine military forces and to treat a war against one as a war against all. Compare **Warsaw Pact.**

Office of Management and Budget (OMB). An office that grew out of the Bureau of the Budget, created in 1921, consisting of a handful of political appointees and hundreds of skilled professionals. The OMB performs both managerial and budgetary functions, and although the president is its boss, the director and staff have considerable independence in the budgetary process. See also **Congressional Budget Office.**

Office of Personnel Management (OPM). The office in charge of hiring for most agencies of the federal government, using elaborate rules in the process.

Olson's law of large groups. Advanced by Mancur Olson, a principle stating that "the larger the group, the further it will fall short of providing an optimal amount of a collective good." See also **interest group.**

OPEC. See **Organization of Petroleum Exporting Countries.**

opinion. A statement of legal reasoning behind a judicial decision. The content of an opinion may be as important as the decision itself.

Organization of Petroleum Exporting Countries (OPEC). An economic organization, consisting primarily of Arab nations, that controls the price and amount of oil its members produce and sell to other nations. The Arab members of OPEC caused the oil boycott in the winter of 1973–74.

original intent. A view that the Constitution should be interpreted according to the original intent of the framers. Many **conservatives** support this view.

original jurisdiction. The jurisdiction of courts that hear a **case** first, usually in a trial. These are the courts that determine the facts about a case. Compare **appellate jurisdiction.**

oversight. The process of monitoring the bureaucracy and its administration of policy, mainly through congressional hearings.

PACs. See **Political Action Committees (PACs).**

parliamentary governments. Governments, like the one in Great Britain, that typically select the political leader from membership in the parliament, the legislature.

participation. See **political participation.**

party. See **political party.**

party competition. The battle of the parties for the control of public offices. Ups and downs of the two major parties are one of the most important elements in American politics.

party dealignment. The gradual disengagement of people and politicians from the parties, as seen in part by shrinking **party identification.**

party eras. Historical periods in which a majority of voters cling to the party in power, which tends to win a majority of the elections. See also **critical election** and **party realignment.**

party identification. A citizen's self-proclaimed preference for one or the other party.

party image. The voter's perception of what the Republicans or Democrats stand for, such as **conservatism** or **liberalism.**

party neutrality. A term used to describe the fact that many Americans no longer have any attitudes one way or the other about the two major political parties. See also **party dealignment.**

party realignment. The displacement of the majority party by the minority party occurring during a **critical election period.** See also **party era.**

patronage. One of the key inducements **machines** use. A patronage job, promotion, or contract is one that is given for political reasons rather than for merit or competence alone. Compare **civil service** and the **merit principle.**

Pendleton Act. Passed in 1883, an act that created a federal **civil service** so that hiring and promotion would be based on merit rather than **patronage.**

per curiam decision. A court decision without explanation, in other words, without an **opinion.**

plaintiff. The participant in a **case** who brings a charge against a **defendant.** Sometimes the plaintiff is the government.

plea bargain. An actual bargain struck between the defendant's lawyer and the prosecutor to the effect that the defendant will plead guilty to a lesser crime in exchange for the state's promise not to prosecute the defendant for the more serious one.

Plessy v. Ferguson. An 1896 Supreme Court decision that provided a constitutional justification for segregation by ruling that a Louisiana law requiring "equal but separate accommodations for the white and colored races" was not unconstitutional.

plum book. Published by Congress, a book listing top federal jobs, or "plums," available for direct presidential appointment, often with Senate confirmation.

pluralist theory. A theory of government and politics emphasizing that politics is mainly a competition among groups, each one pressing for its own preferred policies. Compare **elite and class theory, hyperpluralism,** and **traditional democratic theory.**

pocket veto. A veto taking place when Congress adjourns within ten days of having submitted a **bill** to the president, who simply lets it die by neither signing nor vetoing it. See also **veto.**

policy. See **public policy.**

policy agenda. According to John Kingdon, "the list of subjects or problems to which government officials, and people outside of government closely associated with those officials, are paying some serious attention at any given time."

policy differences. The perception of a clear choice between the parties. Those who see such choices are more likely to vote.

policy entrepreneurs. People who invest their political "capital" in an issue. According to John Kingdon, a policy entrepreneur "could be in or out of government, in elected or appointed positions, in interest groups or research organizations."

policy impacts. The effects a policy has on people and problems. Impacts are analyzed to see how well a policy has met its goal and at what cost.

policy implementation. See **implementation.**

policy voting. Voting that occurs when electoral choices are made on the basis of the voters' policy preferences and on where the candidates stand on policy issues. For the voter, policy voting is hard work.

Political Action Committees (PACs). Funding vehicles created by the 1974 campaign finance reforms. A corporation, union, or some other interest group can create a PAC and register it with the **Federal Election Commission (FEC),** which will meticulously monitor the PAC's expenditures.

political economy. The relationship between government and the economy.

political efficacy. The belief that one's **political participation** really matters, that one's vote can actually make a difference.

political ethics. Matters of right or wrong with respect to government, involving either the actions of individual politicians or policy choices.

political ideology. A coherent set of beliefs about politics, public policy, and public purpose. It helps give meaning to political events, personalities, and policies. See also **liberalism** and **conservatism.**

political issue. An issue that arises when people disagree about a problem and a public policy choice.

political participation. All the activities used by citizens to influence the selection of political leaders or the policies they pursue. The most common, but not the only, means of political participation in a **democracy** is voting. Other means include **protest** and **civil disobedience.**

political party. According to Anthony Downs, a "team of men [and women] seeking to control the governing apparatus by gaining office in a duly constituted election."

political questions. A doctrine developed by the federal courts and used as a means to avoid deciding some cases, principally those involving conflicts between the president and Congress.

political socialization. According to Richard Dawson, "the process through which an individual acquires his [or her] particular political orientations—his [or her] knowledge, feelings, and evaluations regarding his [or her] political world." See also **agents of socialization.**

political system. A set of institutions and activities that link together people, politics, and policy.

politics. According to Harold Lasswell, "who gets what, when, and how." Politics produces authoritative decisions about public issues.

poll taxes. Small taxes, levied on the right to vote, that often fell due at a time of year when poor African-American sharecroppers had the least cash on hand. This method was used by most southern states to exclude African Americans from voting registers. It was declared void by the **Twenty-fourth Amendment** in 1964. See also **grandfather clause** and **white primary.**

polls. See **exit polls.**

pork barrel. The mighty list of federal projects, grants, and contracts available to cities, businesses, colleges, and institutions in the district of a member of Congress.

position taking. According to David Mayhew, one of three primary activities undertaken by members of Congress to increase the probability of their reelection. It involves taking a stand on issues and responding to constituents about these positions. See also **advertising** and **credit taking.**

potential group. All the people who might be **interest group** members because they share some common interest. A potential group is almost always larger than an actual group.

poverty line. A method used to count the number of poor people, it considers what a family would need to spend for an "austere" standard of living.

power. The capacity to get people to do something that they would not otherwise do. The quest for power is a strong motivation to political activity.

Pravda. The national newspaper of the Soviet Communist party. The term is Russian for "truth," and *Pravda's* job is to faithfully mirror changes in Soviet leadership and policy.

precedents. The way a type of **case** has been decided in the past.

presidential approval. An evaluation of the president based on many factors but especially on the predisposition of many people to support the president. One measure is provided by the Gallup Poll.

presidential coattails. The situation occurring when voters cast their ballots for congressional candidates of the president's party because they support the president. Recent studies show that few races are won this way.

presidential debate. A debate between presidential candidates. The first televised debate was between Richard Nixon and John Kennedy during the 1960 campaign.

presidential primaries. Elections in which voters in a state vote for a candidate (or delegates pledged to him or her). Most delegates to the **national party conventions** are chosen this way.

press conference. Meetings of public officials with reporters. President Franklin Roosevelt promised and delivered two press conferences each week.

press secretary. The person on the White House staff who most often deals directly with the press, serving as a conduit of information. Press secretaries conduct daily press briefings.

price supports. The mechanism by which the federal government guarantees the prices of certain agricultural commodities by regularly buying surplus crops in order to keep prices high. In return, farmers agree to limit planting in a given year.

primaries. Elections that select candidates. In addition to **presidential primaries,** there are **direct primaries** for selecting party nominees for congressional and state offices and proposals for **regional primaries.**

print media. Newspapers and magazines, as compared with **broadcast media.**

prior restraint. A government's preventing material from being published. This is a common method of limiting the press in some nations, but it is unconstitutional in the United States, according to the **First Amendment** and as confirmed in the 1931 Supreme Court case of *Near* **v.** *Minnesota.*

privacy. See **right of privacy.**

Privacy Act. A law passed in 1974 stipulating that information collected by one agency of the government cannot be used by another. For example, a driving record cannot be used to deny Social Security benefits.

privileges and immunities clause. A clause in Article IV, Section 2, of the Constitution according citizens of each state some of the privileges of citizens of other states.

probable cause. The situation occurring when the police have reason to believe that a person should be arrested. In making the arrest, the police are allowed legally to search for and seize incriminating evidence. Compare **unreasonable searches and seizures.**

progressive tax. A tax by which the government takes a greater share of the **income** of the rich than of the poor—for example, when a rich family pays 50 percent of its income in taxes, a poor family pays 5 percent. Compare **regressive tax** and **proportional tax.**

project grants. Federal grants given for specific purposes and awarded on the basis of the merits of applications. A type of the **categorical grants** available to states and localities.

proportional representation. An electoral system used throughout most of Europe that awards legislative seats to political parties in proportion to the number of votes won in an election. Compare with **winner-take-all system.**

proportional tax. A tax by which the government takes the same share of **income** from everyone, rich and poor alike—for example, when a rich family pays 20 percent and a poor family pays 20 percent. Compare **progressive tax** and **regressive tax.**

protest. A form of **political participation** designed to achieve policy change through dramatic and unconventional tactics. See also **civil disobedience.**

public interest. The idea that there are some interests superior to the private interest of groups and individuals, interests we all have in common. See also **public interest lobbies.**

public interest lobbies. According to Jeffrey Berry, organizations that seek "a collective good, the achievement of which will not selectively and materially benefit the membership or activities of the organization." See also **lobbying** and **public interest.**

public opinion. The distribution of the population's beliefs about politics and policy issues.

public policy. A choice that **government** makes in response to a political issue. A policy is a course of action taken with regard to some problem.

random digit dialing. A technique used to place telephone calls randomly to both listed and unlisted numbers when conducting a survey. See also **random sample.**

random sample. The key technique employed by sophisticated survey researchers, which operates on the principle that everyone should have an equal probability of being selected for the sample. See also **sample.**

rational-choice theory. A popular theory in political science to explain the actions of voters as well as politicians. It assumes that individuals act in their best interest, carefully weighing the costs and benefits of possible alternatives.

realignment. See **party realignment.**

reapportionment. The process of reallocating seats in the House of Representatives every ten years based on the results of the census.

reconciliation. A congressional process through which program authorizations are revised to achieve required savings. It usually also includes tax or other revenue adjustments.

Red Lion Broadcasting Company* v. *FCC*.** A 1969 case in which the Supreme Court upheld restrictions on radio and television broadcasting, such as giving adequate coverage to public issues and covering opposing views. These restrictions on the **broadcast media** are much tighter than those on the **print media,** based on the rationale that there are only a limited number of broadcasting frequencies available. See ***Miami Herald Publishing Company* v. *Tornillo.

***Reed v. Reed*.** The landmark case in 1971 in which the Supreme Court for the first time upheld a claim of sexual discrimination.

referendum. A state-level method of direct legislation that gives voters a chance to approve or disapprove proposed legislation or a proposed constitutional amendment. See also **initiative petition.**

Regents of the University of California* v. *Bakke*.** A 1978 Supreme Court decision holding that a state university could not admit less qualified individuals solely because of their race. The Court did not, however, rule that such **affirmative action** policies and the use of race as a criterion for admission were unconstitutional, only that they had to be formulated differently. Compare ***Weber* v. *Kaiser Aluminum Company.

regional primaries. A proposal by critics of the **caucuses** and **presidential primaries** to replace those electoral methods with regional primaries held early in the election year.

registration. See **voter registration.**

regulation. The use of governmental authority to control or change some practice in the private sector. Regulations pervade the daily lives of people and institutions.

regulatory agency. See **independent regulatory agency.**

reinforcement. One of three key consequences of electoral campaigns for voters, meaning that the voter's candidate preference is reinforced. See also **activation** and **conversion.**

relative deprivation. A perception by a group that it is doing less well than is appropriate in relation to a reference group. The desire of a group to correct what it views as the unfair distribution of resources, such as income or government benefits, is a frequent motivator for political activism.

representation. A basic principle of **traditional democratic theory** that describes the relationship between the few leaders and the many followers.

republic. A form of government that derives its power, directly or indirectly, from the people. Those chosen to govern are accountable to those whom they govern. In contrast to a direct democracy, in which people make laws themselves, in a republic the people select representatives who make the laws.

responsible party model. A view favored by some political scientists about how parties should work. According to the model, parties should offer clear choices to the voters, who can then use those choices as cues to their own choices of candidates. Once in office, parties would carry out their campaign promises.

retrospective voting. A theory of voting in which voters essentially ask this simple question: "What have you done for me lately?"

revenues. The financial resources of the federal government. The individual income tax and Social Security tax are two major sources of revenue. Compare **expenditures.**

right to privacy. According to Paul Bender, "the right to keep the details of [one's] life confidential; the free and untrammeled use and enjoyment of one's intellect, body, and private property...the right, in sum, to a private personal life free from the intrusion of government or the dictates of society." The right to privacy is implicitly protected by the **Bill of Rights.** See also **Privacy Act.**

right-to-work law. A state law forbidding requirements that workers must join a union to hold their jobs. State right-to-work laws were specifically permitted by the Taft-Hartley Act of 1947.

***Roe* v. *Wade*.** The 1973 Supreme Court decision holding that a state ban on all abortions was unconstitutional. The decision forbade state control over abortions during the first trimester of pregnancy, permitted states to limit abortions to protect the mother's health in the second trimester, and permitted states to protect the fetus during the third trimester.

***Roth* v. *United States*.** A 1957 Supreme Court decision ruling that "obscenity is not within the area of constitutionally protected speech or press."

SALT. See **Strategic Arms Limitation Talks.**

sample. A relatively small proportion of people who are chosen in a survey so as to be representative of the whole.

sampling error. The level of confidence in the findings of a public opinion poll. The more people interviewed, the more confident one can be of the results.

***Schenck* v. *United States*.** A 1919 Supreme Court decision in which Justice Holmes argued that government can restrain free speech only when it provokes a **clear and present danger** to people.

***School District of Abington Township, Pennsylvania* v. *Schempp*.** A 1963 Supreme Court decision holding that a Pennsylvania law requiring Bible reading in schools violated the **establishment clause** of the **First Amendment.** Compare ***Engel* v. *Vitale*.**

search warrant. A written authorization from a court that specifies the area to be searched and what the police are searching for. The Fourth Amendment requires a search warrant to prevent **unreasonable searches and seizures.**

secretary of defense. The head of the Department of Defense and the president's key advisor on military policy; a key **foreign policy** actor.

secretary of state. The head of the Department of State and traditionally the key advisor to the president on **foreign policy.**

select committees. Congressional committees appointed for a specific purpose, such as the Watergate investigation. See also **joint committees, standing committees,** and **conference committees.**

selective perception. The phenomenon that people often pay the most attention to things they already agree with, and interpret them according to their own predispositions.

self-incrimination. The situation occurring when an individual accused of a crime is compelled to be a witness against himself or herself in court. The **Fifth Amendment** forbids self-incrimination. See also ***Miranda* v. *Arizona*.**

Senate Finance Committee. The Senate committee that, along with the **House Ways and Means Committee,** writes the tax codes, subject to the approval of Congress as a whole.

senatorial courtesy. An unwritten tradition whereby nominations for state-level federal judicial posts are not confirmed if they are opposed by the senator from the state in which the nominee will serve. The tradition also applies to courts of appeal when there is opposition from the nominee's state senator, if the senator belongs to the president's party.

seniority system. A simple rule for picking **committee chairs,** in effect until the 1970s. The member who served on the committee the longest and whose party controlled Congress became chair, regardless of party loyalty, mental state, or competence.

separation of powers. An important part of the **Madisonian model** that required each of the three branches of government—executive, legislative, and judicial—to be relatively independent of one another so that one could not control the others. Power is shared among these three institutions. See also **checks and balances.**

Shays' Rebellion. A series of attacks on courthouses by a small band of farmers led by revolutionary war Captain Daniel Shays to block foreclosure proceedings.

shield laws. Laws according a legal right for reporters and other representatives of the media to refuse, under certain circumstances, to respond to orders of legislative committees or court subpoenas to reveal sources of their information.

Simpson-Marzolli Act. An immigration law, named after its legislative sponsors, that as of June 1, 1987, requires employers to document the citizenship of their employees. Civil and criminal penalties can be assessed against employers who knowingly employ illegal immigrants.

single-issue groups. Groups that have a narrow interest, tend to dislike compromise, and often draw membership from people new to politics. These features distinguish them from traditional **interest groups.**

Sixteenth Amendment. The constitutional amendment adopted in 1915 that explicitly permitted Congress to levy an **income tax.**

Sixth Amendment. The constitutional amendment designed to protect individuals accused of crimes. It includes the right to counsel, the right to confront witnesses, and the right to a speedy and public trial.

social policies. Policies that manipulate opportunities through public choice. They include policies related to income and policies related to opportunity.

Social Security Act. A 1935 law passed during the Great Depression that was intended to provide a minimal level of sustenance to older Americans and thus to save them from poverty.

social welfare policies. Policies that provide benefits to individuals, particularly to those in need. Compare **civil rights policies.**

socialized medicine. A system in which the full cost of medical care is borne by the national government. Great Britain and the Soviet Union are examples of countries that have socialized medicine. Compare **Medicaid** and **Medicare.**

solicitor general. A presidential appointee and the third-ranking office in the Department of Justice. The solicitor general is in charge of the appellate court litigation of the federal government.

sound bites. Short video clips of approximately fifteen seconds, which are typically all that is shown from a politician's speech or activities on the nightly television news.

Speaker of the House. An office mandated by the Constitution. The Speaker is chosen in practice by the majority party, has both formal and informal powers, and is second in line to succeed a deceased president.

standard operating procedures. Better known as SOPs, these procedures are used by bureaucrats to bring uniformity to complex organizations. Uniformity improves fairness and makes personnel interchangeable. See also **administrative discretion.**

standing committees. Separate subject-matter committees in each house of Congress that handle **bills** in different policy areas. See also **joint committees, conference committees,** and **select committees.**

standing to sue. The requirement that **plaintiffs** have a serious interest in a **case,** which depends on whether they have sustained or are likely to sustain a direct and substantial injury from a party or an action of government.

stare decisis. A Latin phrase meaning "let the decision stand." The vast majority of cases reaching the courts are settled on this principle.

START. See **Strategic Arms Reduction Talks (START).**

statutory construction. The judicial interpretation of an act of Congress. In some cases where statutory construction is an issue, Congress passes new legislation to clarify existing laws.

Strategic Arms Limitation Talks (SALT). An effort by the United States and the Soviet Union to agree to scale down their nuclear capabilities, with each maintaining sufficient power to deter a surprise attack by the other. The first SALT treaty was signed by President Nixon in 1972. See also **Strategic Arms Reduction Talks (START).**

Strategic Arms Reduction Talks (START). Talks begun in Geneva by President Reagan to follow up on the **Strategic Arms Limitation Talks (SALT)** between the United States and the Soviet Union.

Strategic Defense Initiative (SDI). Renamed "Star Wars" by critics, a plan for defense against the Soviet Union unveiled by President Reagan in 1983. SDI would create a global umbrella in space, using computers to scan the skies and high-tech devices to destroy invading missiles.

street-level bureaucrats. A phrase coined by Michael Lipsky, referring to those bureaucrats who are in constant contact with the public and have considerable **administrative discretion.**

subgovernments. Also known as "iron triangles," subgovernments are composed of key interest group leaders interested in a policy, the government agency responsible for the policy's administration, and the members of the congressional committees and subcommittees handling the policy.

suffrage. The legal right to vote, extended to blacks by the **Fifteenth Amendment,** to women by the **Nineteenth Amendment,** and to people over the age of 18 by the **Twenty-sixth Amendment.**

Super Tuesday. A creation by a dozen or so southern states when they held their **presidential primaries** in early March 1988, hoping to promote a regional advantage as well as a more conservative candidate.

superdelegates. National party leaders who automatically get a delegate slot at the Democratic **national party convention.**

superfund. A $1.6 billion fund created by Congress in the late 1970s and renewed in the 1980s to clean up hazardous waste sites. Money for the fund comes from taxing chemical products.

supply-side economics. An economic theory, advocated by President Reagan, holding that too much income goes to taxes and too little money is available for purchasing, and that the solution is to cut taxes and return purchasing power to consumers. Supply-side economics has widened the gap between government **revenues** and **expenditures.**

supremacy clause. Article VI of the Constitution, which makes the constitution, national laws, and treaties supreme over state laws when the national government is acting within its constitutional limits.

Supreme Court. The pinnacle of the American judicial system. The Court ensures uniformity in interpreting national laws, resolves conflicts among states, and maintains national supremacy in law. It has both **original jurisdiction** and **appellate jurisdiction,** but it, unlike other federal courts, controls its own agenda.

Swann v. Charlotte-Mecklenberg County Schools. A 1971 Supreme Court decision that upheld the right of federal judges to order the busing of students to achieve racially balanced schools.

symbolic speech. Nonverbal communication, such as burning a flag or wearing an armband. The Supreme Court has accorded some symbolic speech protection under the **First Amendment.** See *Texas v. Johnson.*

Taft-Hartley Act. A 1947 law giving the president power to halt major strikes by seeking a court injuction and permitting states to forbid requirements in labor contracts forcing workers to join a union. See also **right-to-work law.**

talking head. A shot of a person's face talking directly to the camera. Because this is visually unappealing, the major commercial networks rarely show a politician talking one-on-one for very long. See also **sound bites.**

tariff. A special tax added to imported goods to raise the price, thereby protecting American businesses and workers from foreign competition.

tax. See **proportional tax, progressive tax,** and **regressive tax.**

tax expenditures. Defined by the 1974 Budget Act as "revenue losses attributable to provisions of the federal tax laws which allow a special exemption, exclusion, or deduction." Tax expenditures represent the difference between what the government actually collects in taxes and what it would have collected without special exemptions.

Tenth Amendment. The constitutional amendment stating that "The powers not delegated to the United States by the Constitution, nor prohibited by it to the states, are reserved to the states respectively, or to the people."

Texas v. Johnson. A 1989 case in which the Supreme Court struck down a law banning the burning of the American flag on the grounds that such action was **symbolic speech** protected by the **First Amendment.**

third parties. Electoral contenders other than the two major parties. American third parties are not unusual.

Thirteenth Amendment. The constitutional amendment passed after the Civil War that forbade slavery and involuntary servitude.

three-fifths compromise. The compromise reached at the Constitutional Convention specifying that representation in Congress and taxation be based on the "number of free persons" and three-fifths the number of "all other persons." Each slave, in other words, was to be counted as three-fifths of a person.

ticket splitting. Voting with one party for one office and another for other offices. It has become the norm in American voting behavior.

tradeoff. The sacrifice of one goal to achieve another.

traditional democratic theory. A theory about how a democratic government makes its decisions. According to Robert Dahl, its cornerstones are equality in voting, effective participation, enlightened understanding, final control over the agenda, and inclusion.

transfer payments. Benefits given by the government directly to individuals. Transfer payments may be either cash transfers, such as Social Security payments and retirement payments to former government employees, or in-kind transfers, such as food stamps and low-interest loans for college education.

trial balloons. An intentional **news leak** for the purpose of assessing the political reaction.

trustee. A legislator who uses his or her best judgment to make policy in the interests of the people. This concept was favored by Edmund Burke. Compare **instructed delegate.**

Twenty-fifth Amendment. Passed in 1951, the amendment that permits the vice-president to become acting president if both the vice-president and the president's cabinet determine that the president is disabled. The amendment also outlines how a recuperated president can reclaim the job.

Twenty-fourth Amendment. The constitutional amendment passed in 1964 that declared **poll taxes** void.

Twenty-second Amendment. Passed in 1951, the amendment that limits presidents to two terms of office.

uncontrollable expenditures. Expenditures that are determined by how many eligible beneficiaries there are for some particular program. According to Lance LeLoup, an expenditure is classified as uncontrollable "if it is mandated under current law or by a previous obligation." Three-fourths of the federal **budget** is uncontrollable. Congress can change uncontrollable expenditures only by changing a law or existing benefit levels.

unemployment rate. As measured by the Bureau of Labor Statistics (BLS), the proportion of the labor force actively seeking work but unable to find jobs. The unemployment rate would be higher if it included what the BLS calls "discouraged workers," people who have become so frustrated that they have stopped actively seeking employment.

union shop. A provision found in some collective bargaining agreements requiring all employees of a business to join the union within a short period, usually thirty days, and remain members as a condition of employment.

unitary government. A way of organizing a nation so that all power resides in the central government. Most governments today, including those of Britain and Japan, are unitary governments. Compare **federalism.**

United Nations (UN). Created in 1945, an organization whose members agree to renounce war and to respect certain human and economic freedoms. The seat of real power in the UN is the Security Council.

United States v. *Nixon.* The 1974 case in which the Supreme Court unanimously held that the doctrine of executive privilege was implicit in the Constitution but could not be extended to protect documents relevant to criminal prosecutions.

unreasonable searches and seizures. Obtaining evidence in a haphazard or random manner, a practice prohibited by the Fourth Amendment. Both **probable cause** and a **search warrant** are required for a legal and proper seach for and seizure of incriminating evidence.

unwritten constitution. The body of tradition, practice, and procedure that is as important as the written **constitution.** Changes in the unwritten constitution can change the spirit of the Constitution. **Political parties** and **national party conventions** are a part of the unwritten constitution in the United States.

veto. The constitutional power of the president to send a **bill** back to Congress with reasons for rejecting it. A two-thirds vote in each house can override a veto. See also **pocket veto** and **legislative veto.**

Virginia Plan. The proposal at the Constitutional Convention that called for *representation* of each state in Congress in proportion to each state's share of the U.S. population. Compare **New Jersey Plan** and **Connecticut Compromise.**

voter registration. A system adopted by the states and requiring voters to sign up well in advance of election day. Although some states permit virtually instant registration for presidential elections, registration dampens voter turnout.

Voting Rights Act of 1965. A law designed to help put an end to formal and informal barriers to African-American **suffrage.** Under the law, federal registrars were sent to southern states and counties that had long histories of discrimination; as a result, hundreds of thousands of African Americans were registered and the number of African-American elected officials increased dramatically.

War Powers Resolution. A law, passed in 1973 in reaction to American fighting in Vietnam and Cambodia, requiring presidents to consult with Congress whenever possible prior to using military force and to withdraw forces after sixty days unless Congress declares war or grants an extension. Presidents view the resolution as unconstitutional. See also **legislative veto.**

Warsaw Pact. A regional security community of the Soviet Union and its Eastern European allies. Compare **North Atlantic Treaty Organization (NATO).**

Water Pollution Control Act of 1972. A law intended to clean up the nation's rivers and lakes. It requires municipal, industrial, and other polluters to secure permits from the **Environmental Protection Agency** for discharging waste products into waters. According to the law, polluters are supposed to use "the best practicable [pollution] control technology."

Watergate. The events and scandal surrounding a break-in at the Democratic National Committee headquarters in 1972 and the subsequent cover-up of White House involvement, leading to the eventual resignation of President Nixon under the threat of **impeachment.**

wealth. The amount of funds already owned. It includes stocks, bonds, bank deposits, cars, houses, and so forth. Throughout most of the last generation, wealth has been much less evenly divided than **income.**

Weber v. *Kaiser Aluminum Company.* A 1979 Supreme Court decision holding that Kaiser's union-management-sponsored training program was intended to rectify years of past employment **discrimination** by the company and was not, therefore, unconstitutional. Justice Brennan's majority opinion was carefully couched to avoid a blanket endorsement of **affirmative action** programs. Compare *Regents of the University of California* v. *Bakke.*

Webster v. *Reproductive Health Services.* A 1989 case in which the Supreme Court held that women did not have a right to an abortion at public expense. Some saw this as a significant limitation on the right to an abortion upheld in *Roe* v. *Wade.*

whips. Party leaders who work with the **majority leader** to count votes beforehand and lean on waverers whose votes are crucial to a **bill** favored by the party.

white primary. One of the means used to discourage African-American voting that permitted political parties in the heavily Democratic South to exclude blacks from primary elections, thus depriving them of a voice in the real contests. The Supreme Court declared white primaries unconstitutional in 1941. See also **grandfather clause** and **poll taxes.**

winner-take-all system. An electoral system in which legislative seats are awarded only to the candidates who come in first in their constituencies. In American presidential elections, the system in which the winner of the popular vote in a state receives all the electoral votes of that state. Compare with **proportional representation.**

writ of certiorari. A formal document issued from the **Supreme Court** to a lower federal or state court that calls up a case.

writ of habeas corpus. A court order requiring jailers to explain to a judge why they are holding a prisoner in custody.

writ of mandamus. A court order forcing action. In the dispute leading to *Marbury* **v.** *Madison,* Marbury and his associates asked the **Supreme Court** to issue a writ ordering Madison to give them their commissions.

Zurcher **v.** *Stanford Daily.* A 1978 Supreme Court decision holding that a proper **search warrant** could be applied to a newspaper as well as to anyone else without necessarily violating the **First Amendment** rights to freedom of the press.

ACKNOWLEDGMENTS

Text Acknowledgments

Page 52: "Power Shift: Economic Status of State Legislators before and after the Revolutionary War" from "Government by the People: The American Revolution and the Democratization of the Legislatures" by Jackson Turner Main in *The William and Mary Quarterly,* July 1966. Reprinted by permission.

Page 221: "Citizens of the World Show Little Knowledge of Geography" from "Two Superpowers' Citizens Do Badly in Geography" by Warren E. Leary, *The New York Times,* November 9, 1989. Copyright © 1989 by the New York Times Company. Reprinted by permission.

Page 347: "Percentage of Groups Using Various Lobbying Techniques" from *Organized Interests and American Democracy* by Kay Lehman Schlozman and John T. Tierney. Copyright © 1986 by Kay Lehman Schlozman and John T. Tierney. Reprinted by permission of HarperCollins Publishers.

Page 624: "Supreme Court Rulings in Which Federal Statutes Have Been Found Unconstitutional" from *The Judicial Process: An Introductory Analysis of the Courts of the United States, England, and France,* Fifth Edition, by Henry J. Abraham. Copyright © 1962, 1975, 1980 by Oxford University Press, Inc.; renewed 1986 by Henry J. Abraham. Reprinted by permission of the publisher.

Page 650: "America's Top Twenty-five Industrial Corporations in Terms of Assets" from *Fortune,* April 23, 1990. Copyright © 1990 by the Time Inc. Magazine Company. All Rights Reserved. Reprinted by permission.

Page 653: "Our Idea, Their Manufacturing" from *Congressional Quarterly Weekly Report,* May 13, 1989. Reprinted by permission.

Page 654: "Still the World's Top Exporter" from *World Economic Outlook,* April 1989. Copyright © 1989 by International Monetary Fund. Reprinted by permission.

Page 659: "The Minimum Wage: 1970-1991" from *The New York Times,* November 1, 1989. Copyright © 1989 by The New York Times Company. Reprinted by permission.

Page 698: "Percent of GNP Spent on Health" from *Comparative World Policy,* Third Edition, by Arnold J. Heidenheimer, Hugh Heclo, and Carolyn Teich Adams. Copyright © 1990 by St. Martin's Press. Reprinted by permission.

Page 701: "Who Pays Medical Bills?" from "Volleyball on Health Care Costs" by Milt Freudenheim in *The New York Times,* December 7, 1989. Copyright © 1989 by The New York Times Company. Reprinted by permission.

Page 708: "Comparing Sources of Electricity: Nuclear, Conventional and Hydro Power" from *Basic Statistics of the Community,* 1989. Reprinted by permission of the Commission of the European Communities.

Page 711: "The Environment: A Higher Priority" from *The New York Times,* July 2, 1989. Copyright © 1989 by The New York Times Company. Reprinted by permission.

Page 756: "The Global Connection and a Personal Computer" reprinted from March 11, 1985 issue of *Business Week* by special permission, copyright © 1985 by McGraw-Hill, Inc.

Photo Acknowledgments

Unless otherwise acknowledged, all photographs are the property of ScottForesman.

Page 4 (left): Tom Stoddart/Katz Pictures/Woodfin Camp & Associates. *Page 4 (center):* AP/Wide World. *Page 4 (right):* Reuters/UPI/Bettmann Newsphotos. *Page 6:* Reuters/UPI/Bettmann Newsphotos. *Page 7:* Jim Argo/Picture Group. *Page 8:* Steve Liss/Gamma-Liaison. *Page 9:* Wright/Reprinted by the *Detroit News. Page 10:* Rob Crandall/Picture Group. *Page 12:* Jim Von Pummelhoff. *Page 14:* Brad Markel/Gamma-Liaison. *Page 15:* Michel Euler/AP/Wide World. *Page 17:* Kok/Gamma-Liaison. *Page 18:* Charles Gupton/Stock Boston. *Page 20:* Brad Markel/Gamma-Liaison. *Page 22:* Ken Alexander. *Page 24:* Gamma-Liaison. *Page 28:* James D. Wilson/Woodfin Camp & Associates. *Page 29:* By Wright for the *Palm Beach Post. Page 31:* By Meyer for © *San Francisco Chronicle.* Reprinted by permission. *Page 32:* Hank Morgan/Science Source/Photo Researchers. *Page 34:* Bill Fitz-Patrick/The White House.

Page 37: New York Public Library, Astor, Lenox and Tilden Foundations. *Page 38 (top):* New York Public Library, Astor, Lenox and Tilden Foundations. *Page 38 (bottom):* Anne S. K. Brown Military Collection, Brown University. *Page 39 (top):* Smithsonian Institution. *Page 39 (bottom):* Library of Congress. *Page 40 (top):* Courtesy West Point Museum Collection. *Page 40 (bottom):* Library of Congress. *Page 41 (top):* Harold Flecknoe/The Airborne Camera. *Page 41 (bottom):* The National Archives.

Page 43: The New-York Historical Society, New York City. *Page 47: National Geographic* photographer, courtesy U.S. Capitol Historical Society (George F. Mobley). *Page 48:* Brown Brothers. *Page 53:* The Bettmann Archive. *Page 54:* Copyright Yale University Art Gallery. *Page 55:* New York Public Library, Astor, Lenox and Tilden Foundations. *Page 56:* James Monroe Memorial Library. *Page 57 (top):* Brown Brothers. *Page 57 (bottom):* Chicago Historical Society. *Page 59:* Universal Press Syndicate. Reprinted by permission. All Rights Reserved. *Page 67:* Courtesy U.S. Capitol Historical Society, *National Geographic* photographer, George F. Mobley. *Page 71:* New York Public Library, Astor, Lenox and Tilden Foundations. *Page 75:* UPI/Bettmann Newsphotos. *Page 78:* By permission of Mike Luckovich and Creators Syndicate, Inc. *Page 81:* Historical Society of Pennsylvania.

Page 85: Stacy Pick/Stock Boston. *Page 90:* U.S. Department of Transportation. *Page 92:* AP/Wide World. *Page 95:* Prints Division/New York Public Library, Astor, Lenox and Tilden Foundations. *Page 97:* UPI/Bettmann Newsphotos. *Page 98:* Stephen Frisch/Stock Boston. *Page 101:* AP/Wide World. *Page 105:* Sepp Seitz/Woodfin Camp & Associates. *Page 109:* Bob Daemmrich/Stock Boston.

Page 119: Chuck Nacke/Picture Group. *Page 121:* Ralf-finn Hestoft/Picture Group. *Page 128 (all):* AP/Wide World. *Page 130:* AP/Wide World. *Page 135:* Bryce Flynn/Picture Group. *Page 136 (left):* AP/Wide World. *Pages 136 (right), 139, 142, 147 (top):* AP/Wide World. *Page 147 (bottom):* By permission of Johnny Hart and by permission of North America Syndicate, Inc. *Page 148:* © 1964 Flip Schulke/*Life Magazine,* Time Warner Inc. *Page 150:* Steve Starr/Picture Group. *Page 155:* UPI/Bettmann Newsphotos.

Page 161: P. F. Gero/Sygma. *Page 164:* Courtesy Lyndon Baines Johnson Library, Austin, Texas. *Page 168:* Library of Congress. *Pages 170, 171:* UPI/Bettmann Newsphotos. *Page 175:* Charles Moore/Black Star. *Page 176:* Lionel J-M Delevingne. *Page 179:* UPI/Bettmann Newsphotos. *Page 182:* By Stayskal for the *Chicago Tribune. Page 185:* Paul Conklin. *Page 189:* UPI/Bettmann Newsphotos. *Page 191:* Randy Taylor/Sygma. *Page 192:* UPI/Bettmann Newsphotos.

Page 195 (top): Library of Congress. *Page 195 (bottom):* UPI/Bettmann Newsphotos. *Page 196 (top):* © 1939, Thomas McAvoy/*Life Magazine,* Time Warner Inc. *Page 196 (bottom):* UPI/Bettmann Newsphotos. *Page 197 (top):* Fred Ward/Black Star. *Page 197 (bottom):* Francis Miller/*Life Magazine,* Time Warner Inc. *Page 198 (top):* Constantine Manos/Magnum Photos. *Pages 198 (bottom), 199 (top):* UPI/Bettmann Newsphotos. *Page 199 (bottom):* Rob Crandall/Picture Group.

Page 203: Reprinted by permission: Tribune Media Services. *Page 204:* Lewis W. Hine Collection/George Eastman House. *Page 206:* Chip Mitchell/Picture Group. *Page 211:* Hella Hammid/Photo Researchers. *Page 215:* UPI/Bettmann Newsphotos. *Page 216:* By Norris for the *Vancouver Sun,* Canada. *Page 227:* UPI/Bettmann Newsphotos. *Page 228:* By Gorrell for the *Richmond News Leader. Page 230:* Jeff Reinking/Picture Group. *Page 232:* John P. Filo/*Valley Daily News,* Tarentum, Pa. *Page 234:* Bruce Roberts/Photo Researchers.

Page 240: AP/Wide World. *Page 245:* The Bettmann Archive. *Pages 248 (left), 248 (right):* UPI/Bettmann Newsphotos. *Page 253:* AP/Wide World. *Page 255 (all):* From *The Party Goes On,* by Xandra Kayden and Eddie Mahe, Jr. Copyright © 1985. Reprinted by permission of Basic Books, Inc., Publishers, New York. *Page 258 (both):* UPI/Bettmann Newsphotos. *Page 263:* Doug Bruce/Picture Group. *Page 267 (left):* John Ficara/Woodfin Camp & Associates. *Page 267 (right):* Cynthia Johnson/Gamma-Liaison. *Page 271 (bottom):* UPI/Bettmann Newsphotos. *Page 271 (top):* Vince Heptig/Picture Group.

Page 277: UPI/Bettmann Newsphotos. *Page 279:* Jim Heemstra/Picture Group. *Page 281:* By Brookins for the *Richmond Times-Dispatch. Page 282:* Gamma-Liaison. *Page 284:* B. R. Atwell. *Page 285:* By Wright for the *Miami News. Pages 289, 294, 298, 300:* AP/Wide World.

Page 307: Stephen Ferry/Gamma-Liaison. *Page 309:* Michael Grecco/Picture Group. *Page 311:* Reprinted by permission of United Feature Syndicate, Inc. *Page 312:* Library of Congress. *Pages 313, 324:* AP/Wide World. *Pages 331, 332:* UPI/Bettmann Newsphotos.

Page 335: Arthur Grace/Sygma. *Page 337:* UPI/Bettmann Newsphotos. *Page 340:* By Stayskal for the *Tampa Tribune. Page 343 (both):* UPI/Bettmann Newsphotos. *Page 349:* Courtesy National Rifle Association. *Page 350:* Distributed by King Features Syndicate, Inc. *Page 355:* Paul Gero/ Sygma. *Page 358:* Paul Conklin. *Page 360:* UPI/Bettmann Newsphotos. *Page 364:* Distributed by King Features Syndicate, Inc. *Page 367:* AP/Wide World.

Page 371: UPI/Bettmann Newsphotos. *Page 373:* AP/Wide World. *Page 374:* Reprinted by permission, Los Angeles Times Syndicate. *Page 376:* UPI/Bettmann Newsphotos. *Page 379:* Acme/UPI/Bettmann Newsphotos. *Page 384:* AP/Wide World. *Page 385:* By Wright in the *Miami News. Page 387:* UPI/Bettmann Newsphotos. *Page 389:* Reprinted by permission: Tribune Media Services. *Page 391:* UPI/Bettmann Newsphotos. *Page 393:* UPI/Bettmann Newsphotos. *Page 396:* CBS News Photo.

Page 399 (top): Library of Congress. *Page 399 (bottom):* White House Historical Association. *Page 400:* Library of Congress. *Page 401:* Courtesy Lyndon Baines Johnson Library, Austin, Texas. *Page 402 (top):* Library of Congress. *Page 402 (bottom):* UPI/Bettmann Newsphotos. *Page 403 (both):* Library of Congress. *Page 404 (top): Harper's Weekly. Page 404 (bottom):* UPI/Bettmann Newsphotos. *Page 405 (top):* Michael D. Sullivan/Paul Conklin. *Page 405 (bottom):* TexaStock.

Page 407: J. L. Atlan/Sygma. *Page 409:* Brookins in the *Richmond Times Dispatch. Page 410:* P. F. Gero/Sygma. *Page 412:* Ken Regan/Camera 5. *Page 419:* AP/Wide World Photos. *Pages 425, 429 (bottom):* UPI/Bettmann Newsphotos. *Page 429 (top):* P. F. Gero/Sygma. *Page 430:* UPI/Bettmann Newsphotos. *Page 432:* AP/Wide World Photos. *Page 436:* Shepard Sherbell/SABA. *Page 437:* Courtesy of the Hispanic Caucus. *Page 448:* UPI/Bettmann Newsphotos.

Page 453: Frank Fisher/Gamma-Liaison. *Page 456:* Auth for the *Washington Post* Writers Group. *Page 460:* Courtesy Lyndon Baines Johnson Library, Austin, Texas. *Page 462:* Alex Webb/Magnum Photos. *Page 471:* UPI/Bettmann Newsphotos. *Page 473:* Reuters/UPI/Bettmann Newsphotos. *Page 476:* Paul F. Gero/Sygma. *Pages 481, 483:* AP/Wide World. *Page 484:* UPI/Bettmann Newsphotos. *Page 486:* AP/Wide World. *Page 488:* Wayne Miller/Magnum Photos. *Page 493:* P. F. Gero/Sygma. *Page 495:* AP/Wide World. *Page 500:* Michael Evans/The White House.

Page 505: AP/Wide World. *Page 508:* UPI/Bettmann Newsphotos. *Page 512:* UPI/Bettmann Newsphotos. *Page 514:* Jefferson Communications. *Page 515:* Bill Gallery/Stock Boston. *Pages 531, 532:* UPI/Bettmann Newsphotos. *Page 539:* John Ficara/Woodfin Camp & Associates.

Page 543: Christopher Brown/Stock Boston. *Page 545:* John Huehnergarth. *Page 552:* Universal Press Syndicate. Reprinted by permission. All Rights Reserved. *Page 560:* Martin Rogers/Stock Boston. *Page 561:* Michael Weisbrot/Stock Boston. *Page 563:* Bob Daemmrich/Stock Boston. *Page 564:* Jonathan Blair/Woodfin Camp & Associates. *Page 566:* Bob Daemmrich/Stock Boston. *Page 568:* UPI/Bettmann Newsphotos. *Page 570:* Stacy Pick/Stock Boston. *Page 573 (left):* Steve Woit/Stock Boston. *Page 573 (right):* Alon Reininger/Contact/Woodfin Camp & Associates. *Page 579:* UPI/Bettmann Newsphotos. *Page 582:* Bob Daemmrich/Stock Boston.

Page 585: Stacy Pick/Stock Boston. *Page 586:* Mark Reinstein/Uniphoto. *Page 596:* Wally McNamee/Woodfin Camp & Associates. *Page 598 (left):* UPI/Bettmann Newsphotos. *Page 598 (right):* Arthur Grace/Stock Boston. *Page 603:* Frank Fournier/Contact Press Images/Woodfin Camp & Associates. *Page 608:* Supreme Court Historical Society. *Page 610:* Wally McNamee/Woodfin Camp & Associates. *Page 614:* UPI/Bettmann Newsphotos. *Page 616:* Supreme Court Historical Society. *Page 618:* UPI/Bettmann Newsphotos. *Page 621:* Bob Daemmrick/Stock Boston. *Page 623:* UPI/Bettmann Newsphotos. *Page 625:* Supreme Court Historical Society.

Pages 629, 630 (top): Library of Congress. *Page 630 (bottom):* Gamma-Liaison. *Page 631 (top):* Paul Conklin. *Page 631 (bottom):* Paul Conklin. *Page 632 (top):* The National Archives. *Page 632 (bottom):* Stephen Brown/Uniphoto. *Page 633 (top):* Harold Flecknoe/The Airborne Camera. *Page 633 (bottom):* The National Archives.

Page 635: Eric Poggenpohl/Folio, Inc. *Page 637:* Larry Lambert/Picture Group. *Page 643:* UPI/Bettmann Newsphotos. *Page 645:* The Bettmann Archive. *Page 646:* UPI/Bettmann Newsphotos. *Page 648:* Copyright 1985 G. B. Trudeau/Universal Press Syndicate. Reprinted with permission. All Rights Reserved. *Page 652:* Danziger/The *Christian Science Monitor. Page 655:* Reprinted with permission, Copley News Service. *Page 656:* Chuck Nacke/Picture Group. *Page 658:* UPI/Bettmann Newsphotos. *Page 660:* The Bettmann Archive. *Page 662:* UPI/Bettmann Newsphotos.

Page 665: Kevin Horan/Picture Group. *Page 667:* UPI/Bettmann Newsphotos. *Page 670:* UPI/Bettmann Newsphotos. *Page 673:* Kevin Horan/Picture Group. *Page 676:* Andrew Popper/Picture Group. *Page 680:* UPI/Bettmann Newsphotos. *Page 681:* P. F. Gero/Sygma. *Page 682:* Courtesy Lyndon Baines Johnson Library, Austin, Texas. *Page 685:* UPI/Bettmann Newsphotos. *Page 690:* Peter Morgan/Picture Group.

Page 693: J. L. Atlan/Sygma. *Page 699:* Nick Pauloff/The Image Bank. *Page 703:* D. Goldberg/Sygma. *Page 705:* © 1989/Universal Press Syndicate. Reprinted by permission. All Rights Reserved. *Page 706:* Mike Peters/*Dayton Daily News. Page 707:* M. L. Miller/Picture Group. *Page 713:* Chuck Nacke/Picture Group. *Page 716:* B. Nation/Sygma. *Page 717:* Tannenbaum/Sygma. *Page 718:* Willis, *San Jose Mercury News. Page 720:* Jack Spratt/Picture Group.

Page 722: David Burnett/Woodfin Camp & Associates. *Pages 724, 729, 730, 733:* UPI/Bettmann Newsphotos. *Page 735:* Patti McConville/The Image Bank. *Page 737:* UPI/Bettmann Newsphotos. *Page 742:* Bryce Flynn/Picture Group. *Page 745:* Reuters/UPI/Bettmann Newsphotos. *Page 748:* UPI/Bettmann Newsphotos. *Page 750:* Chip Hives/Gamma-Liaison. *Page 755:* Reprinted by permission: Tribune Media Services. *Page 760:* Tannenbaum/Sygma. *Page 761:* Dennis Brack/Black Star.

INDEX

Love Canal, 714
Lovejoy, Arthur, 55
Lowery, David, 505, 507, 555
Lowi, Theodore, 342, 369
Luger, Richard, 90
Lukens, Donald, 31
Lunch, William M., 367
Lynch v. *Donnelly,* 130

MacArthur, Douglas, 196, 484
machine, political, 262–63
MacKinnon, Catherine, 134
MacNeil-Lehrer Newshour, 388, 396
MADD (Mothers Against Drunk Driving), 90–91, 104
Madison, James, 48, 51, 53, 55, 60, 63, 68–69, 109, 245, 365–66, 399, 460, 612, 616, 637
Madisonian model, 62–66
Mahe, Eddie, Jr., 252, 273
Mahood, H. R., 356
Main, Jackson Turner, 52, 69
majority leader, *429*
majority rule, *18*
Malanchuk, Oksana, 324–25, 326
Malbin, Michael J., 421, 451
Malcolm X, 163
Manchester, William, 381
mandamus, writ of, 616
mandates, *480*
mandate theory of elections, *323*
Mandela, Nelson, 754
Manhattan Institute, 684
Mann, Thomas E., 416, 421
Mansbridge, Jane J., 75
Mao Zedong (Mao Tse-Tung), 15, 733–34
Mapp, Dollree, 145
Mapp v. *Ohio,* 145
Marbury, William, 616
Marbury v. *Madison,* 64, *76, 617,* 624
March, James, 556
"March against Death," 197
March on Washington (1963), 196
Marchetti, Victor, 132
Marcos, Ferdinand, 6
Marcus, George E., 224
margin of error, 216
Marriott, J. Willard, 294
Marshall, Dale Rogers, 117
Marshall, George, C., 732–33
Marshall, John, 67, 95, 612, 616, 622
Marshall, Ray, 591
Marshall, Thomas R., 461, 621
Marshall, Thurgood, 132, 170, 591, 598, 611–12, 614, 621
Marshall Plan, 732–33
Martin, Luther, 95
Martin, Susan B., 344
Martinez, Robert, 152
Marx, Karl, 14, 637, 660
Mason, Alpheas Thomas, 62
Mason, George, 66, 69
Masotti, Louis, 265
mass media, 213, 370, *372*
in contemporary society, 372–78

democracy and, 395
development of, 378
and presidential press conferences, 378–79
and size of government, 394
socialization through, 213
understanding, 393–94
Matthews, Donald, 425, 427
May, Judith, 560
Mayhew, David R., 417, 451
Mayo Clinic, 151
McAdams, John C., 419
McAdoo, William, 457
McCafferty, Patrick, 324
McCain, John, 336, 375
McCarthy, Joseph, 139, 734
McCarthyism, *734*
McCleskey v. *Kemp, 150*
McClure, Robert D., 299
McConnell, Mitch, 375
McCormick, John, 721
McCormick, Richard P., 333
McCorvey, Norma, 152
McCulloch v. *Maryland, 94*
McDonald, Forrest B., 60, 83
McFarland, Andrew, 346, 369, 721
McGovern, George, 253, 257, 260, 289
McGovern-Fraser Commission, *253–54*
McKinley, William, 247, 311–12, 400
Means, Dennis, 177
media. *See also* mass media; news; television
bias in, 496
broadcast, 384
constitutional change and, 77
interest groups and, 354
news reporting by, 384
policy agenda and, 372, 392
political campaigns and, 276–78, 289–90, 299–300
and the president, 494
print, 381
public opinion and, 391–92
and right to privacy, 377
outside U.S., 380
media events, *374*
Medicaid, 108, 152, 537, 558, 676, *702*
medical care. *See* health care
Medicare, 507, 537, 558, *701*
"medium scrutiny" standard, applied to sexual discrimination, 180
Meese, Edwin, 472, 612
Meharry Medical College, 169
Meier, Kenneth J., 560
Melman, Seymour, 734
melting pot, *205*
Meltzer, Allen, 536
mergers, 651
merit principle, *551*
Merit Systems Protection Board, 552
Mexico
constitution of, 466
presidency of, 466
Miami Herald, 377
Miami Herald Publishing Company v. *Tornillo,* 138
Michel, Robert, 306, 423, 429
Michigan caucus, 281

Middle East, 749–50
Milbrath, Lester, 346, 349
military, 182
women in, 182
military industrial complex, 510, 734
military spending, 510–12
Miller, Arthur H., 324–25, 326
Miller, Gary, 544, 555
Miller v. *California, 133–34*
Mills, C. Wright, 554
Milner, Neal, 148
"minimal effects hypothesis," and the mass media, 391
minority groups, 232–33, 671
income among, 671
political participation of, 232–33
minority leader, *429*
minority majority, 176, *205,* 208
minority plank, in party platform, 290
minority rights, *18*
minority rule, *18*
Mintz, Alex, 741
Miranda, Ernesto, 121, 147–48, 619
Miranda v. *Arizona,* 121, *147,* 614, 618
Miranda card, 148
Miranda warnings, 122
Missouri Compromise, 167, 617
Mitchell, George, 430, 454
Mitchell, John, 198, 465
Mobil Oil, 354
Moderate/Conservative Democrats, 437
Moe, Terry, 544, 555
Molinari, Guy, 438
Mondale, Walter, 228, 253, 278–79, 285, 325, 461
monetarism, *642*
monetary policy, *642–44*
Monroe, James, 245, 732
Monroe Doctrine, 732
Montoya, R. E., 146, 158
Moral Majority, 129, 130, 354, 358
Morgan, James N., 670, 673
Morin, Richard, 202, 219
Morall, John, III, 573
Morris, Gouverneur, 55, 57, 66
Morris, Norval, 578
Morris, Richard B., 83
Mosbacher, Robert, 468
Motion Picture Association of America, 134
Mott, Lucretia, 177
Mueller, John, 226, 235, 491
Muller, Ronald, 662
multinational corporations (MNCs), *650,* 727
municipalities, 112
Munnell, Alicia H., 508
Munn v. *Illinois,* 572
Murray, Alan S., 365
Murray, Charles, 684, 691
Muskie, Edmund, 278
Mussolini, Benito, 405
MX missile, 426, 438, 742–46

NAACP. *See* National Association for the Advancement of Colored People

1913 Sixteenth Amendment to
Constitution ratified, allowing
taxes on income
Seventeenth Amendment to
Constitution ratified, providing
for direct election of Senators
Federal Reserve Act reforms
U.S. banking system

1887 Congress creates the Interstate
Commerce Commission

1917 United States enters World War I

1896 McKinley-Bryan election;
realignment toward
Republicans
Plessy v. *Ferguson,* upholding
"separate but equal" status
for blacks and damaging the
equal protection guarantee

1918 Armistice ends World War I

1919 Congress passes the Eighteenth
Amendment (Volstead Act),
heralding the beginning
of Prohibition

1920 Nineteenth Amendment ratified,
(granting the vote to women)

1898 Spanish-American War

1925 *Gitlow* v. *New York*
(concerning freedom
speech and of the pre

1890   1900   1910   1920   1930

1890 Congress enacts Sherman
Antitrust Act

1908 Supreme Court upholds Oregon
law limiting working hours
for women

"Black Thursday," first phase of stock **1929**
market crash (October 24)

1906 Congress passes
Pure Food and
Drug Act

Near v. *Minnesota* (concerning **1931**
freedom of the press and the
Fourteenth Amendment's
due process clause)

Franklin D. Roosevelt elected president; **1932**
New Deal begins; party realignment,
voter switch to Democrats occurs

25 percent of Americans unemployed **1933**

Congress passes the **1935**
Social Security Act